for the revival of religion from 1821 to 1875.

Tom Cooper

The Memoirs of CHARLES G. FINNEY

The Complete Restored Text

Charles Finney, 1860. From a photograph, colored in oils, taken in Bolton, England. It was pronounced by friends back home to be "a capital likeness." (See the letter from Elizabeth Finney to James and Alice Barlow, 17 September 1860, in Oberlin College Archives; and *The Bolton Chronicle*, 7 April 1860, p. 1.) Original in the possession of Richard Dupuis. Photograph by Edgar Jones Photography, London.

The Memoirs of CHARLES G. FINNEY

The Complete Restored Text

Garth M. Rosell &
Richard A. G. Dupuis
Editors

THE MEMOIRS OF CHARLES G. FINNEY

ACADEMIE BOOKS is an imprint of Zondervan Publishing House,
1415 Lake Drive, S.E., Grand Rapids, Michigan 49506.

Library of Congress Cataloging in Publication Data

Finney, Charles Grandison, 1792–1875.
The memoirs of Charles G. Finney.

Includes index.
1. Finney, Charles Grandison, 1792–1875.
2. Congregational churches–United States–Clergy–
Biography. 3. Evangelists–United States–Biography.
I. Dupuis, Richard A. G. II. Rosell, Garth M.
III. Title.
BX7260.F47A3 1989 285.8'092'4 [B] 87-37244
ISBN 0-310-45920-6

All Scripture quotations, unless otherwise noted, are taken from the HOLY BIBLE: KING JAMES VERSION

Printed in the United States of America

89 90 91 92 93 94 / AF / 10 9 8 7 6 5 4 3 2 1

To
Theresa and Jane

Few men have better earned the right to utter their own thoughts, in their own words.

James Harris Fairchild
Preface to the First Edition

Contents

Illustrations

PLATES

MAPS

Abbreviations and Symbols

ABBREVIATIONS

BR	*Boston Recorder.*
DAB	*Dictionary of American Biography,* ed. Allen Johnson and Dumas Malone. New York: Charles Scribner and Sons, 1928–1937.
DNB	*Dictionary of National Biography,* ed. Leslie Stephen et al. London: Smith, Elder and Co., 1885–1900.
Fairchild	The Reverend James Harris Fairchild, president of Oberlin College and editor of the first published edition of Finney's *Memoirs.*
Fairchild Papers	James Harris Fairchild Papers, Oberlin College Archives, Oberlin, Ohio. Most of the correspondence, consisting of about two-thirds of the papers, has been microfilmed on twenty-five rolls.
Finney Papers	Charles Grandison Finney Letters and Papers, Oberlin College Archives, Oberlin, Ohio. They consist of two groups: File 2/2/1. Personal papers (two boxes). File 2/2/2. Letters and papers (eleven boxes). Most of the contents of boxes 1–9 have been microfilmed on nine rolls.
JHF	James Harris Fairchild, ed., *Memoirs of Charles G. Finney. Written by himself.* New York: A. S. Barnes and Co., 1876. JHF 1, JHF 2, JHF 3, etc., with the corresponding symbol ǀ in the text, mark the beginning of pages 1, 2, 3, etc. of this edition.
Matson	The Reverend Henry Matson, the stenographer used by Finney in the dictation of the *Memoirs.*
MS	Manuscript. MS 1, MS 2, MS 3, etc. are pages 1, 2, 3, etc. of the manuscript. The symbol ǀ in the text indicates the beginning of manuscript pages.
NYE	*The New-York Evangelist* [title varies].

OE — *The Oberlin Evangelist.*

Tappan Papers — Lewis Tappan Papers, Library of Congress, Washington, D.C. These have been microfilmed on seven rolls.

WR — *The Western Recorder* (Utica).

Wright Papers — George Frederick Wright Papers, Oberlin College Archives, Oberlin, Ohio.

SYMBOLS

< > — Finney's handwriting.

[ ] — Dupuis/Rosell editorial insertions.

| — Marks the page divisions both in the original manuscript and in the Fairchild edition; corresponds to the MS and the JHF page numbers in the margins.

Light/**Bold** — Light type represents those portions of the text as published in the Fairchild edition. **Bold type** represents those portions of the manuscript that were either omitted or in any way altered for the Fairchild edition.

Preface

More than a hundred years have passed since *Memoirs of Charles G. Finney* was first published. Since then the book has been reprinted scores of times and has been translated into numerous languages. Thousands of copies have been sold. The continuing popularity of the first edition—prepared after Finney's death by his successor at Oberlin College, President James Harris Fairchild, and used as the basis of all subsequent editions—has made it a familiar sight on the shelves of public and private libraries all over the world.

Like many others who share an interest in Finney's life and work, we had made frequent use of the *Memoirs* in connection with research that we were doing, and we relied on Fairchild's edition. We saw no reason to do otherwise. Fairchild had indicated in his preface that he had chosen to give the material to the public essentially as he had found it. Furthermore, his work had stood for over a century as a recognized part of the standard Finney corpus.

In 1976, however, a series of events occurred that convinced us of the need for a new edition. The sequence started quite by accident. Garth was in Oxford on sabbatical pursuing Finney-related research when a letter arrived from a colleague asking if he knew whether the "one of Chancellor W_____ 's sons" mentioned on page 367 of Finney's *Memoirs* was Clarence Walworth of Rochester, New York. On the chance that the handwritten original manuscript of the "Memoirs" in the Oberlin College Archives might provide the answer, and having felt for some time that the document might also be useful for his own research, Garth wrote to the archivist there to see if he might obtain a copy.

The morning the microfilm arrived, Garth took it with him to the Bodleian Library and, using one of their readers, located the reference to "one of Chancellor W_____ 's sons" and was able to confirm that it was indeed Clarence Walworth. But what really interested him was the discovery that the manuscript pages seemed to be literally covered with editorial markings. To his amazement, he found that whole sections—such as a chapter on Finney's revival labors in Michigan, accounts of his attitude toward black students at Oberlin College, his involvement in the famous Oberlin lynching scandal, his wife's serious illness, to name but a few—had been omitted. Garth recognized, of course, that in preparing an edition for nineteenth-century readers, Fairchild had been confronted with a delicate task. He wanted to be faithful to the original text, written in Finney's characteristically colorful and often outspoken style, yet he had to try to avoid needless offense. As a result, his tendency was to omit potentially controversial passages and to abbreviate individual names, substituting initials in their places. He also tended to tone down or change what he believed to be overly strong language or sections that in his judgment were unnecessarily repetitive. The results reflected nicely Fairchild's cautious sense of propriety. As Garth sat before the microfilm reader, however, he could not help but think that people should know what Finney had originally written.

A growing sense of the importance of making this material available was confirmed by Richard when Garth visited him in his London home a few days later. As we talked and studied the manuscript together, it became clear that the two of us ought to combine our energies and resources in preparing a new edition for the public. Thus began the transatlantic collaboration that has extended now well over a decade. Richard's trips to work with Garth in Boston, Garth's travels to work with Richard in London, and our joint trips to work together on the manuscript in Oberlin have combined to provide regular opportunity for lengthy discussion and review of each other's work.

As the project progressed, we became increasingly indebted to literally scores of colleagues and friends for their generous sharing of information and critique. Some of these are acknowledged in the footnotes. Special mention should be made of the uncommon help that we received from the archivist of Oberlin College, William E. Bigglestone. Without the efficient support that he and his staff provided, this project would not have been possible. We have also received considerable help from William A. Moffett, the director of libraries at Oberlin College, from other librarians and staff there, and from the present archivist, Roland M. Baumann. Of the staffs of the many other libraries and archives that have helped us, we want to mention particularly the librarians and staff of The University of London Library, The British Library, and The Institute of Historical Research. Like others whose research has taken them into the field of nineteenth-century religious history, we owe a special debt to the pioneering work of Timothy L. Smith, William G. McLoughlin, James E. Johnson, and Richard Carwardine; and we have appreciated their encouragement and help. We are also grateful for the patience and enthusiastic support that we received from the personnel associated with Zondervan Publishing House—Stanley Gundry, Ed van der Maas, Len Goss, Louise Bauer, Sandy Draper, Art Jacobs, Dimples Kellogg, Jan Ortiz, Nancy Regan, Gerard Terpstra, Laura Weller, and Nancy Wilson. Special thanks to Craig Noll, whose invaluable expertise and painstaking attention to detail contributed significantly to the quality of this work.

We want to express appreciation too to Gordon-Conwell Theological Seminary for its generous support of this project and to all of the able typists—Barbara Ernst, Lexie Kirkpatrick, Shirley Landmesser, Corrine Languedoc, Kathy Long, Jim McNeil, Heidi O'Shea, Peter Smith, Jean Stacey, Anne Swetland, Connie Tappy, Candace Waldron, and most especially Esther Flewelling—who over the years patiently translated our funny marks and strange scribblings into readable computer printouts. We suspect that Charles Finney would have liked them all. For, as he might have said, they "saw their duty and they did it." Being a family man, Finney would also have appreciated the loving and good-humored support that we received in such abundance from our families. For their sakes especially, we are glad that the book is finally finished.

Working with the original manuscript has been a moving experience. It is our hope that the book may not only be useful to historians but be an inspiration to all who read it.

London — R.A.G.D.
Boston — G.M.R.

Introduction

CHARLES FINNEY AND HIS REVIVAL MEMORIES

Given the immense reputation of Charles Grandison Finney (1792–1875) and the importance of his life and work as preacher, evangelist, pastor, theologian, reformer, educator, and author, it is not surprising that many people eagerly awaited the publication of his autobiography. When it did appear soon after his death, some, like his own grandson William Cochran, were surprised to discover that he had not really written an autobiography at all. It turned out that he had never intended to write one. He had something very different in mind.[1]

Finney was convinced that the evangelization of the world depended on a resurgence of the kind of revivals of religion that had prevailed in America forty years earlier. In the 1820s he had been at the center of religious upheavals of such magnitude that by the year 1831 it had seemed to many people that the Millennium was at hand. The decades that followed had been a time of momentous change. Men and women everywhere had set about trying to perfect society. It was an era of unprecedented reform. Effort and resources had been poured into organizations concerned to bring about a moral revolution in the life of the nation. Those were the years of the temperance reform and the antislavery and peace crusades and the movement for women's rights. It had been a time also of radical social experiment. Innovations in lifestyle had led to a whole range of health reforms and communitarian experiments. As the tide of migration moved westward and new settlements had sprung up, scores of new schools, colleges, and churches had been founded. Prominent in all this ferment was a pervasive religious impulse. A new vitality in theology and in the forms of religious expression was felt throughout the churches, and there had been a huge expansion in the work of home and foreign missions. Most noticeable were the waves of

[1] See *Memoirs of Charles G. Finney. Written by himself* (New York: A. S. Barnes and Co., 1876); and William C. Cochran, *Charles Grandison Finney: Memorial Address Delivered at the Dedication of the Finney Memorial Chapel, Oberlin, June 21, 1908* (Philadelphia: Lippincott, 1908), p. 7. Cochran, who was living with the Finney family while his grandfather was writing his memoirs, wrote:

> The effort to recall the past brought to mind many incidents of his early life, pleasant and otherwise, which he would tell the family and which they supposed would appear in his Memoirs. These were not published until after his death in 1875, and then it was discovered that he had eliminated almost everything which was not directly connected with his conversion and the religious work to which he dedicated his life (pp. 7–8).

religious revival that not only had swept across America but also had carried across the Atlantic and beyond.[2]

Finney had been deeply involved in all these movements. It was apparent, however, as he looked back, that the progress of forty years had done nothing to bring the Millennium any closer. The reason for this seemed clear. The cause of true revivals as Finney understood them had suffered a severe setback. The trouble could be traced back to the autumn of 1826. At that time the revivals Finney had been promoting had begun to come under attack by certain leaders in the church. Since his dramatic conversion in 1821 at the age of twenty-nine, when he abandoned a promising legal career, Finney had been devoting all his energies to evangelism in upstate New York. Extraordinary revivals had spread through Presbyterian and Congregational churches in settlements in the north of the state and swept through towns in Oneida County and along the Erie Canal. But there were reports and rumors that those revivals had been disastrous, that they had resulted in many false conversions and offensive behavior on the part of young converts, that there were undesirable practices like women praying in public meetings, and that the fanaticism of Finney and his followers had brought discredit to the churches. These reports had provoked the opposition of many of the more moderate and influential leaders in the church, particularly Asahel Nettleton, the foremost evangelist in New England, and Lyman Beecher in Boston, one of the most prominent evangelical pastors in the country.

Finney's policy had been to ignore opposition and keep about his revival work. No time was spent counteracting false charges against himself, and he published nothing in reply to the widely publicized attacks by Beecher and Nettleton. This policy appeared to have paid off, for Finney's success was phenomenal. Licensed to preach in 1823 and ordained as a Presbyterian minister in 1824, by 1827 he had risen to national prominence as the most effective evangelist in the West. In spite of the opposition, hundreds were being converted under his ministry. Finney had gone on to introduce his revivals into Pennsylvania, the heartland of Presbyterian orthodoxy, and into the commercial world of New York City, and finally into the conservative and intellectual strongholds of New England, where even Beecher had given him support. It seemed to Finney that "the opposition of Dr. B[eecher] & Mr N[ettleton] had had its day."[3] By 1832 the revival movement had added hundreds of thousands of members to the churches, and Finney had emerged as the leader of the more radical wing of the evangelical church in American.[4]

Success continued to attend Finney's labors as he pursued his evangelistic career. Based from 1832 to 1835 in New York, where he was pastor of one of

[2] Alice Felt Tyler, *Freedom's Ferment: Phases of American Social History to 1860* (Minneapolis: University of Minnesota Press, 1944); Timothy L. Smith, *Revivalism and Social Reform: American Protestantism on the Eve of the Civil War* (Baltimore: Johns Hopkins University Press, 1980); and Kenneth Scott Latourette, *A History of the Expansion of Christianity,* vol. 4, *The Great Century in Europe and the United States of America, A.D. 1800–A.D. 1914* (Grand Rapids: Zondervan, 1970).

[3] MS 409.

[4] See James E. Johnson, "Charles G. Finney and the Great 'Western' Revivals," *Fides et Historia* 6, no. 2 (Spring 1974): 13–30; and Howard A. Morrison, "The Finney Takeover of the Second Great Awakening During the Oneida Revivals of 1825–1827," *New York History* 59, no. 1 (January 1978): 27–53.

the new Free churches, and subsequently in Oberlin, Ohio, where he was professor of theology in the college and pastor in the town, he worked ceaselessly for the revival of religion.[5] Much of his time was spent away, conducting campaigns across the northern states, and for two periods of more than eighteen months in the 1850s he was in Britain. Particularly fruitful were the times he spent in Rochester, New York. A period of six months in the winter of 1830–1831 had ushered in the great revival of 1831–1832. Further campaigns in Rochester in 1842 and 1856 were the precursors of extensive revivals that had spread across the country in 1843-1844 and again in 1857–1858.[6]

Opposition to the Revivals

As the years went by, however, it became increasingly hard to recapture the power of the early revivals. Finney found that all his attempts to broaden and deepen the revival movement met with resistance in the churches. Much of the opposition seemed to be based on prejudice against his early revivals. It was evident that the true nature of those revivals—the methods used and the doctrines taught—had come to be widely misunderstood. The influence of Nettleton and Beecher, Finney believed, as much as anything, had undermined confidence in the revival movement. It became apparent to Finney that it may have been a mistake to allow the early misrepresentations and attacks to go unchallenged. "The fact that no answers were made at the time, left the public abroad and without the range of those revivals, and where the facts were not known, to misapprehend their character."[7]

Finney was made acutely aware of this when he was in Scotland in 1859. Nettleton had died in 1844, and shortly afterward his biography was published.[8] Finney had hoped that the book would reveal the truth behind the opposition, how Nettleton and Beecher had come to misrepresent the early revivals. He was alarmed to find, however, that not only were there no explanations but Nettleton seemed rather to have justified himself in his course. This was bad enough; but when Finney discovered that the book was being used in Scotland to warn British Christians against him, the time had come to speak out.[9] He wrote a long letter to the editor of the Glasgow *Christian News,* much of which was taken up with details about Nettleton and his opposition. Finney pointed out, "Notwithstanding all that Mr Nettleton

[5] Oberlin College was founded in 1833 as "The Oberlin Collegiate Institute." Its name was officially changed to "Oberlin College" in 1850. In this book, "Oberlin College" will normally be used for whatever period is being referred to. See Robert S. Fletcher, *A History of Oberlin College from Its Foundation Through the Civil War* (Oberlin: Oberlin College, 1943), p. 887.

[6] See C. G. Finney, *The Prevailing Prayer-Meeting* (London: Ward, 1859).

[7] MS 281.

[8] Bennet Tyler, *Memoir of the Life and Character of Asahel Nettleton, D.D.* (Hartford: Robins and Smith, 1844).

[9] "Mr. Finney's Career," in Bennet Tyler, *Nettleton and His Labours: Being the Memoir of Dr. Nettleton . . . {with} an introduction: by Rev. Andrew A. Bonar* (Edinburgh: Clark, 1854), p. 449; Alexander MacLeod, *The Truth of the Gospel* (Glasgow: Gallie, 1859), pp. 16–20; "Professor Finney," *The British Standard* (London), 8 April 1859, p. 108; "The Truth of the Gospel," *The Christian News* (Glasgow), 16 April 1859, p. 2; John Moore to the editor, 30 August 1859, *The Christian News,* 3 September 1859, p. 2; and "Mr. Finney's Career and Theology," *The Christian News,* 10 September 1859, p. 5.

wrote and published against me, this is the first time that I have put pen to paper with design to publish a word in reply."[10] Having once broken silence, Finney soon had plans to expose the whole opposition and how it had arisen. Something of the kind needed to be done if the future of revivals was not to be continually overshadowed by the specter of Nettleton.

The situation confronted by Finney in Britain was only one aspect of a much more fundamental problem that was facing him. A generation of Christians was growing up who knew little of the depth of spiritual experience and power of transformed lives that had been the significant feature of the revivals of the 1820s and 1830s. Although many of the new doctrines and measures that had once raised such controversy in the churches had now come to be widely accepted, there was an ignorance of the essential principles behind them that were the motivating force.

Finney was also becoming increasingly aware of a deep concern that was being felt by the friends of revivals about one of the causes of this ignorance. It was eloquently stated in an article in the *Congregational Herald* by a writer who confidently asserted:

> We shall but echo the voice of thousands when we say that Mr. Finney ought to write and publish, or leave behind him, a detailed history of the great revivals in Central New York which occurred in connection with his early labors. Such a work must be largely autobiographical, and should be written, we think, without delay. We are aware this may be thought a remarkable suggestion. We will give our reasons for making it, somewhat after Mr. Finney's own method of sermonizing.
>
> 1. Future generations will be eager to know the whole history of a man who was the means of the conversion of so many thousands of souls, both in this country and in the father land, and who has awakened so general an interest in the whole subject of revivals. That eagerness, as the world moves toward the Millennium, will be vastly greater than that manifested in the history of a conqueror, though he may have been the hero of a hundred battles.
>
> 2. It is evident that no other pen can supply the place of Mr. Finney's in this work. His friends would be partial, and his enemies would not be impartial. No one else can give us a reliable account of his early life. And this reason has greater emphasis as his years increase and his contemporaries are laid in the grave. Mr. F. is already approaching three score and ten.
>
> 3. Many apocryphal stories of his conversion and his early labors, are already afloat, and they will multiply rather than diminish, unless there is some authentic record with which they may be compared.
>
> 4. Unless Mr. Finney himself gives it, the history of those wonderful displays of Divine grace—the early revivals at Rochester, Rome, Whitesboro, Utica, and other places—will, to a degree, be lost to the church. Most of the generation who witnessed them have already passed away, and no one person was with Mr. F. in them all. The facts have never been put on record. They exist nowhere but in Mr. F's memory. It is a solemn duty he owes to the church of Christ to preserve this portion of her history.

[10]Finney to the editor, 10 September 1859, *The Christian News,* 17 September 1859, p. 5.

5. It is understood, or at least it has been asserted, that Mr. Finney in his riper years admits serious mistakes in his early labors. He owes it to posterity to tell precisely what those mistakes were, and "what they were not", that (1.) his admirers may not imitate them, and (2.) that his enemies may not use his own authority to condemn what his mature judgment approved.

6. Such a book, written in Mr. Finney's simple, lucid style, would be read by millions, and, there is reason to believe, would of itself be a means of grace to thousands. The details of his conversion and his Christian experience will preach to a multitude of captivated readers who would not read his sermons.

7. The world will better understand his theology when they have his experience to interpret it, and know the process through which his own mind was carried. We might easily go on to Fifteenthly, but seven good reasons are enough. We entreat Mr. Finney to weigh these reasons; and we charge his immediate friends to see that he does not neglect this work. We should not have said thus much except for the conviction that this important history is in danger of being lost to the world.[11]

The force of these arguments was not lost on Finney. He became onvinced himself of the need for something to be done. Not long after, in peaking of the revivals in which he had been involved, he had this to say:

> Indeed, I doubt if the world has ever witnessed revivals more pure, more powerful, more lasting and desirable in their results than those that have occurred in this country during the last forty or fifty years. If my health will allow, I hope to write some account of the revivals that have occurred under my observation, and since I have been in this ministry, for the purpose, if possible, of disabusing the minds of those who have been prejudiced against those revivals by false reports.[12]

inney's Account of His Revivals

Here, then, was the plan Finney had in mind. But it was to be several years efore he did anything about it. After Finney returned from England in 1860, is health started to deteriorate, and his age began to tell. When he was well nough, his duties in Oberlin College, where he had become the president in 851, and his attempts to promote revival in the community took up all his trength. Then in January 1866, at the height of one of the greatest revivals ver experienced in Oberlin, Finney's health gave way. He became seriously l and had to be confined to bed for three months. It was clear to everyone hat his life might not be prolonged much longer. By the time he had ecovered, the trustees of the college and his colleagues on the faculty etermined to take action. At the trustees' meeting on 26 June 1866, at which inney was present, the following resolution was passed:

> On motion voted that Bretherin H. Cowles and John Keep be appointed a committee to act in connection with a similar committee of the Faculty to confer with *President Finney* with reference to compiling a biographical sketch of his life and preparing it for publication.[13]

[11] Reprinted in *OE,* 21 November 1860, p. 187.
[12] *OE,* 26 November 1861, p. 178.
[13] Oberlin College Board of Trustees, Minutes, 26 June 1866, Oberlin College Archives,

This pressure from his colleagues, at a time when Finney could see that he might not have long to live, appears to have been a deciding factor in persuading him to start work on his narrative.

There was, however, another factor. In 1863 Lyman Beecher died; and two years later his autobiography was published.[14] To his utter amazement Finney discovered that the whole issue of misunderstandings and cover-ups about the early opposition to the revivals was yet again being revived and repeated; and Beecher was presented as justifying that opposition to the day of his death. It was not only the specter of Nettleton that now haunted Finney, but it was the specter of Beecher as well. The shock of reading this book could well have been what galvanized Finney into action.

In response to the resolution of the trustees, Finney had to make up his mind. Shortly afterward, in a document dated 12 July 1866, he put down the following points:

> I have been greatly urged to undertake this work by friends in this country & in Europe. I have not set about it hitherto—1. Because I dislike Auto Biographies. 2. Because, at any rate, I can not bear to write my own. 3. Because I have not had spare time & strength even if I were disposed to undertake it. 4. I have not felt clear that God called me to this work. 5. I have kept no journal & must depend too much on memory to be as accurate as I wish to be in preparing such a work for the press. 6. The events of my own life are, or seem to me to be, of too little importance to be published in [a] book. 6. It does not seem to me that the publick can be much interested in the question of my relations to the great reformatory movements of the present century. 6. So little interest do I feel in having the publick understand the part I have borne in these reforms, that if I know myself I am willing to have future generations remain ignorant of my agency in them. And if no higher reasons existed for the publication than those that relate to myself I would not write a sentence. But far other & higher reasons are urged for undertaking this work. Such as 1. The truth of history demands it. Very much misapprehension has long existed upon the question of the great revivals of the last 50 years & of my relation to them. 2. In consequence of these misapprehensions the cause of revivals has suffered & is likely to continue to suffer a false history of those revivals to go down to the future generations of christians. 2. It is truly urged that no living man can so thoroughly correct history on this subject as I can because I was present in the midst of those great movements of God's Spirit which were early & principally subjects of so much misrepresentation. 3. Much has been written & published to discredit those revivals while their friends & promoters have been too busy in carrying them on to turn aside to defend them by replying to those who misrepresented them. 4. So true is this that it has long been common for good men & friends of revivals to speak of those revivals as having been unhappily marred with much that was wrong & to be greatly lamented. 5. Some great & good men were deceived by opposers of those revivals & committed themselves to the opposition by publishing pamphlets

microfilm. The book containing the faculty records for this period is missing. Finney had resigned from the presidency of the college in August the previous year.

[14] *Autobiography, Correspondence, etc., of Lyman Beecher, D.D.*, ed. Charles Beecher, 2 vols. (New York: Harper, 1864, 1865). A new edition of this work, edited by Barbara M. Cross, was published in 1961 by the Belknap Press of Harvard University Press.

& letters in which there was much that needs correction. 6. The cause of revivals demands the substantial facts in regard to what was called in New England the western revivals & which were stigmatized as being promoted by "New Measures"[.][15]

Here the document ends. It would appear that Finney had now made up his mind to start working on his revival memories.

The "Revival Sketches" in The Advance

There is, however, one more factor of some significance in what was happening at that time. While the committee was trying to persuade Finney to start writing, John Keep, the most senior of the trustees at Oberlin, wrote a letter to Truman Hastings, an elderly lawyer then living in Cleveland.[16] He received the following in reply, dated 20 July 1866:

> For many years I have felt, and often with great pain, that more than one half of the advantages to the church at large which might have resulted from the labor of Mr. Finney have been lost, for the want of a *true,* and *rational* account of them, and of the occasion which gave them *shape.* I rejoice, therefore, at the movement you are about to inaugurate. The task of collecting and collating the facts, will be laborious. Nearly all have died, or become aged, who could have aided you in his earlier revivals, or who could analize the existing hyper Orthodoxy, which his labors providentially designed to meet and overthrow. It is still possible to rescue much that is valuable from the wreck of time. I was daily with Mr. F. at Troy before, during the time, and after he was there. I visited Rome Utica Clinton and Auburn several times during his labors at those places during his administration and became pretty well posted as to the general nature of the work in each place. Scarcely any thing occurred at Troy beyond the sphere of my personal knowledge. I was also familiar with the causes which led to the New Lebanon Convention and with its members (most of them) and with their doings. But these things occurred and transpired many years ago, and it would require a good deal of labor to resuscitate them. Still it can be done with patient effort, time and industry. Many things I remember without effort, others I could recal. In regard to the later labors of Mr. F. in Western New York I know little. Yet I am very generally acquainted there and know how he was esteemed and treated, both by the churches, and by intelligent Laymen outside of the church. But as to detail I know but little. Now I am willing to aid you all I can; but you can doubtless find others that can do far more as well as far better. What little I can do, is at your service. You ask for *names.* In Troy N.Y. I know of but one now living upon whose candor and recollection I could rely, and that one is Silas K. Stow Esqr. Mrs. Genl Gould of Rochester was much there and at New Lebanon, and she might aid you greatly. She read truth and the events almost by intuition, and is a highly intelligent Lady. I know of no one in Oneida County to whom I could refer. I

[15]This document is in Miscellaneous Items, Finney Papers, microfilm, roll 8.

[16]Truman Hastings (1798–1884) was a lawyer in Troy in 1826 when Finney was there and was later in Rochester, where Finney stayed with him for a time in 1855. He was a brother of Finney's old friend and colleague Thomas Hastings, the musician and hymnwriter. See H. H. Kellogg, "The Hasting's Family," *NYE,* 20 January 1881, p. 8; Louis Chapin to G. F. Wright, 10 February 1889, Wright Papers, box 7; and letters of T. Hastings to Finney in the Finney Papers.

could explain about the "whipping" case which made so much noise at one time. I knew the parties.

In Rochester I would refer to Frederick Starr Hon. Addison Gardiner, Samuel Porter, Dr. Shaw Rev. Mr. Ellenwood and George W Parsons, Esqr. Also to Mrs Gould, Mrs R. Lester, &c.

I believe I have among my papers, but where exactly I do not recollect, the "Narrative of the One[i]da Presbytery," giving some account of the labors of Mr Finney in their churches. I may also have some other memorandums, but I cant now tell. On learning the scope of your undertaking more fully, I can at once tell you what I can do.

The work, I think should contain a full "diagnosis" of the Theological Night Mare, under which the Churches were prior to the advent of Mr Finney, as well as of the means he used to break it up. We shall soon need another Finney to break up the new type of the Paralizer of Christian activity in the work of Saving Souls.[17]

It appears from this letter that a project was on foot much more comprehensive than simply getting Finney to write out his story of the revivals. The knowledge that a serious effort was also being made by others may well have contributed to the process whereby Finney decided to do his part in recovering the true history of those early revivals.

This letter of Hastings, however, has further significance. Eighteen months later *The Advance,* a weekly Congregational paper, published a series of ten "Revival Sketches" under the pseudonym "SENEX." These articles give a history of the revival movement under Finney from about 1820 to 1827. They deal with the previous condition of the churches; the theological climate prior to Finney's advent; the revivals from 1820 to 1824, leading up to the Oneida County revivals; the characteristics of the different fields of labor; the revival in Troy, which the writer concentrates on in particular; Finney's measures and the opposition they aroused; and the New Lebanon Convention. The author's explanation of the "whipping" scandal, his occasional use of legal terminology, and the fact that the sketches cover the very things raised by Hastings in his letter indicate, beyond a shadow of a doubt, that their author was Hastings.[18]

A comparison of the narrative of revivals then being written by Finney with the sketches being published shows a definite congruence. Whether there was any collaboration between the two men is not known. It is possible that the "Revival Sketches" were written before Finney had embarked on his undertaking. Hastings wrote in his eighth sketch:

It was the original intention of the writer to give a much fuller detail than has here been attempted of interesting incidents connected with these revivals; but he found that such a course would require a larger space in these

[17] T. Hastings to John Keep, 20 July 1866, Finney Papers, microfilm, roll 5.

[18] The "Revival Sketches" were published in *The Advance* (Chicago) from 5 December 1867 to 23 April 1868. The use, in particular, of the obscure legal term "felo de se," instead of "suicidal," to describe the accusations against Finney and others for the supposed whipping of children to get them to repent, shows the mind of a lawyer at work ("Revival Sketches—No. VIII," *The Advance,* 2 April 1868, p. 2).

> columns, than he felt at liberty to claim. Such a course, might also have seriously interfered with the contemplated labors of another and abler pen.[19]

Hastings is doubtless referring here to Finney. These sketches could have been seen by Finney before he had finished his own, but there is nothing to indicate that they were. Hastings and Finney shared a common perspective on the revivals, so it is not surprising that in many places their accounts are similar or complement each other. The title "Revival Sketches" seems to have an echo in "Revival Memories," published four years later by Finney in *The Independent.*[20]

The Purpose of Finney's Narrative

Although six years his junior, SENEX, like Finney, was an old man and was no doubt subject to the same difficulties in attempting to recollect what happened forty years previously. On the other hand, he clearly made use of contemporary documents, which lends a certain air of objective authenticity to his statements, a feature often missing from the narrative of Finney. The reliability of Finney's memory has troubled many readers of his *Memoirs.* Hastings's sketches help to provide some kind of check on Finney's account. The evidence from these and other sources shows that Finney was often incorrect in his statements. At other times, however, he was surprisingly accurate. His ability to remember, in minute detail, scenes that had transpired forty years earlier is due in part to his frequently repeating them in sermons, lectures, and conversation. Constant recall kept them fresh in his memory. Finney never pretended to have been able to remember the exact words of conversations that he relates.[21] And it is clear that he was not concerned with scholarly accuracy. The transcript that he made of extracts from Lyman Beecher's *Autobiography* and of James Cranbrook's letter have a number of errors that a simple reading through against the originals would have detected.[22] On the other hand, one of the main purposes was historical accuracy. He wrote, "I aim at securing the truth of history."[23] And this is confirmed by alterations that he made to the text in view of errors that were pointed out and research that he did to substantiate his position. Hiram Mead, a later professor in the theological seminary at Oberlin, who knew Finney, wrote: "He certainly placed high value upon historic accuracy. His autobiography shows both his disposition and ability to write a truthful narrative. He might have been a good historian, but he was better adapted to philosophical investigation, and was interested more in metaphysical, than in physical truths."[24]

In aiming at securing "the truth of history," Finney was not aiming at anything like a detailed account of the early revival movements: "I have been obliged, in writing out this Narrative, to give only an outline of what the Lord

[19] "Revival Sketches—No. VIII," *The Advance,* 2 April 1868, p. 2.
[20] See pp. xxxv–xxxvi below.
[21] See MS 161.
[22] See MS 428 and 837–42.
[23] MS 399.
[24] Hiram Mead, "Charles Grandison Finney," *The Congregational Quarterly* (Boston) 19 (January 1877): 16.

has done, without attempting to give such details as would swell my narrative beyond reasonable dimensions." The cases of conversion he described were those of people the public might be more likely to know: "I have not thought best to go into a detailed account of the conversion of persons not known to the general public, unless there was something very striking or interesting that brought out some great principle in the administration of God's government."[25] The particular "truth of history" that concerned Finney was what lay behind the discredit that had come upon revivals. To understand this involved a careful examination of the nature of the opposition and the misunderstandings that had led to it. This in its turn required an understanding of the doctrines and the measures that had been at the heart of the controversy. These were the doctrines and measures that had been at the foundation of the revivals and had led to such remarkable results. Here, then, was Finney's main purpose: to give a sketch of the revivals, including the doctrines preached, the measures used, and the results, to "enable the church hereafter, partially at least, to estimate the power and purity of those great works of God."[26] In this way people might perhaps recapture the spirit of the early revival movement.

This was to be Finney's third great contribution to literature. His two previous major works had in their way also been concerned with the doctrines, the measures, and the results of those revivals. But if his *Lectures on Revivals of Religion* was taken up more with measures and his *Lectures on Systematic Theology* was concerned primarily with the doctrines, then the *Memoirs* preeminently set forth the results.[27]

HISTORY OF THE MANUSCRIPT

It is not clear exactly when Charles Finney started to write his narrative, but it was probably sometime in the summer or autumn of 1866. His grandson William Cochran wrote that he himself was an "inmate" of the Finney family "from the fall of 1866 to the fall of 1869, during which time Mr. Finney was engaged in the preparation of his 'Memoirs.'" Cochran went on to say:

> He was urged to do this by friends in the East who sent out a stenographer to assist him in the work. He was assured that it was of the utmost importance to preserve the record of the wonderful revivals which attended his labors, for the instruction of posterity and the stimulus of like self-sacrificing labor on the part of others. The work was really distasteful to him and he dismissed the stenographer after a few months and destroyed a large part of her work, as it seemed to him to be akin to self-laudation and an attempt to claim the glory which belonged to God alone. His friends persisted and, a year later, another stenographer was employed, with whose assistance the Memoirs were completed, practically as they now appear in print.[28]

[25]MS 922.
[26]MS 5.
[27]C. G. Finney, *Lectures on Revivals of Religion* (New York: Taylor, 1835); and Finney, *Lectures on Systematic Theology* (Oberlin: James M. Fitch, 1846).
[28]Cochran, *Charles Grandison Finney,* pp. 5–6.

Henry Matson, the Stenographer

It is not known who the first stenographer was, and as far as we know, nothing has survived of her work. The second stenographer, however, was the Reverend Henry Matson. Born in 1829 in Ellsworth, Ohio, the son of a carpenter, he had already been a stenographer before entering Oberlin College in 1854. After graduating from the seminary in 1861, he had pastorates in Congregational churches in Massachusetts and Ohio until August 1867, when he returned to Oberlin "and found a congenial task in serving President Finney, who dictated to him his autobiography."[29] In August 1868 he took charge of the Congregational church in Nelson, Ohio, where he remained until September 1872. He then returned to Oberlin and was employed as librarian at the college from 1874 until 1887, when he resigned to devote his time to literary pursuits. He died in Oberlin in 1901.[30]

Although Matson was a stenographer, he may not have been good enough at shorthand to suit Finney. Finney complained of having to dictate the work instead of speaking naturally as he would to an interested audience.[31] But he persevered through the winter and completed dictation of the first draft on 13 January 1868.[32] Matson's fair copy was written in ink on 30-by-19-centimeter sheets of lined white paper. Most sheets had writing on only one side. The manuscript ran to about 893 pages.[33] When it was completed Finney started to revise it. The first 140 pages were completely rewritten and expanded to fill 272 pages.[34] Finney was evidently planning further revision and was still employing Matson in April, when there was a new development.[35]

Loan of the Manuscript to Lewis Tappan

About that time Lewis Tappan heard about the narrative. Tappan had been the pioneer of the Free-church movement in New York and was an old friend of Finney's. He and his brother Arthur were wealthy merchants in New York who had sponsored Finney's revivals there as early as 1829. They were leading evangelical laymen who spent their time and their wealth furthering every good cause. Lewis had been a leader in the antislavery movement and had been critical of Finney's failure to participate actively in that movement.

[29] See biographical details in Matson's handwriting in Alumni Records, file 28/9, box 64, Oberlin College Archives; and *The Oberlin News,* 24 May 1901, p. 1. This obituary gives the date when Finney dictated his memoirs to Matson as 1872, but that is clearly a mistake. *The Congregational Quarterly* 10 (January 1868): 88, 125; and 11 (January 1869): 117, indicates that he was resident at Oberlin in 1867 and 1868 and that the narrative was completed by December of 1868 (see MS 1055).

[30] See *General Catalogue of Oberlin College, 1833–1908* (Oberlin, 1909), Introduction, p. 162, and p. 651.

[31] See Lewis Tappan to Finney, 10 June 1868; and 18 June 1868, where he wrote: "I regret that I had not known & felt as much as I do now on the subject before the amanuensis began his labor, so that a good short-hand writer could have been employed to take down the Narrative as rapidly as you chose to deliver it" (Finney Papers, microfilm, roll 5).

[32] See Finney to E. P. Marvin, 7 February 1868, Finney Papers, file 2/2/2, box 9; and MS 1050.

[33] Page 891 is the last page of the first draft that has survived. But the writing does not end on that page. Two additional pages appear to have been subsequently rewritten (see p. 34 n. 27 [MS 59]).

[34] Pages 141ff. were renumbered accordingly, so that p. 891 became p. 1023.

[35] Lewis Tappan to Finney, 30 April 1868, Finney Papers, microfilm, roll 5.

Henry Matson. The stenographer employed by Finney in the dictation of his memoirs. This photograph was taken some time after 1886. Courtesy Oberlin College Archives.

But they nevertheless had great regard for one another and a deep friendship that lasted over the years.[36]

Tappan learned that Finney had "dictated to an amanuensis 1000 pages of Revival facts," and he was so excited that he wrote to Finney. He offered to pay the fees of the stenographer and encouraged Finney to publish the narrative. He also expressed an interest in reading it. And to his great delight Finney sent it to him. It arrived on 7 May.[37]

There then followed an extensive correspondence in which Tappan expressed his enthusiasm about the work.[38] He made all sorts of suggestions about getting it edited and published, and he offered to help financially and in other ways. But this was all to no avail. Finney refused to let anyone but

[36] See Bertram Wyatt-Brown, *Lewis Tappan and the Evangelical War Against Slavery* (Cleveland: Press of Western Reserve University, 1969); and *DAB*.

[37] John Marsh to Finney, 16 May 1868; and Tappan to Finney, 24 April and 8 May 1868, Finney Papers, microfilm, roll 5.

[38] There are fourteen letters in the Finney Papers written by Tappan to Finney at this time. Tappan refers to eleven letters from Finney, but these are not in the Lewis Tappan Papers in the Library of Congress.

'appan and his wife read it, and he would make no commitment to publish. Iowever, at the suggestion of Joshua Leavitt, another old friend, Tappan did ucceed in persuading Finney to let him make a copy. Finney reluctantly greed, on the condition that Tappan let no one else see it and that he would estroy it or hand it over to Finney on request. So, with the assistance of a oung man, the narrative was copied. On 12 July Tappan could write to 'inney, "My abstract makes 416 pages foolscap. Part is a full copy & part an bridgment."[39]

The manuscript that has come down to us is essentially the draft that was ent to Tappan. But Tappan made a number of suggestions about changes that e thought should be made. On 2 June he wrote:

> *The Narrative needs a name.* Why not say "Narrative of Revivals, by Rev. Charles G. Finney."
>
> It should be divided into Chapters. It should also have an Index.
>
> The paragraphs are not as they should be; some being too long—some too short—while the Narrative is broken up too much into paragraphs where it should not be.
>
> I notice that you make frequent mention of Rev George W. Gale as Brother Gale, and so of other persons, ministers & laymen. Would it not be in better taste to say, after *once* mentioning Mr Gale as brother or Dear Brother, to say, Mr Gale.

'appan also reckoned that the narrative needed correction, "as there are edundancies & other minor errors of various sorts." "There is considerable epetition, and in accordance with your style of preaching this you may itend, but it is worthy of consideration, I think, whether it is so useful in a ook as in the delivery of a sermon."[40] And as an example of how sentence onstruction, punctuation, paragraphing, and other minor changes would iake for easier reading, he set out for Finney's consideration the first page of ie text, showing in parallel columns the original and Tappan's altered ersion.[41]

When Finney received the manuscript back in July, he set about nplementing some of these changes. He may have planned to rewrite the 'hole narrative. Certainly the first sixteen pages were completely revised, sing Matson's help and incorporating some of Tappan's suggestions. But Iatson left Oberlin in August, and Finney may have had to content himself ith making further changes and additions himself.[42] Subsequent alterations re in Finney's handwriting.

[39]Tappan to Finney, 12 July 1868, Finney Papers, microfilm, roll 5.

[40]Tappan to Finney, 11 May and 12 July 1868, Finney Papers, microfilm, roll 5.

[41]Tappan to Finney, 2 June 1868, Finney Papers, microfilm, roll 5. For the text of page 1 as ritten down by Tappan, see p. 1, n. 1 (MS 1).

[42]There are a number of other manuscripts in Matson's handwriting in the Finney Papers, cluding the report of a Masonic meeting and a set of Finney's lecture notes. In a tribute to nney published soon after his death, Matson wrote:

> Mr. Finney seems to me to have been one of those great men of a transition period, who may be said rather to make a new time than to be made by their own. . . .
>
> The one chief lesson of his life is, the singleness and entireness of his devotion to his great work. Called and consecrated by God to the work of saving souls, he gave himself wholly to it. The intensity and constancy of his ardor were surprising. The

The first sixteen pages were expanded to twenty pages, the subsequen pages 17 and following being renumbered 21 and following. A space was lef at the top of the first page above the chapter heading of chapter I. This spac was probably for the title of the narrative, which was never inserted. Finne followed Tappan's suggestion of dividing the narrative up into chapters. I many cases Finney had to rearrange the text to include the headings, an where there was not room on the sheet, he pasted on an additional piece c paper containing the alterations. Finney also inserted paragraph mark throughout the text. In the rewritten pages 1–20, Gale's name was prefixe with "Mr." This change was also made in some other places but not generall throughout the manuscript. Nor did Finney remove any of the redundancie or repetitions that Tappan complained about.[43]

In commenting about Finney's account of Tappan's own conversio Tappan wrote, "Before the Narrative is printed (if it ever gets into type) should like to revise what you say of Ware[44] & myself, that it may be mor correct."[45] Finney must have given Tappan permission to make the necessar changes, for these appear in Tappan's handwriting on pages 555–59 and 64 of the manuscript. Some other marginal notations and comments also i Tappan's handwriting occur in a few places.

One of the major concerns that Finney had was to set the record straigh about the opposition of Lyman Beecher and Asahel Nettleton to the earl revivals in New York State. He evidently had worries about how to deal wit this. He wanted to expose their errors but was concerned about appearing t have a wrong spirit.

Tappan, on the other hand, had no doubts about what Finney ought to d He had been reading the *Autobiography* of Lyman Beecher before Finney se him the manuscript, and he drew Finney's attention to it. Finney must hav written something about this in reply, because Tappan had just started a lette to Finney thanking him for sending the manuscript when he cut short h letter:

> After writing so far your letter of the 5th is received. I think you ought to correct what is wrong in Dr Beecher's statements. Cannot you get Dr Beman to corroborate your correction? I advise that you dictate to the amanuensis a review of Dr B's statement & send it as soon as you can to Dr Beman for his approval.[46]

sacred fire seemed never to burn low. The secret of his life, its innermost spring, its central motive, was this love for souls (H. Matson, "Mr. Finney," *Oberlin Review,* 17 November 1875, pp. 207–8).

[43] Finney had written about repetition in his earlier work on systematic theology:
There is a good deal of repetition in the work. This I judged to be indispensable to perspicuity. Perhaps the reader will not agree with me in this, and may think he should have understood me just as well if I had repeated less. But my experience upon this subject after having taught these truths for years has ripened the conviction that there is no other way of being understood upon such a subject (Finney, *Lectures on Systematic Theology,* p. iv).

[44] Rev. Henry Ware, Jr.

[45] Tappan to Finney, 2 June 1868, Finney Papers, microfilm, roll 5.

[46] Tappan to Finney, 8 May 1868, Finney Papers, microfilm, roll 5. Dr. Beman was Nathan S. Beman, who had been minister of the First Presbyterian Church in Troy, New York, and w living in retirement in Carbondale, Illinois. See *NYE,* 17 August 1871, p. 4.

Finney's concern about this must have been considerable, for Tappan wrote to him on 2 June:

> I think you ought to set the world right with respect to the misstatements of Dr Beecher & Mr Nettleton, but I would do it in a manner to show that these misstate nts resulted from the *peculiarities* of these brethren, the brusque, conservative, habits of one & the timidity, sensitiveness, of the other; and probably the *old age* of both.[47] It would not do to have it appear that you feel wounded on personal grounds, or that you needlessly assail the characters of those useful, but imperfect men. And I would avoid thrusting a pole into a hornet's nest, both as it respects reader & friends. You may smile at my giving such cautions to you, not only in this matter but in others. I feel desirous that the Narrative should be magnanimous; that it should not give undue prominence to what has been said by Doctors B. and N. (By the way Nettleton was not a Doctor, was he?) & that the great body of [Christ]ian people, at this day, should acquiesce in what may be said of Dr B. & Mr N. in the Narrative.

And again on 10 June Tappan wrote:

> I forgot to say that in your allusions to Dr B. and Mr N etc. I saw no evidence of a bad spirit.
>
> As to discrepancies between your recollection of facts, and the remembrances of other people, you are not responsible for their recollections or the want of them. . . .
>
> I put no confidence in Dr B's statements, so far as they differ from yours. His mind was differently constructed. Besides his action was more impulsive than yours. He was a trimmer, & had less respect to the means than the end. I thought everything of him until I knew you. You had system & he jerks. He had some qualities superior to yours. Notwithstanding this he did not always follow his convictions of duty. He believed in the doctrine of expediency to a criminal excess I thought. Of course his fence was in Virginia fashion, while yours was on a straight line.
>
> State the facts, dear Bro. as they lie in your mind, in a right spirit, & fear nothing. If *hornets* buzz about your head never mind. God will take care of the truth.

And in another letter, dated 18 June, Tappan wrote,

> The truth ought to be published, in a mild & [Christ]ian manner, respecting the statements made by Drs B & N. or their representatives, not in a controversial spirit but in accordance with the injunction, "speaking the truth in love," not "as pleasing man but God."

The result of all this correspondence was that Finney wrote some entirely new sections dealing with Beecher and Nettleton's opposition and the statements in their biographies that criticized him. These appear, for example, on pages 396–97, 425–39, 453–54, 698, and 943–46 of the manuscript. It is interesting to note that Finney was revising his *Lectures on Revivals of Religion* about that time and added a significant footnote there also. In the lecture that took the general assembly of the Presbyterian church to task for

[47] At the time of their conflict with Finney, Beecher was fifty-two years old, and Nettleton was forty-four. Finney was thirty-five.

their critical attitude toward the great revival of 1831, he added, "The strange opposition of such men as Dr. Lyman Beecher and Mr. Nettleton had much to do with provoking and sustaining this opposition."[48] These occurrences highlight how central to the whole writing of the narrative was Finney's preoccupation with Beecher and Nettleton.

The new changes required renumbering of the manuscript, so that page 1023 became 1053. Two final pages were then added, bringing the narrative up to date in December 1868.[49] Apart from some changes that appear to have been made in 1872, that seems to have completed the final version.

In 1865 Lewis Tappan's brother Arthur had died, and Lewis prepared a biography of him that was published in 1870. Tappan wrote to Finney to get material for the book, and he received a letter in reply, some of which was published in an appendix. But he also included two pages of extracts that he said Finney had "narrated . . . in a letter to the compiler."[50] However, it is clear that these extracts are taken from pages 670–81 of the manuscript of the narrative. There are some minor changes, and some of it is an abstract, but much of it is word for word the same. So it is possible that we have here some examples of the copy that Tappan had taken. It is interesting that in the list of contents of the chapters at the beginning of the book, this section is called "Mr. Finney's Narrative."[51]

PUBLICATION OF THE MEMOIRS

If Finney's friends had had difficulty persuading him to write his narrative, they had even greater difficulty in persuading him to publish it. While still at work on the manuscript, Finney had written to James and Alice Barlow, friends of his in England, "If this narrative is ever published I do not intend it shall be while I live."[52] Tappan thought he should publish it immediately and tried to persuade him, but Finney refused to yield to pressure. However, the idea was not rejected entirely. He hinted to Tappan that he might publish a revised version. And when he was consulting Tappan soon afterward about getting his other theological works reissued, he included the narrative with them. Tappan offered to help and suggested a plan for financing it, but nothing more was done at the time.[53]

Some years later, however, this scheme was brought forward again. In October 1872 Finney approached Henry Hoyt, a Boston publisher and a deacon at Park Street Church, about reissuing his works, and again he mentioned the narrative. Hoyt's reply was quite enthusiastic. "The work on Revivals, if a new one, written in narrative & from the experience of your life,

[48] Charles G. Finney, *Lectures on Revivals of Religion,* a new edition, revised and enlarged by the author (Oberlin: Goodrich, 1868), p. 275.

[49] See MS 1055.

[50] Lewis Tappan, *The Life of Arthur Tappan* (New York: Hurd and Houghton, 1870), pp. 238–40.

[51] Lewis Tappan died in 1873, but what became of his copy of the narrative after his death is not known. It is not among the Tappan Papers in the Library of Congress.

[52] Finney to J. and A. Barlow, 8 January 1868, Correspondence of Charles G. Finney, 1830–1875, Oberlin College Archives, microfilm.

[53] Tappan to Finney, 18 June and 23 July 1868, Finney Papers, microfilm, roll 5.

would be more decidedly in my line of publications."[54] It is significant that Finney had approached a publishing firm when he did, because there is other evidence that he may have been seriously contemplating publishing his narrative at that particular time.

The "Revival Memories" in The Independent

Early in 1871 Finney received a letter from the office editor of the New York *Independent,* which read:

> It has occurred to me that a rousing article from you, of a religious character would be of service to our readers. What do you say to a brief account of the revivals of thirty and forty years ago in which you took part, with the natural "application" to the needs of the church at the present time. If you like it the columns of the Independent are open to you for an article of reasonable length, or for more than one if disconnected.[55]

This letter must have recalled what Tappan had suggested back in 1868 when he had read the manuscript:

> Sometimes I think it may be best to have the narrative published in one of the weekly "religious" newspapers. The *Advance* or the *Independent.* It would be of immense service to either of them, but it would take a year to publish the narrative in this way, 2 columns a week. I should hesitate about offering it to the Independent lest it should be supposed you & your friends sanctioned the course that paper has taken of late.[56]

Tappan and Finney both thought the religious tone of *The Independent* had declined. For example, the editor had refused to publish all Finney's letters on Freemasonry in 1868. Tappan reckoned it was for fear of losing subscribers, and he was not really sorry: "I did not like very well to see you using such a '*religious* paper' as a channel of communication to the public."[57] So when the invitation came to write for them, Finney was very cautious.[58] Nevertheless, he eventually offered them several articles on various aspects of the Spirit-filled life. In one of these, published on 4 July 1872, he had occasion to describe the revival at Antwerp and "Sodom."[59] This is similar to the account in the manuscript narrative. In the article, Finney makes particular reference to the conversion of Rev. Gorham Cross, the father of Roselle Theodore Cross, the principal of the preparatory department of Oberlin College. In

[54] Henry Hoyt to Finney, 2 November 1872, Finney Papers, microfilm, roll 5; and *NYE,* 7 October 1858, p. 1.

[55] William Hayes Ward to Finney, 21 February 1871, Finney Papers, microfilm, roll 6.

[56] Tappan to Finney, 11 May 1868, Finney Papers, microfilm, roll 5.

[57] Tappan to Finney, 30 April and 12 July 1868, Finney Papers, microfilm, roll 5. Theodore Tilton, the editor of *The Independent,* had earlier announced "with something of a flourish that the *Independent* had ceased to be a Congregational organ and will henceforth be conducted as 'a religious paper' "(*The Lorain County News* [Oberlin], 22 May 1867, p. 2).

[58] See William Hayes Ward to Finney, 27 February 1871, and Henry C. Bowen to Finney, 24 April 1871, Finney Papers, microfilm, roll 6.

[59] "The Enduement of the Spirit," *The Independent* (New York), 4 July 1872, p. 2. Several of these articles were republished in 1944 by Victory Press of London as *Power from on High: A Selection of Articles on the Spirit-filled Life.*

view of this reference it is very interesting to read what R. T. Cross later had to say about Finney:

> His Autobiography which was dictated to an amanuensis in 1867, has proved to be one of the most interesting and useful of all the autobiographies ever written. About five years after it was written and several years before it was printed, it was my privilege to read a large part of the manuscript to Mr. Finney, at his request, and to be frequently interrupted in the reading by his running comments and fuller versions of many of the incidents narrated, especially the scene at "Sodom" (page 101) at which my father, still living, was present as a young man.[60]

This occurred over several days in December 1872.[61] It is therefore of particular interest to find in the new year that Finney embarked on what appeared to be the start of a new series of articles in *The Independent,* with the specific title "Revival Memories." Taking up where he had left off at "Sodom," he wrote two articles describing the revival in Gouverneur and a third on the revival in Philadelphia.[62] These cover the same ground as the manuscript, but as Finney himself stated, they were written independently.[63]

It seems quite significant that, whereas Finney did not offer actual extracts of the narrative to *The Independent,* he did offer the whole of it at the very same time to a publisher. It looks as though Finney had decided at last to go ahead and have it published. But for some reason this was not to be. He does not seem to have taken up Henry Hoyt's offer, and no more "Revival Memories" appeared in *The Independent.* He continued to write for that paper right up to his death in 1875, and several of the articles contain revival reminiscences that were also covered in the narrative. But the narrative itself remained unpublished during his lifetime.

One of the reasons Finney gave for not publishing his narrative was the fear of hurting people. To be faithful to the past as he saw it, he would have to expose people's errors and faults, and he was deeply sensitive to the offense that this would cause. Often in his published sermons and articles he disguised the anecdotes by withholding the names of the participants if there

[60] R. T. Cross, "The Finney Centennial," in *The Advance,* 25 August 1892, p. 668. Finney may have required someone to read the manuscript to him because of the deterioration of his eyesight. It is perhaps significant that about this time in 1872, Gorham Cross and his wife visited the Finneys at Oberlin. See Daniel W. Beaman, "The Crosses at Oberlin," typescript dated 20 April 1963, Alumni Records, file 28/1, "Judson Newell Cross," Oberlin College Archives.

[61] Roselle Theodore Cross, "Memories of Charles G. Finney," typescript, n.d., p. 4, Alumni Records, file 28/1, "Roselle Theodore Cross," Oberlin College Archives (reference from Gertrude Jacob). Cross said that the narrative "had then been written several years and [Finney] wanted to see or hear how it sounded." It seems probable that a number of changes made by Finney in the manuscript in blacker ink and a larger script were done at this time in association with rereading the manuscript. See, in particular, changes in the chapter entitled "Sodom," MS 199 and also MS 177.

[62] See *The Independent,* 23 January 1873, pp. 102–3; 30 January 1873, pp. 134–35; and 24 April 1873, p. 516. A further article entitled "Revival Memories" is in the Finney Papers. It is in the handwriting of Finney's third wife, Rebecca, and was probably written at this time but was not published in *The Independent.* It would appear to be the first in the series, and it deals with the revival in Evans Mills (see Miscellaneous Items, Finney Papers, microfilm, roll 8).

[63] See the unpublished letter dated 10 June 1873 to the editor of the *Examiner and Chronicle,* Miscellaneous Items, Finney Papers, microfilm, roll 8.

was any possibility of someone taking offense. For example, in a later article in *The Independent,* he concludes an anecdote with these words: "I forbear to give names and places, because I would not wound the feelings of relatives and friends of those deceased persons."[64] Yet in the corresponding story in the manuscript of the narrative, the names and places are given in full. Because the narrative was so personal and frank, Finney must have had very grave doubts about the wisdom of publishing the full truth as he recalled it. That this was what turned the balance against publishing is made clear in what Finney said to his wife as he lay dying. Years later she told G. F. Wright, who was working on a biography of Finney, that

> on that last night of his life, he directed me, as his *wisest* thought *then,* to burn his Ms. of the Narrative of Revivals, and the numerous letters that were stored in the Attic. He said he feared there were things in them, that might do more harm by unnecessarily wounding the feelings of good people, than all the *good* that was in them, could atone for. I *did* not burn them.[65]

If Finney felt so strongly, why did Mrs. Finney not comply with his wishes? She must have felt justified in what she did. She mentions that Finney made "replies to my objections." It is possible that she may have dissuaded Finney from such drastic action. James H. Fairchild, in his preface to the first edition of the *Memoirs,* wrote, "He left the manuscript at the disposal of his family, having never decided, in his own mind, that it was desirable to publish it."

Finney died on 16 August 1875. He had made no specific provision for the narrative in his will. He left most of his property to be given "in equal portions share and share alike" to his children, "earnestly requesting and expecting them to use it in a way that will benefit the cause of Christ."[66] The children were Helen, wife of Jacob Dolson Cox, a Civil War general and lawyer in Cleveland; Charles, a lawyer and journalist in California; Norton, a lawyer turned railroad engineer in Wisconsin; and Julia, the wife of James Monroe, an Ohio congressman. They all agreed that the narrative should be published, and they wanted Oberlin College to have the copyright and the profits. The manuscript was therefore presented to the college. It was accepted on 21 October, and James Harris Fairchild, the president of the college, was asked to undertake the task of preparing it for the publishers.[67]

James H. Fairchild, Editor of the First Edition

James H. Fairchild was the obvious choice to edit Finney's narrative. He was born in Stockbridge, Massachusetts, in 1817 and soon after moved with his family to the Western Reserve. After attending high school in Elyria, he entered the first freshman year at Oberlin College in 1834, graduating from the college in 1838 and from the theological department in 1841.

[64] "Hindrances to Revivals," *The Independent,* 16 April 1874, p. 2.

[65] Rebecca Finney to G. F. Wright, 22 October 1889, Wright Papers, box 8. It seems probable that she had intended to underline the word "not," rather than "did."

[66] "Last Will and Testament," dated 8 March 1872, Case No. 1886, Estate Film 20, Court of Common Pleas, Probate Division, Lorain County, Elyria, Ohio.

[67] See Oberlin College Prudential Committee Minutes, 21 October 1875; and "Annual Report of the President to the Trustees for 1875–1876," in Fairchild Papers.

James Harris Fairchild. Finney's successor in the presidency of Oberlin College and editor of the first edition of Finney's *Memoirs*. From an 1875 class album. Courtesy Oberlin College Archives.

During Fairchild's theological course he was responsible for tutoring in classics, and after his graduation he quite naturally slipped into the role of head of the department of languages. Thereafter he was to fill almost every academic post in the college. In 1856 he assisted Finney in the theological department, and in 1859 he became associate professor of theology, finally taking over the job of professor of theology from Finney in 1869. During Finney's presidency much of the detailed administrative work of the college fell on Fairchild's shoulders, and after Finney retired in 1865 Fairchild quite easily slipped into the role of president of the college the next year. He became the ideal man to steer Oberlin through the difficult years of transition after the Civil War. Under Fairchild's administration Oberlin lost some of its more radical and fervent religious character, but it gained in respectability and prestige. Fairchild was successful as a college president and was an able theologian and writer, and he was prominent in the national affairs of the

Congregational church. When he died in 1902 he left behind him a reputation for balance, integrity, and wise and moderate leadership.[68]

By the time Finney died, Fairchild had known him and worked with him for forty years, and he had a great respect for him. As a theologian, Fairchild was generally sympathetic to Finney's theology, and he was a cautious believer in revivals. Moreover, he had himself been involved in the early struggles when Oberlin theology and reform had created such a stir in the land; and he had written a history of the college.[69] So he was well fitted to take on the task of editing Finney's manuscript. Moreover, Finney's children all knew Fairchild well, and they believed he could be relied on to do what was required. But whether Finney would have approved of the choice is not so certain.

The fact that Finney had doubts about Fairchild was well known. For one thing, he was not convinced that he was the right man for the presidency of the college. In Finney's opinion he was altogether too cautious and conservative. He was too much concerned with education, and Finney feared that the high tone of religious piety and revival fervor in the college would suffer at his hands and that the college would cease to be a training place for revival ministers. Fairchild was also critical of the doctrine of sanctification, which had been so important to the older generation of Oberlin leaders, and he played down the importance of the intense revivalism of the early years.[70]

Finney was consequently uncertain about the depth of Fairchild's spiritual experience. Moreover, it is striking that the question of Fairchild's editing the manuscript had already been considered by Finney many years earlier. When Lewis Tappan first heard that Finney had written a narrative of revivals, he wrote to him:

> Are you willing to confide the Ms to two or three friends, in whom you can put confidence, and leave the disposition of it to their judgment? Would you be satisfied to commit it to President Fairchild, Mr. Morgan, Prof. Cowles and myself, or to two of this number or three if you preferred to have three?[71]

Later Tappan wrote,

> I have thought President Fairchild might be a suitable person to prepare the Ms for the press, if he has time & would receive a compensation for it. It is evident, I think, that the amanuensis is not quite scholar enough for doing it. . . .

[68] Albert Temple Swing, *James Harris Fairchild; or, Sixty-Eight Years with a Christian College* (New York: Revell, 1907); John Barnard, *From Evangelicalism to Progressivism at Oberlin College, 1866–1917* (Columbus: Ohio State University Press, 1969); *OE,* 10 September 1856, p. 150; and *DAB*.

[69] See James H. Fairchild, *Oberlin: The Colony and the College, 1833–1883* (Oberlin: Goodrich, 1883).

[70] See Delavan L. Leonard, *The Story of Oberlin: The Institution, the Community, the Ideas, the Movement* (Boston: Pilgrim Press, 1898), p. 292; Edward H. Madden and James E. Hamilton, *Freedom and Grace: The Life of Asa Mahan* (Metuchen, N.J.: Scarecrow Press, 1982), pp. 116–18; J. H. Fairchild, "The Doctrine of Sanctification at Oberlin," *The Congregational Quarterly* 18 (April 1876): 237–59; and Aaron M. Hills, *Life of Charles G. Finney* (Cincinnati: Office of "God's Revivalist," 1902), pp. 229–37.

[71] Tappan to Finney, 24 April 1868, Finney Papers, microfilm, roll 5. John Morgan and Henry Cowles were colleagues of Finney on the faculty.

> Perhaps you may think it best to show this letter to Pres. Fairchild, & get him to write to me.[72]

How Finney replied to Tappan's suggestions is not absolutely clear, but he would seem to have reacted negatively. Tappan's next letter reads:

> In view of all you say I remark,
>
> 1. It has never entered my head that any *material alterations* are required; and I would not allow anyone to suppress or modify anything peculiar to yourself. It was only such small emendations as a near friend, one who sympathized with you in sentiment & action would naturally make, that I thought of.
>
> 2. I have no personal acquaintance with Prest. Fairchild, nor have I known whether he was radical or conservative.
>
> 3. What you say will be considered confidential.[73]

Given these comments, it looks as though Finney may have rejected Tappan's suggestion that Fairchild edit the manuscript. There is no apparent evidence that Finney ever gave Fairchild the manuscript to read. In the sermon that he preached at Finney's funeral, Fairchild recounted incidents and details that appear in Finney's narrative.[74] This might indicate that Fairchild had by then seen the manuscript. But there is no reason to believe that any of his editorial work was carried out until later.

Preparation of the Narrative for Publication

Fairchild wasted no time in starting the editing. According to D. L. Leonard, a historian of Oberlin, in notes that he took of a talk he had with Fairchild in 1897, Fairchild "sent the manuscript to Hastings (he thinks) a connection of Fin[ney']s" to read.[75] This was probably Truman Hastings, the author of the "Revival Sketches" in *The Advance.* D. L. Leonard noted that Fairchild recalled that after Hastings had seen the manuscript, he advised Fairchild to omit a section on Freemasonry in the Oberlin Church.

Fairchild evidently did the editing during the winter vacation that started on 20 November. In early December he was staying in Newburgh, New York, with William McCrea, Esq., and he had the manuscript with him there. Leonard wrote: "Pres[ident Fairchild] went East to revise & stereo-type. Took 3 weeks."[76]

In deciding on an editorial policy, Fairchild was acting on behalf of Finney's family. Their wishes were indicated in a letter from Finney's son-in-law, Jacob Dolson Cox:

> I think reflection has brought all members of the family to the conclusion you express as to the leaving the autobiography *substantially* as written, using judicious power of omission or explanation where there is danger of unnecessary irritation or misunderstanding. Your own judgment as to the

[72] Tappan to Finney, 11 May 1868, Finney Papers, microfilm, roll 5.

[73] Tappan to Finney, 15 May 1868, Finney Papers, microfilm, roll 5.

[74] See the obituary and funeral service in *The Oberlin Weekly News,* 19 August 1875, p. 5.

[75] D. L. Leonard, "Notes upon Talks with Pres. Fairchild," book 2, p. 15, 10 June 1897, R. S. Fletcher Papers, file 30/24, box 1, Oberlin College Archives.

[76] See reverse of MS 746 and 958; and Leonard, "Notes," book 2, p. 15.

methods of doing this will certainly be best. I have a letter from California, from Charley in which he expresses almost exactly your sentiment on this point.[77]

Fairchild's sentiments, which were set out in the preface he wrote for the book, very much reflected what Lewis Tappan had proposed. But that preface obscures the extent to which Fairchild did in fact alter the text. He went far beyond what Tappan had suggested, although it is interesting to observe that many of those suggestions were followed by Fairchild. He changed "Brother" to "Mr." throughout the book, reparagraphed it, and omitted many of the sections that were felt to be unnecessarily repetitious. Tappan had also suggested an index. Although this was not prepared by Fairchild, there may have been plans for one. However, nothing came of it.[78] In his editorial work Fairchild also appears to have gone beyond the changes indicated by the family. Entire sections of material were omitted, including a complete chapter on Finney's labors in Michigan and accounts of revivals in other places; a long section on the notorious Oberlin lynching scandal and Finney's part in the trial; a section on Finney's attitude toward blacks; many revealing passages about the opposition he encountered; a section dealing with his first wife's illness; and the section dealing with Freemasonry, as well as many other sections throughout the book. In all, about 20 percent of the text was omitted or changed. Some of this may have been in order to reduce the length of the book, but much of it was because of its controversial or embarrassing character, and Fairchild was particularly concerned to avoid, if possible, any cause of offense. For the same reason he also omitted names or used only initial letters wherever people might be offended. He also omitted all the underlining Matson had used for emphasis, and he toned down Finney's language, which is often forceful and colloquial. These steps would have brought Finney's manuscript more into conformity with accepted literary taste. Many of the dates that appear in the published version were added by Fairchild, and in two places these were incorrect.

Fairchild's changes were not made all at one time. Evidence shows that he went through the whole manuscript making a few changes before going through in detail making the bulk of the changes.

The edition that Fairchild prepared reflected the sense of cautious propriety and conservative good taste that were such essential elements of Fairchild's personality. And it met with the entire approval of Finney's family,

[77] Cox to Fairchild, 18 November 1875, Fairchild Papers, microfilm, roll 2. Charley was Finney's son Charles.

[78] The matter came up at a faculty meeting of Oberlin College soon after the book was published. The minutes read: "The matter of index to the Autobiography of Pres. Finney by Dr. Pierson of Detroit Mich. was referred to Pres. Fairchild" ("Oberlin College Faculty Records," 21 June 1876, Oberlin College Archives, microfilm). Arthur Tappan Pierson was a Congregational minister in Detroit. A month later he was present in Oberlin for the Memorial Meeting for President Finney and gave an address. Born in a house by Chatham Street Chapel in New York and named after Arthur Tappan, he was a great admirer of Finney. He later became an outstanding evangelical leader and advocate of the Higher Life movement on both sides of the Atlantic. See *Reminiscences of Rev. Charles G. Finney* (Oberlin: Goodrich, 1876), pp. 28–29, 62–67; and *DAB*.

who were relieved that Fairchild had done the editing "so carefully, so discreetly and so lovingly."[79]

The publishers chosen were A. S. Barnes and Company of New York, a firm noted for educational and school books.[80] It was planned to have it stereotyped and produced at the same time in London by Hodder and Stoughton. By the end of the year, the publishers' advertisements were already preparing the religious readership, and the book made its appearance on 27 January 1876.[81] The printed edition follows Fairchild's editing of the manuscript more or less exactly with the exception of a few minor changes.

The title chosen was *Memoirs of Rev. Charles G. Finney. Written by himself.*[82] But this was to cause some confusion. Finney had specifically stated that he was not writing an autobiography. He pointed out in the narrative that he was concerned only with his experiences in revivals of religion. "Narrative of Revivals," the title suggested by Lewis Tappan, or "Revival Memories," the title given by Finney to the articles in *The Independent,* conveys a better impression of the book.[83] It is interesting to note that even before the book appeared off the press, the publishers had used the very name that Finney rejected. The religious papers carried multiple advertisements, in bold type, consisting of the single phrase "PRESIDENT FINNEY'S AUTOBIOGRAPHY."[84]

The faculty of Oberlin College had no objection to the book's being sold by subscription, but the family had given the copyright to Oberlin College with the strict understanding that it should not be sold that way. Finney's son-in-law had written:

> As to the method of "pushing" books by subscription agents, we probably have a kind of 'rabies' on the subject, having been so often galled to the quick by that kind of gentry—but it is simple truth that we should feel as if father himself were disgraced if his memories were crowded upon people in that way.[85]

But there was no need to use subscription agents, for within a month the first edition of 2,500 copies was sold and a second edition was issued.[86] J. D. Cox also passed on to Fairchild another matter that was of particular concern to Finney's son Charles: "By the way, he makes it a sort of condition of his consent to the College publishing the memoirs, that the original MSS should be preserved by the printers & returned so that he may have it." Whether

[79]Julia Monroe to Fairchild, 2 March 1876, Fairchild Papers, microfilm, roll 2.

[80]See J. C. Derby, *Fifty Years Among Authors, Books, and Publishers* (New York: G. W. Carleton and Co., 1884), pp. 575–79.

[81]See, for example, the advertisements in *NYE,* 30 December 1875, p. 5; 20 January 1876, p. 5; and 27 January 1876, p. 5.

[82]The title of the first English edition was *Memoirs of Rev. Charles G. Finney. The American Evangelist. Written by himself.* The text of both editions is the same.

[83]See Tappan to Finney, 2 June 1868, Finney Papers, microfilm, roll 5; Rebecca Finney to G. F. Wright, 22 October 1889, Wright Papers, box 7; and pp. xxxiii–xxxiv above.

[84]For example, *NYE,* 30 December 1875, p. 5; and *The Independent,* 30 December 1875, pp. 3–4, each carried the title in six different places spread across two pages of advertisements.

[85]Cox to Fairchild, 18 November 1875, Fairchild Papers, microfilm, roll 2. See also Oberlin College "Faculty Minutes," 17 November 1875, Oberlin College Archives, microfilm.

[86]See *Oberlin Review,* 8 March 1876, p. 22; and 22 March 1876, p. 32.

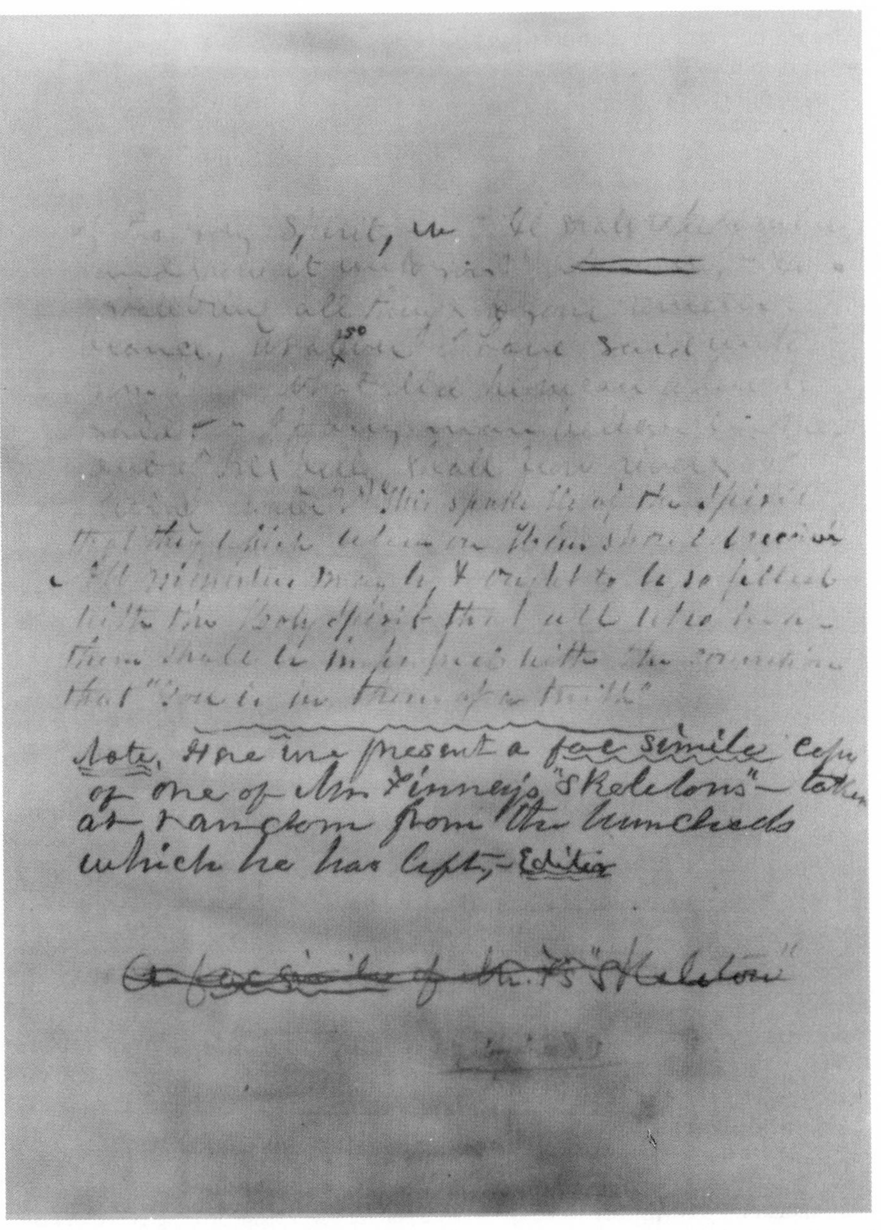
Note. Here we present a fac simile copy of one of Mr Finney's "Skeletons"— taken at random from the hundreds which he has left,— Editor

Reverse of Page 183 of the Manuscript. This photograph shows the handwriting of Henry Matson, the stenographer. It also shows additions in Finney's hand and in the handwriting of James H. Fairchild, editor of the first edition of the *Memoirs*.

Charles ever got the manuscript is not known. D. L. Leonard noted in his talk with Fairchild in 1897 that Fairchild "gave copy to Mrs. Monroe."[87]

It is not known how the manuscript came to Oberlin College Library. It may have been with the bulk of the Finney Papers, which came from the Monroe family in about 1930.[88] It was accessioned in 1948 and was transferred to the archives of the college in 1978.[89]

DESCRIPTION OF THE MANUSCRIPT

The manuscript consists of 1,063 sheets. These are all original sheets except for one that was inserted later by Fairchild (between MS 878 and 879). Each sheet measures 30 by 19 centimeters, but originally the sheets were double. It looks as though they have been divided either by tearing or cutting with a paper knife.

The paper is off-white with faint blue lines, thirty-two lines per page. There are no water marks, but each sheet is faintly embossed at the top left-hand corner with a small circular design of an eagle with wings uplifted, and the letters *GB* below the right claw. The page inserted by Fairchild is the same size, but the paper is thicker.

The paper is of poor quality and very fragile. Owing to deterioration and frequent handling over the years, many of the sheets, particularly in the first few chapters, have become somewhat torn and broken round the edges. At some period, before the manuscript was deposited in the archives, some of the sheets were repaired with library tape. One of the pages (MS 697) that had been torn in two was repaired by Finney. Many of the sheets are marked by dirty fingerprints probably due to handling by the printers.

The writing is in ink on one side of the sheet only, except in the case of eight of the pages, where additions were also made on the reverse. Fairchild also made use of the backs of MS 746 and 958 to write letters; and on the reverse of eight other pages there are various mathematical calculations and other marks. The left-hand margin was used by the printers and also by Lewis Tappan to make comments.

The main narrative is in the handwriting of the stenographer, Rev. Henry Matson, but there are corrections and additions in Finney's own handwriting, amounting to about 5 percent of the text. Some of these changes have been made by pasting an additional piece of paper over a section of the page. Some further corrections were also made by Lewis Tappan.

Matson's text is in ink. For the most part this has faded to a light brown, the covered-up sections remaining darker. In making later alterations in some places, starting from MS 285, he used a darker or even black ink. Finney's additions and alterations were done in a variety of inks, often grayer in color than Matson's. Some changes by Finney in black ink and larger handwriting are thought to have been done some years later in association with rereading the manuscript (see p. xxxvi). In two places (MS 419 and 441) Finney used a

[87]Leonard, "Notes," book 2, p. 15.
[88]See Oberlin College, *Annual Report of the President, 1929–1930,* pp. 24–25.
[89]It is now in the Finney Papers, file 2/2/2, box 10.

pencil to make insertions; and in renumbering MS 111/1–126/22 he used a blue crayon. Lewis Tappan's alterations to the text are in black ink, but he used a pencil for making notes in the margin and on the reverse of some pages. The only occasions when Matson appears to have used a pencil are for a few changes in MS 275–305. A pencil was used also by the Reverend Charles P. Bush, to whom Fairchild sent a section of the manuscript. He crossed out Addison Gardiner's name in some places where Fairchild had failed to do so.

The rest of the pencil alterations that occur in the manuscript appear to have been done by Fairchild. His editorial work is mostly in ink, although there are considerable sections where pencil has been used; and in some places he has gone over pencil alterations in ink. The ink used is normally darker than Matson's or Finney's and is often black. On some pages alterations in pencil and two or three different inks indicate that Fairchild had been through sections of the manuscript several times.

The manuscript also contains details thought to have been added by the printers. Sections varying in length from a paragraph or two to several pages are marked off with names in the left-hand margin in pencil: Annie, Mary, Chad, Albert, Emma, Maggie, Thomas, Petty, Harris, Louise, John, Kate, and Frank. These were the typesetters. Occasionally a number appears by one of these names corresponding with the respective page number of the first printed edition. Many of the printer's galley numbers are also included. These occur at intervals of about eight pages and are either written in full, for example, "Galley 24," "Galley 27," or else abbreviated, "Gal 2," "Gal 4," and so forth. There is no indication in the published edition of the *Memoirs* of who the printers were.

The manuscript has no title. The narrative starts about halfway down the first page with the heading of the first chapter. It is probable that the space above was left for the later insertion of a title that Finney never included.

The pagination indicates that there were basically three stages in the writing of the manuscript:

1. There was a *first draft* of about 893 pages.

2. The first 140 pages were completely rewritten and expanded to fill 272 pages. The rest of the first draft from page 141 on was renumbered so that page 891 became page 1023. There were probably 2 additional pages after this, forming a *revised version* of 1,025 pages, which was the manuscript sent to Lewis Tappan.

3. The revised version was subsequently worked over, and more material was added. Much of the manuscript was again renumbered, so that page 1023 then became page 1053. The last two pages were replaced by two additional pages at the end, forming a *final version* of 1,055 pages.

Because of the changes and insertions and occasional misnumberings, the pagination is quite complex, some pages having had to be renumbered five or six times. In its final form the last page, numbered 1055, is, in fact, the 1,065th page of text.

PRESENT EDITORIAL POLICY

The main concern of the present editors has been to restore the text to the way that Finney left it. Wherever it was altered in any way by Fairchild or it differs from the first published edition of the *Memoirs,* the restoration to the original is in **bold type.** Where Matson or Finney made significant changes, the original is given in the footnotes. No attempt has been made to remove the pieces of paper pasted onto the sheets, but by the use of lighting it has been possible to read what was written underneath, and this is given in the footnotes.

Additions or alterations in Finney's handwriting are marked off with the symbols ‹ ›. But it has not always been practical to indicate where Finney has made an occasional minor change to a letter or punctuation or an underlining. It has sometimes not been possible to tell who made an alteration of this kind, particularly in punctuation. If there is a doubt about a change of any significance, it is indicated in the footnotes.

It is often unclear in the handwritings of both Finney and Matson whether a word should start with a capital letter. These ambiguities are not indicated in the footnotes. Where a word is underlined in the original, it is put in *italics*. In the chapter headings Finney almost always abbreviated the word "chapter" to "chap." These are printed in full. The chapter numbers are in Roman numerals in the manuscript. All entries made by the printers have been omitted.

The paragraphing in the first draft of the manuscript in Matson's handwriting is unclear. The indenting from the left margin varies considerably. In some cases single sentences or short sections are started on a new line and indented to varying degrees. In other places a new sentence is indented far over to the right of the page. Finney went through the manuscript adding the letter *P* to indicate where new paragraphs should start, but it is not clear whether he intended to include any of Matson's apparent paragraphing. In a few places Matson had also inserted the letter *P*. Only Finney's and Matson's paragraph marks have been followed, except where indicated in the footnotes.

Where Fairchild's edition differs significantly from the original manuscript, this is indicated in the footnotes. The page numbers of that edition are given in the margin as JHF 1, JHF 2, JHF 3, and so forth, and the page numbers of the original manuscript are indicated in the margin with MS 1, MS 2, MS 3, and so on. All page divisions are marked off in the text by the symbol ǀ. The text of the edition published by Fleming H. Revell in 1966, entitled *Charles G. Finney: An Autobiography,* has the same page numbers as the first edition. Insertions by the present editors are between brackets [ ]. Quotations from the Bible in the footnotes are from the King James Version.

Preface to the First (Fairchild) Edition

The author of the following narrative sufficiently explains its origin and purpose, in the introductory pages. He left the manuscript at the disposal of his family, having never decided, in his own mind, that it was desirable to publish it. Many of his friends, becoming aware of its existence, have urged its publication; and his children, yielding to the general demand, have presented the manuscript to Oberlin College for this purpose.

In giving it to the public, it is manifestly necessary to present it essentially as we find it. No liberties can be taken with it, to modify views or statements which may sometimes seem extreme or partial, or even to subdue a style, which, though rugged at times, is always dramatic and forcible. Few men have better earned the right to utter their own thoughts, in their own words. These thoughts and words are what the many friends of Mr. Finney will desire. The only changes that seemed allowable, were occasional omissions, to avoid unnecessary repetition, or too minute detail, or, at times, references that might seem too distinctly personal. The narrative is, in its very nature, personal, involving the experiences both of the author and of those with whom he had to do; and to these personal experiences it, in great part, owes its interest and its value. As the narrative presents the memories and heart-yearnings of a veteran pastor, with a passion for winning souls, it is hoped and believed that, in its personal references, it will not be regarded as having transcended the limits of Christian propriety. For the most part, the lapse of time sets aside all question.

Here and there perhaps, the statements in the narrative may seem inadequate, as involving only a partial view of facts. It will be remembered that such partial views belong to all personal observation and opinion, and each one will naturally supply the correction that seems to be demanded.

J.H.F.
OBERLIN COLLEGE, January, 1876.

MS 01
JHF 01

CHAPTER I

My birth and early education.

It[1] has pleased God in some measure to connect my name and labors with an extensive movement of the church of Christ, regarded by some as a new era in its progress. Especially **has this been supposed to be true** in **respect** to revivals of religion. As this movement involved, to a considerable extent, the development of **some modified** views of Christian doctrine which had not been common, and was brought about by **some** changes in the means of carrying forward the work of evangelization, it was very natural that some misapprehension should prevail in regard to these modified statements of doctrine, and the use of these measures; and consequently that to some extent even good men ¦**might** call in question the wisdom of these measures and the soundness of these theological statements, and that ungodly men should be irritated, and for a time should strenuously oppose these great movements.

MS 02

I have spoken of my **name** as connected with these movements, but only as one of the many ministers of Christ, **and others,** who have shared prominently in promoting them. I am aware that by a certain portion of the

[1]The manuscript was originally a continuous narrative with no title or chapter headings and was in the handwriting of Rev. Henry Matson, the stenographer employed by Finney. It was divided up later by Finney into chapters on the advice of Lewis Tappan (see Introduction, p. xxxi). The chapter numbers and headings are all in Finney's handwriting throughout the manuscript, except in the case of chapters I and II. These come within the first twenty pages, which were revised and rewritten subsequently in Matson's handwriting. Chapter I starts halfway down the first page to allow, perhaps, for a title that was never added. The first page was unnumbered.

According to Lewis Tappan, the first page as it was sent to him, before Finney revised it, read:

> It has pleased the great Head of the church in some measure to connect my name & labors with what has been by many regarded as a new era in the onward movements of the church, especially in this country. Especially has this been supposed to be true in respect to revivals of religion. As the change which the Lord introduced in the means of promoting those revivals, and in the type of the revivals themselves, has of course been considerable, it was very natural that much misapprehension should prevail in regard to them, and that the movement should be to a considerable extent misunderstood. I have been urged for a long time, and with increasing urgency, to write some account of the revivals of religion with which my name and labors have been connected in this and other countries.
>
> I have been particularly importuned to do this for the sake of correcting some misapprehensions that have prevailed in respect to the *type* and *results* of those revivals (Tappan to Finney, 2 June 1868, Finney Papers, microfilm, roll 5).

The passages in **bold type** throughout the text are those that were altered or crossed out by James Harris Fairchild, the first editor of the *Memoirs*. They were mostly omitted from the first edition. In the chapter heading the word "My" was crossed out in pencil, and the first letter of "birth" was capitalized. There is some doubt about who made this change, but it would appear to have been done by Fairchild. Words in italics indicate underlining in the original.

church I have been considered an innovator, both in regard to doctrine and measures; and that many have looked upon JHF 02 |me as rather prominent, especially in assailing some of the old forms of theological thought and expression, and in stating the doctrines of the Gospel in many respects in new language, **and introducing other forms of thought**.

I have been particularly importuned, for a number of years, by the friends of those revivals with which my name and labors have been connected, to write a history of them.[2] As so much misapprehension has prevailed respecting them, it is thought that the truth of history demands a statement from myself of the doctrines that were preached, so far as I was concerned, of the measures used, and of the ‹results of›[3] preaching those doctrines and the MS 03 |use of those measures, **as they have been manifest to myself and others for many years.**

My mind seems instinctively to recoil from saying so much of myself as I shall be obliged to do, if I speak honestly of those revivals and of my relation to them. For this reason I have declined, up to this time, to undertake such a work. Of late the trustees of Oberlin college have laid the matter before me, and urged me to undertake **the work.**[4] They, together with numerous other friends in this country and in England, have urged that it was due to the cause of Christ, that a better understanding should exist in the church, than has hitherto existed, in regard especially to the revivals that occurred in central New York and elsewhere, from 182‹1›[5] and onward for several years, ‹because those revivals have been most misrepresented & opposed.›[6] I approach the subject, I must say, with reluctance, for many reasons. **First,** I have kept no diary, and consequently must depend on my memory. It is true, that my memory is naturally very tenacious, and the events that I have witnessed in revivals of religion made a very deep impression on my mind; and **therefore** I remember with great distinctness **many of them,** many more than I shall ‹have time›[7] to communicate **in what** MS 04 |**I shall write**. Every one

[2] There are, for example, extended arguments in favor of such a history, by a writer in *The Congregational Herald,* reprinted in *OE,* 21 November 1860, p. 187.

[3] Brackets ‹ › indicate sections in Finney's own handwriting. The phrase "and of the preaching of" was altered by Finney to "and of the results of preaching."

[4] On 26 June 1866, the trustees appointed Henry Cowles and John Keep a committee to confer with Finney about compiling "a biographical sketch of his life" (Oberlin College "Board of Trustee Minutes," 26 June and 20 August 1866, Oberlin College Archives). In response to this, Finney set out the pros and cons in a paper dated 12 July 1866 (Miscellaneous Items, Finney Papers, microfilm, roll 8).

It was particularly "at the earnest request of Professor Cowles and Dr. Morgan," two of Finney's colleagues on the faculty, that he undertook to write his narrative. At the same time, John Keep, one of the trustees, set about gathering material from other people in connection with compiling the history of the Finney revivals. See "Closing Incidents of Mr. Finney's Life," in *The Oberlin Weekly News,* 20 August 1875, p. 5; and T. Hastings to John Keep, 20 July 1866, Finney Papers, microfilm, roll 5.

[5] Matson had written down the date "1825." The alteration of the *5* to a *1* appears to have been done by Finney. This is the first of a number of changes in blacker ink and larger lettering than most of his writing. It may have been done in 1872 in association with rereading the manuscript (see Introduction, p. xxxvi).

[6] The last phrase of this sentence, "because those revivals have been most misrepresented and opposed," was added by Finney.

[7] The words "think it wise," which were written down by Matson, were altered in black into "have time." The writing appears to be Finney's.

who has **ever** witnessed powerful revivals of religion, is aware that many cases of conviction and conversion are daily occurring, of the greatest interest to the people in the midst of whom they occur. Where **these persons are known and** the facts and circumstances ˡare known, **they often produce** a thrilling effect, and are frequently so numerous that if all the highly interesting facts of even one extended revival, in **one** locality, should be narrated, it would fill a large volume. JHF 03

I do not propose to pursue this course **at all** in what I am about to write. I shall only sketch such an outline as will, upon the whole, give a tolerably clear idea of the type which these revivals took on; and shall only relate a few of the particular instances of conversion which occurred in different places. **Should I do otherwise my narrative would swell to many volumes; whereas I propose, if possible, to condense what I have to say into one volume of moderate size. However interesting may have been the particular cases of conversion that occurred in different places, to persons in their immediate neighborhood, I fear that to persons at a distance it would appear prolix and** ˡ‹**tiresome**›[8] **to enter, with any considerable detail, into the statement of individual cases of conversion.** MS 05

But I shall also endeavor to give such an account of the doctrines which were preached, and of the measures which were used, and **in short** shall mention such facts in **brief** as will **give so much information in respect to them, as to** enable the church hereafter, partially at least, to estimate the power and purity of those great works of God. ‹**Purer & more powerful revivals of religion I never saw than those that have been most spoken against.**›[9]

I hesitate **on another account** to write a **N**arrative of those revivals. I have been **not infrequently** surprized to find how much my own remembrance of facts **that occurred years ago,** differs from the recollection of other persons who **had almost equal facilities for knowing what those facts were at the time. My statements therefore, are very liable to conflict with the recollections of some persons who, at the time, must have understood the facts very nearly as I did myself.** Of course I must state facts as *I* remember them. A great many of those events have been often referred to by myself in preaching, as illustrative of the truths that I was presenting to the people. I have been so often reminded of **these facts**, and have so often referred to them in all the years of my ministry ˡ**since their occurrence**, that I cannot but have strong confidence that I remember them substantially as they occurred. If I shall in any case mis**remember in anything that I state**, or if in any case my recollections differ widely from those of others **who were present in those revivals,** I trust that the church will believe that my statements are in entire accordance with my present remembrance of those facts. I am now seventy five years old.[10] **I of** course remember things that transpired many years ago more definitely than **I do things** of recent MS 06

[8]The word "tedious" here was changed to "tiresome" by Finney.

[9]This sentence was added by Finney but crossed out by Fairchild. After this sentence a paragraph sign *P* in black ink appears, apparently in Finney's handwriting.

[10]Finney was seventy-five years old on 29 August 1867.

occurrence. In regard to the doctrines preached, so far as I was concerned, and the means used to promote **them,** I think I cannot **misremember.**

JHF 04 To give any intelligible account of the part which I was |called to act in those scenes, it is necessary that I should give a little history of the manner in which I came to adopt the doctrinal views which I have long held and preached, and which have been regarded **as in some measure involving a new statement of some of the doctrines of the Gospel, and** by many persons **have been considered** as objectionable. **In order, therefore, to render my narrative intelligible,** I must commence by giving a very brief

MS 07 account of my |birth, and early **location** and education, my conversion to Christ, my study of theology, and **the circumstances of** my entering upon the work of the ministry. I am not about to write an autobiography, let it be remembered; and shall enter no farther into a relation of the events of my own private life than shall seem necessary to give an intelligible account of the manner in which I was **directed, in so far as I have been related** to th‹e›s‹e› great movement‹s›[11] of the church **in this and in other countries ‹in pushing forward reform.›**[12]

I was born in Warren, **in** Litchfield County, Connecticut, **in** 1792.[13] When I was about two years old my father removed to **central New York,** Oneida county, which was at that time to a great extent a wilderness.[14] No religious privileges were enjoyed by the people. **No Sabbath Schools had been established.** Very few religious books were to be had. The new settlers being mostly from New England, almost immediately established common schools; but they had among them very little intelligent preaching of the Gospel. I enjoyed the privileges of a common school summer and winter, until I was fifteen or sixteen years old, I believe; and advanced so far as to be supposed

[11]The phrase "this great movement" was put into the plural by Finney.

[12]The words "in pushing forward reform" were added by Finney.

[13]Finney was born on 29 August 1792. A cairn of stones with a plaque was erected in the western part of the town of Warren in 1922, marking the site of the homestead where he was born. See "President Finney's Birthplace," *The Oberlin Alumni Magazine,* May 1922, p. 11; and October 1922, p. 23; and Florence S. Crofut, *Guide to the History and the Historic Sites of Connecticut,* vol. 1 (New Haven: Yale University Press, 1937), pp. 440–41.

[14]Finney's father, Sylvester Finney (1759–1842), was from an old New England family descended from John Finney, one of the earliest settlers of Plymouth, Massachusetts. He had been a soldier in the Revolutionary Army, but he did not see active service. In 1779 he married Rebecca Rice (1759–1836). She was descended from an old Connecticut family and came from Kent. They had nine children, Charles being the seventh. His daughter Helen described her grandfather as "a farmer in a rather small way, and a good neighbor, a happy, jolly man, beloved by everyone" (H[elen] F[inney] C[ox], "Charles Finney," in Ferdinand Piper, ed., *Lives of the Leaders of Our Church Universal* [Philadelphia: Presbyterian Board of Publication, 1879], p. 730; see also George F. Wright, *Charles Grandison Finney* [Boston and New York: Houghton Mifflin, 1891], pp. 1–2; Franklin C. Clark, "The Bristol Branch of the Finney Family," *The New England Historical and Genealogical Register* [Boston] 60 [1906]: 156; *OE,* 6 July 1842, p. 111; and Sylvester Finney to Commissioners of Pensions, 23 March 1838, Pension Application File, S16114, Military Archives Division, National Archives and Record Service, Washington, D.C.; the signature on this letter is that of Sylvester Finney, but the text is in the handwriting of Charles).

Until 22 September 1798, the family lived on a 109-acre farm, lot number 68, in Brothertown. They were forced to move to the parish of Hanover, now Kirkland, when the state of New York purchased their Brothertown land for £74 sterling, to resettle Indian people. (See "Mortgagors to Mortgagees: F to H," book 1, p. 355, Oneida County Records Building, Utica.)

capable of teaching a common school myself, as common ¦schools were then conducted.[15] MS 08

My parents were neither of them professors of religion, and I believe among our neighbors there were very few **that professed religion**. I seldom heard a **Gospel** sermon **from any person,**[16] unless it was an occasional one from some travelling minister, or some miserable holding forth ‹of›[17] an ignorant preacher **that** would sometimes be found in that country. I recollect very well that the ignorance of the preachers that I heard, **when I heard any at all,** was so **great** that the people would return from meeting and spend a considerable time in irrepressible laughter, **in view of** the strange mistakes ¦which had been made and absurdities which had been advanced. In the neighborhood of my father's residence we had just erected a meeting house and settled a minister, **where I had begun to attend upon a stated ministry,**[18] when my father was induced to remove again into the wilderness skirting the southern shore of lake Ontario, a little south of Sackett's harbor. Here again I lived for several years, enjoying no better religious privileges JHF 05

[15]William C. Cochran, Finney's grandson, wrote:

> Mr. Finney was fitted for this work of teaching, by two years' schooling in the Hamilton Oneida Institute, at Clinton, New York, only a few miles to school from his father's farm in Oneida County. The principal of this school, at that time, was Seth Norton, a graduate of Yale College. . . . He discovered great possibilities in this tall, blue-eyed child of the woods, and seems to have given him unusual attention. He inspired him with an ambition to secure a classical education and evoked an intense love of music.

Apparently Finney walked four miles to school every day, and back to his home at night (William C. Cochran, *Charles Grandison Finney: Memorial Address* [Philadelphia: Lippincott, 1908], pp. 18–19; and Cochran, "Charles Grandison Finney," *The Oberlin Alumni Magazine* 25 [February 1929]: 139; see also L. Nelson Nichols, *History of the Broadway Tabernacle of New York City* [New Haven: Tuttle Morehouse and Taylor, 1940], p. 43). However, no corroborating primary evidence has been found that Finney was ever at Hamilton Oneida Academy.

[16]The omission of the word "Gospel" by Fairchild in the published edition has been most unfortunate. It has resulted in Finney's appearing to present himself and the region in which he grew up as culturally and religiously deprived, which was not the case. See Benjamin B. Warfield, "Oberlin Perfectionism," *The Princeton Theological Review* 19 (January 1921): 8–9.

Finney elsewhere said:

> I had been brought up in great darkness, yet in the midst of a Presbyterian congregation, often listening to Old School preaching. But the strain of it was—"you can and you can't," and it filled my mind with utter confusion, and put every great truth of the gospel out of joint in my mind. It seems to me now, that in all those years of my youth, I never heard one gospel sermon,—not one that I think presented the gospel in its clear and true light. It th[r]ew me headlong into all the absurdities of Old School theology, and there I stumbled along, only getting deeper in the mire (*OE,* 21 January 1846, p. 10).

And in another place he said:

> My situation in regard to early religious instruction, was rather peculiar. I heard no preaching but the strongest form of Old Schoolism, and had to grope my way along through all its absurdities, and think out all my religious opinions in the very face of all the preaching I heard in my earliest years. This led me to think deeply and thoroughly upon the great points of the Christian life (*OE,* 24 June 1846, p. 97).

[17]The word "from" was changed by Finney to "of."

[18]The Finneys are said to have lived from 1796 to 1808 at Pecks Corner, Hanover. The meeting house was built about 1805. Its founding and early history are described in Ada Marie Peck, *A History of the Hanover Society* (Waterville, N.Y.: Waterville Times Print, 1901), chap. 18 (unpaginated). The minister was the Rev. Publius V. Bogue (1764–1836). See Warfield, "Oberlin Perfectionism," p. 9.

than I had in Oneida County.[19] **Almost the only preaching that I heard**
MS 09 **was that of an Elder Osgood, who was a man |of[20] considerable religious zeal, but of very little education.[21] His ignorance of language was so great as to divert the attention of the people from his thoughts to the very comical form of expressing them. For example, instead of saying, "I am," he would say, "I are;" and in the use of the pronouns thee and thou, etc., he would mix them up in such a strange and incongruous manner, as to render it very difficult indeed to keep from laughing while he was either preaching or praying. Of course I received no religious instruction from such teaching.**

When about twenty years old I returned to Connecticut,[22] and from thence went to New Jersey, near New York city, and engaged in teaching. I taught and studied as best I could, and twice returned to New England and attended

[19]The Finney farm, located one mile directly south of Henderson Village, was the family home from 1808 until 1836. Charles lived there from 1808 until 1812. During those years, for two months in the summer and three months in the winter, Finney taught school in a little log building on Smith Road at Stony Creek. A painting of the school hangs in the library of the Henderson High School. See John A. Haddock, *The Growth of a Century* (Philadelphia: Sherman and Co., 1894), p. 573. See also Cochran, *Charles Grandison Finney,* pp. 17–18.

In 1837, after his wife's death, Sylvester Finney left Henderson and moved to Oberlin, where he spent the last years of his life with his son Charles. He remarried and joined the Oberlin Church with his wife, Anna, in 1841. After Sylvester's death in 1842, Anna left Oberlin and died in Strongsville in 1843. The house in Henderson where the Finneys had lived was demolished in 1938. See Oberlin First Congregational Church Records, 1834–1856, p. 25, in Oberlin College Archives, file 31/4/1, box 17; *OE,* 10 May 1843, p. 79; and "Only Ruins Remain of Jefferson County Boyhood Home of Finney, Noted Evangelist," *The Post Standard* (Syracuse), 1 March 1940, p. 15. Cutting in Finney Papers, file 2/2/2, box 9.

[20]At the bottom right-hand corner of page 9, Finney added the word "(*over*)" in parentheses and underlined.

[21]Emory Osgood (1777–1824) was an elder of the First Baptist Church at Henderson from its foundation; and he was the minister there from 1807 to 1823. See "Memoirs of Elder Emory Osgood," *The Western New York Baptist Magazine* (Morrisville, N.Y.) 4 (February 1825): 271–83; and John Peck and John Lawton, *An Historical Sketch of the Baptist Missionary Convention of the State of New York* (Utica: Bennett and Bright, 1837), pp. 181–90. Osgood was responsible for a number of the contemporary reports published in the papers mentioning the earliest revivals in which Finney was involved (see p. 35 nn. 30–31 [MS 60]).

[22]In a letter to P. H. Fowler, Finney explained that he taught school for a time in Henderson, "but there were no schools in which I could push my education." The Hamilton Oneida Institute became a College in 1812, and his former instructor, Seth Norton, was no longer available. So Finney decided to return to Warren, Connecticut, where his Uncle Cyrus Finney lived and where there was an academy. Finney attended the Warren Academy for two years from the fall of 1812. According to W. C. Cochran, "He supported himself by work on his uncle's farm, in summer, and teaching singing school, in winter," where he was successful and popular. He also taught music in the academy. See P. H. Fowler, *Historical Sketch of Presbyterianism Within the Bounds of the Synod of Central New York* (Utica: Curtiss and Childs, 1877), p. 258; Cochran, *Charles Grandison Finney,* pp. 24–25; and Cochran, "Charles Grandison Finney," *The Oberlin Alumni Magazine* 25 (February 1929): 137.

In 1880 Theodore L. Cuyler, the Brooklyn pastor, met an old man from Warren who was a schoolmate of Finney's and who remembered him well: "Finney the schoolboy was the brightest of his class, and after his rustic education was completed, he had worked in a brickyard at making bricks." The man reported to Cuyler that Finney "divided his time between making bricks at Warren and studying books" (T. L. Cuyler, "Pen Portraits of Eminent Preachers," *The Treasury* [New York] 9 [October 1891]: 377; Cuyler, "Under Canvas," *NYE,* 26 August 1880, p. 1; and Cuyler, "Around Mount Bushnell," *NYE,* 15 July 1886, p. 1).

According to Noble B. Strong, a Warren resident, "The last of the Finney family left Warren in 1838" (Strong to G. F. Wright, 11 March 1890, Wright Papers, box 8).

a high school for a season.[23] While attending the high school I meditated going to Yale College. My preceptor was a graduate of Yale **College.**[24] **But** he advised me not to go. He said it would be a loss of time, as I could easily accomplish, **at the rate I was then progressing,** the whole curriculum of study pursued at that institution in two years, whereas it would cost me four years to graduate. He presented such considerations as prevailed with me, and as it resulted, I failed to pursue my school edu‹cation any **further**[25] at that time.[26] However, afterwards I[27] acquired some knowledge of latin, **greek &** **hebrew.**[28] But I was never a classical scholar, **&** never possessed so much

[23]Finney evidently taught school in Mount Pleasant, New Jersey. A "Diary" bought by Finney on 5 November 1814 at Warren and used as an account book has an entry on page 2: "Began School Novr the 21st 1814. Weather verry clear and pleasant—no snow—Mount Pleasant November the 21—1814." Further similar entries run through to 1 July 1816, with notices of his having returned to Connecticut in March and June 1816 (MS, "Account Book, 1814–1820," in Finney Papers, file 2/2/2, box 11).

[24]Noble Strong, whose father attended the Warren Academy with Finney, wrote to G. F. Wright from Warren in 1890:

> Cannot tell who was the principal of the academy when Mr. Finney was here. The academy was started in 1802 and kept up for 50 years and was generally taught by a student from College so that there was a change every year or two. I think there are only four persons living in our town now that remember the time when Mr. Finney attended school here, and neither of them remember who was the principal (Strong to Wright, 11 March 1890, Wright Papers, box 8).

[25]This sentence originally ended here, with the last two and a half words ("cation any farther") on the next page. Finney subsequently added the additional section at the bottom of MS 9, and the word "(*over*)," crossing out "cation any farther" on the top of MS 10. He continued the new section on the reverse of MS 9.

[26]David Bartlett, in a sketch of Finney in 1856, wrote:

> His character as a leader began to develop itself in youth; in sports his associates ranked him among the foremost, yet in school he was studious, and it is remarked by an early acquaintance, that mathematics was to him but a recreation. By the intense vigor of his intellect he was enabled to master easily what other boys did only by close application (D. W. Bartlett, *Modern Agitators; or, Pen Portraits of Living American Reformers* [New York: Miller, Orton, and Mulligan, 1856], p. 152).

Finney's level of education reached at the Warren Academy is indicated by George W. Gale, the Presbyterian minister at Adams, New York:

> He had had but little more than a common education. He had attended an Academy where he got some knowledge of Latin, in addition to English. He had studied some of the higher branches of English education, but nothing very extensively, I should judge, from what he told me, that his education was about what might have been required to enter college, except that he had not studied Greek (G. W. Gale, *Autobiography {to 1834} of George Washington Gale {1789–1861}, Founder of Galesburg, Illinois, and Knox College* [New York: privately printed, 1964], pp. 182–83).

Gale's autobiography is said to be printed "from the text of a typewritten copy of a hand written copy made of the original manuscript by the founder's daughter, Margaret Gale Hitchcock." Most of the original manuscript has apparently been destroyed. A comparison of the printed version with a typewritten version in Knox College Library, Galesburg, shows many minor discrepancies. But neither version is accurate. In quoting from this source, the printed version has been used except where the typewritten version appears to be more accurate.

[27]MS 9 reverse begins here. This page is in Finney's handwriting.

[28]This was during his studies under Rev. George W. Gale of Adams, New York, in 1822 and 1823. The following section had been written by Finney here in the manuscript, but it appears to have been crossed out by him:

> I read several books of Virgil, & Cicero's orations in latin, & my greek testament so far as to pass the usual examination before Presbytery, & so much Hebrew as to be able to satisfy myself of the meaning of a text when I felt in doubt upon the subject. This I did of course with such help as my lexicon & my library furnish.

William C. Cochran pointed out, "His knowledge of Latin, Greek, and Mathematics was as

knowledge of the **de[a]d**[29] languages as to think myself capable of independently criticising our english translation of the bible. **I have seldom ventured to attempt it when I was not sustained by the most respectable authority.**›[30]

MS 10 |**My**[31] ‹**last**› teacher wished me to join him in conducting an Academy in one of the Southern states. I was inclined to accept his proposal, with the design of pursuing and completing my studies under his instruction **during the intervals of teaching.** But when I informed my parents, whom I had not seen for four years, of my contemplated movement south, they both came immediately after me, and prevailed on me to go home with them to Jefferson County, N.Y.[32] After making them a visit I concluded to enter a law office **as a student** at Adams in that county.[33]

JHF 06 |Up to this time I had never enjoyed what might be called religious privileges. I had never lived in a praying community, except during the periods when I was attending the high school in New England; and the religion in that place was of a type not at all calculated to arrest my attention. The preaching **where I attended school** was by an aged clergyman, an excellent man, and greatly beloved and venerated by his people;[34] but he read his sermons in a manner that left no impression whatever on my mind. He had a monotonous, humdrum way of reading what he had probably written many years before.

MS 11 |**But** to give some idea of his preaching let me say, that his manuscript sermons were just large enough to put into a **1‹2› mo.** Bible.[35] I sat in the

good as that of any graduate who had not pursued post-graduate courses; *but* one thing was lacking—he had not received a college diploma" (Cochran, *Charles Grandison Finney,* pp. 26–27).

[29]There is some doubt about the reading of this word. It appears to be "ded." Fairchild altered it to "ancient."

[30]Cochran wrote, "Mr. Finney's knowledge of the Greek Testament and Hebrew Bible was much more intimate and profound than that of most seminary graduates" (Cochran, *Charles Grandison Finney,* p. 29).

[31]Page 10 started with the end of the sentence "cation any farther," which was erased by Finney when he inserted a section on the reverse of page 9. Matson had started the next sentence with the words "My teacher." Finney appears to have changed this to read "One of my teachers" but changed it again to "My last teacher."

[32]In a letter written late in life to P. H. Fowler, Finney wrote, "My mother was infirm, and plead so hard for me to remain near her, that I gave up a further literary course" (Fowler, *Historical Sketch of Presbyterianism,* p. 258). This is one of the few references Finney makes to his mother.

[33]Finney entered the law office of Benjamin Wright (afterward Benjamin Wright and David Wardwell) in 1818. He had arrived in Adams by 13 August 1818 when he attended the Masonic Lodge as a visitor. See Gale, *Autobiography,* p. 182; Fowler, *Historical Sketch of Presbyterianism,* p. 258; and *The National and Freemason* (New York), 20 June 1868, p. 394.

[34]Peter Starr (1744–1829) was the Congregational minister at Warren, Connecticut, from 1772 until his death. See Arthur Goodenough, *The Clergy of Litchfield County* (Litchfield County University Club, 1909), pp. 55–56; and Peter Starr, *A Half-Century Sermon, Delivered at Warren, March 8, 1822* (Norwalk, Conn.: S. W. Benedict [printer], 1828).

The church was built on ground given to the Ecclesiastical Society of Warren by Finney's grandfather, Josiah Finney, and the church was organized originally at his house. See Noble B. Strong to G. F. Wright, 11 March 1890, Wright Papers, box 8.

[35]Matson had written down here, "an 18 mo. Bible." The alteration of the *8* to a *2* in black ink appears to have been done by Finney. This is a reference to the size of the Bible: duodecimo, folded four times, giving twelve leaves and twenty-four pages. See Leonard Montague Harrod,

gallery, and observed that **the parson** placed his manuscript in **about** the middle of his Bible, and inserted **the fo‹ur›** finger‹s›[36] **of each hand** at the places where were to be found the passages of Scripture to be quoted in the reading of his sermon. This made it necessary **for him** to hold his Bible **before him** in both hands, and rendered all gesticulation with his hands impossible. As he proceeded he would read the passages of Scripture where his fingers were inserted, and thus liberate one finger after another until the fingers of both hands were read out of their places. **I observed that w**hen his fingers were all read out, he was near the close of **his** sermon. His reading was altogether unimpassioned and monotonous. **A**nd although the people attended very closely and reverentially to his reading, yet **to me**, I must confess, it was not much like preaching, **or to say the least not much like that which I thought preaching ought to be**.

When we retired from meeting I often heard the people speak well of his sermons; and **not infrequently** they would wonder whether he **made** |any allusion, in what he said, to what **was transpiring there**. It seemed to be always a matter of curiosity to know what he was aiming at, especially if there was anything more in his sermon than a dry discussion of doctrine.[37] And this was really quite as good preaching as I had ever listened to in any place. But any one **may** judge whether such preaching was calculated |to instruct or interest a young man who neither knew or cared anything about religion.

MS 12

JHF 07

When I was teaching school in New Jersey, the preaching in the neighborhood was **at that time almost altogether** in German. I do not think I heard half a dozen sermons in English during my whole stay in New Jersey, which was about three years. **Altogether I was,** when I went to Adams to study law, almost as ignorant of religion as a heathen. I had been **very much** brought up in the woods. I had **paid** very little regard to the Sabbath, and had no definite knowledge of religious truth **whatever**. At Adams, for the first time, I sat statedly for a length of time under |an educated ministry. Rev. George W. Gale, from Princeton, N. J., became, soon after I went there, pastor of the Presbyterian church in that place.[38] His preaching was of the **Old School type**, that is, it was thoroughly Calvinistic; and whenever he came out with the doctrines **as he believed them**, he would preach what **is now** called *hyper*-Calvinism.[39] **‹This however he seldom did.›**[40] He was of

MS 13

The Librarians' Glossary (London: Andre Deutsch, 1971), pp. 272–73. Fairchild altered it to read "a small Bible." The size was probably about 16 by 11 centimeters.

[36] Matson had written down "the fore finger" here. The alteration in black ink to "the four fingers" appears to have been done by Finney. Fairchild changed it to "his fingers."

[37] Matson had written down the following sentence after this: "In some of his remarks he would, once in a while, lead the people to query whether he had not reference to something that was transpiring, or was to transpire, in their midst." It appears to have been crossed out by Finney.

[38] George Washington Gale (1789–1861) was pastor at Adams from 1819 to 1824. He became well known as the originator of the Manual Labor Institute at Oneida, New York, and later as the founder of Knox College in Galesburg, Illinois, a town that was named after him. See Gale, *Autobiography;* Wallace E. Lamb, "George Washington Gale, Theologian and Educator" (Ed.D. diss., Syracuse University, 1949); and *DAB*.

[39] "Old School" and "hyper-Calvinism" refer to the predominant theology in orthodox Christian churches. It was contrasted with the New School theology, a modified form of Calvinism that laid emphasis on the freedom of the will. The differences between these two

course regarded as highly orthodox; but I was not able to gain very much instruction from his preaching. As I sometimes told him, he seemed to me to begin in the middle of his discourse, and to assume many things which to my mind needed to be proved. He seemed to take it for granted that his hearers were theologians, and therefore that he might *assume* all the great and fundamental doctrines of the Gospel. But I must say that I was rather perplexed than edified by his preaching. **However, I attended steadily, and often conversed with him in respect to his teaching, to satisfy myself of his real meaning.**

I had never, until this time, lived where I could attend a stated prayer meeting. As one was held by the church near our office every week, I used to attend **this meeting** and listen to thei**r** prayers **very frequently, and for months together,** as often as I could be excused from business at that hour.[41]

MS 14 ꜝIn studying elementary law I found the old authors frequently quoting Scripture, and referring especially to the Mosaic institutes as authority for many of the great principles of common law. This excited my curiosity so much that I went and purchased a Bible, the first **one** I had ꜝever owned; and whenever I found a reference by the law authors to the Bible, I turned to the passage and consulted it **with** its connection.[42] This soon led to my taking a new interest in the Bible, and I read and meditated on it much more than I had ever done before in my life. However, much of it I did not understand.

JHF 08

Mr. Gale was in the habit of dropping in at our office frequently, and seemed anxious to know what impression his sermons had made on my mind. I used to converse with him freely, and I now think that I sometimes criticised his sermons unmercifully.[43] I raised such objections against his positions as forced themselves upon my attention. **By** conversing with him and asking him questions, I perceived that his own mind was, as I thought, mystified, and that he did not accurately define to himself what he meant by many of the important terms that he used. Indeed I found it impossible to attach any

schools of thought led to major controversies in both the Presbyterian and Congregational churches. See Lewis Cheeseman, *Differences Between Old and New School Presbyterians* (Rochester: Herbert Armstrong, 1848).

[40]This sentence was added by Finney.

[41]In another description of this period in his life, Finney said, "Partly from curiosity and partly from an uneasiness of mind upon the subject, which I could not well define, I began to attend that prayer-meeting" ("Prevailing Prayer," *The Independent* [New York], 5 March 1874, pp. 2–3). And in a sermon preached in London, Finney is reported to have said, "I was in the habit of going to prayer meetings as often as I could, even before I was converted" (*The Penny Pulpit* [London] 1,538 [May–July 1850]: 188).

[42]Finney said on another occasion: "I at first got a Bible and placed it among my law books, to study law out of it. This led me to read portions of the old testament, and from this for a time I derived no benefit. But at length I took up the claims of religion as I would any point of law" (*OE,* 21 January 1846, p. 10). He also said, "I bought my first Bible as a law-book, and laid it by the side of my Blackstone. I studied it as I would any other law-book, my sole object being to find in it the great principles of law" (*OE,* 11 October 1848, p. 146).

[43]P. C. Headley was told that Finney once said to Gale after a church service, "Mr. G—, you don't believe what you preach; were I in your place, holding the truth you declare, I would ring the church-bell, and cry in the streets, 'Fire! fire!' " (P. C. Headley, *Evangelists in the Church* [Boston: Hoyt, 1875], p. 128).

Headley himself was later a minister in Adams, and he gleaned information on Finney's activities there. See also *NYE,* 23 May 1850, p. 81; and 9 January 1879, p. 1.

George Washington Gale. Finney's pastor at Adams, New York, and his theological instructor. Gale later founded Galesburg, Illinois, and Knox College. In George Gale, *The Gale Family Records in England and the United States* (Galesville, Wis.: Leith and Gale, 1866), opposite p. 220. Courtesy The British Library.

MS 15 meaning to many of the terms ˈwhich he used with great formality and frequency. What did he mean by *repentance*? Was it a mere feeling of sorrow for sin? Was it altogether a *passive* state of mind? or did it involve a *voluntary* element? If it was a change of mind, in what respect was it a change of mind? What did he mean by the term *regeneration*? What did such language mean when **spoken of as**[44] a spiritual change? What did he mean by *faith*? Was it merely an *intellectual* state? Was it merely a conviction, or persuasion, that the things stated in the Gospel were true? What did he mean by *sanctification*? Did it involve any *physical change* in the subject, or any *physical influence* on the part of God? I could not tell, nor did he seem to me to know himself in what sense he used these terms, **and the like**. We had a great many interesting conversations; but they seemed rather to stimulate my own mind to inquiry, than to satisfy me in respect to the truth. But as I read my Bible and attended the prayer meetings, heard Mr. Gale preach, and conversed with him, with ˈthe elders of the church, and with others from time to time, I became very restless. A little consideration convinced me that I was ˈby no means in a state of mind to go to heaven if I should die **in that condition**. It seemed to me that there must be something in religion that was of infinite importance; and it was soon settled with me, that if the soul was immortal I needed a great change in my inward state **of mind** to be prepared for happiness in heaven. But still my mind was not made up as to the truth or falsehood of the Gospel and of the Christian religion. The question, however, was of too much importance to allow me to rest in any uncertainty on the subject. I was particularly struck with the fact that the prayers that I listened to **in their prayer meetings**, from week to week, were not, that I could see, answered. Indeed I **could readily** understand **by** their **continued** prayers, and **by the** remarks **they ma‹d›e**[45] in their meetings, that **they** did not regard **their prayers** as answered. When I read my Bible I learned what Christ had said in regard to prayer and answers to prayer. He had said, "Ask and ye shall receive, seek and ye shall find, knock and it shall be opened unto you. For every one that asketh receiveth, and he that seeketh findeth, and to him that knocketh it shall be opened."[46] I read also what Christ affirms, that ˈGod is more willing to give **H**is Holy Spirit to them that ask **H**im than earthly parents are to give good gifts to their children. I heard them pray continually for the outpouring of the Holy Spirit, and as often confess **their leanness, and** that they did not receive what they asked for. They exhorted each other to wake up and be engaged, and to pray earnestly for a revival of religion, asserting that if they did their duty, prayed for the outpouring of the Spirit, and were in earnest, that the Spirit of God would be poured out, that they would have a revival of religion, and that **we who were** impenitent would be converted. But in their prayer and conference meetings they would continually conˈfess, substantially, that they were making no progress **either in prayer or effort, ‹or** in securing a revival of religion.›[47] **Their**

(Margin: JHF 09 · MS 16 · MS 17 · JHF 10)

[44]The words "spoken of as" were not altered in the manuscript, but the published version has "applied to."

[45]The words "would make" were altered by Finney to "made."

[46]Matthew 7:7–8; Luke 11:9–10.

[47]The words "or in securing a revival of religion" were added by Finney.

nconsistency **with their professions**, the fact that they prayed so much and vere not answered, was a sad stumbling block to me. I knew not what to nake of it. It was a question[48] in my mind whether I was to understand that hese persons were not truly Christians, and therefore did not prevail with God; or **whether** I misunderstood the promises and teachings of the Bible on his subject‹, or **whether I** was to conclude that **[the]** bible was not true.›[49] Here was something inexplicable to me; and it seemed, at one time, |**as if** it vould almost drive me into **a state of** skepticism. It seemed to me that the eachings of the Bible did not at all accord with the facts which were before ny eyes. On one occasion, when I was in one of their prayer-meetings, I was sked if I did not desire that they should pray for me. I told them, No, ecause I did not see that God answered their prayers. I said, "I suppose I eed to be prayed for, for I am conscious that I am a sinner; but I do not see hat it will do any good for *you* to pray for me, for you are continually asking, ut you do not receive. You have been praying for a revival of religion ever ince I have been in Adams, and yet you have it not. You have been praying or the Holy Spirit to descend upon yourselves, and yet complaining of your eanness." I recollect having used this expression at that time: "You have rayed enough since I have attended these meetings to have prayed the devil ut of Adams, if there is any *virtue* in your prayers. But here you are praying n, and complaining still."[50] I was quite in earnest in what I said, and not a ttle irritable, I think, in consequence of my being brought so continually face face with religious truth; |which was a new state of things to me. But on urther reading of my Bible it struck me that the reason why their prayers vere not answered was because they did not comply with the revealed onditions upon which |God had promised to answer prayer,[51] that they did ot pray in faith in the sense of *expecting* God to give them the things that ey asked for. **I saw that there were many conditions revealed in the Bible upon which prayer was to be answered, that appeared to be ltogether overlooked by them.** This thought, **however,** for **sometime**[52] y in my mind **in the form of** a confused questioning, rather than in any efinite form that could be stated in words. However, this relieved **my mind**

MS 18

MS 19

JHF 11

[48]Matson wrote down the word as "questions," but Fairchild crossed out the second *s*.

[49]The word "the" before "bible" is not in the original but was inserted by Fairchild. The sense ems to require it, although Finney does on some other occasions use the word "bible" without e definite article. See, for example, MS 240. The whole phrase "or whether I was to conclude at bible was not true" is in Finney's handwriting.

[50]P. C. Headley was told:

> Sometimes, when the bell rang for prayer-meeting, he would say to his fellow-student: "Come, W—, let us go to meeting." At its close, returning to his office, he entertained his friend with an analysis of the petitions offered, in remarks like the following: "Did you notice T—'s prayer? He didn't know what he wanted; his part was Orthodox *duty*. But there was L—, he got hold; he meant something, and believes in God." And so he went round the circle, with a discriminating, if not always just, estimate of the prayers to which he had listened (Headley, *Evangelists,* p. 128).

[51]The sentence originally ended here, and the start of a new sentence followed: "I thought I w that they did not comply with the revealed conditions." This was crossed out by Finney.

[52]The word "sometime" was not altered in the manuscript, but the published edition has "some me." Similar alterations occur in several other places through the book. The words "cannot" IS 68) and "sametime" (MS 240) were altered in the same way.

so far as queries about the truth of the Gospel were concerned;[53] and afte struggling in that way for some two or three years, my mind became quit settled that whatever mystification there might be, either ‹in my own or in my pastor‹'s mind,› or the ‹mind of the› church,[54] the Bible was nevertheless, the true Word of God.[55] This being settled, I was brought fac to face with the question whether I would accept Christ as presented in th Gospel, or pursue a worldly course of life. At this period my mind, as I hav MS 20 ˡsince known, was so much impressed by the[56] Holy Spirit, that I could no long leave this question unsettled; nor could I long hesitate between the tw courses of life presented to me.[57]

[53] Finney later wrote, "I do not think I ever could have been converted if I had not discovere the solution of the question: 'Why is it that so much that is called prayer is not answered?' ("Prevailing Prayer," p. 3).

[54] Here Matson wrote down, "whatever mystification there might be, either of myself, m pastor, or the church," but Finney changed it.

[55] Finney maintained that he still had no true belief in the Bible:

> Nothing in my own experience has ever more surprised me than the deep and strong delusion under which I labored during my early life on this point. I honestly supposed that I believed the Bible to be God's word. For a long time it had been impossible for me to evade the arguments in its favor. Indeed so thoroughly was I convinced on this point, that the first thing I did after my conversion was to make out a skeleton of an argument to prove on legal grounds the truth of the Bible—which I deemed to be unanswerable. If anybody had told me then that I did not believe the Bible, I should have felt that they slandered me most ungenerously and shamefully. But yet mine was then only a mere historical belief, and no act of the heart at all. My will did not bow to the supremacy of Bible truth. Indeed I gave it no place at all in my heart; I did not allow it to have the influence of admitted truth upon my heart or my life. Hence my notion that I believed the Bible to be true was a mere delusion (*OE,* 20 November 1848, p. 185).

[56] The word "the" was written down twice here by Matson, and the first one appears to hav been crossed out by Fairchild.

[57] There has been an impression that at the time of Finney's conversion, there was no revival i Adams (see, for example, Frank G. Beardsley, *A Mighty Winner of Souls, Charles G. Finney: Study in Evangelism* [New York: American Tract Society, 1937], p. 9). But this does not seem t be correct. Finney himself refers to the revival in which he was converted, elsewhere in thes *Memoirs* (MS 588 and 687). He also narrated how he was "present in the first meeting in whic the revival spirit was manifest," and this was before his conversion (see "Prevailing Prayer p. 31). And to George Cragin, a convert of his in New York who knew him well, he onc "declared that he was born in a revival and the atmosphere of one was necessary to his spiritu life" (*Oneida Circular,* 30 August 1875, p. 277).

This is confirmed by the recollections of those who were in a position to know. Rev. Davi Kimball, minister of the Martinsburg Church, who was a member of the same presbytery as (W. Gale and was present at both Finney's licensure and ordination, recalled, "Under the minist of Rev. Mr. Gale, the pastor of the Presbyterian Church at Adams, an interesting reviv occurred; to which Mr. F., at first, like all unconverted persons of reflecting minds, was oppose (D. Kimball, "Rev. Charles G. Finney," *The Independent,* 14 May 1868, p. 6).

In the narrative of the revivals in Oneida County in 1826, the editors wrote about Finney, "H was a subject of the revival in Adams, a few years since, under the preaching of the Rev. M Gale" (*A Narrative of the Revival of Religion in the County of Oneida; particularly in the Bounds of t Presbytery of Oneida, in the year 1826* [Utica: Hastings and Tracy, 1826; reprint, Princeton: D. Barrenstein, 1827], p. 50).

Emory Osgood wrote on 12 January 1822 of the revival in Adams beginning "about fo months since," which would indicate that it had started in September, the month before Finn was converted (see *The Latter Day Luminary* [Philadelphia] 3 [February 1822]: 62; and *Herald Salvation* [Watertown, N.Y.], 30 November 1822, pp. 5–7). But Gale himself wrote of how th revival had probably begun even earlier. In about June 1821 he left with his wife on a trip to vi a sick sister near Troy, New York. During his absence he had arranged for a young man, Jededi urchard from Sackett's Harbor, to take the meetings. Gale had heard of Burchard's success in ɔlding meetings further north in the county although he was not yet licensed to preach. "I ngaged him," Gale wrote, "to conduct our worship on the Sabbath. . . . To prevent him suming duties which did not belong to him, and which also might give offense, I charged him to ad sermons on the Sabbath, but not to do anything that properly and exclusively belonged to a inister" (*Autobiography,* p. 165).

When Gale returned home he "found the state of religion had not retrograded, but rather lvanced." Burchard remained with Gale several weeks, visiting, and attending meetings. Gale rote, "After some weeks, finding that I did not need his services, I advised him to labor in other aces, to help the Baptist church in our Township, and to assist in holding meetings in the ljoining towns, which he did with good results" (*Autobiography,* pp. 163, 166).

ale went on to say:

> The work which was on the advance, although not rapid, for some time, continued to increase in interest. In an adjoining town, where Mr. Burchard was attending a meeting, there was the most visible impression, and there I went every week. . . . The work spread in the town, and a good number of the youth especially were converted. . . . As that part of the town was but three or four miles from Adams most of them united with the church there. The impression seemed deepening at Adams, and numbers were converted, but it seemed to linger specially among the youth. I remarked one day to Burchard, as we were going home from visiting in town, that in a certain town where Mr. Nettleton was laboring, he had remarked that there was one man who stood in the way of the conversion of many in that place. If that man should be converted the spell would be broken, or words like those, and the event proved the truth of his remark. I added, "I believe that we have a similar case. If C. G. Finney (who was then a law student) should be converted the young people in the village, and many others, would give up, for numbers of them are deeply convicted" (*Autobiography,* pp. 174–75).

Burchard's part in this revival led to the widespread belief that he was responsible for Finney's nversion. (See, for example, Joseph I. Foot, "Influence of Pelagianism on the Theological ɔurse of Rev. C. G. Finney, developed in his Sermons and Lectures," *Literary and Theological view* [Boston] 5 [March 1838]: 70; and Franklin B. Hough, *A History of Jefferson County in the ate of New York* [Albany: Munsell, 1854], p. 76.) But Gale went on to say:

> To my surprise, Mr. Finney came one evening late in the fall, into my meeting of inquiry. It was either late in the month of October or the first of November. I mention this time as it was reported that Mr. Burchard was the means directly of his conversion. Mr. Burchard was not in town, nor had he been for some four or six weeks. He had left town at my suggestion and was laboring in neighboring towns ("Autobiography of Rev. G. W. Gale," typescript copy in Knox College Library, Galesburg, Ill., p. 144; the published edition has "five or six weeks" [p. 176]).

nney later told Sylvester Eaton the same thing, that "he utterly disclaims the idea of being a nvert of B. Says, when he was converted, B was not in the place" (Eaton to Edward W. Hooker, January 1836, Hooker Papers on Burchardism in the Congregational Library, Boston). Burchard himself, so Finney apparently told Tryon Edwards, "was often in the habit of ferring to him (Mr F) as one of his (B's) 'spiritual children,' when he knew that such a reference plied an utter falsehood" (Edwards to E. W. Hooker, 1 December 1835, in Hooker Papers). owever, Josiah F. Goodhue of Vermont wrote to Finney:

> I understand that great efforts have been made to fix the impression upon your mind that Mr. B. has been guilty of making a mistatement in saying that you were one of his converts. Permit me to say that I have been much with him, and he has uniformly answered in the negative, saying, if my memory serves me, that your conversion took place in the town of Adams, where he was then preaching a small portion of the time, but he knew not that his labours had any direct connexion with that event, and yet from such a conversation in my own house, it was stated in Rutland association that Mr. B. claimed you as one of his converts, & was guilty of falsehood (Goodhue to Finney, 11 February 1836, Finney Papers, microfilm, roll 3).

Burchard went on to be ordained, largely through the influence of Gale, and became a ominent, if controversial, revivalist. He worked closely with Finney in the early years, but nney subsequently repudiated him and his measures. He died in Adams in 1864 at age seventy-ree and was buried there. See Gale, *Autobiography,* pp. 164–74; and Hooker Papers on ırchardism. See also Fowler, *Historical Sketch of Presbyterianism,* pp. 278–81; John J. Duffy and icholas H. Muller, *An Anxious Democracy: Aspects of the 1830s* (Westport, Conn.: Greenwood, 82), pp. 17–42; and *NYE,* 20 October 1864, p. 1; and 11 February 1869, p. 4.

MS 20
JHF 12

CHAPTER II

My Conversion to Christ.

On[1] a Sabbath evening[2] **just at this time of my history** I made up m mind that I would settle the question of my soul's salvation at-once, that if were possible I would make my peace with God. But as I was very busy in th affairs of the office, I knew that without great firmness of purpose I shoul never effectually attend to the subject. I therefore, then and there resolve as far as possible to avoid all business, and everything that would divert m attention, and to give myself wholly to the work of securing the salvation c my soul. I carried this resolution into execution as sternly and thoroughly as could. I was, however, obliged to be a good deal in the office. But as th providence of God would have it, I was not much occupied either Monday c Tuesday, and had opportunity to read my Bible and engage in prayer most c the time.

MS 21

ˈBut[3] I was very proud without knowing it. I had supposed that I had n much regard for the opinions of others, whether they thought this or that i regard to myself; and I had in fact been quite singular in attending **the** prayer meetings, and in the degree of attention that I had paid to religic while in Adams. In this respect I had been so singular as to lead the churc **repeatedly** to think that I must be an anxious inquirer. But I found, when came to face the question, that I was very unwilliing to have any one kno that I was seeking ˈthe salvation of my soul. When I prayed I would on whisper my prayers, after having stopped the key-hole to my door, lest son ‹one›[4] should discover that I was engaged in prayer. Before that time I h

MS 22

[1] Page 20 ends the section from page 1, which was revised in Matson's handwriting, a replaces a previous section of pages numbered 1–16, the next page having been numbered 1 The word "My" in the chapter title was crossed out in pencil and then recrossed out in ink Fairchild.

[2] This must have been 7 October 1821, since Finney gives the date of his conversion as October, which was a Wednesday. See "Power from on High," *The Independent* (New York), January 1872, p. 1; and MS 33.

[3] Pages 21 to 32 were originally numbered 15 to 26, renumbered 17 to 28 and then 21 to 32 Matson. Page 21 started with the following paragraph in Matson's handwriting, which was cross out after the previous pages had been revised.

> That I would, as far as possible, avoid all business, everything that should divert my attention, and give myself to the work of securing my salvation. Accordingly I avoided, as much as I could, all business on Monday, and on Tuesday. I was obliged to be a good deal in the office; but as the providence of God would have it I was not much interrupted either Monday or Tuesday, and had opportunity to read my Bible and engage in prayer most of the time.

[4] The word "one" was added by Finney.

my Bible |lying on the table ‹with›[5] the law books; and it never had occurred to me to be ashamed ‹of› be‹ing› found[6] reading **my Bible,** any more than I should be ashamed ‹of› be‹ing› found reading any of my other books. But after I had addressed myself in earnest to the subject of my own salvation, I kept my Bible as much as I could out of sight. If I was reading it when anybody came in, I would throw my law books upon it, to create the impression that I had not had it in my hand. Instead of being outspoken, and willing to talk with anybody and everybody on the subject as **I had been in the habit of doing,** I found myself unwilling to converse with anybody. I did not want to see my minister **for two reasons: First,** I did not want to let him know how I felt; and |**secondly,** I had no confidence that he would understand my case, and give me the direction that I needed. For the same reasons I avoided conversation with the elders of the church, ‹or›[7] with any of the Christian people. I was ashamed to let them know how I felt, on the one hand; and on the other, I was afraid they would misdirect me. I felt myself shut up to the Bible.

JHF 13

MS 23

On Monday **and Monday night,** and Tuesday **and Tuesday night,** my convictions increased; but still it seemed as if my heart grew harder.[8] I could not shed a tear; I could not pray. I had no opportunity to pray above my breath; and frequently I felt, if I could be alone where I could use my voice and let myself out, I should find relief in prayer.[9] I was shy, and avoided, as

[5] In making an alteration to the text Matson had crossed out the word "with," which was reinserted by Finney.

[6] "To be found" was changed by Finney here and later in the sentence to "of being found."

[7] The word "and" appears to have been altered to "or" by Finney.

[8] On the Monday evening, to Gale's surprise, Finney went to an inquiry meeting. Gale remembered:

> He came in late, had been in the prayer meeting in the other room. I . . . took him by the hand, and said, looking him in the eye, "You have come in here, I presume, as a spy. You want to get something to make sport of." He looked at me, with an air of solemnity I shall never forget. "No, Mr. Gale," said he, "I have not. I am willing now to be a christian." . . . We sat down together. "Do you think," said he, "there is any hope in my case?" I told him I had not liked his course. . . . I told him he might be converted, but if he were it would be something very similar to God's exercising miraculous power. . . . It was not teaching he needed. It was compliance with what he knew already. As I had conversed with all present I requested them all to kneel, while I prayed with them, as my custom was. He kneeled by my side, deeply impressed. He asked me long afterward if I did not feel the house tremble while we kneeled. He said he trembled so that he thought the house shook. I said I did not notice it (G. W. Gale, *Autobiography {to 1834} of George Washington Gale {1789–1861}, Founder of Galesburg, Illinois, and Knox College* [New York: privately printed, 1964], pp. 176–77).

Finney recalled this occasion:

> True conviction is apt to produce a kind of trembling and a tearless agony of soul. I can well recollect the time when I first went to an enquiry meeting. I trembled so that my very seat shook under me. At that time I had never received such instruction as I needed; for if I had, I should have been converted at once. But in my darkness of mind as to what I had to do, I was in great agony, for I knew full well that God's wrath was upon me and that I was living on the very verge of hell. No wonder therefore that my soul was in great agony—a tearless agony, for I could not get the relief of a single tear, and yet my whole being seemed to tremble and quake to its centre. I was not at this time under particular and special conviction, but only a general conviction of being all wrong (*OE,* 13 October 1852, p. 162).

[9] Finney recalled:

much as I could, speaking to anybody on any subject. I endeavored however to do this in a way that would excite no suspicion in any mind that I was seeking the salvation of my soul.

MS 24 **On** Tuesday night I had become very nervous; and in the ꜜnight a strange feeling came over me as if I was about to die. I knew that if I did ‹I›[10] should sink down to hell. **I felt almost like screaming; nevertheless** I quieted myself as best I could until morning. **In the morning I rose, and at** an early hour started for the office. But just before I arrived at the office something seemed to confront me with questions like these. **Indeed** it seemed as if the JHF 14 ꜜinquiry was within myself, as if an inward voice said to me, "What are you waiting for? Did you not promise to give your heart to God? And what are you trying to do? Are you endeavoring to work out a righteousness of your own?"

Just at this point the whole question of Gospel salvation opened to my mind in a manner most marvellous to me at the time. I think I then saw, as clearly as I ever have in my life, the reality and fulness of the atonement of Christ.[11] I saw that his work was a *finished* work; and that instead of having, or MS 25 needing, any righteousness of ꜜmy own to recommend me to God, I had to *submit myself* to the *righteousness of God through Christ*. **Indeed the offer of** Gospel salvation seemed to me to be an offer of *something to be accepted*, and that it was full and complete; and that all that was necessary on my part, was to get my own consent to give up my sins, and ‹**give**›[12] **myself to** Christ. Salvation, it seemed to me, instead of being a thing to be wrought out by my own works, was a thing to be found entirely in the Lord Jesus Christ, who presented himself before me **to be *accepted***[13] as my God and my Savior.

Without being distinctly aware of it, I had stopped in the street right where the inward voice seemed to arrest me. How long I **had** remained in that position I cannot say. But after this distinct revelation had stood for some little time before my mind, the question seemed to be put, "Will you accept it *now, to-day?*" I replied, "Yes; I will accept it to-day, or I will die in the attempt."

MS 26 North of the village, ꜜand over a hill lay a **grove** of woods,[14] in which I was

> Before my conversion I had never prayed much. For a short time previous, I used to lock my office door, stop the key-hole, and whisper out a short prayer in the greatest perturbation lest somebody should hear my voice, or in some way learn that I was praying. But this answered no purpose; I must pray better than this. I seemed to be bound up and hemmed in on every side, and could not pray (*OE,* 30 January 1856, p. 18).

[10]The word "I" was omitted in the original and appears to have been inserted by Finney.

[11]In another account of his conversion, Finney said:

> This was one of the last things that was cleared up in my mind before I fully committed my soul to trust God. I had been studying the atonement; I saw its philosophical bearings—saw what it demanded of the sinner; but it irritated me and I said—If I should become a Christian, how could I know what God would do with me? Under this irritation I said foolish and bitter things against Christ—till my own soul was horrified at its own wickedness and I said—I will make all this up with Christ if the thing is possible ("God's Love for a Sinning World," *OE,* 22 June 1853, p. 98).

[12]The word "give" was added by Finney.

[13]The underlining of the word "*accepted*" is in black ink and appears to have been added by Finney. The phrase "to be *accepted*" was crossed out by Fairchild.

[14]G. W. Gale, speaking of this place, says, "About half a mile north of the town was a grove, as they are called in Illinois, a woodland of considerable extent" (*Autobiography,* p. 179).

n **almost** the daily habit of walking, more or less, when it was pleasant weather. It was now October, and the time was past for my frequent walks there. Nevertheless, instead of going to the office I turned and bent my course **for that grove of** woods, feeling that I must be alone and away from all human eyes and ears, so that I could pour out my prayer to God. But still my pride must show itself.

As I went over |the hill it occurred to me that some one might see me, and suppose that I was going away to pray. **But I presume that** there was not a person on earth that would have suspected such a thing had he seen me going. But so great was my pride, and so much was I possessed with the fear of man, that I recollect that I skulked along under the fence, till I got so far out of sight that no one from the village could see me. I then penetrated into the woods **for**, I should think, a quarter of a mile, went |over on the other side of the hill, and found a place where some large trees had fallen across each other, leaving an open place between **three or four large trunks of trees.** There I saw I could make a kind of closet. I crept into this place and knelt down for prayer. As I turned to go up into the woods, I recollect to have said, "I will give my heart to God, or I never will come down from there." I recollect repeating this as I went up—"I will give my heart to God before I ever come down again."[15]

JHF 15

MS 27

But when I attempted to pray I found that my *heart* would not pray. I had supposed that if I could only be where I could speak aloud, without being overheard, I could pray freely. But lo! when I came to try, I was dumb: that is, I had nothing to say to God; or at least I could say but a few words, and those without heart. In attempting to pray I would hear a rustling in the leaves, as I thought, and would stop and look up to see if somebody **was** not coming. This I did sev|eral times.[16] Finally I found myself verging fast to despair. I said to myself, "**I find** I cannot pray. My *heart* is dead to God, and *will not* pray." I then reproached myself for having promised to give my heart

MS 28

[15] In another account of these events, Finney said:

I can well recollect a crisis in my own religious history. I felt that there was not another step to take in the direction I was going. I had pursued my worldly interests a long time, all in vain; I had sought God selfishly, but all in vain; and I now betook myself to mighty prayer as I supposed, as if I would pull down blessings at any rate upon my needy soul. Often since, I have looked back with wonder to that moment. I came then to see and I actually said to myself—I may just as well stop this course of seeking now as ever. I hastened away to the woods to pray, pressed with the consideration—I am a selfish man—altogether selfish. I must come to a dead stand in this course; my selfish efforts are of no use, and even my selfish prayers are nothing better than an abomination before God. I had gone out with the determination never to leave the place without giving myself to God. I could see that all had been perfectly selfish, and that now the thing God demanded of me was to desist from any selfishness and give up myself supremely and wholly to Him (*OE,* 4 July 1849, p. 107).

[16] Someone writing in the London *Christian Age* at the time of Finney's death recollected hearing Finney "more than twenty-five years ago" say that he could not feel alone: "Some one was on the other side of the tree. I walked round it, but still felt that some listener, eluding me, was on the other side. In this way I actually walked several times around the tree" (*The Christian Age* [London], 3 November 1875, p. 175).

Finney's own accounts of this incident do not seem to confirm that he walked around a tree. See, for example, *Lectures on Revivals of Religion,* ed. William G. McLoughlin (Cambridge, Mass.: Belknap, 1960), p. 92; and *OE,* 8 November 1848, p. 162.

to God before I left the woods. **I thought I had made a rash promise, that I should be obliged to break. That** when I came to try I found I could not give my heart to God. My inward soul hung back, and there was no going out of my heart to God. I began to feel deeply that it was too late; that it must be that I was given up of God and was past hope. The thought was pressing me

JHF 16 **just at this moment** ‹of›[17] the rashness of my ¦promise, that I would give my heart to God that day or die in the attempt. It seemed to me as if that was binding upon my soul; and yet I was going to break my vow. **I recollect that a** great sinking and discouragement came over me **at this point**, and I felt almost too weak to stand[18] upon my knees.

MS 29 Just at this moment I ¦again thought I heard some one approach me, and I opened my eyes to see whether it were so. But right there the revelation of my pride of heart as the great difficulty that stood in the way, was distinctly ‹shown›[19] to me. An overwhelming sense of my wickedness in being ashamed to have a human being see me on my knees before God, took such powerful possession of me, that I cried at the top of my voice, and exclaimed that I would not leave that place if all the men on earth and all the devils in hell surrounded me. "What!" I said, "such a degraded sinner as I am, on my knees confessing my sins to the great and holy God; and ashamed to have any human being, and a sinner like myself, **know it, and** find me on my knees endeavoring to make my peace with my offended God!" The sin[20] appeared awful, infinite. It broke me down before the Lord. Just at that point this passage of Scripture seemed to drop into my mind with a flood of light: "Then

MS 30 ¦shall ye go and pray unto me, and I will **answer** you. Then shall ye seek me and **shall** find me, when **you** search for me with all your heart."[21] I instantly seized hold of this with my *heart.* I had *intellectually* believed the Bible before; but never had the ‹truth been›[22] in my mind that faith was a *voluntary trust* instead of an *intellectual state.* I was as conscious as I was of my existence of *trusting*‹, at›[23] that moment, in God's veracity. Somehow I knew that that was a passage of Scripture, though I do not think I ‹had›[24] ever read it.[25] I knew that it was God's Word, and God's voice, as it were, that spoke to me. I cried to Him, "Lord, I take thee at thy Word. Now thou *knowest* that I *do* search for thee with all my heart, and that I have come here to pray to thee; and thou

JHF 17 hast promised to hear me." ¦That seemed to settle the question **of the fact** that I could *then, that day,* perform my vow. The Spirit seemed to lay stress

MS 31 upon that idea in the text, "*When* ¦ye search for me with all your heart." The

[17]The word "with" here was changed by Finney to "of."

[18]In the margin at this point the word "keep" is written in pencil. The handwriting appears to be that of Lewis Tappan, who had read the manuscript (see Introduction, p. xxixff.).

[19]This word was originally "made," but it was changed by Finney to "shown."

[20]Matson had at first written down "scene" here but changed it to "sin."

[21]Jeremiah 29:12–13.

[22]The word "idea" here was changed by Finney to "truth been."

[23]The comma and the word "at" were added by Finney.

[24]The word "had" was added by Finney.

[25]In another account Finney seems to indicate that he already knew of the passage. Speaking of himself in the third person, he is reported as saying, "He saw that though this promise was in the Old Testament, and was addressed to the Jews, it was still as applicable to him as to them" (*Lectures on Revivals,* McLoughlin ed., p. 92).

question of *when,* that is of the *present time,* seemed to fall heavily into my heart. I told the Lord that I should take **Him** at **His Word, and** that **He** could not lie; and that therefore I was sure that he heard my prayer, and that **He** would be found of me.

He then gave me many other promises both from the Old and New Testaments, **and** especially some most precious promises respecting our Lord Jesus Christ. I never can, in words, make any human being understand how precious and true those promises appeared to me. I took them one after the other as infallible truth, the assertions of God who could not lie. They did not seem so much to fall into my *intellect* as into my *heart,* to be put within the grasp of the voluntary powers of my mind; and I seized hold of them, appropriated them, and fastened upon them with the grasp of a drowning man.

I continued thus to pray, and to receive and appropriate prom|ises for a long time, I know not how long. **At any rate** I prayed till my mind became so full, that before I was aware of it I was on my feet, and tripping up the ascent toward the road. The question of my being converted had not so much as arisen to my thought. **But** as I went up brushing through the leaves and b**rush,** I recollect saying with great emphasis, "*If I am ever converted, I will preach the Gospel.*"[26] MS 32

I soon reached the road that led to the village, and began to reflect upon what had passed; and I found that my mind had become most wonderfully quiet and peaceful. I said to myself, "What is this? I must have grieved the Holy Ghost entirely away. I have lost all my conviction. I have not a particle of concern about my soul; and it must be that the Spirit has left me." "Why!" thought I, "I never was so far from being concerned about my own salvation in my life." |Then I remembered what I had said to God while I was on my knees. That I had said I would |take[27] **Him** at **His Word;**—and indeed I recollected a good many things that I had said, and concluded that it was no wonder that the Spirit had left me. That for such a sinner as I was to take hold of God's **Word** in that way, was presumption if not blasphemy. I concluded that in my excitement I had grieved the Holy Spirit, and perhaps committed the unpardonable sin. JHF 18 MS 33

I walked quietly toward the village; and so perfectly quiet was my mind that it seemed *as if all nature listened.* It was on the **tenth** of October,[28] and a very pleasant day. I had gone into the woods immediately after an early breakfast; and when I returned to the village I found it was dinner time. **And** yet I had been wholly unconscious of the time that had passed; **for** it **did not**

[26]In another place Finney said:

> I can recollect when religion was repulsive to me because I feared that if I should be converted, God would send me to preach the gospel. But I thought further on this subject. God, said I, has a right to dispose of me as he pleases, and I have no right to resist. . . . A long time I had a secret conviction that I should be a minister, though my heart repelled it. In fact, my conversion turned very much upon my giving up this contest with God, and subduing this repellency of feeling against God's call (*OE,* 5 January 1853, p. 2; and see MS 47–48).

[27]Pages 33 to 45 were originally numbered 29 to 41 and renumbered 33 to 45 by Matson.

[28]The date "1821" inserted here in black ink appears to be in Fairchild's handwriting. It was crossed out again by him.

appear to me **as if** I had been gone from the village but a short time. But how was I to account for the quiet of my mind? I tried to recall my convictions, to get back again the load of sin under which I had been laboring. But all sense MS 34 of sin, all consciousness of present sin or |guilt, had departed from me. I said to myself, "What is this, that I cannot **scare up** any sense of guilt in my soul, as great a sinner as I am?" I tried in vain to make myself anxious about my present state. **I found** I was so quiet and peaceful that I tried to feel concerned about that, lest it should be a **mere** result of my having grieved the Spirit away. But take any view of it I would, I could not be anxious at all about my soul, and about my spiritual state. The repose of my mind was unspeakably great. I never can describe it in words. **No view that I could take, and no effort that I could make, brought back a sense of guilt, or the least concern about my ultimate salvation.** The thought of God was sweet to my mind, and the most profound spiritual tranquility had taken full possession of me. This was a great mystery; but it did not distress or perplex me.

I went to my dinner, and found I had no appetite to eat. I then went to the MS 35 office, and found **Esq. Wright** had gone to dinner.[29] |I took down my bass viol, and as I was accustomed to do, began to play and sing some pieces of JHF 19 sacred music.[30] |But as soon as I began to **play and** sing those sacred words, I began to weep. It seemed as if my heart was all liquid; and my feelings were in such a state that I could not hear my own voice in singing without ‹causing›[31] my Sensibility to overflow. I wondered at this; and tried to suppress my tears, but could not. **I wondered what ailed me that I felt such a disposition to weep.** After trying in vain to suppress my tears, I put up my instrument and stopped singing.

After dinner we were engaged in removing our books and furniture to another office. We were very busy in this, and had but little conversation all the afternoon. My mind, however, remained **all the afternoon** in that profoundly tranquil state. There was a great sweetness and tenderness in my thoughts and **soul**. Everything appeared to be going right, and nothing

[29] Benjamin Wright (1784–1861) opened a law office in Adams in 1808. He was admitted to the bar in 1816 and was a judge from 1829 to 1836. He was "well known all through the county." See Benjamin Wright "biographical details" in file on "War of 1812 Pensioners"; and Grace M. Lansing, "Charles G. Finney," typewritten manuscript dated 1942, Genealogy Department, Watertown Public Library, Watertown, New York.

He is not to be confused with Judge Benjamin Wright (1770–1842) of Rome, New York, the surveyor and chief engineer of the Erie Canal. The latter was said to have been converted during the Rome revival in 1826; however, there is some doubt about this. See *The National Cyclopaedia of American Biography,* vol. 1 (New York: James T. White, 1892), pp. 239–40; *The Circular* (Oneida, N.Y.), 15 November 1869, p. 274; and Abby Bullock to Lydia Finney, 19 January 1828, Finney Papers, microfilm, roll 1.

The abbreviation "Esq." was changed by Fairchild wherever it occurred in the manuscript to "Squire."

[30] Finney played both the violin and the bass viol and was an accomplished musician. He had taught a singing school in Warren, and when he went to Adams he became leader of the choir. His bass viol was purchased with his first earnings. See Helen Finney Cox to W. C. Cochran, 2 April 1908, transcription in Finney Papers, file 2/2/2, box 4; William C. Cochran, *Charles Grandison Finney: Memorial Address* (Philadelphia: Lippincott, 1908), pp. 19–21; and George F. Wright, *Charles Grandison Finney* (Boston and New York: Houghton Mifflin, 1891), p. 18.

[31] The word "setting" here was changed to "causing" by Finney.

seemed to ruffle or disturb me in the least. ꜍Just before evening the thought took possession of my mind, that as soon as I was left alone in the new office **that night**, I would try to pray again. That I was not going to abandon the subject of religion and give it up, at any rate; and therefore, although I no longer had any concern about my soul, still I would continue to pray. MS 36

Just at evening we got the books and furniture adjusted; and I made up in an open fire-place a good **large** fire, hoping to spend the evening alone. Just **as it was** dark **Esq. Wright**, seeing that everything was adjusted, bid me good night and went to his home. I had accompanied him to the door; and as I closed the door and turned around, my heart seemed to be liquid within me. All my **inward** feelings seemed to rise and **pour themselves** out; and the **impression on my mind** was,—"I want to pour my whole soul out to God." The rising of my soul was so great that I rushed into the **Counsel** room, back of the front office, to pray. There was no fire, and no light, in the room; **hence** ꜍**it was dark. N**evertheless it appeared to me as if it **was** perfectly light. MS 37

As I went in and shut the door after me, it seemed as if I met the Lord Jesus Christ *face to face.*[32] It did not occur to me then, nor did it for **sometime** afterward, that it was wholly ꜍a *mental* state. On the contrary, it seemed to me that I **met him face to face, and** saw him as I would see any other man. He said nothing, but looked at me in such a manner as to break me right down at his feet. I have always since regarded this as a most remarkable state of mind; for it seemed to me a reality that he stood before me, and **that** I fell down at his feet and poured out my soul to him. I wept aloud like a child, and made such confessions as I could with my choked utterance. It seemed to me **as if** I bathed his feet with my tears; and yet I had no distinct impression that I *touched* him, that I recollect. I must have continued in this state for a good while; but my mind was too much absorbed with the interview to recollect **scarcely** anything that I said. JHF 20

꜍But I know as soon as my mind became calm enough to break off from the interview, I returned to the front office and found that the fire that I had **just** made of large wood was nearly burned out. But as I **re**turned and was about to take a seat by the fire, I received *a mighty baptism of the Holy Ghost.* Without expect**ing** it, without ever having the thought in my mind that there was any such thing for me, without any recollection that I had ever heard the thing mentioned by any person in the world, **at a moment entirely unexpected by me,** the Holy Spirit descended upon me in a manner that seemed *to go through me,* body and soul. I could feel the impression, *like a wave of electricity,* going through and through me. Indeed it seemed to come in *waves,* and *waves of liquid love*;—for I could not express it in any other way. MS 38

[32]Finney described this in a sermon preached in the Oberlin Church:

I have often in your presence alluded to the circumstances attending my own conversion. When Christ revealed himself to me, I certainly seemed to see him, and to rush and fall at his feet as really as if I were to turn about now and fall at Br. Mahan's feet. I felt a powerful drawing of soul towards him, as if my very soul would be drawn out of me;—I rushed into a private room and there I seemed to meet him. There—so it seemed—was Jesus—the very Savior! (*OE,* 18 March 1846, p. 42).

And yet it did not seem like **water, but rather** ‹**as**›[33] *the breath of God.* I can recollect distinctly that it seemed to *fan* me, like immense wings; **and it seemed to me, as these waves passed over me, that they literally *moved my hair like a passing breeze.***

MS 39 ˡNo words can express the wonderful love that was shed abroad in my heart. **It seemed to me that I should burst.** I wept aloud with joy and love; and I do not know but I should say I literally *bellowed out* the unutterable gushings of my heart. These waves came over me, and over me, and over me one after the other, until I recollect I cried out, "I shall *die* if these waves JHF 21 continue to ˡpass over me." I said to the Lord, "Lord, I cannot *bear* any more." ‹yet I had no fear of death.›[34]

How long I continued in this state, with this baptism continuing to roll over me and go through me, I do not know. But I know it was late in the evening when a member of my choir—for I was the leader of the choir—came into the office to see me. He was a member of the church. He found me in this state of loud weeping, and said to me, "Mr. Finney, what ails you?" I could make him no answer for **sometime**. He then said, "Are you in pain?" I gathered **up** myself as best I could and replied, "No; but ***I am*** *so happy that I cannot live.*"

MS 40 He turned and left the ofˡfice, and in a few minutes returned with one of the elders of the church, whose shop was nearly across the way from our office.[35] This elder was a very serious man; and in my presence had been very watchful, and I had scarcely ever seen him laugh. When he came in I was very much in the state in which I was when the young man went out to call him. He asked me how I felt, and I began to tell him. Instead of saying anything he fell into a most spasmodic laugh. It seemed as if it was impossible for him to keep from laughing *from the very bottom of his heart.* **It seemed to be a spasm that was irresistible.**

There was a young man in the neighborhood who was preparing for college, with whom I had been very intimate. **Mr. Gale, the** minister, as I afterwards learned, had repeatedly talked with him on the subject of religion, and warned him against being misled by me. **Mr. Gale** informed him that I was a very careless young man about religion; and he thought that if he MS 41 associated much with me ˡhis mind would be diverted, and he would not be converted. After I was converted, and this young man was converted, he told me that he had said to Mr. Gale several times when he had admonished him about associating so much with me, that my conversation had often affected him more, religiously, than his preaching. I had, indeed, let out my feelings a good deal to this young man, **whose name was Sears.**[36]

[33]The word "of" here was crossed out and "as" inserted in black ink in what appears to be Finney's handwriting.

[34]The phrase "yet I had no fear of death." was added by Finney in black ink.

[35]This elder was Samuel Bond (see MS 42), one of the six original elders appointed when the church became Presbyterian in January 1821. He had a "cabinet shop," and for fifty years was in partnership with Perley D. Stone, a deacon, and later an elder, of the church. See S. W. Durant, *History of Jefferson County, New York* (Philadelphia: Everts, 1878), p. 260; and *NYE,* 21 September 1882, p. 6.

[36]Charles Cushman Sears (1798–1838) was the schoolteacher at Adams. After his conversion he was baptized at the same time as Finney. He studied for the ministry at Hamilton College and

ˈBut just at the time when I was giving an account of my feelings to this elder of the church, and to the other member who was with him, this young man **Sears** came into the office. I was sitting with my back toward the door, and barely observed that he came in. **However, he came in and** listened with astonishment to what I was saying **to them.** The first I knew he partly fell upon the floor, and cried out in the greatest agony of mind, "Do pray for me!" ˈThe elder of the church and the other member knelt down and began to pray for him; and when they had prayed, I prayed for him myself. Soon after this they all retired and left me alone.

JHF 22

MS 42

The question then arose in my mind, "Why did Elder **Bond** laugh so? Did he not think that I **am** under a delusion, or crazy?" This suggestion brought a kind of darkness over my mind; and I began to query with myself whether it was proper for me—such a sinner as I had been, to pray for that young man. A cloud seemed to shut in over me. I had no hold upon anything in which I could rest; and after a little while I retired to-bed, not distressed in mind, but still at a loss to know what to make of my present state. Notwithstanding the baptism I had received, this temptation so obscured my views that I went to-bed without feeling sure that my peace was made with God.

I soon fell asleep, but almost as soon awoke again on account of the great flow of the love of God that was in my heart. ˈ*I was so filled with love that I could not sleep.* Soon I fell asleep again, and awoke in the same manner. When I awoke this temptation would return upon me, and the love that seemed to be in my heart would abate; but as soon as I was asleep, it was so warm within me that I would immediately awake. Thus I continued, till late at night I obtained some sound repose.

MS 43

When I awoke in the morning the sun had risen, and was pouring a clear light into my room. Words cannot express the impression that this sunlight made upon me. Instantly the baptism that I had received the night before ˈreturned upon me in the same manner. I arose upon my knees in the bed and wept aloud with joy, and remained for **sometime** too much overwhelmed with the baptism of the Spirit to do anything but pour out my soul to God. It seemed as if this morning's baptism was accompanied with a gentle reproof, **as if** the Spirit seemed to say to me, "Will you doubt?" "Will you doubt?" I cried, "No! I *will not* ˈdoubt; I *cannot* doubt." He then cleared the subject up so much to my mind that it was in fact impossible for me to doubt that the Spirit of God had taken possession of my soul.

JHF 23

MS 44

In this state I was taught the doctrine of *justification by faith* as a *present experience.* That doctrine had never taken any such possession of my mind, that I had ever viewed it distinctly as a fundamental doctrine of the Gospel. Indeed, I did not know at all what it meant ‹in the proper sense.›[37] But I could now see and understand what was meant by the passage, "Being

Princeton Theological Seminary. From 1830 until his death he was the principal of Princeton Academy in New Jersey. In 1835 he declined an invitation to fill the professorship of languages at the Oberlin Collegiate Institute. See Gale, *Autobiography,* pp. 181–82; MS notes on Sears in Biography File, Hamilton College Library, Clinton, New York; Oberlin College, "Prudential Committee Minutes," 14 July 1835, Oberlin College Archives; and letters from Sears to Finney in the Finney Papers.

[37]The words "in the proper sense." were added by Finney.

justified by faith, we have peace with God through our Lord Jesus Christ."[38] I could see that the moment I believed while up in the woods, all sense of condemnation had entirely dropped out of my mind; and that from that moment I could not feel a sense of guilt or condemnation by any effort that I could make. My sense of guilt was gone, my sins were gone; and I do not think I felt any more sense of guilt than if I never had sinned. This was just MS 45 the reve|lation that I needed. I felt myself justified by faith; and so far as I could see, I was in a state in which I did not sin. Instead of feeling that I was sinning all the time, my heart was so full of love that it overflowed. My cup ran over with blessing and with love, and I could not feel that I was sinning against God. Nor could I recover the least sense of guilt for my past sins. Of *this* experience I said nothing that I recollect, at the time, to anybody;—that is, this experience of justification, **and so far as I could see, of present sanctification.**[39]

[38] Romans 5:1.
[39] Fairchild crossed out the phrase "and so far as I could see, of present sanctification."

CHAPTER III

MS 45
JHF 24

‹I begin my work with immediate success.›

This[1] morning of which I have just spoken I went down into the office, and there I was having the renewal of these mighty waves of love and salvation flowing over me, when **Esq. Wright** came into the office. I said a few words to him on the subject of his salvation,—**I do not recollect what**. He looked at me with astonish|ment,[2] but made no reply whatever ‹that I recollect›.[3] He dropped his head, and after standing a few minutes left the office. I thought no more of it then, but afterwards found that the remark I made pierced him like a sword; and he did not recover from it till he was converted.[4] MS 46

Soon after **Esq. Wright** had left the office, a Deacon **Barney** came into the office and said to me, "Mr. Finney, do you recollect that my cause is to be tried at ten O'clock this morning? I suppose you are ready." I had been retained to attend his suit as his attorney.[5] I replied to him, "Deacon **Barney**, I have a retainer from the Lord Jesus Christ to plead his cause, and I cannot plead yours." He looked at me with astonishment, and said, "What do you mean?" I told him in a few words that I had enlisted in the cause of Christ; and then repeated that I had a retainer from the Lord Jesus Christ to plead his cause, and that he must go and get somebody else to attend to his law-suit,—I could not do it. He dropped his head; and **after a few moments,** without making any reply, went out. |A few moments later, in passing the window I observed that Deacon **Barney** **stood** in the road, seemingly lost in deep MS 47

[1] MS 45 continues. The heading of this chapter and all the subsequent headings were inserted by Finney. This heading is on a separate piece of paper pasted over a section of the original page. Finney had written down the word "began" in the chapter title, but the *a* was altered to an *i* in black ink. It appears to have been done by Finney himself. Fairchild crossed out the whole title and wrote in *"The Beginning of My Work,"* which he later altered again. The writing covered over, which was crossed out by Finney, reads, "I had related as I had opportunity, what God had done for my soul, my conversion and subsequent baptism of the Holy Ghost."

[2] Pages 46 to 60 were originally numbered 42 to 56 by Matson and were renumbered 46 to 60 by Finney.

[3] The words "that I recollect" were added by Finney.

[4] See MS 60–65.

[5] Finney was not qualified as a lawyer; he was still only an attorney in training. Gale stated:

> He was expecting at the time of his conversion, to be licensed soon in the Supreme Court. He could have been licensed some two or three years before, . . . in the court of "Common Pleas" but he did not choose to do so. He had all the business he wanted, and that was enough to support him, in Justice's Courts. He proposed having all the time he could for study (G. W. Gale, *Autobiography {to 1834} of George Washington Gale {1789–1861}, Founder of Galesburg, Illinois, and Knox College* [New York: privately printed, 1964], p. 182; instead of "proposed" the typescript transcription has "preferred" [p. 149]).

meditation. He went away, as I afterwards learned, and immediately settled
JHF 25 his suit. He then betook himself to ˡprayer, and soon got into a much higher religious state than he had ever been in before.

I soon sallied forth from the office to converse with those whom I should meet about their souls. I had the impression, which has never left my mind, that God wanted me to preach the Gospel, and that I must begin immediately. I somehow seemed to *know* it. If you ask me how I knew it,—I cannot tell how I knew it, any more than I can tell how I knew that that was the love of God and the baptism of the Holy Ghost which I had received. I did somehow know it with a certainty that was past all **doubt, or all** *possibility* of doubt. And so I seemed to know that the Lord commissioned me to preach the Gospel.

When I was first convicted the thought had occurred to my mind that if I was ever converted I should be obliged to leave my profession, of which I
MS 48 ˡwas very fond, and go to preaching the Gospel. This at first stumbled me. I thought I had taken too much pains, and spent too much time and study in my profession to think now of becoming a Christian, if by doing so I should be obliged to preach the Gospel. However, I at last came to the conclusion that I must submit that question to God. **That** I had never commenced the study of law from any regard to God, and that I had no right to make any conditions with **Him**; and I therefore had laid aside the thought of becoming a minister, until it was sprung in my mind, as I have related, on my way from my place of prayer in the woods **down to the village.**[6] But now, after receiving these baptisms of the Spirit I was quite willing to preach the Gospel. Nay, I found that I was unwilling to do anything else. I had no longer any desire to practise law. Everything in that direction was **all** shut up, and had no longer any attractions for me at all. **I found my mind entirely changed and that a complete revolution had occurred within me.**[7] I had no disposition to
MS 49 make ˡmoney. I had no hungering and thirsting after worldly pleasures and amusements in any direction. My whole mind was taken up with Jesus and his
JHF 26 salvation; and the world seemed to me of very little ˡconsequence. Nothing, it seemed to me, could be put in competition with the worth of souls; and no labor, I thought, could be so sweet, and no **enjoyment** so **great**, as **to be employed in** holding up Christ to a dying world.

With this impression, as I said, I sallied forth to converse with any with whom I might meet. I first dropped in at the shop of a shoemaker, who was a pious man, and one of the most praying Christians, as I thought, in the church. I found him in conversation with a son of one of the elders of the church;[8] and this young man was defending Universalism. **Mr. Willard—**

[6]See MS 32.

[7]In a sermon preached in 1858 Finney is reported as saying:

> After my conversion the whole subject of going into court to engross myself in other men's quarrels became unutterably loathesome. I saw that I had never managed a case with real honesty. All I had cared for was to get my case and do well for my client, and my soul turned away from it with loathing. Though pressed very hard to engage again, I refused. Now I do not say that no man can serve God at the bar, but I do say that if he has known God indeed, he will not wish to serve in that sphere. He will beg to be excused (*OE,* 1 September 1858, p. 138).

[8]There were six elders: Abel Clary, Jacob Kellogg, Josiah Hinman, Westwood Wright, William

which was the shoemaker's **name**[9]—turned to me and said: "Mr. Finney, what do you think of the argument of this young man;" and he then stated what he had been saying in defence of Universalism. The answer |appeared to me so ready that in a moment I was enabled to blow his argument to the wind.[10] The young man saw **in a moment** that **I had demolished** his argument; and he rose up without making any reply, and went suddenly out. But soon I observed, as I stood in the middle of the room, that the young man, instead of going along the street, had passed around the shop, **was getting** over the fence, and **steered** straight across the **lots**[11] toward **a grove of** woods. I thought no more of **that** until evening, when the young man came out and appeared to be a bright convert, giving a relation of his experience. He went into the woods, and there, as he said, gave his heart to God.

MS 50

I spoke with many persons that day, and I believe the Spirit of God made lasting impressions upon every one of them. I cannot remember one whom I spoke with, who was not soon after converted. Just at evening I called at the house of a friend where a |young man was employed in distilling whiskey. They had heard that I had become a Christian; and as they were about to sit down to tea, they urged me to sit down and take tea with them. The **heads of the family, both male and female,** were professors of religion. But **the** sister of the lady, who was pres|ent, was an unconverted girl; and this young man of whom I have spoken—a distant relative of the family—was a professed Universalist. He was rather an outspoken and talkative Universalist, and a young man of a good deal of energy of character. I sat down with them to tea, and they **asked** me to ask a blessing. It was what I had never done; but I did not hesitate a moment, but commenced to ask the blessing of God as we sat around th**at** table. I had scarcely more than begun before the state of these young people rose before my mind, and excited so much compassion that I burst into weeping, and was unable to proceed. Every one around the table sat speechless for a short time, while I continued to weep. Directly the young man **shoved** back from |the table and rushed out of the room. He fled to his room and locked himself in, and was not seen again till the next morning; when he came out expressing a blessed hope in Christ. He has been for many years an able minister of **Christ**.[12]

MS 51

JHF 27

MS 52

In the course of the day a good deal of excitement was created in the

Grenell, and Samuel Bond. See S. W. Durant, *History of Jefferson County, New York* (Philadelphia: Everts, 1878), p. 260.

[9]This was probably the E. Willard who subsequently wrote letters to Finney giving news of the progress of religion in Adams (E. Willard to Finney, 28 August 1826 and 12 March 1831, Finney Papers, microfilm, rolls 1, 2).

[10]Finney had thought a good deal about Universalism and even considered becoming a Universalist before his conversion.

> I recollect when I tried and wanted to be Universalist, and for this purpose went to their meetings and heard their arguments; I said to myself, "For very shame, I could never use such arguments; no, not for the shame of admitting and avowing such absurdities!" (*OE,* 9 November 1853, p. 178).

See also *OE,* 26 September 1848, p. 139; 15 February 1854, p. 25; and 30 January 1856, p. 18.

[11]The word "lots" was not changed in the original but appears as "fields" in the published edition.

[12]This sentence had been inserted in the margin in Matson's handwriting. Fairchild crossed it out and reinserted a similar sentence in a space in the text.

village by its being reported what the Lord had done for my soul. Some thought one thing, and some another. At evening, without any appointment having been made that I could learn, I observed that everybody was going to the place[13] where they usually held their conference and prayer meetings. My conversion had created a good deal of astonishment in the village. I afterwards learned that sometime before this some of the members of the church had proposed in a church meeting to make me a particular subject of prayer;[14] and that Mr. Gale had discouraged them, saying that he did not believe I would ever be converted. That from conversing with me he had found that I was very much enlightened upon the subject of religion, and very much hardened. |And furthermore, he said he was almost discouraged. That I led the choir, and taught the young people sacred music; and that they were so much under my |influence that he did not believe, while I remained in Adams, that they ever would be converted.[15]

MS 53

JHF 28

[13]The words "of meeting" here appear to have been crossed out by Finney.

[14]In an 1851 sermon Finney gave another account of this incident. The church held the meeting to decide "what measures should be adopted to secure a revival of religion." It was proposed that "it would be best to pray for the conversion of certain individuals," among whom was Finney (C. G. Finney, *Repentance: Its Nature, Grounds, Necessity, and Infinite Importance* [London: Snow, 1851], p. 33).

[15]In an article published in *The New-York Evangelist* after Finney's death, the writer says:

> It is perhaps needful to preface that before Mr. Finney's conversion he was a reckless, godless, skeptical young man, the leader of the young people, and the ringleader of "fun." His older brother Zenas Finney, told the writer that Charles was a strange, wild sort of boy, "not worth much for work," who was always conjuring up some mischief, or, as Zenas expressed it, "was always full of his tunes." He would leave his work in the field, and his brothers, and perch on the fence near by, where he delighted to "cut up all sorts of antics." He was extremely fond of arguing, and became a champion debater in school-house lyceums. . . .
>
> Mr. Finney was quite a singer, and so quite naturally, while a young lawyer at Adams, became the leader of the choir. Deacon H— was a sober, grave-faced deacon and a "pillar" in the church. The conduct of Mr. Finney and the young folks in the gallery was such as to seriously vex the good people below. The deacon made some pretty severe remarks about Mr. Finney and his conduct; which coming to the ears of the latter, so offended the choir that the next Sabbath they all sat below, and there was nobody in the gallery to do the singing. Mr. Finney came in a conspicuous manner up the aisle, and took a prominent seat in front. The hymn being given out the minister said, "There seems to be no singers in the gallery to-day. Will some-body start the tune?"—looking hard toward Mr. Finney. Mr. Finney thereupon turned partially around, and with a bold gesture toward Deacon H—, said in a stage whisper loud enough to be heard through the church "Deacon H— will lead the singing to-day." The piquancy of this remark can be best appreciated in the light of the well known fact that the good Deacon could not sing any more than a horse. This incident was related to me by a most excellent and pious member of my flock, and a daughter of Deacon H— (H.M.P., "Full of His Tunes," *NYE,* 20 April 1876, p. 2).

Finney himself said on another occasion:

> Now, I had led the singing in that church for a considerable time before I was converted; and he [Gale] told them [the church meeting] that he did not believe they could reach the young people,—for if anything were said to offend me, I should sit below, and that the rest would not sing without me. There it was. I was doubtless a great obstacle in the way of reaching those young people; but, as the Lord would have it, I was the first among them on whom he laid his hand. "Repent," said the Spirit of the Lord to my soul; and when that was done, it was found that the young people actually were under my influence as much as the minister had supposed,—for the whole mass of them rose up, and inquired what they should do to be saved. . . . I used

I found after I was converted that some of the wicked men in the place had hid behind me. One man in particular, a **Mr. Cable,**[16] who had a pious wife, had repeatedly said to her, "If religion is true, why don't you convert Finney? If you Christians can convert Finney, I will believe in religion."

An old lawyer by the name of ‹M›**unson**, living in Adams, when he heard it rumored that day that I was converted, said that it was all a hoax.[17] **That** I was simply trying to see what I could make Christian people believe. However, with one consent the people seemed to rush to the place of worship. I went there myself. **Mr. Gale,** the minister, was there; and nearly all the principal people in the village. ׀No one seemed ready to open the meeting; but the house was packed to its utmost capacity. I did not wait for anybody, but arose and began by saying that I then knew that religion was from God.[18] I went on and told such parts of my experience as it seemed important for me to tell. This Mr. **Cable**, who had promised his wife that if I was converted he would believe in religion, was present. Mr. **Munson,** the old lawyer, was also present. What the Lord enabled me to say seemed to take a wonderful hold upon the people. Mr. **Cable** got up, and pressed through the crowd, and went **off** home, leaving his hat. Mr. **Munson** also left and went home, saying I was crazy. "He is in earnest," said **Munson**, "there is no mistake." **B**ut he is deranged, that is clear."

MS 54

As soon as I had done speaking Mr. Gale, the minister, ‹arose›[19] and made a confession. He said he believed he had been in the way of the church; and then confessed ׀that he had discouraged the church when they had proposed to pray for me. He said also that when he had heard that day that I was converted, he had promptly said that he did not believe it. He said he had **had** no faith. He spoke in a very humble manner.

MS 55

׀I had never made a prayer in public. But soon after **Brother** Gale was through speaking he called on me to pray. I did so, and think I had a good deal of enlargement and liberty in prayer. We had a wonderful meeting that evening; and from that **time** we had a meeting every evening for a long time. The work spread on every side. As I had been a leader among the young people I immediately appointed a meeting for them; which they all attended—that is, all of the class with which I was acquainted. I gave up my

JHF 29

to teach them music, was with them a great deal, and exerted that kind of influence over them which was a snare of death to their souls! (Finney, *Repentance,* pp. 34–35).

[16] According to Franklin B. Hough, there is a record of a Jonathan Cable taking up land at Adams on 29 October 1799 (*A History of Jefferson County in the State of New York* [Albany: Munsell, 1854], p. 72).

[17] Lyman Munson was born probably in the early 1780s. He was admitted to the bar in 1807 and was the first lawyer in Adams. He was a surrogate of Jefferson County in 1816 and again in 1821. In about 1830 he moved to Bristol, Vermont, where he continued to practice law until his death in about 1840 (see Myron A. Munson, *The Munson Record,* vol. 2 [New Haven: printed for the Munson Association, 1895], p. 903; and Durant, *History of Jefferson County,* p. 255). The letter *M* of "Munson" was not clearly a capital letter as written down by Matson. Finney appears to have tried to reform the letter but then crossed it out and inserted a new capital *M* above the name.

[18] It was reported to P. C. Headley that "when he [Finney] announced the change in the public assembly, his first utterance was, while his large expressive eyes glanced over the surprised audience, 'My God, is it I!' " (P. C. Headley, *Evangelists in the Church* [Boston: Hoyt, 1875], p. 129; see also "Early Life of C. G. Finney," *NYE,* 23 May 1850, p. 81).

[19] The words "got up" appear to have been changed in black ink by Finney to "arose."

time to labor for their conversion; and the Lord blessed every effort that was made in a very wonderful manner. They were converted one after another
MS 56 with great rapidity; and |the work continued among them until but one of their number was left unconverted.[20]

The work spread among all classes; and extended itself, not only through the village, but out of the village in every direction.[21] My heart was so full that for more than a week I did not feel at all inclined to sleep or eat. I seemed literally to have meat to eat that the world knew nothing of. I did not feel the need of food, or of sleep. My mind was full of the love of God to overflowing. I went on in this way for a good many days, until **one day standing before the glass and shaving myself, I noticed the look of my own eye, and observed that the pupil was enlarged; and I saw in a moment** that I must rest and sleep, or I should become insane. From that point I was more cautious in my labors; and ate regularly, and slept as much as I could.

I found the **W**ord of God had wonderful power; and I was every day
MS 57 surprized to find that a few words spoken to an individual |would stick in his heart like an arrow.

After a short time I went down to Henderson, where my father lived, and visited him. He was an unconverted man; and only one of the family, my youngest brother, had ever made a profession of religion.[22] My father met me

[20]See MS 74–78. There is some doubt about Finney's claim here. In a letter to Finney from Adams during the revival in 1831, P. D. Stone wrote, "Pray for those who have been your former associates in sin that God will have mercy on them" (Stone to Finney, 25 April 1831, Finney Papers, microfilm, roll 3).

[21]An extract of a letter from a "clergyman in the county of Jefferson, N.Y.," writing from Adams 26 December 1821 and published in the *Ballston Gazette,* was probably written by George W. Gale. It reads:

> The Lord has been, and still is, carrying on a glorious work of grace in this region. You will recollect that I was in haste to get home, on account of some favorable appearances in my congregation before I went away.—These appearances had rather increased, I found, when I returned. I began visiting—Our meetings soon became full and solemn; numbers were awakened, and heard to inquire "what shall I do?" A good number in our bounds have been brought to rejoice in hope. I do not know what number, I presume however, as many as *one hundred.* This has spread into a number of neighboring towns and societies. It soon commenced in the Congregational Society in Rodman, where it has been very powerful as well as in Lorrain, Ellisburgh and Henderson. A powerful revival has commenced both in the Baptist and Congregational societies, in the north part of this town (as reprinted in *BR,* 2 March 1822, p. 34; see also p. 317 n. 86 [MS 589]).

[22]Finney's family consisted of his father, Sylvester; his mother, Rebecca; and their seven children: Sarah, or Salley (1780–1852), who was married to Stephen Whitney and lived in Henderson; Theodotia, or Dotia (1781–1862); Zenas (1783–1874), who became a Christian when over eighty years old; Chloe (born 1785); Harry (born 1790), who worked the family farm; Charles Grandison (1792–1875); and George Washington (1795–1865). There had been two other sons: Sylvester, born in 1787, died in 1798; and Sylvester Rice, born in 1802, died in 1803. George, who ran a flour mill in Henderson, had been converted at the age of twenty. See Howard Finney, Sr., *Finney-Phinney Families in America* (Richmond, Va.: William Byrd, 1957), pp. 44, 84–85; Julia Monroe, "Copy of Records in the family bible of Charles Grandison Finney, in his own hand writing," Miscellaneous Items, Finney Papers, microfilm, roll 8; Salley Whitney to C. G. Finney, 18 October 1833, Finney Papers, microfilm, roll 2; Charles L. N. Camp, notes on the Finney family, MS, Gen. MS. 32101, Connecticut Historical Society Library, Hartford, Connecticut; H. M. Dodd, "The Conversion of Zenas Finney," *NYE,* 9 March 1876, p. 8; the obituary of George W. Finney in *The Congregational Quarterly* (Boston) 7 (July and October

at the gate and said, "How do you do, Charles?" I replied, "I am well, father, body and soul. But father you are an old man, **and** all your children are grown up and have left your house,—and I never heard a prayer in my father's house." Father ˡdropped his head and burst into tears, and replied, "I know it, Charles; come in and pray yourself." JHF 30

I met my youngest brother there. We went in and engaged in prayer. My father and mother were greatly moved; and in a very short time thereafter they were both hopefully converted.[23] I do not know but my mother had had a secret hope before; but if so, none of the family, I believe, ever knew it. I remained in that neighborhood, I think, ˡfor two or three days, and conversed more or less with such people as I could meet with.[24] I believe it was the next Monday night, they had a monthly concert of prayer in that town. There were there a Baptist church that had a minister,[25] and a small Congregational church without a minister.[26] The town was very much of a moral waste, however; and at this time religion was at a very low ebb. My youngest brother attended this monthly concert of which I have spoken, and afterwards gave me an account of it. The Baptists and Congregationalists were in the habit of holding a **U**nion **M**onthly **C**oncert. But few attended, and therefore it was held at a private house. On this occasion they met, as usual, in the parlor of a private house. A few of the members of the Baptist church, and a few Congregationalists, were present. The deacon of the Congregational church was a **thin,** spare, feeble old man by the name of **Montague**. He was quiet in his ways, and had a good reputation for piety; but seldom said much upon the MS 58

1865): 429–30; and William C. Cochran to W. F. Bohn, 8 April 1930, typescript copy in W. F. Bohn Papers, file 3/1/2, box 47, Oberlin College Archives.

Finney later wrote:

> I well recollect, when far from home, and while an impenitent sinner, I received a letter from my youngest brother, informing me that he was converted to God. . . . I was at the time, and both before and after, one of the most careless sinners, and yet on receiving this intelligence, I actually wept for joy and gratitude, that one of so prayerless a family was likely to be saved (C. G. Finney, *Lectures on Systematic Theology* [London: William Tegg, 1851], p. 429).

[23] Finney's parents and brother George were admitted to membership of the Congregational church the next summer (see Gale, *Autobiography,* p. 188). George later entered the ministry and was active in antislavery and temperance work. He died in California in 1865 (see letters of G. W. Finney to Charles Finney in the Finney Papers).

[24] George Gale related in his *Autobiography*:

> Mr. Finney and I went over to Henderson, where his parents lived, to hold meetings. I preached, and Mr. Finney made some remarks and prayed. I urged them then to pledge themselves, by rising up, to labor for the revival of God's work. There was a considerable number of the Baptists present, as well as Congregationalists. . . . A good work commenced there from that time (pp. 187–88; this was probably the same visit that Finney is speaking of here).

It may have been this same visit of "A certain *flaming* preacher, in company with a brother clergyman," that was denounced by Pitt Morse, the Universalist minister, in a letter in the *Religious Inquirer* (Hartford, Conn.), 27 April 1822, p. 100.

[25] The First Baptist Church was formed in 1806 by Emory Osgood, who officiated as pastor till September 1823. See Hough, *History of Jefferson County,* p. 169.

[26] The First Congregational Church was organized in 1810, and a meeting house was built sometime before June 1819 (see William H. Horton, ed., *Part First: Geographical Gazeteer of Jefferson County, N.Y., 1686–1890,* compiled and published by Hamilton Child [Syracuse: Syracuse Journal, 1890], pp. 451–52). This was the church that Finney's parents joined.

MS 59 subject. |He[27] was a good specimen of a New England deacon. He was present, and they called upon him to lead the meeting. He read a passage of Scripture according to their custom. They then sung a hymn, and Deacon Montague[28] stood up behind his chair and led off in prayer. The other persons present, all of them professors of religion and younger people, knelt down around the room. My brother said that Deacon Montague began as usual in his prayer, in a low, feeble voice; but soon began to wax warm and to JHF 31 raise his voice, which became tremulous with emo|tion. He proceeded to pray with more and more earnestness, till soon he began to rise upon his toes and come down upon his heels; and then to rise upon his toes and drop upon his heels again, so that they could feel the jar in the room. He continued to raise his voice, and to rise upon his toes and come down upon his heels more emphatically. And as the Spirit of prayer led him onward, he began to raise his chair together with his heels, and bring that down upon the floor; and soon MS 60 he raised |it[29] a little higher, and brought it down with still more emphasis. He continued to do this, and grew more and more engaged till he would bring the chair down as if he would break it to pieces. In the meantime the brethren and sisters that were on their knees, began to groan, and sigh, and weep, and agonize in prayer. The deacon continued to struggle until he was about exhausted; and when he ceased my brother said that there was nobody in the room that could get off from their knees. They could only weep and confess, and all melt down before the Lord. From this meeting the work of the Lord

[27] On the reverse of page 59 are the following figures in pencil:

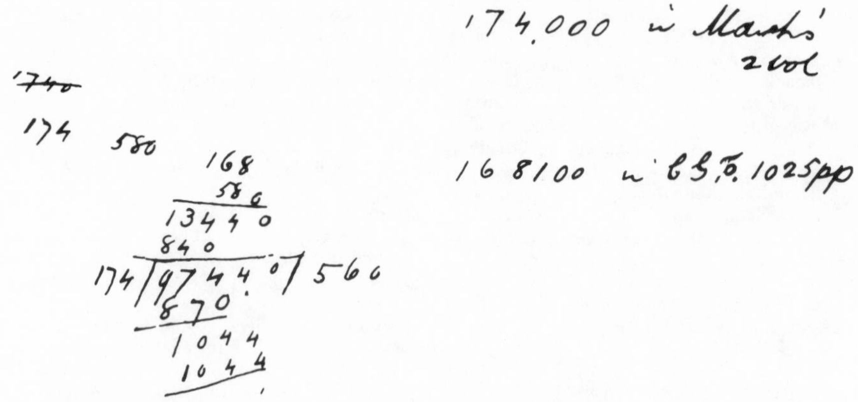

174,000 in Marsh' 2 vol

~~740~~
174 580

168100 in C.G.F. 1025pp

168
580
13440
840
174 | 97440 | 560
870
1044
1044

The handwriting appears to be that of Lewis Tappan. It seems probable from this that the manuscript that was sent to Lewis Tappan had 1,025 pages (see Introduction, p. xxix).

"Marsh" appears to be a reference to Catherine Marsh, *The Life of the Rev. William Marsh, D.D., by His Daughter* (New York: R. Carter and Bros., 1867). This edition was in two volumes but paged continuously and consisting of 580 pages. It appears that Tappan is here comparing the size of the Marsh volumes with the size of Finney's manuscript.

[28] "Montague" here was not crossed out in the manuscript, but the published edition has "M—. "

[29] A dash and number "–61" have subsequently been added in pencil after the page number 60, because the next page was erroneously renumbered 62.

spread forth in every direction all over the town.[30] And thus it spread at that time from Adams as a center, throughout nearly all the towns in the county.[31]

[30]In a private letter from Henderson dated 12 January 1822 Emory Osgood reported:

> The revival in this region began about four months since in the village of Adams, and soon became general. . . . About two months since, it broke out in Henderson. The work has been preceded by the most astonishing spirit of prayer that I ever witnessed, which continues. I cannot describe it to you. Suffice it to say, that, in a number of instances, Christians have prayed all night. . . .
>
> Since the work began in this town I have baptized twelve; and there are six that now stand candidates for baptism, having told their experience to the church. I think as many as fifty have obtained hope; and the work is still spreading in every part of the town, without any abatement.

This letter found its way into print in *The Latter Day Luminary* and was copied into many other religious papers. Pitt Morse, a Universalist minister, at the request of the editor of the Hartford *Religious Inquirer,* looked into the claims Osgood was making and reported back from Henderson on 23 March. He questioned some of Osgood's statistics and opinions on the influence of the revival but conceded:

> That there has been much excitement upon religion in this county is certain.—Many have united to the churches of different denominations. In this town, probably between forty and fifty have united with the Presbyterians, Baptists, and Methodists, within a year past (*Religious Inquirer,* 27 April 1822, pp. 99–101; and *The Latter Day Luminary* [Philadelphia] 3 [February 1822]: 62).

The "clergyman in the county of Jefferson, N.Y." (probably George Gale), writing on 26 December 1821, reported: "In Henderson, the work is peculiarly interesting. The Congregational and Baptist Societies, are perfectly united. There is a wonderful spirit of prayer; and many have been brought to rejoice in hope" (*BR,* 2 March 1822, p. 34).

By February 1822 the work in Henderson was declining, but Adams W. Platt went to the area as a Presbyterian missionary and by August was able to report, "Our church in that place is, on the whole, probably, in a more flourishing state, than it has been at any former time" (*The Sixth Annual Report of the Trustees of the Female Missionary Society of the Western District* [Utica], 1822, p. 9).

[31]George Gale described how the revival spread to the nearby towns of Lorain and Rodman as a result of a visit he made to Lorain to attend a council. At a prayer meeting after the council in the home of the Congregational minister, the Reverend Bliss, Gale described what the Lord was doing in Adams. Deacon Truman was present from Rodman and was so moved that he went back home "with new purpose," and a revival followed in which all but four or five of the fifty families in the village were influenced. "In Lorrain also, a good work commenced from the date of that meeting and in the pastor's family several of his children, some interesting daughters were the subjects of the work" ("Autobiography of Rev. G. W. Gale," typescript copy in Knox College Library, Galesburg, Ill., p. 153; and p. 317 n. 86 [MS 589]).

Franklin B. Hough, in his history of Jefferson County published in 1854, states that Finney's "first ministerial labors were performed in Lorraine. . ." (*History of Jefferson County,* p. 76).

On 28 November 1821 Emory Osgood wrote to the editor of the *Christian Almanack*:

> Our God is doing a great work in this region at the present time. In five towns, viz. Adams, Rodman, Lorrain, Ellisburg, and Henderson, there have been in ten weeks past probably more than 300 souls translated from the kingdom of darkness into the kingdom of God's dear Son. The work is increasing (reprinted in the *Christian Watchman* [Boston], 15 December 1821, p. 3).

But the writer of a letter that was widely publicized in the religious press, dated Watertown, 2 January 1822, to the editor of the *Boston Recorder,* gave a sketch of religion in the area, in which he stated that the revival

> commenced early in the spring, about the same time at Watertown and at Sacket's Harbor. From there it extended to Adams and Rodman; appeared in both of these places about at one time. And now at Ellisburg, Henderson and Lorrain, God is pouring out his Spirit. In short there is scarcely a church or neighborhood, supplied or destitute, in which there is not a number who have commenced the solemn work of seeking the salvation of their souls. The work extends to all Christian denominations. . . . Perhaps only in Rodman can the work be said to have been powerful. In general it is slow rather than rapid—considering the district of the country which it

I have spoken of the conviction of **Esq. Wright**, in whose office I studied law.[32] I have also said that when I was converted it was **up** in a grove where I went to pray. Very soon after my ˡconversion[33] several other cases ‹of conversion›[34] occurred, that were reported to have taken place under similar circumstances; that is, persons went up into the grove to pray, and there made their peace with God.[35] When **Esq. Wright** heard them tell their experience one after the other in our meetings, he thought that *he* had a *parlor* to pray in; and that he was not going up into the woods, **and** have the same story to tell that had been so often told. To this, it appeared, he strongly committed himself. Although this was a thing entirely immaterial in itself; yet ˡit was a point on which his pride had become committed, and therefore he could not get into the kingdom of God.

MS 62

JHF 32

> covers and the population, the number of converts and of the inquiring is not great. . . . Perhaps the whole number of hopeful subjects of this extensive work does not exceed 400. The work is more like the refreshing and silent breeze than the roaring wind—like the gentle dew than the powerful rain (*BR,* 12 January 1822, p. 7).

A report in *The Utica Christian Repository* in February added the town of New Haven to the list of places and gave details of the numbers added to the Presbyterian churches.

> In the society of Adams, under the pastoral care of the Rev. Mr. Gale, between eighty and ninety profess to have experienced religion, forty-four of whom have been added to the church. The north society in the same town, though destitute of the stated ministry, of the word and ordinances, has signally shared in this glorious work. Between sixty and seventy have here also become hopefully pious. In Henderson, between seventy and eighty are rejoicing in hope (*The Utica Christian Repository* 1 [February 1822]: 60).

A further sketch of the revivals in the area was given by Emory Osgood in a letter dated Henderson, 18 February 1822:

> There were some favourable appearances in Sacket's harbour, and Watertown, the latter part of last winter and spring, and a number of souls hopefully converted; but the work seemed not to be general. About September of last year the work commenced in Adams, under the ministry of the Rev. Mr. Gale, (Presbyterian,) aided materially by a young man, candidate for the ministry, by the name of Burchard. The work soon became pretty general, and some of the first characters in the place have been made the rejoicing subjects of grace. The work soon spread into Ellisburgh and Lorain, and many were now made the trophies of all conquering grace. In October, the work broke out in Rodman, under the ministry of Rev. Mr. Spear, and the ministry of Mr. Cornel, a baptist licentiate.

Osgood goes on to describe the spread of the revival to the Baptist church in Adams and to the Congregational church there and at "Handsfield" (Houndsfield Township) and in early November to Henderson (*The American Baptist Magazine* [Boston] 3 [July 1822]: 385–86). In another account in January 1822, Osgood wrote: "In Adams, Lorrain, Ellisburgh, Rodman, Houndsfield and Henderson, according to the best accounts I have obtained from those towns, I think as many as five hundred souls have been regenerated" (Osgood to the board of trustees of the Hamilton Baptist Missionary Society, dated Henderson, 22 January 1822, *The Western New York Baptist Magazine* [Morrisville, N.Y.] 3 [May 1822]: 299). P. H. Fowler stated, "There were supposed to be from 800 to 1,000 converts in Jefferson county" (*Historical Sketch of Presbyterianism Within the Bounds of the Synod of Central New York* [Utica: Curtiss and Childs, 1877], p. 190).

[32] See MS 45–46.

[33] MS 62 was numbered 57 by Matson and renumbered 62 by Finney; it should have been renumbered 61.

[34] The words "of conversion" were added by Finney.

[35] The grove where Finney was converted was to become famous, and other people also went there seeking salvation (see Orson Parker, *The Fire and the Hammer* [Boston: James H. Earle, 1877], p. 257). In later years Finney expressed "deep grief at finding the beautiful grove transformed into a simple field" (John Campbell, "Valedictory Services," *The British Banner* [London], 2 April 1851, p. 220).

I have found in my ministerial experience a great many cases of this kind; where upon some question, perhaps immaterial in itself, a sinner's pride of heart would commit him. In all such cases the dispute must be yielded, or the sinner never will get into the kingdom of God. I have known persons to remain for weeks in great tribulation of mind, pressed by the Spirit; but they could make no progress till the point upon which they were committed was yielded. ˡMr.[36] **Wright's** was the first case of the kind that had ever come to my notice. After he was converted, he said **that** the question had frequently come up when he was in prayer; and that he had been made to see that it was *pride* that made him take that stand, and that kept him out of the kingdom of God. But still he was not willing to admit this, even to himself. He tried in every way to make himself believe, and to make God believe, that he was not proud. One night he said he prayed all night in his parlor that God would have mercy on him; but in the morning he felt more distressed than ever. He finally became enraged that God did not hear his prayer, and was tempted to kill himself. He was so tempted to use his penknife for that purpose, that he actually threw it as far as he could that it might be lost, so that this temptation should not prevail.[37] **One** night, **he said,** on returning from meeting he was so pressed with a sense of his pride, and with the fact that it prevented his going up into the woods to pray, that he was determined to make himself believe, and make God believe, that he ˡwas not proud; and he sought around for a mud puddle in which to kneel down, that he might demonstrate that it was not *pride* which kept him from going into the woods. Thus he continued to struggle for several weeks.

MS 63

MS 64

But one afternoon I was sitting in our office, and **a couple** of the elders of the church **were** with me; when the young man that ˡI met at the shoemaker's shop **as a Universalist, and who was that day converted**, came hastily into the office, and exclaimed as he came, "**Esq. Wright** is converted!" and proceeded to say: "I went up into the woods to pray, and heard some one over in the valley shouting very loud. I went **over** to the brow of the hill where I could look down, and I saw **Esq. Wright** pacing to and fro, and singing as loud as he could sing; and every few moments he would stop and clap his hands with his full strength and shout, "*I will rejoice in the God of my salvation!*"[38] Then he would march and sing again; and then stop, and shout, and clap his hands.["][39] While the young man was telling us this, behold **Esq. Wright** appeared in sight, coming over the hill. As he came ˡdown to the foot of the hill we observed that he met father **Tucker**, as we all called him, an aged Methodist brother. He rushed up to him, and took him right up in his arms. After setting him down and conversing a moment, he came rapidly toward the office. **The moment that he** came in, **we observed that** he was in a profuse perspiration, he was a heavy man;—and he cried out, "**God,** I've got it!" "**God,** I've got it!" slapped his hands with all his might, and fell upon

JHF 33

MS 65

[36]Pages 63 to 81 were originally numbered 58 to 76 by Matson and were renumbered 63 to 81 by Finney.

[37]In another account Finney said it was "for fear he should cut his throat" (*Lectures on Revivals of Religion,* ed. William G. McLoughlin [Cambridge, Mass.: Belknap, 1960], p. 165).

[38]See Habakkuk 3:18.

[39]The quotation mark was omitted here by Matson but was inserted by Fairchild.

his knees and began to give thanks to God. He then gave us an account of what had been passing in his mind, and why he had not obtained a hope before. He said as soon as he gave up that point and went into the woods, his mind was relieved; and when he knelt down to pray the Spirit of God came upon him **with such power as to** fill him with such unspeakable joy, that it resulted in the scene which the young man witnessed. Of course from that time **Esq. Wright** took a decided stand for God.[40]

MS 66 Towards **Spring**[41] the old |members of the church began to abate in their zeal. I had been in the habit of rising early in the morning, and spending a season of prayer alone in the meeting house; and I finally succeeded in interesting a considerable number of brethren to meet me there in the morning for a **morning** prayer meeting. This was at a very early hour; and we JHF 34 were generally together long before it was |light enough to see to read. I persuaded my minister to attend these morning meetings. But soon they began to be remiss; whereupon I would get up in time to go around to their houses and wake them up. Many times I went round and round, and called the brethren that I thought would be most likely to attend, and we would have a precious season of prayer. But still the brethren, I found, attended with **greater** and **greater** reluctance; which fact greatly tried me.[42] One morning I had been around and called the brethren up, and when I returned to the meeting house but few of them had got there. **Brother** Gale, my MS 67 minister, was standing at the door of the church **when I** |**returned. As** I came up **to the church**, all at once the glory of God shone upon and round about me in a manner most marvellous. The day was just beginning to dawn. But all at once a light perfectly ineffable shone in my soul, that almost prostrated me to the ground. In this light it seemed as if I could see that all nature praised and worshipped God except man. This light seemed to be like the brightness of the sun in every direction. It was too intense for the eyes. I recollect casting my eyes down and breaking into a flood of tears, in view of the fact

[40]Gale wrote:

> The change of Mr. Finney, and the decided course that he took, produced an astonishing effect. Mr. Wright, one of the lawyers with whom he was studying, soon after came out decidedly on the cause of Christ, is still living, and has been for many years an esteemed elder of the church (*Autobiography,* pp. 180–81; the typescript copy has the word "side" in the place of "cause" [p. 148]).

Rev. Henry Smith of Camden went over to help Gale and reported on the revival:

> Perhaps one hundred were rejoicing in hope. Many of the first respectability in this pleasant village, including gentlemen of the bar, and one from the bench, had been taught to call Christ, lord, by the Holy Ghost, and gloried in the cross. Commencing in this town, this work of grace extended over a large part of Jefferson County. Perhaps from eight hundred to one thousand souls may be numbered among the subjects (report dated 21 October 1822 in *Sixth Annual Report,* p. 18).

Benjamin Wright was admitted into membership of the Presbyterian church at Adams at the same time as Finney, in January 1822, and subsequently became an elder (see S. N. Bond to Finney, 7 July 1868, Finney Papers, microfilm, roll 5).

Henry Smith's report is the first known account of what could be a reference to Finney's conversion.

[41]This was the spring of 1822.

[42]George Gale recalled: "The number of conversions continued to grow less and less. Our meetings were kept up through the week as well as through the Sabbath, meeting early in the morning as the weather grew mild; but people seemed worn out and business called their attention" (typescript "Autobiography," pp. 163–64).

hat mankind did not praise God. I think I knew something then, by actual xperience, of that light that prostrated Paul on his way to Damascus.[43] It was urely a light such as I could not have endured long. When I burst out into uch loud weeping Mr. Gale **my minister** said, "What is the matter, brother 'inney?" I could not tell him. I found that he had seen no light; and that he aw no reason why I should be in such a state of mind. I therefore said but ttle. I believe |I merely replied, that I saw the glory of God; and that I could ot endure to think of the manner in which **He** was treated by men. Indeed, it id not seem to me at the time that the vision of his glory which I had, was to e described in words. I *wept* it out; |and the vision, if it may be so called, assed away and left my mind calm.

MS 68

JHF 35

I used to have, when I was a young Christian, many seasons of communing ith God which **cannot** be described in words. And not unfrequently those easons would end in an impression on my mind like this: "Go, see that thou ell no man."[44] I did not understand this at the time, and several times I paid o attention to this injunction; but tried to tell my Christian brethren what ommunications the Lord had made to me, or rather what seasons of ommunion I had with **Him**. But I soon found that it would not do to tell my rethren what was passing between the Lord and my soul. They could not nderstand it. They would look surprized, and sometimes, I thought, ncredulous; and I soon learned to keep quiet in regard to those divine nanifestations, and say but little about them.

MS 69

I used to spend a great deal of time in prayer; sometimes, I thought, terally praying "without ceasing."[45] I also found it very profitable, and felt ery much inclined, to hold frequent days of private fasting. On those days I ould seek to be entirely alone with God; and would generally wander off nto the woods, or get into the meeting house, or somewhere away entirely by nyself. Sometimes I would pursue a wrong course in fasting, and attempt to xamine myself according to the ideas of self-examination then entertained by ny minister and the church. I would try to look into my own heart, in the ense of examining my feelings; and would turn my attention particularly to ny motives, and the state of my mind. When I pursued this course I found nvariably that the day would close |without any perceptible advance being nade. Afterwards I saw clearly why this was so. Turning my attention, as I id, from the Lord Jesus Christ, and looking into myself, examining my notives and feelings, my feelings all subsided, of course. But whenever I asted, and let the Spirit take his own course with me, and gave myself up to et him lead and instruct me, I universally found it in the highest degree seful **to me**. I found I could not live without enjoying the presence of God; nd if at any time a **dark streak** came over me, I could not rest, I could not tudy, I could not attend to anything with the least satisfaction or benefit, ntil the medium was again **opened** between my soul and God.

MS 70

JHF 36

I had been very fond of my profession. But as I have said, when I was onverted all was dark in that direction, and I had no more any pleasure in

[43] See Acts 9:3–9.
[44] Matthew 8:4.
[45] 1 Thessalonians 5:17.

attending to law business. I had many very pressing invitations to[46] conduct law suits; but I uniformly refused. MS 71 |I did not dare to trust myself in the excitement of a contested lawsuit; and furthermore, the business itself of conducting other people's controversies appeared odious and **disgusting**[47] to me.

The Lord taught me in those early days of my Christian experience, many very important truths in regard to *the spirit of prayer.* Not long after I was converted a **lady**[48] with whom I had boarded—though I did not board with her at this time **which I am about to mention**—was taken very sick. She was not a Christian, but her husband was a professor of religion. He came into our office one evening, being a brother of **Esq. Wright**,[49] and said to me, "My wife cannot live through the night." This seemed to plant an arrow, as it were, in my heart. **I felt something almost like a cramp seizing me in the region of my heart.** It came upon me in the sense of a burden that crushed me, **and a kind of spasm inwardly,** the nature of which I could not at all understand; but with it came an intense desire to pray for that woman. MS 72 |The burden was so great that I left the office almost immediately, and went up to the meeting house to pray for her. There I struggled, but could not say much. I could only groan with groanings **so** loud and deep **as would have been impossible, I think, for me, had it not been for that terrible pressure on my mind. I** stayed **for** a considerable time in the church in this state of mind, but got no relief. I returned to the office; but I could not sit still. I could only walk the room and agonize. I returned to the meeting house again, and went through the same process of struggling. For a long time I JHF 37 |tried to get my prayer before the Lord; but somehow words could not express it. I could only groan and weep, without being able to express what I wanted in words. I returned to the office again, and still found I was unable to rest; and I returned a third time to the meeting house. At this time the Lord gave me power to prevail. I was enabled to roll the burden upon MS 73 |**Him**; and I obtained the assurance in my own mind that the **lady** would not die, and indeed that she would never die in her sins. I returned to the office. My mind was perfectly quiet; and I soon left and retired to rest. Early the next morning the husband of this woman came into the office. I inquired how his wife was. He, smiling, said, "She **is** alive and to all appearance better this morning." I replied: "Brother **Wright**, she will not die with this sickness; you may rely upon it. And she will never die in her sins." I do not know how I was made sure of this; but it was in some way

[46] Matson had written down "to undertake to," and the word "undertake" was crossed out by Finney. The second "to" was crossed out by Fairchild.

[47] The word "disgusting" was not changed in the manuscript but appears as "offensive" in the published edition.

[48] Here and in many other places through the *Memoirs,* Fairchild altered the word "lady" to "woman." By the 1870s it had become old fashioned to use the term "lady." See Frances J. Hosford, *Father Shipherd's Magna Charta* (Boston: Marshall Jones, 1937), pp. 53–54.

[49] An account book in Finney's handwriting has an entry on p. 7 that reads, "Commenced Boarding with John Wright June 22nd 1818," and it goes on to give the periods when Finney was away until November, when there is an entry (p. 8) that reads, "commenced Boarding with Esquire Wright 9th November 1818." After boarding there and at other places, there is a further entry (p. 13): "commenced Boarding At J. Wright's 4th Sept 1820" (MS, "Account Book, 1814–1820," Finney Papers, file 2/2/2, box 11).

made plain to me, so that I had no doubt that she would recover. **I told him so.** She did recover, and soon after obtained a hope in Christ. At first I did not understand what this exercise of mind that I had passed through, was. But shortly after in relating it to a Christian brother he said to me, "Why that was the *travail* of your soul."[50] A few moments[51] conversation, and pointing me to certain ¦scriptures, gave me to understand what it was. MS 74

Another experience which I had soon after this, illustrates the same truth. I have spoken of one young lady as belonging to the class of young people of my acquaintance, **and who was a member of the choir of which I was leader,** who remained unconverted.[52] This attracted a good deal of attention; and there was considerable conversation among Christians about the case of **this young lady**. She was naturally a charming girl, and very much enlightened on the subject of religion, but remained in her sins. One of the elders of the church and myself agreed to make her a daily subject of prayer—to continue to present ¦her case to a throne of grace morning, noon, and evening, until she was either converted, or should die, or that we should be unable to keep our covenant. I found my mind greatly exercised about her, and more and more as I continued to pray for her. I soon found, however, that the elder **of the church** who had ¦entered into this arrangement with me, was losing his spirit of prayer for her. But this did not discourage me. I continued to hold on with increasing importunity. I also availed myself of every opportunity to converse plainly and searchingly with her on the subject of her salvation. JHF 38 MS 75

After I had continued in this way for sometime, one evening I called to see her just as the sun was setting. As I came up to the door I heard a shriek from a female voice, and a scuffling and confusion inside the door; and stood and waited for the **scuffle** to be over. The lady of the house soon came and opened the door, and held in her hand a portion of a book, which had evidently been torn in two. She was pale and very much agitated. She held out that portion of the book which she had in her hand, and said: "Mr. Finney, don't you think my sister has become a Universalist?" **for she was the sister of the young lady for whom we were praying. On examining** the book **I found it to be a book written in** defence of Universalism. Her sister had detected her ¦reading it—**as she kept it secret**—and tried to get it away from her; and it was this **scuffle** to obtain that book which I heard. **I learned that they had seen me coming up to the door, when the scuffle ensued. The young lady had run up stairs with the other portion of the book in her hand.** I received this information at the door; whereupon I declined to go in. It struck me very much in the same way as had the announcement that the sick **lady** was about to die. It loaded me down with great agony. As I returned to my room, at some distance from that house, I felt almost as if I should stagger under the burden that was on my mind. **I went to my room,** and **there** I struggled, and groaned, and agonized; but could not frame to present MS 76

[50] Isaiah 53:11.

[51] The word "moments" was not altered in the manuscript, but the published edition has "minutes."

[52] See MS 56.

the case before God in words, but only in groans and tears. It seemed to me that the discovery that that young **lady**, instead of being converted was becoming a Universalist, so astounded me that I could not break through with
JHF 39 |my faith and get hold of God in reference to her case.

MS 77 |There seemed to be a darkness hanging over the question, **and** as if a **wall** had risen up between me and God, in regard to prevailing for her salvation. But still the Spirit **of prayer** struggled within me with groanings that could not be uttered. However, I was obliged to retire that night without having prevailed. But as soon as it was light **in the morning** I awoke; and the first thought that I had was to beseech ‹the God› of grace[53] again for that young **lady**. I immediately arose and fell upon my knees. No sooner was I upon my knees than the darkness gave way, and the whole subject opened to my mind and as soon as I plead for her God said to me, "Yes!" "**Y**es!" If he [**h**]ad[54] spoken with an audible voice it would not have been more distinctly understood **and heard,** than **the** "**yes,**" "**yes,**" was **that was** spoken within my soul. It instantly relieved all my solicitude. My mind became **immediately** filled with the greatest peace and joy; and I felt a complete certainty **in my**
MS 78 **mind** |that her salvation was secure.

I drew a false inference, however, in regard to the *time*; which **by the by** was not a thing particularly impressed upon my mind at the time of my prayer. Still I expected her to be converted immediately**. However,** she was not. She remained in her sins for several months. In its proper place I shall have occasion to speak of her conversion.[55] I **however** felt disappointed at the time that she was not converted **immediately**; and was somewhat staggered **in regard to** whether I had really prevailed with God in her behalf.

Soon after I was converted, the man with whom I had been boarding for **sometime**, who was a **M**agistrate and one of the principal men in the place was deeply convicted of sin.[56] ‹H›e had been elected[57] a member of the legislature of the state. I was praying daily for him, and urging him to give his heart to God. His conviction became very deep; but still from day to day he
MS 79 deferred |submission, and did not obtain a hope. My solicitude for him
JHF 40 increased. One afternoon several of his political friends had a pro|tracted interview with him. On the evening of the same day I attempted again to carry his case to God, as the urgency in my mind for his conversion had become very great. In my prayer I had drawn very near to God. I do not remember ever to have been in more intimate communion with the Lord Jesus Christ

[53] Matson had written, "to beseech a throne of grace," but Finney changed it to read, "to beseech the God of grace."

[54] This word is written "ad" in the manuscript. An *h* has been added in pencil.

[55] See MS 99.

[56] This was George Andrus. An entry on p. 12 of Finney's account book reads, "commenced Boarding with George Andrus April 22nd 1819." There are then details of when Finney was away until August. Then an entry (p. 13) records, "commenced Boarding At J. Wright's 4th Sept 1820" (MS, "Account Book, 1814–1820," Finney Papers, file 2/2/2, box 11). There is no further record of where he boarded, but he must have gone back to Andrus's home subsequently.

George Gale described Andrus as "a gentleman of fine appearance, and portly bearing in my congregation, and a regular attendant at church" (*Autobiography,* p. 197).

[57] Matson had originally written down "Soon after my conversion he had been elected," but Finney appears to have crossed out the words "Soon after my conversion" and capitalized the *h* of "he."

than I was at that time. Indeed his presence was so real that I was bathed in tears of joy, and gratitude, and love; and in this state of mind I attempted to pray for this friend. But the moment I did so my mouth was shut. I found it impossible to pray a word for him. The Lord seemed to say to me: "No; I will not hear." An anguish seized upon **my mind**. I thought at first it was a temptation. But the door was shut in my face. It seemed as if the Lord said to me: "Speak no more to me of that matter."[58] It pained me beyond expression. ˡI did not know what to make of it. The next morning I saw him; and as soon as I brought the question **up** of submission to God, he said to me: "Mr. Finney, I shall have nothing more to do with it until I return from the legislature. I stand committed to my political friends to carry out certain measures in the legislature, that are incompatible with my first becoming a Christian; and I have promised that I will not attend to the subject until after I have returned from Albany."[59]

MS 80

From the moment of that exercise the evening before, I had no spirit of prayer for him at all. As soon as he told me what he had done I understood it. I could see that his convictions were all gone, and that the Spirit of God had left him. From that **moment** he grew more careless and hardened than ever. When the time arrived he went to the legislature; and in the Spring he returned an almost *insane* Universalist.[60] I say almost insane, because instead of having formed **such an** opinion from any evidence ˡor course of argument, he told me this. **He** said: "I have come to that conclusion, not because I have found it taught in the Bible, but because such ˡa doctrine is so opposed to the carnal mind. It is a doctrine so generally rejected and spoken against, as to prove that it is distasteful to the carnal or unconverted mind." This was astou**nding**[61] to me. But everything else that I could get out of him was as wild and absurd as this. He remained in his sins, finally fell into decay,[62] and died at last a dilapidated man, and in the full faith of his Universalism ‹**as I have been told**.›[63]

MS 81

JHF 41

[58]Deuteronomy 3:26.

[59]The Forty-fifth Assembly started on 1 January 1822 and finished on 17 April. George Andrus and John Esselstyne were the delegates from Jefferson County. See *Journal of the Assembly of the State of New York: at their Forty-fifth Session begun and held at the Capitol, in the city of Albany, the first Day of January 1822* (Albany: Cantine and Leake [printers], 1822), pp. 5, 1119.

[60]Gale gave an account of this man's conviction and his falling into Universalism: "His father and friends were Universalists living in an adjoining town. They put Universalist books into his hands. He was a man of good sense, had previously expressed his disapproval of their doctrines, attended my church, and was a warm friend of mine. But he imbibed the poison and based his hope upon it." Gale gives the man's father's name as David J. Andrews (*Autobiography*, pp. 197, 199).

[61]This word was not altered in the manuscript, but the published version has "astonishing."

[62]The words "drank too much" here appear to have been crossed out by Finney.

[63]The words "as I have been told" were added by Finney. Gale stated: "He became intemperate; went into business with his father in an adjoining town. They quarreled and it was said fought in a drunken spree. He failed and when I and my wife visited there a year or two before we came west, we were told that he lived in a log house in a neighboring town, very poor" (typescript "Autobiography," p. 162).

MS 81
JHF 42

CHAPTER IV

‹*My first* doctrinal *controversy with my pastor & other events* at Adams›

Soon[1] after I was converted ‹I›[2] called on my pastor, and had a long conversation with him on the Atonement. He was a Princeton student, and of course held the limited view of the Atonement,—that it was made for the elect and available to none else. Our conversation |‹lasted[3] nearly half a day. He held that Jesus suffered for the elect the litteral[4] penalty of the Divine law. That he suffered just what was due to each of the elect on the score of retributive justice. I objected that this was absurd, as in that case he suffered the equivalent of endless misery multiplied by the whole number of the elect. He insisted that this was true. He affirmed that Jesus litterally paid the debt of the elect, & fully satisfied *retributive* justice. On the contrary it seemed to me that Jesus only satisfied ***publick*** justice & that that was all that the government of God could require.[5] I was however but a child in theology. I was but a novice in religion & in biblical learning, but I thought he did not sustain his views from the bible & told him so. I had read nothing on the subject except my bible, & what I had there found upon the subject I had interpreted as I would have understood the same or like passages in a law book. I thought he had evidently interpreted those texts in conformity to an established theory of the atonement. I had never heard him preach the views he maintained in that discussion. I was surprised in view of his positions & withstood them as best I could. He was alarmed, I dare say, at what appeared

MS 82

[1] Chapter IV starts two-thirds of the way down page 81. The chapter heading was written by Finney on a separate piece of paper pasted over a section of the manuscript. The original wording, most of which was covered over and had been crossed out by Finney, reads, "It would be too long a tale should I continue to recount the experiences through which I passed while I remained at Adams."

[2] The *I* appears to have been inserted by Finney.

[3] Pages 82 and 83 were inserted later by Finney.

[4] Fairchild crossed out the second *t* in this word here and later on the page.

[5] This was the governmental theory of the Atonement, as it came to be called, which had been introduced into America particularly through the writings of Jonathan Edwards, Jr., and had become a commonly accepted doctrine among the New School theologians (see Robert L. Ferm, *A Colonial Pastor: Jonathan Edwards the Younger, 1745–1801* [Grand Rapids: Eerdmans, 1976], pp. 114–19). G. F. Wright remarked on the expression "public justice":

> This is a phrase of the younger Edwards, which Finney doubtless adopted from later reading and reflection, and unconsciously interjected in the account of his early experiences. It is pretty certain that he had not then read Edwards, and it is extremely improbable that he independently coined the phrase (*Charles Grandison Finney* [Boston and New York: Houghton Mifflin, 1891], p. 22 n. 1).

.o him to |be my obstinacy. I though[t] that my bible clearly taught that the atonement[6] was made for all men. He limited it to **only** a part. I could not accept this view, for I |could not see that he fairly proved it from the bible. His rules of interpretation did not meet my views. They were much less definite & intelligible than those to which I had been accustomed in my law studies. To the objections which I urged he could make no satisfactory reply. I asked him if the bible did not require all who hear the gospel to repent, believe the gospel and be saved. He admitted that it did require all to believe & be saved. But how could they believe & accept a salvation which was not provided for them. **Unused as I was to theological discussions** we went over **nearly**[7] the whole field of debate between the old & new school divines upon the subject of atonement, as my subsequent theological studies taught me. I do not recollect to have ever read a page upon the subject except what I had found in the bible. I had never, to my recollection, heard a sermon or any discussion whatever upon the **subject. I thought I could see that Mr Gale had a philosophy, a theory to maintain in the light of which he understood the bible.**

JHF 43

MS 83

This discussion was often renewed & continued through my whole course of theological studies under him. He expressed concern lest I should not accept the orthodox faith.› |I[8] believe he had **had** the strongest conviction that I was truly converted; but he felt the greatest desire to keep me within the strict lines of Princeton theology.[9] He had it fixed in his mind that I would be a minister; and he took pains to inform me that if I did become a minister, the Lord would not bless my labors, and His Spirit would not bear witness to my preaching, unless I preached the truth. I believed this myself. But this was not to me a very strong argument in favor of *his* views; for he informed me—but not in connection with this conversation—that he did not know that he had ever been instrumental in converting a sinner. I had never heard him preach particularly on the subject |of the Atonement; **and** |I[10] think he feared to present his particular views to the people. His church, I am sure, did not embrace his views of a limited Atonement. After this we had frequent conversations, not only on the question of the Atonement, but on various theological questions; of which I shall have occasion to speak more fully hereafter.

MS 84

JHF 44
MS 85

I have said that in the Spring of the year the older members of the church began manifestly to decline in their engagedness and zeal for God. This

[6]Finney had written this word with two *t*s. The second *t* was crossed out by Fairchild.

[7]The word "nearly" was not crossed out in the original manuscript but is missing from the published edition.

[8]MS 84 was numbered 77 by Matson and renumbered 83 and 84 by Finney. The following section at the beginning of the page was crossed out by Finney when pages 82 and 83 were inserted in its place: "lasted nearly half a day. I could not accept his view, for I did not believe that it was taught in the Bible. I was soon convinced that he could not sustain it by the Bible. He expressed concern that I was not going to be orthodox in my faith."

[9]Matson had originally written down "orthodoxy" and then changed it to "theology." For Finney, Princeton theology was equivalent to Old School Calvinism, the system that at that time tended to characterize Presbyterian thought. See George M. Marsden, *The Evangelical Mind and the New School Presbyterian Experience* (New Haven: Yale University Press, 1970).

[10]Pages 85 to 110 were originally numbered 78 to 103 by Matson and were renumbered 85 to 110 by Finney.

greatly oppressed me, as it did also the young converts generally. About this time I read in a newspaper an article under the head of, "A revival revived." The substance of it was, that in a certain place there had been a revival during the winter; that in the Spring it declined; and that upon earnest prayer being offered for the continued out-pouring of the Spirit, the revival was powerfully

MS 86 revived. This article set me into a flood of weeping.[11] ǀ‹I[12] was at that time boarding with Mr Gale. I took the article to him. I was so overcome with a sense of the Divine goodness in hearing & answering prayer, & with a felt assurance that He would hear an[d][13] answer prayer for the revival of His work in Adams that I went through the house weeping aloud like a child. Mr Gale seemed surprised at my feelings & my expressed confidence that God would revive His work. The article made no such impression on him as it did on me.

At the next meeting of the young people I proposed that we should observe a closit concert of prayer for the revival of God's work. That we should pray at sunrise, at noon, & at sunset, in our closits›[14] and observe this for one week; when we should come together again and see what farther was to be done. No other means were used for the revival of God's work. But the Spirit of prayer was immediately poured out wonderfully upon the young converts. Before the week was out I learned that some of them, when they

JHF 45 ǀwould attempt to observe this season of prayer, would lose all their strength and be unable to rise from their knees, or even stand upon their knees in their closets; and that some of them would lie prostrate on the floor, and pray

MS 87 with unutterable groanings for the outpourǀing of the Spirit of God. The Spirit was poured out, and before the week ended all the meetings were thronged; and there was as much interest in religion, I think, as there had been at any time during the revival.[15] And here I am sorry to say that a mistake was made, or perhaps I should say a sin committed, by ‹some of›[16] the older members of the church, that resulted in great evil to them.[17] As afterwards learned, a considerable number of the older members of the church resisted this new movement among the young converts. They were jealous of it. They did not know what to make of it; and felt as if the young converts were too forward, were getting out of their places in being so forward and so urgent upon the older members of the church. This state of

[11]The words "It encouraged" followed here at the end of the page. They appear to have been crossed out by Fairchild.

[12]The section on page 86 down to n. 14 in Finney's handwriting was added later on a separate piece of paper pasted onto the sheet. The original wording, which was covered over, reads:

> It encouraged my faith greatly, and led me to pray that the revival in that place might be revived. The meetings had greatly taken off in interest with the exception of the young converts' meeting. At the next meeting of the young converts I proposed to them that we should observe a closet concert for the reviving of the revival. That we should pray at sunrise, at noon, and at sunset in our closets.

[13]This word was spelled "an" by Finney. A *d* appears to have been added by Fairchild.

[14]This ends the section in Finney's handwriting.

[15]In another place Finney recalled this situation and added, "Numerous meetings sprang up, so many persons were inquiring the way of salvation, and Christians were aroused on every side" (*The Prevailing Prayer-Meeting* [London: Ward, 1859], p. 18).

[16]The words "some of" were added by Finney.

[17]Finney inserted here the phrase "as I afterwards learned" but crossed it out again.

mind finally grieved the Spirit of God. **After I left Adams the state of religion run down. Brother Gale, their minister, was soon dismissed, being out of health. He went away to Western, Oneida County, N.Y., and went on a farm, to see if it would not restore his health.**[18]

ˡIt was not long before alienations began to **exist** among those older members of the church, which finally resulted in great evil to those **members** who had allowed themselves to resist this latter revival. The young people held out well. The converts, so far as I know, were almost universally sound, and have been thoroughly efficient Christians. MS 88

In the Spring of the year I put myself under the care of the Presbytery as a candidate for the Gospel ministry.[19] ‹Some of them›[20] urged me to go to Princeton to study theology; but I declined.[21] When they asked me why I would not go to Princeton, I told them, **which was true,** that my pecuniary circumstances forbad it. But they said they would see that my expenses were paid. **But I** still refused to go; and when urged to give them my reasons, I plainly told them that I would not put myself under such an influence as they had been under. That I was confident they had been wrongly educated; and they were not ministers that met my ideal **at all** of ˡwhat a minister of Christ should be. I told them ˡthis reluctantly; but I could not honestly withold it. JHF 46 MS 89

[18] Finney left Adams in April 1824, and Gale left in November. Gale had worked on farms as a young man and had at one time contemplated becoming a farmer. Before settling with his family in Western, he traveled alone for five months in the southern states in an unsuccessful attempt to regain his health (G. W. Gale, *Autobiography {to 1834} of George Washington Gale {1789–1861}, Founder of Galesburg, Illinois, and Knox College* [New York: privately printed, 1964], pp. 225–51).

[19] At this time, the spring of 1822, Finney began studying under Gale, but he was not taken on officially as a candidate for the ministry until more than a year later. Gale indicated what happened:

> After a few months [after his conversion] . . . he came to me and wanted to know what I would think or advise in regard to his leaving the law and studying for the ministry. I said, "I will say to you, as an old minister of my acquaintance said to a young lawyer who came to him with a similar question. It may be best but I would not advise you to turn too short a corner, take time to consider." I told him he might resume his study of Latin and commence the Greek language, and review the studies of moral philosophy and rhetoric, to which he had given some attention. This would do him no harm, but good, whatever conclusions he might come to after he had had time to try his feelings and duly consider the subject. He took this course, and I became his teacher. In the following summer, 1822, the Presbytery met at Adams and I advised him to put himself under their care (*Autobiography,* pp. 184–85).

Gale is incorrect in the date 1822. It was in 1823 that the Presbytery met at Adams. Philemon H. Fowler, quoting the minutes of the St. Lawrence Presbytery, wrote,

> Mr. Finney was taken under the care of the Presbytery with a view to the gospel ministry at Adams, June 25, 1823, and "decided to pursue his studies under the direction of Rev. Messrs. Gale and Boardman" (*Historical Sketch of Presbyterianism Within the Bounds of the Synod of Central New York* [Utica: Curtiss and Childs, 1877], p. 258).

[20] The word "They" here was changed by Finney to "Some of them."

[21] Gale wrote:

> I had written to Andover, to Princeton, and to Auburn, to see if they would admit him as a student and aid him from their funds while in the pursuit of his studies, but getting no encouragement I advised him to this course [i.e. to put himself under the care of presbytery], and to study what should be prescribed, and as long as the Presbytery thought proper (*Autobiography,* p. 185).

They appointed my pastor, ‹**Mr.**› **Gale,**[22] to superintend my studies. He offered me the use of his library, and said he would give what attention I needed to my theological studies.[23] But my studies, so far as he was concerned as my teacher, were little else than controversy.[24] He held to the **Presbyterian**[25] doctrine of original sin, or that the human *constitution* was morally depraved. He held also, that men were utterly unable to comply with the terms of the Gospel, to repent, to believe, or to do anything that God required them to do. That while they were free to all evil, in the sense of being able to commit any amount of sin; yet they were ‹not free›[26] **in regard to all that was** good. That God had condemned men for their sinful *nature*; and for this, as well as for their transgressions, they deserved eternal death, **and were under condemnation**. He held also that the influences of the Spirit of God on the minds of men were *physical*, acting directly upon the substance of the soul. That men were passive in regeneration; and in short he held all those doctrines that logically flow from the fact of a nature *sinful in itself*. These doctrines |I could not receive. I could not receive his views on the subject of atonement, regeneration, faith, repentance, the slavery of the Will, or any of their kindred doctrines. But of these views he was quite tenacious; and he seemed sometimes not a little impatient because I did not receive them without question. He used to insist that if I *would* reason on the subject, I should probably land in infidelity. And then he would remind me that some of the students who had been at Princeton had gone away infidels, because they would reason on the subject, and would not accept the Confession of faith, and the teaching of the Doctors at that school. He furthermore warned me repeatedly, and very feelingly, that as a minister I should never be useful unless I embraced the truth, meaning the truth as he

MS 90

[22]Finney altered the word "Brother" to "Mr." in a number of places on the advice of Lewis Tappan (see Introduction, p. xxxi).

[23]Gale recalled:

> The Presbytery took him under their care, advised as to the general course and appointed the Rev. Geo. S. Boardman and myself a committee to direct and superintend his studies. As he had now no means of support except a little that he had laid up in the practice of law, such as writing and pleading in Justice Courts, which business was now relinquished, I headed a subscription of six months' board in my family. This was followed by others and provision was made. The order of studies was made out by the committee and as I was at Adams, where he must remain, it devolved on me more especially to furnish the topics for essays, hear them and question him in regard to the subjects on which he read. He then entered immediately upon the study of Theology and continued in it, till in the winter of 1824, when the Presbytery met to dissolve my connection with the church ("Autobiography of Rev. G. W. Gale," typescript copy in Knox College Library, Galesburg, Ill., pp. 151–52. By "1824," Gale means 1823–1824).

[24]As a lad, Finney "was extremely fond of arguing, and became a champion debater in school-house lyceums. That power of logical argumentative presentation which characterized his preaching was only this youthful trait *sanctified*" (information from Finney's brother Zenas to "H.M.P." in *NYE,* 20 April 1876, p. 2).

When Finney was studying law he had been similarly involved in controversy. David Kimball, who was ordained by the same presbytery the session before and was present at Finney's licensure, recalled: "While reading law, he disputed the points laid down by his instructor. 'Well, Mr. Finney,' said Judge Wright, 'there are the books and the office; it is of no use for me to try to teach you; you will have your own way' " (*The Independent* [New York], 14 May 1868, p. 6).

[25]Fairchild changed the word "Presbyterian" to "old school."

[26]The words "utterly impotent" here were changed by Finney to "not free."

believed and taught it. ¦I am sure I was quite willing to believe what I found JHF 47 taught in the Bible and told him so. We used to have many protracted discussions; and I would often come from his study greatly depressed and discouraged, **and** saying to myself, "I cannot embrace these views come ¦what MS 91 will. I cannot believe they are taught in the Bible." And several times I was on the point of giving up the study for the ministry altogether.

There was but one member of the church to whom I opened my mind freely on this subject; and that was a[n] ‹Elder›[27] **Hinman**, a very godly, praying man.[28] He had been educated in Princeton views, and held pretty strongly the higher doctrines of Calvinism. Nevertheless as **he and I** had frequent and protracted conversations, he became satisfied that I was right; and he would call on me frequently to have seasons of prayer with me, to strengthen me in my studies and in my **controversy** with **Brother** Gale, and to decide me more and more firmly that, come what would, I would preach the Gospel.[29] Several times he fell in with me when I was in a state of great depression, after coming from **Brother** Gale's study. At such times he would go with me to my room; and sometimes we would ‹continue›[30] till a late hour at night crying to God for light and strength, and for faith to accept and do **H**is perfect will. ¦**The old ‹Elder›**[31] lived more than three miles from the MS 92 village; and frequently he has stayed with me till ten or eleven **O**'clock at night, and then walked home. The dear old man! I have reason to believe that he prayed for me daily as long as he lived. After I got into the ministry and great opposition was raised to my preaching, **which I shall have occasion to relate,** I met **Dea.**[32] **Hinman**, and he alluded to the opposition, and sa‹id›,[33] "O my soul is so burdened that I pray for you day and night. But I am sure that God will help. Go on," he sa‹id›, "go on, **B**rother Finney; the Lord will give you deliverance."

One afternoon ‹Mr.› Gale and I had been conversing for a ¦long time on JHF 48 the subject of the **A**tonement, and the hour arrived for us to attend the **C**onference meeting. We continued our conversation on that subject until we

[27] Matson had written "a Deacon" here, but the word "Deacon" was changed by Finney to "Elder."

[28] This was Josiah Hinman, one of the original elders appointed when the church became Presbyterian in January 1821 (see S. W. Durant, *History of Jefferson County, New York* [Philadelphia: Everts, 1878], p. 260). It may have been this man's conversion from infidelity that Finney described in a sermon. He spoke of "Deacon 'H', whom I well knew in his years of infidelity" (*OE*, 6 July 1853, p. 106).

[29] It was probably Hinman whom Finney was referring to in a description of his own experience before he was converted:

> I can well remember one deacon who used to visit our office. Often however, he seemed to be in an agony of soul; I could often hear him sigh,—could see his struggles of mind;—the tear would start in his eye, and the words falter on his tongue. I used to be searching after the cause of this. . . . After my conversion I could see that I had often given Dea. H. this trouble and anxiety which I had so frequently seen in his countenance. I saw that my folly and sin had caused him this deep grief (*OE*, 30 September 1846, p. 154).

[30] The word "continue" was inserted by Finney in place of "spend."

[31] Matson had written "man," but it was changed by Finney to "Elder."

[32] This was not altered in the manuscript, but the published version has "Elder."

[33] The words "He says" were altered by Finney to "said." A similar alteration was made three lines later.

got into the house. As we were early, and very few persons had arrived, we continued our conversation. The people kept coming in; and **as soon as** they MS 93 **came in** would sit down and listen with the greatest |attention to what we were saying. Our discussion was very earnest, though I trust conducted in a Christian spirit. The people became more and more interested, **as they came,** in hearing our discussion; and when we **said, "It is time** to stop and commence our meeting," they earnestly begged us to proceed with our discussion and let that be our meeting. We did so; and spent the whole evening, I think very much to the satisfaction of those present, and I trust to their permanent edification **on some points.**

After I had been studying theology for a few months, and ‹Mr.› Gale's health was such that he was unable to preach, a Universalist minister came in and began to promulge his objectionable doctrines.[34] The impenitent part of the community seemed very much disposed to hear him; and finally people became so interested that there was a large number **of people** that seemed to be shaken in their minds in regard to the commonly received views of the MS 94 Bible. In this state ‹Mr.› Gale, together with some elders of his |church, desired me to address the people on the subject, and see if I could not reply to the arguments of the Universalist. The great effort of the Universalist was of course to show that sin did not deserve endless punishments. He inveighed against the doctrine of endless punishments as unjust, infinitely cruel, and absurd. God was love; and how could a God of love punish men endlessly? I arose **one night** in one of our meetings and said: "This Universalist preacher holds forth doctrines that are new to me, and I do not believe they are taught in the Bible. But I am going to examine the subject; and if I cannot show that his views are false, I will be a Universalist myself.[''] I then appointed a JHF 49 meeting the next week; at which time I |proposed to deliver a lecture in opposition to his views. The Christian people were rather startled at my boldness in saying that I would be a Universalist if I could not prove that his doctrines were false. However I felt sure that I could. When the evening MS 95 came for my lecture the house was crowded. |I took up the question of the *justice* of endless punishments, and discussed it through that and the next evening. **This settled the question in regard to the *justice* of endless punishments, I believe to the universal satisfaction of those that were present. I know I heard it expressed on every side, that that course of argument was conclusive; and they wondered that Mr. Gale had not taken that subject up, and guarded his people against Universalism.**

The Universalist himself found that the people were convinced that he was wrong, and then he took another tack. ‹Mr.› Gale, together with his school of theology, maintained that the Atonement of Christ was the literal payment of the debt of the elect, a suffering of just what they deserved to suffer; so that the elect were saved upon the principles of exact justice, Christ, so far as they were concerned, having fully answered the demands of the law. The Universalist seized upon this. Assuming that this was the real nature of the

[34]The Universalist minister Stephen R. Smith had been in Adams about this time and lectured on the evening of Sunday, 28 July 1822. His report indicates the activities of Universalists in the area during this period. See *Religious Inquirer* (Hartford, Conn.), 12 October 1822, pp. 195–96.

Atonement, **he** had only to prove that the atonement was made for all men, and then he could show that all men would be saved,[35] |because the debt of all mankind had been literally paid by the Lord Jesus Christ; and **that therefore because of the Atonement,** Universalism would follow on the very ground of justice, for God could not justly punish those whose debt was paid. I saw, and the people saw,—those of them who understood ‹Mr.› Gale's position—that the Universalist had got him into a tight place. For it was easy to prove that the Atonement was made for *all mankind*; and if the nature and value of the Atonement were as ‹Mr.› Gale held, universal salvation was an inevitable result. This again carried the people away; and ‹Mr.› Gale sent for me ‹**&** requested that I should›[36] go on and reply to him **again**. He said **that** he understood the question on the ground of *law* was settled; but now I must answer his argument upon the ground of the *Gospel.* I said to him: "‹Mr.› Gale, I cannot do it without contradicting your views on |that subject, and setting them all aside. With your views of the Atonement he cannot be answered. For if you have **got** the right view of the Atonement, the people can easily see that the Bible |proves that Christ died for all men, for the whole world of sinners; and therefore unless you will allow me to sweep your views of the Atonement all away, I can say nothing to any purpose." "Well," said ‹Mr› Gale, "it will never do to let the thing remain as it is. You may say what you please; only go on and answer him in your own way. If I find it necessary to preach on the subject of the Atonement, I shall be obliged to contradict you." ["]Very well," said I, "let me but show my views, and I can answer the Universalist; and you may say to the people afterward what you please." I then appointed to lecture on the Universalist's argument founded on the Gospel. I delivered two lectures upon the Atonement. In these I think I fully succeeded in showing that the Atonement did not consist in the literal payment of the debt of sinners, in the sense **in** which the Universalist maintained. That it simply rendered the salvation of all men *possible*; and did not of itself lay God under **any** obligation to save *anybody*. That it was not true that Christ suffered just what those for whom he died deserved |to suffer. That no such thing as that was taught in the Bible; and no such thing was true. **But** on the contrary, **that** Christ died simply to remove an insurmountable obstacle out of the way of God's forgiving sinners; so as to render it possible for him to proclaim a universal *Amnesty,* inviting all men to repent, to believe in Christ, and to accept salvation. That instead of **Christ's** having satisfied *retributive* justice, and borne just what sinners deserve, **he** had only satisfied *public* justice, by honoring the law both in his obedience and death; **and therefore** rendering it safe for God to pardon sin, **and** to pardon the sins of any man, and of all men, who would repent and believe in **Christ**. I maintained that Christ in his Atonement merely did that which was necessary as a *condition* of the forgiveness |of sin; and not that which *cancelled* sin, in the sense of literally paying the indebtedness of sinners.

MS 96 — JHF 50 — MS 97 — MS 98 — JHF 51

This answered the Universalist, and put a stop to any farther proceedings

[35]The phrase "since the debt of all had been fully canceled" was added by Finney here but was then crossed out by him.

[36]The words "& requested that I should" were inserted by Finney in place of "to have me."

Page 99 of the Manuscript. This photo shows the incorrect date, March, 1824, that was added by Fairchild. Courtesy Oberlin College Archives.

or |excitement on that subject. But what was very striking, these lectures secured the conversion of the young **lady** for whose **conversion**, as I have said, such earnest and agonizing prayer had been offered.[37] This was very astound**ing**[38] to ‹Mr› Gale; for **here it was manifest** that the Spirit of God had blessed my views of the Atonement. **But he had unceasingly urged that God never would bless that view of the Atonement.** This, I think, staggered him considerably in regard to **whether he was right in** his view. I could see in conversing with him, that he felt very much surprized that this view of the Atonement should be instrumental in converting that young **lady**. **But** after **a great struggle** with ‹Mr.› Gale in pursuing my theological studies, the presbytery was finally called together at Adams to examine me, and if they could agree to do so, to license me to preach the Gospel.[39] I expected a severe struggle with them in my examination; but I found them a good deal |softened.[40] The manifest blessing that had attended my conversations, and my teaching in prayer and Conference meetings, and in these lectures of which I have spoken, rendered them, I think, more cautious than they would otherwise have been in getting into any controversy with me. In the course of my examination they avoided asking any such questions as would naturally bring my views into collision with theirs.

MS 99

MS 100

When they had examined me, they voted unanimously to license me to preach.[41] Unexpectedly to myself they asked me if I received the Confession of faith of the Presbyterian church. I had not examined it;[42]—that is, the large work, containing the Catechisms and **Presbyterian** Confession.[43] This

[37]See MS 74–78.

[38]This word was not altered in the manuscript, but the published edition has "astonishing."

[39]The sentence "This was in March 1824," which appears here in the published edition, was not in the original manuscript and is incorrect. It was added by Fairchild (see photo of the manuscript on p. 52). Finney had written to Philemon H. Fowler, "I was licensed to preach by the Presbytery of St. Lawrence in the spring of 1824"; but Fowler noted, "Adams, Dec 30, 1823 is the exact date of Mr. Finney's licensure, according to the Minutes of the Presbytery" (Fowler, *Historical Sketch of Presbyterianism,* p. 258). See also n. 41 below.

[40]David Kimball, the minister at Martinsburgh, New York, who was the moderator at the licensure, gave some idea of the problem:

> The application for licensure was not at first favorably regarded. He had read theology only a few months with Mr. Gale; and at the previous session, at my own ordination, the presbytery had deferred an application from Mr. Burchard, advising him to read for a year longer with some pastor. Mr. Burchard adroitly evaded the requirement by applying to an association of four ministers, all of whom were members also of presbytery, who licensed, ordained as an evangelist, and dismissed him to our body; and we could not reject him. Mr. Finney's examination proved satisfactory, and we licensed him (David Kimball, "Rev. Charles G. Finney," *The Independent,* 14 May 1868, p. 6).

[41]Finney's license from the St. Lawrence Presbytery dated Adams, 30 December 1823, and attested by David Kimball, moderator, and George S. Boardman, stated clerk, is in the Finney Papers, file 2/2/2, box 9.

[42]The phrase "and really do not know whether I had ever seen the one to which they alluded" written after this appears to have been crossed out by Finney. In MS 467 Finney wrote, "I had never examined it with any attention, and I think I had never read it through."

[43]*The Constitution of the Presbyterian Church, in the United States of America Containing, the Confession of Faith, the Catechisms, the Government and Discipline, and the Directory for the Worship of God. Ratified and adopted by the Synod of New York and Philadelphia, held at Philadelphia, May the 16th, 1788 and continued by Adjournments, until the 28th of the Same Month* (Wilmington, Del.: printed and sold by Bonsal and Niles, 1801).

had made no part of my study. I replied that I received it for substance of doctrine, so far as I understood it. But I spoke in a way that plainly implied, I think, that I did not pretend to know much about it. However, ǀI answered honestly, as I understood it at the time.[44] They heard the trial sermons ǀwhich I had written, on texts which had been given me by the presbytery; and went through with all the ordinary details of such an examination.

MS 101
JHF 52

At this meeting of presbytery I first saw Rev. Daniel Nash, who is generally known as "Father Nash."[45] He was a member of this presbytery. ‹**A**›**t**[46] **Adams a** large congregation assembled to hear my examination. I got in a little late, and saw a man standing in the pulpit speaking to the people, as I supposed. He looked at me, I observed, as I came in; and was looking at others as they passed up the aisles. As soon as I **got to** my seat and listened, I observed that he was praying. **I looked again with** surprize to see him looking all over the house, as if he **was** talking to the people, while in fact he was praying to God. **But of** course it did not sound to me much like prayer. And he was at that time indeed in a very cold and backǀslidden state.[47] **I mention him in this place because** I shall have occasion frequently to mention him hereafter.

MS 102

The next Sabbath after I was licensed I preached for **Brother** Gale.[48] When I came out of the pulpit he said to me: "Mr. Finney, I shall be very much ashamed to have it known, wherever you go, that you studied theology with me." This was so much like him, and like what he had repeatedly said to me, that I made little or no reply to it. I held down my head and felt discouraged, and went my way. He afterwards viewed this subject very differently; and told me that he blessed the Lord that in all our **controversy**, and in all he had said to me, he had not had the least influence to change my views. He very frankly confessed his error in the manner in which he had **spoken to and treated** me; and said that if I had listened to him I should have been ruined as a minister.[49]

[44]Finney referred to this again in MS 466 and 467.

[45]Daniel Nash (1775–1831) was from Cummington, Massachusetts, where he had been a carpenter before preparing for the ministry. In 1809 he was ordained as a Congregational minister with the Union Association, which had just been formed by a division of the Oneida Association. In 1816 he became minister of the Presbyterian church in Stow's Square, Lowville, where he remained until 1823. Besides his pastoral duties, he was also running a farm belonging to his second wife's family. He was twice moderator of the Presbytery of St. Lawrence. He is not to be confused with an Episcopalian priest of the same name. See P. C. Headley, *Evangelists in the Church* (Boston: Hoyt, 1875), pp. 169–75; James H. Hotchkin, *A History of the Purchase and Settlement of Western New York* (New York: Dodd, 1875), p. 110; account of Daniel Nash by his son Seymour W. Nash in *The Circular* (Oneida, N.Y.), 8 June 1868, pp. 92–93; Ralph Birdsall, "Father Nash," *Transactions of the Unadilla Valley Historical Society* 2 (1909): 16–26; and *DAB*.

[46]The words "When the presbytery met," which started this sentence, appear to have been crossed out by Finney.

[47]According to Asa Mahan, Nash was, at this time, "one of the dullest preachers that ever ascended a pulpit in the United States." Finney apparently said that Nash "prayed with his eyes open, and preached with them shut" (Asa Mahan, *Out of Darkness into Light* [London: Wesleyan-Methodist Book-Room, 1882], p. 258).

[48]Gale said that Finney "was licensed six months sooner than he wished, or expected to be, that he might supply the pulpit made vacant by my sickness and dismission" (*Autobiography*, p. 186).

[49]Gale told Richard Steel of Auburn that Finney spoke the truth with such energy that Gale

The fact is that **Brother** Gale's education for the ministry had been entirely defective. ¦He had imbibed a set of opinions, both theological and practical, that were a strait ¦jacket to him. He could accomplish very little or nothing if he carried out his own principles. I had the use of his library, and **ransacked** it thoroughly on all the questions of theology which came up for examination; and the more I examined the books, the more was I dissatisfied. I had been used to the close and logical reasonings of the judges, as I found them reported in our law **books.**[50] But when I went to **Brother** Gale's **Old** School library, I found almost nothing proved to my satisfaction. I am sure it was not because I was opposed to the truth; but I was dissatisfied because the**ir** positions were unsound and not satisfactorily sustained. They often seemed to me to state one thing and prove another, and frequently fell short of logically proving anything. I finally said to ‹Mr.› Gale: "If there is nothing better than I find in your library to sustain the great doctrines taught by our church, I must ¦be an infidel." And I have always believed that had not the Lord led me to see the fallacy of those arguments, and **the manner in which the truth was to be established from the Bible, and** had **He** not so revealed **Him**self to me personally that I could not doubt the truth of the Christian religion, I should have been forced to be an infidel.

MS 103 JHF 53 MS 104

At first, being no theologian, my attitude in respect to his peculiar views was rather that of negation or denial, than that of opposing any positive view to his. I said, "Your positions are not proved." I often said, "They are insusceptible of proof." So I thought then, and so I think now. But after all, he would insist upon it that I ought to defer to the opinions of the great and good men who, after much consultation and deliberation, had come to those conclusions. That it was unbecoming in me, a young man, bred to the profession of law and having no theological education, to oppose my views to those of the great men and profound theologians ¦whose opinions I found in his library. He **insisted** that if I persisted in having my intelligence satisfied on those points with argument, I should **be** an infidel; **and that I ought to accept those opinions, because they were the opinions of men who knew so much more than I did**. ¦He believed that the decisions of the church ought to be respected by a young man like me; and that I should surrender my own judgment to that of others of superior wisdom. Now I could not deny that there was a good deal of force in this; but still I found myself utterly unable to accept doctrine **in the shape of dogma**. If I tried to accept those doctrines as dogmas, I could not do it. I could not be honest in doing it; I could not respect myself in doing it. Often when I left ‹Mr.› Gale, I would go to my room and spend a long time on my knees over my Bible. Indeed I read my Bible on my knees a great deal during those days of con**troversy with**

MS 105 JHF 54

reproved him, telling him that he must not speak so—that he was afraid he was doing more hurt than good. He said that Mr. Finney would grieve over it, weep like a child, saying I will be careful and not do so again; but perhaps at the very next meeting he would be more plain than before, and so it went on. I would chide, and he would weep and be sorry. At last "I let him go on, and I'm glad of it. I done what I could to kill him, but God would not let me" (*NYE*, 9 September 1875, p. 1).

[50]This word appears as "works" in the published edition. It was not altered by Fairchild in the manuscript and appears to have been misread by the typesetter.

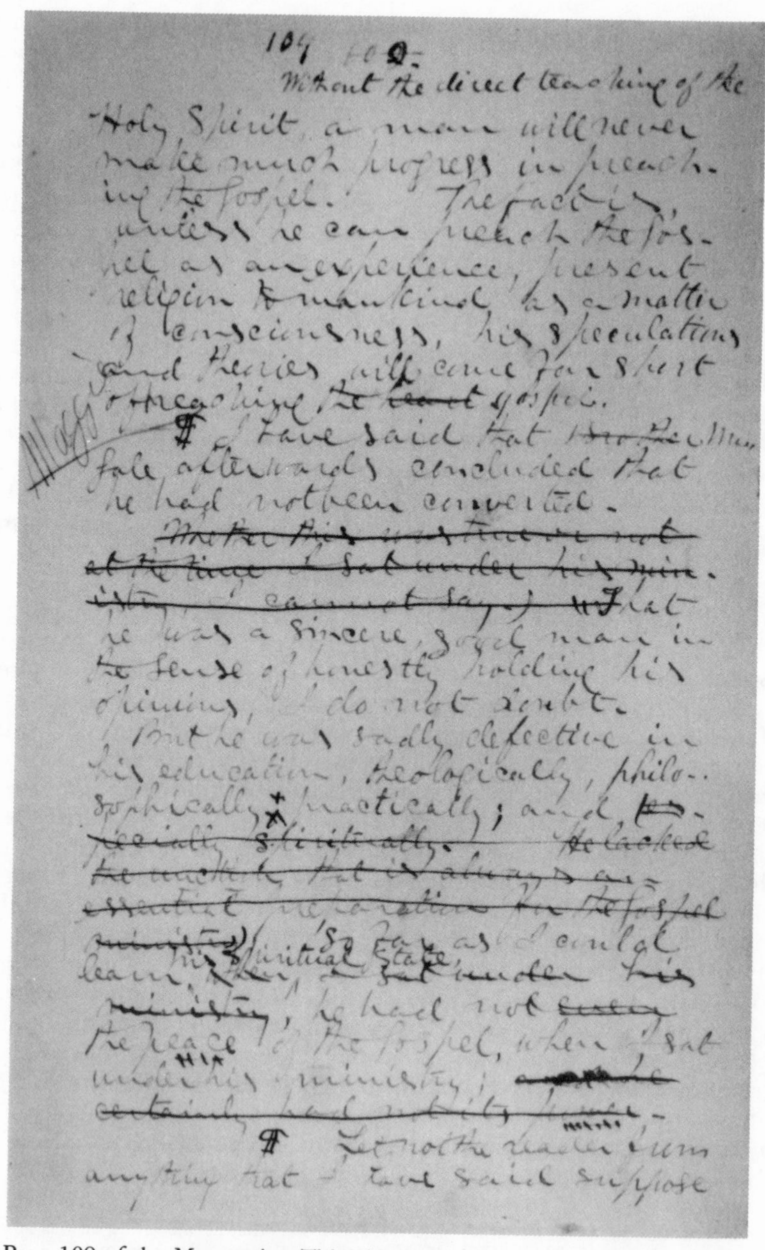
109 ~~102~~

Without the direct teaching of the Holy Spirit, a man will never make much progress in preaching the gospel. The fact is, unless he can preach the gospel as an experience, present religion to mankind, as a matter of consciousness, his speculations and theories will come far short of preaching the ~~[illegible]~~ gospel.

¶ I have said that ~~Mr.~~ Mr. Gale afterwards concluded that he had not been converted. ~~Whether this was true or not at the time I sat under his ministry, I cannot say.~~ That he was a sincere, good man in the sense of honestly holding his opinions, I do not doubt. But he was sadly defective in his education, theologically, philosophically, & practically; and, ~~especially spiritually. He lacked the unction that is always an essential preparation for the gospel ministry.~~ So far as I could learn, his spiritual state, when ~~I sat under his ministry~~, he had not ~~[illegible]~~ the peace of the gospel, when I sat under his ministry; ~~he certainly had not its power~~.

¶ Let not the reader from anything that I have said suppose

Page 109 of the Manuscript. This photo shows that Fairchild crossed out the references to Gale's defective spirituality and power. Courtesy Oberlin College Archives.

‹**Mr**› **Gale**, beseeching the Lord to teach me his own mind on those points. I had nowhere to go but directly to the |Bible, and to the philosophy or workings of my own mind as **they were** revealed in consciousness. My views took on a *positive* type but slowly. **I at** first found myself unable to receive his peculiar views; and **secondly,** gradually formed views of my own in opposition to them, which appeared to me to be unequivocally taught in the Bible.

MS 106

But **I have said that** not only were ‹Mr.› Gale's *theological* views such as to cripple his usefulness; **but** his *practical* views were equally erroneous. Hence he prophesied with respect to my views every kind of evil. **First**, that the Spirit of God would not approve and co-operate with my labors; **Secondly,** that if I addressed men as I **assured** him I intended to, they would not hear me, **it would drive them away**; **Thirdly,** that if they came for a short time, they would soon become **disgusted**, and my congregations would all fall off; **Fourthly,** that unless I wrote my sermons I should immediately become stale and uninteresting, and would not **interest** the people; and **Fifthly,** |that I should divide and scatter **congregations** instead of building **them** up wherever I preached.[51] Indeed I found his views to be almost the reverse of those which I entertained on all such practical questions relating to my duty as a minister. |I do not wonder, and did not at the time, that he was shocked at my views and purposes in relation to preaching the Gospel. With his education it could not be otherwise. He followed out his views with very little practical result. I pursued mine, and by the blessing of God the results were the opposite of those which he predicted. When this fact came out clearly **in my labors**, it completely upset his theological and practical **education** as a minister. This result, as I shall mention in its place, annihilated his hope as a Christian, and finally made him quite another man as a minister.[52]

MS 107

JHF 55

But there was another defect in **B**rother Gale's education, which I regarded as fundamental. If he had ever been converted to Christ, he had failed to re|ceive that divine anointing of the Holy Ghost that would make him a power in the pulpit and in society for the conversion of souls. He had fallen short of receiving the baptism of the Holy Ghost which is indispensable to ministerial success. When Christ commissioned his apostles to go and preach, he told them to abide at Jerusalem till they were endued with power from on high. This power, as every one knows, was the baptism of the Holy Ghost poured out upon them on the day of **p**entecost. This was an indispensable qualification for success in their ministry. I did not suppose then, nor do I now, that this baptism was simply the power to work miracles. The power to work miracles and the gift of tongues were given as signs to attest the reality of their divine commission. But the baptism itself was a divine purifying, **a filling them with the Holy Ghost,** bestowing on them a **vast** divine illumination, filling them with faith and love, with peace and power; so that their words were made sharp in the hearts of God's enemies, **and were** quick and powerful like a two-edged sword. This is an indispensable qualification of a successful minister. **But this part of ministerial**

MS 108

[51] Finney expanded further on this in MS 866–67.
[52] See MS 305–6.

qualification Brother Gale did not possess. And I have often been surprized and pained that to this day so little stress is laid upon this qualification for preaching Christ to a sinful world. MS 109 |Without the direct teaching of the Holy Spirit, a man will never make much JHF 56 |progress in preaching the Gospel. The fact is, unless he can preach the Gospel as an experience, present religion to mankind as a matter of consciousness, his speculations and theories will come far short of [p]reaching the ‹gospel.›[53] I have said that ‹Mr.› Gale afterwards concluded that he had not been converted. **Whether this was true or not at the time I sat under his ministry, I cannot say.** That he was a sincere, good man in the sense of honestly holding his opinions, I do not doubt. But he was sadly defective in his education, theologically, philosophically, practically **and especially spiritually. He lacked the unction that is always an essential preparation for the Gospel ministry.**[54] So far as I could learn his spiritual state, he had not **even** the *peace* of the Gospel, when I sat under his ministry; **and he certainly had not its *power*.** Let not the reader from anything that I have said suppose MS 110 |that I did not love ‹Mr› Gale, and highly respect him. I did both. He and I remained the firmest friends, so far as I know, to the day of his death. I have said what I have in relation to his views, because I think it applicable, I am afraid I must say, to **the great majority** of the ministers even of the present day. I think that their practical views of preaching the Gospel, whatever their theological views may be, are very defective indeed; and that their want of unction, and of the power of the Holy Ghost, is a radical defect in their preparation for the ministry. I say not this censoriously; but still I would record it as a **thing that** has long been settled in my mind, and **as a fact** over which I have long had occasion to mourn. And as I have become more and more acquainted with the ministry in this and other countries, I am persuaded that, with all their training, and discipline, and education, **they are wanting** in practical views of the best way of presenting the Gospel to men; in **their views of** adapting means to secure the end; and especially in their want of the power of the Holy Ghost.

MS 111/1 |I[55] have spoken at considerable length of my protracted controversy with my theological teacher, **Brother** Gale. Upon reflection I think that I should state a little more definitely some of the points upon which we had so much discussion. I could not receive that theological *fiction* of *imputation*. I will state as nearly as I can the exact ground that he JHF 57 |maintained and insisted upon.

[53] Matson had written down the words “of reaching the heart” here, but “heart” was changed by Finney to “gospel.” A *p* in pencil before “reaching” appears to have been added by Fairchild.

[54] Fairchild crossed out these references to Gale's defective spirituality (see photo of the manuscript on p. 56). He also crossed out similar references to Gale's defective mode of preaching in MS 867.

[55] MS 111/1 was numbered 104 by Matson and renumbered 111 by Finney. This was the first of eight additional pages inserted between pages 103 and 104. The original pages 104–9 were then renumbered 112–17 by Matson. Subsequently, they all had to be renumbered again, and this page became 111. However, the numbering became so confused that the numbers *1* to *22* were added in blue pencil to indicate the order of the sheets. This appears to have been done by Finney. This page was numbered 1. It is shown in the manuscript number as 111/1.

When Finney divided up the manuscript into chapters, he headed this page “Chap V. *More of my theological discussions with Mr. Gale.*” But he crossed it out and started chapter V at MS 114/8 instead.

First, he maintained that the guilt of Adam's first transgression is literally imputed to all his posterity; so that they are justly sentenced and exposed to eternal damnation for Adam's sin. Secondly, he maintained that we received from Adam, by natural generation, a nature wholly sinful and morally corrupt in[56] every faculty of soul and body; so that we are totally unable to perform any act acceptable to God, and necessitated ‹by›[57] our sinful nature to **wholly** transgress **His** law in every action of our lives. And this, he insisted, is the estate into which all men fell by the first sin of Adam. For this sinful nature, thus received from Adam by natural generation, all man|kind[58] are also sentenced to, and deserving of, eternal damnation. Then, thirdly, in addition to this, he maintained that we are all justly condemned and sentenced to eternal damnation for our own unavoidable transgression of the law. Thus we find ourselves justly subject to a triple eternal damnation. Then the Second branch of this wonderful imputation is as follows: The sin of all the elect, both original and actual—that is, the guilt of Adam's sin, **so far as the elect are concerned,** together with the guilt of their sinful nature, and also **the** guilt of their personal transgressions, are all literally imputed to Christ; and therefore the divine government regarded him as an embodiment of all the sins and guilt of the elect. **The guilt of Adam's first sin imputed to them, Christ assumed; the guilt of their sinful nature he also assumed; the guilt of their personal transgressions he also assumed,** and **the government of God** treated him accordingly; that is, the Father punished the Son precisely as much as all the elect deserved, **including the desert of the triple damnation which each de|served, and this multiplied by the whole number of the elect. Hence there is no mercy in saving them from the penalty of the law, or in their forgiveness; because,** their debt being thus fully discharged by the ‹punishment›[59] of Christ, they are saved upon principles of *exact justice.* The third branch of this wonderful theological fiction is as follows: First, **The** obedience of Christ to the divine law is literally imputed to the elect; so that in him they are regarded as having always perfectly obeyed the law. Secondly, **his** death for them is also imputed to the elect; so that in him they are regarded as having fully suffered all that they deserve on account of the guilt of Adam's sin |**being** imputed to them, and on account of their sinful nature, and also on account of all their personal transgressions. Thirdly, **thus** by their Surety the elect have first perfectly obeyed the law; and then they have by and in their Surety suffered the full penalty to which they were subject in consequence of the guilt of Adam's sin imputed to them, and also the guilt of their sinful nature, with all their blameworthiness for their personal transgressions. |Thus they have *suffered* in Christ just as if they had not *obeyed* in him. He first perfectly obeys for them, which obedience is strictly imputed to them, so that they are regarded by the government of God as having fully obeyed in their Surety; Secondly, he has

MS 112/2

MS 113/3

JHF 58

MS 114/4

[56]The word "in" had been written down twice by Matson. The first one appears to have been crossed out by Fairchild.

[57]The word "from" here was changed by Finney to "by."

[58]Pages 112/2 to 116/6 were originally numbered 105 to 109 by Matson and renumbered 112 to 116 by Finney. The numbers *2* to *6* were then added in blue pencil.

[59]The word "sufferings" was changed by Finney to "punishment."

suffered for them the penalty of the law, just as if no obedience had been rendered; Thirdly, **then** after the law has been doubly satisfied, the elect are required to repent as if no satisfaction had been rendered; Fourthly, **thus having receiv[ed]**[60] payment in full twice over, the discharge of the elect is claimed to be an act of infinite grace. *Thus the elect are saved by grace on principles of justice.* **That is, grace first obeys the law for the elect; then assumes and pays the debt, as if no obedience had been rendered; and then justice discharges and saves the debter.** So that there is strictly no grace or mercy in our forgiveness; but the whole grace of our salvation is found in the obedience and sufferings of Christ. It follows that the elect may *demand* their discharge on the score of strict justice. They need not pray for pardon ˡor forgiveness; it is all a mistake to do so. This inference is my own; but it follows, as every one can see, irresistibly from what the Confession of faith itself asse[**r**]ts,[61] that the elect are saved on principles of ‹exact›[62] and perfect justice.[63]

MS 115/5

I found it impossible to agree with ‹Mr› Gale on these points. I could not but regard and treat this whole question of imputation as a theological fiction, **somewhat related to our legal fiction of John Doe and Richard Roe.**[64] Upon these points we had constant discussion, in some shape, during the whole course of my study. I do not recollect that ‹Mr.› Gale ever insisted that the Confession of faith taught these principles **right out and out,** as I **afterwards** learned that it did when I came to study it. I was not aware that the ˡrules of the presbytery required them to ask a candidate if he accepted the Presbyterian Confession of faith. **Hence I had never read it; and was not at all aware that ‹Mr› Gale in his discussion with me had only been defending the plain teachings of the ˡConfession of faith on these points.** As soon as I learned what were the unambiguous teachings of the Confession of faith upon these points, I did not hesitate **at all** on all suitable occasions to declare my dissent from them. I repudiated and exposed them. Wherever I found that any class of persons were hidden behind these dogmas, I did not hesitate to demolish them to the best of my ability. I have not caricatured these positions of ‹Mr.› Gale; but have stated them as nearly as I can in the very language in which he would defend them when I presented them to him in controversy. He did not pretend that they were rational, or that they would bear reasoning upon. Hence he insisted that my reasoning would lead me into infidelity. But I insisted that our reason was given us for the very purpose of enabling us to justify the way of God; and that no such fiction of imputation

JHF 59

MS 116/6

[60]This word was written down as "receiving" by Matson.

[61]This word was written "assets," and the *r* appears to have been supplied by Fairchild.

[62]The word "strict" was changed by Finney to "exact."

[63]The Confession of Faith, chapter XI, section III, states: "Christ, by his obedience and death, did fully discharge the debt of all those that are thus justified, and did make a proper, real, and full satisfaction to his Father's justice in their behalf. . ." (*The Constitution of the Presbyterian Church, in the United States of America* [Philadelphia: Perkins, 1850], p. 60).

[64]In cases where it was complicated to determine land titles in the courts and a freeholder wanted to eject a tenant from his land, the device of introducing a fictitious plaintiff and defendant was used. These were called "John Doe" and "Richard Roe." The need for this fiction was done away with by the Common Law Procedure Acts of 1852. See Earl Jowitt, *The Dictionary of English Law* (London: Sweet and Maxwell, 1959).

could by any possibility be true. Of course there were many other points that were so related to these as necessarily to come under discussion, upon ǀwhich[65] we had a good deal of controversy. But our controversy always MS 117 turned upon this as the foundation **upon which all the rest rested**. If man had a sinful nature, then regeneration must consist in a change of nature. If man's nature was sinful, the influence of the Holy Spirit that must regenerate him, must be *physical* and not *moral.* If man had a sinful nature, there was no adaptation in the Gospel to change his nature, and consequently no connection in religion between means and end. This Brother Gale sternly held; and consequently in his preaching he never seemed to expect, nor even to *aim* at converting anybody, by any sermon that I ever heard him preach. ‹And yet he was an able preacher as preaching was then estimated.›[66] The fact is, these dogmas were a perfect straight-jacket to him. If he preached repentance, he must be sure before he sat down to leave the impression on his people that they could not repent. If he called them to believe, he must be JHF 60 sure to inform them that until their naǀture was changed by ǀthe[67] Holy Spirit, MS 118/7 faith was impossible to them. And so his orthodoxy was a perfect snare to himself and to his hearers. *I could not receive it.* I did not so understand my Bible; nor could he make me see that it was taught in the Bible.

When I came to read the Confession of faith, and saw the passages that were quoted to sustain these peculiar positions, I was absolutely ashamed of it. I could not feel any respect for a document that would undertake to impose on mankind such dogmas as those, sustained, for the most part, by passages of Scripture that were totally irrelevant; and not in a single instance sustained by passages **that** in a court of law would have been considered at all conclusive. But the presbytery were all of one way of thinking at that time, **so far as I knew**. They subsequently, however, I believe, all gave in; and when ‹Mr› Gale changed his views, I heard no more from any of the members of the presbytery in defence of these views.

[65] MS 117 was numbered 110 by Matson and renumbered 117 by Finney. Finney did not add the number 7 in blue pencil on this sheet, so the next sheet bears that number.

[66] This sentence was added by Finney.

[67] MS 118/7 was numbered 111 by Matson and renumbered 118 by Finney; the number 7 was added in blue pencil.

THE EARLY REVIVALS, 1824–25

Places where Finney preached from April 1824 to September 1825.

CHAPTER V

MS 114/8
JHF 61

‹*I* commence *preaching as a missionary.*›

‹Having[1] had no regular training for the ministry I did not expect or desire to labor in large towns or cities, or in cultivated congregations. I intended to go into new settlements & preach in school houses, & barns & groves, as best I could. Accordingly›[2] soon after being licensed to preach, for the sake of being introduced to the region where I proposed to labor, I took a commission for six months of a female Missionary Society, located in Oneida County.[3] I went into the northern part of Jefferson County and began my labors at Evans' Mills, in the town of Le Ray.[4] At this place I found two churches, a small Congregational church without a minister,[5] and a Baptist

[1]MS 114/8 was numbered 104 and 112 by Matson; the number *8* was added in blue pencil. More pages may have been added but later removed, for 112 was changed in pencil to 112 1/2 and later to 114, and the next three pages were renumbered 115 to 117. These changes appear to have been made by Finney. Matson had left a space of five lines at the top of the page, perhaps indicating that Finney had intended to insert the further section after page 103. Finney used the space to introduce the beginning of chapter V. The chapter heading and the section down to n. 2 are in his handwriting.

[2]This ends the section in Finney's handwriting.

[3]The Female Missionary Society of the Western District, based in Utica, New York, commissioned Finney on 17 March 1824 for three months' service as a missionary to Jefferson County, New York. The commission and its renewal for an additional three months are contained in letters from the committee to Finney dated 17 March and 29 June 1824 (Finney Papers, microfilm, roll 1). The society's constitution and annual reports can be found at the Oneida Historical Society, Utica. Finney was introduced to the society by Gale, who had been a missionary with the society before he went to Adams. See Wallace E. Lamb, "George Washington Gale, Theologian and Educator" (Ed.D. diss., Syracuse University, 1949), pp. 29–32; and G. W. Gale, *Autobiography (to 1834) of George Washington Gale (1789–1861), Founder of Galesburg, Illinois, and Knox College* (New York: privately printed, 1964), p. 186. See also Mary P. Ryan, "A Women's Awakening: Evangelical Religion and the Families of Utica, New York, 1800–1840," *American Quarterly* 30, no. 5 (Winter 1978): 602–23.

[4]Finney labored in the villages of Evans Mills, Antwerp, and Le Raysville, in Le Ray, a township of about 2,500 inhabitants, from April until October 1824. See Finney's letter to the presiding officer of the Female Missionary Society of the Western District of New York dated Antwerp, 10 June 1824, in *WR,* 6 July 1824, p. 54. This is the earliest known published letter of Finney. It was reprinted in the *Religious Intelligencer* (New Haven), 17 July 1824, p. 111; and in *BR,* 17 July 1824, p. 114. See also S. W. Durant, *History of Jefferson County, New York* (Philadelphia: Everts, 1878), pp. 420–27.

[5]The Le Ray Presbyterian Church, originally a Congregational Society, was organized on 13 January 1814. When Finney arrived it was composed of "hardly more than twenty members." See James H. Keeling, "A History of the First Presbyterian Church of Le Ray, Evans' Mills, Jefferson Co., New York," typescript dated 1939, in the Presbyterian Historical Society, Philadelphia; and Charles Finney, "Revival Memories," unpaginated and undated manuscript in Miscellaneous Items, Finney Papers, microfilm, roll 8.

church with a minister.[6] I presented my credentials to the deacons of the church. They were very glad to see me, and I soon began my labors.[7] They had no meeting house; but the two churches worshipped alternately in a large stone school house.[8] **The school house was so** large, I believe, **as** to accommodate all the children in the village. The Baptists occupied the house **on** one Sabbath, and the Congregationalists **on** the next; so that I could have the house but every other Sabbath **to preach in that place**, but could use **the house** evenings as often as I ˡpleased.[9] I therefore divided my Sabbaths between Evans Mills and Antwerp, a village some sixteen or eighteen miles still farther north. I will relate first some facts that occurred at Evans' Mills during that season, and then give a brief narrative of the occurrences at Antwerp. But as I preached alternately in these two places, these facts were occurring from ˡweek to week in one or the other of these localities. I began, as I said, to preach in the stone school house at Evans' Mills. The people were very much interested, and thronged **en masse** to hear me preach. They extolled my preaching; and the little Congregational church became very much interested, and hopeful that they should be built up, and that there would be a revival. More or less convictions occurred under every sermon that I preached; but still no general conviction appeared upon the public

MS 115/9

JHF 62

[6]The Baptist church was also organized in 1814. The minister was Elder John Blodgett (1792–1876). He started his ministry in 1820 at Champion Village, near Denmark, New York, and held a number of pastorates in the state before moving to Ohio in 1835. He left Evans Mills in December 1825 and moved to Lowville in Lewis County, New York. See Edwin A. Blodgett, *Ten Generations of Blodgetts in America* (Barre, Vt.: Modern Print, 1969), pp. 353–54. Reference supplied by Miss Elizabeth Blodgett of Naples, N.Y.; and Franklin B. Hough, *A History of Lewis County, in the State of New York* (Albany: Munsell and Rowland, 1860), p. 169. Records of both congregations have been lost.

[7]In another account of this revival, Finney mentioned the deacon of the Congregational church as being named Judson, "a very godly man," and the deacon of the Baptist church as McComber, "a man of strong faith, and mighty in prayer, and of a lovely Catholic spirit" ("Revival Memories," roll 8).

In 1889 Finney's daughter Helen, who was living in Cincinnati, sent G. F. Wright, Finney's biographer, an anecdote:

> Until within a year past an old gentleman has lived next door to us, who was a little boy living at "Evans Mills," when father first went there to preach. He said to me, "Your father stopped at my father's house when he came to preach at Evans Mills. I was a little fellow, & had never seen a minister. I imagined him to be a dreadful, solemn being, before whom I would not dare to speak or laugh, & I trembled when he rode up to the house & came in. But a more surprised youngster never lived. Here came, almost bounding in, a young, handsome, bright young man, greeting my father & mother, & all of us, with the utmost cordiality. As he was taking off his overcoat, he said, 'Any praying women around here brother Hopkins'? My father reflected a moment & replied, 'yes, I believe there is one, at the other end of the village.' 'Well, come let us go & see her.' & thrusting his arm in his coat again, he started out at once, without sitting down at all." The old gentleman went on to say, that there was never anything like the state that town was in by the next night (Helen Cox to G. F. Wright, 17 October 1889, Wright Papers, box 7; quotation marks altered to modern usage).

This was the home of Milton W. Hopkins, one of the trustees of the church in Evans Mills. See Hopkins to Finney, 21 August 1825, Finney Papers, microfilm, roll 1; and James Keeling, "History of the First Presbyterian Church of Le Ray," pp. 5–6; cf. also p. 98 n. 14 (MS 185).

[8]In the "Revival Memories" account Finney refers to this as a large "brick" schoolhouse.

[9]Pages 115/9 to 117/11 were originally numbered 105 to 107 and renumbered 113 to 115 by Matson, then renumbered again 115 to 117 by Finney in pencil, and the numbers *9* to *11* added in blue pencil.

mind. I was very much dissatisfied with this state of things; and at one of my evening services, after having preached there two or three Sabbaths and several evenings in the week, I told the people at the close |of my sermon, that I had come there to secure the salvation of their souls. That my preaching, I knew, was highly complimented by them; but that after all, I did not come there to please them but to bring them to repentance. That it mattered not to me how well they were pleased with my preaching, if after all they rejected my Master. That something was wrong, either in me or in them; and that the kind of interest they manifested in my preaching was doing them no good. That I could not spend my time with them unless they were going to receive the Gospel. I then, quoting the words of Abraham's servant, said to them: "Now will you deal kindly and truly with my Master? If you will, tell me; and if not, tell me, that I may turn to the right hand or to the left."[10] I turned this question over, and pressed it upon them, and insisted upon it that I must know what course they proposed to pursue. If they did not purpose to become Christians, and enlist in the service of the Savior, I wanted to know it that I might not labor with them in vain. I said to them: "You admit that what I preach is the Gospel. |You[11] profess to believe it. Now will you *receive* it? Do you *mean* to receive it? Or do you intend to reject it? You must have some mind about it. And now I have a right to take it for granted, inasmuch as you admit that I have preached |the truth, that you acknowledge your obligation at once to become Christians. This obligation you do not deny. But will you *meet* the obligation? Will you *discharge* it? Will you *do* what you admit that you ought to do? If you will not, tell me; and if you will, tell me, that I may turn to the right hand or to the left." After turning this over till I saw they understood it well, and looked greatly surprized at my manner of putting it, I then said to them: "Now I must know your minds. And I want that you who have made up your minds to become Christians, and will give your pledge to make your peace with God immediately, should rise up; but that on the contrary, those of you who are resolved that you will not become Christians, and wish me so to understand, and wish Christ so to understand, should sit still." After making |this[12] plain, so that I knew that they

MS 116/10

MS 117/11

JHF 63

MS 116/12

[10]Genesis 24:49.

[11]The page number *117* is followed by an asterisk in pencil. This appears to have been inserted by Finney. On the reverse side the following marks are made in pencil:

These appear to be examples of proofreaders' symbols for the insertion of quotation marks.

[12]MS 116/12 was numbered 108 and renumbered 116 by Matson; the number *12* was added in blue pencil. After the number *116,* the symbol

understood it, I then said: "You who **now** are willing to pledge to me and to Christ that you will immediately make your peace with God, please **to** rise up. On the contrary, you that mean that I should understand that you are committed to remain in your present attitude, not to accept Christ—**please,** those of you that are of this mind, **to** sit still." They looked at one another, and at me;—and all sat still, just as I expected. After looking around upon them for a few moments I said: "Then you are *committed.* You have taken your stand. You have rejected Christ and his Gospel; and ye are witnesses one against the other, and God is witness against you all. This is explicit, and **that which** you may remember as long as you live,—that you have thus publicly committed yourselves against the Savior, and said, 'We will not have this man Christ Jesus to reign over us.' "[13] This is the purport of what I urged upon them, and as nearly in these words as I can recollect. When I thus

MS 117/13

pressed them they began to look angry, and arose en masse and started ˡfor[14] the door. When they **got fairly under way** I paused. As soon as I stopped

JHF 64

speaking they ˡturned to see why I did not go on. I said: "I am sorry for you; and will preach to you once more, the Lord willing, to-morrow night."

They all left the house except Deacon Mc**Comber,** who was **the** deacon of the Baptist church in that place.[15] I saw that the Congregationalists were confounded.[16] They were few in number, and very weak in faith. I presume that every member of both churches who was present, except **Brother** Mc**Comber,** was taken aback, and concluded that the matter was all over,—that by my *imprudence* I had dashed and ruined all hopeful appearances. **Brother** Mc**Comber** came and took me by the hand and smil‹ing› said:[17] "Brother Finney, you have got them. They cannot rest under this, rely upon it. The brethren are all discouraged," said he; "but I am not. I believe you have done the very thing that needed to be done, and that we shall see the results." I thought so myself, of course. I intended to place them in a position

MS 118/14

ˡwhich,[18] upon reflection, would make them tremble in view of what they had done. But for that evening and the next day they were full of wrath. **Brother** Mc**Comber** and myself agreed upon the spot to spend the next day in fasting

has been inserted in pencil. This appears to have been done by Finney. William Bigglestone has drawn attention to a similar symbol used in the Solomon Spaulding Manuscript. This manuscript in the Oberlin College Archives was reputed to have been written by Solomon Spaulding (or Spalding) in the second decade of the nineteenth century and in some way to have been connected with the origins of the Book of Mormon. The symbol appears to be used there to indicate the insertion of a section at the bottom or the side of the page. See "Solomon Spaulding's Manuscript," *The Oberlin Review,* 24 October 1885, pp. 27–28.

[13] Luke 19:14.

[14] MS 117/13 was numbered 109 and 117 by Matson; the number *13* was added in blue pencil.

[15] John Macomber, who ran a small tannery in Evans Mills, was a charter member and elected officer of the Baptist church. See Durant, *History of Jefferson County,* pp. 422, 428. Matson originally spelled the name "Macomber" in each instance where it appears but subsequently changed it to "McComber." The name is also spelled "McComber" in "Revival Memories," in Rebecca Finney's handwriting, although the first occurrence of it is written "Deacon Macomber, or McComber."

[16] The word "confounded" was originally written as "offended" but was changed by Matson.

[17] Matson had written down "smiled and said," but it was changed by Finney to "smiling said."

[18] Pages 118/14 to 126/22 were originally numbered 118 to 126 by Matson, and the numbers *14* to *22* added in blue pencil.

‹&›[19] prayer, separately in the morning, and together in the afternoon. I learned in the course of the day that they were threatening me,—to "ride me on a rail," "to tar and feather me," "and to "give me a walking paper"," as they said. Some of them cursed me; and said that I had put them under oath, and made them swear that they would not serve God,—that I had drawn them into a solemn and public pledge to reject Christ and his Gospel. This was no more than I expected. In the afternoon **Brother McComber** and I went into a grove together, and spent the whole afternoon in prayer. Just at evening the Lord gave us great enlargement, and **gave us** victory. ‹B›oth[20] of us felt assured that we had prevailed with God; and that that night the power of God would be revealed among the people. As the time came for meetˡing, we left the woods and ˡwent to the village. The people were already thronging ‹to›[21] the place of worship; and those that had not already gone, seeing us go through the village turned out of their stores and places of business, threw down their ball clubs where they were playing **ball** upon the green, and packed the house to its utmost capacity.

MS 119/15
JHF 65

I had not taken a thought with regard to what I should preach,—indeed, this was common with me at that time. **I was full of** the Holy Spirit, and I felt confident that when the time came for action I should know what to preach. As soon as I found the house packed, so that no more could get in, I arose, and I think without any formal introduction of singing opened upon them with these words: "Say to the righteous that it shall be well with him; for they shall eat the fruit of their doings. Wo to the wicked! it shall be ill with him; for the reward of his hands shall be given him."[22] **I say I *opened upon* them with these words.** The Spirit of God came upon me with such power, that it was like ˡopening a battery upon them. For more than an hour, and perhaps for an hour and a half, the Word of God came through me to them in a manner that I could see was carrying all before it. It was a fire and a hammer breaking the rock; and as the sword that was piercing to the dividing asunder of soul and spirit. I saw that a general conviction was spreading over the whole congregation. Many of them could not hold up their heads. I did not call that night for any reversal of the action they had taken the night before, nor for any committal of themselves in any way; but took it for granted, during the whole of the sermon, that they were committed against the Lord. **At the close** I appointed another meeting, and dismissed.

MS 120/16

As the people withdrew I observed a **lady lying** in the arms of some of her friends, who were supporting her, in one part of the house; and I went to see what was the matter **with her**, supposing that she was in a fainting fit. But I soon found that she was not fainting, but that she ˡcould ˡnot speak. There was a look of the greatest anguish in her face, and she made me understand that she could not speak. I advised the **ladies** to take her home and pray with her, and see what the Lord would do. They informed me that she was a sister

MS 121/17
JHF 66

[19] Finney appears to have crossed out the word "in" here and inserted "&."
[20] Matson had originally written down "We both." Finney crossed out the "We" and changed the *b* of "both" into a capital *B*.
[21] The word "for" here was changed by Finney to "to."
[22] Isaiah 3:10–11.

of the **great** missionary, **William Goodell of Constantinople;**[23] and that she was a member of the church in good standing, and had been for several years.[24]

That evening, instead of going to my usual lodgings I accepted an invitation and went home with a family where I had not before stopped over night. Early in the morning I found that I had been sent for to the place where I was supposed to be several times during the night, to visit families where they were under awful distress of mind. This led me to sally forth among the people; and everywhere I found a state of wonderful conviction of sin and alarm for their souls. After lying in **this** speechless state about sixteen hours, **Miss Goodell**'s mouth was opened, and a new song was **put in** her **mouth**. She was |taken from the horrible pit of mir‹y›[25] clay, and her feet were set upon a rock; and it was true that many saw it and feared. It occasioned a great searching among the members of the church. She declared that she had been entirely deceived. That for eight years she had been a member of the church, and thought she was a Christian. But during the sermon the night before she saw that she had never known the true God; and when his character arose before her mind as it was then presented, her hope "perished," as she expressed it, "like a moth." She said such a view of the holiness of God was presented, that like a great wave it swept her away from her standing, and annihilated her hope in a moment.[26]

MS 122/18

I found at this place a number of deists; **and** ‹some of them›[27] **were** men of high standing in the community. One of them was a keeper of a hotel in the village;[28] and ‹others› were[29] respectable men, and of more than average intelligence. But they seemed banded together to resist the revival. When I |ascertained |exactly the ground **that** they took, I preached a sermon to meet their wants—for on the Sabbath they would attend my preaching. I took this for my text: "Suffer me a little, and I will show you that I have yet to speak **in** God's behalf. I will bring my knowledge from afar, and I will ascribe righteousness to my Maker."[30] I went over the whole ground, so far as I understood their position; and God enabled me to sweep it clean. As soon as I had finished and dismissed the meeting, the hotel keeper, who was the

JHF 67 MS 123/19

[23] William Goodell (1792–1867) was a graduate of Dartmouth College and Andover Theological Seminary. He went to the Near East in 1825 under the auspices of the American Board of Commissioners for Foreign Missions. In 1831 he started a new mission at Constantinople among the Armenians, where he translated the Bible into Armenian. He returned to America in 1865. See *DAB*.

[24] She was the oldest sister of William Goodell. In the congregation were also another brother and a sister who were already converted. See Finney, "Revival Memories," roll 8.

[25] Matson had written down "mire and." Finney changed it to "miry."

[26] Finney also said she told him:

> I saw that I had never known God. When you described his holiness, I saw that I had not the least degree of it myself, and indeed, that I did not *wish* to have any. I knew then that my character was utterly unlike God's. Then all my Christian hope perished. My whole soul drew back from God, as if it refused to have any thing more to do with a being so holy and pure. Then followed convictions of my own sin and guilt—a fearful conflict—until grace triumphed and my soul bowed (*OE*, 27 October 1854, p. 170).

[27] The word "they" was changed by Finney to "some of them."

[28] This may have been Capt. John Hoover. See Durant, *History of Jefferson County*, p. 422.

[29] The words "they were all" were changed by Finney to "others were."

[30] Job 36:2–3.

leader among them, came frankly up to me, and taking me by the hand said: "Mr. Finney, I am convinced. You have met and answered all my difficulties. Now I want you to go home with me, for I want to converse with you." I heard no more of their infidelity; and if I remember right, that class of men were nearly or quite all converted.[31]

There was one old man in this place,—**I cannot recollect his name**—who was not only an infidel, but a great railer at religion, **and** was very ˡangry at the revival movement. I heard every day of his railing and blaspheming, but took no public notice of it. He refused altogether to attend meeting. But in the midst of his opposition, and when his excitement was great, while sitting one morning at the table he suddenly fell out of his chair in a fit. **It proved to be a fit** of apoplexy. A physician was immediately called, who, after a brief examination, told him that he could live but a very short time; and that if he had anything to say, he must say it at once. He had just strength and time, as I was informed, to stammer out, "Don't let Finney pray over my corpse." This was the last of his opposition in that place.

MS 124/20

During that revival my attention was called to a sick woman in the community, who had been a member of a Baptist church, and was well-known in the place; but people had no confidence in her piety. She was fast failing with the consumption; and they begged me to call and see her, **and see if I could ˡnot undeceive her.** I went, and had a long conversation with her. She told me a dream which she had when she was a girl, which ˡmade her think that her sins were forgiven. Upon that she had settled down, and no argument could move her. I tried to persuade her that there was no evidence of her conversion in that dream. I told her plainly that her acquaintances affirmed that she had never lived a Christian life, and had never evinced a Christian temper; and I had come to try to persuade her to give up her false hope, and see if she would not now accept Jesus Christ that she might be saved. I dealt with her as kindly as I could, but did not fail to make her understand what I meant. But she took great offence; and after I went away complained that I tried to get away her hope and distress her mind. **That** I was cruel to try to distress a woman as sick as she was in that way,—to try to disturb the repose of her mind. She died not long afterwards. But her death, **in thinking of it,** has often reminded ˡme of Dr Nelson's book called, "The Cause and Cure of infidelity."[32] When this woman came to be actually dying, her eyes were opened; and before she left the world she seemed to have such a glimpse of the character of God, and of what heaven was and of the holiness required to dwell there, that she shrieked with agony, and exclaimed that she was going to hell. In this state, as I was informed, she died.

MS 125/21
JHF 68

MS 126/22

While at this place, one afternoon a Christian brother called on me and wished me to visit his sister, who, as he informed me, was fast failing with consumption, and was a Universalist. Her husband, he said, was a Universal-

[31] John Hoover was later a member of the church and an officeholder. See Keeling, "History of the First Presbyterian Church of Le Ray," p. 6.

[32] David Nelson, *The Cause and Cure of Infidelity,* was first published in New York by John S. Taylor in 1837 and went through many editions. David Nelson was an acquaintance of Finney's. See C. G. Finney, *Repentance: Its Nature, Grounds, Necessity, and Infinite Importance* (London: Snow, 1851), p. 50; and *OE,* 6 June 1855, p. 90.

ist, and had led her into Universalism.[33] He said he had not asked me to go and see her when her husband was at home, because he feared that he would abuse me, **and was confident that he would,** as he was determined that his wife's mind should not be disturbed on the question of universal salvation, MS 127 **but that she should be left to die in that belief. |He[34] said that her husband was gone at that time, and begged me to go and see her.** I **did so,** and found her not at all at rest in her views of Universalism; and **after conversing sometime** with her, she gave up these views entirely. **I think she declared that she had never been settled in them; but at any rate she gave them up,** and appeared to embrace the Gospel of Christ. I believe she held fast to this hope in Christ till she died.

JHF 69 At evening her husband returned, and learned from her|self what had taken place.[35] He was greatly enraged, and swore he "would kill Finney."[36] As I learned afterwards he armed himself with a loaded pistol, and that night went to meeting where I was to preach. Of this, however, I knew nothing at the time. The **preaching** that evening was in a school house out of the village. The house was very much packed, almost to suffocation. I went on to preach with all my might;[37] and almost in the midst of my discourse I saw a powerful looking man, about in the middle of the house, fall from his seat. As he sunk MS 128 down he groaned, and then cried**, or bellowed,** that |he was sinking to hell. He repeated that several times. The people knew who he was; but he was a stranger to me. I think I had never seen him before. Of course this created a great excitement.[38] It broke up my preaching; and so great was his anguish that we spent the rest of our time in praying for him. When the meeting was dismissed his friends helped him home.[39] The next morning I inquired for him; and found that he had spent a sleepless night, **and was** in great anguish of mind **all night**, and that at the early dawn he had gone forth, they knew not whither. He was not heard from till about ten **O'**clock in the morning. I was passing up the street, and saw him coming **from out of the village, and** apparently from a grove at some distance from the village. He was on the opposite side of the street when I first saw him, and coming toward me. When he recognized me he came across the street to meet me. When he came near enough, I saw that his countenance was all in a glow. I said to him, "Good MS 129 morning, Mr. **Comstock.**" |"Good morning," he replied. "And," said I, "how

[33] This was Sackett Comstock (see MS 128). His blacksmith shop was on the corner of Main and Noble Streets in Evans Mills (see Durant, *History of Jefferson County,* p. 422). In another place Finney called Comstock the "leading man" among the Universalists in the place (see *OE,* 11 October 1848, p. 145).

[34] Pages 127–34 are numbered by Matson.

[35] Finney recollected she cried out to her husband as he entered, "O my dear husband, you are in the way to hell—your Universalism will ruin your soul forever!" (*OE,* 11 October 1848, p. 145).

[36] Finney was later told: "his rage was kindled against me. 'Where is he now?' said he. 'Gone to the meeting,' was the reply. 'I'll go there and shoot him,' he cried" (*OE,* 11 October 1848, p. 145).

[37] Finney remembered that he was preaching from the text "Ye serpents, ye generation of vipers, how can ye escape the damnation of hell!" (*OE,* 11 October 1848, p. 145).

[38] In another description of this scene, Finney wrote that "his howling was electrical. I could preach no more. He was quite overcome" ("Revival Memories," roll 8).

[39] In another account Finney said the man's friends "carried him" home (*Repentance,* p. 65).

do you feel in your mind this morning?" "O I do not know," he replied; "I have had an awfully distressed night. But I could not pray there in the house; and I thought if I could get alone, where I could pour out my voice with my heart, I could pray. In the morning I went into the woods," **said he**; "but when I got there I found I could not pray **as I thought I could.** I thought I could give myself to God; but **I found that** I could not. I tried and tried till I was discour|aged," he continued. "Finally I saw that it was of no use; and I told the Lord that I found myself condemned and lost; that I had no heart to pray to **Him**, and no heart to repent; that I found I had hardened myself so much that I could not give my heart to **Him**, and therefore I must leave the whole question to **Him**. I was at **His** disposal, and could not object to **His** doing with me just as it seemed good in **His** eyes, for I had no claim to **His** favor at all. I left the **whole** question |of my salvation or damnation wholly with the Lord." "Well, what followed?" I inquired. "Why," said he, "I found I had lost all my conviction. I got up and came away, and my mind was so still and quiet that I found the Spirit of God was grieved away, and I had lost my conviction." **Said he: "I came along the street, and found that my convictions were so gone that I could not account for it unless the Holy Spirit had left me.** "But," said he, "when I saw you my heart began to burn and grow hot within me; and instead of feeling as if I wanted to avoid you, I felt so drawn that I came across the street to see you." But I should have said that when he came near me he leaped and took me right up in his arms, and turned around once or twice and then set me down. This preceded the conversation that I have just related. After a little farther conversation I left him **without expressing any opinion with respect to his religious state. However, he** soon came into a state of mind that led him to indulge a hope. We heard no more of his opposition.[40]

JHF 70

MS 130

|At this place I again saw father Nash, the man who prayed with his eyes open at the meeting of presbytery when I was licensed. After he was **there** at presbytery he was taken with inflamed eyes, and for several weeks **he** was shut up in a dark room.[41] He could neither read nor write, and gave himself up almost entirely to prayer, **as I learned**. He had a terrible overhauling in his whole Christian experience; and as soon as he was able to see with a double black veil before his face, he sallied forth to labor for souls.[42] When he came to Evans' Mills he was full of the power of prayer. He was another

MS 131

[40] "Deacon S. Comstock" of "Le Roy, N.Y." is listed as donating three dollars to Oberlin College in 1847. This may be the same man (*OE*, 19 January 1848, p. 15).

[41] According to Finney, Nash "was almost entirely blind for about six months." See Finney's letter to P. C. Headley about Daniel Nash dated 7 July 1875, in P. C. Headley, *Evangelists in the Church* (Boston: Hoyt, 1875), pp. 170–71.

[42] Nash referred to this as his "second conversion." His son Seymour wrote:

> Soon after his [second] conversion, he felt that God called him to leave his family and farm, and give himself wholly to the work of saving souls. This, I presume, he thought he could do without injury to his family, as, in one way and another they were all well provided for, so far as their temporal wants were concerned. . . . He made occasional visits to his family to look after their wants, frequently bringing home with him, sums of money for this purpose, which he had received by way of contribution, in places where he had labored; but he never made it his permanent home with them again. He felt that his home was in God, and in the work he had given him to do (*The Circular* [Oneida, N.Y.], 8 June 1868, pp. 92–93).

man altogether from what he had been at any former period of his Christian JHF 71 life. I found that he had "a praying list," as he called it, of the ᑊnames of persons whom he made subjects of prayer every day, and sometimes many times a day. And praying with him, and hearing him pray in meeting, I found that his gift of prayer was wonderful, and his faith almost miraculous.[43] There MS 132 was a man by the name of **Dresser**,[44] who kept a ᑊlow tavern in a corner of the village, whose house was the resort of all the opposers of the revival. The bar-room was a place of blasphemy; and he was himself a most profane, ungodly, abusive man. He went railing about the streets respecting the revival; and would take particular pains to swear and blaspheme **if he saw a Christian, for the sake of hurting his feelings.** One of the young converts lived almost across the way from him; and he told me that he meant to sell and move out of that neighborhood, because every time he was out of doors and **Dresser** saw him, he would come out and swear, and curse, and say everything he could to ‹wound›[45] his feelings. He had not, I think, been **to** any of our meetings. Of course he was ignorant of the great truths of religion, and despised the whole Christian enterprize. Father Nash heard us speak of this Mr. **Dresser** as "a hard case;" and immediately put his name upon his praying MS 133 list.[46] He remained in town a day or two, and went on his way; having ᑊin view another field of labor.[47] Not many days **subsequent to this**, as we were holding an evening meeting with a very crowded house, who should come in but this notorious **Dresser**? His entrance created a considerable movement

[43]Nash's remarkable exploits in prayer became legendary, and he had many imitators, especially among the young converts. But he was also strongly condemned as being fanatical. He was largely responsible for popularizing the "Prayer of Faith," which became an essential feature of the New Measures revivals. In the last few years of his life, when his health had deteriorated, he devoted much time to writing on the subject. More than thirty articles that appeared in *The New-York Evangelist* anonymously in the eighteen months before his death were from Nash's pen. John Humphrey Noyes considered that "Father Nash was the highest type and best representative of the old revival spirit. In him the faith of the New Measure school reached its highest point." See "The Praying Man of Long Ago," *NYE,* 7 July 1892, p. 5; Gale, *Autobiography,* pp. 278–81; Josephus Brockway, *A Delineation of the Characteristic Features of a Revival of Religion in Troy, in 1826 and 1827* (Troy, N.Y.: Adancourt [printer], 1827), pp. 54–57; Asa Mahan, "The Prayer of Faith," *The Advance* (Chicago), 21 May 1868, p. 1; "Father Nash's Doctrine," *The Circular,* 7 July 1873, pp. 220–21; "Rev. Daniel Nash," *NYE,* 21 January 1832, p. 379; and "The Old Revival," *The Circular,* 8 June 1868, pp. 92–93.

[44]That is, Aaron Dresser. See Keeling, "History of the First Presbyterian Church of Le Ray," p. 3.

[45]The word "hurt" was changed by Finney to "wound."

[46]In another account of this incident Finney added: "The case weighed on his mind, when he was asleep and when he was awake. He kept thinking about him, and praying for him for days. And the first we knew of it, this ungodly man came into a meeting, and got up and confessed his sins, and poured out his soul" (*NYE,* 10 January 1835, p. 6).

[47]At this time Nash was also working for the Female Missionary Society of the Western District, in the area of Carthage and Wilna (see *The Eighth Annual Report of the Trustees of the Female Missionary Society of the Western District* [Utica], 1824, pp. 15–16). He subsequently labored with Finney in revivals in Gouverneur and DeKalb.

> In the midst of the great revival in Rome, Oneida County, he came to me and labored in prayer and conversation with great effect. He followed on to Utica, and afterwards in Troy and New Lebanon. . . . After we parted at New Lebanon, I went to Wilmington, Delaware, and from there to Philadelphia, to which places he did not follow me. He labored about in many places in central and northern New York, and gave himself up to almost constant prayer, literally praying himself to death at last (Finney's letter to P. C. Headley in Headley, *Evangelists,* p. 170).

and excitement in the congregation. People feared that he had come in to make a disturbance. The fear and abhorrence of him had become very general among Christians, I believe; so that when he came in some of the people got up and retired. I knew his countenance, and kept my eye upon him. I very soon became satisfied that he had not come in to oppose, and that he was in great anguish of mind. He sat and writhed upon his seat, and was very uneasy. He soon arose, and tremblingly—**for he trembled from head to foot**—asked if he might say a few words. I ꜝtold him that he might. He then proceeded to make one of the most heart-broken confessions that I almost ever heard. His confession seemed to cover the whole ground,—of his treatment of God, and of his treatment ꜝof Christians, and of the revival, and of everything good. This thoroughly broke up the fallow ground in many hearts. It was the most powerful means that could have been used, just then, to give an impetus to the work. **Dresser** soon came out and professed a hope, abolished all the revelry and profanity of his bar-room; and from that time, as long as I **stayed**[48] there, and I know not how much longer, **they held** a prayer meeting in his bar-room nearly every night.[49]

JHF 72

MS 134

[48]This word appears as "staid" in the published edition, but it was not altered in the manuscript.

[49]James H. Keeling wrote:

> I find this in the records of the church. "July 6, 1824. Pursuant to notice given, the Church met at Aaron Dresser's barn, and was constituted by prayer by Rev. C. G. Finney." And his ministry here continued for about ten months. His stipend was according to the books, "On motion Resolved that we agree to employ the Rev. Chas. G. Finney to preach half of the time in said Society at the rate of two hundred dollars a year commence and be paid from the 20 of Feb. last" ("History of the First Presbyterian Church of Le Ray," p. 4).

MS 134
JHF 73

CHAPTER VI

‹*More Concerning the revival & its results*›

‹A[1] little way from the Village of Evans' Mills was a settlement of germans, where there was a german church with several Elders, a considerable membership, but no minister, & no regular religious meetings›.[2] Once each year they were in the habit of having a dutch minister come up from the Mohawk valley, to administer the ordinances of baptism and the Lord's Supper. He would catechize their children, and receive such of them as had made the required attain|ments in knowledge. This was the way in which they were made Christians. They were required to commit to memory the catechism, and to be able to answer certain doctrinal questions; whereupon they were admitted to full communion in the church. After receiving the Communion they took it for granted that they were Christians, and that all was safe. This is the way in which that church had been organized and continued.

MS 135

But mingling, as they did more or less, in the scenes that passed in the village, they requested me to go out there and preach. I consented; and the first time I preached I took this text: "Without holiness no man shall see the Lord."[3] The settlement turned out en masse; and the school house where they worshipped was filled to its utmost capacity.[4] I began by showing what

[1]The heading of the chapter and the first few lines down to n. 2 are in Finney's handwriting on a piece of paper pasted onto the middle of page 134. Underneath the paper, in Matson's handwriting, are the words: "A little way from the village of Evans' Mills was a small settlement of Germans, where there was a German church with several elders and a considerable membership. They had no minister, and no regular religious meetings." In the chapter heading Finney wrote "Chapter" as "Capt." Pages 134 to 148 were numbered by Matson.

[2]This ends the section in Finney's handwriting.

The German Reformed Church of Evans Mills was formed in 1822. No house of worship was ever constructed, and no church records remain. In his report to the Female Missionary Society of the Western District in Utica, Finney called this a "settlement of High Dutch people." He observed, "The people are for the most part unlearned, and many of them unable to read the sacred Scriptures in any language" (*The Eighth Annual Report of the Trustees of the Female Missionary Society of the Western District* [Utica], 1824, p. 17; this report by Finney, dated 30 September 1824, is in fact a combination of a report sent after his first assignment of three months and a second report after his second three months). In a report in *WR*, 3 August 1824, p. 64, it is also called "a Dutch Reformed Church." Alexander H. Van Brockelin, Peter Hoover, John C. Walradt, and Richard Hoover were elders at the time. Many of the original church members are buried in a small cemetery on Carr Road, three-quarters of a mile from the schoolhouse.

[3]Finney appointed this meeting soon after his arrival at Evans Mills, according to his report. The text is from Hebrews 12:14.

[4]The schoolhouse, now a private home, is located a mile and a half north of Evans Mills on the corner of Call and Dutch Settlement roads.

oliness was *not.* Under this head I took everything that they considered to e religion, and showed that it was not holiness at all. **They could nderstand English well.** |**Then** in the second place I showed what holiness s›.[5] I then showed, thirdly, what **was** intended by seeing the Lord; and then, hy those that had no holiness |could never see the Lord—why[6] they could ever be admitted to **His** presence and ‹be›[7] accepted of **Him.** I then oncluded with such pointed remarks as were intended to make the subject o home. And it did go home by the power of the Holy Ghost. The sword of e Lord slew them on the right hand and on the left. In a very few days it was ound that the whole settlement was under conviction;—elders of the church nd all were in the greatest consternation, feeling that they had no holiness.[8] t their request I appointed a meeting for inquiry to give instruction to quirers. This was in their harvest time. I held the meeting at one **O**'clock in e afternoon, and found the house literally packed. People had thrown down e implements with which they were gathering their harvest, and had come to the meeting. |As many were assembled as could ‹be› pack‹ed in›[9] the ouse. I took a position in the center of the house, as I could not move ound among them; and asked them questions, and encouraged them to ask uestions. They became very much interested; and were very free in asking uestions, and in answering the questions which I asked them. I seldom ever tended a more interesting or profitable meeting than that.[10]

MS 136

JHF 74

MS 137

I recollect that one woman came in late, and sat near the door. When I me to speak to her, I said, "You look unwell." "Yes, she replied, "I am very ck. I have been in bed until I came to meeting. But I cannot read; and I anted to hear God's **W**ord so much that I **have** got up and come to eeting." "How did you come?" I inquired. She replied, "I came on foot." How far is it?" was the next inquiry. "We call it three miles," she said. **This**

[5] Matson had written down the word "*was*" underlined. This was crossed out and "is" inserted black ink. It appears to be in Finney's handwriting.

[6] The words "that in that sense" have been crossed out in black ink. It appears to have been ne by Finney.

[7] The word "be" was added by Finney.

[8] Finney's report at the time read:

> After this, I made it a practice to preach a third discourse among them, on the Sabbath, once in two weeks. . . . And, blessed, forever blessed, be the God of our salvation, the word has taken surprising effect. The state of feeling there at present, is so interesting and affecting, that any but a heart of stone, must be moved in view of the simplicity and deep anxiety which they almost universally manifest. The work of the blessed Spirit is so deep among them, that the clearness of their views, with respect to the Divine justice, in casting them off forever, is truly astonishing. As my duties were so abundant, that it was impossible for me to visit their families, the last time I preached among them, I appointed the next day, at 1 o'clock, P.M. to meet them at their usual place of worship, for the purpose of familiar conversation with them upon the state of their minds (*Eighth Annual Report,* p. 17).

[9] Matson had written the word "pack" here, but it was changed by Finney to "be packed in."

[10] Finney reported this meeting at the time:

> It was a moving scene. The house was crowded, and I conversed a few moments with each one, which occupied several hours. A deep and universal feeling seemed to pervade the whole assembly. Those that were truly pious among them, poured forth their tears of mingled joy, gratitude, and deep solicitude for their anxious and distressed neighbors (*Eighth Annual Report,* p. 17).

had well nigh broken me[11] **down.** On inquiry I found that she was unde
MS 138 conviction of sin, |and had a most remarkably clear apprehension of he
character and position before God. She was soon after converted, and
remarkable convert she was. My wife ‹said›[12] that she was one of the mos
JHF 75 remarkable women in prayer that she ever heard pray; |and that she repeate
more Scripture in her prayers than any person she ever heard **pray**.

I[13] addressed another, a tall, dignified looking woman, and asked her wha
was the state of her mind. She replied immediately that she had given he
heart to God; and went on to say that the Lord had taught her to read, sinc
she had learned how to pray. I asked her what she meant. She said she neve
could read, and never had known her letters. But when she gave her heart t
God she was greatly distressed that she could not read God's Word. "But
thought," she said, "that Jesus could teach me to read; and I asked him if h
MS 139 would not please to teach me ‹to read› his Word."[14] |Said she; "I though
when I had prayed that I could read. The children have a Testament; and
went and got **the Testament,** and I thought I could read what I had hear
them read." "But," said she, "I went over to the School ma'am, and asked he
if I *did* read right; and she said I did. And since then," said she, "I can rea
the Word of God for myself." I said no more; but thought there must be som
mistake about this, as the woman appeared to be quite in earnest, and quit
intelligent, in what she said. I took pains[15] afterwards to inquire of he
neighbors about her. They gave her an excellent character; and they a
affirmed that it had been notorious that she could not read a syllable unt
after she was converted. I leave this to speak for itself. There is no use i
theorizing about it. Such, I think, were the undoubted facts.[16]

But this revival among these[17] Germans resulted in the conversion of th
whole church, ‹I believe,›[18] and of nearly the whole community of Ge

[11] Matson had originally written down "her" here but changed it to "me."

[12] Matson had written, "My wife said—for I afterward brought my wife there—. " Apart fro
the first two words this appears to have been crossed out by Finney in black ink, and the wo
"said" reinserted by him. Finney was married to Lydia Andrews in October 1824. See MS 20

[13] This sentence had started, "In questioning I finally," but apart from the first *I*, it appears t
have been crossed out by Finney in black ink.

[14] The words "to read" were added by Finney.

[15] The word "therefore" after this appears to have been crossed out by Finney in black in

[16] In Finney's account of this incident given in a lecture in 1837 he stated:

> At the time, I thought it was a miracle; but since the facts which have been developed within a few years, respecting the indestructableness of the memory, I have thought this case might be explained in that way; and that she had probably been told the names of letters and their powers, when young, and now the Spirit of God, in answer to her prayer, had quickened her mind, and brought it all to her remembrance, so that she could read the Bible.

He then cited some other similar examples.

> It is plain from this, that even unintelligible sound may be so impressed on the memory, as afterwards to recur with entire distinctness. I suppose that was the case with this poor German woman, and that the Spirit of God, in answer to her fervent prayer, so refreshed her memory as to recall the sounds and forms of letters, she had been told when a child, and thus enable her at once to read the Bible (*Lectures to Professing Christians* [London: Milner, 1839], pp. 259–60).

[17] The word "these" was not altered by Fairchild on the manuscript, but the published editio
has "the."

[18] "I believe" was added by Finney.

mans.[19] |It was one of the most interesting revivals that I ever saw. While I was laboring at this place the presbytery were called together to ordain me, which they did.[20] Both churches were so strengthened, and their numbers so greatly increased, that they soon went forward and built |each of them a commodious stone meeting house, and I believe have had a healthy state of religion there since that time.[21] I have not been there for many years. MS 140 JHF 76

I have only narrated some of the principal facts that I remember as connected with this revival. But I would further say respecting it, that a wonderful spirit of prayer prevailed among Christians, and great unity of feeling. The little Congregational church, as soon as they saw the results of the next evening's preaching, recovered themselves; for they had been scattered, discouraged, and confounded the night before. They rallied and took hold of the work as best they could; and though a feeble and |inefficient band, with one or two exceptions, still they grew in grace, and in the knowledge of the Lord Jesus Christ during that revival. MS 141

The woman of whom I have spoken as a German woman, and as being sick when she came to the meeting of inquiry, united with the Congregational church. I was present and received her to the church. A very affecting incident I recollect occurred at the time she gave a relation of her Christian experience. There was a mother in Israel belonging to that church by the name of Schofield;[22] a very godly woman, of ripe age, and of quite ripe piety. We had been sitting for a long time and hearing the narration of the experience of one after another who came forward as candidates for admission to the church. At length this dutch woman arose and related her experience. It was one of the most touching, childlike, interesting Christian experiences that I ever listened to. As she was going on with her narrative I observed that |old Mrs. Schofield rose up from her place, and, as the house was crowded, crowded her way around as best she could. At first I supposed she was going out of doors. I was so occupied myself with the woman's narrative, that I was barely conscious of Mrs. Schofield's moving in that direction. As soon as she came near to where the dutch woman stood relating MS 142

[19] In Finney's second report dated Evans Mills, 30 September 1824, he wrote:

> The work in the Dutch settlement, of which mention was made in my former report, is still slowly progressing, owing, probably to the fact, that it has not been subject to so much sectarian influence as at other places. It has been powerful and affecting in that place and has extended its influence to an adjoining neighborhood, where it now goes on with great power (*Eighth Annual Report,* pp. 18–29).

[20] Gathered in formal session at the Methodist meeting house in Evans Mills on 1 July 1824, the Presbytery of St. Lawrence ordained Finney as an evangelist. Rev. A. W. Platt presided, Rev. I. Clinton preached the sermon, Rev. G. S. Boardman delivered the charge, Rev. S. F. Snowden offered the prayer, and Rev. E. Bliss and W. B. Stowe led devotions (P. H. Fowler, *Historical Sketch of Presbyterianism Within the Bounds of the Synod of Central New York* [Utica: Curtiss and Childs, 1877], p. 258).

[21] The Presbyterian church, located on Church Street, was completed in 1826; and the Baptist church, on Main Street, shortly after.

[22] Abigail Schofield was the wife of Elisha Schofield, of Ingerson's Corner. He had been in the army during the Revolutionary War and in 1814 founded the church in his home. He and his wife were charter members. See James H. Keeling, "A History of the First Presbyterian Church of Le Ray, Evans' Mills, Jefferson Co., New York," typescript dated 1939, in the Presbyterian Historical Society, Philadelphia, p. 2; and S. W. Durant, *History of Jefferson County, New York* (Philadelphia: Everts, 1878), p. 427.

her experience, she stepped forward, and threw her arms around her neck and burst into tears and said, "God bless you, my dear sister! God bless you!"

JHF 77 ¹The **dutch** woman responded with all her heart;—and such a scene as followed, so unpremeditated, so natural, so childlike, so overflowing with love,—it melted the congregation on every side to tears. They wept on each others necks. It was too moving a scene to be described in words.

The Baptist minister and I seldom **came in contact**, though sometimes we were enabled to attend meeting together. He preached there but one half of MS 143 the time, and I the other half; consequently I was generally away when ¹he was there, and he was generally absent when I was there. He was a good man, and worked as best he could to promote the revival.[23]

The doctrines preached were those which I have always preached as the Gospel of Christ. I insisted upon the voluntary total moral depravity of the unregenerate; and the unalterable necessity of a radical change of heart by the Holy Ghost, and by means of the truth. I laid great stress upon prayer as an indispensable condition of promoting the revival. The atonement of Jesus Christ, his divinity, his divine mission, his perfect life, his vicarious death, his resurrection, repentance, faith, justification by faith, and all the kindred doctrines were discussed as thoroughly as I was able, and pressed home, and were manifestly made efficacious by the power of the Holy Ghost. The means used were simply preaching, prayer and conference meetings, much private prayer, much personal conversation, and meetings for the instruction of MS 144 earnest inquirers. ¹These and no other means, were used for the promotion of that work. There was no appearance of fanaticism, no bad spirit, no divisions, no heresies, no schisms. Neither at that time, nor certainly so long as I was acquainted at that place, was there any result of that revival to be lamented, nor any feature of it that was of questionable **validity**.

I have spoken of cases of intensified opposition to this revival. One JHF 78 circumstance I found had prepared the ¹people for this opposition, and had greatly embittered it. I found that region of country, what in the western phrase would be called, "a burnt district."[24] There had been a few years

[23] In another account Finney described him as "an able, and lovely minister of Christ. He was truly a man of an excellent, and catholic spirit, and as might be expected, his church, much larger than that of the Congregationalists, partook largely of his spirit" ("Revival Memories," in Miscellaneous Items, Finney Papers, microfilm, roll 8).

[24] The use of fire as an analogy for revival was common at that time; and the expression "burnt over" to describe an area where the fires of revival caused "moral desolation and ruin" was "the strong language of Dr. Beecher." His use of the expression "burnt over" or "burned over" (he spelled it both ways) in his published letters may have been particularly responsible for the expression gaining currency. It was applied at that time "to the western sections of the State of New York, during the great revivals of 1826–27." See *Revivals of Religion, Considered as Means of Grace; A Series of Plain Letters to Candidus, from his friend Honestus* (Ithaca, N.Y.: Mack & Andrus [printers], 1827), p. 18; *The Christian Examiner* (Boston) 4 (May–June 1827): 243–44; *Letters of the Rev. Dr. Beecher and Rev. Mr. Nettleton on the New Measures* (New York: G. and C. Carvill, 1828), pp. 94–99; Beecher to Nettleton, 30 January 1827, in the *Christian Intelligencer and Eastern Chronicle* (Gardiner, Maine), 6 April 1827, p. 53; Lyman Beecher, *To the Congregationalist Ministers and Churches of Connecticut. Copy of a Letter from the Rev. Dr. Beecher, to the Editor of the Christian Spectator, Boston, December 18th, 1827* (n.p., n.d.); and *NYE*, 8 April 1837, p. 58. Finney's use of the expression here has led to the phrase "the Burned-over District" being applied by historians to much wider areas of upstate New York, and even to large tracts of the northern states that were affected by the revival and reform movements of the antebellum

revious a wild excitement passing through that region, which they called a evival of religion, but which turned out to be spurious. **The preaching, as I nderstood, had been by the Methodist brethren.** I can give no account of t except what I heard from Christian people and others. It was reported as aving been a very extravagant excitement; and resulted in a reaction so xten|sive and profound, as to leave the impression on many minds that eligion was a mere delusion. A great many men seemed to be settled in that onviction. Taking what they had seen as a specimen of a revival of religion, hey felt justified in opposing anything looking toward the promoting of a evival **of religion**. I found that it had left among Christian people some ractices that were offensive, and calculated rather to excite ridicule than any erious conviction of the truth of religion. For example, in all their prayer neetings I found a custom prevailing like this: Every professor of religion felt : a duty to testify for Christ. They must "take up their cross," and say omething in meetings. One would arise and say in substance: "I have a duty o perform which no one can perform for me. I arise to testify that religion is ood; though I must confess that I do not enjoy it at present. I have nothing n particular to say, only to bear my testimony;—and I hope you will pray for ne." |This concluded, the **individual** would sit down, and another would rise nd say about to the same effect. "Religion is good—I do not enjoy it. I have othing else to say, but I must do my duty. I hope you will all pray for me." 'hus the time would be occupied, and the meeting would pass off with very ttle **more** that was interesting than such remarks as these. Of course the ngodly would make sport of this. It was in fact ridiculous and repulsive. But **o was** the impression riveted[25] in the public mind that this was the way to old a prayer and Conference meeting, and that it |was the duty of every rofessor of religion whenever an opportunity was **given** to give such estimony for God, that I was obliged, for the purpose of getting rid of it, to old no such meetings. I appointed every meeting, consequently, for reaching. When we were assembled, I would begin by singing, and then pray nyself. I would then call on one or two others to pray, naming them. Then I vould name a |text and talk for a while. **And** then when I saw that an npression was made, I would stop and ask one or two to pray that the Lord night fasten that on their minds. I would then proceed with my talk, and after little stop again and ask some one or two to pray. **And** thus I would proceed **hrough the meeting,** not throwing the meeting open at all ‹f›o‹r›[26] remarks n the part of the brethren and sisters. Then they would go away without eing in bondage, feeling that they had neglected their duty in not bearing estimony for God. Thus ‹most of›[27] our prayer meetings were not so in ame. **Appointing them** for preaching, it was not expected that they would

MS 145

MS 146

JHF 79

MS 147

eriod. See Whitney R. Cross, *The Burned-over District: The Social and Intellectual History of nthusiastic Religion in Western New York, 1800–1850* (Ithaca, N.Y.: Cornell University Press, 950); and Marvin S. Hill, "The Rise of Mormonism in the Burned-over District, Another iew," in *New York History* 61 (October 1980): 411–16.

[25] The word "riveted" was not altered by Fairchild in the manuscript, but the published edition as "rooted."

[26] Finney changed the word "to" to "for."

[27] The words "most of" were added by Finney.

be thrown open for every one to speak; and in this way I was enabled to overcome that silly method of holding meetings that created so much **repellence and** mirth on the part of the ungodly. After the revival took thorough hold in this place, and those things occurred that I have named, opposition ceased so far as I could learn, **entirely**.[28]

MS 148 |I spent more than six months at this place and at Antwerp, laboring between the two places; and for the latter part of the time I heard nothing of open opposition. I have spoken of the doctrines preached. I should add that I was obliged to take much pains in giving instruction to inquirers. The practice had been, I believe universal, to set anxious sinners to praying for a new heart, and to using means for their own conversion. The directions they received either assumed, or implied, that they were very willing to be Christians, and were taking much pains to persuade God to convert them. I JHF 80 tried to make them under|stand that God was using the means with them, and not they with **Him**; that God was willing, and they were unwilling; that God was ready, and they were not ready. In short, I tried to shut them up to present faith and repentance as the thing which God required of them,— MS 149 present and instant submission to **His** will, present and instant |acceptance[29] of Christ. I tried to show them that all delay was only an evasion of present duty; that all praying for a new heart, was only trying to throw the responsibility of their conversion upon God; and that all efforts to do duty while they did not give their hearts to God, were hypocritical and delusive **and no doing of duty at all**. During the whole six months that I labored in that region, I rode on horseback from town to town, and from settlement to settlement, in various directions, and preached the Gospel as I had opportunity. When I left Adams my health had run down a good deal. I had coughed blood; and at the time I was licensed my friends thought that I could live but a short time. **Brother** Gale charged me when I left Adams not to attempt to preach more than once a week, and then to be sure not to speak more than half an hour at a time. But instead of this I visited from house to MS 150 house, attended prayer meetings, and |preached and labored every day and almost every night through the whole season.[30] Before the six months were

[28]The report of the state of religion in St. Lawrence Presbytery presented on 3 February 182 reads:

> In May a missionary sent out by the "Female Missionary Society of the Western District" began his labors here. Great opposition was at first manifested, but the Lord poured out his spirit and solemn times ensued. In the midst of the work, party spirit began to appear. But Christians adopted a measure which we would ever recommend in such cases. When any altercation arose between individuals, notice was given to a few of the nearest neighbors, and a number immediately collected for a prayer meeting. Thus party spirit was overcome, as to its immediate injurious effects. The solemnity increased, and the work became general. In this work there were many interesting cases. Infidelity gave way, and many who had established themselves in heretical principles, trembled, bowed, and became humble believers in the doctrines of the Gospel of Christ. The number of hopeful converts is about eighty. Thirty have united with the Presbyterian church (*WR*, 29 March 1825, p. 50).

[29]Pages 149–54 were first numbered 148 to 153 in error and had to be changed by Matson

[30]After his first three months Finney reported back to the Female Missionary Society of the Western District in Utica: "I have spent in the execution of your commission, 12 Sabbaths preached 77 discourses, attended 36 prayer, and 13 conference meetings, and made 469 family visits." And at the end of his second three months, he reported on a further 12 Sabbaths

completed my health was entirely restored, my lungs were sound, I coughed no more blood, and could preach two hours and two hours and a half, and longer, without feeling the least fatigue. I think my sermons generally averaged nearly or quite two hours. I preached out of doors—I preached in barns—I preached in school houses; and a glorious revival spread all over that new region of country.[31]

All through the earlier part of my ministry especially, I used to meet from ministers with a great many rebuffs and reproofs, particularly in respect to my manner of preaching. I have said that Mr. Gale, when I preached for him immediately after I was licensed, told me that he should |be |ashamed to have anyone know that I was a pupil of his.[32] The fact is, their education had been so entirely different from mine, that they disapproved of my manner of preaching very much. They would reprove me for illustrating my ideas by reference to the common affairs of men of different pursuits around me; for I was in the habit of doing so. Among farmers I illustrated truth by reference to their occupation; among mechanics, and every class of men,—I borrowed my illustrations from their own occupations. I tried also to use such language as they would understand. I addressed them in the language of the common people. I sought to express all my ideas in the fewest words, and in words that were in common use; and I studiously sought to avoid the use of any word that would not be understood by the common people without reference to their dictionaries. Before I was converted I had had a different |tendency. In writing and speaking I had sometimes allowed myself to use ornate language. But when I came to preach the Gospel my mind was so ‹anxious›[33] to be thoroughly understood, that I studied in the most earnest manner on the one hand to avoid what was vulgar, and on the other to express my thoughts with the greatest simplicity of language. This was extremely contrary to the notions that at that time, and even yet, prevail among the

MS 151
JHF 81

MS 152

"preached seventy-seven times, attended eighteen conference, twenty-seven prayer, and nine church meetings. Administered the Lord's Supper four times, made three hundred and seventy family calls" (*Eighth Annual Report,* pp. 18–19).

[31] By mid-June a report had appeared in the papers: "At the village of Evans's Mills, Leray, a powerful work began about three weeks since, but of the probable number of those who are the subjects of it, I have not been informed" (letter by Emory Osgood dated Henderson, 16 June 1824, to the publishers of the *Christian Watchman* [Boston], 26 June 1824, p. 115; reprinted in the *Religious Intelligencer* [New Haven], 8 July 1824, p. 79). About the same time Finney himself wrote from Antwerp about his labors, to the president of the Female Missionary Society:

> The blessed work has been exceedingly powerful in the village of Evans' Mills, indeed to the hopeful conversion of the great mass of the inhabitants of every rank and sex. It is now spreading in almost every direction. . . . Antwerp is 13 miles from Evans' Mills. The Lord has owned his work here also. But as the work has been so powerful at Evans' Mills, I have found it impracticable to spend much time with *this people,*—in visiting from house to house as yet (letter dated Antwerp, 10 June 1824, in *WR,* 6 July 1824, p. 54).

When the St. Lawrence Presbytery presented its report the next February on the state of religion within its bounds, it was "chiefly made up of notices of revivals." Details are given of revivals in Orleans, Carthage and Wilna, Leyden, Denmark, Brownville, Martinsberg, Cape Vincent, Le Ray, Antwerp, and Lowville (*WR,* 29 March 1825, p. 50).

A gap of four lines was left here in the manuscript by Matson before continuing with the next section.

[32] See MS 102 and also MS 156, 157.

[33] Finney crossed out the word "set" here and inserted "anxious."

great mass of ministers. In reference to my illustrations they would say, "Why don't you illustrate from events of ancient history, and take a more dignified way of illustrating your ideas?" To this of course I replied, that if my illustrations brought forward anything that was new and striking, the illustration itself would rather occupy the minds of the people than the truth which I wished to illustrate. **I told them that I wished to illustrate truths** MS 153 **by illustrations |so familiar to every one, that the fact which I used to illustrate would not *dwell* in the minds of the people, but would simply be the medium through which the truth would shine on them.** And in respect to the simplicity of my language I defended myself by saying, that my object was not to cultivate a style of oratory that should soar above the heads of the people, but to make myself understood; and that therefore I would use any language **that would best make myself understood,** and that did not involve vulgarity **and obscenity.**

About the time that I left Evans' Mills our presbytery met, and I attended JHF 82 the meeting. I left **my** revival work |at the particular request of some brethren, and went over to the presbytery. The brethren had heard of my MS 154 manner of preaching—those of them who had not heard me preach. |The[34] presbytery met in the morning, and went on with the transaction of business; and after our recess for dinner, as we assembled in the afternoon, the mass of the people came together and filled the house. I had not the remotest thought of what was in the minds of the brethren of the presbytery. I therefore took my seat in the crowd, and waited for the meeting of presbytery to be opened. As soon as the congregation **were** fairly assembled, one of the brethren arose and **observed**: "The people have come together manifestly to hear preaching; and I move that Mr. Finney preach a sermon." This was seconded, and **immediately** unanimously carried. I saw in a moment that it was the design of the brethren of the presbytery to put me on trial, that they might see if I could do as they had heard that I did, get up and preach on the spur of the

[34]On the reverse of MS 154 is the following in pencil:

10
8
5
6
29 Annie

A. Greger

This appears to be the name and signature of one of the typesetters. The handwriting is the same as the figures on the reverse of MS 181 and 759. The name "Annie" appears on all three pages in the margin.

moment, without any previous preparation. I made no apology or objection to preaching; for I must say that my heart was full of it, and that I ¦*wanted*[35] to preach. I arose and stepped into the aisle; and looking up to the pulpit, I saw that it was a high, small pulpit, up against the wall. I therefore stood in the aisle and named my text: "Without holiness no man shall see the Lord."[36] The Lord helped me to preach **as** I walked up and down the broad aisle; and the people were evidently interested and much moved. But after the meeting one of the brethren stepped up to me and said: "Brother Finney, if you come up our way, I should like to have you preach in some of our school districts. I should not like to have you preach in our church. But we have got school houses in some of the **remote** districts, away from the village—I should like to have you preach in some of those." I mention this to show what their ideas were of my method of preaching. But how completely they were in the dark in regard to the results of that method of address¦ing people! They used to complain that I let down the dignity of the pulpit; that I was a disgrace to the ministerial profession; that ¦I talked like a lawyer at the bar; that I talked to the people in a colloquial manner; that I *said you*, instead of preaching *about* sin and sinners, and saying *they*; that I said *hell*, and with such an emphasis as often to shock the people.[37] Furthermore, that I urged the people with such vehemence, as if they might not have a moment to live; and sometimes they complained that I *blamed* the people ‹t›o‹o›[38] much. One Doctor of divinity told me that he felt a great deal more like *weeping* over sinners, than *blaming* them. I replied to him that I did not wonder, if he believed that they had a sinful nature, and that sin was entailed upon them and they could not help it. After I had preached **sometime**, and the Lord had everywhere added his blessing, I used to say to ministers whenever they contended with me about my manner of preaching, and desired me to adopt their ideas and preach as they did, that I dared[39] not make the change they desired. I said: "Show me a more excellent way. Show me the *fruits* ¦of your ministry; and if the **fruits of your ministry** so far exceed mine as to give me evidence that you have found **out** a more excellent way **than I have**, I will adopt your views. But do you expect me to abandon my own views and practices and adopt yours, when you yourselves cannot deny that, whatever errors I may have fallen into, or whatever imperfections there may be in my preaching in style, and in everything else,—yet the *results* **unspeakably surpass the results of yours?"** I would say to them: "I intend to improve all I can. But I never can adopt your **practices and** manner of preaching the Gospel, until I have higher evidence that you are right and I am wrong." **Still I was often addressed in such a way by them that I should have been extremely mortified, had it not been that my mind was fully made up that they had been spoiled in**

MS 155

JHF 83

MS 156

MS 157

[35]Pages 155–58 were numbered by Matson.

[36]Hebrews 12:14 reads, "Follow peace with all men, and holiness, without which no man shall see the Lord."

[37]The underlinings in this sentence were crossed out by Fairchild, but he later reunderlined the words "you" and "they" and put them in quotation marks. The underlinings were not included, however, in the published version.

[38]The word "so" appears to have been changed to "too" by Finney.

[39]This word was written as "dareed" but was altered by Fairchild to "dared."

their education. They used to complain oftentimes that I was guilty of *repetition* in my preaching. I would take the same thought and turn it over
MS 158 ˡand over, and illustrate it in various ways. I assured them that I thought it was necessary to do so to make myself understood; and that I could not be
JHF 84 persuaded ˡto relinquish this practice by any of their arguments. **But** then they would say, "You will not interest the *educated* part of your congregations." But facts soon silenced them on this point. They found that under my preaching judges, and lawyers, and educated men were converted by scores; whereas under their methods such a thing seldom occurred.

CHAPTER VII

MS 158
JHF 85

‹*Further remarks upon ministerial Education*›

‹In[1] what [I] say[2] upon this subject I hope my brethren will not impute to me any other motive than a kind & benevolent regard for their highest usefulness. I have always taken their criticisms kindly & given them credit for benevolent intentions. Now I am an old man & many of the results of my views & methods are known to the publick. Is it out of place in me **now** to speak freely to the ministry upon this subject?[3] In reply to their objections I have sometimes told them what a judge of the supreme court remarked to me upon this subject. "Ministers" said he ["]do not exercise good sense in addressing the people. They are afraid of repetition. They use language not well understood by the common people. Their illustration[s] are not taken from the common pursuits of life. They write in to[o] elevated a style & read without repetition ˡ&›[4] are not understood by the people. Now", said he, "if lawyers should take such a course **as that**, they would ruin themselves and their cause. When I was at the bar," he added, "I used to take it for granted, when I had before me a jury of respectable men, that I should have to repeat over my main positions about as many times as there were **jury men** in the jury box. I learned that unless I did so, **and** illustrated, and repeated, and turned the main points over—the main points of law and of evidence—**unless I did this over and over, said he, I expected to** lose my cause. "Our object," he said, "in addressing a jury is *to get their minds settled before they leave the jury box.* **N**ot to make a speech in language but partially understood by them; not to let ourselves out in illustrations entirely above their apprehensions; not to ˡdisplay our oratory, and then let them go. *We are set on getting a verdict. Hence we are set upon being understood.* We mean to *convince* them; and **if**

MS 159

JHF 86

[1] This section of page 158 was written by Finney on two separate pieces of paper pasted onto the bottom of the page. The first piece carries the section down to n. 3, and the second piece carries the remainder. The wording that is covered up stops in midsentence and reads:

> In reply to such objections I have often told them what one of the judges of the Supreme Court said to me. He said: "Ministers do not exercise good sense in addressing the people. They are afraid of repetition. They are afraid of descending in their language to the common people, and of using language and illustrations that are familiar to them. They go in to the pulpit and rise over the heads of the people in their style. They write their sermons and slide right along without repetition and they

After "Supreme Court" Matson had written down "of Massachusetts," but this appears to have been crossed out by Finney. Pages 158 to 168 were numbered by Matson.

[2] Finney wrote down "In what Say." The capital *S* looks like a capital *I*.

[3] This ends the section on the first piece of paper pasted onto the sheet.

[4] The symbol *&* was inserted by Finney at the start of page 159.

MS 160 they have prejudices, to overcome their prejudices; if[5] |they have doubts as to the law, to[6] make them understand it, and rivet it in their minds. In short, we expect to get a *verdict,* and to get it *upon the spot*; so that when they go to their room to see if they are agreed it will be found that they have understood us; and that they have been convinced by the facts and arguments presented to them,—and that they have *all* been convinced. And if we do not take this pains to urge every thought, and every word, and every point home, so as to lodge it in their convictions, we are sure to lose our cause. We must overcome their prejudices; we must overcome their ignorance; we must try to overcome even their *interest,* if they have any, against our client."[7]

"Now," said he, "if ministers would do this, the effects of their preaching would be unspeakably different from what they are. They go into their studies and write a sermon; they go into their pulpit and read it. But those that listen to it but poorly understand it. Many words are used that will not MS 161 be understood until they go home and consult their |dictionaries. They do not address the people expecting to convince them, and to get their verdict in favor of Christ upon the spot. They seek no such object. They rather seem to aim at making fine literary productions, and displaying great eloquence and an ornate use of language." Of course I do not profess, at this distance of time, to give the exact language used by the judge; but I have given his remarks in substance, as made to me at the time. I have often told ministers of this.[8]

I never entertained the least hard feeling toward my brethren for the roughness with which they often treated me. I knew that they were very anxious to have me do good; and really supposed that I should do much more good and much less evil, if I should adopt their views. But I was of a different opinion.

I could mention many facts illustrative of the views of ministers, and of the manner in which they used to snub me and treat me. When I was preaching JHF 87 in Philadelphia, for example, |Dr Hewitt, the celebrated temperance agent MS 162 from Connecticut, |came to Philadelphia and heard me preach.[9] He was indignant at the manner in which I let down the dignity of the pulpit. His principal conversation, however, was with Brother Patterson, with whom at that time I labored.[10] He insisted upon it that I should not be allowed to

[5] Fairchild crossed out "if" here and inserted it at the top of the next page.

[6] The word "to" was not altered in the manuscript, but the published version has "we."

[7] The next sentence was indented on a new line. Matson apparently intended to start a new paragraph, although Finney added no paragraph mark.

[8] Finney had referred to these remarks of the judge in his "Lecture No. XII on Revivals of Religion," *NYE,* 21 February 1835, p. 30. He gave a similar account then.

[9] Nathaniel Hewit (1788–1867) graduated from Yale College in 1808. After studying law he was a student at Andover Theological Seminary and was ordained in 1815. He served in Presbyterian churches at Plattsburg, New York, and Fairfield, Connecticut, until 1827, when he resigned to become the agent of the American Temperance Society. He was considered to be the "Luther of the early Temperance Reformation." In 1831 he went on a temperance mission to England. Subsequently he was a minister in Bridgeport, Connecticut, and was one of the founders of Hartford Theological Seminary. See Franklin B. Dexter, *Biographical Sketches of the Graduates of Yale College,* vol. 6 (New Haven: Yale University Press, 1912), pp. 202–7; *The National Cyclopaedia of American Biography,* vol. 11 (New York: White, 1901), p. 357; and George W. Bungay, *Pen Portraits of Illustrious Abstainers,* vol. 1 (New York: National Temperance Society and Publishing House, 1881), pp. 191–94.

[10] James Patterson, a Princeton graduate, was the minister at the First Presbyterian Church of

preach till I had a *ministerial* education. That I should stop preaching and go to Princeton and learn theology, and get better views of the way in which the Gospel should be preached. **But from Brother Patterson's account of the matter, Dr Hewitt did not get much consolation from him; for Brother Patterson turned upon the ministers as they were educated, and with their views, and compared the results of their preaching with the manifest results of mine.**[11]

Let not anything I say on this ‹subject›[12] leave the impression on any mind, that I thought either my views or my methods perfect, for I had no such thought. I was aware that I was but a child. I had not enjoyed the advantages of the higher schools of learning. And so conscious had I been all along that I lacked those qualifications that would make me ˡacceptable, especially to ministers, and I feared to the people in **populous** places, that I had never had any higher ambition or purpose than to go into the new settlements and places where they did not enjoy the Gospel. Indeed I was often surprized myself, in the first years of my preaching, to find it so edifying and acceptable to the most educated classes. This was more than I had expected,—greatly more than my brethren had expected; and more than I had dared to hope myself. I always endeavored to improve in everything in which I discovered myself to be in error. But the longer I preached, the less reason had I to think that my error lay in the direction in which it was supposed to lie by my brother ministers. MS 163

The more experience I had; the more I saw the results of my method of preaching; the more I conversed with all classes, high and low, educated and uneducated, the more was I confirmed in the fact that God had led me, had taught me, had given me right conceptions in regard to the best manner of winning souls. I say that ˡ*God* taught me; and I know it must have been so, for surely I never had obtained these notions from man. And I have often thought that I ˡcould say with perfect truth as Paul said, that I was not taught the Gospel by man but by the Spirit of Christ himself.[13] And I was taught it by the Spirit of the Lord in a manner so clear and forcible, that no arguments of my ministerial brethren, with which I was plied so often and so long, had the least weight with me. MS 164 JHF 88

the Northern Liberties of Philadelphia from 1814 until his death. See W. B. Sprague, *Annals of the American Pulpit,* vol. 4 (New York: R. Carter and Bro., 1859), pp. 423–28. Finney preached for him in 1828. See chapter XVIII.

[11]Finney was probably speaking of this incident in his "Lecture No. XI on Revivals of Religion":

> Two ministers were one day conversing about a certain minister whose labors were greatly blessed in the conversion of some thousands of souls. One of them said, "That man ought not to preach any more; he should stop and go to" a particular theological seminary which he named, "and go through a regular course of study." He said the man had "a good mind, and if he was thoroughly educated, he might be very useful." The other replied, "Do you think he would be more useful for going to that seminary? I challenge you to show by facts that any are more useful who have been there. No, sir, the fact is, that since this man has been in the ministry, he has been instrumental in converting more souls than all the young men who have come from that seminary in the time" (*NYE,* 14 February 1835, p. 26).

[12]The word "occasion" here was changed by Finney to "subject."

[13]Galatians 1:11–12.

I mention this as a matter of duty. For **still** I am solemnly impressed with the conviction, that the schools are to a great extent spoiling the ministers. Ministers in these days have great facilities for obtaining information on all theological questions. And are vastly ‹more› learned,[14] so far as theological, historical, and Biblical learning is concerned, than they perhaps ever have been in any age of the world. Yet with all their learning, *they do not know how to use it.* They are, after all, like David in Saul's armor ‹**to a great extent.**›[15] MS 165 |A man can never learn to preach except *by preaching.* But one great thing above all others ministers need, and that is *singleness of eye.* ‹If they›[16] have a reputation to ‹secure & to›[17] nurse, they will do but little good. Many years ago a beloved pastor of my acquaintance left home for his health, and employed a young man just from the Seminary to fill his pulpit while he was absent. **He** wrote and preached as splendid sermons as he could. The pastor's wife finally ventured to say to him: "You are preaching over the heads of our people. They do not understand your language or your illustrations. You bring too much of your learning into the pulpit." He replied: "I am a young man. I am cultivating a style. I am aiming to prepare myself for occupying a pulpit and surrounding myself with a cultivated congregation. I cannot descend to your people. I must cultivate an elevated style." I have had my MS 166 thought and my **mental** eye upon this man |ever since. I am not aware that he is yet dead. **But** I have never seen his name connected with any revival, amidst all the great revivals that we have had from year to year since that time; JHF 89 |and I never expect to unless his views are radically changed, and unless he addresses the people from an entirely different stand-point, and from entirely different motives. **The fact is if ministers have a single eye, and intend to reach and to save the people, they will feel the necessity of being understood. They will not be satisfied with setting the crowd agape with their great eloquence and splendid education; but they will come down to them, and will try to understand their language and accommodate their addresses to their capacities and positions, to their modes of thought and language.** I could name ministers who are yet alive, old men like myself, who were greatly ashamed of me when I first began to preach because I was so undignified in the pulpit; used language **in such common** MS 167 **use;** addressed the people with such directness, and |**said "*you*;" and** because I aimed not at all at ornament, or at supporting the dignity of the pulpit. **But I heard at second-hand much more in this direction from ministers, than was spoken directly to my face. Now I wish to be distinctly understood as insisting that in the main, if not universally, those ministers were honest, and very solicitous for my usefulness. They of course verily thought that their views and ways were right and mine were wrong. It was not because of any quarrel they had with me as a man or a Christian; but they lamented my want of ministerial education, which prevented**

[14] Matson had written, "And ministers in these days are vastly better learned," but it was altered by Finney.

[15] 1 Samuel 17:38–39. The phrase "to a great extent" was added by Finney.

[16] An ink smudge on the manuscript obscured the first two words of the sentence, so they were written in again by Finney.

[17] The words "secure & to" were added by Finney.

me, as they supposed, from maintaining the dignity of the pulpit and of the profession.

Dear brethren they were; and I always felt in the kindest manner toward them, and do not know that in a single instance I was ruffled or angry at what they said. **I did not wonder they thought so.** I was from the very first aware that I should meet with this opposition; and that there was this wide gulf in our views, and would be in **our** practices, between myself and other ministers. ˡI[18] seldom felt **as if** I was one of them, or **as if** they regarded me as really belonging to their fraternity. I was bred a lawyer. I came right forth from a law office to the pulpit, and talked to the people as I would have talked to a jury. **All this was exceedingly opposed to the manner in which they had been educated, and to all their views and feelings. Of course I was a speckled bird. I was a foreigner, an interloper, a man that had come into the ministry without being brought in under the regular course of training.** It was very common, as I learned, among ministers in my earlier years of preaching to agree among themselves that if I were **allowed** to succeed in the ministry it would bring the schools into disrepute. **The theological seminaries would be thrown into the shade**; and men would come to think it hardly worth while to support them with their funds, if a man could be accepted as a successful preacher without them. Now I never had a thought of **opposing or throwing into the shade any** college or theological seminary;—though I did think, ˡ‹&[19] think now that in certain respects they are greatly mistaken in their modes of training their students. 1. They do not encourage them to talk to the people & accustom themselves to extemporaneous addresses to the people in the surrounding country while pursuing their studies. Men can not lear[n] to preach by study without practice. The students should be encouraged to exercise, & prove, & *improve* their gifts & calling of God by going out into any places open to them & holding Christ ˡup to the people in earnest talks. They must thus learn *to preach.* Instead of this the students are required to write what they call sermons, & present them for criticism. To preach, i.e. read them to the class & the Professor. Thus they *play* preaching. **But to whom are they addressed? Not to the class, but to a congregation of saints & sinners.** No man can preach in this manner. These so called sermons, will of course, under the criticism they **will** receive degenerate in[to][20] literary essays. The people have no respect for such sermons as *sermons.* This reading of elegant literary essays is not to them *preaching.* **It is reading.** It is gratifying to literary taste, but[21] not spiritually edifying. It does not meet the wants of the soul. It is not calculated to win souls to Christ. The students are taught to cultivate a fine elevated style of writing. As for real eloquence & that gushing, impressive, & persuasive oratory that **would** naturally flow from an educated man whose soul **was** on

MS 168

MS 169

JHF 90

[18] Finney added the word "over" and circled it at the bottom right of page 168.

[19] Page 169 is inserted in Finney's handwriting on the reverse side of MS 168 and evidently replaces a previous page 169.

[20] The letters *to* appear to have been added by Fairchild.

[21] Finney wrote the word "but" twice here in the manuscript. Fairchild crossed out the second one.

fire with his subject, **&** who **was** free to pour out his heart **extemporaneously** to a waiting **&** earnest people they have none of it.›

MS 170 |A[22] reflecting mind will feel as if it were infinitely out of place to present in the pulpit to immortal souls hanging upon the verge of everlasting death, such specimens of learning and rhetoric. They know that men do not do so on any subject where they are really in earnest. The Captain of a fire company, when a city is on fire, does not read to his company an essay, or exhibit fine specimens of rhetoric, when he shouts to them and directs their movements. MS 171 It is a question of urgency, and he intends that |every word shall be understood. He is entirely in earnest with them; and they feel **as if** criticism would be out of place in regard to the language he uses. **It is a question of too much importance and urgency for his company to expect that he is going to trim his language, and speak to them under such circumstances with all the fine drapery and furniture of a studied and ornate discourse.** So it always is when men are entirely in earnest **about a thing.** Their language is direct, simple, **in point.** Their sentences are short, cogent, powerful. The appeal is made directly **to them** for *action*; and hence all such discourses take effect. This is the reason why the ignorant Methodist preachers, and **formerly** the earnest Baptist preachers produced so much more effect than our most learned theologians and **splendid** divines. They JHF 91 |do so now. The **mere efforts** of a common exhorter will often move a congregation far beyond anything that those splendid exhibitions of rhetoric **will do.** ‹*Great* sermons lead the people to praise the *preacher*. *Good* preaching MS 172 leads the people to praise the Saviour.›[23] |Our theological schools would be of much greater value than they are if there **was much more about them that was** *practical.* I heard ‹a› theological teacher[24] *read* a sermon on the importance of extemporaneous preaching. His *views* on that subject were correct; but his *practice* entirely contradicted them. He seemed to have studied the subject, and to have attained to practical views of the highest importance. But yet I have never known one of his students in practice to adopt those views; **and surely he does not do it himself**. I have understood that he says that if he were to begin his life as a preacher **anew**, he would practice according to his present views; and that he laments that his education was wrong in this respect, and consequently his practice has been wrong. In our school **here**[25] our students have been led—not by myself, I am bound to say—to think that they must write their sermons; and very few of them,

[22] Pages 170–83 were numbered by Matson. This page starts with the following passage, which was crossed out by Finney:

> convert souls to Christ. I believe he seldom preaches a sermon that would seem to have been written for that purpose. He takes the greatest possible pains with his sermons; and I should think had spent as much as six weeks on each of them before he ventures to present them to the public. They are manifestly designed to be *great sermons*. But they are, after all, anything but what a sermon ought to be to convert the mass of minds to Christ. The fact is, the people of plain common sense have no respect for such preaching *as preaching*.

[23] The last two sentences were added by Finney.

[24] Matson had written here, "I heard the same theological teacher to whom I have referred," but Finney changed it. This appears to have been a theological teacher referred to on the original page 169, which was discarded.

[25] Oberlin College, Ohio.

notwithstanding all I could say to them, have the courage to launch out, |and MS 173 commit themselves to extemporaneous preaching. They have been told again and again: "You must not think to imitate Mr. Finney. You cannot be **Mr.** Finneys." ‹M›inisters[26] do not like to get up and talk to the people as best they can, and break themselves at once into the habit of *talking* to the people. They must *preach*; and if they must preach in the common acceptation of the term, they must write. Hence according to that view I have never preached. Indeed, people have often said to me: "Why, you do not *preach.* You *talk* to the people." A man in London went home from one of our meetings greatly convicted. He had been a skeptic; and his wife seeing him greatly agitated, said to him, "Husband, have you been to hear Mr. Finney preach?" He replied: "I have been to |Mr. Finney's meeting. He don't *preach; he only* JHF 92 *explains what other people preach.*" This, in substance, I have heard over and over again. "Why!" they say, "anybody could preach as you do. You just |*talk* MS 174 to the people. You talk as if you were as much at home as if you sat in the parlor." Others have said: "Why it don't seem like *preaching*; but it seems as if Mr. Finney had taken me alone, and **were**[27] conversing with me face to face."

Ministers generally avoid preaching what the people before them will understand as addressed particularly to *them.* They will preach to them *about* other people, and the sins of other people, instead of addressing them and saying, "*You* are guilty of these sins;" and "the Lord requires this of *you.*" They often preach *about* the Gospel instead of preaching the Gospel. They often preach *about* sinners instead of preaching *to* them. They studiously avoid being *personal*, in the sense of making the impression on any one present that **they mean him or her**. Now I have thought it my duty to pursue a different course; and I always *have* pursued a different course. **I have intended to make every person present feel as if I meant him and her. And** I have often said: |"Do not think I am talking *about* anybody else; but I mean *you*, MS 175 and *you*, and *you*." **Now** ministers told me at first that people would never endure this; but would get up and go out, and never come to hear me again. But this is all a mistake. Very much in this, as in everything else, depends on the *spirit* in which it is said. If the people see that it is said in the spirit of love, with a yearning desire to do them good; if they cannot call it an ebullition of personal animosity, but if they see, and cannot deny that it is telling the truth in love, that it is coming right home to them to save them individually,— there are very few **people** that will continue to resent **this**. If at the time they feel pointed at, and rebuked; nevertheless the conviction is upon them that they needed it, and it will surely *ultimately* do them great good.

I have often said to people when I saw that they looked |offended: "*Now* JHF 93 you resent this, and you will go away and say that you will not come again; but you *will*. Your own convictions are on my side. You know that what I tell you is true; and that I tell it |for your own good; and that you cannot continue to MS 176 resent it." And I have always found this to be true. **I have very seldom**

[26]"The fact is, that ministers" was changed by Finney to "Ministers."

[27]The word "were" is not altered in the original but was changed to "was" in the published version.

found individuals staying away permanently from our meetings because they were offended at my plainness.

My experience has been, that even in respect to personal popularity, "honesty is the best policy" in a minister. That if he means to maintain his hold upon the confidence, and respect, and affection of any people, he must be faithful to their souls. He must let them see that he is not courting them for any purpose of popularity, but that he is trying to save their souls. Men are not fools. They have no solid respect for a man that will go into the pulpit and preach smooth things. They cordially despise it in their inmost souls. And let no man think that he will gain permanent respect, that he will be permanently honored by people, unless as an ambassador of Christ he deals faithfully with their souls.

The great argument in opposition to my views of preaching the Gospel MS 177 was, that I should not ¦give nearly so much instruction to the people as I should if I wrote my sermons. They said I should[28] not study; and consequently, although I might succeed as an Evangelist, where I labored but a few weeks or months in a place,—still it would never do for a *pastor*[29] to preach extemporaneously.

Now I have the best of reasons for believing that preachers of written sermons do not give their people so much instruction as they think they do. The people do not *remember* their sermons. I have in multitudes of instances heard people complain,—"I cannot carry home anything that I hear from the pulpit." They have said to me in hundreds of instances: "We always remember what we have heard you preach. We remember your text, and the manner in which you handled it; but written sermons we cannot remember."

JHF 94 ¦I have been a pastor now for many years,—indeed ever since 1832, ‹40› years;[30] and I have never heard any complaint that I did not instruct the MS 178 people. I do not believe it is true that my peo¦ple are not as well instructed, so far as pulpit instruction is concerned, as those people are who sit under the preaching of written sermons. It is true that a man may write his sermons without studying much; and so it is true that he may preach extemporaneously without much study or thought. Many written sermons that I have heard manifested anything but profound, accurate thought. My habit has always been to study the Gospel, and the best application of it, all the time. I do not confine myself to hours and days of writing my sermons; but my mind is *always* pondering the truths of the Gospel, and the best ways of using them. I go among the people and learn their wants. I then in the light of the Holy Spirit take a subject that I think will meet their present necessities. I think intensely on, and pray much over[31] the subject on Sabbath morning, for

[28]This word was not changed in the manuscript but was changed to "would" in the published edition.

[29]The word "*pastor*" was underlined in black ink and appears to have been done by Finney. See also n. 30.

[30]The number *40* is written in black ink and replaces the word "thirty-five" written down by Matson. It appears to have been done by Finney. This change may have been made at the time that Roselle T. Cross read the manuscript over to Finney in 1872 (see p. xxxvi). That year Finney finally resigned from the pastorate of the First Congregational Church in Oberlin.

[31]The phrase "and pray much over" was inserted in the text by means of an asterisk and written in the margin. Fairchild crossed it out and rewrote it in the text.

example, and get my mind full of **the subject**, and then go and pour it out to the people. Whereas one great difficulty with a written ser|mon is, that a man MS 179 after he has written it needs to think but little of the subject. He needs to *pray* but little. He perhaps reads over his manuscript Saturday evening or Sabbath morning. But he does not feel the necessity of being powerfully anointed, that his mouth may be opened and filled with arguments, and that he may be enabled to preach out of a full heart. He is quite at ease. He has only to use his eyes and his voice, and he can preach in his way; **that is, he can read a written sermon**. It may be a sermon that has been written for years; it may be a sermon that he has written, every word of it, within the week. But on Sabbath day there is no *freshness* in it. It does not come necessarily new and fresh, and as an anointed message from God to his heart, and through his heart to the people. I am prepared to say most solemnly, that I think I have studied all the more for not having written my sermons. I |have been obliged JHF 95 to make the subjects upon which I preached familiar to my thoughts, to fill |my mind with **the subject**, and then go and talk **it** off to the people. I simply MS 180 note the heads upon which I wish to dwell in the briefest possible manner, and in language not a word of which I use, perhaps, in preaching. I simply jot down the order of my propositions and positions which I propose to take, and in a word sketch an outline of the remarks an[**d**] inferences with which I conclude.

But unless men will try it, unless they will begin and talk to people as best they can, keeping their hearts full of truth and full of the Holy Ghost, they will never make extemporaneous preachers.[32] I believe that half an hour's earnest talk to the people from week to week, **and from time to time,**—if the talk be pointed, direct, earnest, logical, will really instruct **the people** more than the two labored sermons that those who write get off to their people on the Sabbath. I believe the people would remember more of what is said, be more interested in it, and would carry it away with them to be pondered, vastly more than they do what they get from the labored |written[33] MS 181 sermons **which they hear**.

[32]The words "But really" that started the next sentence appear to have been crossed out by Finney.

[33]On the reverse side of MS 181 are two sets of figures in pencil. The number *61* has been multiplied by *26*, and *71* has been multiplied by *26*. This appears to be in the same handwriting as the entries on the reverse of MS 154 and 759.

Just above I have spoken of my method of preparing for the pulpit in more recent years. When I first began to preach, and for some twelve years of my earliest ministry, I wrote not a word; and was most commonly obliged to preach without any preparation whatever except what I got in prayer.[34] Oftentimes I went into the pulpit without knowing upon what text I should speak, or a word that I should say. I depended on the occasion and the Holy Spirit to suggest the text, and to open up the whole subject to my mind; and certainly in no part of my ministry have I **ever** preached with greater success and power **than I did when I preached in that way**. If I did not preach from *inspiration,* I don't know how I did preach. It was a common experience with me, and has been during all my ministerial life, that the subject would open up to my mind in a manner that was surprizing to myself. It seemed that JHF 96 I could ˡsee with intuitive clearness just what I ought to say; and whole MS 182 platoons of thoughts, ˡwords,[35] and illustrations, came to me as fast as I could deliver them. When I first began to make skeletons, I made them *after*, and not *before* I preached. It was to preserve the outline of the thought which had been given me on occasions such as I have just mentioned. I found when the Spirit of God had given me a very clear view of a subject, I could not retain it **after preaching** to be used on any other occasion unless I jotted down an

[34] William C. Cochran stated that Finney "never wrote but two sermons in his life and that was at the very outset of his career." He had to present two written sermons to the presbytery for his licensure (Cochran, *Charles Grandison Finney: Memorial Address* [Philadelphia: Lippincott, 1908], p. 64; see also MS 372). But there was also an occasion at Antwerp when Finney wrote a sermon. The story was told to G. F. Wright by Gorham Cross. After some weeks, Finney was embarrassed by a report to the effect that he did not have the necessary ability to compose "a creditably written sermon." The people "heard said that he was a lawyer and could petty fog but could not write."

> Stung by these suspicions, he attempted to demonstrate their injustice by preparing a sermon after the regulation style. But, as the motives inducing him to take this course were not of the most exalted nature, his carefully prepared effort was likely to prove an ignominious failure in the delivery. He was quick to discern the danger, however, and, taking time by the forelock, seized the notes that were impeding his eloquence and flung them under the pulpit out of sight, and then launched forth with his accustomed freedom in extemporaneous argument and exhortation. Finney was ever after an ardent advocate of extemporaneous speaking (George F. Wright, *Charles Grandison Finney* [Boston and New York: Houghton Mifflin, 1891], p. 23; see also G. F. Wright, Notebook no. 1, pp. 95–96, Wright Papers, box 25; and Austin Phelps, *My Note-Book: Fragmentary Studies in Theology and Subjects Adjacent Thereto* [London: T. Fisher Unwin, 1891], p. 94).

Two other written sermons were found in the Finney Papers by James Robert Emmel, one dated 17 March 1827 and the other dated 2 January 1852, and were transcribed by him. They cannot now be found in the Finney Papers. See J. R. Emmel, "The Persuasive Techniques of Charles Grandison Finney as a Revivalist and Social Reform Speaker, 1820–1860" (Ph.D. diss., Pennsylvania State University, 1959), pp. 397–437.

[35] On the reverse side of MS 182 the following, in pencil, appears to be written by Lewis Tappan: "225 words on page; 25 minutes writing a page; Began again at 1/2 past 7." MS 183 has a count of 226 words. The phrase "25 minutes" may refer to the time taken to write a page of the copy or abstract of the memoirs that Tappan was making (see Introduction, p. xxxi). Each of the foolscap pages of the copy would have contained, on the average, about two and a half pages of the memoirs manuscript.

outline of the thoughts.[36] But after all, I have never found myself able to use old skeletons in preaching, to any considerable extent, without remodeling them, and having a fresh and new view of the subject given me by the Holy Spirit. I almost always get my subjects on my knees in prayer; and it has been a common experience with me upon receiving a subject from the Holy Spirit, to have it make so strong an impression on my mind as to make me tremble so that I could with difficulty write. When subjects are thus given me that seem to go through me body and soul, I can in a few moments make out a skeleton that shall enable me to retain the view presented by the Spirit; and I find that such sermons always tell with great power upon the people.

ˡ**And**[37] some of the most telling sermons that I have ever preached in Oberlin, I have thus received after the bell had rung for church; and I was obliged to go and pour them off from my full heart without jotting down more than the briefest possible skeleton, and that sometimes not covering half the ground that I covered in my sermon. MS 183

I tell this, not boastfully, but because it is a fact, and to give the praise to God and not to any talents of my own. Let no man think that those sermons which have been called so powerful were productions of my own brain, or of my own heart, unassisted by the Holy Ghost. They were not mine, but from the Holy Spirit in me.

And let no man say that this is **boasting of** a higher inspiration than is promised to ministers, or than ministers have ˡa right to expect. For I believe that all ministers, called by Christ to preach the Gospel, ought to be, and may be in such a sense inspired, as to "preach the Gospel with the Holy Ghost sent down from heaven."[38] What else did Christ mean when he said, "Go and disciple all nations;—and lo I am with you always, even unto the end of the world?"[39] What did he mean when he said, speaking of[40] the Holy Spirit— JHF 97

[36]By the summer of 1830, when he was in Troy, New York, Finney was already using the system of keeping the headings of his sermons on small cards. He often had requests to borrow them. See R. H. Hurlbut to Finney, 1 February 1831, Finney Papers, microfilm, roll 2; E. N. Kirk to Finney, 15 April 1831, Finney Papers, microfilm, roll 3; and John Moore to Finney, 30 April 1850, Finney Papers, microfilm, roll 4.

By the time Finney delivered his lectures on revivals in 1834, he was writing a skeleton beforehand, "carefully prepared and so compact, that it can be written on one side of a card" (Joshua Leavitt, introduction to *Lectures on Revivals of Religion*). When he was preaching in the Broadway Tabernacle in 1836, he "usually preached from a 'brief' lying before him. But though extempore in their dress, they were not unstudied, as to their matter or their form." A deacon of the church reported:

> In yonder study, the first pastor of the Tabernacle had a huge slate upon which he would sketch an outline of a sermon, as the architect sketches his plan, the painter his groups. This done, he would betake himself to prayer, or pace the room in earnest thought. By-and-by, perhaps the whole plan would be effaced, and another substituted for it; or, the first would be recast in the vigorous mold of a mind kindled by prayer, till it came forth glowing with the fire of the Holy Ghost. Then he was ready for the pulpit (Joseph P. Thompson, *The Last Sabbath in the Broadway Tabernacle: A Historical Discourse* [New York: Calkins and Stiles, 1857], p. 15).

About seven hundred of Finney's sermon outlines from about 1853 until his death are in the Finney Papers, microfilm, rolls 7–9.

[37]At the foot of the page Matson wrote the word "over" in brackets and inserted an addition on the reverse of the sheet.

[38]1 Peter 1:12.

[39]Matthew 28:19–20.

"He shall take of mine and show it unto you?" **And also,** "He shall bring all things to your remembrance, whatever I have said unto you[?]"[41] What did he mean when he said, "If any man believe in me, out of his belly shall flow rivers of living water?"[42] ‹"This spake **He** of the Spirit that they which believe on **Him** should receive."[43] All ministers may be & ought to be, so filled with the Holy Spirit that all who hear them shall be impressed with the conviction that "God is in them of a truth"›[44]

[40]Here begins MS 183, reverse. After the end of the text of this page of the manuscript, Fairchild wrote:

> *Note.* Here we present a *fac simile* copy of one of Mr. Finney's "skeletons"—taken at random from the hundreds which he has left,—*Editor*

The words "Note" and "Editor" have a double underscore in the original. See the illustration on p. xliii. Between pages 96 and 97 of the first edition of the *Memoirs,* Fairchild included a facsimile of the skeleton of Finney's sermon on Matthew 5:13–16, entitled "Christians the Light." This is Undated Sermon Outline, no. 588, Finney Papers, microfilm, roll 8.

[41]John 16:15.

[42]John 7:38. The section following this was added by Finney.

[43]John 7:39.

[44]Acts 14:25.

CHAPTER VIII

MS 184
JHF 98

‹Revival at Antwerp›

I[1] must now give some account of my labors and their results, at Antwerp, a village[2] north of Evans' Mills.[3] I arrived there the first time in April, and found that no religious services of any kind were held in that town. The land in the town‹ship›[4] belonged to a Mr. Parish, a rich landholder residing in Ogdensburgh.[5] To encourage the settlement of the town‹ship› he had built them a brick meeting house.[6] But the people had no mind to keep up public worship; and therefore the meeting house was locked up, and the key was in the possession of a Mr. Copeland, who kept the village hotel.[7]

I very soon learned that there was a Presbyterian church in that place, consisting of but few members.[8] They had some years before tried to keep up a meeting at the village on Sabbath. But one of the elders who conducted

[1] Pages 184–208 were numbered by Matson. The chapter number and heading of page 184 are in Finney's handwriting and are written in the space left by Matson, who had started the first sentence on the fourth line of the page.

[2] After the word "village," Matson had written down, "about sixteen or eighteen miles, as I have said," but it appears to have been crossed out by Finney.

[3] Antwerp was thirteen miles from Evans Mills. First settled in 1802, it became a separate community in 1810. The town records, dating from 1811, are in the office of the town clerk. Finney was in Antwerp from April to October of 1824.

[4] Matson had written down "town" here and in the next sentence, but Finney altered it in each case to "township."

[5] David Parish was a prominent financial entrepreneur from an English family, with extensive business interests in Europe. He came to America in 1806. Among his financial adventures he invested in large tracts of land in New York with a view to improving them and building up prosperous communities. In 1816 he returned to Europe, and his younger brother, George, who died in 1839, managed the properties in his absence and lived in the house in Ogdensburg. But financial disaster in Europe resulted in David's suicide in 1826. See Raymond Walters, Jr., and Philip G. Walters, "David Parish: York State Land Promoter," *New York History* 26, no. 2 (April 1946): 146–61; and Franklin B. Hough, *A History of St. Lawrence and Franklin Counties, New York* (Albany: Little, 1853), pp. 600–605. The Parish family records and furniture are housed in the Remington Museum, Ogdensburg, New York.

[6] Franklin B. Hough recorded in 1854: "In 1816, a committee consisting of John Howe, Silvius Hoard, and Samuel Randall, were appointed to take charge of the church when completed. This was the present brick church, erected at the expense of David Parish, for the use of the town, at a cost of $9692.26" (*A History of Jefferson County in the State of New York* [Albany: Munsell, 1854], p. 86). The original building still stands on Maple Avenue.

[7] Clewly and Polly Copeland ran the "Copeland House," the hotel in which Finney boarded.

[8] The First Presbyterian Church of Antwerp was organized in July 1819 by the Reverend Isaac Clinton. It had ten members: Isaac Clinton; William Randall, Sr.; Percival Hawley and his wife; Eliza Hough; Hosea Hough; Edward Foster and his wife; Polly Copeland; and Francis Eaton. See parish "Record Book" of the First Presbyterian Church of Antwerp (handwritten document held by the congregation), p. 1.

their Sabbath meetings lived about five miles out of the village, and was MS 185 obliged, |in[9] approaching the village, to pass through a Universalist settlement. The Universalists had broken up their village meeting by rendering it impossible for Deacon Randall, as they called him, to get through their village and get to meeting.[10] They would even take off the wheels of his carriage; and finally they carried their opposition so far that he gave up attending meetings at the village; and all religious services at the village, or in the town‹ship so far as I could learn›[11] were relinquished altogether.

I found Mrs. Copeland, the landlady, a pious woman. There were two other pious women in the village; a Mrs. Howe,[12] the wife of a merchant, and JHF 99 a Mrs. Randall, the wife |of a physician in the village.[13] It was on Friday, if I remember right, that I arrived there. I called on those pious women and asked them if they would like to have a meeting.[14] They said that they would, but they did not know that it would be possible. Mrs. Howe agreed to open her parlor that evening for a meeting, if I could get anybody to attend. I went about and invited the people, and secured the attendance, I think, of some MS 186 thirteen in her |parlor. I preached to them; and then said that if I could get the use of the village school house, I would preach on Sabbath. I got the consent of the trustees; and on the next day an appointment was circulated around among the people, for a meeting at the school house on Sabbath morning.[15]

In passing around the village I heard a vast amount of profanity. I thought I had never heard so much in any place that I had ever visited. It seemed as if the men in playing ball upon the green, and in every business place that I stepped into, were all cursing and swearing, and damning each other. I felt as if I had arrived upon the borders of hell. I had a kind of awful feeling, I recollect, as I passed around the village on Saturday. The very *atmosphere* seemed to me to be poison; and a kind of *terror* took possession of me. I gave myself to prayer on Saturday, and finally urged my petition till this answer came: "Be not afraid to speak, and hold not thy peace; for I am with thee, and

[9]The number *186* is written in black ink in the upper lefthand corner of the page. This appears to be in Lewis Tappan's handwriting. It is crossed out in pencil.

[10]William Randall, Sr., a charter member of the church.

[11]Finney altered the word "town" to "township" and added "so far as I could learn."

[12]This was probably the wife of John Howe, one of the founders of the church in 1816. See Hough, *History of Jefferson County,* p. 86.

[13]Samuel Randall had taken up land in Antwerp in 1808 and was town clerk in 1812. In 1817 he was elected to the Jefferson County Medical Society, but he was also a merchant. He died in 1831 at age forty-seven "of a lingering disease." See Hough, *History of Jefferson County,* pp. 86–87, 400; and *WR,* 29 November 1831, p. 191.

[14]It was probably this occasion that G. F. Wright refers to. When Finney first arrived in the town, Gorham Cross, as a lad,

> was at the house of the deacon of the church upon Finney's arrival. As soon as he had taken off his overcoat, he asked what praying persons there were in the neighborhood. He was informed that there were very few. Two or three women in humble circumstances were mentioned, however, who were of recognized piety. His instant reply was, "I must see them," and he immediately put on his overcoat and set out to look them up. This will illustrate what was his universal practice in subsequent years (*Charles Grandison Finney* [Boston and New York: Houghton Mifflin, 1891], pp. 29–30; see also p. 64 n. 7 [MS 114/8]).

[15]The meeting was held in Antwerp's second schoolhouse, a wooden structure completed on "the hill" in 1816.

no man shall set on thee to hurt thee. For I have much people in this city." Acts 18:9, 10. |‹This›[16] completely relieved me of all fear. I found, however, that the Christian people there were really afraid that something serious might happen if religious meetings were established in that place again. MS 187

I spent Saturday very much in prayer; but passed around the village enough to see that the appointment that had been given out for preaching at the school house was making a considerable excitement. On Sabbath morning I arose and left my lodgings in the hotel; and in order to get alone, where I could let out my |voice as well as my heart, I went up into a grove of woods at some distance from the village, and continued for a considerable time in prayer.[17] However, I did not get relief, and went up a second time; but the load upon my mind increased, and I did not get relief. I went up a third time, and then the answer came. I found that it was time for meeting, and went immediately to the school house. I found it packed to its utmost capacity. |I had my little pocket Bible in my hand, and read to them this text: "God so loved the world that He gave His only begotten Son that whosoever believeth in him might not perish but have everlasting life."[18] I cannot remember much that I ‹said›;[19] but I know that the point on which my mind principally labored, was the treatment which God received in return for His love. The subject affected my own mind very much; and I preached and poured out my soul and my tears together. I saw several of the men there from whom I had the day before heard the most awful profanity. I pointed them out in the meeting, and told what they said—how they called on God to damn each other. Indeed I let loose my whole heart upon them, and my tears flowed most copiously. I told them they seemed "to howl blasphemy about the streets like hell hounds;" and it seemed to me that I had arrived "on *the very verge of hell*." Everybody knew that what I said was true, and they quailed under it. They did not appear offended; but |the people wept about as much as I did myself. I think there were scarcely any dry eyes in the house. JHF 100 MS 188 MS 189

Mr. Copeland, the landlord, had refused to open the meeting house in the morning. But as soon as these first services closed, he arose and said to the people that he would open the meeting house in the afternoon. The people scattered and carried the information in every direction; and in the afternoon the meeting house was nearly as much packed as the school house had been in the morning. Everybody was out at meeting; and the Lord let me loose upon them in a wonderful manner. My |preaching seemed to them to be something new. Indeed it seemed to myself *as if I could rain hail and love upon them at the same time*; or in other words, that I could rain upon them *hail in love*. It seemed as if my love to God, in view of the abuse which they heaped upon Him, sharpened up my mind to the most intense agony. I felt like rebuking them with all my heart, and yet with a compassion which they could JHF 101

[16] Matson had written here: "I did not recollect where the passage was, but afterwards found it in my Bible. However it." Finney later crossed it out and inserted the word "This."

[17] In his account in *The Independent* in 1872, Finney commented, "I could not express the agony of my soul in words, but struggled with much groaning, and, I believe, with many tears, for an hour or two, without getting relief" (*The Independent* [New York], 4 July 1872, p. 2).

[18] John 3:16.

[19] Matson had written down "preached," but Finney crossed it out and wrote "said."

MS 190 not mistake. I never knew that they accused me of severity; al|though I think I never spoke with more severity, perhaps, in my life. But the labors of this day were effectual to the conviction of the great mass of the population.[20] From that day, appoint a meeting when and where I would **in that neighborhood** anywhere round about, and the people would throng to hear.

The work immediately commenced and went forward with great power. I preached ‹**thrice**›[21] in the village church on Sabbath, attended a prayer meeting at intermission, and generally preached somewhere in a school house in the neighborhood ‹at 5. P.M.›[22] On the third Sabbath that I preached there an aged man came to me as I **came out of** the pulpit, and asked me if I would not go and preach in a school house in his neighborhood, saying that they had never had any services there.[23] **He told me that it was about three miles in** MS 191 **a certain direction.** He wished me to come |as soon as I could. I appointed the next day, Monday, at five O'clock in the afternoon. It was a warm day. I left my horse at the village and thought I would walk down, so that I should have no trouble in calling along on the people in the neighborhood of the school house **on my way**. However before I **got to** the place, having labored so hard on the Sabbath I found myself very much exhausted, and sat down by the way and felt as if I could scarcely proceed.[24] I blamed myself for not having taken my horse.

When I arrived at the appointed hour I found the school house full; and I could only get a standing place near the door, **which stood open,—and the windows were all open**. I read a hymn;—and I cannot call it singing, for JHF 102 they seemed |never to have had any church music in that place. However, they *pretended* to sing. But it amounted to about this: each one *bawled* in his own way. My ears had been cultivated by teaching church music; and their MS 192 horrible |discord distressed me so much that at first I thought I must go out. I finally put both hands over my ears and held them with **the** full strength **of my arms**. But this did not shut out the discords. **I held my head down over my knees, with my hands on my ears, and shook my head, and tried as**

[20]The population was about 2,250.

[21]Finney crossed out "twice" and inserted "thrice." This was unaltered by Fairchild, but the published edition has "twice." Finney's alterations here and in some other places in this chapter are in black ink and appear to have been made in 1872 in association with rereading the manuscript (see Introduction, p. xxxvi; and n. 39 below). In the account published in *The Independent* that year he also mentions preaching "three times" (see n. 24 below).

[22]Matson had originally written down "in the evening" here, but Finney changed it. It was followed by a sentence that appears also to have been crossed out by Finney: "The meeting house was not lighted; and the inhabitants were too much scattered, and the roads too new, to hold evening services at the village meeting house." Finney had added the words "in the evening" in his own handwriting, which he also crossed out. These changes are in black ink and were probably done in 1872.

[23]This was Theodore Cross, the father of Gorham Cross, according to a statement by Aaron M. Hills. (See nn. 37 and 39 below; *The Congregational Year Book* [Boston], 1896, p. 23; and Aaron Merrit Hills, *Life of Charles G. Finney* [Cincinnati: Office of "God's Revivalist," 1902], pp. 54–55. Hills was a student at Oberlin College while Roselle T. Cross, a grandson of Theodore Cross, was principal of the preparatory department there.) Theodore Cross became a trustee of the newly formed Methodist church in Antwerp in 1832 (see Hough, *History of Jefferson County,* p. 95).

[24]In his *Independent* article, Finney wrote: "I had preached three times in the village, and attended two prayer-meetings on the Lord's Day" (*The Independent,* 4 July 1872, p. 2).

far as possible to get rid of the horrible discords that seemed almost to make me mad. I stood it however until they were through; and then I cast myself down on my knees almost in a state of desperation, and began to pray. The Lord opened the windows of heaven and the Spirit of prayer was poured out, and I let my whole heart out in prayer.

I had taken no thought with regard to a text upon which to preach; but waited to see the congregation, **as I was in the habit of doing in those days, before I selected a text.** As soon as I had done praying, I arose from my knees and said: "Up, get ye out of this place; for the Lord will destroy this city."[25] I ‹**said**›[26] I did not recollect where that text was; but I |told them very nearly where they would find it, and then went on to explain it. I ‹**said**› that there was such a man as Abraham, and ‹**also**›[27] who he was; and that there was such a man as Lot, and who he was; their relations to each other; their separating from each other on account of differences between their herdmen; and that Abraham took the hill country, and Lot settled in the vale of Sodom. I then told them how exceedingly wicked Sodom became, and what abominable practices they fell into. I told them that the Lord decided to destroy Sodom, and visited Abraham and informed him what **He** was about to do. That Abraham prayed to the Lord to spare Sodom if **He** found so many righteous there; and the Lord promised to do so for their sakes. That then Abraham besought **Him** to save it for a certain less number; and the Lord said **He** would spare it for their sakes. That he kept on reducing the number until he reduced the number of righteous persons to ten; and God promised him that if **He** found ten right|eous persons in the city, **He** would spare it. Abraham |made no farther request, and Jehovah left him. But it was found that there was but one righteous person there, and that was Lot, Abraham's nephew. "And the men said to Lot, **H**ast thou here any besides? Son-in-law, and thy sons, and thy daughters, and whatsoever thou hast in the city, bring them out of this place; for we will destroy this place, because the cry of them is waxen great before the face of the Lord; and the Lord hath sent us to destroy it. **And Lot went out and spake unto his sons-in-law, which married his daughters, and said, Up, get you out of this place, for the Lord will destroy the city. But he seemed as one that mocked unto his sons-in-law." Gen. 19:12–14.**

MS 193 | MS 194 | JHF 103

While I was relating these facts I observed the people looked as if they were angry. Many of the men were in their shirt sleeves; and they looked at each other and at me, as if they were ready to **pitch into** me and chastise me **for something** on the spot. I saw their strange and |unaccountable looks, and could not understand what I was saying that had offended them. However it seemed to me that their anger arose higher and higher as I continued the narrative. As soon as I had finished the narrative I turned upon them and said, that I understood that they had never had a religious meeting in that place; and that therefore I had a *right* to take it for granted, and was *compelled* to take

MS 195

[25] Genesis 19:12–14.

[26] Finney crossed out the words "told them" and inserted "said." Fairchild changed it back to "told them." The same thing was done in the next sentence.

[27] Finney added the word "also," but Fairchild crossed it out.

it for granted, that they were an ungodly people. I pressed that home upon them with more and more energy, with my heart full to bursting.

I had not spoken to them in this strain of direct application, I should think more than a quarter of an hour, when all at once an awful solemnity seemed to settle down upon them; **and a some thing**[28] **flashed over the congregation,—a kind of *shimmering*, as if there was some agitation in the atmosphere itself.** The congregation[29] began to fall from their seats; **and** MS 196 **they fell** in every direction, |and cried for mercy. If I had had a sword in each hand I could not have cut them off their seats as fast as they fell. Indeed nearly the whole congregation were either on their knees or prostrate, I should think, in less than two minutes from this first shock that fell upon them. Every one prayed for himself, who was able to speak at all. **I,** of course was obliged to stop preaching, for they no longer paid any attention. I saw the JHF 104 old man who had in|vited me there to preach sitting about in the middle of the house, and looking around with utter amazement. I raised my voice almost to a scream to make him hear, and pointing to him said, "Can't you pray?" He instantly fell upon his knees, and with a stentorian voice poured himself out to God; but he did not at all get the attention of the people. I then spake as loud as I could, and tried to make them attend to me. I said to them, "You are not in hell yet; and now let me direct you to Christ." For a few MS 197 moments I tried to hold forth the Gospel to them; but scarcely |any of them paid any attention. My heart was so overflowing with joy at such a scene that I could hardly contain myself. **A little way from where I stood was an open fire-place. I recollect very well that my joy was so great, that I could not help laughing in a most spasmodic manner. I knelt down and stuck my head into that fire-place, and hung my pocket handkerchief over my head, lest they should see me laugh; for I was aware that they would not understand that it was irrepressible, holy joy that made me laugh.** It was with much difficulty that I refrained from shouting, and giving glory to God.

As soon as I could sufficiently control my feelings I turned to a young man who was close to me, and was engaged in praying for himself, laid my hand on his shoulder, thus getting his attention, and preached in his ear Jesus. As soon as I got his attention to the cross of Christ he believed, was calm and quiet for MS 198 a minute or two, and then broke out in praying for the others. |I[30] then turned to another and took the same course with him, with the same result;—and then another, and another. In this way I kept on until I found the time had arrived when I must leave them, and go and fulfil an appointment in ‹the village›.[31] I **then** told them **so. I** asked the old man who had invited me there to remain and take charge of the meeting while I went to[32] **another place.**

[28]The words "that looked as if there was a *glimmer*" followed on here but appear to have been crossed out in black ink by Finney, probably in 1872 (see n. 21 above).

[29]The words "were startled, and" after this appear also to have been crossed out by Finney.

[30]On the reverse side of MS 198, "173 words" is written in pencil. This appears to be in the handwriting of Lewis Tappan. The number of words on this page as sent to Lewis Tappan was probably 175.

[31]The words "another place" were changed by Finney to "the village." This change and the alteration in the next sentence in black ink appear to have been made in 1872 (see n. 21 above).

[32]Here the words "preach in" appear to have been crossed out by Finney.

He did so. But there was too much interest, and too many wounded souls, to dismiss the meeting; and so it was held all night. In the morning there were still those there that could not get away; and they were carried to a private house in the neighborhood to make room for the school. In the afternoon they sent for me to come down there, as they could not yet break up the meeting.

When I went down the second time I got an explana|tion of the anger manifested by the congregation during the introduction |of my **first** sermon there. I learned that the place was called Sodom,—but I knew it not; and that there was but one pious man in the place, and him they called Lot. This was the old man that invited me there. The people supposed that I had chosen my subject, and preached to them in that manner, because they were so wicked as to be called Sodom. This was a striking coincidence; but so far as I was concerned, it was altogether accidental. JHF 105 MS 199

I have not been in that place for many years. A few years since I was laboring in Syracuse in the State of New York.[33] Two gentlemen called upon me one day; one **quite** an elderly man, **another perhaps a man of** ‹47›[34] years of age. The younger man introduced the older one to me as ‹**Deacon**›[35] **White, and** elder in his church; saying that he had called on me to give a hundred dollars to Oberlin college.[36] The older man in his turn introduced the younger; saying, "This is |my minister, the Rev. Mr. Cross.[37] He was converted under your ministry." Whereupon **Brother** Cross said to me: Do you remember preaching at such a time in Antwerp, and in such a part of the town in a school house in the afternoon, and that such a scene—describing it—occurred there? I said, "I remember it very well, and can never forget it while I remember anything." "Well," said he, "I was then but a young man, and was converted in that meeting."[38] He has been many years a successful minister. Several of his children have obtained their education in our college MS 200

[33]This was in February 1853. See Finney to Hamilton Hill, 17 February 1853, Letters Received by Oberlin College 1822–1866, microfilm, roll 14.

[34]Matson had written down the word "fifty" here, but it was changed by Finney to "47." This change and the one in the next sentence may have been made by Finney in 1872 in connection with a visit of the man concerned, Rev. Gorham Cross, to Oberlin, and a rereading of the manuscript to Finney by the son of Gorham Cross (see nn. 37 and 39 below). Gorham Cross would have been about forty-five in 1853, when they were in Syracuse. But Finney was under the impression that the date he was in Syracuse was "in 1856, I think." See the account, also written in 1872, in *The Independent,* 4 July 1872, p. 2.

[35]The word "elder" here was changed by Finney to "Deacon."

[36]Orson White was a founding member and deacon of the First Congregational Church in Richville. See Hough, *History of St. Lawrence and Franklin Counties,* p. 293. Finney wrote at the time to the treasurer of Oberlin College: "Deacon Orson White of Richville, St. Lawrence co. N. York has just left with me for the Oberlin college the inclosed $100. bill" (Finney to Hamilton Hill, 17 February 1853).

[37]Gorham Cross (1808–1895) came from New Hampshire to Jefferson County in 1820, where he became a school teacher. From 1840 until his death he was a Congregational minister in and around Richville, New York. See Roselle T. Cross, *My Children's Ancestors* (Twinburg, Ohio: Champlin Press, 1913), pp. 20–28; and *The Congregational Year Book,* 1896, p. 23.

[38]According to Francis A. Strough of Akron, Ohio, Cross was a village blacksmith and an atheist, and he had gone into Finney's meeting at Antwerp "to throw him out of the school house window" but was soundly converted. Strough was later ordained to the ministry by Cross. See Strough to E. H. Wilkins, 12 October 1933, Alumni Records, file 28/1, box 60, "Gorham P. Cross," Oberlin College Archives.

in Oberlin.[39] As nearly as I can learn, although that revival came upon them so suddenly, and was of such a powerful type, the converts were sound and the work permanent and genuine. I never heard of any disastrous reaction as having taken place.

I have spoken of the Universalists having prevented Deacon **Randall** from MS 201 attending ˡreligious[40] meetings on Sabbath in the village of Antwerp by taking JHF 106 off the wheels of his ˡcarriage. When the revival got its full strength Deacon **Randall** wanted me to go and preach in that neighborhood. I appointed to preach **there** on **the** afternoon **of a certain day**, in their school house. When I arrived I found the school house filled; and Deacon **Randall** sitting near a window, by a stand with a Bible and hymn book on it. I sat down beside him; then arose and read a hymn, and they sung after a fashion—or **rather *bawled***. I then engaged in prayer, and had great access to **a** throne of grace. I then arose and took this text: "Ye serpents, ye generation of vipers, how can ye escape the damnation of hell?"[41] I saw that Deacon **Randall** was very uneasy; and **very** soon **he** got up and went and stood in the door**, it being warm weather**. As there were some boys near the door, I supposed at the time that he had gone **there for the sake of** keeping the boys still. But I MS 202 afterwards learned that it ˡwas through fear. He thought that if they **pitched** upon me, he would be where he could escape. From my text he concluded that I was going to deal very plainly with them; and he had been made quite nervous with the opposition which he had met with from them, and wanted to keep out of their reach. I proceeded to pour myself out upon them with all my might; and before I was through there was a complete upturning of the very foundations of Universalism, I think, in that place.[42] It was a scene that

[39] Six of his seven children were educated at Oberlin; most notably, Rev. Roselle T. Cross, who was principal of the preparatory department at Oberlin from 1869 to 1874. He later pioneered Congregationalism in Colorado. Roselle Cross recollected that Finney "often told the story about preaching in a district called Sodom near Antwerp, New York, and always brought in about my father being there and about his children being at Oberlin. My father was sixteen at the time and was deeply convicted but did not date his conversion at that time" (R. T. Cross, "Memories of Charles G. Finney," typescript in Alumni Records, file 28/1, 'Roselle Theodore Cross," Oberlin College Archives).

When Roselle Cross was married in Oberlin in 1869, Gorham Cross and his wife went to Oberlin and visited Finney. A further visit in 1872 may have been the occasion for Roselle Cross to read much of the manuscript over to Finney and for Finney to make a number of changes in this chapter. See Charles G. Finney, "The Enduement of the Spirit," *The Independent,* 4 July 1872, p. 2; Walter S. Hopkins et al., *The Bible and the Gold Rush: A Century of Congregationalism in Colorado* (Denver: Big Mountain Press, 1962); and Daniel W. Beaman, "The Crosses at Oberlin," typescript dated 20 April 1963, Alumni Records, file 28/1, box 60, "Judson Newell Cross," Oberlin College Archives.

[40] On the reverse side of MS 201 are the following calculations in pencil, which appear to be in Lewis Tappan's handwriting.

24/150/6	42
144	6
6	242

Also on the reverse of page 201 and upside down are some marks in ink and a "?" in the handwriting of Lewis Tappan.

[41] Matthew 23:33.

[42] Finney's attacks against the Universalists while he was preaching in Jefferson County drew

almost equalled that of which I have spoken in Sodom. The revival penetrated to every part of the town, and some of the neighboring towns shared in the blessing. The **revival** was very precious in this place.

When we came to receive the converts, after a great number had been examined and the day approached for their admission, I found that several of them had been **raised** in Baptist families, and asked them if they would not prefer to be immersed.[43] They said *they* had no choice; but their parents would prefer to have them ˡimmersed. I told them I had no objection to immersing them if they thought it would please their friends better, and themselves as well. ˡAccordingly when Sabbath came I **appointed** to baptize by immersion during the intermission. We went down to a stream that runs through the place; and there I baptized **by immersion**, I should think a dozen or more. **But do all I could I could not secure very much solemnity. I observed that the unconverted standing upon the shores laughed,—and that it excited their merriment not a little, especially when I immersed the females.**

MS 203

JHF 107

When the hour for afternoon services arrived, we went to the meeting house; and there I baptized a great number of persons by taking water in my hand and applying it to the forehead. The administration of the ordinance in **that place** was so manifestly owned and blessed of God, as to do **more** to **convince** that that mode of baptism was acceptable to Him, **than anything I could have said. Under the administration of that ordinance in the meeting house the people were intensely solemn, ˡand wept on every side. It seemed to have been a common remark, and to have struck almost every one in that way, that God put his seal upon that mode of baptism. The contrast was so great between that scene and that which passed at the river, as to make a very decided impression.** Among the converts was also a considerable number whose friends were Methodists.[44]

MS 204

On Saturday I learned that some Methodist people were saying to the converts, "Mr. Finney is a Presbyterian. He believes in the doctrine of election and predestination; but he has not preached it here. He *dare* not preach it, because if he should the converts would not join his church.["] This determined me to preach on the doctrine of election **on** Sabbath morning previously to their joining the church. I took my text, and went on to show, First, what the doctrine of election is not; Secondly, what it is; Thirdly, that it

strong criticism from Rev. Pitt Morse, the Universalist minister in Watertown. Morse published a letter addressed to Finney in *The Herald of Salvation*, in which he wrote:

> I am informed, from a source which is entitled to the fullest confidence, that you have recently made the following statements concerning me, viz: "*That I have no more religion than your horse; that I am the wickedest man in all this country; that I do not believe what I preach; and that I told you I did not believe what I preached.*

Morse ridiculed the accusations, accusing Finney of lying, and demanded an apology. He ended with a final P.S.: "If you are subject to paroxisms of *insanity*, you are altogether excusable, and no acknowledgement nor apology, other than a statement of this fact, is required" (*The Herald of Salvation* [Watertown, N.Y.], 28 August 1824, pp. 102–3).

[43] A Baptist society was organized in Antwerp in 1824.

[44] As a result of Finney's ministry, 41 new members were added to the Presbyterian church, 12 by letter of transfer and 29 by profession of faith. If one counts the 45 baptized infants, the church had 101 members when Finney left in October 1824. See entry for 21 February 1825 in the parish "Record Book" of the First Presbyterian Church of Antwerp, p. 20.

is a doctrine of the Bible; **F**ourthly, that it is the doctrine of reason; **F**ifthly, that to deny it is to deny the very attributes of God; **S**ixthly, that it ‹oppose**d**›[45] no obstacle in the way of the salvation of the non-elect; **S**eventhly, |[MS 205 [1]] that all men **might** be saved if they **would**; and **L**astly, that it **was** the only hope that *anybody* **would** be saved**,** and concluded with remarks. The Lord made it exceedingly clear to my own mind, and so clear to the people that I believe it convinced the Methodists themselves. I never heard a word said against it, or a word of dissatisfaction with the argument. While I was preaching I observed a Methodist sister with whom I had become acquainted, and whom I regarded as an excellent Christian woman, weeping as she sat near the pulpit stairs. I feared that I was hurting her feelings. After **dismissing** |[JHF 108] the meeting[46] she remained sitting and weeping; and I went to her and said to her, "Sister, I hope I have not injured your feelings." "No," said she, "you have not injured my feelings, Mr. Finney; but I have committed a sin. No longer ago than last night my husband, who is an impenitent man, was arguing this very question with me; and maintaining, as best he could, the doctrine of election." Said she, "I resisted it, and told him that it was not true. And now," **said** |[MS 205 [2]] **she,**[47] "to-day you have convinced me that it *is* true; and instead of forming any excuse for my husband, or anybody else, it is the only hope I can have that he will be saved, or anybody else." I heard no farther objection to the converts joining a church that believed in the doctrine of election.

There were a great many interesting cases of conversion in this place. **But** there were two very striking cases of instantaneous recovery from insanity during this revival. As I went into meeting in the afternoon of one Sabbath, I saw several ladies sitting in a pew with a **lady** dressed in black**,** who seemed to be in great distress of mind; and they were partly holding her and preventing her from going out. As I came in one of the ladies came to me and told me that she was an insane woman. **T**hat she had been a Methodist; had, as she supposed, fallen from grace; ‹which had led to›[48] despair, and finally **into** insanity. Her husband was an intemperate man, and lived several miles from the village; and he had brought her down and left her at meeting, and had |[MS 206] himself[49] gone to the ‹**Hotel.**›[50] I said a few words to her; but she replied that she must go. **T**hat she could not hear any praying, or preaching, or singing. **T**hat hell was her portion, and she could not endure anything that made her think of heaven. I cautioned the ladies privately to keep her in her seat, if they could without her disturbing the meeting. I then went into the pulpit and read a hymn. As soon as they began **to sing** she struggled hard to get out. But the ladies |[JHF 109] obstructed her passage; and kindly, but persistently

[45] Matson had written down the word "threw" here, but Finney changed it to "opposed."

[46] This phrase was not altered in the manuscript but was changed to "After the close of the meeting" in the published edition.

[47] This page was numbered 205 in error by Matson, and the words "should be 206 call it 205½" were added by Lewis Tappan, who had read the manuscript.

[48] The words "and had fallen into" were changed by Finney to "which had led to."

[49] After page number 206 Lewis Tappan wrote in the words "should be 207." Fairchild crossed them out.

[50] The word "Tavern" was originally written down by Matson, but Finney crossed it out and wrote in "Hotel." Fairchild then crossed out "Hotel" and wrote in "tavern" again.

resisted her escape. After a few moments she became quiet; but seemed to avoid hearing, or attending at all to the singing. I then prayed. For some little time I heard her struggling to get out; but before I had done she became quiet, and the congregation was still. The Lord gave me a great spirit of prayer,—and a text; for I had no text **before** settled upon **in my mind**.

I took my text from Hebrews: "Let us come boldly to **a** throne of grace, that we may obtain mercy and find grace to help in time of need."[51] My object was to encourage faith, in ourselves, and in her, and |‹in[52] ourselves MS 207 for her. When I began to **preach**[53] she at first made quite an effort to get out. But the ladies kindly resisted, & she finally sat still, but held her head very low & seemed determined not to attend to what I said. But as I proceeded **I observed that** she began gradually to raise her head & to look at me from within her long black bonnet. She looked up more & more until she sat upright & looked me in the face with intense earnestness. As I proceeded to urge the people to be bold in their faith, to launch out & commit themselves with the utmost confidence to God through the atoning sacrifice of our great High Priest all at once she startled the congregation by uttering a loud shriek, she then cast herself almost from her seat held her head very low & I could see that she "trembled very exceedingly."[54] The ladies in the pew with her partly supported her & watched her with manifest prayerful interest & sympathy. As I proceeded she began to look up again & soon sat upright with face wonderfully changed, indicating triumphant joy and peace. There was such a **halo** upon her countenance as I have seldom seen in any human› |face.[55] Her joy was so great that she could scarcely contain herself till MS 208 meeting was over; and then she soon made everybody understand around her that she was set at liberty. She glorified God, and rejoiced with amazing triumph. About two years after I met with her, and found her still full of joy and **triumph**.

|The other case of recovery **from insanity**, was that of a **lady in the town**, JHF 110 who had also fallen into despair and insanity. I was not present when she was restored; but was told that it was almost or quite instantaneous, by means of a baptism of the Holy Spirit. Revivals of religion are sometimes accused of making people mad. The fact is, men are naturally mad on the subject of religion; and revivals rather *restore* them than make them mad. During this revival we heard much of opposition to it from Gouverneur, a town about twelve miles, I believe, farther north. We heard that the wicked threatened to come down and mob us, and break up our meetings. |However, of course, we MS 209 paid no attention to that; and I mention it here only because I shall have occasion soon to notice a revival **in that place**. Having received the converts,

[51] Hebrews 4:16.

[52] Page 207 in Finney's handwriting replaces a previous page.

[53] The word "preach" is not altered in the text, but the published edition has "pray."

[54] This is a quotation from Genesis 27:33.

[55] The first three words on page 208 were crossed out by Fairchild and inserted at the end of the previous page.

and having labored in **that place** together with Evans' Mills, until the fall of the year, I sent and procured for them a young man by the name of Deming, whom they settled as pastor.[56] I then suspended my labors at ‹Antwerp.›[57]

[56]Rufus Romeo Deming (1792–1868) graduated from Hamilton College in 1821. He probably went to Antwerp first as a missionary in September 1824. After five weeks he reported: "Since coming to this place, I have had the happiness to see the number in the church increase from sixteen to fifty-six. A body of ruling elders also, has been duly elected and ordained. . . . The precious work of grace commenced among this people some months since and is still continued." Deming served the church until January 1826, when he was succeeded by Rev. James Sandford. Deming continued to be active as a home missionary with a ministry devoted to strengthening the churches in central and northern New York. (See *Hamilton College Bulletin* 16, no. 1 [November 1932]: 28; *The Eighth Annual Report of the Trustees of the Female Missionary Society of the Western District* [Utica], 1824, p. 16; and *NYE,* 7 May 1868, p. 5.) Franklin Hough states, "The Society was reorganized October 5, 1826" (*History of Jefferson County,* p. 94). Deming's name is spelled "Deming" in the manuscript and was not altered but appears as "Denning" in the published version.

[57]The words "that place" were changed by Finney to "Antwerp." Finney's report of his labors there, dated 30 September 1824, states that the church, when he arrived, consisted of sixteen members, "three of these only, were males. Forty-one has been added by your missionary; eleven of whom, are male heads of families" (*Eighth Annual Report,* p. 18).

"The Report of the State of Religion within the Bounds of the Presbytery of St. Lawrence," presented on 3 February 1825 under the heading "Antwerp," reported: "The power of God in the salvation of sinners has also been manifested in this place under the labors of the individual who spent some part of his time in Le Ray. About thirty have been added to the church" (extract in *WR,* 29 March 1825, p. 50).

MS 209
JHF 111

CHAPTER IX

‹*Return to Evans' Mills*›

‹I[1] was at this time earnestly pressed to remain at Evans' Mills, & finally gave them encouragement that I would abide with them at least one year.›[2] Being engaged to marry, I went from there **in October** to Whitestown, Oneida County, and was married.[3] My wife had made preparations for housekeeping; and a day or two after our marriage I left her and returned to Evans' Mills to obtain conveyances to transport ‹**her**›[4] goods to that place. I told her that she might expect me back in about a week. The fall previous to this I had preached a few times ˡin the evening at a place called Perch River, MS 210

[1] The chapter heading and the first sentence in Finney's handwriting are on a separate piece of paper pasted onto the middle of page 209. The section covered over reads: "At Evans' Mills they were very solicitous to have me settle there as pastor. I finally gave them encouragement that I would remain at least for one year." Pages 209–23 were numbered by Matson.

[2] Finney was ordained on 1 July 1824, and on 6 July he was settled as part-time pastor at Evans Mills (see p. 77 n. 20 [MS 140] and p. 73 n. 49 [MS 134]).

[3] The following notice appeared in *The Western Recorder*: "Married—At Whitesboro', October 5th, by Rev. Adams W. Platt, Rev. Charles G. Finney, of Adams, Jefferson Co., to Miss Lydia R. Andrews, of Whitesboro'" (12 October 1824, p. 83).

Lydia Root Andrews (1804–1847) of Whitestown was the eighth of ten children born to Nathaniel Andrews, a Revolutionary Army pensioner of New Britain, Connecticut, and his wife Jerusha Sage. Converted at the age of eleven under the ministry of Rev. John Frost in Whitesboro, she had met Finney when she was eighteen and had been praying for his conversion. See Julia Finney Monroe, "Some statistics concerning the Finney Family," undated manuscript in Miscellaneous Items, Finney Papers, microfilm, roll 8; *OE,* 5 January 1848, pp. 3–4; and Leonard I. Sweet, *The Minister's Wife* (Philadelphia: Temple University Press, 1983).

As well as getting married on that day, Finney attended the Synod of Albany meeting in Utica.

There were rumors later that Finney had two wives. Stephen Hull wrote to William Lapham warning him against Finney:

> This noted Finney's Character it is said is very bad (I know nothing personally) I have been informed that he was bred a Lawyer has had two wives without loosing any has had a child laid to him by a third female since he was married (Hull to Lapham, 2 October 1827, Finney Papers, microfilm, roll 1).

Ephraim Perkins likewise wrote, "He has had two wives, both of whom are now living" (Perkins to A. Bancroft, 10 June 1826, copy in Correspondence Files of the American Unitarian Association, Andover-Harvard Theological Library, Harvard Divinity School).

George W. Gale also wrote that Finney was said to have been "a very wicked man before his conversion; that was the common report," although Gale himself did not support that view (*Autobiography {to 1834} of George Washington Gale {1789–1861}, Founder of Galesburg, Illinois, and Knox College* [New York: privately printed, 1964], p. 183).

In the course of writing *The Story of Oberlin,* D. L. Leonard had talks with President James H. Fairchild, during which he made the following notes of what Fairchild told him: "Fin[ney] had [a] wo[man] & child before bec[oming a Christia]n. He supported [th]em. [He] said [i]t wasn't his" (D. L. Leonard, "Notes upon Talks with Pres. Fairchild," book 2, p. 19, 1 July 1897, R. S. Fletcher Papers, file 30/24, box 1, Oberlin College Archives).

[4] Here Matson had written down "our," but Finney crossed it out and inserted "her." Fairchild later crossed out "her" and wrote "our" again.

still farther Northwest from Evans' Mills about a dozen miles. I spent one Sabbath at Evans' Mills, and intended to return for my wife about the middle of that week. But a messenger from Perch River came up that Sabbath, and said there had been a revival working its way slowly among the people ever since I preached there; and he begged me to go down and preach at least once more **there**. I finally sent an appointment to be there **on** Tuesday night. But I found the interest so deep that I stayed and preached **on** Wednesday night, and **on** Thursday night; and I finally gave up returning that week for my wife, and continued to preach in that neighborhood.[5]

The revival soon spread in the direction of Brownville; a village **of considerable size** several miles, I think, in a south western direction from that place. **I** finally, under the pressing invitation of the minister and church at Brownville, went there and spent the winter.[6] |**I wrote** to my |wife that such were the circumstances that I must defer coming for her until God seemed to open the way; **for I could not leave so interesting a work to gratify myself or her**. At Brownville there was a very interesting work. But still the church was in such a state that it was very difficult to get them into the work. **The policy pursued in collecting the church had been such, that I found in the eldership Presbyterians, Baptists, Methodists, and I know not what. The same was true, so far as I could learn, of the membership of the church; and some of them were Universalists.**[7] I could not find much that seemed to me to be sound-hearted piety. **A**nd the policy of the minister was really such as to forbid anything like a general sweep of a revival. I labored there that winter with great pain, and had many serious obstacles to overcome. Sometimes I would find that the minister and his wife were away from our meetings, and would learn afterwards that they had stayed away to attend a party. |I was the guest at that place of a Mr. **Ballard**, one of the

MS 211
JHF 112
MS 212

[5] Perch River was a small hamlet in an agricultural district, with a Baptist church. Samuel W. Durant mentions a "protracted meeting in 1825–26, when between sixty and seventy were added to the church. A society was legally organized on April 25, 1825" (S. W. Durant, *History of Jefferson County, New York* [Philadelphia: Everts, 1878], p. 306).

[6] The Presbyterian church at Brownville had been organized in 1818. In September of 1820 Noah M. Wells (1782–1880) was installed as pastor. He was a graduate of Union College, New York, and had been a member of the General Assembly in 1813. In June of 1825 he went to the Presbyterian church in Detroit. Subsequently, he held various pastorates in the West. See Franklin B. Hough, *A History of Jefferson County in the State of New York* (Albany: Munsell, 1854), p. 106; and *NYE,* 27 May 1880, p. 1.

George Gale spoke of Wells as "a very popular and pleasant man with whom I often exchanged, his people not being willing he should exchange much except with me" ("Autobiography of Rev. G. W. Gale," typescript copy in Knox College Library, Galesburg, Ill., p. 181).

[7] Rev. Warren Skinner, the Universalist minister of Cavendish, Vermont, described a sermon in which Finney probably referred to these Universalists in Brownville:

> For an introduction to his subject, he indulged himself for about the space of five minutes, in a most violent invective against Universalists—After having in this manner disgorged a copious quantity of gall, wormwood or something else equally bitter, he said he should treat his subject in the following manner, viz: 1. Speak of the new birth, or regeneration, and show what it was. 2. Show its necessity. 3. Show its effects, or consequences.

Skinner was writing the sermon out some years after he heard it, to give readers of the Vermont *Watchman and Repository* some idea of "Finneyism." This is the earliest of Finney's sermons known to have been reported (reprinted in the *Christian Intelligencer and Eastern Chronicle* [Gardiner, Maine], 14 August 1829, p. 129; and in the *Trumpet and Universalist Magazine* [Boston], 10 October 1829, pp. 58–59).

elders of the church, and the most intimate and influential friend of the minister.[8]

One day as I came down from my room and was going out to call on some inquirers, I met Mr. **Ballard** in the hall, and he said to me, "Mr. Finney, what should you think of a man that was praying week after week for the Holy Spirit, and could **not** get **it**?" I replied that I should think he was praying from *false motives*. "But from what motives," said he, "*should* a man pray? If he wants to be *happy*, is that a false motive?" I replied, "Satan might pray with as good a motive as that;" and then quoted the words of the Psalmist: "Uphold me with thy free **Spirit**. Then will I teach transgressors thy ways, and sinners shall be converted unto thee."[9] "See!" said I, "the Psalmist did not pray for the Holy Spirit that he might be *happy*, but that he might be *useful*, and that sinners might be converted to Christ."[10] I said this and turned |and went immediately out; and **I observed that** he turned very short and went back to his room. I remained out till dinner time; and when I returned he met me and immediately began to confess. "Mr. Finney," said he, "I owe you a confession. I was angry when you said that to me; and I must confess that I hoped I should never see you again. What you said," he con|tinued, "forced the conviction upon me that I never had been converted,—that I never had had any higher motive than a mere selfish desire for my own happiness." **Said he,** "I went away after you left the house, and prayed to God to take my life. I could not endure to have it known that I had always been deceived.[11] I have been most intimate with our minister. I have journeyed with him, and slept with him, and conversed with him, and have been more intimate with him than any other member of the church; and yet I saw that I had always been a deceived hypocrite. The mortification |was intolerable; and," said he, "I wanted to die, and prayed the Lord to take my life." However, he was all broken down then, and from that time became a new man.[12] That conversion did a great deal of good. I might relate many other interesting facts connected with this revival; but as there were so many things that pained me in regard to the relation of the pastor to it, and especially of the pastor's wife, I will forbear.[13]

MS 213

JHF 113

MS 214

[8] Finney spoke of him in another place as "altogether a leader in the church, and very intimate with the ministers who frequented the place" (*OE,* 27 October 1854, p. 170).

[9] Psalm 51:13.

[10] In one of his accounts of this conversation Finney represents the man as asking him these questions directly about himself, rather than seemingly about a third person. See *Lectures on Revivals of Religion,* ed. William G. McLoughlin (Cambridge, Mass.: Belknap, 1960), pp. 96–97.

[11] In an earlier account of this incident Finney recalled: "In the first gush of feeling he prayed that God would cut him down and send him to hell, lest he should have to confess his sin and shame before all the people" (*OE,* 11 October 1848, p. 147).

[12] Some years later Daniel Nash wrote to Finney from Watertown, New York:

> During the 14 weeks that I have been here, I have not seen Ballard of Brownville; but I hear that he has become worldly, & carnal, is Boardmanized, & rails against me, tho' I have not seen him for more than 3 years. I am told his wife has become gay, & fond of dress—wears false curles, & does not know whether she should be glad to see Finney, or not (Nash to Finney, 6 August 1830, Finney Papers, microfilm, roll 2).

[13] An unpleasant division arose in the church, and several influential members left and united in an Episcopal organization. Noah Wells left the church and the Presbyterians reorganized on 16 May 1825. See Hough, *History of Jefferson County,* pp. 106-7; and letter of the Reverend Ebenezer H. Snowden in *The Baltimore Literary and Religious Magazine* 4 (May 1838): 236.

Early in the Spring **of the year** I left Brownville with my horse and cutter to go after my wife. I had been absent six months **after** our marriage; and as mails then were between us, we had seldom been able to exchange letters.[14] I drove on some fifteen miles, and the roads were very slippery. My horse was smooth shod, and I found I must have his shoes re-set. I stopped at Le Ray-ville, a small village about three miles south of Evans' Mills.[15] While my

MS 215 horse was being shod, the people finding that ˡI was there, ran to me and wanted to know if I would not preach.[16] **They urged me so hard that I agreed to preach**[17] at One O'clock in the school house,—for they had no meeting house.[18] At One O'clock the house was packed; and while I preached the Spirit of God came down with great power upon the people. So great and manifest was the out-pouring of the Spirit, that in compliance with their earnest entreaty I concluded to spend the night there and preach again in the

JHF 114 evening. But the work increased more and more; ˡand in the evening I appointed another meeting in the morning, and in the morning I appointed another in the evening; and soon I saw that I should not be able to go any farther after my wife. I told a brother that if he would take my horse and cutter and go after my wife, I would remain. He did so; and I went on preaching, from day to day, and from night to night; and there **we had** a

MS 216 powerful revival. I should have said that while I was at Brownville ˡGod revealed to me all at once in a most unexpected manner, the fact that He was going to pour out His Spirit at Gouverneur, and that I must go there and preach. Of the place I knew absolutely nothing, except that in that town there

Wells went to Detroit. He evidently had no hard feelings toward Finney, for five years later he was expressing the wish that Finney would visit that region. See Philip Andrews to Finney, 14 February 1830, Finney Papers, microfilm, roll 2.

[14]G. F. Wright who, as a student, had known Finney, commented on this incident in his biography:

> It would be doing the keenest injustice to Finney to attribute this long separation from his wife, so soon after their marriage, to any indifference of feeling. It is to be taken purely as an index of the strength of his devotion to the ministerial work to which he felt himself called. For, throughout his life, he was passionately devoted to his family, and was never separated from them except upon occasion of necessity, and then with much self-sacrifice and solicitude (*Charles Grandison Finney* [Boston and New York: Houghton Mifflin, 1891], pp. 38–39).

[15]This was usually spelled Le Raysville. It was within the township of Le Ray. See *Map of Jefferson County, New York* (Philadelphia: Shields, 1855).

[16]Finney had preached in Le Raysville before, while he was at Evans Mills. He reported on the revival there after his first three months:

> Several very interesting cases of hopeful conversion have occurred there, and appearances indicate a general movement among the "dry bones" in that valley where Satan has held his seat. The work has commenced among the first class in society, in point of talent and influence.

But three months later, on 30 September, Finney had to report, "It is greatly to be feared that the blessed work is fast yielding to the benumbing influence of sectarian feeling" (*The Eighth Annual Report of the Trustees of the Female Missionary Society of the Western District* [Utica], 1824, pp. 17, 19).

[17]This phrase was not crossed out by Fairchild but is not in the published edition.

[18]The schoolhouse was probably the one built in 1805–1806, located on the old Bedlam Road. A 1913 photograph from a newspaper clipping in an old scrapbook shows a single-story structure about fifteen by twenty feet. The ruins of this building near the ghost town of Le Raysville, about three miles from the center of Evans Mills, have now been removed to make way for the United States Army expansion of Fort Drum (information from Commissioner John D. Waldron of Unadilla, New York).

was so much opposition manifested to the revival in Antwerp the year before. I can never tell *how* or *why* the Spirit of God made that revelation to me. But I knew then, and I have no doubt now, that it was a direct revelation from God to me. I had not thought of the place, that I know of, for months; but when engaged in prayer, the thing was all shown to me as clear as light that I must go and preach in Gouverneur, and that God would pour out His Spirit there.

Very soon after this I saw one of the members of the church from Gouverneur, who was passing through Brownville. I told him what God had revealed to me. He stared at me as if he supposed that I was insane. But I charged him to go home and tell the brethren what I said, and to prepare themselves for my coming and ¦for the outpouring of the Lord's Spirit. From him I learned that they had no minister. That there were two churches, and two meeting houses in the town standing near together. That the Baptists had a minister, and the Presbyterians no minister. That an elderly minister lived there who had formerly been their pastor, but had been dismissed;[19] and that they were having in the Presbyterian church no regular Sabbath services. From what he said I gathered that religion was in a very low state; and he himself was as cold as an iceberg.[20] MS 217

¦But now I return to my labors in Le Rayville. After laboring there a few weeks, the great mass of the inhabitants were converted; and amongst the rest Judge Canada, a man in point of influence standing head and shoulders above all the people around him.[21] My wife arrived, of course, a few days after I JHF 115

[19]James Murdock (1755–1841) of Saybrook, Connecticut, was graduated at Yale in 1774. After pastorates in Vermont and Lewis County, New York, he came to the Presbyterian church in Gouverneur in 1820 and was dismissed on 2 December 1824. Serious loss of hearing prevented him from doing further regular ministerial work, but in 1825 he returned to Lewis County, where he continued for a number of years to supply destitute churches. See Franklin B. Dexter, *Biographical Sketches of the Graduates of Yale College,* vol. 3 (New York: Holt, 1903), pp. 532–33; G. Cross to Finney, 24 April 1873, Finney Papers, microfilm, roll 6; and "Narrative of the late Revival in Gouverneur, St. Lawrence County, New York," *WR,* 26 September 1826, pp. 154–55.

Harvey D. Smith, in a manuscript history of the Presbyterian church in Gouverneur, wrote:

> Mr Murdock labored faithfully in this field four years, instructed and habituated the church in discipline, and church order, instituted the weekly prayer-meeting and monthly concert. It is believed that his example and preaching in conjunction with the prayers and efforts of the faithful of the church, prepared the way for that signal revival which was experienced here in 1825 (quoted in Mary H. Smith to Finney, 14 April 1873, Finney Papers, microfilm, roll 6).

[20]The church had been without regular preaching since 1 January 1825. The "Narrative" in *The Western Recorder* reported on the state of religion at this time:

> Those who were inimical or indifferent to religion, composed a great majority in society; though it cannot be said that much hostility was exhibited; it rather seemed that the world wished to forget that there was such an institution as the christian religion. Darkness—gross darkness prevailed: Vice and immorality triumphed. By the multitude, the Sabbath was neglected, and almost disregarded: The house of God was deserted; and the church assembled in a school house, and mourned because so few came to her solemn feasts (26 September 1826, p. 154).

[21]This was Samuel C. Kanady, a Jefferson County attorney in 1805 and a judge in 1820 (see Luther J. Dorwin, "Bench and Bar of Jefferson County," *Geographical Gazeteer of Jefferson County, New York, 1684–1890,* comp. Hamilton Child [Syracuse: Child, 1890], pp. 50–53; and letters from Kanady to Finney in the Finney Papers). George Gale, in a letter to Finney, refers to Kanady as "Judge Canada" (Gale to Finney, 4 March 1827, Finney Papers, microfilm, roll 1).

sent for her; and we accepted the invitation of Judge **Canada** and his wife to become their guests. But after a few weeks ‹the people›[22] urged me to go and MS 218 preach ˡin a Baptist church in the town of Rutland, where Rutland joins Le Ray.[23] I made an appointment to preach there one afternoon. The weather had become warm, and I walked over through a pine grove about three miles to their place of worship. I arrived early, and found the house open but nobody there. I was warm from having walked so far, and went in and took my seat near the broad aisle **and about** the center of the house. Very soon people began to come in and take their seats here and there, scattered over the house. Soon the number **coming in was such** that they were coming continually. I sat still; and being an entire stranger there no person came in that I knew, and I presume that no person that came in knew me.

Bye and bye a young **lady** came in who had ‹two or›[24] three tall plumes in her bonnet. **She** was rather gaily dressed; was **rather** slender, tall, dignified, and decidedly handsome. I observed as soon as she came in **at the door** that MS 219 she waved her head and gave a ˡvery graceful motion to her plumes, **and thought she must have practiced that motion before her looking glass.** She came as it were sailing around, and up the broad aisle toward where I sat, mincing as she came, at every step waving her great plumes most gracefully, **and rolling her eyes to indicate that she was** looking just enough to see the impression she was making. For such a place the whole thing was so peculiar that it struck me very much. **As the Lord would have it, she came up the broad aisle and took a seat** directly behind me, in which at the time nobody was sitting. **She and I** were **sitting close** together, but each **of us** occupying a separate slip. **I moved along a little so that I could turn around, and by putting my elbow on the back of my seat could pretty easily survey her motions and looks and see what she was about. She still kept up the graceful motion of her head, and kept her body moving just enough to** MS 220 **wave ˡher plumes; and it was evident that she was as full of pride, and of herself, as she could be. After sitting for a short time in that way, I turned around and looked at her. Every part of her dress indicated the greatest vanity.**[25] I turned partly around and looked at her from head to foot; **casting my eye from her feet up to her bonnet, and then down again, then up again, then down again.** She saw that I was observing her so JHF 116 critically, and looked a little abashed. In a **very** low voice I said ˡto her: **"Don't you** ‹believe that›[26] **God thinks you look pretty? Why how pretty God must think you do look! Don't you think all the people will think you look so very nice?" And then I said to her still more** earnestly, "Did you come in here to divide the worship of God's house? to make people

[22] Here Finney changed the word "they" to "the people."

[23] A survey in *The Western Recorder* indicated that Rutland had a population of about five thousand at this time, and that the "Baptists are numerous and have preaching." The Presbyterian minister was Rev. Adams W. Platt, a friend of Finney's, who had officiated at his wedding (3 August 1824, p. 64).

[24] The words "two or" were added by Finney.

[25] The following sentence was written down here by Matson but appears to have been crossed out by Finney before being recrossed out by Fairchild: "I think her cheeks must have been painted."

[26] Here Finney crossed out the word "think" and inserted the words "believe that."

worship you to get their attention away from God and **His** worship?" This made her writhe; and I followed her up in a voice so low that nobody else heard me, but I made her hear me distinctly. |She quailed under **it**, and could not hold up her head. She began to tremble, and **her plumes were all in a shake.** When I had said enough to fasten the thought of her insufferable vanity on her mind, I arose and went into the pulpit. As soon as she saw me go into the pulpit, and that I was the minister that was about to preach, her **manifest** agitation began to increase,—so much so as to attract the attention of those around her. The house was soon full, and I took a text and went on to preach. MS 221

The Spirit of the Lord was evidently poured out on the congregation; and at the close of the sermon I did what I do not know I had ever done before, called upon any who would give their hearts to God to come forward and take the front seats. **And I cannot remember that I ever did this again anywhere until I did it in Rochester, N.Y.**[27] The moment I made the call this young **lady** was the first to arise. She burst out into the aisle, and came forward, like a person in a state of desperation. |She seemed to have lost all sense of the presence of anybody but God. She came rushing forward to the front seats, until she finally fell in the aisle and shrieked with agony. A large number arose in different parts of the house and came forward; and a goodly number appeared to give their hearts to God upon the spot, and among the **rest** this young **lady**. On inquiry I found that she was **regarded as** rather the belle of **that** place. That she was an agreeable girl; but was regarded by everybody as very **proud** and dressy. MS 222

After I left that place—and many years after—I saw a man who called my attention to that meeting. I inquired after this young **lady**. He informed me that he knew her well. That she still resided there, was married, and was a very useful woman; and had always been a very earnest Christian **from that time.**

I preached a few times at this place, and then the ques|tion of Gouverneur came up again; and God seemed to say to me, "Go to Gouverneur,—|the time has come." Brother Nash had come **to me** a few days before this, and was spending **sometime** with me **at that place**. At the time of this last call to Gouverneur, I had some two or three appointments ahead in that part of Rutland. I said therefore to brother Nash, "You must go to Gouverneur and see what is there, and come back and make your report." He started the next morning; and after he had been gone two or three days returned, saying, That he found a good many professors of religion under considerable exercise of mind, and that he was confident that there was a good deal of the Spirit of the Lord among the people; but that they were not aware what the state of things really was. I then informed the people where I was preaching that I was called to Gouverneur, and could make no more appointments to preach in that place. I requested Brother Nash to return immediately, informing the people that they might expect me on a certain day **in** that week. JHF 117 MS 223

[27] Finney records his use of the practice there and the rationale for it in MS 569 and 570. This sentence was crossed out by Fairchild.

MS 224
JHF 118

CHAPTER X

‹Revival at Gouverneur›

Brother[1] Nash accordingly returned the next day, and made **an** appointment ‹**for me**›[2] **to meet the church on the day that I had appointed to be there.**[3] I had to ride nearly thirty miles, I believe, to reach the **appointment**. In the morning it rained very hard; but the rain abated in time for me to ride to Antwerp. While I was getting dinner at that place the rain came on again, and literally poured until **considerably** late in the afternoon. It seemed in the morning before I started, and at noon, **as if** I should not be able to reach my appointment. However, **it** abated again in time for me to ride rapidly to Gouverneur. I found that the people had given up expecting me that day in consequence of the great rain. Before I reached the village I met a Mr. **Smith**, one of the principal members of the church, returning from the church meeting to his house, which I had just passed **at the time I met him.**[4] He stopped his |carriage, and addressing me said, "Is this Mr. Finney?" After my reply in the affirmative he says: "Please to go back to my house. **F**or I shall insist on your being my guest; **and you have rode so far, and** are fatigued, and the roads are so bad, you will not have any meeting tonight." I replied that I must fulfil my appointment. **I** asked him if the church meeting had adjourned. He said it had not when he left; and he thought it possible I might reach the village before they would dismiss. I rode rapidly on, alighted at the meeting house door, and hurried in.[5] Brother Nash stood in front of the

MS 225

[1]Pages 224–62 were numbered by Matson.

[2]Finney added the words "for me."

[3]Finney and Nash labored in Gouverneur from the end of April until September 1825. There was some doubt in Finney's mind about the date that he went there. When his other account of the revival was published some years later in the columns of *The Independent*, questions were raised about his truthfulness as a historian. As a result, a number of Finney's friends did some research into the accuracy of his statements. After examining the results, Finney concluded: "I sent Father Nash a few days before me, in the last of April, and arrived myself, either in the last of April, or about the first of May" (unpublished letter dated 10 June 1873, in the handwriting of Finney's third wife, Rebecca, from Finney to the editor of the *Examiner and Chronicle*, in Miscellaneous Items, Finney Papers, microfilm, roll 8).

Finney's account of the revival is in *The Independent* (New York), 23 January 1873, pp. 102–3; and 30 January 1873, pp. 134–35.

[4]Capt. Benjamin Smith had moved to Gouverneur from Putney, Vermont, in 1823 with his wife, Lucy. Four other brothers and two sisters also moved there within a few years. See *Oneida Circular*, 24 March 1873, pp. 100–101.

[5]This was the Presbyterians' second meeting house, completed in 1824. See Jay S. Corbin, ed., *Centennial Souvenir History of Gouverneur* (Watertown, N.Y.: Hungerford-Holbrook, 1905), p. 174.

pulpit, **and had** just risen up to dismiss the meeting. On seeing me enter he held up his hands and waited till I came near the ǀpulpit, and then he took me right in his arms. After thus embracing me he introduced me to the congregation. In a word I informed them that I had come to fulfil my appointment; and, the Lord willing, I should preach at a certain hour which I named.[6] JHF 119

ǀWhen the hour arrived the house was filled. The people had heard enough for and against me to have their curiosity excited, and there was a general turning out. The Lord gave me a text, and I went into the pulpit and let my heart out to the people. The Word took powerful effect. That was very manifest to everybody, I think. I dismissed the meeting, and that night got some rest. MS 226

The village hotel was at that time kept by a Dr. **Spencer, an Unitarian in sentiment, and** an avowed Universalist.[7] The next morning **I found the village excited; and** I went out, as usual, to call on the people and converse with them about their souls. After making a few calls I dropped into a tailor's shop, where I **saw that** a number of people **were assembled; and I thought that they were** discussing the subject of **my** sermon the night before. **I found this to be the fact.** Dr **Spencer** at that time I had never heard of; but I found him among the number at this tailor's shop, and defending his Universalist sentiments. As I went in the remarks that were made immediately opened the conversation; ǀand Dr **Spencer** stepped forward, manifestly sustained by the whole influence of his comrades, to dispute the positions that I had ‹advanced›[8] **the night before**, and to maintain, as opposed to them, the doctrine of Universal Salvation. Somebody introduced him to me, **and told me who he was**; and I said to him: "Doctor, I should be very happy to converse with you about your views; but if we are going to have a conversation, we must first agree upon the method upon which we are going to discuss." I was too much used to discussing with Universalists to expect any good to come from it unless certain terms were agreed upon and adhered to in the discussion. I proposed, therefore, **First,** that we should take up one point at a time and discuss it **until** we had settled it, or had no more to say upon ǀit, and then another, and another, confining ourselves to the point immediately in debate; Secondly, that we should not interrupt each other, but each one should be at liberty to give his views upon the point without interruption **from any one**; and Thirdly, that there should ǀbe no caviling **and** mere banter, but that we should observe candor and courtesy, and give to every argument due weight, on whichsoever side it was presented. I knew they were all of one way of thinking; and I could easily see that they were banded together, and had come together that morning for the sake of sustaining each other in their views. MS 227 JHF 120 MS 228

[6] In another account, Finney wrote: "I preached that evening." See *The Independent,* 23 January 1873, p. 103.

[7] Dr. John Spencer from Windsor, Connecticut, arrived in Gouverneur in 1809 and was for several years the only doctor within many miles. He was one of the trustees of the Presbyterian church. See Franklin B. Hough, *A History of St. Lawrence and Franklin Counties, New York* (Albany: Little, 1853), pp. 309–13.

[8] Here the word "maintained" was changed by Finney to "advanced."

Having settled the preliminaries we commenced the argument. It did not take long to demolish every position that he assumed, **and to drive him from step to step**. He really knew but little of the Bible. He had a way of disposing of the principal passages, as he remembered them, that are generally arrayed against the doctrine of Universalism. But as Universalists always do, he dwelt mainly on the utter injustice of endless punishments. I soon showed him, and those around him, that he had but slender ground to stand on so far as the Bible was concerned; and very soon **forced him on the ground**, that MS 229 whatever the Bible said about |it, endless punishments **were** unjust, and that therefore if the Bible threatened men with endless punishments, **the Bible** could not be true. This settled the question so far as the Bible was concerned. In fact I could easily see that they were all skeptics, and would not at all give in because they saw that the Bible contradicted their views. I then closed in with him on the *justice* of endless punishments. I saw that his friends became agitated, and felt as if the foundations were giving way under them. Pretty soon one of them went out; and as I proceeded another went out, and finally they *all* forsook him, seeing, as they must have done one after the other, that he was utterly wrong. He had been their leader; and God gave me thus an opportunity to use him entirely up in the presence of his followers. When he JHF 121 had nothing more to say, I urged |the question of immediate attention to salvation **upon him with warmth**[9] and very kindly, bid him good morning, MS 230 and went away. |**I felt very**[10] sure that I should soon hear from that conversation again. The Doctor's wife was a Christian woman, and a member of the church. She told me a day or two after, that the Doctor came home from that conversation apparently greatly agitated, though she did not know where he had been. He would walk the room, and ‹then›[11] sit down, but could not **sit**. He would thus walk and sit alternately; and she could see in his countenance that he was greatly troubled. She said to him, "Doctor, what is the matter?" "Nothing," was his reply. But his agitation increased; and she inquired again, "Doctor, do tell me what is the matter!" She **mistrusted** that he had somewhere fallen in with me; and she said **therefore**, "Doctor, have you seen Mr. Finney this morning?" This brought him to a stand; and he burst into tears and exclaimed, "Yes! and he has turned my weapons on my own MS 231 head!" His agony became intense; and as soon |as the way was opened for him to speak out, he surrendered himself up to his convictions and soon[12] after expressed hope in Christ. ‹In a few days›[13] his companions **that had embraced his views** were brought in one after the other, till I believe the revival made a clean sweep of them.[14]

[9]The order of the words was not changed in the original manuscript, but the published edition reads, "I urged upon him with warmth, the question of immediate attention to salvation."

[10]The word "very" was not altered in the manuscript but was omitted from the published version.

[11]Finney changed the word "would" to "then."

[12]Matson had written down the words "very soon," but Finney crossed out the word "very."

[13]Finney changed the words "Very soon" to "In a few days."

[14]A report of the beginning of the work was carried in the *Religious Intelligencer* (New Haven) and later published in other papers:

A letter from a gentleman in DeKalb, St. Lawrence co., (N.Y.) says "One of the most astonishing works of divine grace that I ever heard of has lately taken place in the town

I have said that there was a Baptist and a Presbyterian **church**, each having a meeting house standing upon the green not far apart; and that the Baptist church had a pastor,[15] but the Presbyterian **church** had none.[16] As soon as the revival broke out and attracted general attention, the Baptist brethren began to oppose it. They spoke against it, and used very objectionable means indeed to arrest its progress. **Their own children attended our meetings, and numbers were converted. They carried their opposition to such lengths, that I have known them to come into our meetings when we were kneeling in prayer, and take their young people off from their |knees, and take them out of meeting and forbid them to return.**[17] This encouraged a set of young men to join hand in hand to strengthen each other in opposition to the work.[18] The Baptist church was quite influential; and the stand that they took greatly emboldened the opposition, and seemed to give it a peculiar bitterness and strength, as might be ex|pected. Those young men **that joined hand in hand—and there were a good many of them—** seemed to stand like a bulwark in the way of the progress of the work;[19] **and they were manifestly sustained by the Baptist church, and sundry of them by their own parents who belonged to that church.** In this state of things Brother Nash and myself, after consultation, made up our minds that

MS 232

JHF 122

> of Gouverneur, a small town adjoining this—More than 100 persons have within a few days been brought under deep conviction (18 June 1825, p. 45).

Dr. Spencer apparently renewed his opposition following the revival. See Mary H. Smith to Lydia Finney, 19 March 1826, Finney Papers, microfilm, roll 1.

[15]The Baptist church was organized in 1810. The minister, Rev. Noah Barrell, had recently arrived and was to remain there for three years before moving to Perry, in Genessee County. See "Souvenir Journal Celebrating the 160th Anniversary of the First Baptist Church of Gouverneur, N.Y.," mimeographed history dated 1971, in Gouverneur Historical Society; and *Christian Watchman* (Boston), 11 January 1828, p. 7.

[16]The Presbyterian church was organized in 1817. The church has handwritten record books dating from 1820. See Sarah H. A. Parker, *A Brief Historical Sketch of the First Presbyterian Church* (Gouverneur, N.Y.: Cox, 1918).

[17]In Finney's account published in *The Independent* in 1873, he refers to this as happening on one occasion only. It brought a denial from James W. Putnam: "no one ever heard of any persons causing their children to rise from prayer, and leave his congregation." See *Examiner and Chronicle* (New York), 27 February 1873, p. 4; and *The Independent*, 30 January 1873, p. 139.

[18]Among the "roughs," as they were called, was a man named Raymond Austin; and probably Benjamin Smith's nephew, Henry Smith, whom he had adopted; and another nephew, Harvey Smith, whom he had also brought from Putney.

Local reminiscences of the pranks of these young people were published in the *Oneida Circular*, 24 March 1873, pp. 100–101. See also *Oneida Circular*, 10 February 1873, p. 51; "The Gouverneur Pastor's Testimony," *Examiner and Chronicle*, 13 March 1873, p. 5; and Finney's unpublished letter dated 10 June 1873 to the editor of the *Examiner and Chronicle*, in Miscellaneous Items, Finney Papers, microfilm, roll 8.

[19]In his account in *The Independent*, Finney wrote, "The young men who had banded together to resist the revival were among the most influential in the place." This drew forth a comment from a man who told James W. Putnam:

> I suppose I was one of those young men to whom Mr. Finney referred. I was in those days, a very wild boy, and said, with others, that I did not want the religion Finney preached. He was such an overbearing man, such an egotistical man, that we determined not to have anything to do with him, or his meetings. In fact, he did not know how to use people decently. He would go into our families, and if we did not happen to think alike, he would tell us that we were on the direct road to hell. But as for us young men banding together, there is no truth in it (*Examiner and Chronicle*, 27 February 1873, p. 4).

that thing must be overcome by prayer, and that it could not be reached in any other way. We therefore retired to a grove and gave ourselves up to prayer until we prevailed; and we felt confident that no [MS 233] |power which earth or hell could interpose, would be allowed **to** permanently stop the revival.

The next Sabbath, after preaching morning and afternoon myself—for I did the preaching altogether, and **B**rother Nash gave himself up almost continually to prayer—we met at five **O**'clock in the church for a prayer meeting. The meeting house was filled. Near the close of the meeting **B**rother Nash arose and addressed that company of young men who had joined hand in hand to resist the revival. I believe they were all there, and sat braced up against the Spirit of God. It was too solemn for them really to make ridicule of what they heard and saw; and yet their brazen-facedness and stiff-neckedness **was** apparent to everybody. Brother Nash addressed them **in a** very **warm manner**, and pointed out the guilt and danger of the course they were taking. Toward the close of his address he waxed exceeding warm, and said to them: "Now, mark me, young men! [MS 234] |God will break your ranks in less than one week, either by converting some of you, or by sending some of you to hell. ***And*** *He will do this as certainly as the Lord is my God*!"[20] He was standing where he ‹brought›[21] his hand down on the top of the pew before him so as to make it thoroughly jar. He sat immediately down, **held down** his head, and groaned with pain. The house was as still as death, and most of the people held down their heads. I could see that the young men were agitated. **However** I regretted that **B**rother Nash had gone so far. He had committed himself that God [JHF 123] |would either take the life of some of them and send them to hell, or convert some of them within a week. **I was afraid that in his excitement he had said what would not turn out to be true, and that would embolden the young men all the more in their opposition.** However **I think it was** on Tuesday morning of the same week, [MS 235] |the leader of these young men came to me in the greatest distress of mind. He was all prepared to ‹submit;›[22] and as soon as I came to press him he broke down like a child, confessed, and manifestly gave himself to Christ. Then he said, "What shall I do, Mr. Finney?" I replied, "Go immediately to all your young companions and pray with them, and exhort them at once to turn to the Lord." He did so; and before the week was out, nearly if not all ‹of›[23] that class of young men were hoping in Christ.[24]

There was a merchant living in the village by the name of **Hervey D**

[20] In another account of this incident, Finney is reported as saying that Father Nash made a declaration which startled me, and almost shocked himself. Yet as he said afterwards, he dared not to take it back for he did not know how he came to say it, and perhaps the hand of God might be in it,—"Young men, said he, God will break your ranks within one week, or He will send some of you to hell" (*OE,* 3 March 1847, p. 35).

[21] Matson had written down the word "pounded" here, but Finney changed it to "brought."

[22] Finney crossed out the words "break down" and inserted "submit."

[23] Matson wrote down the words "quite all" here, but Finney crossed out "quite" and inserted the word "of."

[24] John Humphrey Noyes suggests that his own religious conversion and work with the Oneida Community grew out of a visit to Putney by two of these converted "roughs," Harvey and Henry Smith. See *Oneida Circular,* 10 February 1873, pp. 51–52.

Smith.[25] He was a very amiable man, **and** a gentleman, but a deist. His wife was the daughter of a Presbyterian minister.[26] She was his second wife; and his first had also been the daughter of a**n Old School** Presbyterian minister. He had thus married into two ministers' families. His fathers-in-law had taken the greatest pains |to secure his conversion to Christ. He was a reading, reflecting man. Both of his fathers-in-law were **O.S.**[27] Presbyterians, and had put into his hands the class of books that **taught** their peculiar views. This had greatly stumbled him; and the more he had read the more **was he**[28] fixed in his convictions that the Bible was a fable.[29] His wife**, Mrs. Smith,** urgently entreated me to come **and see** and converse with her husband.[30] She informed me of his views, and of the pains that had been taken to lead him to embrace the Christian religion. But she said he was so firmly settled in his views, she did not know that any conversation could meet the case.[31] Nevertheless, I promised **her that I would** call and see him**. I** did so. His store was in the front part of the building in which they resided. She went into the store and requested him to come in. He declined. He said it would do no good. That he had talked with ministers enough.|That he knew just what I would say beforehand, |and he could not spend the time; beside, it was very repulsive to his feelings. She replied to him, "Mr. **Smith**, you have never been in the habit of treating ‹ministers›[32] who called to see you in this way. I have invited Mr. Finney to call and see you to have a conversation on the subject of religion; and I shall be greatly grieved and mortified if you decline to see him." He **loved and** greatly respected his wife; and she was indeed a gem of a woman. To oblige her he consented to come in. Mrs. **Smith**

MS 236

MS 237

JHF 124

[25] Harvey Douglas Smith (1789–1864) came to Gouverneur from Poultney, Vermont, and was not related to the Putney Smiths. According to the *National Union Catalog,* he was the author of *Family Register of the Descendants of Nathaniel Smith, jr. to which is prefixed some notices of his Ancestors* (Utica: D. Bennett, 1849). See *Oneida Circular,* 24 March 1873, p. 100; and *NYE,* 1 December 1864, p. 4.

[26] His wife was Mary H. Smith. She was the daughter of Rev. John B. Preston of Rupert, Vermont. She became a Christian at the age of sixteen. When she went to Gouverneur with her husband, she joined the Presbyterian church, where she was a member for more than sixty years. She died in 1884 at age eighty-four. See her obituary in *NYE,* 25 December 1884, p. 5; and letters from her to Finney in the Finney Papers.

[27] Old School.

[28] This was not changed in the manuscript but was changed in the published edition to "he was."

[29] In an earlier account of this incident Finney said that Smith had read "almost every book then extant on the inspiration of the Scriptures—had disputed, and caviled, and often thought himself to have triumphed over believers in the Bible, and in fact he was the most subtle infidel I ever saw" (*OE,* 11 October 1848, p. 145).

[30] In the account in *The Independent,* Finney wrote, "I had been there but a few days when she called on me" (23 January 1873, p. 103).

[31] Finney's article on the revival in an 1873 issue of *The Independent,* in which he described the deism and skepticism of Harvey D. Smith, evidently caused some distress. Smith's widow wrote to Finney that it

> struck painfully upon the ear of his friends, who had only known him as a true believer in the word of God—And possibly he never expressed to anyone but myself the infidel doubts that troubled him, and which I communicated to you, that you might more readily understand his case. But I consider your account correct, in all essential particulars (Mary Smith to Finney, 14 April 1873, Finney Papers, microfilm, roll 6).

[32] Matson wrote down the word "persons" here, but Finney changed it to "ministers." This may have been one of the changes made in 1872 (see p. 100 n. 21 [MS 190]).

introduced me to him, and left the room. I then said to him: "Mr. **Smith**, I have not come in here to have any dispute with you at all; but if you are willing to converse, it is possible that I may suggest something that may help you over some of your difficulties in regard to the Christian religion, as I probably have felt them all myself."[33] As I addressed him in great kindness, MS 238 he immediately seemed to feel at-|home with me, and sat down near me and said: "Now, Mr. Finney, there is no need of our having a long conversation on this point. We are both of us so familiar with the arguments **pro and con**, that I can state to you in a very few minutes just the objections to the Christian religion on which I rest, and which I find myself utterly unable to overcome. I suppose I know beforehand how you will answer them, and that the answer will be utterly unsatisfactory to me. But if you desire it I will state them." I begged him to do so; and he began, as nearly as I can recollect in this way: "You and I *agree* in[34] believing in the existence of God." "Yes." "Well, we agree that He is infinitely wise, and good, and powerful." "Yes." "We agree that He has in our very creation given us certain irresistible convictions of right and wrong, of justice and injustice." **I said,** "Yes." "Well, we agree, then, that whatever contravenes our irresistible convictions of justice cannot MS 239 be from God." "Yes," I said. |"What according to our irresistible convictions JHF 125 is neither wise nor good, cannot be from |God." "Yes," I said; "we agree in that." "Well now," said he, "the Bible teaches us that God has created us with a sinful nature, or that we come into existence totally sinful and incapable of any good; and this in accordance with certain preestablished laws of which God is the author. That notwithstanding this sinful nature **that** is utterly incapable of any good, God commands us to obey Him and to be good, when to do so is utterly impossible to us; and He commands this on pain of eternal death." I replied, "Mr. **Smith**, have you **got** a Bible? Will you not turn to the passage that teaches this?" "Why, there is no need of that," he says; "you admit that the Bible teaches it." "No, I do not," **I said,** "believe any such thing." "Then," he continued, "the Bible teaches that God has imputed Adam's sin to all his posterity—that we inherit the guilt of that sin by nature, and are exposed to eternal damnation for the guilt of Adam's sin." "Now," MS 240 said he, "I do not |care who says it, or what book teaches such a thing, I know that such teaching cannot be from God. This is a direct contradiction of my irresistible convictions of right and justice." "Yes," I replied, "and so it is directly in contradiction ‹of›[35] my own." "But now," said I, "where is this taught in the Bible?" He began to quote the catechism, as he had done before. "But," I replied, "that is catechism; **that is** not Bible." "Why," said he, "you are a Presbyterian minister, **ar'n't** you? I thought the catechism was

[33]In another account Finney recalled saying: "Don't understand me as having called here to have a quarrel with you, and provoke a dispute. I only wish at your wife's request to converse with you if you are perfectly willing, upon the great subject of divine revelation." This passage is in a sermon by Finney published in *OE,* 8 June 1853, p. 89. The whole sermon, entitled "The Sinner's Excuse Answered," is an elaboration of the discussion that Finney had with Harvey Smith. It was one of a number of sermons preached at Oberlin from 1845–1861 that were reported by Henry Cowles, the editor of *The Oberlin Evangelist,* and reprinted in a volume, *Sermons on Gospel Themes* (Oberlin: Goodrich, 1876).

[34]Matson wrote the word "in" twice here, but it was not altered in the manuscript.

[35]Here Finney changed the word "to" to "of."

good authority for you." "No," I said; "we are talking about the Bible now—whether the Bible is true. Can you say that this is the doctrine of the Bible?" Oh, he said, if **I was** going to deny that it **was** taught in the Bible,—why that **was** taking such ground as **he** never knew a Presbyterian minister to take. He then proceeded to say that the Bible commanded men to repent, but at the **sametime** taught them that they could not repent; commanded them to obey and believe, and yet at the **sametime** taught them that |this was impossible. I, MS 241 of course, |closed with him again, and asked him where these things were JHF 126 taught in the Bible. He quoted catechism; but I would not receive it. The Bible taught also, **he went on to say,** that Christ died only for the elect; and yet it commanded all men everywhere, whether elect or non-elect, to believe on pain of eternal death. "The fact is," said he, "the Bible in its commands and teachings contravenes my innate sense of justice at every step. *I cannot, I will not receive it*!" He became very positive and warm. But I said to him: "Mr. **Smith**, there is a mistake in this. These are not the teachings of the Bible. They are the traditions of men rather than the teachings of the Bible." "Well then," said he, "Mr. Finney, do tell me what you *do* believe!" This he said with a considerable degree of impatience. I said to him, "If you will give me a hearing for a few moments, I will tell you what I do believe."

I then began and told him what my views of both |law and **G**ospel were**, in** MS 242 **short order**. He was intelligent enough to understand me easily and quickly. In the course of an hour, I should think, I took him over the whole ground of his objections. He became intensely interested; and I saw that the views that I was presenting were new to him. When I came to dwell upon the **A**tonement, and showed that it was made for all men,—dwelt upon its nature, its design, its extent, and the freeness of salvation through Christ, I saw his feelings rise till at last he put both hands over his face, threw his head forward upon his knees, and trembled all over with emotion. I saw that the blood rushed to his head, and that the tears began to flow freely. I **got** quickly **up** and left the room without saying another word. I saw that an arrow had transfixed him, and I expected him to be converted immediately. It turned out that he was converted before he left the room.

Very soon after **I left his** |**room** the meeting house bell tolled for a prayer MS 243 and conference meeting. I went into the meeting; and soon |after meeting JHF 127 commenced Mr. and Mrs. **Smith** came in. His countenance showed that he had been greatly moved. The people looked around and appeared surprized to see Mr. **Smith** come into a prayer meeting. He had always been in the habit of attending worship on the Sabbath, I believe; but **for him** to come into a prayer meeting, and that in the daytime, was something new. For his sake I took up a good deal of the time at that meeting in remarks, to which he paid the utmost attention. His wife afterwards told me, that as he walked home when the prayer meeting was over he said **to her**, "My dear, where has all my infidelity gone? I cannot recall it. I cannot make it look as if it had any sense in it. It appears to me as if it always had been perfect nonsense. And how I could ever have viewed the subject as I did, or respected my own arguments as I did, I cannot |imagine.[36] It seems to me," said he, "as if I had MS 244

[36]This page and the first two lines of page 245 appear to replace a previous page 244.

been called to pass judgment on some splendid piece of architecture, some magnificent temple; and that as soon as I came in view of one corner of the structure I fell into disgust, and turned away and refused to inspect it farther. I condemned the whole without at all regarding its proportions. Just so I have treated the government of God."[37] She said he had always been particularly bitter against the doctrine of endless punishments. But on this occasion **on which** they were walking home he said, that for the manner in which he had treated God he deserved endless damnation. His conversion was very clear and decided. He warmly espoused the cause of Christ, and enlisted heartily in the promotion of the revival. He joined the church, and soon after became ‹a deacon›;[38] and to the day of his death, as I have always been told, was a very useful man.

After the conversion of Mr. **Smith**, and of that class of young men to whom I have alluded, I thought it was time, if possible, to put a stop to the opposition of the Baptist church and minister. I therefore had an interview

JHF 128 first with **the** deacon of the Baptist church, who had been very |bitter in his

MS 245 oppo|sition, and said to him, "Now you have carried your opposition far enough. You must[39] be satisfied that this is the work of God." **Said I,** "I have made no allusion in public to **any** opposition **made by yourself or by any of your people, or your minister;** and I do not wish to do so, or to appear to know that there is any such thing **as this. B**ut you have gone far enough; and I shall feel it my duty, if you do not stop immediately, to take you in hand and expose your opposition from the pulpit." Things had got into such a state that I was sure that both God and the public would sustain me in carrying out the measure that I proposed, **if the Baptists continued their opposition**. He confessed, and said that he was sorry; and promised that he would make confession, and that he would not oppose the work any more. He said that he had made a great mistake, and had been deceived; but that he also had been very wicked about it. He then went after his minister, and I had a long

MS 246 conversation with them together. **His** minister confessed that |he had been all wrong; that he had been deceived, and had been wicked; and that his sectarian **prejudices** had carried him too far. He hoped that I would forgive him, and prayed God to forgive him. I told him that I should take no notice whatever of the opposition of his church, provided they stopped it; which they promised to do. But I then said to him: "Now a considerable number of the young people, whose parents belong to your church, have been converted." If I recollect right, as many as forty of their young people had **at that time** been converted in that revival. "Now," said I, "if you go to proselyting, that will

[37] An account of the incident given by Finney in 1848 has Smith saying to his wife: You have long known me as a strong-hearted infidel; but my infidelity is all gone. I cannot tell you what has become of it—it all seems to me as the merest nonsense—I cannot conceive how I could ever have believed and defended it. I seem to myself like a man called to view some glorious and beautiful structure, in order to pass his judgment upon it; but who presumes to judge and condemn it after having caught only a dim glimpse of one obscure corner. Just so have I done in condemning the glorious Bible and the glorious government of God (*OE,* 11 October 1848, p. 145).

[38] The words "an elder" appear to have been changed by Finney to "a deacon." This may have been one of the changes made in 1872 (see p. 100 n. 21 [MS 190]).

[39] This ends the first two lines inserted at the top of page 245 when page 244 was rewritten.

hurt the feelings of the Presbyterians, and create a sectarian feeling in both churches, and will be worse than any opposition which you have offered." I said to him, "In spite of your opposition the work has gone on; because the Presbyterian brethren have kept clear of a sectarian spirit, and have had the Spirit of prayer. But if you go to ˡproselyting, it will destroy the Spirit of prayer, and will stop the revival immediately." He knew it, he said; and therefore he would say nothing about receiving ˡany of the converts, and would not open the doors of the church for their reception until the revival was over; and then, without any proselyting, let the converts all join which church they pleased. **This, I told him, was what I wanted them to do.**[40] MS 247 JHF 129

This was on Friday. The next day, Saturday, was the day for their monthly Covenant meeting. When they **got together**, instead of **his** keeping his word he threw the doors of the church open and invited the converts to come forward and tell their experience and join the church. As many as could be persuaded to do so told their experience; and the next day there was a great parade in baptizing them.[41] The minister sent off immediately and secured the help of one of the most proselyting Baptist ministers that I ever knew. He came ˡin and began to preach and lecture on baptism. They **ransacked** the town for converts in every direction; and whenever they could **get** any one to join they would get up a procession, and march, and sing, and make a great parade in going to the water and baptizing them.[42] This so grieved the Presbyterian church as to destroy their spirit of prayer and faith, and the work came to a dead stand-**still**. For six weeks there was not a single conversion. **In the meantime the subject of baptism was rung throughout the place, and the whole excitement of the revival fell into that channel.** All, both saints and sinners, were discussing the question of baptism; **for this was lectured upon nearly every day by this old proselyting minister.**[43] MS 248

[40]The Reverend Noah Barrell gave an account of this meeting between Finney and himself in a long letter to the editor of the *Examiner and Chronicle,* who gave a précis for his readers. Finney made the comment: "Brother Barrell's account of his interview with me differs marvelously from *my* recollection of the interview." Finney then contested a number of the points Barrell was making. See *Examiner and Chronicle,* 13 March 1873, pp. 4–5; and Finney's letter dated 10 June 1873 to the editor of the *Examiner and Chronicle,* Miscellaneous Items, Finney Papers, microfilm, roll 8.

[41]The *Christian Watchman* carried details from a letter of Moses Rowley Esq., of Gouverneur: "17 were recently baptized, and added to the Baptist church, and a number were expected to be baptized on the last Lord's Day, June 26" (*Christian Watchman,* 2 July 1825, p. 119).

[42]Noah Barrell wrote on 12 July 1825: "I have baptized forty, that have united with this little branch of Zion, and expect to baptize many more" (*Christian Watchman,* 22 July 1825, p. 131). And Moses Rowley wrote on 31 August: "There has not been a Sabbath since the 5th of June, but what more or less have been baptized. Last Sabbath there were five. Some others also have related their christian experience, and expect to be baptized next Sabbath (*Christian Watchman,* 16 September 1825, p. 162).

A letter dated 19 September 1825 stated, "I believe that for 15 weeks past, the Baptist Church in this place, have been to the water side every Sabbath, besides once or twice on week days" (*The American Baptist Magazine* [Boston] 6 [August 1826]: 247).

[43]Matson wrote down the following sentence after this: "His name was Freeman, a man whom I had known before I was converted." But it appears that Finney later crossed it out and also crossed out the name "Freeman" in all the places where it subsequently occurred. This was probably Joshua Freeman, who was pastor of the Baptist church in Adams around the time Finney was converted. See Franklin B. Hough, *A History of Jefferson County in the State of New*

There ‹**were**›[44] a considerable number of men, and some of them MS 249 prominent men, in ˡthe village, that had been under strong conviction and appeared to be near conversion, who had been entirely diverted by this discussion of baptism; and indeed, this seemed to be the universal effect. Everybody could see that the revival had stopped; and that the Baptists, although they had opposed the revival from the beginning, were bent upon having all the converts join their church. However, I think that a majority ‹of› **the**[45] converted could not be persuaded to be ‹immersed›,[46] although nothing had been said to **any of** them on the other side. I finally said to the people on Sabbath **day**: "You see how it is—that the work of conversion is JHF 130 suspended, and we do not ˡknow that a conversion has occurred now for six weeks; and you know the reason." I did not tell them at all how the pastor of the Baptist church had violated his word, nor allude to it; for I knew that it MS 250 would do no good, **and** much hurt, ˡto inform the people that he had been guilty of taking such a course. But I said to them: "Now I do not want to take up a Sabbath in preaching on this subject; but if you will come on Wednesday afternoon at **One O**'clock, and bring your Bibles and your lead pencils to mark the passages, I will read to you all the passages in the Bible that relate to the *mode* of baptism; and I will give you as nearly as I understand **it**, the views of our Baptist brethren on all those passages, together with my own, and you shall judge for yourself where the truth lies." When Wednesday came the house was crowded. I saw **a considerable** number of the Baptist brethren present. I began and read first in the Old Testament, and then in the New, all the passages that had any refere[**n**]ce[47] to the mode of baptism, so far as I knew. I gave the views that the Baptists had of those texts, and the reasons for MS 251 their views. I then gave my own views, ˡand my reasons for them. I saw that the impression was decided and good, and that no bad spirit prevailed; and the people appeared satisfied in regard to the mode of baptism. **I found that it took me just three hours and a half to read and explain those passages of Scripture.** The Baptist brethren, so far as I know, were quite satisfied that I stated their views fairly, and as strongly as they could state them themselves, and also their reasons for them. Before I dismissed the meeting I said: "If you will come to-morrow, at the same hour, at **One O**'clock, I will read to you all the passages in the Bible that relate to the *subjects* of baptism, and pursue the same course as I have done to-day." The next day the house was crowded, if possible more than the day before. Quite a number of the principal Baptist brethren were present; and I observed ‹the› old **Elder**,[48] the great proselyter, MS 252 sitting in the congregation. After going ˡthrough with the introductory

York (Albany: Munsell, 1854), p. 77; and extract of a letter from Emory Osgood dated Henderson, 18 February 1822, in *The American Baptist Magazine* 3 (July 1822): 386.

[44] Finney changed the word "was" to "were." Fairchild then changed it back to "was."

[45] Matson had written down the phrase "that had then been," but Finney changed it to "of the." Fairchild subsequently changed it to "of those."

[46] Finney changed the word "baptized" to "immersed." This may be one of the changes made by Finney in 1872 (see p. 100 n. 21 [MS 190]).

[47] Matson omitted the letter *n* from the word "reference," but Fairchild added it.

[48] Matson wrote down "old Elder Freeman" here. Finney later crossed out the name "Freeman" and changed the phrase to "the old Elder." He made similar changes in several other places where the name occurs.

services, I arose and |commenced my reading. At this point ‹the› Elder[49] JHF 131 arose and said, "Mr. Finney, I have an appointment, and cannot stay to hear your readings. But I shall wish to answer you; and how shall I know what course you take?" I replied to him: "Elder, I have before me a little skeleton, whereon I quote all the passages that I shall read, and note the order in which I discuss the subject. You can have my skeleton, if you please, and reply to it." He then went out, and as I supposed went away to attend his appointment. I then **began in Genesis. I** took up the covenant made with Abraham; and read every thing in the Old Testament that directly bore upon the question of the relation of families and of children to that covenant. I gave the Baptist view of the passages that I read together with my own, with the reasons **pro and con** as I had done the day before. I then took up the New Testament, |and went through with all the passages in that **that related** to the MS 253 subject. The people waxed very mellow; and the tears flowed very freely when I held up that covenant as still the covenant which God makes with parents and their household. The congregation was much moved and melted. **I found that it took me just three hours and a half to read and expound the passages relating to the *subjects* of baptism.** Just before I was through, the deacon of the Presbyterian church had occasion to go out with a child that had s‹a›t[50] with him during the long meeting. He told me afterwards that as he went into the vestibule of the church he found ‹the old› Elder[51] sitting there with the door ajar, and listening to what I was saying, and absolutely weeping himself.[52]

When I was done the people thronged around me on every side, and with tears thanked me for so full and satisfactory an exhibition of that subject. I should have said that the meeting |was attended, not only by members of the MS 254 church, but by the community generally.[53] **Those two readings settled the subject of baptism. I was told that as the people went out one of the principal of the unconverted men in the village, who had been under conviction and had been diverted by this discussion on baptism, said to ‹the› Elder:[54] "Elder, you ought to be ashamed of yourself. You have**

[49] Matson wrote down the words "Elder Freeman" here, but Finney later crossed out the name "Freeman" and changed it to "the Elder."

[50] Matson wrote down the word "sit," but it appears to have been changed by Finney to "sat."

[51] Matson wrote down the words "Elder Freeman" here, but Finney changed them to "the old Elder."

[52] The presence of Elder Freeman in Gouverneur and this incident in particular were denied by the Baptists after Finney's account in *The Independent* was published. Finney wrote to the deacon concerned and received a reply, which he quoted in his unpublished letter to the editor of the *Examiner and Chronicle*:

> This same Deacon writes under date of May 24th 1873. "You need not doubt, that I saw Elder Freeman weeping, in the vestibule of the church, as I told you." In reference to leading out the little child, he says "James, the little one whom I led out of church, as you may recollect, died at Watertown in 1846" (Finney's letter dated 10 June 1873 to the editor of the *Examiner and Chronicle,* in Miscellaneous Items, Finney Papers, microfilm, roll 8).

See *The Independent,* 30 January 1873, p. 135; and the *Examiner and Chronicle,* 27 February 1873, p. 4; and 13 March 1873, p. 5. The original letter from the deacon is not preserved in the Finney Papers.

[53] Fairchild crossed out the rest of this page, and it was omitted from the published edition.

[54] Matson wrote down the words "Elder Freeman," but Finney crossed out the name "Freeman" and altered it to read "the Elder."

come here as a religious teacher, and have been teaching us continually by your lectures that this covenant made with Abraham was a covenant of works and not of grace. And here you have been getting up all this excitement through your ignorance of the teachings of the Bible on the subject of baptism. And yet you are a professed Baptist, and don't understand the subject yourself. "I have heard what *you* have said," said he, "and I have heard Mr. *Finney*; and it is perfectly plain that you are
MS 255 **wrong and** ¦**that he is right."** ‹The old› **Elder**[55] **left the place, I believe, immediately. I am not aware that any more of the converts united with the Baptist church.** The question was intelligently settled, and soon the people ceased to talk about it. In the course of a few days the Spirit of prayer
JHF 132 returned, and the revival was revived and went on again ¦with great power. Not long after the ordinances were administered, and a large number of the converts united with the church.[56] **Several Baptist families who had attended my readings were convinced; and came and united with the Presbyterian church, and I baptized their children.**[57]

I have already intimated that I was a guest of Mr. **Benjamin Smith**. He had a very interesting family. **By** his wife, called by everybody "Aunt Lucy," **he** had no children. **But** they had from time to time, through the yearnings of
MS 256 their hearts, adopted one child after another until they had ten;[58] ¦and they were so nearly of an age that at the time **of the commencement of this revival** his family was composed of himself, and "Aunt Lucy," his wife, and ten young people, I think about equally divided, young men and young women. They ‹were all› soon converted,[59] and their conversions were very striking. They were bright converts, and very intelligent young people; and a happier and more lovely family I never saw than they were when they were all

[55] Matson wrote down the words "Elder Freeman," but later Finney crossed out the name "Freeman" and changed it to "The old Elder."

[56] According to Mary Smith, the records of the Presbyterian church read:

> July 10th sabbath noon, when 12 more related their Ch[ristian] ex[perience], and with those previously examined and approved to the number of 63 in all, publicly professed their faith in Christ and sat down for the first time to the Sacramental table of our Lord. Communion administered by Rev C. G. Finney, assisted by Rev Daniel Nash (M. Smith to Finney, 13 May 1873, Finney Papers, microfilm, roll 6).

[57] Noah Barrell informed the editor of the *Examiner and Chronicle* that no member of his church left to join the Presbyterian church. This is confirmed by the recollections of Mary H. Smith: "I do not certainly know if any of them were ever communicants in the Baptist Ch" (Smith to Finney, 14 April 1873, Finney Papers, microfilm, roll 8; and *Examiner and Chronicle,* 13 March 1873, p. 5).

But Finney wrote: "I understood they were Baptists, as this writer does, but I did not know whether or not they had joined the Baptist church in that place, and never thought to raise the question" (unpublished letter to the editor of the *Examiner and Chronicle,* 10 June 1873, p. 3, in Miscellaneous Items, Finney Papers, microfilm, roll 8).

During Finney's stay in Gouverneur, 92 members were added to the Presbyterian church, raising total membership to 152. All of these came on "profession of the faith," and Finney baptized 29 of them. In addition he baptized 38 infants. See "Presbyterian Church Archives: Minutes and Congregational Meetings, 1820–1955," of the First Presbyterian Church, Gouverneur, New York, filed in the archives of the Presbyterian Historical Society, Philadelphia.

[58] Two of these children were Henry and Julia, the children of Joseph, a brother of Benjamin Smith. Another was Harvey, the son of his brother Jonathan. See *Oneida Circular,* 10 February 1873, p. 51; and 24 March 1873, p. 100.

[59] Finney changed the phrase "They soon became converted, every one of them" to "They were all soon converted."

converted. But Aunt Lucy had been converted under other circumstances, when there was no revival; and she had never before seen the freshness, and strength, and joy of converts **converted** in a powerful revival. Their faith and love, their joy and peace, completely stumbled **Aunt Lucy**. She began to think that she was never converted; and although she had given herself heart and soul to the promotion of the work, yet right in the midst of it she fell into despair in spite of all that could be said or done. MS 257 |She concluded that she never had been converted, and of course that she never could be. This introduced into the family a matter of great pain and concern. Her husband thought she would go deranged. The young people, who all regarded her as a mother, were filled with concern about her; and indeed the house was thrown into mourning. **Brother Smith** gave up his time to converse and to pray with her, and to try to revive her hope. I had several conversations with her; but in the great light which the experience of those young converts, to which she was daily listening, threw around her, she could not be persuaded to believe either that she ever was converted, or ever could be. JHF 133 |This state of things continued day after day till I began myself to think that she would be deranged. The street on which they lived was a thickl‹y›[60] settled street, almost a village for some three miles in extent. The work had **gone on** on that street until there was but one adult unconverted person left.[61] MS 258 |He was a young man by the name of **Bela Hough**, and was almost frantic in his opposition to the work. Almost the whole neighborhood gave themselves to prayer for this young man, and his case was in almost everybody's mouth. One day I came in and found Aunt Lucy taking on very much about **Bela Hough**. "Oh dear!" she said; "what *will* become of him? Why, Mr. **Smith**! he will certainly lose his soul! What *will* become of him?" She seemed to be in the greatest agony lest that young man should lose his soul. I listened to her for a few moments, and then looked gravely at her and said: "Aunt Lucy, when you and **Bela Hough** die, God will have to make a partition in hell and give you a room by yourself." She opened her large blue eyes, and looked at me with a reproving look:—"Why Mr. Finney!" said she. "Just so, ‹I said.›[62] Do you think God will be guilty of so great an impropriety as to put you and **Bela Hough** in the same place? Here *he* is, raving against God; and *you* are almost insane in feeling the abuse which he heaps upon God, and MS 259 |with the fear that he is going to hell. Now can two such persons, in such opposite states of mind, do you think, be sent to the same place?" I calmly met her reproving gaze, and looked her steadily in the face. In a few moments her features relaxed, and she smiled, the first time for many days. "It is just so, my dear," said Mr. **Smith**,—"just so. How can you and **Bela Hough** go to the same place?" She laughed and said, "We cannot." From that moment her despair

[60] Here Matson wrote "thickled." Finney scratched out the *d* and part of the *l* and altered the word. It then could have been misread as "thicky," and was clarified by Fairchild.

[61] Noah Barrell stated in a letter dated Gouverneur, 12 July 1825: "On the main road that runs thro' this town, there are very few houses where prayer and praises are not heard; and in this village there is but one solitary family but what give testimony that salvation has come to their houses" (*Christian Watchman,* 22 July 1825, p. 131).

[62] Finney added the words "I said."

cleared up; and she came out clear, and as happy as any of the young converts.[63] This **Bela Hough** was afterwards converted.

JHF 134 ˡAbout three quarters of a mile from Mr. **Smith**'s lived a Mr. **Martin**,[64] who was a strong Universalist, and for a considerable time kept away from our meetings. One morning Father Nash, who was at the time with me at Mr. **Smith**'s, rose up, as his custom was, at a very early hour; and went back to a MS 260 grove some fifty rods, perhaps, from the road, to have a ˡseason of prayer alone. It was before sunrise; and Brother Nash, as usual, became very much engaged in prayer. It was one of those clear mornings, on which it is possible to hear sounds a great distance. Mr. **Martin** had **arisen** and was out of doors at that early hour in the morning, and heard the voice of prayer. He listened, and could distinctly hear Father Nash's voice. He knew it was prayer, he afterwards said; though he could not distinguish much that was said. He however said that he knew *what* it was, and *who* it was. **But** it lodged an arrow in his heart. He said it brought a sense of the *reality* of religion over him, such as he never had experienced before.[65] The arrow was fastened. He found no relief till he found it in believing in Jesus.[66] I do not know the number **that was** converted in that revival. It was a large farming town, settled by well-to-do inhabitants.[67] The great majority of them, I am confident, were in that MS 261 revival ˡconverted to Christ.[68] **After I left, as I have been informed, the**

[63] Nearly three years later Henry Smith wrote to Finney about his "Aunt Lucy's" failing health, and finally her death (on 17 March 1828), when

> it pleased the Lord to deliver her from her troubles & trials. Yes "*Aunt Lucy*" [MS torn] gone—of her death I can say but little as I was absent at this time also. She however died very happily. She you [*sic*] has always been subject to clouds & darkness. Four days before her death these were dispelled, & her path continued to shine brighter & brighter until the perfect day (Henry H. Smith to Finney, 19 April 1828, Finney Papers, microfilm, roll 2).

The date is written "19 April 1827," but this is a mistake. The context clearly indicates that it was written in 1828.

[64] This was Nathaniel Martin. See *Oneida Circular*, 24 March 1873, p. 101.

[65] Finney had had a similar experience before his own conversion. He was returning home from a legal appointment when he heard a man praying in a schoolhouse. "That praying did more to impress my mind with the subject of religion, than all I had heard before, from my birth" (*OE*, 2 July 1845, p. 107).

[66] Stephen R. Leonard on a visit to Gouverneur from the Oneida Community in 1873 was told by Daniel Keyes, who had been in Gouverneur during the revival, that

> Martin was a Universalist and deadly opposed to the revival. Father Nash was bent on his conversion, and retired day after day to the grove back of Benjamin Smith's house to pray for him. At last he came into the house one day saying that his prayer had been answered. There had been no visible change in Martin up to this time; but Father Nash was positive that "there was no mistake." Sure enough, Martin was shortly converted, and he afterward became a talented Congregational preacher (*Oneida Circular*, 24 March 1873, p. 101).

[67] Gouverneur's population was about 1,250 at that time.

[68] Contemporary accounts of the revival give some idea of the numbers that were said to be converted:

> The work continued about five months, and then did not wholly cease.—More than 200, in this town, besides many in adjoining towns, indulged hopes of having been born again. Since the 1st April, 1825, ninety-one by profession, and seven by certificate, have been added to our church [the Presbyterian Church].—About the same number to the Baptist and Methodist churches ("Narrative of the late Revival in Gouverneur, St. Lawrence Co., New York," *WR*, 26 September 1826, p. 155).

Another report reads:

Baptists dismissed their minister, he having become very unpopular from the course he pursued toward that revival. They gave up their own separate meetings, and went over to the Presbyterian meeting house as a body; and they worshipped with them, if I remember rightly, some ‹year or› two[69] before they revived their own separate meetings.[70] I have not been in that place for many years. But I have often heard from there; and have always understood that there has been a very healthful state of religion in that place, and that they have never had anything like a discussion on the subject of baptism since.[71]

The doctrines preached in promoting that revival were those that I have preached everywhere. The total moral **and** voluntary depravity of unregenerate man; the necessity of a radical change of heart, through the truth, by the agency of the Holy Ghost; the divinity and humanity of our |Lord Jesus Christ; his vicarious atonement, equal to the wants of all mankind; the gift, divinity and agency of the Holy Ghost; repentance, faith, justification by faith, sanctification |by faith; persistence[72] in holiness as a condition of salvation,— **and** indeed all the distinctive doctrines of the Gospel were stated and set forth with as much clearness, and point, and power, as **was** possible to me under the circumstances. A great spirit of prayer prevailed;[73] and after the

MS 262

JHF 135

> A great revival of religion commenced here in April last. . . . About 158 persons during the last four months, have united to the Baptist and Congregational Churches in this town, besides a small number with the Methodists, and others have experienced religion who have made no covenant profession (letter dated 19 September 1825, in *The American Baptist Magazine,* n.s., 6 [August 1826]: 247).

Benjamin Smith wrote in December 1825, mentioning Finney's part "in the work of grace which God hath wrought in bringing more than 200 souls from darkness to light" (Smith to Finney, 22 December 1825, Finney Papers, microfilm, roll 1). A further report stated: "The town of Gouverneur has been favored with a very extensive revival. It is supposed that between two and three hundred have there experienced a saving change of heart" ("A Narrative of the State of Religion within the bounds of the Presbytery of Ogdensburgh for the year ending January 3, 1826," *WR,* 31 January 1826, p. 17).

[69] Finney changed the phrase "two or three years" to "year or two." He may have done this in 1872 (see p. 100 n. 21 [MS 190]).

[70] This information, which Finney also gave in his article in *The Independent,* 30 January 1873, p. 135, was denied in articles in the *Examiner and Chronicle,* 27 February 1873, p. 4; and 13 March 1873, p. 5. Finney's response to these denials reads:

> I said in my article that after I left, the Baptist church dismissed their minister, and worshipped for some time, with the Presbyterians. I derived my information on this point some years after I left Gouverneur, from parties whose veracity I did not at all question. But as this is denied by some of the Baptist brethren at Gouverneur, it is probable that I was misinformed (Finney letter dated 10 June 1873 to the editor of the *Examiner and Chronicle,* Miscellaneous Items, Finney Papers, microfilm, roll 8).

On Finney's recommendation, the Presbyterian church called the Reverend Richard C. Hand as its pastor. This young graduate of Andover Seminary served the congregation from 1825 to 1833. See Benjamin Smith to Finney, 22 December 1825, Finney Papers, microfilm, roll 1; and Parker, *Sketch of the First Presbyterian Church,* p. 9.

[71] Gorham Cross reported to G. F. Wright that he went to Gouverneur six years after the revival and found that the place was very religious and that it was impossible to get up a ball or to have a circus. See G. F. Wright, Notebook no. 1, p. 95, Wright Papers, box 25; and Wright, *Charles Grandison Finney* (Boston and New York: Houghton Mifflin, 1891), pp. 60–61.

[72] Matson wrote this word as "persisistence," but Fairchild corrected it.

[73] S. R. Leonard was informed "that for months during the summer and fall of the revival year one could scarcely go out at any hour of the night without hearing individuals or companies of individuals praying in the fields and groves in several directions at the same time" (*Oneida Circular*, 24 March 1873, p. 101).

discussion on baptism, a spirit of most interesting unity, brotherly love, and Christian fellowship prevailed. I never had occasion, finally, to rebuke the opposition of the Baptist brethren publicly. In my readings on the subject of baptism the Lord enabled me to maintain such a spirit that no controversy was started, and no controversial spirit prevailed. The discussion produced no evil results; but great good, and, so far as I could see, only good.[74]

[74]The progress of the revival among the Baptists was reported in the papers. Moses Rowley wrote on 31 August, "Sixty-six have been added by baptism, and a number by letter; so that our little church, which before consisted of about 93 members, now consists of about 175" (*Christian Watchman*, 16 September 1825, p. 162; see also n. 68 above).

CHAPTER XI

MS 263
JHF 136

‹*Revival at De Kalb*›

From[1] **this place** I went to De Kalb; another village still farther north, some sixteen miles, I think.[2] Here **was** a Presbyterian church and minister; but the church was small, and the minister seemed not to have a very strong hold upon the people.[3] However, I think he was decidedly a good man. I began to hold meetings in De Kalb in different parts of the town. The village was small, and the people were very much scattered. The country was new, and the roads were new and bad. But a revival commenced immediately, and went forward with a good deal of power for a place where the inhabitants were so much scattered.[4] A few years before there had been a revival there under the labors of the Methodists.[5] It had been attended with a good deal of excitement; and many cases had occurred of what the Methodists call "*falling* under the power of God." This the Presbyterians had resisted, and in consequence a bad state of feeling had **exis|ted** between the Methodists and MS 264

[1] Pages 263–65 were numbered by Matson.

[2] It is probable that Finney went to De Kalb in August of 1825, before he had finished at Gouverneur. He may even have made a brief visit in late July. A letter dated 26 July 1825 is addressed to him there. See J. W. McAuley to Finney, 26 July 1825, Finney Papers, microfilm, roll 1. See also Ephraim Perkins, *A "Bunker Hill" Contest* (Utica: printed for the Author, 1826), p. 65; and Moses Rowley, letter dated Gouverneur, 31 August 1825, in *Christian Watchman* (Boston), 16 September 1825, p. 162.

[3] This was Thomas Kennan (1773–1853). Originally from Vermont, he was the minister in De Kalb until about 1833, when he went to Norwalk, Ohio. See Thomas Lathrop Kennan, *Genealogy of the Kennan Family* (Milwaukee: Cannon, 1907), p. 25.

Gorham Cross, a later minister in De Kalb, told G. F. Wright that Finney called the minister "Cannon" and was reported to have said that "he would either make him roar or would spike him" (G. F. Wright, Notebook no. 2, p. 96, Wright Papers, box 25).

[4] *The New York Observer* gave a report from the United Domestic Missionary Society:

> A letter from De Kalb, St. Lawrence co. one of our missionary stations, dated Dec. 13, 1825, states, that a revival of religion commenced there in August last, the fruits of which, before the end of September following, were the hopeful conversion of sixty souls. More recently we have been informed by an esteemed correspondent in that county, that the work of grace is still advancing in De Kalb, and that in that single town, embracing only 131 families, and 766 souls, more than 70 have, in the judgment of charity, become the children of God (reprinted in *WR,* 21 February 1826, p. 30).

In January 1826 the Presbytery of Ogdensburgh reported: "In the town of De Kalb, the divine Spirit has been carrying on a revival of the work of the Lord. There, about fifty have hopefully passed from death to life" ("A Narrative of the State of Religion within the bounds of the Presbytery of Ogdensburgh for the year ending January 3, 1826," *WR,* 31 January 1826, p. 17).

[5] The Methodists were the first religious organization in De Kalb. A revival there in about 1817 or 1818 resulted in forty or fifty joining the Methodist church. The First Presbyterian Church was formed in 1817. See Franklin B. Hough, *A History of St. Lawrence and Franklin Counties, New York* (Albany: Little, 1853), pp. 292–93.

the Presbyterians; the Methodists accusing the Presbyterians of having opposed the revival among them because of these cases of falling **under the power of God.** As nearly as I could learn there was a good deal of truth in this, and the Presbyterians had been decidedly in error. I had not preached long, before one evening, just **before** the close of my sermon, I observed a man[6] fall from his seat near the door, and **that** the people **were** gathered around him to take care of him. From what I saw I was satisfied that it was a JHF 137 case of "falling under the power of God," as the Methodists would ᑊexpress it, and supposed that it was a Methodist; **and** I must say that I had a little fear that it might reproduce that state of division and alienation that had before existed. But on inquiry I learned that it was one of the principal members of the Presbyterian church that had fallen. And it was remarkable that during MS 265 [1] this revival there were several cases of this ᑊkind among the Presbyterians, and none among the Methodists. This led to such confessions and explanations among the members of the different churches as to secure a state of great cordiality and good feeling among them.

While laboring at De Kalb I first became acquainted with **John Fine Esq**, of Ogdensburgh.[7] He heard of the revival in De Kalb, and came to see it. He was wealthy, and very benevolent. He proposed to employ me as his missionary to work in the towns throughout that county, and he would pay me a salary. However, I declined to pledge myself to preach in any particular place, or to confine my labors within any given lines. **Brother Fine** spent several days with me in visiting from house to house, and in attending our meetings. He had been educated in Philadelphia, an **O.S.**[8] Presbyterian; and was himself an elder in the Presbyterian church in Ogdensburgh. **When he left De Kalb** he left **with a lady, with whom I was staying,** a letter for me. MS 265 [2] ᑊ**On**[9] **opening it I found in it** three ten dollar bills. A few days later he came up again and spent two or three days, and attended our meetings and became very much interested in the work. When he went away he left another letter **as before**, containing three ten dollar bills. Thus I found myself possessed of sixty dollars; with which I immediately purchased a **one horse** buggy. Before this time, though I had a horse, I had no carriage; and my young wife and myself used to go a good deal on foot to meeting.

The revival took a very strong hold of the church in this place; and among others **it thoroughly broke up the heart of** one of the elders of the church, JHF 138 by the name of **Burnett.**[10] **He got** thoroughly broken up and broken ᑊdown,

[6]Here Matson wrote down "young man," and "young" appears to have been crossed out by Finney.

[7]John Fine (1794–1867), a graduate of Columbia College, moved to St. Lawrence County in 1815 as a lawyer. He was appointed a judge in 1824 and went on to become a judge of the supreme court. In 1839 he was elected to Congress and in 1845 to the state senate. He also became prominent in the Presbyterian church and served as a delegate to the General Assembly, where he had considerable influence. See Hough, *St. Lawrence and Franklin Counties*, p. 586; and *The National Cyclopaedia of American Biography*, vol. 4 (New York: James T. White, 1897), p. 399.

[8]Old School.

[9]This page was originally numbered 265 in error. It should have been 266, and the words "make it 265½" were added by Lewis Tappan.

[10]Matson had spelled the name with one *t*, and in each case an additional *t* appears to have

and became quite another man. The impression deepened on the public mind from day to day. One Saturday just before evening a German merchant tailor from Ogdensburgh, by the name of **Father,**[11] called on me and informed me |that[12] **Esquire Fine** had sent him from Ogdensburgh to take my measure for a suit of clothes. I had begun to need clothes, and had once not long before spoken to the Lord about it, that my clothes were getting shabby; but it had not occurred to me again. **Brother Fine**, however, had observed it; and sent this man, who was a Roman Catholic, to take my measure **for a suit of clothes.**[13] I asked him if he would not stay over the Sabbath, and take my measure **on** Monday morning. I said, "It is too late for you to return to-night; and if I allow you to take my measure to-night, you will go home to-morrow." He admitted that he expected to. I **told him**, "Then you shall not take it. If you will not stay till Monday morning, I will not be measured for a suit of clothes." He remained. The same afternoon there were other arrivals from Ogdensburgh; **a village on the St. Lawrence, and some sixteen miles still farther north from De Kalb.** Among the **other arrivals** was an **E**lder **Smith**, who was a brother elder in the |same church with **Mr. Fine. Mr. Smith**'s son, an unconverted young man, came with him; **and several other persons from Ogdensburg came up to attend the meeting.** Elder Smith attended meeting in the morning, and at the intermission was invited by **E**lder **Burnett** to go home with him and get some refreshment. Elder **Burnett** was full of the Holy Spirit; and on the way home he preached to **E**lder **Smith,** who was at the time very cold and backward in religion. Elder **Smith** was very much penetrated by his words. Soon after they entered the house the table was spread, and they were invited to sit down and take some refreshment. As they drew around the table **E**lder **Smith** said to **E**lder **Burnett:** "How did you get this blessing?" Elder **Burnett** replied: "I stopped *lying to God.*" Said he, "All my Christian life I have been making pretences, and asking God for things that I was not on the whole willing to have; |and I had gone on and prayed as other people prayed, |and often had been insincere, and really lied to God." He continued: "As soon as I made up my mind that I never would say anything to God in prayer that I did not really *mean*, God answered me; and the Spirit came down, and I was filled with the Holy Ghost." At this moment Mr. **Smith**, who had not commenced to eat, shoved his chair back from the table, and fell on his knees and began to confess how *he* had lied to God; and how he had played the hypocrite, in his *prayers* as well as in his *life.* The Holy Ghost fell upon him immediately, and filled him as full as he could hold. **The first that I knew anything of it was as follows:** The people had assembled for **afternoon** worship, and I was standing in the pulpit reading a hymn. I heard somebody talking very loud, and approaching the house **of worship,** the door and windows being open. Directly two men came in. Elder

MS 266

MS 267

JHF 139

MS 268

been added by him. The letters *ur* in the name here have been clarified in black ink, possibly by Finney in 1872 (see p. 100 n. 21 [MS 190]).

[11]The letters *er* in the name here have been clarified in black ink, possibly by Finney in 1872 (see p. 100 n. 21 [MS 190]).

[12]Pages 266 to 272 were numbered by Matson.

[13]Fairchild crossed out the words "for a suit of clothes" in the manuscript, but they appear in the published version.

MS 269 **Burnett** I knew; the other man was a stranger. As soon |as he came in at the door he lifted his eyes to me, came straight into the desk **to me**, and took me **right** up in his arms:—"*God bless you*!" said he; "*God bless you*!" He then began and told me, and told the congregation, what the Lord had just done for his soul. His countenance was all in a glow; and he was so changed in his appearance, that those that knew him were perfectly astonished at the change. His son, who had not known of this change in his father, when he saw and heard him rose up and was hastening out of the church. His father cried out: "Do not leave the house, my son; for I never *loved* you before." He went on to speak; and the power with which he spoke was perfectly astonishing. The people melted down on every side; and his son broke down almost immediately. Very soon this Roman Catholic tailor, Mr. **Father**, rose up **in the congregation** and said: "I must tell you what the Lord has done for *my* MS 270 soul." "I was brought up," **said he,** "a Roman Catholic; and I never dared |to JHF 140 read my Bible. I was told that if I did, the |devil would carry me off bodily. Sometimes when I dared to look into it, it seemed as if the devil was **peaking** over my shoulder, and had come to carry me off. "But," said he, "I see it is all a delusion." And he went on to tell what the Lord had done for **his soul right** there on the spot,—what views the Lord had given him of the way of salvation by Jesus Christ. It was evident to everybody that he was converted. This made a great impression on the congregation. I could not preach. The whole course of the meeting had taken on a type which the Lord had given it. I sat still and saw the salvation of God. **One after another told what the Lord had done for their souls, and the work went on.** All that afternoon conversions were multiplied in every part of the congregation. As one after another **arose** and told what the Lord had done, and was doing, for their souls, the impression increased; and so spontaneous a movement by the Holy MS 271 Ghost in convicting and |converting sinners I had scarcely ever seen. The next day this **Elder Smith** returned to Ogdensburgh. But as I understood he made many calls on the way, and conversed and prayed with many families; and thus the revival was extended to Ogdensburgh. **I never knew anything like the number of conversions that occurred in this place at that time; but it must have been very large in proportion to the number of settlers in that new town.**

In the early part of October the Synod to which I belonged met in Utica. I took my wife, and we went down to Utica to attend the Synod, and to visit her father's family **who lived** near Utica.[14] **Brother** Gale, my theological

[14]There is a confusion here in Finney's mind about the occasion of this visit to his father-in-law's home in Whitesboro. In this year, 1825, the Synod of Albany met at Troy, not Utica, and Finney is not known to have been present. It was the year before that it had met at Utica in early October. On that occasion Finney had planned his wedding for Tuesday, 5 October, and attended the synod in the evening. But on the occasion he is speaking of here, George W. Gale stated that Finney was visiting his father-in-law "for a short visit to recruit his health," and it was late September (G. W. Gale, *Autobiography {to 1834} of George Washington Gale {1789–1861}, Founder of Galesburg, Illinois, and Knox College* [New York: privately printed, 1964], p. 256). See also Synod of Albany, "Minutes, 1812–1828," p. 230, in Presbyterian Historical Society; *WR,* 12 October 1826, p. 83; *A Narrative of the Revival of Religion in the County of Oneida; particularly in the Bounds of the Presbytery of Oneida, in the year 1826* (Utica: Hastings and Tracy, 1826; reprint, Princeton: D. A. Borrenstein, 1827), p. 13; William E. Knox, *Semi-Centennial. A Sermon,*

teacher, had left Adams not long after I left it myself; and had removed **on**‹to›[15] a farm in the town of Western, Oneida County, where he was endeavoring to regain his health,[16] and was employed in teaching some young men who proposed to prepare themselves ¦to preach the Gospel.[17] I spent a few days at the Synod at Utica, and then set out on my return to my former field of labor in St. Lawrence County. We had not gone more than a dozen miles when we met **Brother** Gale in his carriage, on his way to Utica.[18] He leaped from his carriage and said: "God bless you, Brother Finney! ¦I was going down to the Synod to see you. You must go home with me; **and** I cannot be denied. I do not believe that I ever was converted; and I wrote the other day to Adams to know where a letter would reach you, as I wanted to open my mind to you on the subject.[″][19] He was so importunate that I consented; and we drove immediately to Western.[20]

MS 272

JHF 141

¦In[21] reflecting upon what I have said of the revivals of religion in Jefferson and St Lawrence Counties, I am not quite sure that I have laid as much stress as I intended upon the manifest agency of the Holy Spirit in those revivals. I

MS 273

Preached in the First Presbyterian Church, Rome, N.Y., September 29, 1850, upon its Fiftieth Anniversary (Rome, N.Y.: Sandford, 1851), p. 13; and MS 209.

[15]The letters *to* appear to have been added by Finney.

[16]Gale recorded that he had left Adams on 9 November 1824. Before settling in Western he left his family in Troy and traveled in the southern states for five months to recuperate, but still he was not well. The family moved to Western about 1 August 1825. Gale had been brought up on farms as a boy, and before he turned to the ministry he had contemplated becoming a farmer (*Autobiography*, pp. 221, 225–54).

[17]Elias Cornelius, reporting on the Oneida Institute after a visit in the summer of 1829, wrote:

> The Rev. Mr. Gale, the Principal, belongs to that numerous class of ministers who have made shipwreck of a sound constitution by too close an application to study, in early life. He became convinced, that the same cause still operates to the injury of many students, and that nothing but vigorous exercise can remedy the evil. With these views, he resolved upon making an experiment in a private manner, with a class of six young men, whom he was fitting for college. He agreed to board and instruct them free of expense provided they would labour for him in the field, three hours every day (*Quarterly Register and Journal of the American Education Society* [Boston] 2 [November 1829]: 65).

At the time of Finney's visit, however, this experiment was not yet in operation. In a historical sketch, also written in 1829, Gale remarked,

> that in the spring of 1826, after the late glorious work of God in this part of our country, or rather while it was in progress, there being a considerable number of young men of excellent spirit and promise of that revival, it was thought to be a favourable opportunity to commence the plan.

Gale was proud to acknowledge that it was his pioneering work that led to the Manual Labor Movement in America. See *Quarterly Register and Journal of the American Education Society* 2 (November 1829): 112; Gale, *Autobiography*, p. 277; and Herman R. Muelder, *Fighters for Freedom: The History of Anti-Slavery Activities of Men and Women Associated with Knox College* (New York: privately printed, 1964) p. 253.

[18]According to Gale, it was to Rome to visit friends, rather than to Utica, that he and his wife were traveling. Gale recalled that Finney said, "I heard at Rome that you were here, and I turned out of my course to see you" (*Autobiography*, pp. 254–55). Keith Hardman, however, has drawn attention to another anomaly: Gale refers to the Finneys as having a child with them. But their first child, Helen, was not born until 10 June 1828. So Gale could also have been mistaken about the occasion. See Keith J. Hardman, *Charles Grandison Finney, 1792–1875: Revivalist and Reformer* (Syracuse: Syracuse University Press, 1987), pp. 68 and 458 n. 21.

[19]The quotation mark is inserted in the manuscript in pencil.

[20]This ends the revision that replaced the first 140 pages of the first draft of the manuscript.

[21]Pages 273–78 were first numbered 141–46 and then renumbered 273–78 by Matson.

wish it to be distinctly understood in all that I shall say in my narrative of the revivals that I have witnessed, that I always in my own mind, and practically, laid the utmost stress upon this fact underlying, directing, and giving efficiency to the means, without which nothing would be accomplished. I have said, more than once, that *the spirit* of *prayer* that prevailed in those revivals was a very marked feature of them. It was common for young converts to be greatly exercised in prayer; and in some instances so much so that they were constrained to pray whole nights, and until their bodily strength was quite exhausted, for the conversion of souls around them. There was a great pressure of the Holy Spirit upon the minds of Christians; and they seemed to bear about with them the burden of immortal souls. They manifested the greatest solemnity of mind, and the greatest watchfulness in all their words

MS 274 and actions. It was very common to find Christians, |whenever they met in any place, instead of engaging in conversation, to fall on their knees **and engage** in prayer. Not only were prayer meetings greatly multiplied and fully attended, not only was there great solemnity in those meetings; but there was a mighty spirit of secret prayer. Christians prayed a great deal, many of them

JHF 142 spending many hours in private prayer. It was also the case that |two would take the promise, "If two of you shall agree on earth as touching anything that they shall ask, it shall be done for them of my Father which is in heaven,"[22] and **retire to** make some particular person a subject of prayer; and it was wonderful to what an extent they prevailed. Answers to prayer were so manifestly multiplied on every side, that no one could escape the conviction that God was daily and hourly answering prayer. If anything occurred that **was in danger of marring** the work, if there was any appearance of any root of bitterness springing up, or any tendency to fanaticism or disorder **in any respect**, Christians would take the alarm and **immediately** give themselves to

MS 275 prayer that God would direct and control all things; and **in many instances** |it was surprizing to see to what extent, and by what means, God would remove obstacles out of the way in answer to prayer.[23] In regard to my own experience, I will say that unless I had the Spirit of prayer I could do nothing. If even for a day or an hour I lost the Spirit of grace and supplication, I found myself unable to preach with power and efficiency, or to win souls by personal conversation. In this respect my experience **at that time** was what it has always been **since—I found myself having more or less power in preaching and in personal labor for souls just in proportion as I had the Spirit of prevailing prayer. I have found that unless I kept myself—or have been kept—in such relations to God as to have daily and hourly access to Him in prayer,[24] my efforts to win souls were abortive; but that when I could prevail with God in prayer, I could prevail with man in preaching, exhortation, and conversation.**

I have stated that my last field of labor in St Lawrence County was in

MS 276 **De Kalb, and that the revival there was powerful |for the scattered**

[22] Matthew 18:19.

[23] See, for example, p. 80 n. 28 (MS 147).

[24] The word "that" written here by Matson was crossed out in pencil before the whole section was crossed out by Fairchild in ink. This is the first of a number of alterations in pencil that appear to have been made by Matson.

population that then existed in that new region of country. For several weeks before I left De Kalb to go to the Synod **in Oneida County of which I have made mention**, I was very strongly exercised in prayer, and had an experience **then** that was somewhat new to me **at the time**. I found myself so much exercised, and so borne down with the weight of immortal souls that I was constrained to pray without ceasing. **I could not rest in the house, and was obliged to retire to the barn frequently through the day, where I could unburden my soul and pour my heart out to God in prayer. I had wonderful faith given to me at that time, and had** some experiences that alarmed me. **When alone I would wrestle and struggle, and my faith would rise till** I would say to God that He had made a promise to answer prayer, and I could not, and would not, be denied. **I would be so wrought up as to use such strong language to God in prayer,—**I felt so certain that He would hear me, and that faithfulness to His promises and to Himself rendered it impossible that He should not hear and answer, |that frequently I found myself saying to Him, "I hope thou dost not think that I can be denied. I come with thy faithful promises in my hand, and I cannot be denied." **At that time the Spirit of God made such an application of the promises to my mind, and so revealed their real meaning, as to lead me to understand better how to use them, and to what cases they were especially applicable, than I had ever understood before. I had been in the habit from my first conversion of having the Spirit in prayer lead me to such an appreciation of the promises, as I never should have gotten by any study of my own. I had very frequently had the promises so applied, had so applied and used them, as to find that they had a much wider application in their spirit than a mere critical examination of their letter would have warranted. I was led frequently to see that the New Testament writers quoted the promises of the Old Testament in such a way as to cover much more ground than the mere letter of the promises would have warranted. But this experience of |mine at De Kalb was extraordinary in this respect.** I cannot tell how absurd unbelief looked to me, |and how certain it was in my mind that God would answer prayer,—**and** those prayers that from day to day and from hour to hour I found myself offering in such agony and faith. I had no idea **in my mind** of the shape the answer would take, the locality in which the prayers would be answered, or the exact time of the answer. My impression was that the answer was near, even at the door; and I felt myself strengthened in the divine life, put on the harness for a mighty conflict with the powers of darkness, and expected soon to see a far more powerful outpouring of the Spirit of God in that new country where I had been laboring.

MS 277

MS 278

JHF 143

THE ONEIDA COUNTY REVIVALS, 1825–26

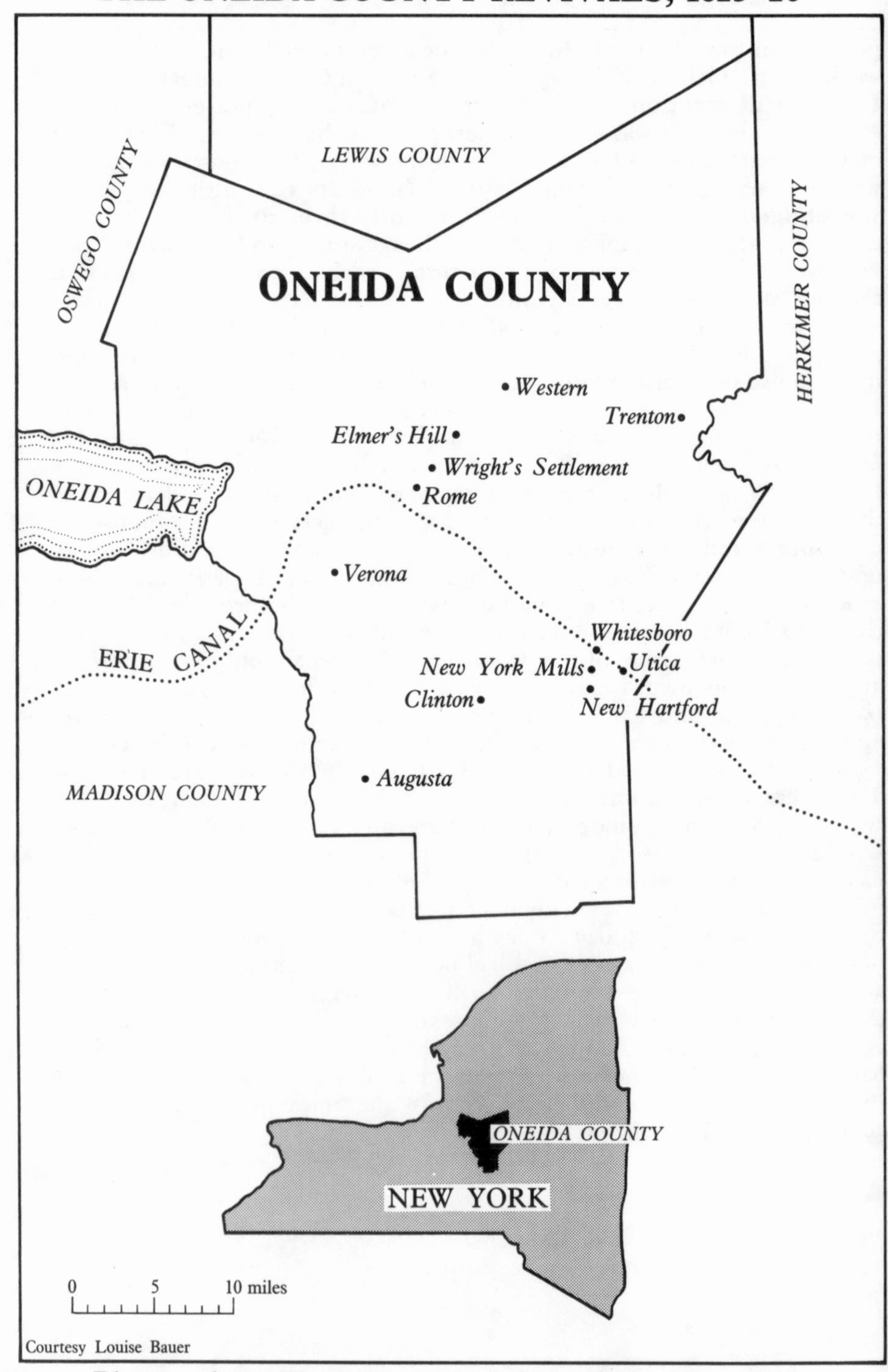

Places where Finney preached from September 1825 to May 1826.

CHAPTER XII

MS 278
JHF 144

‹*Revival at Western.*›

‹I[1] have spoken of my turning aside to Western, as I was returning from the Synod at Utica.[2] At this place commenced that series of revivals afterwards called the western revivals. So far as I know these revivals first attracted the notice & excited the opposition of **Mr. Nettleton[3] & Dr. Beecher›[4] ˡand raised the cry of "New Measures." Those of us who labored in those revivals have never been able to learn the true source of this opposition. That those brethren were grossly deceived by information that they received from some source, we were sure. We regarded them as good men, and true; but we knew that somebody was giving them most unreliable information. I shall not mention in this place the efforts that we made to acquaint ourselves with the authors of those reports, or letters, or whatever they may have been, by which those brethren were led to publicly oppose those revivals. But we failed to get at the source of this opposition.**[5] The churches in that region were mostly

MS 279

[1]This section of page 278 is in Finney's handwriting on a separate piece of paper pasted over the original sheet near the bottom. The section covered over reads: "I have related my turning aside to Western, Oneida County as I was returning from the Synod at Utica. Here at Western that series of revivals commenced which for many years were known as the 'Western revivals.' So far as I know the revivals in this county first. . . ." The sentence continues to the bottom of the page and was crossed out by Finney: "attracted the attention and excited the opposition of Dr Nettleton and Dr Beecher." Lewis Tappan pointed out to Finney that Nettleton was not a doctor. See Tappan to Finney, 2 June 1868, Finney Papers, microfilm, roll 5. Pages 278–307 were first numbered 146–75 and then renumbered 278–307 by Matson.

[2]See MS 271–72.

[3]Asahel Nettleton (1783–1844) was the most prominent of the early revivalists of the Second Great Awakening in New England. He was a graduate of Yale and was licensed as a Congregationalist preacher in 1811. He worked mainly in Connecticut with great success until 1822, when ill health curtailed his labors. As a strict Calvinist, he was opposed to the "New Haven Theology," and in 1834 he helped to found Hartford Theological Seminary. See Sherry P. May, "Asahel Nettleton: Nineteenth Century American Revivalist" (Ph.D. diss., Drew University, 1969); and *DAB*. See also, John F. Thornbury, *God Sent Revival: The Story of Asahel Nettleton and the Second Great Awakening* (Welwyn, Herts, and Grand Rapids: Evangelical Press, 1977).

[4]Lyman Beecher (1775–1863) was one of the leading clergymen in America. He was a graduate of Yale and a student of Timothy Dwight. Ordained as a Presbyterian, he had risen to prominence in the Congregational church in Litchfield, Connecticut, and was soon to move to Boston, where he led the Evangelical revival. In 1832 he again became a Presbyterian and went west to head up Lane Seminary and the fight to establish New School Presbyterianism. He was the father of a brilliant family, notably Henry Ward Beecher and Harriet Beecher Stowe. See *Autobiography, Correspondence, etc., of Lyman Beecher, D.D.*, ed. Charles Beecher, 2 vols. (New York: Harper, 1863, 1865); and *DAB*.

[5]See MS 413-21.

Presbyterian. There were in that county, however, three Congregational ministers who called themselves "The Oneida Association," who at the time published a pamphlet against those revivals.[6] Thus much we knew; but as the pamphlet made no public impression that we could learn, no notice, so far as I MS 280 **know**, was ever taken of it **in public**.[7] |We thought it likely that that association had much to do with the opposition that was raised in the east. The leader **of them**, Rev. William R Weeks,[8] as was well known, **was a man that** embraced and propagated the peculiar doctrines of Dr Emmons, and insisted very much upon what he called "The divine efficiency scheme."[9] His peculiar views on this subject **we could see** naturally led him to be suspicious

[6]The pamphlet Finney refers to was the *Pastoral Letter of the Ministers of the Oneida Association, to the Churches Under Their Care, on the Subject of Revivals of Religion* (Utica: Ariel Works, 1827). The ministers concerned in its production were John D. Pierce (spelled "Peirce" on p. 2), Ralph Robinson, and William R. Weeks.

The pamphlet drew attention to "a few of those things which appear to us to be evils in themselves, or more or less connected with danger, at the present time." They were set out under the following headings: 1. Indifference on the subject of Revivals; 2. Neglect to discriminate between true religion and false; 3. Insensibility to danger; 4. Condemning in the gross, or approving in the gross; 5. Indifference to instruction; 6. Calling men hard names; 7. Making too much of any favourable appearances; 8. Ostentation and noise; 9. Going to particular places to obtain the Spirit, or to be converted; 10. Not guarding against false conversions; 11. The hasty acknowledgment of persons as converted; 12. Injudicious treatment of young converts; 13. Suffering the feelings to control the judgment; 14. Giving heed to impulses, impressions, or supposed revelations; 15. Allowing any body and everybody to speak and pray in promiscuous meetings, as they feel disposed; 16. Wrong means of exciting fear; 17. Trying to make people angry; 18. Talking much about opposition; 19. The affectation of familiarity with God in prayer; 20. Language of profaneness; 21. Disregard of the distinctions of age or station; 22. Censuring, as unconverted, or as cold, stupid, and dead, those who are in good standing in the visible church; 23. Praying for persons by name in an abusive manner; 24. Imprecations in prayer; 25. Denouncing as enemies to revivals those who do not approve of everything that is done; 26. Female prayer and exhortation; 27. Loud groaning, speaking out, or falling down, in time of publick or social worship; 28. Taking the success of any measure, as an evidence that those measures are right, and approved of God; 29. Disorderly and disorganizing measures.

[7]In fact, the *Pastoral Letter* may have had considerable influence. P. H. Fowler says it "voyaged with them [slanderous reports] to almost every door in the land" (*Historical Sketch of Presbyterianism Within the Bounds of the Synod of Central New York* [Utica: Curtiss and Childs, 1877], p. 273). And James Richards wrote to Asahel Nettleton, "Mr. Williston's Sermon, and the pastoral letter from Oneida Association, have done much to correct the prevailing errors, and are destined to do still more" (letter dated 23 June 1827, in Gardiner Spring, *Personal Reminiscences*, vol. 1 [New York: Scribner, 1866], p. 230; and Bennet Tyler, *Memoir of the Life and Character of Rev. Asahel Nettleton, D.D.*, 2d ed. [Hartford, Conn.: Robins and Smith, 1845], pp. 267–68).

The Oneida Association letter was printed in full in *The Christian Advocate* (Philadelphia), June and July 1827; and in *The Hopkinsian Magazine* (Providence, R.I.) 2 (June–August 1827). See also *WR*, 19 June 1827, p. 99.

[8]William Raymond Weeks (1783–1848) was stated supply at Paris Hill Congregational Church. He was a graduate of Princeton and Andover and held various part-time pastorates and school-teaching appointments until he was called to Paris Hill in 1820. In 1832, after a year in Utica, he moved to Newark, New Jersey, where he continued school teaching and pastoral work until 1846, when his health failed. See W. B. Sprague, *Annals of the American Pulpit*, vol. 4 (New York: R. Carter and Bro., 1859), pp. 173–76.

[9]Nathanael Emmons (1745–1840), the Congregational minister of Franklin, Massachusetts, for over fifty years, was one of the most important of the teachers of the New England theology, evolving his system from that of Samuel Hopkins. But the central place he gave to the sole causality of God in all exercises of the mind, both holy and sinful, virtually took away any freedom and responsibility from man. See Frank H. Foster, *A Genetic History of the New England Theology* (Chicago: University of Chicago Press, 1907), pp. 343–45; and *DAB*.

of whatever was not connected with those **peculiar** views in preaching and in the means that were used to promote a revival. He seemed to have little or no confidence in any conversions that did not bring men to embrace his **peculiar** views of divine efficiency and divine sovereignty; and as those of us who labored in those revivals had no sympathy with his **peculiar** views in that respect, it was very natural for him to have but little confidence in the genuineness of those revivals. But ˡwe never supposed that the whole of the opposition **of Brother Nettleton and Dr Beecher** could have originated in representations made by any of the members of that association.[10] JHF 145

ˡNo public replies were made to the letters **of Dr Beecher** that found their way into the public prints, nor to anything that was published in opposition to the revivals **at the time.** Those of us who were engaged in them had our hands too full, and our hearts too full, to turn aside to reply to letters, or reports, or publications that so manifestly misrepresented the character of the work. The fact that no answers were made at the time, left the public abroad and without the range of those revivals, and where the facts were not known, to misapprehend their character. So much misapprehension came to exist that it had been common for good men in referring to those revivals to assume, that although they were upon the whole revivals of religion; yet that they were so conducted that great disorders were manifest in them, and that there was much to deplore in their results.[11] MS 281

[10] Some of the earliest opposition came from the Universalists. They attacked Finney and his revivals and held up to ridicule the fanatical goings on, in reports and stories published in their papers. A supporter of the revival movement from Buffalo saw Universalism as the chief threat:

> I doubt not you have heard that there is a Universalist paper printed in this village. It is called "*Gospel Advocate*," (what perversion of words!). This is the fountain whence all the little streams, that are poisoning our very existence, flow,—the common centre around which all the advocates of error revolve, and the medium through which they promulgate their ribald jests, and low scoffs at religion and its followers.

He goes on to point out how the magazine's circulation had grown in three years to 1,700 copies per week:

> the print is circulated far and wide, and is fast poisoning public opinion, and turning men from righteousness to the more natural courses of vice (letter from "Timothy," dated Buffalo, 17 January 1826, in *WR,* 31 January 1826, p. 20).

See the *Gospel Advocate* (Buffalo), 13 January 1826, pp. 3–5; 3 March 1826, p. 64; and 2 June 1826, p. 165. See also the *Evangelical Restorationist* (Troy, N.Y.) 1 (December 1825): 68; *The Universalist* (Philadelphia), 2 January 1826, pp. 308–9; and the *Gospel Herald* (New York), 20 May 1826, p. 7.

[11] Elizabeth Thomson, daughter of Rev. Israel Brainerd of Verona, in reminiscing about Finney and these early revivals, wrote:

> At first all stood amazed and glorified God. At length persons of ill-balanced minds and scanty knowledge of Bible truth, began to glorify Mr. Finney. To them it was plain *he* had caused the revival, he had converted souls; and as the work progressed and extended, it was believed it would never cease. What man had done, man could do; therefore those staid pastors who had not wrought such revivals, must be in fault. The Church was suffering from the delinquency of its shepherds. These must be prayed for and labored with.
>
> Soon little conclaves of brethren and sisters were held for the purpose of praying for the conversion of their pastors. Persons whom they had baptised in infancy, and received into the Church in maturer years, wrote anonymous letters to their pastors, asking them to create and continue a revival; or if not, to resign, and not to stand in the way of souls. Some, with more frankness, if not with more grace, went to their pastors personally, and reproached them that the former revivals had ever ceased. Conservative minds saw and deprecated the injustice of such a construction of God's dealings

Left: Asahel Nettleton. The foremost evangelist of the earlier phase of the Second Great Awakening in New England. He was highly critical of Finney and his New Measures. In Bennet Tyler, *Memoir of the Life and Character of Asahel Nettleton, D.D.* (Hartford, Conn.: Robins and Smith, 1844), frontispiece. Courtesy The British Library.

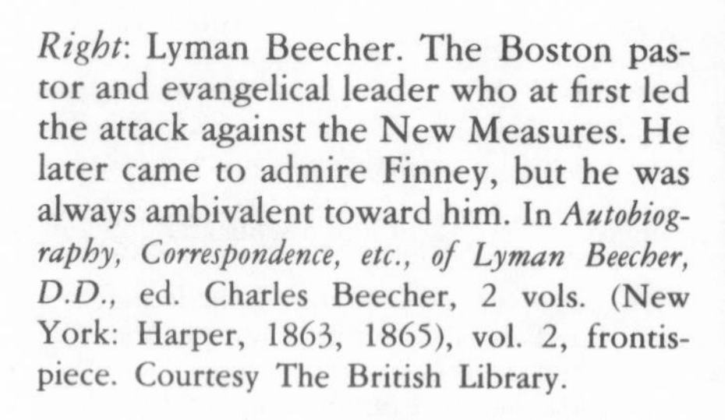

Right: Lyman Beecher. The Boston pastor and evangelical leader who at first led the attack against the New Measures. He later came to admire Finney, but he was always ambivalent toward him. In *Autobiography, Correspondence, etc., of Lyman Beecher, D.D.*, ed. Charles Beecher, 2 vols. (New York: Harper, 1863, 1865), vol. 2, frontispiece. Courtesy The British Library.

Now all this is an entire mistake. I shall relate as fairly as I can the characteristics of those revivals, the measures that were used in promoting them, and disclose to **my** best ability[12] ¦their real character and results; understanding well, as I do, that there are multitudes of living witnesses who can attest the truth of what I say, or if in anything I am mistaken can correct me. MS 282

And now I will turn to Western, where these revivals **first** commenced in Oneida County.[13] I have said that **Brother** Gale had **moved on‹to›**[14] a farm in Western; and was employing some young men in helping to cultivate the farm, and was engaged in teaching them, and endeavoring to regain his health.[15] I went directly to his house, and for several weeks was his guest. We arrived there **on** Thursday, I think,[16] and **on** that afternoon there was a stated prayer meeting in the school house near the church. They had no settled minister, and **Brother** Gale was unable to preach,—indeed, he did not go there to preach, but simply for his health. I be¦lieve they **never** had a minister **for more than** a part of the time; and for sometime previous to my going there I think they had had no stated preaching in the Presbyterian church **at all**. There were three elders in the **Presbyterian** church, ¦and a few members; but the church was very small, and religion was at low water mark. There seemed to be no life, or courage, or enterprize on the part of Christians, and nothing was doing to secure the conversion of sinners or the sanctification of the church.[17] In the afternoon **Brother** Gale invited me to go to the prayer JHF 146 MS 283

with his people. They revolted at the ingratitude thus shown to honored and beloved and faithful men. Words and prayers waxed warm. Brother rose in spirit against brother, and not seldom, children against parents.

At first the difference of opinion was not so much in relation to doctrine, though some new views of truth had been introduced. It was more in respect to measures, modes of conducting meetings, of the wisest method of addressing the unconverted, and especially the tone and manner of prayer. The more conservative referred to scriptural example as enjoining reverence and humility in devotion. Others, believing that what they stigmatized as formal prayers were neither heard nor answered, cited the apparent effect of loud, emotional, and familiar addresses to the ear of the Most High, as indicative of divine approval. Not of Mr. Finney, but of some of his followers, could these loud prayers be cited.

Inevitably a spirit of antagonism spread, from which arose opposing factions, the advance guard of the hosts that ultimately named themselves "Old" and "New School," and from thence, strengthened by other forces, came the division of the American Presbyterian Church in 1837. . . . Speaking of this unhappy event in later times, Dr. Lyman Beecher said "The Oneida revivals did it" (Mrs. G. W. Thomson, "Early Labors of President Finney," *NYE,* 9 December 1875, p. 2).

[12]The order of the words here was not changed in the manuscript but reads, "and disclose, to the best of my ability," in the published version.

[13]Some sources indicate that the revival may have started first at Vernon Centre in August 1825. See, for example, *A Narrative of the Revival of Religion in the County of Oneida; particularly in the Bounds of the Presbytery of Oneida, in the year 1826* (Utica: Hastings and Tracy, 1826; reprint, Princeton: D. A. Borrenstein, 1827), p. 9; and *BR,* 6 January 1826, p. 2.

[14]The letters *to* appear to have been added by Finney.

[15]See MS 271.

[16]In his report to the Oneida Presbytery the next year, Gale wrote: "On the last of September, 1825, the Rev. Charles G. Finney arrived in town" (Oneida Presbytery *Narrative*, p. 13). The last Thursday in September was the 29th.

[17]*The Western Recorder* reported:

This town has, till lately been a perfect moral desert. Its inhabitants had been a prey to sectarian dissensions and to almost every species of error and heresy. Universalism had

meeting, and I went. They asked me to take the lead of the meeting; but I declined, expecting **only** to be there[18] for that afternoon, and preferring to hear them pray and talk than to take part in the meeting myself. The meeting was opened by one of the elders reading a chapter in the Bible; then a hymn, which they sung. After this he made a long prayer, or perhaps I should say an exhortation, or gave a narrative—I hardly know what to call it. He told the Lord how many years they had been holding that prayer-meeting weekly, and that no answer had been given to their prayers. He made such statements and confessions as greatly shocked[19] me. After he had done another elder took up the same **thing**. He read a hymn, and after singing engaged in a long prayer, MS 284 in which he ˡwent over very nearly the same ground, making such **additions and** statements as the first one had omitted. Then followed the third elder in the same strain. By this time I could say with Paul that my spirit was stirred within me.[20] They had got through and were about to dismiss the meeting. But one of the elders asked me if I would not make a remark before they dismissed.[21] I arose and took their statements and confessions for a text; and it seemed to me at the time **as if** God inspired me to give them a terrible searching. When I arose I had no idea what I should say; but the Spirit of God came upon me **with such power, that** I took up their prayers, and JHF 147 statements, and confessions, and dissected them. I ˡshowed them up, and asked if it had been understood that that prayer meeting was a mock prayer meeting—whether they had come together professedly to mock God by implying that all the blame of what had been passing all this time was to be ascribed to His sovereignty. At first I observed that they all looked angry. Some of them afterwards said that they were on the point of getting up and MS 285 ˡgoing out. But I followed them up on the track of their prayers and confessions until the elder, who was the principal man among them, and

> flourished there; and a regular clergyman of any denomination, we believe, has never been settled among them (13 December 1825, p. 196).

G. W. Gale drew a similar picture of the low state of religion and the infidelity among the people. The Presbyterian church had been formed by a missionary ten years before:

> The Presbyterian house of worship was respectable for size and appearance, but needed repairing. The membership was not numerous, and the church was without a pastor. I was unable to preach but I met with them on the Sabbath, had a sermon read, prayed with them, and visited the members, aided also in the discipline of some who had walked disorderly. In this was I enabled to be of some service to the cause (*Autobiography {to 1834} of George Washington Gale {1789–1861}, Founder of Galesburg, Illinois, and Knox College* [New York: privately printed, 1964], p. 253).

[18] The order of the words was not changed in the manuscript, but in the published version it reads, "expecting to be there only."

[19] This word is spelled "schocked" in the manuscript, and the first *c* is crossed out in pencil. This may have been done by Matson.

[20] Acts 17:16 reads, "Now while Paul waited for them at Athens, his spirit was stirred in him, when he saw the city wholly given to idolatry."

[21] Thomas C. Hartshorn recollected, "A short distance up the valley were the homes of the Braytons . . . where this memorable revival was inaugurated at a Wednesday evening prayer-meeting, at which Father Brayton invited young Finney to 'make a few remarks' " (*NYE,* 19 November 1885, p. 6).

George Brayton, Sr., was a wealthy businessman and leading citizen in Western and was one of the deacons of the church. He was at one time a member of the state senate. He died in 1837 at age sixty-five. See S. W. Durant, *A History of Oneida County, New York* (Philadelphia: Everts and Faris, 1878), p. 595; and *NYE,* 15 April 1837, p. 64.

opened the meeting, bursting into tears exclaimed, "Brother Finney, it is all true!" He fell upon his knees and wept aloud. This was the signal for a general breaking down. Every man and woman present went down upon their knees. There were probably not more than a dozen present; but they were the leading influences in the church. They all wept, and confessed, and broke their hearts before God. This scene continued, I presume, for an hour; and a more thorough breaking down and confession I have seldom ever witnessed. As soon as they recovered themselves enough they besought me to remain and preach to them on the Sabbath. I regarded it as the voice of the Lord, and consented to do so. This was on Thursday at night. On Friday my mind was greatly exercised. I went off frequently[22] into the church to engage in secret prayer, and |had a mighty hold upon God. The news was circulated, and on (MS 286) Sabbath I had the church full of hearers. I preached all day, and God came down with great power upon the people. It was manifest to everybody that the work of grace had begun. I made appointments to preach in different parts of the town in school houses, and at the center, during the week; and the work increased from day to day. In the meantime my own mind was much exercised in prayer; and I found that the spirit of prayer was prevailing, especially among the female members of the church. Mrs. Brayton[23] and Mrs. Harris,[24] the wives of two of the elders |of the church, I found almost (JHF 148) immediately were[25] greatly exercised in prayer. Each of them had families of unconverted children; and they laid hold in prayer with an earnestness that to me gave promise that their families must be converted. Mrs. Harris, however, was a woman of very feeble health, and had not ventured out much to any meeting for a long time. However, as the day was pleasant, she was out at the prayer-|meeting to which I have alluded, and seemed to catch the (MS 287) inspiration of that meeting, and took it home with her.

It was on the next week, I think, that I called in at Mr. Harris', and found him pale and agitated. He said to me, "Brother Finney, I think my wife will die. She is so exercised in her mind that she cannot rest day or[26] night, but is given up entirely to prayer." "She has been all the morning," said he, "in her room groaning and struggling in prayer; and I am afraid it will entirely overcome her strength." Hearing my voice in the sitting room she came out from her bedroom, and upon her face was a most unearthly, heavenly glow. Her countenance was lighted up with a hope and a joy that were plainly from heaven. She exclaimed, "Brother Finney, the Lord has come! This work will spread over all this region! A cloud of mercy overhangs us all; and we shall see such a work of grace as we have never yet seen." Her husband looked

[22] Matson inserted the word "frequently" in black ink. It appears to be the first of a number of alterations that he made in black ink.

[23] Sarah Brayton was the wife of George Brayton, Sr. "She was long an ornament to the church of God." She died in 1841 in her sixty-fourth year. See *NYE*, 29 May 1841, p. 87; and Durant, *History of Oneida County*, p. 595.

[24] She was the wife of John Harris, who was an "elder in the Presbyterian church from 1826." See Durant, *History of Oneida County*, p. 595.

[25] The order of the words was not changed in the manuscript, but the published version reads, "were, almost immediately."

[26] Matson had written down "nor," but the *n* has been crossed out in pencil. This may have been done by Matson.

MS 288 surprized, confounded, and knew not what to say. It was new to |him, but not to me. I had **seen** such scenes before; and believed that prayer had prevailed, nay, I felt sure of it in my own soul. The work went on, spread, and prevailed, until it began to exhibit unmistakable indications of the direction in which the Spirit of God was leading from that place. **From that place to** Rome was **about** nine miles, I believe. About half way was a small village called Elmer's Hill. There was a large school house where I held a weekly lecture; and it JHF 149 soon became manifest that the work was spreading in the |direction of Rome and Utica. There was a settlement north east of Rome, about three miles, called Wright's settlement.[27] Large numbers of persons came down to attend the meetings at Elmer's Hill from Rome and from Wright's settlement; and the work soon began to **manifest itself as** taking effect among them.[28]

But I must relate a few of the incidents that occurred in the revival at Western. Mrs. **Brayton, the wife of one of the elders,** to whom I have MS 289 already alluded, had a large family of unconverted children. One of |the sons was, I believe, a professor of religion, and lived at Utica; the rest of the family were at home.[29] They were a very amiable family; and the eldest daughter especially had been manifestly regarded by the family as almost perfect. I went in several times to converse with her; but I found that the family were so tender of her feelings that I could not strip away her self-righteousness; **for** she had evidently been made to believe that she was almost, if not quite, a Christian. Her life had been so irreproachable that it was very difficult to convict her of sin. The second daughter was also a very amiable girl; but she did not ‹**so**›[30] regard herself as to be compared with the eldest in respect to amiability and **morality** of character. One day when I was talking with **Sarah**, the eldest, and trying to make her see herself as a great sinner notwithstanding her morality, **Cynthia**, the second daughter, said to me, "Mr. Finney I think that you are too hard upon **Sarah**. If you should talk so to *me*, I should MS 290 feel that I deserved it; but I don't think that *she* does." |After being defeated several times in my attempts to secure the conviction and conversion of **Sarah**, I made up my mind to bide my time, and improve some opportunity when I should find her away from home, or alone. It was not long before **I had an** opportunity **to find her away from home**. I entered into

[27]Wright's Settlement was named after Judge Benjamin Wright's family. They had settled there about 1789. See Franklin B. Hough, *A History of Jefferson County in the State of New York* (Albany: Munsell, 1854), p. 453.

[28]*The Western Recorder* reported on the revival in Western:

> The excitement under the labours of Rev. Mr. Finney, has become great and extensive; and a general aspect of seriousness pervades the whole town. The hopeful subjects of the work, we understand are becoming numerous; and in one instance five are mentioned as belonging to a single family. The work is also extending to the north part of Rome, as far as Wright's Settlement and great hopes are still entertained respecting it (13 December 1825, p. 196).

[29]The Braytons had nine children. The two eldest, Milton and Hervey, were twins. They had been converted under the Methodists (see Gale, *Autobiography*, p. 255). Milton lived in Utica and was a merchant in partnership with Truman Parmelee. He subsequently returned to Western, where he became an elder in the church. He was active in various religious enterprises and died in Westernville in 1880 at age seventy-nine. He corresponded with Finney for many years. See Moses Bagg, *Pioneers of Utica* (Utica: Curtiss and Childs, 1877), p. 612; *NYE,* 5 May 1881, p. 5; and letters of Milton Brayton to Finney in the Finney Papers.

[30]Finney added the word "so."

conversation with her, and by God's help stripped the covering from her heart, and she was brought under powerful conviction for sin. The ꞋSpirit pursued her with mighty power. The family were surprized and greatly distressed for **Sarah**; but God pushed the question home till, after a struggle of a few days she broke thoroughly down, and came out into the kingdom as beautiful a convert as perhaps I have ever seen.[31] Her convictions were so thorough that when she came out she was strong in faith, clear in her apprehension of duty and of truth, and immediately became a host in her power for good among her friends and acquaintances.[32]

JHF 150

In the meantime **Cynthia**, the second daughter, became Ꞌvery much alarmed about herself, and very anxious for the salvation of her own soul. The mother, **Mrs. Brayton,** seemed to be in real travail of soul day and night. I called in to see the family almost daily, and sometimes two or three times a day. One of the children after another was converted; and we were expecting every day to see **Cynthia** come out a bright convert. But for some reason she lingered. It was plain the Spirit was resisted; and one day I called to see her and found her in the sitting room alone. I asked her how she was getting on, and she replied, "Mr Finney, I am losing my conviction. I do not feel nearly as much concerned about myself as I have done." Just at this moment a door was opened and Mrs. **Brayton** came into the room; and I told her what **Cynthia** had **just** said. It shocked her so that she groaned aloud, and fell prostrate on the floor. She was unable to rise, and struggled and groaned out her prayers in a manner that immediately Ꞌindicated to me that **Cynthia** must be converted. She was unable to say much in words, but her groans and tears witnessed the extreme agony of her mind. As soon as this scene had occurred the Spirit of God manifestly came upon **Cynthia** afresh. She ‹fell› upon her knees,[33] and before she arose she broke down; and became to all appearance as thorough a convert as **Sarah** was.[34] The **Brayton** children, sons and daughters, were all converted at that time, I believe, except the youngest, a little child, **who was afterwards converted.** ‹One of the sons has preached the gospel for many years.›[35]

MS 291

MS 292

[31] In another account of the girl's conversion Finney said that when she saw that she was selfish, she exclaimed: "I have sown to the winds and I must reap the whirlwind. My whole heart is selfish. I see that I might as well make no efforts for salvation as to make selfish ones, and that truly I have but one right and hopeful way, and that is, to renounce my selfishness at once and forever" (*OE,* 4 July 1849, p. 107).

[32] Sarah Brayton became the wife of Rev. George S. Boardman of Watertown, New York. She died in 1849 at the age of forty-five. See *NYE,* 2 August 1849, p. 123.

[33] Matson wrote down "She also groaned upon her knees" and changed it in black ink to "She also threw herself upon her knees." Finney crossed out "also threw herself" and inserted the word "fell."

[34] In 1834 Cynthia Brayton became the first wife of John B. Jervis, the canal and railroad engineer. She died in Western in 1839, a devoted Christian. See *NYE,* 25 May 1839, p. 83; and *DAB.*

[35] This sentence was added by Finney. It was reported that "Mr. George Brayton, and his sons, Henry, George, Milton, and Isaac" were converted. The Brayton family became prominent in Western and were staunch supporters of the Presbyterian church. See *The Circular* (Oneida, N.Y.), 15 November 1869, p. 274; Gale, *Autobiography,* pp. 255–56; Durant, *History of Oneida County,* pp. 595–96; and correspondence from the family in the Finney Papers.

Isaac Brayton, born 1812, the next to the youngest child, was minister of the First Presbyterian Church in Watertown, New York, from 1837 to 1864. See Alfred Nevin, ed., *Encyclopaedia of the*

JHF 151 |Among other incidents I recollect that ‹of›[36] a young lady in a distant part of the town ‹who›[37] came to the meeting at the center almost every day; and I had conversed with her several times and found her deeply convicted, and indeed almost in despair. I was expecting to hear from day to day that she had been converted; but she remained stationary, or rather despair increased upon her day after day. This led me to suspect that something was wrong MS 293 at-home. I asked her if her parents were |Christians. She said they were members of the church. I asked her if they attended meetings. She said, "Yes, on the Sabbath." "Do not your parents attend meetings at other times?" "No," was the reply. "Do you have family prayers at home?" "No Sir," she said. "We used to have; but we have not had family prayers for a long time." This revealed to me the stumbling block at once. I inquired when I could probably find her father and mother at-home. She said almost any time, as they were seldom away from home. Feeling that it was infinitely dangerous to leave this case as it was, I went the next morning to see the family. The young lady was, I think, an only child; at any rate she was the only child at home. I found ‹her›[38] bowed down, dejected, and sunken in despair. I said to the mother, "The Spirit of the Lord is striving with your daughter." "Yes," she said, "she didn't know but he was."[39] I asked her if she was praying for her. MS 294 She gave me an answer that led me to understand |that she did not know what it was to pray for her. I inquired for her husband. She said that he was in the field at work. I asked her to call him in. He came, and as he came in I said to him, "Do you see the state that your daughter is in?" He replied that he thought she felt very bad. "And are you awake, and engaged in prayer for her?" His answer revealed the fact that if he was ever converted he was a miserable backslider, and had no hold upon God whatever. "And," said I, JHF 152 "you do not have family prayers." "No Sir.["] "Now," said I, "I |have seen your daughter day after day bowed down with conviction, and I have learned that the difficulty is here at-home. You have shut up the kingdom of heaven against your daughter. You neither enter yourself, nor will you suffer her to enter. Your unbelief and worldly mindedness prevent the conversion of your daughter, and will ruin your own soul. Now you must repent. I do not intend to leave this house until you and your wife repent, and get out of the way of MS 295 your daughter. |You must establish family prayer, and build up the altar that has fallen down. Now my dear Sir, will you get down here on your knees, you and your wife, and engage in prayer? And will you promise that from this time you will do your duty, set up your family altar, and return to God?" I was so earnest with them that they both began to weep. My faith was so strong that I did not trifle when I told them that I would not leave the house until

Presbyterian Church in the United States of America (Philadelphia: Presbyterian Encyclopaedia Publishing Co., 1884), p. 94.

An obituary of George Brayton, Sr., states: "Few men have done so little evil and so much good. . . . His numerous family, all of which have professed faith in Christ, his neighbors, the poor and the church, rise up and call him blessed" (*NYE,* 15 April 1837, p. 64).

[36]Finney added the word "of."

[37]Finney added the word "who."

[38]Finney crossed out the words "the young lady" and inserted "her."

[39]This was not changed by Fairchild in the manuscript, but in the published edition it reads, "I don't know but he is."

they would repent, and establish their family altar. I felt that the work must be done, and done *then*. I cast myself down upon my knees and began to pray; and they knelt down and wept sorely. I confessed for them as well as I could, and tried to lead them to God, and to prevail with God in their behalf. It was a moving scene. They both broke down their hearts, and[40] confessed their sins; and before we rose from our knees the daughter got into liberty, and was manifestly converted. She arose rejoicing in Christ. Many answers to prayer, and many scenes of great interest **transpired** in this revival.

|There was one passage of my own experience that, for the honor of God, I must not omit to relate in this connection. I had preached and prayed almost continually during the time that I had been at Mr. Gale's. As I was accustomed to use my voice in prayer, **and pray aloud,** for convenience' sake, that I might not be heard, I had spread a buffalo **skin**[41] on the hay-loft; where I used to spend much of my time when not abroad visiting, or engaged in preaching, in secret prayer to God. **Brother** Gale had admonished me several times that if I |did not take care I would go beyond my strength and break down. But the Spirit of prayer was upon me, and I would not resist him; and gave him scope, and let out my strength freely in pouring my soul out to God **in prayer**. It was November, and the weather was becoming cold. **Brother** Gale and I had been out visiting inquirers with his horse and buggy. We came home and went into the barn and put out the horse. **After the horse was unharnessed,** instead of going |into the house I crept up into the hay loft to pour out my burdened soul to God in prayer. I prayed until my burden left me. I was so far exhausted that I fell down **upon the buffalo skin** and lost myself in sleep. **When my mind was relieved and the burden gone,** I must have fallen **to** sleep almost instantly, ‹I judge›[42] from the fact that I had no recollection of any time elapsing **at all** after the struggle in my soul was over. **Brother Gale went into the house; and I remained in the barn so long that he became alarmed.** The first I knew **he** came climbing up into the hay loft, and said, "Brother Finney, are you *dead*?" I awoke, and at first could give no account **of** why I was there asleep, and could form no idea **of** how long I had been there. But this I knew, that my mind was calm and my faith unwavering. The work would go on, of that I felt assured.

MS 296 · JHF 153 · MS 297

|I have already said that I was ordained to the ministry by a presbytery. This was years before the division of the Presbyterian church into what is known as the Old and New School Assemblies.[43] The **Edwardean** doctrine[44] of **Moral** and **Natural**[45] ability and inability was held by the Presbyterian church almost universally in the region where I commenced my ministry. ‹I

MS 298

[40]Matson inserted the word "and" in pencil.

[41]This was not changed in the manuscript by Fairchild, but in the published version it reads, "robe."

[42]The words "I judge" were added by Finney.

[43]See MS 140. The division in the Presbyterian church took place in 1837.

[44]That taught by Jonathan Edwards (1703–1758), of Northampton, Massachusetts. He was a renowned theologian and philosopher and was briefly, at the end of his life, president of the College of New Jersey, now Princeton University. See *DAB*.

[45]The words "Moral and Natural" were unchanged in the manuscript, but appear as "natural and moral" in the published edition.

must here repeat also that Mr.› Gale,[46] who, by direction of the presbytery, had attended somewhat to my theological studies,[47] held firmly to the doctrine of the sinner's inability to obey God; and the subject as he presented it in his preaching—as was the case with most of the Presbyterian ministers of that day—left the impression upon the people that they must wait God's time. If they were elect, in due time the Spirit would convert them; if they were non-elect, nothing that they would do for themselves, or that anybody JHF 154 else would do for them, would ever ‹savingly› benefit them.[48] |They held the doctrine that moral depravity was constitutional, and belonged to the very nature; that the will, though free to do evil, was utterly impotent to all good; MS 299 |that the work of the Holy Spirit in changing the heart was a physical operation on the substance or essence of the soul; that the sinner was passive in regeneration till the Holy Spirit had implanted a new principle in his nature, and that all efforts on his part were utterly unavailing; that properly speaking there were no *means* of *regeneration*, this being a physical re-creation of the soul by the direct agency of the Holy Ghost; that the atonement was limited to the elect, and that for the non-elect to be saved was an utter impossibility. In my studies and controversies with ‹Mr› Gale I had maintained the opposite of this. I assumed that moral depravity was,[49] and must be, a voluntary attitude of the mind; that it did and must consist in the committal of the will to the gratification of the ‹desire, or as the bible expresses it, of the lusts of the flesh,›[50] as opposed to that which the law of God requires. In consistency with this I maintained that the influence of the Spirit of God upon the soul of man was *moral*, that is *persuasive*; that Christ represented him as a teacher; that his work was to convict and convert the sinner by ‹Divine teaching &›[51] moral persuasion. I held also that there were MS 300 |*means* of ‹regeneration›,[52] and that the truths of the Bible were in their nature calculated to lead the sinner to abandon his wickedness and turn to God. I held also that there must be an *adaptation of means to the end to be secured*: that is, that the intelligence must be enlightened the unreasonableness of moral depravity must be set before the sinner, and its wickedness and ill-desert clearly revealed to him; that when this was done the mission of Christ could be understood by him, **and could be strongly presented** that taking this course with the sinner had a *tendency* to convert him to Christ; and that JHF 155 when this was faithfully and prayerfully done, we had a right to |expect the Holy Spirit to co-operate with us.[53]

[46] Matson started this sentence with "Brother Gale," but Finney crossed out the word "Brother" and wrote in "I must here repeat also that Mr."

[47] The phrase "was from Princeton, and of course" after this was crossed out by Finney.

[48] Matson had written down, "would ever benefit them at all," but Finney crossed out "at all" and inserted the word "savingly."

[49] The past tense of the verb here and in several other places in this section was not altered in the manuscript but was changed to the present tense in the published version.

[50] Finney added this phrase in place of the word "sensibility."

[51] Finney inserted "a Divine teaching & persuasion" but crossed out again the words "a" and "persuasion."

[52] Finney crossed out the word "conversion" and wrote in "regeneration."

[53] The words "giving effect to our feeble effort" appear after this in the published version but are not in the manuscript.

Furthermore, I held that the Holy Spirit operates in the preacher clearly revealing these truths in their proper order to him, and enabling him to set them before the people in such proportion and in such order as was calculated to convert them. I understood then, as I do now, the charge and promise which Christ gave to the apostles and to the church, to be applicable in the present day: "Go and disciple |all nations, baptizing them in the name of the Father, and of the Son, and of the Holy Ghost; and lo I am with you alway, even unto the end of the world."[54] MS 301

This I regarded as a charge committed to *me*, to *all ministers*, and to *the church*; with the express *promise* that when we go forth to this work with a single eye, and with a prayerful spirit, Christ will be with us by his Spirit, giving efficiency to our efforts to save souls. It appeared to me then, as it ever has since, that the great failure of the ministry and of the church in promoting religion consisted, in great measure, in the want of a suitable adaptation of means to that end. I had sat under ‹Mr.› Gale's preaching for years, and could never see any adaptation in his preaching to convert anybody. It did not appear to me as if that could have been his *design*. I found the same was true of all the sermons that I heard anywhere. I had on one occasion spoken to ‹Mr› Gale on this subject, and said to him that of all the causes that were ever plead the cause of religion, I thought, had the fewest able advocates; and |that if advocates at the bar should pursue the same course in pleading the cause of their clients that ministers do in pleading the cause of Christ with sinners, they would not gain a single case. MS 302

But at that time ‹Mr› Gale could not see it; for what connection was there between means and end upon his view of what ‹regeneration›[55] consists in, and the manner in which the Holy Spirit change‹s› the ‹heart›?[56]

As an illustration, soon after I began to preach, in the |midst of a powerful revival, a young man from the theological Seminary at Princeton, came into the place. The former pastor of the church where I was laboring, an elderly gentleman, lived there, and had a great curiosity to hear this young man preach. The church had no pastor at the time; I therefore had the sole charge of the pulpit, and was conducting things according to my own discretion. He said he had known the young man before he went to college, and he desired very much to see what proficiency he had made, and wanted I should let him preach. I said I was afraid to set |him to preach, lest he should mar the work by not preaching that which was needed at the time. "O," said the old gentleman, "he will preach the truth; and there is no connection in religion, you know, between means and ends, and therefore there is no danger of his marring the work." I replied, "That is not my doctrine. I believe there is as much connection between means and ends in religion as in nature; and therefore I cannot consent to let him preach." I have often found it necessary to take substantially the same course in revivals of religion, and sometimes by doing so I have found that I gave offence; but I dared not do otherwise. JHF 156 MS 303

[54] Matthew 28:19–20.

[55] Finney changed the word "conversion" to "regeneration."

[56] Matson wrote down, "induces the change in the mind." Finney altered it to read, "changes the heart."

In the midst of a revival of religion, and when souls needed peculiar instruction, adapted to their present condition and their present wants, I dared not put **A, or B, or C,** into the pulpit where I had the charge, to preach any of his great sermons,—and generally too, **one** not at all adapted to the wants of the people. For this course I have frequently been accused of supposing that I could preach better than others. MS 304 |And I confess I did suppose that I could meet the wants of the people better than those that knew less about **their wants**, or than those that would preach their old written sermons to them; and **it was for this reason that** I supposed that Christ had put the work into my hands in such a sense that I was under obligation to adapt means to ends, and not call upon others who knew little of the state of things to attempt, **under such circumstances**, to instruct the people. I did in these cases just as I would be done by. JHF 157 |I would not allow myself to go in where another man was laboring to promote a revival, and suffer myself to be put in his place when I knew little or nothing about the state of the people.

I have said that[57] at Western I was the guest of ‹Mr› Gale, and that he had come to the conclusion that he was never converted. He told me the progress of his mind: that he had firmly believed, as he had so frequently urged upon me, that God would not bless my labors because I would not preach what he regarded as the truths of the Gospel. MS 305 **I have also said elsewhere |that a short time after I was licensed I preached once in his pulpit,[58] and gave my own views of the Gospel and the way to preach it; and that he told me after the sermon that he should be ashamed to have it known that he had had any connection with teaching me theology. He supposed, and had insisted, that I need not expect the Spirit of God to accompany my labors.** But when he found that the Spirit of God did accompany my labors, it led him to the conclusion that he was wrong; and this led him to such an overhauling of his whole state of mind, and of his views as a preacher, as resulted in his coming to the conclusion that he had never been converted, and did not understand the Gospel himself. During the revival in Western he attended nearly all the meetings; and before many weeks he told me he had come into an entirely different state of mind in regard to his own soul, and had changed his views of the Gospel, and thought I was right. He said he thanked God that he had had no influence with me to lead me to adopt MS 306 |his views—that I should have been ruined as a minister if ‹he› had ‹*prevailed.*›[59] From this time he became a very efficient worker, so far as his health would permit, in the revival in that region of country. The doctrine upon which I insisted, that the *command* to obey God *implied* the *power* to do so, created in some places considerable opposition at first. Denying also, as I did, that *moral* depravity **was** *phys{i}cal*,[60] or the depravity of the *nature*, and maintaining, as I did, that it **was** altogether *voluntary*, and therefore that the Spirit's

[57]The word "that" was inserted by Matson in pencil.

[58]See MS 102 and 150-51. Here Matson had originally written down, "that the short time I preached after I was licensed I preached in his pulpit," but he changed it. This section was crossed out by Fairchild.

[59]Here Matson had written down, "if I had," but Finney altered it to "if he had *prevailed*."

[60]"*Phys-*" was written at the end of one line and "*cal*" at the beginning of the next. Fairchild inserted the *i*.

influences **were** those of *teaching, persuading,* convicting, and ‹of course›[61] a *moral* influence—**these doctrines were to a great extent new ‹to many.›**[62] Indeed as late as 1832, when I was laboring in Boston for the first time, Dr Beecher said that he never had heard the doctrine preached before that the |Spirit's influences **were** moral as opposed to physical.[63] ‹Therefore,›[64] to a considerable extent, ministers and[65] Christians regarded that doctrine as virtually a denial of the Spirit's influence altogether; and hence, although I ever insisted very much, and incessantly, upon the divine agency in conviction and |‹regeneration›,[66] and in every Christian exercise, yet it was a long time before the cry ceased to be heard that I denied the agency of the Holy Ghost in regeneration and conversion. It was said that I taught *self*-conversion, *self*-regeneration; and not unfrequently was I rebuked for addressing the sinner as if the blame of his impenitence all belonged to himself, and for urging him to immediate submission. However, I persisted in this course, and it was seen by ministers and Christians that God owned it as **His** truth, and blessed it to the salvation of thousands of souls. **I shall have occasion to advert to this subject again in other places, and for the present drop it and return to my narrative.** I have spoken of the meetings at Elmer's Hill, and have said that people from Rome and Wright's settlement began to come in large numbers; and that the manifest effect of the **W**ord upon those that came **from other places** plainly indicated **to me** that the work was rapidly extending in that direction.[67]

JHF 158

MS 307

[61] Finney crossed out "altogether" and inserted "of course."

[62] Finney added the words "to many." Fairchild altered the end of this sentence to read, "I was regarded by many as teaching new and strange doctrines."

[63] Beecher soon came to adopt this theory himself. Bennet Tyler, writing to Dr. John Witherspoon in 1837, affirmed that Beecher "maintains, as I happen to know from repeated conversations with him on the subject, that the Holy Spirit never operates *directly* on the heart in regeneration (except perhaps in the case of infants, idiots &c.) but only through the medium of truth and motives—that the influence of the Spirit is a *persuasive* influence, analogous to the influence which one man exerts over the mind of another" (*Letters on the Origin and Progress of the New Haven Theology. From a New England Minister to one at the South* [New York: Robert Carter and Ezra Collier, 1837], pp. 91–92).

[64] Matson started this sentence with the word "But." Finney changed it to "Therefore."

[65] The word "Calvinistic" here appears to have been crossed out by Finney.

[66] Here Finney changed the word "conversion" to "regeneration."

[67] See MS 288. Rev. William E. Knox, a later minister of the church in Rome, recalled in 1851 that the revival at Western

> had not been many weeks in progress when several young persons from Wright's Settlement, attracted to the meeting by perhaps better motives than those of curiosity, returned home under deep religious convictions. The fact was communicated on Thanksgiving day to Mr. Gillett by a member living in the settlement, and he went the same evening to a meeting previously appointed at Deacon Allen Wright's, (who had brought him the information,) when to his astonishment he found the room thronged by anxious inquirers for salvation. For a month the religious interest continued to spread in the settlement, and was confined to it (W. E. Knox, *Semi-Centennial. A Sermon, Preached in the First Presbyterian Church, Rome, N.Y., September 29, 1850, upon its Fiftieth Anniversary* [Rome, N.Y.: Sandford, 1851], p. 14).

The following start of a sentence was written by Matson at the bottom of the page: "At this time Rev. Moses Gillett, pastor of the Congregational." Finney crossed it out when he started a new chapter on the next page.

MS 308
JHF 159

CHAPTER XIII

‹Revival at Rome›

‹At[1] this time Rev. Moses Gillett,[2] Pastor of the congregational›[3] church in Rome,[4] hearing of what the Lord was doing in Western, came in company with a Miss Huntington, one of the prominent female members of his church,[5] to see the work that was going on. They were both greatly impressed with the work of God. I could see that the Spirit of God was stirring them up

[1] Pages 308–40 were numbered 176–208 and renumbered 308–40 by Matson. The chapter heading and part of the first sentence of page 308 down to n. 3 were inserted by Finney. Henrietta Matson, an Oberlin College student in the 1850s, wrote: "The revival in Rome, N.Y., was one of the most remarkable of those early times. Mr. Finney sometimes told this wonderful story, 'The Revival at Rome,' to the students, and it always produced such an impression that there was the most intense interest" (Henrietta Matson, *Recollections of Rev. Charles G. Finney* [Nashville: Pentecostal Mission, n.d.], p. 37; copy in Oberlin College Library).

[2] Moses Gillett, or Gillet (1776–1848), a graduate of Yale College, was ordained and installed as the first pastor of the Congregational church in Rome in 1807. He remained as its pastor until 1837, during which time the congregation grew from thirty-four to over five hundred. He subsequently supplied the pulpits of vacant churches in Moscow and Sweden in western New York until 1844, when he returned to Rome in feeble health (see F. B. Dexter, *Biographical Sketches of the Graduates of Yale College,* vol. 5 [New York: Holt, 1911], pp. 662–63; and James H. Taylor, *Historical Discourse* [Rome, N.Y.: published by the Session, 1888], pp. 8–11). In early letters he signed his name "Gillet" (with one *t*), but he signed a letter in 1837 "Gillett" (see Letters of Gillet to Finney, 1827–1832, in the Finney Papers; and Gillett to Finney, 4 May 1837, Letters Received by Oberlin College 1822–1866, microfilm, roll 4).

[3] This section in Finney's handwriting continues on with the words "church in Rome," which duplicated what Matson had written down. Finney therefore crossed out the words again but omitted crossing out "church."

[4] Organized in 1800, the congregation joined the Oneida Congregational Association in 1812 and the Oneida Presbytery in 1818. Church records dating from 1806 are kept in a vault in the church basement. See Elizabeth M. Evans, *The First One Hundred and Fifty Years: 1800–1950* (Rome, N.Y.: First Presbyterian Church of Rome, 1950).

[5] Catherine Huntington (1797–1856) was the eldest daughter of Henry Huntington of Rome. She had been converted in about 1815 under the preaching of Gardiner Spring of New York and had become a zealous Christian and superintendent of the Sunday school. P. H. Fowler described her experience at this time: "Religion took the entire possession of her soul, and became both a master passion and a controlling principle. . . . Probably no actor in those memorable scenes, was more powerfully exercised during the great revival in the village of Rome, in 1826, than she." In 1833 she married William Williams, the Utica printer and chairman of the Oneida Sunday School Union. See Philemon H. Fowler, *The Voice of the Dead. A Sermon: on the occasion of the death of Mrs. Catharine Huntington Williams, Preached September 21, 1856* (Utica: Curtiss and White, 1856), pp. 19–20; John Camp Williams, *An Oneida County Printer: William Williams, Printer, Publisher, Editor* (New York: Scribner, 1906); *WR,* 9 July 1833, p. 111; and Catherine Huntington to Lydia Finney, undated letter, Finney Papers, microfilm, roll 2, no. 415. This letter is listed in the calendar of the Finney Papers under the date 15 September 1829, but it appears to have been written about February 1826. See also subsequent letters from her to the Finneys in the Finney Papers. Her name sometimes appears to be spelled "Catharine."

to the deepest foundations of their minds. After a few days **Brother** Gillett[6] and Miss **Huntington** came up again. Miss **Huntington** was a very devout and earnest Christian girl. On their second coming up **Brother** Gillet says to me, "Brother Finney, it seems to me that I have **got** a new Bible. I never before understood the promises ‹as I do now›;[7] I never got hold of them before. I cannot rest," sa‹id›[8] he; "my mind is full of the subject, and the promises are new to me."[9] This conversation, protracted as it was for sometime, gave me to understand that the Lord was preparing him for a great work in his own congregation.

Soon after this, and when the revival was in its full strength at Western, Mr. Gillett per|suaded me to exchange a day with him. I consented reluctantly. On the Saturday before the day of our exchange, on my way to Rome, I greatly regretted that I had consented to the exchange **at that time.**[10] I felt that it would greatly mar the work in Western, because **Brother** Gillett would preach some of his old sermons, which I knew very well could not be adapted to the state of things.[11] However **I knew** the people were praying; and **that** it would not *stop* the work, although it might *retard* it. I went to Rome and preached three times on the Sabbath.[12] To |me it was perfectly manifest that the Word took great effect. I could see during the day that many heads were down, and that a great number of them were bowed down with deep conviction for sin. I preached in the morning on the text, "The carnal mind is enmity against God;"[13] and followed it up with something in the same direction in the afternoon and evening—**I do not recollect the texts.** I waited on Monday morning till **Brother** Gillett returned from Western. I told

MS 309

JHF 160

[6]Matson spelled Gillet's name with one *t* as far as MS 332, where he started spelling it with two *t*s. He appears to have added a second *t* in most cases later. In several places this was not done. In this particular place Matson appears to have added two additional *t*s.

[7]Finney added the words "as I do now."

[8]Finney changed the word "says" to "said."

[9]On another occasion Finney spoke of this incident: "I shall never forget how that man would say to me time after time, with deep emotion—'I have a new Bible. How striking the promises are. It seems to me as though I had never read them before. So *rich* they are, so full, so precious!'" (*OE,* 17 July 1844, p. 114).

[10]Finney began in Rome on 25 December 1825, the last Sunday of the year. Rome and Western were about nine miles apart. See Moses Gillet's account of the revival in *A Narrative of the Revival of Religion in the County of Oneida; particularly in the Bounds of the Presbytery of Oneida, in the year 1826* (Utica: Hastings and Tracy, 1826; reprint, Princeton: D. A. Borrenstein, 1827), pp. 15–20.

[11]George W. Gale remembered that Finney "after much solicitation" agreed on an exchange with Gillet. "It was in the height of the revival at Western. We were very sorry and so was he [Finney]." Gale continued:

> He said if I had been with him he should not probably have consented, but he could not alone resist Mr. Gillet. He was a very good man but a very different one from Mr. Finney. Moderate in his delivery and much tied to his notes. We were, however, reconciled to it after reflection. He knew it was wrong to limit God, and to lean upon an arm of flesh. It might result in great good to the people of Rome also. Prayer was offered that God would help Brother Gillet. He came and prayer seemed to be answered. He preached as if under a new baptism of the Spirit (*Autobiography {to 1834} of George Washington Gale {1789–1861}, Founder of Galesburg, Illinois, and Knox College* [New York: privately printed, 1964], pp. 262–63).

[12]On the Saturday afternoon after his arrival he attended a prayer meeting, which he described. See MS 332–33.

[13]Romans 8:7.

MS 310 him what my impressions were in respect to the |state of the people. He did not seem to realize that the work was beginning with such power as I supposed. But he wanted to call for inquirers, if there were any in the congregation, and **that I should** be present at the meeting. I have said before that the means that I had all along used thus far in promoting revivals, were much prayer, secret and social, public preaching, personal conversation, and visitation from house to house **for that purpose**; and when inquirers became multiplied I appointed meetings for them, and invited those that were inquiring to meet **where I gave them** instructions suited to their necessities. These were the means, and the *only* means, that I had thus far used in attempting to secure the conversion of souls. **Brother** Gillett **knew this, and wanted to call a** meeting of inquiry, **and wanted me to be present**. I told him I would; and that he might circulate information through the village that there would be a meeting of inquiry on Monday evening. I would go to Western, and return just at evening**, and take the people by surprize**; it
MS 311 being un|derstood that he was not to let the people know that he expected me to be present.[14] The meeting was called at the house of one of his deacons. When we arrived we found the large sitting room **in the front part of the house** crowded to its utmost capacity. ‹Mr.› Gillett looked around with surprize and manifest agitation; for he found that the meeting was composed of many of the most intelligent and influential members of his congregation, and especially was largely composed of the **first class of** young men in the town. We spent a little while in attempting to converse with them; and I soon
JHF 161 saw that the feeling was so |deep that there was danger of an outburst of feeling that would be almost ‹uncontrolable.›[15] I therefore said to ‹Mr.› Gillett, "It **won't** do to continue the meeting in this shape. I will make some remarks such as they need, and then dismiss them; **enjoin[in]g[16] it upon them so far to suppress their feelings as not to make any outcries in the streets as they are going home**."

MS 312 Nothing had been said or |done to create any excitement in the meeting. The feeling was all spontaneous. The work was with such power that **only** a few words of conversation would make the stoutest men writhe on their seats as if a sword had been thrust in‹to›[17] their hearts. It would probably not be possible for one who had never witnessed such a scene to realize what the **power**[18] of the truth sometimes is **in the hands** of the Holy Ghost. It was indeed a sword, and a two-edged sword. The pain that it produced when searchingly presented in a few words of conversation, would create a distress that seemed unendurable. ‹Mr.› Gillett became very much agitated. He

[14] According to George W. Gale, Finney did not return to Western. "We expected him on Monday, and still more on Tuesday, but he did not come. On Wednesday morning as we heard nothing I told my wife I would go down to Rome and see what was the matter" (*Autobiography*, p. 263).

[15] The word "uproarious" here was changed by Finney to "uncontrolable." Fairchild added an *l*.

[16] Matson had written down "enjoing" here. Fairchild corrected it before crossing out the section.

[17] The letters *to* appear to have been added to the word "in" by Finney.

[18] This word was not changed by Fairchild in the manuscript, but the published version has "force."

turned pale; and with a good deal of **agitation**[19] he said, "What shall we do?" "What shall we do?" I put my hand on his shoulder and **said** in a whisper, "Keep quiet, Keep quiet, ‹**Mr.**›[20] Gillett." I then addressed them in as gentle but plain a manner as I could; calling their attention at once to their only remedy, and assuring them that it was a present and all-sufficient remedy. I pointed them to Christ as the Savior of the world; and kept on ¦in this strain as long as they could well endure it, which indeed was but a few moments. **Brother** Gillet became so agitated that I stepped up to him and taking him by the arm I said, "Let us pray." We knelt down in the middle of the room where we had been standing. I led in prayer in a low, unimpassioned voice; but interceded with the Savior to interpose his blood then and there, and to lead all these sinners to accept the salvation which he proffered and to believe to the saving of their souls. The agitation deepened every moment; and as I could hear their sobs, **and breathing,** and sighs, I closed my prayer and rose ¦suddenly from my knees. They all arose, and I said: "Now please go home without speaking a word to each other. **Say nothing**—try to keep silent, and do not break out into any boisterous manifestation of feeling; **and as you cannot talk or speak to each other and still control your feelings, please to** go without saying a word, to your rooms."

MS 313

JHF 162

At this moment, a young man by the name of **Wright**, a clerk in ¦Mr. **Huntington**'s store,[21] being one of the first young men in the place, so nearly fainted that he fell on some young men that stood near him; and they all of them partially swooned away, and fell together. This had well-nigh produced a loud shrieking; but I hushed them down, and said to the young men, "Please set that door wide open, and go out; and let **them** all retire in silence." They did as I requested.[22] They did not shriek; but they went out sobbing and sighing, and their sobs and sighs could be heard till they got out into the street. This Mr. **Wright** to whom I have alluded, **afterward told me that he was obliged to hold his mouth with the full strength of his arms till he got home, his distress was so great. He** kept silence till he entered the door where he lived; but he could contain himself no longer. He shut the door, fell upon the floor, and burst out into a loud wailing in view of his awful condition. This brought the family around him **very quick**, and scattered conviction among the whole of them.

MS 314

I afterwards learned that similar scenes occurred ¦in **several** families.

MS 315

[19]This word was not changed by Fairchild in the manuscript, but the published version has "excitement."

[20]Matson had written the word "Brother" here, and Finney changed it to "Mr.," in line with Lewis Tappan's suggestion (see p. xxxi above). However, since this is reported speech, Finney probably should have left it as it was. Fairchild therefore changed it back to "Brother."

[21]This may have been Benjamin H. Wright, who married Henrietta, a daughter of Henry Huntington. The firm of George Huntington and Co. was established by George Huntington about 1793 with the assistance of his brother Henry. Originally in the mercantile business, they dealt largely in real estate, with an interest in the manufacture of iron and cotton. See Elijah B. Huntington, *A Genealogical Memoir of the Huntington Family in this Country* (Stamford, Conn.: published by the author, 1863), pp. 134, 195.

[22]The next sentence started with the word "However," which appears to have been crossed out by Finney, who failed to give the next word a capital *T*. It was supplied by Fairchild.

Several, as it was afterwards ascertained, were converted at the meeting, and went home so full of joy that they could hardly contain themselves.[23]

The next morning, as soon as it was fairly day, people began to call at Mr. Gillett's to have us go and visit their families; whom they represented as being under the greatest conviction. We took a hasty breakfast, and started out. As soon as we were in the streets, the people ran out from many houses and begged us to go into their houses. As we could visit but one place at a time, when we went into **one** house the neighbors would rush in and fill the largest JHF 163 room. We would stay and give them instruction |for a short time, and then go to another house, and the people would follow us. We found a most extraordinary state of things. Convictions were so deep and universal that we MS 316 would sometimes go into a house and find some in a kneeling |posture, some prostrate on the **carpet, some bathing the temples of their friends with camphor, and rubbing them to keep them from fainting, and as they feared from dying**. We visited, and conversed, and prayed in this manner from house to house till noon. I then said to Mr. Gillett, "This will never do; we must have a meeting of inquiry. We cannot go from house to house; and we are not meeting the wants of the people at all." He agreed with me; but the question arose, where shall we have the meeting? A Mr. **Flint**, a religious man, at that time kept a hotel on the corner at the center of the town.[24] He had a large, **long** dining room; and Mr. Gillett said, "I will step in and see if I cannot be allowed to appoint the meeting of inquiry in his dining room.["] Without difficulty he obtained consent, and then went immediately to the public schools and gave notice that at **One O'clock** there would be a meeting of inquiry at Mr **Flint's** dining room. We went home and took **a hasty**[25] MS 317 dinner and started for the meeting.[26] |We saw people hurrying, and some of

[23] Matson wrote the following sentence after this: "They said that they were obliged to hold their hands over their mouths to keep from shouting hallelujah in the streets as they went home." The word "hallelujah" was crossed out by Matson, and the rest of the sentence appears to have been crossed out by Finney.

Gillet reported:

> Monday evening, the last week in December, a meeting of inquiry was held for convicted sinners. Mr. Finney came here that evening, and remained four weeks, and was a distinguished instrument in promoting the revival. The meeting of inquiry was at a private house, and a prayer-meeting at a school-house at the same time. The room was filled with inquiring sinners. After prayer, personal conversation, and a short address, we dismissed them. Instead of retiring, they partly fell upon each other, and gave vent to their feelings in sobs and groans. It was with difficulty we prevailed upon them to retire. From this time the excitement became general in the village (Oneida Presbytery *Narrative*, p. 16).

[24] This was Amos Flint. He was said to have "led an unblemished Christian life" until he died in 1869 at age eighty-one in Nyack, New York (*Utica Herald*, 6 November 1869, reprinted in *The Circular* [Oneida, N.Y.], 15 November 1869, p. 274).

[25] This was not changed in the manuscript by Fairchild, but the published version has "our."

[26] George Gale, who placed these events on Wednesday rather than Tuesday, recollected:

> I arrived at Mr. Gillet's a little before dinner, when he and Mr. Gillet had just come in from visiting. Both expressed a great deal of satisfaction that I had come. Said Finney, "You never saw such a state of things. In some of the families we have visited today some of the young ladies are unable to sit up, and young men and old ones can attend to no business. Last night (after we were alone he told me) Brother Gillet was frightened. After the meeting some of the young people wrung their hands and fell upon each other's necks. We had to send them home." . . . Mr. Finney also remarked, "We have appointed a meeting of inquiry to be held in the large dining room at one of

them actually running to the meeting. They were coming from every direction. By the time we were there the room, though a large one, was crammed to its utmost capacity. **Persons of both sexes and of all ages** crowded the apartment.[27] This meeting was very much like the one we had had the night before. The feeling was overwhelming. **The Word of God was truly the sword of the Spirit; and** some men of the strongest nerves were so cut down by the remarks which were made that they were unable to help themselves and had to be taken home by their friends. This meeting lasted till nearly night. It resulted in a great number of hopeful conversions, and was the means of greatly extending the work on every side.[28]

I preached that evening, and ‹Mr. Gillet›[29] appointed a meeting for inquiry the next morning in the court house. ˡThis was a much larger room than the dining hall, though it was not so central. However at the hour the court house was crowded **to its utmost** ˡ**capacity**; and we spent a good part of the day in giving instructions. **We adapted our instructions as much as possible to the state of the people**, and the work went on with wonderful power. I preached again in the evening, and ‹Mr. Gillett›[30] appointed a meeting of inquiry the next morning at the church; as no other room in the village was then large enough to hold the inquirers. **That** evening, if I rightly remember the order of things, we undertook to hold a prayer and conference meeting in a large school house. But the meeting was hardly begun before the feeling deepened so much that, to prevent an undesirable outburst of overwhelming feeling, I proposed to Mr. Gillett that we should dismiss the meeting, and request the people to go in silence, and Christians to spend the evening in secret prayer, or in family prayer, as might seem most desirable. Sinners we exhorted not to sleep until they gave their hearts to God. After this the work became so general that I preached every night, I think, for twenty nights in succession, and twice on the Sabbath. Our prayer meetings ˡduring this time **were held in the church. In** the daytime the prayer meeting was held **on** one part of the day, and a meeting for inquiry, **on another** part **of the day**. Every

JHF 164

MS 318

MS 319

the hotels. We have just sent out to the schools of the village. It is appointed at 1:00 o'clock. It is but short notice but I presume there will be a good many present. We have also requested professors to come into the adjoining sitting room for prayer. I want you to go with me into the meeting of inquiry while Brother Gillet leads the prayer meeting" (*Autobiography*, pp. 263–64).

[27] Gale wrote:

We went to the hotel at the hour appointed and found many gathering. The professors occupied the room adjacent with Brother Gillet, and Mr. Finney and I went into the other room, where I judged, from passing my eye over the assembly there were about seventy persons present of different ages and classes, the youth and the man of years, and men of all occupations, the merchant, the mechanic, and the professional man, the lawyer and the doctor. As many as fifty more came in after I entered, I should judge, filling the room, in short.

Gale went on to describe the meeting in detail. See *Autobiography*, pp. 264–65.

[28] Gale wrote:

I returned that night, but as often as I could go down I did. From the day I have named the work went on with power. No room in the village would contain the multitude who flocked to the meeting of inquiry. They were obliged to go to the church, where meetings of this kind were held three times a week (*Autobiography*, p. 266).

[29] Finney added the words "Mr. Gillett."

[30] Finney added the words "Mr. Gillett."

day, if I remember aright, after the work had thus commenced, we held a prayer meeting and a meeting for inquiry, and preaching in the evening. There was a solemnity covering the whole place, an awe that made everybody feel that God was there. Ministers came in from neighboring towns, and expressed great astonishment at what they saw and heard, as well they might.[31] Conversions multiplied so rapidly that we had no way of learning who they were. I therefore every evening, at the close of my sermon, requested all who had been converted that day to come forward and report themselves in front of the pulpit, that we might have a little conver|sation with them. We were every night surprized by the numbers ‹& class of persons› that came forward.[32] At one of our morning prayer meetings the lower part |of the church was full. I arose and was making some remarks to the people, when an unconverted man, a merchant, came into the meeting. He came along till he found a seat ‹in front of me &› near where I stood speaking.[33] He had s[a]t[34] but a few moments when he fell from his seat as if he had been shot. He writhed and groaned in a terrible manner. I stepped to the pew door, and saw that it was altogether an agony of mind. A skeptical physician sat near him. He stepped out of his slip, and came and examined this man who was thus distressed. He felt his pulse, and examined the case for a few moments. He said nothing, but turned away and leaned his head against a post that supported the gallery, and manifested great agitation of mind. He said afterwards that he saw at once that it was distress of mind, and it took his skepticism entirely away. He was soon after hopefully converted. We

JHF 165

MS 320

[31] George Gale mentioned in particular the case of Rev. Henry Smith of Camden, New York, who went to Rome and was deeply affected. Catherine Huntington also mentioned this case, among others, in a letter to Rev. Gardiner Spring of New York, dated 22 February 1826: "There is a glorious revival in—, where Mr. Smith is settled. He came to Rome, and got the Spirit, and carried it home with him" (*Personal Reminiscences of the Life and Times of Gardiner Spring,* vol. 1 [New York: Scribner, 1866], p. 223; Gale, *Autobiography*, p. 266; see also H. H. Kellogg's report in the Oneida Presbytery *Narrative,* p. 21; and p. 317 n. 85 [MS 589]).

Another minister was Noah Coe, of New Hartford, who spent two days in Rome with an elder from his church. See Coe's account in the Oneida Presbytery *Narrative*, p. 28. See also *OE,* 17 January 1849, p. 10.

[32] Matson had written down here, "the numbers that came forward, and at the class of people that came forward," but Finney altered it.

Catherine Huntington wrote:

> I do not know the number of converts in our town; it may be four hundred. Two evenings since, when those were requested to come forward who had obtained hopes within about thirty-six hours, between twenty and thirty presented themselves. Usually every other evening the ministers made the request, that they might see who they were, and shake hands with them (*Reminiscences of Gardiner Spring*, p. 222; see also MS 324).

A report in the *Missionary Herald* reads:

> At Rome, in Oneida county, there has been one of the most remarkable revivals of religion ever known in that section of country. Within the space of eight weeks, not less than 400 became hopefully pious. During one week, it is said, scarcely any secular work was done, so intent were the people on the great concerns of the soul. It was a sort of sabbatical week (*The Missionary Herald* [Boston] 22 [May 1826]: 160).

[33] Here Matson had written down, "found a seat near where I stood speaking, in front of me." Finney altered it.

[34] The word "set" appears to have been altered to "sat" by Fairchild.

engaged in prayer for the man who fell in the pew; and before he left |the house ‹I believe›[35] his anguish passed away, and he rejoiced in Christ. MS 321

Another **skeptical** physician, a very amiable man but a skeptic, had a little daughter **Hannah**, and a **very** praying wife.[36] Little **Hannah**, a girl perhaps eight or nine years old,[37] was strongly convicted of sin, and her mother was greatly interested in her state of mind. But her father was at first quite indignant. He said to his wife, "The subject of religion is too high for *me*. I never could understand it. And do you tell me that that little child understands it so as to be intelligently convicted of sin? I do not believe it. I know better. I cannot endure it. It is fanaticism; it is madness." Nevertheless the mother of the child held fast in prayer. The doctor made these remarks, as I learned, with a good deal of spirit. Immediately he took his horse and went several miles to see |a patient. On his way, as he afterwards remarked, that subject **was on** his mind in such a manner that it was all open to his understanding; and the whole plan of salvation by Christ was so clear |to him that he saw that a child could understand it.[38] He wondered that it had ever seemed so mysterious to him. He regretted exceedingly that he had said what he had to his wife about little **Hannah**, and felt in haste to get home that he might take it back. He soon came home, **but** another man; told his wife what had passed in his own mind; encouraged dear little **Hannah** to come to Christ; and both father and daughter have since been earnest Christians, and have lived long and done much good.[39] JHF 166 MS 322

But in this revival, as in others that I have **seen**, God did some terrible things in righteousness. On one Sabbath ‹**whilst**›[40] I was there, as we came out of the pulpit and were about to leave the church, a man came in haste to Mr. Gillett and myself and requested us to go to a certain place, saying that a man had fallen down dead there. I was engaged in conversing with somebody, and ‹Mr› Gillett went alone. When I was through with the |conversation I went to Mr. Gillett's house, and he soon returned and related this fact. Three men who had been opposing the work had met that Sabbath day and spent the day in drinking and ridiculing the work.[41] They went on in this way until one MS 323

[35] Finney added the words "I believe."

[36] In another account of this incident Finney calls him "Dr. B"; and George Gale indicates that it was Dr. Arba Blair (1781–1863), the "leading physician in Rome." He went there from Warren, Massachusetts, in 1803 and was licensed to practice in 1805. He became eminent in obstetrics and was a popular and successful doctor. See *OE,* 3 December 1856, p. 194; Gale, *Autobiography*, p. 26; and J. V. Cobb, "Notice of Dr. Arba Blair, of Rome," *Medical Society of the State of New York, Transactions*, 1863, pp. 443–46.

[37] In a sermon in London, Finney called Hannah "one of the most beautiful little children I ever beheld." See *The Penny Pulpit* 1,570 (July–September 1850): 199.

[38] Matson had written down after this the phrase, "as well it could understand anything else." Finney added the word "as" after "well" but crossed the whole phrase out.

[39] Arba Blair became "an active and leading member of the Presbyterian Church, and for a number of years one of its ruling elders." He was also prominent in the antislavery movement in the state. See Cobb, "Notice of Dr. Arba Blair," p. 446; and *NYE,* 31 October 1835, p. 257; and 7 May 1836, p. 75.

[40] Matson had written the word "that," but it was crossed out and the word "whilst" inserted by Finney.

[41] In an earlier account of this incident, Finney recalled that they were "a small class of hard drinkers who seemed determined to resist every call from God to repent. On the Sabbaths they would get together for drinking and reveling" (*OE,* 9 May 1849, p. 74).

of them suddenly fell **down** dead. When ‹Mr› Gillett arrived at the house and the circumstances were related to him he said, "There! there is no doubt but that man had been stricken down by God, and has been sent to hell." His companions were speechless.[42] They could say nothing; for it was evident to them that their conduct had brought upon him this awful stroke of divine indignation.

As the work proceeded it gathered in nearly the whole population. Nearly every one of the lawyers, merchants, and physicians, and **nearly** all the principal men,—and indeed nearly all the adult population of the village were brought in, **and** especially those who **had** belonged to Mr. Gillett's JHF 167 congrega|tion. He said to me before I left, "So far as my congregation is MS 324 concerned, the **Millennium** is come |already. My people are all converted. Of all my past labors I have not a sermon that is suited at all to my congregation, for they are all Christians." Mr. Gillett afterwards reported that during the twenty days that I spent at Rome there were five hundred conversions in that town, **or an average of twenty five per day.**[43] **At evening when I requested that any who had been converted during the day should come forward and report themselves, the people would remain standing instead of retiring, to see who came forward to report themselves as having been converted; and the utmost astonishment was expressed by those present when they saw who came forward.**[44]

During the progress of this work a good deal of excitement sprung up in Utica, and some were disposed to ridicule the work at Rome. Mr. **Henry Huntington**, who lived at Rome, was a very prominent citizen, and **perhaps I may say stood** at the head of society there in point of wealth and **of** MS 325 intelligence.[45] But he was **skeptical**; or perhaps I should say he |held

[42] In the earlier account Finney said that Gillet

> found the fallen man yet warm, but actually dead; and turning to the surrounding company of his associates, said, "There—who of you can doubt that this man has gone right down to hell!" This case made a deep and thrilling impression (*OE,* 9 May 1849, p. 74).

[43] Moses Gillet's report dated 30 October 1826 is printed in Oneida Presbytery *Narrative,* pp. 15–20. He writes, "Four lawyers, four physicians, and all the merchants who were not professors before, and men of the first respectability in the place, are hopeful converts."

The revival led to the famous occasion on 12 March 1826, when 176 people were admitted to church membership. Albert Barnes, the Bible commentator and Presbyterian leader, who grew up in Rome, recorded: "Among those, were nearly all the merchants of the place, and *all the lawyers*. Since the fall of man, was such a thing ever known before, that all the lawyers in any place were converted to the faith of the Saviour?" One of the young trainee lawyers converted at the time was Thomas Brainerd, later to become an eminent Presbyterian minister (*NYE,* 16 September 1875, p. 4; see also *BR*, 17 March 1826, p. 42).

[44] See MS 319. This perhaps served a similar function to the anxious seat or the altar call of the Methodists, which Finney had first used in Rutland and then in Rochester in 1830–1831. See MS 221, 569, and p. 306 n. 33 (MS 570).

[45] Henry Huntington (1766–1846) was a graduate of Dartmouth, and he abandoned a legal career to take up commercial pursuits. He was president of the bank of Utica for more than twenty-five years. He had represented the Western District of the state in the state senate and had also been a member of the state assembly. See E. B. Huntington, *Memoir of the Huntington Family*, p. 133; and *NYE,* 22 October 1846, p. 171.

Franklin Hough wrote that at the time of Henry Huntington's death he was "the wealthiest man in the county; he had a high standing in community, and filled several important offices" (*American Biographical Notes* [Albany: Munsell, 1875], p. 219).

Unitarian views. He was a very moral and respectable man, **and a man highly educated**; and **he** held his peculiar views unobtrusively, saying very little to anybody about them. The first Sabbath I preached there Mr. **Huntington** was present; and he was so astonished, as he afterwards told me, at my preaching, that he made up his mind that he would not go again. He went home and said to his family: "That man is mad, and I should not be surprized if he set the town ‹on› fire."[46] He stayed away from the meeting for some two weeks. In the meantime the work became so great as to confound his skepticism, and he was in a state of great perplexity. He was president of a bank in Utica, and used to go down to attend the weekly meeting of the directors **on a certain day**.[47] On one of these occasions one of the directors began to rally him on the state of things in Rome, as if they were all running mad there. Mr. **Huntington** remarked, "Gentlemen, say what you will, there is something |very remarkable in the state of things in Rome. Certainly no human power or eloquence has produced what we see there. I cannot understand it. You say it will soon subside. No doubt the ***degree*** of feeling that is now in Rome must soon subside, or the people will become insane. But, gentlemen," said |he, "there is no accounting for that state of feeling by any philosophy, unless there be something divine in it." After Mr. **Huntington** had stayed away from the meeting about two weeks, a few of us assembled one afternoon to make him a special subject of prayer. The Lord gave us strong faith in praying for him; and we felt the conviction that the Lord was working in his soul.[48] That evening he came to meeting. When he came into the house, ‹Mr› Gillett whispered to me as we sat in the pulpit and said, "Brother Finney, Mr. **Huntington** has come. I hope you will not say anything that will offend him." |"No," said I, "but I shall not spare him." In those days I was obliged to preach altogether without premeditation; for I had not an hour in a week, **in which I was able to be out of my bed,** which I could take to arrange my thoughts beforehand. **It was very common with me to wait till the congregation was assembled, and let the appearance of the state of things suggest my subject.**[49] **At the time I speak of I do not think I had a subject in my mind upon which I intended to speak**

MS 326

JHF 168

MS 327

[46]Matson had written down the word "afire" here, but Finney changed it to "on fire."

[47]Hough stated: "From the year 1812 until his death he was president of the Bank of Utica, going from Rome to Utica twice a week to attend to the affairs of the bank" (*American Biographical Notes*, p. 219).

[48]This may have been the meeting George Gale remembered, when Daniel Nash was present. Nash had followed Finney to Rome and was completely weighed down with a burden for souls:

> At a prayer meeting which I attended in Rome at the early stage of the revival, he [Nash] cried out while an individual was praying (it being a private prayer meeting of ministers and deacons in which prayer was offered for some prominent individuals), "Do you pray for Henry Huntington" (the rich banker of Rome) "I shall die" and fell down upon the floor ("Autobiography of Rev. G. W. Gale," typescript copy in Knox College Library, Galesburg, Ill., p. 223).

[49]Matson had written the following section after this, which appears to have been crossed out by Finney:

> Up to that time I never had made a skeleton, or carried a scrap of anything into the pulpit prepared to deliver, except on one occasion which I have already related [see MS 101], when I preached a sermon which I wrote when I was studying theology. Indeed, I believe I had preached one of those sermons in ‹Mr› Gale's pulpit; but those were exceptional cases.

when Mr. Huntington came in. When therefore I saw my congregation together, I chose my subject and preached. The Word took a powerful hold; MS 328 and, as I hoped and intended, it took a ˡpowerful hold of Mr. Huntington himself. I think it was that very night, when I requested at the close of the meeting all those who had been converted that day and evening to come forward and report themselves, this Mr. Huntington was one who came deliberately, solemnly forward, and reported himself as having given his heart to God. He appeared humble and penitent, and I have always supposed was truly converted to Christ.

The state of things in the village and in the neighborhood round about was such that no one could come into the village without feeling awe-stricken, and the solemn impression that God was there in a peculiar and wonderful manner. As an illustration of this I will relate an incident. The sheriff of the county resided in Utica. There were two court houses in the county, one at Rome and the other at Utica; consequently the sheriff, Broadhead by name, had much business at Rome.[50] He afterwards told me that he had heard of the MS 329 state of things at Rome; and he, together with others, ˡhad a good deal of JHF 169 laughing in the hotel where he boarded about what they had heard. ˡBut one day it was necessary for him to go to Rome. He said that he was glad to have business there, for he wanted to see for himself what it was that people talked so much about, and what the state of things really was in Rome. He drove on in his one horse sleigh, as he told me, without any particular impression upon his mind at all until he crossed what was called the old canal, a place about a mile, I think, from the town. He said as soon as he crossed the old canal an awful impression came over him, an awe so deep that he could not shake it off. He felt as if God pervaded the whole atmosphere. He said that this increased the whole way till he came to the village. He stopped at Mr. Flint's hotel, and the hostler came out and took his horse. He observed, he said, that the hostler *looked* just as he himself *felt*, as if he were afraid to speak. He went into the house, and found the gentleman there with whom he had business. MS 330 ˡHe said they were manifestly all so much impressed they could hardly attend to business. He said that several times in the course of the short time he was there, he had to arise from the table abruptly and go to the window and look out, and try to divert his attention, to keep from weeping. He observed, he said, that everybody else appeared to feel just as he did. Such an awe, such a solemnity, such a state of things he had never had any conception of before. He hastened through with his business and returned to Utica; but, as he said, never to speak lightly of the work at Rome again. A few weeks later at Utica

[50]Charles C. Brodhead (1772–1852), from New Paltz, near Kingston, New York, was a surveyor, employed initially in laying out the lands and negotiating with the Indians in upstate New York. He was appointed sheriff of Oneida County in 1800 and moved to Utica that year. Much of the layout of Utica was due to him; and he was responsible for surveying the stretch of the proposed Erie Canal between Albany and Rome. In his prime he was very sociable and popular, but as he advanced in years, he became more of a recluse. He was increasingly prone to extreme moodiness, living as a bachelor in public boarding houses, until he died, a solitary old man. See Moses Bagg, *Pioneers of Utica* (Utica: Curtiss and Childs, 1877), pp. 104–11.

he was hopefully converted; the circumstances of which I shall relate in **its** proper place.[51]

I have spoken of Wright's settlement, a village north east of Rome some two or three miles. The revival took powerful effect there, and converted the great mass of the inhabitants.[52] The means that were used at Rome were such as I had used before, and no others: ˡpreaching, public, social, and private prayer, exhortations and personal conversation. It ˡis difficult to conceive so deep and universal a state of religious feeling with no instance of disorder, or tumult, or fanaticism, or anything that was objectionable, as was witnessed at Rome. There are many of the converts of that revival scattered all through the land, living to this day; and they can testify that in those meetings the greatest order and solemnity prevailed, and the utmost pains were taken to guard against everything that was to be deplored. The Spirit's work was so spontaneous, so powerful, and so overwhelming, as to render it necessary to exercise the greatest caution and wisdom in conducting all the meetings in order to prevent an undesirable outburst of feeling that soon would have exhausted the sensibility of the people and brought about a reaction. But no reaction followed, as everybody knows who is acquainted with the facts. They kept up a sunrise prayer-ˡmeeting for several months, and I believe for more than a year afterwards, at all seasons of the year, that was very fully attended, and was as full of interest as perhaps a prayer meeting could well be. The moral state of the people was so greatly changed that **Brother** Gillet often remarked that it did not seem like the same place. **Indeed, it had made a clean sweep.** Whatever of sin was left was obliged to hide its head. No open immorality could be tolerated there for a moment. I have **only** given a very faint outline of what passed at Rome. **To give a** faithful description of all the moving incidents that were crowded into that revival, would make a volume of itself.

MS 331 JHF 170 MS 332

I should say a few words in regard to the spirit of prayer which prevailed at Rome at this time. I think it was on the Saturday that I came down from Western to exchange with ‹Mr› Gillett, that I met the church in the afternoon in a prayer meeting in their house of worship. I endeavored to make them understand that God would immeˡdiately answer prayer provided they fulfilled the conditions upon which he had promised to answer prayer; and especially if they believed in the sense of *expecting* **Him** to answer their ˡrequests. I observed that the church were greatly interested in my remarks, and their countenances manifested an intense desire to see an answer to their prayers. Near the close of the meeting I recollect making this remark. **It was before there were railroads. I said to the church,** "I really believe, if you will unite this afternoon in the prayer of faith to God for the immediate outpouring of **His** Spirit, that you will receive an answer from heaven sooner than you would get a message from Albany by the quickest ‹post that **you**

MS 333 JHF 171

[51] See MS 342–44. The word "its" was not crossed out by Fairchild, but the published version has "the."

[52] Moses Gillet reported on Wright's Settlement: "In about four weeks, forty might be numbered as hopeful converts to Christ" (Oneida Presbytery *Narrative*, p. 16; see also W. E. Knox, *Semi-Centennial. A Sermon, Preached in the First Presbyterian Church, Rome, N.Y., September 29, 1850, upon its Fiftieth Anniversary* [Rome, N.Y.: Sandford, 1851], p. 14).

could send›."[53] I said this with great emphasis, and felt it; and I observed that the people were startled with my expression of earnestness and faith in respect to an immediate answer to prayer. The fact is, I had so often seen this MS 334 result in answer to prayer, that I made the remark without ˡany misgiving. Nothing was said by any of the members of the church at the time; but I learned after the work had begun, that three or four members of the church,—**Mr. George Huntington,**[54] **brother of Henry Huntington, and two or three other brethren,**—called in at Mr. Gillett's study, and felt so impressed with what had been said about speedy answers to prayer that they determined to take God at His Word, and see whether He would answer while they were yet speaking. One of them told me afterwards that they had wonderful faith given them by the Spirit of God to pray for an *immediate answer*; and he added, "The answer *did* come quicker than we could have got an answer from Albany by the quickest post we could have sent."[55] Indeed the town was full of prayer. Go where you would you heard the voice of prayer. Pass along the streets, and if two or three Christians happened to be together they were praying. Wherever they met they prayed. Wherever there was a sinner unconverted, especially if he manifested any opposition, you MS 335 would find some ˡtwo or three brothers or sisters agreeing to make him a particular subject of prayer; **and it was very remarkable to see to what an extent God would answer prayer immediately**.

There was the wife of an officer in the United States army residing at JHF 172 Rome, the daughter of[56] a prominent citizen ˡ‹of›[57] that place.[58] This lady

[53]Finney wrote in the phrase "post that you could send" to replace the words "method of conveyance that exists," which had been written down by Matson.

[54]George Huntington (1770–1842) was the first of the Huntington family to move to Rome from Norwich, Connecticut, and he became "the patriarch of the village." He was elected supervisor at the first town meeting in 1796, was appointed a judge in 1798, and had been a member of the state assembly at various times since 1811. He and his wife joined the church in 1808. See Huntington, *Memoir of the Huntington Family*, p. 134; S. W. Durant, *A History of Oneida County, New York* (Philadelphia: Everts and Faris, 1878), pp. 187, 189, 364; and Knox, *Semi-Centennial*, p. 12. His eldest daughter, Hannah, was married to Rev. Henry Smith of Camden, New York.

[55]Catherine Huntington wrote at the time to Gardiner Spring: "The prayer of faith has been much dwelt upon this winter; and many Christians, I believe, have had new views on the subject. In many cases, the answers to prayer have been wonderful and astonishing" (*Reminiscences of Gardiner Spring*, p. 222).

[56]Here Matson wrote in the name "Judge Hathaway," but it appears to have been crossed out by Finney.

[57]Here Finney replaced the word "in" with the word "of."

[58]Joshua Hathaway (1751–1836), a graduate of Yale College, had gone to Rome from Vermont in 1795. As a lawyer, he held at various times many prominent positions and was judge of the Court of Common Pleas from 1821. He was married and had daughters, one of whom may have been married to an army officer. See F. B. Dexter, *Biographical Sketches of the Graduates of Yale College,* vol. 4 (New York: Holt, 1907), pp. 550–51.

It is more probable, however, that Finney is referring here to Susannah Huntington (1795–1837), who was married in 1815 to Major James S. Dalliba. After being taken prisoner in the War of 1812, Dalliba was responsible for erecting the arsenal and barracks in Rome in 1813. In 1824 he resigned from the army and became proprietor of an iron factory at Port Henry. He died in 1833. His wife, Susannah, was the eldest daughter of Gurdon Huntington (1768–1840), who was a merchant in Rome, and a brother of George and Henry. See Huntington, *Memoir of the Huntington Family*, p. 195; John W. Barber,*Historical Collections of the State of New York* (New York: Clark, Austin, 1851), p. 229; George W. Cullum, *Biographical Register of the Officers and*

manifested a good deal of opposition to the work, and as was reported said some strong things against it; and this led to her being made a particular subject of prayer. This had come to my knowledge but a short time before the event occurred which I am about to relate. I believe in this case,—some of the principal **ladies**[59]—made this lady a particular subject of prayer, as she was a **woman** of prominent influence in the place. She was an educated lady, ‹**&**›[60] **was a woman** of great force of character and of strong will; and of course she made her opposition felt. But almost as soon as this was known, and the spirit of prayer was given for her in particular, the Spirit of God took ˡher case in hand. One evening almost immediately after I had heard of her case, and perhaps the evening of the very day that the facts came to my knowledge, after the meeting was dismissed and the people had retired, ‹Mr.› Gillett and myself had remained to the very last conversing with some persons who were deeply bowed down with conviction. As they went away and we were about to retire, the sexton came hurriedly to us as we were going out and said, "There is a lady in yonder pew that cannot get out, ‹she›[61] is helpless. Will you not come and see her?" We returned, and lo![62] down in the pew[63] was this lady of whom I have spoken, perfectly overwhelmed with conviction. The pew had been full, and she had attempted to retire with the others that went out; but as she was the last to go out she found herself unable to stand, and sunk down upon the floor, and did so without ˡbeing noticed by those that preceded her. We **helped her up,** had some conversation with her, and found that the Lord had stricken her with unutterable conviction of sin. After praying with her, and giving her the solemn charge to give her heart immediately to Christ, I left her; and **Brother** Gillett, I believe, helped her home. It was a few rods to her house. We afterwards learned that when she got home she went into a chamber by herself and spent the night. It was a cold winter's night. She locked herself in and spent the night alone. ˡThe next day she expressed hope in Christ, and so far as I have known proved to be soundly converted.

MS 336

MS 337

JHF 173

I think I should mention also the conversion of Mrs. Gillett during this revival. She was a sister of the missionary Mills, who was one of the **first**

Graduates of the U. S. Military Academy, from 1802 to 1867, vol. 1 (New York: James Miller, 1879), pp. 117–18; Gale, *Autobiography*, pp. 267–68; and letters of Catherine Huntington Williams to Lydia Finney, 20 March 1837, and to Anne Dalliba, 21 March 1837, Finney Papers, microfilm, roll 3.

The officer in charge of the arsenal when Finney was there was Lt. James Simonson, who was said to have been so apprehensive that he would be seriously affected by the revival, "that he would not go through the streets on foot, but always went on horseback, and at full speed" (*The Circular* [Oneida, N.Y.], 15 November 1869, p. 275; and Cullum, *Register of Officers*, pp. 130–31).

[59] Matson had written down here, "I believe the *ladies* in this case,—some of the principal ladies—. " Finney crossed out the words "the *ladies*" but omitted to cross out the dashes.

[60] The words "and belonged to an influential family" appear to have been crossed out by Finney, who inserted the symbol *&* here.

[61] Finney replaced the word "that" with "she."

[62] Matson had originally written the word "low" but changed it to "lo!"

[63] The following sentence appears to have been crossed out by Finney: "—I forget whether she was lying prostrate, or whether her head was leaned upon the seat and she was sitting upon the floor—. "

missionaries of the American Board.[64] She was a beautiful woman, considerably younger than her husband, and his second wife.[65] She had been, before Mr. Gillett married her, under conviction for several weeks, and had become almost deranged. She had the impression, if I recollect right, that she
MS 338 was not one of the elect, and ˡthat there was no salvation for her. Soon after the revival began in Rome she was powerfully convicted again by the Spirit of the Lord. She was a **lady** of refinement, and fond of dress; and, as is very common **for ladies**, wore about her head and upon her person some trifling ornaments,—nothing, however that I should have thought of as being any stumbling block in her way at all. Being her guest I conversed repeatedly with her as her convictions increased; but it never occurred to me that her fondness for dress could stand in the way of her being converted to God. But as the work became so powerful her distress became alarming; and Mr. Gillett, knowing what had formerly occurred in her case, felt quite alarmed lest she should get into that state of despondency in which she had been years before. She threw herself upon me for instruction. Every time I came into the house, almost, she would **immediately** come to me and beg me to pray for her, and tell me that her distress was more than she could bear. She was
MS 339 evidently going fast to despair; but I could ˡsee that she was depending ‹too much on me›;[66] **and I** therefore tried to avoid her. **But every time I came into the house from visiting among the anxious, as soon as she heard me come in she would immediately throw herself upon my prayers and instructions, as if she expected something from me.**

It went on thus **from day to day**, until one day I came into the house and turned into the study. In a few moments, as usual, she was before me, begging me to pray for her, and complaining that there was no salvation for her. I got up abruptly and left her without praying with her, and saying to her that it was
JHF 174 ˡof no use for me to pray for her, that she was depending upon my prayers. When I did so she sunk down as if she would faint. I left her ‹alone› notwithstanding,[67] and went abruptly from the study to the parlor. In the course of a few moments she came rushing across the hall into the parlor, with her face all in a glow, exclaiming, "O Mr. Finney! I have found the Savior! I
MS 340 have found the Savior! ˡDon't you think that it was the ornaments in my hair

[64] This was the American Board of Commissioners for Foreign Missions (ABCFM). Samuel John Mills (1783–1818), while a student at Andover Theological Seminary, had been largely responsible for the ABCFM being formed, and although he never went out as a missionary with that organization, his missionary efforts entitle him to be considered the "father of foreign missionary work in the United States" (see *DAB*; and Clifton J. Phillips, *Protestant America and the Pagan World: The First Half Century of the American Board of Commissioners for Foreign Missions, 1810–1860* [Cambridge, Mass.: Harvard University Press, 1969]). Mrs. Gillet was his sister Harriet, who died in 1869 at age eighty-four (see *NYE,* 22 April 1869, p. 5).

[65] Mrs. Elizabeth Thomson, the daughter of Rev. Israel Brainerd of Verona, recollected that Harriet "was so beautiful and engaging and pious, that had she been a queen, her fame would have been handed down in history as an elegant woman" (*NYE,* 6 July 1876, p. 2).

[66] Matson had written, "she was depending in an improper manner on me, on my prayers and instructions." Against this in the left-hand margin is written in pencil in what appears to be Lewis Tappan's handwriting, "say too much on him." This was crossed out by Finney and the text altered accordingly.

[67] Here Matson had written down, "I left her notwithstanding, left her alone," but Finney altered it.

that stood in the way of my conversion? I have found when I prayed that they would come up before me; and I would be tempted, as I supposed, to give them up. But," said she, "I thought they were trifles, and that God did not care about such trifles. This was a temptation of Satan. But the ornaments that I wore, continually kept coming up before my mind whenever I attempted to give my heart to God. When you abruptly left me," she said, "I was driven to desperation. I cast myself down and lo!, these ornaments came up again; and I said, I will not have these things come up again, I will put them away from me forever." Said she, "I renounced them, and hated them as things **coming and** stand[**ing**][68] in the way of my salvation. As soon as I promised to give them up, the Lord revealed himself to my soul; and O!" said she, "I wonder I have never understood this before. This was really the great difficulty with me before when I was under conviction, my fondness ‹for dress **&** and I did not know it.["]›[69]

[68] The word "stand-", with a hyphen, is at the end of the line, but the letters *ing* were omitted on the next line. Fairchild added them.

[69] Finney added the words "for dress & I did not know it" when he introduced the new chapter heading on the next page. The quotation marks appear to have been added by Fairchild.

MS 341
JHF 175

CHAPTER XIV

‹*Revival at Utica New York*›

When[1] I had been at Rome about twenty days, one of the elders of Mr. Aikin's church in Utica,[2] a very prominent and a very useful man, died; and I went down to attend his funeral.[3] Mr Aikin[4] conducted the funeral exercises; and I learned from him that the spirit of prayer was already manifest in his congregation, and in that city. He told me that one of his principal ladies had been so deeply exercised in her soul about the state of the church and of the ungodly in that city, that she had prayed for two days and nights almost incessantly, until her strength was quite overcome; that she had literal travail of soul to such an extent that when her own strength was exhausted she could not endure the burden of her mind unless somebody was engaged in prayer with her, upon whose prayer she could lean—some one who could express her desires to God. I understood this, and told Mr. Aikin that the work had already begun in her heart. He recog|nized it, of course; and wished me to commence labor with him ‹&›[5] his people immediately. I soon did so, and be sure the work began ‹at once›.[6] The Word took immediate effect, and the place became filled with the manifested influence of the Holy Spirit. Our meetings were crowded every night, and the work spread and went on powerfully, especially in the two Presbyterian congregations; of which Mr.

MS 342

[1]The chapter heading is written on a separate slip of paper pasted onto the top of the page. Under the pasted section is the original number 209, renumbered 341 by Matson. Also covered over are the words: "for dress; and I did not know it. Of course there was great joy in that house."

[2]Samuel Clark Aikin, or Aiken 1790–1879), was graduated from Andover Theological Seminary in 1817 and became pastor of the First Presbyterian Church in Utica in 1818. In 1835 he moved to Cleveland, Ohio (see the obituary by Anson Smyth, *NYE*, 9 January 1879, p. 1; and *General Catalogue of the Theological Seminary, Andover, 1808–1908* [Boston: Todd, 1909], p. 46). Fairchild altered the spelling of Aikin's name to "Aiken." It is often spelled that way in contemporary sources, and he appears to have spelled it himself with an *e* later in life, but in his letters at this time, he signed his name "Aikin."

[3]This was Andrew Merrell, a partner in the publishing firm of Merrell and Hastings, who published *The Western Recorder*. He died on 25 January 1826 at age thirty-five. See his obituary in *WR*, 31 January 1826, p. 19.

[4]Matson had written down here, "I was introduced to Mr. Aikin, who," but he changed it to "Mr. Aikin."

[5]Matson had written here the symbol *&*, which Finney clarified by writing his symbol over it.

[6]Here Finney changed the word "immediately" to "at once." Finney started working at Utica about 1 February 1826. See Aikin's report in *A Narrative of the Revival of Religion in the County of Oneida; particularly in the Bounds of the Presbytery of Oneida, in the year 1826* (Utica: Hastings and Tracy, 1826; reprint, Princeton: D. A. Borrenstein, 1827), p. 30.

Aikin was pastor **of one**,[7] and Mr. Brace **was pastor** of the other.[8] I divided my labors between the two congregations.

Soon after I commenced in Utica I observed to Mr. Aikin that Mr. **Broadhead,** of whom I have made ˡmention,[9] did not attend the meetings as I saw. But **it was but** a few evenings **before** just **before I began** to preach, **while sitting in the pulpit,** Mr. Aikin whispered to me **and told me** that Mr. **Broadhead** had come in. He pointed him out to me as he made his way up the aisle to his seat. I took my text and proceeded to address the congregation. I had spoken but a few moments when I observed Mr. **Broadhead** rise up in his ‹slip›,[10] turn deliberˡately around, wrap his great coat about him, and kneel down. I observed that it excited the attention of those that sat near, who knew him, and produced a considerable sensation in that part of the house. The sheriff continued on his knees during the whole service. He then retired to his room **in** the hotel in which he boarded. He was a man perhaps fifty years old, and **a bachelor**. He afterwards told me that his mind was greatly burdened when he went home and brought up the subject to which he had been listening. I had pressed the congregation to accept Christ just as he was presented in the Gospel. The question of the present acceptance of Christ, and the whole situation in regard to the sinner's relation to him and his relation to the sinner, had been the subject of discourse. He said that he had treasured up in his mind the points that had been made, and that he presented them solemnly before himself, and said, "My soul, will you consent to this? Will you accept of Christ, and give up sin, give up yourself? And will you do it *now*?" ˡHe[11] said he had thrown himself, in the agony of his mind, upon his bed. He made this point with himself, and conjured his soul,

JHF 176

MS 343

MS 344

[7]The First Presbyterian Church in Utica had originally been organized in 1803, in combination with the church in Whitesboro. They were separated in 1813. The original church was built in 1807, but at the time of Finney's visit there were plans for a new church. See *A Brief History of the First Presbyterian Church and Society in Utica* (Utica: William Williams, 1829).

[8]The Second Presbyterian Church had been formed in May 1824. It was taken over by Aikin's new assistant, Samuel William Brace (1790–1878), and a new church was built in 1825. Brace was from Vermont and was a fellow student of Aikin's at Andover. He had been a minister at Phelps, New York, when he was called to Utica. After four years he moved to Skaneateles, and in 1843 he moved to Binghamton. He retired in 1845 or 1846 to Utica, where he continued supplying pulpits and doing agency work (Moses Bagg, *Pioneers of Utica* [Utica: Curtiss and Childs, 1877], pp. 460, 598–601; and P. H. Fowler, *Historical Sketch of Presbyterianism Within the Bounds of the Synod of Central New York* [Utica, N.Y.: Curtiss and Childs, 1877], pp. 209–12).

Until the completion of their new church, the congregation worshiped in the First Presbyterian Session Room on Hotel Street. The new church was completed in August 1826. Known as the Bleecker Street Church, it was considered acoustically to be one of the finest churches in the country. Thomas W. Seward wrote, "It was the favorite place for conventions of every kind. In many respects it may be said to have been the counterpart as well as contemporary of the old Broadway Tabernacle of New York" ("The Bleecker Street Church, Utica," *Transactions of the Oneida Historical Society of Utica,* 1887–1889, pp. 143–58).

There was some doubt about the real commitment of S. W. Brace to the New Measures. He was considered by some to be "an *anti*-revival minister." See John Frost to Finney, 22 March 1827, Finney Papers, microfilm, roll 1; and S. W. Brace to Asahel Nettleton, 6 December 1832, Nettleton Papers, Hartford Seminary.

[9]See MS 328–30.

[10]Here Matson had written down the words "his seat," but Finney crossed them both out and inserted "slip."

[11]Pages 344 to 346 were at first renumbered 343 to 345 in error and then corrected by Matson.

to accept "*now* and *here*." Right there, he said, his distress left him so suddenly that he fell asleep and did not ‹a›wake[12] for several hours. When he did awake he found his mind full of peace and rest in Christ; and from this moment he became an earnest worker for Christ among his acquaintances.[13]

I have said that he boarded at a hotel, which was at that time kept by a Mr. **Shepard.**[14] The Spirit took powerful hold in that house. Mr. **Shepard** himself, **the keeper of the hotel,** was soon made a subject of prayer and JHF 177 |became converted; and a large number of his family and of his boarders.[15] Indeed that largest hotel in the town became a center of spiritual influence, and many were converted there. The stages as they passed through stopped at the hotel; and so powerful was the impression in the community that I heard MS 345 of several cases of persons that just stopped **to dine, |or breakfast, or sup** ‹or to spend a night›[16] being powerfully convicted and converted before they left the town. Indeed, both in this place and in Rome it was a common remark that nobody could be in the town, or pass through it, without being aware of the presence of God; that a divine influence seemed to pervade the place, and the whole atmosphere **seemed** to be instinct with a divine life.

A merchant from Lowville, **in Lewis county,** came to Utica to **get some goods,** ‹**&**›[17] do some business in his line. He stopped at the hotel where Mr. **Broadhead** boarded. He found the whole conversation in the town was such

[12]Finney altered the words "wake up" to "awake."

[13]He was later to become a leader in the Presbyterian churches in Utica. He was one of the founders of the Oneida Evangelical Association, which was to start employing Finney in December 1826; and he was a vice-president of the Utica Bible Society and the Western Sunday School Union. See *WR,* 3 June 1828, p. 91; and 9 July 1833, p. 111; J. Burchard to Finney, 17 October 1827; and M. Brayton to Finney, 30 October 1827, in Finney Papers, microfilm, roll 1.

Moses Bagg wrote:

> When past middle life, and under the influence of the revival that attended the preaching of Rev. Mr. Finney, Mr. Brodhead made a profession of religion, and became beyond doubt a sincere and humble follower of his Saviour. He united with the Presbyterian Church, and when shortly afterwards the Reformed Dutch Church was organized, he attached himself to it and was one of its ardent supporters. Yet so emotional and impulsive was he, so little were his feelings under control, that his surliness would betray itself in the most unseemly times and places; and even his church associates were not beyond the range of his testy outbursts (*Pioneers of Utica*, p. 110).

[14]According to Moses Bagg,

> Abraham Shepard of New London, Conn., assumed charge of Bagg's [Hotel], and kept it two or three years, when he kept the United States (1828) the Utica Hotel (1829), and the Coffee House (1832–33). Then, after a short experience as a dealer in lumber, he engaged in the sale of crockery. In 1845 he was a resident of the place, but without occupation. . . . His subsequent home was in Troy. He was a man of mild deportment and gentlemanly bearing (*Pioneers of Utica*, p. 614).

[15]Moses Bagg listed his family:

> One of his daughters became the wife of John A. Collier of Binghampton, one married John T. Kirkland, of Cleveland, and another the Rev. John W. Fowler, pastor of the First Presbyterian Church of Utica. He had three sons, Edward, who studied law and resided abroad; Henry, who died young; and William, a merchant of Troy (*Pioneers of Utica*, p. 614).

Abraham Shepard was later a director of the Western Sunday School Union. See *WR,* 9 July 1833, p. 111.

[16]Finney added the phrase "or to spend a night."

[17]This is another case where Finney appears to have written over Matson's symbol *&*. See n. 5 above.

as greatly to annoy him, for he was an unconverted man. He was vexed, and said he could do no business there, it was all religion; and he resolved to go home. He could not go into a store but **what** religion was intruded upon him, and he could do no business with them. That evening he would go home. These remarks had been made in the presence of some of the young converts who boarded at the hotel, and I think especially in the presence of Mr. **Broadhead**. As the stage was expected to leave late at night, he ˡwas observed to go to the bar just before he retired to pay his bill; saying that Mr. **Shepard** would not probably be up when the stage passed through, and he wished therefore to settle his bill before he retired. Mr. **Shepard** said that he observed while he was settling his bill that his mind was very much exercised,[18] and he suggested to several of the gentleman boarders that they should make him a subject of prayer. They took him, I believe, to Mr. **Broadhead**'s room, and conversed with him, and prayed with him, and before the stage came **along** he was a converted man. And so concerned did he feel immediately about the ˡpeople of his own place, that when the stage came **along** he took passage and went immediately home. As soon as he arrived at-home he told his family **what the Lord had done for his soul**, and called them together and prayed with them. **Being** a very prominent citizen, and very outspoken, and everywhere proclaiming what the Lord had done for his soul, it immediately produced a very solemn impression in Lowville, and soon resulted in a great revival in that place.

MS 346

JHF 178

ˡIt was in the midst of the revival in Utica that we first heard of the opposition to those revivals that was springing up in the east.[19] Mr. Nettleton wrote some letters to Mr. Aikin, with whom I was laboring, in which it was manifest that he was very much mistaken with regard to the character of those revivals. Mr. Aikin showed me those letters, and they were handed around among the ministers in the neighborhood, as they were intended to be. Among them was one in which Mr Nettleton stated fully what he regarded as objectionable in the conduct of those revivals;[20] but as no such things were done in those revivals, or had been known at all **as he complained of**, we took no other notice of **those** letters than to read them and let them pass. Mr. Aikin, however, replied privately to one or two of them, assuring Mr Nettleton that no such things were done.[21] **I said that no such things were done as he complained of.** I do not recollect now whether **he mentioned** the fact that **occasionally females** would pray in the social meetings.

MS 347

[18] Matson had originally written down the word "agitated" but changed it to "exercised."

[19] Finney was initially in Utica from February to May of 1826, but he returned there at various times, particularly in September and November, and again in January 1827. It was during the summer of 1826 that reports from the area started to alarm the New England ministers.

[20] Nettleton's first letter to Aikin was dated 13 January 1827. Nettleton had also written what came to be known as the "Historical Letter," a copy of which was sent to Aikin (see MS 418). Another letter dated 15 February 1827, sent to John Frost, was also for Aikin and Noah Coe, and other letters were sent to members of the Oneida Presbytery. See *Religious Intelligencer* (New Haven), 15 December 1827, pp. 456–59; 22 December 1827, pp. 463–68; and 5 January 1828, pp. 498–500. Letters were also sent by Lyman Beecher (see n. 96 below).

[21] Two letters of Aikin to Nettleton, dated 4 February and 7 May 1827, are in the Nettleton Papers, Hartford Seminary, but owing to their poor condition and the difficulty of deciphering them, copies have not been available for study.

Whether he made that complaint or not,[22] it is true that in a few instances ladies, and some very prominent ladies, who were strongly pressed in spirit, MS 348 would lead ǀin prayer in their social meetings which we held daily from house to house.[23] No opposition that I know of was manifested to this either at Utica or at Rome; nor was it a thing that I had myself introduced, for I had no agency in introducing that among their people, and do not know whether it had existed there before or not. Indeed it was not a subject of much conversation or thought, so far as I know, among the people in the neighborhood where it occurred.[24]

JHF 179 I have already said that Mr. Weeks, who maintained the ǀmost offensive doctrines on the subject of divine efficiency, was known to be opposed to those revivals.[25] For the information of those who may not know that any such doctrines were ever held, I would say that Mr. Weeks, and those that agreed with him, held that both sin and holiness were produced in the mind by a direct act of Almighty power; that God made men sinners or holy at His sovereign discretion, but in both cases by a direct act of almighty power, an act as irresistible as that of creation itself; that in fact God was the only MS 349 ǀproper agent in the universe, and that all creatures acted only as they were moved and compelled to act by an irresistible act of omnipotence; that every sin in the universe, both of men and of devils, was the result of a direct act of irresistible power on the part of God. This they attempted in a most sophistical way to prove by the Bible. Mr. Weeks' idea of conversion or regeneration was, that God who had made men sinners, made them also in regenerating them to approve of this, to admit that He had a right to do it for His glory, and to send them to hell for the sins which He had directly created in them, or compelled them to commit by the force of Omnipotence. In conversions that did not bring sinners to accept this view of the subject, he had no confidence. Those that have read Mr. Weeks' nine sermons on the subject, will see that I have not misrepresented his views.[26] However, as this

[22]This was one of the chief complaints in Nettleton's letters.

[23]Samuel Aikin made a particular point of mentioning "various small circles for prayer" at which "females, in some cases, though more seldom than we could wish, have taken a part" (Oneida Presbytery *Narrative*, p. 33.)

[24]Theodore Weld, whose conversion Finney describes in MS 359–67, wrote to Angelina Grimke, his future wife and one of the pioneers in the women's rights movement:

> and the very week that I was converted to Christ in the city of Utica during a powerful revival of religion under brother Finney—and the first time I ever spoke in a religious meeting—I urged females both to pray and speak if they felt deeply enough to do it, and not to be restrained from it by the fact that they were *females*. I made these remarks at a meeting when not less than two hundred persons were present of both sexes, and *five* ministers of the gospel at least, and I think more. The result was that seven females, a number of them the most influential female christians in the city, confessed their sin in being restrained by their sex, and prayed publickly in succession at that very meeting. It made a great deal of talk and discussion, and the subject of female praying and female speaking in public was discussed throughout western New York (letter dated 26 August 1837 in Gilbert H. Barnes and Dwight L. Dumond, eds., *Letters of Theodore Dwight Weld, Angelina Grimké Weld, and Sarah Grimké, 1822–1844*, vol. 1 [Gloucester, Mass: Peter Smith, 1965], pp. 432–33).

[25]See MS 280.

[26]William R. Weeks, *The Doctrine of the Universal Decrees and Agency of God, Asserted and Vindicated: Nine Sermons from Ephesians 1.11* (Plattsburgh, N.Y., 1813). A second edition was

view of Mr. Weeks was embraced to a considerable extent by ministers and professors of religion in that region, his known opposition, together with that of some other ministers, greatly emboldened and increased the opposition.[27] |The work, however, went on with great power, converting all classes, until Mr. Aikin reported the hopeful conversion of five hundred in the course of a few weeks, most of them, I believe, belonging to his own congregation.[28] Revivals **at that time** were comparatively a new thing in that region; and the great mass of the people had not become convinced that they were the work of God. They were not *awed* by them |as they afterwards became. It seemed to be extensively the impression that those revivals would soon pass away, and would prove to have been but a mere excitement of animal feeling. I do not mean that those that were interested in the work had any such idea.

MS 350

JHF 180

One circumstance occurred in the midst of that revival that made a powerful impression. The Oneida presbytery met there while the revival was going on in its full strength.[29] Among others there was an aged clergyman **by the name of Southard ‹I believe›**,[30] a stranger to me.[31] **He** was very much annoyed by the heat and fervor of the revival. He found the public mind all |absorbed on the subject of religion; that there was prayer and religious conversation everywhere, even in the stores and other public places. **Mr. Southard** had never seen a revival, and had never heard what he heard there. He was a Scotchman, and I believe had not been very long in this country.[32] On Friday afternoon, before presbytery adjourned, he arose and made a violent speech against the revival as it was going on. What he said greatly shocked and grieved the Christian people who were present.[33] They felt like

MS 351

published in 1819 by Miller and Huchens of Providence, Rhode Island, and a third edition was published in 1839 in Newark, New Jersey.

[27] Philemon H. Fowler reckoned that Finney exaggerated the influence of Weeks, whereas in fact, "that divine stood almost entirely alone, with little or no countenance from his surrounding brethren" (*Historical Sketch of Presbyterianism*, p. 216).

[28] This was reported in the Oneida Presbytery *Narrative*. Aikin gives a figure of five hundred converts but does not indicate that "most of them" belonged to his own congregation. "More than a hundred" had joined the Presbyterian church, and there were an additional fifty adults, who for various reasons had not joined the church, as well as many children (p. 31).

[29] The Oneida Presbytery met in 1826 at Utica, from Wednesday, 6 September, to Friday, 8 September. For the report of the meetings, see "Minutes of the Oneida Presbytery," 5:55–59, manuscript in Presbyterian Historical Society. At this meeting Finney's membership was transferred from the Presbytery of St. Lawrence to the Presbytery of Oneida.

[30] Finney added the words "I believe."

[31] This was, in fact, Rev. James Southworth, stated supply for the Presbyterian Church in Plainfield, Otsego County, New York. He was a man of about fifty years of age. In his early ministry he had labored in Otsego County before becoming pastor of the Congregational Church in Bridgewater, Oneida County, New York. He was there around 1810 for several years and was one of the founders of the Oneida Bible Society at that time. Later he labored in the neighboring town of Plainfield. He was the father of Tertius D. Southworth, the successor in Dr. Emmons's pulpit in Franklin, Massachusetts. See Bagg, *Pioneers of Utica,* p. 285; *Minutes of the General Assembly of the Presbyterian Church in the United States of America* (Philadelphia), 1825, p. 309; *The Congregational Quarterly* (Boston) 18 (April 1876): 333; and *WR,* 10 October 1826, p. 163.

[32] An obituary states that he "was a native of Canajoharie, Montgomery Co. He was born of poor parents; and his education for a time was greatly neglected. Possessing, however, an uncommonly vigorous mind, he so far overcame these obstacles, as to rise to a very respectable standing among his brethren in the ministry" (*WR,* 10 October 1826, p. 163).

[33] In another account of this incident, Finney stated that he himself was not present at the meeting ("Hindrances to Revival," *The Independent* [New York], 16 April 1874, p. 2).

falling on their faces before God, and crying to **Him** to prevent what he had said from doing any mischief. The presbytery adjourned just at evening. Some of the members went home and others remained over night. Christians gave themselves to prayer. There was a great crying to God that night that he would counteract any evil influence that might result from that speech **which** MS 352 **had been made by Mr. Southard.** ˡThe next morning **Mr Southard** was found dead in his bed.[34] **This again produced a great shock, but on the right side. It more than counteracted all the influence which Mr. Southard's speech had had in presbytery.** In the course of these revivals persons from a distance, in almost every direction hearing what the Lord was doing, or being attracted by curiosity and wonder at what they heard, came to **witness what was doing,** ‹&› many of them ‹were› converted to Christ.[35] Among **others** Dr. Garret Judd, who soon after went to the Sandwich islands as a missionary, and has been well-known to lovers of missions for many JHF 181 years, was one.[36] He belonged to the congregation of Mr. ˡWeeks, to whom I have referred. His father, old ‹Dr› Judd, was an earnest Christian man.[37] He came down to Utica and sympathized greatly with the revival.

About the same time **of the conversion of Dr Judd** a young **lady,** Miss **Fanny Thomas,** from some part of New England, came to Utica under the MS 353 following circumstances.[38] She was teaching ˡa high school, in the neighborhood of Newburgh, N.Y.[39] As much was said in the newspapers about the

[34]*The Western Recorder* reported: "We stop the press to announce the sudden death of Rev. Mr. Southworth, one of the members of the Oneida Presbytery. He was found dead in his bed." He died on Sunday, 17 September. The date of his death, however, does not coincide with the meetings of the presbytery, which were ten days earlier. He died at his home in Bridgewater. See *WR,* 19 September 1826, p. 151; 10 October 1826, p. 163; and the Oneida Presbytery "Minutes," p. 60.

[35]Here Matson had written down "to witness what the Lord was doing, and were many of them, converted to Christ," but Finney altered it.

[36]Gerrit Parmele Judd (1803–1873), born in Paris, New York, went to Fairfield Medical College. His conversion was on 11 April 1826, and he sailed as a missionary doctor to Honolulu in November of 1827. From about 1833 he became increasingly involved in secular and political affairs in Hawaii, so that in 1842 he left the mission. He became minister of foreign affairs in 1843, minister of the interior in 1845, and minister of finance in 1846. He was "the prime minister in fact, if not in name" and was the trusted adviser of the king. He married another friend of the Finneys, Laura Fish. See *DAB*; Gerrit P. Judd IV, *Dr. Judd, Hawaii's Friend: A Biography of Gerrit Parmele Judd (1803–1873)* (Honolulu: University of Hawaii Press, 1960); and letters from the Judds to Finney, in the Finney Papers. Judd's Christian name was originally spelled "Garret" by Matson, but he appears to have altered it, inserting an additional *r* so that it was misread as "Garnet" by the typesetters.

[37]Elnathan Judd (1773–1845) was a physician in Paris, New York, for thirty years. After difficulties with Mr. Weeks's church in 1826, the Judd family transferred their membership to the New Hartford church. His wife, Betsey, was a sister of Thomas, Truman, and Orlando Hastings. (See Judd, *Dr. Judd*, pp. 5–11; for a eulogy on his Christian character see *The New York Observer*, 27 September 1845, p. 153.) Matson had written "Mr. Judd," and Finney changed it to "Dr Judd."

[38]Fanny Hinckley Thomas (1798–1883) was from Westfield, Massachusetts, and graduated from the academy there. She apparently had worked as a pioneer missionary among the poor in New York. See Addison Gulick, *John Thomas Gulick* (Chicago: University of Chicago Press, 1932), pp. 3–5; and Patricia Grimshaw, "Christian Woman, Pious Wife, Faithful Mother, Devoted Missionary: Conflicts in Roles of American Missionary Women in Nineteenth-Century Hawaii," *Feminist Studies* 9, no. 3 (Fall 1983): 510.

[39]The school was in Middletown, Orange County, New York, about twenty-one miles west-southwest of Newburgh. See the letter of M. H. Corwin in *NYE,* 7 July 1864, p. 4.

revival in Utica **and that region**, Miss **Thomas** among others became filled with astonishment **and wonder**, and with a desire to go and see for herself what it meant. She dismissed her school for ten days, and took the stage for Utica. As she passed through Genesee st. to the hotel **where she stopped**, she observed on one of the signs the name of **Briggs Thomas**.[40] She was an entire stranger, and did not know that she had an acquaintance or relative **in that place**. But after stopping a day or two at her hotel, and inquiring who **Briggs Thomas** was, she **thought he might be a relative, and** dropped him a note saying that the daughter of a Mr. **Thomas**, naming her father, was at the hotel, and would be pleased to see him.[41] Mr. **Thomas** waited upon her and found that she was a distant relative of his, and invited her immediately to his house. She accepted his invitation, ׀and he being an earnest Christian man, immediately took her to all the meetings and tried to interest her in religion. She was greatly surprized at all that she saw, and a good deal annoyed. She was an energetic, highly cultivated, and proud young lady; and the manner in which people conversed with her, and pressed upon her the necessity of immediately giving her heart to God, very much disturbed her. **Especially did** the preaching which she heard from night to night **take** a deep hold upon her. The guilt of sinners was largely insisted upon; and their desert and danger of eternal damnation, **was** made prominent in what she heard. This aroused her opposition; but still the work of conviction went powerfully on in her heart. In the **mean time** I had not seen her to converse with ׀her, but had heard from Mr. **Thomas** of her state of mind. After writhing under the truth for a few days she called at my lodging.[42] She sat down upon the sofa in the parlor. I drew up my chair in front of her, and began to press her with the claims of God. ׀She referred to my preaching that sinners deserved to be sent to an eternal hell, and said that she could not receive it,—that she did not believe that God was such a **Being**. I replied, "Nor do you yet understand what sin is in its true nature and ill desert; if you did, you would not complain of God for sending the sinner to an eternal hell.["][43] I then spread out that subject before her in conversation as plainly as I could. **I soon saw that the conviction was ripening in her mind.** Much as she hated to believe it, still the conviction of its truth was becoming irresistible. I conversed in this strain

MS 354

JHF 182

MS 355

[40] Briggs White Thomas (1788–1874) arrived in Utica from Connecticut in 1804. After a short residence in Canada and Ogdensburg he started in a mercantile business in Utica with his brother-in-law, Anson Thomas, in about 1815. The partnership lasted for fifteen years. He was subsequently associated with Truman Parmelee and Milton Brayton. In 1833 he went to Albany, but being unsuccessful he returned to Utica. In later life he was a clerk in a bank. He was active in the Presbyterian church and in Sunday school work. The store he and Anson Thomas built was "on the site of the First National Bank and extended around the corner into Catherine Street." See Bagg, *Pioneers of Utica*, pp. 182, 184, 379–81.

[41] Her father was John Thomas of Westfield, Massachusetts. See "Vital Statistics" of P. J. Gulick, in *The Congregational Quarterly* 20 (April 1878): 444.

[42] In another account Finney is reported as saying: "Soon a friend with whom she was boarding said to me, 'We have a dreadful case at our house. You must come and see her.' I went." The subsequent events are then reported as happening at Mr. Thomas's house rather than at Finney's lodging. This appears to be confirmed by Daniel Nash in a letter to Finney. He wrote of "Fanny H. Thomas, converted at Deac. Thomas' Utica, when we were there" (*OE,* 21 November 1855, p. 186; and Nash to Finney, 26–28 November 1831, Finney Papers, microfilm, roll 3).

[43] The quotation marks here appear to have been inserted by Fairchild.

for sometime until I saw that she was ready to sink under the ripened conviction; and then I turned and said a few words about the place which Jesus holds, and what was the real situation of things in regard to the salvation of those who thus deserved to be damned. Her countenance waxed pale‹. I›n a moment ‹after›[44] she threw up her hands and shrieked, and then fell forward ‹upon›[45] the arm of the sofa, and let her heart break. |I think she had not wept at all before. Her eyes were dry, her countenance haggard and pale, her sensibility all locked up; but now the flood-gates were opened she let her whole gushing heart out before God.[46] I had no occasion to say any more to her. She soon arose and went to her own lodgings. She almost immediately gave up her school, offered herself as a foreign missionary, was married to a Mr. Gulick,[47] and went out to the Sandwich islands, I think at the same time that Dr Judd went out.[48] Her history as a missionary is pretty well known. She has been a very efficient missionary, and has raised several sons who also are missionaries.[49] **One of them was at our house a few months since, and has gone on a mission to Mexico.**[50] **I was refreshed to hear his account of**

MS 356

[44]Here Matson had written down: "Her countenance waxed pale in a moment; she threw up her hands," etc. But Finney changed it, adding the word "after."

[45]Here Finney changed the word "on" to "upon."

[46]Finney said also, "Almost her first words as she broke silence again were 'I'll be a missionary!' " (*OE,* 21 November 1855, p. 186).

[47]Peter Johnson Gulick (1797–1877) from Freehold, New Jersey, was a graduate of Princeton, where he had roomed with James Brainerd Taylor. He was married to Fanny Thomas on 5 September 1827. See Rufus Anderson, *A Heathen Nation Evangelized. History of the Sandwich Island Mission* (Boston: Congregational Publishing Society, 1870), pp. 85, 364; and Alfred Nevin, ed., *Encyclopaedia of the Presbyterian Church in the United States of America* (Philadelphia: Presbyterian Encyclopaedia Publishing Co., 1884), p. 285.

[48]They embarked from Boston with the Judds and twelve other missionaries for Hawaii on 3 November under the auspices of the American board. Theodore Weld, who was among the friends at the farewell celebration, recollected Lyman Beecher being there to see them off. When the missionaries were gathering before the departure, Laura Judd wrote to the Finneys:

> O you remember Fanny Thomas, now Mrs Gulick, one of our happy number, she is well, we are very sociable when together. I shall leave you to guess the most common topic. She said to me last evening, "How is it that Boston people are sending Finneyites on Missions? I should not suppose they would dare to" (Laura Judd to Charles and Lydia Finney, 30 October 1827, Finney Papers, microfilm, roll 2; and *Autobiography, Correspondence, etc., of Lyman Beecher, D.D.,* ed. Charles Beecher, 2 vols. [New York: Harper, 1863, 1865], 2:312-13.

Jonathan S. Green, the brother of Rev. Beriah Green, and his wife were also in the party. The arrival in the Sandwich Islands of a group of missionaries so recently involved in the scenes of the revivals of western New York may have had some significance in preparing the way for the revival in Hawaii in the 1830s. The first wave of that revival appears to have started on the island of Kauai in 1832, where the Gulicks were laboring. See the letter from a missionary (possibly Gerrit Judd) to Finney, dated October 183[2] in the *Religious Intelligencer,* 13 April 1833, p. 734; and the letters of P. J. Gulick in *The Missionary Herald* (Boston) 29 (November 1833): 403–4; and 32 (November 1836): 429; see also pp. 313 n. 67 (MS 580).

[49]The "missionary Gulicks" were well known. Their six sons and a daughter became missionaries. Another son, named Charles Finney Gulick, also planning to be a missionary, died at age nineteen, while a student. Several of the grandchildren went to Oberlin College. See, e.g., Frances Gulick Jewett, *Luther Halsey Gulick: Missionary in Hawaii, Micronesia, Japan, and China* (London: Stock, 1895); and P. J. Gulick to Finney, Sandwich Isles, 24 December 1835, Finney Papers, microfilm, roll 3. See also *The Independent,* 23 February 1854, p. 61; and the articles entitled, "A Missionary Family," in *NYE,* 2 June 1864, p. 1; 30 November 1871, p. 6; and 8 October 1874, p. 1.

[50]This was Theodore Weld Gulick (1837–1924), the sixth of the Gulick brothers. He had been studying at Union Theological Seminary and was on his way out to Mexico under the

the spirit and labors of his mother as a missionary in the Sandwich islands. With his father, Mr. Gulick, I have no personal acquaintance,[51] but his mother I shall not soon forget.

While making it my home in Utica I preached considerable[52] in New Hartford, a village ǀfour miles south of Utica. There was a precious and powerful work of grace, a Mr. Coe being ǀat the time pastor of the Presbyterian church.[53] I preached also at Whitesboro, another beautiful village, four miles west of Utica;[54] where also was a powerful revival. The pastor, Mr. John Frost, was an efficient, powerful laborer in the work.[55]

MS 357

JHF 183

Another circumstance occurred which I must not fail to notice. There was a Cotton Manufactory on the Oriskany creek, a little above Whitesboro, a place now called New York mills. It was owned by a Mr. Wolcott, an unconverted man, but a gentleman of high standing and good morals.[56] My

auspices of the American and Foreign Christian Union. He was in Oberlin on 12 September 1867 and spoke at the Thursday Lecture. See *Hawaiian Mission Children's Society, 16th Annual Report*, 1868, p. 8; *73rd Annual Report*, 1925, p. 67; and *The Lorain County News* (Oberlin), 18 September 1867, p. 3. Information from Margaret S. Ehlke.

[51] Although Finney had never met P. J. Gulick up until this time, they corresponded. But in April 1871 Gulick visited Finney in Oberlin. See letters of Gulick to Finney in the Finney Papers; and Roselle T. Cross, "Memories of Charles G. Finney," typescript, n.d., Alumni Records, file 28/1, "Roselle Theodore Cross," Oberlin College Archives.

[52] Here Matson had written down "a considerable," but the word "a" appears to have been crossed out by Finney. Compare this with the sentence referred to in p. 209 n. 29 (MS 399).

[53] Noah Coe (1786–1871) was a graduate of Yale and Andover and was ordained in 1811 in Chester, New York. In 1814 he moved to New Hartford Presbyterian Church, where he remained until 1835. He later labored in Congregational churches in Connecticut and New York. See *Obituary Record of Graduates of Yale College Deceased during the academical year ending in July 1871 . . .* (New Haven: Yale College, 1871), p. 4.

Coe reported on the revival in New Hartford: "The labours of Mr. Finney and Mr. Nash, the former of whom preached six sermons, and attended the same number of meetings of inquiry, were greatly blessed; as in these meetings of inquiry, it was not uncommon for two or three in every meeting to submit their hearts to Christ" (Oneida Presbytery *Narrative,* pp. 28–29).

[54] Whitesboro and New Hartford were villages in the township of Whitestown.

[55] Matson had written this sentence in the margin. Fairchild altered it and then crossed it out. Then he entered the altered version in the text.

John Frost (1788–1842) was a graduate of Middlebury and Andover, and he was ordained in 1810. He was involved in work on behalf of foreign missions until he was called to Whitesboro in 1813. He took over the Presbyterian church when it was divided from the Utica church, and he remained pastor until he resigned in 1833 to work for the Oneida Institute. He subsequently became pastor of the Presbyterian church in Elmira, New York. See transcription of an obituary from a local paper in *Records of the First Presbyterian Church of Whitesboro, New York*, ed. Royden W. Vosburgh for the New York Genealogical and Biographical Society (New York, 1920), pp. 200–202. Reference supplied by Leonard I. Sweet.

Aikin, Frost, and Coe were the leading triumvirate in the Oneida Presbytery. They were most prominent in sponsoring Finney and the New Measure revivals, Frost and Coe being on the committee responsible for preparing the Oneida Presbytery *Narrative*. See Hiram H. Kellogg, "Reminiscences— 'Aiken, Frost, and Coe'," *NYE,* 3 April 1879, p. 1.

In John Frost's report of the revival, he wrote: "We lament that Mr. Finney could not have spent a little time with us; but his labours were needed elsewhere. The few lectures he preached while at Utica were useful" (Oneida Presbytery *Narrative*, p. 27).

[56] This was Benjamin S. Wolcott, Jr. His father, Benjamin S. Wolcott, Sr., had worked at the Cumberland Mill in Rhode Island, where the new Arkwright process had been introduced. In 1808 he had been invited by the newly formed Oneida Manufacturing Society in Whitestown to come and take charge of erecting a mill. This was the first cotton factory in the state of New York. He was joined in 1809 by his son, and together they completed the mill. Soon after

brother in law, Mr **George Andrews,** was at that time superintendent of the factory.[57] I was invited to go and preach ‹at that place›[58] and went up one evening and preached in the village school house, which was **of** large **size** and was crowded **to its utmost capacity.**[59] The **W**ord, I could see, took powerful effect among the people, especially among the young people who were at work in the factory. The next morning after breakfast I went into the factory

MS 358 to look through it. ¦As I went through **the factory** I observed there was a good deal of agitation among those **that** were busy at their looms, and their mules, and other implements of work. On passing through one of the apartments where a great number of young ‹women›[60] were attending to their **spinning or** weaving, I observed a couple of ‹them›[61] eyeing me, and speaking very earnestly to each other; and I could see that they were a good deal agitated, although they both laughed.[62] I went slowly toward them. They saw me coming, and were evidently much ‹excited.›[63] **The thread of one of them broke**, and I observed that her hands trembled so that she could not mend it. I approached slowly, looking on each side at the machinery as I passed, but observed that this girl grew more and more agitated, and could not proceed with her work. When I came within eight or ten feet of her I looked solemnly at her. She observed it, and was quite overcome, and sunk down, and burst into tears.[64] **That** impression caught almost like powder; and

operations began his father returned to the East, and Benjamin Wolcott, Jr., was made superintendent, or "agent."

In 1825 Benjamin Wolcott, Jr., took control of the company and built a factory village, renaming it New York Mills, which by 1845 was the tenth largest producer of cotton yarn in the United States. He was to become the leading industrialist in the area, a philanthropist of note, and an elder in the Presbyterian church. His daughter Elizabeth was also converted about this time. See Moses M. Bagg, "The Earliest Factories of Oneida, and their Projectors," *Transactions of the Oneida Historical Society,* 1881, pp. 112–24; Mary P. Ryan, *Cradle of the Middle Class* (New York: Cambridge University Press, 1981), pp. 9–10, 43–47; and *NYE,* 14 November 1895, p. 18.

[57] George Andrews (born 1793) was the eldest brother of Finney's wife, Lydia.

[58] The words "at that place" were added by Finney.

[59] Benjamin Wolcott had helped to get a Methodist meeting started at the factory village. Many of the other families there were involved with the Presbyterian church at Whitesboro. See Ryan, *Cradle of the Middle Class,* pp. 47–48.

[60] Here Finney changed the word "ladies" to "women."

[61] Here Finney changed the words "young ladies" to "them."

[62] In other accounts of this incident Finney said that the people who worked there all knew him by sight and knew who he was but that he knew none of them. See *Lectures on Revivals of Religion,* ed. William G. McLoughlin (Cambridge, Mass.: Belknap, 1960), pp. 18–19; and *The Independent,* 18 January 1872, p. 1.

[63] Here Finney changed the word "agitated" to "excited."

[64] The effect of Finney's look upon this woman was used by John Bate in his book *Influence of Mind on Mind* as an example of the powerful unconscious influence that eyes can have. Bate quoted from the account in *The Independent,* which demonstrates the point even more forcefully:

> As I approached nearer to those who had recognized me, they seemed to increase in their manifestations of lightness of mind. Their levity made a peculiar impression upon me; I felt it to my very heart. I stopped short and looked at them; I know not how, as my whole mind was absorbed with the sense of their guilt and danger. As I settled my countenance upon them, I observed that one of them became very much agitated. A thread broke. She attempted to mend it; but her hands trembled in such a manner that she could not do it. I immediately observed that the sensation was spreading, and had become universal among that class of triflers. I looked steadily at them; until one after another gave up, and paid no more attention to their looms (*The Independent,* 18

in a few moments nearly all in the room were in tears.[65] This feeling spread through the factory. Mr. Wolcott, the owner of the establishment, was present, and seeing the state of things, he said to the superintendent, "Stop the mill, and let the people attend to religion; for it is more important that our souls should be saved than that this factory run." The gate was immediately shut down, and the factory stopped;—but where should we assemble? The superintendent suggested that the mule room was large; and the mules being run up, we could assemble there. We did so, and a more powerful meeting I scarcely ever saw. It went on with great power. The building was large, and had a great many people in it from the garret to the cellar. The revival went through the mill with astonishing power, and in the course of a few days nearly all in the mill were hopefully converted.[66]

JHF 184
MS 359

January 1872, p. 1; and J. Bate, *Influence of Mind on Mind* [London: T. Woolmer, 1883], pp. 104–5).

There are numerous anecdotes describing the way Finney looked at people and the effect it had on them. His eyes were one of the most noticeable features of his person, commanding attention and never forgotten. "His eye was as piercing as a hawk's, and yet with nothing either fierce or sinister in its glance" (W.H., "The Late Rev. Charles G. Finney," *NYE,* 30 September 1875, p. 2).

John Ellis wrote:

> [It] seemed to look you through and through and hold you with its fascination under its continued scrutiny, till you felt that your very soul was being searched. And no one in a vast congregation could escape its penetrating and magnetic power. The thoughtless were sobered by it, the uninterested were attracted into attention, the scoffer quailed before it, and into every heart this piercing glance opened a way for the entrance of the truths uttered by the great soul that looked through it into your soul. Again this piercing eye would beam with tenderness and gentleness, or fill with tearful yearning and entreaty (John M. Ellis, "On Certain Elements of President Finney's Power as a Preacher," in James Brand and John M. Ellis, *Memorial Addresses on the Occasion of the One Hundredth Anniversary of the Birth of President Charles G. Finney* [Oberlin: Goodrich, 1893], pp. 33–34).

Finney said about himself in the mill: "The eye of this individual, his solemn countenance, his compassionate feeling, rebuked the levity of the young woman, and brought her under conviction of sin; and this whole revival followed, probably in a great measure, from so small an incident" (*Lectures on Revivals,* McLoughlin ed., p. 19).

[65] Finney, in the account in *The Independent*, added, "I had not spoken a word; and the noise of the looms would have prevented my being heard if I had" (18 January 1872, p. 1).

[66] Charles Giles, the Methodist minister at the factory village, who also appears to be describing this incident, although making no mention of Finney, reckoned, "This sudden and convincing work of grace widened the influence of religion in the neighborhood, and strengthened and gladdened the hearts of the righteous" (*Pioneer: A Narrative of the Nativity, Experience, Travels and Ministerial Labours of Rev. Charles Giles, etc.* [New York: Lane and Sandford, 1844], pp. 308–16).

Giles also gave further reports of the development of the work among the Methodists there in the *Christian Advocate and Journal* (New York), 7 April 1827, p. 122; and 7 December 1827, p. 54. See also Amelia A. Norton to Lydia Finney, 24 May 1827, and H. Norton to Finney, 30 April 1827, Finney Papers, microfilm, roll 2; and Noah Coe's report in the Oneida Presbytery *Narrative*, p. 29.

Apparently the York Mills Methodist Church was organized with about one hundred members, the majority of them converts of the revival. A Presbyterian church was eventually organized in March 1830. See *The Circular* (Oneida, N.Y.), 15 November 1869, p. 275; *WR*, 28 March 1830, p. 47; and C. B. Austin, "Walcott Memorial Church of New York Mills, N.Y.," *NYE,* 11 August 1881, p. 8.

Another similar incident was reported in a letter from G. Baker dated New York Mills, 21 April 1830, when the factory was again stopped. The "agent" is by this time described as "a pious and benevolent member of the Presbyterian church" (*Christian Advocate and Journal and Zion's Herald* [New York], 14 May 1830, p. 146).

As much has been said about the hopeful conversion of Theodore Weld at Utica, it may be well for me to give a correct **version of that matter.**[67] He MS 360 had an aunt living |in Utica, who was a very praying, godly woman.[68] He was the son of an eminent clergyman in New England,[69] and his aunt thought he was a Christian. He used to lead her family in its worship. Before the commencement of the revival he had become a member of Hamilton college at Clinton. The work at Utica had attracted so much attention that many persons from Clinton, and among the rest some of the professors of the college, had been down to Utica and had reported what was doing there, **which had produced** a good deal of excitement.[70] **Theodore** Weld held a

[67]Theodore Dwight Weld (1803–1895) was to become famous as one of the leaders of the antislavery movement (see Robert H. Abzug, *Passionate Liberator: Theodore Dwight Weld and the Dilemma of Reform* [New York: Oxford University Press, 1980]; and *DAB*). Weld's own account of his conversion, written down probably by Charles Beecher "soon after hearing it from his own lips," was published in *Autobiography of Lyman Beecher,* 2:310–12. When Weld's account was reprinted in the *Cleveland Herald*, S. C. Aiken wrote to the editor, "I doubt very much whether he ever made this statement, certainly not in the form in which it appears in the book." Aiken pointed out a number of statements that Weld reputedly made that were either erroneous or gave a false picture of the incident. Weld's reported account differs in some respects from Finney's (S. C. Aiken to the editor of the *Cleveland Herald*, 24 February 1865, reprinted in *The Lorain County News,* 8 March 1865, p. 1).

[68]Sophia Clark was the daughter of Royal Flint of Hartford, Connecticut. In 1812 she became the second wife of Erastus Clark (1768–1825), who was an older brother of Weld's mother. Erastus Clark was a leading lawyer and politician in Utica. His first wife, who died in 1810, had been a pioneer reformer among women in the area and had founded the organization that was to become the Female Missionary Society of the Western District. Her name was also Sophia (née Porter), which has caused confusion.

The second Mrs. Clark was described by Moses Bagg as "a lady of extreme gentleness and sweetness of disposition combined with much strength of character and unusual culture." She was also prominent in reform work. She had just been left a widow with three young children by the death of her husband the previous November. She was still living in 1851. See Nathaniel Goodwin, *Genealogical Notes or Contributions to the Family History of Some of the First Settlers of Connecticut and Massachusetts* (Hartford, Conn.: Brown, 1856), pp. 27, 31; Bagg, *Pioneers of Utica*, pp. 65, 230; and Mary P. Ryan, "A Women's Awakening: Evangelical Religion and the Families of Utica, New York, 1800–1840," *American Quarterly* 30, no. 5 (Winter 1978): 602–23.

[69]His father was Ludovicus Weld (1766–1845), a Harvard graduate who had been minister of the Congregational church in Hampton, Connecticut, since 1792. In March 1824 he had resigned because of ill health and had taken a farm in Fabius, New York, but continued a ministry at large in the Presbyterian churches. His wife was Elizabeth Clark (1792–1853), and Theodore Dwight was the third of four children. See "Congregational Churches and Ministers in Windam County, Ct.," *The Congregational Quarterly,* 2 (April 1860): 181–82; Charles Frederick Robinson, *Weld Collections* (Ann Arbor: privately printed, 1938), p. 123; and Abzug, *Passionate Liberator*.

[70]The professors at this time were Henry Davis, the president; Josiah Noyes; Theodore Strong; and John Monteith. Monteith, in particular, was a fervent Finney supporter and did much to promote the revival in the college. See *Catalogue of the Officers and Students of Hamilton College, December 1st 1824*; W. J. Cameron, "John Monteith, First President of the University of Michigan," *Michigan History Magazine* 28 (1944): 573–85; and W. H. Cowley, "Notes on the Life of John Monteith, 1788–1868," photocopy of a typescript dated 20 March 1975 in Hamilton College Library.

The excitement created by the revival soon led to trouble in the college. Finney went himself to Clinton for several weeks at the end of May, but he and his supporters in the college and on the board of trustees were strongly opposed by Henry Davis, the president. The conflict led to near disaster for Hamilton College. There was a loss of confidence in the college by the New Measures party, who switched much of their support to the Oneida Institute. See Henry Davis, *A Narrative of the Embarrassments and Decline of Hamilton College* (Clinton, N.Y., 1833); *Baltimore Literary and Religious Magazine* 4 (May 1838): 236; and David K. McMillan, "To Witness We Are

very prominent place among the students of Hamilton college, and had a very great **degree of** influence. Hearing what was going on at Utica he became very much excited, and his opposition **became** ‹greatly›[71] aroused. He became quite outrageous in his expressions of opposition to the work, as I understood.[72] This fact became known in Utica; and his aunt, with whom he had boarded, became very anxious about him. To me he was an entire stranger. His aunt wrote him, and ˡ**wanted he should** come home and spend a sabbath, hear the preaching, and become interested in the work. ˡHe at first declined, but finally got some of the students together and told them that he had made up his mind to go down to Utica; that he knew it must be fanaticism or enthusiasm; that he knew it would not move him, they would see that it would not. He came **home** full of opposition, and his aunt soon learned that he did not intend to hear me preach. **Brother** Aikin had occupied the pulpit in the morning, and I in the afternoon and evening.[73] His aunt learned that he intended to go to Mr. Aikin's church in the morning when he expected Mr. Aikin to preach; but that he would not go in the afternoon or evening, because he was determined not to hear me **preach**. In view of this **Brother** Aikin suggested that I should preach in the morning, **as he wanted much to have Weld hear me.**[74] I consented, and we went to meeting. Mr. Aikin took the introductory exercises, as usual. Mrs. **Clark** came to meeting with her family, and among **others** Mr. Weld. She took pains to have him so seated in the slip that he could not ˡwell get out without herself and one or two other members of the family stepping out before him; for she feared, as she said,

JHF 185

MS 361

MS 362

Living: A Study of Charles Finney and the Revival of Religion in and about Utica, New York, During the Winter and Spring of 1826" (B.D. thesis, Union Theological Seminary, 1961), chap. 4.

[71] Finney wrote in the word "greatly" to replace the words "very much."

[72] In another account of this incident, in a sermon preached in London in 1851, Finney spoke of Weld (although not by name) as a "young man . . . of great talents—in fact, of the greatest ability I ever saw in so young a man." Finney gave additional details at this point in the story. "He was pursuing his studies at a college some few miles from his home" (speaking of his aunt's home),

> but had returned on a visit. He was much disturbed by the influence of the revival, and went back to college with his mind by no means at ease on the subject, although he was greatly opposed to it. . . . After he had been back a few days, they sent for him home again, hoping that he would be converted. His college companion had been converted before he came back (*Repentance: Its Nature, Grounds, Necessity, and Infinite Importance* [London: Snow, 1851], pp. iv, 22–23).

This sermon was preached in Whitefield's Tabernacle, London, where the minister was John Campbell. In his foreword to the sermon, Campbell stated that it was published "from the Notes of an accomplished Shorthand Writer" and "its substantial accuracy in all the main features is indubitable."

[73] Thomas W. Seward, a witness of the revival, recalled Finney's preaching:

> He was chary, rather than prodigal of sermons; preaching only in the afternoon or evening of Sundays. In this respect, he practiced a wise reserve which undoubtedly told upon the general work of reform with great effect (*A Memorial of the Semi-Centennial Celebration of the Founding of the Sunday School of the First Presbyterian Church* [Utica: Roberts, 1867], p. 126).

[74] The word "preach" here appears to have been crossed out by Finney. Weld is reported to have said that his aunt went over to Aikin's house and told him that Weld was going to church in the morning. But the statement also makes it appear as if it was his aunt who engineered the switch and then pretended to know nothing about it. Aikin denied that Weld's aunt would ever have played such an "underhand game" (*The Lorain County News,* 8 March 1865, p. 1).

that he would **get up and** go out when he saw that I was going to preach. I knew that his influence among the young men of Utica was very great, and that his coming there would have a powerful influence to make them band together in opposition to the work. Mr. Aikin pointed him out to me as he came in and took his seat. After the introductory exercises I arose and named this text, "One sinner destroyeth much good."[75] I had never preached from it, or heard it preached from; but it came home with great power to my **own** mind, and **as was my custom in such cases, I took that for my text**. I began to preach, and to show in a great many instances how one sinner might destroy much good, and how the influence of one man might destroy a great many souls. I suppose that I drew a pretty vivid picture of Weld, and of what JHF 186 his influence was, and what mischief |he might do. Once or twice he made an MS 363 effort |to get out; but his aunt perceiving it would throw herself forward and lean on the slip in front and engage in ‹silent› prayer,[76] and he could not get out without arousing and annoying her, and therefore he remained in his seat till meeting was out. The next day I called **into** a store in Genesee street to converse with some **young men and** people there, as it was my custom to go from place to place **to converse with people**; and who should I find there but Weld?[77] He fell upon me **in a** very unceremonious **manner**, and I should think for nearly or quite an hour talked to me in a most abusive manner. I had never heard anything like it. I got an opportunity to say but very little to him myself, for his tongue ran incessantly. He was very gifted in language. It soon attracted the attention of all that were in the store, and the news ran along the streets and the clerks gathered in from the neighboring stores; **and quite a large number of young men ran in and** stood to **listen to** what he had to MS 364 say. All business ceased in the store |**where we were**, and all gave themselves up to listening to his vituperation. **I could only once in a while get an opportunity to say anything to which he would attend.**[78] But finally I appealed to him and said, "Mr Weld, are you the son of a minister of Christ, and is this the way for you to behave?" I said a few words in that direction, and I saw that it stung him; and **he,** throwing out something very severe, immediately left the store **and went out**. [79] I went out also, and **went down** to Mr. Aikin's, where for the time I was lodging. I had been there but a few

[75] Ecclesiastes 9:18.

[76] Matson had written down here, "engage herself in prayer," but Finney changed it to "engage in silent prayer."

[77] In his own account of this incident, Weld is said to have indicated that it was not an accidental meeting: "Next day I was sitting in a store. One of the partners was in the revival, and he slipped out and told Finney. In he came, and began to talk" (*Autobiography of Lyman Beecher*, 2:312).

[78] One thing Finney evidently said was: "Puke it up, Mr. W—, puke it up!" (according to a writer, who appears to be speaking about Weld, in *The Liberator* [Boston], 17 May 1834, p. 79). David Kimball also mentioned this comment:

> Mr. Finney often addressed sinners in severe terms. "Puke it all up! You will feel better after it," said he to a moral young man, son of a clergyman, who had come into Utica on purpose to insult him (*The Independent,* 14 May 1868, p. 6).

[79] According to another account by Finney: "he went away in a rage, declaring that he was not going to stay and hear this vituperation. As if it was the minister, instead of himself, that had been scolding" (*Lectures on Revivals,* McLoughlin ed., p. 168).

moments[80] when somebody called at the door; and as no servant was at hand I went to the door myself. **Indeed I was sitting in the parlor alone at the time, and got up to open the front door**; and who should come in but Mr. Weld?[81] He looked as if he would sink. He began immediately to make the most humble confession and apology for the manner in which he had treated me, and expressed himself in the strongest terms of self-condemnation.[82] I took him kindly by the hand and had a little conversation with him, assured him that I had laid up nothing against him, and exhorted him **strongly** to give ˈhis heart to God. I believe I prayed with him before he went. He left, and I heard no more of him that day. ˈThat evening I preached, I think, at New Hartford, and returned late in the evening. The next morning I heard that he went to his aunt's greatly impressed and subdued. She asked him to pray in the family. He said that he was at first shocked at the idea. But his enmity arose so much, that he thought that was one way in which he had not yet expressed his opposition, and therefore he would comply with her request. He knelt down and began and went on with what his aunt intended should be a prayer; but from his own account of it, it was the most blasphemous strain of vituperation that could well be uttered. He kept on in a most wonderful **strain** until they all became convulsed with feeling and astonishment, and he kept on so long that the light went out, **and finally** closed. His aunt attempted to converse with him, and to pray with him; but the opposition of his heart was terrible. She became frightened at the state of mind which he manifested. She pray**ed** with ˈhim, **conjured** him to give his heart to God, **and then** retired.[83] He went to his room; and **he** walked his room by turns, and by turns he lay upon the floor. He continued the whole night in that terrible state of mind, angry, rebellious, and yet so convicted that he could scarcely live. Just at daylight, while walking back and forth in his room, he said a pressure came upon him that crushed him **right** down to the floor; and with it a voice that seemed to command him to repent, to repent *now*. He said it broke him down **on** the floor, and there he lay **broken to pieces,** until late in the morning his aunt coming up found him upon the floor calling himself a thousand fools,[84] and to all human appearance with his heart all broken to pieces. The next night he **got up** in meeting; and **wanted to know** if he might make confession. I **told him Yes,** and he made public confession

MS 365

JHF 187

MS 366

[80] It was "Less than half an hour" in another account (*Lectures on Revivals,* McLoughlin ed., p. 168).

[81] Weld's account states:

> I went, and rung at Aikin's door. A girl came. I stood in the entry, and she called Mr. Finney. He came down stairs. It was rather dim light, so he put his hand up over his eyes to see. Did not recognize me till just as he reached the bottom of the stairs. "Ah!" said he, "is it not enough? Have you followed a minister of the Lord Jesus to his own door to abuse him?" (*Autobiography of Lyman Beecher,* 2:312).

[82] According to David Kimball's reference to this meeting:

> The sister of the young man compelled him to go back and apologize for his ungentlemanly and unchristian conduct. "I have nothing to do with it," said Mr. F., "it is between you and God!" (*The Independent,* 14 May 1868, p. 6).

[83] In the 1851 version Finney said: "at last, he jumped up and ran away to his bedroom, and, casting himself down, declared he would not repent" (*Repentance*, p. 24).

[84] The 1851 version has: "ten thousand fools and wretches for his past enmity against God" (*Repentance*, p. 25).

before the whole congregation. He said it became him to remove the stumbling-block which he had cast before the whole people; and he wanted
JHF 188 opportunity to 'make the most public confession he could. He did make a
MS 367 very humble, 'earnest, broken-hearted confession. From that time he became a very efficient helper in the work.[85] He labored diligently; and being a powerful speaker and much gifted in prayer and labor, he was instrumental for several years in doing a great deal of good, and in the hopeful conversion of a great many souls. His health became enfeebled by his great labors. He was obliged to leave college, and he went on a fishing excursion to the coast of Labrador. He returned the same earnest laborer as before he went away, with health renewed. I found him for a considerable time an efficient helper where I was attempting to labor. **I shall have occasion to mention him in other connections, and therefore will say no more of him at present.**[86]

I have said that no public replies were made to the things that found their way into print in opposition to these revivals, that is, to nothing that was written by Dr Beecher or Mr Nettleton.[87] I have also said that a pamphlet

[85]Weld is reported as saying: "That put an end to my studying. I was with him [Finney] in his meetings, speaking and laboring, all that summer" (*Autobiography of Lyman Beecher*, 2:312).

[86]Lewis Tappan, who read the manuscript, wrote to Finney:

> After giving an account of T. D. Weld's supposed conversion you say you will recur to the subject again; but I do not recollect that you have said anything of him since. As his exercises appeared to be so remarkable, how will it appear as the Narrative leaves the matter, considering his change of views? (Tappan to Finney, 2 June 1868, Finney Papers, microfilm, roll 5).

Finney does speak of Weld in one place later (MS 384–85), which was deleted by Fairchild, but he adds no further remarks about him. Weld went on to acquire a national reputation as a temperance and antislavery lecturer. He also was one of the leaders in the manual labor and reform movements that led to the establishment of Oberlin College. But when the holiness revival shook Oberlin in the late 1830s, Weld was unable to go along with Finney and the Oberlin leaders in the direction they were taking. In 1838 he married the Quaker women's rights advocate, Angelina Grimke, and his Evangelical faith gave way to a broad liberalism. After he retired from leadership in the antislavery movement in the 1840s, he concentrated his energies in pioneering educational work with children. In later life he abandoned all formal religion, although he gave his support to the Unitarians. See Milton Brayton to Finney, 14 July 1850, Finney Papers, microfilm, roll 4; Gilbert H. Barnes, *The Antislavery Impulse, 1830–1844* (Gloucester, Mass.: Peter Smith, 1957); James A. Thome, "Baptism of the Holy Ghost," and Asa Mahan, "The Sequel," *Divine Life and International Expositor of Scriptural Holiness* (New York) 4 (March 1881): 163–65 (reference supplied by James E. Hamilton); and F.J.G., "In Memoriam," *The Woman's Journal* (Boston), 9 February 1895, p. 45.

[87]The first of these publications was part of a letter from Beecher to Nettleton dated 30 January 1827 in which Beecher criticized the revivalists. This was published in the *Boston Evening Gazette* and reprinted in many of the religious journals in March and April 1827; and it was passed among the members of the Oneida Presbytery as a printed sheet. See, e.g., Mary S. Wright to Lydia Finney, 29 March 1827, Finney Papers, microfilm, roll 1. The original is in the Nettleton Papers, Hartford Seminary.

Nettleton reviewed a sermon of Finney's in a letter to Rev. Gardiner Spring of New York dated 4 May 1827, which was published in *The New York Observer* and in pamphlet form and was also extensively reprinted in other papers.

Extracts from Nettleton's letter to Aikin, 13 January 1827, were published in the *Christian Register* [Boston], 13 October 1827, pp. 161–62, and copied and commented on elsewhere before Nettleton published the letter officially in *The New York Observer* in December (see *Letters of the Rev. Dr. Beecher and Rev. Mr. Nettleton, on the "New Measures" in Conducting Revivals of Religion* [New York: Carvill, 1828]). Although there were many comments in the papers about these letters, it was not until they were published officially in *The New York Observer* that John Frost and Samuel Aikin went into print publicly with replies (see *The New York Observer*, 9 February 1828, pp. 21–22; and 16 February 1828, p. 25).

was published by the ministers that composed the Oneida Association, |in opposition to the work.[88] To this, I believe, no public answer was given. I recollect that a Unitarian minister, residing at Trenton in that county, published an abusive pamphlet, in which he greatly misrepresented the work, and made a personal attack upon myself.[89] To this the Rev. Mr. Wetmore, one of the members of the Oneida Presbytery, published a reply.[90] MS 368

This revival occurred in the winter[91] and Spring of 1826. When the converts had been received into the churches throughout the county, Rev. John Frost, pastor of the Presbyterian church at Whitesboro, published a

[88]See MS 279.

[89]Ephraim Perkins was the author of *A "Bunker Hill" Contest, A.D. 1826. Between The "Holy Alliance" for The Establishment of Hierarchy, and Ecclesiastical Domination Over The Human Mind, on the one side; And the Asserters of Free Inquiry, Bible Religion, Christian Freedom and Civil Liberty on the other. The Rev. Charles Finney, "Home Missionary," and High Priest of the Expeditions of the Alliance in the Interior of New York; Head Quarters, County of Oneida* (Utica: printed for the author, 1826).

Perkins was not the Unitarian minister of Trenton (the Reverend Isaac B. Pierce was), but he was a farmer and horsebreeder and a member of the Unitarian church there. See Tyler Owen Hendricks, "Charles Finney and the Utica Revival of 1826: The Social Effect of a New Religious Paradigm" (Ph.D. diss., Vanderbilt University, 1983), p. 235.

In a letter to Aaron Bancroft dated Trenton, 10 June 1826, Perkins described himself as "a farmer, much embarrassed by the change of times having bought a large farm in the highest times and am now under a heavy debt" (manuscript copy in Correspondence File of the American Unitarian Association, Andover-Harvard Theological Library, Harvard Divinity School; the letter is referred to in an unpublished manuscript by David K. McMillan).

This letter, sent to the president of the American Unitarian Association, was written by Perkins to alert the Unitarians in the East about Finney and his revivals. It contained a strong attack on Finney and his activities and a denunciation of the whole movement. Perkins also asked for help in getting material he had written condemning the revivals published.

Bancroft sent a copy of the letter with a cover note dated Worcester, 20 June 1826, to Ezra S. Gannett, secretary of the American Unitarian Association, who was also assisting Rev. Henry Ware, Jr. in editing the *Christian Register*, in Boston. See William C. Gannett, *E. S. Gannett, Unitarian Minister in Boston, 1824–1871. A Memoir* (Cambridge, Mass.: Roberts, 1875), p. 113.

On 5 August part of what Perkins had written appeared in the *Christian Register*. On 12 August it was followed by a letter highly critical of Finney written by Rev. Henry Ware, Jr. It was probably this letter that first alerted Beecher to the troubles in the West. It led to bitter exchanges in the papers that were intensified after the publication of *A "Bunker Hill" Contest*. See, e.g., *WR*, 12 September 1826, p. 1; and 3 October 1826, p. 158; *BR*, 22 September 1826, p. 151; *Christian Register* (Boston), 30 September 1826, p. 154; and *Letters of Beecher and Nettleton*, p. 81.

[90]Oliver Wetmore (1774–1852) was the Presbyterian minister at Trenton. His reply, dated 1 December 1826, was published as an appendix to the second edition of Oneida Presbytery *Narrative*, pp. 63–88.

Wetmore stated that Finney was only once in Trenton: "While at Utica, he rode out in a week day and preached twice." Wetmore reckoned that Perkins was the mouthpiece for others, one of whom may have been Rev. Henry Ware, Jr., of Boston. This was denied, however, in a pamphlet reviewing the "Oneida Revival," and also by Perkins himself in a subsequent pamphlet he wrote to substantiate his case. See James Carnahan Wetmore, *The Wetmore Family of America, and Its Collateral Branches* (Albany: Munsell and Rowland, 1861), p. 334; John Ware, *Memoir of the Life of Henry Ware Jr., by his Brother*, vol. 1 (Boston: Munroe, 1846), pp. 200–203; *A Calm Review of the Spirit, Means, and Incidents of the Late "Oneida Revival," as exhibited in various Presbyterian Societies*, by "A Calm Observer" (Utica: printed for the author, by Danby and Maynard, 1827), p. 23; and Perkins, *Letter to the Presbytery of Oneida County . . .* (Utica: printed for the author, by Danby and Maynard, 1827), p. 3.

[91]Matson had written down "the latter part of the winter," but "latter part of the" appears to have been crossed out by Finney.

pamph[l]et[92] giving some account of the revival, and stated, if I remember right, that within the bounds of that Presbytery the converts numbered three thousand.[93] I have no copy of any of these pamphlets. I have said that the work spread from Rome and Utica as from a center in every direction. Ministers came from a considerable distance, and spent more or less time in JHF 189 attending the meetings, and in various ways ˡhelping forward the work. I spread my own labors over as large a field as I could, and labored more or less MS 369 throughout the bounds of the presbytery.[94] ˡI cannot now remember all the places where I spent more or less time.[95] The pastors of all those churches sympathized deeply with the work; and like good and true men laid themselves upon the altar, and did all they could to forward the great and glorious work; and God gave them a rich reward.

With regard to the doctrines preached in those revivals, I would say that the doctrine of total moral depravity was thoroughly discussed, and urgently pressed upon the people; the spirituality and authority of the divine law was also made prominent; the doctrine of the atonement of Christ as sufficient for all men, and the free invitations of the Gospel based thereon, were held forth in due proportions. All men were represented as by nature dead in trespasses and sins, as being under condemnation and the wrath of God abiding on them. Then they were pointed to the cross of Christ, and every inducement presented to lead them to a total renunciation of self-righteousness, and of all selfishness MS 370 **in every form, and to a present thorough committal of themselves ˡand of their all to the Lord Jesus Christ. Ministers and Christians who had adopted the literal interpretation of the Presbyterian Confession of faith, had found it very difficult to deal with inquiring sinners. In general they did not like to tell them that they had nothing to do. They would therefore instruct them to use the means of grace, to pray for a new heart, and wait for God to convert them. In this revival we discarded all this teaching;** and instead of telling sinners to use the means of grace and pray for a new heart we called on them to make themselves a new heart and a new spirit, and pressed the duty of instant surrender to God. We told them the Spirit was striving with them to induce them *now* to give

[92] Matson omitted the *l* from "pamphlet."

[93] This was the Oneida Presbytery *Narrative*. The committee who made the report, consisting of John Frost, Moses Gillett, and Noah Coe, emphasized:

> *More than three thousand are indulging hope that they have become reconciled to God through the Redeemer.* About half this number have already united with the Presbyterian and Congregational churches, and a large portion of the remainder with the Baptist and Methodist churches. Never before have the churches in this region been blessed with so great a shower of divine grace (Oneida Presbytery *Narrative*, p. 41).

[94] The following sentence was added by Finney at the bottom of MS 368 and the top of MS 369 but appears to have been crossed out again by him: "All the Pastors took hold of the work like true and faithful men of God and were very [MS 369] laborious and efficient in carrying the blessed work forward. I never labored with a more earnest and useful class of ministers in this or any other country."

[95] Finney is known to have preached also in Verona, Augusta, and Trenton. See Mrs. G. W. Thomson, "Early Labors of President Finney," *NYE*, 9 December 1875, p. 2; Samuel Moss to Finney, 8 February 1827, Finney Papers, microfilm, roll 1; and the Oneida Presbytery *Narrative*, p. 75. The latter gives reports of revivals in other churches in the presbytery where Finney may have preached.

him their hearts, *now* to believe, and to enter *at once* upon a life of **submission and** devotion to Christ, of faith and love and Christian obedience. We taught them that while they were praying for the Holy Spirit they were constantly resisting him; and that if they would at once yield to their own convictions of duty, they would be |Christians. MS 371 We tried to show them that everything they did or said before they had submitted, believed, given their hearts to God, was all sin, was not that which God required them to do, but was simply deferring repentance and resisting the Holy Ghost. Such teaching as this was of course **resisted** by many; **but** nevertheless **the teaching** was **insisted upon, and** greatly blessed by the Spirit of God. Formerly it had been supposed necessary that a sinner should remain under conviction a long time; and it was not uncommon to hear old professors of religion say that they were under conviction **so** many months or years before they found relief; and they evidently had the impression that the longer they were under conviction the greater was the evidence that they were truly converted. We taught the opposite of this. I insisted that if they remained long under conviction they were in danger of becoming self-righteous, in the sense that they would think that they had prayed a great deal, and |done a great deal to persuade God to JHF 190 save them; |and that finally they would settle down with a false hope. MS 372 We told them that under this protracted conviction they were in danger of grieving the Spirit of God away, and when their distress of mind ceased a reaction would naturally take place, they would feel less distress and perhaps **comfortable in their minds**, from which they were in danger of inferring that they were converted; that the bare thought that they were possibly converted might create a degree of joy which they might mistake for Christian joy and peace; and that this state of mind might still farther delude them by being taken as evidence that they were converted.

We tried thoroughly to dispose of this false teaching, **that it was necessary that sinners should remain a great while under conviction**. We insisted then, as I have ever done since, on immediate submission as the only thing that God could accept at their hands; and that all delay, under any pretext whatever, was rebellion against God. It became very common, **through** this teaching, for persons to be convicted and |converted in the MS 373 course of a few hours, and sometimes in the course of a few minutes. Such sudden conversions were alarming to many good people; and of course they **feared and** predicted that they would fall away, and prove not to be soundly converted. But the event proved that among those sudden conversions were some of the most **powerful** Christians that ever have been known in that region of country; and this has been in accordance with my own experience through all my ministry.

I have said that Mr. Aikin privately replied to some of Mr. Nettleton's and Dr Beecher's letters.[96] Some of Dr Beecher's letters at the time found their

[96] See MS 347. Apart from the letters that Nettleton wrote to Aikin, there were other letters written by Nettleton and Beecher to Aikin, Frost, Beman, Coe, and Gillett. Most notably, Beecher wrote a letter to Beman dated January 1827 that was also meant for Finney. This was subsequently published in *The New York Observer* and was reprinted in the pamphlet *Letters of Dr. Beecher and Mr. Nettleton*. Parts of Aikin's letter of 20 April 1827 to Beecher were published in *Autobiography of Lyman Beecher*, 2:91, 93, 94. See H. Norton to Finney, 30 April 1827, Finney

way into print, but no public notice was taken of them. Mr. Aikin's replies, which he sent through the mail, seemed to make no difference with the opposition of either Mr. Nettleton or Dr Beecher. From a letter which Dr Beecher wrote about this time to Dr Taylor of New Haven,[97] it appeared that some one had made the impression upon him that the brethren engaged in promoting those revivals were untruthful. MS 374 JHF 191 |In[98] |that letter he asserted that the spirit of lying was so predominant in those revivals, that the brethren engaged in promoting them could not be at all believed. This letter of Dr Beecher to Dr Taylor found its way into print.[99] **I have somewhere among my papers a copy of this letter, as I have also some of Mr. Nettleton's letters.**[100] If **Dr Beecher's letter** should **ever** be published **again**, the people of the region where those revivals prevailed **will** think it very strange that Dr Beecher should even in a private letter ever have written such things of the ministers and Christians engaged in promoting those great and wonderful revivals. ‹**In another place I must say more of Dr. Beechers and Mr Nettletons opposition to those glorious revivals**›[101]

Papers, microfilm, roll 1. Some of these letters were eventually published in *The New York Observer* in December 1827.

[97] Nathaniel William Taylor (1786–1858) was a graduate of Yale and a student of Timothy Dwight. In 1812 he became pastor of the First Congregational Church in New Haven and was professor of theology at Yale from 1822 until his death. He was the leading exponent of the New England theology. See Sidney E. Mead, *Nathaniel William Taylor, 1786–1858: A Connecticut Liberal* (Chicago: University of Chicago Press, 1942); and *DAB*.

[98] Chapter XV starts at the bottom of page 374.

[99] Finney appears to be referring to a private letter, which "was subsequently, in a surreptitious manner, given to the world, in the form of an 'Address' " (see *Autobiography of Lyman Beecher*, 2:103). It was published under the title *To the Congregational Ministers and Churches of Connecticut. Copy of a letter from the Rev. Dr. Beecher, to the Editor of the Christian Spectator, Boston, December 18th, 1827* (Boston: 1827). Beecher wrote:

> I do know, as incident to these new measures, there is a spirit of the most marvellous duplicity and double-dealing and lying, surpassing anything which has come up in my day. I call no names. I cast no implications of *designed* falsehood. I leave all this for God to decide. But, that the system is maintained by a most active and inveterate circulation of falsehood I am sure (p. 2).

And, after a eulogy on Nettleton, he continued:

> Now, that such a man as he, should be traduced, and exposed to all manner of evil falsely, in order to save from deserved reprehension such a man as Finney, (who, whatever talents or piety he may possess, is as far removed from the talent, wisdom, and judgment, and experience of Nettleton, as any corporal in the French army was removed from the talent and generalship of Bonaparte,) is what neither my reason, nor my conscience, nor my heart will endure (p. 4).

Although the *Christian Spectator* was considered to be N. W. Taylor's paper, he was not the editor, and this letter was not addressed to him. It was addressed to John Mitchell (1794–1870), who was the editor from 1824 to 1839. Mitchell protested strongly that the letter had been published without his knowledge or consent. See *Religious Intelligencer,* 1 August 1835, pp. 134–36; and *Obituary Record of Graduates of Yale College Deceased from July, 1859, to July, 1870. Presented at the Annual Meetings of the Alumni* (New Haven: Tuttle, Morehouse, and Taylor, 1870), pp. 345–46. See also p. 228 n. 127 (MS 436).

[100] There is no copy of Beecher's letter to Mitchell among the Finney Papers, and there is only a copy of Nettleton's letter to John Frost, 15 February 1827, Finney Papers, microfilm, roll 1.

[101] Finney added further sections on the opposition of Beecher and Nettleton on MS 396–99 and MS 425–39. This sentence here together with the chapter heading of chapter XV are written in Finney's handwriting on a separate strip of paper pasted onto page 374.

CHAPTER XV

MS 374
JHF 192

‹Revival at Auburn in 1826.›

‹Dr[1] Lansing Pastor of the first Pres. church at Auburn came to Utica to witness the revival there &›[2] urged me to go out and labor for a time with him.[3] In the summer of 1826[4] I complied with his request, and went there and labored with him for a season.[5] Soon after I went to Auburn, I found that some of ǀthe professors in the theological seminary in that place were taking an attitude hostile to the revival.[6] I had before known that ministers east of Utica were a considerable number of them **writing letters to each other,** holding a correspondence with reference to those revivals, and taking an attitude of hostility to them. MS 375

Some of them took the ground that it would greatly injure the colleges and theological seminaries if I were allowed to pass through the churches and preach, when I had neither a collegiate nor a regular theological education. Of course all sorts of false reports were circulated, and things were said too absurd and ridiculous to notice. I in no instance attempted any reply. I had too much to do to turn aside to say anything about opposition. Although articles frequently appeared in the newspapers against me and my labors, I never did more than to look

[1]The chapter heading and the section in Finney's handwriting down to n. 2 are written on a separate piece of paper pasted onto page 374. The section covered over reads: "Amongst the ministers that visited Utica whilst I was at that place was the Rev. Dr Lansing of Auburn. He became very much interested in the work in Oneida County, and." Pages 374–91 were first numbered 242–59 and then renumbered 374–91 by Matson.

[2]This ends the section in Finney's handwriting.

[3]Dirck Cornelius Lansing (1785–1857) was a graduate of Yale and had been a minister in Onondaga and Saratoga before settling in Auburn in 1816. As well as being the minister, he was a trustee and lecturer at Auburn Theological Seminary. In 1829 he moved to Utica and in 1833 to New York. He became one of the leaders in the New School Presbyterian church. See Joseph P. Thompson, *The Faithful Preacher: A Discourse Commemorative of the Late Dirck C. Lansing* (New York: Calkins and Stiles, 1857).

The Presbyterian church at Auburn originally had been formed in 1811 as a Congregational church but became Presbyterian in 1814 and joined the Cayuga Presbytery. The church building was erected in 1817. See James H. Hotchkin, *A History of the Purchase and Settlement of Western New York and the Rise, Progress and Present State of the Presbyterian Church in that Section* (New York: Dodd, 1848), pp. 344–45.

[4]In the original the words "or '27" appear here but were crossed out by Finney.

[5]Finney was in Auburn from late June until late August 1826.

[6]James Richards (1793–1843), the president of Auburn Theological Seminary, was at this time particularly hostile to Finney's measures. See W. B. Sprague, *Annals of the American Pulpit,* vol. 4 (New York: Carter and Bro., 1859), p. 104; and John Q. Adams, *A History of Auburn Theological Seminary, 1818–1918* (Auburn: Auburn Seminary Press, 1918), pp. 74–75. See also p. 334 n. 37 (MS 615).

them over to see what of justice or injustice there was in them. In no case did I make any reply.[7] However, until I arrived at Auburn I was not fully aware of the amount of opposition I was destined to meet from the MS 376 ministry: not the ministry in the region where I had |labored, but from ministers where I had not labored, and who knew personally nothing of me, but were influenced by the false reports which they heard, **and by some mysterious influence originating somewhere, which neither myself nor any of my friends could understand.**[8] But soon after I arrived at Auburn I learned from various sources that a system of espionage was being carried on, that was destined to result, and *intended* to result, in an extensive union of ministers and churches to hedge me in, and prevent the spread of the revivals in connection with my labors.

Nathan S. S. Beman. The minister of the First Presbyterian Church, Troy, New York, and a leader in the emerging New School party within the Presbyterian church. He was one of Finney's chief supporters in the revivals of 1826–1827. From an engraving in *The Evangelical Magazine and Missionary Chronicle* (London) 19 (October 1841): opposite p. 477. Courtesy The British Library.

About this time I was informed that Mr. Nettleton had said that I could go no farther east,—that all the New England churches especially were closed

[7] Albert B. Dodd of Princeton Theological Seminary, a severe critic of Finney's methods, made the following comment, however: "Mr. Finney, we are told, makes it his rule never to reply to any attacks upon him,—it should have been added, save by bitter vituperations from the pulpit. A very convenient principle this" (in a review of Finney's *Lectures on Revivals of Religion* in the *Biblical Repertory and Theological Review* [Princeton] 7 [October 1835]: 651).

[8] One of Nettleton's informants was a student at Auburn Theological Seminary, Charles E. Furman (1801–1880), who was later to have pastorates mainly in Monroe County, New York, and to settle in Rochester in 1854. He was later to be one of Finney's supporters. See his letters to Nettleton, 19 October and 16 November 1826, in Nettleton Papers, Hartford Seminary; Samuel Blatchford to James Richards, 29 January 1827, in Simon Gratz Collection, case 8, box 36, The Historical Society of Pennsylvania; *NYE,* 24 June 1880, p. 6; and p. 325 n. 112 (MS 604). See also MS 399 and p. 209 n. 30.

against me. Mr. Nettleton came and made a stand at Albany;[9] and a letter from Dr Beecher fell into my possession in which he exhorted Mr. Nettleton to make a manful stand against me ˡand the revivals in central New York; **and** that when the judicatures, as he called them, of New England met, ˡ"they would all speak out and sustain him in his opposition."[10] But for the present I must return to what passed at Auburn. My mind became, soon after I went there, very much impressed with the extensive working of that system of espionage of which I have spoken. ‹**Rev.**›[11] Mr. Frost, of Whitesboro, had come to a knowledge of the facts to a considerable extent, and communicated them to me. I said nothing publicly, or as I recollect privately, to anybody on the subject, but gave myself to prayer. I looked to God with great earnestness day after day to be directed, **that He would** show me the path of duty and give me grace to ride out the storm.

JHF 193
MS 377

I shall never forget what a scene I passed through one day in my room at Dr Lansings **in Auburn, soon after my arrival there.** The Lord showed me as in a vision what **I had to pass through**. He drew so near to me while I was engaged in prayer that *my flesh literally trembled on my bones*. I shook from head to foot, **like a man in an ague fit,** under a full sense of ˡthe presence of God. At first, and for sometime, it seemed more like being on the top of Sinai, amidst its full thunderings, than in the presence of the cross of Christ.

MS 378

Never in my life, that I recollect, was I so awed and humbled before God as **I was** then. Nevertheless, instead of feeling like fleeing, I seemed drawn nearer and nearer to God,—seemed to draw nearer and nearer to that Presence that filled me with such unutterable awe and trembling. After a season of great humiliation before **Him**, there came a great lifting up. God assured me that **He** would be with me and uphold me; that no opposition should prevail against me; that I had nothing to do but to keep about my work, and wait for the salvation of God **in regard to all this matter.** The sense of God's presence, and all that passed between God and my soul at that time, I can never describe. It led me to be perfectly trustful, perfectly calm, and to have ˡnothing but the most perfectly kind feelings toward all the brethren that were misled, and were arraying themselves against me. ˡI felt assured that all would come out right, that my true course was to leave everything to God and keep about my work. **I did so**; and as the storm gathered and the opposition increased, I never for one moment doubted how it would result. I was never disturbed by it, I never spent a waking hour in thinking of it, when to all outward appearance it seemed as if all the churches of the land, except where I had labored, would unite to shut me out of their pulpits. This was indeed the avowed determination, as I understood, of the

JHF 194
MS 379

[9]This sentence started with the words "About this time," which Finney crossed out. Nettleton went to Albany in the first week of November 1826 and was there for about four months. See J. P. Cushman to Finney, 6 November 1826, Finney Papers, microfilm, roll 1; and MS 395–96.

[10]This was Beecher's letter of 30 January 1827. The extract reads: "Stand fast brother, and you shall have all New England to back you in due time. If it become necessary all our judicatures will speak out next spring, though I hope it will not be." The editor of the *Christian Register,* who published the letter, added a note: "By Judicatures we suppose that Dr. Beecher means Presbyteries, Synods, General Assembly, Associations etc." (*Christian Register* [Boston], 26 March 1827, p. 46).

[11]Finney inserted "Rev.," but Fairchild crossed it out.

men that led in the opposition. They were so deceived that they thought there was no effectual way but to unite **against me**, and as they expressed it, put **me** down. But God assured me that they could not put me down. A passage in the **20th** chapter of Jeremiah was repeatedly set home upon me with great power. It reads thus: "O Lord, thou hast deceived me and I was deceived." In the margin it reads *enticed*. "Thou art stronger than I, and hast prevailed: I am
MS 380 in derision daily, every |one mocketh me. For since I spake, I cried out, I cried violence and spoil; because the word of the Lord was made a reproach unto me, and a derision daily. Then I said, I will not make mention of him, nor speak any more in his name. But his **W**ord was in my heart as a burning fire shut up in my bones, and I was weary with forebearing, and I could not stay. For I heard the defaming of many, and fear was on every side. Report, say they, and we will report it. All my familiars watched for my halting, saying, **P**eradventure he will be enticed, and we shall prevail against him, and we shall take our revenge on him. But the Lord is with me as a mighty terrible one; therefore my persecutors shall stumble, and they shall not prevail. They shall be greatly ashamed, for they shall not prosper; their everlasting
JHF 195 confusion shall never be forgotten. But O Lord of |hosts that triest the righteous, and seest the reins and the heart, let me see thy vengeance on
MS 381 them; for unto thee have I opened my cause." **Jeremiah,** 20:7–12. |I do not mean that this passage literally described my case, or expressed my feelings; but there was so much similarity in the case that this passage was often a support to my soul. **Indeed, as I said,** the Lord did not allow me to lay the opposition to heart **at all, to be fearful of the results, or to be at all angry with the brethren who were leading on in that direction.** I can truly say, so far as I can recollect, I never had an unkind feeling toward Mr Nettleton or Dr Beecher, or any leading opposer**s** of the work during the whole of their opposition.

I recollect having had a peculiar feeling of horror in respect to the pamphlet published, and the course taken by William R Weeks, to whom I have made **an** allusion.[12] **I felt no personal resentment; but there appeared to me to be an artfulness, a mock candor, and a determination in his case, of which I do not recollect to have spoken; but I do recollect distinctly to have frequently felt a kind of shudder in view of his taking such an attitude.** Those who are acquainted with the history of Mr. Weeks
MS 382 recol|lect that soon after this he began to write a book which he called "The pilgrim's progress in the nineteenth century." This was published in numbers, and finally bound up in a volume; with which many of the readers of this narrative may be familiar.[13] **So far as I can learn he carried his opposition**

[12] See MS 279–80.

[13] *The Pilgrim's Progress in the Nineteenth Century* (New York: Davis, 1826) appeared under the pseudonym "Bunyanus." It had appeared previously in installments in *The Utica Christian Repository* (a magazine edited by Weeks) from 1824 to 1826 and was reprinted in other journals. Further installments were published in the *Repository* and in *The Hopkinsian Magazine* (Providence, R.I.) from May 1828 to March 1829. A greatly enlarged edition was published posthumously in 1848 by M. W. Dodd of New York, and another edition in 1849 by Crocker and Brewster in Boston.

to those revivals to the day of his death.[14] **He could not maintain his standing, however, in Oneida County, where he was pastor when I was laboring there. He was dismissed from that congregation soon after, and went to Newark, N.J., and engaged in teaching school. He gathered around him, as I have been told, a very few followers and believers in his doctrine, and continued to preach till the day of his death.** He was a man of considerable talent, and I must hope a good man; but as I think much deluded in his philosophy, and exceedingly out of the way in his theology. I do not mention him because I wish to say any evil of him, **nor** of his book **entitled "The pilgrim's progress in the nineteenth century**;" but merely |to say that he never ceased, so far as I can learn, to offer more or less MS 383 opposition, direct and indirect, to revivals that did not favor **more or less distinctly** his peculiar views. He took much pains, without naming him, to defend the course which Mr. Nettleton took in putting himself at the head of the opposition to those revivals.[15] But God has disposed of all that influence. I have heard nothing of it now for many years.

Notwithstanding the attitude that some of the professors at Auburn were taking, in connection with so many ministers abroad, the Lord soon revived **His** work in Auburn. ‹**Rev.**›[16] Mr. Lansing had a large congregation, and a very intelli|gent one. The revival soon took effect among the people, and JHF 196 became powerful. It was at that time that Dr **Steele** of Auburn, who still resides there, was so greatly blessed in his soul as to become quite another man. Dr **Steele** was an elder in the Presbyterian church when I arrived there.[17] He was a very timid and doubting kind of Christian, and had |but MS 384 little Christian efficiency because he had but **very** little faith. He soon, however, became deeply convicted of sin, and descended into the depths of humiliation and distress, almost to despair. He continued in this state for weeks, until one night in a prayer-meeting he was quite overcome with feelings, and sunk down helpless on the floor. Then God opened his eyes to the reality of his salvation in Christ.[18] ‹This occurred just after I had left

[14]Weeks later attacked revivals in his *Letter on Protracted Meetings addressed to the Church in Paris, 24 Feb 1832* (Utica: Williams, 1832). See also his letter to Rev. Charles Simmons, of Wareham, Massachusetts, dated Newark, 17 May 1841, in *BR,* 11 June 1841, p. 93; and p. 206 n. 16 (MS 397).

[15]In *The Pilgrim's Progress of the Nineteenth Century*, Nettleton appears under the guise of "Mr. Meek." His revivals are contrasted with those conducted by "Mr. Bold," who is Finney. In chapter 32 the two pilgrims "Thoughtful" and "Ardent" are accosted by "Bold" and attend one of his revival meetings in "Westerley street" (Oneida County). They witness his methods and those of two converts of his whom they meet and find many of them "very objectionable" (Weeks, *Pilgrims Progress* [New York: Dodd, 1848], p. 235; the copy of this book in the library of Hamilton College, Chilton, New York, has pasted into the front a handwritten key to some of the characters).

[16]"Rev." was inserted by Finney but crossed out by Fairchild.

[17]Richard Steel (born 1795) came to Auburn in 1817. He was a "Druggist Merchant" and a prominent Presbyterian layman. He had been made an elder in 1824. See letters from him to Finney in the Finney Papers; and Charles Hawley, *The History of the First Presbyterian Church, Auburn, N.Y.* (Auburn: Dennis, 1869), p. 42.

[18]The following section down to n. 20, in Finney's handwriting, is written on a separate piece of paper pasted onto the sheet. The writing underneath reads: "He spoke out after he was relieved and said, 'Brother Finney, they have buried the Savior! But Christ is risen!' The manner in which he spoke this was very impressive. The Lord gave him such a won-."

Auburn & gone to Troy, N. York to labor.[19] **Br. Steel** soon followed me to Troy & the first time I saw him there he exclaimed with an emphasis peculiarly his own "Br. Finney they have buried the Saviour, but Christ is risen." He received such a won›derful[20] baptism of the Holy Ghost, that he has been the rejoicing and the wonder of God's people **who have known him ever since.**

Partly in consequence of the known **opposition to** my labors on the part of many ministers, a good deal of opposition sprung up in Auburn, and a number of the leading men in that large village took strong ground **in opposition to** the work.[21] **In the meantime Theodore Weld, of whom I**

MS 385 **have spoken, ¦came there and spent several days.[22] As a specimen of the opposition, one of the leading opposers met Weld one day in the streets, and said to him, "Weld, I have promised that I will kick you, and I will be as good as my word," and stepped up to him and kicked him. Weld took very little notice of it, and it passed by.** But the Spirit of the Lord was among the people with great power. **There were many very striking incidents at that time in that place.**[23]

I recollect that one Sabbath morning while I was preaching I was describing the manner in which some men would oppose their families, and if possible prevent their being converted. I gave so vivid a description of a case of this kind that I said, "Probably if I were acquainted with you, I could call some of you by name who treat your families in this manner." At this instant a **gentle**man cried out in the congregation, "Name me!" and then threw his

JHF 197 head forward on the seat before him, and it was plain that he trembled ¦with

MS 386 great emotion. ¦It turned out that he was treating his family in this manner, and that morning had done the same things that I had named **without being acquainted with any of the facts**. He said his crying out, "Name me!," was so spontaneous and irresistible that he could not help it.[24] ‹But I fear he was never converted to Christ.›[25]

[19]This experience happened about four weeks after Finney left Auburn. It is described by Richard Steel in *Reminiscences of Rev. Charles G. Finney* (Oberlin: Goodrich, 1876), p. 35. For further reminiscences by Steel of Finney's revivals in Auburn, see P. C. Headley, *Evangelists in the Church* (Boston: Hoyt, 1875), pp. 138–39, 141–43; and *NYE,* 9 September 1875, p. 1; and 16 December 1880, p. 6.

[20]The section in Finney's handwriting ends in the middle of the word "wonderful."

[21]Other accounts of the revival and contemporary reports stress the opposition in Auburn. See, e.g., *Christian Advocate* (New York), 9 September 1826, p. 2; Henry Fowler, *History of the Church of Christ in Auburn* (Auburn: Scribner, 1868), p. 32; and Headley, *Evangelists,* p. 138.

[22]See MS 359–67.

[23]An abstract of one of the sermons preached by Finney at Auburn is contained in the pages of a diary found in the Autograph Collection at Oberlin College. It is one of the earliest known reports of a sermon by Finney. The discourse on Genesis 6:3 was given on the evening of Tuesday, 1 August 1826. The writer was a twenty-nine-year-old student at the theological seminary, but his name is not known. The sixteen-page section of the diary runs from 1 August to 2 September 1826, and Finney's discourse is on pp. 1–7 (Finney Papers, file 2/2/2, box 9). It was transcribed by Roy Alan Cheesebro in "The Preaching of Charles G. Finney" (Ph.D. diss., Yale University, 1948), pp. 271–73.

[24]In an earlier account of this incident Finney recalled that the man said afterwards that he had no idea of speaking out, but Finney had "described him so perfectly, that he really thought he was going to call him by name" (*Lectures on Revivals of Religion*, ed. William G. McLoughlin [Cambridge, Mass.: Belknap, 1960], p. 229). William C. Cochran reported a very similar incident and pointed out that Finney knew of hundreds of similar cases.

There was a hatter by the name of **Hawley**[26] residing at this time in Auburn. His wife was a Christian woman; but he was a Universalist, and an opposer of the revival. He carried his opposition so far as to forbid his wife attending our meetings; and for several successive evenings she remained at-home. One night as the warning bell rang for meeting half an hour before the assembly met Mrs. **Hawley** was so much exercised in mind about her husband that she retired for prayer, and spent the half hour in pouring out her soul to God. She told **Him** how her husband behaved, and that he would not let her attend meeting, **&c.**, and drew very ˡnear to God. As the bell was tolling for the people to assemble she came out of her closet, as I learned, and found that her husband had come in ‹from›[27] the shop, and as she entered the sitting room, he asked her if she would not go to meeting; and said that if she would go he would accompany her. He afterwards informed me that he had made up his mind to attend meeting that night to see if he could not get something to justify his opposition to his wife, or at least **get** something to laugh about and sustain him in ridiculing the whole work. When he proposed to accompany his wife she was very much surprized, but prepared herself, and they came to meeting. Of all this I knew nothing at the time of course. **But I went to meeting, as was common with me in those days, without having made up my mind at all as to the text from which I should preach.** MS 387

I had been visiting and laboring with inquirers the whole day, and had had no time whatever to arrange my thoughts, or even settle upon a text. ˡDuring the introductory services a text occurred to my mind, **just before I was to rise and preach**. It was the words of the man with the unclean spirit, who cried out "Let us alone."[28] I took those words and went on to preach, and endeavored to ˡshow up the conduct of those sinners that wanted to **be let**[29] alone, that did not want to have anything to do with Christ. The Lord gave me power to give a very vivid description ‹of› the course th‹at class of men› were pursuing.[30] In the midst of my discourse I observed a person fall from his seat near the broad aisle, who cried out in a most **unearthly and** terrific manner. The congregation were very much shocked and the outcry of the man was so great that I stopped preaching and stood still. After a few moments I requested the congregation to sit still, **and** I **would** go down and speak with the man. I found **it** to be this Mr. **Hawley** of whom I have been speaking. MS 388 JHF 198

In most of these cases, he had no actual knowledge of wrong-doing. He simply had—what he said all ministers should have to be effective—a thorough knowledge of human nature and the courage to denounce sin, though the sinner sat right before him (*Charles Grandison Finney: Memorial Address* [Philadelphia: Lippincott, 1908], pp. 62–63).

[25] Here Matson had written down, "He was very soon after hopefully converted," but Finney crossed it out and added, "But I fear he was never converted to Christ."

[26] In each case where the name "Hawley" appears, Matson had written "Hall" but changed it, except for the last time in MS 389, where it was spelled "Hawley."

[27] Here Matson had written down, "out of." In place of "out" Finney wrote "from," and the word "of" appears to have been crossed out by Fairchild.

[28] Mark 1:24 or Luke 4:34.

[29] The words "be let" were not altered in the original, but they appear as "let be" in the published edition.

[30] Here Matson had written down, "of that class of men, together with the course they were pursuing," but Finney changed it.

The Spirit of the Lord had so powerfully convicted him that he was unable to sit on his seat. MS 389 |When I **got to** him he had so far recovered his strength as to be on his knees with his head on his wife's lap. He was weeping aloud like a child, confessing his sins, and accusing himself in a terrible manner. I said a few words to him, to which he seemed to pay but little attention. The Spirit of God had **got** his attention so thoroughly that I soon desisted from all efforts to make him attend to what I said. When I told the congregation who it was they all knew him and his character, and it produced tears and sobs in every part of the house. I stood for some little time to see if he would be quiet enough for me to go on with my sermon; but his loud weeping rendered it impossible. I can never forget the appearance of his wife as she sat and held his face in her hands upon her lap. There **were** in her face a holy joy and triumph that words cannot express. We had several prayers, and then I dismissed the meeting. **They** helped Mr. **Hawley** to his house. He immediately wished them to send for certain of his companions, MS 390 |with whom he had been in the habit of ridiculing the work of the Lord in that place. He could not rest until he had sent for a great number of them and had **an opportunity to** make confession to them, which he did with a very broken heart. He was so overcome that for two or three days he could JHF 199 |not get about town, and continued to send for such men as he wished to see that he might confess to them, and warn them to flee from the wrath to come. As soon as he was able to get about he took hold of the work with the utmost humility and simplicity of character, but with great earnestness. Soon after he was made an elder,[31] or deacon, **I do not recollect which**; and he has ever since been a very exemplary and useful Christian. His conversion was so marked and so powerful, and the results were so manifest **to everybody**, that it did very much to silence opposition.

There were several wealthy men in the town who took offence at Dr Lansing and myself and the laborers in that revival, and ‹after I left they›[32] MS 391 |got together and formed a new congregation. Most of these **men** were at the time unconverted men. Let the reader bear this in mind, for in its proper place I shall have occasion to notice the results of this opposition and formation of a new congregation, and the conversion **at another time** of nearly every one of those opposers.[33]

While at Auburn I preached more or less in the neighboring churches round about; and the revival spread in various directions to Cayuga **on the banks of Cayuga lake**,[34] and to Skaneateles **on the banks of Skaneateles lake**. This was, **I think,** in the summer and Autumn of 182‹6›.[35]

[31] Here the words "of the church" appear to have been crossed out by Finney.

[32] Finney added the words "after I left they."

[33] See MS 609. Henry Fowler wrote:

> The conservatives did not approve of Mr. Finney, nor of Dr. Lansing, because he sustained Mr. Finney. At a meeting of brethren called to consider differences and to devise a mode of harmonious action, the conservatives insisted on the dismissal of Dr. Lansing, and as the other party would not hear to this, and was a majority, they withdrew, and with marked energy, built the Second Church (*Church of Christ in Auburn*, p. 18).

[34] After the revival in Cayuga, thirty-one were reported as being added to the church, bringing

Revival at Auburn in 1826

ǀ‹Soon[36] after my arrival at Auburn a circumstance occurred of so striking a character that I must give a brief relation of it. My wife & self were guests of Dr. Lansing the Pastor of the church. The church was much conformed to the world & were accused by the unconverted of being leaders in dress & fashion & worldliness. As usual I directed my preaching to secure the reformation of the church & to get them into a revival state. On sabbath I had preached as searchingly as I was able to the church in regard to their attitude before the world. The word took deep hold of the people. At the close of my address I called, as usual, upon the Pastor to pray. He was much impressed with the sermon & the very manifest impression upon the congregation. Instead of immediately engaging in prayer, he made a ǀshort but very earnest address to the church confirming what I had said to them. At this moment a man arose in the gallery & said in a very deliberate & distinct manner, "Mr. Lansing I do not believe that such remarks from you can do any good whilst you wear a ruffled shirt & a gold ring on your finger, & whilst your wife & the ladies of your family sit as they do before the congregation dressed as leaders in the fashions of the day." It seemed as if this would kill the Dr. outright. He made no reply, but cast himself across the side of the pulpit & wept like a child. The congregation was almost as much shocked & affected as himself. They almost universally dropped their ǀheads upon the back of the seat in front of them & many of them wept on every side. With the exception of the sobs & sighs the house was profoundly silent. I waited a few moments & as Dr. Lansing did not move I arose & offered a short prayer & dismissed the congregation. I went home with the Dear wounded Pastor, & when all the family were returned from church he took the ring from his finger, it was a slender gold ring that could hardly attract notice. He said his first wife when upon her dying bed took it from her finger & placed it upon his with a request that he should wear it for her sake.[37] He had done so without a thought of its being a stumbling-block. Of his ruffles he said he had worn ruffles from his childhood & did not think of them as anything improper. Indeed he could not remember when he began to wear them & of course thought nothing about them. "But," said he, "if these things are an occasion of offense to any I will not wear them."[38] He was a precious Christian man & an excellent Pastor.

MS 392

JHF 200

MS 393

the membership in 1827 to seventy-seven members. See Hotchkin, *The Purchase and Settlement of Western New York*, p. 347.

[35]Matson had written "1827," but Finney changed the 7 to a 6. The section below, which appears after this, was crossed out by Finney when he inserted three additional pages between MS 391 and 392:

> There were a great many very interesting incidents in this revival, and also many interesting facts in regard to the manner in which it spread in every direction throughout an extensive region. In the fall of this year I was invited by the Rev. Dr Beman to go to the city of Troy to labor with him. At Troy I spent the fall and winter, and the revival was powerful at that place. I have already said that Mr.

[36]This is the first of three new pages in Finney's handwriting, inserted between MS 391 and 392. An additional seventeen pages were inserted by Finney in various places before MS 440.

[37]His first wife, Jane Vander Heyden, whom he had married in 1805, died in 1812 at age thirty-eight. See F. B. Dexter, *Biographical Sketches of the Graduates of Yale College,* vol. 4 (New York: Holt, 1907), p. 678.

[38]Henry Fowler reported another dramatic occasion. Once when Lansing was preaching, he took off his cloak and two rings and dropped them all into the area below, saying, "Thus do I cast off all these poor adornments of this mortal body" (*Church of Christ in Auburn*, p. 8).

Almost immediately after this the church were disposed to make to the world a publick confession of their backsliding & want of a christian spirit. Accordingly a confession was drawn up covering the whole ground. It was JHF 201 submitted to the church for their approval & then read before ˡthe congregation the church arose & stood, many of them weeping, while the confession was read.[39] From this point the work went forward with greatly MS 394 increased power. ˡThe confession was evidently a heart work & no sham, & God most graciously & manifestly accepted it & the mouths of gainsayers were shut. **The opposition to this work on the part of some of the unconverted was very bitter, & was much encouraged by the mistaken attitude of many ministers whose opposition they plead as a justification of their own.** The fact is that to a great extent the churches & ministers were in a low state of grace & those powerful revivals took them by surprise. I did not much wonder then, nor have I since, that those wonderful works of God were not well understood & received by those who were not in a revival state.[40]

There were a great many interesting conversions **around** in Auburn & vicinity & also in all the neighboring towns throughout that part of the state, as the work spread in every direction. In the Spring of 1831, I was again in Auburn & saw another powerful revival there. The circumstances were peculiar, & deeply interesting & will be related in their appropriate place in this **N**arrative.›[41]

In a 19 June 1843 lecture on pastoral theology to the students at Oberlin College, Finney dealt with "clerical habits." One of the students, William Westervelt, took notes of the lecture. Among the items for the students to consider when they became pastors Westervelt noted: "2) Avoid wearing ruffels; 3) wearing rings should be avoided; 4) Breast pins should not be worn even if given by a dying friend" ("Pastoral Lectures by Pres. Finney," in William A. Westervelt Papers, file 30/120, box 1, Oberlin College Archives).

Finney is also reported as saying in a sermon:

> After I became a Christian, though no one spoke to me about it, yet I was ashamed of my ruffles and of my great bunch of watch-seals and keys. I could see that I had worn them for mere show. At once I ceased to care for those vain things. When young converts obtain a pure heart, all they want in the line of dress and adornment is only so much as will make them most useful (*OE,* 1 September 1858, p. 138).

[39] Finney wrote this sentence as it is printed here.

[40] Fifty-four were admitted to membership of the First Church as a result of the revival. This was a smaller number than in some previous years and may have reflected the difficulty Finney had in Auburn. See Hawley, *First Presbyterian Church, Auburn,* pp. 46–47; and *WR,* 21 November 1826, p. 187.

[41] See MS 608–16.

CHAPTER XVI

MS 394
JHF 202

‹Revival at Troy›

‹Early[1] in the Autumn of this year 1826, I accepted an invitation from Rev. Beeman & his Session to labor with them in Troy for the revivals of religion.[2] At Troy I spent the fall & winter & the revival was powerful in that city.[3] I have already said that Mr.› ǀNettleton[4] had been sent by Dr Beecher, as I understood, to Albany to make a stand against the revivals that were MS 395

[1]The chapter heading of page 394 and the section to the bottom of the page is in Finney's handwriting.

[2]Nathan Sidney Smith Beman (1785–1871), from New Lebanon, New York, was a graduate of Middlebury College, where he was later a tutor. In 1812 he went to Georgia, where he achieved prominence not only as a Presbyterian minister but as a teacher, becoming the president of Franklin College. In 1823 he was called to the First Presbyterian Church in Troy. This was the largest and one of the wealthiest churches in the area, having a membership of about 1,200. He remained there for forty years. In 1845 he also became president of Rensselaer Polytechnic Institute. In 1831 he was moderator of the General Assembly; and when the Presbyterian church split in 1837, he led the New School party. See Owen Petersen, *A Divine Discontent: The Life of Nathan S. S. Beman* (Macon, Ga.: Mercer University Press, 1986); and *DAB*.

He was at this time

> a man of marked ability . . . and was already making himself felt throughout the whole Presbyterian Church by his able discussions of the fundamental doctrines of their belief. . . . His power as an advocate on the floor of the General Assembly had also much to do in strengthening and solidifying this party (G. F. Wright, *Charles Grandison Finney* [Boston and New York: Houghton Mifflin, 1891], p. 53).

Finney named his second child, and eldest son, Charles Beman, in honor of him. But in later life the son took his father's name, Charles Grandison (see p. 404 n. 92 [MS 703]). The spelling "Beeman" here in the text by Finney was corrected to "Beman" by Fairchild.

A revival had already started in Troy. It originated in January 1826 with the conversion of a young man in Beman's congregation while on a trip to Williamstown, Massachusetts. Nearly thirty people had been converted and were actively involved in measures to bring about a revival, and Beman had written to Finney in June to invite him. But after leaving Auburn in late August, Finney had returned to Utica. After further repeated attempts by Beman to get him to go, Finney eventually went at the end of September (see Senex, "Revival Sketches—No. VI,"*The Advance*, [Chicago], 20 February 1868, p. 2; and letters of Beman to Finney, 9 June, 30 August, 23 and 25 September 1826, Finney Papers, microfilm, roll 1). Finney preached his first sermon there on the morning of Sunday, 1 October. The entomologist Asa Fitch (1809–1879) was at that time a student at the Rensselaer School, and he attended the service. Fitch noted, "His sermon was good but it was delivered too furiously, & his gestures too violent." Fitch attended the Presbyterian church during the revival and made further notes on Finney's preaching. See Asa Fitch "Diary," vol. D., p. 127, 1 October 1826, in Asa Fitch Papers, Yale University Library; Samuel Rezneck, "The Religious Life and Struggles of a New York Scientist, 1809–1879," *New York History* 53, no. 4 (October 1972): 411–36; and *DAB*.

[3]Finney was based there until early April of 1827, with various periods away in Utica, Whitesboro, Rome, and New Lebanon.

[4]Pages 395 and 396 were originally numbered 260 and 261, renumbered 392 and 393 by Matson, and then changed to 395 and 396 by Finney.

spreading in central New York.[5] I had had the greatest confidence in Mr. Nettleton, though I had never seen him. I had had the greatest *desire* to see him, so much so that I had frequently dreamed of visiting him and obtaining from him **information** in regard to the best means **in regard to** promoting a revival. **I wanted exceedingly to see him, and** felt like sitting at his feet, almost as I would at the feet of an apostle, from what I had heard of his success in promoting revivals. At that time my confidence in him was so great that I think he could have led me almost or quite at his discretion. Soon after my arrival at Troy I went down to Albany to see him. He was the guest of a family with which I was acquainted.[6] I spent part of an afternoon with him, and conversed with him in regard to his doctrinal views **on some subjects,** especially **those** held by the Dutch and Presbyterian churches in regard to the MS 396 **voluntariness or involuntariness** |of moral depravity, **and kindred topics.** I found that he entirely agreed with me, so far as I had opportunity to converse with him, on all the points of theology upon which we conversed. Indeed there had been no complaint by Dr Beecher or Mr. Nettleton of our *teaching* JHF 203 in those revivals. They did not complain at all that we did not |teach what they regarded as the true Gospel. What they complained of was something that they supposed was highly objectionable in the *measures* that we used.[7] ‹Our

[5] See MS 376. It is probably more correct to say that Nettleton went to Albany on his own initiative, and only after talking with Finney did *he* write to Beecher and urge *Beecher* to make a stand. An editorial note in the Hartford *Watchman* states:

> In 1826, when an effort was made by the friends of new measures at the west, to introduce them into the churches in Albany, the ministers of that Presbytery sent a delegate to the Rev. Mr. Nettleton, then laboring in a revival in Jamaica, on Long Island, requesting him to come and aid them in their efforts to exclude those measures, which they deemed highly injurious to the cause of pure revivals. The advocates of the new measures in Albany, had already denounced the Rev. Dr. Chester as cold, and stupid, and dead, and an enemy to revivals, and prayed for him as such. But finding that the labors of Mr. Nettleton in connexion with the settled pastors were followed by an interesting work of grace, the new measure men went to Dr. Chester, stating that they were entirely satisfied with his, (Dr. Chester's) preaching, and that if he would dismiss Mr. Nettleton, and receive Mr. Finney, he would now have a good opportunity to establish his reputation as a friend to revivals. This information Dr. Chester himself communicated to his brethren in the ministry at the time (*The Watchman* [Hartford, Conn.] 1 [16 May 1836]: 78).

See also Sherry P. May, "Asahel Nettleton: Nineteenth Century American Revivalist" (Ph.D. diss., Drew University, 1969), pp. 46, 196.

[6] Finney went to Albany to see Nettleton in December 1826. Nettleton was staying with Rev. Henry R. Weed (1789–1870), a Princeton graduate who was minister of the First Presbyterian Church. See n. 9 below and *The American Annual Cyclopaedia and Register of Important Events of the Year 1870* (New York: D. Appleton and Co., 1872), p. 585.

[7] The section that follows, to the bottom of MS 396, in Finney's handwriting, is on a separate piece of paper pasted over the original sheet. The writing underneath reads:

> I stayed that evening and heard Mr. Nettleton preach, the only time that I ever heard him preach. When we went to meeting I was a little surprized to find that he was anxious not to be seen with me; hence Judge Cushman, who went with me from Troy, and I went and sat in the gallery, and did not appear anywhere with Mr. Nettleton. I found his mind was made up to have no connection with my labors whatever, but to resist them. As Troy was so near to Albany, we soon began to feel in Troy the influence of Dr Beecher's

The last seven words forming the last line of the page are exposed below the pasted piece of paper. The last sentence had been crossed out by Finney when he rewrote it at the end of MS 397.

conversation was brief upon every point upon which we touched. I observed that he avoided the subject of promoting revivals. When I told him that I intended to rema[i]n[8] in Albany & hear him preach in the evening he manifested uneasiness & remarked that I must not be seen with him.[9] Hence Judge Cushman who accompanied me from Troy & who was in college with Mr. N. & myself went to meeting & sat in the gallery.[10] I saw enough to satisfy me that I could expect no advice or instruction from him, & that he was there to take a stand against me. I soon found I was not mistaken. |Since[11] writing the last paragraph[12] my attention has been called to a statement in the biography of Mr. Nettleton to the effect that he tried in vain to change my views & practices in promoting revivals of religion.[13] I can not think that Mr Nettleton ever authorized such a statement for certainly he never attempted to do it. As I have said, at that time he could have moulded me at discretion but he said not a word to me about my manner of conducting revivals nor did he ever write a word to me upon the subject. He kept me at arm's length & although as I have said we conversed on some points of theology then much discussed, it was plain that he was unwilling to say any thing regarding revivals & would not allow me to accompany him to meet-

MS 397

[8]Finney had omitted the *i* from "remain," but Fairchild corrected it in pencil.

[9]John Frost recollected Finney speaking afterward about this interview with Nettleton. Finney said that

> he was more anxious to see and converse with him than with any man living; that he told him he wished to have a free and full conversation with him on the subject of revivals, but he appeared unwilling to enter fully into the subject and to give his views. Mr. N., he said, assigned various reasons for declining a free conversation—that his health was too feeble, and then that he had an engagement to preach in the evening. Mr. Finney said he would stay and hear him, and would converse with him when he was able. Mr. N. stated that he expected to leave town the next day, and go into the country. Mr. F. said he should like that still better, and would go with him wherever he pleased, and would stay as long as he pleased. Mr. N. then said he expected some person to go with him. From all this Br. Finney said he concluded that he did not wish to enter into a free and full conversation with him. Mr. F. appeared to be much disappointed and grieved.—This conversation with Mr. F. was before Mr. Aikin received his letter from Mr. Nettleton (John Frost to S. C. Aikin, January 1828, in a letter from Aikin to the editors of *The New York Observer*, 16 February 1828, p. 25).

A note from T. Hastings in the same letter, dated Utica, 28 January 1828, says:

> This certifies that soon after Mr. Nettleton's arrival at Albany, I called upon him at the house of the Rev. Mr. Weed, for the purpose of introducing Mr. Finney to his acquaintance, who was very desirous of profiting by his knowledge and experience on the subject of revivals. After a short interview had taken place between the gentlemen, I learned from Mr. Finney that the nature of the interview had been entirely unsatisfactory; and that as to the subjects of highest interest, Mr. N. had preserved a mysterious silence. I spent more than a week for the purpose of bringing about a *special* interview; but to no effect.

[10]John Paine Cushman (1794–1848) graduated from Yale in 1807 and took up law in Troy. In 1816, the same year that he was elected to Congress, he joined the Presbyterian church and two years later was made an elder. He was to become a judge of the Third District in 1838. See Henry W. Cushman, *A Historical and Biographical Genealogy of the Cushmans* (Boston: Little, Brown, 1855), pp. 318–34.

[11]This page was inserted by Finney and numbered 397, necessitating the renumbering of the subsequent pages. He made the alterations on the next five pages.

[12]This section on MS 396 and 397 in Finney's handwriting was written after the manuscript had been sent to Lewis Tappan to read (see Introduction, p. xxxiii).

[13]Bennet Tyler, *Memoir of the Life and Character of Rev. Asahel Nettleton, D.D.*, 2d ed. (Hartford, Conn.: Robins and Smith, 1845), p. 238.

ing.[14] This was the only time I saw him until I met him in the convention at New Lebanon.[15] At no time did Mr. N. ever try to correct my views in relation to revivals. **After I heard more of his views & practices in promoting revivals I was thankful to God that he never did influence me upon that subject.**[16]

As Troy was so near Albany we soon began to feel in Troy the influence MS 398 of Dr. Beecher's› ˡletters[17] over some of the leading members of Dr Beman's

[14]Finney wrote, "This he told me to my face," after this but then crossed it out. Nettleton explained in a letter to Lyman Beecher shortly after this why he did not attempt to receive Finney or to try and mold him:

> I could not do it without sanctioning all that he had done, and joining with disorganizers all over the world; for my name was already in their service at the West; and besides, if I should not succeed, it would ruin us both, and if I should have succeeded, the disorganizers would say I had spoiled him.

Lyman Beecher's son Charles, however, noted: "The truth seems to be that Mr. Nettleton's mind was made up before he visited Albany" (*Autobiography, Correspondence, etc., of Lyman Beecher, D.D.,* ed. Charles Beecher, 2 vols. [New York: Harper, 1863, 1865], 2:93–94).

[15]Finney had "two short interviews" with Nettleton at this time. See Aikin's letter in *The New York Observer*, 16 February 1828, p. 25; and Tyler, *Memoir of Rev. Asahel Nettleton*, pp. 238, 249. The New Lebanon Convention was in July 1827. See MS 409–24.

[16]Finney preached a sermon in Troy on Sunday, 4 March 1827, while the presbytery was in session. Members of the presbytery requested its publication, and Finney "hastily sketched down the principal thoughts." It was published as *A Sermon Preached in the Presbyterian Church at Troy, March 4, 1827, by the Rev. Charles G. Finney, from Amos III.3: "Can two walk together except they be agreed?"* (Troy: Tuttle and Richards, 1827). It was the first of Finney's sermons to be published. Although it had previously been preached in Utica in January, and apparently before Finney had read Nettleton's letter to Aikin (dated 13 January 1827), Nettleton took it as a personal attack on himself and wrote a severe criticism in a letter to Dr. Gardiner Spring. These "Remarks" dated Durham, 4 May 1827, were published in *The New York Observer* and in pamphlet form and were reprinted in the *Religious Intelligencer* (New Haven), 2 June 1827, pp. 11–13; and 9 June 1827, pp. 28–30. Years later Finney wrote: "I remember that Mr Nettleton did write an article in which he criticised a sermon of mine. . . . His objection was however so trivial that I never noticed it, and cannot remember what it was" (Finney to the editor, 10 September 1859, *The Christian News* [Glasgow], 17 September 1859, p. 5). The purpose of Nettleton's critique was to show the difference between true and false zeal and to give a warning against spiritual pride.

Another review of the sermon appeared in the *Albany Christian Register* and was reprinted in *The Hopkinsian Magazine* (Providence, R.I.), November 1827 to February 1828, and elsewhere. It was written by "Novanglus," who was presumed to have been William R. Weeks. John Frost wrote to Finney after seeing Lyman Beecher in Boston in November 1827: "Weeks Dr B. told me has written a review of your sermon. Said he had a part of it. I have not seen it. It seems after all that you must have a tug with the *Orthodox Devil* on Paris Hill (Frost to Finney, 12 November 1827, Finney Papers, microfilm, roll 1).

The sermon and reviews received considerable notice in the press, and there was concern among Finney's friends about how to deal with the damage being done to the cause of revivals by these attacks. See *Religious Intelligencer,* 23 June 1827, p. 59; *WR,* 22 May 1827, p. 83; 14 August 1827, p. 129; 30 October 1827, p. 175; *Christian Advocate* (Philadelphia), n.s., 5 (December 1827): 553–68; n.s., 6 (January 1828): 29–36; *Personal Reminiscences of the Life and Times of Gardiner Spring,* vol. 1 (New York: Scribner, 1866), pp. 230–37; Weeks to Nettleton, 6 July 1827, in Nettleton Papers, Hartford Seminary; and letters to Finney from N. S. S. Beman, 26 May 1827; E. Jennings, 17 July 1827; and J. P. Cushman, 23 January, 19 February, and 1 and 3 March 1828, Finney Papers, microfilm, roll 1.

The reviews were republished in *Letters of the Rev. Dr. Beecher and Rev. Mr. Nettleton, on the "New Measures" in Conducting Revivals of Religion. With a Review of a Sermon by Novanglus* (New York: Carvill, 1828). Finney's sermon was reprinted in Philadelphia by William F. Geddes, and another edition was brought out in 1828 by Hiram Ferry at Northampton, Massachusetts. It was later included in Finney's *Sermons on Important Subjects* (New York: Taylor, 1836).

[17]Pages 398 to 400 were originally numbered 262 to 264 and renumbered 394 to 396 by Matson, then changed to 398 to 400 by Finney.

church. This opposition increased, and was doubtless fomented by an out‹side›[18] influence, until finally it was determined to complain of Dr Beman, and bring his case before the presbytery.[19] **They did so,** and for several ˡweeks the presbytery sat and examined the charges against him.[20] In the meantime I went on in my labors in the revival.[21] Christian people continued praying mightily to God. I kept up preaching and praying incessantly, and the revival went on with increasing power; Dr. Beman, in the meantime being under the necessity of giving almost his entire attention to his case **which was** before the presbytery. When the presbytery had examined the charges and specifications I think they were nearly or quite unanimous in dismissing the whole subject, and justifying the course which he had taken. The charge was not for *heresy*, nor were the specifications for heresy, I believe, but for things conjured up by the enemies of the revival, and by those who were misled by an outside influence.[22] In the midst of the

JHF 204

[18]Matson had written the word "outward" here, but Finney changed it to "outside."

[19]See MS 399. The opposition had started before Finney went to Troy and was led by Josephus Brockway, lay member of the Congregational church in Middlebury, Vermont, who had been living in Troy since May 1826 and who was a regular attender at Beman's church. He was the author of the anonymous pamphlet *A Brief Account of the Origin and Progress of the Divisions in the First Presbyterian Church in the City of Troy; containing, also, Strictures upon the New Doctrines broached by the Rev. C. G. Finney and N. S. S. Beman, with a Summary Relation of the Trial of the Latter before the Troy Presbytery. By a number of the late Church and Congregation* (Troy: Tuttle and Richards, 1827). See Senex, "Revival Sketches—No. VII," *The Advance,* 12 March 1868, p. 2.

[20]Finney stated elsewhere that the trial lasted six weeks. The case came before the presbytery at the end of January 1827 and was referred to the synod. But in fact there were continued attempts to get rid of Beman right through 1827 and into 1828. The case came before the General Assembly in Philadelphia while Finney was there in May 1828. Finney was kept abreast of the proceedings through letters when he was not in Troy, particularly from John P. Cushman. See *Lectures on Revivals of Religion*, ed. William G. McLoughlin (Cambridge, Mass.: Belknap, 1960), pp. 285, 291; and Eric N. Newberg, "The Civil War in Zion; Charles Grandison Finney, Lyman Beecher, and the Popularization of American Protestantism During the Second Great Awakening, 1795–1835" (M.A. thesis, Pacific School of Religion, 1974), pp. 151–55.

Martin Townsend, a later minister of the church, reckoned that "the whole life of the First Presbyterian Church for the first ten years of Dr. Beman's ministry, was one of an almost unbroken series of controversies between the doctor and some of his congregation." See *Proceedings of the First Presbyterian Church, Troy, N.Y., Dec 30 and 31, 1891* (Troy: Troy Times, 1892), p. 22.

[21]One of the two surviving sermons written by Finney in his own handwriting was preached on 17 March 1827, probably at Troy. It was from Acts 20:35 and was entitled "The Blessedness of Benevolence." This cannot now be found in the Finney Papers, but it was transcribed by James Robert Emmel in "The Persuasive Techniques of Charles Grandison Finney as a Revivalist and Social Reform Speaker, 1820–1860" (Ph.D. diss., Pennsylvania State University, 1959), pp. 397–420.

[22]Brockway's pamphlet caused a storm of controversy. Attention was drawn to inaccuracies in Brockway's statements about the trial in a pamphlet *A Contrast of Josephus Brockway's Testimony and Statement by a Brief Remarker* (Troy: Tuttle and Richards, 1827). But Brockway only reiterated his charges against Beman in *Mr. Brockway's Apology to the Reverend Nathan S. S. Beman, with the facts in the case* (Troy: Troy Sentinel, 1827). See John R. Tufft, "The Influence of the Theology of Charles G. Finney on the Presbyterian Church in the United States of America" (S.T.M. thesis, Biblical Seminary in New York, 1949), chap. 4.

Brockway also wrote a letter to Finney, drawing attention to his offensive doctrines and measures. It was anonymous, but he admitted authorship in another pamphlet, *A Delineation of the Characteristic Features of a Revival of Religion in Troy, in 1826 and 1827* (Troy: Adamcourt, 1827), p. 58.

When the great revival occurred fours years later at Troy in the winter of 1830–1831, there was, according to J. P. Cushman, a great "softening" in the feelings of church members toward

MS 399 revival **my wife was in a state of health that demanded** |that I should leave Troy for a week or two and visit **her** at Whitesboro, **Oneida County.**[23] While I was gone **the** Rev. Horatio Foote was invited by **Brother** Beman to preach.[24] I do not know how often he preached; but this I recollect, that he gave great offence to the already disaffected members of the church. He bore down upon them with the most searching discourses, as I learned.[25] A few of them finally made up their minds to withdraw from the congregation. They did so, and established another congregation; but this was after I had left Troy, I do not recollect how long.[26] **This** effort to break Dr Beman down **being an utter failure**, considerably discomfitted[27] the outside movement in

each other in Troy. "Even Brockway told Br. Gant two days since that he could give the hand of fellowship" (J. P. Cushman to Finney, 31 December 1830, Finney Papers, microfilm, roll 2).

[23] Finney went to Whitesboro about the end of December and did not return to Troy until after January 23. See John P. Cushman to Finney, 12 January and 23 January 1827, Finney Papers, microfilm, roll 1.

[24] Horatio Foote (1796–1886) was a graduate of Union College in 1820 and Auburn Theological Seminary in 1824. He had become a Presbyterian minister in Kingston, Ontario, but he was itinerating in the state of New York when Finney went to Troy. In the 1830s he was to be notorious as an evangelist throughout the northern states and New England before becoming a Congregational minister in Illinois. See *The Congregational Year Book* (Boston), 1887, p. 24; and William H. Collins and Cicero F. Perry, *Past and Present of the City of Quincy, and Adams County, Illinois* (Chicago: Clarke, 1905), p. 600.

[25] Josephus Brockway gives details of the offensive preaching and rude behavior of Foote at this time. Brockway adds:

> This, too, is the man who introduced, I believe, the expression in prayer, *Ferret* them out, O Lord, *hunt* them; they must be *ferreted* out. This went the rounds; for such pretty expressions were catched with a wonderful alacrity (*Features of a Revival in Troy*, p. 58).

From Brockway's account, Foote's preaching and behavior would appear to have been no more offensive than Finney's or Beman's. In William R. Weeks, *The Pilgrim's Progress in the Nineteenth Century* (New York: Davis, 1826), Foote appears under the name "Wild." See p. 197 n. 15 (MS 383).

[26] The Second Presbyterian Church was formed on 25 September 1827 with fifty members, of whom forty-five were from the First Church, with Mark Tucker as pastor. See John P. Cushman to Finney, 25 September 1827, Finney Papers, microfilm, roll 1; and William H. Hollister, Jr., *Second Presbyterian Church of Troy, N.Y. Historical Sketch* (Troy: published by direction of the Session, 1917), pp. 5–7.

Although there is general agreement that the withdrawal of disaffected members from the First Church was connected with the New Measures of Beman and Finney, a later pastor of the Second Church, William Irvin, maintained that Finney was not really correct in attributing its formation to the trouble in the First Church. Initial steps toward a new church had been taken as early as February 1826:

> It is no doubt true that there were such differences of opinion and feeling, and that some who entertained them left the First Church and joined the Second. But the facts already stated show plainly that this church was fairly inaugurated as an enterprise and formed as a Society before Mr. Finney was invited to Troy: and it is pleasant to feel assured that the church had its origin in no such disagreement among Christians and Presbyterians, but as the consequence of natural and healthful growth (*Centennial Sermon Preached by William Irvin, Pastor, July 2, 1871, being the Church's Semi-Centennial* [Troy: Whig Publishing Company, 1876], pp. 3–6).

See also Martin I. Townsend, "Historical Address," in *Proceedings of the Centennial Anniversary of the First Presbyterian Church, Troy, N.Y., Dec 30 and 31, 1891* (Troy: Troy Times, 1892), pp. 19–20; A. J. Weise, *History of the City of Troy* (Troy: Young, 1876), p. 156; James E. Johnson "The Life of Charles Grandison Finney" (Ph.D. diss., Syracuse University, 1959), pp. 135–36; and Senex, "Revival Sketches—No. IX," *The Advance,* 16 April 1868, p. 2.

[27] This word was spelled "discomfitted" by Matson, and one of the *t*s was crossed out by Fairchild.

opposition to the revival. A great many very interesting incidents occurred during this revival that I must pass in silence, lest they should appear to reflect too severely on the opposers of the work. **To give, however, a hint at the *nature* of the opposition, as I aim at securing the truth of history, I would remark that among other things that were done, it was found that one of the leaders in the opposition from New England had come to Troy, and was attending the young converts prayer-meeting and taking notes of all their expressions, and of whatever occurred in the meeting of these young converts.[28] He did not appear among any of the friends of the revival; nor did he attend any of the meetings, as I could learn except in this stealthy manner. He was evidently a spy, sent in, or came in on his own motive, to spie out of the land. However he did not get hold of anything that was ever published to my knowledge; nor so far as I know was there anything objectionable in those meetings, or in any of our meetings, that he could make public to the injury of the revival. This was a ministerial brother, who had labored a considerable with Brother Nettleton.[29] ‹I did not see him nor did the Pastor. He manifestly came not as a friend.›[30] But I will not attempt to uncover** ˡ**many things that greatly grieved the people of God and the Holy Spirit.** MS 400

In this revival there was a very earnest spirit of prayer, **as in all the rest that had preceeded it.** We had a prayer-meeting from house to house daily at eleven O'clock. At one of those meetings I recollect that a Mr. Stowe, cashier of a bank ˡin that city, was so pressed by the spirit of prayer, that when the meeting was dismissed he was unable to rise from his knees, as we had all just been kneeling in prayer.[31] He remained upon his knees, and writhed and groaned in agony. He said, "Pray for —, **who was** president of the bank of which he was cashier. This president was a **rich, but an** unconverted man. JHF 205

[28]At this point in the manuscript an asterisk and the word "over" indicate the insertion of a section on the reverse of the page. This side then ends with the words "But I will not attempt to uncover." MS 399, reverse, was edited by Fairchild and then crossed out by him in the manuscript.

[29]This sentence is so written in the original. Cf. the sentence referred to in p. 181 n. 52. The next two sentences are in Finney's handwriting.

[30]Nettleton refers to a number of ministers who visited Troy and witnessed the revival at this time, namely: Edward Dorr Griffin, David Porter, Eliphalet Nott, Mark Tucker, and Elias Cornelius. One of these may be the man to whom Finney is referring. See Nettleton to S. C. Aikin, 13 January 1827, in *Letters of Beecher and Nettleton,* p. 9; and Nettleton to John Frost, 15 February 1827, copy in Finney Papers, microfilm, roll 1.

Truman Hastings drew attention to what may be the same incident:

> It was also charged against the promoters of these revivals, that they inculcated the duty of parents to compel, when necessary, their children to repent, by the application of the rod. This proposition was so absurd as absolutely to defy credence. It was deemed necessary, therefore, to get up a *fact* to sustain it. Hence the cruel espionage which resulted in a wanton and wicked stab to the maternal heart of one of the most intelligent, refined and delicate ladies of the county. It is needless to say that the story itself was the patch-work of a spy (Senex, "Revival Sketches—No. VIII," *The Advance,* 2 April 1868, p. 2).

This is the end of the addition that was inserted on the reverse of page 399. The words "But I will not attempt to uncover" end the page.

[31]This was Silas K. Stow, cashier of the Troy City Bank. See *The Troy Directory, for the Year 1836–7,* p. 109; and T. Hastings to J. Keep, 20 July 1866, Finney Papers, microfilm, roll 5.

When it was seen that his soul was in travail for that man, the praying people knelt down and wrestled in prayer for his conversion. As soon as the mind of **the cashier** was so relieved that he could go home, we all retired; and soon after the president of the bank, for whom we prayed, expressed hope in Christ. He had not **previous to** this, I believe, attended any of the meetings, and it was not known that he was concerned about his salvation. But prayer prevailed, and God soon took his case in hand.

MS 401 |‹The[32] father of **the** judge **Cushman** who was at **Troy**[33] with me, was **at that time** living with his son whose guest I was at the time. The old gentleman had been a judge in Vermont.[34] He was **a** remarkably correct **man** in his outward life. **A** venerable man whose house in Vermont had been the home of ministers who visited the place, & he was to all appearance quite satisfied with his amiable & selfrighteous life. His wife had told me of her anxiety for his conversion[35] & his son **J. P. Cushman** had repeatedly expressed fear that his father's selfrighteousness would never be overcome & that his natural amiability would ruin his soul. One sabbath morning the Holy Spirit opened the case to my apprehension & showed me how to reach it. **I** in a few moments had the whole subject in my mind. I went down stairs & told the old lady & her son **J. P.** what I was about to do & exhorted them to pray earnestly for **the old judge**. I followed out the **Divine** showing **& as I was assured** the word took such powerful hold of him that he spent a sleepless night **& in the morning looked haggard, pale & ill**. His wife informed me that he had spent a night of anguish—that his selfrighteousness was thoroughly annihilated, & that he was almost in dispair. His son had told me that he had JHF 206 |long prided himself as being better than members of the church. He soon became clearly converted & lived a christian life to the end.[36] **Very many like conversions occurred.**›[37] MS 402 |Before[38] I left Troy a young lady, a

[32] MS 401. This page in Finney's handwriting was inserted after MS 400 and was numbered 401, and the subsequent pages were renumbered 402, etc.

[33] Fairchild altered this to "Albany."

[34] Isaac Cushman (1759–1842) had been a farmer in Connecticut during the American Revolution before moving to Guildhall, Vermont, in 1809, where he continued to farm until ill health caused him to retire and move to Troy. He was "a Judge of Probate in Vermont for eight years from 1816; and a member of the Council of Censors in 1820." See Cushman, *Genealogy of the Cushmans,* pp. 178–79.

[35] Sarah Cushman (d. 1832) was the sister of Judge Elijah Paine of Williamstown, Vermont.

[36] An obituary notice by Beman states: "He removed to this city in 1827, and soon after made a public profession of religion, by uniting with the First Presbyterian Church, of which he remained, till his death, a consistent and worthy member" (reprinted in Cushman, *Genealogy of the Cushmans,* p. 179).

[37] The *Troy Review* carried notices of the revival and its results. A meeting for inquiry had been established by Beman in February 1826 that had continued on through the time Finney was there and was attended by 20 to 160 persons each week. By the time Finney left, more than 100 had joined the Presbyterian church. The ages of the converts ranged from sixteen to eighty-seven, the oldest being a captain who had commanded a company at the battle of Bunker Hill in the Revolution (*BR,* 2 March 1827, p. 34; and *Religious Intelligencer,* 7 April 1827, p. 716). Truman Hastings recollected in 1868:

> The subjects of this revival cannot be enumerated; it embraced both citizens and strangers. It cannot be doubted that many hundred were truly converted to God. The good work continued nearly eighteen months; and the First Presbyterian Church in Troy became, and ever since has been a large, influential and active body, in every

Miss Seward, from New Lebanon in Columbia County, who was an only daughter of one of the deacons or elders of the church in New Lebanon, came to Troy, as I understood, to purchase a dress for a ball which she wished to attend.[39] She had a young lady relative in Troy, who was numbered among the young converts, and was a zealous Christian. She invited Miss Seward to attend with her all the meetings. This aroused the enmity of her heart. She was very restive; but her cousin plead with her to stay from day to day and to attend the meetings, until before she left Troy she was thoroughly converted to Christ.

As soon as her eyes were opened and her peace was made with God, she went immediately home, and began her labors for a revival in that place. Religion in New Lebanon was at that time in a very low state. The young people were nearly all unconverted; and the old members of the church were in a very cold and inefficient state. Miss Seward's father had become very formal; and for a long time religious matters had been in a great measure neglected in that place.[40] They had an aged ˡminister,[41] a good man, I trust, but a man that did not seem to know how to perform revival work.[42]

MS 403

good word and work ("Revival Sketches—No. VII," *The Advance,* 12 March 1868, p. 2).

The revival also swept through the Troy Female Seminary. The pioneer women's rights leader Elizabeth Cady Stanton, at that time a sixteen-year-old pupil at the school, recalled that it went through the seminary "like an epidemic, attacking in its worst form the most susceptible." She herself was "one of the first victims" but came to look back with horror on Finney's methods: "such preaching worked incalculable harm to the very souls he sought to save" (*Eighty Years and More {1815–1897}: Reminiscences of Elizabeth Cady Stanton* [London: T. Fisher Unwin, 1898], pp. 41, 43). The principal of the seminary, Emma Willard, was also displeased. Finney disapproved of the dancing that had been introduced as a beneficial form of exercise; and Gloriana Huntington, another pupil, "had to tell Mrs. Willard all about it and the consequence is that Mrs. Willard has no very good opinion of Mr. Finney—she considers his conduct as an attack upon her school and an insult to herself" (Gloriana Huntington to Benjamin Huntington, 15 October 1826, transcription in Robert Samuel Fletcher Papers, file 30/24, box 1, Oberlin College Archives). Gloriana Huntington was a daughter of Henry Huntington of Rome. Elizabeth Cady later married Henry B. Stanton, a Finney convert from Rochester, New York.

[38] Page 402 was originally numbered 265 and renumbered 397 by Matson; renumbered 400, renumbered again 401, and changed to 402 by Finney.

[39] Sarah T. Seward was the daughter of Deacon Abram Seward. She qualified as a teacher at Frances Willard's Seminary in Troy; and in 1833, with her brother Jason, she moved to Rochester, New York, where she started the Rochester Female Seminary. In 1841 she married General Jacob Gould of Rochester, a shoe manufacturer who had been mayor of Rochester in 1836. She died in 1875. See Daniel Nash to "Deacon Abram Seward," 22 October 1827, Finney Papers, microfilm, roll 1; William F. Peck, *Semi-Centennial History of the City of Rochester* (Syracuse: Mason, 1884), pp. 672–73; Blake McKelvey, "On the Educational Frontier," *The Rochester Historical Society, Publication Fund Series*, vol. 17, 1939, pp. 24–26; McKelvey, "Private Educational Enterprise Since the Mid-Century," in *ibid.*, p. 155; and John Livingston, *Portraits of Emminent Americans Now Living,* vol. 1 (New York: Cornish, Lamport, 1853), pp. 75–78. See also the letters of Sarah Seward to the Finneys in the Finney Papers.

[40] John T. Avery, who was converted in the revival in New Lebanon, wrote, "The town had churches, composed principally of godly women, while most of their husbands were trusting in their morality" ("Remarks of Rev. John [T.] Avery, of Cleveland, Ohio," in *Reminiscences of Rev. Charles G. Finney* [Oberlin: Goodrich, 1876], p. 29).

[41] Page 403 was originally numbered 266 and renumbered 398 by Matson; then renumbered 401, changed to 402, and renumbered again 403 by Finney.

[42] The minister was Silas Churchill (1769–1854), a Yale graduate who went to the New Lebanon Presbyterian Church in 1795. He was minister there for forty-two years. See F. B. Dexter, *Biographical Sketches of the Graduates of Yale College*, vol. 4 (New York: Holt, 1907), pp.

Miss Seward first began at home, and besought her father to give up his "old prayer," as she expressed it, and wake up, and be engaged in religion. As she was a great favorite in the family, and especially with her father, her conversion and conversation greatly affected him. He was very soon aroused, and became quite another **sort of a** man, and felt deeply that they must have a revival of religion. **Sarah, this** daughter, **also** went to the house of her pastor, and began with a daughter of his who was in her sins.[43] She was soon JHF 207 converted; and they two united in prayer for a revival of |religion, and went to work from house to house in stirring up the people. In the course of a week or two there was so much interest excited that **Sarah** came out herself to Troy to beg me to go **out** there to preach.[44] She was requested to do so by the pastor and by members of the church. I went out and preached.[45] The Spirit of the Lord was poured out, and ‹the› revival soon ‹went› forward with great power.[46] Very interesting incidents occurred al‹most every day. **Powerful** MS 404 conversions were multiplied[47] |**&** a great **&** blessed change came over the religious aspect of the whole place. **The most cultivated & influential of the inhabitants were converted.**[48] Here we **had gotten** out of the region poisoned by the influence of the opposition raised by Dr. B. **&** Mr. N.[49] consequently we heard but little of opposition at this place during the revival

536–37. The supporters of the revival in the congregation were always dissatisfied with Churchill, feeling that he was never fully committed to the New Measures. See John Kendall to Finney, 18 June 1828, Finney Papers, microfilm, roll 2; and 4 February 1835, Finney Papers, microfilm, roll 3.

[43]This was Rhoda C. Churchill. She became the wife of the Reverend Edwards A. Beach of Stephentown. See letters from her to the Finneys in the Finney Papers.

[44]John Avery recollected, "It was a case of such mark that it interested the whole community" (*Reminiscences of Finney,* p. 29).

[45]Finney first went to New Lebanon about 18 February 1827 but stayed for only a day or two. Then he went again on 10 March for about a week. He was persuaded to return on 8 April, and he remained until the end of May. See letters from Silas Churchill to Finney, Finney Papers; and Charles Churchill, "Book of Memoranda," Silas Churchill Papers, Presbyterian Historical Society. The "Book of Memoranda" of Charles, the nineteen-year-old son of the pastor, gives the dates and texts and some details of many of Finney's sermons at this time. Reference from Leonard I. Sweet.

[46]This sentence originally read, "The Spirit of the Lord was there poured out, and a revival soon commenced that went forward with great power," but Finney altered it.

[47]The end of MS 403 and the start of MS 404 were altered by Finney. The section down to n. 50 appears to have originally read: "Very interesting incidents occurred al/most daily, powerful conversions; and at this place very little open opposition was made so far as I can recollect. There were some individuals who at first opposed; but I do not recollect that any opposition was made by any of the members of the church." The alterations were made by Finney on two separate pieces of paper pasted over this section of the page. Before Finney pasted on the first strip, he started to make the alteration at the top of the page, with the words "& a great & blessed change came over the religious aspect." The rest of the sentence ("of the whole place") and further additions were written on the first strip of paper. But when it was pasted onto the page, it covered up the previous part of the sentence, which had to be rewritten in at the top of the strip. In rewriting it, Finney added the word "of," which thus appears twice. The first strip ends at n. 48.

The pagination changes of MS 404 were covered over, so Finney rewrote in the page number 404 at the top of the page. Pages MS 404 to 424 were originally numbered 267–287 and renumbered 399–419 by Matson, then changed to 420–422 and again renumbered 404–424 by Finney.

[48]Finney added a section at this point that he later crossed out: "Amongst others I recollect the very striking conversion [of] a Dr. Wright who up to that time was a skeptic. He had been steadfast." This ends the section on the first strip of paper. It is followed by the second strip.

[49]That is, Dr. Beecher and Mr. Nettleton.

especially from professors of religion.›[50] Everything seemed to go on harmoniously, so far as I know, in the church. They were soon led to feel that they greatly needed a revival, and seemed to be very thankful that God had visited them. Most of the prominent men in the community were converted.

Among these was a Dr **Wright**, who was said to be an infidel, **and I suppose he was. He was a man very much respected in his profession, and a good deal gifted in conversation.**[51] He at first manifested a good deal of hostility to the revival, and declared that the people were mad. But he was made a particular subject of prayer by **this** Miss **Seward**, and some others who laid hold upon his case; and who had great faith that notwithstanding his fiery opposition he would soon be converted. **On o**ne Sunday morning he came to meeting,[52] and I could see that those who felt for him were **bowed down**. Their heads were down, ˡand they were in a prayerful state during nearly the whole sermon. It was plain, however, before night that the Doctor's opposition began to give way. He listened through the day, and that night he spent in a deeply exercised state of mind.[53] The next morning he called on me, subdued like a little child, and confessed that he had been all wrong; **but** was very frank in opening his heart and declaring the change that had come over him. It was plain ˡthat he was another man; and from that day he took hold of the work and went forward with all his might.[54]

MS 405

JHF 208

There was also a Mr. **Tilden**, a merchant **of that place**, probably the most prominent and wealthy citizen of the town at that time, but a **s**keptic.[55] I recollect one evening I preached on the **subject**, "The carnal mind is enmity against God."[56] He was present. He had been a very moral man in the common acceptation of that term, and it had been very difficult to fasten anything upon his mind that would convict him of sin. His wife was a

[50]This ends the section in Finney's handwriting on the second strip of paper.

[51]This sentence was not crossed out by Fairchild in the manuscript, except for the words "a good deal," which were changed by him to "quite." It was omitted from the published edition. In John Avery's account of Dr. Wright's conversion, he states that Wright was "a man in many things like Mr. Finney" (*Reminiscences of Finney*, p. 30).

[52]This was 15 April 1827. Finney preached morning, afternoon, and evening on that day. See Churchill, "Book of Memoranda"; and John Avery, in *Reminiscences of Finney*, p. 30.

[53]Avery recollected, "We learned subsequently that the doctor was so affected that he sprang from his bed at midnight, saying to his wife, 'I can not live so, and I will not if there is any way to get out of it.' He went to his Unitarian neighbor, who had been converted, and got advice from him" (*Reminiscences of Finney*, p. 31).

[54]Avery wrote in 1876: "This physician became one of the most faithful and childlike of Christians, and has continued faithful to this hour. He is a venerable-looking man; and in a recent revival, as deacon of the church, he held the vase while eighty were baptized" (*Reminiscences of Finney*, p. 31; see also Rhoda Churchill to Lydia Finney, 15 March 1828; Thomas Kendall to Finney, 15 March 1828; and Sarah Seward to Lydia Finney, 15 March 1828, Finney Papers, microfilm, roll 1).

[55]Elam Tilden (1781–1842) was a manufacturer of medicines and chemicals and was also postmaster of the village. His family had moved from Lebanon, Connecticut, in 1790 and had named the place New Lebanon. The Tilden home became the resort of Martin van Buren, Silas Wright, and other prominent politicians. His political wisdom was greatly valued by the Democrats. He was the father of Samuel J. Tilden, mayor of New York City and the presidential nominee for the Democratic party in 1878. See Alexander C. Flick, *Samuel Jones Tilden* (New York: Dodd, Mead, 1939).

[56]Romans 8:7. Finney preached from this text on Tuesday evening, 9 April, in the meeting house. See Churchill, "Book of Memoranda."

Christian woman, and the Lord had converted his daughter.[57] The state of
MS 406 things in the town and in his family had so far inter|ested him that he would come to meeting and hear what was said. The next day after this sermon on moral depravity, he confessed himself convinced. He told me it came home to him with resistless power. He saw it was all true, and assured me his mind was made up to serve the Lord the rest of his life.[58] I recollect also that **the Rev.** John T Avery, a noted evangelist, who has labored in many places for many years, was present at that meeting.[59] His family lived in New Lebanon. He was born and brought up there; and was at this time a lad perhaps fifteen or sixteen years of age. The next morning after that sermon was preached,[60] he came to me **one of the dearest little ‹fellows›[61] and** converts that I have ever seen. He began and told me what had been passing in his mind for several days; and then he added, "I was completely *rolled up* in the sermon, and it carried me right along. I could understand it. I gave up; I gave all to Christ." ‹This he said in a manner not to be forgotten.›[62] But why should I multiply cases. I might spend hours in relating incidents, and the conversion
MS 407 of particular individuals. But I must not |enter too much into particulars, **or this narrative will be swelled to undue proportions.**[63]

But I must mention a little incident connected somewhat with the opposition that had been manifested at Troy. The presbytery of Columbia had a meeting somewhere within its bounds while I was at New Lebanon; and
JHF 209 being |informed that I was laboring in one of their churches, appointed a

[57] Elam Tilden's wife was Polly Younglove Jones (1782–1860). The daughter that Finney mentions was probably Mary Tilden. See Rhoda Churchill to Lydia Finney, 4 May 1828; and E. Tilden to Finney, 28 November 1827, Finney Papers, microfilm, roll 1.

[58] Thomas Kendall, Jr., of New Lebanon wrote to Finney some months later: "Mr. Tilden stands, as when you was here, halting, he does not yet unite with the church" (Kendall to Finney, 15 March 1828, Finney Papers, microfilm, roll 1).

[59] John Thomas Avery (1810–1896) was the seventh of eight children born to William and Phebe Avery. The parents had come to New Lebanon in about 1791. In 1820 the father died, and eventually Phebe and the children moved to Galesburg, Illinois, where she died in 1844. After John was converted, he attended Oneida Institute and the Troy Seminary under Beman, before becoming a pastor in Syracuse. He was well known as a powerful evangelist in western New York. After 1839 he made his home in Cleveland, Ohio, where he was for a time pastor of the Plymouth Church. See Elroy M. Avery and Catharine H. Avery, *The Groton Avery Clan,* vol. 1 (Cleveland, 1912), pp. 313, 500; and Avery to Theodore D. Weld, 13 December 1893, Weld-Grimke Papers, William L. Clements Library, University of Michigan.

A discussion on "Evangelists and Pastors" in the columns of *The New-York Evangelist* in 1883 threw doubt on the value of Avery's work, but E. Colton considered he was "second only to Mr. Finney himself" (see *NYE,* 11 January 1883, p. 6; 25 January 1883, p. 2; 8 February 1883, p. 2; and 29 March 1883, p. 2). Finney himself described Avery as "the ablest evangelist I know of" in a letter to Edwin Lamson, 23 February 1864, Correspondence of Charles G. Finney, 1830–1875, microfilm, Oberlin College Archives.

[60] Avery recalled that it was after a sermon preached from "the text, 'He that is ashamed of me before men,' etc." This sermon, from Mark 8:38, was preached on Sunday evening, 11 March. See Avery, in *Reminiscences of Finney,* p. 31; and Churchill, "Book of Memoranda."

[61] Here Finney changed the word "boys" to "fellows."

[62] Finney added this sentence.

[63] It was while Finney was in New Lebanon that he "first set foot as a missionary in New England." He preached in Dalton, Hinsdale, and Peru in Berkshire County, Massachusetts. See E. Jennings to Finney, 5 May and 17 July 1827; and Silas Churchill to Finney, 20 June 1827, Finney Papers, microfilm, roll 1. His real debut in New England, however, was not until the autumn of 1831, when he went to Providence and then to Boston.

committee to visit the place and inquire into the state of things; for they had been led to believe from Troy and other places, and from the opposition of Mr. Nettleton and the letters of Dr Beecher, that my method of conducting revivals was so very objectionable that it was the duty of presbytery to inquire into it. They appointed two of their number, as I afterwards understood, to visit the place; and they attempted to do so. As I afterwards learned, though I do not recollect to have heard it at the time, the news reached New Lebanon of this action of **that** presbytery; and **they** feared that it might create some division and make some disturbance, if this committee came. Some of the most engaged Christians made this a particular subject of prayer; and for a day or two before the time when they were ˡexpected, they prayed much that the Lord would over-rule this thing, and not suffer it to divide the church, or introduce any element of discord. They were expected to **come and** be there on the Sabbath, and attend the meetings. But **on** the day before a violent snow-storm set in; and the snow fell so deep that **although they started to come** they found it impossible to get through, were detained over the Sabbath, and on Monday, **or as soon as they could,** found their way back to their own congregations. Those brethren were the Rev. **Joel Benedict** and the Rev. Mr. **Chester**. Mr. **Chester** was pastor of the **presbyterian** church at Hudson, N.Y;[64] and **the Rev.** Mr. **Benedict** was pastor of the **presbyterian** church in Chatham, a village some fifteen or sixteen miles below Albany **on the Hudson river**.[65]

MS 408

Soon after I received a letter from **Brother Benedict**, informing me that the presbytery had appointed him one of a **C**ommittee to visit me and make some inquiry in regard to my mode of conducting revivals, and inviting me to come and spend a Sabbath with him and preach for him.[66] I did so. As I understood **afterwards** his report to the presbytery was, that it was ˡunnecessary and useless for them to take any farther action in the case; that the Lord was in the work, ˡand they should take heed lest they be found fighting against God. I heard no more of opposition from that source. I have never doubted that the presbytery of Columbia were honestly alarmed at what they had heard. I have never called in question the propriety of the course which they took; and I ever admired their manifest honesty in receiving testimony from sources **that quieted their fears**.[67] **And** so far as I

MS 409
JHF 210

[64]This was William Chester (b. 1796), at one time secretary of the Presbyterian Board of Education. See *Minutes of the General Assembly of the Presbyterian Church in the United States of America* (Philadelphia), 1825, p. 308; and 1831, p. 218; and Edward Strong, "Genealogy of the Chester Family," *The New England Historical and Genealogical Register* (Boston) 22 (1868): 340. See also W. B. Sprague, *Annals of the American Pulpit,* vol. 4 (New York: Carter and Bro., 1859), pp. 401–10.

[65]Joel Tyler Benedict (1772–1833) was admitted to the bar in 1794 but turned to the ministry in 1803. He was called to New Concord (Chatham) in 1815. See Henry M. Benedict, *The Genealogy of the Benedicts in America* (Albany: Munsell, 1870), pp. 139–41. In the manuscript the names "Chatham" and "Hudson" were originally left blank and filled in later by Matson.

[66]This letter is not in the Finney Papers.

[67]The words "that quieted their fears" were not altered in the manuscript, but in the published edition these words were omitted, and the sentence ends, "receiving testimony from proper sources."

know they thereafter sympathized with the work that was going on.[68] ‹**The opposition of Dr. B. & Mr N. had had its day.**›[69]

About this time a proposition was made by some‹body, I know not who›,[70] to hold a convention or consultation on the subject of conducting revivals.[71] Correspondence was entered into between the western brethren who had been engaged in those revivals, and the eastern brethren who had been opposing them. It was finally agreed to hold the convention on a certain day, I think in Ju‹ly›,[72] in New Lebanon where I ‹had been laboring.›[73] I ‹had› left MS 410 New Lebanon,[74] and **went up and** spent a short time |at the village of Little Falls, on the Mohawk **river**, near Utica.[75] Some very interesting incidents occurred there during my short stay; but nothing so marked as naturally to find a place in this narrative, as I was obliged to leave after a very short stay in that place, and return to New Lebanon to attend the convention.

It would seem that the *design* of this meeting has since been, by many, very much misunderstood. I find there is an impression in the public mind that some complaint had been alleged against myself; and that this meeting was for the trial of myself as complained of before a council. But this was by no means the case. I had nothing to do with getting up the convention. Nor was I any more particularly concerned in its results, than any of the members that attended. The design was to get at the facts of those revivals that had been so much opposed, to consult in reference to them, compare views, and see if we could not come to a better understanding than had existed between the

[68] Joel Benedict became a firm supporter of Finney. See letters of Joel Benedict to Finney; G. W. Gale to Finney, 6 June 1827, Finney Papers, microfilm, roll 1; and *Letters of Beecher and Nettleton,* p. 42.

[69] Finney added this sentence. "Dr. B. and Mr N." are Dr. Beecher and Mr. Nettleton.

[70] Here Matson had written down, "by some ministers,—I think by Dr Beecher himself,—" but Finney changed it.

[71] Lyman Beecher may have been the first to propose a convention. The idea was passed on to the western ministers by John Frost. Subsequently the proposal was taken up by Beman, who went to Boston to confer with Beecher. Beman wrote in a letter to Finney and J. P. Cushman, "We have a plan on foot to bring Brs. Nettleton and Finney together which I can fully disclose when I have seen Dr. B." (Beman to Finney and J. P. Cushman, undated letter in Finney Papers, microfilm, roll 6). However, Beecher later stated: "Beman came on to Boston to propose a convention for purposes of explanation. I fell in with it; sat down and wrote to ten or a dozen others to go by all means" (*Autobiography of Lyman Beecher,* 2:100). The convention was arranged by Beman and Beecher. See Beecher's letters to Beman, January 1827, and to Nettleton, 30 January 1827, in *Letters of Beecher and Nettleton*; and *The Christian Examiner* (Boston) 6 (March 1829): 108; John Frost to Finney, 22 March 1827, Finney Papers, microfilm, roll 1; and G. W. Gale, *Autobiography (to 1834) of George Washington Gale (1789–1861), Founder of Galesburg, Illinois, and Knox College* (New York: privately printed, 1964), pp. 293–94.

[72] Matson had written the word "June," but Finney changed it to "July."

[73] The convention was held from 18 to 26 July 1827 at the house of Mr. Betts in New Lebanon. The full proceedings were sent only to *The New York Observer*, but they were copied into many other religious papers and widely commented upon. See *The New York Observer*, 4 August 1827, pp. 122–23; and *BR,* 3 August 1827, p. 122.

[74] Matson had written down, "where I was then laboring. In the meantime I left New Lebanon." Finney changed it.

[75] Finney went to Little Falls about the middle of June 1827 and returned to New Lebanon to preach on Sunday, 15 July. The minister at Little Falls was Stephen W. Burritt. James Boyle, another evangelist, had also been helping Burritt before Finney went there. See Burritt and Boyle to Finney, 12 May 1827; and Burritt to Finney, 18 September 1827, Finney Papers, microfilm, roll 1.

eastern opposers of the revivals and the brethren who had been instrumental in promoting them.

JHF 211 MS 411

ꜜI arrived in New Lebanon a ꜜday or two before the convention met. On the day appointed the ‹invited members›[76] arrived. They were not men that had been appointed by any ecclesiastical bodies; but they had been invited by the brethren most concerned, east and west, to come together for consultation. None of us were men representing any churches or ecclesiastical bodies whatever. We came together with no authority to act for the church, or any branch of ‹it›;[77] but simply, as I have said, to consult, to compare views, to see if anything was wrong in fact; and if so, to agree to correct what was wrong on either side. For myself I supposed that as soon as the brethren came together and exchanged views, and the facts were understood; that the brethren from the east who had opposed the revivals, especially Dr Beecher and Mr. Nettleton, would see their error, and that they had been misled, and that the thing would be disposed of; for I was certain that the things of which they complained in their letters had no foundation in fact. Of the brethren that composed this convention I can remember the following: From the east there were Dr Beecher and Mr. Nettleton, ꜜ**Rev.** Dr Joel Hawes from Hartford,[78] **Rev.** Dr Dutton from New Haven,[79] **Rev.** Dr Humphrey president of **William's** college,[80] Rev. Justin Edwards of Andover,[81] and a considerable number of **eastern**[82] brethren whose names I do not recollect.[83] From the west, that is from central New York where those revivals had been in progress, there were **Rev.** Dr Beman of Troy, Dr Lansing **from** Auburn,

MS 412

[76]Matson had written the word "delegates," but Finney changed it to "invited members."

[77]Finney substituted the word "it" for "the church."

[78]Joel Hawes (1789–1867) was a graduate of Andover and was pastor of the First Congregational Church in Hartford from 1818 until his death. He was an advocate of revivals but opposed the New Measures. Later, however, he cooperated with Finney. See *Appletons' Cyclopedia of American Biography*, 7 vols. (New York: Appleton, 1888), 3:119; and MS 883–90.

[79]Finney was probably referring to Aaron Dutton (1780–1849), who was minister at Guilford, a town about thirteen miles east of New Haven. But he is not listed among those who attended the conference. See *Appletons' Cyclopedia*, 2:275–76.

[80]Heman Humphrey (1779–1861), a Yale graduate, had been a Congregational minister in Fairfield, Connecticut, and Pittsfield, Massachusetts. In 1823 he became president of Amherst College (not Williams), where he remained for twenty-two years. He was a conservative revivalist (see *DAB*). Fairchild had written "Amherst (?)" in pencil over the name "William's." He later crossed out "William's" and the question mark in ink.

[81]Justin Edwards (1787–1853) was a graduate of Williams College and Andover Theological Seminary and, while still a student, became the pastor of the South Congregational Church in Andover. He was active in tract, temperance, and Sabbath reform. In 1836 he became president of Andover Theological Seminary. See Sprague, *Annals of the American Pulpit*, 2:572–85.

[82]The word "eastern" appears as "other" in the published edition. It was not changed in the manuscript, however, except that Fairchild capitalized the initial letter.

[83]The only other person strictly from the East was Caleb J. Tenney (1780–1847), of Wethersfield; but there were two from New York State who were perhaps in sympathy with the eastern ministers, notably Dr. Asahel S. Norton (1771–1833), of Clinton, who had invited Finney to preach for him in 1826, and Henry R. Weed of Albany. Truman Hastings wrote that Weeks and Norton "were invited as was generally supposed, not because of any special experience in revivals of religion; but because of their prominence as clergymen, and because it was believed that they had knowledge of many important facts connected with the revivals in their county, which might be drawn into question" (Senex, "Revival Sketches—No. X," *The Advance*, 23 April 1868, p. 2).

Mr. Aikin of Utica,[84] **Rev.** Mr. Frost of Whitesboro, **Rev. Moses** Gillett **from** Rome, **Rev.** Mr. Coe **from** New Hartford,[85] **Rev. George W** Gale **from** Western, **Rev. William R.** Weeks of Paris Hill, and perhaps some others whose names I do [**not**][86] now recollect, and myself.[87]

We soon discovered that some policy was on foot in organizing the convention on the part of Dr Beecher. However we regarded it not. The convention was organized, and I believe **the Rev.** Dr Humphrey presided as JHF 212 **M**oderator. There |was not the least unkindness of feeling, that I know of, existing **in** the members of the convention toward each other. It is true that the members from the west regarded with suspicion Mr. Weeks, as I have already intimated, as being the man who was responsible, in a considerable MS 413 |degree for the misapprehension of the eastern brethren.[88] As soon as the convention was duly organized, and the business before us was stated and understood, the inquiry was raised by the brethren from the west in regard to the source whence Dr Beecher and Mr. Nettleton had received their information. We had been particularly solicitous to find out who it was that was misleading those brethren, and giving them such a view of the revivals as to make them feel justified in the course they were taking. **To make this discovery was a prime idea with us.** We wanted to know whence all this mysterious opposition had proceeded. We therefore raised the inquiry at once, and wished to know of those brethren from what source they had received their information as touching those revivals. It was discovered at once that this was an embarrassing question. I should have observed before, and now wish to be distinctly understood to say, that no opposition had been manifested by any of the ministers from the east who attended the convention, except Dr Beecher and Mr. Nettleton. It was not difficult to see from the outset that Dr Beecher felt himself committed, and that his MS 414 |reputation was at stake; that as his letters, some of them, had found their way into the public prints, he would be held responsible for them should they not prove to have been called for. It was very plain that he and Mr. Nettleton were both very sensitive. It was also very apparent that Dr Beecher had secured the attendance of these most influential of the New England ministers in order to sustain himself before the public, and justify himself in the course he had taken. As for Mr. Nettleton, Dr Beecher had assured him that he would be sustained by New England, and that all the New England church

[84] Aikin arrived on the second day.

[85] Noah Coe is not listed as being present nor even as having been invited. However, George W. Gale also remembered him being there (Gale, *Autobiography*, p. 294).

[86] The word "not" does not appear in the original manuscript. It was inserted by Fairchild.

[87] Henry Smith (1789–1828) of Camden, who was a friend of Finney's, and Silas Churchill, the minister of New Lebanon, were also present. Joel Benedict arrived near the end of the convention. According to the minutes of the convention a number of other ministers had also been invited who were not present, namely: David Porter of Catskill, New York; Alvan Hyde of Lee, Massachusetts; Samuel Tomb of Salem, New York; Eliphalet Nott, president of Union College, Schenectady; Thomas McAuley and Gardiner Spring of New York; James Patterson and Thomas H. Skinner of Philadelphia; and Edwin Dwight of Richmond, Massachusetts.

[88] G. W. Gale considered that Weeks had "doubtless been as instrumental as any other man in exciting unfavorable impressions abroad against the work of God here" (Gale to Finney, 14 March 1827; this letter is listed in the calendar of the Finney Papers under 11 March 1827, microfilm, roll 1).

judicatories would speak out in his favor and sustain him.[89] **As I have said, we at the very outset raised the question where those brethren had obtained the information upon which they had based their opposition, and to which they had so fully referred in their letters.** ˡWhen the question was raised Dr Beecher replied: "We have not come here to be catechized; and our spiritual dignity forbids us to answer any such questions." For myself I thought this was strange, that when such letters had ˡbeen written and published as had appeared in opposition to those revivals, when such things had been affirmed as facts which were no facts at all, and when such a storm of opposition had been raised throughout the length and breadth of the land, and we had come together to consider the whole question, that we were not allowed to know the source from which their information had been obtained. **We had been totally misrepresented, and as a consequence much evil had resulted to the cause of Christ. We wished to know, and thought we had a *right* to know, the source from which all this misapprehension had arisen.** But we found ourselves utterly unable to learn anything about it. The convention sat several days;[90] but as the facts came out in regard to the revivals, **Brother** Nettleton became so very nervous that he was unable to attend several of our sessions.[91] He plainly saw that he was losing ground, and that nothing could be ascertained that could justify the course that he was taking. This must have been very visible also to Dr Beecher. I should have said before, that when the question came up how ˡthe facts were to be learned about those revivals, Dr Beecher took the ground that the testimony of those brethren from the West, who had been engaged in promoting them, should not be received; that as we were in a sense parties to the question, and had been ourselves the objects of his censure, it was like testifying in our own case; that we were therefore not admissible as witnesses, and the facts should not be received from us. But to this the brethren from the east would not listen for a moment. Dr Humphrey very firmly remarked that we were the best witnesses that could be produced; that we knew what we had done, and what had been done, in those revivals of religion; that we were therefore the most competent[92] and the most credible witnesses; and that our statements were to be received without hesitation by the convention. To this, so far as I know, ˡthere was a universal agreement, with the exception of Dr Beecher and Mr. Nettleton.

JHF 213

MS 415

MS 416

JHF 214

This decision, however, it was very plain at the time, greatly affected both Dr Beecher and Mr Nettleton. They saw that if the facts came out from the brethren who had witnessed the revivals, who had been on ˡthe ground and knew all about them, they might entirely overrule all the misapprehensions and all the misstatements that had been made and entertained upon the subject. Our meeting was very fraternal throughout, there was no sparring or

MS 417

[89]See MS 376–77.

[90]The convention sat from Wednesday, 18 July, to Saturday, 21 July, and the following Monday, 23 July, through to the afternoon of Thursday, 26 July. See minutes of the convention in *The New York Observer*, 4 August 1827, pp. 122–23.

[91]Nettleton left on Saturday of the convention and did not return until the convention was almost over.

[92]This word was spelled "cọmpentent" by Matson but was corrected by Fairchild.

bitterness manifested; but with the exception of the two brethren whom I have named, Dr Beecher and Mr. Nettleton, the brethren from the east appeared candid and desirous to know the truth, and glad to learn particulars of the western revivals.

There were several points of discussion during the convention, especially one on the propriety of **females** taking any part in social meetings.[93] Dr Beecher brought up that objection and argued it at length, insisting upon it that the practice was unscriptural and inadmissible. To this Dr. Beman replied in a very short address, showing conclusively that this practice was familiar to the apostles; and that in the eleventh chapter of Corinthians the apostle called the attention of the church to the fact that Christian **females** had given a shock to eastern **prejudice** by their practice of taking part and praying in MS 418 their religious meetings without their ˡveils. He showed clearly that the apostle did not complain of their taking part in the meeting, but the fact that they did so laying aside their veils; which had given a shock **to their prejudices**, and **given** occasion to heathen opposers **to complain that Christian women appeared publicly in their assemblies and took part in them, especially prayed in them, without being covered with their veils. He** did not **attempt to** reprove the practice of their praying, but simply admonished them to wear their veils when they did so. To this reply of Dr Beman no answer was made or attempted. It was manifestly too conclusive to admit of any re‹futation.›[94]

JHF 215 Near the close of the convention Mr. Nettleton came in ˡmanifestly very much agitated; and said that he would now give the convention to understand the reasons he had for the course he had taken. He had what he called "a historical letter," in which he professed to give the reasons, and state the facts,[95] upon which he had founded his opposition. I was glad to hear the announcement that he wished to read this letter to the convention. A copy of MS 419 it ˡhad been sent to Mr. Aikin when I was laboring with him in Utica, and Mr. Aikin had given it to me. I had it in my possession at the convention, and should have called it up in due time, had not Mr. Nettleton done so. **It appeared in the sequel that Mr. Nettleton had no idea that I had a copy of the letter, or that I had ever seen it.** He went on to read the letter. It was a statement, under distinct heads, of the things of which he complained; and which he had been informed were practiced in those revivals, and especially by myself. It is evident that the letter was aimed at me particularly. Though perhaps I was seldom mentioned **by name** in ‹it. Y›et[96] the things complained of were so presented that there was no mistaking the design, **and that the things complained of were charged to me**. The convention listened attentively to the whole letter, which was as long as a sermon. Mr.

[93] This subject occupied the convention from the afternoon of Thursday, 19 July, until Friday afternoon.

[94] The word "reply" was changed by Finney to "refutation."

[95] Matson had written "to give all the reasons, and state all the facts," but Finney crossed out the word "all" in both places.

[96] Matson had written down, "by name in the letter; yet," but it was changed by Finney. This was not altered in the manuscript, but the order of the words was changed in the published edition.

Nettleton then observed that the convention had before them the facts upon which he had acted, and which he supposed had called for and justified his proceedings.

When he sat down I arose |and expressed my satisfaction that that letter had been read; and remarked that I had a copy of it, and should have read it in due time if Mr. Nettleton had not done so. I then affirmed that so far as I was personally concerned, not one of those facts mentioned there and complained of, was true.[97] **I had done no such thing.** And I added, "All the brethren are here with whom I have performed all these labors, and they know whether I am chargeable with any of these things in any of their congregations. If they know or believe that any of these things are true of me, let them say so now and here, **and I will immediately confess them.**" They all at once affirmed, either by expressly saying so, or by their manifest acquiescence, that they knew of no such |thing. Mr. Weeks was present. **I have said that we had supposed that some or many of those things communicated to Brother Nettleton had been given him by Mr. Weeks.** I expected, therefore, that if anything was said in reply to my explicit denial of all the facts charged in Mr. Nettletons letter with respect to myself, that it would come from Mr. Weeks. |**I did not know but he supposed himself in possession of all the facts, which he would there relate.** I supposed **also** that if he had written to Dr Beecher or Mr. Nettleton affirming those facts, that he would feel called upon then and there to speak out and justify what he had written. But he said not a word. No one there pretended to justify a single sentence in Mr. Nettleton's historical letter, that related to myself. This of course was astounding to Mr. Nettleton and Dr Beecher. If any of their **pretended** facts had been received from Mr. Weeks, no doubt they expected him to speak out and justify what he had written. But he said nothing intimating that he had any knowledge of any of the facts that Mr. Nettleton had presented in his letter.[98] The reading of this letter, and what immediately followed, prepared the way for closing up the convention.

MS 420 · JHF 216 · MS 421

And now follow some things that I am sorry to be obliged to mention. **Brother** Justin Edwards had been present during all the discussions; and had attended, I believe, all the sessions of the convention. He was a very intimate friend of Dr Beecher and Mr. Nettleton, and he must have |seen clearly how the whole thing stood. **Whether at the request of Dr Beecher,** I do not know, near the close of the convention he brought in a string of resolutions, in which, from step to step he **had** resolved to disapprove of such, and such, and such measures in the promotion of revivals.[99] He **had gone** over in his

MS 422

[97] Matson had originally written "applicable to myself" after the word "was," but he replaced it with the word "true."

[98] The accusations in Nettleton's historical letter appeared to have been taken from the Oneida Association *Pastoral Letter* that had been written by Weeks (see p. 142 n. 6 [MS 279]). Frost, Aikin, and Gale were appointed some months later, on 8 February 1828, by the Presbytery of Oneida, to inquire of William Weeks "whether he has evidence that any member of this Presbytery used any of the exceptionable expressions quoted" by him in that letter. The committee subsequently reported that "he refused to give them any information" on the subject (P. H. Fowler, *Historical Sketch of Presbyterianism Within the Bounds of the Synod of Central New York* [Utica: Curtiss and Childs, 1877], pp. 274–75).

[99] Edwards started to introduce his resolutions on the second day, and most of the convention was taken up discussing them.

resolutions nearly, if not quite, every specification contained in Mr. Nettleton's historical letter, disapproving of all the things which Mr Nettleton had complained **of in that letter.** When he had read his resolutions, it was said immediately by several of the brethren from the West: "We approve of these resolutions; but what is their *design*? It is manifest that their design is to make the public impression that such things have been practiced; and that this
JHF 217 convention, condemning those practices, condemns the brethren that ǀhave been engaged in those revivals; and that this convention justifies, therefore, the opposition that has been made **to those revivals.**" Dr Beecher insisted that the design of the resolutions was entirely *prospective*; that nothing was
MS 423 asserted or implied with respect to the past, ǀbut that they were merely to **act** as *land-marks*, and to let it be known that the convention disapproved of such things if they ever should exist, with no implication whatever that any such things had been done.

It was immediately replied, that from the fact that such complaints **have** gone abroad, and it **is** publicly known that such charges **have** been made, **and such things complained of,** it **is** evident that these resolutions were designed to **cover the retreat of** the brethren ‹who had made› this opposition,[100] and to make the impression that such things have been done in those revivals as **are** condemned in these resolutions; **and therefore to justify the opposition of Dr Beecher and Mr. Nettleton, so much of which has found its way to the public.** It was indeed perfectly plain that such was the meaning of those resolutions on the part of **Dr** Beecher and Mr. Nettleton. The brethren from the **west** said: "Of course we shall vote for these resolutions. We believe in these things as much as you do, and we as
MS 424 much disapprove of the practices condemned in these resoǀlutions as you do yourselves; therefore we cannot help voting for them. But **we *do* say,** we believe that they are intended to justify this opposition, to have a *retrospective* rather than a *prospective* application." However we passed the resolutions, I believe unanimously;[101] and I recollect saying that for my part I was willing that these resolutions should go forth, and that all the facts should be left to the publication and adjudication of the solemn judgment. I then proposed that before we dismissed we should pass a resolution against lukewarmness in religion, and condemning it as strongly as any of the practices mentioned in **any** of the resolutions. Dr Beecher declared that there was no danger of lukewarmness at all; whereupon the convention adjourned sine die.[102]

[100]Matson had written down, "of the brethren that led the way of this opposition," but Finney changed it.

[101]Of the twenty-five propositions originally put forward by Edwards, eight were either amended or withdrawn and alternative motions presented by other people. In two of the cases Edwards himself "declined voting." Eighteen of the propositions were passed unanimously. In the other cases no negative votes were actually cast, but several members "declined voting." See *The New York Observer*, 4 August 1827, pp. 122–23.

[102]A paragraph at the bottom of the page follows here in the manuscript:

> The manner in which the whole proceedings, when published, impressed the public, I need not mention. The reaction upon Brother Nettleton was overwhelming. Late in the fall of the same year I met him in the city of New York. He had come there to publish in a pamphlet form the letters that he

This paragraph was crossed out by Finney when he inserted four new pages to replace page 423.

ˡ‹How[103] the publication of the whole proceedings was received by the publick I need not say. In the 2 ˡVol. of the Biography of Dr. Beecher page 101, I find the following note by the Editor.[104] He says, "A careful perusal of the minutes of this convention has satisfied us that there was no radical difference of views between the western brethren & those from N. England; & that but for the influence of one individual the same settlement might have been made there[105] which was afterward effected at Philadelphia." This is no doubt true. The fact is that had not Mr Nettleton listened to false reports & got committed against those revivals no convention would have been held upon this subject or thought of. It was all the more wonderful that he should [have][106] credited such reports as he had so often been made the subject of manifold misrepresentations. But he was nearly worn out, had become exceedingly nervous & was of course fearful & easily excited & withal had the infirmity attributed to him By Dr. Beecher in his Biography of never giving up his own will. I am sure that I say this with entirely kind feelings toward Mr. N. I never entertained or had any other.

MS 425
JHF 218

After this convention the reaction of publick feeling against Br. Nettleton was overwhelming. Late in the fall of the same year I met him in the city of N. York.[107] He told me he was there to give his letters against the western revivals to the publick in pamphlet form.[108] I asked him if he would publish his "historical letter["] which he read before the convention. He said he must publish his letters to justify what he had done. I told ˡhim if he published that letter it would react to his ruin as all who were acquainted with those revivals would see that he was acting without a valid reason. He replied that he should publish his letters & would risk the reaction. He published several other letters but that one he did not publish so far as I could learn. If it had been true the publication of it would have made the impression that his opposition had been called for. But as it was not true it was well for him that he did not publish it.

MS 426

ˡHere I must take a slight notice of some things I find in Dr. Beechers Biography about which I think there must have been some misunderstanding. The Biography represents him as having justified his opposition to those revivals that is to the manner in which they were conducted until the day of his death & as having maintained that the evils complained of were real & were corrected by their opposition. If this was his opinion after that convention he must still have believed that the brethren who testified at that Convention that no such things had been done were as he had previously written to Dr. Taylor a set of liars, & he must have wholly rejected our united testimony. But as he & Mr Nettleton were exceedingly anxious to

JHF 219

[103]Pages 425 to 439 were inserted by Finney after having sent the manuscript to Lewis Tappan to read (see Introduction, p. xxxiii). This page is the first of four that were initially inserted to replace the page number 423 (previously numbered 280 and 420).

[104]*Autobiography of Lyman Beecher,* 2:101.

[105]The original from which Finney is quoting has "then and there."

[106]Finney omitted the word "have" in the original. Fairchild inserted it.

[107]Finney was in New York for a few days early in December 1827 on his way to Wilmington, Delaware.

[108]They were published first of all in *The New York Observer* and then as *Letters of Beecher and Nettleton.*

justify their opposition if they still believed those statements in **Mr N's** "historical letter" to be true why did they not publish it & appeal to those who MS 427 were on the ground & witnessed the revivals? Had the letter been |true[109] its publication would have been their justification. If the[y][110] still believed it true why was it not published with Mr **N's** other letters? That the developments made at that convention has shaken the confidence of Dr B. in the wisdom & justice of Mr **N's** opposition **to those revivals** I had infered from the fact that during my labors in Boston a year & a half after the convention[111] & after Mr N's letters were published Dr. B. in speaking of that convention remarked that after that he "would not have had Mr. N. come to Boston for a thousand dollars."[112] Is it possible that until his death Dr. B. continued to believe that the **P**astors of those churches where those revivals occurred were liars & not to be believed in regard to facts which must have been within their personal knowledge. **What will those Churches say to this?**

I find in the **B**iographies of Dr. B. & Mr. N. much complaint of the bad spirit that prevailed in those revivals. Their mistake lies in their attributing a spirit of denunciation to the wrong side. I never heard the name of Dr. B. or Mr. N. mentioned during those revivals in publi**c**k that I recollect & certainly JHF 220 not censoriously. |They were never even in[113] private conversation spoken of to my knowledge with the least bitterness. The friends & promoters of those revivals were in a sweet **c**hristian spirit & as far as possible from being MS 428 denunciatory. If they had been in a |denunciatory spirit those blessed revivals could never have been promoted by them & the revivals could never have turned out as gloriously as they did. No, the denunciation was on the side of the opposition. A quotation from Dr. B's **B**iography will illustrate the animus of the opposition. 2. **vol.** page 101. Dr. B. is represented as saying to me at the convention at New Lebanon, "Finney I know your plan & you know I do; you mean to come to Connecticut & carry a streak of fire to Boston. But if you attempt it, as the Lord liveth I'll meet you at the state line & call out all the artillerymen & fight every inch of the way to Boston & then I'll fight you there."[114] I do not remember this, but, as Dr. B. does let it illustrate the *spirit* of his opposition.[115] The fact is, he was grossly deceived at every step. I had

[109]Page 427 was numbered 247 in error by Finney and changed in pencil to 427, possibly by the typesetter.

[110]Finney omitted the letter *y* from "they." Fairchild inserted it.

[111]Finney is incorrect in the dating here. He was in Boston in August 1831, about four years after the convention. See MS 633.

[112]Nathan Beman was under a similar impression. When Beecher's letters were brought before the General Assembly in 1837, as evidence of the bad influence of the New Measures revivals, Beman replied,

> There was a convention held at New Lebanon, growing out of this correspondence, where the brethren had an opportunity of conferring together freely; and Dr. Beecher has since declared to me, that he had been misinformed with regard to many things; and that he was a great deal nearer to me than he was to Mr. Nettleton, who had put him up to write the letter; and the accusatory matter was all satisfactorily answered (*NYE*, 17 June 1837, p. 99).

[113]The word "in" was written twice by Finney. Fairchild crossed out the second one.

[114]Finney has made some minor changes in the punctuation in copying this extract.

[115]Finney had evidently remembered it a few years later when he was invited to Boston to hold a revival. He wrote to John Starkweather that in his hearing Dr. Beecher "most solemnly

no design nor desire to go to Connecticut nor Boston. The above & many other things I find in his Biogaphy show how completely he was deceived & how utterly ignorant he was of the character & motives & doings of those who had labored in those glorious revivals. I write these things with no pleasure. I find much in this Biography that surprises me, & leads me to the conclusion that by some mistake Dr. B. has been misunderstood & misrepresented. But I pass by other matters.[116] ˡAfter this convention I heard no more of the opposition of Dr. Beecher & Mr Nettleton. **As I shall relate Mr. N. published a pamphlet of his letters designed to justify himself. But they fell dead from the press, I believe, for I scarcely heard them spoken of.** Opposition in that form had spent itself. The results of the revivals **that had been so opposed** were such as to shut the mouths of gainsayers & convince every body that they were indeed pure & glorious revivals of religion, & as far from any thing objectionable as any revivals that ever were witnessed in this world. Let any one read the Acts of the Apostles **in the promotion of** the revivals of their day & ˡthen read what they say in their epistles of the reaction, backsliding & apostacies that followed. Then let the[m][117] find out the truth respecting the glorious revivals of which I have been writing, their commencement, progress, & results, which have been more & more manifest for nearly forty years, & they can not fail to see that these revivals were **much more pure & resulted much more favorably than those. Indeed I have never witnessed a revival anywhere of the results of which such complaints could be justly made as were made by the Apostles of the revivals of their day. This ought to be, & so it is.** Revivals should increase in purity & power as intelligence increases. ˡThe converts in Apostolic times were either Jews with all their prejudice & ignorance or degraded heathen. The art of printing had not been discovered. Copies of the old testament & of the written word of God were not to be had except by the rich who were able to purchase manuscript copies. Christianity had no literature that was accessible to the masses. The means of instruction were not at hand. With so much darkness & ignorance, with so many false notions of religion. With so much to mislead & debase & **such limited means of instruction** & so few facilities for sustaining a religious reformation it was not to be expected that revivals of religion should be so pure & free from errors **to be lamented as they should be expected to be in these latter days, with all our bibles & means of instruction.** We have & preach

MS 429

JHF 221

MS 430

pledged himself to use his influence to oppose me if I came to New England." Beecher also recalled, "About the same time Catharine saw him [Finney], and he said to her, 'Your father vowed solemnly at the New Lebanon Convention he would fight me if I came to Boston, and I shall never go there till he asks me'" (*Autobiography of Lyman Beecher*, 2:108; and Finney to Starkweather, 8 August 1831, Finney Papers, microfilm, roll 3).

[116] At this point, at the bottom of page 428, Finney started a new paragraph that originally led in to page 424 (which therefore had to be renumbered 429 but was finally numbered 441). The paragraph reads: "After this convention I remained in N. Lebanon & preached for a short time. I am not aware that the convention produced any disastrous influence upon the state of religion there. After a short time as I came." Finney later crossed this section out and incorporated the information at the start of a new chapter on a new sheet of paper (MS 440). Page 429 is the first of eleven additional pages that Finney inserted after MS 428.

[117] Finney omitted the letter *m* from the word "them." Fairchild supplied it.

the same gospel that Apostles preached. We have every facility for guarding against error in doctrine & practice & for securing a sound gospel religion. The people amongst whom these great revivals prevailed were an intelligent cultivated people. They had not only secular but religious education abounding in their midst. Nearly every Church had an educated, **& an** able and faithful pastor. These pastors were well able to judge of the **ability,** soundness, & discretion of an evangelist whose labors they wished to enjoy. They were well able to judge of the propriety of the measures **they saw fit to** MS 431 **employ.** |God[118] set his seal to the doctrines that were preached & to the means that were used to carry forward that great work **of God** in a most striking & remarkable manner. The results are now found in all parts of the land. The converts of those revivals are still living & laboring for Christ & JHF 222 |souls in almost or quite **in** every state in this union. It is **no flattery to them** to say that they are amongst the most intelligent & useful Christians in this or any other country.[119] **The measures used to promote these revivals were in no proper sense objectionable. They were simply preaching, prayer & such meetings for instruction, prayer & confession as were plainly demanded by the necessities of the people. There was no wildness, no appearance of fanaticism or of heresy. No bad or denunciatory spirit amongst the converts, indeed I never saw nor heard nor read of revivals of religion more free from every thing deplorable than were these revivals which mysteriously excited or rather were the occasion of so much opposition at the time from some good but mistaken men. So much was said & written about new measures that it seems to have been taken for granted that there was very much to deplore in the means used to promote that blessed work of the Holy Spirit. This is an entire** MS 432 **mistake.** As I have since labored extensively in this country & in |**Europe &** no exceptions have been taken to my measures it has been assumed & asserted that since the opposition made by Mr. Nettleton & Dr. Beecher I have been reformed & have given up the measures they complained of. This **again** is an entire mistake.[120] I have always & everywhere used all the

[118]This page was numbered 431 by Finney. It was then changed to 432, possibly as a result of misreading the previous page as 431. Consequently, the subsequent pages to 437 had to be renumbered. But then this page was renumbered 431 again, so the other pages also had to be changed back again.

[119]Philemon Fowler's considered judgment was similar:

> notwithstanding the fears expressed at the time and the predictions ventured, and the warnings given, the converts of the "Oneida County revivals" have as generally persevered and run as well as professing Christians elsewhere, and during their generation they constituted largely the strength of the communions they joined (*Historical Sketch of Presbyterianism*, p. 270, and see also pp. 276–77).

[120]Before Finney was invited to Boston in 1831 Beecher had written to him:

> We have understood, & we believe that those things which are past, which we regarded with chief solicitude, have ceased to exist, to any extent—as would now justify the withholding of confidence from you, & a cordial fellowship as to the main body of your doctrine & instructions (Beecher to Finney, 2 August 1831, Finney Papers, microfilm, roll 3).

But Finney wrote concerning this letter to John Starkweather:

> that while Dr. Beecher expressed the kindest feeling toward me he was particular to inform me that the change in his sentiments towards me was founded on a supposed revolution or reformation in my views & practices. Now it would be uncandid in me

measures I used in these revivals, & have often added other measures **such as the anxious seat** whenever I have deemed it expedient. I have never seen the necessity of reformation in this respect. Were I to live my life over again, I think that with the experience of more than forty years in revival labors I should under the same circumstance use substantially the same measures that I did then. And let me not be understood to take credit to myself. No indeed. It was no wisdom of my own that directed me. I was made to feel my ignorance & dependence & led to look to God continually for His guidance. I had no doubt then nor have I ever had that God led me by his Spirit to take the course I did. So clearly did he lead me from day to day that I never did nor could doubt that I was Divinely directed. **It is altogether a mistake to suppose that the opposition of Dr. B. & Mr. N. made me ashamed of what I had done as Dr. B's Biography represents & that I reformed ˡ& that consequently their opposition ceased.**[121] **I may safely appeal to all who heard me in those revivals & who witnessed the measures that I used, & who have since heard me & seen my measures in every place, to say whether I have not always & every where employed the measures that I employed in Central New York in those great revivals, & in many places I have added other measures as in my judgment they were demanded.** That the brethren who opposed those revivals were good men I do not doubt. That they were, **by somebody,** misled & grossly & most injuriously deceived I have just as little doubt. If they died under the belief that they had just reason for what they did, & wrote, & said & that they corrected the evils of which they complained they died grossly deceived in this respect. It is not for the safety of the church, the honor of revivals or the glory of Christ that posterity should believe that those evils existed & were corrected by such a spirit & in such a manner as has been represented. I should have remained silent had not so marked an effort been made to perpetuate & confirm the delusion that the opposition ˡto those revivals was justifiable & successful. The fact is **they were** neither.[122]

MS 433

JHF 223

ˡI have no doubt that Dr. B. was led by somebody to believe that his opposition was called for. From his Biography it appears that at Philadelphia the next Spring after the convention it was agreed by himself, Dr. Beman &

MS 434

> [to] encourage this idea & not frankly to acknowlege th[at] in this he is mistaken, that my views in regard to doctrine & revivals of religion are not that I know of materially changed. I hope that like other men I make some advances in knowledge & gain advantage from experience, but to encourage the idea that my views of doctrine or of measures (under similar circumstances) are changed were to do wrong. I have always supposed & do now believe that Dr. Beecher has been but very imperfectly acquainted with my real views & practices, but if [he] has understood them & has been opposed to what I really have been I have no reason to doubt but that he would feel so still should he come in contact with me (Finney to John Starkweather, 8 August 1831, Finney Papers, microfilm, roll 3).

[121] Beecher recalled: "The excesses we had complained of, though real, were effervescent and evanescent. The men were beginning to be ashamed of them themselves. They soon sobered down" (*Autobiography of Lyman Beecher*, 2:104.) And speaking specifically of Finney in 1835, Beecher said: "Mr. Finney has, since that time, gained knowledge by experience. He has reformed some of his measures, which I supposed to be of dangerous tendency, and he is doing, as I hope, much good, with but few attendant evil consequences" ("Trial of Dr. Beecher," reprinted in *NYE,* 26 September 1835, p. 244).

[122] Finney reiterates this point even more forcibly in MS 454.

others to drop the subject & publish no more in regard to those revivals.[123] The truth is that all the controversy & all the publishing had been on the side of the opposition. Previously to the meeting at Philadelphia Mr. Nettleton had published his letters & I saw nothing further in print upon the subject. I was not a party to the agreement entered into at Philadelphia[124] **nevertheless** had not Dr. B's Biography reopened this subject with the manifest design to justify the course that he took & rivit the impression upon the publick mind that in making that opposition to those revivals he performed a great & good work I should not feel called upon to say what I can not now be justified in withholding. I write from personal knowledge & to me it matters not who may have given to Dr. B. the supposed facts upon which he acted. **They doubtless were in substance the same as those mentioned in Mr. N's "historical letter" read by him to the convention.** Those asserted facts were no facts as I stated before the convention to which statement every brother with whom I had labored assented. This was proof if any thing can be MS 435 proven by ¹human[125] testimony. This testimony it would seem Dr. B. did not believe, if his biographer has not misrepresented him. And what will the churches in Oneida county say to this. Will they, can they believe that such men as Rev. Dr. Aikin, Rev. John Frost, Rev. Moses Gillett, Rev. Mr Coe & the other men from that county who attended that convention deliberately falsified upon a subject which was within their own personal knowledge? **They can never believe it.** It matters not who Dr. B's informants were. Certainly none of the Pastors where those revivals prevailed ever gave him any information that justified his course & no other men understood the JHF 224 matter as ¹well as they did. I submit that as the convention decided they were the best possible witnesses of what was said & done in their own congregations & their testimony was unanymous that no such things were done as were charged **in Mr. N.s "historical letter." We never could learn from whom Dr. B. & Mr N. received their information. This was suspicious. If the things were true which were affirmed by their correspondents why conceal their names? Had they a right to receive their testimony & act upon it in such a publick manner & yet refuse to** MS 436 **give their names?** ¹I[126] had read the strong & even terrible charges against the brethren who labored in those revivals, contained in Dr. B's letter to Dr. Taylor, in which he states that his correspondence will justify what he was doing & writing against those brethren.[127] When I learned that this matter

[123]This agreement was in the form of a resolution dated Philadelphia, 27 May 1828, and signed by Lyman Beecher, Dirck C. Lansing, S. C. Aikin, A. D. Eddy, C. G. Finney, Sylvester Holmes, Ebenezer Cheever, John Frost, Nathan S. S. Beman, Noah Coe, E. W. Gilbert, and Joel Parker. It was published in the *Philadelphian* and reprinted in many other papers. See, e.g., the *Religious Intelligencer,* 14 June 1828, p. 41; and p. 249 n. 29 (MS 470).

[124]It may be true that Finney played little part in the discussions that led to the resolution. Beecher does not mention him in a list of people with whom he conferred; nevertheless, his name is listed as being among the signatories. See *Autobiography of Lyman Beecher*, 2:104.

[125]Page 435 starts with an additional "by," which was inserted by Finney.

[126]Page 436 was changed to 438 (possibly in error) instead of 437 and renumbered 436 again by Finney.

[127]See p. 192 n. 99. Beecher wrote in this letter:

> And I am also certain, (for I have tried it for more than one whole year, thoroughly, as my correspondence will show, if ever called for,) that no kindness and magnanimity on

was to be spread before the publick in the Drs Biography I hoped that, at last, we should get at the authors of those reports through the publication of his correspondence. But I see nothing in his correspondence to justify his course. Are these charges still to be virtually repeated & stereotyped & the correspondence by which they are said to be justified, concealed? If as it seems Dr. B. until the day of his death continued to reject our united testimony may we not know by whose counter testimony ours is impeached?[128]

On page 103, of the 2. Vol. of Dr. B's Autobiography we have the following. "In the spring of 1828, said Dr. Beecher, in conversation on the subject, I found out that Mr. Finneys friends were laying their plans to make an impression on the general assembly, that held its session at Philadelphia, & to get one of their men into[129] Mr. Skinners place.[130] Skinners church had just asked me to preach for them & I wrote back that I would supply, if they wished, while the Assembly was in Session. That blocked somebody's wheels. I staid till the close when Beman preached half a day. That defeated their plans. They failed." What this means I can not say. In reading the above, & what follows to the end of the chapter, |together[131] with what I find elsewhere on this subject in this biography, I stand amazed in view of the suspicions & delusions under which Dr. B's mind was laboring. If any of my friends were trying to get into Dr. Skinner's pulpit which he had vacated, I have no recollection of ever having |heard of it.[132] I was, at that time, a minister in the presbyterian church, & was preaching in Philadelphia when the Assembly was in Session, & Dr. Beecher was there. **I wonder how much Dr. B's influence with the members of that assembly had to do with the mysterious opposition to revivals which soon after appeared in that body & which I felt called to notice in my lectures on revivals.[133] I kept**

MS 437

JHF 225

our part will be appreciated,—but as it ceases to oppose the new measures and falls in. And nothing will reclaim, but, OPEN and DECIDED RESISTANCE (*To the Congregational Ministers and Churches of Connecticut. Copy of a letter from the Rev. Dr. Beecher, to the Editor of the Christian Spectator. Boston, December 18th, 1827* [Boston, 1827], p. 3).

[128]This originally ended the additional section inserted by Finney starting from MS 429. It formed the end of the chapter. The first page of the new chapter (MS 440), then numbered 429, was renumbered 437; and when this page was changed to 438, the first page of the new chapter was changed to 439. However, Finney subsequently added a further section at the bottom of this page and on three new pages.

[129]The original quotation has the word "in," not "into."

[130]Thomas Harvey Skinner was minister of the Fifth Presbyterian Church in Philadelphia. In March 1828, just before the General Assembly in May, he was called to Boston. See *DAB* and MS 469.

[131]Pages 437 to 440 were inserted by Finney.

[132]There appears to have been some truth in what Beecher says. Samuel Brace, who was staying with Skinner in June 1827, wrote to Nettleton about the trouble being stirred up by Finneyites in Skinner's church. He reckoned that "there is now going forward a plan from *abroad* to foist somebody in here who is only waiting for an opportunity to come" (Brace to Nettleton, 12 June 1827, Nettleton Papers, Hartford Seminary). It is possible that Nathan Beman himself is the man referred to. A notice of changes that had occurrred in the churches in Philadelphia appeared under the title "Changes in Philadelphia" in the *Religious Intelligencer* in 1837: "The Fifth Presbyterian Church . . . has experienced various vicissitudes. The attempt to press a call for Dr. Beman as successor to Dr. Skinner, was the beginning of evils which have been perpetrated for several years" (4 February 1837, p. 576).

[133]Finney took the General Assembly to task in his lecture "On Hindrances to Revivals" given

about my revival work in Philadelphia & elsewhere without being diverted or agitated by what Dr. B. & Mr N. were saying or doing, & with no thought whatever of having any controversy with them. I was as ignorant as a child of all this management revealed in **Dr. B**'s biography. **It seems that the Dr. & Mr N. were suffering under a vast amount of excitement, suspicion & misapprehension in regard to my motives, plans, & labors, & the plans, & motives of those whom they regarded as my committed friends, whilst I was attending to my revival work without any plan or motive whatever but to go when & where the Lord called me to work. This work I pursued without interruption except the few days I was at the convention.** I shared none of the terrors & distractions that seem to have so much distessed Dr. B. & Mr. N. If any of my friends were sharing in the state of mind in which **Dr. B. & Mr N.** were I knew it not. MS 438 |The truthful record of my labors up to the time of the Convention & from that time onward will show how little I knew of or cared **about** what Dr. B. & Mr N. were saying or doing about me. I bless the Lord that I was kept from being diverted from my work by their opposition & that I never gave myself any uneasiness about it. When at Auburn as I have related, God had given me the assurance that **He** would overrule all opposition without my turning asid**[e]**[134] to answer my opposers. This I never forgot. Under this **D**ivine assurance I went forward with a single eye & a trustful spirit & now when I read what agitations suspicions, & misapprehensions possessed the minds of **Dr. B. & Mr N.** I stand amazed at their delusions & consequent anxieties respecting myself & my labors. **God kept me full of love & faith & filled my heart & hands with most successful labors.** At the very time that Dr. B. was in Philadelphia managing with members of the general assembly as related in his biography I was laboring in that city & had been for several months, in different churches in the midst of a powerful revival of religion as ignorant of Dr. B's errand there **as a babe. He was there it seems to influence the general assembly against me & to keep some friend of mine from occupying the pulpit vacated by Dr.** MS 439 **Skinner. I wonder who that friend was, & |how**[135] **much credit he deserved, for this service.**[136] I can not be too thankful that God kept me from being agitated & changed in my spirit, or views of labor by all **that was passing in the ranks of** the opposition **in** those days. **As I have said I**

in New York in March of 1835. He remarked, "No doubt there is a jubilee in hell every year, about the time of the meeting of the General Assembly." See *NYE,* 14 March 1835, p. 42.

When Finney was revising his *Lectures on Revivals of Religion* in 1868, about the same time that he was revising his narrative, he added a note: "The strange opposition of such men as Dr. Lyman Beecher and Mr. Nettleton had much to do with provoking and sustaining this opposition" (Finney, *Lectures on Revivals of Religion* [Oberlin: Goodrich, 1868], p. 275). There is also in the Finney Papers an "Appendix," which was probably written for this new edition, consisting of four foolscap sheets in Rebecca Finney's handwriting, giving an explanation of the nature of the opposition of the General Assembly and Finney's reasons for drawing attention to it at that time. This appendix, however, was not published (Finney Papers, microfilm, roll 9).

[134] Finney omitted the *e*.

[135] Page 439 starts with an additional *&* put in by Finney.

[136] After the word "deserved," Finney originally wrote, "& how much reward he will have in heaven for this service. But I must resume my narrative from the close of the Convention at New Lebanon." He crossed out these words and substituted "for this service."

neither heard nor felt much of the opposition after the convention. I knew from Mr. Nettleton himself that he felt keenly the reaction of publick sentiment against him. I knew that he & Dr. B. had been misinformed & misled & had got into a bad scrape but not until I had seen their biographies was I aware how much trouble & perplexity it cost them to get out of it.›[137]

[137]This ends the section from the bottom of MS 436 that was inserted by Finney at the end of the chapter. It required the next page to be renumbered 440.

MS 440
JHF 226

CHAPTER XVII

‹*Revival in Stephentown.*›

‹After[1] this Convention I remained a short time in New Lebanon. I do not think the convention injured the religious state of the people in that place. It would have done so had any facts come out to justify the opposition which they knew had been made to the revivals that had been the subject of discussion, but as it turned the church in New Lebanon were, I believe, edified & strengthened by what they knew of the Convention. Indeed every thing had been conducted in a spirit tending to edify rather than stumble the people. Soon after the adjournment of the Convention on Sabbath day as I came› ˡout[2] of the pulpit, a young lady by the name of Sackett, from Stephentown, was introduced to me.[3] She asked me if I could not go up to their town and preach. I replied that my hands were full, and that I did not see that I could. I saw her utterance was choked with deep feeling; but as I had not time to converse with her then I went to my lodging. Soon after I made inquiry about Stephentown, which was north of and adjoining New Lebanon. Many years before a wealthy individual had died and given to the presbyterian church in that place a fund, the interest of which was sufficient to support a pastor.

MS 441

Soon after this a Mr. Bogue, who had been a chaplain in the revolutionary army, was settled there as pastor of the church.[4] He remained until the church ran down under his influence, and he finally became an open infidel.[5]

[1]Page 440 was originally numbered 429 by Finney. It replaced what he had written at the end of MS 428 when he started the new chapter. It required the next page to be renumbered 430. As further pages were added, this page had to be renumbered 437, 439, and 440.

[2]Written in Finney's handwriting and encircled in pencil on the upper left corner of MS 441 are the words "2nd page of this chap." It was originally numbered 289 and renumbered 421 by Matson and then changed to 424 and renumbered 429, 430, and 441 by Finney. He appears to have started to alter the number 430 to 441 but then crossed it out and inserted 441.

[3]This was Sunday, 22 July 1827. Cf. MS 442–43 and n. 8 below. Maria Sackett was the daughter of Benjamin Sackett of Stephentown. See Juliet Pardee to Lydia Finney, 17 January 1828, Finney Papers, microfilm, roll 1.

[4]Aaron Jordan Bogue (1752–1826) was a graduate of Yale College and is said to have served as a chaplain in the Revolution. He was a minister in Connecticut and Massachusetts before moving to Stephentown in 1800. In 1809 he left the Stephentown church and supplied other churches in New York; and after being a chaplain in the War of 1812, he returned to New Lebanon where he continued to live. See Virgil T. Bogue, *Bogue and Allied Families* (Holly, Mich.: Herald Printers, 1944), pp. 37–39; and F. B. Dexter, ed., *Biographical Sketches of the Graduates of Yale College*, 3d ser. (New York: Holt, 1903), pp. 518–19.

[5]Bogue's pastorates all seem to have been disastrous because of the "neglect with which he treated his official duties." Time spent in "secular pursuits," "meddling in politics," and "relapse

This had produced a most disastrous influence in that town. ¦He remained among them openly hostile to the Christian religion. After he had ceased to be pastor of the church, they had had one or two ministers settled. Nevertheless the church **ran down**, and the state of religion grew worse and worse; until finally they had **quit** their meeting house, as so few attended meeting, and held their ¦services[6] on the Sabbath in a small school house which stood near the church. The last minister they had had affirmed that he stayed until not more than half a dozen people in the town would attend **his preaching** on the Sabbath; and although there was a fund for his support, and his salary was regularly paid, yet he could not think it his duty to spend his time in laboring in such a field. He had therefore been dismissed. No other denomination had taken possession of the field so as to excite any public interest, and the whole town was a complete moral waste. Three elders of the **p**resbyterian church remained, and about twenty members. The only unmarried person in the church was this Miss **Sackett** of whom I have spoken. Nearly the whole town was in a state of impenitence.[7] It was a large, rich farming town, with no **large** village in it. JHF 227 MS 442

On the next Sabbath Miss **Sackett** met me again as I came out of the pulpit, and begged me to go up there and preach; and asked me if I knew anything of the state of things there. I informed her that I did; but I told her I did not know how I could go. She appeared greatly affected; too much so to converse, ¦for she could not control her feelings. **This state of things**, with what I had heard, began to take hold of me; and my mind began to be stirred **to its deepest foundations** in respect to the state of things in Stephentown. I finally told her that if the elders of the church desired me to come, she might have a notice given out that I would come up, the Lord willing, and preach in their church the next Sabbath at five **O**'clock in the afternoon. This would allow me to preach twice in New Lebanon, after which I could ride up to Stephentown ¦and preach at five **O**'clock. **Saying** this seemed to light up her countenance and lift the load from her heart. She went home and had the notice given. Accordingly the next Sabbath, after preaching the second time one of the young converts at New Lebanon offered to take me up in his carriage **to Stephentown**.[8] When he came in his buggy to take me **up** I asked MS 443 JHF 228

into intemperate habits" are given as causes of his troubles. See Dexter, *Graduates of Yale*, p. 519.

[6]Pages 442–452 were originally numbered 290–300, renumbered 422–432 by Matson, and then changed to 442–452 by Finney.

[7]N. S. S. Beman, in a widely published report, reviewing the history of the revival in the church, stated:

> I preached in Stephentown twice in the month of June last [1826], and *then* all was desolation. The Church was reduced to a mere handful—probably there were not more than *twenty* resident members—and the congregation was scattered and almost extinct. A deserted sanctuary proclaimed the fearful condition and prospects of that people. Divisions of long standing and of a painful character had wasted the heritage of God. In August last their Pastor was dismissed, having been installed within the period of a year, and his predecessor having been dismissed within *two* years (*The New York Observer*, 15 December 1827, p. 198).

[8]This was 5 August. Charles Churchill's "Book of Memoranda" (Silas Churchill Papers, Presbyterian Historical Society) indicates that he attended Finney's preaching in the morning and afternoon and "in Steventown at 5 o'clock," so he may have been the young convert who took Finney there in his carriage.

him, "Have you a steady horse?" "O yes!" he replied, "perfectly so;" and smiling asked, "What made you ask the question?" "Because," I replied, "if MS 444 the Lord wants me to go to Stephentown, the devil will prevent |it if he can; and if you have not a steady horse he will try to make him kill me." He smiled, and we rode on; and strange to tell before we got there that horse ran away twice, and came near killing us. His owner expressed the greatest astonishment, and said he had never known such a thing before. However in due time we arrived in safety at Mr. **Sackett**'s, the father of Miss **Sackett** whom I have mentioned; **who** lived about half a mile from the church in the direction ‹of›[9] New Lebanon, **so that we had to pass the house**. As we went in we met Maria—for that was her name—who tearfully **and** yet joyfully received us, showed me to a room where I could be alone, **and** as it was not quite time for meeting, ‹**I**› soon after heard her,[10] **as I sat alone,** praying in a room over my head. When it was time for meeting we all went, and found **the congregation** very large. **I preached.** The congregation was **very** solemn and attentive, but nothing very particular occurred that evening. I **went and** spent the night at Mr. **Sackett**'s; and this Maria seemed to be praying over MS 445 **the** room **in which I was** nearly all night. |I could hear her low, trembling voice, interrupted often by sobs and manifest weeping. I had made no appointment to come again; but before I left in the morning she plead so hard that I consented to have an appointment made for me for five **O**'clock the next Sabbath. When I came up on the next Sabbath nearly the same things occurred **that had** before; but the congregation was more crowded**,** and as JHF 229 the house was old, for fear the galleries |would break down they had been strongly propped during the week. I could see a manifest increase of solemnity and interest the second time **that** I preached there. I then left an appointment to preach again. At the third service the Spirit of God was poured out on the congregation.

There was a Judge **Platt** that lived in a small village in one part of the town, who had a large family of unconverted children.[11] At the close of the service as I came out of the pulpit, Miss **Sackett** stepped up to me **at the pulpit stairs** and pointed me to a pew—the house had then the old square pews—in MS 446 which sat a young **lady** greatly overcome with her |feelings. I went in to speak to her, and found her to be one of the daughters of this Judge **Platt**.[12] Her convictions were very deep. I sat down by her and gave her instructions**,** and I think before she left the house she was converted. She was a very intelligent, earnest young **lady**, and became a very useful Christian.[13] She was afterwards the wife of the evangelist Underwood, who has been so well known in many

[9]Here Matson had written "from," but Finney changed it to "of."

[10]Matson had written ". . . time for meeting; and soon after I heard her," but Finney altered it.

[11]This was Henry Platt, Sr., who died in 1842 at the age of seventy-eight. He served as an elder in the Presbyterian church for twenty-eight years and had twelve children, one of whom had died in infancy. See his obituary in *NYE,* 27 October 1842, p. 171.

[12]This was Henrietta Platt.

[13]Her father wrote a few months later: "Henrietta goes on her religious Course something beyond those of her age & Sex full of life and animation in the Cause." And John P. Cushman wrote in June of "Henrietta as much engaged apparently as ever." See Henry Platt to Finney, 7 April 1828, and J. P. Cushman to Finney, 12 June 1828, Finney Papers, microfilm, roll 2.

of the churches, in New Jersey especially, and in New England.[14] She and **Maria Sackett** seemed immediately to unite their prayers. But I could not see, as yet, much movement among the older members of the church. They stood in such relations to each other that a good deal of repentance and confession had to pass among them as a condition of their getting into the work.

The state of things in Stephentown now demanded that I should leave New Lebanon, and take up my quarters **in Stephentown**. I did so. The Spirit of prayer in the meantime had come powerfully upon me, as **he** had been for sometime **on Miss Sackett**. The praying power so manifestly spreading and in|creasing, the work soon took on a very powerful type; so much so that the word of the Lord would cut the strongest men down and render them entirely helpless **when set home by the Holy Ghost.**[15] I could name many cases of this kind. One of the first that I recollect was on Sabbath when I was preaching on the text, "God is love."[16] There was a |man by the name of **Jowles**, a man of strong nerves and of considerable prominence as a farmer in the town.[17] He sat **down** almost immediately before me, **as his pew was** near the pulpit. The first that I observed was that he fell, and **seemed as if he was in a fit. He** writhed in agony for a few moments, **and groaned with deep feeling**; but afterwards became still, and nearly motionless, but entirely helpless. He remained in this state until the meeting was out, **and they took him** home. He was very soon converted, and became **a powerful instrument** in **influencing** his friends **to come** to Christ.[18] **It was common afterwards for cases similar to this one to occur in those revivals.**

MS 447

JHF 230

In the course of this revival Zebulon R. Shipherd, a celebrated |lawyer from Washington County, N.Y., being in attendance upon the court at Albany, and hearing of the revival at Stephentown, so disposed of his business

MS 448

[14] Almon Underwood (1809–1887) was a graduate of Union College who studied theology with N. S. S. Beman in Troy. He was the Presbyterian minister of Poughkeepsie, New York, from 1837 to 1844 and pastor of the First Presbyterian Church in Newark, New Jersey, until 1850. He then became a Congregational evangelist, living on in Newark until 1859, when he moved to Irvington, New Jersey. He was a strong advocate of the Oberlin doctrine of sanctification. He married Henrietta in 1834. She was his first wife and died in 1843, leaving a daughter and a son, Rev. Henry Beman Underwood. See *The Congregational Year Book* (Boston), 1888, p. 42; *NYE*, 6 June 1844, p. 92; William Chapin to Finney, 5 June 1850, and 6 February 1851, Finney Papers, microfilm, roll 4; and *The Congregational Quarterly* (Boston) 18 (July 1875): 436.

[15] *The Western Recorder* reported:

> A correspondent at the east writes to a clergyman in Utica, that the revival in Stephentown has become more powerful than it ever had been in New-Lebanon; and that the work had recently extended to Hancock Village, Mass. In New-Lebanon, also, there is still much sensibility on the subject of religion, and much earnest prayer for the continued outpouring of the Spirit upon the churches (9 October 1827, p. 162).

[16] 1 John 4:8.

[17] It is possible that this was Stephen Van Renselaer Jolls (1776–1882), a farmer, who was said to have been converted under Finney in Stephentown in 1827. Jolls had moved there from Rhode Island with his father when he was four years old. After his conversion he joined the Presbyterian church and was an elder for many years. See *NYE*, 13 April 1882, p. 5.

[18] J. P. Cushman wrote to Finney some months later: "Mr. Jowles has been ill, but his soul glows with intense love to God & the souls of men" (Cushman to Finney, 12 June 1828, Finney Papers, microfilm, roll 2).

as to come out and labor with me in the revival.[19] He was an earnest Christian man, attended all the meetings, and enjoyed them greatly. He was there when the November elections occurred through the State. I looked forward to the election day with considerable solicitude, fearing that the excitement of that day would greatly retard the work **that was going on**. I exhorted Christians to watch and **to** pray greatly, that the work might not be arrested by any excitement that should **be got up** on that day.[20] On the evening of election day I preached. When I came out of the pulpit after preaching, **this** Mr. Shipherd **of whom I have spoken,**—who, by the **by,** was the father of J. J. Shipherd who established Oberlin[21]—beckoned to me from a pew where he sat to come to him. It was a pew in the corner of the house, at the left hand of the pulpit. I went to him and found one of the gentlemen who had sat at the MS 449 table to receive votes during the day, so overcome with conviction of sin |as to be unable to leave his seat. I went in and had some conversation with him,

[19]Zebulun Rudd Shipherd (1768–1841) was from North Granville, New York, where he lived until about 1830, when he moved to Moriah, New York. He was "a lawyer, a judge, a prominent Free Mason, and a member of Congress for one term, and clearly was one of the ablest and most prosperous men of his locality." He was elected as a Federalist to the Thirteenth Congress (1813–1815) and was a trustee of Middlebury College in Vermont from 1819–1841 (see Lyman B. Hall, "Notes on the Founders of Oberlin College," *The Oberlin Alumni Magazine* 4, no. 5 [February 1908]: 170–75; and *Biographical Dictionary of the American Congress, 1774–1927* [Washington, D.C.: U.S. Government Printing Office, 1928], p. 1521). Finney evidently knew him before this time. See Shipherd to Finney, 8 May 1827, Finney Papers, microfilm, roll 1. An apparently earlier letter from Shipherd written to Finney in Stephentown, 20 February 1827, is misdated and should probably have been dated 1828.

[20]This was the election for the state legislature in mid-November, "which in almost every county has turned upon the presidential question." The campaign of Andrew Jackson for the presidency the next year was arousing the country to a high pitch of political excitement. See *WR,* 13 November 1827, p. 183; and 20 November 1827, p. 187.

[21]John Jay Shipherd (1802–1844) was the third son of Z. R. Shipherd. He attended Pawlet Academy in Vermont and planned to go to Middlebury College and become a minister, but his studies were interrupted when an accidental dose of poison seriously affected his health. However, he was able to continue studying under Rev. Josiah Hopkins of New Haven, Vermont, and was eventually ordained as a Congregational minister in 1827. In 1828 he became the general agent for the Vermont Sabbath School Union and then in 1830 moved west.

While Shipherd was pastor of the Presbyterian church in Elyria, Ohio, he became associated with an old classmate, Philo P. Stewart, in a scheme for founding a colony and school to be a center of evangelization of the West. The enterprise was named Oberlin in honor of Jean Frederic Oberlin, the Strasbourg pastor who pioneered communities in the Vosges region of France, and whose life story had recently been published. The pioneer colony was formed in 1833 on a tract of virgin forest nine miles from Elyria. In 1835 the Oberlin Collegiate Institute was put on a firm foundation by the addition of Asa Mahan as president and Finney as professor of theology. Shipherd then moved on to attempt further educational experiments and founded Olivet College in Michigan in 1844. The Oberlin Collegiate Institute was officially renamed Oberlin College in 1850. See Robert Samuel Fletcher, *A History of Oberlin College from Its Foundation Through the Civil War* (Oberlin: Oberlin College, 1943), and *DAB*.

On 3 December 1827 Shipherd wrote to his brother Fayette,

> I have lately recd an earnest invitation from Stephentown by way of father & Mr. Finney to visit that place immediately & preach as candidate for settlement. All the *first* men *now* hopefully pious. A glorious work going on & widespread desolation around them.

Shipherd turned down the request (Shipherd to Fayette Shipherd, 3 December 1827, in Bragdon Family Papers, University of Rochester Library, Rochester, New York).

It is interesting to note that Finney had also been reading *The Life of John Frederic Oberlin* and had named his second son Frederic Norton in honor of him. See William C. Cochran, *Charles Grandison Finney: Memorial Address* (Philadelphia: Lippincott, 1908), p. 76; and p. 290 n. 41.

and prayed with him, and he was manifestly converted. A considerable portion of the congregation had in the meantime set[22] down **while this was passing**. As I came out of the pew and was about to retire, my attention was called to another pew **on** the right hand side of the pulpit, where was |another of those men that had been prominent at the election, and had been receiving votes, precisely in the same condition of mind. He was too much overpowered by the state of his feelings to leave the house. I went and conversed with him also; and if I recollect he was converted before he left the house. I mention these cases as specimens of the type of the work in that place.[23] JHF 231

I have mentioned the family of **Mr. Platt** as being large. I recollect there were sixteen members of that family, children and grandchildren, hopefully converted; all of whom, I think, united with the church before I left.[24] There was another family in the town by the name of **Moffitt**; |which was also a large and very influential family, one of the most so of any in town.[25] Most of them lived scattered along on a street which, if I recollect right, was about five miles **long, a farming country pretty thickly settled**. On inquiry I found there was not a religious family on that whole street, and not a single house in which family prayer was maintained. I made an appointment to preach in a school house on that street, and when I arrived **found** the house very much crowded. I took for my text, "The curse of the Lord is in the house of the wicked."[26] The Lord gave me a very clear view of the subject and I was enabled to **point out in a clear way the manner in which the curse of the Lord is in the house of the wicked**. I told them that I understood that there was not a praying family in that whole district. The fact is, the town was in an awful state. The influence of Mr. **Bogue**, their former minister **and** now an infidel, had borne its legitimate fruit; and there |was but very little conviction of the truth and reality of religion left among the impenitent in that town. This meeting that I have spoken of resulted in the conviction of nearly all that were present, I believe, at the meeting. The revival spread in that neighborhood; and I recollect that in this **Moffit** family there were seventeen ‹hopeful›[27] conversions.[28] MS 450 MS 451

[22]The word "set" was changed by Fairchild to "sat."

[23]A correspondent of the *Albany Christian Register* wrote about the work: "Such has been the overwhelming power of truth upon the conscience, that cases have repeatedly occurred in the sanctuary, where sinners have been pressed down by the spirit, and remained so until joy succeeded sorrow" (reprinted in *WR*, 4 December 1827, p. 194).

[24]Henry Platt himself had become a Christian about 1806, and his wife, Martha, had been converted under Dr. John Chester of Albany. Their eight surviving children were all said to be Christians in 1842. See *NYE*, 27 October 1842, p. 171; and 3 March 1864, p. 5. Henrietta Platt wrote to Mrs. Finney, "My brothers Henry and Edwins families are in good health & appear to be steadfast in the faith—Edwin manifests considerable zeal in the service of his blessed Master" (Henrietta Platt to Lydia Finney, 25 April 1828, Finney Papers, microfilm, roll 2).

[25]According to the calendar of the Finney Papers, a letter from John Wadsworth dated 15 November 1827 (now missing) was addressed to Finney at "Moffit's Store P.O. (Stephentown) N.Y." But *An Atlas of the State of New York containing a map of the State of the Several Counties* (New York: Burr, 1829) gives "Moffit's Store" as the "P.O." (Post Office) at New Lebanon.

[26]Proverbs 3:33.

[27]Finney added the word "hopeful." There is a question mark in pencil over the word "seventeen." This may have been inserted by Lewis Tappan, leading Finney to add the word "hopeful" before "conversions." The question mark was crossed out by Fairchild.

[28]Some months later Finney was told, "The Moffits are doing well—some fears as respects

But there were several families in the town who were quite prominent in JHF 232 influence, who did not attend the meet|ings. It seemed that they were so much under the influence of Mr. **Bogue**, that they were determined not to attend. However in the midst of this revival, this Mr. **Bogue** died a horrible death; and this put an end to his opposition.[29] I have said there were several families in town that did not attend meeting; and I could devise no means by which they could be induced to attend. Miss **Seward, of whom I have spoken as living in** New Lebanon, **and as being** converted at Troy, heard MS 452 that these families did not attend, and came up to Stephentown; |and[30] as her father was a man very well known and very much respected, she was received with respect and deference in any family that she wished to visit. She went and called on one of these families. I believe she was acquainted with their daughters. **At any rate on the Sabbath she** induced them to accompany her to meeting. They soon became so interested that they needed no influence to persuade them to attend. **They continued to do so.** She then went to another, with the same result, and to another; and finally, I believe secured the attendance of all those families that had stayed away. These families were nearly or quite all—**I do not recollect which**—converted before I left the town. Indeed nearly all the principal inhabitants of the town were gathered into the church **before I left**, and the town was morally renovated.[31] I have

Eber but I have heard nothing serious" (Henry Platt to Finney, 7 April 1828, Finney Papers, microfilm, roll 2).

[29]The date of Aaron Bogue's death was 30 June 1826. It is noted in *WR,* 25 July 1826, p. 119. This was while Finney was in New Lebanon and before he went to Stephentown.

[30]After the page number 452 Fairchild added "–3" to indicate to the printers to omit the next page and proceed to 454.

[31]A correspondent of the *Albany Christian Register* wrote:

> The more aged inhabitants and heads of families in unusual numbers are among the trophies of divine and sovereign mercy. . . . In some cases whole families are the hopeful subjects of renewing grace. The subjects of the work are of almost all ages, from the hoary head of seventy-eight, to the youth of twelve years old (reprinted in *WR,* 4 December 1827, p. 194).

Another report stated:

> The revival in this place has been and still is overwhelming. The church consisted, I believe of about 20 members. *Seventy-eight* have been added; among whom are almost all the first men in the community. . . . I have never seen any place take a more thorough breaking up. Almost every adult person belonging to the congregation is hoping, and many who did not formerly belong to it. The work is still spreading (reprinted from the *Boston Recorder and Telegraph* in *WR,* 11 December 1827, p. 198).

According to Finney, there were 150 conversions. See Anson G. Phelps, "Diary," 16 December 1827, microfilm in New York Public Library.

After he left Stephentown early in December 1827, Finney wrote to Alexander B. Johnson, who was the secretary of the Oneida Evangelical Association, the society for whom Finney was working:

> "Your society may have the satisfaction of having been instrumental in rescuing the church and society at Stephentown (P.A.) from the brink of ruin, and throwing around them prospects for time and eternity a radiance which had never before cheered and encouraged their hearts; and they are about settling a young man of whom they speak in the highest terms" (copied by A. B. Johnson into his manuscript "Autobiography," 1864, vol. 5, p. 251, in Hamilton College Library, Clinton, New York).

The week that Finney left Stephentown, Edwards A. Beach arrived to take over the work and was soon settled as minister. See John P. Cushman to Finney, 21 and 22 December 1827, Finney Papers, microfilm, roll 1; and Rhoda Churchill to Charles and Lydia Finney, 18 June 1828, Finney Papers, microfilm, roll 2.

never been there since **I left at** that time, which was in the fall of 182‹7›.[32] But I have often heard from there, and the revival produced permanent results. The converts turned out to be sound; and the church has maintained a good degree of spiritual vigor, **I believe, ever since.**

MS 453 |‹**The[33] doctrines preached & measures used in this revival were the same that I had used wherever I had labored. The meetings were uniformly characterized by perfect order, & great solemnity. The[r]e were no indications of wildness, extravigance, heresy, fanaticism or of any thing deplorable. The convention at New Lebanon had not resulted favorably to the opposition of Dr. B. & Mr. N.[34] Consequently we heard nothing of opposition sustained by their authority, either at Stephentown or elsewhere after this.** MS 454 |As elsewhere the striking characteristics of this revival were 1. **The prevalence of** a mighty Spirit of prevailing prayer. 2. Overwhelming conviction of sin. 3. Sudden & powerful conversions to Christ. 4. Great love & abounding joy of the converts. **5. Intelligence & stability of the converts.** 6. Their great earnestness, activity, & usefulness in their prayers & labors for others. This revival occurred in the town adjoining New Lebanon & immediately after the Convention. The opposition had at that convention rec^d[35] JHF 233 |its death blow. I have seldom labored in a revival with greater comfort to myself & with less opposition than in Stephentown. At first the people chafed a little under the preaching but with such power was it set home by the Holy Spirit that I soon heard no more complaint. **Dr. Beechers Memoir represents that we had become ashamed of our measures & reformed & gives himself & Mr Nettleton credit for this. So they laid this flattering unction to their souls. But this is an entire mistake & I can truly say that their opposition never made me ashamed, never convinced me that I was wrong in doctrine or practice, & I never made the slightest change in conducting revivals as a consequence of**

[32] Matson had originally written "1828," but the *8* was changed to a 7. The writing appears to be Finney's.

[33] Finney inserted two new pages, numbered 453 and 454, between page 452 and the next page, which had been numbered 433, requiring that page to be renumbered 455. MS 453 begins with a section that appears to have been crossed out by Finney. It reads:

> Conviction of sin was very profound in this as in the other revivals I have mentioned. I recollect that one evening whilst I was preaching, & the house was much crowded, just as I was rebuking profanity the most profane man in town came in. He only got within the door as the rebuke fell upon his ear & was carried home by the Holy Spirit with such power that he resolved upon the instant to stop swearing or to cut out his tongue. The conviction was effectual; he soon expressed a hope in Christ.
>
> Judge Platt was a merchant. My wife & self were his guest for the time. I one day dropped into his store & found a prominent citizen there inculcating the doctrines of Universalism. I invited him to my room & soon succeeded in driving him from his refuge of lies. He had taught his family those errors & they were of course unconverted. He attended meeting that evening, & went home so broken down in heart that finding his family in bed he went to the rooms of different members & confessed his sins & errors & soon he, & I believe the adult members of his family were hopefully converted to Christ.

Fairchild omitted the whole of page 453.

[34] That is, Dr. Beecher and Mr. Nettleton.

[35] That is, "received."

their opposition. I thought I was right. I think so still. I thought their opposition was impertinent & assuming, uncalled for & injurious to themselves, & the cause of God. I think so still, but I should not have said it in this narrative had not their biographies compelled me to speak my mind.›

CHAPTER XVIII

MS 455
JHF 234

‹*Revival at Wilmington,* **Delaware**›

While[1] laboring at New Lebanon the preceding summer, **the** Rev. Mr. Gilbert of Wilmington, Delaware, whose father resided in New Lebanon, came there on a visit.[2] **A very affecting incident had occurred in the revival at New Lebanon touching a brother of this Mr. Gilbert. This brother was very much disturbed—so much so that, being impenitent he finally left the place declaring, as I understood, that he would not return until the revival was over. He had been gone but a short time before they heard of his death; which, if I recollect right, had occurred in a tragic manner.** Mr. Gilbert was very **Old**-School in his theological views, but a good and earnest man. His love of souls over-ruled all **sticklishness**[3] on nice questions of theological difference **of opinion** between him and myself. He heard me preach in New Lebanon, and saw the results; and he was very earnest that I should come **that fall**[4] and aid him in Wilmington, **Delaware**.[5] As soon as I could see my way clear to leave Stephentown, therefore, I went to Wilmington and engaged in labors with **Brother** Gilbert.[6]

[1]Pages 455–501 were originally numbered 301-47, were renumbered 433-79 by Matson, and then were changed to 455–501 by Finney. After the number 455, Fairchild had added, "–6," indicating to the typesetters to proceed after this page directly to page 457, omitting page 456.

[2]Eliphalet Wheeler Gilbert (1793–1853), the eldest son of Elisha Gilbert (1768–1857), was born in New Lebanon and educated at Union College and Princeton Theological Seminary. He was called to the pastorate of the Second Presbyterian Church in Wilmington in 1818. In 1829 the church split and he continued as pastor of the new Hanover Street Church until 1834, when he was called to the presidency of Newark College. He had a further period with the same church from 1835 to 1840. See Homer W. Brainard et al., *The Gilbert Family* (New Haven, 1953), p. 312; George H. Ryden, "The Founding of the University of Delaware and Its First President, Dr. E. W. Gilbert," in *Delaware Notes*, 8th ser., 1934, pp. 31–39; and *DAB*.

[3]The word "sticklishness" was not crossed out in the manuscript, but the published edition has "difficulty."

[4]The words "that fall" were not crossed out in the manuscript but did not appear in the published edition.

[5]Gilbert wrote letters to Finney on 19 October and 12 November describing the condition of the churches in the Wilmington area and pleading with Finney to go there (Finney Papers, microfilm, roll 1).

[6]Finney preached his farewell sermon to the Stephentown church on the evening of Sunday, 2 December 1827. The next day he left for Troy. After spending a few days there, he and Mrs. Finney left for Wilmington. They traveled via New York, where they spent some days at the home of Zephaniah Platt and his family, conferring with leaders of the churches there. They then traveled south to Wilmington, arriving the second week of December. See N. S. S. Beman's letter dated 11 December 1827, *The New York Observer*, 15 December 1827, p. 198; Anson G.

MS 456 **ˡBut before I cease speaking of Stephentown I should say, that both there and at New Lebanon the same means, and no other, were used that had been used and blessed in the revivals in central New York. The same spirit of powerful and prevailing prayer was manifested there; the Word had the same prodigious power imparted to it by the Holy Ghost; and the conversions were of the same general type. The converts were clear, strong, zealous, and united. There was no appearance of heterodoxy among them, no tendency to fanaticism or anything objectionable that I ever perceived. I know not that any complaint was ever made in any quarter of there being anything disastrous or out of the way in those revivals. They were remarkably pure and powerful, and lasting in their results. If I recollect I received at one time about two hundred of the converts ‹into›[7] the communion of the church.[8] I shall never forget the interest taken by the young converts in the Miss Sackett of whom I have spoken. She seemed to be regarded by them with peculiar affection.** MS 457 **They had known of her instrumentality in ˡgetting me to go there, and they had seen her earnest soul pouring itself out in every direction for their salvation. They clung to her and around her in a very affectionate manner. She was young, and unaffected and simple-hearted as a child. But she was over-done. Her strength soon began to fail; and she lived, I believe, but a few months after the revival closed.[9] But as I said, I went to Wilmington, Delaware, and engaged with Brother Gilbert.** I soon found that his teaching had placed the church in a position that rendered it impossible to promote a revival among them till their views could be corrected. They seemed to be afraid to make any effort, lest they should take the work out of the hands of God. They had the oldest of the Old School views of doctrine; and consequently their theory was that God would convert sinners in His own time; and that therefore to urge them to immediate repentance, and in short to attempt to promote a revival, was to attempt to

Phelps, "Diary," 16 December 1827, microfilm in New York Public Library; Rhoda C. Churchill to Lydia Finney, 3 December 1827; J. P. Cushman to Finney, 7 December and 21 December 1827, and Zephaniah Platt to Finney, 20 December 1827, Finney Papers, microfilm, roll 1.

[7]Here Finney changed the word "at" to "into."

[8]Finney's figure of two hundred received into the church is probably too high. According to the correspondent of the *Albany Christian Register*, "Fifty-five were added to the church on the 4th inst," that is, 4 November 1827 (reprinted in *WR*, 4 December 1827, p. 194). And Beman reported on the admissions at the meeting of 2 December: "*Twenty-three* persons were admitted to the Church, making, with the former admissions since the revival commenced, *one hundred and one*" (*The New York Observer*, 15 December 1827, p. 198). That was Finney's last Sunday in Stephentown. A letter dated Stephentown, 28 December 1827, written by a Baptist, speaks of fifty-nine being added to the Baptist church and continues:

> The Presbyterian Society has been greatly augmented of late, in this town, under the labours of the Rev. G. Finney. Nearly one hundred persons have been added to them—some by *immersion*, and others by *sprinkling*. Mr. Finney immersed three men, and afterwards sprinkled an infant child of one of them. He also sprinkled a lady, who had been sprinkled in her infancy (*Christian Secretary* [Hartford, Conn.], 5 January 1828, p. 198).

[9]Maria Sackett commenced a school in the spring of 1830, but her health declined through the summer and fall, and she died of consumption at the end of the year. See letters to Lydia Finney from Sarah Seward, 29 November 1830; Henrietta Platt, 22 January 1831; and Rhoda C. Beach, 5 March 1831, Finney Papers, microfilm, roll 2.

make men Christians by human agency and **in** human strength, and thus to dishonor God by taking the work out of **H**is hands. ¦I observed also that in their prayers there was no urgency for an immediate outpouring of the Spirit; and that this was all in accordance with the views in which they had been educated. MS 458

It was plain that nothing could be done unless **Brother** Gilbert's views could be changed upon this subject.[10] I there¦fore spent hours each day in conversing with him on his peculiar views. We talked the subject all over in a brotherly manner; and after laboring with him in this way for two or three weeks, I saw that his mind was prepared to have my own views brought before his people. The next Sabbath I took for my text, "Make to yourselves a new heart and a new spirit; for why will ye die?"[11] I went thoroughly into the subject of the sinner's responsibility; and showed what a new heart **was** not, and what it **was**. I preached about two hours; and did not sit down till I had gone as thoroughly over the whole subject as very rapid speaking would enable me ‹to do›[12] in that length of time. The congregation became intensely interested, and great numbers rose and stood on their feet in every part of the house. ¦The house was **crowded to its utmost capacity**, and there were strange looks in the assembly. Some looked offended **and disgusted**, others intensely interested. Not unfrequently when I brought out strongly the contrast between my own views and the views in which they had been instructed, some laughed, some wept, some were manifestly angry; but I do not recollect that anyone left the house. It was a strange excitement. In the meantime **Brother** Gilbert **sh**oved[13] himself from one end of the sofa to the other behind me **in the pulpit**. I could hear him breathe and sigh, and could not help observing that he was himself in the greatest **excitement**.[14] However I knew I had him, in his convictions, fast; but whether he would make up his mind to withstand what would be said by his people, I did not know. I was preaching to please the Lord, and not man. I thought **at the time** it might be the last time I would ever preach there; but **thought that at** all events **I would** tell them the truth, and the whole truth on that subject, whatever the result might be. JHF 235 MS 459

I **had** endeavored ¦to show that if man were as helpless as their views represented him to be, he was not to blame for his sins. If he had lost in Adam all power of obedience, so ¦that obedience had become impossible to him, and that not by his own act or consent but by the act of Adam, it was mere nonsense to say that he could be blamed for what he could not help. I had endeavored also to show that in that case the atonement was no grace, but really a debt due to mankind on the part of God for having placed them in a MS 460 JHF 236

[10] Finney was so discouraged that he thought of returning north again immediately. See, e.g., Helen Platt to Lydia Finney, 17 December 1827; Zephaniah Platt to Finney, 26 December 1827; and J. P. Cushman to Finney, 21 December 1827, Finney Papers, microfilm, roll 1.

[11] Ezekiel 18:31.

[12] The words "to do" appear to have been inserted by Finney.

[13] The word "shoved" was not changed in the manuscript but appeared as "moved" in the published edition.

[14] In another account of this incident, Finney explained, "It was not that he dissented from the doctrine preached, but he felt so intensely anxious for the effect it might have on the people" (*OE*, 23 December 1857, p. 202).

condition so deplorable and so unfortunate. Indeed the Lord **had** helped me to show up, I think, with irresistible clearness the peculiar dogmas of **O**ld Schoolism and their inevitable results. When I was through I did not call upon **Brother** Gilbert to pray, for I dared not; but prayed myself that the Lord would set home the **W**ord, make it understood, and give a candid mind to weigh what had been said, and to receive the truth and reject what might be erroneous. I then dismissed the assembly and went down the pulpit stairs, MS 461 **Brother** Gilbert follow|ing me **down**. The congregation withdrew very slowly, and ‹many›[15] seemed to be standing and waiting for something in almost every part of the house. The aisles were cleared pretty nearly; and the rest of the congregation seemed to remain in a waiting position as if they supposed they should hear from **Brother** Gilbert upon what had been said. Mrs. Gilbert, however, went immediately out **and went home**.[16] As I came down the pulpit stairs I observed **a couple of** ladies sitting on the left hand of the aisle through which we must pass, to whom I had been introduced, and knew **they** were particular friends and supporters of **Brother** Gilbert. I saw that they looked partly grieved, and partly offended, and greatly astonished. The first we **came to**, who was near the pulpit stairs, took hold of **Brother** Gilbert as he was following behind me, and said to him, "Mr. Gilbert, what do you think of that?" She spoke in a loud whisper. He replied in the same MS 462 manner, "It is worth five hundred dollars." That greatly gratified me, |and affected me very much. She replied "Then you have never preached the Gospel." "Well," said he, "I am sorry to say I never have." We passed along, JHF 237 and then the other lady said to him about the |same things; and **also he to her**. That was enough for me; I made my way to the door and went out. Those that had gone out were standing many of them in front of the house discussing vehemently the things that had been said. As I passed along the streets going to Mr. Gilbert's, where I lodged, I found the streets full of excitement and discussion. The people were comparing views; and **from the things that I heard,** from the **sentences** that escaped from those that did not observe me as I passed along, I saw that the impression was decidedly in favor of what **I** had been say**ing**.

When I arrived at Mr. Gilbert's his wife accosted me as soon as I entered by saying, "Mr. Finney, how dared you preach any such thing in our pulpit?" I replied, "Mrs. Gilbert, I did not dare to preach anything else; it is the truth of MS 463 God." |She replied: "Well, it is true that God was in justice bound to make an atonement for mankind. I have always felt it, though I never dared say it. I believed that if the doctrine preached by Mr. Gilbert was true, God was under obligation, as a matter of justice, to make an atonement; and to save me

[15]Finney added the word "many."

[16]Lydia Hall (Monro) Gilbert was the eldest daughter of Dr. George Monro of New Castle, Delaware, and subsequently of Wilmington, where he was an elder in the church. She was a granddaughter, on her mother's side, of John Haslet, a well-known Revolutionary Army colonel. Lydia was Gilbert's first wife, whom he married in 1819, "a lady of great intelligence and consistent and elevated piety. She proved a most efficient auxiliary to him in his work. She became the mother of six children,—five daughters and one son." She died in 1843 at age forty-nine "of a rapid consumption" after "years of feeble health." See W. B. Sprague, *Annals of the American Pulpit*, vol. 4 (New York: Carter and Bro., 1859), p. 597; and *NYE*, 9 March 1843, p. 39.

from those circumstances in which it was impossible for me to help myself, and from a condemnation which I did not deserve." Just at this moment Mr. Gilbert entered. "There!" said I, "Brother Gilbert, you see the results of your preaching here in your own family;" and then repeated to him what his wife had just said. He replied: "I have sometimes thought that my wife was one of the most pious women that I ever knew; and at other times I have thought that she had no religion at all." "Why!" I exclaimed, "she has always thought that God *owed* her, as a matter of *justice* the salvation provided in Christ; how can she be a Christian?" This was all said by each of us with the greatest solemnity and earnestness. ˡUpon my making the last remark she got up and left the room. The house was very solemn; and for two days, I believe, I did not see her. She then came out clear, not only in the truth, but in the ˡstate of her own mind; having passed through a complete revolution of views and experience.[17] MS 464 JHF 238

From this point the work went forward. The truth was worked out admirably by the Holy Spirit. **Brother** Gilbert's views became greatly changed; and also his style **and mode** of preaching, and manner of presenting the Gospel. So far as I know, until the day of his death his views remained corrected, **and** New School as opposed to the Old School views which he had before maintained.[18] The effect of this sermon upon many of Mr. Gilbert's church members was very peculiar. I have spoken of the lady who asked him what he thought of it. She afterwards told me that she was so offended to think that all her views of religion were so overthrown, that she promised herself she never would pray again. She had been in the habit of so far justifying herˡself because of her sinful nature, and had taken in her own mind such **views** as **I have represented** Mrs. Gilbert **as expressing, that what she had heard of** my preaching on that subject had completely subverted her views, her religion and all. She remained in this state of rebellion, if I recollect right, for some six weeks before she would pray again. She then broke down, and became thoroughly changed in her view and religious experience. And this, I believe, was the case with a large number of that church. MS 465

[17]When she died in 1843, *The New-York Evangelist* published a long eulogy on her Christian character: "Protracted meetings and revivals of religion found in her a ready sympathy, and a heart, and hand, and tongue ready for action in any scriptural mode; and she was never happier than when directly engaged in seeking the conversion of some individual soul" (*NYE,* 9 March 1843, p. 39).

It was probably Mrs. Gilbert to whom the Reverend John Holt Rice of Union Seminary was referring in a letter to Dr. Archibald Alexander of Princeton, written after Finney had moved to Philadelphia: "We hear that Finney is making a noise in Philadelphia. He has certainly got G— and D— fully with him, and Mrs. G— is beyond any of them" (letter dated 4 March 1828, *The Watchman* [Hartford, Conn.], 13 June 1836, p. 95). "D—" was probably Joshua N. Danforth, a Presbyterian minister in New Castle, Delaware, who was a Finney supporter. Finney preached there in December 1827. Soon after this, Danforth left his church to become an evangelist. See Gilbert to Finney, 19 October and 21 November 1827; and Danforth to Finney, 13 November and 26 December 1827, Finney Papers, microfilm, roll 1; and *BR,* 13 June 1828, p. 95.

[18]Gilbert came out in support of the New School theology, and when the Presbyterian church split in 1837, he was chosen as permanent clerk of the New School General Assembly. See James Wood, *Old and New Theology; or, An exhibition of those differences with regard to Scripture doctrines, which have recently agitated and now divided the Presbyterian church* (Philadelphia: Wm. S. Martien, 1838), p. 179.

James Patterson. The minister of the First Presbyterian Church of the Northern Liberties, Philadelphia. This is an 1837 engraving by John Rubens Smith, from a painting by Bass Otis. Courtesy The Historical Society of Pennsylvania.

In the meantime I had been induced to go up and preach for **Brother** Patterson, at Philadelphia, twice each week.[19] I went up on the steamboat and

[19]James Patterson (1779–1837) was a graduate of Jefferson College and of Princeton. In 1813 he went to the First Presbyterian Church of the Northern Liberties in Philadelphia. Up to that time the church was connected with the Second Presbyterian Church, and both were under the joint charge of Dr. Jacob J. Janeway and Rev. Thomas H. Skinner. But it was thought that the Northern Liberties field needed the whole time and energies of one man. It was located "in the suburbs of the city, among the poor, the illiterate, the animalized, the stupid, the heathenish." Patterson had particular success among the poor and carried on a city mission work comparable with that of Thomas Chalmers in Glasgow, Scotland. "Rough and uncouth in his manner, he was suited to his location." He remained there until his death. See Sprague, *Annals of the American Pulpit*, pp. 423–28; and Robert M. Patterson, *Historical Sketch of the Synod of Philadelphia and Biographical Sketches* (Philadelphia: Presbyterian Board of Publication, 1876), pp. 74–75.

So successful had he been in building up the church that, at the time Finney went there, it was the largest church in Philadelphia and one of the largest in America, with nearly a thousand members (see *Minutes of the General Assembly of the Presbyterian Church in the United States of America* [Philadelphia], 1827 and 1828). Patterson had tried to get Finney to go in April 1827 but without success, so he renewed his invitation in December. See Patterson to Finney, 20 April and 14 December 1827, Finney Papers, microfilm, roll 1.

preached in the evening, and returned the next day and preached at Wilmington; thus alternating my evening services between Wilmington and Philadelphia. **By boat these cities were about** forty miles **apart**. The work took so much effect in Philadelphia as to convince me that it was my duty to leave **Brother** Gilbert to carry on the work, **under God,** in Wilmington, while I gave my whole time to labor in **the large city of** Philadelphia.[20]

|**Brother** James Patterson, with whom I first labored in Philadelphia, held the views of theology then held at Princeton **Theological Seminary**, |since known as the theology of the **O**ld School **p**resbyterians. But he was a godly man, and cared a great deal more for the salvation of souls than for nice questions about ability and inability, or any of those points of doctrine upon which the old and new school **p**resbyterians differ. His wife held the New England views of theology; that is, she believed in a general as opposed to a restricted atonement, and agreed with what was called New England orthodoxy as distinguished from Princeton orthodoxy.[21] It will be remembered that at this time I belonged to the **p**resbyterian church myself. I had been licensed and ordained by a presbytery composed mostly of men educated at Princeton. **I have already related the struggle that I had with some of the members of that presbytery, and especially with my theological teacher, the Rev. George W Gale.** I have also said that when I was licensed to preach the Gospel, I was asked whether I received the **p**resbyterian confession of faith as containing |the substance of Christian doctrine.[22] I replied that I did so far as I understood it. But not expecting to be asked any such question I had never examined it with any attention, and I think I had never read it through. **In my controversy with Brother Gale we had made no use of a confession of faith; it was with the views of**

MS 466
JHF 239
MS 467

[20] In another account of the Philadelphia revival Finney said that it was "late in the autumn of 1827" that he went to labor with Patterson ("Revival Memories," *The Independent* [New York], 26 April 1873, p. 516). Finney's correspondence indicates that it was about 15 January 1828 that he finally left Wilmington. Cf. Patterson to Finney, 12 January 1828; E. W. Gilbert to Finney, 17 January 1828; and Emily Curtiss to Lydia Finney, 15 January 1828, in the calendar of the Finney Papers, but written on "Monday morning," which was probably Monday, 14 January, Finney Papers, microfilm, roll 1. Gilbert and the converts in the revival in Wilmington very much regretted that Finney left them, and they kept writing, begging him to return. Gilbert reckoned Finney had paid them "only half a visit before, & that too, in a most unfavorable season."

Soon after Finney's departure, the congregation became divided over the question of building a new church, and the revival atmosphere subsided. But Gilbert and the majority of the congregation decided to form a new church, and their new building, the Hanover Street Church, the largest in the state, was opened in 1829. See Gilbert to Finney, 11 February and 27 February 1828, Finney Papers, microfilm, roll 1; and 22 April 1829, Finney Papers, microfilm, roll 2; and Theophilus K. Jones, "Recollections of Wilmington from 1845 to 1860," *Historical and Biographical Papers of the Historical Society of Delaware* 5, no. 52 (1909): 11. Finney visited Wilmington again in June 1831, where he conducted a protracted meeting in Gilbert's church in association with Dr. Skinner of Philadelphia and Joel Parker of New York. See *Religious Intelligencer* (New Haven), 4 August 1832, p. 155.

[21] His wife, Sarah, whom he married in 1813, was the eldest daughter of Halsted Coe, of Newark, New Jersey, "a lady of highly respectable connections—in whom he found in every respect a most congenial spirit, and an efficient helper in his work. They had ten children,—six sons and four daughters." See Sprague, *Annals of the American Pulpit*, p. 25; and Joseph G. Bartlett, *Robert Coe, Puritan* (Boston: published for private circulation by the author, 1911), p. 118.

[22] See chapter IV and MS 100.

Princeton that I supposed myself to be combatting him on certain points. However, when I read the confession of faith and pondered it, I saw that although I could receive it, as I now know multitudes of presbyterians do, as containing the substance of Christian doctrine **as taught in the Bible,** yet **that** there were several points upon which I could not put the same construction that was put on them at Princeton; and I accordingly, everywhere gave the people to understand that I did not accept that construction **of the confession of faith**; or **at any rate,** if that was the true construction **of the confession of faith upon those points**, I entirely differed from **it**. I suppose that **Brother** Patterson understood this before I went to labor with MS 468 him, as when |I took that course in his pulpit he expressed no surprize. Indeed, he did not at all object to it.

The revival took such **powerful**[23] hold in his congregation as greatly to interest him; and as he saw that God was blessing the word as I presented it, he stood firmly by me, and never in any case objected to anything that I advanced. Sometimes when we returned from meeting Mrs. Patterson would JHF 240 smil|ingly remark: "Now you see, Mr. Patterson, that Mr. Finney does not agree with you on those points upon which we have so often conversed." He would always, in the greatness of his Christian faith and love, reply: "Well, the Lord *blesses* it." The interest became so great that our congregations were packed at every meeting.[24] One day **Brother** Patterson said to me: "Brother Finney, if the presbyterian ministers in this city find out your views, and what you are preaching to the people, they will hunt you out of the city as they would a wolf." I replied: "I cannot help it. I can preach no other doctrine; and if they must drive me out of the city, let them do it and take the responsibility. But I do not believe that they can get me out."

MS 469 |However, the ministers did not take the course that he predicted by any means; but nearly all **of them** received me to their pulpits. When they learned what was going on at **Brother** Patterson's church**,** and that many of their own church members were greatly interested, **and many of their own congregation stirred up,** they invited me to preach for them;[25] and if I recollect right, I preached in all of the presbyterian churches except that of Arch street.[26]

[23]The word "powerful" was not crossed out by Fairchild in the manuscript but is omitted in the published version.

[24]Already by the beginning of February, Finney was "the great topic of conversation" in Philadelphia (see Samuel I. Prime, *Memoirs of the Rev. Nicholas Murray, D.D.* [New York: Harper, 1863], p. 91). In May, James Patterson reported on the state of the work in a letter to the *Philadelphian*: "The Rev. Mr. Finney is labouring with me at present, and his preaching has been remarkably owned of God. Our anxious meetings, held always once and sometimes twice a week, have been attended usually, for *many* weeks past, by from 100 to 140 persons" (reprinted in *WR,* 13 May 1828, p. 78).

[25]Patterson recorded the presence of members from other churches in the anxious meetings:

> From the middle of February last, some hundreds have attended them of the different religious persuasions in this city—Methodists, Baptists, Episcopalians, etc. etc. . . . Many, from time to time, gave evidence, as we thought, of a saving change of heart; and have disappeared, and will probably connect themselves with different churches in this city (*WR,* 13 May 1828, p. 78).

[26]The Arch Street Church at Third and Arch Streets was the meeting house of the Second Presbyterian Church. This was one of the largest and most prestigious Presbyterian churches in America and was under the pastoral charge of Rev. Jacob J. Janeway. It was the church where Ashbel Green had been minister, and it was always a bastion of Old School conservative

There were a great many wonderful cases of conversion connected with the revival in Philadelphia, and many cases of extreme bitterness on the part of individual opposers. I have said that I met Mr. Nettleton in New York in the fall after the New Lebanon Convention, and that he had come there to publish his letters.[27] I was then on my way to Wilmington, and spent a few days with my friends in New York. Mr. Nettleton did publish his letters, and they were immediately sent and circulated in Philadelphia. This was no doubt intended to forestall my labors there.[28] I suppose that in some ˡinstances opposition was encouraged by those letters; yet I recollect that they reacted upon Brother Nettleton in that city.[29] When they were read, people said: MS 470

Presbyterianism. See *The National Cyclopaedia of American Biography,* vol. 13 (New York: James T. White, 1906), pp. 498–99.

Finney probably did not preach in *all* the remaining Presbyterian churches. The local *Directory* lists twelve, but according to Keith J. Hardman, the "Records" of the Presbytery of Philadelphia in the Presbyterian Historical Society list as many as sixteen throughout the area (see *Desilver's Philadelphia Directory and Stranger's Guide* [Philadelphia], 1828, appendix, p. 13; and K. J. Hardman, *Charles Grandison Finney, 1792–1875, Revivalist and Reformer* [Syracuse: Syracuse University Press, 1987], p. 467 n. 17). On MS 479 Finney states that he preached in "nearly all," and elsewhere he wrote, "I preached more or less in several of the Presbyterian and Dutch churches in the city" (*The Independent,* 24 April 1873, p. 516).

In March 1828 it had been reported that Finney had preached in five of the churches. One of these was probably the Fifth Presbyterian Church, where Thomas H. Skinner, the minister, had left early in March and the church was without a pastor. Another was the Sixth Presbyterian Church under Rev. John H. Kennedy. (See *BR,* 14 March 1828, p. 63; D. L. Dodge to Finney, 11 March 1828; and E. W. Gilbert to Finney, 27 January, 27 February, and 14 March 1828, Finney Papers, microfilm, roll 1.) Finney also preached in the First Presbyterian Church of the Southwark district, under Rev. Charles Hoover, where it was reported that "as many as 80 persons are more or less impressed: about 25 of whom have obtained a hope." See *Christian Watchman* (Boston), 21 March 1828, p. 47; *BR,* 13 June 1828, p. 95; and E. H. Gillett, *History of the Presbyterian Church,* vol. 2 (Philadelphia: Presbyterian Publication Committee, 1864), pp. 357–58.

It was a particular surprise when Finney was invited to preach in the First Presbyterian Church for James P. Wilson. David L. Dodge wrote to Finney from New York: "Dr. Wilson having taken you into his pulpit it has almost petrified opposition here. He has more weight here than perhaps any minister in the Presbyterian Church" (Dodge to Finney, 25 February 1827 [in error for 1828]; and Zephaniah Platt to Finney, 10 March 1828, Finney Papers, microfilm, roll 1). Finney also preached in the Mariner's Church, where Alfred H. Dashiel was the stated supply, and for Rev. William Ramsey of the Second Presbyterian Church of the Southwark District. See Oliver Smith to Finney, 24 July 1828; and Ramsey to Finney, 23 November 1829, Finney Papers, microfilm, roll 2.

[27] See MS 425.

[28] Nettleton's letter to Aikin of 13 January 1827, together with a cover letter, was published first by him in *The New York Observer,* 8 December 1827, before it came out in the pamphlet *Letters of the Rev. Dr. Beecher and the Rev. Mr. Nettleton, on the New Measures in conducting Revivals of Religion. With a Review of a Sermon by Novanglus* (New York: Carvill, 1828). Thomas Hastings, the publisher of *The Western Recorder* in Utica, New York, commented to Finney that the pamphlet had been published "as *we* suppose, for the express purpose of fencing you away from the South" (Hastings to Finney, 25 December 1827, Finney Papers, microfilm, roll 1). Just after Finney had seen him in New York, Nettleton went south for his health. He stayed in Philadelphia at the invitation of Thomas Skinner. And while Finney was in Wilmington, Nettleton was in Philadelphia. Nettleton left on 11 January 1828 and continued south, a few days before Finney moved to Philadelphia. See letters to Finney from D. L. Dodge, 18 December 1827; E. W. Gilbert, 19 October 1827; and James Patterson, 12 January 1828, Finney Papers, microfilm, roll 1.

[29] Lyman Beecher wrote to Nettleton on 28 May 1828 from Philadelphia, warning him that any further controversy would react against him. Beecher had been conferring with the leading

"Why! if Mr. Finney is wrong, Mr. Nettleton is the great and leading offender; for he has held these same views, and used these measures for many years. Why is he now condemning the course of Mr. Finney? We had better hear Mr. Finney for ourselves."

Philadelphia was at that time a unit, almost, in regard to the views of theology held at Princeton. **Rev.** Dr Skinner held to some extent what have since been known as New School views; and differed enough from the tone of theology round about him to be suspected **by the presbyterian churches about him** as not altogether sound **in the sense in which they understood** orthodoxy.[30] I have ever regarded it as a most remarkable thing, that so far as I know my **orthodoxy** did not prove a stumbling block in that city, was **not** openly called in question by any of the ministers or churches **that I heard of.**

MS 471 I preached in the Dutch church to Dr. Livingston's congregation;[31] ˡand I found that he sympathized with my views, and encouraged me with all his influence to go on and preach the preaching that the Lord had bidden me. I

JHF 241 did not hesitate everywhere and on all ˡoccasions, to present my own views of theology, and those which I had everywhere presented to the churches.

ministers involved in the controversy, who were in Philadelphia for the General Assembly, and he told Nettleton that "the opinion of everyone is to forbear farther publication, if possible." Beecher and Beman and a number of other ministers, including Finney, published a statement the same day, agreeing "to cease from all publications, correspondences, conversations, and conduct designed or calculated to keep those subjects before the public mind" (*Autobiography, Correspondence, etc., of Lyman Beecher, D.D.*, ed. Charles Beecher, 2 vols. [New York: Harper, 1863, 1865], 2:103–7; and see p. 228 n. 123 [MS 434]). A Universalist editorial spoke of the disruption caused by the revivals, breaking out after the New Lebanon Convention "into an open rupture" through the publication of the *Letters of Nettleton and Beecher*. It was claimed to be well known that Beecher had "to go all the way from Boston to Philadelphia to see Mr Finney, and make confessions to him, that the raging flame might longer be smothered" (*Trumpet and Universalist Magazine* [Boston], 8 August 1829, p. 22).

[30]Thomas Harvey Skinner (1791–1871) was training to be a lawyer before deciding to enter the Presbyterian ministry. He was ordained at Philadelphia in 1813 and became copastor with Dr. Jacob J. Janeway of the prestigious Second Presbyterian Church. But his adoption of New School views led to a bitter controversy in which he was accused of being a Hopkinsian. So in 1816 he withdrew from the church with seventy of the members to become minister of the Fifth Presbyterian Church on Locust Street. In 1823 a new church on Arch Street was built. He left Philadelphia early in March 1828 because of ill health and accepted a call to Boston, but his health deteriorated even further, so he returned to Philadelphia in August. In 1832 he became a professor at Andover Theological Seminary, and subsequently he was minister of the Mercer Street Presbyterian Church in New York and a professor in the Union Theological Seminary, which he helped to found. See George L. Prentiss, *A Discourse in Memory of Thomas Harvey Skinner, D.D., LL.D.* (New York: Randolph, 1871); and *DAB*.

[31]Gilbert Robert Livingston (1786–1834) was the minister of the First Dutch Reformed Church. This church had been formed in 1813 from the English-speaking portion of the Old German Reformed Church, which had broken away in 1806. It was one of two Dutch Reformed churches in Philadelphia. Finney preached there on 12 February 1828, but by the second week in March he had left. See Edward T. Corwin, *A Manual of the Reformed Church in America, 1628–1878*, 3d ed. (New York: Reformed Church in America, 1879), pp. 350–51, 626; and E. W. Gilbert to Finney, 27 January, 27 February, and 14 March 1828, Finney Papers, microfilm, roll 1.

An extract of a letter from Philadelphia "to a gentleman in New York," dated 11 March 1828, and published in *The New York Observer*, reported: "In Mr. Livingston's congregation the excitement is increasing, and 50 or 60 attend the inquiry meetings" (reprinted in the *Christian Watchman*, 21 March 1828, p. 47). In February 1829 the revival was still going on in the church, with sixty or seventy attending the inquiry meetings, and Finney was informed in frequent letters of the continuing work over the next two years. See Oliver Smith to Finney, 21 February 1829, Finney Papers, microfilm, roll 2.

Brother Patterson was himself, I believe, greatly surprized that I met **with** no open opposition from the ministers or churches on account of my theological views. Indeed, I did not present them at all in a controversial way, but simply **presented** them in my instructions to saints and sinners in a way so natural as not, perhaps, to excite very much attention except **to** discriminating theologians. But many things that I said were new to the people. For example, one night I preached on this text: "There is one God, and one Mediator between God and men, the man Christ Jesus, who gave himself a ransom for all to be testified in due time."[32] This was a sermon on the atonement, in which I took the ˡviews that I have always held of its nature and of its universality; and stated as strongly as I could those points of difference between my own views and those that were held by limited atonement theologians. This sermon attracted so much attention, and excited so much **feeling**, that I was urged to preach on the same subject in other churches. **But** the more I preached upon it, the more desirous people were to hear; and the excitement became so general that I preached on that subject seven different evenings in succession in as many different churches.[33] **I heard of no open opposition to the views which I presented; and this was to me, and to Brother Patterson, a very remarkable fact.**

MS 472

It would seem that the people had heard much said against what was called Hopkinsianism; the two great points of which were that man ought to be willing to be damned for the glory of God and that God was the author of sin. In preaching I sometimes noticed these points, and took occasion to denounce Hopkinsianism; and said that they appeared ˡto have too much of it in Philadelphia.[34] That their great neglect in attending to the salvation of their souls looked very much as if they were willing to be damned; and that they must hold that God was the author of sin, for they maintained that their

MS 473

[32] 1 Timothy 2:5.

[33] The First Presbyterian Church of Southwark was one of the churches where Finney preached the sermon. The Reverend Charles Hoover, the pastor, was present but had some difficulties with Finney's presentation and wrote to him for clarification. He thought Finney had presented Christ merely as an Arbitrator and not as a Mediator (Hoover to Finney, 5 February 1829, Finney Papers, microfilm, roll 2).

[34] Because Finney preached New School doctrines, he was himself being labeled "Hopkinsian." In a letter to Theodore Weld at this time, he wrote: "The fact is, that here we are all hereticks, Alias Hopkintians who dont sit quietly down in a corner of the Triangle and wait God's time." The orthodox doctrines of original sin, inability, and a limited atonement were attacked by Samuel Hopkins and his followers and were labeled "The Triangle" in a series of pamphlets written by Samuel Whelpley in 1816 and 1817. These modifications of Calvinism as well as other aspects of Hopkins's theories were accepted by Finney (e.g., the understanding of holiness or love as "universal disinterested benevolence"). These ideas had become commonly accepted by many of the more moderate clergy. But because of the objectionable features that Finney speaks about here, he refused to be identified with Hopkinsians. See Finney to Weld, 27 March 1828, in Gilbert H. Barnes and Dwight L. Dumond, eds., *Letters of Theodore Dwight Weld, Angelina Grimké Weld, and Sarah Grimké, 1822–1844,* vol. 1 (Gloucester, Mass.: Peter Smith, 1965), p. 10; William G. McLoughlin, *Modern Revivalism: Charles Grandison Finney to Billy Graham* (New York: Ronald, 1959), pp. 44–47; Frank Hugh Foster, *A Genetic History of the New England Theology* (Chicago: University of Chicago Press, 1907), p. 152; and James Brand and John M. Ellis, *Memorial Addresses on the Occasion of the One Hundredth Anniversary of the Birth of President Charles G. Finney* (Oberlin: Goodrich, 1893), pp. 13–14. It is interesting to note that Finney himself later came to conclusions about being willing to be damned for the glory of God similar to those of Hopkins when he experienced a spiritual crisis in Boston in 1843. See MS 777.

JHF 242 nature was sinful. This I turned over and over, and these two points I |dwelt upon. I heard again and again that the people said: "Well, he is no Hopkinsian.["] Indeed I felt it my duty to expose, **and found it *necessary* to expose,** all those hiding places of sinners, and to hunt them out from under those peculiar views of orthodoxy in which I found them entrenched.[35] The revival spread, and took a powerful hold. All our meetings for preaching **and** prayer, and **meetings** for inquiry, were crowded. There were a great many more inquirers than we could well attend to.[36] It was late in the fall **before** I MS 474 took my lodgings in Philadelphia,[37] and I continued |to labor **on** there without any intermission until **about the first of** August **the next Summer.**[38]

I have said that there were some cases of very bitter opposition on the part of individuals. **I recollect that** in one case, a man whose wife was very deeply convicted **in view of the situation of her soul**, was so enraged that he came in and took his wife out of meeting by force. Another case I recollect as a very striking one, of a German whose name I cannot now **recollect**. He was a tobacconist.[39] He had a very amiable and intelligent wife; and was himself, as I afterwards found when I became acquainted with him, an intelligent man. He was, however, a skeptic, and had no confidence in religion at all. His wife, however, came to our meetings, and became very much concerned about her soul; and after a severe **mental** struggle of many days, she was thoroughly converted. As she attended meetings **very**[40] frequently, MS 475 and became very much interested, it soon attracted the attention of |her husband, and he began to oppose her being a Christian. He **was a man**, as I learned **of** hasty temper, and a man of athletic frame, and of great resolution

[35] Matson had written another sentence after this, which was crossed out by Finney: "This of course led me to expose most thoroughly the nature and bearing of the peculiar views that had been taught at Princeton."

[36] Finney lamented the lack of helpers in his letter to Theodore Weld:

> The good work of God is deepening and spreading in this AntiRevival city. . . . We want 10 times as much help as we have. 100dreds are willing to be visited, and anxious to be, whom we can not go and see. . . . I am called upon by anxious persons almost continually some days, and often requested to go and visit anxious persons and am not able, on account of my health and multiplied duties. O how much I want your help and that of 20 others who understand revivals (Barnes and Dumond, *Letters of Theodore Dwight Weld,* pp. 10–11).

[37] The Finneys were staying with Mr. Abraham Martin, an accountant, and his wife, at 113 Wood Street in Philadelphia. They remained there while Mrs. Finney gave birth to their first child, Helen Clarissa, on 10 June 1828, and then returned via New York to Mrs. Finney's parents' home in Whitesboro. See *Desilver's Philadelphia Directory,* p. 115; E. W. Gilbert to Finney, 14 March 1828, Finney Papers, microfilm, roll 1; Maria Cushman to Lydia Finney, 27 May 1828; and Caspar Schaeffer to Finney, 21 July 1828, Finney Papers, microfilm, roll 2.

[38] It was about mid-July 1828 when the Finneys left Philadelphia to travel north. See MS 480.

[39] In another account of this incident Finney wrote: "I have not seen him since, and of late years I have forgotten his name. Being a German name and new to me, it has entirely escaped my mind" ("Revival Memories," *The Independent,* 24 April 1873, p. 516). There are many tobacconists with German names listed in *Desilver's Philadelphia Directory*. One of these was Peter Hess (or Hesse), a "cigar maker" living in the Northern Liberties area in 1828. He may be the man referred to, for his name also appears some years later in a list of signatures of members of the First Presbyterian Church of the Northern Liberties in a letter to Finney inviting him to take part in a protracted meeting. See Members of the First Presbyterian Church of the Northern Liberties to Finney, 5 March 1835, Finney Papers, microfilm, roll 3.

[40] The word "very" was not crossed out in the manuscript but does not appear in the published edition.

and fixedness of purpose. As **she** became more and more interested his opposition increased, till finally he forbade her attending meetings any more. She then called to see me, and asked my advice with regard to what course she should take. I told her that her first obligation was to God; that she was undoubtedly under obligation to obey **His** commands, even if they conflicted with the commands of her husband; and that while I ˡadvised her to avoid giving him offence if she could **help it** and do her duty to God, still in no case to ‹omit›[41] what she regarded as her duty to God for the sake of complying with his wishes **as an infidel**. I told her that as he was an infidel his opinions on religious subjects were not to be respected, and that she could not safely follow his advice. She was well aware of this. He was a man that paid no attention to religion at all except to oppose it. ˡIn accordance with my advice she attended the meetings as she had opportunity, and **got** instructions; and she soon **got** into the liberty of the Gospel, had great faith and peace of mind, and enjoyed much of the presence of God. This highly displeased her husband; and he finally went so far as to threaten her life if she went to meeting again. She had so frequently seen him angry that she had no confidence that he would fulfil his threat. She told him calmly that whatever it cost her, her mind was made up to do her duty to God; that she felt it her duty to avail herself of the opportunity to get the instruction she needed; and that she must attend those meetings whenever she could do it without neglecting her duty to her family. One Sabbath evening, when he found she was going to meeting he renewed his threat that if she went he would take her life. She told me afterwards that she had no thought that it was anything but a vain threat. She calmly replied to him that her duty was plain; that there was no reason why she ˡshould remain at-home at that time but simply to comply with his unreasonable wishes; and that to stay at-home under such circumstances would be entirely inconsistent with her duty to God and to herself. She therefore went to meeting. When she returned from meeting she found him in a great rage. As soon as she entered the door he locked it after her and took out the key, and then drew a dagger and swore he would take her life. She ran up stairs. He caught a light to follow her. The servant girl, **being frightened,** blew out the light as he passed by her. This left them both in the ˡdark. She ran up and through the rooms in the second story, found her way into the kitchen and **down** [**the**][42] cellar. He could not follow her in the dark, and she got out of the cellar window and went off to a friend's and spent the night. Taking it for granted that he would be ashamed of it before morning, she went home early, and **went into** the house and found things in the greatest disorder. He had broken some of the furniture, and acted like a man distracted. ˡHe again locked the door as soon as she was fairly in the house; and drawing a dagger he threw himself upon his knees and held up his hands, and took the most horrible oath that he would then take her life. She looked at him with astonishment and fled. She ran up stairs, but it was light and he followed her. She ran from room to room till finally she entered the last, from which there was no escape. She turned around and faced him. She threw

JHF 243

MS 476

MS 477

JHF 244

MS 478

[41] Here Finney changed the word "avoid" to "omit."

[42] The word "the" is not in the original. Fairchild altered it to "and then to the cellar."

herself upon her knees as he was about to strike her with his dagger, and lifted up her hands to heaven and cried for mercy upon herself and upon him. At this point God arrested him. She said he looked at her for a moment, dropped his dagger, and fell upon the floor and cried for mercy himself. He then and there broke **right** down, confessed his sins to God and to her; and begged God, and begged her, to forgive him. **Of course she did forgive him; and I trust God forgave him.** From that moment he was a wonderfully MS 479 changed man. He became one of the most earnest Christian converts. ˡHe was greatly attached to myself; and some year or two after, as he heard that I was to come to Philadelphia in a certain steamboat, he was the first man in Philadelphia that met and greeted me.[43] I received him and his wife into the church before I left Philadelphia, and baptized their children. I have not seen or heard from them for many years.

But while there were individual cases of singular bitterness and opposition to religion **arising out of false views**, still I was not annoyed or hindered by anything like public opposition ‹**as I had been by Dr. B. & Mr. N.**›[44] The JHF 245 ministers **behaved** kindly; and in no instance that I recollect, did ˡthey speak publicly, if indeed they did privately, against the work that was going on. **The number of converts must have been very great.**[45] After preaching in **Brother** Patterson's church for several months, and more or less in nearly all the presbyterian churches in the city, it was thought best that I should take up a central position, and preach steadily in one place. In Race street there was a MS 480 large German church,[46] ˡthe pastor of which was a Mr. Helfenstine.[47] The

[43] Finney was in Philadelphia again in June 1832 and preached in the Fifth Presbyterian Church (see Elizabeth White to Lydia Finney, 15 October 1832, Finney Papers, microfilm, roll 3). The letter from members of Patterson's church to Finney dated 5 March 1835, containing Hess's name and inviting Finney to take part in a protracted meeting, was probably given to Finney while he was on another visit to Philadelphia. See p. 386 n. 10 (MS 679).

[44] That is, Dr. Beecher and Mr. Nettleton. This phrase was added by Finney and crossed out by Fairchild.

[45] An indication of the revival interest is given in reports of the service held in Patterson's church on Sunday, 25 May, when 87 were admitted to the church, about 80 of them on profession of faith, 33 being baptized.

> Mr Finney preached in the morning. In the afternoon the sacrament of the Lord's supper was administered. . . . Mr. Beman, of Troy, and Mr. Finney, made addresses to the church and congregation. The scene was very impressive. Not less than 2000 persons were present. A large number of the ministers of the General Assembly were among the audience.
>
> Many had to commune standing, the crowd was so great and so compact that it was difficult to move them, and multitudes went away who could not get into the house.
>
> Several households were also presented to be baptized, at the same time with the parents; but the crowd was so great, it seemed impracticable to accomplish it, and the baptism of the households was deferred (see *WR,* 3 June 1828, p. 90; and *BR,* 6 June 1828, p. 90).

By August it was reported that 119 had been added to Patterson's church since the revival commenced (*BR,* 8 August 1828, p. 127).

[46] The German Reformed Church at the corner of Fourth and Race streets was built in the latter part of the eighteenth century. It had been one of the first German Reformed churches to make the transition to the English language, thus opening the way for the introduction of New Measures revivalism. See Samuel Helffenstein, Jr., "Recollections of the German Reformed Church of Race Street, Philadelphia," *The Reformed Church Monthly* (Philadelphia) 2, no. 5 (June 1869): 280–91; and Marion Bell, *Crusade in the City: Revivalism in Nineteenth-Century Philadelphia* (Lewisburg, Pa.: Bucknell University Press, 1977), p. 63.

elders of the congregation, together with their pastor, requested me to occupy their pulpit.[48] **That** was then, I think, the largest house of worship in the city. **In that church I continued to preach statedly for many months.** It was always crowded; and it was said it seated three thousand people when the house was packed and the aisles were filled.[49] I had an opportunity to preach to a great many Sabbath School teachers. Indeed it was said that the Sabbath School teachers throughout the city generally attended my ministry.[50] About midsummer of 1829 I left for a short time and visited my wife's

[47] Samuel Helffenstein, Sr. (1775–1866), was the most outstanding member of an illustrious family of German Reformed pastors. He had been the minister of the Race Street Church since 1799. He was at the center of a number of controversies over the introduction of the English language. These had caused considerable disruption, and more than half the membership had seceded. Although he was not fully in sympathy with the new revivalism, the church was in a very weak state, and he consented to have Finney hold meetings in his church. See Charles E. Schaeffer, "The Helffenstein Family," *Bulletin of the Theological Seminary of the Evangelical and Reformed Church* 26, no. 3 (July 1955): 21–28; and Donald E. Harpster, "Controversy in the German Reformed Church in Pennsylvania, with Emphasis on Nineteenth Century Philadelphia" (Ph.D. diss., Pennsylvania State University, 1976), pp. 26–39, 58–61.

[48] Friends and sponsors of Finney proposed to the Race Street Church that he should be invited, and this was finally arranged while he was away from Philadelphia in July. The formal invitation, presented to him on his return in mid-August, was to preach for six months on Sunday afternoons and evenings and on Thursday evenings. See John B. Frantz, "Revivalism in the German Reformed Church in America to 1850, with Emphasis on the Eastern Synod" (Ph.D. diss., University of Pennsylvania, 1961), p. 89; Caspar Schaeffer to Finney, 21 July and 4 August 1828; and Oliver Smith to Finney, 24 July 1828, Finney Papers, microfilm, roll 2.

[49] Finney preached in Race Street Church from mid-August until early January 1829. He was assisted for some weeks by the pastor's son, Jacob Helffenstein, who recollected: "From all parts of the city people flocked to hear him, and his earnest appeals were made effective to the conversion of some hundreds, who united with different branches of the Christian church." This was one of the first revivals of religion to be reported in the German Reformed churches. See Jacob Helffenstein, "C. G. Finney on 'New Measures.' Views of a Contemporary Minister," *NYE,* 20 July 1876, p. 6; and John B. Frantz, "The Return to Tradition: An Analysis of the New Measure Movement in the German Reformed Church," *Pennsylvania History* 31, no. 3 (July 1964): 314–15.

[50] James Patterson had been the first to establish a real Sabbath school association in Philadelphia in 1815, with 100 scholars, and his enthusiasm soon led to the work's spreading. In 1817 the Philadelphia Sunday and Adult School Union was formed. This grew to become national and so large in scope that it was reorganized as the American Sunday School Union in 1824. By the time the Philadelphia City Sabbath School Union held their second anniversary on 1 April 1828, while Finney was in town, it was estimated that there were 53 schools with 519 teachers and 6,125 scholars in Philadelphia. When Finney left the city in July, Oliver Smith wrote to him, "I think I can safely say that the great body of the pious youth, [and] comprehending Sabbath School teachers, are pleased with your labors: and with that kind of preaching which is called *revival* preaching." See Joshua N. Danforth, "Sketches of the Life of Rev. James Patterson," *NYE,* 13 February 1851, p. 25; report of the American Sunday School Union reprinted in *The Western Luminary* (Lexington, Ky.), 11 February 1829, p. 255; *BR,* 11 April 1828, p. 58; and 25 April 1828, p. 67; and Oliver Smith to Finney, 24 July 1828, Finney Papers, microfilm, roll 2.

Toward the end of the year the Sunday school teachers were making a concerted effort to improve their effectiveness. A concert of prayer on the last Monday evening of the year was attended by 700–800 teachers, and the highlight was the "Teacher's Fast Day" on 29 January 1829. It was estimated that about 1,000 Sunday school teachers attended, with 200–300 unable to get in. During the meeting, which lasted three and one-half hours, the mass of teachers rededicated their lives through a renewal of their covenant. One observer wrote to Mrs. Finney, "I never witnessed such wrestling for souls: all appeared to feel the awful responsibilities resting upon them." The occasion was considered "one of the most solemn transactions in which the Sunday School Teachers of this or any other place have ever engaged in." The enthusiasm eventually declined, but the Sunday school movement generally came to adopt the aims and the

parents in Oneida County, N.Y,. and then returned to Philadelphia and labored there until about midwinter.[51] I do not recollect exact dates, but think that in all I labored in Philadelphia about a year and a half.[52] In all this time there was no abatement of the revival that I could see. The converts became numerous in every part of the city; so numerous that I never had any MS 481 knowledge, nor could I form any just estimate of their number.[53] |I never had labored anywhere where I was received more cordially; and where Christians, and especially converts, appeared better than they did there. There was no jar or schism among them that I ever knew of; and I never heard of any disastrous influence resulting from that revival.[54] In a great city

methods of the new revival movement. See *The American Sunday School Magazine* (Philadelphia) 6 (February 1829): 49–50; and (April 1829): 115–16; Elizabeth White to Lydia Finney, 28 and 29 January 1829; Joseph Naglee to Finney, 31 December 1829, Finney Papers, microfilm, roll 2; and Fred J. Hood, *Reformed America: The Middle and Southern States, 1783–1837* (University: University of Alabama Press, 1980), pp. 186–90. Finney was made a life member of the American Sunday School Union on 10 April 1828 and of the Young Men's Bible Association of Philadelphia on 19 May 1828 (certificates in Finney Papers, microfilm, roll 2).

[51]There is a question mark in pencil over the 9 of "1829," which may have been inserted by Lewis Tappan. It was crossed out by Fairchild. It was not in 1829 but in mid-July 1828 that the Finneys returned to Whitesboro. They traveled via New York, where Finney preached on Sunday, 20 July, for Dr. Gardiner Spring to a "densely packed" audience at the Brick Church. Back in Whitesboro, Finney also spent some days in Troy and preached in Rome before returning to Philadelphia in mid-August, leaving Mrs. Finney with their daughter, Helen, in Whitesboro.

On the way back to Philadelphia, Finney conferred in New York with leading ministers and laymen about the possibility of returning there later. He also preached in the pulpit of the Laight Street Church while the pastor, Dr. Samuel H. Cox, was away. See letters to Finney from Oliver Smith, 24 July 1828; Zephaniah Platt, 6 August 1828; David McClure, 16 August 1828; Sarah Seward, 8 September 1828; H. Norton, 16 September 1828; and Arthur Tappan, 25 September 1828; also Catherine Huntington to Lydia Finney, 19 August and 27 August 1828, Finney Papers, microfilm, roll 2; Lewis Tappan, "Journal," 20 July 1828, in Tappan Papers, microfilm, roll 1; *Personal Reminiscences of the Life and Times of Gardiner Spring,* vol. 1 (New York: Scribner, 1866), pp. 225–26; *NYE,* 30 September 1875, p. 2; and *Memorials of William E. Dodge*, comp. and ed. David Stuart Dodge (New York: Randolph, 1887), p. 210.

Mrs. Finney went back to join her husband in Philadelphia in October 1828. See Mary Ann Beebe to the Finneys, 26 October 1828, Finney Papers, microfilm, roll 2.

[52]Finney was in Philadelphia for about a year, from January 1828 to January 1829; but he may have been thinking of the whole time he was down in Pennsylvania.

[53]After eight months the papers were still giving favorable notices of the revival. The *Philadelphian* reported:

> We are informed that the revival still continues to progress, in the Rev. Mr. Patterson's congregation. One hundred and nineteen have been added to his church, since its commencement;—and among the fruits of this season of refreshing, many others are numbered, who have attached themselves to other churches, both in and out of the city (reprinted in the *Religious Intelligencer,* 16 August 1828, p. 190).

The writer of a letter dated Philadelphia, 14 August 1828, in the *Christian Watchman,* similarly reported the continuation of the revival "ever since last winter" and added:

> I was at a meeting last Sabbath evening, where there were fifty came forward, after the public exercises, to be prayed for, some of whom were in the greatest possible distress. Among the number were two of our City Physicians, ten other males, and 38 females (22 August 1828, p. 135).

In December Finney was able to report: "Probably more than 100 in the anxious room last night. We had to fetch in additional seats, until the room was full. Several professed submission" (Finney to Jacob Helffenstein, 9 December 1828, Finney Papers, file 2/2/2, box 9). There was a renewal of the revival in Patterson's church the next January. See the *Christian Watchman,* 6 February 1829, p. 23.

[54]Although things may have appeared to go smoothly while Finney was in Philadelphia, his

converts may be greatly multiplied, and yet you cannot estimate the greatness of the revival, as you could in a small town where you are acquainted with all the inhabitants.

There were a great many **very**[55] interesting facts connected with this revival. I recollect that a young **lady,** who was the daughter of a **Baptist** minister of the **Old** School stamp, attended my ministry at Mr. Patterson's church, and became awfully convicted. Her convictions were so deep that she finally ˡfell into a most distressing despair. She told me **that** she had been taught from her childhood by her father, that if she was one of the elect she would be converted in due time; and that until she was converted and her nature changed by the Spirit of God, she could do nothing for herself but to read her Bible and pray for a new heart. ˡWhen she was quite young she had been greatly convicted of sin, but had followed her father's instruction, had read her Bible and prayed for a new heart, and thought that was all that was required of her. She waited to be converted, and thus for evidence that she was one of the elect. In the midst of her great struggle of soul on the subject of her salvation, something had come up relative to the question of marriage; and she promised God that she never would give her hand **in marriage**[56] to any man till she was a Christian. When she made the promise she said that she expected God would very soon convert her. But her convictions passed away. She was not converted; and still that promise to God was upon her soul, and she dared not break it. When she was about eighteen years of age a young man proposed to make her his wife. She **consented**, but as that vow was upon her she could not consent to be married until she was a Christian. She said they greatly loved each other, and he urged her **to consent** to be married without delay. But without telling him her real reason, she ˡkept deferring it from time to time. **She thus put him off from time to time** for some five years, if I recollect right, waiting for God to convert her**, and hoping that it would take place**. Finally, in riding **out**[57] one day the young man was thrown

JHF 246

MS 482

MS 483

revival was to lead to considerable conflicts. In the Race Street Church the state of things was greatly improved, but the congregation became dissatisfied with Helffenstein and wanted Finney back as pastor. A number of the prorevivalists left to form a new church, and Helffenstein was eventually forced to resign. It was several years before the church recovered. The introduction of "New Measures" into the German Reformed churches was to cause a major disturbance until the 1840s. See David Van Horne, *A History of the Reformed Church in Philadelphia* (Philadelphia: Reformed Church, 1876), pp. 71–72; and Frantz, "Revivalism in the German Reformed Church."

After Finney left Philadelphia, some of the revival-minded Christians started an "Association for the Promotion of Revivals," or the "Revival Association," as it was called. They wanted to form an independent Revival Church and hoped Finney would help to start it. At the same time the Race Street Church was also trying to get Finney to go there again. But the different factions and personality clashes and lack of unity among the leaders so discouraged Finney that he declined all invitations. When he did visit the area again in June 1832, it was in Skinner's church that he preached. See the correspondence about this in the Finney Papers, particularly letters to Finney from Caspar Schaeffer, Thomas Elmes, Benjamin T. Neal, Oliver Smith, David McClure, and Nehemiah Dodge, Finney Papers, microfilm, rolls 2, 3.

[55]The word "very" was not crossed out in the manuscript but was omitted from the published version.

[56]The words "in marriage" were not crossed out in the manuscript but do not appear in the published version.

[57]The word "out" was not crossed out in the manuscript but was omitted from the published edition.

from a carriage and instantly killed. This aroused the enmity of her heart against God. She accused God of dealing hardly with her. She said that she had been waiting for Him to convert her, and had been faithful to her promise not to get married until she was converted; that she had kept her lover for years waiting for her to get ready, **and she had been waiting for God to convert her,** and now behold! God had cut him off, and she was still JHF 247 unconverted. She had learned that the young man was a Universalist; ¦and now she was greatly interested to believe that Universalism was true, and would not believe that God had sent him to hell; and if He had sent him to hell, she could not be reconciled to it at all. Thus she had been warring with God for a considerable time before she came to our meetings, supposing that MS 484 the blame of her ¦not being converted was chargeable upon God and not upon herself. When she heard my preaching and found that all her refuges of lies were torn away, and saw that she ‹should› have ‹given her heart to God› long before,[58] and all would have been well, she saw that she herself had been entirely to blame, and that the instructions of her father on all those points had been entirely wrong; and remembering as she did how she had blamed God, and what a blasphemous attitude she had maintained before Him, she very naturally despaired of mercy. I reasoned with her and tried to show her the long-suffering of God, and encouraged her to hope, to believe, and to lay hold upon eternal life. But her sense of sin was so great that she seemed unable to grasp the **subject**, and sunk down deeper and deeper into despair from day to day. After laboring with her a great deal I became greatly distressed about her case. **As soon as** meeting **was out** she would **come and** follow me home with her despairing complaints, and would exhaust me by MS 485 appeals to my ¦sympathy and Christian compassion for her soul. After this state of things had continued for many weeks, one morning she called upon me in company with an aunt of hers, who had become greatly concerned about her, and who thought her on the very verge of a desperate insanity. I was myself of the opinion that it would result in that if she would not believe. Catharine—for that was her name[59]—came into my room in her usually despairing way; but with a look of wildness in her face that indicated a state of mind that was unendurable;[60] and at the moment I think it was the Spirit of God that suggested to my mind to take an entirely different course with her JHF 248 from what I had ever taken. ¦I said to her: "Catharine, you profess to believe that God is good." "Oh yes!" she said, "I believe *that*."[61] "Well, you have often told me that His goodness forbids Him to have mercy on you—that your sins have been so great that it would be a dishonor to Him to forgive you MS 486 and save you. You have often confessed to me that you believed ¦that God would forgive you if He wisely could; but that your forgiveness would be an

[58] Here Matson had written "that she would have been converted long before had she submitted to God," but Finney changed it.

[59] She may have been Catharine W. Knowles, one of three sisters from Peach Hill, who were all converted during this revival. See letters from Catharine, Mary, and Sarah Knowles in the Finney Papers.

[60] Matson had started a new sentence here with the words "Her aunt was with her," which appear to have been crossed out by Finney.

[61] The underlining of the word "*that*" appears to have been done by Finney.

injury to Him, to His government, and to His universe, and therefore He cannot forgive you." "Yes," she said, "I believe that." I replied: "Then your difficulty is that you want God to sin, to act unwisely and injure Himself and the universe for the sake of saving you." She open[e]d[62] and set her large blue eyes upon me, and looked partly surprized and partly indignant. But I proceeded: "Yes! you are in great trouble and anguish of mind because God will not do wrong; because He will persist in being good whatever may become of *you*. You go about in the greatest distress of mind because God will not be persuaded to violate His own sense of propriety and duty, and save you to His own injury and that of the entire universe. You think yourself of more consequence than God and all the universe; and cannot be happy unless God makes Himself **unhappy,** and everybody else, in making you happy." ˡI pressed this upon her. She looked with the utmost astonishment at me, and after a few moments she submitted. She seemed to be almost instantly subdued like a little child. She said: "I accept it. Let God send me to hell if He thinks that is the best thing to be done. I do not want Him to save me at His own expense and at the expense of the Universe. Let Him do what seemeth Him good." I got up instantly and left the room; and to get entirely away from her I went out and got into a carriage and **went off riding**. When I returned she had gone of course; but in the afternoon she and her aunt returned to declare what God had done for her soul. She was filled with joy and peace, ˡand one of the most submissive, humble, beautiful converts that I **almost ever saw**. MS 487 JHF 249

Another young **lady**, I recollect—**who was by the by** a very beautiful girl, perhaps twenty years old—called to see me under great conviction of sin. I asked her, among other things, if she was ˡconvinced that she had been so wicked that God might in justice send her to hell. She replied in the strongest language: "Yes! I deserve a *thousand* hells." She was gaily, and I think richly, dressed. I had a very thorough conversation with her, and she broke down in heart and gave herself to Christ. She was a very humble, broken-hearted convert. I learned that she went home and gathered up a great many of her artificial flowers and ornaments, with which she had decked herself, and of which she was very **proud**, and passed through the room with them in her hand. They asked her what she was going to do with them. She said she was going to burn them up. Said she, "I will never wear them again." "Well," they said to her, "if you will not wear them you can sell them; don't burn them." But she said: "If I sell them **to anybody** else **they** will be as **proud of them, and as** vain of them, as I have been myself; I will burn them up." And she actually put them into the fire. MS 488

ˡA few days after ‹this›[63] she called on me and said that she had, in passing through the market, I think that morning, observed a very richly dressed lady in the market. Her compassions were so stirred that she went up to her and asked if she might speak to her. The lady ‹replied›[64] that she might. She said to her, "My dear **M**adam, are you not proud of your dress? **A**nd are you not MS 489

[62] Matson omitted the second *e* in "opened."
[63] Finney added the word "this."
[64] Finney crossed out the words "said to her" and inserted "replied."

vain, and neglecting the salvation of your soul?" She said that she herself burst into tears as she said it, and told the lady a little of her own experience, how she had been attached to dress, and how it had well-nigh ruined her soul. "Now," said she, "you are a beautiful lady, and are finely dressed—are you not in the same state of mind that I was in myself?" She said the lady wept, JHF 250 and confessed that that had been her snare; and |she was afraid that her love of dress and society would ruin her soul. She confessed that she had been MS 490 neglecting the salvation of her soul, because she |did not know how to break away from the circle in which she moved. The young lady wanted to know if I thought she had done wrong in what she said to the lady. I told her No! that I wished all Christians were as faithful as she; and that I hoped she would never cease to warn her own sex against that which had so nearly ruined her own soul.

In the Spring of 1829,[65] when the Delaware was so high, the lumbermen came down with their rafts from the region of the high land where they had been getting the lumber out during the winter. At that time there was a large tract of country along the northern region of Pennsylvania, called by many "the lumber region," that extended along up toward the head waters of the Delaware river. Many persons were engaged in getting out lumber there summer and winter. Much of this lumber was floated down in the Spring of the year, when the water was high, to Philadelphia. They would get out their MS 491 lumber when the river was low; and when |the snow went off, and the Spring rains came on, they would throw it into the river and float it down to where they could build rafts, or otherwise embark it for the Philadelphia market. Many of the lumbermen were raising families in that region, and there was a large tract of country there at that time unsettled and unoccupied except by these lumbermen. They had no schools, and at that time had no churches or religious privileges at all. I knew a minister who told me he was born in that lumber region; and that when he was twenty years old he had never attended a religious meeting, and did not know his alphabet.

These men that came down with lumber attended our meetings, and quite a number of them were hopefully converted. They went back into the wilderness and began to pray for the outpouring of the Holy Spirit, and to tell JHF 251 the |people around them what they had seen in Philadelphia, and to exhort them to attend to their salvation. Their efforts were immediately blessed, MS 492 |and[66] the revival began to take hold and to spread among those lumbermen. It went on in a most powerful and remarkable manner. It spread to such an extent that in many cases persons would be convicted and converted who had not attended any meetings, and who were almost as ignorant as heathen. Men who were getting out lumber and were living in little shanties there alone, or where two or three or more were together, would be seized with such conviction that it would bring them into such a state as would lead them to wander off and inquire what they should do, and they would be converted, and thus the revival spread. There was the greatest simplicity manifested by

[65]Finney meant the spring of 1828, since he had left Philadelphia by the spring of 1829.
[66]Page 492 was numbered 238 and renumbered 469 (in error) and corrected to 470 by Matson, and changed to 492 by Finney.

the converts. An aged minister who had been somewhat acquainted with the state of things, related to me as a **specimen** of what was going on there the following fact. He said one man in a certain place, had a little shanty by himself where he slept nights, and was getting out his shingles |during the day. MS 493 He began to feel that he was a sinner, and his convictions increased upon him until he broke down, confessed his sins, and repented; and **that** the Spirit of God revealed to him so much of the way of salvation that he evidently knew the Savior. But he had never attended a prayer-meeting, or heard a prayer that he recollected **of**, in his life. His feelings became such that he finally felt constrained to go and tell some of his acquaintances, that were getting out lumber in another place, how he felt. But when he arrived he found that they felt, a good many of them, just as he did; and that they were holding prayer-meetings. He attended their prayer meetings and heard them pray, and finally prayed himself; and this was the form of his prayer: "Lord, you have got me down, and I hope you will keep me down. And since you have had so good luck with me, I hope you will try other sinners." I have said that this work began in the **S**pring of 1829.[67] |In the Spring of 1831 I was |at Auburn again. JHF 252 MS 494 Two or three men from this lumber region came there to see me, and to inquire how they could get some ministers to go in there. They said that not less than five thousand people had been converted in that lumber region; that the revival had extended itself along for eighty miles, and there was not a single minister of the **G**ospel there. I have never been in that region; but from all I have ever heard about it, I have regarded that as one of the most remarkable revivals that occurred in this country. It was carried on **so** independently of the ministry, among a class of people **so** ignorant **as relates** to all **scholarship**; and yet so clear and wonderful were the teachings of God, that I have always understood the revival was remarkably free from fanaticism, or wildness, or anything that was objectionable. I may have been misinformed in some respects, but report the matter as I have understood it. "Behold how great a matter a little fire kindleth!"[68] The spark that was struck into the hearts of those few lumbermen |that came to Philadelphia, spread MS 495 over that forest, and resulted in the salvation of a multitude of souls.[69]

I found **Brother** Patterson to be one of the truest and holiest men that I have ever labored with. His preaching was quite remarkable. He preached with great earnestness; but there was no connection **often** in what he said,—**or** very little **connection—with** his text. He has often said to me: "When I preach, I preach from Genesis to Revelations." He would take a text, and after making a few remarks upon it, or perhaps none at all, some other text would be suggested to him upon which he would make some very pertinent and striking remarks, and then another text; and thus his sermons were made up of pithy and striking remarks upon a great number of texts as they arose in

[67]This should probably be 1828 (see n. 65 above).

[68]James 3:5.

[69]The conditions in the back country seemed to be conducive to the spread of revival. About this time, or soon after, the Albright Methodists (or Evangelical church) and the Campbellites (or Disciples of Christ) flourished in that area. See Thomas R. Cox, ed., "The Diary of William Langdon for 1855: A Pennsylvania Lumber Raftsman's Year," *Journal of Forest History* 26, no. 3 (July 1982): 124–39; and information from Thomas R. Cox.

his mind. He was a tall man, of striking figure and powerful voice. He would preach with the tears rolling down his cheeks, and with an earnestness and pathos that was very striking.[70] MS 496 JHF 253 |It was impossible to hear him preach without being impressed with a sense of his intense earnestness and his great honesty. I only heard him preach occasionally; and when I first did so was pained, thinking that such was the rambling nature of his preaching that it could not take effect. However, I found myself mistaken. I found that notwithstanding the rambling nature of his preaching, his great earnestness and unction fastened the truth on the hearts of his hearers; and I think I never heard him preach without finding that some persons were deeply convicted by what he said.[71] He always used to have a revival of religion every winter up to the time when I labored with him. I think he told me he had had a revival every winter for fourteen winters in succession.[72] He had a praying people. When I

[70]Thomas Brainerd described him:

> At least six feet in height, and so lank that he seemed still taller; eyes black, and set deep in his head; coal black, straight hair; skin dark, and complexion so pale as often to seem cadaverous; high cheek bones and large mouth;—all wrought by labour, responsibility, nervous sympathy and feeble health, into an expression grave—almost sad;—his eyes often streaming with tears, and his voice in its higher tones, shrill, piercing, lugubrious or severe, he seemed like an old prophet of Israel risen from the dead,—a messenger from another world, come to warn the wicked to flee the wrath to come (Sprague, *Annals of the American Pulpit,* p. 426).

[71]Thomas Brainerd recalled him in the pulpit:

> His sermons were seldom written out. He delighted to get some novel, startling thought, that "came right home," as he was wont to say; and then carry it out by illustrations drawn from every day life. His efforts were very unequal; sometimes marked by crudeness and bad taste; but in listening to him nearly a whole year, I remember no discourse that had not some original touches; nor one that did not seem to make a good moral impression on his congregation. . . . In direct and personal efforts to convert sinners to God, perhaps he has had no superior in this land since the days of Whitefield (Sprague, *Annals of the American Pulpit*, p. 427).

[72]Patterson's constant efforts for revival were renowned. He used Finneyite measures long before Finney was converted, and he was the center of a circle of young revivalists and workers. His biographer, Robert Adair, wrote:

> Mr. Patterson's ministry, especially from the time of his settlement in Philadephia, was characterized by glowing zeal, and intense and incessant activity. . . . There were many revivals of religion, and some of them of great power, in connection with his labours; and to produce and maintain such a state of things his efforts, both in and out of the pulpit, seem to have been specially designed (Sprague, *Annals of the American Pulpit*, p. 425).

See also Bruce Laurie, *Working People of Philadelphia, 1800–1850* (Philadelphia: Temple University Press, 1980), chap. 3.

The long series of revivals seems to have been particularly prominent in 1816, 1821, and 1822, and they were carried on afterward throughout Patterson's ministry. It was noteworthy that by August 1828, 1,270 members had been added to his church since he started his ministry. See *BR*, 15 August 1828, p. 131. See also Bell, *Crusade in the City*, pp. 52, 56.

Thomas Brainerd wrote of Patterson's work among the poor and illiterate:

> He must gain their attention. He must draw them to church. Hence he circulated advertisements; pasted pious placards on the walls; announced novel subjects; took wonderful texts, and wrought out queer illustrations. And when, by the help of God, he had roused and attracted the multitude, he felt that the case was urgent; that he must, at all hazards, and by any means lawful, however novel, bring them to submit to God. Revival excitements first filled his church; and he had a tendency perhaps to suppose that these alone were periods of blessing; and for the recurrence of these he mainly laboured and prayed. . . .

was laboring with him I recollect that for two or three days, at one time, here seemed to be something in the way. The work seemed to be in a measure suspended; and I began ˡto feel alarmed lest something had grieved the Holy Spirit. One evening at prayer-meeting while this state of things was becoming manifest, one of his elders arose and made a confession. He said: "Brethren, the Spirit of God has been grieved, and I have grieved him. I have been in the habit," said he, "of praying for **Brother** Patterson, and for the preaching, on Saturday night until midnight. This has been my habit for many years, to spend Saturday night till midnight in imploring the blessing of God upon the labors of the Sabbath. Last Saturday night," he continued, "I was fatigued, and omitted it. I thought the work was going on so pleasantly and so powerfully, that I might indulge myself, and go to bed without looking to God for a blessing on the labors of the Sabbath. On the Sabbath," said he, "I was impressed with the conviction that I had grieved the Spirit; and I saw that there was not the usual manifestation of the influence of the Spirit upon the congregation.[73] I have felt convicted ever since; ˡand have felt that ˡit was my duty to make this public confession. I do not know," said he, "who beside myself has grieved the Spirit of God; but I am sure that I have done so."

MS 497

MS 498
JHF 254

I have spoken of **Brother** Patterson's orthodoxy. When I first began to labor with him I felt considerably tried, in some instances, with what he would say to convicted sinners. For example: the first meeting for inquirers that we had, the number in attendance was very large. We spent **sometime** in conversing with **individuals**, and moving around from place to place giving instructions. The first I knew **Brother** Patterson arose, and in a very excited manner said: "My friends, you have turned your faces Zionward, and now I exhort you to press forward." He went on in an exhortation of a few moments, in which he made distinctly the impression that they were now in the right way; and that they had only to press forward as they were doing then, and they would be saved. His remarks pained me exceedingly; for they seemed ˡto me to **make a self-righteous impression**—to make **them think** that they were doing very well, **and doing their duty;** and if they continued to do their duty, as they were then doing, **and would press forward,** they would be saved. This was not my view of their condition at all; and I felt **in trouble,** pained to hear such instructions given, and perplexed with the question how I should counteract it. However, **as soon as he sat down,—or**

MS 499

He was always burdened with this responsibility—to save sinners. He worked himself; he made his elders, his church-members work. "Work, work, work!" was the burden of his appeals through the press, of his exhortations to his ministerial brethren, and of his sermons and lectures. . . . He started scores of little meetings, where his church-members might exhort and pray (Sprague, *Annals of the American Pulpit*, p. 427).

Of this particular revival in which Finney labored, Patterson wrote in March 1828:

Never has there been in my church, for the fourteen years I have been here, so much attention to the subject of religion. Some of the richest and proudest of the congregation have been brought to sue for mercy at the feet of Jesus. The preaching takes hold specially of the thinking part of society. Hundreds have been awakened, and a goodly number have been led to rejoice in hope (Joshua N. Danforth, "Sketches of the Life of Rev. James Patterson," *NYE,* 13 March 1851, p. 41).

[73] There is a question mark in pencil in the margin against the end of this sentence. It may have been inserted by Lewis Tappan.

perhaps I should say at the close of the meeting when, according to my custom, I summed up the results of our conversation and made an address to them, I alluded to what **Brother** Patterson had said; and remarked that they must not misunderstand what he had said. That what he had said was true of those that had really turned to God, and set their faces Zionward by giving their hearts to God. But they must not think of applying this to those of them who were convicted, **and** had not yet repented, believed, and given their MS 500 hearts to God. ᑊThat instead of *their* faces being turned Zionward, they were really turning their backs upon Christ **yet**; that they were still resisting the JHF 255 Holy Spirit; that they were still in the way to ᑊhell. That every moment they resisted they were waxing **worse and** worse;[74] and that every moment they remained impenitent, without submission, repentance, and faith,[75] they were **sinning against greater light**. The Lord gave me a very clear view of this subject. **Brother** Patterson listened with the greatest possible attention. I never shall forget with what earnestness he looked at me, and with what interest he saw the discriminations that I made. I kept on in my address until I could see, and until I felt, that the impression made by what **Brother Patterson** had said had not only been corrected, but that a great pressure was bearing upon them to **immediately** submit. I then called upon them to kneel down, and then and there commit themselves forever to the Lord; renouncing MS 501 ᑊall their sins, and giving themselves up to the disposal of sovereign goodness, with faith in the Lord Jesus Christ. I explained to them as plainly as I could the nature of the Atonement, and the salvation presented in the Gospel. I then prayed with them, and have reason to believe that a great number of them were converted on the spot. After this I never heard anything from **Brother** Patterson that was at all objectionable, **or trying to my feelings,** in giving instruction to inquiring sinners. Indeed I found him remarkably teachable, and his mind open to just discriminations. He seemed particularly quick to get hold of those truths that needed to be presented to inquiring sinners; and I presume to the day of his death he never again presented such a view of the subject as the one to which I have alluded, **that at the time distressed me so much**. I respect and reverence his very name. He was a lovely Christian man, and a faithful minister of Jesus Christ.[76]

[74]The words "waxing worse and worse" were not altered in the manuscript, but the published version reads, "waxing worse."

[75]Matson wrote down the following phrase here: "they were waxing worse than ever before, because," which appears to have been crossed out by Finney.

[76]Of all the revivalists that Finney worked with, Patterson was probably the one with whom he was in most sympathy. When Finney's health broke down in 1833 and he planned to go on a trip to South America, he invited Patterson to go with him. See "Victory over the World," *OE,* 5 November 1845, p. 177; and Patterson to Finney, 2 January 1834, Finney Papers, microfilm, roll 3. An obituary of Patterson stated, "Probably no preacher since the days of Whitefield, has been more invariably blessed in *direct* efforts to convert souls to God" (*BR,* 1 December 1837, p. 191).

CHAPTER XIX

MS 502
JHF 256

‹*Revival at Reading*›

As[1] I found myself in Philadelphia in the heart of the Presbyterian church, and where Princeton views were almost universally embraced, I must say still more emphatically than I have done, if possible, that the greatest difficulty I met with in promoting revivals of religion was the false instruction given to the people, and especially to inquiring sinners. Indeed in all my ministerial life, in every place and country where I have labored, I have found this difficulty to a greater or less extent; and I am satisfied **that the people are misled to such an extent** that multitudes are living in sin who would immediately be converted if they were truly instructed. The foundation of the error of which I speak is the dogma that human nature is sinful in itself; and that therefore sinners are entirely unable to become Christians. It is admitted, either expressly or virtually, that sinners *may* want to be Christians; and that they really *do* want to be Christians, and often *try* to be Christians.

It had been the practice, and still is to some extent, when ministers preached repentance, and urged the people to repent, to save their orthodoxy |by telling the **sinner in conclusion** that **he** could not repent any more than **he** could make a world. But the sinner *must* be set to do *something*; and with all th‹eir›[2] orthodoxy, they could not bear to tell **the sinner** that he had *nothing* to do. They must therefore set him self-righteously to pray for a new heart. **Strange enough, while they would tell him that he was totally depraved, that every act of his life and every thought of his heart ‹and every faculty and part of his soul and body were›[3] sinful, still in this utterly depraved condition they would tell him that he must have a new heart; and assuming that he wanted a new heart, that he was anxious for a new heart, but being unable to make to himself a new heart they would set him to pray for it.** They would sometimes tell him to do his duty, to press forward in duty, **etc.**, to read his Bible, to use the means of grace;— in short, they would tell him to do anything and everything but the very thing which |God commanded him to do. God commanded him to repent *now*, to believe *now*, to make to him a new heart *now*. But they were afraid to urge God's claims in this form, because they were |continually telling the sinner

MS 503

JHF 257

MS 504

[1] Pages 502–36 were numbered 348–82 and then 480–514 by Matson and 502–36 by Finney.

[2] Finney changed the word "this" to "their."

[3] Finney added the phrase "and every faculty and part of his soul and body were" in the margin. Fairchild crossed the whole sentence out.

that he had no ability whatever to do these things. **They would therefore compromise with him; and instead of calling on him to repent, to believe, to change his heart, to submit and turn immediately to God, they would tell him to do something else, and set him to perform mere outward works, and call that his duty; and encourage him to expect if he would press on in duty in this respect, he would be converted.**

As an illustration of what I have found in this and other countries, more or less ever since I have been in the ministry, I will refer to a sermon that I heard from the Rev. Baptist Noel, in England, a good man, and orthodox in the common acceptation of the term.[4] His text was: "Repent and be converted, that your sins may be blotted out when the times of refreshing shall come from the presence of the Lord."[5] In the first place he represented repentance not as a *voluntary*, but as an *involuntary* change,—as consisting in sorrow for sin, a mere state of the sensibility. He then insisted upon its being the sinner's

MS 505 duty to repent, and |urged the claims of God upon him. But he was preaching to an orthodox congregation; and he must not, and did not fail to remind them that they could not repent; that although God required it of them, still he knew that it was impossible for them to repent only as He gave them repentance. "You ask, then," he said, "what you shall do." "Go home," said he in reply, "and pray for repentance; and if it does not come pray again for repentance; and still if it does not come, keep praying till it does come." Here he left them. The congregation was large and the people very attentive; and I actually found it difficult to keep from screaming to the people *to repent*; and not to think that they were doing their duty in merely *praying* for repentance.

‹A›t[6] the time I was in Philadelphia, and indeed throughout all my ministerial life, I have found it very common for ministers and professors of religion to assume the inability of sinners to do what God required them to do, and to encourage them to do something else. They

MS 506 **did not dare encourage the sinner to remain |perfectly still and wait God's time without doing anything; but would tell him, as I have said, to use the means of grace and pray that God would change his heart, and in the performance of duty to press forward and wait God's time to convert ‹him.›**[7]

Such instructions always pained me exceedingly; and much of my labor in the ministry has consisted in correcting such views, and in pressing the sinner immediately to do just what God commands him to do. When he has inquired of me if the Spirit of God has nothing to do with it, I said, "Yes: as a matter of fact you *will* not do it of yourself. But the Spirit of God is *now* striving with

JHF 258 you to lead |you to do just what he would have you do. He is striving to lead

[4] The Honorable Baptist Wriothesley Noel (1798–1873) was a leading evangelical minister in England. Born of an aristocratic family, he read for the bar but turned to the ministry in the Church of England, where he soon rose to leadership among the evangelical clergy. In 1849 he caused a sensation by becoming a Baptist. As minister of the John Street Chapel in London, he was very prominent and successful. He wanted Finney to preach for him, and like others, he was stimulated by Finney's preaching in London to undertake revival meetings himself. He did have some success. See *DNB*; E. Finney to Henrietta Bissell, 22 April 1850, Finney Papers, microfilm, roll 4; and *The Christian Journal* (Glasgow), n.s., 2 (March 1851): 138.

[5] Acts 3:19.

[6] Matson had started this sentence, "However at," but Finney altered it.

[7] Finney altered the words "be converted" to "convert him."

you to repentance, to lead you to believe; and is striving with you, not to secure the performance of mere outward acts, but to change your heart." The church, to a very great extent, have instructed sinners to begin on the *outside* in religion; and by what they have called an outward performance ˡof duty, to secure an inward change of their will and affections. But I have ever treated this as totally **absurd, as heretical, entirely** unorthodox, and in the highest degree dangerous. **I have ever taught that until the sinner's *heart* was changed, there could be no virtue in any of his outward actions.**[8] **That no self-righteous, outward efforts could secure the favor of God; and that until the sinner changed his *heart* all his outward efforts were hypocrisy, ‹a delusion and an abomination.›**[9]

MS 507

Almost innumerable instances have occurred in which I have found the results of this teaching of which I have complained, to be a **universal** misapprehension **of the sinner's duty**; and I think I may say I have found thousands of sinners of all ages who are living under this delusion, and would never think themselves called upon to do anything more than merely to pray for a new heart, live a moral life, read their Bibles, attend meeting, use the means of grace, and leave all the responsibility of their ‹conversion and› salvation[10] **upon** God.

ˡFrom Philadelphia, in the winter of 1829,[11] I went to Reading, a city about forty miles west of Philadelphia.[12] At this place an incident occurred, which I shall mention in its place, that was a striking illustration of the kind of teaching to which I have alluded, and of its natural results.[13] In Reading there were several German churches and one presbyterian church.[14] The pastor of

MS 508

[8]The section following, to the end of the paragraph, was inserted on the reverse side of MS 507 in Matson's handwriting. He used an asterisk and the word "over" to indicate the insertion. It replaces the phrase "until his heart was changed from all mere efforts of selfishness, from seeking to do something in a self-righteous way to obtain the favor of God," which was crossed out. The section on the reverse was omitted by Fairchild.

[9]Here Matson had first written down, "were hypocrisy, and an abomination." He changed it to read, "were hypocrisy, a delusion and an abomination." But the change made it difficult to read, so Finney crossed it out and wrote "a delusion and an abomination." This ends the section on the reverse of MS 507.

[10]Here Matson had first written "their salvation and conversion," but Finney altered it to read, "their conversion and salvation."

[11]Fairchild altered this to read, "1829–30."

[12]Finney had completed less than five months of his agreement with the Race Street Church when he sent a letter on 5 January 1829 to the consistory of the church, indicating that he had a duty to labor in different places. This was accepted at their quarterly meeting, and a resolution was passed thanking him for his services (see Charles Schnider to Finney, 5 January 1829, Finney Papers, microfilm, roll 2).

Finney went to Reading on 9 January. It seems that initially he was not planning to remain there long, so he did not take his family with him. The date of Finney's arrival in Reading is given in a letter written by Finney on 19 September 1872 to Louis Richards: "I have a memorandum kep[t] by my former wife, from which I learn that I arrived at Reading the 9th of January 1829 & left for Lancaster the 7th of May making our stay in Reading about 4 months." Louis Richards was a member of the Presbyterian church in Reading and somewhat of a local historian. He had become interested in Finney's revival, which had taken place thirteen years before Richards's birth. He struck up a correspondence with Finney that led him to do some research into the revival. His five letters to Finney are preserved in the Finney Papers, and Finney's three letters to him were published in "A Religious Revival in Reading, 1829," *Historical Review of Berks County* 15 (October 1949): 148–50. See also *WR,* 24 February 1829, p. 30.

[13]See MS 520.

[14]German churches had been established in Reading in the middle of the eighteenth century.

the latter was the Rev. Dr Greer.[15] At his request, and that of the elders of the church, I went out to labor there for a time.[16] I soon found, however, that neither Dr Greer, nor any of his people, had any just idea of what they needed, or what a revival really was. None of them had ever seen a revival, so far as I could learn.[17] Besides, all revival efforts for that winter had been forestalled by an arrangement to have a ball ‹every alternate week›[18] which was attended by many of the members of the church, one of the leading
JHF 259 elders in Dr Greer's church being one of the managers.[19] I could ˡnot learn that Dr Greer had ever said anything against this. They had no preaching
MS 509 during the ˡweek, and I believe no religious meetings of any kind. When I found what the state of things was, I thought it my duty to tell Dr Greer that those balls would very soon be given up, or I should not be allowed to occupy his pulpit. That those balls, attended by his church members, and headed by one of his elders, would not long consist with my preaching.[20] **However,** he said, "Go on; take your own course." I did so; and preached three times on the Sabbath, and four times, I think, during the week, for about three weeks, before I said anything about any other meetings. We had no prayer meetings, I believe, for the reason that the lay members had never been in the habit of taking part in such meetings. However, on the third Sabbath, I think, I gave notice **in my services on the Sabbath, and Sabbath evening,** that a meeting for inquiry would be held in the lecture room in the basement of the church on Monday evening. I stated as clearly as possible the object of the meeting,
MS 510 and mentioned the class of persons that I desired to attend; inviting ˡthose, and those only, that were seriously impressed with the state of their souls, and

The Lutheran church, Holy Trinity, was under the pastoral charge of Rev. Henry A. Muhlenberg, and there was a German Reformed church under Rev. William Pauli. See Israel Daniel Rupp, *History of the Counties of Berks and Lebanon* (Lancaster, Pa.: Hill, 1844), pp. 435–49.

[15] John Ferguson Grier (1783–1829) was a part-time minister. He was called to Reading as a teacher in the academy and lay preacher to the Presbyterians there. Elders had been appointed in 1813, and in 1814 Grier was ordained and a church was formed. They worshiped in the academy building until the Old White Church was built in 1823. See Raymond W. Albright, *Two Centuries of Reading, Pa., 1748–1948* (Reading: Historical Society of Berks County, 1948), p. 125.

[16] Grier had first written to Finney in March 1828, begging him to go and saying that the church consisted of nearly one hundred members and that "Three gentlemen of the Bar" were recently ordained as elders. Further pressure was put on him to go at the end of December. See letters to Finney from Grier, 31 March and 29 December 1828, and from F. A. Strale, 29 December 1828, Finney Papers, microfilm, roll 2. The three lawyers were William Bell, William Darling, and Elijah Deckert. John McKnight, Samuel Baird, and Lewis Reese were also elders. See letter signed by them in *The Berks and Schuylkill Journal* (Reading), 4 April 1829, p. 3.

[17] *The Western Recorder* reported that Reading "contained about 10,000 inhabitants, has never before witnessed a revival. Religion and morals in the place had degenerated to a degree almost beyond parallel" (24 February 1829, p. 30).

[18] Matson had written "a weekly ball," but Finney changed it to "a ball every alternate week."

[19] This was John McKnight. He was one of the original elders ordained over the church in 1813 and was responsible for bringing Grier to Reading. He had gone to Reading in 1808 to be the first cashier of the bank and was a prominent citizen. A notice of his death in March 1855 speaks of him as "Cashier of the Office of Discount and Deposit of the Bank of Pennsylvania. He was the oldest cashier in the State" (*The Independent* [New York], 15 March 1855, p. 85; and see Finney to Louis Richards, 6 September 1872, "Religious Revival in Reading," p. 149; and Albright, *Two Centuries of Reading*, pp. 125, 131, 183).

[20] Finney also recollected, "I said to Grier 'in less than one month I shall preach myself out of your pulpit or Mr McKnight out of his balls.' And so it was. Br. McKnight like a good man accepted the truth & I heard no more of his attending balls" (Finney to Richards, 6 September 1872, "Religious Revival in Reading," p. 149).

had made up their minds to immediately **attend** to the subject, and desired to receive instruction on the particular question of what they should do to be saved. Dr Greer made no objection to this, as he had left everything to my judgment. But I do not think he had an idea that many, if any, would attend such a meeting, under such an invitation, as to do so would be to make an open acknowledgment that they were anxious for the salvation of their souls, and had made up their minds to **immediately** attend to the subject. Monday was rather a snowy, cold day. I think I observed that conviction was taking hold of the congregation; yet I felt doubtful how many would attend a meeting of inquirers, **a thing entirely new and unheard of in that place**. However, when evening came I went to meeting. Dr Greer came in, and behold! the lecture room, a large one—I ¦think nearly as large as the body of the church above—¦was full; and on looking around Dr Greer observed that most of the impenitent persons in his congregation were present; **and, to his great surprize**, the most respectable and influential **portion of his congregation were present**. He said nothing publicly. He said to me: "I know nothing about such a meeting as this; take it in your own hands, and manage it in your own way." I opened the meeting by a short address, in which I explained to them what I wished, that is to have a few moments conversation with each of them, and to have them state to me frankly how they felt on the subject,—what their convictions were; what their determinations were; what their difficulties were. I told them that if they were sick and called a physician, he would wish to know their symptoms, and that they should tell him how they were and how they had been. I said to them: "I cannot adapt instruction to your present state of mind unless you reveal it to me. ¦The thing, therefore, that I want, is that you reveal, in as few words as you can, your exact state of mind at the present time. I will now pass around among you, and give each of you an opportunity to say, in the fewest words, what your state of mind is." **I then passed around.** Dr Greer said not a word, but followed me around, and stood or sat by me and heard all that I had to say. He kept near me, for I spoke to each one in a low voice so as not to be heard by others than those in the immediate vicinity. I found a great deal of conviction and feeling in the meeting. They were greatly pressed with conviction. **A more solemn meeting of inquiry I have scarcely ever attended.** Conviction had taken hold of all classes, the high and the low, the rich and the poor. Dr Greer was greatly moved. Though he said nothing, still it was evident to me that his **excitement** was intense. To see his congregation in such a state as that, was what he had never had any conception of. ¦I saw that with difficulty, at times, he controlled his emotions. **Still he said not a word.** When I had spent as much time as was allowed me in ¦personal conversation, I then went back to the desk, and gave them an address; in which, according to my custom, I summed up the results of what I had found that was interesting in the **revelations** that they had made to me. Avoiding all personalities I took up the representative cases, and dissected, and corrected, and taught them. I tried to strip away their misapprehensions and mistakes, to correct the impression that they had that they must simply use means and wait for God to convert them; and in an address of perhaps half or three quarters of an hour, I set before them the whole situation as clearly as I possibly could. **I then**

JHF 260
MS 511
MS 512
MS 513
JHF 261

called on them to submit and to believe, to consecrate themselves and all they had then and there, to Christ. I then prayed with them. **I then** called MS 514 on those that felt prepared to submit, |and who were willing then and there to pledge themselves to live wholly to God; **who were** willing **then and there** to commit themselves to the sovereign mercy of God in Christ Jesus; who were willing **then and there** to give up all sin, to renounce it forever **in every form,**—to kneel down, **and not to expect that my prayers were going to save them; but when** I prayed to commit themselves to Christ, and inwardly to do what I exhorted them to do. I called on those only to kneel down who were willing to do what God required of them, and what I presented before them. Dr Greer looked very much surprized at the test I put, and the manner in which I pressed them to instant submission. **I was careful to discriminate, so that they should not kneel down unless they were entirely in earnest. I saw that the Spirit of God was pressing them so hard, that if I could make them understand exactly what God wanted them to do, many of them would no doubt be led by the Spirit of God to do it then and there.**

MS 515 |As soon as I saw that they thoroughly understood me I called on them to kneel, and knelt myself. Dr Greer knelt by my side, but said nothing. I presented the case in prayer to God, and held right to the point of now submitting, believing, and consecrating themselves to God. There was an awful solemnity pervading the congregation; and the stillness of death, with the exception of my own voice in prayer, and the sobs, and sighs, and weeping that were heard more or less throughout the congregation. After spreading the case before God **I** arose from **my knees, and they all arose.** Without saying anything farther I pronounced the blessing and dismissed them. Dr Greer took me cordially by the hand, and smiling said, "I will see you in the JHF 262 |morning." He went his way, and I went to my lodgings. At about eleven O'clock, I should judge, a messenger came running over to my lodgings, and MS 516 called me, and said that |Dr Greer was dead. I inquired what it meant. He said he had just retired, and was taken with a fit of apoplexy, and died immediately.[21] He was greatly respected and beloved by his people, and I am

[21] He died about 2:00 A.M., Tuesday, 27 January 1829. Samuel Baird, one of the elders, wrote a letter that day to Rev. E. S. Ely about Grier's death, in which he said:

> A few Sabbaths ago, while employed in prayer, he stated, in words to this effect, from the pulpit:—That could he but witness a revival of religion in this borough, he would be prepared joyfully to yield up his spirit, and exclaim, in the words of Simeon of old, "Lord, now lettest thou thy servant depart in peace, for mine eyes have seen thy salvation."
>
> About fifteen days ago, the Rev. Mr. Finney came on to Reading, to assist him in his ministerial labours, and by his powerful exhibition of divine truth, produced a great awakening in the minds of multitudes. An anxious meeting was held last evening in the session-house of our church, and appearances were so encouraging, that Dr. Grier returned from it full of holy joy and the most animated expectations, and declaring that he now verily believed the Spirit of God had come down among his people.
>
> He retired to bed at a late hour, slightly indisposed with a cold, but too slightly to excite any apprehensions. About two o'clock in the morning, his bereaved wife was awakened from her sleep, as she believes, by the sound of something unusual in his respiration. And before a light could be obtained, or a physician called, his spirit had winged its flight to eternity (letter sent for publication to the *Philadelphian* and copied into *WR,* 10 February 1829, p. 22, and other papers).

persuaded ‹he›[22] *deserved* to be. He was a man of thorough education, and I trust of earnest piety. But his theological education had not at all fitted him for the work of the ministry, that is to win souls to Christ. He was beside rather a timid man. He did not like to face his people, and resist the encroachments of sin as he needed to do. His sudden death was a great shock, and became the subject of constant conversation throughout the town. Although I found a goodly number had, to all human appearance, submitted at the meeting on Monday evening; still the death of Dr Greer, under such extraordinary circumstances, proved a **sad** diversion of the public mind for a week or more. |But after his funeral was over, and the usual evening services MS 517 got into their proper channel, the work took on a powerful type, and went forward in a most encouraging manner.

Many very interesting incidents occurred in this revival. I recollect on one very snowy **evening**, when the snow had already fallen deep, and was drifting in a terrible manner under a fierce gale of wind, I was called up about midnight to go and visit a man who, they informed me, was under such awful conviction that he could not live unless something could be done for him. The man's name was **Buck**.[23] He was a stalwart man, very muscular, a man of great force of will and strength of nerve, **and** physically a **proud** specimen of humanity. His wife was a professor of religion; but he had **been a Gallio, and** "cared for none of these things."[24] He had been **to** meeting that evening, and the sermon had |torn him to pieces. He went home in a terrible |state of MS 518 JHF 263 mind, his convictions and distress increasing till it overcame his bodily strength; and his family feared **that** he would die **unless something could be done for him**. Although it was in the midst of such a terrific storm, they dispatched a messenger for me. **I arose and prepared myself for the storm, and went into the street.** We had to face the storm, and walk perhaps fifty or sixty rods. I heard his moanings, **and perhaps I should almost say** howlings, before I got near the house.[25] When I entered I found him sitting on the floor, his wife, I believe, supporting his head,—and what a look on his face! It was indescribable. **Used** as I was to seeing persons under great convictions, I must confess that his appearance gave me a tremendous shock. He was writhing in agony, grinding his teeth, and literally gnawing his tongue for pain.[26] He cried out to me, "O Mr Finney! I am lost! I am a lost soul!" **and added several |things that still increased the shock upon my nerves. I** MS 519 **recollect exclaiming,** "If this is conviction, what is hell?" However I recovered myself as soon as I could, and sat down by **him and gave him instructions**. At first he found it difficult to attend; but I soon **got his attention** to the way of salvation through Christ. I pressed the Savior upon

[22] Finney added the word "he."

[23] This was Amos Buck. He was the first convert in Reading. See Louis Richards to Finney, 16 September 1872, Finney Papers, microfilm, roll 6.

[24] Acts 18:17. In another account of this incident Finney said, "He had a praying wife and praying sister, and they gathered their souls in the might of prayer close about him as a party of men would hem in a wild bull in a net" (*OE*, 14 September 1853, p. 146).

[25] In one account Finney is reported as saying, "While yet sixty rods from his house I heard his screams and wailings of woe." However, in another account in 1835 Finney is reported as giving a figure of twenty rods. See *OE*, 14 September 1853, p. 146; and *NYE*, 5 September 1835, p. 232.

[26] Finney added "drawing blood" in another account. See *OE*, 24 June 1846, p. 99.

his attention and upon his acceptance. His burden was soon removed. He was ‹persuaded›[27] to trust the Savior, and he came out free and joyful in hope.[28]

Of course from day to day I had my hands, my head, and my heart entirely full. I had no pastor to help me, and the work spread on every hand. The elder of the church to whom I have alluded as being one of the managers of their stated balls, soon broke down his heart before the Lord, and entered into the work; and as a consequence his family were soon converted.[29] The work made a thorough sweep in the families of those members of the church that entered into the work.[30]

MS 520 ǀI said that in this place a circumstance occurred that illustrated the fact of that Old School teaching of which I have complained. Very early ‹one›[31] morning a lawyer belonging to one of the most respectable families in the JHF 264 town, called at my room in the greatest agitation of mind.[32] ǀI saw he was a man of first-rate intelligence, and a gentleman; but I had nowhere seen him to know him. He came in and introduced himself, and said he was a lost sinner,—that he had made up his mind that there was no hope for him. He then informed me that when he was in Princeton college, he and two of his classmates became very anxious about their souls. They went together to Dr Ashbel Green, the then president of that college, and asked him what they should do to be saved.[33] He said the Doctor told them he was very glad to have them come and make the inquiry; and then told them to keep out of all

[27]Here Finney changed the word "enabled" to "persuaded."

[28]According to Louis Richards, "Mr Amos Buck died in Alabama in 1841, in his 60th year. He was an exemplary member of the M[ethodist] E[piscopal] Church" (Richards to Finney, 15 October 1872, Finney Papers, microfilm, roll 6).

[29]John McKnight's wife was named Ellen. Amelia Norton wrote to Mrs. Finney, "What a *lovely creature* she is"; and Finney remembered, "The McKnights were a lovely family." One of their sons was Col. C. B. McKnight, who was living in Reading when Louis Richards wrote to Finney, his father having died some years before (Amelia Norton to Lydia Finney, 4 July 1829; Ellen McKnight to Lydia Finney, 8 September 1829, Finney Papers, microfilm, roll 2; Richards to Finney, 3 September 1872, Finney Papers, microfilm, roll 6; and Finney to Richards, 6 September 1872, "Religious Revival in Reading," p. 149). John McKnight remarked to another elder, Elijah Deckert, "that he would go 5 miles on foot" to hear Finney preach (Deckert to Finney, 2 November 1829, Finney Papers, microfilm, roll 2).

[30]Finney wrote to Theodore Weld that the revival "is particularly powerful among the *men* and those of the higher class of society." The same points were made in reports of the revival, where it was stated that a majority of the converts were men (see *WR*, 24 February 1829, p. 30; 24 March 1829, p. 46; and *The Western Luminary* [Lexington, Ky.], 22 April 1829, p. 332). On the other hand, E. W. Gilbert was told by a student from Auburn Theological Seminary, who was an eyewitness, that the ratio of women to men converted, was nine to one. See Finney to Theodore Weld, 30 March 1829, in Weld-Grimke Papers, William L. Clements Library, University of Michigan; and Gilbert to Finney, 18 March 1829, Finney Papers, microfilm, roll 2.

[31]Finney wrote the word "one" in place of the words "in the" written down by Matson.

[32]This was Levi Bull Smith (d. 1880). He was a graduate of Princeton of the class of 1824. His sister was the wife of another lawyer in Reading, William Darling, and his wife was a niece of Amos Buck. See Finney to Louis Richards, 6 and 19 September 1872, "Religious Revival in Reading," pp. 149–50; Louis Richards to Finney, 16 September 1872, Finney Papers, microfilm, roll 6; and *General Catalogue of Princeton University, 1746–1906* (Princeton: published by the University, 1908), p. 137.

[33]Ashbel Green (1762–1848) was one of the most eminent ministers of the Old School Presbyterian church. He was president of Princeton from 1812 to 1822. Later he became editor of the *Christian Advocate* in Philadelphia and was critical of Finney's theology and measures. See *DAB*; and *Christian Advocate* (Philadelphia), n.s., 5 (December 1827): 553–68; and n.s., 6 (January 1828): 29–36.

bad company, to read their Bible statedly, and to pray God to give them a new heart. [MS 521] |"Continue this," he **says,** "and press forward in duty, and the Spirit of God will convert you; or else he will leave you, and you will return back to your sins again." "Well," I inquired, "how did it terminate?" "O," said he, "we did just as he told us to do. We kept out of bad company, and prayed that God would make us a new heart. But after a little while our convictions wore away, and we did not care to pray any longer." "We lost all interest in the subject," **said he;** and then bursting into tears**,** "My two companions," **said he,** "are in drunkards' graves, and if I cannot repent I shall soon be in one myself."[34] This remark led me to observe that he had indications of being a man that made too free use of ardent spirits. However this was early in the morning; and he was entirely free from drink; and in terrible anxiety about his soul.[35] I tried to instruct him, and to show him the error that he had fallen into under such instructions as he had received; ‹**&**›[36] that he had resisted and grieved [MS 522] |the Spirit by waiting for God to do what **He** had commanded *him* to do. I tried to show him that in the very nature of the case God could not do for him what he required him to do. God required him to repent, and God could not repent *for* him; required him to believe, but God could not believe for him; God required him to submit, but could not submit for him.[37] I then tried [JHF 265] |to make him understand the agency that the Spirit of God has in giving the sinner repentance and a new heart. That it **was** a divine **moral** persuasion. That the Spirit **led** him to see his sins, urged him to give them up, **made him see his guilt and his danger, and urged him** to flee from the wrath to come. He presents to him the Savior, the atonement **and** plan of salvation, and urges him to accept it. I asked him if he did not feel this urgency upon himself, in these truths revealed in his own mind; and **an urgent** call now to submit, to believe, to make himself a new heart. "O yes!," he said, "O yes! I see [MS 523] |and feel all this. But am I not given up of God? Is not my day of grace past?" I said to him, "No! It is plain that the Spirit of God is still calling you, **still convicting you,**[38] still urging you to repentance. **Y**ou acknowledge that you feel this urgency in your own mind." He inquired: "Is this, then, what the Spirit of God is doing, to show me all this?" I assured him

[34]The Princeton College *Catalogue* gives the names of two of Smith's classmates who had died before this time: Johnson Clarke in 1825 and George Washington Baker in 1826. A third, James Lawrence Boggs, died some time in 1828. See *General Catalogue of Princeton University,* p. 136.

[35]In his instructions to Christians on how to approach "careless sinners," Finney advised: "Be sure that the person is perfectly sober. . . . If they have been drinking beer, or cider, or wine, so that you can smell their breath, you may know there is but little chance of producing any effect on them" (*NYE,* 7 February 1835, p. 21).

[36]An ink blot on the paper nearly obscured the word "and," so another *&* was inserted by Finney.

[37]In another account of this incident Finney is reported as saying:

> I told him, ["]your president was probably a good man, but he taught you just what the devil wished you to be taught. Instead of at once accepting Christ, believing the truth, breaking down before him, he set you to read the Bible and to pray, thus throwing all the responsibility upon God. You were waiting for God to convert you without your co-operation. That was just what the devil wanted." "Oh! I see it!" said he, "I see it!" (sermon of 28 August 1850 in *The Penny Pulpit* [London] 1,570 [July–September 1850]: 198).

[38]The words "still convicting you" were not crossed out in the manuscript but do not appear in the published version.

that it was; and that he was to understand this as a divine call, and as evidence conclusive that he was not abandoned, and had not sinned away the day of grace, but that God was striving to save him still. I then asked him if he would respond to the call, if he would come to Jesus; if he would lay hold upon eternal life then and there. He was an intelligent man, and the Spirit of God was upon and teaching him, and making him understand every word that I said. When I saw that the way was fully prepared, I called on him to kneel down and submit; and he did so, and to all human appearance became a

MS 524 thorough convert right upon the spot.[39] ¦"Oh!" he afterwards said, "if Dr. Green had only told us this that you have told me, **if we had only had right instruction,** we should all have been converted immediately. But my friends and companions are lost; and what a wonder of mercy it is that I am saved!"

Now this instruction of Dr Green, in substance, has been given by thousands of ministers to inquiring sinners for scores and scores of years past; and is still in substance the instruction that is given by many of the leading ministers in the church of God of all denominations. I do regard it as utterly erroneous; and I fear that it has been instrumental in ruining hundreds of thousands of souls.

I recollect a very interesting incident in the case of a merchant in Reading, **who was a very respectable man, and** one branch of whose business was the making of whiskey. He had just been fitting up a very large distillery at a good deal of expense. He had constructed it with all the **modern** improvements,

MS 525
JHF 266 ¦on a large ¦scale, and was going deeply into the business. But as soon as he was converted he gave up all thought of going any farther with that **branch of** business. It was a spontaneous conclusion of his own mind. He said at once, "I shall have nothing to do with that. I shall tear my distillery down. I will neither work it, nor sell it to be worked." His wife was a good woman, and a sister to **the Mr. Buck,** whose conversion I have mentioned on that stormy night. The merchant's name was **O'Brien.**[40] The revival took a powerful hold in his family, and several of them were converted. I do not recollect now how many there were; but I think every impenitent person in his household was converted. His brother also, and his brother's wife—and I know not how many, but quite a large circle of relatives—were among the converts.[41] But Mr. O'**Brien** himself was in feeble health, and was rapidly **hurried out of this**

MS 526 **world** with the consumption.[42] I visited him frequently, ¦and found him full

[39]Louis Richards wrote in 1872 that Levi Smith had been for many years a pious member of the Protestant Episcopal church. His daughter became the second wife of Rev. Elias J. Richards, a Finney convert from Utica, who subsequently became a minister of the church in Reading. See Louis Richards to Finney, 13 August and 15 October 1872, Finney Papers, microfilm, roll 6.

[40]This was Dennis O'Brien. His wife was Nancy O'Brien. See Louis Richards to Finney, 15 October 1872, Finney Papers, microfilm, roll 6; and letters from her to Lydia Finney in the Finney Papers.

[41]His brother was Thomas O'Brien. Louis Richards wrote to Finney:

> Thomas O'Brien remembers that on the evening on which he experienced a hope, after church you walked up the street with him arm in arm, and he felt so glad that he had met his Savior that he wanted to tell everybody about it. The argument which took hold of him, he said, was that Christ had always been willing to save him, but that the unwillingness was all on his own part (Richards to Finney, 16 September 1872, Finney Papers, microfilm, roll 6).

[42]He died "of pulmonary consumption" on Sunday, 12 April 1829. See *The Berks and Schuylkill Journal,* 18 April 1829, p. 3.

of joy. We had been examining candidates for admission to the church, and ‹a›[43] large number were to be admitted on a certain Sabbath; **and** among the **rest** those members of his own family, and those relatives of his that had been converted. Sabbath morning came. It was soon found **that** Mr. O'Brien could not live through the day. He called his wife to his bed-side and said to her, "My dear, I am going to spend the Sabbath in heaven. Let all the family go, and all the friends, and unite with the church below; and I will join the church above.["] Before meeting time he was dead. Friends were called in to lay him in his shroud. **His** family and relatives gathered around his corpse, and then turned away and came to meeting; and, as he had desired, united with the church militant while he went to unite with the church triumphant. **This was a most affecting scene, and a moving fact to mention at the communion table.** Their pastor had but just gone |before; and I think it was that morning I had said to Mr. O'**Brien** , "Give my love to **B**rother Greer when you get to heaven."[44] He smiled |with holy joy and said to me, "Do you think I shall know him?" I said, ["]Yes, undoubtedly you will know him. Give him my love, and tell him the work is going on gloriously." "I will, I will," said he. **I do not recollect the number of his family and relatives that united that day; but they were a goodly number.** His wife sat at the communion table, **and manifested in** her countenance **such** mingled joy and sorrow **as might be expected on an occasion like that**. There was a kind of holy triumph manifested **by his relatives and friends** as their attention was called to the fact that the husband, and father, and brother, and friend, was sitting that day at the table of Jesus on high, while they were gathered around his table on earth.

MS 527

JHF 267

There was much that was moving and interesting in that revival in a great many respects. It was among a population that had had no conception of |revivals of religion. The German population supposed themselves to have been made Christians by baptism, and especially by receiving **their** communion. Nearly every one of them, if asked when they became Christians, would reply that they took their communion of Dr **Muhlenberg**, or some other German divine, **at such a time**.[45] And when I asked them if they thought that was religion, they would say, **Y**es, they supposed it was. Indeed that was the idea of Dr **Muhlenberg** himself. In walking with him to the grave of Dr Greer, on the occasion of his funeral, he told me he had made sixteen

MS 528

[43]Finney inserted the word "a."

[44]This was one of a number of things that Finney said that shocked the local people. He was accused in the press of using irreverent language, praying for people by name in public, telling a woman she would go to hell, speaking disrespectfully of other pastors, encouraging children to disobey their parents, and encouraging women to evangelize their neighbors in a way that was considered insulting. See letter to the "Elders of the Presbyterian Church," signed by "Luther" in *The Berks and Schuylkill Journal,* 18 April 1829, p. 3; see also Charles Yrigoyen, Jr., "The Second Great Awakening and Finney's Revival in Reading," *Historical Review of Berks County* 38 (Spring 1973): 65–73.

[45]Henry Augustus Philip Muhlenberg (1782–1844) had gone to Reading in 1803 as minister of Trinity Lutheran Church, where he became a successful and prominent minister. In 1828 ill health caused his resignation, but he continued to preach to his congregation until March 1829, when his successor, Jacob Miller, was installed. He was then elected to Congress and became a distinguished Democratic politician, being appointed the first American minister to Austria in 1838. He died during the 1844 campaign to elect him as governor of Pennsylvania (see *DAB*).

hundred Christians by baptism and giving them the communion since he had been pastor of that church. He seemed himself to have no other idea of ‹becoming›[46] a Christian than simply to learn the catechism, and to be baptized and partake of the communion. The revival had to **struggle with** that view of things; and **at Reading** the influence was at first almost altogether in that direction. It was held, as I was informed,—and I have no MS 529 doubt of it—that ˡfor them to begin to think of being religious by being converted, and to establish family prayer, or to give themselves to secret prayer, was not only fanaticism, but was virtually saying that their ancestors had all gone to hell, for they had done no such thing. The German ministers JHF 268 would ˡpreach against all those things, as I was informed by those that heard them, and speak severely of those that forsook the ways of their fathers, and thought it necessary to be converted, and to maintain family and secret prayer.[47]

[46]Here Finney changed the word "being" to "becoming."

[47]In another account of this situation Finney is reported as saying:

> I have frequently been told, when labouring amongst them—"Oh! I'm a Christian already." "Are you indeed? Who made you a Christian?" "Dr. Millenberg," was the reply in one case. "Well, but do you call that religion?" I have asked, "Oh, yes, that is *our* religion." Now, every drunkard I met in the streets had been to the communion, said his catechism, learned his lesson, and been received into the bosom of the church. So fatal and deep was their prejudice that it was astounding to see the masses in such a position. Their minister, for instance, would make such appeals to them as this, if there was any great revivals of religion in the neighborhood—"Why do you go to hear such preaching as that? If you embrace that religion you will turn against your fathers, and you may as well say your fathers are gone to hell! Did they pray and do such and such things? Did they tell their religious 'experience,' and how they were 'converted?' Will you turn against your fathers, give them all up, and proclaim by your conduct that they are all gone to hell?" In this way they were harangued from Sabbath to Sabbath (sermon of 5 January 1851 in *The Penny Pulpit* 1,969 [16 October 1852]: 95).

The low state of religion attributed by Finney to the Lutherans was shared to some extent by the German Reformed church. Both traditions of the German-speaking churches were largely antagonistic to the new revival measures. In 1842 German Reformed theologian John Williamson Nevin described his church as it had been earlier:

> By many the church was neglected altogether except on a few sacramental or other solemn occasions, which were supposed sufficient to make up for all ordinary neglect of ordinances. . . . Confirmation was looked upon as a privilege to which all were entitled at a certain age, on the condition of a mere outward preparation in the way of learning the catechism. Great value was attached to it as the seal and certificate of membership in the Church, although in most cases it had little force subsequently as a bond upon the soul in favor of righteousness. To be confirmed and then to take the sacrament occasionally, was counted by multitudes all that was necessary to make one a good christian, if only a tolerable decency of outward life were maintained besides, without any regard at all to the religion of the heart. True serious piety indeed was too often treated with open and marked scorn. In the bosom of the Church itself, it was stigmatized as *Schwaermerei Kopfhaengerei*, or miserable drivelling methodism. The idea of the new birth was considered a pietistic whimry. Experimental religion, in all its forms, was eschewed as a new fangled invention of cunning imposters, brought in to turn the heads of the weak and to lead captive silly women. Prayer meetings were held to be a spiritual abomination. Family worship was a species of saintly affectation, barely tolerable in the case of ministers, (tho' many of *them* also gloried rather in having no alter in their houses,) but absolutely disgraceful for common christians. To show an awakened concern on the subject of religion, a disposition to call upon God in daily secret prayer, was to incur certain reproach. . . .

The great majority, I think, of Dr Greer's congregation were converted ‹in this revival.›[48] At first I had considerable difficulty in getting rid of the influence of the *daily press*. I think there were two or more daily newspapers published there at the time.[49] I learned that the editors were drinking men, and were not infrequently carried home, on public occasions, in a state of intoxication. The people were a good deal under the influence of the daily press,—I mean the German population particularly.[50] These editors began to give the |people religious advice, and to speak against the revival, and the preaching, **etc**.[51] This threw the people into a state of perplexity. It went on from day to day, and from week to week, till finally the state of things became such that I thought it my duty to notice it. I therefore went into the pulpit when the house was crowded **to its utmost capacity**,[52] and took for my text: "Ye are of your father the devil, and the lusts of your father ye will do."[53] I then went on to show in what way sinners would fulfil the desires of the devil, pointing out a great many ways in which they would **do** his dirty work, and do for him what he could not do for himself. After I had got**ten** the subject well before the people, I applied it to the course pursued by the editors of those daily papers. I asked the people if they did not think that those editors were fulfilling the desires of the devil—if they did not believe the devil desired them to do just what they did. I then asked them if it was suitable and decent for men of their character to attempt to give religious instruction to the people. I told the people what I under|stood their character to be, **that they were often carried home from places of public debauch in a state of intoxication;** and I turned my hand upon them pretty heavily, that such men

MS 530

MS 531

The picture, it must be acknowledged, is dark; but not more so than the truth of history would seem to require. It must be taken indeed only in a general way (*Weekly Messenger* [Chambersburg, Pa.], 10 August 1842, pp. 1433–34).

[48]Finney added the words "in this revival."

[49]There were no daily papers published in Reading at this time; all were weeklies. The oldest weekly was *The Berks and Schuylkill Journal*, a Whig newspaper. *The Chronicle of Times* was the other English paper. There were also two German papers, *Der Readinger Adler* and *Der Readinger Democrat*.

[50]George Getz was the editor of *The Berks and Schuylkill Journal* (see Louis Richards to Finney, 16 September 1872, Finney Papers, microfilm, roll 6). *Der Readinger Adler* was edited at this time by the eminent German economist Georg Friederich List (1789–1846). He edited the paper from the summer of 1826 until 1830, and he was responsible for making it one of the most influential papers in Pennsylvania and a powerful organ of the Democratic party. It was popularly styled "the Berks County Bible." See William Notz, "Frederick List in America," *American Economic Review* 16, no. 2 (June 1926): 249–65.

[51]According to Finney: "Hundreds of false & absurd stories were put in circulation about me," and articles appeared in the *Chronicle* and *Journal* denouncing him. One report, in particular, had national coverage. When the election took place in mid-March for the office of town constable, a number of people voted for Finney in derision. As a result it was widely reported in the papers that he had been elected. There was so much malicious gossip in the community that the elders of the Presbyterian church found it necessary to come to his defense in a statement in the *Journal*. See Finney to Richards, 6 and 19 September 1872, "Religious Revival in Reading," p. 149; *The Chronicle of Times* (Reading), 24 March 1829, p. 2; 31 March 1829, p. 3; *The Berks and Schuylkill Journal*, 4 April 1829, p. 3; 18 April 1829, p. 3; *Gospel Herald and Universalist Review* (New York), 25 April 1829, p. 137; 20 June 1829, p. 201; and 21 November 1829, p. 380; *Trumpet and Universalist Magazine* (Boston), 23 May 1829, p. 186; and Yrigoyen, "Second Great Awakening."

[52]The words "to its utmost capacity" were not crossed out in the manuscript but do not appear in the published version.

[53]John 8:44.

should attempt to instruct the people in regard to their duties to God, and their ‹neighbors.›[54] I said if I had a family in the place I would not have such JHF 269 ꜝa paper in the house, I should fear to have it under my roof; **that** I should consider it too filthy to be touched with my fingers, and would take the tongs and throw it into the street. **As I learned, that** in some way **their** papers got into the street the next morning pretty plentifully. I neither saw nor heard any more of their opposition. **The daily press was from that time, I believe, entirely silent, and the work went on.** I continued in Reading until late in the Spring. **I do not know the number of converts; for, as I have said, I never was in the habit of counting or publishing the number of converts.** There were many very striking conversions; and so far as I know Dr Greer's congregation was left entirely united, greatly encouraged and strengthened, and with large additions made to their number. I have never been in that place since.

MS 532 ꜝFrom Reading I went to Lancaster, Pa., **then and** ‹until his death› the home of the late president Buchanan.[55] The presbyterian church at Lancaster had no pastor, and I found religion in a very low state.[56] They had never had a revival of religion, and manifestly had no just conception of what it was, or of the appropriate means of securing it. I remained at Lancaster but a very short time. However the work of God was immediately revived, the Spirit of God being poured out almost at once upon the people. I was the guest of an aged gentleman by the name of **Kirkpatrick**, who was one of the elders of the church, and indeed the leading **and most influential** man in the church.[57] **He**

[54]Matson had written "religious duties" here, but Finney changed it to "neighbors."

[55]Finney was at Lancaster from 7 May until 15 June 1829. See Finney to Louis Richards, 19 September 1872, "Religious Revival in Reading," p. 149.

James Buchanan (1791–1868) was the fifteenth president of the United States, from 1857 to 1861. At the time Finney was in Lancaster, Buchanan was a wealthy lawyer and congressman, who had just played a prominent part in getting President Jackson into the White House. He lived in Lancaster until 1849, when he purchased Wheatland, a country estate nearby (see Philip S. Klein, *President James Buchanan* [Philadelphia: Pennsylvania State University Press, 1962]). Matson had written down, "then and now the home of the late president Buchanan." But Buchanan died on 1 June 1868, and when Finney came to revise the manuscript he had to change it to "then and until his death," etc.

[56]The church had a membership of 116 with 300 to 500 worshiping on a Sunday morning. But the previous pastor, Rev. William Ashmead (1798–1829), had just left in April. His health had been poor for two or three years, with hemorrhage of the lungs, and he had been away recuperating the previous winter. There was no prospect of a replacement for him, which was the reason why the church approached Finney for help. See William Kirkpatrick to Finney, 15 April 1829, Finney Papers, microfilm, roll 2; and "Memoir of the Rev. William Ashmead," *Christian Advocate* 8 (January 1830): 13–16.

E. W. Gilbert wrote to Finney: "They are a people indifferent to all religion—, & I have understood from a member of Pby. have had thoughts of shutting up their church for a year at least!" (Gilbert to Finney, 29 April 1829, Finney Papers, microfilm, roll 2 [dated 22 April 1829 in the calendar of the Finney Papers]). James Patterson's opinion of the place was, "It is a hard field to cultivate & I fear Mr. Ashmead has not been plain enough & honest enough & faithful enough for that people" (Patterson to Finney, 14 May 1829, Finney Papers, microfilm, roll 2 [dated 12 May 1829 in the calendar of the Finney Papers]). Finney himself reckoned that he was in "a cold, desolate region in the land of moral darkness" (Milton Brayton to Finney, 27 May 1829, Finney Papers, microfilm, roll 2).

[57]William Kirkpatrick (1759–1838) was in the mercantile business and was prominent as a philanthropist. He lived in Lancaster for nearly forty years. See William F. Worner, "Society for the Promotion of Industry and Prevention of Pauperism," in *Papers Read Before the Lancaster*

was a very wealthy man, and in point of influence stood head and shoulders above any member of the church. A fact occurred in relation to him while I was in his family that revealed the real state of things in a religious point of view in that church. A former pastor of the church invited Mr. **Kirkpatrick** to join ‹and› **to** hold the office of elder.[58] I should say that the facts I am about to communicate respecting |this event, were related to me by himself. One Sabbath evening after hearing a couple of very searching sermons, the old gentleman could not sleep. He was so greatly exercised in his mind that he could not endure it until morning. He called me up in the middle of the night, stated what his convictions were, and then said that he knew he had never been converted. He said that |when he was requested to join the church and become an elder, he knew that he was not a converted man. But the subject was pressed upon his **attention** till he consulted Rev. Dr **Cathcart**, an aged minister of a presbyterian church not far from Lancaster,[59] **and** stated to him the fact that he had never been converted, and yet that he was desired to join the church that he might become an elder. Dr **Cathcart**, in view of all the circumstances, advised him to join and accept the office,—which he did. His convictions at the time I speak of were very deep. I gave him such instructions as I thought he needed, pressed him to **immediately** accept the Savior, and dealt with him just as I would with |any other inquiring sinner. It was a very solemn time. He professed at the time to submit and accept the Savior. Of his subsequent history I know nothing. He was certainly a gentleman of high character, and never to my knowledge did anything outwardly to disgrace the position which he held.[60] Those who are

MS 533

JHF 270

MS 534

County Historical Society 35, no. 6 (1931): 130–31; and information from Lancaster County Historical Society.

[58] Here Matson had written down, "A former pastor of the church finding in the church no male member suitable to hold the office of elder, invited Mr. Kirkpatrick to join." This was altered by Finney.

According to an obituary of William Kirkpatrick, he had become an elder more than thirty years before his death. The minister at Lancaster at that time was Rev. Nathaniel Welshard Semple (1752–1834). He was minister from 1781 for forty years and was succeeded by William Ashmead in 1821. See *NYE,* 27 October 1838, p. 171; and Catherine Courtney and John D. Long, "A History of First Presbyterian Church of Lancaster, Pennsylvania," *Journal of the Lancaster County Historical Society* 90, no. 1 (Hillarymas 1986): 15–18.

[59] Robert Cathcart (1759–1849) was born in Ireland and educated in Glasgow. He came to America in 1790. He was minister of the Presbyterian church in York, Pennsylvania, from 1793 until he resigned in 1837. See Robert M. Patterson, *Historical Sketch of the Synod of Philadelphia* (Philadelphia: Presbyterian Board of Publication, 1876), pp. 83–84; and *NYE,* 13 May 1837, p. 80.

[60] His obituary states:

> He also served the church both as a Trustee and its Treasurer. His place in the house of God and in the meetings for prayer was seldom vacant. The church always found him ready to aid with his purse in her pecuniary difficulties, and at all times a liberal supporter of the gospel. The various benevolent and religious societies, to whose funds he was a constant and large contributor, will greatly feel his loss. Having been entrusted with a considerable portion of this world's goods, as a faithful steward he dispensed them freely and judiciously. No real object of charity ever applied in vain for aid, if he knew it to be such. His house was the home of hospitality. Many of the public as well as private servants of Christ, will look back with pleasure to the kind and affectionate treatment they received from this aged disciple. The poor around him will mourn the loss of their favorite place of resort; and the church, one of its most staunch pillars. . . . He indulged no very strong confidence, but an humble, and often

acquainted with the state of the church of which Dr **Cathcart** was pastor in regard to eldership at that time, will not wonder at the advice which he gave to Mr. **Kirkpatrick**.

Some very striking[61] **things** occurred during my short stay at Lancaster. **Among others I will mention this.** One evening I preached on a subject that led me to insist **as thoroughly as I could** upon the immediate acceptance of Christ. The house was very much crowded, literally packed. At the close of my sermon I made a strong appeal to the people to decide **then and there**; and I think I called on those whose minds were made up, and who would then accept the Savior, to rise up, that we might know who they were, and that we might make them subjects of prayer. As I learned the next day, MS 535 there were **a couple of** men **who were acquainted with** |**each other,** sitting near one of the doors of the church. **One of them** was very much affected under the appeal that was made, and could not avoid manifesting very strong emotion, which was observed by his neighbor. However, the man did not rise JHF 271 up, nor give his heart to God. I had pressed **this** thought upon |them **with all my might**, that that might be the last opportunity that some of them would ever have to meet and decide this question. **That** in so large a congregation it was not unlikely that there were those there who would then decide their everlasting destiny one way or the other. It was not unlikely that God would hold some of them to the decision that they then **and there** made, **to all eternity**. After the meeting was dismissed, as I learned the next day, the two men **of whom I have spoken** went out together, and one said to the other, "I saw you felt very deeply under the appeals Mr. Finney made." "I did," he replied. "I never felt so before in my life; and especially when he reminded us that that might be the last time we should ever have an opportunity to accept MS 536 the offer of mercy." |They went on conversing in this way for some distance, and then separated, each one going to his own home. It was a dark night, and the one who had felt so deeply, and so pressed with the conviction that he might then be rejecting his last offer, fell over the curbstone and broke his neck, **thus making it plain that it was in fact his last offer**. This was reported to me the next day **after it occurred**. I established prayer-meetings in Lancaster, and insisted upon the elders of the church taking part in them.[62] This they did at my earnest request, although, as I learned, they had never been accustomed to do it before. The interest seemed to increase from day to day, ‹**&**›[63] hopeful conversions multiplied. I do not recollect now why I did not remain longer than I did; but I left at so early a period as not to be able to give anything like a detailed account of the work there.[64]

humbling hope. Yet no one acquainted with his life can doubt that he was a sincere and devoted Christian (*NYE*, 27 October 1838, p. 171).

[61] The word "striking" was altered in pencil, probably by Fairchild, to "startling." He later crossed out the phrase.

[62] There were five elders of the church. See William Kirkpatrick to Finney, 15 April 1829, Finney Papers, microfilm, roll 2.

[63] The word "and" was originally written here but was covered by some spilled ink. Since the original word could no longer easily be read, Finney added the symbol *&*.

[64] The following section after this, at the bottom of the page, was crossed out by Finney when he started a new chapter on the next page: "From Lancaster, about midsummer, I should think I returned to Oneida County, and spent a short time at my father-in law's. I think it was at."

CHAPTER XX

MS 537
JHF 272

‹Revivals in Columbia and New York City›

‹From[1] Lancaster, about mid-summer, I returned to Oneida County N. York, & spent a short time at my father-in-law's.[2] I think it was at›[3] that time during my stay in Whitestown,[4] that a circumstance occurred **which has been one** of great interest **to me**, and which I will relate. A messenger came from the town of Columbia in Herkimer County, requesting me to go down and assist in a work of grace there which was already commenced. Such representations were made to me as induce‹d›[5] me to go. However I did not expect **when I went** to remain there, as I had other ‹& more pressing calls for labor›.[6] I went down, however, to see, and to lend such aid as I was able for a short time.[7] ‹At Columbia was a large german Church the membership

[1] Pages 537–43 were originally numbered 383–89, then 515–21 by Matson, and changed to 537–43 by Finney. The chapter heading and first three lines of page 537 down to n. 3 are in Finney's handwriting on a separate piece of paper pasted onto the top of the sheet. This strip of paper projects above the page, lengthening it by an inch. It obscures the original page numbers written by Matson.

[2] The date "1830" was inserted after "mid-summer" by Fairchild but is not correct. Finney left Lancaster with his wife and daughter on 15 June 1829 (see Finney to Louis Richards, 19 September 1872, in "A Religious Revival in Reading, 1829," *Historical Review of Berks County* 15 [October 1949]: 149). On the way, they spent some time in Troy, where Finney preached. Then they went to Albany for some weeks in July. Finney assisted the Reverend Edward N. Kirk, pastor of the newly organized Fourth Presbyterian Church. Mrs. Finney was back in Whitesboro on 1 August, but Finney went up "North," so he was possibly visiting his parents in Henderson. See letters to Finney from Joab Seeley, 9 July 1829; Thomas Kendall, 12 July 1829; E. N. Kirk, 29 July 1829; Oliver Smith, 12 October 1829; and to Lydia Finney from Catherine Huntington, 1 August 1829; and Charlotte Bliss, 15 August 1829, Finney Papers, microfilm, roll 2.

[3] This ends the section in Finney's handwriting.

[4] Here Matson had written down, "Whitesboro," but he changed it to "Whitestown." Mrs. Finney's parents lived in Whitesboro, which was a village in the township of Whitestown. See David M. Ellis, "Whitestown: From Yankee Outpost to Cradle of Reform," *New York History* 65, no. 1 (January 1984): 32–59.

[5] Here Matson had written "to induce," but Finney altered it to "induced."

[6] Here Matson had written "as I had other places in my mind," but Finney altered it.

[7] The section that follows to n. 9 is in Finney's handwriting on a separate piece of paper pasted onto the bottom of the page. It leaves exposed the first part of a section that Finney crossed out. It reads, "Columbia was a large farming town, where there was a German church; the membe‹rs of› which had been originally received, not upon examination of their Christian faith and conversion to Christ, but upon." An ink blot in the middle of this section had obscured some letters, so Finney reinserted them. The section covered up by the pasted strip of paper continues, "condition that they learned their catechism and complied with certain rules of the church, where upon they were received of course, consequently the church had been made up almost altogether of unconverted members. Still nearly all the adult population were members of the church; and both church and congregation for a country place were very large."

of which had been rec^d[8] according to their custom, upon examination of their *doctrinal knowledge* instead of their christian experience. Consequently the church had been composed mostly, as I was informed, of unconverted persons. Both the church & the congregation were large.›[9] Their p[**astor was** MS 538 **a**] young man |by the name of **Hongin**.[10] He was of German descent, ‹**&**›[11] from Pensylvania.

He gave me th‹e following› account[12] of himself and of the state of things in Columbia. He said he studied theology with a German Doctor of divinity at the place where he lived, who did not encourage experimental religion at all. He said that one of his fellow students was religiously inclined, and used to pray in his closet. Their teacher, **the old Doctor, mistrusted** this, and in some way came to a knowledge of the fact. **The old Doctor warned him** JHF 273 against it, as a very dan|gerous practice, and said he would become insane if he **pursued such a course**,[13] and he should be blamed himself for allowing a student to take such a course. Mr. **Hongin** said that he himself had no religion. He had joined the church in the common way **in which they joined those churches at that time;** and had no thought that anything else was requisite, so far as piety was concerned, to become a minister. But his mother was a pious woman. She knew better, and was greatly distressed **in mind** that MS 539 a son of hers should enter the sacred ministry who had |never been converted. When he had received a call to the church in Columbia and was about to leave home, his mother had a very serious talk with him, impressed upon him the fact of his responsibility, and said some **very pungent** things that bore upon his conscience. He said that this conversation of his mother he could not get rid of; that it bore upon his mind heavily, and his convictions of sin deepened until he was nearly in despair. This continued for many months. He had no one to consult, and **therefore he** did not open his mind to anybody. But after a severe and protracted struggle he was converted, came into the light, saw where he was and where he had been, and saw the condition of his church and of all those churches which had admitted their members in the way in which he had been admitted. His wife was unconverted. He immediately gave himself to labor for her conversion, and under God he soon secured it. His soul was full of the subject; and he read his Bible, and prayed and preached MS 540 with all his might. But he was a young convert, and had had |no instruction such as he needed, and he felt at a loss what to do. He rode about the town and conversed with the elders of the church and with the principal members, and satisfied himself that one or two of his leading elders, and several of his female members, knew what it was to be converted. After much prayer and

[8]That is, "received."

[9]This ends the section in Finney's handwriting on the pasted strip. The line of writing that follows is at the bottom of the original sheet. This has been torn, and part is missing, but Fairchild had rewritten the line above the tears.

[10]Jacob W. Hangen (1805–1843) was the minister at Columbia and Warren until 1832, when he went to Mapletown and Currytown. See Edward T. Corwin, *A Manual of the Reformed Church in America, 1628–1878*, 3d ed. (New York: Reformed Church in America, 1879), p. 585.

[11]Finney inserted the symbol *&* here.

[12]Finney changed the word "this" to "the following."

[13]The words "pursued such a course" were not changed in the manuscript but appear as "persisted in it" in the published version.

consideration he made up his mind what to do. On the Sabbath he gave them notice that there would be a meeting of the church on a certain day |during the week for the transaction of business, and wished all the church especially to be present. His own conversion, and preaching, and visiting, and conversing around the town had already created a good deal of excitement, so that religion came to be the common topic of conversation; and his call for a church-meeting was responded to, so that **when they met** on the day appointed the church were nearly all present. He then addressed them in regard to the real state of the church, and the error **that** had **been** fallen into in regard to the conditions on which members had been received. |He made a speech to them, partly in German and partly in English, so as to have all classes understand as far as he could; and after talking until they were a good deal **excited** he **then** proposed to disband the church and form a new one, insisting upon it that this was essential to the prosperity of religion. He had an understanding with those members of the church that he was satisfied were truly converted, that they should lead in voting for the disbanding of the church. **I do not know but one of them made the motion and the others seconded it. At any rate,** the motion was put, whereupon the converted members arose as requested. They were very influential members **of the church**, and the people looking around and seeing these on their feet, rose up, and finally they kept rising till the vote was nearly or quite unanimous. **He** then said: "There is now no church in Columbia; and we propose to form one of Christians, of people who have been converted." He then before the congregation related his own experience; and called on his wife, and she did the same. |Then the converted elders and members followed one after another, as long as any could come forward and relate a Christian experience. These they proceeded to form into a church. He then said to the others: "Your church relations are dissolved. You are out in the world; and until you are converted and in the church you cannot have your children baptized, and you cannot partake of the ordinances of the church.["] This created a great panic; for according to their views it was an awful thing not to partake of the |sacrament, and not to have their children baptized, for this was the way in which they themselves had been made Christians. Mr. **Hongin** then labored with all his might. He visited, and preached, and prayed, and held meetings, and the interest increased.[14] Thus **it** had been going on for sometime when he heard that I was in Oneida County, and sent the messenger for me. I found him a warm-hearted young convert. He listened to my preaching with almost irrepressible joy. I found the congregation **very**[15] large and interested; and |so far as I could judge, the work was in a very prosperous, healthful state. That revival continued to spread until it reached and converted nearly all the inhabitants of the town. Galesburg in Illinois was settled **with** a colony from Columbia, who were nearly, **if not quite,** all converts, I believe, of **that**

JHF 274

MS 541

MS 542

JHF 275

MS 543

[14] *The Western Recorder* reported: "We learn that a powerful work of grace has been in progress since November last in Columbia, Herkimer county, and is now more powerful than ever. Converts aged from 11 to 80 years—infidels whose race was nearly run—have been brought to the foot of the cross" (31 March 1829, p. 50).

[15] The word "very" was not crossed out by Fairchild but does not appear in the published version.

revival.[16] I have told facts as I remember them as related to me by Mr. Hongin. I found his views evangelical and his heart warm; and he was surrounded by a congregation as thoroughly interested in religion as could well be desired. They would hang on my lips as I held forth to them the Gospel of Christ, with an interest, an attention, and a patience, that was in the highest degree interesting and affecting. Mr. Hongin himself was like a little child. He was as teachable, and humble, and earnest a young convert as ever I saw. That work continued for over a year, as I understood, spreading, and spreading throughout that large and interesting population of farmers.

MS 544 After I returned to Whitestown I was invited to visit ˈthe[17] city of New York.[18] Pains had been taken, as I afterwards learned, to prevent my going to the city of New York. Under the influence partly of Mr. Nettleton, as I was informed, an understanding had been entered into by the Presbyterian ministers not to invite me to their churches.[19] I

[16] Fairchild had inserted here: "The founder of the colony & of Knox College, located there, was Mr. Gale, my former pastor at Adams." Galesburg was started as a Christian colony in 1836 through the efforts of Gale, after whom it was named. It was the result of his experience at Oneida Institute and his dream of spreading manual labor colleges as centers of Christian reform throughout the West. Knox College, which he founded there in 1837, was a continuation of the movement that had produced the Oneida Institute, Lane Theological Seminary in Cincinnati, and the Oberlin Collegiate Institute. Gale himself visited Oberlin in the fall of 1835 to learn about operations there before moving to Illinois. See Hermann R. Muelder, *Fighters for Freedom* (New York: Columbia University Press, 1959); and E. E. Calkins, *They Broke the Prairie* (New York: Scribner, 1937), p. 60.

Gale lists many of the early colonists and where they came from in *A Brief History of Knox College*. Although most of them were from the area surrounding Oneida County, only one, Isaac Mills, is listed as coming specifically from Columbia. He went out in 1836, among a group of thirty-seven of the earliest settlers, in a converted canal boat. Gale wrote:

> Col. Isaac Mills, a farmer of Columbia, Herkimer County, N.Y., was with his family converted to Christ from Universalism in the great revivals of 1825–6. He was a liberal and holy man, also an elder in the church. He left every comfort of life in the hope of doing more good in this mission colony (Gale, *A Brief History of Knox College* [Cincinnati: Clark, 1845], pp. 12–13).

Unfortunately, the appalling conditions of the journey resulted in the death of Mills and two others. See Martha F. Webster, *Seventy-Five Significant Years: The Story of Knox College, 1837–1912* (Galesburg, Ill.: Wagoner, 1912), chap. 6.

A number of other settlers came from around Russia and Norway, further north in Herkimer County, including Gale's cousin Silvanus Ferris, who became the most important person after Gale in building up Knox College and the community. E. P. Chambers, a son of one of the earliest settlers, said: "In all that part of the State of New York from which the Galesburg colonists came, there was a deep and ardent religious sentiment created through the powerful revivals resulting from the preaching and efforts of the Rev. Chas. G. Finney" (E. P. Chambers, "Incidents of Earliest Days," undated typescript, Knox College Library, Galesburg, Ill., p. 9).

[17] Page 544 was originally numbered 390, then renumbered 522 by Matson and changed to 544 by Finney. Finney renumbered the next page 546 instead of 545, and "–5" appears to have been added in pencil by Fairchild after "544."

[18] After being in Columbia, Finney spent some time in Rome in September and October, where a revival was reported. See H. H. Kellogg to Finney, 26 September 1829; M. Gillet to Finney, 26 October 1829, Finney Papers, microfilm, roll 2; *WR*, 13 October 1829, p. 163; and Anson G. Phelps, "Diary," 25 October 1829, on microfilm in New York Public Library.

It was probably during this visit of Finney to Rome that Daniel D. Whedon, then a law student, was converted. "So radical was the alteration in his feelings that he never entered the law-office again." He was to become an eminent Methodist theologian, teacher, and Bible commentator. See Daniel D. Whedon, *Essays, Reviews, and Discourses. With a biographical sketch by his son, J. S. Whedon, and his nephew, D. A. Whedon* (New York: Phillips and Hunt, 1887), p. 12; and *DAB*.

[19] There seems to have been an impression at the time among Finney's friends that men like

never inquired into this, and it may not be a fact.[20] **‹I knew nothing of it until long after.›** [21] **But at any rate,** Anson G. Phelps, since well-known as a great contributor by will to the leading benevolent institutions of our country,[22] hearing that I **was not** invited to the pulpits of the city, hired a vacant church in Vandewater st., and sent an urgent request **for me** to come there and preach.[23] I did so, and there we had a powerful revival. I found Mr.

Gardiner Spring and Samuel H. Cox, the leading moderate Presbyterian ministers in New York, may have been turned against Finney by Nettleton, although David L. Dodge, the New York merchant, reckoned that Nettleton was not entirely successful in getting the full support of either Dr. Spring or all the clergy. But after Finney's visit there in December 1827, there was some easing of the tension, and he had repeated assurances that he would be welcomed to New York and that pulpits would be opened to him. See letters to Finney from Dodge, 18 December 1827; Ward Stafford, 31 December 1827; Z. Platt, 10 March 1828, Finney Papers, microfilm, roll 1; Eli Sawtell to Finney, 3 April 1828, Finney Papers, microfilm, roll 2; and the letter of Nettleton to Gardiner Spring, 4 May 1827, in *Letters of the Rev. Dr. Beecher and Rev. Mr. Nettleton, on the "New Measures" in Conducting Revivals of Religion* (New York: Carvill, 1828), pp. 25–41.

It is not true that he had no invitations. Gardiner Spring certainly never took to Finney or the New Measures; however, he tried to keep an open mind and did invite Finney on one occasion to preach for him. Finney also preached in his church on at least one occasion when Spring was absent. And the session of Dr. Cox's church also invited him although the pastor was absent. He also had repeated invitations from the Reverend Ward Stafford of the Bowery Presbyterian Church, backed up by members of his congregation, including Anson G. Phelps. Finney turned these invitations down because of internal dissensions in the church. See letters to Finney from D. L. Dodge, Z. Platt, W. Stafford, A. G. Phelps, and E. N. Sawtell from December 1827 through 1828 in the Finney Papers; *Personal Reminiscences of the Life and Times of Gardiner Spring,* vol. 1 (New York: Scribner, 1866), pp. 220–23; "Remarks of Prof. John Morgan, D.D., of Oberlin," in *Reminiscences of Rev. Charles G. Finney* (Oberlin: Goodrich, 1876), p. 57; and p. 256 n. 51 (MS 480).

[20] A question mark has been penciled in, in the margin next to this sentence. This appears to have been done by Lewis Tappan.

[21] "I knew nothing of it until long after" was added later by Finney. In fact, Finney may have already been suspicious of some kind of a conspiracy from the time of his first visit to New York. In answer to a letter from Finney dated 25 December 1827, Ward Stafford wrote, "As to your being regarded as 'an intruder' and 'obstacles being thrown in your way' and your 'hands' 'tied' you need have no apprehensions" (Stafford to Finney, 31 December 1827, Finney Papers, microfilm, roll 1).

[22] Anson Greene Phelps (1781–1853) was one of the leading metal importers and manufacturers in New York. Well known as a wealthy philanthropist, he took a prominent lead in many of the religious and reform movements of the period. See Richard Lowitt, *A Merchant Prince of the Nineteenth Century: William E. Dodge* (New York: Columbia University Press, 1954); and *DAB*. Phelps left about a half million dollars to various philanthropies. The American Bible Society, the American Board of Commissioners for Foreign Missions, and the American Home Missionary Society received a hundred thousand dollars each. See *NYE,* 8 December 1853, p. 194.

[23] William E. Dodge wrote:

> My father-in-law, Mr. Anson G. Phelps, became deeply impressed with the feeling that a great blessing would follow if Mr. Finney could be induced to come to New York, but found his pastor, Dr. Gardiner Spring, as well as other prominent ministers doubtful of the propriety of introducing a man into their pulpits about whom there was so much said and such difference of opinion existed (*NYE,* 8 January 1880, p. 4).

Phelps arranged for Finney, together with Beman, Aikin, and Lansing, to meet with leaders of the churches in New York in August 1828 to prepare the way. Phelps himself, together with Arthur Tappan, another merchant, then transferred to the reorganized Bowery Church, where Phelps became a trustee and deacon. When troubles developed there, he and Tappan and a party of others split off and formed a new organization.

The Vandewater Street Church had been under the care of the presbytery but was in considerable financial difficulty. Their pastor had resigned in June 1829, and some proposed to disband the church. The building was therefore unoccupied pending the sale of the property.

JHF 276 Phelps very much engaged in the work, ¹and not hesitating **at all** at any expense that was necessary to promote it. The church which he hired could **not** be had for **more than** three months.[24] Accordingly Mr Phelps, **at his own expense,** before the three months were out, purchased a church in Prince st., near Broadway. This church had been built by the Universalists, MS 546 and was sold to Mr. ¹Phelps,[25] who bought and paid for it himself.[26] From Vandewater st. we went therefore to Prince st. , and there formed a church, mostly of **the converts** that had been converted during our meetings in Vandewater st.[27] I continued my labors in Prince st. for some months, I think until quite the latter part of summer.[28] **Many very interesting conversions took place, as persons came from every part of the city and attended our meetings.** I was very much struck, during my labors there with the piety of Mr. Phelps. While we continued at Vandewater st., myself and wife, with our only child, were guests in his family.[29] I had observed that while Mr. Phelps was a man literally loaded with business, somehow he preserved a highly spiritual frame of mind; and that he would come directly from his business to our prayer-meetings, and enter into them with such spirit as to show clearly

Phelps was advised not to purchase but to hire the church. He obtained possession about the beginning of October, and the new church was organized by the presbytery on 14 October.
Phelps's "particular & urgent request" for Finney to go to the Vandewater Street Church was conveyed to Finney in an October 12 letter from Aikin while Finney was preaching in Rome. Finney and his family arrived in New York on Saturday, 17 October, and he commenced preaching the next day. See Jonathan Greenleaf, *A History of the Churches, of All Denominations, in the City of New York* (New York: French, 1846), pp. 163–64; letters to Finney from Oliver Smith, 22 January 1829; Aikin, 12 October 1829; and Amy Bullock, 18 October 1829, Finney Papers, microfilm, roll 2; and Phelps, "Diary," August to November 1828.

[24] Nathan Beman wrote to Finney in New York, on 23 October 1829: "I presume you have had a *high fever* because the house could not be had more than 3 months—as I am appraised by Mr. Phelps that it is *sold*" (Beman to Finney, 23 October 1829, Finney Papers, microfilm, roll 2).

[25] Pages 546–59 were originally numbered 391–404, were renumbered 523–36 by Matson, and then were changed to 546–59 by Finney.

[26] The church was on the corner of Prince and Marion streets. It had been built about five years previously by the Prince Street Universalist Society. Abner Kneeland, the well-known freethinker, had, for a time, been the minister there. See Greenleaf, *History of the Churches,* , pp. 168–69; *WR,* 2 November 1830, p. 175; and *DAB.*

[27] The Union Church had been formed on 13 October 1829 with 35 original members, just before Finney started at Vandewater Street. The new church in Prince Street was dedicated on Sunday, 27 December 1829, with Dr. S. H. Cox preaching the first sermon in the morning and Finney preaching in the afternoon and evening. Finney normally preached three times each Sunday and gave a lecture on Thursday evenings. By the end of February the revival had taken hold, and 40 were attending the anxious meeting. On 10 January, 34 members were added (21 by profession), and in May another 50. A report at the end of May stated that 103 people had joined the church by profession and 42 by letter as a result of the revival. Another 35 were added in July. Details of the revival and the texts of Finney's sermons during January and February are recorded by Anson Phelps in his diary. See *NYE,* 29 May 1830, p. 35; and Phelps, "Diary."

[28] The Finneys were in New York until the end of July 1830. Finney did not confine his labors to the Prince Street Church; he preached, e.g., late in March 1830 in the Presbyterian church in Poughkeepsie for the Reverend A. Welton. See Poughkeepsie Session to Finney, 29 March 1830, Finney Papers, microfilm, roll 2; and *BR,* 6 April 1831, p. 54.

[29] The Phelps family had moved from 32 Cliff Street to Fourth Street, near the Bowery, in April 1829. After staying with them there, the Finneys boarded with William Rockwell, a dry-goods merchant, and his family at 10 Charlton Street. See Phelps, "Diary," 24 April and 3 May 1829; letters to Lydia Finney from Charlotte Bliss, 12 March 1830, and from A. A. Norton, 2 July 1830, Finney Papers, microfilm, roll 2; *Longworth's American Almanac* (New York), 1829; and letters from the Rockwells to the Finneys in the Finney Papers.

that his mind was not absorbed in business to the exclusion of spiritual things. As I watched him from day to day, I became more and more interested in his interior life as it was manifested ˡin his outward life.[30] One night I had occasion to go down stairs, I should think about twelve or one O'clock at night, to get something for our little child. I supposed the family were all **in bed**; but to my surprize I found Mr. Phelps sitting by his fire in his night **gown**, and ‹saw›[31] that I had broken in upon his secret devotions. I apologized by saying that I supposed he was in bed. He replied: "Brother Finney, I have a great deal of business pressing me during the day, and have but little time for secret devotion. **And** my custom is, after having a nap at night, to arise and have a season of communion with God." After his death, which occurred not many years ago, it was found that he had kept a journal during these hours in the night **in which he was up, composed of** several manuscript volumes. This journal ˡrevealed the secret workings of his mind, and the real progress of his interior life.[32] **This fact greatly interested and affected me, and made me still farther acquainted with what had excited so much of my attention and admiration when I was a member of his own family.**

MS 547

JHF 277

ˡ**Of course** I never knew the number converted while I was in Prince and Vandewater streets; but **I know the number was** large.[33] There was one case of conversion that I must not omit to mention. A young **lady** visited me one day under great conviction of sin. On conversing with her I found that she had many things upon her conscience. She had been in the habit, as she told me, ‹**of pilfering**›[34] from her very childhood. She was the daughter, and the only child, I think, of a widow lady; and she had been in the habit of ‹tak›ing[35] from her schoolmates and others handkerchiefs, and breastpins,

MS 548

[30] William W. Newell wrote of Phelps at this time:

> During his life he was constantly employed in enterprises useful to his fellow-men. He was actively engaged in temperance and revival work. He established a prayer-meeting at his own house, No. 32 Cliff Street. He purchased the Universalist Church in Prince Street. There he placed a godly minister with whom he labored for souls. In my young days I first met him at those meetings. But the special point now before us is his intense devotion to the spiritual interests of his own household. The supreme aim of Mr. Phelps and his godly wife was the early conversion of their children. His prayers and instructions at the family altar were very direct and fervent. The weekly prayer-meeting at his house was a blessing to the children. So was the maternal association where mothers pleaded God's promises for their children. His children were instructed and urged to yield themselves at once to Christ. . . . His five daughters and his only son, Anson G. Phelps, Jr., all confessed Christ before they were fourteen years old. Nearly all his twenty-five grandchildren, and most of his great-grandchildren of suitable age, are in the church (W. W. Newell, *Revivals: How and When?* [New York: Armstrong, 1882], p. 101).

[31] Here Finney changed the word "found" to "saw."

[32] Seven volumes of his diary, covering the years 1806–1807 and 1817–1853, were preserved by his family. There is a microfilm copy in the New York Public Library.

[33] A report in May stated, "It is supposed by some, who have been most favourably situated for making an estimate, that more than 200 have been hopefully renewed by the power of the Holy Ghost" (*NYE,* 29 May 1830, p. 35).

[34] Matson had written "She had been in the habit of pilfering, as she told me." Finney crossed out the words "of pilfering" and wrote in after "as she told me" the words "of taking" but altered it to "of pilfering." Fairchild changed it back to Matson's wording.

[35] Finney altered the word "pilfering" to "taking."

and pencils, and whatever she had an opportunity to steal. She made confession respecting some of these things to me, and asked me what she should do about it. I told her **that** she must go and return them, and make confession to those from whom she had taken them. This of course greatly tried her; yet her convictions were so deep that she dared not keep them, and she began the work of making confession and restitution. But as she went MS 549 forward with it she **kept remembering** |more and more instances of the kind, and kept visiting me frequently and confessing to me her thefts of almost every kind of **an** article that a young **lady** could use. I asked her if her mother knew that she had these things. She said, **Y**es; but that she had always told her mother that they were given her. She said to me on one occasion: "Mr. Finney, I suppose I have stolen a million of times. I find **among my things** things that I know I stole, but I cannot recollect from whom." I refused altogether to compromise with her, and insisted on her making restitution **wherever she could remember, or in any wise learn where she had gotten anything that she had stolen. When she came to me with her confessions, she would afterwards, when she had done what I had told her,** come to me and report what she had done. I asked her what the people said. She replied: "Some of them say I am crazy; some of them say that I am a JHF 278 fool; and some of them are very much affected." |"Do they all forgive you?" I asked. "O yes!" said she, "they all forgive me; but some of them think that I had better not do as I am doing."

MS 550 |One day she informed me that she had a shawl which she had stolen from a daughter of Bishop Hobart, then **B**ishop of New York, whose residence was on St. John's square, and near St. John's church.[36] As usual I told her she must restore it. A few days after she called and related to me the **facts**. She said she folded up the shawl in a paper, and went with it and rung the bell at the Bishop's door; and when the servant came she handed him the bundle directed to the Bishop. She made no explanation, but turned immediately away and ran around the corner into another street, lest some one should look out and see which way she went, and find out who she was. But after she got around the corner her conscience smote her, and she said to herself, "I have not done this thing right. Somebody else may be suspected of having **done it** unless I make known to the Bishop who did it.["] **Whereupon** she turned around, went immediately back, and inquired if she could see the Bishop. Being informed that she could she was conducted to his study. She then MS 551 confessed to him—told him about the shawl |and all that had passed. "Well," said I, "and how did the Bishop receive you?" "Oh," said she, "when I told him he wept, laid his hand on my head, and said he forgave me and prayed God to forgive me." "And have you been at peace in your mind," said I, "about that transaction since?" "O yes!" said she. This process continued for weeks, and I think for months. This girl was going from place to place in all parts of the city, restoring things that she had stolen, and making confession.

[36]John Henry Hobart (1775–1830) was a leading theologian of the High Church Anglican party. He was made bishop of New York in 1816 and was also rector of Trinity Church. He lived at 50 Varick Street, which ran along the east side of St. John's Square. The incident described here took place shortly before his death. He died on 14 September 1830 while on a tour of the western part of the state. See *DAB*; and *Longworth's American Almanac*, 1829, p. 293.

Sometimes her convictions would be so awful that it seemed as if she would be deranged.

One morning she sent for me to come to her mother's residence. I did so, and when I arrived I was introduced to her room and found her with her hair hanging over her |shoulders, her clothes **but slightly put on**, walking the JHF 279 room in an agony of despair, and with a look that was frightful because it indicated that she was well-nigh deranged. Said I, "My dear child, what is the matter?" She held in her hand as she was walking a little Testament. |She MS 552 turned to me and said, "Mr. Finney, I stole this Testament. I have stolen God's **W**ord; and will God ever forgive me? I cannot recollect which of the girls it was that I stole it from. I stole it from one of my schoolmates, and it was so long ago that I had really forgotten that I had stolen it. It occurred to me this morning; and it seems to me that God can never forgive me for stealing **His W**ord." I assured her that there was no reason for her despair. "But," said she, "what shall I do? **for** I cannot remember where I got it." I told her, "Keep it as a constant[37] remembrance**r** of your former sins, and use it for the good you may now get from it." "Oh," said she, "if I could only remember where I got it, I would instantly restore it." "Well," said I, "if you can ever recollect where you got it, make an[38] instant restitution, either by restoring that or giving **her** another as good." "I will," said she. All this process was exceedingly affecting to me; but as it proceeded, the state of mind that resulted from these transactions was truly wonderful. A depth of humility, a deep knowledge of herself and |her own depravity, a brokenness MS 553 of heart and contrition of spirit and finally a faith, and joy, and love, and peace like a river, succeeded; and she became one of the most delightful young Christians that I have **almost ever seen**. When the time drew near that I expected to leave New York, I thought that some one ought to be acquainted with her **in the church that** could watch over her. Up to this time whatever had passed between us had been a secret sacredly kept to myself. But as I was about to leave I narrated the fact to **Brother** Phelps, and the narration affected him greatly. He said, "Brother Finney, introduce me to |her. I will be JHF 280 her friend; I will watch over her for good." He did so, as I afterwards learned. I have not seen the young **lady** for many years and I think not since I related the fact to Mr. Phelps. But when I returned from England the last time, in visiting one of Mr. Phelps' daughters, **now a married lady in New York city,**[39] in the course of the conversation **in some way** this case was alluded to **by her**. I then inquired: "Did your father introduce you to that young **lady**?" "Oh yes!" she replied, "we all knew |her;"—meaning, as I supposed, all the MS 554 daughters of the family. "Well, what do you know of her?" said I. "O," said she, "she is a very earnest Christian woman. She is married, and her husband is in business in this city. She is a member of the church, and lives in **such a** street," pointing to the place, not far from where we then were. I inquired,

[37] Matson had originally written the word "sad" here, but he changed it to "constant."

[38] The word "an" appears to have been inserted in the manuscript by Lewis Tappan.

[39] This was probably Melissa, the wife of William E. Dodge, a partner in the firm of Phelps, Dodge, and Co. But Phelps had three married daughters living in New York. See Phelps to Finney, 20 March 1848, Finney Papers, microfilm, roll 2. Finney and his wife were in New York in August 1860.

"Has she always maintained a consistent Christian character?" "O yes!" was the reply. "She is an excellent, praying woman." In some way I have been informed—and I cannot recollect now the source of the information—that **that** woman said that she never had had a temptation to pilfer from the time of her conversion—that she had never known what it was to have the desire to do so. This revival prepared the way in New York for the organization of the free presbyterian churches in the city.[40] Those churches were composed afterwards largely of the converts of that revival. Many of them had belonged to the church in Prince st. **After I left the congregation in Prince st., the Rev. Herman Norton was settled as their pastor.[41] After he left for some reason the house of worship was sold, and the church was ultimately broken up, the members uniting with other churches.[42]**

MS 555 ¹At this point of my narrative, in order to render intelligible many things that I shall have to say hereafter, I must give a little account of a circumstance connected with[43] the conversion of **Brother** Lewis Tappan, and his connection afterwards with my own labors.[44] **I shall give the** account[45] **as** I received

[40]The Free-church movement was an attempt to democratize the churches. It was an extension of the New Measures revival movement adapted to the largely untouched poorer classes and disadvantaged sections of the cities. Lewis Tappan, who was the leading spirit behind the movement, described its evolution in his "History of the Free Churches in the City of New York," which was published in Andrew Reed and James Matheson, *A Narrative of the Visit to the American Churches of the Deputation from the Congregational Union of England and Wales,* vol. 1 (London: Jackson and Walford, 1835), pp. 500–517. See also Charles C. Cole, "The Free Church Movement in New York City," *New York History* 34 (1953): 284–97.

[41]Herman Norton (1799–1850) was a graduate of Hamilton College and Auburn Theological Seminary. After working as an evangelist in New York State and New Jersey, he looked after the church in Reading, Pennsylvania, when Finney left in May 1829. He was installed at Prince Street on 22 October 1830 and remained there until April 1835. He was later involved in work among Roman Catholics and was secretary of the American Protestant Society. See *The Independent* (New York), 28 November 1850, p. 194; and 5 December 1850, p. 199; *Quarterly Register of the American Education Society* (Boston) 8 (May 1836): 322; and P. H. Fowler, *Historical Sketch of Presbyterianism Within the Bounds of the Synod of Central New York* (Utica: Curtiss and Childs, 1877), pp. 615–17.

He and his wife Amelia (Flint) Norton were very close friends of the Finneys, whose third child was named Frederic Norton, after Herman Norton. See letters from the Nortons to the Finneys in the Finney Papers. Frederic, who may have spelled his name with a final *k* in later years, was usually known by his second name, Norton.

[42]It was pointed out in an obituary of Herman Norton that the Union Church

> was unfortunate in the location of its house of worship, in Prince-Street, just under the eaves of the Roman Catholic Cathedral; and when at length they disposed of the property with the intention of building in a better situation, the commercial crash of 1837 came suddenly upon them, and so frustrated all calculations that the church finally concluded to dissolve (*The Independent,* 28 November 1850, p. 194).

Jonathan Greenleaf gave the reason for the sale of the property as heavy debts.

> The church with its pastor retired to a hall, resolving to keep on, but after struggling for a year, Mr. Norton resigned his charge in April 1835. The church, though weakened by dismissions, still kept together, supplying themselves as best they could, until April 1838, when they were dissolved by presbytery (Greenleaf, *History of the Churches*, p. 169).

[43]The words "a circumstance connected with" were added by Lewis Tappan. Finney had sent the manuscript to Lewis Tappan to read, and Tappan had obtained permission from Finney to make some alterations to the text. See Introduction, p. xxxii; and n. 51 below.

[44]Lewis Tappan (1788–1873) was a prominent New York merchant and was to become well known as an abolitionist. See Bertram Wyatt-Brown, *Lewis Tappan and the Evangelical War Against Slavery* (Cleveland: Press of Western Reserve University, 1969); and *DAB*.

[45]The words "of his conversion" here appear to have been crossed out by Tappan.

Left: Arthur Tappan. A New York merchant and leader in many benevolent reform movements. He gave liberal financial support to Finney and to Oberlin College in its early years. Engraving in [Lewis Tappan], *The Life of Arthur Tappan* (New York: Hurd and Houghton, 1870), frontispiece. Courtesy Oberlin College Archives.

Right: Lewis Tappan. He was Finney's wealthy New York friend and pioneer of the Free-church movement in the 1830s. He read the manuscript of Finney's *Memoirs* and made some alterations. From an 1846 daguerreotype in *The Independent* (New York) 65 (December 1908):1350. Courtesy Oberlin College Archives.

it from himself.[46] **It** occurred before I was personally acquainted with him, under the following circumstances. He was a Unitarian and lived in Boston. His brother Arthur, then a very extensive dry goods merchant in New York, was orthodox, and an earnest Christian man.[47] The ˡrevivals through central New York had created a good deal of excitement among the Unitarians; and **the newspapers, and especially** their **own,** had a good deal to say against

JHF 281

[46]In March 1846 Tappan had sent to Finney a copy of a detailed account of these circumstances leading up to his conversion, which he had written in a long letter to Rev. John Ware and published in the *Christian Register* (Boston), 28 February 1846, p. 33. See Tappan to Finney, 7 March 1846, in Lewis Tappan, "Letter Book," Tappan Papers, microfilm, roll 3; and n. 51 below.

[47]Arthur Tappan (1786–1865) was in the silk-jobbing business in New York and became a wealthy man. He was a prominent supporter of the great religious and educational reform movements and became active in the antislavery movement. *The Life of Arthur Tappan* (New York: Hurd and Houghton, 1870) was written by his brother Lewis. See *DAB*.

them. Especially were there strange stories in circulation about myself, representing me as a half-crazed fanatic.[48] These stories had been related to Lewis Tappan by **Rev. Henry Ware Jr** a leading Unitarian minister of Boston, and he believed them.[49] They were credited by many of the **leading** Unitarians in New England and throughout the state of New York. While

MS 556 these stories were in circulation Lewis Tappan visited |his brother Arthur in New York, and they fell into conversation in regard to those revivals. Lewis called Arthur's attention to the strange fanaticism connected with these revivals, especially **of** what was said of myself.[50] He asserted that I gave out publicly that I was "the **B**rigadier **G**eneral of Jesus Christ."[51] This and like reports were in circulation, and Lewis insisted upon their truth. Arthur utterly discredited them, and told Lewis that they were all nonsense and false, and that he ought not to believe any of them.[52] Lewis relying upon the statements

[48]The Boston *Christian Register*, which Tappan himself helped to edit at that time, was the main Unitarian newspaper. Stories started appearing there in August 1826 and were copied into other papers, particularly Universalist publications. See, e.g., the *Christian Register* (Boston), 5 August, p. 122; 12 August, p. 130; and 30 September, p. 154; Tappan, "Diary," 1826, p. 76, Tappan Papers, microfilm, roll 1; p. 189 n. 89 (MS 368), p. 143 n. 10 (MS 280), and n. 60 below.

[49]Matson had written down, "These stories had come to the ears of Lewis Tappan, and he believed them." It was altered by Lewis Tappan.

Next to W. E. Channing, Henry Ware, Jr. (1794–1843), was the leading Unitarian minister in New England. From 1817 until his health failed in 1828, Ware was pastor of the Second Unitarian Church in Boston. He then became a professor in the Harvard Divinity School and was a well-known editor and theologian. See *DAB*.

Early in July 1826 Ware had gone to the Utica area and there discovered the revival excitement. At Trenton he heard many stories about Finney and the revivals, and as a result he wrote to Ezra Gannett, the editor of the *Christian Register* in Boston, relaying the stories. The letter was communicated by Gannett to the executive committee of the Unitarian Association, of which Tappan was a member, and it was then published in the *Christian Register*, 12 August 1826, p. 130. Tappan related that he heard the statement also made by Ware

> on his return from his journey, respecting Mr. Finney and fully believing that my friend Rev. Henry Ware Jr. had given a true statement of facts, as related to him, or as having come under his notice, I, at once, in common with my Unitarian associates, credited every word of it (Lewis Tappan to John Ware, 10 February 1846, in *Christian Register,* 28 February 1846, p. 33).

See also John Ware, *Memoir of the Life of Henry Ware, Jr. by his brother,* vol. 1 (Boston: Munroe, 1846), pp. 200–204.

The publication of this memoir, reviving the long-since discredited stories about Finney, prompted Tappan's letters to John Ware in defense of Finney. See n. 51 below and *Christian Register,* 9 May 1846, p. 74.

[50]Here Matson had written down, "Lewis ridiculed them, and called Arthur's attention to the strange fanaticism, especially of myself," but Tappan changed it.

[51]Matson had written down, "the Major General of Jesus Christ, sent out to make war with the devil," but Tappan changed it to "the Brigadier General of Jesus Christ." He wrote to Finney on 2 June 1868:

> The report brought to Boston by Rev. Henry Ware, that you said you were a Major General of J. C. etc (Brigadier G. it should be) is mentioned in the Memoir of H. W. by his brother, Dr. John Ware; with some qualification, but still improperly. After the publication of this work, I had some correspondence with Dr. Ware on the subject, in which I urged him to make some corrections in another edition, but I think he did not.
>
> Before the Narrative is printed (if it ever gets into type) I should like to revise what you say of Ware & myself, that it may be more correct (Tappan to Finney, 2 June 1868, Finney Papers, microfilm, roll 5).

[52]Matson had written down, "and that he must not believe any of them," but Tappan altered it.

of Mr Ware[53] proposed to bet five hundred dollars that he could prove these reports to be true; especially the one **that I gave out myself as "the Brigadier General of Jesus Christ."**[54] Arthur replied: "Lewis, you know that I do not bet; but I will tell you what I will do. If you can prove by credible testimony that that is true, and that the reports about Mr. Finney are true, I will *give* you five hundred dollars. I make this offer to lead you to investigate. I want you to know that these stories are false, and that ˡthe source whence they come is utterly unreliable."[55] Lewis, not doubting that he could bring the proof, inasmuch as these things had been so[56] ‹confidently asserted by the Unitarians, wrote to Rev. Mr. **Pierce**[57] Unitarian minister at Trenton falls, N. York to whom Mr. **Ware** had refered him,[58] **&** authorized him to expend five hundred dollars, if need be, in procuring sufficient testimony that the story was true; such testimony as would lead to the conviction [**of**][59] a party in a court of justice. ˡMr. **Pierce** accordingly undertook to procure testimony, but after great painstaking was unable to furnish any except what was contained in a small **universalist** newspaper printed in Buffalo, in which it had been asserted that Mr. Finney claimed that he was a **Brigadier General** of Jesus Christ.›[60] Nowhere could he get the least

MS 557

JHF 282

[53]Matson had started this sentence, "Lewis became excited, and," but Tappan altered it.

[54]Matson had written the end of this sentence to read, "the Major General of Jesus Christ, sent out and commissioned especially to make war upon the devil," but Tappan changed it.

[55]In another account Lewis Tappan said that he told Arthur in return, "If I do not prove it to be true, I will give you five hundred dollars" ("Stories About Mr. Finney, the Oberlin Revivalist," *The Evening Post* [New York], 15 July 1859, p. 1).

[56]The section following from here to n. 60 is in Finney's handwriting on a separate piece of paper pasted onto the sheet. It covers up a section that originally read:

> confidently asserted by the Unitarians, wrote to all the Unitarian ministers and leading men, he said, from Buffalo to New York, desiring them to furnish the proof that these stories were true. He found that no one of them knew them to be true. They had heard in one town that I had said so in another town, and, in writing to that town, they did not know that I had said any such thing there, but had heard that I had said so in another town.

Most of this was crossed out by Lewis Tappan, and the changes made were almost exactly copied out by Finney.

[57]Isaac B. Pierce.

[58]The word "refered" was spelled "referred" by Tappan underneath the piece of paper pasted on the sheet. In another account Tappan wrote:

> I addressed a letter to the Unitarian clergyman in Oneida county, who replied that the statement made to Mr. Ware was undoubtedly correct; that it had been widely circulated, and was generally believed. In my reply, I told him of my engagement with the orthodox gentleman in New York; that I wanted evidence of the truthfulness of the story, such evidence as would be necessary in a court of question; and I authorized him to procure it, regardless of expense ("Stories About Mr. Finney," p. 1).

[59]Tappan had written the word "of" underneath. Fairchild inserted it here.

[60]This ends the section in Finney's handwriting. The Buffalo newspaper was the *Gospel Advocate*. A number of articles ridiculing and denouncing Finney and the revivals appeared from January 1826 through 1827. The particular article referring to Finney calling himself the "Brigadier General of Jesus Christ" is in the issue for 13 January 1826, p. 5. It was in fact taken from *The Evangelical Restorationist,* a Universalist magazine published in Troy, New York, where it first appeared in vol. 1 (December 1825), p. 68. The article, under the heading "Original Anecdote," reads:

> A zealous fanatic by the name of Finney, a Presbyterian preacher in Jefferson county, N.Y., publickly declared, not long since, that he was one of the *Brigadier General's of Jesus Christ*, with a special commission from the court of heaven to preach the gospel, and all that did not believe him would be *eternally damned!!* In one of his meetings he

proof that **these things, which were reported that I had said, were** true. **They** had **all** heard, and **they** believed, that I had said these things somewhere; but as he followed **them** up from town to town by his correspondence, he could not learn that they **really** had been said anywhere. This in connection with other matters[61] he said led him to reflect seriously upon the nature of the opposition, and upon the source whence it had come. Knowing as he did what stress had been laid upon these stories by the MS 558 Unitarians, and |the use they had made of them to oppose the revivals in New York and other places,[62] his confidence in them was greatly shaken. Thus his prejudices against the revivals and orthodox people became softened, **and his confidence in the Unitarian opposition to those revivals utterly shaken.[63] He was led to review the theological publications of the Orthod[o]x[64] & Unitarians, with great care & seriousness, & the result was that he felt constrained to abandon his Unitarian views & embrace those of the orthodox.** The mother of the Tappans was a very godly, praying woman.[65] She had never had any sympathy with Unitarianism. She had lived a very praying life, and had left a **very**[66] strong impression upon her children.

When the confidence of Lewis Tappan with regard to the Unitarian doctrines and their opposition to revivals and measures for the conversion of men, was thus shaken, his ears became open to the truth, and it resulted in his conversion to Christ. He had felt strong in his opposition, confident that the extravagances said to attend those revivals were all true and that Unitarianism was true. His brother Arthur was very anxious to have him have confidence in the orthodox belief, and very anxious to bring him under evangelical influence so as

further declared himself commissioned to make war with the *devil*; and that he was not ignorant of the *machinations* and *devices* of that *evil being*, nor of his *power*, neither indeed of his *size*; which he asserted was "*bigger than the whole of this world!*" At this last Polyphemian monster of an expression, a young man in the congregation, had the unblushing impudence to *smile*; whereupon the *Brigadier General*, suddenly breaking off from preaching, demands, in a voice of thunder; "*Young man, what are you laughing at?*" "Sir, I did but just smile, and I don't know as I am obliged to tell *you* what I smiled at." "*I insist on it you shall tell! what were you laughing at?*" "I think Sir, I understood you to say, *the devil was bigger than all this world?*" "*I did say so.*" "I would merely wish to inquire, then, *how large Mary Magdalene was?*"

[61] The words "in connection with other matters" are in the handwriting of Lewis Tappan.

[62] Lewis Tappan changed the word "revival" to "revivals in New York and other places."

[63] In another account Tappan wrote:

My informant [Isaac Pierce], Mr. Ware, and myself, had been egregiously imposed upon, to our no little chagrin and mortification. On stating to my orthodox friend in this city [Arthur Tappan] the result of my labors and those of Mr. Ware's friend, and acknowledging my forfeiture, he laughed, and "forgave me the debt," while I learned a useful lesson ("Stories About Mr. Finney," p. 1).

The sentence following was inserted in the manuscript by Lewis Tappan and was erased by Fairchild, who substituted a similar but shorter sentence.

[64] Tappan appears to have omitted the letter *o* from "Orthodox."

[65] Their mother was Sarah (Holmes) Tappan (1748–1826). An account of her devoted Christian life was written by Lewis Tappan and published as the *Memoir of Mrs. Sarah Tappan: taken in part from the Home Missionary Magazine of November, 1828, and printed for distribution among her descendants* (New York: West and Trow, 1834).

[66] The word "very" was not crossed out in the manuscript but does not appear in the published version.

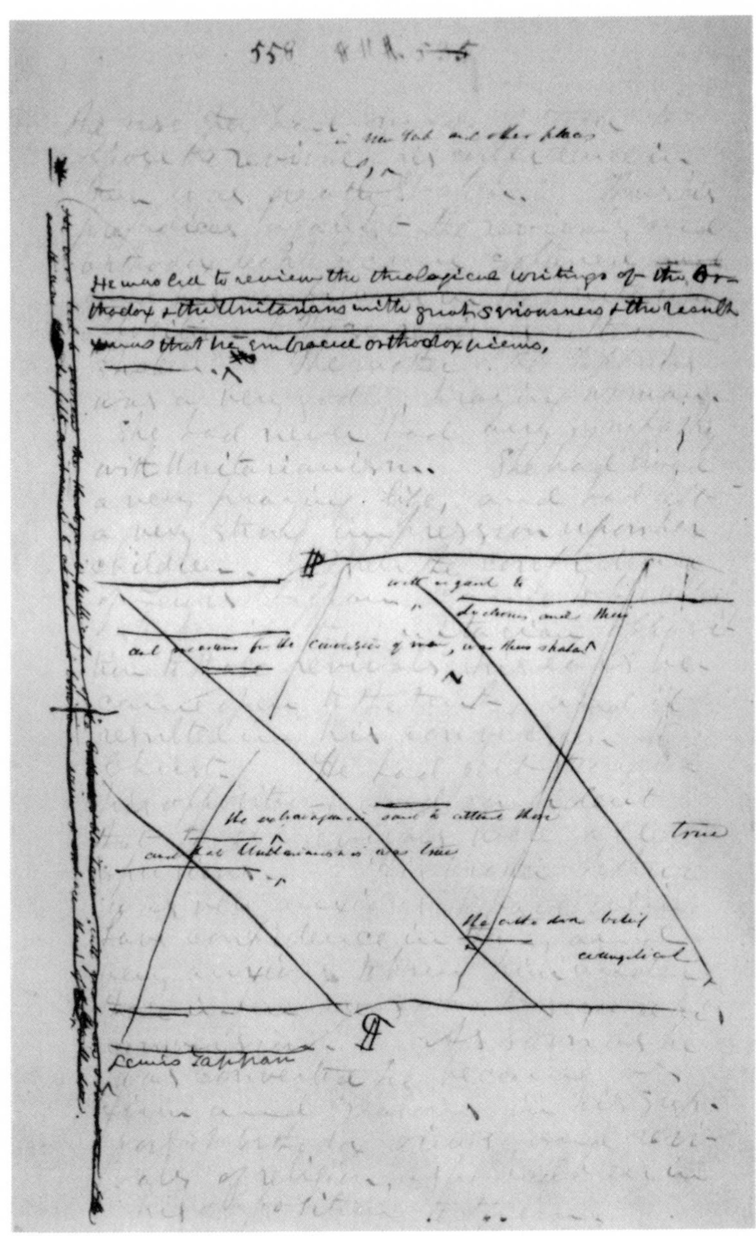

558

He was led to review the theological writings of the Orthodox & the Unitarians with great seriousness & the result was that he embraced orthodox views,

Lewis Tappan

Page 558 of the Manuscript. This page shows alterations in Lewis Tappan's handwriting. Courtesy Oberlin College Archives.

to secure his conversion.[67] As soon as **he** was converted he became as firm and zealous in his support of **O**rthodox views and revivals of religion, as he had been in his opposition to them.

MS 559 |**He came to New York and went into partnership with Arthur, I believe, soon after his conversion.**[68] **I became acquainted with him, and was considerably acquainted with his brother Arthur.** About the time that I left New York, after my first labors there in Vandewater **st.** and Prince st., **Brother** Tappan and some other good brethren became dissatisfied with the state of things in New York and[69] after much prayer and consideration, concluded to organize a new **C**ongregation, and introduce new **means** for the conversion of men.[70] They obtained a place to hold worship,[71] and called the Rev. Joel Parker, who was then pastor of the Third Presbyterian church in JHF 283 Rochester, to come to their aid.[72] **Brother** Parker |arrived in New York and

[67]This section from the beginning of the paragraph, which was omitted by Fairchild, had been altered by Lewis Tappan. It originally read:

> When the confidence of Lewis Tappan came to be utterly shaken in the Unitarian opposition to those revivals, his ears became open to the truth, and it resulted in his conversion to Christ. He had felt strong in his opposition, and confident that those revivals were all spurious. His brother Arthur was very anxious to have him have confidence in them, and very anxious to bring him under their influence so as to secure his conversion.

[68]Tappan left Boston for New York on 28 January 1828. See Tappan, "Diary," Tappan Papers, microfilm, roll 1.

[69]The words "became dissatisfied with the state of things in New York and" were added by Tappan.

[70]Here Matson had written down, "concluded to get up a kind of city missionary movement," but Tappan changed it. In fact, the city mission work pioneered by Thomas Chalmers in Glasgow, Scotland, influenced Lewis Tappan and Dr. James C. Bliss, a member of the Dutch Reformed church, as they formulated the idea of Free churches. A number of features were introduced in the hope of bringing the gospel to bear particularly on the poorer classes of society in the cities. Pew rents and class distinctions in seating were done away with; ministers were supported by free gifts rather than by salaries; lay participation was encouraged through the organization of the whole congregation into classes for Bible study and Sunday schools; canvassing of the district was undertaken, and tracts were widely distributed; the meetings were mostly of a social nature in which all could participate; and theological and sectarian controversy was avoided by concentrating on a basic gospel message.

The first steps at organization were taken in May 1830, when Tappan, Bliss, and three others met at Tappan's house, together with Rev. Joel Parker of Rochester, who was in the city attending the May Anniversaries. At this meeting they formed an Association of Gentlemen and decided to organize a church. The proposed plan was then set out in *The New-York Evangelist,* 29 May 1830, p. 35. See also Bliss, Tappan, and Benjamin H. Folger to Absolom Peters, 14 June 1830, in American Home Missionary Society Papers, Dillard University, New Orleans; Tappan, "History of the Free Churches," pp. 501, 509–15; Joseph P. Thompson, *The Last Sabbath in the Broadway Tabernacle: A Historical Discourse* (New York: Calkins and Stiles, 1857), pp. 7–9; Tappan, "Diary," 19 April 1857, p. 205, Tappan Papers, microfilm, roll 2; Louis Chapin to G. F. Wright, 1 February 1890, Wright Papers, box 8; and George Cragin, "The Free Church of Old Times," *The Free Church Circular* (Oneida, N.Y.), 7 February 1850, pp. 19–20.

[71]The First Ward in the city was chosen as the first area to evangelize. George Cragin, one of the converts in the Union Church, who transferred to the new church, recalled: "An old unsightly building, on a back street, near the City Hotel, was procurred, and rudely fitted up as a place of worship" (Cragin, "Free Church," p. 20). This was a room formerly occupied as a lecture room by Rev. John B. Romeyn's church in Thames Street near Broadway. It could hold about four hundred persons (see *NYE,* 26 June 1830, p. 51).

[72]Joel Parker (1799–1873) was a graduate of Hamilton College in 1824. After studying at Auburn Theological Seminary, he organized the Third Presbyterian Church in Rochester. After three years in New York he went to New Orleans but returned in 1838 as pastor of the

began his labors, I think about the time that I closed my labors at Prince st.[73] **This left his church in Rochester vacant. They formed** a First Free ‹presbyterian›[74] church in New York about this time, and **the Rev. Joel** Parker **was** its pastor.[75] They labored especially[76] among that class of the population that had not been in the habit of attending meetings anywhere, and **they** were very successful.[77] They finally fitted up the upper story of some ware-houses in Dey st.[78] ‹that would hold a good congregation and there they continued their labors.›[79]

Broadway Tabernacle. For two years he was president of Union Theological Seminary, but in 1842 financial difficulties necessitated his resignation. He had further pastorates in Philadelphia, New York, and Newark, New Jersey. See *DAB*.

[73]Parker started at Thames Street on 27 June 1830, preaching to a congregation of forty people. Cragin recalled that he "entered the city with all the zeal and devotion of a missionary on heathen ground" (Cragin, "Free Church," p. 20; and Tappan, "History of the Free Churches," p. 502).

[74]Finney added the word "Presbyterian."

[75]The First Free Church was formed on 22 September 1830 with sixteen members, and Parker was installed as pastor on 27 October (Tappan, "History of the Free Churches," p. 503; and *NYE*, 23 October 1830, p. 119).

[76]Here Tappan changed the word "mostly" to "especially."

[77]The meetings gradually increased until nearly four hundred were filling the hall and the passages. By mid-February 1831 the crowds were so great that they had to move to the Masonic Hall in Broadway, the largest and most central hall in the city, until a new place of worship was ready. See Tappan, "History of the Free Churches," p. 503; and *NYE*, 19 February 1831, p. 187.

[78]Here Matson had written "Dye," but Tappan changed it to "Dey." (The word was also spelled "Dye" by Louis Chapin in a letter to G. F. Wright, 1 February 1890, Wright Papers, box 8.) The rest of the sentence to the end of the page was added by Finney from the top of the next page when he pasted in a piece of paper with a new chapter heading there.

[79]The new place of worship, which was purchased on the northwest corner of Dey and Washington streets, had consisted of four large brick stores leased out to grocers. The upper floors were converted into one large hall that could hold between eight hundred and one thousand people. New leases, with clauses forbidding the sale of spirits, resulted in a change of tenants for the ground floor stores. The congregation moved in on 16 October 1831 and immediately commenced a protracted meeting. So many new members resulted that a decision was made to start a second Free church.

Parker continued at Dey Street until October 1833 and was succeeded by Rev. Jacob Helffenstein. By February 1835, 753 members had been admitted, 493 of these on profession of faith. The church continued at Dey Street until February 1838, when it was absorbed into the Broadway Tabernacle. See Tappan, "History of the Free Churches," pp. 504–5; and Greenleaf, *History of the Churches*, p. 180.

THE ROCHESTER REVIVAL, 1830–31

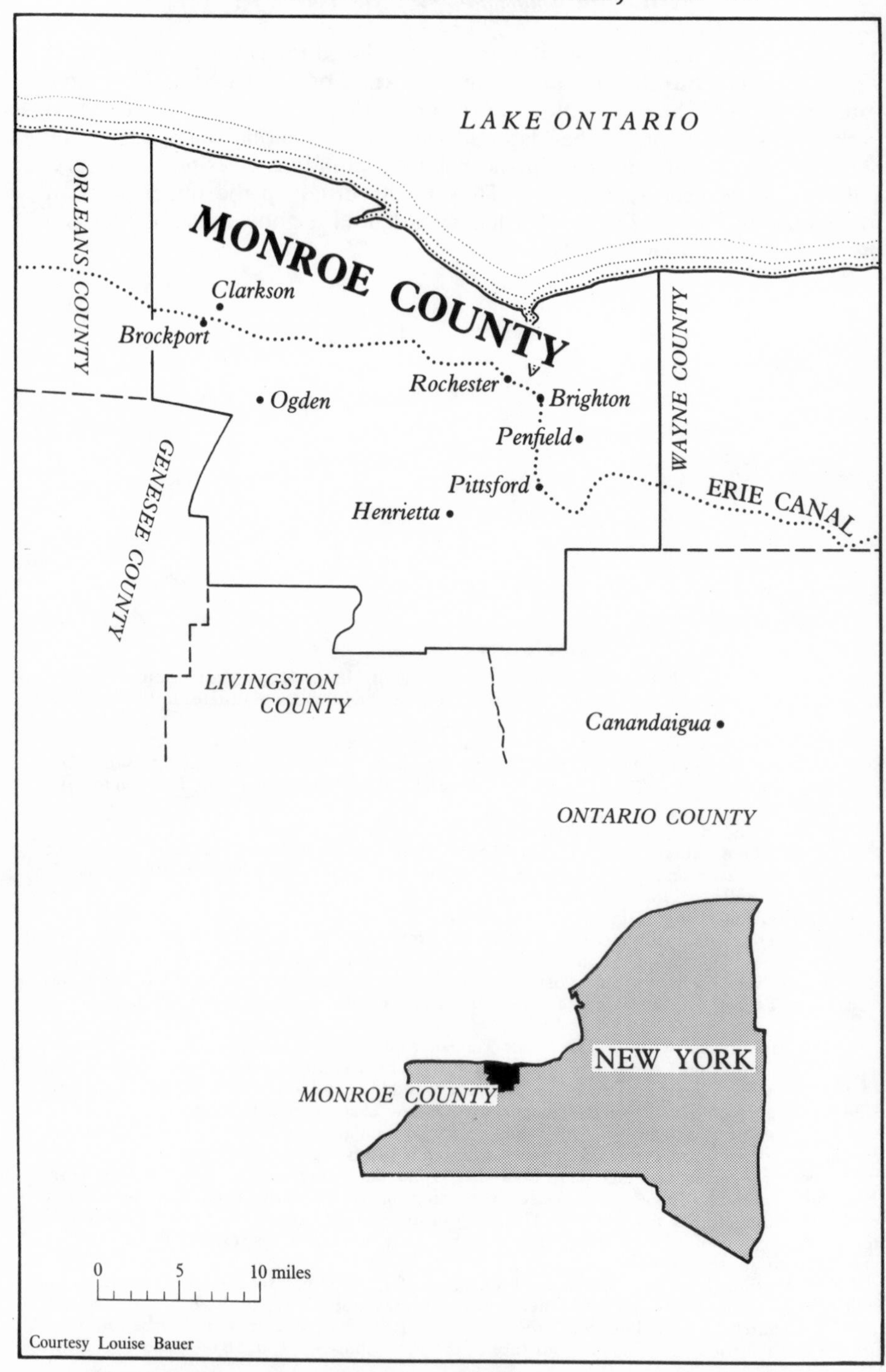

Places where Finney preached from September 1830 to March 1831.

CHAPTER XXI

MS 560
JHF 284

‹Revival in Rochester **New York** 1830.›

I[1] went from New York **and** spent a few weeks in Whitestown,[2] **being solicited in the meantime to return to Philadelphia, and also to New York**;[3] and as was common, **I was** pressed to go in many directions, **and** was greatly at a loss what was my duty.[4] But ‹among others›[5] a **pressing** invitation was received from the third presbyterian church in Rochester, of which **Brother** Parker had been pastor, to go there and supply them for a season.[6] I inquired into the circumstances, and found that on several accounts it was a very unpromising field of labor **at that time**. There were but three presbyterian churches in Rochester. The third church, that extended the invitation **to me**, had no minister, and religion was in a low state. The second

[1] Pages 560–90 were originally numbered 405–35 and then 537–67 by Matson, and changed to 560–90 by Finney. The chapter heading of page 560 is on a separate piece of paper pasted over the sheet. Underneath are Matson's page numbers and the number 560 written by Finney. Finney had crossed out the first three lines of the text and inserted a new chapter heading that read, "‹Chap. XXI *Revival at Rochester New York, in 1830 & 31.*›" The section crossed out reads, "that would hold considerable of a congregation; and there they held their meetings." The next sentence began with the word "But" in Matson's handwriting. This was also crossed out by Finney.

[2] Finney also made a visit to Henderson to see his father and to Adams, leaving there about 20 August 1830. See George W. Finney to Charles Finney, 22 October 1830, Finney Papers, microfilm, roll 2; and Lydia [Whitney] Finney to Charles and Lydia [Andrews] Finney, 20 August 1830, details given in the calendar of the Finney Papers. The letter is now missing.

[3] The German Reformed Church in Philadelphia had been trying to get Finney back since July 1830. The Union Church in New York also wanted him back. See letters to Finney from Joseph Naglee, 12 August 1830; Caspar Schaeffer, 31 August 1830; and Anson G. Phelps, 2 September 1830, Finney Papers, microfilm, roll 2.

[4] There is a pressing invitation from John Brooks of Salem, Massachusetts, dated 26 August 1830, in the Finney Papers, microfilm, roll 2.

[5] Here Matson had written "But at the time." Finney altered it.

[6] The Third Presbyterian Church had been formed by Josiah Bissell, Ashbel Riley, and some others from the First and Second churches who wanted a place of worship on the less fashionable east side of the Genesee River and one devoted to revivals and reform. Joel Parker started preaching as a student there in December 1826, and the church was formed in February 1827. Bissell had tried in vain to get Finney to go there in September 1829. Then when Joel Parker left for New York in June 1830, he recommended Finney to the church. See "Historical Questionaires of the Presbyterian Churches of the Synod of New York," vol. 4 (1932), pp. 47–49, typescript in The Presbyterian Historical Society, Philadelphia; Levi Parsons, comp., *History of Rochester Presbytery* (Rochester: Democrat-Chronicle Press, 1889), pp. 251–52; "An Incident of Finney's Labors," *NYE,* 11 February 1886, p. 6; and "The Brick Church, Rochester," *NYE,* 16 December 1875, pp. 2–6.

Their meeting house on the northeast corner of Main and Clinton streets was sold to the Second Baptist Church in 1834. See Henry O'Reilly, *Settlement in the West: Sketches of Rochester* (Rochester: Alling, 1838), pp. 286–87.

presbyterian church, or "the Brick church," as it was called, had a pastor, an excellent man;[7] but in regard to his preaching there was considerable division in the church, and he was restive and about to leave.[8] MS 561 ‹There[9] was a controversy existing between an elder of the third **Presbyterian** Church[10] **&**

[7]This was William James (1797–1868). "Billy" James was the youngest of twins born to the wealthy Albany merchant, William James, by his first wife. He was thus an uncle of Henry James, the novelist, and William James, the psychologist. He graduated from Princeton in 1816, and after pastorates in New York City and Clarkson, New York, he was called to Rochester in 1826. He remained until October 1831, when he moved to Schenectady. But in 1832 he made his home in Albany. Although he had a brief pastorate there, being wealthy after the death of his father, he was chiefly engaged in philanthropic activities and withdrew from ministerial life. From an early period, concern for sanctification and holiness became the all-absorbing passion of his life. See Katharine B. Hastings, "William James (1771–1832) of Albany, N.Y., and His Descendants," in *The New York Genealogical and Biographical Record* 55 (April 1924): 104, 108–9; Henry B. Stanton, *Random Recollections* (New York: Harper, 1887), p. 40; Stanton to T. D. Weld, 4 August 1832, in Gilbert H. Barnes and Dwight L. Dumond, eds., *Letters of Theodore Dwight Weld, Angelina Grimké Weld, and Sarah Grimké, 1822–1844* (Gloucester, Mass.: Peter Smith, 1965), p. 83; and Henry Neill, "View of Mr. James's Character and Life," in *Grace for Grace: Letters of Rev. William James, of Albany, U.S.A.* (London: Hodder and Stoughton, 1875), pp. 282–90.

The Second Presbyterian Church had been organized in 1825 as an offshoot of the First Church. In 1826 James was called as the first pastor, and in 1828 a large brick meeting house seating 1,250 people was completed. In 1833 the church was reorganized under the name of the Brick Presbyterian Church. The building, however, was demolished in 1860 because of constant problems with dampness due to faulty construction. See Louis Chapin, "Historical Sketch," in *Fiftieth Anniversary of the Organization of the Brick Church, Rochester, N.Y.* (Rochester: Andrews, 1876), pp. 7–19; Orlo J. Price, "The Life and Times of Brick Church," *The Rochester Historical Society, Publication Fund Series* 14 (1936): 83–96; and "Rochester Revival—New Brick Church," *NYE,* 12 April 1860, p. 2.

[8]He in fact resigned a few weeks later on 14 October 1830 and was dismissed to the Albany Presbytery on 4 February 1831. Finney listed his dismissal as one of many obstacles that seemed to be put in the way by Satan to stop the revival. See *Lectures on Revivals of Religion*, ed. William G. McLoughlin (Cambridge, Mass.: Belknap, 1960), p. 34; and Chapin, "Historical Sketch," p. 15.

[9]The section at the top of MS 561 down to n. 14 was written by Finney on a separate piece of paper pasted on to the top of the sheet. It replaced a section, part of which was covered over. This includes the page numbers 406 and 538 written by Matson and the number 561 written by Finney and part of the text in Matson's handwriting:

> There was a good deal of sour feeling between the members of the third church and the members of the first church, which was then under the pastoral care of the Rev. Dr Penny. Things had been carried so far between these two churches, that one of the elders of the third church had brought charges

The text continues below where the piece of paper ends:

> against Dr Penny, the pastor of the first church, before the presbytery, and they were about having a trial. This, and many other matters of difference and jangling among the churches of Rochester at that time, rendered it an exceedingly uninviting field of labor when viewed from a certain standpoint.

This was crossed out by Finney.

[10]This was Josiah Bissell, Jr. (1790–1831), who was reputed to be the most zealous layman in Rochester. He had come there in 1815 and engaged in merchandising and building. He led in the promotion of Bible distribution, Sabbath schools, Sunday observance, and other reforms, and he was an advocate of the principle of "Pioneerism," or the refusal to do business with anyone but Christians. He was also well known as the founder of the Pioneer Packet and Stage Companies, which did no business on Sundays. He built the first wooden church occupied by the Third Presbyterian Church and became the leading elder and superintendent of the Sunday school. His zeal was such that "Worldlings thought him fanatical or even insane." See Edward R. Foreman, "The Bissells, Father and Son," *The Rochester Historical Society, Publication Fund Series* 6 (1927): 332–35; Blake McKelvey, "Civic Medals Awarded Posthumously," *Rochester History* 22, no. 2 (April 1960): 7; and Lewis Tappan, "Josiah Bissell, Jun.," *NYE,* 23 April 1831, pp. 222–23.

the **Pastor** of the first church[11] that was about to be tried before the **Presbytery**.[12] This **&** other matters had **created an** unchristian **state of** feeling to[13] **considerable** extent in both churches **&** altogether it seemed a forbidding field of labor at that time.›[14] The friends at Rochester were exceedingly anxious to have me go there—I mean the members of the third church. Being left without a pastor they felt as if there was great danger that they would be scattered, and perhaps annihilated as a church unless something could be done to revive religion amongst them.[15] With these pressing invitations before me **from so many points of the compass,** I felt, as I ꜝhave ꜝoften done, greatly perplexed. I remained at my father-in-law's, and considered the subject until I felt that I must take hold and work somewhere. Accordingly we packed our trunks and went down to Utica, about seven miles distant **from my father-in-law's,** where I had many praying friends. We arrived there in the afternoon,[16] and in the evening a **considerable** number of the leading brethren, in whose prayers and wisdom I had a great deal of confidence, at my request met for consultation and prayer in regard to my next field of labor. I laid all the facts before them in regard to Rochester; and so far as I was acquainted with them, the leading facts in respect to the **leading** fields to which I was invited at that time. Rochester seemed to be the least inviting of them all.

JHF 285
MS 562

After talking the matter all over, and having several seasons of prayer interspersed with **our** conversation, the brethren gave their opinions one after another in relation to what they thought it wise for me to do. They were unanimous in the opinion that ꜝRochester was too uninviting a field of labor to be put at all in competition with New York or Philadelphia, and some other fields to which I was then invited. They were firm in the conviction that I should go east from Utica, and not west. At the time this was my own impression and conviction; and I retired from this meeting, as I supposed

MS 563

[11]Joseph Penney (1793–1860) was the second minister of the First Presbyterian Church, which had been organized in 1815. Penney was from Ireland and was educated in Dublin and at Glasgow University. He was installed at Rochester in 1822 and was to remain until 1832. After three years in Jonathan Edwards's old church in Northampton, Massachusetts, he became president of Hamilton College until 1839, when he moved to New York. He had recently returned from a visit to Ireland in 1829, where he was instrumental in introducing temperance reform, which led to the first temperance organizations in Britain. See Henry O'Reilly, *Settlement in the West*, pp. 277–79; *NYE*, 12 April 1860, p. 6; and McKelvey, "Civic Medals," pp. 8–9.

[12]The controversy between Joseph Penney and Josiah Bissell had been going on for more than a year. It apparently revolved around Bissell's extreme zeal. His original dispute was with James of the Second Church, who was opposed to Bissell's reforming zeal. Bissell had attempted to get James dismissed, and his intermeddling had caused disaffection in that church. Penney had come to James's defense. Penney was "a conservative balance against the emotional excesses of Josiah Bissell and his associates" (McKelvey, "Civic Medals," p. 9). See also Blake McKelvey, *Rochester the Water-Power City, 1812–1854* (Cambridge, Mass.: Harvard University Press, 1945), pp. 132–35, 188–89; and "Church Difficulties," *The Craftsman* (Rochester), 9 March 1830, pp. 30–31.

[13]Finney omitted the indefinite article.

[14]This ends the section in Finney's handwriting.

[15]The Third Church had started with 22 members and had been built up to a membership of 207 by the time Parker left. However, it was reported that sometimes his congregation was only 30 to 50. See "Rev. Joel Parker," *NYE,* 3 July 1830, p. 55; and *The Craftsman,* 9 March 1830, p. 30.

[16]This was about the second week in September 1830.

Third Presbyterian Church, Rochester. Finney preached here during the great revival of 1830–31 and again in 1842 after it had become the Second Baptist Church. Engraving in Henry O'Reilly, *Settlement in the West* (Rochester: Alling, 1838), opposite p. 280. Courtesy The British Library.

settled not to go to Rochester but to New York or Philadelphia. This was before railroads existed; and when we parted that evening I expected to take the canal boat—which was the most convenient way for a family to travel—and start in the morning for New York. But after I retired to my lodging the question was presented to my mind under a different aspect. Something seemed to question me—"What are the reasons that deter you from going to Rochester?" I could readily enumerate them; but then the question returned—"Ah! but are these *good* reasons? Certainly you are *needed* at Rochester *all the more* because of these difficulties. Do you shun the |field because there are so many |things that need to be corrected, because there is so much that is *wrong*? But if all was right, you would not be needed." I soon came to the conclusion that we were all wrong; and that the reasons that had determined us *against* my going to Rochester, were the most cogent reasons *for* my going. **I concluded that I was more needed at that time in Rochester than in any of the fields that were open to me.** I felt ashamed to

JHF 286
MS 564

shrink from undertaking the work because of its difficulties; **because** it was strongly impressed upon my **mind** that the Lord would be with me, and that that was my field. My mind became entirely decided before I retired to rest, that Rochester was the place to which the Lord would have me go. I informed my wife of my decision; and accordingly early in the morning, before the people were **up much** in the city, the packet **canal** boat came along, and we embarked and went westward instead of eastward, **and made our way to Rochester**. The brethren in Utica were greatly surprized when they learned |of this change in our destination, and awaited the result with a good deal of (MS 565) solicitude, **as I learned**. We arrived in Rochester early in the morning,[17] and were invited to take up our lodgings for the time with **Brother** Josiah Bissel, who was the leading elder in the third church, and who was the person that had complained to the presbytery respecting Dr Penny.[18] ‹On my arrival I met my cousin **Frederic Star**[**r**] in the street who invited me to his house.[19] He was an Elder in the first **Pres.** Church, & hearing that I was expected at Rochester was very anxious to have his **P**astor Dr. Penny meet & converse with me & be prepared to cooperate with me in my labors. **As** I declined his kind invitation **to go to his house**, informing him that I was to be the guest of Mr Bissell he called on me **immediately** after breakfast & informed me that he had arranged an interview between myself & Dr. Penny, at his house **at that hour**. I hastened to meet the **Dr.** & we had a cheering Christian interview. When I commenced my labors Dr. Penny attended our meetings &

[17] Finney started supplying the pulpit of the Third Church from Friday, 10 September 1830, and he remained until 6 March 1831. See Parsons, *History of Rochester Presbytery*, p. 252.

[18] The section following to the end of the page is in Finney's handwriting on a separate piece of paper pasted onto the bottom of the sheet. It replaces a section that continued at the top of the next page. The part of the text covered up reads:

> Josiah Bissell was a very warm-hearted, thorough, energetic Christian man. He had a year or two before established a line of Sabbath-keeping stages from Albany to Buffalo, as the old line travelled on the Sabbath. This he had done at great expense and self-sacrifice, and had brought upon himself a storm of opposition from the friends of the old line. When I commenced my labors in the third church, there was at first no apparent sympathy with my labors manifested by the members of the other churches or by the ministers. But very soon things began to change. The leading members of the other churches came in and heard. Dr Penny came and heard;

The text continues at the top of the next page:

> and brother William James, from the second church, came and heard. It was soon apparent that a better state of feeling was springing up.

This was crossed out by Finney.

[19] Frederick Starr (1799–1869) was a son of Platt Starr, a clothier and hotelkeeper in Warren, Connecticut, whose uncle was Rev. Peter Starr, the minister there. His mother was Lucinda (Finney) Starr (1763–1836), a younger sister of Finney's father Sylvester. Frederick was a schoolmate of Finney's in Warren, and at age twenty he went to New York and became a clerk in a bookstore. In 1822 he moved to Rochester, where he became a furniture and piano manufacturer and was prominent in the affairs of the town. He was a founder and elder of the First Presbyterian Church, but in 1856 he joined the Washington Street Church. Although fairly conservative, he supported the benevolence and reform movements. He was a man "of uncompromising Christian principle, of great energy of character, and deservedly wide influence." His father and mother also moved to Rochester in 1826. (See Burgis Pratt Starr, *A History of the Starr Family, of New England* [Hartford, Conn.: Case, Lockwood, and Brainerd, 1879], pp. 451–53; James Logan McElroy, "Social Reform in the Burned-Over District: Rochester, New York, as a Test Case, 1830–1854" [Ph.D. diss., State University of New York at Binghamton, 1974], p. 232; and "Death of Mrs. Frederick Starr," *NYE*, 4 January 1883, p. 8.) Finney's spelling of the name as "Star" is evidently an error, for he spells it correctly later.

soon invited me to his pulpit.[20] **Mr Starr** exerted himself to bring about a
JHF 287 good understanding be|tween the **Pastors & Churches**[21] & a great change soon manifested itself in the attitude & spiritual state of the **Churches**.›[22]

MS 566 |There[23] were very soon some very marked conversions. ‹T›he wife[24] of a prominent lawyer in **that** city, was one of the first converts **that was much known in the city**. She was a **lady** of high standing, **well-known,** a lady of

[20]Dr. Penney probably at first opposed Finney's going to Rochester. Mary Allen, the schoolteacher, recollected:

> It is well known that Mr. Finney was opposed by many of the ministers of this State. He came to Rochester in the midst of opposition. Many were opposed to his being invited to preach in the pulpit of the Third Church. . . . Mr. B— [Bissell], favored his coming, and Dr. Penny, the devoted and learned clergyman of the First Church, remarked to me, on first hearing him, that he was glad to sit at his feet and learn (Mary B. Allen King, *Looking Backward; or, Memories of the Past* [New York: Randolph, 1870], p. 120).

[21]Louis Chapin, a clerk in Josiah Bissell's canal boat firm and a convert in this revival, wrote to G. F. Wright: "Such was the state of feeling between the pastors or their congregations that neither of the 3 ministers was an acceptable preacher in any but his own church" (Chapin to Wright, 1 February 1890, Wright Papers, box 8; and Alfred Nevin, ed., *Encyclopaedia of the Presbyterian Church in the United States of America* [Philadelphia: Presbyterian Encyclopaedia Publishing Co., 1884], p. 1096).

[22]The state of things at Rochester may not have been as bad as Finney imagined. A widely published report in the *Rochester Observer* stated:

> It is now four weeks since the Rev. Mr. Finney commenced his labors with us. At that time there was evidently more feeling and more of the spirit of prayer in all of the churches than had existed for some time previous, and some solitary cases of conversion to encourage the hopes and gladden the hearts of Christians (reprinted in *NYE,* 23 October 1830, p. 119).

The Methodist minister Gleazen Fillmore also wrote that there had been increasing interest that reached a climax at a camp meeting in Henrietta at the end of August 1830: "From this meeting we may date a powerful reformation in Rochester. After sixteen had professed conversion in our congregation, the Rev. Mr. Finney commenced his labours in the Presbyterian congregations, and the work became general through the village" (letter dated 1 March 1831 in *Christian Advocate and Journal* [New York], 25 March 1831, p. 118).

Asa Mahan, at that time minister of nearby Pittsford, recalled:

> In the spring and summer of 1830, months before Mr. Finney came to Rochester, and before it was known that he had thought of doing so, a visible change, from no known cause, came over the public mind. Scoffing at sacred things, and bitter opposition to religious truth, spontaneously disappeared. Our congregations on the Sabbath gradually increased, while an unwonted solemnity rested upon them in all sacred exercises. This was attended with occasional conversions in various directions. These facts I heard referred to by various ministers. They made manifest the gathering of the cloud far in the heavens above us, while the windows of heaven were not yet opened (Asa Mahan, *Autobiography, Intellectual, Moral, and Spiritual* [London: Woolmer, 1882], p. 221).

[23]The section at the top of page 566 was crossed out by Finney when he replaced it with a new section on the previous page.

[24]This sentence originally started, "Mrs. Sela Matthews, the wife," but the name was crossed out by Finney. "?Sela?" is written in the margin in pencil. The writing appears to be Lewis Tappan's.

Mary P. Mathews was the wife of Selah Mathews (1807–1861), a rising young lawyer who went into partnership with his uncle, Gen. Vincent Mathews, and became one of the most prominent lawyers in Rochester. In the 1850 Census Schedule she is listed as age forty-four, a year older than her husband. See George H. Humphrey, "Changes in Practice of the Law in Rochester," *The Rochester Historical Society, Publication Fund Series* 4 (1925): 209–11; William F. Peck, *Semi-Centennial History of the City of Rochester* (Syracuse: Mason, 1884), p. 149; letters of the Mathews to the Finneys in the Finney Papers; and "Population Schedules of the Seventh Census of the United States, 1850," City of Rochester, 3rd Ward, Dwelling 586, The National Archives and Records Service, microfilm, roll 530.

culture and extensive influence. Her conversion was a very marked one. The first that I saw her a **lady** friend of hers came with her to my room, and introduced her. The lady who introduced her was a Christian woman, who had found that she was very much exercised in her mind, and persuaded her to come and see me. Mrs. ‹———›[25] had been a gay, worldly woman, and very fond of society. She af**ter**wards told me that when I first came there she greatly regretted it, and feared there would be a revival; **and if so it** would greatly interfere with the pleasures and amusements that she had promised herself that winter. |On conversing with her I found that the Spirit of the Lord (MS 567) was indeed dealing with her in an unsparing manner. She was bowed down with great conviction of sin. After considerable conversation with her, **I pressed her hard**[26] **then and there to give herself to Christ**—to renounce sin, and the world, and self, and everything for Christ. I saw that she was a very proud woman, and this struck me as rather the most marked feature of her character. At the conclusion of our conversation we knelt down to pray; and my mind being full of the subject of the pride of her heart as it was manifested, I very soon introduced the text, "Except ye be converted and become as little children, ye shall in no wise enter into the kingdom of heaven."[27] **This I seemed to be led to by the Spirit of prayer almost irresistibly.** I turned this subject over in prayer; and **I** almost immediately heard Mrs. **Matthews**,[28] as she was kneeling by my side, repeating that text: "Except ye be converted and become as little children"—"as *little children*"—"Except ye be converted *and become as little children*." |I observed that her (MS 568) mind was taken with that, and the Spirit of God was pressing it upon her heart. I therefore continued to |pray **and** hold that subject before her mind, (JHF 288) and holding her up before God as needing that very thing[29] to be converted,—to become as a little child. **I besought the Lord to convert her, to make her as a little child, to put away her pride and her loftiness of spirit and bring her down into the attitude of a little child.** I felt that the Lord was answering prayer. I felt *sure* that **He** was; **and had no doubt, I believe, in my mind, that the Lord was** doing the very work that I asked him to do. Her heart broken down, her sensibility gushed forth, and before we rose from our knees she was indeed a little child. When I stopped praying and opened my eyes and looked at her, her face was turned up toward heaven, and the tears streaming **over her face**; and she was in the attitude of praying that she might be made a little child.[30] She rose up, became peaceful, settled into a joyous faith, and retired. |From that moment she was out- (MS 569)

[25] The name "Matthews" was written down by Matson but appears to have been crossed out by Finney. Fairchild reinserted the initial *M* and a dash.

[26] A question mark has been written in pencil in the margin against this phrase. It appears to have been inserted by Lewis Tappan.

[27] Matthew 18:3.

[28] The name "Matthews" was not crossed out by Finney here. Apart from the initial *M*, it was crossed out by Fairchild.

[29] The words "in order" here appear to have been crossed out by Finney.

[30] Mrs. Mathews recalled how Finney appeared to her then: "I shall never forget the heavenly appearance which his face exhibited to me, when I first looked up, and exclaimed that I felt that I could love God" (letter to Lydia Finney, 22 March [probably 1833], "Undated Letters," Finney Papers, microfilm, roll 7).

spoken in her religious convictions, and zealous for the conversion of her friends.[31] Her conversion of course produced much excitement among that class of people to which she belonged.

I had never, I believe ‹except in rare instances›,[32] until I went to Rochester, used as a means of promoting revivals, what has since been called "the anxious seat."[33] I had sometimes asked persons in the congregation to stand up; but this I had not frequently done. However, in studying upon the subject I had often felt the necessity of some measure that would bring sinners to a stand. From my own experience and observation I had found, that with the higher classes especially, the greatest obstacle to be overcome was their fear of being known as anxious inquirers. They were too proud to take any position that would reveal them to others as anxious for their souls. I had found also that something was needed **more than I had practiced** to make the impression on them that they were expected **then and there** to give up their |hearts; **and** something that would call them to act, and act as publicly before the world as they had in their sins; something that would commit them publicly to the service of Christ; **some public manifestation or demonstration that would declare to all around them that they abandoned a sinful life then and there, and committed themselves to Jesus Christ.** When I had called them simply to stand up in the public congregation, I found that this **had** had[34] a very good effect; and so far as it went it answered the purpose for |which it was intended. But after all I had felt for **sometime** that something more was necessary to bring them out from among the mass of the ungodly to a public renunciation of their sinful ways, and a public committal of themselves to God.

MS 570

JHF 289

At Rochester, if I recollect right, I first introduced this measure.[35] This was years after the cry had been raised of "**N**ew **M**easures." A few days after the

[31] After her conversion she became particularly involved in the abolition movement and was one of the founders of the abolitionist Bethel Free Church. Her husband was also active in religious and reform movements, particularly temperance. They were looked upon as "the greatest *Finneyites* in this village" (Mary Mathews to the Finneys, 19 October 1831, Finney Papers, microfilm, roll 3). See also James L. McElroy, "Social Control and Romantic Reform in Antebellum America: The Case of Rochester, New York," *New York History* 58, no. 1 (July 1977): 29–36.

Selah Mathews became city recorder in 1841 and a federal judge in 1847. He and his wife subsequently moved away from Evangelical perfectionism, and when Finney visited Rochester again in 1855 they "kept distant though he was then an elder in the Third" (Louis Chapin to G. F. Wright, 10 February 1890, Wright Papers, box 8). See also Nancy A. Hewitt, "The Perimeters of Women's Power in American Religion," in *The Evangelical Tradition in America,* ed. Leonard I. Sweet (Macon, Ga.: Mercer University Press, 1984), pp. 233–56.

[32] Finney added the words "except in rare instances."

[33] Finney records having first used this measure at Rutland in 1824 (MS 221). When he was in Rome in 1825, his invitations to people were not calls for decision making but were for the purpose of meeting them. The calls may, however, have served both functions. See MS 319 and 324.

[34] The tense of the verb was not altered in the manuscript, but one "had" was omitted from the published edition.

[35] It is possible that Finney was influenced by the Methodist practice of calling people to the altar, which had already been used effectively in Rochester. See Richard Carwardine, "The Second Great Awakening in the Urban Centers: An Examination of Methodism and the 'New Measures,'" *Journal of American History* 59, no. 2 (September 1972): 338–39.

conversion of Mrs. [36] I made a call, I think for the first time, upon all that class of persons whose convictions were so ripe that they ˡwere willing **then and there** to renounce their sins and give themselves to God, to come forward to certain seats which I requested to be vacated, and offer themselves up to God while we made them subjects of prayer. A much larger number came forward than I expected, and amongs**t others ‹another›** prominent lady;[37] and several others of her acquaintance, and belonging to the same circle of society, came forward. This increased the **excitement and** interest among that class of people; and it was soon seen that the Lord was aiming at the conversion of the highest classes of society. My meetings soon became thronged with that class. The lawyers, physicians, merchants, and indeed all the most intelligent **class of society**, became more and more interested, and more and more easily influenced **to give their hearts to God**.[38] Very soon the work took effect extensively among the lawyers in that city.[39] There has

MS 571

[36] The name "Matthews" appears to have been crossed out by Finney. Fairchild reinserted the initial letter *M* and a dash.

[37] Matson had written down, "and amongst others a prominent lady, a Mrs. General Riley." Finney altered it. A penciled question mark in the margin against the name appears to have been inserted by Lewis Tappan.

This was Charlotte (Stillson) Riley. She was the sister of Betsey Ann Stillson, who had been the first wife of Gen. Ashbel W. Riley (b. 1794). She became Riley's second wife in 1827. He was one of the pioneers of the village and a distinguished and prominent citizen. As a member of the Third Church, he and Josiah Bissell were known as "the make or break team." He was a man of great energy and enterprise and later devoted his life largely to the temperance cause, in which he was compared with Theobald Matthew. He became a major general in the militia service in the 1830s and was always known by his title after that. His second wife died in 1870. See "Gen. A. W. Riley," *Rochester Historical Society Publications* 1 (1892): 105; Orlo J. Price, "One Hundred Years of Protestantism in Rochester," *Centennial History of Rochester* 3 (1933): 250; "Rochester's Half-Century," *NYE*, 19 June 1884, p. 8; and Peck, *Semi-Centennial History*, pp. 127, 669.

[38] Reports of eyewitnesses at the time laid stress on the "great numbers of the first standing & influence," who were the subjects of the revival. "Men of the first business talent, men of wealth, most of the professional men of the place, as well as those who were poor, obscure, or vicious, are numbered among its hopeful subjects" (letter dated Rochester, 24 December [1830], in Heman Ely Collection, box 1, folder A, New York Historical Society). See also *WR*, 23 November 1830, p. 186.

Another report refers to a crowded prayer meeting for young converts in which the ten prayers offered were made by "a Brigadier General—Sheriff of the County—two Colonels—two Physicians—two Lawyers & two Merchants" ("Copy of a letter from a gentleman in Utica to a Clergyman in Boston," 7 February 1831, in Clark Collection, Congregational Library, Boston).

The reports published by the editor of the *Rochester Observer* stressed the same thing. All classes benefited by the revival,

> but were we to mention any one description of persons as having shared in it more largely than another, it would be young heads of families. Of these great numbers have arranged themselves on the Lord's side. We can say too—and facts will abundantly warrant us in saying it—that we have never known as large a proportion of men of wealth, talents and influence—those who move in the highest circles of society—brought to submit to the Gospel terms of salvation, and to lay all at the feet of the Saviour. They are those who are in the prime of life, and vigor of manhood (*Rochester Observer*, 12 November 1830, p. 2; see also 24 December 1830, p. 2).

The research of Paul Johnson reaches the same conclusion: "New church members came disproportionately from among businessmen, professionals, and master workmen." Of these, master workmen represented the most prominent group. "Of those whose birth dates are known, the median age of Finney's converts was thirty years" (P. Johnson, *A Shopkeeper's Millennium: Society and Revivals in Rochester, New York, 1815–1837* [New York: Hill and Wang, 1978], pp. 103–4, 188).

[39] In 1890 Louis Chapin was able to jot down from memory the names of twelve lawyers who

always been a large number of the leading lawyers of the state resident at
MS 572 Rochester. ˡThe work soon got hold of numbers of those. They became very anxious, and came freely to our meetings of inquiry; and numbers of them came forward to the anxious seat, as it has since been called, and publicly gave their hearts to God.

I recollect one evening after preaching, three of them followed me to my room, all of them deeply convicted; and all of them had been, I believe, on the anxious seat, but were not clear in their minds, and felt that they could not
JHF 290 go home until they were convinced their ˡpeace was made with God. I conversed with them, and prayed with them; and I believe, before they left they all found peace in believing in the Lord Jesus Christ. I should have said that very soon after the work commenced, the difficulties between **Brother** Bissel and Dr Penny were healed; and all the distractions and collisions that had existed there were adjusted, so that a spirit of universal kindness and fellowship pervaded all the churches **so far as I could learn**.

MS 573 ˡ**The work continued to increase, and** I ‹had an appointment› in the first church.[40] There had been a military parade in the city that day. The militia had been called out, and I had feared that the excitement of the parade might divert the attention of the people and mar the work of the Lord.[41] The house was **very much packed,** filled **to its utmost capacity** in every part. Dr Penny had introduced the services, and was engaged in the first prayer, when I heard something which I supposed to be the report of a gun, and the jingling of glass as if a window had been broken **by it**. My thought was that some careless **one of the trainers** on the outside had fired so near the window as to break a pane of glass. But before I had time to think again, Dr Penny leaped from the pulpit over me, for I was kneeling **and leaning upon** the sofa behind him. The pulpit was in the front of the church, between the two
MS 574 doors.[42] ˡThe **back end** of the church **came up to** the brink of the canal. The congregation in a moment fell into a perfect panic, and rushed for the doors and the windows as if they were all distracted. One elderly **lady** held up a window in the rear of the church, where several, as I was informed, leapt out into the canal. The rush was terrific. Some jumped over the galleries into the aisles below; **some actually ran from slip to slip on the tops of the pews;**[43] they ran over each other in the aisles. I stood up in the pulpit, and not knowing what had happened **I** put up my hands and cried at the top of my voice, "Be quiet! Be quiet!"[44] Directly a couple of **ladies** rushing up into the

became ministers from among those who were converted, as well as three physicians and seven students (Chapin to G. F. Wright, 10 February 1890, Wright Papers, box 8).

[40] Here Matson had written down, "The work continued to increase, and I was soon invited to occupy the pulpit of the first church." Finney altered it and also crossed out a sentence further down the page. See n. 41.

[41] Finney crossed out a sentence that followed here. It read, "On that evening I had an appointment in the first presbyterian church."

[42] According to William F. Peck, the Rochester historian, "Unlike the arrangement in most churches, the pulpit was at the front of the auditorium and all the pews were so arranged as to face it directly" (Peck, *Semi-Centennial History*, p. 118).

[43] This section was not crossed out by Fairchild in the manuscript but was omitted in the published edition.

[44] Charles P. Bush, a witness to the scene, recollected that Finney "stretched out his long arm over the surging throng, and cried at the top of his voice: 'Keep still! Keep still! there is no

pulpit, one on the one side and the other on the other side, caught hold of me in a state of distraction.[45] Dr Penny ran out into the streets, and they ˈwere JHF 291 getting out in every direction as fast as **they could.** As I did not know that there was any danger, the scene looked so ludicrous to me that I could scarcely refrain from laughing. ˈThey MS 575 rushed over each other in the aisles, so that in several instances I observed men **picking themselves up, and as they rose throwing weaker ones as they had stumbled upon them off "heads and points."[46] They got out of the house as soon as they could.** Several were considerably hurt, but no one killed. But the house was strewed with all sorts of, **especially female** apparel. **Some of them had their dresses torn off around near the bottom; and** bonnets, shawls, gloves, handkerchiefs, and parts of dresses, were scattered in every direction. **I learned that a large quantity of female apparel, parts of female dress, was left in the aisles and scattered about the house.**[47] The **gentlemen** had very generally gone out without their hats, I believe; and many persons had been **wounded and made sore by** the awful rush.

‹I afterwards› learned[48] that the walls of the church had been settling for some time, the ground being **made** very damp **by** its proximity to the canal. **The church was built of stone, and was consequently very heavy; the ground was clay, and ˈthe building had settled.** MS 576 It had been spoken of in the congregation as not in a satisfactory state; and some were afraid that either the tower would fall, or the roof, or the walls of the building, would come down.[49] Of this I had heard nothing myself.[50] The **noise that I heard was**

danger.' But there *was* danger, and the people would not keep still. The house was emptied in a few moments" (C. P. Bush, "Mr. Finney in Rochester and Western New York," in *Reminiscences of Rev. Charles G. Finney* [Oberlin: Goodrich, 1876], p. 10). Bush was one of the students at the Rochester High School who later became a minister. See MS 580.

[45] Robert L. Stanton, who witnessed the scene, recalled that "a few rushed up the pulpit stairs, clung to the ministers, and cried aloud for mercy" ("The Great Preacher," *The Independent* [New York], 23 September 1875, p. 5). Stanton was in the gallery and saw that the building was safe. He stood and watched and was among the last to leave.

[46] *The Oxford English Dictionary* gives the meaning of the expression "heads and points": "Said of nails, wedges, etc. placed alternately in opposite directions, so that the head of one lies against the point or edge of the next; hence transferred sense of persons lying."

[47] Stanton recalled:

> It was the time when "Navarino bonnets" were in fashion. After the house was emptied of people, crushed Navarinos, shawls, fans, slippers, reticules, gloves, hats, and all the *et ceteras* were brought out into the vestibule, and made a promiscuous pile of demoralized wearing apparel as large as a small hay-stack (*The Independent,* 23 September 1875, p. 5).

[48] The sentence began, "I learned," but Finney crossed out the "I" and inserted the words "I afterwards."

[49] Stanton pointed out:

> Its walls had settled and the side walls leaned outward slightly; but architects had pronounced it entirely safe and the usual congregation had worshiped in it for many years. A few, however, were afraid of it. On seeing the immense audience that evening, their fears were a little excited; but as the service went on, apprehensions were allayed (*The Independent,* 23 September 1875, p. 5).

According to Louis Chapin, a historian of the churches in Rochester and one of those in the stampede: "The walls were built on *rock* but there being no truss in the roof its pressure spread the top of the walls" (Chapin to G. F. Wright, 10 February 1890, Wright Papers, box 8).

[50] Finney had inserted at this point: "The weight in the gallery spread the walls, the roof spread," but he crossed it out.

made by a timber **in** the roof,[51] falling end downwards, and breaking through the **plastering right** above the lamp in front of the organ. **The plastering broke the lamp, which created the jingling of glass that I heard. The people of the city being afraid of the house, took the alarm and rushed out, as I have described. Dr Penny said that when the timber fell, he opened his eyes as he was leading in prayer, and saw what was done; and thinking that no doubt the roof was** ‹falling›,[52] **he leaped from the pulpit and got out as soon as he could.** On examining the house it was found that the walls **of the house** had spread in such a manner that there was indeed danger of the roof falling in. The pressure each night in the gallery was MS 577 so great as to spread the walls on each side |until there was real danger **of the peoples being injured.** At the time this occurred, I greatly feared, as I suppose others did, that **it would mar the work; it created so great an excitement, and withal rendered it impossible to hold our meetings any more in that house.** But **it seemed not to mar the work.**[53] The Spirit of the Lord had taken hold of the work in earnest, and nothing seemed to stay it.

The Brick church was thrown open to us, **and its pastor about that time took his dismission and went to another field.**[54] From that time ‹our meetings› alternated[55] between the second and third **presbyterian** churches, the people of the first church and congregation attending as far as they could get into the house;[56] **and** the three **presbyterian** churches, and indeed JHF 292 Christians of every denomination |generally seemed to make common cause, **and entirely united in their efforts,**[57] and went to work with a will to pull sinners out of the fire. We were obliged to hold meetings almost continually. I preached nearly every night, and three times on the Sabbath.[58] We held our

[51] This was evidently "a loose bit of scantling left by some careless workman among the timbers of the roof" (Bush, "Mr. Finney in Rochester," p. 10). Stanton, however, noted: "On examination, a small piece of scantling, not at all connected with the frame of the roof, was found resting upon the broken lath where the plastering fell. Whether it was thrown there designedly, to break up the meeting, or fell there in some other way was never satisfactorily determined" (*The Independent,* 23 September 1875, p. 5).

[52] Finney changed the words "giving in" to "falling."

[53] Stanton reckoned that the catastrophe "was regarded by many as a sort of judgment on that church, that they might be driven out to meet with other congregations" ("Remarks of Rev. R. L. Stanton," in *Reminiscences of Finney,* p. 26). "The First and Second church people had been somewhat estranged. This brought them together" (*The Independent,* 23 September 1875, p. 5).

[54] The catastrophe in the First Church happened on the evening of 1 October, and William James resigned on 14 October 1830. See Parsons, *History of Rochester Presbytery,* pp. 244, 246.

[55] Matson had written "I alternated," but Finney changed it to "our meetings alternated."

[56] After the disaster, First Church was closed until supports for the roof could be set up in the middle aisle. Buttresses were subsequently added. In the meantime, St. Paul's Episcopal Church, which had no rector, was made available for their use for a time (see O'Reilly, *Settlement in the West,* p. 279; and Parsons, *History of Rochester Presbytery,* p. 244). Finney also preached "a few times in the first Baptist & the Methodist churches" (L. Chapin to G. F. Wright, 10 February 1890, Wright Papers, box 8).

[57] Fairchild omitted the phrase "and entirely united in their efforts." But the unity among Christians was noted early on in the revival: "The most perfect harmony prevails between the different Presbyterian churches" (*Rochester Observer,* 15 October 1830, reprinted in *WR,* 19 October 1830, p. 167, and elsewhere). See also *WR,* 28 December 1830, p. 206.

[58] Finney preached ninety-eight sermons during his six months in Rochester.

> Every sermon for two or three weeks was addressed to Christians,—scarce a word to sinners in all that time. . . . The Church being thus shaken as by an earthquake, and aroused to pray fervently for God's blessing on the efforts contemplated for the saving

meetings of inquiry, after the work took ˡon such a powerful type, very frequently in the morning. One morning I recollect we had been holding a meeting of inquiry, and a gentleman was present and was converted there who was the son-in-law of a very praying, godly woman belonging to the third church. She had been very anxious about him, and had been spending much time in prayer for him. When he returned from the meeting of inquiry he was full of joy, and peace, and hope. She had been spending the time in earnest prayer that God would convert him at that meeting. As soon as she met him and he declared his conversion to her, and from his countenance she saw that it was really so, it overcame her, and she swooned away and fell dead. **This was a very striking fact, and served rather to increase the solemnity. Another man that lived on the west side of the river, and below the city a mile or more, was under great conviction for several days, and finally was suddenly and powerfully converted. The reaction in his mind ˡwas so great, and his joy so overwhelming, that he also fell dead.** MS 578 MS 579

There was at that time a high school in Rochester,[59] presided over by a Mr. **Benedict**,[60] the son of **Abner Benedict**, then pastor of the church at Brighton near Rochester.[61] Mr. **Benedict** was a skeptic, but was at the head of a very large and flourishing **high** school.[62] As the school was made up of both sexes, a Miss **Allen** was his assistant and associate in the school at the time.[63] Miss **Allen** was a Christian woman. The students attended the

of souls, Mr. Finney was prepared to preach to sinners (C. P. Bush, "Charles G. Finney," *NYE,* 26 August 1875, p. 4).

See also Parsons, *History of Rochester Presbytery*, p. 252. A number of these sermons were noted down by Bradford King, one of the converts, in his "Diary," pp. 52–81, University of Rochester Library.

[59]The high school had been started in 1828 and was a flourishing school with three hundred pupils. It was later reorganized as the Rochester Seminary under Gilbert Morgan in 1832, and in 1838 Chester Dewey became the principal. It was one of the best schools in western New York. In 1839 it became the Rochester Collegiate Institute. See Blake McKelvey, "On the Educational Frontier," *The Rochester Historical Society, Publication Fund Series* 17 (1939): 16–28; and King, *Looking Backward,* pp. 116, 119.

[60]Farand Northrop Benedict (1803–1880) was a graduate of Hamilton College. After studying law for two years he practiced civil engineering and then became principal of the high school. He left in 1831 to go to an academy in Virginia. Subsequently he became professor of mathematics and civil engineering at the University of Vermont. See Henry M. Benedict, *The Genealogy of the Benedicts in America* (Albany: Munsell, 1870), pp. 222–24.

[61]Abner Benedict (1781–1830) had been a schoolteacher and Congregational pastor in New Jersey before becoming an evangelist in western New York. He was a younger brother of Joel T. Benedict (Benedict, *Genealogy of the Benedicts*, pp. 141–42; see also n. 65 below.

Brighton was at that time a separate village three miles southeast of Rochester. It was one of the first places to which the revival spread. Finney went there to preach for Benedict during the revival. See *Rochester Observer*, 15 October 1830, reprinted in *WR,* 19 October 1830, p. 167; and letters from Benedict to Finney in the Finney Papers.

[62]According to Mary Allen he "thought more of his mathematical attainments than of his soul. He told me that he sometimes thought over a problem in mathematics during the whole time of family worship, without hearing a word of Scripture or prayer" (King, *Looking Backward*, pp. 119–20).

[63]Mary B. Allen (born c. 1799) had taught school in Vermont before moving to New York State in 1826. From 1828 until the spring of 1830 she was the female principal of the Monroe Academy at Henrietta. Then she started a school in Pittsford, where she was friendly with the minister, Asa Mahan, and his wife. She took up the appointment of female principal at the high school in Rochester about two weeks before Finney went there. She remained seven years and afterward opened her own seminary. Failing sight compelled her to relinquish teaching in about

religious services, and many of them soon became deeply anxious about their souls. One morning Mr. Benedict found that his classes could not recite. When he came to have them before him they were so anxious about their souls that they wept, and he saw that they were in such a state that it very much confounded him. He called his female associate, Miss Allen, and told her that the young lads and young men were so exercised about their souls that they could not recite; and asked if they had not better send for Finney to give them instruction. She afterwards in|formed me of this, and said that she was very glad to have him make the inquiry, |and most cordially advised him to send for me. He did so, and the revival took a tremendous hold of that school.[64] Mr Benedict himself was soon hopefully converted, and nearly every person in the school was converted.[65] But a few years since Miss

MS 580
JHF 293

1863. Three years later she married another Rochester teacher, Moses King, and she was still living in Rochester as a widow in 1890. See her autobiography, *Looking Backward*; Louis Chapin to G. F. Wright, 10 February 1890, Wright Papers, box 8; and Peck, *Semi-Centennial History*, pp. 308–11.

[64] Mary Allen recalled the details of the story in her autobiography. Mr. Benedict "had about sixty of the young gentlemen in his room, all of whom, with the exception of two, who were professors of religion, tried to do and think as he did. One of these two was Mr. A—, who ever since has been a successful evangelist, both in this and the Western States." Finney had been preaching for two weeks, and the revival had taken hold.

> The principal of the school was opposed to the students leaving their studies to attend meeting, but Mr. A— felt great anxiety for the conversion of his class-mates. One Monday morning, the third week after the meetings began, he called on Mr. Finney, and asked what he could do for them.
>
> "Talk with them," said Mr. Finney, "and pray for them."
>
> "There is no time in school," said Mr. A—, "and I can't get access to them out of school."
>
> "Go and talk with them now," said Mr. Finney; "you have half an hour before school is called, and I will pray for you," and kneeling down, he commenced, while Mr. A— was leaving the room.
>
> He said a few words to them before the school opened, and at eleven o'clock Mr. Benedict came into my room, and with some excitement, said "I don't know what ails the young men in my room. We can't get along at all this morning. They can't one of them go through with a proposition at the board."
>
> "Why," said I; "what is the matter with them?"
>
> "Half of them are crying," he said "and say they are troubled about their souls." And he added, "Do you think I had better send for Finney to talk and pray with them?"
>
> "Yes," I replied, "and invite him into my room also."
>
> This last was just what I desired. He did so. Thus God answered prayer. . . .
>
> The revival continued for months. All the teachers and a large number of the scholars were hoping in Christ (King, *Looking Backward*, pp. 120–21, 123).

[65] Miss Allen goes into considerable detail in relating how Mr. Benedict was eventually converted. But he was evidently disillusioned later with Finney and the revival. When the excitements occasioned by Jedediah Burchard were causing a stir in Vermont in 1835, Professor James Marsh wrote to Nathan Lord from the college at Burlington:

> Professor F. N. Benedict of this college was at Rochester at the time, when Mr Finney kept up the same state of things, as we have here now, for nearly a year. . . . The church, in which Mr. F laboured, had been formed by the excitable members from two other churches uniting. They kept the whole town in commotion, & a large school, which Mr. Benedict was teaching, was entirely broken up for months, a number of young men preparing for the ministry, & aided by the Education Society, were induced to leave their studies, & commence preaching at once, & all further prosecution of sound knowledge discouraged, as incompatible with the duty of Christians in this age. They numbered about 2,000 converts in the city, & talked of nothing less, than the immediate approach of the millennium. . . . Professor B.s father was the pastor of a church in the suburbs of Rochester of about 200 members, had had frequent revivals,

Allen informed me that more than forty persons that were then converted in that school had become ministers; **and I am not sure but she said that more than forty of them had become foreign missionaries.**[66] That was a fact that I had not known before. She named many of them to me at the time, **and a** large **proportion** of them, **certainly,** had become foreign missionaries.[67] After remaining a few weeks at Josiah Bissel's, we took lodgings in a more central position, at the house of Mr **Beach,** a lawyer of the city, who was a professedly Christian man.[68] His wife's sister was with them, and was an impenitent girl.[69] She was **a girl** of fine appearance, a‹n exquisite› singer,[70] a

> & the ch[urc]h was in a flourishing healthful state. This system was crowded in against the will of his father, it distressed & agitated him, & as his son believes was the occasion of his death. However multitudes were added to the church, & *now* that church is literally disorganized, & there is no church there (James Marsh to Nathan Lord, December 1835, James Marsh Collection, University of Vermont Library).

See also John J. Duffy, ed., *Coleridge's American Disciples: The Selected Correspondence of James Marsh* (Amherst: University of Massachusetts Press, 1973), pp. 185–86; and King, *Looking Backward*, pp. 123–24.

[66]There is a penciled question mark in the margin against the last part of this sentence. It appears to have been inserted by Lewis Tappan.

It was in November 1859 that the Finneys learned about these events from Miss Allen. She was on a trip to Europe and met the Finneys when they were in Edinburgh, Scotland. Mrs. Finney noted the details in her journal at the time: "Miss Allen said she could count 40 in that school at that time who had become ministers and missionaries beside many in the female department who had been most actively useful—some as teachers some as ministers' wives—some as missionaries" ("A Journal Kept by Mrs. Elizabeth Ford Atkinson Finney during a Visit to England in 1859–1860," pp. 54–55, manuscript in Special Collections, Oberlin College Library). These details differ in some respects from those in Miss Allen's account.

According to Louis Chapin, who had read the published edition of Finney's *Memoirs*, "Miss A— . . . overestimated the number of students in Benedict's High School who became ministers. There were a good number." (The part of the sentence referring to "foreign missionaries" was not in the published version that Chapin read.) Miss Allen herself wrote in her autobiography, "twenty or more became ministers of the gospel." See Chapin to G. F. Wright, 10 February 1890, Wright Papers, box 8; and King, *Looking Backward*, p. 121.

[67]Miss Allen gives details of a number of the students in her autobiography. One of those who went there soon after the revival was Fidelia Church, who married Titus Coan, the missionary to Hawaii. Coan and Miss Church were both involved in the revivals and knew Finney at this time. They went out to Hawaii in 1834. The great revival there, which reached its peak in 1837, probably owed a good deal indirectly to the Finney revivals, through the labors of the Coans, Judds, Gulicks, and others. Coan later wrote: "I have seen great and powerful awakenings under the preaching of Nettleton and Finney, and like doctrines, prayers and efforts seemed to produce like fruits among this people" *Life in Hawaii: An Autobiographical Sketch* [New York: Randolph, 1882], pp. 14, 29; letters of Fidelia Church to Titus Coan, 1831–1832, in Coan Papers, New York Historical Society [information from Margaret S. Ehlke]; and MS 356).

Roselle T. Cross remembered a meeting in the Second Church in Oberlin in June 1870 when "the Communion was administered by Mr. Finney and Titus Coan, the great Hawaiian missionary. Probably no two men then living had led more souls to Christ. It was an impressive communion service" (R. T. Cross, "Memories of Charles G. Finney," typescript, n.d., p. 4, Alumni Records, file 28/1, "Roselle Theodore Cross," Oberlin College Archives).

A. H. Strong also mentioned that "forty of the converts entered the ministry." But he was referring to the whole of Rochester, not just the high school. See Strong, *Christ in Creation and Ethical Monism* (Philadelphia: Williams, 1899), p. 365.

[68]This was Elisha Beach (see Louis Chapin to G. F. Wright, 10 February 1890, Wright Papers, box 8). At the end of their stay in Rochester the Finneys were boarding with the Mathews (see Mary Mathews to Lydia Finney, 24 and 25 April 1831, Finney Papers, microfilm, roll 3). For a time Finney apparently "had his Quarters" in the Eagle Hotel (see Augustus H. Strong, "Reminiscences of Early Rochester," *The Rochester Historical Society, Publication Fund Series* 4 [1925]: 294).

[69]This was Mary Selkrigg, "of Scotch descent." See L. Chapin to G. F. Wright, 10 February 1890, Wright Papers, box 8; and Peck, *Semi-Centennial History*, p. 656.

MS 581 cultivated lady; and, as we soon learned, was |engaged in marriage to ______, who was then judge of the supreme court of that state.[71] He was a very proud man, and resisted the anxious seat, and spoke against it.[72] **However he was** absent a good deal from the city in holding court, and was not that winter converted. A large number of the lawyers, however, were converted; and the young lady to whom he was engaged was converted.[73] I mention this because ‹the› Judge afterwards married her;[74] which no doubt led to his own conversion in a revival which occurred some ten years later; the leading particulars of which I shall mention in another part of my narrative ‹**in the order of time.**›[75]

This revival made a great ‹change› in the moral ‹state & subsequent› history of Rochester.[76] The great majority of the leading men and women in the city were converted. A great number of very striking incidents occurred that I shall not soon forget. One day ‹the lady who first visited me &› whose conversion I have mentioned, ‹called on› me[77] in company with a friend of MS 582 hers with whom she |wished me to converse. I did so, but found her to all appearance very much hardened, and rather disposed to trifle with the subject. Her husband was a merchant, and they were persons of high JHF 294 |standing in the community. When I pressed her to attend to the subject, she said she would not do it because her husband would not attend to it, and she was not going to leave him. I asked her if she was willing to be lost because her husband would not attend to it; and if it was not folly to neglect her soul because he did his. She replied very promptly: "If he goes to hell I want to go. I want to go where he does. I do not want to be separated from him at any

[70] Matson had written "a beautiful singer, and," but Finney changed it to "an exquisite singer."

[71] The words "Judge Addison Gardiner" here appear to have been crossed out by Finney. Addison Gardiner (1797–1883), a native of New Hampshire, went to Rochester in 1822 and became the first justice of the peace there. In 1825 he was appointed district attorney for the county, and he was made a circuit judge in 1829. In 1844 and again in 1846 he was lieutenant governor of the state. At the reorganization of the judicial system in 1847, he became one of the first judges of the court of appeals, serving until 1855, when he voluntarily retired. See *In Memoriam: Addison Gardiner, 1797–1883* (privately printed, 1884); and Peck, *Semi-Centennial History*, pp. 653–56.

[72] John Ingersoll, who was supplying the pulpit at the time in Manlius, New York, wrote to Finney: "Colo. Gardiner, one of the Deacons of this Church feels a deep solicitude for the soul of his son living in Rochester, Judge Gardiner. The Deacon has repeatedly and with much consultings, requested me to write you requesting you to go and see him. Do go" (Ingersoll to Finney, 19 November 1830, Finney Papers, microfilm, roll 2, punctuation supplied).

[73] According to Louis Chapin this happened soon after Finney went to board at Elisha Beach's house. She

> was seriously affected and manifested stubborness and affected indifference, but the next morning he [Finney] met her coming into the hall singing to herself: "Jesus with all thy saints above: My tongue would bear her part &c" and said "Mary, when did you become a Christian." She replyed "I don't know that I am a Christian, but I have made up my mind to serve the Lord" (Chapin to G. F. Wright, 10 February 1890, Wright Papers, box 8).

[74] Matson had written "Judge Gardiner," but Finney altered it to "the Judge." They were married in 1831.

[75] See MS 741–47. Finney added the phrase "in the order of time."

[76] Here Matson had written down, "This revival made a great turning point in the moral history of Rochester," but Finney changed it.

[77] Here Matson had written "One day the Mrs. Matthews, whose conversion I have mentioned, visited me," but Finney changed it.

rate." It seemed that I could make **but** very little if any impression upon her. **She had made up her mind to cleave to her husband; and if he did not attend to the salvation of his soul she would not.**[78] But from night to night I had been making appeals to the congregation, and calling forward those that were prepared to give their hearts to God; and large numbers were converted every evening.

MS 583

|As I learned afterwards, when this **lady** went home her husband said to her: "My dear, I mean to go forward to-night, and give my heart to God." "What!" said she. "I have to-day told Mr. Finney that I would not become a Christian, or have anything to do with it. **That** you did not become a Christian, and I would not; and that if you went to hell, I **would** go with you." "Well," said he, "I do not *mean* to go to hell, I have made up my mind to go forward to-night, and give my heart[79] to Christ." "Well," said she, "then I will not go to meeting. I do not want to see it. And if you have a mind, after all, to become a Christian, you may; I won't." When the time came he went to meeting alone. The pulpit was between the doors in the front of the church.[80] The house was a good deal crowded; but he finally got a seat near one of the aisles in quite the back part of the church. At the close of the meeting, as **was my custom then,** I called for those that were anxious and whose minds were made up, to come forward, and take certain seats, and **occupy a certain space about** |**the pulpit, where we could commend them to God in prayer. It afterwards** appeared that **after he went to** meeting **she went herself; but not knowing where he was, she** passed up the other aisle, and **took** a seat almost opposite **to** him in the extreme part of the house. When I made |the call he started immediately. She was watching **to see where he was, and saw him ‹rise to go forward›.**[81] **As soon as she** saw him on his feet, and **crowding** his way along **through** the crowded aisle **to get to the place where they were to have seats,** she also started down the other aisle **toward the pulpit. To their mutual surprize** they met in front of the pulpit, and knelt down as subjects of prayer. ‹A› larger[82] number obtained hope on the spot; but this husband and wife did not. They went home, too proud to say much to each other about what they had done, and spent a very restless night. The next day about ten O'clock, **I should think,** he called to see me, and was shown into my room. My wife occupied a front room on the second floor; and I a room in the rear **of the house, at the head of the stairs** on the same floor. |While I was conversing with him, the servant informed me that a lady was waiting in Mrs. Finney's room to see me. I excused myself for a few moments, and requested him to wait while I went in to see her. I found that it was the **lady** who but the day before had been so stubborn, and the wife of the **gentle**man who was in my room. Neither of them knew that the other had called to see me. I conversed with her, and found that she was on

MS 584

JHF 295

MS 585

[78] Here Matson had written "—her mind was made up." This appears to have been crossed out by Finney.

[79] Here Finney crossed out the word "up."

[80] This was the First Presbyterian Church. See n. 42 above.

[81] Finney altered the word "start" to "rise to go forward."

[82] Finney altered the word "The" to "A." The *r* at the end of "larger" was crossed out by Fairchild.

the very verge of submitting to Christ. I had learned that he was also, to all appearance, in the same state. I then returned to him **in my own room,** and said **to him,** "I am going to pray with a lady in Mrs. Finney's room; and we will go in there, if you please, and all join in prayer together." He followed me; and **who should the lady turn out to be but** his own wife! They looked at each other with surprize, but were both greatly affected, each to find the other there. We knelt down to pray. I had not proceeded far in my prayer before she began to weep, and to pray audibly for her husband. I stopped and MS 586 |listened, and found that she had lost all concern for herself, and was struggling in an agony of prayer for his conversion. His heart seemed to break and give way, and just at this time the bell rang for our dinner. I thought it would be well to leave them together alone. I therefore touched my wife, and we rose silently and went down to dinner, leaving them in prayer. We took a JHF 296 hasty dinner and returned, and |found them as mellow, and as humble, and as loving as could be desired.

I have not said much as yet of *the spirit of prayer* that prevailed in this revival, which I must not omit to mention. When I was on my way to Rochester, as we passed through a village some thirty miles east of Rochester, a brother minister whom I knew seeing me on **board** the canal boat, jumped **on** to have a little conversation with me, intending to ride but a little way and **jump off and** return. He however became **so** interested in conversation, and MS 587 upon finding where I was going he made |up his mind to keep on and go with me to Rochester; **and he did so. He almost immediately fell under great conviction, and the work was very deep with him.** We had been there but a few days when this minister became so convicted that he could not help weeping aloud at one time as he passed along the street. The Lord gave him a powerful spirit of prayer, and his heart was broken. As he and I prayed much together, I was struck with his faith in regard to what the Lord was going to do there. I recollect he would say, "Lord, I do not know how it is; but I seem to know that thou art going to do a great work in this city." The Spirit of prayer was poured out powerfully, so much so that some persons stayed away from the public services to pray, being unable to restrain their feelings under preaching.

And here I must introduce the name of a man, whom I shall have occasion to mention frequently, Mr. Abel Clary. He was the son of a very excellent MS 588 man, and an elder of the church where I was converted.[83] |He was converted in the same revival in which I was. He had been licensed to preach; but his spirit of prayer was such, he was so burdened with the souls of men, that he

[83] Abel Clary was one of the early pioneers in Jefferson County, moving from Conway, Massachusetts, to Adams in about 1803. He was made an elder of the Adams church on 27 January 1821. He was the father of Rev. Dexter Clary. See S. W. Durant, *History of Jefferson County, New York* (Philadelphia: Everts, 1878), p. 269; and A. L. Chapin, "Dexter Clary," *The Congregational Quarterly* (Boston) 18 (July 1876): 357.

According to Finney, he was an elderly man who took alcohol, on the advice of doctors, because of the state of his appetite. But when the temperance question became an issue, he was able to give up alcohol. "On being asked what he thought of giving up alcohol, 'Oh!' he said, 'I am renewing my youth; it was the devil who made me think I could not do without it!' " (Finney, "Total Abstinence a Christian Duty," *The Penny Pulpit* [London] 1,548–49 [July–September 1850]: 25–26).

was not able to preach much, his whole time and strength being given to prayer. The burden of his soul would frequently be so great that he was unable to stand, and he would writhe and groan in agony **in a most wonderful manner.** I was well acquainted with him, and knew something of the wonderful spirit of prayer that was upon him. ᴵHe was a very silent man, as almost all are who have that powerful spirit of prayer. The first I knew of his being at Rochester, a gentleman who lived about a mile west of the city called on me one day, and asked me if I knew a Mr. Abel Clary, a minister. I told him that I **did** know him well. "Well," said he, "he is at my house, and has been there for so **long a time,"—I forget how long, but nearly from the first of my being in Rochester. Says he,** "I don't know what ᴵto think of him." I said, "I have not seen him at any of our meetings.[''] "No," he replied, "he cannot go to meeting, he says. He prays nearly all the time, day and night," **said he,** "and in such an agony of mind that I do not know what to make of it. Sometimes he cannot even stand on his knees, but will lie prostrate on the floor **and groan; and then throw himself upon the bed and roll from side to side,** and groan and pray in a manner that quite astonishes me." **I inquired what he said. He replied, "He does not say much. He cannot go to meeting he says; but his whole time is given to prayer."**[84] I said to the brother, "I understand it; please keep still. It will all come out right; he will surely prevail." I knew at the time a considerable number of men who were exercised in the same way. A Dea. **Pond,** of Camden, Oneida county;[85] a Dea. **Truman,** of Rodman, Jefferson County;[86] a Dea. **Baker** of Adams in the same county; this Mr. Clary, and many others among the men, ᴵand[87] a large number of women, partook of the same Spirit,

JHF 297

MS 589

MS 590 [1]

[84] The words "and sometimes it seems as if he will die with agony" followed here in the original but appear to have been crossed out by Matson.

[85] This was Billious Pond (1781–1874). He emigrated with his parents to Oneida County from New England when he was a child and settled in Camden. He became deacon of the Presbyterian church of which Henry Smith was the pastor. He was one of those who had visited the revival at Rome in 1826 (see p. 162 n. 31 [MS 319]) and had returned "with their loins girded for active service" (G. W. Gale, *Autobiography {to 1834} of George Washington Gale {1789–1861}, Founder of Galesburg, Illinois, and Knox College* [New York: privately printed, 1964], p. 267).

H. H. Kellogg knew him well as a man "gifted in exhortation and mighty in prayer. During the revivals which prevailed so extensively through central New York from 1826 to 1836, he was ever welcomed by evangelists, pastors, and churches as a most able, modest, and discreet lay laborer." At the age of fifty-five and with only a common school education he was ordained, and for nearly forty years he was a minister in Illinois. See H. H. Kellogg's letter in *NYE,* 25 February 1875, p. 6.

[86] George W. Gale refers to Truman in his autobiography. While the revival in which Finney was converted was occurring in Adams, Gale went to a council held in Lorain, about six or seven miles south of Adams.

> As it stormed, and we could not return that night, we held a prayer meeting at the house of the pastor, Rev. Mr. Bliss. In the course of the meeting I took occasion to relate what the Lord had done and was doing in Adams. Deacon Truman of the Congregational Church in Rodman, a town east of Adams, was then a member of the Council. He listened with a deep interest and remarked, "I shall go home with new purpose." He did so, and the pastor, my excellent friend and neighbor, the Rev. Mr. Spear, was sick. The Deacon labored day and night visiting with others through the congregation. The Lord blessed the efforts in which the pastor was able soon after to unite and a glorious work followed ("Autobiography of Rev. G. W. Gale," typescript copy in Knox College Library, Galesburg, Ill., pp. 152–53).

[87] Page 590 was originally numbered 435, renumbered 567 by Matson, and then changed to 590 by Finney. Finney also renumbered the next page 590, in error.

and spent a great part of their time in prayer. **Brother, or as we called him,** Father Nash, **a minister** who in several of my fields of labor came to me and aided me, was another of those men that had such a powerful spirit of prevailing prayer. This Mr Clary continued in Rochester as long as I did, and did not leave it until after I had left. He never, that I could learn, appeared in public, but gave himself wholly to prayer.

There were a good many cases in Rochester in which people were exercised with this spirit of agonizing travail of soul. I have said that the moral aspect of things was greatly changed by this revival. It was a young city, full of thrift and enterprize, and full of sin. The inhabitants were intelligent and enterprizing in the highest degree; but as the revival swept through the town and converted the great mass of the most influential people both **male** JHF 298 and **female,** ¦the change in the order, sobriety, and morality of the city was wonderful.[88]

MS 590 [2] ¦At[89] a subsequent period, which I shall mention in its place, I was conversing with a lawyer who was converted at this revival of which I have been speaking, and who soon after had been made district attorney of the city, **the same that some call prosecuting attorney**. His business was to superintend the prosecution of criminals. From his position he was made thoroughly acquainted with the history of crime in that city. In speaking of the revival in which he was converted, he said to me many years afterwards: "I have been examining the records of the criminal courts, and I find this striking fact, that whereas our city has increased since that revival three-fold, there **is** not one third as many prosecutions for crime as there had been up to that time.[90]

"Thus crime," he says, "has *decreased* two thirds, and the population has *increased* two thirds. This is," he said, "the wonderful influence that that revival **had** had upon the community."[91] Indeed by the power of that revival

[88]The moral reformation of the city and its leadership in the religious and reform movements of the subsequent decades was the subject of frequent comment both at the time and afterward by visitors and in the reminiscences of its citizens. Out of a population of about 10,000 in 1831, there were thought to be 800 converts. Some 1,200 united with the churches of the Rochester Presbytery, 635 of these becoming members of the churches in the town. See Orlo J. Price, "The Significance of the Early Religious History of Rochester," *The Rochester Historical Society, Publication Fund Series* 3 (1924): 165–87.

An article "Reform in Rochester, N.Y." stated:

> Among the other improvements effected the past year, indicating the prosperous condition of our village, there is none perhaps that marks more distinctly the progress of improvement, than the fact that our Circus building has been converted into a Tallow Chandler's Shop, and our old Theatre into a Livery Stable (reprinted from the *Rochester Observer* in the *Religious Intelligencer* [New Haven], 18 February 1832, p. 605).

Theaters were considered to be places of corruption and vice. No attempt was made to establish another for seven years, and it was not possible to sustain any permanent theater in Rochester until the late 1850s. See Susan M. Ogden-Malouf, "American Revivalism and Temperance Drama: Evangelical Protestant Ritual and Theatre in Rochester, New York, 1830–1845" (Ph.D. diss., Northwestern University, 1981), pp. 175–86.

[89]Finney erroneously renumbered this page 590 instead of 591; and "½," in pencil, appears to have been added by Fairchild.

[90]Matson began the next sentence on a new line, indented slightly and with a new set of quotation marks, indicating a new paragraph, although Finney did not insert a paragraph sign.

[91]Asa Mahan recorded that, during the progress of the revival in Rochester in 1842, "the most

public sentiment has been molded. The public affairs |of[92] the city have been, MS 591 in a great measure in the hands of Christian men. The **great weight of character** has been on the side of Christ, **and their public business had been conducted accordingly.**

Among other conversions I must not forget to mention that of **Samuel D. Porter**, a prominent citizen **in** that place.[93] He was at the time a bookseller, and in partnership with a Mr. Everard Peck,[94] **who was the father of our late Professor Peck.**[95] Mr. **Porter** was an infidel; not an atheist, but a disbeliever in the divine authority of the Bible. He was a reader and a thinker, a man of keen, shrewd mind, strong will, and most decided character. He was, I believe, a man of good outward morals, and a gentleman highly respected. He came to my room early one morning and said to me, "Mr. Finney, there is a great movement here on the subject of religion, but I am a skeptic; and I want you to prove to me that the Bible is true." The Lord enabled me at once to discern his state of mind so far as to decide the course I should take with

full and careful census of crime in the city during the interval [between the two revivals], and during a corresponding number of years prior to the first revival, was taken by the most competent men, the individual who had been for many years prosecuting attorney for the city superintending the whole investigation." After speaking of the results of the investigation, Mahan continued: "Nor did an individual in the city question the deduction, that the exclusive cause of this wonderful difference was that revival of religion" (A. Mahan, "Rev. C. G. Finney," *The Banner of Holiness* [London], 30 September 1875, p. 22). C. P. Bush made a similar comment: "The courts had little to do, and the jail was nearly empty for years afterwards" ("Mr. Finney in Rochester," p. 15).

[92] Pages 591–606 were originally numbered 437–52 and then renumbered 569–84 by Matson. Finney then changed them to 591–606.

[93] Samuel Drummond Porter (1808–1881) went to Rochester in 1827. He was to become one of the leading activists in the religious, benevolence, and reform movements, particularly in antislavery. He was one of those who left First Church to help form the Bethel Church in 1836. He married another Finney convert, Susan Farley. They were also prominent in civic affairs. See McElroy, "Social Reform in the Burned-Over District," pp. 222, 236; and Amy Harmer-Croughton, "Anti-slavery Days in Rochester," *The Rochester Historical Society, Publication Fund Series* 14 (1936): 121–22.

[94] Everard Peck (1791–1854) from Berlin, Connecticut, was the first bookseller and publisher to go to Rochester, settling there in 1816. He became a leading citizen in the village. He was already a Christian and was prominent in the reform movements. In 1831 he took up banking and became involved in railroads and insurance. He was also largely responsible for the founding of Rochester University. In his will he left, among other bequests, one thousand dollars to Oberlin College. See Madeleine B. Stern, "Books in the Wilderness (Part II): Some Nineteenth Century Upstate Publishers," *New York History* 31, no. 4 (October 1950): 417–23; Donald B. Gilchrist, "The First Book Printed in Rochester," *The Rochester Historical Society, Publication Fund Series* 9 (1930): 276; and *OE,* 15 March 1854, p. 47.

His first wife, Chloe, was a sister of S. D. Porter, and his second wife, a sister of Porter's wife, Susan. See *WR,* 21 December 1830, p. 203; and S. D. Porter to Finney, 1 March 1851, Finney Papers, microfilm, roll 4.

[95] Henry Everard Peck (1821–1867) was a pupil at the Rochester High School and was converted during the revival in Rochester in 1842. He graduated from Bowdoin College in 1841 before training for the ministry at Oneida Institute and the Oberlin Collegiate Institute, where he graduated in 1845. In 1847 he became pastor of the State Street Congregational Church in Rochester. He returned to Oberlin in 1851 as professor of sacred rhetoric and took over the professorship of mental and moral philosophy following the departure of Asa Mahan. In 1865 he went to Haiti as United States commissioner and consul general, but he died in 1867 of yellow fever. His remains were later buried in Oberlin. See "Henry E. Peck," *The Rochester Historical Society, Publications* 1 (1892): 106; *The Lorain County News* (Oberlin), 3 July 1867, p. 2; Peck, *Semi-Centennial History*, p. 291; and James A. Podgett, "Diplomats to Haiti, and Their Diplomacy," *Journal of Negro History* 15 (July 1940): 271–74.

MS 592 him. I said to him: |"Do you believe in the existence of God?" "Oh yes!" he said, "I am not an Atheist." "Well, do you believe that you have treated God JHF 299 as you ought? Have you respected **His** authority? |Have you loved **Him**? Have you done that which you thought would please **Him**, and with the *design* to please **Him**? Don't you admit that you ought to love **Him**, and ought to worship **Him**, and ought to obey **Him**, according to the best light you have?" "O yes!" he said, ["]I admit all this." "But have you done so?" I asked. "Why **No**," he answered, "I cannot say that I have." "Well then," I replied, "why should I give you farther information, and farther light, if you will not do your duty and obey the light you already have?" "Now," said I, "when you will make up your mind to live up to your convictions, to obey God according to the best light you have; when you will make up your mind to repent of your neglect thus far, and to please God just as well as you know how the rest of your life, I will try to show you that the Bible is from God. Until then it is of MS 593 no use for me to do any such thing." I did not sit down, and I |think[96] had not asked him to sit down. He replied, "I do not know but that is fair," and retired.[97] I heard no more of him until the next morning **early,** soon after I arose, he came to my room again; and as soon as he **came in** he slapped his hands and said: "Mr. Finney, God has wrought a miracle!" "I went down to the store," he continued, "after I left your room, thinking of what you had said; and I made up my mind that I would repent of what I knew was wrong in my relations to God, and that hereafter I would live according to the best light I had. And when I made up my mind to this," said he, "my feelings so overcame me that I fell; and I do not know but I should have died if it had not been for Mr. **Peck**, who was with me in the store."[98] From this time he has been, as all who know him are aware, a praying, earnest Christian man. **I mention this case particularly because this same Mr. Porter has been** for many years one of the trustees of Oberlin College, has stood by us through all our trials, and has aided us with his whole influence, **and his purse**.[99]

MS 594 |**The[100] means used for the promotion of this revival were precisely the same that had been used in all the revivals that I had witnessed before, with the exception, as I have said, of what has since been termed "the anxious seat." I found, as I expected, that this was a great power for good. If men who were under conviction refused to come forward**

[96]The number "–602" was added after page number 593 by Fairchild, indicating to the printers to proceed to page 603, omitting pp. 594–602.

[97]Finney used this incident in his pastoral theology lectures at Oberlin College in 1843 to illustrate how a pastor should deal with certain kinds of questions. The brief notes taken down by a student, William Westervelt, read: "Mr Porter came in and said tell me if the Bible is true. I shant. Do you live up to the light you have—according to your ideas. No. What do you want to do more" ("Pastoral Lectures by Pres. Finney," William A. Westervelt Papers, file 30/120, box 1, Oberlin College Archives).

[98]Everard Peck wrote about the revival to his father-in-law in January 1831: "Saml. is indulging a trembling hope that he is a subject of the work—his views on religious subjects have manifestly changed & we cannot but hope that he has been made a subject of Divine Grace" (Peck to Samuel Porter, 11 January 1831, manuscript in Porter Family Papers, University of Rochester Library).

[99]Porter was a trustee of Oberlin College from 1844 to 1876.

[100]Pages 594–602 have some alterations by Fairchild, but they were omitted from the published edition.

publicly and renounce their sins and give themselves to God, this fact disclosed to them more clearly the pride of their hearts. If, on the other hand, they broke over all those considerations that stood in the way of their doing it, it was taking a great step; and as I found continually was the very step that they needed to take. And when the truth was explained to them, and they were made intelligent, and the very duty to be performed was placed before them before they were pressed to come forward, in great numbers of instances, as was afterwards ascertained,[101] they indeed did as they promised to do, and this was one of the means used by the Spirit of God to bring them to a present submission ‹to,›[102] and acceptance of Christ. I had been long of opinion that a principal reason ˡwhy so few were converted while under the voice of the living preacher was, that they were not brought to the point, and instant submission demanded of them. Ministers had been in the habit of preaching to sinners sermons pointing out to them their duty; but then in all probability admonishing them at the close that their nature must be changed by the Spirit of God or they could do nothing. Ministers had been so much afraid of dishonoring the Spirit of God as to think it their duty to call the sinner's attention to his dependence on the Spirit of God at the close of every sermon, and every exhortation to repentance. MS 595

The doctrine that sin was constitutional and belonged to the very nature, that the very nature itself must be changed by direct physical influence exerted by the Holy Spirit, compelled ministers who believed it to remind sinners of their inability to do what God required and what in their sermons they urged them to do; and thus just at the point where the sinner needed to think of Christ, of his duty, of the thing important to be *done*, his attention was turned back to see whether any divine influence was going to change ˡhis nature, and let the Spirit of God act upon his nature like an electric shock while he remained passive. Thus the sinner's mind was mystified; and under such preaching it was no wonder that few souls were converted. The Lord convinced me that this was no way to deal with souls. He showed me clearly that moral depravity must be *voluntary*; that the divine agency in regeneration must consist in teaching the soul, in argument, in persuasion, entreaty. That therefore the thing to be done was to set the sinner's duty clearly before him, and depend on the Spirit's teaching to urge him to do it; to set Christ before him, and expect the Holy Spirit to take of the things of Jesus and show them to the sinner; to set his sins before him, and expect the Holy Spirit to show him his awful wickedness, and lead him voluntarily to renounce his sins. I saw therefore clearly that to cooperate with the Spirit of God as an intelligent agent in this work, I must present the truths to be believed, the duties to be done, and the reasons for those duties. ˡThis is the very thing that the Spirit is doing, MS 596 MS 597

[101] Here Matson had written "and has frequently been and is ascertained," which appears to have been crossed out by Finney.

[102] The word "to" appears to have been inserted by Finney.

to make the sinner see and understand the force of the reasons urged by the minister, the truth of the facts stated, and to give the sinner a realizing sense of those truths which the minister presents to him, to induce him to *act*. Therefore to me it was, and is plain, that to divert the sinner's attention, just at that point, to his dependence on the Spirit of God, was necessarily to hinder rather than to help forward the ‹work of› [the] Spirit.[103] It is the minister's duty to urge him, and the office of the Spirit to make this urgency effectual to overcome his voluntary opposition. Therefore to me it was plain that it was totally unphilosophical and absurd when calling on the sinner to do his duty, to tell him that he could not, to remind him that he was dependent on the Spirit of God, that his nature must be changed, and all those things which in their very nature were calculated to prevent his taking the very step which the Spirit of God was urging him to take. This kind of teaching MS 598 leads the sinner to resist the ˡSpirit of God, to wait for God to do something and to change his heart before he turns to God. The fact is, the fundamental error consists in supposing that a change of heart is a *physical* instead of a *moral* change; that is, a change in the nature instead of a change in the voluntary committal and preference of the mind.

By the kind of teaching of which I am speaking, sinners were constantly stumbled, and almost never converted under the voice of the living preacher. If they were convicted of sin and ever converted, it must of necessity have been when they forgot their theory in which they had been instructed, left entirely out of view their inability, and for the moment their dependence on the Spirit of God, and acted upon their convictions and complied with the urgency of the Spirit's teaching. It is the Spirit's office first to convict the sinner of sin, of righteousness, and of judgement to come; and when taught their need of the Savior, to present the Savior in his divine nature, his offices and relations, his MS 599 atonement and ˡmercy, his willingness, his readiness, his ability to save unto the uttermost. Thus Christ promises the Holy Spirit as a *teacher*, to lead men by a divine moral persuasion to renounce their sins, and give themselves to God. That of which the sinner is conscious under his agency is not the personal presence of any divine agency in his mind. But he sees the truth clearly, so sees it that it makes a deep impression. His difficulties are cleared up, his errors are corrected, his mind is enlightened, the truth presses his conscience, and he feels an urgency upon his spirit immediately to submit to God. It is the *truth* that engages his attention. If he is a reader of his Bible, he will infer of course that this urgency that is upon him is from the Spirit of God. It is often well that he should be told that this is the way in which the Spirit of God works with him; that in resisting the truths that are before his mind, he is resisting the Holy Ghost; and that in accepting these truths MS 600 cordially, he yields to divine teaching. ˡBut he should understand

[103]Here Matson had written down, "to help forward the Spirit." Finney added the words "work of." The second "the" was later added by Fairchild.

distinctly that the Spirit's work is not to convert him while he is passive, while he is waiting God's time; but that the Spirit of God converts or turns him by inducing him to turn himself; that the act of submission is his own act, and the Spirit is persuading him to do this; that faith is his own act, and the Spirit of God gives faith only by so presenting the truths to be believed with such a divine clearness and persuasiveness, as to lead the sinner to trust the Savior. That he gives us faith by inducing us to believe; and that he leads us to perform every duty, to repent, to believe, to submit, to love, by presenting the truths which are calculated to lead to these acts in so clear a light as to overcome our reluctance, and induce us voluntarily, with all sincerity and with all our hearts to turn to God, to trust Him, to love Him, to obey Him. With these views of the subject I saw clearly that just at the point where the sinner is thoroughly instructed, and while under the voice of the living preacher with the strong pressure of truth set home by the Holy Ghost |upon him, MS 601 something was needed to induce him to act then and there upon his convictions. I concluded then, and have always thought since, that to call the sinner right out from the mixed multitude to take a stand for God, to be as open and frank in his renunciation of sin before the world as he had been in committing it; to call him to change sides, to renounce the world and come over to Christ, to renounce his own righteousness and accept that of Christ,—in short to do just that which constitutes a change of heart, was just what was needed. I was not disappointed in the use of this measure. I have always found it a thing greatly needed; and I might relate scores of instances in which proud men, after resisting it for a time, saw the propriety and necessity of it, and themselves came forward to the anxious seat and gave themselves to God. And I have often been told that they believed if they had not been called on to take that step, and if they had not taken it or something equivalent to it, |they never should have been converted. MS 602 If I labor for the conversion of a sinner, I must say to him the things that the Spirit of God wants him to believe and to understand. I need to present before him the considerations that ought to influence his present action. In this way I co-operate with the Spirit of God; for this is the very thing the Spirit of God is endeavoring to secure, *his present action in accordance with the claims of God.* And I never feel as if I had done my duty till I have pressed every consideration upon the sinner's mind that seems to me at the time to be essential to his rightly understanding his duty and doing it.

In another place, when I come to speak of the next great revival in Rochester in which I was present, the truths that I am now stating will be seen to be exemplified in the conversion of ‹the› Judge ‹I have mentioned.›[104] In this revival at Rochester I am not aware that there was ever any complaint of any fanaticism, or anything that was to be deplored in its results. The revival was so powerful, it gathered in such great numbers |of the most influential class in society, it made so clean a MS 603

[104] Finney altered the words "Judge Gardiner" to "the Judge I have mentioned."

sweep, that it created a great excitement far and near. Some persons JHF 300 wrote letters from ᑊRochester at the time to their friends giving an account of the work, which were read in various churches throughout several states, and were instrumental in producing great revivals of religion. Many persons came in from abroad to witness the great work of God, and were converted.[105] I recollect that a physician was so attracted by what he heard of the work, that he came from Newark, N.J. to Rochester to see what the Lord was doing, and was himself converted there.[106] He was a man of talents and high culture and has been for years an ardent Christian laborer for immortal souls.[107]

One evening I recollect when I made a call for the anxious to come forward and submit, a man of the first influence in a neighboring town came forward himself, and several members of his family, and gave themselves to God. Indeed the work spread like waves in every direction.[108] I preached in as MS 604 ᑊmany places around about as I had time and strength to do, while my main labors were in Rochester. I went to Canandaigua and preached several times. There the work took effect, and many were converted.[109] The pastor, the

[105]The presence of large numbers of people from a distance was a feature particularly noted in the newspaper accounts of the revival. See, e.g., *Rochester Observer*, 5 and 22 October, 12 November, and 24 December 1830; 17 February, 3 and 31 March 1831.

[106]Lewis Tappan wrote in ink in the margin of the manuscript against this sentence, "Did not Dr Ward then live in Albany?" Isaac Moreau Ward (1806–1895) was born in Bloomfield, New Jersey. Educated at Yale and Rutgers Medical College, he practiced medicine in Newark from 1828 until 1841, when he moved to Albany. He was the first president of the New York State Homoeopathic Medical Society in 1849 and was called to the chair of obstetrics in the Homeopathic College of Medicine in Philadelphia in 1853. In 1857 he moved to New York, where he helped to organize the New York Homeopathic Medical College. (Identification and information is from Carl A. Lane of the New Jersey Historical Society.)

This man's conversion was referred to in a report at the time:

> An infidel Dr. a man of distinction from Bloomfield (N Jersey) feeling some concern about his soul, and hearing of Mr Finney said, "I am determined to see him"—he came to Rochester, was introduced to Mr Finney told him frankly the state of his mind—was asked why he left home without repenting of his sins—was pressed to immediate repentance & submission—was prayed for; and the same day hopefully converted—and is yet in the place, laboring for his new *Master* ("Copy of a letter from a gentleman").

[107]He was active in the establishment of the First Free Presbyterian Church of Newark, and he established a daily prayer union. He was also one of the founders of the Howard Mission for the poor in New York.

[108]*The New-York Evangelist* reported that "almost every town within forty or fifty miles of Rochester is favored more or less with the special presence of the Lord" (26 February 1831, p. 191).

[109]The Congregational church in Canandaigua was formed in 1800. Originally orthodox, it became a stronghold of Unitarianism until about 1817, when it reverted to orthodoxy under the ministry of Evan Johns. When Ansel Eddy took over in 1823, there were about one hundred members. The church had a powerful revival in 1826, adding more than one hundred new members. In November 1830 there were signs again of a revival. About that time Eddy visited Pittsford, where he met Finney at Asa Mahan's church. He became so much of a convert to Finney's ideas that he caused some trouble by preaching one of Finney's sermons to his own church. But the revival "did not become general till about the middle of January." It was about that time that Finney was invited there.

The revival "continued with various degrees of interest until the approach of summer, and resulted in the conversion of about one hundred." See *A Narrative of the Late Revivals of Religion Within the Bounds of Geneva Presbytery* (Geneva, N.Y.: Merrell, 1832), pp. 9–10; James H. Hotchkin, *A History of the Purchase and Settlement of Western New York* (New York: Dodd, 1848), pp. 33, 399; Ansel D. Eddy's letters in *WR,* 19 December 1826, p. 202; and 26 December 1826,

Rev. Ansel Eddy, entered heartily into the work.[110] A former pastor, an elderly man, an Englishman by birth, also did what he could to forward the work.[111] **I went and preached at several places around about, the names of which I cannot now recollect.[112] But I recollect distinctly that wherever** I went the Word of God took immediate effect;[113] and it seemed only necessary to present the law of God and the claims of Christ in such relations and proportions as were calculated to secure the conversion of men, and they would be converted by scores. The greatness of the work at Rochester at that time attracted so much of the attention of ministers and Christians throughout the state of New York, throughout New England, and in many parts of the United States, that the very *fame* of it was an efficient instrument in the hands of the Spirit of God in ˡpromoting the greatest revival of religion throughout the land that this country had than ever witnessed.[114] Years after this in conversing with Dr Beecher about this powerful revival and its results, he remarked: "That was the greatest work of God, and the greatest ˡrevival of religion, that the world has ever seen in so short a time. MS 605 JHF 301

p. 206; *NYE,* 26 February 1831, p. 191; Josiah Hopkins to Finney, 19 November 1830; and letters of Eddy to Finney, Finney Papers, microfilm, roll 2.

[110]Ansel Doane Eddy (1798–1875) was a graduate of Union College and was a law student for two years, but then he turned to the ministry and studied theology at Andover. Canandaigua was his first pastorate. He began there about 1823 and stayed there for about ten years. Subsequently he moved to Newark, New Jersey, and then went west to Chicago. In 1843 he was moderator of the New School Presbyterian General Assembly (see letter of Samuel H. Gridley in *NYE,* 18 February 1875, p. 1). The church at Canandaigua was Congregational; Eddy, however, was a Presbyterian.

[111]This was Evan Johns (1763–1849). He was from Pembrokeshire, Wales, where he started preaching at age nineteen. He came to America in 1801, and after pastorates in Connecticut, he went to Canandaigua in 1817. After Eddy took over the church in 1823, Johns continued to live in Canandaigua, where he was "known as a man of books, a scholar and antiquary." See *The Independent,* 17 May 1849, p. 95.

[112]Other places where Finney is known to have preached were Clarkson, Brockport, Ogden, Henrietta, and Penfield. At Pittsford he usually gave a lecture in Asa Mahan's church on Wednesdays. He may also have preached in Lockport and perhaps some other places around Rochester. The minister at Clarkson was Charles E. Furman, who had written letters to Nettleton from Auburn Theological Seminary in 1826 criticizing Finney's revival there. He had now become favorably impressed with Finney. See p. 194 n. 8 (MS 376) and Clarkson to Finney, 26 November 1830, Finney Papers, microfilm, roll 2. See also the extensive correspondence with ministers and members of these churches in the Finney Papers; and *Rochester Observer*, 24 December 1830, p. 2; *NYE,* 23 April 1831, p. 223; and 16 January 1879, p. 8; David G. Hale, "'Achan in this Church': Rev Joseph Myers in Brockport, 1828–32," *Western Monroe Historical Society Annual Report* (Brockport), 1980–82; Nancy Ann Hardesty, "'Your Daughters Shall Prophesy': Revivalism and Feminism in the Age of Finney" (Ph.D. diss., University of Chicago, 1976), p. 75; and William C. Walzer, "Charles Grandison Finney and the Presbyterian Revivals of Central and Western New York" (Ph.D. diss., University of Chicago, 1945), p. 163.

The ministers from a number of these churches helped Finney during an extended Four Days' Meeting held in Rochester at the end of February. See *Rochester Observer*, 3 March 1831, p. 2.

[113]Finney wrote to E. N. Kirk of Albany at the time: "I have preached in several of the towns. In every instance, the Lord has come down & commenced a work upon the spot" (Finney to Kirk, 1 November 1830, Special Collections, University of Rochester Library).

[114]The position of Rochester as the significant radiating center of the awakening of 1830–1831 was confirmed by a survey at the time:

> The *recent revivals of religion*, as they have been termed, appear to have commenced in the western part of New York, in Rochester and the surrounding region, in the autumn of 1830. During the next three or four months, the work spread rapidly, and extended itself over a considerable portion of the State ("The Recent Revivals of Religion," *The Spirit of the Pilgrims* [Boston] 4 [August 1831]: 408).

One hundred thousand," he remarked, "were reported as having connected themselves with churches as the results of that great revival. This," he said, "is unparallelled in the history of the church and of the progress of religion."[115] He spoke of this having been done in one year, and said that in no year during the Christian era had we any account of so great a revival of religion.

From the time of the New Lebanon convention of which I have spoken, open and public opposition to revivals of religion ‹was› less and less ‹manifested›;[116] and especially did I meet with much less personal opposition than I had met with before. It gradually but greatly subsided. At Rochester I felt nothing of it.[117] Indeed the waters of salvation had risen so high, revivals had (MS 606) 'become so powerful and extensive, and people had had time to become acquainted with them and their results in such measure, that men were afraid to oppose them as they had done. Ministers had come to understand them better, and the most ungodly sinners had been convinced that they were

[115]In another account Finney is reported as having quoted Beecher as saying, "This is the greatest revival of religion that has been since the world began"; and Finney added, "Taking the whole of that time, or perhaps from 1830 to 1835, there could not have been fewer than 200,000 that were converted" (Finney, *The Prevailing Prayer-Meeting* [London: Ward, 1859], p. 22). Herman Norton also stated in a sermon in January 1832 that it was calculated that 100,000 people had been converted. See Anson G. Phelps, "Diary," 2 January 1832, microfilm, New York Public Library.

These figures have been considered to be far too high. But researchers at the time and since tend to confirm the scale of the awakening. A widely publicized report in the *Boston Recorder* stated that an inspection of the papers for the first four months of 1831 revealed 362 places that had reported revivals, 150 of these being in New York State. The total number of converts where figures were given was 10,620. The report pointed out: "The summary is necessarily imperfect, for many places are known to have been visited which are not named in the papers. In more than half the places named, the number of converts or of additions to the churches is not given" (4 May 1831, p. 7).

The survey in *The Spirit of the Pilgrims* quotes the secretary of the American Education Society, "who has paid particular attention to the subject and has the best means of forming a judgment," as saying that as many as a "thousand congregations in the United States have been visited within six months, to a greater or less extent, with revivals of religion; and that the whole number of conversions is probably not less than fifty thousand" (4 [August 1831]: 409). See also Preston Franklin Strauss, "The Revivals of Religion in the State of New York (1825–1835) Under the leadership of Charles G. Finney," typescript, n.d., chap. 10, in Speer Library, Princeton Theological Seminary; and J. Edwin Orr, *The Eager Feet: Evangelical Awakenings, 1790–1830* (Chicago: Moody, 1975). Asa Mahan put the figure at 200,000 during "the space of a single year, including portions of the years 1830 and 1831" (*Autobiography*, p. 216).

[116]Here Matson had written "grew less and less," but Lewis Tappan wrote in the margin of the manuscript, "not *grew*," and Finney changed it to "was less and less manifested."

[117]Asa Mahan pointed out: "The first result" of Finney's preaching in Rochester "was the disappearance of all opposition to Mr. Finney and the work of God under his influence, and unity of spirit in prayer and labours for the conversion of sinners, such as had characterized no preceding work of grace" (*Autobiography*, p. 222).

Theodore Weld also wrote to Finney at the time, "the influence which the revival at R and vicinity has had to do away prejudice against you is beyond calculation" (Weld to Finney, dated 2 March 1831 in the calendar, Finney Papers, microfilm, roll 2). Finney wrote to E. N. Kirk of Albany:

> I hear of no cavilling nor opposition, as yet from Ministers nor [Chris]tians of any denomination. Sinners have from the beginning of this work, been so awed that I have heard very little of opposition from any quarter. Indeed they so entirely overdid the matter in their opposition at Troy & Albany & in that region that ever since, as in this place, people have seemed to stand amazed & said "*what could all that opposition mean*" (Finney to Kirk, 1 November 1830, Special Collections, University of Rochester Library).

indeed the work of God. So manifestly were the great mass of the conversions sound, the converts really regenerated and made new creatures, so profoundly were individuals and whole communities reformed, and so permanent and unquestionable were the results, that the conviction became nearly universal that they were the work of God. There were so many instances of conversion that were so striking, such characters converted, and all classes, high and low, rich and poor, so thoroughly were subdued by these revivals, as almost entirely to silence open opposition.[118] Had I time I might fill a volume with the relation of the most striking instances of conversions that have occurred under my own observation for many, many ‹years & in many places.›[119]

[118]Henry B. Stanton reported that the revival in Rochester "began with the judges, the lawyers, the physicians, the bankers, and the merchants, and worked its way down to the bottom of society, till nearly everybody had joined one or the other of the churches controlled by the different denominations" (*Random Recollections*, p. 41).

Another report stated:

> The number who present themselves for prayers, when opportunity is given is from 100 to 300. All denominations in Rochester are united in this work. Part of the meetings are held in the Episcopalian Church already 200 have been united to that Church & 30 more are expected to unite soon. The Methodists & Baptists have shared largely in the work. 300 have already united with the Presbyterian Churches. The subject [*sic*] of the work in Rochester are supposed to be about 2,500, and the work is still in progress. Among the late converts, are 14 Lawyers, 24 Merchants & Physicians, one General 3 Colonels one Sheriff, one Cashier of the Bank, these are mentioned only to show the character of the work, and to take away a reproach, which has been cast upon revivals, that none but children & weak women were its fruits. An unusual numbers [*sic*] of heads of families are among the converts ("Copy of a letter from a gentleman").

[119]The word "years" was originally on the next page, but Finney crossed it out when he inserted a new chapter heading there. He wrote the word in here, adding "& in many places."

MS 607
JHF 302

CHAPTER XXII

‹Another revival at Auburn New York›

During[1] the latter part of the time that I was at Rochester my health was poor. I was overdone, and some of the leading physicians, I learned **afterwards**, had made up their minds that I never would preach any more.[2] **About the closing up of my** labors in Rochester at this time **the** Rev. Dr Wisner of Ithaca[3] came down and spent **sometime in Rochester**, witnessing and helping forward the work.[4] In the meantime I was invited to many fields;[5]

[1] Pages 607–43 were originally numbered 453–89 and renumbered 585–621 by Matson and changed to 607–43 by Finney.

[2] In fact, reports of his being sick were already spreading by the middle of November (see William F. Curry to Finney, 15 and 19 November 1830; and John Ingersoll to Finney, 19 November 1830, Finney Papers, microfilm, roll 2). There are frequent references over the next four months in his correspondence to his being sick and worn out, to physicians advising him to stop preaching, and to offers of homes where he could go away to rest. In December the *Rochester Observer* announced, "We still enjoy the ministerial labors of Rev. Mr. Finney, but they have considerably impaired his health" (24 December 1830, p. 2).

[3] William Wisner (1782–1871) had been a lawyer for ten years before turning to the ministry. He studied at Princeton Theological Seminary and then went to the Presbyterian church in Ithaca in 1816. There he became a prominent and active minister, pioneering total abstinence among the churches in the Synod of Geneva and building up his church from fifteen members to eight hundred. In May 1831 he was to be installed over the Second Presbyterian Church in Rochester, where he remained until 1835. During his pastorate there, seven hundred were added to the church. Theodore Cuyler once heard him say that "he could enumerate about twelve hundred hopeful conversions under his preaching." After four years in St. Louis he returned to Ithaca in 1839, retiring ten years later. See James H. Hotchkin, *A History of the Purchase and Settlement of Western New York* (New York: Dodd, 1848), pp. 410–11; Judith M. Wellman, "The Burned-Over District Revisited: Benevolent Reform and Abolitionism in Mexico, Paris, and Ithaca, New York, 1825–1842" (Ph.D. diss., University of Virginia, 1974), pp. 85–94; W. Wisner, *Incidents in the Life of a Pastor* (New York: Scribner, 1852); and *NYE,* 19 January 1871, pp. 1–2.

[4] Wisner had known Finney for some years. Toward the end of 1830 his church experienced a powerful revival, and he tried to get Finney to come to Ithaca to help him. Finney may have planned to go, and was in fact rumored to have left Rochester and gone there, but there seems to be no actual evidence that he went. See letters from Wisner on the revival in *WR,* 14 December 1830, p. 198; 4 January 1831, p. 2; and 16 January 1831, p. 6; and letters to Finney from the Presbytery of Chenango, 6 November 1830; from S. Brown, 6 January 1831; and from Wisner from 22 October 1830 through 3 January 1831, Finney Papers, microfilm, roll 2.

Finney attempted to get Wisner to move from Ithaca to Rochester in January, a move that he eventually made later in the year. Wisner was probably in Rochester on this occasion for Sunday, 20 February, and was one of those helping at the Four Days' Meeting. See Wisner to Finney, 18 January 1831; and J. Hopkins to Finney, 19 February 1831, Finney Papers, microfilm, roll 2; and *Rochester Observer*, 3 March 1831, p. 2.

[5] Whitney Cross has noted more than ninety letters in the Finney Papers sent to Finney while he was in Rochester, from communities as far apart as Ohio and Boston, begging for his services. A large number of requests came from New York City. See W. Cross, *The Burned-Over District* (Ithaca: Cornell University Press, 1950), pp. 155–56.

and among others I was ‹urged›[6] by Dr Nott,[7] President of **Columbia**[8] College, to go and labor with him and‹, if possible,›[9] secure the conversion of his numerous students.[10] I made up my mind to comply with his request.[11] In company with Dr Wisner and Josiah Bissel, **of whom I have spoken,** I started in the stage in the Spring of the year[12] when the going was exceedingly bad. I left my wife and children for the time at Rochester, as the **going** was too dangerous and the journey too fatiguing for them **to undertake.**[13] When we arrived at Geneva Dr Wisner insisted on my going home with him to rest awhile. I declined, |and said I must keep about my work. He pressed me very hard to go, and finally told me that the physicians in Rochester had told him to take me home with him, for I was going to die; that I would never labor any more in revivals, for I had the consumption and could live but a little while. I replied that I had been told this before, but that

MS 608

[6]Here Finney changed the word "invited" to "urged."

[7]Eliphalet Nott (1773–1866) was a graduate of Rhode Island College. As minister of the First Presbyterian Church in Albany from 1798, he was renowned as a preacher and educator before becoming president of Union College in Schenectady in 1804. He had a remarkable career as president, spanning sixty-two years, being prominent not only as an educator, reformer, and writer but also as an inventor in the field of heat engineering. He had visited Troy during the great revival in 1826 and had been invited to the New Lebanon Convention but did not attend. See Codman Hislop, *Eliphalet Nott* (Middletown, Conn.: Wesleyan University Press, 1971); and *Letters of the Rev. Dr. Beecher and the Rev. Mr. Nettleton, on the "New Measures" in Conducting Revivals of Religion* (New York: Carvill, 1828), p. 9.

[8]Matson wrote "Columbia" here, but a question mark was inserted in pencil in the margin of the manuscript. It appears to be in Lewis Tappan's handwriting. The name was corrected by Fairchild to "Union" College.

[9]Finney added the words "if possible."

[10]Finney told Tayler Lewis in May 1874: "As an Evangelist I was repeatedly and earnestly invited to labor with Dr. Nott in his College" (C. Van Santvoord and Tayler Lewis, *Memoirs of Eliphalet Nott, D.D., LL.D.* [New York: Sheldon, 1876], p. 226). Although there are no letters from Nott in the Finney Papers, there are some from the students of the college. Two from a "Committee in behalf of the pious Students" indicated that the president was "strongly in favour" of Finney going. They pointed out that there were about two hundred students, twenty or thirty of whom were "professors" of religion (letters dated 8 and 18 February 1831; and Nelson Slater to Finney, 22 February 1831, Finney Papers, microfilm, roll 2). There was already "an interesting state of religious feeling" in the college, and a revival had begun. See *Christian Watchman* (Boston), 4 March 1831, p. 34.

[11]Finney was ready to leave Rochester, for the town was "now supplied with ministers," and he replied to the "pious Students" committee that he would go (see their letter of 18 February 1831; and S. Brown to Finney, 9 February 1831, Finney Papers, microfilm, roll 2). He had evidently planned to go to Union College and to Albany on his way to New York. See letters of Finney to G. W. Gale, 16 February 1831; and T. D. Weld, 17 March 1831, in Weld-Grimke Papers, William L. Clements Library, University of Michigan.

[12]Here Fairchild added the date "1831," which is correct. Finney preached his last sermon in Rochester on Sunday, 6 March, and left the next day. See Levi Parsons, comp., *History of Rochester Presbytery* (Rochester: Democrat-Chronicle Press, 1889), p. 252; and H. Ely to Finney, 5 March 1831, Finney Papers, microfilm, roll 2.

[13]The Finneys had two children. Charles was one year old; and Helen, who was not yet three, had recently been very ill and had nearly died. Lydia was "almost worn out with care and watching." See S. Brown to Finney, 9 February 1831; and N. Andrews to Charles and Lydia Finney, 14 March 1831, Finney Papers, microfilm, roll 2; and Finney to T. Weld, 16 February 1831, in Weld-Grimke Papers. The Finneys had also been planning to go to New York and stay with Arthur Tappan, but he was unable to have the whole family at that time. See Finney to Weld, 17 March 1831, Weld-Grimke Papers; and Joshua Leavitt to Finney, 28 February 1831, Finney Papers, microfilm, roll 2.

it was a mistake. That the Doctors did not understand my case; **and** that I was only fatigued, and a little rest would bring me up.[14]

JHF 303 Dr Wisner finally gave up his importunity, and I passed ˡon in the stage to Auburn. The going was so very bad that sometimes we could not get **any** more than two miles an hour **in the stage**, and we had been two or three days in going from Rochester to Auburn.[15] As I had many dear friends in Auburn, and was very much fatigued, I made up my mind to stop there and rest till the next stage. I had paid my fare quite through to Schenectady; but could stop MS 609 over for one or more days, **if I chose, and then take the stage again**. ˡI stopped at the house of **Brother Theodore Spencer**,[16] a son of Chief Justice **Spencer of that State**.[17] He was an earnest Christian man, and a very dear friend of mine; consequently I went to his house instead of stopping at the hotel, and concluded to rest there till the next stage. In the morning, after sleeping quietly **for a time** at **Brother Spencer**'s, I had risen and was preparing to take the stage **as it** was **expected along** in the **fore**part of the day, when a gentleman came in with the request for me to remain, signed by that large number of influential men of whom I have spoken before as resisting the revival in that place in 182‹6›.[18] **This was in the Spring of 1831. In 182‹6›, when Dr Lansing was there,** these men had set themselves against the revival, and carried their opposition so far as to break from Dr Lansing's congregation and form a new one.[19] In the meantime Dr Lansing

[14]Finney was reported as saying, on one occasion:

> Since I have been in the ministry, I have been pressed, I cannot say how many times, to *spare* myself and take more rest, and take more care of myself. But Jesus Christ laid down his life, and I can afford, if necessary, to lay down mine. It is not the point *how long* any-one lives, but *what he does*. If a man is endeavoring to spare his own health, and to make that a primary object, setting it before his duty,—he is not doing very much. . . .
>
> To preserve one's life is a duty, when it can be done consistently with other and more important duties. But it is often our duty to sacrifice life, or at least, to risk it; and the man who cannot do this, will never accomplish very great things. The work must be done, come life or come death (*The Penny Pulpit* [London] 1,570 [July–September 1850]: 195).

[15]Finney arrived in Auburn on Wednesday, 9 March. See J. W. Adams to Finney, 10 March 1831, Finney Papers, microfilm, roll 2.

[16]Theodore Spencer (1800–1870) had originally been destined for the army and was trained at West Point Military Academy, but he changed to law and became a lawyer in Auburn. He was district attorney at the time of Finney's visit. He had been converted during Finney's previous revival in Auburn and had become an elder in the First Church. Subsequently he became a Presbyterian minister, but his health prevented him from doing much preaching. As secretary of the American Home Missionary Society for central and western New York, he developed a special ministry as a pastoral counselor. See P. H. Fowler, *Historical Sketch of Presbyterianism Within the Bounds of the Synod of Central New York* (Utica: Curtiss and Childs, 1877), pp. 651–55.

In 1836 Spencer was invited to Oberlin to become professor of law in the college and pastor of the church, but he did not accept. See Oberlin College Faculty Minutes, 5 October 1836, Oberlin College Archives, microfilm.

[17]Ambrose Spencer (1765–1848) was a lawyer in Albany. He became chief justice in 1819 and mayor in 1824. In 1829 he was elected to Congress. See *DAB*.

[18]See MS 391. Here and in three other places in this and the next paragraph, Matson had written the date "1827," but Finney altered the 7 to a 6 in each case.

[19]Sixty-six members of the First Church were dismissed and formed the Second Presbyterian Church in November 1830 under the pastoral charge of Daniel C. Axtell. Among the reasons assigned for the formation of a second society was "that in consequence of dissatisfaction that had

had been called to another field of labor,[20] and **the** Rev. Josiah Hopkins of Vermont was settled as pastor of the first church **in Dr Lansing's place.**[21] The paper to which I have alluded contained an earnest ˡappeal to me to stop and labor for their salvation, signed by a long list of unconverted men, most of them among the most prominent citizens in the city. This was very striking to me. In this paper they alluded to the opposition they had formerly made to my labors, and besought me to overlook it and stop and preach the Gospel to them. This request did not come from the pastor, nor from his church, but from those who had formerly led in the opposition to the work **in 182‹6›.**[22] But the pastor and members of his church[23] pressed me with all their

MS 610

arisen among many on account of certain measures adopted to promote revivals of religion, a new and separate organization would be desirable" (Hotchkin, *History of Western New York*, pp. 345–46).

[20]Lansing had been repeatedly called to the Second Presbyterian Church in Utica and finally went in June 1829. He remained there until 1832, when he went to New York. See Charles Hawley, *The History of the First Presbyterian Church, Auburn, N.Y.* (Auburn: Dennis, 1869), p. 44.

[21]Josiah Hopkins (1785–1862) had been minister of the Congregational church in New Haven, Vermont, for twenty-one years before moving to Auburn in July 1830. He was minister of the First Presbyterian Church, Auburn, until ill health caused his retirement in 1846. See Timothy Hopkins, *John Hopkins of Cambridge, Massachusetts, 1634, and Some of His Descendants* (Stanford, Calif.: Stanford University Press, 1932), pp. 338–39.

He was the author of *The Christian's Instructor* (Middlebury, Vt., 1825), which became a very popular book to give to young converts. Finney used it, and when a new edition was to be published, he was asked by Hopkins on behalf of the publisher, Henry Ivison of Auburn, to write a recommendation. The book went through many editions. See Oliver Smith to Finney, 21 February 1829, Finney Papers, microfilm, roll 2; Hopkins to Finney, 4 March 1833, Finney Papers, microfilm, roll 3; Finney to H. Ivison and Co., 9 March 1833, in "Recommendations," *The Christian's Instructor*, 2d ed., rev. and enl. (Auburn: Ivison, 1833), pp. 3–4; and n. 22 below.

Hopkins also trained a number of students for the ministry, one of whom was John J. Shipherd, one of the founders of Oberlin College. See p. 236 n. 21 (MS 448); and letters of Hopkins to Finney in the Finney Papers.

[22]The letter that Finney refers to is apparently the one dated Auburn, 15 March 1831, and signed by fifty-eight people (Finney Papers, microfilm, roll 2). Finney, however, appears to be confused about when the letter was given to him and about its contents. According to Richard Steel, a member of the First Presbyterian Church at the time, Finney had been "prevailed upon to stay over four or five days" and had already preached "a few times,"

> and, although he had paid his fare in the stage and directed the driver to call for him at two o'clock the next morning, at the house where he stopped (a private residence) a petition was got up signed by non-professors, some of whom were among the most prominent citizens of the place, urging him not to leave. That request was sent to his room, after he had retired to bed; and it is said he uttered a groan, and after a while sent word down to those who were waiting, "Go to the stage office, and withdraw my name from the list of passengers." He then remained for say three or four weeks (Richard Steel to P. C. Headley, in Headley, *Evangelists in the Church* [Boston: Hoyt, 1875], pp. 138–39).

The letter, written about a week after Finney arrived in Auburn, reads:

> To the Rev: Charles G. Finney,
>
> We the undersigned, feeling in some measure the importance of the salvation of the Soul, and believing that God has been graciously pleased to bless your labours as a preacher of the Gospel, do earnestly request, that, should it be consistent with your duties elsewhere, you would continue to give us the benefit of your instructions for a longer period.
>
> Auburn 15th March 1831.

The list of signatures is headed by George E. Pomeroy, and the second name is H. Ivison, the publisher. See n. 21 above.

[23]Here Matson had written down, "But as soon as the pastor and members of his church heard

influence to remain and preach and comply with the requests of these men.[24] JHF 304 They ˡappeared as much surprized as I was myself at the change in the attitude of those men. I went to my room and spread the subject before God, and soon made up my mind what to do.[25] I told the pastor and his elders that I was very much fatigued, and nearly worn out; but that upon certain conditions MS 611 I would remain. I would preach twice ˡupon the Sabbath and two evenings during the week;[26] but that they should take all the rest of the labor upon their own hands. That they must not expect me to attend any other meetings than those at which I preached; and that they must take the labor of instructing inquirers ‹& conducting the prayer & other meetings.›[27] I knew that they understood how to labor with sinners, and *could* well trust them to perform that part of the work. I furthermore stipulated that neither they nor their people should visit me, except in extreme cases, at my lodgings; for that I must have my days, Sundays excepted, that I might rest, and also my evenings, except those when I preached.[28] There were three preaching services on the Sabbath, one of which was filled by Brother Hopkins. I preached in the morning and evening, I think, of each Sabbath, and he in the afternoon.

The Word took immediate effect. On the first ‹or second› Sabbath evening that I preached,[29] I saw that the Word was taking such powerful hold that at the close I called for those whose minds were made up to come right MS 612 forward, publicly renounce their sins, and give themselves to Christ. ˡA good

of it they were filled with earnest joy in view of the event, and." This appears to have been altered by Finney.

[24] Hopkins had been to Rochester in early November and had met Finney there. Soon after, a revival "with overwhelming interest" began in a Sabbath school taught by Richard Steel, one of Hopkins's church members, and was given "an astonishing impulse" through a Three Days' Meeting near the end of February, when there were thought to be one hundred conversions. Hopkins and others had tried to get Finney to go there and help. See *WR,* 8 March 1831, p. 38; and 12 July 1831, pp. 110–11, where a widely publicized account of the revival by Josiah Hopkins, dated 23 June, was reprinted from the *Vermont Chronicle*; and see letters to Finney from Hopkins, (Palmer?) Holley, M. L. R. Perrine, and Richard Steel in January and February 1831, Finney Papers, microfilm, roll 2.

Soon after Finney arrived, he wrote to Weld: "Br. Hopkins & people first made a set upon me to stay. Next a Committee from the Seminary backed them up, & lastly a written request was sent in signed by a great number of the impenitent modestly but earnestly urging me to stay" (Finney to Weld, 17 March 1831, in Weld-Grimke Papers).

[25] Edwin Benedict, a student at Auburn Theological Seminary at the time, recalled:

> Mr. Finney came from west of Cayuga Lake and stayed over night. His stopping at Auburn to labor was still a matter of doubt, and I remember distinctly that prayer was offered in the sunrise meeting that the Lord would direct whether he should remain or pass on to some other field ("Fifty Years Ago: The great revival in Auburn," *NYE,* 31 March 1881, p. 6).

[26] That was on Tuesday and Friday evenings. See Benedict, "Fifty Years Ago."

[27] Here Matson had written down, "the labor of instructing inquirers into their own hands," but Finney changed it.

[28] Just before Finney left Rochester he had received a letter from Theodore Weld: "How is your health—how lungs and throat. Do for Jesus sake *be careful, be careful.* I do know that your *room conversation* when I was in Rochester was the *worm at the root.* Why not have certain hours in the day and write Sanctum upon them" (Weld to Finney, dated 2 March 1831 in the calendar, Finney Papers, microfilm, roll 2).

[29] Here Matson had written "On the very first Sabbath evening that I preached," but Finney changed it. The first Sabbath was 13 March. Finney is probably therefore referring to Sunday, 20 March.

deal to my own surprize, and very much to the surprize of the pastor and many members of the church, the first man that I observed as coming forward and leading the way, was the man that had led, and exerted more influence than any other one man, in the opposition to the revival **when I was there in 182‹6›**. He came forward promptly, followed by a large number of the persons who had signed that paper; and th‹at› evening[30] there was such a demonstration made as to produce a general **excitement** throughout the place.

I have spoken of ‹**Rev**› **Abel** Clary as the praying man who ˡwas at Rochester.[31] He had a brother, a physician, living in Auburn.[32] I think it was the second Sabbath that I was at Auburn this time **that** I observed in the congregation the solemn face of this **Rev. Abel** Clary. He looked as if he was borne down with an agony of prayer. Being well-acquainted with him, and knowing the great gift of God that was upon him, the Spirit of prayer, I was very glad to see him there. He sat in the pew ˡwith his brother, the Doctor, who was also a professor of religion, but who knew nothing by experience, I should think, of his brother Abel's great power with God. At intermission, as soon as I came down from the pulpit **Brother** Clary, with his brother **the Doctor**, met me at the pulpit stairs, and the Doctor invited me to go home with him and spend the intermission and get some refreshment. I did so. After arriving at his house we were soon summoned to the dinner table. We gathered about the table, and Dr Clary turned to his brother and said, "Brother Abel, will you ask a blessing?" Brother Abel bowed his head and began audibly to ask a blessing. **But a** sentence or two **had escaped him** when he broke instantly down, moved suddenly back from the table, and fled to his **bed**chamber. The doctor supposed he had been taken suddenly ill, and rose up and followed him. In a few moments he came down and said, "Mr. Finney, Brother Abel wants to see you." Said I, "What ails him?" Said he, "I do not know; but he says *you* know."[33] ˡHe appears in great distress, but I think it is the state of his mind." I understood it in a moment, **and got up** and went to his room. **He was in one of his seasons of travail of soul.** He lay groaning upon the bed, **and tossing from side to side**; the Spirit making intercession for him and in him with groanings that cannot be uttered. **That is, his desires were altogether too great to be expressed in words, and his groans could be heard all over the house.** I had **no more than fairly got into** the room when he made out to say, "*Pray*, Brother Finney." I knelt down and helped him in prayer by leading his soul out for conversion of sinners. I continued to pray until his distress passed away, and then I returned to the dinner table. ˡ**I think that Brother Clary did not make his appearance at the dinner table again, and I do not recollect that I spoke with him again that day. But** I understood that this was the voice of God. I saw the

JHF 305

MS 613

MS 614

JHF 306

[30] Finney changed "the very first evening" to "that evening."

[31] See MS 587–90. Finney added the abbreviation "Rev."

[32] This may have been Joseph Clary, who was admitted to the Jefferson County Medical Society in 1811. See Franklin B. Hough, *A History of Jefferson County in the State of New York* (Albany: Munsell, 1854), p. 399.

[33] Matson put quotation marks at the end of the sentence at the bottom of page 613, but the quotation continues at the top of the next page.

Spirit of prayer was upon him, and I felt his influence upon myself, and took it MS 615 for granted that the work would **take** on **a** powerful **type**. It did so. ᑊI believe, but am not quite sure, that every one of those men that signed that paper, making a long list of names, was converted during that revival. But a few years since Dr **Steele** of Auburn wrote to me to know if I had preserved that paper, wishing, as he said, to ascertain whether every one of the men that signed it was not at that time converted.[34] The paper has been mislaid; and although it is probably among my numerous papers and letters, and may sometime be found, yet I could not at the time answer his inquiry **to his satisfaction. But of this I am confident, that nearly if not quite all of those men were converted; and they have been, I believe, among the most earnest and useful Christians in that city ever since.**

I stayed at this time at Auburn six Sabbaths,[35] preaching, as I have said, twice on the Sabbath, and twice during the week, and leaving all the rest of the labor for the pastor and members of the church.[36] Here, as at Rochester, MS 616 there was at this time little or no open opposition.[37] Ministers ᑊand Christians took hold of the work, and every-body that had a mind to work found enough to do, and good success in **their** labors. The pastor told me afterwards that he

[34]Dr. Steel's letter is not in the Finney Papers.

[35]The sixth Sabbath was 17 April. Hopkins stated that Finney was in Auburn helping for seven weeks. See *WR,* 12 July 1831, p. 110.

[36]While he was at Auburn, Finney preached in other places in the area. He visited Skaneateles, where the minister was Samuel Brace, who had been at Utica during the 1826 revival. Finney preached there on the evening of Thursday, 31 March. Brace, who had been somewhat ambivalent toward Finney, considered that his labors were "of a cast entirely different from what they were in Dr. Lansing's day" in 1826 (see Brace to Asahel Nettleton, 6 December 1832, Nettleton Papers, Hartford Seminary; p. 173 n. 8 [MS 342]; Brace to Finney, 29 March 1831; and Hopkins to Finney, 31 March 1831, Finney Papers, microfilm, roll 2). Finney may also have visited William Wisner at Ithaca on Saturday, 9 April (Wisner and Joseph Esty to Finney, 5 April 1831, Finney Papers, microfilm, roll 3).

Finney also visited Geneva at the invitation of the minister Eliakim Phelps, to help in a Three Days' Meeting that started on 12 April (see Phelps to Finney, 6 April 1831, Finney Papers, microfilm, roll 3; Finney to G. S. Boardman, 9 April 1831, Simon Gratz Manuscripts, Historical Society of Pennsylvania, Philadelphia; and Elizabeth Stuart Phelps, *Austin Phelps: A Memoir* [London: Nisbet, 1891], pp. 25–26). The report of these meetings in *The New-York Evangelist* mentions that "The Rev. Mr. Finney preached three very powerful sermons." This report was also published in other papers. It is curious that the versions in the Boston papers (*BR,* 27 April 1831, p. 67; and *Christian Watchman*, 29 April 1831, p. 66) both omitted this sentence about Finney. The *Boston Recorder*, however, printed it in another notice on 11 May 1831, p. 74. See *NYE,* 23 April 1831, p. 223.

Finney may also have preached on 20 April at Cayuga Village. See John Clark to Finney, 18 April 1831, Finney Papers, microfilm, roll 3.

[37]During the 1826 revival in Auburn there had been considerable opposition from Dr. James Richards, principal of the theological seminary (see MS 374–75). But Hopkins had written to Finney to say: "The opposition are becoming more and more *mum*. Dr. Richards himself has been heard (inter nos) to say all this difference is nothing & he wishes it were buried for ever" (J. Hopkins to Finney, 3 February 1831, Finney Papers, microfilm, roll 2). And again: "Dr. Richards does not lift a finger nor move an eye nor wag his tongue to oppose you. He wishes—yes from the bottom of his heart that all the opposition he has ever shown were blotted from remembrance" (Hopkins to Finney, 15 February 1831, Finney Papers, microfilm, roll 2).

A critique of three of Finney's sermons, showing the inconsistencies in his views of endless punishment and the Atonement, was published by Ulysses F. Doubleday, the bookseller and politician who denied reports that he had been converted from Universalism in the revival ("Mr. Finney at Auburn," *The Evangelical Magazine and Gospel Advocate* [Utica], 30 April 1831, pp. 138–39).

found that in the six weeks that I was there, five hundred souls had been converted.[38] The means that were used were the same that had been used at Rochester. **In this revival there was no appearance of fanaticism, or anything witnessed, that I know of to be regretted.** This revival seemed to be only a *wave* of divine **influence** reaching Auburn from the center at Rochester, whence such a mighty influence had gone out over the length and breadth of the land.

Near the close of my labors here a messenger arrived from Buffalo with an earnest request that I should visit that city.[39] **Auburn, I believe, is about the same distance east of Rochester that Buffalo is west.**[40] The revival in Rochester had prepared the way in Auburn, as in every other place **all** round about, and had also prepared the way **at** Buffalo. At Buffalo, the messenger[41] informed me, the work had begun, and a few souls ˡhad been hopefully converted; but they felt **as if** other means needed to be used **than those that were on the spot**, and they urged me so hard, that from Auburn I **returned** back through Rochester to Buffalo.[42] I spent but ˡabout one month, I think,

MS 617

JHF 307

[38]According to Edwin Benedict: "Some four to six hundred of all ages and previous modes of life were gathered to the evangelical churches of the village and immediate vicinity" (*NYE,* 31 March 1881, p. 6). Charles Hawley wrote, "During his stay of about two months, Mr. Finney preached in no other pulpit than this, but the results were by no means limited to this congregation." And he added, "The fact remains that this church owes to these palmy days of its increase, much of its character, influence, its sinew and strength" (Hawley, *History of the First Presbyterian Church,* pp. 50, 54–55). Hopkins reported in May that 146 had been added to the First Church, 70 to the Second Church, 70 to the Methodists, and more than 100 to the Baptists. See *WR,* 12 May 1831, p. 78; and *Christian Watchman,* 29 July 1831, p. 121.

[39]Two delegates had arrived from Buffalo on 7 April (see Finney to G. S. Boardman, 9 April 1831, Gratz Manuscripts), but Finney is referring to Alvan Ingersoll, who arrived about 18 April armed with a petition from Sylvester Eaton, the minister of the Presbyterian church, and signed by his six elders and fifty other people. These included the trustees of the church and many of the most influential men in Buffalo, mostly "impenitent sinners." Ingersoll had also got support from Joseph Penney and five others at Rochester on the way, who added their recommendation (letter dated 15 April 1831; and Eaton to Finney, 16 April 1831, Finney Papers, microfilm, roll 3).

Mrs. Finney and the children probably arrived from Rochester with Ingersoll. See Selah Mathews to Finney, 19 April 1831; and Mary D. Mathews to Lydia Finney, 24 April 1831, Finney Papers, microfilm, roll 3.

[40]Auburn and Buffalo were both reckoned to be about sixty-five miles from Rochester.

[41]Matson had at first written the word "minister" here, but he changed it to "messenger." Ingersoll was not ordained but was thinking of preparing for the ministry. See Alvan Ingersoll to Finney, 1 April 1831, Finney Papers, microfilm, roll 2.

[42]Finney was evidently put off continuing east to New York because of a lack of unity among the clergy about inviting him. A letter from Rev. Henry G. Ludlow of Spring Street Church strongly advised him not to go for this reason (Ludlow to Finney, 16 March 1831, Finney Papers, microfilm, roll 2). It is clear from a large correspondence at this time that Finney was extremely cautious of entering any new field unless he had the unanimous support of the ministers. See also M. L. R. Perrine to Gardiner Spring, 9 April 1831, in *Personal Reminiscences of the Life and Times of Gardiner Spring,* vol. 1 (New York: Scribner, 1866), pp. 223–25. Finney was considering going north at this time to Henderson, New York, where his father was very ill.

Theodore Weld also wrote to him: "I don't believe, I cannot & I will not that you had better go to New York City *now.* Why not go to Buffalo & to the intermediate towns between there & Rochester. Once get that region thoroughly soaked and all hell can't wring it dry you know." See Finney to Boardman, 9 April 1831, Gratz Manuscripts; and Weld to Finney, in the calendar dated 2 March 1831, Finney Papers, microfilm, roll 2. In fact, Finney had been interested in the state of things in Buffalo for some time. He had had repeated urgent requests from the minister, Sylvester Eaton, backed up by others, for several months, and he had asked visitors to send back reports. There was already a considerable revival under way, and they had had a Four Days' Meeting, and many converts were reported. He had, moreover, promised that he would go. See

at Buffalo; during which time a large number of persons were hopefully converted. The work at Buffalo, as at Auburn and Rochester, took effect very generally among the **higher** classes.[43] **Among the converts at Buffalo, I believe the** Rev. Dr Lord then a lawyer, was converted at that time.[44] Also **at that time,** Mr. **Heacock,**[45] the father of **the present** Rev. Dr Heacock of Buffalo,[46] **was converted.** There were many circumstances connected with his conversion that I have never forgotten. He was one of the most wealthy and influential men in Buffalo, and a man of outwardly good morals, fair character, and high standing as a citizen, but an impenitent sinner. His wife was a Christian woman, and had long been praying for him, and hoping that

MS 618 he would be converted.[47] |But when I began to preach there,[48] and insisted

letters to Finney from Sylvester Eaton, Alvan Ingersoll, Edward Corning, Calvin and John Wadsworth, and Samuel Johnson, in the Finney Papers; and *NYE,* 23 April 1831, p. 223.

A sermon on Saturday, 23 April, may have been the last that Finney preached before leaving with his family for Buffalo. Reports of seven sermons and parts of two others, from the end of March to 23 April 1831, taken down by Charles Churchill, are preserved in a notebook, "Sermons Preached by Charles G. Finney, Auburn, 1831," in Silas Churchill Papers, the Presbyterian Historical Society, Philadelphia (reference from Leonard I. Sweet).

[43] The *Western Recorder* reported: "The church at Buffalo, we understand, is now enjoying the labours of Rev. Mr. Finney. The work had, by the latest accounts, become deep and powerful. Some of the numerous subjects are from the conspicuous ranks in society" (3 May 1831, p. 71).

[44] John Chase Lord (1805–1877) was the son of Rev. John Lord of Madison County, New York. He was a graduate of Hamilton College and had gone to Buffalo in 1825, where he was admitted to the bar in 1828 (*NYE,* 26 April 1877, p. 2). Before Finney went to Buffalo he was told by John Wadsworth in a letter from Buffalo that Lord had been converted "the week before last" (J. Wadsworth to Finney, 4 April 1831, Finney Papers, microfilm, roll 3). Richard Steel, however, related that Lord "was then a lawyer there, and prominent as a young man, and very successful in his profession; but on hearing Mr. F. preach his second sermon, I think, he went forward for prayers, consecrated himself to Christ, left his law office, and after three years' study in the seminary at Auburn went forth to preach the gospel, and has preached in Buffalo over one third of a century" (Headley, *Evangelists,* p. 142).

In 1835 Lord became minister of the Pearl Street Church, reorganized later as the Central Presbyterian Church, where he remained until his retirement thirty-eight years later. He was an Old School Presbyterian, and when Finney's doctrine of perfectionism began to be spread abroad, he became bitterly opposed to Oberlin and was an outspoken critic. See Sherlock Bristol to H. Hill, 19 October 1843, Letters Received by Oberlin College 1822–1866, microfilm, roll 9; J. C. Lord, "Finney's Sermons on Sanctification and Mahan on Christian Perfection," *The Biblical Repertory and Princeton Review* 13 (April 1841): 231–50; Lord, *The Doctrine and Order of the Presbyterian Church; or, The points of difference between the old and new school. A Sermon* (Buffalo: R. D. Foy, 1843); and "Modern Perfectionism," *The New York Observer,* 26 September 1840, p. 155.

[45] Reuben Heacock (1788–1854), a native of Derby, Connecticut, had been an Indian trader before settling as a resident in Buffalo in 1811. He went into business with Seth Grosvenor, who married his sister and became one of the leaders in civic and Indian affairs. He was also a member of the state legislature. "He had that superabundant and restless energy which required a large amount of business and even of difficulty to expend itself on" (*NYE,* 4 May 1854, p. 69; and Ketchum, *History of Buffalo,* pp. 241–43).

[46] Grosvenor Williams Heacock (1822–1877) was pastor of the Lafayette Street Church from 1845 until his death. The church was "numerically and morally the product of revivals enjoyed for the last twenty-five years under the faithful and earnest ministry of its founder and only pastor, Rev. Grosvenor W. Heacock, D.D." See *NYE,* 13 May 1869, p. 4; and 19 December 1895, p. 8.

[47] He was married to the sister of Seth Grosvenor.

[48] Finney preached in the Brick Church, built by the First Church in 1827, the largest church building west of the Genesee River. Rev. Sylvester Eaton was the minister there from 1828 to 1834. See Walter McCausland, "Buffalo's First Church and Its People," *Niagara Frontier* 8, no. 2 (Summer 1961): 40–41.

that the sinner's "*cannot*" is his "*will not*," that the difficulty to be overcome was the voluntary wickedness of sinners, and that they were wholly unwilling to be Christians,—Mr. Heacock rebelled very decidedly against such teaching. He insisted upon it that it was false in his case; for he was conscious of being willing to be a Christian, and that he had long been willing. As his wife informed me of the position that he occupied, I did not spare him; but from night to night, and from day to day, I hunted him from his refuges, and answered all his objections, and met all his excuses. He became more and more excited. He was a man of strong will; and he declared that he *did not*, and *would not*, believe such teaching. He said so much in opposition to the teaching as to draw around him, to some extent, some men with whom he had no sympathy at all except in their opposition to the work. But I did not hesitate to press him in every sermon, in one shape or another, with his unwillingness to be a Christian.

After his conversion |he told me that he was shocked and ashamed when he found out that some scoffers had taken refuge behind him. One evening he said he sat right across the aisle from a notorious scoffer. He said that repeatedly while I was preaching this man, with whom he had no sym|pathy at all on any other subject,[49] would look to him and smile, and give great indications of his fellowship with his opposition to the revival.[50] He said that on discovering this his heart rose up with indignation; and he said to himself, "I am not going to be in sympathy with that class of men; I will have nothing to do with them." MS 619 JHF 308

However that very night at the close of my sermon I pressed the consciences of sinners so hard, and made so strong an appeal to them to give up their voluntary opposition and come to Christ, that he could not contain himself. As soon as meeting was out, altogether |contrary to his custom, he began to resist and to speak against what had been said before he got out of the house. The aisles were full, and people were crowding around him on every side. Indeed he made some profane expressions, as his wife informed me, which very much disturbed her, as she felt that by his opposition he was very likely to grieve the Spirit of God away and lose his soul. However that night he could not sleep. He afterwards told me that he scarcely slept at all. His mind was so exercised that he rose as soon as there was any light, left his house and went off to a considerable distance where there was then a grove of wood, and not far from where he had some water works which he called "the hydraulics."[51] There in that grove he knelt down to pray. He said MS 620

[49] Here Matson had written down, "on any other subject." It was not altered in the manuscript, but in the published edition it appears as "on other subjects."

[50] The following section was originally written after this by Matson but appears to have been crossed out by Finney: "—would look to him and smile, and try to make him understand that he was with him in his views and feelings of the work and in his opposition to it."

[51] Heacock "was principally instrumental in developing the hydraulic power in the eastern part of the city by means of a canal from the rapids of the easterly branch of the Buffalo Creek, which before the general use of steam, was used for manufacturing purposes" (Ketchum, *History of Buffalo*, p. 243). The canal was completed in 1828, and the area became known as "The Hydraulics." It was in the vicinity of Seneca and Emslie streets. Heacock organized the Buffalo Hydraulic Association.

he had felt during the night as if he must get away by himself, so that he could speak aloud and let out his voice and his heart, as he was pressed beyond endurance with the sense of his sins, and with the necessity of immediately MS 621 making ¦his peace with God. But to his surprize and mortification when he knelt down and attempted to pray, he found that his *heart* would not pray. He had no words; he had no desires that he could express in words. He said that it appeared to him that his heart was as hard as marble, and that he had not the least feeling on the subject. He stood upon his knees disappointed and JHF 309 confounded, and found that if he opened ¦his mouth to pray he had nothing in the form of prayer that he could sincerely utter. In this state it occured to him that he could say the Lord's prayer. So he began, "Our Father which art in heaven." He said as soon as he uttered it he was convicted of his hypocricy in calling God his Father. When he uttered the petition, "Hallowed be thy name," he said it almost shocked him. He saw that he was not sincere, that his words did not at all express the state of his mind. He did not care to have God's name hallowed. Then he uttered the next petition, "Thy kingdom MS 622 come." Upon this, he said, he almost choked. He saw that ¦he did not want the kingdom of God to come; that it was hypocritical in him to say so, and that he could not say it as really expressing the sincere desire of his heart. And then came the petition, "Thy will be done on earth as it is done in heaven." He said his heart rose up against that, and he could not say it. Here he was brought face to face with the will of God. He had been told from day to day that he was opposed to this will; that he was not willing to accept it; that it was his voluntary opposition to God, to His law, and His will, that was the only obstacle in the way of his conversion. This consideration he had resisted and fought like a tiger. But here on his knees, with this Lord's prayer in his mouth, he was brought face to face with that question, and he saw with perfect clearness that what he had been told was true: that he was not willing that God's will should be done; and that he did not do it himself because he *would not*. Here the whole question of his rebellion, in its nature and its extent, was brought so strongly before him, that he saw ‹it would cost him›[52] MS 623 a mighty struggle to give up that voluntary opposition to God.[53] ¦And then, he said, he gathered up all the strength of his will, and cried ‹aloud›,[54] "*Thy*

By the year 1832 the Hydraulics had expanded to a community of 500 and the milling enterprises consisted of a sawmill, grist mill, pail factory, woolen mill, shoe last factory, hat body factory, and brewery. The settlement of mill workers in the vicinity naturally led to the establishment of grocery and drygoods stores, meat markets, blacksmith shops, shoemakers, etc. The city limit of Buffalo at that time was at Jefferson Street (Frank J. Lankes, "The Hydraulics," *Niagara Frontier* 2, no. 1 [Spring 1955]: 7–9).

[52]The words "he would have" were changed by Finney to "it would cost him."

[53]In another account of this incident Finney said:

But what should he do? I think he said he sweat with agony. It seemed as if his sins would crush him. He saw where the difficulty lay; the whole difficulty lay in his unwillingness; and a load of guilt was pressing him down to death.

But just here it occurred to him, "Why should I not be willing? Why should not God's will be done? Ought not his will to be done? Is not his will perfect? Should not all his creatures submit to his will? Whose will should govern? Is it not right, is it not safe, is it not altogether best that I, and that all beings, should do the will of God?"

Such considerations flashed over his mind (*OE*, 31 July 1861, pp. 121–22).

[54]The words "cried at the top of his voice" were changed by Finney to "cried aloud."

will be done on earth as it is done in heaven." He said he was perfectly conscious[55] that his will went with his words; that he accepted the will of God, and the *whole* will of God; ˡthat he made a full surrender to God, and accepted Christ just as he was offered in the Gospel. He gave up his sins, and embraced the will of God as his universal rule of life. The language of his heart was, "Lord, do with me as seemeth thee good. Let thy will be done with me, and with all creatures on earth, as it is done in heaven.[”][56] He said he prayed freely, as soon as his will surrendered, and[57] his heart poured itself out like a flood. **The** rebellion **of his mind** all passed away, his feelings subsided into a great calm, and a sweet peace seemed to fill all his soul. He rose from his knees and went to his house and told his anxious wife, who had been praying for him so earnestly, what the Lord had done for his soul; and confessed that ˡhe had been all wrong in his opposition, and entirely deceived as it respected his willingness to be a Christian. From that time he became an earnest laborer for the promotion of the work of God. His subsequent life attested the reality of the change, and he lived and died a useful Christian man.[58] **Judge Wilkinson was also converted at that time, if I am not mistaken;**[59] **and many other prominent men, and women not a few.**[60] From Buffalo I went in June, I think, to my father-in-law's, in Whitestown. I spent a part of the

JHF 310

MS 624

[55]The words "at that moment" appear to have been crossed out by Finney.

[56]The quotation marks were omitted by Matson and were not inserted in the manuscript by Fairchild, but they appear in the published version.

[57]A comma and the symbol & appear to have been inserted by Finney in place of the words "He said," which had started a new sentence here. Matson then inserted the word "and" and crossed out Finney's symbol.

[58]An obituary states:

> He was brought to Christ under the preaching of Rev. Mr. Finney in 1831; and throughout the rest of his life remained an earnest friend of revivals, always ready to engage in special efforts for the conversion of sinners.
>
> The change wrought by his own conversion was marked and decided. He was ever ready with liberal contributions to benevolent objects. He loved the church of God; and amid multiplied business engagements, never failed to be in his place at the prayer-meeting. His example in this respect may justly be held up for the imitation of Christian men of business.

He became an elder in Dr. Lord's church but spent the last years of his life under his son's ministry (*NYE,* 4 May 1854, p. 69).

[59]Samuel Wilkeson (1781–1848), of Scotch-Irish descent, moved to Buffalo after the War of 1812 and was one of those chiefly responsible for building up the ruined town. As trader, ship owner, contractor, iron founder, and manufacturer he rapidly became a leading citizen. But he is known mainly as the man who built the harbor, thus ensuring that Buffalo became the western terminus of the Erie Canal. In 1821 he was appointed a judge and in 1824 a state senator. In 1836 he became mayor. He also became an elder in the Presbyterian church. See John C. Lord, "Samuel Wilkeson," *Buffalo Historical Society Publications* 4 (1896): 71–85; and *DAB.*

[60]A historian of the church reported:

> For two weeks the church was packed, pews, aisles, and pulpit steps. The galleries cracked with the weight of the crowds and additional supports had to be placed under them. From the day-break prayer meeting and mid-day services to the evening conference, throughout every week day the people gathered in multitudes to hear this wonderful man, all sects sharing the interest aroused (*Manual of the First Presbyterian Church of Buffalo, N.Y.* [Buffalo: First Presbyterian Church, 1912], p. 19).

See also Samuel M. Welch, *Home History, Recollections of Buffalo during the decade from 1830 to 1840, or Fifty Years Since* (Buffalo: Peter Paul, 1891), p. 244. Sixty-two were added to the church on 24 July. Richard Steel, however, made the comment: "At Buffalo his preaching was blessed, not however so wonderfully as in some localities: but the fruits there have been remarkably permanent" (Headley, *Evangelists,* p. 142).

summer in journeying for recreation, and for the restoration of my health and strength.[61]

Early in the **Autumn** of 1831 I accepted an invitation to hold what was then called "a protracted meeting," or a series of meetings, in Providence, **R. I.**[62] I labored mostly in the church of which **the** Rev. Dr Wilson was at that time pastor.[63] I think I remained there about three weeks, holding meetings every evening, and preaching three times on the Sabbath. The Lord poured out **His**

MS 625 Spirit ¹immediately upon the people, and the work of grace commenced and **progressed** in a most interesting manner **for the short time that I at that time spent in that city**. However my stay was too short to secure so general a work of grace in that place as occurred afterwards in 1842, when I spent some two months there; the particulars of which I shall relate in its proper

[61]Finney left Buffalo early in June 1831, arriving in Vienna, Ontario County, on 10 June, where he preached in the afternoon, leaving the next morning for the East. Mrs. Finney and the children had evidently gone on independently. See Laura Boyle to Lydia Finney, 11 June 1831, Finney Papers, microfilm, roll 3.

On 12 July 1831, *The Western Recorder* reported, "Rev. Mr. Finney, after preaching a few sermons in Utica and vicinity, has set his face toward New England" (p. 111). He spent some time in Albany preaching "about every night" and also preaching in Troy, Lansingburgh, and Waterford (see Finney to T. D. Weld, 21 July 1831, Weld-Grimke Papers; and *NYE,* 23 July 1831, p. 275). He then went on to New York about 25 July, where he stayed with Herman Norton and his wife until the second week in August, preaching seven times in the Union Church before going to Providence (Finney to John Starkweather, 8 August 1831, copy in Finney's handwriting in Finney Papers, microfilm, roll 3; and Anson G. Phelps, "Diary," 4 September 1831, microfilm, New York Public Library).

[62]"Protracted meetings" were a new measure for conducting revivals introduced in 1830. A few years before this, meetings lasting three or four days had become an effective measure. Finney stated that they were first called "conferences of churches." The first "Four Days' Meeting" for revival was said to have been held by William C. Walton in Alexandria, Virginia, just south of Washington, D.C., in October 1828, with help from James Patterson, Reuben Post, and Joshua N. Danforth. The so-called protracted meeting was an extension of this into a campaign, with several ministers cooperating and meetings for preaching and prayer and inquiry arranged through the day for many days at a time. See "Measures in Revivals," *NYE,* 2 March 1843, p. 34; *OE,* 29 January 1845, p. 19; "Four Days Meetings," *The Western Luminary* [Lexington, Ky.], 30 January 1828, p. 244; the review of the *Memoir of William C. Walton, NYE,* 1 July 1837, p. 106; and Reuben Post to Finney, 4 November 1828, calendar of the Finney Papers, microfilm, roll 1.

The meetings in Providence commenced on Wednesday, 10 August, and continued through to the close of the Sabbath. Eleven Congregational clergy took part, and the schedule included:

> Prayer meetings at 5 o'clock, each morning. Meetings for prayer and exhortation, each day at 9 o'clock, A.M. Preaching at 10 o'clock. Prayer meeting at 2 o'clock, P.M. Preaching at 3. Prayer meeting a quarter before seven. And preaching at half past seven o'clock in the evening.

Finney was there from the commencement and preached "every evening, with *great acceptance* to crowded assemblies" (*NYE,* 10 September 1831, p. 302).

[63]James Wilson (1760–1839) was a native of Ireland. In 1791 he happened to be on a journey through Providence when he was invited to preach by the pastor of the Beneficent Congregational Church. As a result, he stayed on for two years assisting the pastor, Joseph Snow. But he had been a Methodist in Ireland, and when he was ordained by the society in 1793, there was opposition on doctrinal grounds. Snow and members of the church withdrew to form a separate society, which became the Richmond Street Congregational Church. Wilson continued as minister of the Beneficent Congregational Church until his death (see William R. Staples, "Annals of the Town of Providence," *Rhode Island Historical Collections* 5 [1843]: 449–54). There is no apparent evidence that Wilson was ever a Doctor of Divinity. Finney may have confused him with Dr. James P. Wilson, the minister at the First Presbyterian Church in Philadelphia, where Finney had preached in 1828.

connection.[64] There were many **very** interesting conversions at that time; |and several of the men who have had a leading Christian influence in that city from that time to the present day, were **at that time** converted. This was also true of the **ladies:** many **among them** very interesting cases of conversion occured.[65] **Among them** I remember with great distinctness the conversion of one young lady, which I will in brief relate. I had observed in the congregation on the Sabbath a young **lady** of great personal beauty, sitting in a pew with a young **gentle**man who I afterwards learned was her brother. She had a very intellectual, and a very earnest look, and seemed to listen to every word I said with the utmost attention and seriousness. I was the guest |of **Brother** Josiah Chapin;[66] and in going from the church with him to his own house, I observed this young **gentlemen** and **lady** going up the same street. I pointed them out to **Brother** Chapin, and asked him who they were. He informed me that **it was** a Mr. and a Miss **Ainsworth, that they were** brother and sister, and remarked that she was considered the most beautiful girl in Providence. I asked him if she was a professor of religion, and he said, **N**o. I told him I thought her very seriously impressed, and asked him if he did not think it would be well for me to call and see her. He spoke discouragingly in regard to that, and thought it would be a waste of time, and that possibly I might not be cordially received. He thought that she was a girl so much caressed and flattered, and that her surroundings were such, that she probably entertained but little serious thought in regard to the salvation of her soul. But he was mistaken; and I was right in supposing that the Spirit of the Lord was striving with her. I did not call upon her; but a few days after **I first spoke to |Brother Chapin respecting her** she called to see me. I knew her at once, **asked her to be seated,** and inquired of her in regard to the state of her soul. She was very thoroughly awakened; but her real convictions of sin were not ripened into that state that I wished to see, and which I thought was necessary before she could be really brought intelligently to accept the righteousness of Christ. I therefore spent an |hour or two—for her call was considerably protracted—in trying to show her the depravity of her heart. **I asked her if she was not proud, and vain, and self-righteous. She thought she was not. I asked her many searching questions, such as these. I asked her if**

JHF 311

MS 626

MS 627

JHF 312

[64] See MS 733–35.

[65] One lady, however, was reported by a resident in Providence as

> laboring under a most wretched form and degree of insanity, brought on by attending the four days meeting while FINNEY was in this town. Her uncle tells me he thinks it will terminate her existence. She is much emaciated. All reason and sense of decency are lost (letter dated 24 November 1831 in Abner Kneeland's paper, *Boston Investigator*, 2 December 1831, p. 141).

The words "among them" were inserted later by Matson. Fairchild crossed them out and inserted them instead after the word "conversion," where Matson may have intended to insert them. The next sentence begins with "Among them," and this was crossed out in what appears to be Fairchild's handwriting.

[66] Josiah Chapin (1788–1881) was a farmer's son from Uxbridge, Massachusetts. He went to Providence in 1815 and became the leading cotton merchant in the area. In 1839 he was joined in the firm by his son, William C. Chapin, who became a wealthy Rhode Island politician. The father retired in 1844 to a farm, having amassed a large fortune. See entry in *Dorr Obituaries* in Rhode Island Historical Society Library, Providence; and letters from the Chapins to Finney in the Finney Papers.

she had never been envious. She replied that she was not aware that she had. I asked her then if there was any young lady of her acquaintance that she thought more beautiful than herself. She at first recoiled from **this** searching question, **but there was a spirit of candor that pretty soon brought her to acknowledge that she did not know any young lady that** MS 628 **she thought was more beautiful than she was. |I asked her if she did not think she should be envious or jealous if she thought there was any young lady more beautiful than she was. She thought she should not. I asked her if she knew any young lady that she thought was more *amiable* than herself. She said that she did know of one at least, that she thought was more amiable than herself; but she was not aware that she had any envy or jealousy in respect to her. I put a great many such like questions for the purpose of forcing her to think and reflect in that direction.** Her convictions seemed to ripen as I conversed with her; and she became more and more profoundly serious **as I put the searching questions to her.** When I had said to her what I thought was necessary to secure a ripened and thorough conviction under the influence of the Spirit of God, she got up with a manifested feeling of dissatisfaction and left me. I was confident the Spirit of God had so thoroughly taken hold of her case that what I said to her would not be shaken off, but on the contrary that it would work the MS 629 conviction that I sought to produce. |Two or three days afterwards she called on me again. I could see at once that she was greatly bowed down in her spirit. As soon as she came in she sat down and threw her heart open to me. With the utmost candor she said to me, "Mr. Finney, I thought when I was here before that your questions and treatment of me were pretty severe. But," said she, "I see now that I am all that you represented me to be. Indeed," said she, "had it not been for my pride and regard for my reputation, I should have been as wicked a girl as there is in Providence. I can see," said she, "clearly, that my life has been restrained by pride and a regard to my reputation, and not from any regard to God, or His law or Gospel. I can see that God has made use of my pride and ambition to restrain me from disgraceful iniquities. I have been petted and flattered, and have stood upon my dignity, and have maintained my reputation from purely selfish motives." MS 630 She went on spontaneously and |owned up, and showed that her convictions were thorough and permanent. She did not appear to be excited, but calm, and in the highest degree rational in everything that she said. It was evident, however, that she had a fervent nature, a strong will, and an uncommonly well-balanced and cultivated intellect. **Indeed, at the time I thought that I had never seen a more thoroughly interesting case of conviction than** JHF 313 **hers.** After conversing with her for **sometime** and giving her |as thorough instruction as I could, we bowed before the Lord in prayer; and she, to all human appearance, gave herself unreservedly to Christ. She was in a state of mind at this time that seemed to render it easy for her to renounce the world. She has always been a very interesting Christian. Not many years after her conversion she was married to a wealthy gentleman in the city of New York.[67] For several years I had no direct correspondence with her. Her

[67] According to the index "Marriages in Providence," Mary W. Ainsworth was married to

husband took her into a circle of society with which I had no particular acquaintance; and until after he died I did not ꞌrenew my acquaintance with her. Since then I have had much Christian correspondence with her, and have never ceased to be greatly interested in her religious life.[68] I mention this case because I have ever regarded it as a wonderful triumph of the grace of God over the fascinations of the world. **It is probable that there was no lady in the country more flattered than she was, more caressed, more respected, and more the idol of society. But** the grace of God was too strong for the world, even in a case like this, in which every worldly fascination was surrounding her. **She has never that I can learn faltered in her Christian course.** While I was at Providence, the question of my going to Boston was agitated by the ministers and deacons of the several Congregational churches of that city.[69] I was not myself aware of what they were doing there. **But** Dr Wisner, then pastor of the Old South church, came over to Providence and attended our meetings.[70] I afterwards learned that he was sent over by the ministers "to spy out the land and bring back a report."[71] I

MS 631

Charles W. Milbank on 28 May 1835 (p. 71, Rhode Island Historical Society Library). Charles W. Milbank was a brewer with the firm of C. and S. Milbank in New York. "Mary W. Milbank, widow of Charles W.," is listed as living at 213 Madison Street in *Trow's New York City Directory* for 1856–1857, p. 575.

[68] There are no letters from her to Finney in the Finney Papers. However, Finney wrote to his daughter Julia in November 1868: "Ainsworth Milbank has made us his anual [*sic*] visit since I wrote you. His mother & family were all well" (Finney to James and Julia Monroe, 17 November 1868, Finney Papers, microfilm, roll 5).

[69] In May and again in July, Finney had received invitations from the Union Congregational Church in Essex Street to supply their pulpit while the pastor was off sick. Finney replied: "I am ready to go to Boston, if the ministering brethren are prepared to receive me; otherwise I must decline." He wanted the "hearty concurrence" of the Boston ministers (S. V. S. Wilder to Finney, 6 May 1831; Committee for Supplying Union Church to Finney, 2 August 1831, Finney Papers, microfilm, roll 3; and Asa Rand, "Letter to Dr. Beecher," *The Volunteer* [Boston] 2 [July 1833]: 378). Union Church therefore arranged a meeting for 1 August of all the orthodox Congregational ministers, together with about twenty deacons and lay representatives, to consider Finney's replies.

At the same time, Finney had met Lyman Beecher's daughter, Catharine (probably at the home of the Nortons in New York, where he was staying), and told her, "Your father vowed solemnly at the New Lebanon Convention he would fight me if I came to Boston, and I shall never go there till he asks me" ("Trial of the Rev. Dr. Lyman Beecher for Heresy," *The Christian Examiner and General Review* [Boston] 19 [September 1835]: 124; *Autobiography, Correspondence, etc., of Lyman Beecher, D.D.*, ed. Charles Beecher, 2 vols. [New York: Harper, 1863, 1865], 2:108; and Catharine Beecher to Finney and Amelia Norton, 2 August 1831, Finney Papers, microfilm, roll 3).

At the meeting in Boston the laymen all voted for Finney to be invited, but the ministers led by Beecher and Wisner voted against it. The next day (2 August) Beecher wrote to Finney to tell him of the meeting and to dissuade him from going to Boston at that time. So when the deacons of Union Church independently renewed their invitation again, Finney made it quite clear that he would not go unless Beecher changed his attitude (Beecher to Finney, 2 August 1831; and Finney to John Starkweather, 5 August 1831, copy in Finney's handwriting, Finney Papers, microfilm, roll 3).

[70] Benjamin Blydenburg Wisner (1794–1835) was a graduate of Union College, Schenectady, where he later became a tutor before training for the ministry at Princeton Theological Seminary. He was called to the Old South Church in Boston in 1820 and remained until ill health in 1832 caused him to retire. He then became secretary of the American Board of Commissioners for Foreign Missions until his death. See William B. Sprague, *Annals of the American Pulpit,* vol. 2 (New York: Carter and Bro., 1857), pp. 682–87.

[71] This appears to be a reference to Numbers 13:17.

Park Street Church, Boston. This church was known as "Brimstone Corner." Finney preached here in 1831 and again in the 1850s. Courtesy Park Street Church.

had several conversations ˡwith him, and he manifested an almost enthusiastic interest in what he saw and heard in Providence.[72] About the time he was there **there were** some very striking conversions. MS 632

The work at Providence was of a peculiarly searching character as it respected professors of religion. Old hopes were terribly shaken, and there was a great shaking among the dry bones in the different churches.[73] So terribly was **one of the** deacons of one of the churches searched on one occasion, that he said to me as I came out of the pulpit, "Mr. Finney, I do not believe there are ten real Christians in Providence. We are ˡall wrong," said he, "we have been deceived." **Mr. Josiah Chapin was thoroughly blessed in that revival.[74] He was converted about that time; but whether it was just after I got there, or just before, I cannot recollect. Among other gentlemen that were converted I recollect a Mr. Barstow, who has since been a prominent Christian man in that city;[75] a Mr. Green also, who was cashier of one of the banks.[76]** Dr Wisner, I believe, was thoroughly convinced that the work ˡwas genuine, and for the time, extensive; and that there was **nothing to complain of as unchristian, or anything** to be deplored.[77] After Dr Wisner returned to Boston I soon received a request JHF 314 MS 633

[72] According to P. C. Headley, Wisner did not make himself known to Finney till he had heard three sermons. He then went to him and said, "I came here a heresy-hunter; but here is my hand, and my heart is with you" (*Evangelists,* p. 164).

[73] This included the Baptist churches. See C. Allyn Russell, "Rhode Island Baptists, 1825–1831," *Rhode Island History* 28, no. 2 (May 1969): 35–36.

[74] Although he had attended the Beneficent Congregational Church for many years, Chapin did not become a member until 1831. He then started to be active in mission and Sunday school work and was one of the chief founders and the first deacon of the new High Street Congregational Church in 1834. He returned to the Beneficent Church in 1849, where he became a deacon and continued to be active in Christian work and in helping to found new churches. See J. G. Vose, "Deacon Josiah Chapin," *Providence Journal,* 7 May 1881, clipping in Rhode Island Historical Society, Providence.

[75] This was Amos Chafee Barstow (1813–1894). He was to become a wealthy businessman engaged in the manufacture of stoves and furnaces, as well as being involved in banking. He was frequently a member of the state legislature and in 1870 was speaker of the house. In 1852 he became mayor of Providence. The New York *Independent* noted that he

> was more than a prominent member of the financial world. He was an earnest and active Christian man, interested in every good work. He was an earnest advocate of temperance principles, and in 1847 was the candidate of the temperance party for Mayor. While in the General Assembly he was chairman of the committee in charge of temperance interests and worked hard to secure the passage of the Maine Law. In December, 1859, he was chairman of a meeting of antislavery men and made a speech in favor of John Brown, whose execution took place on that day. He was especially interested in work among the Indians, having been appointed by President Grant a member of the Board of Indian Commissioners in 1875 and chairman of the Board in 1878, which position he held for several years. He was one of the most influential and honored corporate members of the American Board, and gave largely to foreign missions as also to all forms of church and charitable work. At the age of twenty-six he was chosen superintendent of the Sunday-school and held that position for twenty-six years (13 September 1894, p. 12).

See also p. 21, and "To the Friends of the Late President Finney," undated circular for the "Finney Professorship," in portfolio of Finney materials, Oberlin College Library.

[76] This was probably Luke Green. He is listed in Providence *Directories* from 1832 to 1852 as "cashier of Weybosset Bank." His name also appears among a list of people in Providence who donated money to Oberlin College (see *OE,* 31 March 1847, p. 50).

[77] Wisner had been assisting at the protracted meeting at Providence, and left on the Saturday

from the Congregational ministers and churches to go to that city and labor.[78] Dr Lyman Beecher was at that time pastor of the Bowdoin st. church;[79] and his son, Edward Beecher, was either pastor or stated supply at Park st.[80] A Mr. Green was pastor of the Essex st. church, but had gone to Europe for his health; and that church was without any stated supply at the time.[81] Dr Fay was pastor of the Congregational church in Charlestown;[82] and Dr Jenks was

(12 August). He arrived at his house on Monday afternoon, where the ministers were holding their weekly meeting and were waiting for him. P. C. Headley said:

> Quietly laying aside his travelling wardrobe, and directing his attention especially to Dr. Beecher, he said, "When Dr. Beecher preaches, he has prepared himself, and makes a profound impression; but what the next blow will be we cannot tell. Mr. Finney strikes home, and repeats the blow on the same spot, only harder, until the driven wedge splits the log, and there is no help for it" (*Evangelists,* p. 164).

According to Beecher, Wisner "told the ministers that he was satisfied, and he thought that we ought to yield to the wishes of the churches. We assented accordingly." Wisner evidently proclaimed Finney to be "the holiest man, he had ever seen" ("Trial of Lyman Beecher," p. 124; Wisner to Finney, 16 August 1831, Finney Papers, microfilm, roll 3; and Joseph I. Foot, "Theological Origin of the Prevailing Deficiency of the Churches in Spirituality," *Literary and Theological Review* [New York] 6 [September 1839]: 317).

[78] A messenger went to Finney from the Union Church with a letter written on 15 August by Wisner and signed by the ministers to the "Committee for supplying Union Church," indicating their change of mind. He also had a messenger from the Park Street Church; and he received a letter from Wisner dated 16 August formally inviting him to Boston (letters in Finney Papers, microfilm, roll 3).

[79] The Hanover Street Church, where Beecher had gone in 1826, was destroyed by fire in February 1830, and the new church was built in Bowdoin Street, the name of the church being changed accordingly. Beecher remained there until September 1832, when he was called to the presidency of Lane Theological Seminary in Ohio (Martin Moore, *Boston Revival, 1842: A Brief History of the Evangelical Churches of Boston* [Boston: John Putnam, 1842], p. 44).

[80] Edward Beecher (1803–1895) was the third of Lyman Beecher's children. He was a graduate of Yale and Andover Theological Seminary and went to Park Street Church in 1826. In October 1830 he was appointed the first president of Illinois College in Jacksonville but did not take up the appointment until eighteen months later. He wrote to G. F. Wright about Finney:

> I was pastor of Park St church when he was first invited to preach in Boston, & I invited him to preach for me. He complied with my request, & preached to a crowded house the most impressive & powerful sermon I ever heard. It rings in my ears to this day. His text was Rev. 22:17. "Whosoever will let him take the water of life freely." Those who have heard him can conceive of his train of thought but no one can form any conception of the power of his appeal. It rings in my ears even to this day. As I was preaching myself, I did not hear him again. But I met good results in all who heard him, & have ever honoured & loved him, as one as truly commissioned by God to declare his will, as were Isaiah, Jeremiah, Ezekiel or Paul (E. Beecher to G. F. Wright, 6 November 1889, Wright Papers, box 7).

See also *Julian M. Sturtevant: An Autobiography* (New York: Revell, 1896), pp. 176–78.

[81] Samuel Green (1792–1834) was at Harvard and Andover Theological Seminary; and after three years in Reading, Massachusetts, he went to the Union Church in Essex Street in 1823. He was there until early 1831, when "an organic affection of the throat" prevented further ministerial work (*The New York Observer*, 6 December 1834, p. 193).

In April 1831 Green was given six months' leave from his charge to regain his health, but he was away for more than a year, traveling in Britain and Europe. He was not sufficiently recovered to be able to resume pastoral duties, and after many unsuccessful attempts to regain his health, he had to retire in March 1834, shortly before his death. Finney met him in New York in December 1832 (John S. Ropes, "Samuel Green," *The Congregational Quarterly* [Boston] 8 [July 1866]: 235–37; and John Gulliver to Finney, 15 December 1832; and 9 January 1833, Finney Papers, microfilm, roll 3).

[82] Warren Fay (1784–1864) was installed in the Charlestown church in 1820 and was apparently an eminent Boston minister for over twenty-five years and a member of the Prudential Committee of the American Board of Commissioners for Foreign Missions. But he had evidently

pastor of the Congregational church in Green st. **Boston.**[83] I do not recollect who were the pastors of the other churches at the time.[84] I began my labors by preaching around in the different churches on the Sabbath, and on week evenings I preached in Park st.[85] I soon saw that the Word of God was taking effect, and that the interest was increasing from day to day. **However,** I perceived also ˡthat there needed to be a great searching amongst professed Christians. I could not learn that there was amongst them anything like the Spirit of prayer that had prevailed in the revivals at the West and in New York city. There seemed to be a peculiar type of religion there, **that had not** that freedom and strength of faith **in it that** I had been in the habit of seeing in New York. I therefore began to preach some searching sermons to Christians. Indeed I gave out on the Sabbath that I would preach a series of sermons to Christians in Park st. on certain evenings of the week. But I soon found that these sermons were not at all palatable to the Christians of Boston. It was something they never had been used to; **therefore** the attendance at Park st. **was** less and less, especially on those evenings when I preached to professed Christians. This was *new to me*. I had never before seen professed ˡChristians shrink back, as they did at that time in Boston, from searching sermons. But I heard again and again of speeches like these: "What will the Unitarians ˡsay if such things are true of us who are orthodox?" "If Mr. Finney preaches to us in this way, the Unitarians will triumph over us, and say that at least the orthodox are no better Christians than Unitarians." It was evident that they somewhat resented my plain dealing. **I was soon informed by Dr Wisner that my manner of dealing with professors of religion was directly opposite to that of Dr Beecher. That the standard which he set up was a very low one; and that he was letting down the standard of**

MS 634

JHF 315

MS 635

"long indulged in secret sin," and in 1839 he was charged with adultery. Although he made a full confession of his crimes, he was dismissed. See D. M. Bennett, *The Champions of the Church: Their Crimes and Persecutions* (New York: Bennett, 1878), p. 978; Lewis Tappan to George Whipple, 18 December 1843, in Letter-book, Tappan Papers, microfilm, roll 3; and *NYE,* 31 August 1839, p. 139.

[83] William Jenks (1778–1866) was a well-known biblical and oriental scholar and was the author of the popular *Comprehensive Commentary* of the Bible. He had been instrumental in founding the Green Street Church and was pastor there from 1826 to 1845 (*DAB*).

[84] The other ministers who attended the meetings to consider inviting Finney to Boston were Joy H. Fairchild (who gained notoriety in 1844 by making a suicide attempt in connection with another sexual scandal) of the Evangelical Congregational, or Phillips's Church, South Boston, and George W. Blagden of the Salem Street Church. See letter from the Boston ministers to the Committee for Supplying Union Church, 15 August 1831, Finney Papers, microfilm, roll 3; "Churches and Ministers in Boston," *BR,* 2 February 1831, p. 19; and *Remarkable Incidents in the Life of Rev. J. H. Fairchild,* 3d ed. (Boston: printed for the Author, 1856). The other Congregational churches were the Pine Street Church, without a minister at that time, and the Mariner's Church, where Jonathan Greenleaf officiated. See Moore, *Boston Revival, 1842,* pp. 53–56.

[85] Finney went to Boston about the last day of August 1831, but he was not satisfied with the arrangements. It was therefore resolved at a meeting of the ministers and church representatives on 5 September that he should be invited as "a general laborer" among the Evangelical churches. A subscription was also to be raised to meet the expenses of his family for six months. Finney accordingly left the next day to get his family. See Boston Ministers and Churches to Charles Scudder, 5 September 1831; J. Wilson to Finney, 5 September 1831, Finney Papers, microfilm, roll 3; and Asa Rand, "Letter to Dr. Beecher," *The Volunteer* 2 (July 1833): 378. Finney generally preached two evenings a week in Park Street.

orthodox piety and preaching in such a way that left the doors open too wide altogether to the orthodox Christian church. He said that he felt, and they had felt in Boston for sometime, that getting the people into the churches under so low a standard of preaching was calculated to do them great mischief. This was the feeling, at the time, of Dr Wisner; and I believe a feeling very extensively entertained by the orthodox people. I suppose that it was owing to this fact that my searching sermons so astonished and ˡeven offended **multitudes of professed Christians.**[86] However as the work went forward this state of things changed greatly; and after a few weeks they would listen to searching preaching, and came to **highly** appreciate it.

MS 636

I found in Boston, as I had everywhere else, that there was a method of dealing with inquiring sinners that was very trying to me. I used sometimes to hold meetings of inquiry with Dr Beecher in the basement of his church. One evening when there was a large attendance, and a feeling of great searching and solemnity among the inquirers, at the close, as was my custom, I made an address in which I tried to point out to them exactly what the Lord required of them. My object was to bring them to renounce themselves and their all, and give themselves and all they possessed to Christ **then and there**. I tried to show them that they were not their own, but were bought with a price, and pointed out to them the sense in which they were expected to forsake all that they had and deliver everything to Christ as belonging to him. I made this point as clear as I possibly could, and saw that the ˡimpression upon the inquirers seemed to be very deep. I was about to call on them to kneel down while we presented them to God in prayer, when Dr Beecher arose and said to them: "You need not be afraid to give up all to Christ, your property and all, for he will give it right back to you."[87] Without making any just discriminations at all as to the sense in which they were to give up their possessions, and the sense in which the Lord would allow them ˡto retain

MS 637

JHF 316

[86]In a letter to E. P. Marvin in 1873, Finney wrote:

> Is not the fastidiousness of city churches and their unwillingness to hear sound preaching, due to the trimming policy of the pastors themselves? The policy, which you reject, of attempting to win sinners to Christ, without the schoolmaster, is working great mischief in the church. Dr. Lyman Beecher started it. When I labored in Boston, in 1831 & 2, I found the churches there would not bear searching at all. Dr. Beecher expressed disapprobation of my preaching so much of what he called reprehension. And *his* teaching, especially in the latter part of his life, has gone to seed in Henry Ward. Dr. Wisner, then of the Old South, informed me, that they felt keenly, that the Dr. was preaching a very low standard of piety. H. Ward is preaching a much lower standard still (Finney to E. P. Marvin, 15 April 1873, Finney Papers, file 2/2/2, box 9).

Henry Ward Beecher was Lyman Beecher's son and the well-known minister of Plymouth Church, Brooklyn.

Asa Rand, an editor in Boston, had a different view of Finney's preaching:

> He did indeed, while among us, aim to adapt his operations to the sober, considerate character of our people. But, even in their mitigated form, the thoroughly evangelical churches and ministers of New England could not endure his preaching or his measures. They were disgusted with his philosophical speculations, his denunciatory spirit, his irreverence in worship, his vulgarity, his rashness, and his arrogance (Rand, "Letter to Dr. Beecher," p. 377).

[87]And he apparently added, "He is willing you should enjoy the world." In narrating this in one of his lectures on revivals of religion, Finney is reported as then exclaiming, "Miserable!" (*NYE,* 7 February 1835, p. 22).

them, he simply exhorted them not to be afraid to give up all, as they had been urged to do, as the Lord would give it right back to them. I saw that he was making a false impression, and I felt in an agony. I saw that his language was calculated to make an impression the direct opposite of the truth. After he had finished his remarks, as wisely and carefully as I could, I led them to see that in the sense in which God required them to give up their possessions He would never give them back, and they must not entertain such a thought. I tried to say what I said in such a way as not to appear to contradict Dr Beecher, but yet thoroughly to correct the impression that I saw he had made. |I told them that the Lord did not require them to relinquish all their possessions, to quit their business, and houses, and possessions, and never to have possession of them again; but *to renounce the ownership of them*, to understand and realize that these things were not theirs, but that they were God's. That they were never to treat these things as belonging to themselves *as it respected God*. That in respect to men these things were theirs, not belonging to others; but as respected God He required them not to regard themselves, or anything they possessed, as belonging to themselves. He therefore required them to renounce all claim to these, or anything else, as it respected their relation to Him. That his claim was absolute, and his property in themselves and in everything else so entirely above the right of every other being in the universe, that what He required of them was to use themselves and everything else for Him and His glory and as belonging to Him; and never to think that they had a right to use their time, their strength, their substance, their influence, or anything else which they possessed as if it were their own and not the Lord's. MS 638

Dr. Beecher made no objection to |what I said either at the time, or ever, so far as I know; and it is therefore probable that he did not mean anything inconsistent with this in what he said. And yet he said that which was calculated to make the impression that God would restore their possessions to them, in the sense in which they had relinquished them and given them up to Him. MS 639

The ‹members›[88] of the orthodox churches of Boston at this time generally, I believe, received my views of doctrine without question. I know that Dr Beecher did; for he told me |that he had never seen a man with whose theological views he so *entirely* accorded as he did with mine.[89] There was one point of my orthodoxy ‹however›[90] to which many of them at the time JHF 317

[88] Here Matson had written "people," but Finney changed it to "members."

[89] Before Finney arrived in Boston, Beecher wrote to him, "But especially because with very little difference, & that more on points of discretion unessential, you and I are, as much, perhaps even more, *one* than almost any two men whom God has been pleased to render conspicuous in his church" (Beecher to Finney, 2 August 1831, Finney Papers, microfilm, roll 3). And during Finney's stay in Boston, according to Asa Rand, Beecher "repeatedly declared in public his full accordance with views which had been advanced. Once he did so with evident emotion, confessing the mistakes of his own ministry" ("Letter to Dr. Beecher," p. 378). Beecher himself was reported as saying, "It will be long before I again hear so much truth with as little to object to, in the manner of its exhibition, in the same space of time" (Bennet Tyler, *Letters on the Origin and Progress of the New Haven Theology* [New York: Carter and Collier, 1837], p. 92).

[90] Finney added the word "however."

objected. There was a Mr. Rand,[91] who published, I think, a periodical in Boston at that time,[92] who wrote an earnest article against my views on the subject of the divine agency in regeneration.[93] I preached that the divine agency was that of teaching and persuasion, that the influence was a *moral* and not a *physical* one. President Edwards had held the **reverse of this**; and Mr. Rand held with President Edwards that ˡthe **Divine** agency exercised in regeneration was a physical one, that it **was** a change of **the** *nature*[94] instead of a change in the *voluntary attitude and preference of the soul.*[95] Mr. Rand regarded my views on this subject as quite out of the way, **and wrote and published a pretty severe article at the time I was there in opposition to this view**. There were some other points of doctrine upon which he dwelt in a critical manner, such, for example, as my views of the voluntary nature of moral depravity, and the sinner's activity in regeneration. Dr Wisner wrote a reply, and justified my views, with the exception of those that I maintained on the persuasive or moral influence of the Holy Spirit.[96] He was not then

MS 640

[91] Asa Rand (1783–1871) was a graduate of Dartmouth College and was ordained in 1809. After thirteen years as a Congregational minister in Maine, he became a publisher and editor. From 1822 to 1825 he edited the *Christian Mirror* and was then associated with Nathaniel P. Willis in producing the *Boston Recorder* and *Youth's Companion* until 1831. In April 1831 he was publishing the *Education Reporter* before launching *The Volunteer*. In 1833 he established a bookstore and printing office in Lowell, where he published the *Lowell Observer*. In 1837 he went back into the pastoral ministry. See Francis S. Drake, *Dictionary of American Biography* (Boston: Osgood, 1876), p. 72; and *BR,* 20 April 1831, p. 62.

[92] *The Volunteer: devoted to the promotion of Revivals, Evangelical Doctrines, and Congregationalism,* was a monthly periodical published in Boston from August 1831 to July 1833. It advocated the Edwardean theology and moderate revivalism against the new theological speculations of Yale Divinity School and the New Measures revivalism of Finney.

[93] The article that appeared in the fifth issue of *The Volunteer* (1 [December 1831]: 136–56) was in two parts. The first, "Depravity and Regeneration," consisted of an abstract of a sermon preached by Finney from Ezekiel 18:31, together with a philosophical and theological criticism. The second part, "The Agency of the Spirit in Conversion," contained the main criticism. There was such a demand for the article that it was republished in pamphlet form in January 1832 with the title *The New Divinity Tried, Being an Examination of a Sermon Delivered by the Rev. C. G. Finney, on Making a New Heart* (Boston: Light and Harris, 1832). It was substantially the same as the original article but contained some amendments to the sermon abstract "from the skeleton used by the preacher on its delivery."

Finney became concerned about the "garbled extracts" that had been given to the public "by note-takers and reviewers," who he felt had "entirely misrepresented" the doctrine of the sermon. So in 1834 he wrote a new version entitled "Sinners bound to change their own hearts." This was published as a separate sermon in December 1834 by John S. Taylor and also by S. W. Benedict of New York (see *NYE,* 27 December 1834, p. 207). It also appeared as the first of a series of "Doctrinal Sermons" published in 1835 by the same publishers under the title *Sermons on Various Subjects*. This was republished in various editions. The sermon then appeared again in *Sermons on Important Subjects* in 1836.

[94] Apart from crossing out the underlining of the word "nature," Fairchild made no alteration to the text here, but in the published edition it appears as "that it produced a change of nature."

[95] A second article by Rand carried an analysis of the philosophical system of Jonathan Edwards, comparing it with that of Asa Burton (the "Taste System"), of Nathanael Emmons (the "Exercise System"), and of Samuel Hopkins (the "Hopkinsian"). Rand maintained that Finney's theories did not agree with any of these systems of New England theology but were akin to the Wesleyan, or Arminian, system. ("A Vindication of 'The New Divinity Tried,'" *The Volunteer* 1 [March 1832]: 242–56; and April 1832, pp. 265–88).

[96] Wisner, who had heard the sermon by Finney and had borrowed the "skeleton" from him, wrote to Rand indicating changes that needed to be made in the abstract. His letter was published over the initial *W* in the next issue of *The Volunteer* (1 [January 1832]: 186–88). Then when Rand's amended pamphlet appeared, Wisner produced an anonymous reply, *Review of "The New*

prepared to take the ground against President Edwards, and the general orthodox view of New England, that the Spirit's agency was not physical, but only moral. Dr Woods of Andover[97] also published an article in one of the periodicals—I believe it was one that was at the time published at Andover—under the title, "The Holy Ghost the author of regeneration."[98] This was, I think the title; |at any rate the design was to prove that regeneration was the work of God. He quoted of course that class of scriptures that assert the divine agency in the work of changing the heart. To this I made no reply in writing; but in my preaching I said that that was only a half truth. That the Bible just as plainly asserted that regeneration was the work of man; and I quoted those passages that affirmed that. Paul said to one of the churches that *he* had begotten them, that is regen|erated them, for the same word is used as where regeneration is ascribed to God.[99] It was easy therefore to show that God had an agency in regeneration, and that His agency was that of teaching or persuasion. It was also easy to show that the *subject* had an agency: that the acts of repentance, faith, and love were his own; and that the Spirit persuaded him to put forth these acts by presenting to him the truth. As the truth was the instrument, that the Holy Spirit was one of the agents; and that a preacher, or some human, intelligent, and designing agent generally also co-operated in the work.[100] |There was

MS 641

JHF 318

MS 642

Divinity Tried"; or, An Examination of Rev. Mr. Rand's Strictures on a Sermon by the Rev. C. G. Finney, on Making a New Heart (Boston: Peirce and Parker, 1832). In reply to this, Rand wrote "A Vindication of 'the New Divinity Tried,'" which was published in *The Volunteer* for March and April 1832. That was also published as a pamphlet. Wisner then brought out a second pamphlet, *Reply to Mr. Rand's Vindication of "The New Divinity Tried," Published as an Appendix to the Second Edition of a "Review" of the Same* (Boston: Peirce and Parker, 1832). This was also anonymous. Wisner's purpose in defending Finney was to show that he was in reality orthodox and did not differ from "the standard divines of New England." Rand, however, later wrote, "I have reason to believe, though I cannot prove it, that when Dr. Wisner felt bound to write pamphlets in his defence, Mr. F. frankly told him to let it alone, because he *did* differ widely from 'The New England Divinity'" (Rand, "Letter to Dr. Beecher," p. 378).

[97] Leonard Woods (1774–1854) was an eminent Congregational minister. He had been professor of theology at the Andover Theological Seminary since 1808. See *DAB*.

[98] Finney is probably referring to *The Biblical Repository*, a quarterly periodical edited by Edward Robinson. But the article was not published in that periodical. It may have been written in connection with a memorable visit that Finney made to Andover. He was taken there by Beecher soon after he went to Boston, and he preached on the evenings of Monday, Tuesday, and Wednesday, 26–28 September, in the Old South Church, where Milton Badger was pastor. It was during the anniversary week of Andover Theological Seminary, and the excitement was so great that some of the anniversary exercises had to be suspended while everyone went to hear him. See David B. Coe, "Milton Badger," *The Congregational Quarterly* 17 (January 1875): 5; G. F. Wright, *Charles Grandison Finney* (Boston and New York: Houghton Mifflin, 1891), pp. 71–74; Frank Hugh Foster, *The Life of Edwards Amasa Park* (New York: Revell, 1936), pp. 59–60; and *BR*, 28 September 1831, p. 155; and 5 October 1831, p. 158.

In *The Works of Leonard Woods, D.D.*, vol. 2 (Boston: John P. Jewett, 1851), are three lectures on regeneration and the Holy Spirit. In the index in vol. 5, a section of one of the lectures (pp. 557–70) is referred to as "Regeneration, Holy Spirit the author of."

[99] See 1 Corinthians 4:15. The Greek word used here comes from the root γεννάω. In referring to the use of this word to ascribe regeneration to God, Finney may have had in mind either the third chapter of John's Gospel or various references throughout the First Epistle of John. While the theme of regeneration is clearly central to the Johannine material, some scholars doubt whether it can be appropriately used in interpreting this section of the Corinthian correspondence (information from Gordon Fee).

[100] Asa Rand's abstract of Finney's sermon contained the summary of this teaching:

nothing at all unchristian, that I recollect, in any of the discussions that we had at that time; nothing that grieved the Spirit or produced any unkind feelings among the brethren.[101] After I had spent some weeks in preaching about in the different congregations, I consented to supply Mr. Green's church in Essex st. statedly for a time. I therefore concentrated my labors upon that field.[102] We had a blessed work of grace; and a large number of persons were

> There is a sense in which a sinner does make a new heart. There is also a sense in which God does it; another, in which a preacher does it; and another in which the truth or the word of God does it. The bible employs expressions regarding conversion, in these four different ways. It is ascribed to the subject, the sinner himself; he changes his own heart. It is ascribed to the instrument, or the preacher; he converts sinners and saves souls from death. It is ascribed to the means, or the word; men are begotten by the word of truth. It is ascribed to God, or the Spirit; they are born again by the Spirit. A person is walking near Niagara Falls, and sees a man approaching from the opposite direction towards the precipice, who seems to be lost in a reverie. He is advancing directly to the verge of the precipice, unconscious of danger and heedless of his footsteps. He has just raised his foot to step off, when the other spies his danger and cries out, *Stop!* He is roused, turns at the critical moment, and is saved. People gather round, and the rescued man in great agitation relates the occurrence. "*That man*," says he, "has saved my life." "But how?" "O he called to me at the very moment I was stepping off, and *that word, stop*, snatched me from destruction. *O if I had not turned* that instant, I should have been dashed to pieces. O it was *the mercy of God* that kept me from a horrid death." This illustrates the use of those four kinds of expression in the bible, in reference to the conversion of a sinner (Asa Rand, "Depravity and Regeneration," *The Volunteer* 1, no. 5 [December 1831]: 138–39).

[101]The controversy, however, was becoming part of the wider conflict that was being waged within Congregationalism. Leonard Woods was in the forefront of the struggle to preserve the New England theology from the inroads of the New Divinity of Nathaniel W. Taylor. As the pamphlets of Rand and Wisner were reviewed in the periodical press, Rand carried on the debate in the pages of *The Volunteer* after Finney left Boston. Finney had become identified with Taylor in the battle. See Donald Moore Scott, "Watchmen on the Walls of Zion: Evangelicals and American Society, 1800–1860" (Ph.D. diss., University of Wisconsin, 1968), pt. 2.

Leonard Woods was to be an outspoken critic of Finney again later when the Oberlin theology began to agitate the churches. See Woods, "Examination of the Doctrine of Perfection, as held by Rev. Asa Mahan, President of the Oberlin Collegiate Institute, Rev. Charles Fitch, and others agreeing with them," *American Biblical Repository* (Andover, Mass.) 5 (January 1841): 166–89; and April 1841, pp. 406–38; see also *NYE,* 25 February 1837, p. 33; and 4 March 1837, p. 38.

[102]Asa Rand's understanding of the course of Finney's career in Boston was quite different:

> At length it was manifest, that this career was not acceptable to the churches; and that if it were continued, the revival powers of Mr. F. were likely to fail him in Boston. It was therefore concluded to withdraw him suddenly from Park street, and discontinue his efforts as a general preacher, confining his labors principally to Union Church which had first invited him to the city. After this, he could seldom be obtained for any public occasion in the country. About this time, some of the pastors rather showed a conviction, that the man was not likely to exert a very salutary influence in the city. One at least "put down his foot," and would sanction his plans no further. Even Dr. Wisner bolted, and objected to *measures*, whatever he might think of *sentiments*. Still Dr. Beecher adhered to Mr. Finney; conducted protracted meetings with him in both their houses, with scarcely any other aid; extolled him and his labors at a public meeting of the Conference of the Churches, pronouncing him to be "a glorious man;" and was openly in strict intimacy with him till he departed (Rand, "Letter to Dr. Beecher," pp. 378–79).

Rand also threw doubt on Wisner's claim that Finney had gone to Boston "by the invitation of the churches, (or some of them,) and their pastors."

> Probably the six pastors *consented* to his coming, after he had been invited. Three of them have for months past, as we are informed, decidedly dissented from him; and two only, Drs. Beecher and Wisner, have fully upheld him. We always understood that *one* church only, out of eight, invited him. We doubt whether any other ever acted as a

converted in different parts of the city. **Indeed the work was more or less extensive throughout the city.**[103] **There my third child was born that winter.**[104] I had become fatigued, as I had labored **more than**[105] ten years as an evangelist, without anything more than a few days or weeks of rest **at a time** during the whole period. The ministerial brethren were true men, had taken hold of the work as well as they knew how, and labored faithfully and efficiently in securing good results. By this time a second free church had been formed in New York city. **Brother** ‹Joel›[106] Parker's ˡchurch, the first free church, had grown so large that a colony had gone off and formed a second church, to which **the** Rev. Mr. Barrows, ‹of late› **a** professor at Andover, had been preaching.[107] Some earnest brethren wrote to me from MS 643

body with respect to hearing or approving him; and we believe, that for four months before he left the city, not more than two churches could have been persuaded to invite him to their pulpits as a temporary supply ("The New Divinity," *The Volunteer* 1, no. 12 [July 1832]: 379).

[103]In June 1832 it was reported that the revival was still continuing "with no sensible interruption." One hundred fifty members had been added to the Essex Street Church, fifty or sixty were about to join, and "a large number who have become hopefully pious, who are expected to come forward hereafter." The report added that "the labors of the Rev. Mr. Finney among the church and congregation have been remarkably blessed." There were also large additions to other Congregational churches and the Baptists and Methodists. See *Religious Intelligencer* (New Haven), 30 June 1832, p. 79.

P. C. Headley reckoned, "It was estimated that not less than three thousand souls were converted during the time he was in Boston" (*Evangelists,* p. 164), but this claim has not been substantiated. G. F. Wright stated that Finney's preaching in Boston "was not followed either at this time or at any other, by such a general movement as in some other places" (*Charles Grandison Finney,* p. 106).

[104]Frederic Norton Finney (1832–1916) was born on 7 March 1832.

[105]Fairchild altered the words "more than" to "about."

[106]The name "Joel" was added by Finney.

[107]After a year, the First Free Church had grown from three families to a membership of over 200, with a Sunday school of over 300 students and 25 teachers. While the new meeting house on Dey Street was being prepared, the Tappans hired the Masonic Hall, and they were getting congregations of 800 to 1,200 people. It was decided that a colony from the First Free Church should form a new church and continue to occupy the Masonic Hall when the First Church took possession of their new premises on 16 October 1831. The new society was officially organized as the Second Free Presbyterian Church on 14 February 1832 with three elders and 36 members. The Broadway Hall was hired for their use. See MS 559; *BR,* 12 October 1831, p. 164; letters of Tappan to Finney from February to April 1831; and Joel Parker to Finney, 13 and 15 February 1832, Finney Papers, microfilm, roll 3.

Elijah Porter Barrows (1805–1888), a Yale graduate, was principal of the Hartford Grammar School for six years before moving to the Second Free Church. He wrote to Finney from Hartford: "I was once an opposer of you and your measures, but as I did it ignorantly through unbelief, the Lord has been pleased to enlighten my eyes. I am now employed by a few friends in the capacity of a city Missionary." He moved to New York in April 1832 and supplied the church in the Broadway Hall until 1 June, and then in July went to the church in Westminster, Connecticut, as pastor. In July 1835 he succeeded Joel Parker at the First Free Church in New York. In May of that year he turned down an appointment as professor of Old Testament literature at the new theological department at the Oberlin Collegiate Institute, an appointment he was to accept thirty-seven years later. But in 1837 he went to Western Reserve College as professor of sacred literature. In 1853 he was appointed professor of Hebrew at Andover Theological Seminary, where he remained until 1866. In 1869 and 1870 he was teaching at Union Theological Seminary before moving to Oberlin in 1871, where he became professor of Hebrew and Old Testament literature. He retired in 1880 and died in Oberlin. See Barrows to Finney, 19 February 1831, Finney Papers, microfilm, roll 2; *Obituary Record of Graduates of Yale University* (New Haven), 1889, pp. 487–88; *The National Cyclopaedia of American Biography,* vol. 10 (New York: White, 1909), pp. 102–3; *Religious Intelligencer,* 8 December 1832, pp.

New York proposing to lease a theater and fit it up for a church, upon condition that I would come there and preach.[108] They proposed to get what was called the "Chatham st. theater," in the heart of the most irreligious population of New York.[109] **It was not far from the "five points," and was** JHF 319 **a place of resort highly discreditable to the city.**[110] It was ˡowned by men who were very willing to have it transformed into a church.[111] **My family**

445–46; Oberlin College Board of Trustees, Minutes, 29 May 1835, p. 33, Oberlin College Archives, microfilm; *Oberlin Review*, 25 September 1888, pp. 4–5; and L. Tappan to Finney, 19 April 1832, Finney Papers, microfilm, roll 3.

Matson had written "now a professor at Andover," but Finney changed the "now" to "of late." Barrows had recently left Andover.

[108]The moving spirits behind this proposal were Lewis Tappan and William Green, Jr. They were strongly supported by a group of men who were mostly members of the First and Second Free churches, such as James C. Bliss, Rev. Joel Parker, Edward Corning, Arthur Tappan, Stephen Brown, Anson G. Phelps, S. V. S. Wilder, and others (see Joel Parker to Finney, 14 March 1832; and letters of Lewis Tappan to Finney, 16 March to 14 April 1832, Finney Papers, microfilm, roll 3). This was originally planned to be a Third Free Church.

[109]Chatham Gardens was a popular resort in the early 1820s, and Henry Barrière's theater, which opened there in 1824, enjoyed considerable success for a few years. But competition from the new Bowery Theatre and other resorts resulted in a decline in its fortunes. In spite of repeated renovations and changes of management, it proved impossible to retain popular support. In January 1830 the lease passed to William Blanchard, the equestrian manager, who was able to achieve some success with his circus and dramatic entertainments. But the Chatham Garden Theatre never regained its former prestige. Actor Thomas Hamblin, who had recently taken over the Bowery Theatre, was manager when the last theatrical performances were given in March 1832. See Joseph N. Ireland, *Records of the New York Stage, from 1750 to 1860* (New York: Morrell, 1866); and George C. D. Odell, *Annals of the New York Stage* (New York: Columbia University Press, 1927), vol. 3.

[110]The Five Points was a district in southern Manhattan where five streets intersected to form a large open space. It was an area of squalid, overcrowded lodging houses, saloons, and dance halls and was considered to be "the most depraved few acres in North America." See Carroll Smith Rosenberg, "Protestants and Five Pointers: The Five Points House of Industry, 1850–1870," *The New York Historical Society Quarterly* 48, no. 1 (January 1964): 327. According to Lewis Tappan, Chatham Garden Theatre had been

> the pest of the neighborhood. The price of admission ranged from two shillings down to one; and it was frequented by the lowest classes of society. Round about it were from twenty to thirty grog shops, and every night was made hideous with scenes of debauchery (see Joseph P. Thompson, *The Last Sabbath in the Broadway Tabernacle* [New York: Calkins and Stiles, 1857], p. 10; and Lewis Tappan, "Journal," 19 April 1857, p. 205, Tappan Papers, microfilm, roll 2).

[111]There is a question mark in the margin in pencil against this sentence. It appears to be in the handwriting of Lewis Tappan.

The theater was owned by "the heirs of George Janeway, deceased." A Rev. Janeway, representing the proprietors, "expressed much interest in the project, and in being relieved from his involuntary oversight of a concern which he could not approve. He has aided the plan by every means in his power and has contributed $500 towards annulling the former lease" (*The Christian Index* [Philadelphia], 21 April 1832, p. 256).

It was leased until May 1834 to William Blanchard. Tappan and Green apparently called on him in his rooms in the theater and, introducing themselves, proposed to him to sell his lease.

> "What for?" he bluntly asked. "For a church." "A w-h-a-t!" "A church, sir." With open mouth and eyes, he said, "You mean to make a c-h-u-r-c-h here!" And then with one of those mysterious revulsions of feeling, the tears started from the hardened man's eyes, and he added, "You may have it, and I will give one thousand dollars towards it," and he did (Henry Fowler, *The American Pulpit* [New York: J. M. Fairchild, 1856], p. 35).

Tappan wrote to Finney at the time: "We made Janeway feel ashamed of having such property and he felt a desire to be rid of it. We talked to the Lessee (Blanchard, the great Circus man) until he wept, & said he would aid us in converting the place into a church. He seemed to be under conviction of the H[oly] S[pirit]." The theater had been sublet to Thomas Hamblin until 1 May,

had then become so large that I could not well take them with me while laboring as an Evangelist, and my strength had become a good deal exhausted; and on praying and looking the matter over a good deal, I concluded that I would accept the call from the Second Free Church, and labor for a time at least, in New York.[112]

Chatham Garden Theatre, New York. This shows the theater as it was in 1825. It was converted into a chapel in 1832 and was used as a center for evangelical reform while Finney was pastor between 1832 and 1836. Engraving in George C. D. Odell, *Annals of the New York Stage*, vol. 3 (New York: Columbia University Press, 1927), opposite p. 120. Courtesy The British Library.

and he let Tappan have it without any compensation (Tappan to Finney, 22 March 1832, first letter; and 11 April 1832, Finney Papers, microfilm, roll 3).

[112] Finney went up from Boston toward the end of March to see the buildings and to confer with Lewis Tappan and others. It was considered best to drop the plan for a third Free church and for the new Chatham Street Chapel to be the home of the Second Free Church, who would invite Finney. See Tappan to Finney, 22 March 1832, and the second letter dated 7 April 1832; A. Rockwell to Lydia Finney, 28 March 1832; and E. Corning to Finney, 27 April 1832, Finney Papers, microfilm, roll 3. Finney had three children under five years of age—Helen, Charles, and Norton.

MS 644
JHF 320

CHAPTER XXIII

‹Labors & revivals in New York City in 1832, & onward.›

‹Mr.[1] Lewis Tappan with other Christian bretheren leased the Chatham Street theater & fitted it up for a Church, & as a suitable place to accommodate the various Charitable societies in holding their anniversaries.[2] They called me to, & I accepted the pastorate of the second free Presbyterian church.›[3] I left Boston in April, and commenced labors in that theater at that time.[4] The Spirit of the Lord was immediately poured out upon us, and we

[1] Pages 644–54 were numbered 490–500 and then 622–32 by Matson and changed to 644–54 by Finney. The chapter heading and the first two sentences of page 644, down to n. 3, are in Finney's handwriting on a separate piece of paper pasted onto the sheet. The section covered up by the pasted strip reads as follows: "Mr. Lewis Tappan was a leader in this movement, as he had been in forming the First church. He, together with several other men of property, leased the theater in Chatham st. for a term." The text continues below the pasted strip, "of years, and fitted it up for a church." This was crossed out by Finney. After the word "property," Tappan had inserted a cross and written in the margin, "Say Christian brethren, some of whom contributed in order to secure a good place in which the annual meetings of the Bible, Tract & other societies could be held." This was crossed out by Finney.

[2] Tappan had written elsewhere:

> The expense of fitting up the theatre for a house of God, and converting the saloons into lecture and Sabbath school rooms, was nearly 7000 dollars, and about half of that sum was contributed by members of other churches, on condition that the Chapel might be occupied by the public at the religious anniversaries (*NYE,* 21 February 1835, p. 29).

A new ten-year lease was negotiated and taken out in the name of William Green, Jr. On 11 April work started to convert the theater into a chapel that would seat 2,500 people. By 23 April enough of it was completed to hold a service of consecration. This was arranged for 5:30 in the morning to allow businessmen and their employees to attend. "To the surprise of all, eight hundred persons were present at the hour," which was possibly an overestimate, although Joshua Leavitt reckoned there were between one and two thousand. See Lewis Tappan, *The Life of Arthur Tappan* (New York: Hurd and Houghton, 1870), p. 210; Henry Fowler, *The American Pulpit* (New York: J. M. Fairchild, 1856), p. 36; Joseph P. Thompson, *The Last Sabbath in the Broadway Tabernacle* (New York: Calkins and Stiles, 1857), p. 11; and Leavitt to Finney, 28 April 1832, Finney Papers, microfilm, roll 3. See also Susan Hayes Ward, *The History of the Broadway Tabernacle Church* (New York: Trow, 1901), p. 24.

[3] This ends the section in Finney's handwriting.

[4] Finney in fact appears to have remained in Boston until 2 May (see Warren Fay to Finney, 30 April 1832, Finney Papers, microfilm, roll 3). The essential work on the conversion of the theater was completed by anniversary week. On the preceding Sunday, 6 May, the building was opened for public worship as the "Chatham Street Chapel," with Finney preaching morning and evening, administering the sacraments in the afternoon. It was estimated that two thousand or even three thousand attended the evening service, with many unable to get in. The week following, the chapel was packed with crowded meetings of the Benevolent Societies. See Fowler, *American*

had an extensive revival that Spring and Summer.[5] About midsummer the cholera ‹appeared›[6] in New York for the first time. **This was in the Summer of 1832. A** great many Christian people fled into the country. **The panic became great.** The cholera was very severe in the city that summer, more so than it ever has been since; and it was especially fatal in the part of the city where I resided.[7] I recollect counting from the door of our house five hearses drawn up at the same time at different doors within sight**, to remove the dead.**[8] I remained in New York until quite the latter part of summer, |not being willing to leave the city while the mortality was so great‹.[9] B›ut I found that the influence was undermining my health, and in the latter part of summer went into the country for two or three weeks.[10] On my return I was installed as pastor of the church.[11] During the installation services I was taken

MS 645

Pulpit, p. 36; *BR*, 16 May 1832, p. 79; and "Letters from John Pintard to his Daughter Eliza Noel Pintard Davidson, 1816–1833," *New York Historical Society Collections* 73 (1941): 49–51.

Finney continued to preach at the invitation of the Second Free Church, who had use of the chapel, but he was not at that time the pastor. The official invitation to be pastor, signed by Joel Parker, James C. Bliss, and William Green, Jr., was not issued until 1 June 1832 (Finney Papers, microfilm, roll 3). Finney held himself free to conduct revivals elsewhere, and in mid-June he visited Philadelphia and helped in a protracted meeting in Wilmington, Delaware. See George Cragin, "The 'Free Church of Old Times.' No. 2," *The Free Church Circular* (Oneida, N.Y.), 27 February 1850, p. 60; p. 254 n. 43; *Religious Intelligencer* (New Haven), 4 August 1832, p. 155; and E. W. Gilbert to Finney, 1 June 1832, Finney Papers, microfilm, roll 3.

[5] According to Lewis Tappan, there was a moral change in that part of the city. Within three months every grog shop in the area had to close (*Christian Register* [Boston], 28 February 1846, p. 33).

[6] The words "broke out" were changed by Finney to "appeared."

[7] The first cholera cases in New York appeared in June, and by around July 20 the epidemic reached its height, with the death rate at over a hundred per day. As many as two-thirds of the population, including many of the ministers, left the city. See Charles E. Rosenberg, *The Cholera Years* (Chicago: University of Chicago Press, 1962), pp. 25, 32, 34; S. B. Halliday, *Winning Souls: Sketches and Incidents During Forty Years of Pastoral Work* (New York: Ford, 1874), pp. 37–43; and Margaret C. Barnet, "The 1832 Cholera Epidemic in New York," *Medical History* 16 (January 1972): 27–39.

[8] The Finneys had moved to 177 Grand Street at the beginning of July. Lydia Finney wrote to her parents on 15 July:

> The report from the board of health states 84 deaths and 133 near cases during the last 24 hours. As we were going to church in the morning, we saw a corpse just put into a coffin only a few doors from us. A little farther on we met a hearse followed by one carriage with only 2 or 3 individuals in it. Before we arrived at the *Chapel*, met a 2 horse close carriage filled with coffins. The City is in great consternation, and multitudes are fleeing in every direction (Lydia Finney to Nathaniel and Jerusha Andrews, 15 July 1832, Finney Papers, microfilm, roll 3).

[9] Matson had written a semicolon here, but Finney altered it to start a new sentence.

[10] The Finneys went to Whitesboro early in August but had to stay with Lydia's brother George in New York Mills because her father had sold the family farm. See Lydia and Charles Finney to Nathaniel and Jerusha Andrews, 15 and 17 July 1832; Silas Mathews to Finney, 11 August 1832; L. Tappan to Finney, 17 and 18 August 1832; Luther Myrick to Finney, 3 September 1832; and Sylvester Finney to Charles Finney, 9 October 1832, Finney Papers, microfilm, roll 3. Before he returned to New York in mid-September, Finney also visited Utica. See Charles Hastings to Finney, 24 September 1832, Finney Papers, microfilm, roll 3.

[11] Finney was installed on 28 September 1832 by a commission appointed by the Third Presbytery, consisting of the Reverends Joel Parker, Samuel H. Cox, John Woodbridge, and Elihu Baldwin. The sermon was preached by Joel Parker. See John P. Prall, "Rev. C. G. Finney in New York: A Reminiscence," *NYE*, 16 September 1875, p. 2.

Finney had been transferred from the roll of the Oneida Presbytery to the Third Presbytery of New York on 28 June 1832. See the Oneida Presbytery "Records, 1825–1833," 5:350–51, The Presbyterian Historical Society, Philadelphia.

ill, and soon after I got home it was plain that I was seized with the cholera. The gentleman at the next door was seized about the same time **of night**, and before morning he was dead.[12] **I however recovered. But the** means **that were** used for my recovery **had given** my system a terrible shock, from

JHF 321 which it took me long to recover.[13] ˡHowever, toward Spring I was able to preach again. I invited **a couple of** ministerial brethren to help me in holding a series of meetings. We **alternated. One of us would preach one night, and the other the next, and so on.** For two or three weeks but very little was accomplished. I saw that it was not the way to promote a revival there, and I drew the meeting in that form to a close.

MS 646 ˡOn the next Sabbath I made **an** appointment to preach every evening during the week. **I did so**, and a revival immediately commenced and became very powerful. I continued to preach for twenty evenings in succession, beside preaching on the Sabbath. **One of the elders, who gave himself up to visit among inquirers, kept a note-book, in which he set down the names of those persons in which the case seemed to be a clear conversion to Christ.** My health was not yet vigorous **enough to continue to preach every night;** and after preaching twenty evenings **in succession** I suspended that form of my labors; **and** the converts **that were** known to us numbered five hundred, **as Father Smith, as we called him, one of the elders, assured us.**[14] **This made** our church so large that very soon a colony was sent off to

[12]In another account of this, Finney said, "A man of the strongest constitution occupied a room adjacent to mine; was attacked the same hour that I was, and within a few hours was a corpse" (*OE,* 9 May 1849, p. 74).

[13]By late October he was well enough to receive visitors. See *NYE,* 27 October 1832, noted in James E. Johnson, "The Life of Charles Grandison Finney" (Ph.D. diss., Syracuse University, 1959), p. 194.

[14]In March 1833 Finney wrote to Rev. George B. Cheever, "Between 4 & 500 whose names & places of residence we know, have recently indulged the hope of eternal life in our meetings, besides we have reason to believe that many more, whom we do not know have been converted" (Finney to Cheever, 15 March 1833, in Cheever Family Papers, American Antiquarian Society, Worcester, Mass.).

Oliver Smith (1774–1837) was from Providence, Rhode Island. From 1799 to 1807 he lived in Franklin, Massachusetts, where he became a Christian and joined Nathanael Emmons's church. He then moved to Philadelphia. Although he was a busy merchant, much of his time was spent in Christian work, particularly among the youth. He cooperated closely with Finney during the revival there in 1828. In 1830 he moved to New York, where he pioneered city missionary work until 1835, when he went to Cincinnati. There he continued his work among children.

> At one time, he had, he says, about 1000 youth under his instruction, distributed in Bible classes over the city, whom he met and instructed every week. . . . While we make no computation, it may be safely said, that few laymen have ever accomplished as much for the souls of men (*NYE,* 8 July 1837, p. 112; see also Joel Parker to Finney, 11 November and 8 December 1830, Finney Papers, microfilm, roll 3; and letters from Smith to Finney in the Finney Papers).

Finney also kept a record of those who joined the church. Edmund Watts, an apprentice who attended Finney's ministry at that time, wrote in 1875:

> In a letter I received from Mr. Finney, not long since, he said he had a record of all the persons who united with the church (Chatham-street chapel) while he was pastor, and it gave him great pleasure to look over it, and mark the names of those whom he learned incidentally had died, and also to note the continuance of others in Christian work. Not long since I notified him of the death of an intimate friend of mine who died during the war, and of the record he had left behind for the Master's followers. It gave him great pleasure, and he wrote in response that my friend had united with the church

form another church; and a suitable building was erected for that purpose on the corner of Madison and Catharine sts.[15] The work continued to go forward in a very interesting manner. We held meetings of inquiry once or twice a week, and sometimes oftener, and found that ˡevery week a goodly number of conversions was reported. The church were a praying, working people. They were thoroughly united; **and after being well-instructed** in regard to labors for the conversion of sinners, were a most devoted and efficient church of Christ. They would **take hold and** go out into the highways and hedges, and bring people to hear preaching whenever they were called upon to do so. Both men and women would undertake this work.[16] When we wished to give notice of any extra meetings, little slips of paper, on which was printed an invitation to attend the services, would be carried from house to house by the members of the church **in every direction,** especially in that part of the city in which Chatham st. chapel, as we called it, was located. By distributing these slips, and **giving an** oral invitation **to such as they saw and had an opportunity to speak with**, the house could be filled any evening in the week. Our ladies were not afraid to go and gather in all classes from the neighborhood round about **into our meetings**. ˡIt was something new **in that part of the city** ˡto have religious services in that theater, instead of such scenes as had formerly been enacted there. **When they transformed it into a church ‹as before said›[17] they called it,[18] Chatham st chapel.[19]**

MS 647

JHF 322

MS 648

in February, 1833 ("Reminiscences of Rev. C. G. Finney," *NYE,* 2 September 1875, p. 2).

[15]This church was the Fourth Free Presbyterian Church formed on 5 January 1834 by thirty-five members from the Second Free Church. On the site where the new church was built, there had been an old brewery. This had been fitted up as a chapel and used until 1835, when it was pulled down. The new church was opened for public worship on 3 January 1836. The first minister was Arthur Granger in 1834, followed by Isaac N. Sprague until April 1836, and then Joel Mann. See Jonathan Greenleaf, *A History of the Churches, of All Denominations, in the City of New York* (New York: French, 1846), pp. 175–77.

The Third Free Church had been formed in December 1832 by another group of thirty-five members of the First and Second churches, "early converts of Mr. Finney, and all of them unmarried." Dirck C. Lansing of Utica was called to the pastorate, and a church was built at the corner of Houston and Thomson streets (Cragin, "'Free Church,' No. 2," pp. 60–61).

[16]George Cragin, one of Finney's New York converts who had been in the First Free Church and transferred to the Third, looked back to this period:

> We had been daily and diligently instructed by Mr. F., that the way to keep our hopes bright and our souls happy, was to labor constantly for the salvation of sinners, and not hesitate for a moment to go out into the streets and lanes of the city, and lay hold of every sinner we met and tell him he must repent and give his heart to God, or he would go to hell. Willing to *do* any thing to keep bright hopes, not a few followed his advice. Persons would allow themselves to be addressed in a rather rude way, provided the spirit of the language was gentle and persuasive. This band of young zealots organized themselves into committees of two each, to take their turn in visiting the purlieus of theatres, ale-houses, and the like places; and not without success. Instances occurred where dissipated fathers of poor families would be picked up, taken to the meeting where others of our band were praying, converted, and then sent home rejoicing in God, to the perfect astonishment of their families. Such were among the motives urged, to keep alive the spirit of proselyting among the Free churches (Cragin, "'Free Church,' No. 2," p. 60).

[17]The words "said before" were written in pencil in the margin against this sentence. They appear to have been written by Lewis Tappan. Finney first added the words "as before said" at the beginning of the sentence, but he crossed them out and added them here instead. Fairchild crossed out the whole sentence.

There were three rooms, **one over the other,** connected with the front part of the theater, long, large rooms, which were fitted up for prayer-meetings and for a lecture room. **It was said that** these rooms had been used for very **vile** purposes while the main building was occupied as a theater.[20] But **these rooms,** when fitted up for our purpose, were exceedingly convenient. There were three tiers of galleries; and those rooms were connected with th**ose tiers of the** gallery respectively, one above the other. I instructed my church-members to scatter themselves over the whole house, and to keep their eyes open in regard to any that were seriously affected under preaching, and if possible to detain them after preaching for conversation and prayer. They were true to **this** teaching, and on the lookout at every meeting to see with whom the Word of God was taking |effect; and they had faith enough to dismiss their fears, and to speak to any **one before they retired, if possible,** whom they saw to be affected by the Word. In this way the conversion of a great many souls was secured. They would invite them into **one of** those rooms **that we had fitted up for prayer, for the Sabbath School, and for lecture rooms, where** we could converse and pray with them, and thus gather up the results of every sermon. **The members became exceedingly efficient in this respect; and I could hardly wish for better helpers to secure the conversion of sinners than I found in them. ‹They [were] wise & in real earnest.›**[21]

MS 649

A case which I this moment recollect, will illustrate the manner in which the members would work. The firm of Naylor and Co., who were at that time the great Cutlery Manufacturers in Sheffield, Eng., had a house in New-York, and a partner by the name of **Hutchinson.**[22] Mr. **Hutchinson** was a worldly

[18]Here Finney crossed out the words "instead of Chatham st. theater."

[19]There had been some discussion about what to call the new chapel, in view of the different uses to which it would be put. Lewis Tappan wrote to Finney:

> The music Soc'y have been desirous from the beginning to designate the house by a name significant of their objects—such as Handel Hall or something like it. We declined of course. The object then was to fix upon some name (they objected to the word church or chapel) of an indefinite meaning. We suggested Chatham Hall, and they were pleased with it. As they have Exeter Hall in London, where all the anniversaries are held, we thought Chatham Hall as good a name. On receiving your letter we again considered the subject. *Tabernacle* is not liked here. The Society will not give up the name Chatham Hall. So as you, and others, object to this we shall call it Chatham Chapel or Chatham street Chapel (is not the latter best, to avoid alliteration?) (Tappan to Finney, 19 April 1832, Finney Papers, microfilm, roll 3).

[20]Theaters at this time were regularly used as places of prostitution. The upper gallery, or "third tier," where the seats were cheapest, and the associated saloon or barrooms were well known as places where clients could meet prostitutes. The barroom of the Chatham Theatre was converted into "a room for social prayer," and it was a striking fact at the time that at the first prayer meeting "the first man who knelt there, with strong emotion uttered these words of supplication: 'O Lord, forgive my sins. The last time I was here Thou knowest I was a wicked actor on this stage. O Lord have mercy on me' " (Fowler, *American Pulpit*, pp. 36–37; see also Claudia D. Johnson, "That Guilty Third Tier: Prostitution in the Nineteenth Century American Theaters," *American Quarterly* 27, no. 5 [December 1975]: 575–84).

[21]This sentence was added by Finney, but the word "were" had been omitted.

[22]After the dissolution of the leading Sheffield firm of Naylor and Sanderson in 1829, George P. Naylor entered into partnership with John Hutchinson and others to form the firm of Naylor, Hutchinson, Vickers and Co. Hutchinson had been a coach builder in Sheffield and moved to New York soon after joining the partnership. See Sanderson, Brothers & Co., "To the Importers

man, had travelled a great deal, and had resided in several of the principal cities of Europe. One of the clerks of ˡthat establishment had come to our meetings and been converted, and felt very anxious for ‹the›[23] conversion of Mr. **Hutchinson**. The young man for **sometime** hesitated about asking him to attend our meetings, but he finally ventured to do so; and in compliance with his earnest entreaty Mr. **Hutchinson** came one evening to meeting. ˡAs it happened he sat **on the opposite side of** the broad aisle over against where Mr. Tappan sat. Mr. Tappan saw that during the sermon he manifested a good deal of emotion; and seemed **so** uneasy **that several** times he **seemed** on the point of going out. Mr. **Hutchinson** afterwards acknowledged to me that he was several times on the point of leaving, because he was so affected by the sermon. **However** he remained till the blessing was pronounced. Mr. Tappan kept his eye upon him, and as soon as the blessing was pronounced **crowded across the aisle, and** introduced himself as **being** Mr. Tappan, a partner of Arthur Tappan and **Co.**, a firm well-known to everybody **then** in New York. I have heard Mr. **Hutchinson** himself relate ˡthe facts with great emotion. He said that Mr. Tappan stepped up to him and took him gently by the button of his coat, and spoke very kindly to him, and asked him if he would not remain for prayer and conversation. He tried to excuse himself and to get away; but Mr. Tappan was so gentlemanly and so kind, that he could not well get away from him. He was importunate, and as Mr. **Hutchinson** expressed it, "he held fast **at** my button, so that," said he, "an ounce weight at my button was the means of saving my soul." The people retired, and Mr. **Hutchinson,** among others, was persuaded to remain. According to our custom we had a thorough conversation; and Mr. **Hutchinson** was either then, or very soon after, hopefully converted.[24]

MS 650

JHF 323

MS 651

When I first went to Chatham st. **C**hapel I informed the brethren that I did not wish to fill up the house with Christians from other churches, as my object was to gather from the world. I wanted to secure the conversion of the ungodly to the utmost possible extent. We therefore gave ourselves to labor for that class of persons, and ˡby the blessing of God with good success. Conversions were multiplied so much, that our church would soon become so large that we would send off a colony. **Our church was, when I went there, the second church.** When I left New York I think we had seven free churches, whose members were laboring with all their might to secure the salvation of souls.[25] ˡThey were supported mostly by collections that were

MS 652

JHF 324

and Consumers of Steel," Sheffield, March 1832, typescript copy, Sheffield Central Library; *Longworth's American Almanac* for 1830–1832; and information from Sheffield Central Library.

[23]The word "the" was written originally by Matson in such a way that the stroke of the *t* appeared to have crossed out the word. It was rewritten in by Finney.

[24]In about 1838 Hutchinson moved to Williamsburgh, Long Island, where he became a member of the church there. He had suffered financial disaster in the crash of 1837, but he continued with the firm of Naylor and Co. until about 1844. In 1850 he was in England, where the Finneys met up with him again. See John Hutchinson to Finney, 17 November 1838, Finney Papers, microfilm, roll 3; *The New York City and Co-partnership Directory* for 1843–1846; *The Independent* (New York), 4 April 1850, p. 55; and Elizabeth Finney to Angelina Atkinson and Julia Finney, 1 April 1850, Finney Papers, microfilm, roll 4.

[25]By the beginning of 1835 the first four Free churches had received over 1,500 into membership. But opposition to the system of free seats and the New Measures by most of the clergy and influential laymen of the city and the espousal of radical abolitionism curtailed the

taken up from Sabbath to Sabbath **by carrying the contribution boxes around among the people.** If at any time there was **any** deficiency in the treasury **to pay all our expenses,**[26] there were a number of brethren of property who would at once supply the deficiency from their own purses, so that we never had the least difficulty in **supplying** the pecuniary **wants of the congregation.**

A more harmonious, prayerful, and efficient people I never knew than were the members of those free churches.[27] They were not among the rich, although there were several men of property belonging to them. In general MS 653 they were gathered ˡfrom **among** the middle and lower classes of **New York citizens.** This was what we aimed to accomplish, to preach the Gospel especially to the poor.[28] When I first went to New York I had made up my mind on the **subject** of **the** slavery **question**, and was exceedingly anxious to arouse public attention to the subject.[29] I did not, however, turn aside to make it a hobby, or divert the attention of the people from the work of converting souls. Nevertheless in my prayers and preaching I so often alluded

popularity of the Free-church cause, and the Fifth and Sixth churches were never successfully established. The Seventh Free Church was the Broadway Tabernacle. See L. Tappan, *Letter to the Convention of Ministers and Representatives of the Evangelical Branches in the Church in Brooklyn* (New York: Gray and Green, 1866), pp. 5–6; and Charles C. Cole, "The Free Church Movement in New York City," *New York History* 35 (1953): 284–97. L. Nelson Nichols lists four other churches organized between 1837 and 1840 that operated as Free churches for a few years (L. N. Nichols, *History of the Broadway Tabernacle of New York City* [New Haven: Tuttle, Morehouse, and Taylor, 1940], p. 69).

[26]Written in the margin in pencil against this phrase are the words "seldom anything sufficient." This appears to be in Lewis Tappan's handwriting.

[27]A writer who witnessed these revivals recalled:

> Probably no man, since the days of Whitfield [*sic*], ever stirred the minds of men in this city so widely and deeply, in their relations to practical and personal religion, as this great and good man. Preaching and praying were his only weapons. He surrounded himself with an atmosphere of prayer, and a body of devoted, praying, and working Christians, male and female, such as New York had never before seen, and probably never since. His pulpit and church here were a centre of holy and soul-converting influences, that were diffused in every direction, through the length and breadth of the land, and the impulse of his New York life and labors is still perpetuated and embodied in our churches and in various forms of Christian activity (W.H., "The Late Rev. Charles G. Finney," *NYE,* 30 September 1875, p. 2).

[28]The revival movement was channeled to these sections of the population also by means of missions like the Tract and Female Moral Reform Societies. See Carroll Smith Rosenberg, *Religion and the Rise of the American City: The New York City Mission Movement, 1812–1870* (Ithaca, N.Y.: Cornell University Press, 1971).

[29]Finney is referring here to the question of the immediate abolition of slavery, which had begun to be agitated by William Lloyd Garrison and others. Gradual emancipation and the American Colonization Society's policy of shipping the slaves back to Africa had been considered the most viable way of dealing with slavery. But Finney came out publicly, with other leaders of the antislavery movement, against the Colonization Society. He refused to give communion to slaveholders, and he proclaimed slavery to be a sin and immediate abolition of all forms of slavery to be the duty of the slaveholders, the church, and the government. See *The Liberator* (Boston), 13 July 1833, p. 109; *NYE,* 8 November 1834, p. 179; and Anne C. Loveland, "Evangelicalism and 'Immediate Emancipation' in Antislavery Thought," *Journal of Southern History* 32 (May 1966): 172–88. Finney said:

> Before I went to the Mediterranean I had taken the stand in my congregation in New York City that no slave holder could come to our communion. In that vast congregation some slaveholders of professed piety were almost always present, and the rebuke was being solemnly felt. The example was exerting a decidedly good influence (*OE,* 18 August 1852, pp. 130–31).

to slavery and denounced it, that a considerable excitement came to exist among the people.[30]

While laboring at Chatham st. some events occurred connected with the presbytery that led to the formation of a Congregational church, and to my becoming its pastor. A member came to us from one of the old churches; and we were soon informed that before **this man** came **to us** he had committed a **crime** for which he needed to be disciplined. I supposed that since **we had been misled in receiving** ¦**him,**[31] **as** he had been recommended to us as a member in good standing, and **it appeared that the crime** had been committed before he left that church, that it belonged to them to discipline him**, and that the crime did not come within our jurisdiction**. The question was brought before the third presbytery of New York, to which I

MS 654 [1]

[30]There is a question mark in pencil in the margin against the last part of this sentence. It appears to have been inserted by Lewis Tappan.

Prominent abolitionist James A. Thome drew attention to the crucial role played by Finney at this time in the antislavery movement. He considered that the cause of emancipation had been brought to birth at the first anniversary meeting of the American Antislavery Society held in New York in May 1834. This birth he likened to the birth of Christ. And the inn or stable where it happened was the Chatham Street Chapel. The place was auspicious. It was no great temple:

> It was a sort of Caravansera, an extemporized inn, where unclean and hideous creatures, worse than four-footed beasts, had been wont to herd for nightly orgies. . . . It had been recently converted into a rude chapel, for Charles G. Finney, the revivalist, the harbinger of this reform, to preach in, and to preach from, to city and nation the arousing gospel of immediate repentance of sin and complete redemption in Christ. We do not disparage the revival of which Mr. Finney was the honored instrument, when we say it ushered in this Christian reform. Of this, subsequent church history will have a grateful record to make (J. A. Thome, "The Antislavery Movement: Its Past and Present," address delivered before the Church Anti-Slavery Society on its anniversary, 6 May 1861, in the Church of the Puritans, New York; newspaper cutting in Tappan Papers, microfilm, roll 7).

See also George Cragin, "The 'Free Church of Old Times.' No. 3," *The Free Church Circular,* 26 March 1850, p. 74.

The research of Gilbert H. Barnes led the way toward a better understanding of the significant role played by Finney in the antislavery movement. While he inspired many of the leaders and gave a powerful impetus to the doctrine of immediatism, Finney was critical of the inflammatory methods of some abolitionists. He wrote to T. D. Weld:

> One most alarming fact is that the absorbing abolitionism has drunk up the spirit of some of the most efficient revival men & is fast doing so to the rest, & many of our Abolition brethren seem satisfied with nothing less than this. This I have been trying to resi[s]t from the beginning as I have all along foreseen that should that take place, the church and world, ecclesiastical and state leaders will become embroiled in one common infernal squabble that will roll a wave of blood over the land. The causes now operating are in my view as certain to lead to this result as a cause is to produce its effect, unless the publick mind can be engrossed with the subject of salvation and make abolition an appendage just as we made temperance an appendage of the revival in Rochester (Finney to Weld, 21 July 1836, Weld-Grimke Papers, William L. Clements Library, University of Michigan; this letter is published in Gilbert H. Barnes and Dwight L. Dumond, eds., *Letters of Theodore Dwight Weld, Angelina Grimké Weld, and Sarah Grimké, 1822–1844,* vol. 1 [Gloucester, Mass.: Peter Smith, 1965], pp. 318–20, but there are errors in the transcription).

See also G. H. Barnes, *The Antislavery Impulse, 1830–1844* (Gloucester, Mass.: Peter Smith, 1957); Ben Williams, "Charles G. Finney's Revivalism and the Early Abolition Movement" (M.A. thesis, Harding College Graduate School of Religion, 1972); James D. Essig, "The Lord's Free Man: Charles G. Finney and His Abolitionism," *Civil War History* 24, no. 1 (March 1978): 25–45; and Lawrence T. Lesick, *The Lane Rebels* (Metuchen, N.J.: Scarecrow, 1980).

[31]MS 654 [1] was numbered 500, renumbered 632 by Matson, and changed to 654 by Finney. Finney also renumbered the next page 654 in error.

then belonged, and they decided that he was under our jurisdiction, and that it belonged to us to take the case in hand and discipline him. We did so. But JHF 325 soon another case occurred in which a **lady** came ˡfrom one of the **other** churches and united with us, and we found that she had **committed a crime** before she came to us, **for** which **she needed to be** disciplined. In accordance with the ruling of the presbytery in the other case we went forward and excommunicated her. She appealed from the decision of the Session to the presbytery; and they decided that the **crime** was not committed under our MS 654 [2] jurisdiction, and ruled in a ˡmanner[32] directly opposite ‹to their former ruling›.[33] I expostulated, and told them that I did not know how to act; that the two cases were precisely similar, and that their rulings in the two cases were entirely inconsistent and opposed to each other. Dr Cox replied that they would not be governed by their own precedent, or by any other precedent; and talked so warmly and pressed the case so hard, that the presbytery went with him.[34] **I then told them that *we* could not get along that way; for they would not abide by their own decisions, and we knew not how to act.**

Soon after, the question came up of building the Tabernacle in Broadway. The men that built it, and the leading members who formed the church there, built it with the understanding that I should be its pastor, and they formed a Congregational church.[35] I then took my dismission from the presbytery, and became pastor of that Congregational church.[36] But I should have said that MS 655 **the second or third year after I went to Chatham st.** ˡ**chapel,**[37] I was

[32] MS 654 [2] was numbered 501, renumbered 633 by Matson, and then incorrectly numbered 654 by Finney. A ½ appears to have been added by Fairchild.

[33] Here Matson had written down, "from what they had before in the other case," but Finney crossed it out and inserted "to their former ruling."

[34] Samuel Hanson Cox (1793–1880) was minister of Laight Street Presbyterian Church. He was a prominent New School leader and educator. See *DAB*.

[35] George Cragin, a member of the Third Free Church, recalled that he had been invited "to unite with Wm. Green, I. M. Dimond, S. W. Benedict, and other prominent friends of the Free Church cause, in organizing another Free Church *especially* for Mr. Finney" (*The Free Church Circular,*26 March 1850, p. 75).

Isaac M. Dimond (1803–1862), one of Finney's staunchest supporters, was a silversmith. He was a convert in the First Free Church and had been one of the young men chiefly responsible for forming the Third Free Church. He and William Green, Jr., contributed the bulk of the $66,500 needed. The church was formed of 118 members, with the help of a colony from Chatham Street Chapel, on 13 March 1836. See Thompson, *Last Sabbath in Broadway Tabernacle*, pp. 12–13; Ward, *History of the Broadway Tabernacle,* pp. 27–28; "Necrology: Sarah C. Capen Putnam '39," *The Oberlin Alumni Magazine* 3 (November 1906): 91–92; and *NYE,* 21 February 1835, p. 29; and 1 January 1863, p. 5.

[36] Finney resigned from the Third Presbytery on 13 March 1836 and was installed as pastor of the Broadway Tabernacle on 10 April. See Nichols, *History of the Broadway Tabernacle,* pp. 62–63. On 18 January 1837 a convention was held at the Broadway Tabernacle, at which Finney was present, when the New York City Congregational Association was formed. Finney became a member of that body, but within three months he took his dismission, when he gave up the pastorate of the tabernacle. He was dismissed to join the Association of the Western Reserve but delayed joining until 1844 "for the very purpose of cultivating fraternal relations with [his] Presbyterian brethren" (*OE,* 24 September 1856, p. 156; and see copy of extract from the minutes of the meeting of the New York City Association, 5 April 1837, by Joshua Leavitt, Finney Papers, file 2/2/2, box 9; *NYE,* 28 January 1837, p. 17; and p. 390 n. 32 [MS 685]).

[37] Pages 655–72 were originally numbered 502–17. Matson renumbered them 634–51, and Finney changed them to 655–72.

Broadway Tabernacle, New York. This building was built for Finney in 1836 to his own design. He was pastor here until April 1837, at which time he left for Oberlin. This is the earliest known engraving of the church. In Joseph P. Thompson, *Memoir of David Hale* (New York: Wiley, 1850), opposite p. 62. Courtesy The British Library.

obliged to leave and take a voyage to sea.[38] I went up the Mediterranean in a small brig in the midst of winter.[39] We had a very stormy passage, my state

[38]Finney had never recovered since having cholera. In March 1833 he had thought of going on a trip to England with Anson G. Phelps, but nothing came of it. Then in June he and his family left the city for the summer and went to Milford, New York, where he did some preaching and wrote some tracts for the new Revival Tract Society. Tracts number 6, 7, 14, and 15 were possibly written by him, and he may also have written tracts for the American Tract Society. (See Phelps "Diary," 24 March 1833, and Phelps to Finney, 19 August 1833; American Tract Society to Finney, 6 February 1833; William Green, Jr., to Finney, 25 June 1833, 9 July 1833; L. Tappan to Finney, 10 July 1833; T. Drown to Finney, 1 January 1833, Finney Papers, microfilm, roll 3; and *NYE,* 10 May 1834, p. 76.) But Finney was still unwell when he returned to New York at the beginning of October, and he had plans to go on a boat to the Sandwich Islands and to Argentina. Finally he decided to go to the Mediterranean. See D. Greene to Finney, 22 November 1833; and James Patterson to Finney, 2 January 1834, Finney Papers, microfilm, roll 3.

[39]Finney sailed from New York on 20 January. The following notice appeared in *The New-York Evangelist*:

> Rev. C. G. Finney.—The numerous friends of Mr. Finney, are informed that he sailed from this port on Monday the 20th ult., in the Brig Padang, for Smyrna, Asia Minor, with a favorable wind. His health has been declining for several months. Though able to be out in pleasant weather, he has not preached for several weeks. His arduous

room was small, and I was on the whole very uncomfortable; and the voyage did not much improve my health. I spent some weeks at Malta, and also **at** Sicily. I was gone about six months, **and then returned.**[40] On my return I found that there was a great excitement in New York. The members of my church, together with other abolitionists in New York, had held a meeting on the fourth of July, and had had an address on the subject of slaveholding. **This had excited a** mob;[41] ‹**& this**›[42] was the beginning of that series of

JHF 326 mobs that spread in many directions whenever and wherever ˡthere was an Anti-slavery gathering, **and addresses made** against the abominable institu-

MS 656 tion of slavery. However, I went forward ˡin my labors in Chatham Street. The work of God immediately revived **on my return,** and **went forward** with great interest, numbers being converted at almost or quite every meeting.[43] I continued to labor thus in Chatham street, and the church

> labors for so many years have much affected his health. Still it is believed he has no chronic disease. He needs rest; . . . It will depend on the effects of the outward passage how far Mr. Finney will proceed in his travels. He hopes to be able to visit the missionary stations on the Mediterranean Sea; and probably he will visit Palestine (reprinted in *Religious Intelligencer,* 8 February 1834, p. 575).

During Finney's absence, Rev. John Ingersoll supplied the pulpit. He was installed as associate pastor on 2 April 1834 and remained until February 1835, when he resigned. See Herman E. Kittredge, *Ingersoll: A Biographical Appreciation* (London: Watts, 1911), pp. 17–18.

[40]Finney arrived back in Boston on 14 July 1834 (see *The Boston Morning Post,* 15 July 1834, p. 2).

[41]This meeting and its disruption by a mob was widely reported in the press. See, e.g., *The Liberator,* 12 July 1834, p. 110. Matson had written at this point: "and Brother Lewis Tappan was hunted so by the pro-slavery zealots that he was obliged to spend the nights away from home where they could not find him." Against this section Lewis Tappan had written in ink in the margin of the manuscript: "This is an error. Did not leave my house until the evening before the furniture was burned." Finney accordingly crossed out the section. These riots started on 9 July. Lewis Tappan's house was attacked and ransacked, and the riot spread to the houses and churches of other abolitionists in the city. See letter of Tappan to Theodore Weld, 10 July 1834, in Barnes and Dumond, *Letters of Theodore Dwight Weld,* pp. 153–56; "Dreadful Riots," *The Emancipator,* 15 July 1834, p. 2; and Linda K. Kerber, "Abolitionists and Amalgamators: The New York City Race Riots of 1834," *New York History* 48 (January 1967): 28–39.

[42]Finney inserted the words "& this" in place of the word "This."

[43]Finney had spent the late summer of 1834, after his Mediterranean trip, with his family in Western. While there he heard from Lewis Tappan, "Our church has been a good deal distracted about the Slavery Question, & but few sinners have been converted" (Tappan to Finney, 18 July 1834, Finney Papers, microfilm, roll 3). And when Finney arrived in New York in November 1834, he found a heart-breaking situation in the church. Before he had gone on his Mediterranean trip, he believed that the stand he had taken against slavery, and the example he had set of refusing communion to slaveholders,

> was exerting a decidedly good influence. But when I came back, I soon found that a strange state of things had come about. Everything was hot and fiery. I felt bound to tell them plainly that they were casting out devils through Beelzebub, and by getting his spirit were really doing his work. This would never do. The cause of love and of human well-being could not be built up by uncharitableness and hate (*OE,* 18 August 1852, p. 131 [misnumbered 132]).

Edmund Watts, then a lad in Chatham Street Chapel, recalled that Finney had left the church in the hands of an assistant (John Ingersoll) during a powerful revival, when he went on his voyage:

> To leave, under such circumstances, cost him a great sacrifice. He had scarcely reached the Island of Malta, when the spirit of envy and discord crept into the church, the Holy Spirit was grieved, the revival ceased, the church had grievously backslidden, and none inquired the way of life. A few faithful ones besought the Lord in prayer and kept the flock together as best they could. The minister then in charge (a good man) became discouraged, and the condition of the church was alarming. In the midst of this sad

continued to flourish and to extend its influence and its labors in every direction, until the Tabernacle in Broadway was completed.[44] The plan of the interior of that house was my own. I had observed the defects of churches in regard to sound; and was sure that I could give the plan of a church in which I could easily speak to a much larger congregation than any house would hold that I had ever seen. An architect was consulted, and I gave him my plan.[45] But he objected to it that it would not appear well, and feared that it would injure his reputation to build a church with such an interior as that. **However, I insisted on it, and** told him that if he would not build it on that plan he was not the man to superintend its construction at all. It was finally built in ˡaccordance with my ideas; and it was **altogether the** most **spacious,** commodious, and comfortable place to speak in **that I have ever seen of its size.**[46] MS 657

In this connection I must relate the origin of the New York Evangelist. When I first went to the city of New York, and *before* I went there, the New York Observer, in the hands of Mr. Morse, had gone into the controversy

> state of affairs Mr. F. returned. I shall never forget his expression when he came in and saw but the remnant of a congregation that crowded the church when he left. He turned a withering look upon the minister, and with this question, "Where is the church I left in your charge?" buried his face in his hands and shed bitter tears. The scene was fearful. It was but a short time, however, before the scattered flock was gathered, the meetings were crowded, the church was revived, and the Holy Spirit blessed his labors in the salvation of souls (E. Watts, letter dated 16 June 1876, in *Reminiscences of Rev. Charles G. Finney* [Oberlin: Goodrich, 1876], pp. 37–38).

Although Finney was unwell, he preached on Sundays and gave a lecture on Friday evenings. He also found time to write sermons for publication (see Finney to Lydia Finney, 10 and 26 November 1834, Finney Papers, microfilm, roll 3). These started to be published as monthly sermons by John S. Taylor of New York in December 1834 (see *NYE,* 27 December 1834, p. 207); and they were published in different editions by him and also by S. W. Benedict and Co. of New York in 1834 and 1835 under the title *Sermons on Various Subjects.* In 1836 further sermons were added, making twelve in all, which were published by John S. Taylor as *Sermons on Important Subjects.* The publisher made it appear as if there were three editions; however, only two thousand copies were ever printed. Taylor told William Green "that the 1st 2d & 3d Edition was inserted as a 'trick of the Trade' to induce the public to believe that they sold well." Due to the failure of Taylor's firm in the financial crash of 1837, Finney never received much in the way of payment for what copies were sold. See W. Green to Finney, 19 March 1840, Finney Papers, microfilm, roll 4.

On Sunday evening, 11 January 1835, Finney began a series of doctrinal sermons, which he preached for eight weeks. These were taken down by Joshua Leavitt at the time, and his notes were published in *The New-York Evangelist* from 1 August 1835 through 30 October 1835.

[44]The building of the Broadway Tabernacle was started in May 1835 and completed in April 1836. See Ward, *History of the Broadway Tabernacle,* pp. 28–29.

[45]This was Joseph Ditto, who had been the "foreman" responsible for the work done on the Dey Street warehouse for the First Free Church, and on the Chatham Street Chapel. He was a member of the Second Free Church. In 1839 he left New York to take up a two-year contract constructing locks on the Genesee Canal. See Lewis Tappan to Finney, 11 April 1832; and Caroline Brown to Lydia Finney, 28 January 1839, Finney Papers, microfilm, roll 3; and Thompson, *Last Sabbath in Broadway Tabernacle,* p. 13.

[46]It was described by J. Alexander Patten:

> The building was one hundred feet square, with a spacious gallery around the entire circuit, and would hold three thousand people. While the chief design was the extension of the free church plan, it was proposed also to provide suitable accommodation for the May anniversaries and other public meetings. From the number of important meetings held here during the twenty-one years of its existence, the building became famous throughout the whole country (J. A. Patten, *Lives of the Clergy of New York and Brooklyn* [New York: Atlantic, 1874], p. 556).

originating in Mr. Nettleton's opposition to the revivals in central New York.[47] **He** had sustained Mr. Nettleton's course, and refused to publish anything on the other side. **Anything that** Mr. Nettleton **or** his friends **would write**, Mr. Morse would publish in the **New York** Observer; but if any reply was made by any of **my friends, or of** the friends of those revivals, he would not publish it.[48] In this state of things **the** friends **of those revivals** had no organ through which they could communicate with the public to correct misapprehensions.[49] Judge Jonas Platt, of the Supreme Court, was

JHF 327 then living in New York, and was a friend of mine.[50] His son and ˡdaughter

MS 658 had been hopefully converted in the revival at Utica.[51] ˡConsiderable **pains were taken** by the friends of those revivals to get a hearing on the question in debate. **But it was** all in vain; **the New York Observer would not publish**

[47]Sidney Edwards Morse (1794–1871)—journalist, author, and inventor—started the *New York Observer* in 1823 and continued as proprietor and editor until 1858. See *DAB*.

[48]The paper did support the opponents of the New Measures revivalism and had published the letters of Nettleton and Beecher in December 1827. And in this connection David L. Dodge wrote to Finney:

> Mr. Aikin I learn is about to reply to Mr. N. & will offer it for publication in the observer but I do not believe they will publish it. I do not think the time is very distant when we shall have a strictly religious periodical in the City—one of a decided & independent character. It is greatly needed—almost every publication is governed by popularity. We want one on the side of revivals & deeply experimental & practical. The state of things has not yet come to the point to sustain it (Dodge to Finney, 18 December 1827, Finney Papers, microfilm, roll 1).

The New York Observer did, however, publish Aikin's letter and also one from John Frost, in February 1828. See MS 396–97.

The paper, although owned by Sidney E. Morse and Richard C. Morse, was edited by the young Gerard Hallock, soon to be the well-known editor of the *Journal of Commerce* (see *DAB*). According to John Frost: "N[ettleton] sent him a communication some time ago, in answer to the letters [of Aikin and Frost] denying that he had made such charges & he has recently recd. a review of the letters which I presume is from W[eeks?] but has written to him declining to publish." Hallock was determined to publish no more from either side. See Frost to Finney, 2 May 1828, Finney Papers, microfilm, roll 2.

[49]In fact, they had *The Western Recorder* published in Utica, New York, and edited by Thomas Hastings, which they did to some extent use. But, as Nathan Beman pointed out, its circulation was limited, and a paper located in New York City itself was considered essential. See *NYE*, 1 January 1880, p. 8.

[50]Jonas Platt (1769–1834), the son of Zephaniah Platt, the founder of Plattsburg, had been a most eminent Oneida County judge of the supreme court and a member of Congress. In 1823 he retired from the bench and went to live in Utica, where he carried on a legal practice with his son Zephaniah. He had two sons and six daughters. Soon after the revival in Utica in 1826, he went to live in New York. See *The National Cyclopaedia of American Biography*, vol. 11 (New York: James T. White, 1901), p. 161; Oswald P. Backus, "The Early Bar of Oneida County," *Proceedings of the New York State Historical Association* 14 (1915): 324–26; and Moses Bagg, *The Pioneers of Utica* (Utica: Curtiss and Childs, 1877), pp. 567–70.

[51]Finney is referring here to Zephaniah and Helen. Zephaniah Platt (1796–1871) was a graduate of Hamilton College, and after practicing law in Utica, he went soon after the revival there in 1826 to New York. His father went there to live with him. Zephaniah later moved to Detroit, where he became attorney general of the state of Michigan and was subsequently a judge in South Carolina. See *The American Annual Cyclopaedia and Register of Important Events of the Year 1871*, p. 573.

Helen Platt was married in 1829 to Truman Parmelee, a dry-goods merchant of Utica. They moved to New York about 1830 and then went to New Orleans, where they were active in Joel Parker's church, returning to New York in 1836. After Parmelee's death in 1845 she became, by a second marriage, Mrs. Bell of Staten Island. See Bagg, *Pioneers of Utica*, pp. 570, 613; *NYE*, 21 April 1829, p. 63; and 5 February 1846, p. 23; and letters of the Platts to the Finneys in the Finney Papers.

anything except on one side. Judge Platt found one day, pasted on the inside cover of one of his old law books, a letter written by one of the **then** New York **pastors** against **the labors of**[52] Whitefield at the time he was in this country.[53] That letter of the New York pastor struck Judge Platt as so strongly resembling the opposition made by Mr. Nettleton, that he sent it to the New York Observer and wished it published as a literary curiosity, it having been written nearly a hundred years before. Mr. Morse refused to publish it, assigning as a reason that the people would **apply** it **as being a parallel** to the opposition of Mr. Nettleton.[54] **After waiting for sometime**, some of the friends of the revivals in New York assembled and talked the matter over of establishing a new paper that should deal fairly with those questions.[55] They finally **did so**. I assisted them in getting out the ¦‹first[56] MS 659

[52]The words "the labors of" were not crossed out by Fairchild in the manuscript but were omitted from the published version.

[53]Elsewhere Finney says it was "a piece of old newspaper" with the letter printed on it and that it was from a "Presbyterian" pastor. See *The Independent,* 6 February 1873, pp. 161–62; and *NYE,* 7 March 1835, p. 38. George Whitefield (1714–1770), the Methodist evangelist, visited America several times between 1739 and his death, which occurred in America. See *DAB*.

[54]On another occasion when Finney spoke of this letter he linked it with a similar attack on Whitefield by Charles Chauncy, the leading Congregational minister in Boston. Chauncy's *Seasonable Thoughts on the State of Religion in New England* (Boston, 1743), published after Whitefield's first two visits to America, was the most comprehensive attack on the revival movement. It was followed in 1744 and 1745 by two letters to Whitefield. See *NYE,* 7 March 1835, p. 38. See also *The Independent,* 17 April 1857, p. 61.

Although Chauncy was not the author of the letter referred to here by Finney, it is of interest that Chauncy's attack was specifically used at the time of the New Measures controversy by the protagonists. Because of a similarity in the revival methods of Whitefield and of the New Measures under Finney, a reviewer in *The Christian Examiner* made use of Chauncy's book expressly to correct the "prevailing errors" of the New Measures. This article, "The Revival Under Whitefield," by James Walker, was drawn to Finney's attention by John Frost. See *The Christian Examiner* (Boston) 6 (November–December 1827): 464–95; and Frost to Finney, 2 May 1828, Finney Papers, microfilm, roll 2.

It was probably Chauncy's book that John P. Cushman also referred to when he wrote to Finney: "I have Chauncy, & were I in the habit of writing, could astonish Dr Beecher by a *parallel* between him & Chauncy in the course pursued by them in relation to Whitfield Tenant Edwards & Beman & Finney & Western brethren. Dr. B's attack in his note to Edrs of Observer is bitter & without excuse" (Cushman to Finney, 23 January 1828, Finney Papers, microfilm, roll 1).

[55]William E. Dodge recollected:

> A meeting was called at the office of Zephaniah Platt, at the corner of Exchange Place and New Street, of some ten or twelve gentlemen, among whom I remember Anson G. Phelps, Arthur Tappan, Lewis Tappan, Z. Platt, Mr. Betts and Rev. Noah C. Saxton and myself. At this meeting it was resolved to start such a paper; and as Mr. Finney, Mr. Nettleton, and Mr. Saxton were all evangelists, it was determined to give it that name—particularly as it was to be the advocate of Revivals. . . . A subscription of a few thousand dollars was raised, and Mr. Saxton . . . was engaged to edit the new paper, and Mr. Platt was to manage the finances, and a Mr. Beach to take charge of the general business, getting subscribers, sending off papers, etc. ("The Origins of the Evangelist," *NYE,* 8 January 1880, p. 4).

The promoters of the paper called themselves "An Association of Gentlemen" and were the publishers in the early years. They were for the most part wealthy merchant and banking friends of Arthur Tappan, who collaborated over a number of projects, including the founding of the First Free Church in New York. See Bertram Wyatt-Brown, *Lewis Tappan and the Evangelical War Against Slavery* (Cleveland: Press of Western Reserve, 1964), pp. 61, 73 n. 2; and Theodore L. Cuyler, "A Glorious Group," *NYE,* 16 January 1896, p. 4.

[56]The section from the top of MS 659 down to n. 57 is on a separate piece of paper pasted onto the sheet. It replaces a section that read:

number, in which I invited ministers & lay men to consider, & discuss several questions in theology, & also questions relating to the best means of promoting revivals of religion.›[57]

The first editor of this paper was a Mr. Saxton, a young man who had formerly labored a good deal with Mr. Nettleton, but who strongly disapproved of the course he had been taking in opposing what he then called "the western revivals."[58] This young man continued in the editorial chair about a year, and discussed with considerable ability many of the questions that had been proposed for discussion. The paper changed editors two or three times perhaps in the course of as many years; and finally the Rev. Joshua Leavitt was called to and accepted the editorial chair.[59] He, as everybody knows, was and is an able editor. The paper soon went into

> first number, and in getting out a prospectus; and proposed in the first number for discussion, to which I invited the attention of ministers and of Christians generally, several topics, principally relating to the best means for promoting revivals, and also specifying several theological questions that I should like to have considered.

Finney changed the first section that was covered over to read, "first number, and ‹in that number I invited discussion upon certain questions of theology› to which I invited the attention of." This was covered over and the remaining section crossed out.

[57]This ends the section in Finney's handwriting. The full title of the paper was *The New-York Evangelist. Devoted to Revivals, Doctrinal Discussions, and Religious Intelligence Generally*. It was a four-page weekly, and the first issue was published on 6 March 1830. There is an article on p. 2 signed "Investigator," which lists a number of questions for discussion under the headings "Revivals," "Prayer," and "Regeneration." Although this could be the article to which Finney refers, it does not quite fit his description, nor is he otherwise known to have used a pseudonym. The article starts, "Having seen the prospectus of the Evangelist, I would beg leave to suggest the following subjects for discussion in its future numbers." The "prospectus" mentioned was issued on 1 March, but that would not have been referred to as "the first number" (see *NYE,* 6 November 1879, p. 4). However, in December 1829 a specimen copy was being taken round by Edward Beach, the agent, to raise support and subscriptions. It was "issued in advance as a sample of what it was intended [the paper] should be in the future." This may be the "first number" referred to by Finney. No copy of this issue has been located. See E. A. Beach, "A Memory of Fifty Years Ago," *NYE,* 1 January 1880, p. 8.

[58]Noah C. Saxton had been a very successful evangelist in New England until his health broke down in 1829, with bleeding from the lungs. After passing the winter in New York, he was persuaded by the promoters of the paper to become the proprietor. He carried on the editorial work until ill health necessitated giving it up in July 1831. In 1832 he bought the *Rochester Observer* and edited it for a short time under the title *The American Revivalist and Rochester Observer*, but he died of consumption the following year. See William E. Dodge, "The Evangelist Forty Years Ago," *NYE,* 6 January 1870, p. 4; and letters of Saxton to Finney in Finney Papers.

[59]Owing to Saxton's ill health and occasional absences, he was helped out by Joshua Leavitt, who edited about half the issues in 1830. Saxton gave up editing in July 1831, and William Beach became the proprietor, probably in association with Zephaniah Platt and Oliver Ellsworth Huntington, a New York merchant. The editor was Samuel Griswold. He continued until December 1831, when Leavitt took over. Griswold became editor of the *Rochester Observer* after Saxton's death. See *NYE,* 16 July 1831, p. 27; 30 July 1831, p. 277; 17 December 1831, p. 359; 8 January 1880, p. 4; and *The Congregational Quarterly* (Boston) 18 (July 1876): 627.

Joshua Leavitt (1794–1873), the prominent reformer and editor, was at that time the general agent of the American Seamen's Friend Society. He ran the *Evangelist* as part owner and editor from 17 December 1831 until 1837, when he became editor of *The Emancipator*. From 1848 he was associated with the New York *Independent*. See Hugh H. Davis, "The Reform Career of Joshua Leavitt, 1794–1873" (Ph.D. diss., Ohio State University, 1969); *DAB*; and *NYE,* 17 December 1831, p. 359; and 29 July 1837, p. 122. According to Finney's recollection, Leavitt had been offered the editorial chair at the beginning. "It was a new enterprise, and, for some reason, he at first declined to take the editorial charge. After, however, becoming acquainted with its design and spirit, he accepted" (Finney, "Dr. Leavitt's Death," *The Independent,* 6 February 1873, p. 162).

extensive circulation, and proved itself a medium through which the friends of revivals as ˡthey then existed could communicate their thoughts to the public.[60] ˡI have spoken of the building of the Tabernacle, and of the excitement in New York on the subject of slavery. When the Tabernacle was in the process of completion, its walls being up and the roof on **and they were doing off the interior**, a story was set in circulation that it was going to be "**An A**malgamation church," in which colored and white people were to be compelled to sit **together,** promiscuously **mingled together all** over the house. Such was the state of the public mind in New York at that time that this report created a great **deal of** excitement, and somebody set the building on fire. The firemen were in such a state of mind that they refused to put it out, and left the interior and roof to be consumed. However the gentlemen who had undertaken to build it went forward and completed it.[61]

MS 660

JHF 328

As the excitement increased on the subject of slavery **and anti-slavery, Brother** Leavitt espoused the cause of the slave, and advocated it in the **N.Y.** Evangelist.[62] I watched the discussion with a good deal of attention and anxiety. ˡ**But about this time my health so failed that I was obliged, as I have already intimated, to take a voyage to sea.**[63]**When I went away** I admonished **Brother** Leavitt to be careful and not go too fast in the discussion of the **A**nti-slavery question, lest he should destroy his paper.[64] **I returned in**

MS 661

[60]There was difficulty in getting the paper established. Nine months after the start, the circulation was about three thousand, but the managers were in financial difficulties, needing another two thousand subscribers to make the paper viable (see Z. Platt to Finney, 18 January 1831, Finney Papers, microfilm, roll 3). Under Joshua Leavitt's editorship the paper became successful. After he left at the end of July 1837, Rev. Nathaniel E. Johnson, pastor of the Third Free Presbyterian Church in New York, took over as editor. The paper then became the organ of New School Presbyterianism and less the voice of independency and aggressive revivals.

[61]In speaking here of the building of the Broadway Tabernacle, which was completed in April 1836, Finney has jumped ahead in time. It had not begun to be built until the year after the events he is about to describe took place.

[62]Finney wrote: "Dr. Leavitt was early and thoroughly converted to the doctrines of the Abolitionists. He confessed that this conversion produced almost as radical a change in him as his first conversion to Christ" (*The Independent,* 6 February 1873, p. 162; see also 3 July 1873, p. 847). John Humphrey Noyes, who knew Leavitt from the days when they both lived in Putney, Vermont, reckoned: "He was, by his first love and by the labors of his most effectual manhood, preeminently a Revival man." He was drawn away from his "true life-labor" to the antislavery cause—"a local and inferior reform"—by William Lloyd Garrison. Noyes saw this as a tragedy ("Doubtful Success," *Oneida Circular*, 3 March 1873, p. 76).

Oliver Johnson, the Garrison abolitionist, editor, and historian of the antislavery movement, wrote:

> One powerful ally of our cause at this time was "The New York Evangelist," then edited by the Rev. Joshua Leavitt. It had a considerable circulation, and exerted a wide influence among the "New School" Presbyterians, who were active in the revivals that occurred in connection with the labors of the Rev. Charles G. Finney. It advocated the cause with zeal and earnestness, and many clergymen and laymen were led by it to declare themselves Abolitionists. When Mr. Leavitt withdrew from "The Evangelist" to become editor of "The Emancipator," the anti-slavery tone of the former became quite feeble, in compliance, no doubt, with the well-understood desire of the larger number of its readers (O. Johnson, *William Lloyd Garrison and His Times; or, Sketches of the Anti-Slavery Movement in America* [Boston: Houghton Mifflin, 1881], pp. 156–57).

[63]See MS 655.

[64]Finney also recalled, "Before I left, we consulted upon that subject; and he resolved to keep within bounds, and not bring on a reaction, to the ruin of his paper" (*The Independent,* 6 February 1873, p. 162).

about six months with my health but very little improved. On my homeward **bound** passage my mind became exceedingly exercised on the question of revivals. I feared that they would decline throughout the country. I feared that the opposition that had been made to them had grieved the Holy Spirit. My own health, it appeared to me, had nearly or quite broken down; and I knew of no other Evangelist that would take the field, and aid pastors in revival work. This view of the subject distressed **my mind** so much that one day I found myself unable to rest. My soul was in an utter agony. I spent almost the entire day in prayer[65] in my state room; or walking the deck in **such** ‹agony› **as to wring my hands, and almost to gnaw my tongue, as it**
MS 662 **were, ‹with› pain**[66] |in view of the state of things. In fact I felt *crushed* with the burden that was on my soul. There was no one on board to whom I could open my mind or say a word.

It was the Spirit of prayer that was upon me; that which I had often before
JHF 329 experienced in *kind*, but perhaps |never before to such a degree for so long a time. I besought the Lord to go on with **H**is work, and to provide **H**imself with such instrumentalities as were necessary. It was a long summer day in the early part of July. After a day of unspeakable wrestling and agony in my soul, just at night the subject cleared up to my mind. The Spirit led me to believe that all would come out right, and that God had yet a work for *me* to do. That I might be at rest **on the subject**; that the Lord would go forward with **H**is work, and give me strength to take any part in it that **H**e desired. But I had not the least idea **of** what the course of providence would be. On **my** arriving at New York I found, as I have said, the mob excitement on the subject of
MS 663 slavery very intense. |I **spent** but a day or two in New York, and went into the country to the place where my family were spending the Summer.[67] On my return to New York in the fall[68] **Brother** Leavitt came to me and said: "Brother Finney, I have ruined the Evangelist. I have not been as prudent as you cautioned me to be, and I have gone so far ahead of public intelligence and feeling on the subject, that my subscription list is rapidly failing;[69] and we shall not be able to continue its publication beyond the first of January, unless *you* can do something to bring the paper back to public favor again. I told him my health was such I did not know what I could do; but I would make it a subject of prayer. He said if I could write a series of articles on revivals, he had no doubt it would restore the paper immediately to public favor. After considering it a day or two, I proposed **to him** to preach a course of lectures

[65]Here Finney crossed out the words "there on my knees."

[66]The last part of this sentence had originally been written, "or walking the deck in such pain as to wring my hands, and almost to gnaw my tongue, as it were, for pain and agony," but Finney changed it.

[67]Mrs. Finney and the children had left New York at the beginning of June and had gone to her brother's home at York Mills. She then visited her relatives in Adams. But after Finney returned, they moved to a farm belonging to a Mr. Dann in Western (see letters to Lydia Finney at this period in the Finney Papers). Finney was still unwell and had serious thoughts of giving up preaching for a time and buying the farm. See Finney to Lydia Finney, 10 November 1834, Finney Papers, microfilm, roll 3.

[68]Finney returned to New York about the beginning of November 1834.

[69]In his article on Leavitt, Finney said that Leavitt "came to me, and said that he had over-estimated the amount of pressure that the public would bear on the subject of abolition" (*The Independent,* 6 February 1873, p. 162).

to my people on revivals of religion, **and that** he might report **them** for his paper. He caught at this at once. Says he, "That is the very thing!" and in the ˡnext number of his paper he advertised the course of lectures.[70] This had the effect he desired, and he soon after told me that the Subscription list was very rapidly increasing; and stretching out his long arms he said, "I have as many new subscribers every day as would fill my arms with ˡpapers to supply them each a single number." He had told me before that his subscription list had fallen off at the rate, **he found,** of sixty **per** day. But now he said it was increasing more rapidly than it ever had decreased.[71]

MS 664

JHF 330

I began the course of lectures immediately and continued them through the winter preaching one each week.[72] **Brother** Leavitt could not write short-hand, but would sit and take notes, abridging what he wrote in such a way that he **would** understand it himself; and then the next day he would sit down and fill out his notes and send them to the press. I did not see what he had reported until I saw it published in his paper. I did not myself write the lectures, of course; they were wholly extemporaneous.[73] I did not make up my mind, from time to time ˡwhat the next lecture should be until I saw his report of my last. **When I saw his report** I could see what was the next question that would naturally need discussion. Brother Leavitt's reports were meag**er** as it respects the matter contained in the lectures. They averaged, if I remember right, not less than an hour and three quarters in their delivery. But all that he could catch and report, could be read, probably, in thirty minutes.[74]

MS 665

[70]The lectures were not advertised until the day after the first had been given. An advertisement appeared at the same time as the report of the first lecture in *The New-York Evangelist* for 6 December 1834, p. 194. They were advertised the same day in *The New York Observer*, 6 December 1834, p. 195.

[71]Leavitt reported that 2,500 people subscribed for the paper when the lectures were in progress. The demand was so great that several thousand extra back numbers had to be printed to supply to new readers. See *NYE,* 14 February 1835, p. 26; and 9 May 1835, p. 74; 2 January 1836, p. 3; and 9 January 1836, p. 7. The papers were also hung up daily outside the *Evangelist* office on a bulletin board. Edmund Watts, who was a lad at the time, recollected that being small, he could never read them because of the crowds, "so intense was the anxiety of the people to know the way of salvation." So he saved enough to subscribe for the paper for six months. See P. C. Headley, *Evangelists in the Church* (Boston: Hoyt, 1875), p. 149; and *NYE,* 2 September 1875, p. 2; and 2 June 1881, p. 4.

[72]The first lecture was given on Friday, 5 December 1834. They were published weekly in *The New-York Evangelist* from 6 December 1834 through 2 May 1835. See Ward, *History of the Broadway Tabernacle,* p. 27.

[73]Leavitt explained the situation of the lectures to his readers:

> They are seen by no person but the editor and the printers, until they come out in the paper. It is but justice to the preacher to state this, for it is to be presumed that some statements and positions are often presented either in a less guarded or less impressive position in our brief sketches, which in the sermon itself would be entirely unobjectionable. We have Mr. Finney's consent to our publication of these notes, *as our notes*. Our readers will therefore make all allowances for their being notes, *unrevised*, such as we can take without stenography, and written out by the aid of memory (*NYE,* 24 January 1835, p. 14).

[74]According to Matthew Hale Smith,

> Dr. Leavitt commenced the system of reporting sermons as they were delivered from the pulpit. The celebrated lectures of Mr. Finney, in Chatham Theatre, reported by Dr. Leavitt, attracted so much attention that professional reporters were brought from

Charles Finney, 1834. An oil painting by Frederick R. Spencer in the Oberlin College Library. Photograph by Anne Pearson.

These lectures were afterwards published in a book, and called "Finney's Lectures on Revivals."[75] Twelve thousand copies of them were sold as fast as they could be printed.[76] And here for the glory of Christ I would say, that

> Washington to do the same thing for other papers (M. H. Smith, *Sunshine and Shadow in New York* [Hartford, Conn.: Burr, 1868], p. 650).

In reminiscing about Leavitt after his death, Finney wrote:

> With what ability and pungency he reported those lectures is well-known. . . . And to this day I cannot read them over without feeling the fire and unction with which they were written. Dear, blessed Brother Leavitt! I can almost say that I loved him as my own soul. Even now I cannot think of him as I then knew him without tears (*The Independent,* 6 February 1873, p. 102).

[75]The *Lectures on Revivals of Religion* were issued jointly by Finney and Joshua Leavitt and published in New York by Leavitt, Lord and Co. on 15 May 1835. See agreement between Finney, Leavitt, and the publisher, 19 March 1835, Finney Papers, microfilm, roll 3; and *NYE,* 16 May 1835, p. 80.

[76]The first twelve thousand copies were printed in six editions of two thousand each. The financial crash of 1837 put an end to further editions in America, and "the stereo type plates were lost sight of" until 1847. A new edition was brought out by C. H. Peirce of Boston in 1848.

they have been reprinted in England and France;[77] they were translated into Welch,[78] and on the Continent were translated into French[79] and I believe German,[80] and were very extensively circulated throughout Europe and the colonies of Great Britain.[81] They **are**,[82] I presume, to be found wherever the

Beginning in 1838, however, many editions were published in Britain. See *NYE,* 30 December 1847, p. 206.

[77]The seventh edition was published in January 1838 by Thomas Tegg and Son of London as *Lectures on Revivals of Religion.* This was probably the first to be published in England. It sold two thousand copies in six months. Further editions followed rapidly. The thirteenth edition was brought out in May of 1840.

An edition with an introduction was said to have been brought out, about 1838, by the Reverend Robert Aitken, the Methodist turned High Church Anglican revivalist, "vindicating and enforcing Mr. Finney's plan of conducting the work of God" (Edwin F. Hatfield, *St. Helena and the Cape of Good Hopes* [New York: Fletcher, 1852], pp. 30–31; and see "A Tractarian Revivalist," *NYE,* 21 December 1854, p. 202; and p. 487 n. 40 [MS 825]).

[78]They were translated into Welsh from the seventh English edition by Rev. Evan Griffiths of Swansea. *Darlithiau ar Adfywiadau Crefyddol,* gan y Parch. Charles G. Finney (Abertawy: E. Griffiths, 1839). Finney followed up the publication of his *Lectures on Revivals* with *Sermons on Important Subjects* (New York: Taylor, 1836). This book, published by Thomas Tegg in London in 1839, was also translated into Welsh by Evan Griffiths and published in 1841. See Thomas Rees, *Miscellaneous Papers on Subjects Relating to Wales* (London: Snow, 1867), pp. 50–51.

[79]They were translated into French from the ninth English edition by Ami Bost, *Discours de Finney sur les reveils religieux* (Paris: Delay, 1844). See Alexandre Vinet, *Lettres de Alexandre Vinet et de quelques-uns de ses correspondents,* vol. 2 (Lausanne: Bridel, 1882), pp. 207, 298–99.

[80]There is no known translation into German at this time. The earliest appears to have been an edition referred to by Paulus Scharpff: "Professor Theodor Christlieb's (Bonn) German edition of 1879 was of great help in stimulating church fellowship and co-operation in Germany" (P. Scharpff, *History of Evangelism,* trans. Helga Bender Henry [Grand Rapids: Eerdmans, 1966], pp. 109–10). There was a translation from Finney's lectures by F. Hahn, *Charles G. Finney, über geistliche Erweckungen. Aus seinen Reden, nebst einem kurzen Abriss seines Lebens* (Basel: Spittler, 1885), and the complete lectures were translated by E. von Feilitzsch and published in Dusseldorf by C. Schaffnit in 1903.

[81]The ninth edition of the *Lectures on Revivals of Religion*, published by Thomas Tegg in 1839 in London, was published in association with R. Griffin and Co., Glasgow; Tegg and Co., Dublin; and J. and S. A. Tegg, Sydney and Hobart in Australia. The widespread distribution of Finney's works at that time is also reflected in the experience of David Livingstone, the missionary explorer. On the way out to Africa in December 1840, the boat went via Brazil. Livingstone wrote to George Drummond, a missionary in Tahiti:

> Have you seen Finney's work on Revivals of Religion? If you have it please to read it. . . . I was so well pleased with Finney, that when in Rio, I purchased another of his works & gave 12/– for what I should have got in London for 4/– (David Chamberlain, *Some Letters from Livingstone, 1840–1872* [London: Oxford University Press, 1940], p. 20).

The calendar of the Finney Papers describes the contents of a letter, now missing, received by Finney from "P. Boucher," dated Brussels, Belgium, 3 August 1839: "Desire to translate some of Finney's lectures into French to be distributed gratis to evangelists in France, Belgium and Switzerland. Asks Finney to secure the money for this in America." This was Philippe Boucher, a friend of Rev. E. N. Kirk. He was a pastor of the French Reformed Church and chaplain to the king of the Netherlands, and he had recently been in America trying to collect funds to erect a church in Belgium. Whether anything came of this scheme is not known. See *NYE,* 1 August 1837, p. 53.

When Professor Edwards A. Park of Andover Theological Seminary visited Berlin in 1843, he found that his friend Frederick Godet, the great Swiss theologian, had a copy of Finney's *Lectures on Revivals* in his library. Godet was at that time tutor to Prince Frederick (later Emperor Frederick III of Germany). Godet apparently told Park, "This book has had more influence over my life than any other" (John H. Barrows, "Oberlin College—a Christian Opportunity," *Education* [Boston] 19 [June 1899]: 588; and G. F. Wright, *Charles Grandison Finney* [Boston and New York: Houghton Mifflin, 1891], pp. 311–12).

[82]The word "are" was not altered in the manuscript, but the published version has "were."

English language is spoken, **or wherever the French language is spoken.** After they had been printed in Welch, the Congregational ministers of the MS 666 principality of Wales at one of their public meet|‹ings[83] appointed a committee to inform me of the great revival that had resulted from the translation of those lectures into the Welch language. This they did by JHF 331 letter›.[84] One publisher in London informed |me that his father had published eighty thousand volumes of them.[85] **They are stereotyped in England, and I believe on the continent. I do not know into how many languages they have been translated. But I mention this particularly as being an answer to prayer.** These revival lectures, meag**er** as was the report of them, and feeble as they were in themselves, have been instrumental, as I have learned, in promoting revivals **of religion** in England, and Scotland, and Wales, on the Continent in various places, in Canada **east** and **west**, in Nova Scotia, in some of the islands of the sea,[86]**—and in fact throughout the British colonies and dependencies. When I have been** in England and Scotland, I have often been refreshed by meeting with ministers and laymen in great numbers that MS 667 had been converted, directly |or indirectly, through the instrumentality of those **revival** lectures. I recollect the last time that I was **there** one evening

[83]The section from the top of the page 666 to n. 84 is in Finney's handwriting on a separate piece of paper pasted onto the sheet. This covered up a section which read, "ings appointed a committee to draft a communication to me, in which they very kindly testify of the great revival of religion that had resulted." The text continued below the pasted strip: "from publishing those lectures in Welch." This was crossed out by Finney.

[84]This ends the section in Finney's handwriting. The letter, signed by ten ministers from North Wales, dated 27 February 1840, is in the Finney Papers. When Rev. John Campbell was compiling his *Valedictory Services and Farewell Sermon of Professor Finney* (London: Snow, 1851), he considered this letter and another written to Finney from ministers in South Wales important enough historically to include in an appendix. There were "many thousands" converted in that revival (see Thomas Rees, *History of Protestant Nonconformity in Wales*, 2d ed. [London: Snow, 1883], pp. 429–30). The *Valedictory Services* are published in the appendix in this volume (see pp. 639–70).

[85]Finney elsewhere wrote, "One house in London published 80,000 copies in English." He is probably referring to Thomas Tegg (1776–1845) and his son William (1816–1895), the London publishers (see Finney, *Lectures on Revivals of Religion* [Oberlin: Goodrich, 1868], p. v; and *DAB*). The first editions of the *Lectures* to appear in England were the seventh, eighth, and ninth, in 1838 and 1839, which were published by Thomas Tegg. His son was the publisher of Finney's *Systematic Theology* in 1851. Henry Ward Beecher, in a letter written in 1850 after his return from England, where he had seen Finney, wrote of the circulation of the *Lectures on Revivals* as being very great, "one publisher, Mr. Johnson of Manchester, having issued 80,000" (*The Independent*, 21 November 1850, p. 190).

Thomas Johnson started book selling and publishing in Liverpool in 1829 and was the printer and publisher for Thomas Tegg of the early English editions of the *Lectures on Revivals of Religion* and also of the *Lectures to Professing Christians*. He later went to Manchester, where he joined the publishing business of his father, Samuel Johnson; the twelfth edition of the *Lectures on Revivals of Religion* was published there in 1846. He was said to have published 150,000 copies of these books, his most successful printing venture. On his retirement his son, W. T. Johnson, continued the business in Manchester. See Henry Curwen, *A History of Booksellers, the Old and the New* (London: Chatto and Windus, 1873), pp. 454–56. Information from the archivist, Liverpool Record Office.

[86]Finney's *Lectures on Revivals of Religion* was being read and used as sermons by missionaries in the Sandwich Islands (Hawaii) as early as 1836 during the period leading up to the great revival there in 1838–1839. (See Margaret S. Ehlke, "Enthusiastic Religion and the Lives of Titus and Fidelia Coan, Missionaries to Hilo" [M.A. thesis, University of Hawaii, 1986], pp. 88, 125–26.) Finney had thought of going to the Sandwich Islands himself as a missionary in 1836 (see G. P. Judd to Finney, 28 April 1837, Finney Papers, microfilm, roll 3).

three very prominent ministers of the Gospel introduced themselves to me after the sermon, and said that when they were in college they got hold of my revival lectures, which had resulted in their becoming ministers. I found persons in England in all the different denominations, who had not only read those revival lectures, but had been greatly *blessed* in reading them.[87] When they were first published in the New York Evangelist the reading of them resulted in revivals of religion in multitudes of places throughout this country.[88] **‹This looks egotistical. But›**[89] **let the reader remember my agony at sea, the** long day of **travail of soul that I spent in** praying that God would do something to forward the work of revival, and enable me, if **He** desired to do it, to take such a course as to help forward the work. I felt certain then that my prayers would be answered; and I have regarded all the **revival work** that I have since been able to accomplish, **and all the results of preaching and publishing those lectures, as well** |**as all else that I have been in any wise instrumental in accomplishing for the Zion of God,** as in a very important sense an answer to the prayers of that day. **It has always been my experience, when I have a day or season of great travail of soul for any object, if I *pursue* the subject, and continue my pleadings until I prevail and my soul is at rest,—that in answer to such prayers God not only gives me what I ask, but exceedingly above all that I at the time had in my mind. God has been answering the prayers of that day on shipboard, for more than thirty years.**[90]

MS 668

Nobody but myself can appreciate the wonderful manner in which those agonizing throes of my soul on that occasion have met with the divine response. Indeed it was God the Holy Ghost making intercession in me. The prayer was not properly mine, but the prayer of the Holy

[87] *Lectures on Revivals* was circulated much more extensively in England and Scotland than in America. Rev. John Campbell, the leading Congregational editor in London, writing shortly before Harriet Beecher Stowe's all-time best seller, *Uncle Tom's Cabin*, swept the country, reckoned that Finney's *Lectures on Revivals* "have had a more extensive circulation than any other American publication on this side of the Atlantic" (*The Christian Witness* [London] 9 [March 1852]: 129; and see *The Independent,* 20 March 1851, p. 47).

Alexander Strachan, a Methodist writing in 1848, was critical of the *Lectures* but acknowledged their popularity:

> His work has been published in all the intermediate sizes, between the 8vo. and the 24 mo.: and at almost all the intermediate prices, between ten shillings and ten pence. It has been spread over the whole kingdom, and read with avidity by all denominations of Christians: but none, perhaps, have bestowed upon it a more extensive patronage than the Wesleyans. The book has become so great a favourite with many, that to speak disapprovingly of either the author or his work, is to run some risk of being put down as an enemy to the progress of Christ's kingdom (A. Strachan, *Recollections of the Life and Times of the Late Rev. George Lowe* [London: Mason, 1848], pp. 248–49).

[88] *The New-York Evangelist* noted at the time a number of cases of individuals being blessed by the reading of *Lectures on Revivals*, and of revivals occurring. See 28 March 1835, p. 51; 25 April 1835, p. 65; 27 June 1835, p. 104; 28 November 1835, p. 273; see also 6 October 1881, p. 2; *Baltimore Literary and Religious Magazine* 4 (May 1838): 236; and Aaron Williams to Absolom Peters, 1 April 1835, in William W. Sweet, *Religion on the American Frontier*, vol. 3, *The Congregationalists* (Chicago: University of Chicago Press, 1939), pp. 21–22.

[89] Finney inserted a paragraph sign *P* at the beginning of the sentence but later crossed it out as well as the word "Now" that started the sentence. He added the words "This looks egotistical. But."

[90] After the word "thirty" Finney inserted "five" but crossed it out again.

Spirit. It was for no righteousness or worthiness of my own at all. The **Spirit** of prayer came upon me as a sovereign grace, bestowed upon me without the least merit, and in despite of all my sinfulness. He pressed my

MS 669 ˡsoul in prayer until I was enabled to prevail; and through infinite riches of grace in Christ Jesus I have been many years witnessing the wonderful results of that day of wrestling with God. ‹In answer to that day's agony **He** [**h**]as continued to give me the Spirit of prayer.›[91]

JHF 332 ˡ‹Soon after›[92] I returned to New York I commenced my labors[93] in the Tabernacle.[94] The Spirit of the Lord was poured out upon us, and we had a **continuous** precious revival as long as I continued to be pastor of that church. While in New York I had many applications from young men to take them as students, **and give them some of my views** in theology. I however had too much on my hands to undertake such a work. **However, in doing off the Tabernacle** the brethren who built **it** had this in view; and prepared a room under the **orchestra**, which we expected to use for prayer-meetings, but more especially for a theological lecture room. The number of applications had been so large that I had made up my mind to deliver a course

MS 670 of theological lectures in that room each year, and let ˡsuch students as chose attend them gratuitously. But about this time, and before I had opened my lectures in New York, the breaking up **occurred** at Lane Seminary, **the particulars of which are too well known to need to be narrated here.**[95] When this occurred **Brother** Arthur Tappan proposed to me **that I should come West somewhere long enough to get those young men that had left Lane Seminary into the ministry. He made the proposition** that if I would **come West and** take rooms where I could **instruct them**, and **would** give them my views in theology and prepare them for the work of preaching throughout the West, he would **foot the bills and** be at the entire expense of the undertaking. He was very earnest in this **request.**[96] But I did not know how to leave New York; and **furthermore** I did not see how I could

[91]This sentence was added by Finney. The word "has" is written "cas."

[92]Matson had written down the word "When" here, but Finney changed it to "Soon after."

[93]Finney crossed out the words "soon afterwards" here.

[94]This was after his first summer in Oberlin in 1835. He arrived in New York the second week of December. Finney was released from Chatham Street Chapel on 2 March 1836 and installed in the Broadway Tabernacle on 10 April 1836. See *NYE,* 19 December 1835, p. 204; and Samuel D. Alexander, *The Presbytery of New York, 1738 to 1888* (New York: Randolph, 1887), p. 107.

[95]With the spread of antislavery feeling in the North, the subject came up for discussion among the students at Lane Seminary, the Presbyterian theological school in Cincinnati, Ohio, on the border of the slave states. In a series of intense debates under the leadership of Theodore Weld in February 1834, the majority of the students were converted to "immediate abolitionism" and set to work to achieve it. The stir created in the neighborhood alarmed the trustees, who without consulting the faculty or the president, Dr. Lyman Beecher, forbade the subject to be discussed further; whereupon, in the fall, about 75 of the 103 students in the seminary left. Most of these had returned home or gone to other schools, but in November 1834 "about a dozen" had come together in a house in Cumminsville, a few miles from Cincinnati, and with the help of money from Arthur Tappan, were continuing their studies. See Lesick, *Lane Rebels.*

It was the section of the manuscript from here to MS 681 that Lewis Tappan used in the biography of his brother, *Life of Arthur Tappan,* pp. 238–40. See Introduction, p. xxxiv.

[96]In another account Finney said, "Mr. Lewis Tappan, Mr. William Green, Rev. Joshua Leavitt, a Mr. Higgins, and a few others, agreed with Mr. Tappan and joined in urging me to come West" (*The Oberlin Weekly News,* 20 August 1874, p. 4).

accomplish the wishes of Mr. Tappan, although I strongly sympathized with him in regard to helping those young men. **Most, and perhaps nearly all of them,** were converts in those great revivals in which I had taken more or less part.[97] |While this subject was under consideration, ‹Rev.›[98] J. J. Shipherd, and **the** Rev. Asa Mahan **from** Cincinnati, arrived in New York to persuade me to **come** to Oberlin as professor of theology.[99] **Brother** Mahan had been one of the trustees of **the theological** seminary **that had exploded near Cincinnati.**[100] |**Brother** Shipherd had **formed**[101] a colony, **some of whom were on the ground, in** Oberlin; and had obtained a charter **wide** enough for a University, **but at that time its corporate name was, "The Oberlin Collegiate Institute."**[102] **Brother** Mahan had never been in Oberlin. The trees had been removed from the **public** square, some **log** houses had been **built; and they had had the previous season a few scholars here, and had opened the** preparatory or academic department of the institution.[103]

MS 671

JHF 333

The proposal they laid before me, was to come on and take those students that had left Lane Seminary, and teach them theology. They had themselves proposed to **come here** in case I would **come.**[104] This proposal met the views of **Brothers** Arthur and Lewis Tappan, and many of the friends |of[105] the slave who sympathized with Mr. Tappan in his wish to have those young men instructed and **got** into the ministry **as soon as possible.** We had several consultations on the subject. The brethren in New York who were interested in the question offered if I would **come** and spend half of each year in

MS 672 [1]

[97] Prominent among the students who were converted through Finney's revivals were Charles P. Bush, Marius R. Robinson, Henry B. and Robert L. Stanton, and T. D. Weld. See Lesick, *Lane Rebels,* p. 72.

[98] Matson had written "Brother" here, but Finney changed it to "Rev."

[99] Asa Mahan (1799–1889), holiness teacher and college president, was at this time minister of the Sixth Presbyterian Church in Cincinnati. He was president of Oberlin College from 1835 to 1850. See Asa Mahan, *Autobiography, Intellectual, Moral, and Spiritual* (London: Woolmer, 1882); Edward H. Madden and James E. Hamilton, *Freedom and Grace: The Life of Asa Mahan* (Metuchen, N.J.: Scarecrow, 1982); and *DAB*..

Shipherd and Mahan arrived in New York early in January 1835. See Barnes and Dumond, eds., *Letters of Theodore Dwight Weld,* p. 197. Finney said, "This was the first I had ever heard of Oberlin" (*The Oberlin Weekly News*, 20 August 1874, p. 4). Reports of the college had appeared in the papers, but Finney had been away for much of 1834, and if he had seen them, they would probably have meant nothing to him.

[100] Fairchild had written here "—the only one I think that had resisted the prohibition of free discussion."

[101] The word "formed" was not altered in the manuscript, but it appears as "founded" in the published edition.

[102] The charter, granted by the Ohio legislature on 28 February 1834 is printed in the *General Catalogue of Oberlin College, 1833–1908* (Oberlin: Oberlin College, 1909), pp. 13–14. See Robert S. Fletcher, *The History of Oberlin College from Its Foundation Through the Civil War* (Oberlin: Oberlin College, 1943), p. 124. The name was changed to Oberlin College in 1850.

[103] The colony was in a more developed state than Finney indicates. Fairchild, who was one of the students at the time that Finney arrived in Oberlin, altered the manuscript here to read, "The trees had been removed from the College square, some dwelling houses and one College building had been erected & about a hundred pupils had been gathered in the preparatory or academic department of the institution."

[104] See the letter from H. B. Stanton and G. Whipple to Finney, 10 January 1835, Finney Papers, microfilm, roll 3.

[105] MS 672 [1] was originally numbered 519 and renumbered 651 by Matson. Finney changed it to 672 and also numbered the next page 672 in error.

Oberlin, to endow the institution so far as the professorships were concerned, and to do it immediately. I had understood that the trustees of Lane Seminary had acted "over the heads" of the faculty, and in the absence of several of them had passed the obnoxious resolution that had caused the students to leave.[106] I said therefore to **Brother** Shipherd, **as he was the agent with whom I had to do,** that I would not go at any rate unless two **propositions** were conceded **to** by the trustees. One was that the **trustees** should never interfere with the internal regulations of the school, but should leave that entirely to the discretion of the faculty. The other was, that we should be allowed to receive colored people on the same conditions that we ¦did[107] white people, that there should be no discrimination made on account of color; **and that this question should be left also entirely to the faculty.** When these conditions were forwarded to Oberlin the trustees were called together, and **they had** a great struggle to overcome their own prejudices and the prejudices of the ¦community, **and** pass resolutions complying with the conditions **upon which I would come.**[108] This difficulty being removed, the

MS 672 [2]

JHF 334

[106]Among the resolutions passed by the trustees on 6 October 1834 was a standing rule forbidding students from holding meetings, giving addresses, or being absent from the seminary without faculty permission; an order to disband the antislavery society that had been formed by the students; and another order giving the executive committee of the trustees the "power to dismiss any student from the Seminary, when they shall think it necessary so to do; & to make any rules & regulations . . . which they may deem expedient." These enabled the trustees to interfere with the internal management of the seminary in the absence of the president and others on the faculty. The students, many of them mature men, considered such "gag laws" and threatened expulsions to be manifestations of the spirit of slavery, which they were not prepared to tolerate (Lesick, *Lane Rebels,* p. 126).

[107]MS 672 [2] was originally numbered 520 and 652 by Matson. Finney incorrectly renumbered it 672 instead of 673, so Fairchild added "½" after 672.

[108]Shipherd sent details of Finney's conditions to the trustees of Oberlin College in a letter dated 19 January 1835, and on 9 and 10 February the trustees met to consider them. There was strong feeling in the community and among the students against any resolution that would admit blacks to the institute. At a previous trustees' meeting on 1 January such a proposal had been turned down. Unless they changed their minds, Shipherd threatened to resign (Oberlin College Board of Trustees Minutes, 1 January 1835, Oberlin College Archives, microfilm; Fletcher, *History of Oberlin College,* pp. 170–78; and p. 396 n. 66).

The meeting, with nine trustees present, was held at Shipherd's house in Oberlin amid intense excitement. The significant proposal was:

> That the question in respect to the admission of Students into this Seminary be in all cases left to the decision of the Faculty & to them be committed also the internal management of its concerns, provided always that they be holden amenable to the Board & not liable to censure, or interruption from the Board so long as their measures shall not infringe upon the laws or general principles of the Institution (Oberlin College Board of Trustrees Minutes, 9 February 1835, Oberlin College Archives, microfilm).

The situation hung in the balance, with the trustees about equally divided over the motion. Mrs. Shipherd recollected:

> My room was adjoining, and all their deliberations were easily heard. As there was a difference of opinion expressed with some warmth, a couple of our sisters retired for prayer, while I remained to give the progress of the discussion. They would call occasionally to inquire, and I kept them posted, until at length, Father Keep, who had just been elected president of the board, threw in the casting vote, and came to my room, to relieve our minds (Mrs. E. R. Shipherd to W. W. Patton, 1 September 1875, in William W. Patton, *Prayer and Its Remarkable Answers* [Chicago: Goodman, 1876], pp. 176–77).

According to Richard M. Luker, the resolution that was passed was a radical departure from the normal trustee control of colleges at that period. It created a new form of governance that

friends in New York were called together to see what they could do about endowing the institution. In the course of an hour or two they had a subscription filled **that endowed** eight professorships; **which** was supposed **to be all that** the institution would need for several years, ‹**for Professors**›.[109]

But these subscriptions were in such a form that when the great commercial crash came in 1837, the men failed, nearly every one of them, who had subscribed, and thus our endowment fund fell to the ground. But after this endowment fund was subscribed, I felt a great difficulty **in my mind** in giving up that admirable place for preaching the Gospel, **which was always** ˡ**crowded**[110] **when I preached to its utmost capacity. But** I felt assured that in this enterprize we should have great opposition from many sources. I therefore told **Brother** Arthur Tappan that my mind did not feel at rest upon the subject. That we should meet with great opposition because of our anti-slavery principles, **throughout the land;** and that we could expect to get but very scanty funds to put up our buildings, **to provide ourselves with apparatus** and to procure all the **parepharnalia** of a college. **We wanted a library, apparatus, etc., and we had nothing. That we were what were called New School in theology; that we were revivalists, and believed in pushing revival measures wherever we could.** That therefore I did not see my way clear, after all, to commit myself; unless something could be done that should guarantee us the funds that were indispensable.

MS 673

enabled Oberlin College to pioneer coeducation and equal educational opportunities for blacks. It has come to be known as the "Finney Compact" and remains the basis of governmental policy at Oberlin College. See Richard M. Luker, "The Western Reserve and a Legacy for Higher Education: Faculty Self-Governance at Oberlin College Under the Finney Compact, 1834–1846" (Ed.D. diss., University of Akron, 1985). At the same meeting in which the resolution was passed, Finney was appointed professor of theology.

[109]Matson had written the words "at least in that direction," but Finney crossed them out and inserted "for Professors." They formed a Professorship Association "engaging to pay quarterly the interest on eighty thousand dollars, sufficient for the salaries of eight professors, at six hundred dollars each." It was intended finally to pay the principal and thus secure the permanent endowment of the institution (J. H. Fairchild, *Oberlin: The Colony and the College* [Oberlin: Goodrich, 1883], p. 65).

The contributors were mostly wealthy New York merchants and businessmen: Arthur and Lewis Tappan and another partner in their firm, William E. Whiting; William Green, Jr.; Isaac M. Dimond, the jeweler; Israel W. Clark and Seth B. Hunt, partners in the dry-goods business; Thomas S. Williams, another merchant; John Lovejoy, a dentist; Claiborne W. Cain, a watchmaker; Edward Prime, a broker in the firm of Prime, Ward, and King; J. W. Higgins; George M. Tracy; C. Morris; Dr. Lewis Hallock; John H. Browning; and Cornelius Baker. Lewis Tappan was the president until the middle of August 1835, when he handed the presidency over to William Green, Jr. The secretary was I. W. Clark, and for the first two years the treasurer was Rufus Leavitt of the firm of J. W. and R. Leavitt and Co., merchants. Leavitt then turned his responsibilities over to Alfred Smith, who worked for the Fulton Bank and was later to be an agent for Finney's property in New York. See Letters of Rufus Leavitt and Alfred Smith, 1835–1837 in Letters Received by Oberlin College, 1822–1866, microfilm, rolls 2–4; Reports of the Professorship Association in Treasurer's Office, "Miscellaneous Archives," file 7/1/3, dated 9 October 1835, in box 2, and 21 April 1836, in box 3, Oberlin College Archives; Lewis Tappan to J. J. Shipherd, 19 August 1835, copy in Tappan Papers, microfilm, roll 6; and *Longworth's New York Directory* (New York), 1835–1838.

[110]Pages 673–76 were originally numbered 521–24 and renumbered 653–56 by Matson and then changed to 673–76 by Finney.

Brother Arthur Tappan's heart was as large as all New York, and I might say, as large as the world. **He was a small man in stature, but he had a** MS 674 **mighty heart.** When I laid the case thus be|fore him he said: "Brother Finney, my income**, I will tell *you* on this occasion,** averages about a hundred thousand dollars a year. Now if you will go to Oberlin, take hold of that work, and go on and see that the buildings are put up, and a library and everything provided,"—**said he,** "I will pledge **to give** you my entire income, except what I need to provide for my family, till you are beyond pecuniary want." Having perfect confidence in **B**rother Tappan I said, "That will do. Thus far the difficulties are out of the way." But still there was a great difficulty in **my** leaving my church in New York. I had never thought of having my labors at Oberlin interfere with my revival labors and preaching. It JHF 335 was therefore agreed between myself and **my** church that I |should spend my winters **there**, and my summers **here** at Oberlin. That they would be at the expense of my going and coming; **and that I would come out here in April, and return there in November ‹of each year.›**[111]

When this was arranged ‹I took my family & arived in Oberlin **in May**.›[112]

[111]Finney added the words "of each year." At the trustees' meeting of 10 February 1835, when Finney was appointed professor of theology, it was also resolved that "he have liberty to be absent 4 or 5 months of each year" (Oberlin College Board of Trustees Minutes, 10 February 1835, Oberlin College Archives, microfilm). At Oberlin the long vacation was in the winter to allow students to get work teaching in schools. This arrangement continued until 1877.

[112]Finney added the words "I took my family & arrived in Oberlin in May" after he had inserted a new chapter heading at the top of the next page. Finney left New York on Tuesday, 5 May, and arrived in Oberlin about 17 May 1835. See Arthur Tappan to J. J. Shipherd, 6 May 1835, copy in Tappan Papers, microfilm, roll 6; and J. J. Shipherd to Fayette Shipherd, 17 May 1835, in Bragdon Family Papers, University of Rochester Library.

CHAPTER XXIV

MS 675
JHF 336

‹*Early Labors in Oberlin.*›

The[1] students from Lane Seminary came **here,**[2] and the trustees put up barracks, **or shanties,** in which they were lodged.[3] **When it was known that this college was opened, the** students thronged to us from every direction.[4] After I was engaged to come **here**, the brethren **here** wrote requesting me to bring a large tent to hold meetings in, as there was no room **here** large enough to accommodate the people. I made this request known to some of my brethren, who told me to go and get a tent made, and they would "**foot the bills.**" I went and engaged the tent, and they handed me the money to pay for it. **But just at this time the brethren here fearing that the tent might be a snare, inasmuch as we should be pressed so much to go and preach and use the tent throughout all this new country, so that we should be in danger of leaving our main work here for the sake of performing evangelical labor in the towns and counties around us,— they therefore wrote to me** ˡ**that**[5] **I had better drop the idea of getting the tent. I informed the brethren who had given me the money, and asked them what I should do with it. They told me that they would not take it back, but advised that it should be given either to the funds of the college, or to some other benevolent enterprize, I am not certain which. However I disposed of it according to their views, and thought no more about it until a very short time before I was to leave for Oberlin, when lo! another request came from the brethren here saying that they did not see how they could do without the tent, and therefore**

MS 676

[1] Finney inserted the chapter heading and crossed out the first sentence, which read, "I took my family and came to Oberlin in the Spring of the year." He replaced it with a similar sentence at the foot of the previous page.

[2] Twenty-nine of the Lane Rebels enrolled at Oberlin College. See Lawrence T. Lesick, *The Lane Rebels* (Metuchen, N.J.: Scarecrow, 1980), p. 172.

[3] The "barracks" was a single-story wooden building 144 feet long by 24 feet wide, divided into twenty compartments, with a kitchen at one end. Each compartment had its own door and could house two students. The building was made of timber with the outside battening of slabs with the bark still on. It was officially known as Cincinnati Hall but was often referred to as "Slab Hall" or "Rebel Shanty" (A. L. Shumway and C. de W. Brower, eds., *Oberliniana* [Cleveland: Home Publishing Co., 1883], p. 18; and J. H. Fairchild, *Oberlin: The Colony and the College* [Oberlin: Goodrich, 1883], p. 67).

[4] Nearly three hundred students attended at one time or another during 1835, and considerably more than that attended the next year. See Robert S. Fletcher, *The History of Oberlin College from Its Foundation Through the Civil War* (Oberlin: Oberlin College, 1943), p. 186.

[5] Finney numbered the next page 678 in error, so "−7" was added after page number 676 in ink. This appears to be Fairchild's addition.

wished me to get it. I felt chagrined at this; but as I knew the hearts and pockets of my friends in New York were thoroughly opened, and that they were thoroughly committed to carry this project forward, I mentioned this last request to them. They said without the least hesitation, "Get the tent made, and we will give you the money to pay for it."

I then went and ordered it again a circular tent a hundred feet in MS 678 diameter, with all the **parephranalia of** putting it up.[6] |At[7] the top of the **center** pole which supported the tent, was a streamer, upon which was written in very large characters, "Holiness to the Lord."[8] This tent was of great service to us. When the weather would permit we spread it upon the square every Sabbath, and held public services in it. **We held** several of our earliest Commencements in it. It was used to some extent for holding protracted meetings in the region round about, **but never so as to interfere with our public labors here.**[9]

I have spoken of the **agreement** of **Brother** Arthur Tappan to supply us with funds, to the extent of his whole income, till we were beyond pecuniary want. **The understanding of Brother Tappan and myself was a *private* one, a promise made to me individually as a condition of my coming**

[6]The tent cost seven hundred dollars and was sent off to Finney at Oberlin on 22 May. It could hold three thousand people (see *NYE,* 23 May 1835, p. 83). This was not the only tent on order. The Reverend Ralph W. Gridley ordered one about the same time to be used by home missionaries in Illinois to evangelize the greater Mississippi Valley. See the references in *NYE* from 2 May 1835, p. 21, through 17 October 1835, p. 258; and 5 August 1837, p. 127.

[7]Pages 678–709 were originally numbered 525–56 and renumbered 657–88 by Matson. Finney changed them to 678–709.

[8]Fairchild pointed out that it was the manufacturers who thought the structure was unfinished without a flag upon the central mast,

> and accordingly sent a blue streamer with the millennial inscription, "Holiness to the Lord." This seemed to the people too pretentious, especially as the millennium had not yet come; and it was never raised except at the first putting up of the tent (J. H. Fairchild, *Oberlin: Its Origin, Progress, and Results* [Oberlin: R. Butler, 1871], p. 56).

An eyewitness recalled the morning when the tent was first spread on the college campus:

> It was a lovely morning, not a cloud obscured the clear blue sky. Just breeze enough to keep the flag floating, displaying the sacred words inscribed on the whole length of the streamer, in large beautiful white letters,—"*Holiness to the Lord*". The flag was made of blue silk, & nearly three yards in length. It was broad at the base where it was fastened to the flagstaff, tapering down the whole length. It was a grand, impressive sight. It seemed that the people ought "to take off their shoes for the place on which they stood was Holy Ground" (Martha H. Pierce to Henry Matson, 18 July 1884, Alumni Records, file 28/1, "John Tappan Pierce" folder, Oberlin College Archives).

[9]The tent may have been used only twice for revivals in the neighborhood. The first time was in September 1835, when Mahan and the senior theological class took the tent to Dover and Wakeman (see *NYE,* 28 November 1835, p. 273; and H. B. Hall, "When It Was First Used," *The Oberlin News*, 16 June 1903, p. 5). The second time was in the summer of 1836 near Mansfield, Ohio. See Asa Mahan, *Autobiography, Intellectual, Moral, and Spiritual* (London: Woolmer, 1882), p. 124.

After First Church was built in 1843, the tent was no longer used. It was sold to the Western Antislavery Society in 1847 for three hundred dollars, and it was used extensively after that for meetings in the West. According to Henry Matson, "The dilapidated remnants, during the war, were sold at a high price for paper rags and the money contributed for the education of the Freedmen." See Samuel Brooke to Hamilton Hill, 22 June 1847, Letters Received by Oberlin College, 1822–1866, microfilm, roll 11; Oberlin College Semi-Centennial Fundraising Leaflet, 1883, Oberlin College Archives. Information from Marlene Merrill.

Page 680 of the Manuscript. This manuscript page shows Fairchild's alteration of Finney's description of the location of Oberlin. Oberlin College Archives.

here. He said: "I want your institution to be known; therefore I want your trustees to send out agents over the country, and into the cities, and make the objects and wants of the institution known. Collect what MS 679 **money ˡyou can, and spread the knowledge of your enterprize through your agencies as far as you can.[10] I do not want you to spread an abolition flag; but carry out your design of receiving colored students upon the same conditions that you do white ones; and see to it that the work be not taken out of the hands of the faculty and spoiled by the trustees, as was the case in Cincinnati. Just let it be known that you thus receive students, and work your way on as best you can. Go on and put up your buildings as fast as you can; and whatever your deficiency of funds may be, after making efforts through your agents, you may draw on me and I will honor your draft to the extent of my income from year to year.**

I came on the ground with this understanding. But it was farther understood between **Brother Tappan and myself** that his pledge should not be known to the trustees, lest they should fail to make due efforts as he JHF 337 MS 680 desired, not merely to collect funds, but to make the ˡwants and objects ˡof the institution known throughout the land. In accordance with this understanding the work here was pushed as fast as it could well be, considering that we were in the heart of a great forest, and in a **mud hole, as this whole neighborhood then was. The location of the institution was unfortunate, ill-considered, hastily decided upon; and had it not been for the good hand of God in helping us at every step, the institution would have been a failure because of its ill-judged location. It has cost us ‹many› thousand dollars[11] to overcome the natural obstacles in the way of planting a college here.[12]**

[10]John J. Shipherd had great difficulties in his attempts to raise funds: "*Finneyism Abolitionism* &c are excuses of multitudes for not giving funds, & again there is some doubt whether we are sufficiently imbued with Abolitionism." Finney himself went with Shipherd about March down to Philadelphia to try and raise funds:

> & returned without money enough to pay our fare. The city of brotherly love is filled with contentions to the exclusion of benevolence, & as the O. C. Institute is to afford an assylum for the rebelious students late at Lane Sem. it ought not to be sustained &c (J. J. Shipherd to Fayette Shipherd, 1 April 1835, Bragdon Family Papers, University of Rochester Library).

[11]Here Matson had written down, "It has cost us hundreds of thousands of dollars," but he appears later to have crossed out the words "hundreds of." Finney subsequently altered it again, adding the word "many."

[12]J. H. Fairchild, who omitted this section from the published edition, looked back after fifty years and reflected on the location of Oberlin:

> In the broader view it is not difficult to see that Oberlin was placed where it should have been. . . . As to the exact locality, the result must be accepted as a vindication. The desirable thing was to secure a community around the college in general sympathy with its educational work, and with little attraction for other interests which might bring in undesirable influences. If the site had been more inviting, the sudden and rapid growth which took place would have attracted men with an eye to business, and an era of land speculation might have afflicted the college and the town. Other institutions have suffered such calamities. If the place had been attractive to manufacturers, and large establishments had sprung up with many workmen, the tone of society would have been changed, and saloons and similar nuisances would have multiplied upon us. The educational work would have been greatly marred. To a great

We had only fairly **got under way, and in the process** of putting up our buildings, and had arranged to need a large amount of money, when the great commercial crash prostrated **Brother** Tappan, and nearly all the men who had subscribed for the fund for the support of the faculty. The commercial crash went over the country, and prostrated the great mass of wealthy men.[13] |It left us not only without funds for the support of the faculty, but **fifty**[14] thousand dollars in debt, without any prospect, that we could see, of obtaining funds from the friends of the college in this country. **Brother** Tappan wrote me at this time, acknowledging expressly the promise he had made me, expressing the deepest regret that he was prostrated and wholly unable to fulfil his pledge.[15] Our necessities were then great, and **in** human view it would seem **as if** the college must be a failure. MS 681

The state was then strongly democratic in politics, and utterly opposed to our enterprize because of its Abolition character. The towns around us were **so** hostile to our movement **as to oppose in every way they could, going so far as to threaten** to come and tear down **what** buildings **we had put up**. A democratic legislature was in the meantime endeavoring to get some hold of us that would enable them to abrogate our charter.[16] In this state of things there was of course a great crying to |God among the people here. In the meantime my revi[v]al[17] lectures had been very extensively circulated in England; and we were aware that the British public would strongly sympathize with us if they knew our objects, our prospects, and our condition. We therefore **fitted out** an agency composed of Rev. John Keep[18] MS 682

extent the world has yielded the Oberlin tract to the uses for which it was selected and consecrated (Fairchild, "The Divine Hand in the Oberlin Enterprise," *Jubilee Notes* [Oberlin], November 1883, p. 48).

[13]This was the financial crash of 1837. There had been warning signs since early in 1836, and by the early months of 1837 it was clear that America was in the throes of a major depression that was to last for several years. In May the new treasurer of the Professorship Association, Alfred Smith, informed the treasurer of Oberlin College:

> Nearly all our merchants are bankrupts. Such times were never known among us. More than 200 of our heaviest Merchants in this city have failed within a few weeks. Among the failures are A. Tappan & Co, J. W. & R. Leavitt, Leavitt Lord & Co, C. Baker & Co. Cutter Buckley & Hunt successors of Clarke & Hunt, A. G. Phelps Dodge & Co and a multitude of other good men. It is of no use to urge the payment of the dues at such a time as this. It would be unbecoming in me so to do. Our only recourse is to wait untill money affair is easier (Alfred Smith to Levi Burnell, 12 May 1837, Letters Received by Oberlin College, 1822–1866, microfilm, roll 4).

See also Samuel Rezneck, "The Social History of an American Depression, 1837–1843," *American Historical Review* 40, no. 4 (July 1935): 662–87.

[14]Fairchild, who was familiar with the financial situation, changed this figure to "thirty."

[15]This letter is not in the Finney Papers.

[16]Attempts to repeal the charter were first made in 1836 and continued for the next six sessions in the Ohio legislature. See Clayton S. Ellsworth, "Ohio's Legislative Attack upon Abolition Schools," *Mississippi Valley Historical Review* 21 (December 1934): 379–86.

[17]Matson had written this word as "revial." Fairchild corrected it.

[18]John Keep (1781–1870) graduated from Yale and was ordained a Congregational minister in 1805. After successful pastorates in Blandford, Massachusetts, and Homer, New York, he moved to Cleveland in 1833, where he organized the First Congregational Church. In 1834 he was elected a trustee and president of the board of the Oberlin Collegiate Institute, and in 1836 he became their financial agent. But the financial crash of 1837 necessitated further pastoral work until he went on the deputation to England in 1839. After he returned to America he resumed pastoral work in Ohio before moving permanently to Oberlin in 1850, when he again became a

and Mr Wm Dawes,[19] **and got** for them letters of recommendation, and JHF 338 expressions of confidence in our enterprize, from some of the **principal ˡmen in the United States.**[20] They went to England and laid our objects and our wants before the British public.[21] They generously responded, and gave us **ten**[22] thousand pounds Sterling. This very nearly canceled[23] our indebtedness.

Our friends scattered throughout the northern states, who were abolitionists and friends ‹of›[24] revivals, generously aided us to the extent of their ability. But we had to struggle with poverty and many trials for a **number** of years. Sometimes we did not know from day to day how we were to be MS 683 provided for. ˡ**Especially was this true of myself.**[25] **The endowment fund had failed, and the faculty were altogether unprovided for.** But with the blessing of God we helped ourselves as best we could. At one time I saw no means of providing for my family through the winter. **A** thanksgiving day **had been appointed by the executive of the state; which** came and found us so poor that I had been obliged to sell my travelling trunk, which I used in my

financial agent for the college. See J. H. Fairchild, "John Keep," *The Congregational Quarterly* (Boston) 13 (April 1871): 209–24; and F. B. Dexter, *Biographical Sketches of the Graduates of Yale College,* vol. 5 (New York: Holt, 1911), pp. 513–17.

[19]William Dawes (1799–1888) was a wealthy businessman. He had been a builder in Hudson and a member of First Church as well as treasurer of Western Reserve College. When he learned about Oberlin he decided to move there with his family and devote his time and his wealth to furthering the interests of the college and the reform movements that it promoted. Asa Mahan, the president of Oberlin College, considered that the financial assistance that he brought to the college saved it at that time. He became an agent for the college in 1837 without salary and later became a trustee and member of the Prudential Committee. He was particularly attached to Asa Mahan, and after Mahan left in 1850, Dawes turned his back on Oberlin and threw in his lot with Mahan and the new university being started in Cleveland. Dawes was appointed the leader of the deputation to England. See Richard M. Luker, "The Western Reserve and a Legacy for Higher Education: Faculty Self-Governance at Oberlin College Under the Finney Compact, 1834–1846" (Ed.D. diss., University of Akron, 1985), pp. 249–52; Asa Mahan, *Out of Darkness into Light* (London: Wesleyan-Methodist Book-Room, 1882), pp. 214–15; Mahan, *Autobiography,* p. 275; D. L. Leonard, "A Legacy from President Fairchild," *The Oberlin News*, 6 March 1903, p. 4; and Fletcher, *History of Oberlin College.*

[20]Thirty-nine letters from twenty-one prominent ministers and reformers in America, recommending their mission to friends in Britain, were copied by John Keep into a credential book. These included letters from Lewis Tappan, Joshua Leavitt, E. N. Kirk, Amos A. Phelps, David Lee Child, H. C. Howells, James C. Fuller, George Beecher, William A. Alcott, and Sylvester Graham. The deputation also took with them two copies of a parchment document setting out the claims of the Oberlin Institute, written by Theodore D. Weld and signed by thirty-five leading reformers, including Arthur and Lewis Tappan, William Lloyd Garrison, James G. Birney, Gerrit Smith, Wendell Phillips, Joshua Giddings, John G. Whittier, and the Grimké sisters. See Marlene Merrill, "Early Fund Raising: Weld Appealed to British," *The Observer* (Oberlin College) 3 (29 October 1981): 3. The documents are all preserved in the Oberlin College Archives.

[21]They left America on 20 May 1839 and returned in November 1840. See Fletcher, *History of Oberlin College*, chap. 29, "Oberlinizing England."

[22]Fairchild corrected this figure to "six."

[23]The word "canceled" was not altered in the manuscript but was changed to "cancelled" in the published edition.

[24]Here Finney changed the word "to" to "of."

[25]Finney owned property in New York that he had probably purchased when he was to be the pastor of the Broadway Tabernacle. This was rented out, but he received very little money from it at that time. He was also receiving no money from the sale of his books because of the failure of the firm that published them. See letters to Finney from S. Brown, 24 February 1838, and 28 January 1839, Finney Papers, microfilm, roll 3; and 19 March 1840, roll 4.

evangeli**cal** labors, to supply the place of a cow which I had lost. I rose on the morning of Thanksgiving, and spread our necessities before the Lord.[26] I finally concluded by saying that if help did not come, I should assume that it was best that it should not, and would be entirely satisfied with any course that the Lord would see it wise to take. I went and preached, and enjoyed my own preaching as well, I think, as I ever did. I had a blessed day to my own soul; and I could see that the people enjoyed it exceedingly. |**When** the meeting **was out** I was detained a little while in conversation with some brethren, and my wife **came** home. When I **came home and entered** the gate, she **came to the door and stood** in the open door with a**n open** letter in her hand. As I approached she smilingly said, "The answer has come, **M**y dear;" and handed me the letter containing a check from **Brother** Josiah Chapin of Providence, **R.I.,** for two hundred dollars. He had been here the previous summer with his wife. I had said nothing about my wants at all, as I never was in the habit of mentioning them to anybody. But in the letter containing the check he said he had learned that the endowment fund had failed, and that I was in want of help. He intimated that I might ex|pect more from time to time.[27] He continued to send me six hundred dollars a year for several years; and on this I managed to live.[28] |I should have said that agreeably to my arrangement in New York, I spent my summers **here** and my winters **there** for two or three years.[29] We had a blessed reviving whenever I returned to preach there. We also had a revival here ‹continually›.[30] Very few students came here then without being converted. But my health soon became such that I found I must relinquish one of these fields of labor. But the interests **of the institution here** seemed to forbid utterly that I should leave it.[31] I therefore took **my** dismission from my church in N.Y.; and the

MS 684

JHF 339

MS 685

[26]This was Thanksgiving Day of 1837. See William C. Cochran, *Charles Grandison Finney: Memorial Address* (Philadelphia: Lippincott, 1908), p. 92.

[27] The earliest letter from Josiah Chapin in the Finney Papers is dated 22 November 1837 and is for the transfer of one hundred dollars. It acknowledges a letter dated 10 November from Finney. Chapin's letter presupposes that he had already decided to pay Finney's salary. Asa Mahan appears to be writing of this event in *Out of Darkness into Light*. When it was clear that the endowment of the college had failed, Mahan took action:

> Knowing that Professor Finney's health and circumstances would not permit him to continue with us unless his salary was promptly paid, and knowing that the large fortune of a mutual friend of his and my own had not suffered in the national calamities, I visited him, and, after full consultation, he agreed to pay regularly the salary under consideration (p. 214).

[28]He continued to send money to Finney until May 1846. His son, William C. Chapin, continued to provide assistance and became one of the largest benefactors to Oberlin College. See W. Chapin to Finney, 9 May 1846; and Willard Sears to Finney, 9 April 1846, Finney Papers, microfilm, roll 4; and Fletcher, *History of Oberlin College,* p. 896.

[29]Finney spent the summers of 1835 and 1836 in Oberlin before moving there permanently in the spring of 1837.

[30]Finney changed the words "every season" to "continually." The period from 1835 to 1840 was said to have been one of continual revival. See "History of Revivals in Oberlin," *OE,* 24 September 1856, p. 157.

[31]Matson had originally written the following section after this but altered it:

> I therefore took my dismission; and from that time I spent my vacations in laboring abroad in the capacity of an Evangelist, in promoting revivals, in such fields as were open to me. The six months of the year that I was to have spent in New York, after I had taken my dismission from there, I spent in laboring abroad to promote revivals of religion.

six months **of the year that** I was to have spent in New York, I spent in laboring **abroad** to promote revivals of religion.[32]

MS 686 ˡThe lectures on revivals of religion were preached while I was still pastor of the presbyterian church in Chatham st. chapel. The two following winters I **preached** lectures to *Christians* ‹in the Broadway Tabernacle›[33] which were also reported by **Brother** Leavitt, and published in the New York Evangelist.[34] These also have been printed in a volume in this country and in Europe.[35] Those sermons to Christians were very much the result of a searching that was going on in my own mind. I mean, that the Spirit of God was showing me many things in regard to the question of sanctification that led me to preach those sermons to Christians. Many Christians regarded those lectures as rather an exhibition of the law than of the Gospel. But I did not, and do not, so regard them. For me the law and Gospel have but one rule of life; and every violation of the spirit of the law is also a violation of the spirit of the Gospel. But I have long been satisfied that the higher forms of Christian experience are attained only as a result of a terribly searching application of God's law to the human conscience and heart. The result of my MS 687 labors up to that ˡtime had shown me more clearly than I had known before JHF 340 the great ˡweakness of Christians, and that the older members of the church as a general thing were making very little progress in grace. I found that they would fall back from a revival state, even sooner than young converts, **by far**. It had been so in the revival in which I myself was converted. **And I had often observed that many of the older members of the church would fall back into a state of comparative apathy and indifference much sooner than young converts.** I saw clearly that this was owing to their early teaching; that is, to the views which they had been led to entertain when they

[32]Finney was granted a dismission from the Broadway Tabernacle at a meeting of the church on 6 April 1837, following his resignation from the New York City Congregational Association the previous day. The reason Finney gave for requesting dismission was "the state of his health." See letter of J. H. Colton to Finney, 7 April 1837, Finney Papers, microfilm, roll 3; and copy of extract from the minutes of the meeting of the New York City Association, 5 April 1837, by Joshua Leavitt, Finney Papers, file 2/2/2, box 9.

The next winter, 1837–1838, Finney spent conducting meetings in Cleveland. See letters of Finney to Levi Burnell, 15 December 1837; 9 January and 6 February 1838, Letters Received by Oberlin College, 1822–1866, microfilm, rolls 4, 5.

[33]Finney added the words "in the Broadway Tabernacle."

[34]Finney and his family were in New York from mid-December 1835 until 3 May 1836. The Broadway Tabernacle was not in fact completed at that time, so the church was still occupying the Chatham Street Chapel. He gave the lectures on Friday evenings, commencing on 25 December 1835 and continuing until 11 March 1836, when hoarseness prevented him from continuing (see *NYE,* 19 December 1835, p. 284; 9 April 1836, p. 58; and 7 May 1836, p. 76). The eleven lectures were published in the *Evangelist* from 26 December 1835 to 12 March 1836. Then the next winter Finney was in New York at the new Broadway Tabernacle from mid-November 1836 until mid-April 1837. See *NYE,* 19 November 1836, p. 186; and 15 April 1837, p. 62. Lectures were given on Thursday evenings from 5 January 1837 until early April. The sixteen lectures were published in the *Evangelist* from 7 January to 15 April 1837.

[35]They were published in April 1837 by John S. Taylor of New York as *Lectures to Professing Christians*. In England they were first published in 1839 as the third edition by Milner and Co. of London, with an introduction by Joseph Barker. They were also published at that time in London by G. Wightman and Thomas Tegg. A facsimile of the first edition was published by Garland Publishing of New York and London in 1985 in"The Higher Christian Life" series, under the editorship of Donald W. Dayton.

were young converts. I was also led into a state of great dissatisfaction with my own want of stability in faith and love. To be candid and tell the truth, I must say to the praise of God's grace **that**[36] He did not suffer me to backslide to anything like the same extent to which manifestly many Christians did backslide. But I often felt myself weak in the presence of temptation; and needed frequently to hold days of fasting and prayer, and to spend much time in overhauling my own religious |life in order to retain that communion with God, and that hold upon the divine strength, that would enable me efficiently to labor for the promotion of revivals of religion. MS 688

In looking at the state of the Christian church as it had been revealed to me in my revival labors, I was led earnestly to inquire whether there was not something higher and more enduring than the Christian church was aware of; whether there were not promises, and means provided in the Gospel, for the establishment of Christians in altogether a higher form of Christian life. I had known **considerable** of the view of sanctification entertained by our Methodist brethren.[37] But as their **view** of sanctification seemed to me to relate almost altogether to states of the sensibility, I could not receive their teaching.[38] However, I gave myself earnestly to search the Scriptures, and to

[36]The word "that" was not crossed out by Fairchild but was omitted from the published edition.

[37]In his first lecture on Christian perfection preached in the Broadway Tabernacle in February 1837, he stated:

> I have recently read Mr. Wesley's "Plain Account of Christian Perfection," a book I never saw until lately. I find some expressions in it to which I should object, but I believe it is rather the expression than the sentiments. And I think, with this abatement, it is an admirable book (*NYE,* 25 February 1837, p. 34).

Finney also refers to the "Life of Mrs. Hester Ann Rogers" in another of his lectures at that time (*NYE,* 8 April 1837, p. 58).

J. H. Fairchild, speaking of the inquiries going on at Oberlin on the subject, wrote:

> The view was essentially that of the Wesleyan experience of perfect love, and biographies of Wesleyans were eagerly sought for, in which these experiences were portrayed, as of the Wesleys, Fletcher, Carvosso, Hester Ann Rogers, as well as the experiences of President and Mrs. Edwards and J. B. Taylor. Mr. Finney was about leaving for his winter in New York, but these new ideas went with him, and gave tone to his experience and his preaching there (*Colony and College,* p. 91).

It is perhaps significant that these were the books that John Humphrey Noyes particularly cites as influencing him in the direction of perfectionism. *The Perfectionist* was at the time being read by students at Oberlin. See J. H. Noyes, *Confessions of Religious Experience* (Oneida Reserve, N.Y.: Leonard, 1849), p. 10.

[38]The emphasis on "sanctification of the sensibility" was, however, an aspect of the Wesleyan doctrine that particularly appealed to Asa Mahan. The Methodist idea of sanctification as a "second blessing" also was prevalent at that time at Oberlin. The earliest formulation of the Oberlin doctrine of sanctification can be seen as a Wesleyan phase. See J. H. Fairchild, "The Doctrine of Sanctification at Oberlin," *The Congregational Quarterly,* 18 (April 1876): 241–44; and James W. Lee, "The Development of Theology at Oberlin" (Ph.D. diss., Drew University, 1953), pp. 10–12. Asa Mahan wrote, "The *terms* by which we designated it were those by which it had been presented since the times of Wesley and Fletcher, namely, Christian Perfection, Entire Sanctification, and Full Salvation" (*Autobiography,* p. 367).

The Methodists, however, while welcoming the Oberlin teaching on the experience of Christian perfection, took issue with Finney, in particular, on his legal phraseology, which George Peck believed, "seems to tend toward a confounding of the law and the gospel—of the covenant of works and the covenant of grace; and makes salvation predicable of obedience to the law, contrary to the doctrine of St. Paul" (G. Peck, *The Scripture Doctrine of Christian Perfection Stated and Defended* [New York: Lane and Tippett, 1845], p. 242). See also the criticisms of Finney's theology by the Methodist Francis Hodgson in *An Examination of the System of New*

read whatever came to hand upon the subject, until my mind was satisfied that ‹an› altogether higher[39] and more stable form of Christian life was attainable, and was the privilege of all Christians. MS 689 |This led me to preach in the Broadway Tabernacle two sermons on Christian perfection. Those sermons are now JHF 341 |included in the volume of lectures preached to Christians. In those sermons I defined what Christian perfection was, and endeavored to show that it is attainable in this life, and the sense in which it is attainable. **I said those sermons were published in the N.Y. Evangelist.**[40] **So far as I know they did not startle the christian church as anything heretical; for until sometime after I came to Oberlin I never heard the question of the truth of those sermons raised in any quarter.**[41] But about this time the question of Christian perfection in the Antinomian sense of the term, came to be agitated a good deal at New Haven,[42] at Albany,[43] and somewhat in N.Y. city.[44] I examined their views. **I read and examined pretty thoroughly**

Divinity; or, New School Theology (New York: Lane, 1840). The copy of this book in New College Library, Edinburgh, has the following inscription on the flyleaf: "In ref[erenc]e to this Vol[ume] Mr Finney stated to me that he had not read it & that its pub[licatio]n had occasioned him no more pain than if he had heard that there was a flea somewhere in Canada. Jan[uar]y 1859." The handwriting is that of the Wesleyan Methodist minister John Moore, one of Finney's most ardent disciples in England and a devoted friend.

Although Finney rejected the Wesleyan teaching of the cleansing of the depraved human nature in entire sanctification, this was the only real point of disagreement over the doctrine. In general,

> in regard to the attainability of the experience of entire sanctification, the prerequisites of attainment, the conditions of attainment, and the results of entering into this experience, both the Wesleyans and Finney are in substantial, if not absolute agreement (Paul Rader, "A Study of the Doctrine of Sanctification in the Life and Thought of Charles G. Finney" [B.D. thesis, Asbury Theological Seminary, 1959], p. 103).

[39] Matson had written "altogether a higher," but Finney changed it to "an altogether higher."

[40] The sermons were entitled "Christian Perfection" and appeared in *NYE,* 25 February 1837, pp. 34–35; and 11 March 1837, p. 42.

[41] Finney also wrote: "Whatever was thought of them, I heard not a word of objection to the doctrine from any quarter. If any was made, it did not, to my recollection, come to my knowledge" (*Lectures on Systematic Theology* [London: William Tegg, 1851], p. 571).

[42] It was agitated among members of the Free church in New Haven under James Boyle and particularly by John Humphrey Noyes, a theological student at the seminary, who openly advocated sinless perfection and declared himself saved from sin on 20 February 1834. See George W. Noyes, ed., *Religious Experience of John Humphrey Noyes* (New York: Macmillan, 1923).

[43] The group at Albany emerged about 1831 under the leadership of John B. Foot. Members of Rev. E. N. Kirk's church and some of the students in the Troy and Albany Theological School run by N. S. S. Beman and Kirk appear to have been involved. There was considerable proselytizing by this group in 1832 and 1833, and a number of perfectionist groups were established in Massachusetts and in New York State. A Universalist minister wrote at the time:

> Mr Kirk's church, in Albany, is said to be approaching a state of perfection not generally preached up by this gentleman and his associate revivalists. Several of them claim to be divinely inspired, and through faith, to possess the power of working miracles. Where will they end? (*Evangelical Magazine and Gospel Advocate* [Utica], 19 May 1832, p. 159; see also Whitney R. Cross, *The Burned-Over District* [Ithaca, N.Y.: Cornell University Press, 1950], pp. 192, 195, 240; and Asa Mahan, *Scripture Doctrine of Christian Perfection* [London: Partridge and Oakey, 1849], p. 65n).

[44] Perfectionism first appeared in New York. James Latourette, who had broken away from the Methodist church in 1828, became the leader of a congregation who advocated a form of Wesleyan perfectionism. From there it spread to Albany. See *The Witness* (Putney, Vt.), 25 September 1839, p. 75.

their periodical entitled, "The Perfectionist."[45] But I could not accept **their peculiar views.**[46] Yet I was satisfied that the doctrine of sanctification in this life, and *entire* sanctification in the sense that it was the privilege of Chris|tians to live without known sin, was a doctrine taught in the Bible, and that abundant means were provided for the securing of that attainment. MS 690

The last winter that I spent in New York the Lord was pleased to visit my soul with a great refreshing.[47] After a season of great searching of heart he brought me, as he has often done, into a large place, and gave me much of that divine sweetness in my soul of which President Edwards speaks as **an** experience **of his own soul.**[48] That winter I had a thorough breaking up, so much so that sometimes for a considerable period I could not refrain from loud weeping in view of my own sins, and of the love of God in Christ. Such seasons were frequent that winter, and resulted in the great renewal of my spiritual strength, and enlargement of my views in regard to the privileges of Christians and the abundance of the grace of God.[49] It is well known that my **own** views on the **subject**[50] of sanctification have been the subject of a good deal of criticism.

|To be faithful to history I must say some things that I would otherwise pass by in silence. **This** college[51] was established by Mr. Shipherd very much MS 691

[45] Matson had originally written "Christian Perfection," here, but he crossed it out and wrote in "The Perfectionist." This paper was first published on 20 August 1834 at New Haven by James Boyle with assistance from John H. Noyes. It was the first of a series of periodicals that Noyes was involved in publishing that were to be the main organ of the perfectionist groups.

[46] The views that some of the perfectionists advocated were connected with sexual irregularities and the abandonment of all forms of organization and government, including religious observances. This "antinomianism" was particularly prevalent in 1835 and 1836 (see Noyes, *Religious Experience,* chap. 19, "Antinomianism"). These ideas were repudiated by Noyes himself.

Finney said early in 1837 in his first lecture on Christian perfection: "I disclaim, entirely, the charge of maintaining the peculiarities, whatever they be, of modern Perfectionism. I have read their publications, weeping, and have had much knowledge of them as individuals, and I cannot assent to their views" (*NYE,* 25 February 1837, p. 34). Later in April he met J. H. Noyes in New York and expressed some confidence in him and an interest in his views. See *The Witness* (Ithaca, N.Y.), 20 August 1837, p. 2. Asa Mahan pointed out that as soon as their "Satanic morals" were understood, it "reduced the sect to the limits of some five or six hundred members" (*Autobiography*, p. 324).

[47] This was from November 1836 to April 1837. See n. 34 above.

[48] Jonathan Edwards described his experience in *A Treatise Concerning Religious Affections,* first published in Boston in 1746 and frequently republished. See also *NYE,* 11 March 1840, p. 45.

[49] Finney later wrote that it was then that

> the question came fully up whether the grace of God was sufficient *as a matter of fact* for the entire sanctification of Christians in this life, . . . The question in this shape had never come fairly and fully before my mind as a subject of distinct consideration till the last winter of my residence in N.Y. (*OE,* 17 July 1839, p. 124).

Finney had gone to New York straight from Oberlin, and the scenes of the great revival, where the possibility of a higher Christian life had become a central issue. As Fairchild stated, "These new ideas went with him, and gave tone to his experience and his preaching there" (Fairchild, *Colony and College,* p. 91; and MS 706–9).

Asa Mahan had accompanied Finney to New York and was assisting him at the Broadway Tabernacle. He wrote that "brother Finney and myself came to New York, and spent most of the winter together in prayer and the study of the Bible" (Mahan, *Scripture Doctrine of Christian Perfection*, p. 184; and *NYE,* 19 November 1836, p. 186).

[50] The word "subject" here was not altered in the manuscript, but the published edition has "question."

[51] That is, Oberlin College.

against the feelings and wishes of the men most concerned in building up **Hudson** College.[52] Mr. Shipherd once informed me that **Brother Coe, who was then** the principal agent of that college, asserted to him that he would do JHF 342 all he could to put this college down.[53] As |soon as they heard at Hudson that I had received a call **at** Oberlin as professor of theology, the trustees elected me as professor of theology at **Hudson**; so that I held the two invitations at the same time.[54] I did not, in writing, commit myself to either, but came on to survey the ground and then decide upon the path of duty.[55] That **Spring** the general assembly of the Presbyterian church held their **May** meeting at Pittsburgh. When I arrived at Cleveland I was informed that two of the professors from Hudson had been waiting at Cleveland for my arrival, designing to have me go first at any rate to Hudson.[56] But I had been delayed

[52]The Western Reserve College at Hudson, Ohio, had been established in 1826 and was beginning to get under way. So the presence of another school within fifty miles was considered an intrusion; it threatened to draw off patronage and potential students. The new college was attacked from the start in the *Ohio Observer*, which acted as the organ of Western Reserve College. See C. H. Cramer, *Case Western Reserve* (Boston: Little, Brown, 1976); Fletcher, *History of Oberlin College*, pp. 429–30; and Fairchild, *Oberlin: Its Origin,* p. 34.

[53]Harvey Coe (1785–1860) was the agent in raising funds for Western Reserve College. He had been a missionary on the reserve since 1814 and was for some years the only settled pastor in that part of the country. He was one of the founders of the college and was on the board of trustees until his resignation in 1855. See J. Gardner Bartlett, *Robert Coe, Puritan: His Ancestors and Descendants, 1340–1910* (Boston: published by the Author, 1911), pp. 289–90; P. H. Fowler, *Historical Sketch of Presbyterianism Within the Bounds of the Synod of Central New York* (Utica: Curtiss and Childs, 1877), p. 297; and *NYE,* 29 March 1860, p. 7.

[54]Finney was appointed professor of theology at Oberlin at the meeting of the board of trustees on 10 February 1835 (see Oberlin College Board of Trustees Minutes, 10 February 1835, Oberlin College Archives, microfilm). He was informed of the appointment by a letter from the chairman of the trustees, John Keep, dated 15 February 1835 (Finney Papers, microfilm, roll 3).

Finney's appointment at Western Reserve College, made at a trustees' meeting on 6 May 1835, was to the post of professor of pastoral theology and sacred rhetoric. The official invitation was in a letter from the president of the college, George E. Pierce, dated 12 May 1835. The letter is missing from the Finney Papers, but there is a typescript transcription in R. S. Fletcher Papers, file 30/24, box 5, Oberlin College Archives. See also *NYE,* 30 May 1835, p. 87; and Carroll Cutler, *A History of Western Reserve College, during its first half-century 1826–1876* (Cleveland: Crocker, 1876), p. 39.

[55]Although Finney may have given no definite written acceptance, he had provisionally agreed to accept the appointment at Oberlin. On the basis of this, Mahan and Shipherd were able to go ahead and make arrangements in New York in January; and at the meeting of the trustees on 6 April 1835, "a communication from the Rev. Charles G. Finney of New York City, signifying his acceptance of Professor of Theology" was presented. This was over a month before Finney arrived in Oberlin. Even before this it was announced in the press that he had accepted the appointment. See *NYE,* 21 March 1835, p. 67; and 11 April 1835, p. 59; Mahan, *Autobiography,* p. 196; and Oberlin College Board of Trustees Minutes, 6 April 1835, Oberlin College Archives, microfilm. Finney also wrote to George Pierce, indicating that he might accept the appointment to Western Reserve College on certain conditions. See Pierce to Finney, 12 May 1835, typescript in Fletcher Papers, Oberlin College Archives.

[56]At the Western Reserve trustees' meeting of 7 May it was

> Resolved that President Pierce, Professor Folsom, Rev. John Seward and Harmon Kingsbury be a Committee to confer with the Board of Trustees of the Oberlin Institute and with Mr. Finney, and if possible to secure his acceptance of the above appointment and thus instead of having the feeling and resources of the churches on the Reserve divided on two Theological Seminaries so near each other as Hudson and Oberlin, unite public sentiment and patronage in favor of the Theological Seminary established at Hudson (quoted in Luker, "Western Reserve," p. 166).

on **the lake**[57] by adverse winds, and the brethren |who had been waiting for MS 692 me at Cleveland had **left** to be at the opening of the general assembly, and had left word with a brother to see me immediately on my arrival, and by all means to get me to go to Hudson.[58]

But in Cleveland I found a letter awaiting me from **Brother** Arthur Tappan of New York.[59] He had in some way become acquainted with the fact that strong efforts were making to induce me to go to Hudson rather than to Oberlin. Hudson, at that time, ‹had›[60] **their** buildings and apparatus, and **it** was already an established college.[61] **It had reputation and influence;** Oberlin had nothing. It had no **public** buildings, and was composed of a little colony settled **right** in the woods; and just beginning to put up their own houses, and clear away the immense forest and make a place for a college. **They** had, to be sure, **their** charter, and **a few**[62] students on the ground; but **in comparison with Hudson it was as nothing.** This letter of Brother Tappan was written to put me on my guard against supposing that I could be instrumental in securing at Hudson what we desired to secure at Oberlin.[63] |I MS 693

[57] Fairchild changed this in the manuscript to "Lake Erie."

[58] George E. Pierce, the president of Western Reserve College, wrote on 12 May to Finney:

> We can meet and consult. And I hope you will reach Hudson before I leave for Pittsburg next week Tuesday [i.e., 19 May]. . . . You will notice that a Committee of our Board has been appointed to consult with you and with the Board at O with the hope of securing your acceptance of the appointment and the discontinuance of a Theological Seminary at O. In behalf of that Committee I would suggest an interview with yourself at Hudson as soon as convenient after your arrival in Oberlin, Ohio. Or shall we meet you at Cleveland?

This letter was sent to Finney "care of Rev. John Keep, Cleveland, Ohio" (Pierce to Finney, 12 May 1835, typed transcription in Fletcher Papers). The General Assembly opened on 21 May 1835. See *Minutes of the General Assembly of the Presbyterian Church*, 1835.

[59] This letter is not in the Finney Papers.

[60] Here Matson had originally written down, "Hudson, at that time, had," but he altered it to read, "They had at Hudson, at that time." Finney then changed it back again.

[61] George Pierce had pointed out to Finney the advantages of going there. It had recently had "a pleasant season of refreshing influence. Of its 85 students all but 6 are now hopefully pious. It has two well built College edifices, and is to have a building for a Chapel and public rooms erected this summer. The situation is very delightful, in a pleasant village central on the Reserve, and near many places of growing importance" (Pierce to Finney, 10 April 1835, Finney Papers, microfilm, roll 3).

[62] Fairchild altered "a few" to read "perhaps a hundred."

[63] This letter was probably written on 6 May 1835, the day after Finney left New York. Finney had left unexpectedly, so Arthur Tappan was unable to warn him in person. But the next day Tappan wrote a letter to J. J. Shipherd and another to John Keep, chairman of the board of trustees of Oberlin College, warning them of the plans of Western Reserve College, in the hope that Finney would be dissuaded from accepting their offer. His letter to Finney was probably written at the same time (A. Tappan, letters to J. J. Shipherd and John Keep, 7 May 1835, Letters Received by Oberlin College, 1822–1866, microfilm, roll 2).

According to the reminiscences of an old resident of Hudson:

> I think it was about this time that Arthur Tappan offered to give quite a sum to help endow our college if they would be liberal on the anti-slavery question, i.e. liberal to the anti-slavery element, and admit females on equal terms with males, and appoint Charles Finney as one of its professors. The students of Lane Seminary in Cincinnati, which had just been suspended, proposed to come to Hudson if they were allowed to express their opinion in the slavery question. But the trustees refused to accept either offer under those conditions. Tappan gave to Oberlin College the sum he had offered Western Reserve. . . .
>
> The gift of Tappan to Oberlin raised strong opposition to that College by Western Reserve College and by the Congregational Church here, with its minister (Lora Case,

left my family at Cleveland, hired a horse and buggy, and came out to Oberlin without going to Hudson.[64] I thought at least that I would see Oberlin first. JHF 343 When I ar|rived at Elyria I found some old acquaintances there, whom I had known in central New York. They informed me that the ‹Trustees of›[65] **Hudson** thought that if they could secure my presence at Hudson, it would at least in a great measure defeat Oberlin; and that at Hudson there was an **O**ld **S**chool influence of sufficient power to compel me to fall in with their views and course of action. **This they informed me they had learned from an agent of Hudson who had been at Elyria.** This was in precise accordance with the information which I had received from **Brother** Tappan. I came **here** and saw that there was nothing to prevent the building up of a college on the principles that seemed to me not only to lie at the foundation of all success in establishing a college here at the West; but on principles of reform such as I MS 694 knew were |dear to the hearts of those who had undertaken the support and building up of Oberlin College. The brethren that were here on the ground were heartily in favor of building up a school on radical principles of reform. I therefore wrote to the trustees of Hudson declining to accept their invitation, and took up my abode at Oberlin.[66] I had nothing ill to say of Hudson, and I knew no ill of it. **However the policy seemed to be pursued that had been avowed by Brother Coe, of putting Oberlin college down, or rather *keeping* it down.**

Very soon the cry of **A**ntinomian perfectionism was heard, and this charge brought against us. Letters were written, and **E**cclesiastical bodies were

Hudson of Long Ago: Progress of Hudson During the Past Century. Personal Reminiscences of an Aged Pioneer [Hudson, Ohio: Hudson Library and Historical Society, 1963], p. 27).

[64] Lydia Finney's parents were at that time living in Cleveland. Finney arrived in Oberlin about 17 May 1835. See J. J. Shipherd to Fayette Shipherd, 17 May 1835, Bragdon Family Papers, University of Rochester Library.

[65] Matson had written "people at," but Finney changed it to "Trustees of."

[66] Western Reserve College also sent a deputation "directly to Oberlin, to propose a transfer of the entire establishment, professors and students in a body, to Hudson" (Fairchild, *Oberlin: Its Origin,* p. 35). Carroll Cutler, a professor at Western Reserve College from 1860, and a later president, wrote: "There is no report of the committee on record, nor did Mr. Finney do President Pierce and the Board the honor to reply to the letter which informed him of his election and most cordially urged his acceptance." Cutler added a footnote:

> Mr. Finney in his Memoirs, p. 343, says that he ["]wrote to the Trustees of Hudson declining to accept their invitation." In this he is mistaken. The Records of the Trustees imply that he did not write them. At a meeting August 24th 1835, the following action was taken: "Whereas the Rev. Charles G. Finney has entered on the duties of Professor in another institution, therefore,
>
> Resolved, That the chair of Pastoral Theology and Pulpit Eloquence in Western Reserve College be and it is hereby declared vacant."
>
> It was also well known and a matter of common fame here at the time that he did not answer the call which was cordially made him (Cutler, *History of Western Reserve College,* p. 39).

Finney wrote a formal letter of acceptance to the trustees of Oberlin College, dated 30 June 1835, in which he reiterated his conditions of accepting the position: (1) that he should have leave of absence a part of each year "to labor either as Pastor or as an Evangellist," (2) that sufficient funds should be procured "to put the Institution beyond the pressure of pecuniary embarrassments," and (3) that "the Trustees give the internal control of the school into the hands of the Faculty & leave it to their discretion to admit or reject those who in their judgment shall be proper subjects for admission or rejection irrespective of color" (Finney to the Trustees of Oberlin College, 30 June 1835, Finney Papers, microfilm, roll 3).

visited, and much pains taken to represent our views here as entirely heretical. Such representations were made to ecclesiastical bodies throughout the length and breadth of the land, as to lead many of them to pass resolutions warning the churches against the influence of Oberlin theology.[67] There seemed to be a general union of ministerial influence against us. ˈWe understood very well here what had set this on foot, and by what means all this excitement was raised. But we said nothing. We **kept still on that subject, and** had no controversy with those brethren that we were aware were taking pains to raise such a powerful public sentiment against us.[68] I may not enter into particulars, but suffice it to say that the weapons that were thus ˈ**taken to put us down** reacted **upon themselves** most disastrously, **and finally resulted in** a change of nearly all the members of the faculty at Hudson, and the general management of the college fell into other hands.[69] I

MS 695

JHF 344

[67] During the years 1840–1845 the newspapers frequently reported the pronouncements and attacks against Oberlin from presbyteries and Congregational associations. These were often reviewed in *The Oberlin Evangelist.* D. L. Leonard and Barbara Zikmund have described the action taken by many of them; e.g., the presbyteries of Huron, Grand River, Richland, and Cleveland in the neighborhood of Oberlin; Detroit in Michigan; Newark in New Jersey; and a number of New York State presbyteries: Troy, Chenango, North River, Rochester, and Geneva. The Congregational General Associations of Connecticut and New York, the Fox River Congregational Union in Illinois, and the Marietta Association in Ohio also rejected Oberlin theology and Oberlin ministers.

Barbara Zikmund has pointed out that "the churches that were most distressed over Oberlin theology were the very churches which had benefitted so extensively from Finney's earlier revivals" (Zikmund, "Asa Mahan and Oberlin Perfectionism" [Ph.D. diss., Duke University, 1969], p. 204; and see also pp. 199–226; and D. L. Leonard, *The Story of Oberlin* [Boston: Pilgrim, 1898], pp. 254–57).

[68] Writing in 1847, Finney said:

> Perhaps it is not best that the public should be made acquainted with the springs of influence that have stirred up and put in motion all this hurricane of ecclesiastical and theological opposition to Oberlin. It is unpleasant to us to name and disclose it, and perhaps the cause of truth does not at present, at least, demand it (Finney, "Recent Discussions on the Subject of Entire Sanctification in this Life," *The Oberlin Quarterly Review* 2 [May 1847]: 472).

[69] Although the college did gain a measure of success under the presidency of Edward Pierce (1834–1855), the theological department suffered disastrously and had to be discontinued in 1852. The college had already suffered severe disruption in 1833, owing to the refusal of the trustees to tolerate the abolition stance of the previous president and some of the faculty. Continuing personality conflicts and crippling financial problems resulted in the resignation of three of the faculty in 1852. This led to a public outcry and bitter recriminations that nearly ruined the college. President Pierce resigned in 1855; and four of the trustees, including Harvey Coe, went at the same time. The new president, Henry L. Hitchcock, and the new trustees were able to pull the college back from the brink of bankruptcy. In 1880 the college moved to Cleveland and became Western Reserve University. See Frederick C. Waite, *Western Reserve University: The Hudson Era* (Cleveland: Press of Western Reserve University, 1943); "Western Reserve College," *The Independent* (New York), 17 August 1854–19 April 1855; and Fletcher, *History of Oberlin College*, p. 431.

At the Oberlin College commencement exercises in August 1858, President Finney presided, and President Hitchcock of Western Reserve College was present and addressed the college literary societies. The editor of *The Oberlin Evangelist* observed:

> It struck us as a thing of some interest that then for the first time the President of Oberlin and the President of Hudson sat side by side in the same pulpit, participating in the same exercises, before the same audience. This was in Oberlin, and by invitation from Oberlin. We have reason to think, this fraternal advance received an equally cordial response from the President of Western Reserve College. For our part, we

scarcely ever heard anything said ***here*** at that time against Hudson, or at any time. We kept about our own business, and felt that in respect to opposition from that quarter our strength was to sit still; and we were not mistaken. We felt confident that it was not God's plan to suffer such **kind of** opposition to prevail. I wish to be distinctly understood, that I am not at all aware that any MS 696 of the present leaders and managers of that college have sym|pathized with what was at that time done, or that they so much as know the course that was then taken.[70]

I have often been asked what it was that stirred such an excitement all at once on the subject of sanctification; and what it was that led people to regard my views on that subject as heretical after I came here, when my views on that subject had been fully known and published in the city of New York, and circulated in the N.Y. Evangelist, before this talk about our being Antinomian perfectionists was heard of.

The ministers far and near carried their opposition a great ways. At that time a convention was called to meet at Cleveland, to consider the subject of Western education, and the support of Western Colleges.[71] The call had been

> rejoice in this indication that, as between these Institutions, an era of fraternity is opened which will be as enduring as their existence (1 September 1858, p. 140).

[70]Carroll Cutler, in his history of Western Reserve College, written just after the publication of Finney's *Memoirs* in 1876, had this to say:

> President Finney in his Memoirs (pp. 343–4) seems to say that all the prejudice against Oberlin, which pervaded the whole land, was caused by evil and groundless reports set in motion by this College. No doubt some partisans of this College were too ready to take up any reproach against their neighbor. But it is to be remembered that Mr. Finney himself had many violent opponents long before he went to Oberlin, on the ground of his theological opinions and his methods of conducting revivals, and they had not ceased their original hostility. The new circumstances into which he placed himself added new grounds of opposition. Mr. Finney at the head of a theological school, and leading an abolition movement, and fathering the new heresy of co-education of the sexes, must expect to draw upon himself and his Institution far more prejudice and hostility than plain Mr. Finney the revivalist. . . . The friends of Lane Seminary also were doubtless prepared at least to listen to suspicions and to let them pass on without diminution. President Mahan's doctrine of perfection caused wide and deep opposition and prejudice not here only, but among multitudes of sober-minded people who had no interest in this College, and that opposition necessarily came down upon the Institution of which he was the head. . . . But happily those prejudices have passed, and we of the present day here are glad that we know nothing of them except as matters of history (Cutler, *History of Western Reserve College*, pp. 40–41).

The editor of *The Oberlin Evangelist* pointed out about the time of the resignation of President Pierce from Western Reserve College "that an over-ruling Providence has mainly quieted all antagonism between the rival interests of Western Reserve and Oberlin Colleges; and that Oberlin graduates are now admitted to Congregational churches without prejudice or opposition, and are doing a noble work for the peace, purity and strength of the churches" ("Congregationalism in Ohio," *OE,* 4 July 1855, p. 111).

[71]The "Western Convention of Presbyterian and Congregational Clergymen" was held in Cleveland from 20 to 25 June 1844, "the avowed object of which was to promote the prosperity of religion" (John Keep, *Congregationalism and Church Action* [New York: S. W. Benedict, 1845], p. 69; see also the reports of the proceedings in *NYE,* 4 July 1844, pp. 105–6; and 11 July 1844, pp. 109–10).

The subject of "Ministerial Education" came up during the morning session of Monday, 24 June, when the Society for the Promotion of Collegiate and Theological Education at the West was adopted. This society had been formed after a previous Convention of Western Churches in Cincinnati in June 1842, through the efforts of Theron Baldwin, with strong support from Lyman

so worded that we went out from **here**, expecting to take part in the proceedings of the convention.[72] When we arrived there we found Dr Beecher on the ground;[73] and soon saw that a course of proceedings was on foot to shut out Oberlin brethren, and those that sympathized with Oberlin, from ¦the[74] convention. I was therefore not allowed a seat in the convention as a member, yet I attended several of its sessions **before I came home.**[75] I recollect hearing it distinctly said by one of the ministers, **a Mr. Lathrop,** who was then, **or had been, pastor of the church at Elyria, I think,**[76] that he regarded Oberlin doctrines and influence as worse than those of Roman Catholicism. That speech was a representative one, and seemed to be about the view that was entertained by that body.[77] I do not mean by all of them, by

MS 697

Beecher. It emerged as a result of the depressed conditions among the western colleges following the financial crash of 1837. Oberlin, however, was not one of the colleges originally invited to cooperate or to receive assistance. It was not until 1863 that any help was given to Oberlin students. See "Western College Society," *The American Journal of Education* (New York) 15 (June 1865): 261–64.

Students of Oberlin College had also been refused aid by the American Education Society since 1838. Finney, however, was of the opinion that Oberlin should be self-supporting, and that the students should not receive aid from the Education Society, but he "yielded to the wishes of his colleagues." See "Oberlin Collegiate Institute and the Education Society," *OE,* Extra no. 1, 20 November 1839, p. 2.

[72] The Committee of Correspondence, consisting of Lyman Beecher and four other ministers, sent out the invitation to the Second Western Convention, dated Cincinnati, 25 March 1844:

> They do, therefore, hereby respectfully invite their brethren of the Presbyterian and Congregational denominations throughout the States of Ohio, Indiana, Illinois, Kentucky, Tennessee, and Michigan, the territories of Wiskonsin and Iowa, Western New York, and Northern and Western Pennsylvania, to be fully represented in said Convention. They hope that their Congregational brethren, within the specified bounds, will feel precisely as cordial and free as Presbyterians to move and act in the matter (*The New York Observer*, 20 April 1844, p. 61).

[73] Lyman Beecher was the chairman of the convention.

[74] The manuscript sheet 697 was torn in two about a third of the way down but was repaired by pasting on a strip of similar paper on the back. Since the edges of the tear did not exactly meet, the separated letters were joined up by Finney.

[75] Edward H. Fairchild, who was present, recollected:

> The Conference with which the Oberlin church was connected was not invited to send representatives. But Pres. Mahan and Prof. Finney were present, and a motion was made and advocated by Dr. Duffield of Detroit, that they be invited to sit as corresponding members. This was voted down by a considerable majority (E. H. Fairchild, *Historical Sketch of Oberlin College* [Springfield: Republic, 1868], p. 19).

The resolution admitted only delegates from presbyteries, "and Associations or Consociations of Orthodox Congregationalists, who sympathize with the operations of the Am. Home Miss. Society, and the A.B.C.F.M." This effectively excluded the Oberlin church, which was critical of those missionary societies for their failure to take a firm stand on antislavery. See Frederick I. Kuhns, *The American Home Missionary Society in Relation to the Antislavery Controversy in the Old Northwest* (Billings, Mont., 1959), pp. 5–11.

[76] Daniel Whiting Lathrop (1798–1883) had helped to organize the Presbyterian church in Elyria and was its first pastor from 1824 until John J. Shipherd took over the church in 1830. According to Shipherd, Lathrop was "at the head of ministers on the Reserve." For six years he was an agent of the American Home Missionary Society in Ohio. In 1848 he moved to New Haven. See E. B. Huntington, *A Genealogical Memoir of the Lo-Lathrop Family in this Country* (Ridgefield, Conn.: Huntington, 1884), pp. 153–54; and Shipherd to Fayette Shipherd, 15 October 1830, Bragdon Family Papers, University of Rochester Library.

[77] A report, probably by Henry Cowles, one of the faculty of the Oberlin Collegiate Institute who was present, indicated that the chief charge against Oberlin was

> that our influence is worse than Romanism; in particular, that our students and Faculty preach without pay; that we draw out people to hear us;—and that thereby churches

any means. Some **of our students,** who had been educated **here** in theology, were so related to the churches and the convention, that they were admitted to seats **in that body as they had** come there from different parts of the JHF 345 country.[78] ¹These were very outspoken upon the principles and practices of Oberlin, so far as they were called in question. The object of the convention evidently was to hedge in Oberlin on every side, and crush us by a public sentiment that would refuse us all support.[79] But let me be distinctly MS 698 understood to say, that I do not in the ¹least degree blame the members of that convention, or but very few of them; for I knew that they had been misled, and were acting under an entire misapprehension of the facts. ‹Dr. L. Beecher was the leading spirit in that convention.›[80]

The policy that we pursued **here** was to let opposition alone.[81] We kept about our own business, and always had as many students as we knew what to do with. Our hands were always full of labor, and we were always greatly encouraged in our efforts. A few years after the meeting of this convention, one of the leading ministers who was there came and spent a day or two at our house. He said to me among other things: "Brother Finney, Oberlin is to us a great wonder." Said he, "I have, for many years been connected with a college as one of its professors. College life and principles, and the conditions upon which colleges are built up, are very familiar to me. We have always thought," said he, "**speaking of colleges,** that colleges could not exist unless they were patronized by the ministry. We knew that young men who were about to go MS 699 to ¹College would generally consult their pastors in regard to what colleges they should **go to; and generally young men that wished to go to College did so in accordance with their views.** Now," said he, "the ministers almost universally arrayed themselves against Oberlin. They were deceived by the cry of **A**ntinomian perfectionism, and in respect to your views of reform; and ecclesiastical bodies united, far and near, congregational, and **p**resbyterian, and of all denominations. They warned their churches against you, they discouraged young men universally, **if consulted,** from coming **here;** and still

are divided, and pastors unsettled. We are accused of lacking ministerial courtesy (*OE,* 3 July 1844, p. 111).

[78]There was a discussion at the start of the convention "in regard to admitting the delegates from the Eastern Conference of Michigan as members . . . on account of the impression that they were tinctured with Oberlinism." The two delegates referred to were Revs. Harvey Hyde and Edward H. Fairchild. Hyde replied "that Oberlinism was not a general thing: indeed it was more than probable but one man in that Conference entertained it." He was referring to Fairchild, an Oberlin graduate, who reckoned he himself was "the only Oberlin man in the Convention." See *NYE,* 4 July 1844, p. 105; and Fairchild, *Historical Sketch of Oberlin College,* p. 19.

[79]John Keep wrote: "Professor Finney and his associates were excluded, and the Convention permitted these men and their views to be defamed, without suffering them to be heard in reply" (*Congregationalism and Church Action,* p. 69). According to E. H. Fairchild:

> Much of the time was spent in denouncing Oberlin, and the chief object of the Convention seemed to be to destroy its influence, and exclude it from the pale of orthodoxy. . . . At this Convention the opposition to Oberlin culminated. From that time it gradually declined, till now it may be said to have disappeared (*Historical Sketch of Oberlin College,* pp. 19–20; see also *OE,* 11 September 1844, p. 150).

[80]Finney added this sentence later.

[81]E. H. Fairchild wrote that "there were a hundred attacks upon Oberlin where there was one reply. And with one or two exceptions, the members of the Faculty were, by nature and by grace, averse to controversy" (*Historical Sketch of Oberlin College,* p. 20).

the Lord has built you up. You have been supported with funds better than almost any college |in the **land;**[82] you have had by far more students **than any other college in the west, or even in the east;** and the blessing of God has been upon you, so that your success has been wonderful. Now," said he, "this is a perfect anomaly in the history of colleges. The opposers of Oberlin have been confounded, and God has stood by you and sustained you through all this opposition, so that you have hardly felt it." JHF 346

|It is difficult now for people to realize the opposition that we met with when we first established this **C**ollege. As an illustration of it, and as a representative case, I will relate a laughable fact that occurred about the time of which I am speaking. I had occasion to go to Akron, **Summit Co.,** to preach on the Sabbath.[83] I went with a horse and buggy. On my way, beyond the village of Medina, I observed in the road before me a **lady** walking with a little bundle in her hand. As I drew near her I observed **it** was an elderly **lady** nicely dressed, but walking, as I thought, with some difficulty on account of her age. As I came up to her I reined up my horse, and asked her how far she was going on that road. She told me; and I then asked if she would accept a seat in my buggy and ride. "O," she replied, "I should be very thankful for a ride, for I find I have undertaken too long a walk;" **and then explained how she came to undertake so long a walk.** I helped her into my buggy, **and then took a seat beside her** and drove on. I found her a very intelligent **elderly** lady, and very free and home-like in her conversation. After riding for some distance |she **asked,** "May I ask to whom I am indebted for this ride?" I told her who I was. She then inquired from whence I came. I told her I was from Oberlin. This announcement startled her. She made a motion as if she would sit as far from me as she could; and turning and looking earnestly at me, she said, "From Oberlin! why," said she, "our minister said he would just as soon send a son to State-prison as to Oberlin!" Of course I smiled and soothed the old lady's fears, if she had any; and made her understand she was in no danger from me. I relate this simply as an illustration of the spirit that pre|vailed very extensively when this college was first established. Misrepresentations and misapprehensions abounded on every side; and these misapprehensions extended into almost every corner of the United States. MS 700 MS 701 JHF 347

However there was a great number of laymen, and no inconsiderable number of ministers on the whole, in different parts of the country, **that** had no confidence in this opposition, who sympathized with our aims, our views, our efforts, and who stood firmly by us |through thick and thin; and knowing, as they did, the straitness to which, for the time, we were reduced because of this opposition, they gave their money and their influence freely to help us forward. I have spoken of **Brother** Chapin of Providence, as having for several years sent me six hundred dollars a year on which to support my family. When he had done it as long as he thought it his duty,—which he did, indeed, until financial difficulties rendered it inconvenient for him longer to do so,—**Brother** Willard Sears of Boston took his place, and for several years suffered me to draw on him for the same amount annually, that Mr. Chapin MS 702

[82] Fairchild altered the word "land" to "West."
[83] A revival in Akron was reported in *OE,* 22 April 1840, p. 70.

had paid.[84] In the meantime efforts were constantly made to sustain the other members of the faculty; and by the grace of God we rode out the gale. After a few years the panic in a measure subsided.

President Mahan, Professor Cowles,[85] Professor Morgan,[86] and myself, published on the subject of sanctification. We established a periodical, "The Oberlin Evangelist,"[87] and afterwards, "The Oberlin Quarterly;"[88] in which

[84]Willard Sears (1803–1890) was a deacon of the Free Church in Boston. He had gone there in 1822 and become apprenticed as an organ builder but soon afterwards formed a partnership with his brother, Eben Sears, as a contractor and builder. During his lifetime he built thirty churches in Boston. He was later involved in putting up the first buildings in San Francisco and in organizing the Northern Pacific Railroad Company. He was a liberal patron of Oberlin College and on the board of trustees from 1845 to 1862. He started paying Finney's salary in 1846, discontinuing in 1852. See his obituary in the *Boston Evening Transcript*, 26 June 1890, transcription in Alumni Records, file 28/3, box 71, Oberlin College Archives; *Brief History of the First Free Congregational Church* (Boston: Dow and Jackson, 1845); and Sears to Finney, 9 April 1846; and 25 September 1852, Finney Papers, microfilm, roll 4.

[85]Henry Cowles (1803–1881), from a farming family in Norfolk, Connecticut, was a graduate of Yale College and Divinity School. In 1828 he was ordained by the Hartford Consociation as a missionary to the Western Reserve. After pastorates in Ashtabula and Sandusky, he spent five years at Austinburg, where he had considerable success. In 1835 he went to Oberlin College, where he was professor of Latin and Greek and later professor of Hebrew and Old Testament in the seminary. He became the full-time editor of *The Oberlin Evangelist* in 1848 and continued in that position until the paper ceased publication in 1862. He then devoted the remainder of his life to writing a commentary on the whole Bible. He reported more than a hundred of Finney's sermons at Oberlin, which he read first to Finney and then published in *The Oberlin Evangelist*. See *In Memoriam: Rev. Henry Cowles, D.D.* (Oberlin: n.p., 1883); and "Remarks of Rev. Henry Cowles, D.D., of Oberlin," in *Reminiscences of Rev. Charles G. Finney* (Oberlin: Goodrich, 1876), p. 60.

[86]John Morgan (1802–1884), a native of Cork, Ireland, had come to America with his family when he was about ten years old, settling in Philadelphia and then in New York. He trained as a printer, and while living in Utica, New York, in the family of his employer, William Williams, he became a Christian. After graduating from Williams College in 1826 with the highest honors, he went to New York, where he taught in a girls' school and studied theology under Dr. Samuel H. Cox. It was there that he got to know Finney and sat under his preaching. In 1833 he took charge of the preparatory department of Lane Seminary. During the antislavery disruptions there, he was sympathetic with the students and was dismissed. He then went to Oberlin at the same time as Finney and became professor of New Testament literature until he retired in 1881. He and Finney were lifelong friends. Fairchild wrote, "For many years he was associated with Mr. Finney in the pastorship of the church, preaching once on the Sabbath, and more in Mr. Finney's absence or ill health." See J. H. Fairchild, "Memorial Address. With a Sketch of the Life and Character of Prof. John Morgan, D.D.," *The Oberlin Review*, 25 October 1884, pp. 30–33; "Remarks of Prof. John Morgan, D.D., of Oberlin," in *Reminiscences of Finney,* p. 57; Joshua Leavitt and C. G. Finney, Recommendation of John Morgan, 9 May 1833, Lane Seminary Records, Cincinnati Historical Society; Fletcher, *History of Oberlin College*, p. 29; and Fairchild, *Colony and College*, p. 284.

[87]*The Oberlin Evangelist* started publication with a specimen number on 1 November 1838 and then appeared fortnightly from 1 January 1839 until 17 December 1862, when it ceased publication because of lack of support during the Civil War. It was compiled by an association made up of the Prudential Committee, the faculty of Oberlin College, and others. Horace C. Taylor was the first editor until 1844. Henry Cowles then took the main responsibility and was appointed full-time in 1848. Finney was never an editor. Its circulation gradually rose to nearly five thousand. See Fletcher, *History of Oberlin College*, p. 419.

[88]*The Oberlin Quarterly Review*, edited at first by Asa Mahan and William Cochran, was started in August 1845. It was designed to provide a vehicle for more lengthy and scholarly articles, which would not be suitable for *The Oberlin Evangelist*, but it never attained large-scale circulation and was discontinued after May 1848.

On 8 May 1846, William Cochran, one of the editors, who was married that day to Finney's daughter, Helen, left Oberlin for New York to take up the editorship of *The New-York*

we disabused the public in a great measure in regard to what our real views were.[89] |In 1846 I published two volumes on Systematic theology; and in this work I discussed the subject of entire sanctification more at large.[90] After this MS 703

Evangelist. Finney wrote to him, "The brethren set upon me so hard after you left that I consented to have my name go on to the Quarterly as associate editor." He was editor with Mahan from November 1846 (Finney to W. Cochran, 8–19 May 1846, Charles G. Finney Correspondence 1830–1875, Oberlin College Archives, microfilm).

[89]The first publication on the subject of sanctification was an address given by Asa Mahan to the "Society of Inquiry" at Oberlin on 4 September 1838. It was entitled "Is Perfection in Holiness Attainable in This Life?" and first appeared in *The Cleveland Observer*, 13 September 1838. It was also printed in the first issue of *The Oberlin Evangelist*, 1 November 1838, pp. 1–6. Mahan used this address as the basis of the principal chapter of his book, *The Scripture Doctrine of Christian Perfection*, published in 1839 by the Methodist publisher, D. S. King, of Boston. This was a book of sermons preached in the Marlboro Chapel in Boston in the winter of 1837–1838. It became the classical exposition of Oberlin perfectionism in its early period. It was widely reviewed and frequently reissued. Mahan continued to expound the doctrine in sermons and articles and further books. He was the main promoter of the early Wesleyan form of Oberlin perfectionism, and his later life was largely devoted to the propagation of the subject. See Zikmund, "Asa Mahan and Oberlin Perfectionism."

Henry Cowles wrote a series of articles on holiness in the first volume of *The Oberlin Evangelist* in 1839, that was brought out as a separate volume, *Holiness of Christians in the Present Life* (Oberlin: Steele, 1840).

John Morgan wrote two articles for the first volume of *The Oberlin Quarterly Review*. One was "The Gift of the Holy Ghost" in the first issue, August 1845, pp. 90–118, which was published later as a separate pamphlet with an introduction by Finney, entitled *The Gift of the Holy Ghost According to the Teaching of Scripture* (Oberlin: Goodrich, 1875). The other was "The Holiness Acceptable to God," which was published in the third issue, February 1846, pp. 317–64, and was reprinted at the time as a separate pamphlet with that title by James M. Fitch of Oberlin.

Finney wrote a series of twenty-two lectures in the first volume of *The Oberlin Evangelist* in 1839. (This was republished by Timothy L. Smith under the title *The Promise of the Spirit* [Minneapolis: Bethany Fellowship, 1980].) A further series of nine lectures on sanctification in *The Oberlin Evangelist* from January to April 1840 was reissued as a separate book entitled *Views of Sanctification* (Oberlin: Steele, 1840). Finney also published two series of letters to the churches in 1839 and 1840 through the medium of *The Oberlin Evangelist*, designed to raise the standard of holiness in the land. Many of Finney's sermons that dealt with sanctification were published in *The Oberlin Evangelist*. He also published "Recent Discussions on the Subject of Entire Sanctification" in *The Oberlin Quarterly Review* 2 (May 1847): 449–72.

Fairchild wrote:

> The idea was much the same under these varying forms of expression, namely, that there is an experience attainable in the Christian life, subsequent in general to conversion, in which the believer raises to a higher plane, secures new views of Christ and His salvation, obtains victory over weakness which had before marred his character, and attains a stability to which he was before a stranger ("The Doctrine of Sanctification at Oberlin," *The Congregational Quarterly* [Boston] 18 [April 1876]: 240–41).

After a few years the doctrine of sanctification at Oberlin underwent modification, particularly under the impact of the theory of the "simplicity of moral action," and the Wesleyan emphasis on a second blessing was more or less abandoned, particularly by Finney. But Finney continued to advocate the Oberlin doctrine in its modified form throughout his life. It was considered by some that the decline of spirituality at Oberlin in later years was due to the resignation of President Mahan in 1850 and the abandoning of the Wesleyan emphasis on the need for an experience of sanctification. And in 1893 Sherlock Bristol, one of the early students, wrote to Fairchild:

> Let me express to you . . . my fear that the advice which since Finneys death has prevailed at Oberlin,—not to make *a speciality of seeking this baptism* of the Holy Ghost;—nor deem its reception indispensable to the preacher & the efficient worker, has exerted a sad & baleful influence (Bristol to Fairchild, 25 March 1893, Fairchild Papers, microfilm, roll 21; see also A. M. Hills, *Life of Charles G. Finney* [Cincinnati: Office of "God's Revivalist," 1902], pp. 218–38).

[90]Finney's *Lectures on Systematic Theology* were to have been in three volumes. The first volume

work was published, it was reviewed by a Committee of the presbytery of Troy, N.Y.[91] **To this review I replied, and heard no more criticism from that quarter.**[92] Then Dr Hodge of Princeton published in the Biblical Repertory a lengthy criticism upon my theology.[93] This was from the Old-JHF 348 School standpoint. |**I replied, and heard no more from that quarter.**[94] Then Dr Duffield, of the New School Presbyterian church living at Detroit, reviewed me professedly from the New-School stand-point, though his review was far enough from consistent New-schoolism.[95] **However, to this I**

was never written. It would probably have been an expansion of his *Skeleton of a Course of Theological Lectures* (Oberlin: Steele, 1840). Melvin Dieter has pointed out that those "skeletons" were marked "Vol. 1" and that a note on the last page (p. 248) reads: "The remaining Volumes will be issued as soon as they can be prepared for the press." No further volumes at that time were published. Volume 2 of the *Lectures on Systematic Theology, embracing Lectures on Moral Government, Together with Atonement, Moral and Physical Depravity, Regeneration, Philosophical Theories, and Evidences of Regeneration*," was published in Oberlin by James M. Fitch in 1846. Volume 3, "*embracing Ability (natural, moral and gracious,) Repentance, Impenitence, Faith and Unbelief, Justification, Sanctification, Election, Reprobation, Divine Purposes, Divine Sovereignty, and Perseverance*," was published in 1847.

Out of 612 pages in volume 3, the section on sanctification took up pages 166–424. Part of that section (pp. 245–312), dealing with the relations of Christ to the believer, was published as a separate book under the title *Guide to the Savior; or, Conditions of attaining to and aiding in entire holiness of heart and life* (Oberlin: Fitch, 1848).

[91]The "Action of the Troy Presbytery," signed by Thomas J. Haswell and N. S. S. Beman, Troy, 29 June 1841, was published in *The New York Observer* and *The New-York Evangelist*, on 10 July 1841, and later copied into *The Oberlin Evangelist*, 15 September 1841, pp. 145–47.

[92]Finney's reply was refused by *The New-York Evangelist* and was therefore published in *the Oberlin Evangelist*, 15 September 1841, pp. 147–49. It was noted that no answer was made by the Troy Presbytery to Finney's reply. See *OE*, 28 August 1844, p. 162; and 23 October 1844, p. 175. On seeing the name of Beman at the bottom of the Troy Presbytery statement, Finney wrote in his reply: "I cannot however refrain from saying, that when I saw the name of one whom I greatly loved, and with whom I had often taken sweet counsel, attached to that report, my heart felt a kind of spontaneous gushing, and I almost involuntarily exclaimed, '*Et Tu Brute!*'" According to Asa Mahan, Beman could not be persuaded to read Finney's reply (Mahan to Finney, 5 January 1850, Finney Papers, microfilm, roll 4).

It is of interest that Finney's son, Charles Beman, who was named after Beman, changed his name to Charles Grandison when he graduated from Oberlin College in 1851. See p. 203 n. 2 (MS 394); and Alumni Records, "Charles Grandison Finney Jr.," file 28/1, Oberlin College Archives.

[93]Charles Hodge (1797–1878) was professor of theology at Princeton Theological Seminary. He was a graduate of Princeton College and Seminary and was a professor there all his life. He was the most eminent conservative Presbyterian theologian in America and a staunch defender of Calvinism and the Westminster Confession. He was the founder and editor of the *Biblical Repertory and Princeton Review*. See Archibald A. Hodge, *The Life of Charles Hodge* (London: Nelson, 1881); and *DAB*. Hodge's "Review of Finney's *Lectures on Systematic Theology*" is in *Biblical Repertory and Princeton Review* 19 (April 1847): 237–77.

[94]"An Examination, by Prof. C. G. Finney, of the Review of Finney's Systematic Theology published in the Biblical Repertory, N.J., April 1847," *The Oberlin Quarterly Review* 3 (August 1847): 23–81. This was also published as a separate pamphlet, *The Reviewer Reviewed; or, Finney's Theology and the Princeton Review* (Oberlin: Fitch, 1847). When Hodge came to write his own *Systematic Theology*, which was published in 1873, he repeated the same criticisms. He made no reference to Finney's "Examination" of Hodge's "Review," nor to the revision that Finney made to his *Systematic Theology* in 1851. G. F. Wright commented, "There is no evidence that Dr. Hodge read anything from President Finney's pen later than April, 1847, the date of his review of the first edition of Finney's Lectures on Theology." See G. F. Wright, "Dr. Hodge's Misrepresentations of President Finney's System of Theology," *Bibliotheca Sacra* (Andover, Mass.), 2d ser., 33 (April 1876): 391–92.

[95]George Duffield (1794–1868) had been Finney's successor at the Broadway Tabernacle, New York. He went to the First Presbyterian Church in Detroit in 1838 and was the most

replied; since which, criticisms upon our theology here have not met my eye that I recollect,—that is, nothing has been said, so far as I know, impugning our orthodoxy.[96] **‹My replies are published as an appendix to the English Edition of my Theology.›**[97]

I have thus far narrated the principal facts connected with the establishment and struggles of **our** school **here** so far as I have been concerned with them. And being |the professor of theology, the theological opposition was directed, of course, principally toward myself; which has led me of necessity to speak more freely of my relations to it all than I otherwise should have done. But let me not be misunderstood. I am not contending that the brethren who thus opposed were wicked in their opposition. No doubt the great mass of them were really misled, and acted according to their views of right as they then understood it. I must say for the honor of the grace of God, that none of the opposition that we met with ruffled our spirits here, or disturbed us in such a sense as to provoke us into a spirit of controversy or ill feeling, **that I am aware of.**[98] We were well aware of the pains that had been taken to lead to these misapprehensions, and could easily understand how it was that we were opposed in the spirit and manner in which we were assailed.

MS 704

During these years of smoke and dust of misapprehension and opposition from without, the Lord was blessing us richly *within*. We not only prospered in our own souls here as a church, but |we had a continuous revival. **It varied in its strength and power at different times; but we were at no time in a state that would not have been regarded as a revival state in any other place than this.**[99] Our students were converted by scores **from year to year**;

MS 705

prominent Presbyterian minister in Michigan. See *DAB*. Duffield's review was in *A Warning against Error, being the Report of a Committee, adopted by the Presbytery of Detroit, at their Session at Northville, Mich., September 29, 1847. Approved by the Synod of Michigan, at their Session at Kalamazoo, Oct. 18, 1847. And ordered to be published for the benefit of the churches under their care* (Detroit: Willcox, 1847). He also wrote "Review of Finney's Theology," which appeared in four parts in *The Biblical Repository and Classical Review* (New Haven), 3d ser., 4 (1848); 5 (1849).

[96] Finney published "A Reply to the 'Warning against error' . . .," *The Oberlin Quarterly Review* 3 (May 1848): 373–417, which was also reprinted as a pamphlet, *A Reply to Dr. Duffield's "Warning against Error"* (Oberlin: Fitch, 1848). The first part of Duffield's "Review" had by then appeared, but Finney stated: "I have seen Dr. Duffield's review of my Theology in the Biblical Repository. That is only an expression and a dilation of the Warning against Error, to which I have in the foregoing article replied. All I need to say in reply to such a production is, that if he has enlightened anyone by what he has written, I shall be happy to know it" (p. 47).

[97] This sentence is in Finney's handwriting. The replies are in his *Lectures on Systematic Theology* (London: Tegg, 1851), pp. 916–96.

[98] William H. Ryder, who had lived in Oberlin as a boy and was in the college before and after the Civil War, wrote to G. F. Wright, Finney's biographer:

> One thing that I came to admire much in Mr. Finney,—as I grew older and understood him better,—was that, with all his intensity, he was very free from partisanship. In the days of Oberlin's unpopularity, when the Churches feard him and the missionary Societies would not accept his pupils,—I never heard him utter any bitter words. . . . He saw good things in the men whose views he condemned,—and even the sinner whom he harried dreadfully in his sermon, found him a genial companion (W. H. Ryder to G. F. Wright, 10 April 1890, Wright Papers, box 8).

[99] Reports of the state of religion in Oberlin and the special efforts to promote revivals were carried in *The Oberlin Evangelist* from 1839 to 1862. They indicate that the period from 1835 to 1840 was the most intense, with the autumns of 1836, 1837, and 1838 being the most remarkable. "The power of those revivals reached this entire people. It did not indeed convert

and the Lord overshadowed us continually with the cloud of his mercy. Gales of divine influence swept over us from year to year, **leaving us His** fruits **among us abundantly of** love, joy, peace, long-suffering, gentleness, JHF 349 **temperance,** goodness, faith.[100] I have always attributed our success in this good work entirely to the grace of God. It was not wisdom or goodness of our own that has achieved this success. Nothing but continued divine influence pervading the community, sustained us under our trials, and kept us in an attitude of mind in which we could be efficient in the work we had undertaken. We have always felt that if the Lord **forsook us by H**is Spirit, no outward circumstances could make us truly prosperous. We have had trials MS 706 amongst ourselves. Frequent subjects of public discussion have come up; and we have **frequently**[101] spent days, and even weeks, in discussing great questions of duty and expediency on which we have not thought alike. But these questions have none of them permanently divided us. Our principle has been to accord to each other the right of private judgment. We have generally come to a substantial agreement on subjects upon which we have differed; and when we have found ourselves unable to see alike, the minority have submitted themselves to the judgment of the majority, and the idea of rending the church to pieces because in some things we could not see alike has never been entertained by us. We have to a very great extent preserved "the unity of the Spirit in the bond of peace;"[102] and perhaps no community has existed for such a length of time, and passed through such trials and changes as we have, that has on the whole **preserved** a greater spirit of **unity,** Christian forbearance, and brotherly love.

When the question of entire sanctification first came up here for public MS 707 discussion, and when the subject first attracted the general attention of the church, we were in the midst of a powerful revival.[103] When the revival was going on hopefully, one day President Mahan had been preaching a searching

all, but it left none outside the pale of its influence. So much cannot be said of any revivals enjoyed since" (*OE,* 8 June 1853, p. 92).

There was a slackening off in the early 1840s when revivals generally occurred only in the winter. But revival influence remained central to the operations of the college up until the 1858 revival, and there were powerful revivals frequently after that. The numbers admitted to the church in Oberlin averaged fifty per year for the years 1835 to 1856. See *OE,* 26 September 1856, p. 157; and Norman Rovick, "The Impact of Religious Revivalism upon Five Selected Ohio Colleges of the Mid-Nineteenth Century" (M.A. thesis, Ohio State University, 1965), pp. 73–78.

Asa Mahan wrote, "During the fifteen years in which I remained President of Oberlin College, no year passed without from one to three general revivals, some of the most powerful being in midsummer" (*Out of Darkness into Light,* p. 184). In 1857 it was reported, "Oberlin has had a revival every year during the twenty-three years of its history—and Pres. Finney states that no month has occurred without some conversions" (*The Independent,* 12 March 1857, p. 3).

[100]The words "See Bible" inserted in the margin in pencil at this point appear to be in the handwriting of Lewis Tappan. Galatians 5:22–23 reads, "But the fruit of the Spirit is love, joy, peace, longsuffering, gentleness, goodness, faith, meekness, temperance: against such there is no law."

[101]Fairchild altered the word "frequently" to "sometimes."

[102]Ephesians 4:3.

[103]This was October 1836. Finney's duties and health restricted him mainly to conducting the meetings of inquiry. The responsibility for doing the preaching fell on Asa Mahan. See Mahan, *Scripture Doctrine of Christian Perfection,* p. 180; and *Out of Darkness into Light,* p. 132.

Asa Mahan. The president of the Oberlin Collegiate Institute from 1835 to 1850 and a leading exponent of the Oberlin doctrine of perfection. An 1842 oil painting in the Oberlin College Library. Photograph by Richard A. G. Dupuis.

discourse.[104] I observed in the course of his preaching that he had left one point untouched, that appeared to me of great importance in that connection. He would often ask me when he closed his sermon if I had any remarks to |make, and he did on this occasion. I arose and pressed the point that he had omitted. It was the distinction between desire and will. From the course of thought he had presented, and from the attitude in which I saw that the congregation was at the time, I saw, or *thought* I saw, that the pressing of that distinction just at that point would throw much light upon the question whether they were really Christians or not, whether they were really consecrated persons, or whether they merely had desires without being in fact

JHF 350

[104]The sermon was on the first Sabbath after the special meetings for revival had started. He preached on the text from Hosea 10:1, "Israel is an empty vine; he bringeth forth fruit unto himself" (Mahan, *Out of Darkness into Light*, p. 132).

willing to **do the will of** God.[105] When this distinction was made clear just in that connection, I recollect the Holy Spirit fell upon the congregation in a MS 708 most remarkable manner.[106] ¦A large number of persons dropped down their heads, and some **of them** groaned so that they could be heard **all over** the house. It cut up the false hopes of deceived professors on every side. Several **of them** arose on the spot, and said that they had been deceived, and that they could see wherein; and this was carried to such an extent as greatly astonished me, and indeed produced a general feeling of astonishment, I think, in the congregation.[107] **However it was reality, and very plainly a revelation of the state of the heart of the people made by the Spirit of God.** The work went on with power; and old professors **either** obtained **a** new hope or were reconverted in such numbers, that a very great and

[105]Mahan's recollection of this event is as follows:

> In the discourse I pressed upon professing Christians the fact, that the reason why they were "bringing forth fruit unto themselves," and not unto God—in other words, that the reason, and only reason, of the low state of piety among us—was that individuals were not "*aiming* to do any better than they were doing," and that here was the ground of "the Lord's controversy" with them. Brother Finney, perceiving the searching and convicting power of the truth, arose at the close of the discourse, and remarked, that if there were any self-deceived professors present, they would escape the pressure of the truth upon their consciences by falling back upon their *good desires*. "If we are not living as we should, we *desire* thus to live," they will say. He then showed that in mere desires, that did not induce the serious *aim* or *intent* to do what God requires—that is, did not issue in real obedience—there is no religion at all. "If there are any professors of religion present," he added, "who now see that their hopes are not well founded, let them signify it by rising" (*Out of Darkness into Light,* pp. 132–33).

Henry Cowles, in a report of the revival dated 30 November 1836, drew attention to the same point:

> Great pains was taken to point out the distinction between the almost Christian and the real Christian—between those who have *desires* and those who really and fully *design*. It was shown that men may desire heaven, and desire Christ as the means of gaining heaven, without ever designing and determining to serve Christ and serving him wholly. Here was a distinction which many were conscious they had never made (reprinted from the *Ohio Observer* in *NYE,* 24 December 1836, p. 207).

[106]Fergus Ferguson, Jr., of Scotland, in a review of Finney's *Memoirs*, commented, "We do not recollect of ever having read before of the work of grace being helped forward by what may be called the clearing up of a metaphysical difficulty, or rather the making of a nice metaphysical distinction" (*The Evangelical Repository* [Glasgow], 6th ser., 3 [June 1877]: 284).

[107]Mahan described the scene:

> To our amazement, quite one-third of the professors present arose, and asked us to tell them "what they should do to be saved." The other portion of the church, with almost one voice, and that from all parts of the assembly, implored us to tell them how they might cease to live at their present "dying rate," and attain to the revealed "liberty of the sons of God" (*Out of Darkness into Light,* p. 133).

Henry Hammond, however, who was a student at the time, stated later: "I well remember that scene, and have no doubt that a large proportion of those students were mistaken in their hasty judgments against themselves." According to Hammond, "There were indeed some sensitive and over conscientious souls who were not so much benefited by Mr. Finney's preaching; nor was he always most useful when he thought himself so" (H. L. Hammond, "The First Decade," in *The Oberlin Jubilee, 1833–1883,* ed. W. G. Ballantine [Oberlin: Goodrich, 1883], p. 204). Fairchild recalled that

> it was not a rare thing for a large portion of the congregation, after a searching sermon by Prof. Finney or Pres. Mahan, to rise up in acknowledgment that they had reason to apprehend that they were deceived as to their Christian character, and to express their determination not to rest until their feet were established upon the Rock ("Doctrine of Sanctification at Oberlin," p. 238).

important change c‹a›m‹e›[108] over the whole community. President Mahan had been greatly blessed among others, with some of our professors. **Brother Mahan** came manifestly into an entirely new form of Christian experience at that time.[109] ‹In a meeting a few days› after this[110] one of our theological students arose and put the inquiry,[111] whether the Gospel did not provide for Christians all the conditions of an established faith, ¦and hope, and love; MS 709 whether[112] there was not something better and higher than Christians had generally experienced; in short, whether sanctification was not attainable in this life, that is sanctification in such a sense that Christians could have unbroken peace, and not come into ¦condemnation, or have the feeling of JHF 351 condemnation or a consciousness of sin.[113] Brother Mahan immediately answered, "Yes." What occurred at this meeting brought the question of sanctification prominently before us as a *practical* question. We had no theories on the subject, no philosophy to maintain, but simply took it up as a Bible question. In this form it existed amongst us as an *experimental* truth, which we did not attempt to reduce to a theological formula; nor did we attempt to explain its philosophy until years afterwards. But the discussion **and settling** of this question **here** was a great blessing to us, and to a great number of our students who are now scattered in various parts of the **United States, and in Missionary stations in** different parts of the world.[114]

[108]Here Finney changed the words "was coming" to "came."

[109]Mahan described the change that came about on the afternoon of the next day when he went to one of the professors and told him that he was seeking to discover "the *secret* of the piety of Paul," and how as he was speaking he suddenly arose with the joyful exclamation, "I have found it!" (*Out of Darkness into Light*, p. 134). A student describing the revival wrote to a friend on 26 October:

> The President and some of the Professors were seemingly overwhelmed with the view they had of Christ and themselves, and acknowledged they had not preached Christ as faithfully as they ought. Many professing Christians for a time gave up their hopes and were in great distress. Professor Finney, in his remarks to day, was so much affected in speaking of the relation we sustain to Christ, that he could not proceed, and sat down and wept like a child. The whole congregation were melted into tears (M[olliston]. M. C[lark], "Interesting State of Things at Oberlin. Extract of a letter from a member of the Institution to a gentleman in Buffalo," *Religious Intelligencer* [New Haven], 26 November 1836, p. 413).

[110]Matson had started the sentence, "Soon after this," but Finney changed it.

[111]Here Matson had written "in meeting," but Finney crossed it out.

[112]This word is written "whethere" in the manuscript and was unaltered.

[113]According to Asa Mahan, it was Sereno Wright Streeter (1810–1880) who asked this question. He had been at the Oneida Institute and Lane Seminary and was one of a number of students who had just graduated from the theological department at Oberlin and was about to go out as an antislavery agent. He was later a Presbyterian minister. See Mahan, *Autobiography*, p. 322; and John L. Myers, "Antislavery Activities of Five Lane Seminary Boys in 1835–1836," *Bulletin of the Historical and Philosophical Society of Ohio* 21, no. 2 (1963): 107–10.

Fairchild appears to be speaking of the same incident in *College and Colony*, p. 90, but he does not identify the student by name. D. L. Leonard, however, in talking with Fairchild about the incident, wrote the name "William Dewey" in his notebook. Dewey was a member of the college but was not a theological student at the time. It was possibly a different occasion that was referred to by Fairchild. See D. L. Leonard, "Notes on Talks with Pres. Fairchild," Notebook 1, pp. 26, 32, 124, 144, R. S. Fletcher Papers, file 30/24, box 1, Oberlin College Archives.

[114]At a reunion at Oberlin in 1860, S. W. Streeter, then a pastor in Michigan, is reported as giving

> a very touching allusion to those rich and wonderful effusions of the Spirit which fell upon us, bathing the whole College and community in the waters of salvation, showing

how, as the students, having mostly closed the studies of the season 1836, tarried in this Jerusalem, and in connection with prayer long-protracted, united, and most earnest, were indeed endowed with power from on high. Those who were here then will never forget the searching power of the truth and Spirit of God upon almost all hearts, nor how, after the searching out of dark hearts, and the wreck of many doubtful and many worthless hopes, Jesus was revealed as one mighty to save. This revelation of the power and grace of a divine Redeemer was the glory of those refreshings. It seemed little to say they can never be forgotten (*OE,* 29 August 1860, p. 144).

MS 710
JHF 352

CHAPTER XXV

‹*Matters at Oberlin.*›

Before[1] I return to my revival record, in order to give any knowledge of the connection of things in our history here and my own labors, I must dwell a little more upon the progress of the anti-slavery or abolition movement, not only here but elsewhere as connected with my own labors. I have spoken of the state of public feeling on this subject all around us when we first came here, and said that we were opposed by the whole region of country around us, and that even the democratic legislature of this state endeavored to get hold of something that would justify them in abolishing our charter because of our anti-slavery sentiments and action.[2] As might be supposed, when colored students first came here there was a considerable excitement about their being received into our families and sitting at our tables, and in regard to their sitting promiscuously at the tables in the boarding hall. Very soon after I arrived—which was about the time, I think, of the arrival of the first colored students here—the question came up in the form of a request from some[3] of the white boarders in the boarding hall that the colored students in the hall might have a table by themselves; whereupon I made a motion, to which the faculty all consented, that any of the white students who were unwilling to sit ˡat the table with the colored students in the hall, might have a table by themselves. This put the few in the hall that took that ground in an awkward position. But still they could not complain. But we were determined, if there was any separation, that it should not be by giving the colored students a table by themselves, but those that objected to sitting with them. Although this action of the faculty did not set very comfortably, I suppose, upon those students, still it was in such shape that they could not object to it.[4] In the meantime different members of the faculty took colored students to board; and we suffered them to sit at our own tables, making no distinction on account of color.[5] The same

MS 711

[1] Pages 710–23 were numbered 557–70, then 689–702 by Matson, and changed to 710–23 by Finney. The chapter heading of page 710 was inserted by Finney. The title was not altered by Fairchild in the manuscript, but the published edition has "Labors in Boston and Providence."

[2] See MS 681.

[3] Fairchild had altered the word "some" to "a few," before crossing out the whole section.

[4] There is no reference to this action in the faculty minutes.

[5] The reformer and writer Caroline Dall, who stayed with the Finneys during her tour of western colleges in the mid-1860s, noted that "President Finney has never been without a

was done by all the leading families[6] **in the place, I believe. In our preaching and public instruction we aimed to correct this feeling that had existed here, and almost universally prevailed, of prejudice against color. It soon subsided; and now for years the people in their public assemblies seem to be hardly aware of any distinction between them. Colored people sit where they please; and nothing is said, or so far as I know, thought about it.** It was at first reported on every side of us **around about**, that we intended to encourage marriage between colored and white MS 712 students, and even |to *compel* them to intermarry; and that our object was to introduce a universal system of miscegenation.[7] A little fact will illustrate the feeling that existed among **even intelligent farmers** in the neighborhood. I had occasion to ride out a few miles soon after we came **here,**[8] **to get some currant bushes. A** farmer **to whom I went** looked very sullen and suspicious when he found who I was and from whence I came, and intimated to me that he did not want to have anything to do with the people of Oberlin. That our object was to introduce amalgamation of the races,[9] and compel the white and colored students to intermarry. That we also intended to **introduce the connection** of church and state, and that our ideas and projects were altogether revolutionary and abominable.[10] He was quite **serious** about this. But **I must say** the thing was so ridiculous that **I could not reply to him with any degree of seriousness, and therefore did not reply at all.** I knew that if I attempted **it** I should laugh him in the face. We JHF 353 had reason at an early day **to be seriously** apprehensive that a |mob from a MS 713 |neighboring town would come and destroy our buildings.

But we had not been here long before circumstances ‹occurred›[11] that created a reaction in the public mind. This place became one of the points **of** "the underground railroad," as it **was** called, where escaped slaves on their way to Canada, would take refuge for a day[12] until the way was open for them to proceed. Several cases occurred in which **they** were pursued by slaveholders, and **the** hue and cry was raised, not only in this neighborhood but in the neighboring towns, by their attempting to **force** the slaves back into slavery. **At one time I recollect several slaves had been secreted here;**

colored student at his table" (Caroline H. Dall, *The College, the Market, and the Court* [Boston: Lee and Shepard, 1868], p. 25).

[6] Fairchild altered the words "all the leading families" to "other families," before erasing the whole section.

[7] Here Matson had originally written "miscegeneration, or less properly miscegenation," but he changed it.

[8] Finney crossed out the words "in the Spring of the year." In a later account of this incident Finney remembered that it was "a year or two after I came here [to Oberlin]" and that it was "out on to the ridge, toward Elyria" ("Remarks of Ex-President Finney," at the Dedication of Council Hall in Oberlin, *The Oberlin Weekly News,* 20 August 1874, p. 4).

[9] Matson had written down the word "sexes" here, but he changed it to "races."

[10] In the other account Finney said: "The man was very cross when he found I was from Oberlin, and snapped out, 'You're going to compel the young men to marry "nigger wenches" over there, and you're going to try and unite church and state'" ("Remarks of Ex-President Finney," p. 4).

[11] Finney changed the word "arose" here to "occurred."

[12] Here Matson had written "a day or so," but the "or so" appears to have been crossed out by Finney. Fairchild then inserted "or two." Fairchild was a young member of the faculty at the time when most of the slaves were coming through the town.

of which, however, at the time I knew nothing until the row occurred. The slaveholders arrived in pursuit of them. The slaves took the alarm; and advised by some of their friends—I do not know by whom—started across the lots ‹&›[13] woods toward the lake, the slaveholders following as best they could ascertain which way they had gone. In the meantime the friends of the slaves, some on foot and some on horseback, went in different directions; and making the impression that they themselves were in pursuit of the slaves, they all got very mixed |up;[14] and while some cried *this way*, and some *that* way, the slaves through fields of high standing corn and through woods made their escape. MS 714

But scenes like this soon aroused public feeling in the towns around about, and began to produce a reaction. It set the farmers and people **in the surrounding region** to study more particularly into our aims and views, and our school soon became known, and **became better** appreciated; and it has resulted, **so far as I know,** in a state of universal confidence and good feeling between Oberlin and the surrounding[15] **towns and counties. So much hostility to us had been excited through the length and breadth of the land, that editors very extensively seemed to seize with avidity upon anything that would "spite" Oberlin, and[16] give it as wide a circulation as they could.**

Among other curious circumstances that occurred, with which editors at the time made a great show of opposition, but which finally reacted and resulted in our favor, I will relate the following: A young man from Kentucky, I think, came here to study; and while on probation, and before he was known to any considerable extent here, he laid a plan to seduce |one[17] of our young ladies.[18] She was a very estimable, modest girl. The young man had, I believe, been a writing master, and could use his pen in a masterly manner. He wrote this young lady a letter, in which he drew a very vile picture with his pen; and MS 715

[13] Matson had written the symbol & here. Finney tried to write the symbol more clearly, crossed it out, and inserted his own symbol.

[14] Fairchild added the figures "–731" after the page number 714, indicating to the printers to go straight to page 731, omitting all the intervening pages. The section that Fairchild wished to omit was later cut out of the manuscript. The bottom part was cut off MS 714 and the top part off MS 731, and the bottom of MS 731 was then joined to the top of MS 714, originally with a pin, and subsequently by pasting. A section of the original text was thus obscured. The sections cut off were kept and labeled.

[15] The section from here down to n. 16 was covered up by the piece of MS 731 pasted over it.

[16] The section from here to the bottom of the page is on the part of the sheet that was cut off. This was retained along with the words "real bottom of 714" written in pencil in the margin in an unidentified handwriting.

[17] Page 715 and the following pages down to MS 730 were not marked by Fairchild and were omitted from the published edition.

[18] This happened in May 1840. The young man was Horace Norton from Crawfordsville, Indiana, a son of Dr. Greenleaf Norton. In April 1839, at age seventeen, he had moved to Oberlin from Ripley, Ohio, where the family then lived. He was a student in his second year in the preparatory department of the college. H. C. Taylor, a theological student, wrote that Norton "was a stranger to us all. Some did not even know his name till then." And Finney apparently told Norton's father that "he had never seen him in his life." See Greenleaf Norton, *An Exposure of the Proceedings of the Late Mob at Oberlin, in a Letter Addressed to the Faculty of Oberlin Collegiate Institute* (Ripley, Ohio: Edwards, 1841), p. 6; *General Catalogue of Oberlin College, 1833–1908;* and *OE,* extra no. 3, 24 February 1841, p. 19.

couched the letter in such language, and gave it such shape, that it was calculated to produce the very worst effect upon her. He requested that she should reply to A.B. ______ I do not recollect the direction that she was requested to give to the letter. She was of course very much shocked, and gave this letter to the lady Principal of the institution; and this lady showed it to her husband, who was one of the members of the faculty.[19] Soon after he wrote another letter of the same character, with as loathsome a picture as could well be drawn—I mean loathsome to a[20] pure mind; and shaped altogether in such a manner as to lay before her the strongest temptation to bad conduct, and urged her again to reply and direct as he had before requested.[21] This letter immediately passed into the hands of the lady Principal, and through her hands into the hands of the Faculty. Of course this aroused the attention ˡof the Faculty, and they were on the look out.[22] We had a very trustworthy young man at that time as our Postmaster.[23] After these two letters had been received the subject was laid before the Postmaster, and of his own accord he undertook to ascertain from whom those letters came. I think he kept the letters that had been received by ‹her›,[24] that he might compare them with the hand-writing of anything of the kind that should come through his hands again. Soon a letter directed to this young lady came into the post office. He saw that it was the same hand-writing, and opened the letter, and found it to be another of those abominable epistles.[25] That aroused to the utmost his indignation. I

MS 716

[19] Alice Welch Cowles (1804–1843) was principal of the female department from 1836 to 1840 and a member of the Women's Board of Managers from 1837 to 1843. She was the leader in Oberlin and one of the leaders in the country of the Female Moral Reform movement. She died soon after this time, of consumption. Henry Cowles, her husband, was professor of Old Testament literature. See *OE,* 25 October 1843, p. 175; and Robert S. Fletcher, *The History of Oberlin College from Its Foundation Through the Civil War* (Oberlin: Oberlin College, 1943), pp. 301–8.

[20] Matson had at first written down the word "any" here, but he crossed it out and wrote "a."

[21] Henry Cowles described the letters: "Their language was most obscene and insulting, yea even positively bestial; and then, to crown all, they were lined all round the margin with pictoral representations of the vilest imaginable kind. Yet no reader of this description will conceive of the thing nearly as bad as it is" (*OE,* extra no. 3, 26 February 1841, p. 17). According to Cowles this letter was sent to another girl.

[22] Norton wrote letters to more than one female student. It is probable that the first letter to come into the hands of Professor Cowles was addressed to Mary L. Ingalls early in May 1840, and the second to Jane D. L. Isham. According to Cowles, both recipients were "daughters of respectable Presbyterian ministers." Letters were sent to others, including Sarah A. Bidwell and a Miss Owen. See Oberlin College Faculty Minutes, 29 July and 13 August 1840, Oberlin College Archives, microfilm; "Lynching at Oberlin," *Independent Treasury* (Elyria, Ohio), 10 August 1842; and *OE,* extra no. 3, 24 February 1841, p. 17.

[23] The postmaster is listed as Grosvenor D. Reed in Wilbur H. Phillips, *Oberlin Colony: The Story of a Century* (Oberlin: Oberlin Printing, 1933), pp. 64, 313. He held the office from 11 December 1839 to 11 June 1841.

[24] The word "him" here was changed by Finney to "her."

[25] According to a statement by Horace C. Taylor, one of the conspirators involved in the affair, the postmaster knew nothing of the letters in the hands of the faculty and became involved in the affair independently. He noticed that a letter addressed to a young lady had obscene pictures that had not been entirely concealed by the folding. He also noticed two other letters in the same handwriting addressed to two other ladies and opened them all (*OE,* extra no. 3, 24 February 1841, p. 18).

believe without consulting any one he replied to the letter himself, as if he was the young lady to whom it had been addressed. He recognized the two former letters, and so shaped his answer that he wrote again. The Postmaster ‹thus›[26] opened a correspondence with him.[27] It soon resulted in an appointment to meet at a certain place in the village, at a certain hour of the night, and then to go and spend the night together; the vile young man supposing that his correspondence was with the young lady ˈherself, whereas she was entirely ignorant of what was transpiring between the Postmaster and the young man.[28] ‹We had here at that time an energetic young man & woman who were under an engagement to marry & who had come here to first complete their education. They were of good reputation & possessed in a high degree the confidence of the community. To this young man the postmaster & the few who were in the secret applied to assist in the detection of the villain who had spread this snare for a worthy young lady. The young man arranged with his affianced to play the part of the young lady to whom the vile letters had been directed, so far as to secure his detection & arrest.›[29] She consented to go. In the meantime several of our most estimable young men had been consulted, and one of our youngest professors, and they agreed to go and arrest him and deal with him as wisdom should direct.[30] ‹The time for the appointed meeting arrived. It

MS 717

[26]Finney inserted the word "thus" in place of "this."

[27]According to Taylor, the postmaster and "a friend" devised the plan of intercepting the letters. Robert S. Fletcher, the historian of Oberlin College, has stated that the letters were intercepted by Taylor himself, who was acting postmaster at the time, but Taylor denied any knowledge of the affair at that stage: "In this intercepting and opening the letters I had no hand, though I should have done as they did in the same circumstances." Norton's father listed "the Postmaster" and "a Deputy Postmaster" among the conspirators rumored to be involved. See *OE*, extra no. 3, 24 February 1841, p. 18; Fletcher, *History of Oberlin College*, p. 444; and Norton, *Exposure*, p. 9.

[28]This lady was evidently Sarah A. Bidwell, a student attending the literary course at the college. According to testimony given to the faculty by Isaac Judkins, another student, Norton admitted to him that he had sent two letters to Miss Bidwell "signed 'Junius' or 'Julius' and had received answers signed Julia" (Oberlin College Faculty Minutes, 29 July 1840, Oberlin College Archives, microfilm).

The section from here down to n. 29 is in Finney's handwriting on a separate piece of paper pasted onto the sheet. It replaces a section of the original text, which read:

> When the assignation was made and all the preliminaries settled, a young man who had come here to study, and was engaged to a young lady who had come here to study, was consulted in regard to securing the consent of this young lady to whom he was engaged to go and meet that wretch, and enable the young men to get hold of him. When the young lady was consulted, being a girl of very resolute character, strong will, and fearless,

Finney altered the phrase "to a young lady who had come here to study" to read, "to a young lady who had ‹also› come to study."

[29]The section in Finney's handwriting ends here on the separate piece of paper. It left the words "character, strong will, and fearless," which Finney had crossed out, uncovered. The young man was probably Edward Henry Fairchild (1815–1889), brother of James Harris Fairchild. He was a student in the seminary and an assistant teacher in the preparatory department. His fiancée was Maria B. Babbitt (1816–1888), a student in the college. They were married on 31 August 1841. According to E. H. Fairchild, his fiancée was one of the women to whom letters were sent. See Edward H. Fairchild, *Historical Sketch of Oberlin College* (Springfield: Republic, 1868), p. 11; *OE*, 1 September 1841, p. 143; and *The Oberlin Review*, 15 October 1889, p. 42.

[30]It was at this point that Horace Taylor said he was consulted. The professor was Timothy B.

was a dark night. The hour appointed for the meeting was, I believe, ten oclock.[31] The arrangement was that they should meet at a certain corner in the village when he should reveal himself by a certain signal & she should take his arm & accompany him to the place he had prepared for their lodging.›[32] The young man boarded at the hotel, and was very

MS 718 **little known at the time.[33] He had taken his bed from |the room, and carried it a little way out of the village, and spread it under the shelter of a large tree that had been thrown down with a very high[34] root turned up, that cut off the sight of the road and the village altogether.[35] The young man conducted ‹his›[36] young lady to within a few rods of where they were to meet. It was very dark, and he secreted himself within hearing, and the young lady went a little forward and waited for the signal of his approach. Soon she heard the signal and returned it. They met. He gave her his arm, and they walked hastily toward the place where he had prepared his bed. The young men who were to arrest him being aware of the whole plot, had secreted themselves a little way from where they were to leave the road and turn into the woods. He was armed with a pistol, and had in him the real southern spirit. When they arrived at the point where the young men were secreted, they surrounded him. He undertook to use his pistol; but they seized it, and no one was hurt.[37] After considerable conversation ‹&**

Hudson, the professor of Latin and Greek. As a student he had transferred from Western Reserve College to Oberlin in 1835, on account of his antislavery principles, and was a leader in the reform movements. But he had recently been discovered attending a theater in the company of tutor William Cochran while they were delegates at a teachers' meeting in Columbus. The affair was hushed up, but they had made a full confession and had tendered their resignations, which were about to come before the board of trustees. See *OE,* extra no. 3, 24 February 1841, pp. 18–20; J. A. Thome to Theodore Weld, 20 June 1840, in Gilbert H. Barnes and Dwight L. Dumond, eds., *Letters of Theodore Dwight Weld, Angelina Grimké Weld, and Sarah Grimké, 1822–1844,* vol. 1 (Gloucester, Mass.: Peter Smith, 1965), pp. 844–45; Oberlin College Board of Trustees Minutes, 27 August 1850, Oberlin College Archives, microfilm; and R. S. Fletcher, *History of Oberlin College*, pp. 185, 690.

The section from here down to n. 32 is in Finney's handwriting and was written on a second piece of paper pasted onto page 717. It covers up a further section of the text that originally read:

> When the hour for them to meet arrived the young man who was first consulted took the young lady to whom he was engaged by the arm and led her near to the spot where she was to meet the vile wretch, where he supposed he was going to meet a young lady with whom he had been corresponding.

Finney altered part of this sentence to read: ". . . took ‹his young› lady by the ‹hand› and led her. . . ."

[31] This was the evening of Saturday, 25 July 1840. The time was significant because reports later spread that the affair had been happening in the early hours of Sunday morning and had thus been a violation of the Sabbath. But it was pointed out that the meeting had been planned for 10:00 the evening before, and the whole proceedings were over and the students back in their lodgings shortly before or shortly after midnight (*OE,* extra no. 3, 24 February 1841, pp. 21–22).

[32] This is the end of the section in Finney's handwriting.

[33] He had been staying during this time in Oberlin at a public boarding house run by Harvey Gibbs. See Norton, *Exposure*, p. 15; and *OE,* extra no. 3, 24 February 1841, p. 17.

[34] Matson had written the words "and sheltering" after this, but Finney crossed them out.

[35] Matson had written down after this the sentence: "They were to meet at just 10 O'clock, I think." Finney crossed it out.

[36] Here Finney changed the word "the" to "his."

[37] According to his father, Norton had "nothing with which to defend himself but a walking cane of some brittle wood." His father, on the other hand, when he later came to Oberlin was

prayer›[38] they concluded to whip him; and appointed on[e][39] of their number, one of our most amiable ˡyoung men, to ply the lash.[40] It tried his feelings exceedingly to do it; nevertheless he put on his back the assigned number of strokes with a rawhide with which they had furnished themselves.[41] They then let him go; he, at the time, I believe, acknowledging the justice of the course they had pursued with him.[42] MS 719

The fact is, there was no law of the land that would take hold of him, and inflict any punishment at all upon him in this case; and these young men, I have no doubt, acting under a sense of duty, took the case in their own hands, and administered what they supposed to be a moderate and merited chastisement. As this school was one in which young men and women were associated together in all their studies,[43] these young men supposed justly that an act of this kind should meet with decided public disapprobation; and thought that this young man should be made an example, to teach young men that if they came here and attempted to seduce any of our young ladies, what they might expect. However these young men had acted on their own responsibility, without consulting anybody that I know of out of their own circle. But when the father of the young man came to be acquainted ˡwith the facts, he was stirred up MS 720

reported as arriving "with pistols bowie knife etc." (Norton, *Exposure*, p. 11; and J. H. Fairchild to Mary Kellogg, 8 February 1841, Fairchild-Kellogg Letters, 1838–1841, Oberlin College Archives, microfilm). See also George N. Allen to Caroline M. Rudd, 5 and 13 January 1841, George N. Allen Papers, file 30/67, Oberlin College Archives.

[38]Finney added the words "and prayer."

[39]The word "one" is spelled "on" in the manuscript.

[40]James H. Fairchild wrote: "My brother Henry was the one that gave the 25 lashes! He was chosen to the service by the company." Norton's father stated that Samuel D. Cochran, a theological student, had been appointed, but declined, and E. H. Fairchild volunteered instead (J. H. Fairchild to Mary Kellogg, 13 October 1840, Fairchild-Kellogg Letters; and Norton, *Exposure*, pp. 13–14). E. H. Fairchild's own account of the incident reads:

> Some unknown person wrote several anonymous letters, of the vilest character imaginable, to several virtuous ladies, the friends and companions of young men here, and one of them, a *special* friend of one of the young men; and he, fired with indignation at the villainous insult to his betrothed, with the aid of a few others, one night, entrapped the fellow, flogged him, and sent him out of town (*Historical Sketch of Oberlin College*, p. 11).

[41]Norton's father described it as a "large 'cowhide.'" Twenty-five lashes on the naked back were applied (Norton, *Exposure*, p. 14).

[42]Norton was given a dollar and told to leave Oberlin immediately. He wandered through the night and next day made his way to Wellington, nine miles from Oberlin. There he stayed until he could settle up his affairs and get money to return home. On the advice of friends he returned to Oberlin a week later to make a public confession, which he claimed was denied him. But on 6 August he wrote a letter of confession and apology, justifying the punishment. This was read at a public meeting and later published as part of the faculty's statement about the affair. See *OE*, extra no. 3, 24 February 1841, p. 20; and Norton, *Exposure*, pp. 14–17.

Norton was expelled from the college at a faculty meeting on 28 July 1840, but no action was taken against the other students involved in the affair. In 1868 E. H. Fairchild wrote: "It was reported and believed that the young man died of the injuries received. But he is still alive, and is a good and useful man" (Fairchild, *Historical Sketch of Oberlin College*, p. 11).

[43]The Oberlin Collegiate Institute was the first college to attempt the experiment of coeducation, conferring the first degrees on three women in 1841. See Frances J. Hosford, *Father Shipherd's Magna Carta: A Century of Coeducation in Oberlin College* (Boston: Marshall Jones, 1937).

to irrepressible wrath.[44] He came here in a very blustering and abusive spirit.[45] He learned the facts, and could not justify his son, though he felt himself disgraced by the whipping which his son had received rather than by the crime which he had committed; and therefore instead of thanking us, as was really his duty, for administering this most merited chastisement upon his son, he took great pains to stir up the whole country against us for this deed.[46] The public mind was at that time in a state favorable to seize hold of any such occurrence to put down Oberlin. The papers teemed with opposition to Oberlin, and the wrath of the press was greatly excited at the whipping; though so far as I heard, no words of reprobation fell upon the ears of the criminal, or of any one else, for his crime. A great crime, it was assumed, had been committed in punishing him; but the crime that had most justly demanded this punishment, was left out of view. We, as usual, kept still, and kept about our business.

When the court met at Elyria the Grand Jury found bills of MS 721 **indictment against the young men that had been |engaged in this thing.[47] They subpoenied many persons in Oberlin, to come before them as witnesses, and in this way discovered, I believe, all the young men who had taken part in it save one. The first I knew, however, of this**

[44]This was Dr. Greenleaf Norton. He lived in Ripley, Ohio, until soon after his son went to Oberlin College in 1839 and then moved to Crawfordsville, Indiana. See Norton, *Exposure.*

[45]This was on 4 January 1841. Dr. Norton recalled: "At the 'Oberlin House' I accidentally met with Prof. Finney and Whipple, in company with Mr. Gibbs and one of the Oberlin Agents, who had just returned from England" (Norton, *Exposure*, p. 24).

[46]According to one report, as he was traveling to Oberlin, Dr. Norton was "scattering printed handbills on the way, misrepresenting the case & inflaming the people against O[berlin]" (G. N. Allen to Caroline M. Rudd, 13 January 1841, Allen Papers, file 30/67, Oberlin College Archives). He distributed a printed circular, dated 1 January 1841, and later published his *Exposure.* He also took the Oberlin students to court over the affair.

[47]The trial was held in the Court of Common Pleas in Elyria. It was to have started on 20 July 1841 but may have been postponed due to the sickness of one of the witnesses. See J. H. Fairchild to Mary Kellogg, 19 July 1841, Fairchild-Kellogg Letters; and the report of the trial in the *Independent Treasury,* 10 August 1842. The constitution of the state of Ohio required that no one should be put on trial without the previous judgment of a grand jury that that one ought to be tried. On the opening of a court the grand jurors would be sworn in and given a charge, and after a foreman was appointed they would "retire to a private apartment to attend to their duties." They were required to hear all the complaints and examine all the witnesses, and if they thought there should be a trial,

> they draw up a writing, in which they charge the person with the offence of which they think he is guilty. This is called an *indictment.* It is signed by the foreman, endorsed "a true bill," and carried by the jury into court. If the person has not before been arrested, he may now be arrested, to be put upon trial (Andrew W. Young, *First Lessons in Civil Government; including a comprehensive view of the Government of the State of Ohio, . . .* [Cleveland: Younglove, 1846], p. 97).

There were about fifteen young men involved in the "lynching," but only five were put on trial. These were Horace C. Taylor, E. Henry Fairchild, Samuel D. Cochran, Timothy B. Hudson, and another theological student, James Steele. See J. H. Fairchild to Mary Kellogg, 10 April 1841, Fairchild-Kellogg Letters; and Oberlin College Faculty Minutes, 28 September 1840, Oberlin College Archives, microfilm. In the report in the *Independent Treasury*, the name of William Cochran is given. This may be a mistake for his brother S. D. Cochran, since William is not otherwise known to have been involved. See also Fletcher, *History of Oberlin College*, p. 445 n. 52. A search made by William Bigglestone revealed that the court records for that period are missing. There is an index of defendants, but neither of the Cochrans is listed.

proceeding it came to my ears by my being myself subpoenied as a witness before the Grand Jury. I went. I observed as I went in that the District Attorney, who was with the Grand Jury, was a person that I knew, and was an avowed skeptic. The foreman of the Jury I had understood to be another; and indeed as I observed the Grand Jury I saw that they were made up very much of leaders of the opposition to Oberlin, and of men who were no less opposed to religion than to Oberlin—that is, there were several of them, if I was not entirely misinformed, who were skeptics. The District Judge, who presided over the court, was also a skeptic, and also one of the side judges. Thus a majority of the court, and I think a majority of the Grand Jury, were skeptics. The same was true of the Sheriff and Deputy Sheriff, I think. At any rate I was informed that it was true of the Deputy Sheriff, who was in attendance upon the Grand Jury. Of course I found myself surrounded by not altogether a ˡpleasant moral atmosphere. The foreman of the Grand Jury informed me of the object of my being sent for; and after administering the usual oath told me whom they had indicted, and asked me if I knew of any other persons in Oberlin who had been connected with that affair. I replied that I did know of one, who from his own confession to me as his pastor, I knew had been connected with it. But that he had gone out of the state: not that he had run away or gone away to escape prosecution; but he had gone home to his friends, and so far as I knew he expected to remain at-home. The foreman then asked me what his name was. I replied that the young man was a member of the church of which I was pastor, and at the time of the occurrence was a member of my family; that after the occurrence, learning how the people felt here about the mistake that they had made, his conscience troubled him, and that he then confessed to me his connection with the affair;—and I then said, "I do not know as I ought to be called upon to testify in this case, and reveal the young man's name." However, I did not refuse to testify; I only made the remark, as nearly as I can recollect, as I have stated it. They did not urge me to give his name; indeed, ˡthey said no more, but very politely dismissed me. I left the room and went immediately to the hotel to get my horse and return home. But while waiting at the hotel for my horse to be brought to the door, I learned from the conversation of those that were there that the Grand Jury had said they "would set[48] until they had examined every man in Oberlin, if need be, to find out every one who had had any connection with that affair." I learned that the impression existed in Elyria, and in the minds of the Grand Jury themselves, that the people of Oberlin wished to cover the matter up, and were not willing to have the laws of the land executed. I observed as I rode home that there was a good deal of excitement in the minds of the people; and I made up my mind that I would return in the morning and go in to open court and consult the judges in regard to my duty, and to the law upon that point.

MS 722

MS 723

[48] Matson wrote the word "set." He probably should have written "sit." Later on where he used that same word, Finney changed it to "sit." See n. 54 below.

Accordingly the next morning, although very rainy, and very muddy, it being late in the fall, I got on my horse[49] and rode through the rain and mud to Elyria. I went immediately into the court room, and found the court busily engaged in the trial of some cause that had excited a good deal of interest, and hence the ˡcourt[50] room was well filled with spectators. I went to one of the gentlemen of the bar with whom I had some acquaintance, took him a little one side and requested him to ask the court to give me a hearing for a few moments, as I had an important question to lay before them. He very deferentially and appropriately made the communication that I desired to the court. They immediately suspended business; and the presiding Judge remarked, that Professor Finney who was present had a communication to make to the court, and that business would be suspended for a few moments to hear what he had to say. I then told them what had happened the day before, before the Grand Jury; and the question that I had to present to them was, whether law or equity required me to give that young man's name to the Grand Jury. I then stated what I understood to be the law upon that subject. I said that men have consciences; and people may differ as they please in regard to many other questions, there could be no difference of opinion upon this, that all men and women have consciences, and that often very embarrassing cases of conscience arise in which advice is needed. That in such cases, as they must exist in society and in every ˡcommunity,[51] the public weal demanded that there should be some persons protected by the law from becoming public informers, to whom persons could go for advice. I said that I knew how this had been abused by the Roman Catholics in their confessional, and how the law had been settled in regard to them. But I said that although the law in this country does not recognize the union of church and state, yet it does recognize the pastoral relation; and it ought to protect this relation to the extent of protecting the community, and also the pastor when he has been consulted as pastor in regard to cases of conscience where advice is needed. I enlarged upon this at discretion, and occupied considerable time in stating my views and the reasons for them. Indeed, it might be said that I *preached* to the court and those that were present. I felt as if it was a good occasion to represent our sentiments at Oberlin. I told the court the reasons of my returning to Elyria, what I had heard at the public house the day before, and that I was satisfied they entirely misunderstood the Oberlin people. I assured the court that we were a law-abiding people; that we had not as a people approved of the course taken by the young men; and that we did not wish to shield them from

MS 724

MS 725 [1]

[49]Here Matson had written down, "into my buggy," but he changed it to "on my horse."

[50]MS 724 was originally numbered 572 by Matson. It should have been numbered 571, but the sheet with that number was later used for MS 740. It appears that Matson had numbered the sheets in advance before he wrote on them. He missed out sheet 571, so that sheets 572–88 had to be renumbered 571–87. They were later renumbered 703–19 by Matson before being changed to 724–39 by Finney. But see n. 52 for Finney's misnumbering.

[51]This page is MS 725 [1]. The next page was also renumbered 725 in error by Finney.

|the[52] operation of criminal law, but were entirely willing that justice should take its course, and were disposed rather to aid in the administration of justice than to throw obstacles in the way. In short I represented to them Oberlin views and feelings on the subject, and said that we merely desired that the young men should have a fair trial, and an opportunity to spread before the court when they were tried the provocation under which they had acted and the reasons for their conduct. The court did not seem at all weary of listening to what I had to say. The attention was universal, respectful, and I thought solemn. I then said to the judges, "Now if your honors are of opinion that it is my duty as a citizen to go and give the Grand Jury the name of that young man, I will do it immediately." I then sat down, and the presiding Judge said that they were very much obliged to me for returning and giving ‹an›[53] expose of my views and of the whole subject. That the court entirely accorded with me in opinion; and said that they had had a false impression in regard to the opinions of Oberlin in this matter, and were very happy to be set right on this subject. That my statement had greatly relieved their minds and feelings; |and the view that I had presented was one with which they unitedly agreed. He concluded by remarking that it was a question for the Grand Jury, and asked me if I was not willing to go and make the same statement in substance to the Grand Jury in the room below. I said that I should be glad to have an opportunity to do so; and I thought I observed that the court felt that it might do the Grand Jury good. I then proceeded to the Grand Jury room. I found them all present as the day before, the Deputy Sheriff and skeptic, standing at the door in attendance upon the Grand Jury, the skeptical Prosecuting Attorney sitting by the table with the foreman of the Grand Jury; and I observed, as I did the day before, that so far as I knew the Grand Jury, there was a very large element of skepticism on religious subjects found among them. I then stated to them in substance what I had stated to the court above, what I had learned the day before of the state of feeling in the neighborhood, and of the Jury itself; and that it was their determination to s‹i›t[54] until they had examined every person in Oberlin, if need be, to find out all the persons that had been connected with that transaction. I then stated my views as I had done to the court, |and gave them as nearly as I could the same view of the case throughout. I observed the same profound attention and effect in the Grand Jury room that had been produced in the court. When I was through, the foreman after consulting a moment with the District Attorney, replied in substance as the court had done above. He expressed great satisfaction at my returning and giving them my view of the subject, as he agreed with me entirely in the view I had taken of my duty; and he expressed the opinion that the Jury did not think it my

MS 725 [2]

MS 726

MS 727

[52] MS 725 [2] was changed to 725 in error by Finney. It should have been 726.

[53] Matson had written down the word "my" here, but Finney changed it to "an."

[54] Here Matson had written down the word "set," but it appears to have been altered to "sit" by Finney. The same word occurred earlier but was not altered. See n. 48 above.

duty to give the name of the young man, and that they did not require it. As I left the room, the Deputy Sheriff, who was standing inside and had heard what had been said, followed me out into the hall. He took hold of my arm with very manifest excitement and said: "Mr. Finney, your coming back and saying what you have is worth a thousand[55] dollars." As I returned to the hotel after my horse, the court above had a recess for dinner. The presiding Judge, who was then a stranger to me, introduced himself to me, and said he was very happy to meet me; and expressed regret that they had so entirely misapprehended the views, and feelings, and action of the people of Oberlin. He said: "We have MS 728 been deceived ¹respecting you there; and now I for one want to become better acquainted with you;" and then added, "When I come out to hold court here again," naming the time, "may I not bring my wife and leave her at your house while I attend court here, that she may become acquainted with you, and that I myself may become acquainted with some of your people?" I most cordially invited him to come, and assured him that I would bring or send him out every day to attend court, and bring him back to his wife in the evening. A few weeks after that I spent a few days in Cleveland in preaching to the people. This was his residence. I observed him in the congregation, and soon learned that he was very seriously weighing the question of his soul's salvation. I had a protracted conversation with him, and found the state of his mind not only very interesting, but as I thought very hopeful. I urged him to immediately accept the Savior, his skepticism being, to all appearance, entirely gone. He received all I had to say with great tenderness, and renewed his promise to come out with his wife when he next held his court in Elyria. But before that time he was in his grave, so that I saw MS 729 him no more. ¹Before I left Elyria at the time I have spoken of, I learned that the Grand Jury had adjourned sine die. That after my statement they were entirely satisfied that they had no reason to make any farther inquiry, and having no other business before them they dissolved.[56]

[55]Here Matson had originally written "ten thousand," but he changed it to "a thousand."

[56]The trial was held over two days in the October 1841 session of the court. The jury found the young men guilty and "gave a verdict . . . of *fifteen hundred dollars*! This was for damages to the person flogged!" This was the civil suit. There was also a criminal suit in which "the *court* inflicted a penalty of *fifty dollars* upon one of the young men, and *one hundred dollars* upon each of the others." Five in all were indicted (*OE*, 10 November 1841, p. 181). The verdict in the civil court was later appealed against in the Supreme Court and the penalty reduced to $550. See *OE*, 17 August 1842, p. 134.

Horace Taylor, one of the accused, who had been licensed to preach by the Huron Presbytery, had his license revoked because of his part in the affair. Three years later he was on trial again. He was then editor of *The Oberlin Evangelist* and an assistant postmaster in the village. He was also a trustee of the college and on the Prudential Committee. In December 1843 he was discovered to have been stealing from the post office and from the funds of the *Evangelist*, and also to have seduced his housekeeper and procured an abortion. He was sentenced to a year in jail and a fine of $275. See R. Braden Moore, *History of Huron Presbytery* (Philadelphia: Fell, 1892), pp. 107–8; and Fletcher, *History of Oberlin College*, pp. 447–48.

Timothy Hudson, another of the accused, had remained as a tutor in the college but finally resigned his position in August 1841, about the time of the trial. He became an antislavery lecturer but in 1847 returned to Oberlin again as professor of Latin and Greek. It was largely through him that the college procured a $100,000 endowment in 1852. In 1858 he was killed by

After this there was a most remarkable change in the views and feelings of the leading men in the opposition in the region around about us. The next winter, for example, after ‹this court›,[57] one of the side judges, a democrat and as I had understood a skeptic, was a member of the legislature, in which a plot was on foot to try to take away our charter. This judge, who had been present at the time I have spoken of, stood, as we were told, manfully and boldly in defence of Oberlin; and told them that the impressions that had gone abroad in respect to our views and our character as a school, were altogether erroneous. And as I understood, these remarks had a leading influence in diverting the legislature from their purpose.

Thus one event after another occurred that made the community around us better acquainted with us and with our views, until the prejudice was entirely done away. ¦But what effect ‹had›[58] the trial of the young men? And especially how did the outrageous comments and denunciations of the press, far and near, ‹have upon›[59] our school? Did it keep the young ladies and gentlemen from coming here to school? No indeed! It was found that it had produced an entirely opposite effect. It was found that people reasoned thus. They had been afraid, and much pains had been taken to make them afraid, of trusting their daughters in a school where young ladies and gentlemen recited in the same classes, ate in the same boarding hall, and were in all respects associated as they were here. It was of course regarded as an experiment, and by many as an experiment of a very questionable nature. But the result of all this bluster and opposition, especially in relation to this prosecution and the cause of it, was that people reasoned in this way: Well, if there is such a public sentiment as this at Oberlin, if an attempt to seduce one of those young ladies brings upon the offender that kind of retribution, there is the very place for our daughters. We can send them there with more safety than ¦anywhere else. If the young men of that college will themselves give a young man such a thorough castigation who attempts any such thing, such a public sentiment must be favorable to chastity, and to the protection of our daughters when away from home. There was therefore a continual increase of our students, and especially of females; and the relative number of ladies in our college seemed to increase from year to year.[60]

MS 730

MS 731

a railway train. See Oberlin College Board of Trustees Minutes, 18 and 20 August 1841, Oberlin College Archives, microfilm; and *The Independent* (New York), 8 April 1858, p. 1.

[57] Matson had written the words "these remarks," but they were crossed out and the words "this court" inserted by Finney.

[58] Finney inserted the word "had." The sentence originally read, "But what was the effect of this action of the court and of our young men, and of the trial of the young men that succeeded, upon our college?" It was altered by Finney.

[59] The words "have upon" were inserted by Finney in place of the word "affect."

[60] J. H. Fairchild wrote to his fiancée six months after the trial of the students:

> The poor fellows have sufficiently atoned for the crime I think—But they take it all very calmly. Indeed they have not lost the confidence of any who know them—They go out to preach almost every Sabbath in Cleveland, Ohio City & other towns in the vicinity & are received as kindly as ever.—One singular fact is that the female part of community exculpate them from all blame,—I do not recollect now a single instance in

Indeed, in the providence of God almost all the onsets that were made against us through the press, ‹by other methods of attack›,[61] resulted in our favor. We kept still, and kept about our own business, and let the smoke and dust clear away in God's own best time.[62]

In the meantime the excitement on the subject of slavery was greatly agitating the eastern cities as well as the west and the south.[63] Our friend **and brother,** Willard Sears, of Boston, was braving a tempest of opposition there. And in order to open the way for a free discussion on that subject in Boston, and for the establishment of religious worship where a pulpit should be open to the free discussion of all great questions of reform,[64] he had purchased the MS 732 Marlborough hotel on Washington st.,[65] and had connected |with it a large

which they have been censured by a lady. They frequently receive letters from ladies in New England & other parts of the country thanking them for the deed,—And some parents have sent their daughters to O. for education who hesitated to do it before,—Notwithstanding the violent opposition to O. on this account & others, our buildings are crowded with students (Fairchild to Mary Kellogg, 27 April 1841, Fairchild-Kellogg Letters, 1838–1841, Oberlin College Archives, microfilm).

A survey done in 1853 pointed out: "The proportion of ladies has been increasing since the second year." In 1835, out of 276 students, there were 73 women (26.4 percent of the total). About the time of the lynching in 1840 there were 484 students, 166 of them women (34.3 percent). In 1851 the numbers had risen to 571, with 241 women (42.2 percent). The next year, owing to the introduction of a new scholarship system, the numbers nearly doubled to 1,020, with 459 women (45.0 percent). By 1860 the number of students had reached 1,311, a figure not surpassed until 1882, and 508 of these were women (38.7 percent). Then came the Civil War and a drop in numbers to 859 in 1862. But the proportion of women increased, reaching 54.6 percent in 1864. In 1867, about the time Finney started writing his memoirs, the number of students was 1,134, with 494 women (43.6 percent). See "History of Oberlin College," *OE,* 11 May 1853, p. 78; and *General Catalogue of Oberlin College, 1833–1908* (Oberlin, 1909), Introduction, pp. 117–19.

[61] Here Matson had written down, "and in other ways." Lewis Tappan had written in ink in the margin, "other ways or otherwise." Finney therefore altered it to "by other methods of attack."

[62] This ends the section starting with MS 714, which was omitted by Fairchild. The page was cut here, and the bottom half was pasted to the top half of MS 714. The words "bottom of 731" are written in pencil at the bottom left side of the page.

[63] The first letters of the words "eastern," "west," and "south" were underlined three times in pencil. This appears to have been done by Fairchild to indicate to the printers to use capital letters, which is how they are written in the published edition.

[64] A Free church had been formed in Boston by Finney supporters, many of them from the Essex Street Church. It was organized on 16 July 1835 under great difficulties and without the recognition of many of the Congregational ministers. Three years later it numbered about two hundred members. See William Dawes to Finney, 10 August 1838, Finney Papers, microfilm, roll 3; *BR,* 17 July 1835, p. 115; 24 July 1835, p. 117; and 1 August 1835, p. 214; and *Brief History of the First Free Congregational Church* (Boston: Dow and Jackson, 1845).

[65] Sears did not purchase the Marlborough (or Marlboro) Hotel at this time. Amasa Walker, the wealthy Boston businessman turned political economist and reformer, was the leading spirit in its purchase, and he related the details:

For several years after the anti-slavery agitation commenced it was quite difficult to get any place for meetings. The churches (in Boston especially) were hermetically sealed. I recollect the young men of the Bowdoin Street Church wished to hold a prayer meeting for the slaves and applied to "the Committee" for the use of its vestries, but it was denied, although I offered $5 per evening.

One year, I cannot recollect which (but I think about 1836), we were utterly unable to procure a room and met in a loft of a stable in the rear of the Marlboro Hotel. It was rudely fitted up, but answered our purpose pretty well; and what was more, it brought about an important movement—for feeling the great emergency in which we were placed without any hall in Boston that could be had for free discussion, the project was started of building or buying one. A subscription was opened among the friends of the chapel for public worship, and for reform meetings that could not find an entrance anywhere else.[66] This he had done at great expense. In 1842 I was strongly urged to go and occupy **that** Marlborough chapel and preach for a few months.[67] I went and began my labors, and preached with all my might for two months. The Spirit of the Lord was immediately poured out, and there **became** a general agitation among the dry bones. I was visited at my room almost constantly dur|ing every day of the week by inquirers from **various congregations in** all parts of the city, and many were obtaining hopes from day to day. JHF 354

At this time Elder Knapp, well-known **as a** Baptist **R**evivalist,[68] was laboring in Providence, **R.I., and met with persistent opposition in that city from his Baptist brethren.**[69] **When the work was in a very hopeful**

> object and I think I made the first, and recollect I put down $1000. The effort proved so far successful, that we formed a company and purchased the Marlboro Estate for that purpose.
>
> . . . I was Chairman of the Board and of course had to take the laboring oar so far as financial affairs were concerned (James P. Munroe, *A Life of Francis Amasa Walker* [New York: Holt, 1923], pp. 18–19).

Later, in 1844, Sears bought the property. See Sears to Finney, 2 May 1844; and 18 August 1845, Finney Papers, microfilm, roll 4; and p. 455 n. 37 (MS 772).

[66]The Marlborough Estate in the center of Boston had been a hotel "where a vast quantity of intoxicating drink was sold; in the rear of which was a large stable, in whose upper loft was a great gambling establishment." In 1836 it was purchased "and placed under the care of an incorporated company, most of whom are members of the Free Church." After being renovated and enlarged it was opened in July 1837 as a "Temperance House" in which the boarders lived together as a Christian family community. On the second floor it incorporated a large chapel that could seat 2,500 people and that was described as "the most spacious and convenient hall, with seats, in New England." The interior was modeled after the Broadway Tabernacle. See "Marlboro Hotel and Chapel, in Boston," *NYE,* 30 June 1838, p. 103; and "The Boston Free Church," *NYE,* 25 November 1837, p. 191.

[67]The Free Church had been built up with the help of Asa Mahan from Oberlin, who had been there the three previous winters. But his preaching on the doctrine of perfection had caused difficulties. The minister, Amos A. Phelps, had left, and the church and congregation were small. See letters of David Cambell to Levi Burnell from 1839 to 1840, Letters Received by Oberlin College, 1822–1866, microfilm; John Gulliver to Finney, 18 February 1839, Finney Papers, microfilm, roll 3; *OE,* 22 May 1839, p. 12; *The Liberator* (Boston), 31 January 1840, p. 19; and *BR,* 19 June 1840, p. 99.

Finney left Oberlin for Boston at the beginning of October 1841, and in December, about the time Finney left Boston, Martin Moore commenced laboring with the church. Moore pointed out: "Owing to the state of br. Finney's health, and to previous engagements of the chapel for other purposes, the church were unable to hold meetings more than three or four evenings in a week" (M. Moore, *Boston Revival, 1842* [reprint, Wheaton, Ill.: Roberts, 1980], p. 61; *OE,* 13 October 1841, p. 166; and J. J. Shipherd to Fayette Shipherd, 16 October 1841, Bragdon Family Papers, University of Rochester Library).

[68]Matson had written the word "Evangelist" here but changed it to "Revivalist."

[69]Jacob Knapp (1799–1874), ordained as a Baptist in 1825, became an itinerant evangelist in 1832. He was a fiery preacher, whose denunciations of sin caused considerable disturbances, and vast crowds attended his meetings all over the northern states. He was said to have preached sixteen thousand sermons and baptized four thousand persons. See *Appletons' Cyclopaedia of American Biography,* vol. 3 (New York: Appleton, 1888), p. 560; and Jacob Knapp, *Autobiography of Elder Jacob Knapp* (New York: Sheldon, 1868).

Knapp had gone to Providence about 1 November 1841 to labor in the Third Baptist Church and was there until the end of December. According to J. D. Fulton, "There was determined opposition to his efforts, on the part of several distinguished ministers." Knapp himself singled out the First and Pine Street churches "with their great resources of influence, if not openly opposing, at least withholding their sympathies, and practically giving us the cold shoulder." However, when the revival got under way he was invited to preach in Pine Street. "Many of the

way at Boston, he was invited by the Baptist brethren at Boston to come and labor there. He therefore left Providence **amid a storm of opposition,** and came to Boston.[70] **Brother** Josiah Chapin and many others were **at that time** insisting very strongly upon my coming and holding |meetings in Providence. MS 733 I felt very much indebted to **Brother** Chapin for what he had done for Oberlin, and **for me** personally **in sending me money from time to time to support my family at Oberlin during the season of our very great depression in regard to funds.** It was a great trial for me to leave Boston at this time. However, after seeing **B**rother Knapp and informing him of the state of things **in Boston, and assuring him that a great work was begun and was spreading throughout the city, and that things were in a most hopeful way,** I left and went to Providence.[71] This was the time of the great revival in Boston. It **progressed** wonderfully, especially among the Baptists, and more or less throughout the city.[72] The Baptist ministers took hold with **B**rother Knapp, and many Congregational brethren were greatly blessed, and the work was very extensive.[73]

members of Congregational and Episcopal churches came in with us, and the work extended over the city" (Knapp, *Autobiography*, pp. 122–23; and Justin D. Fulton, *Memoir of Timothy Gilbert* [Boston: Lee and Shepard, 1866], p. 71).

[70]Knapp caused a great deal of antagonism in Providence through his denunciation of sinners. He particularly enraged the Universalists when he slandered a woman from the pulpit. The resulting court case gave him considerable notoriety. See Knapp, *Autobiography*, p. 123; and Fulton, *Memoir of Timothy Gilbert*, p. 71. When he arrived in Boston at the end of December, it was by no means with the full support of the Baptists. Five of the Baptist churches cooperated in inviting him, but two churches did not invite him into their pulpits. "One of these with its pastor, was decidedly unfriendly to the whole movement from beginning to end" (Asa Wilbur, *An Examination of the Comparative Statistical Results of the Labors of Elder Jacob Knapp in the State of Massachusetts* [Boston: Heath and Graves, 1855], p. 4).

Robert W. Cushman, minister of the Bowdoin Square Baptist Church, reluctantly surrendered his church for Knapp to use. But he was very critical of the revival and its results. See Robert W. Cushman, *A Calm Review of the Measures Employed in the Religious Awakening in Boston in 1842* (Boston: Skinner, 1846).

[71]Finney wrote to Henry Cowles in Oberlin: "I shall probably leave Boston soon to spend a little time in Providence & perhaps some in N. York before I return. . . . Maffitt & Knapp & Kirk will be left on the ground here. Knapp has begun to day. Kirk is to be here in two weeks" (Finney to Cowles, 23 December 1841, Charles G. Finney Correspondence, 1830–1875, Oberlin College Archives, microfilm). John Newland Maffit, the Methodist revivalist, had gone to Boston shortly before Finney and was being very successful. Edward Norris Kirk, the Congregationalist minister, preached mostly at Park Street Church. See *NYE,* 17 February 1842, p. 26.

[72]According to Knapp "2000 persons were added to the churches composing the Boston Baptist Association during that year. Hundreds were added to churches of other denominations, and many came in from the surrounding villages and were converted." It was at this time that the Tremont Theater had to be sold and was converted into a place of worship. Knapp was in Boston until mid-March 1842 (Knapp, *Autobiography*, p. 128).

[73]Martin Moore indicated that more than four thousand people were added to the Boston churches in 1842 (*Boston Revival, 1842*, p. 141). Knapp also preached in the Marlborough Chapel, where there were "hundreds of inquirers and a multitude of conversions." Amasa Walker wrote in March:

> We never had so interesting a time in Boston as the present in regard to religion. Bro Knapp has just closed his labours. Bro. Kirk is now here. All the Churches of all the evangelical denominations are crowded & so general [a] feeling of interest & awakening was never before known. Bro. Finney's labours contributed greatly to this glorious result. I wish he could be here now, to hear & see of the fruits of his labours (Walker to William Dawes, 19 March 1842, Letters Received by Oberlin College, microfilm, roll 8; see also *OE,* 16 March 1842, p. 46).

In the meantime I **began** my labors in Providence, **R.I.**[74] The work began almost immediately **there**, and the interest visibly increased from day to day. There were many striking cases of conversion, among **which** was an elderly gentleman whose name I do not **now**[75] recollect. His father had been a Judge of the Supreme Court in 'Massachusetts, if I mistake not, many years before. MS 734 This old gentleman **was living in Providence, and was a skeptic. He** lived not far from the church where I was holding my meetings in High st. After the work had gone on for **sometime**, I observed a very venerable looking gentleman come into meeting, **and that he** paid very strict attention to preaching. My friend Mr. Chapin immediately noticed him, and informed me who he was, and what his religious views were. He said he had never been in the habit of attending religious meetings; and he expressed a very great interest in the man, and in the fact that he had been drawn out to meeting. I observed that he continued night after night to come; and could 'easily JHF 355 perceive, as I thought, that his mind was very much agitated, and deeply interested on the question of religion. One evening as I came to the close of my sermon, this **aged,** venerable **gentleman, tall and with gray hair, and with a decidedly intellectual look,** rose up and **addressing me** asked **me** if he might address a few words to the people. I replied in the affirmative. He then spoke in substance as follows: "My friends and neighbors, you are probably surprized to see me 'attend these meetings. You have known my MS 735 skeptical views, and that I have not been in the habit of attending religious meetings for a long time. But hearing of the state of things in this congregation I came in here; and I wish to have my friends and neighbors know that I believe that the preaching we are hearing from night to night is the Gospel. I have altered my mind," said he; "I believe this is the truth, and the true way of salvation. I say this," he added, "that you may understand my real motive for coming here; that it is not to criticize and find fault, but to attend to the great question of salvation, and to encourage others to attend to it." He said this with much emotion, and sat down.

There was a very large Sabbath School room in the basement of the

The New England correspondent of *The New-York Evangelist*, however, in a full account of the revival, dated Boston, 8 February 1842, wrote:

> Mr. Finney does not seem to have made much impression in the Chapel. He was listened to with interest and profit by many of the members of the other churches. Some of them were quickened by what they heard. There were also quite a number of conversions at the Chapel. But after all, the effort was not a successful one (*NYE,* 17 February 1842, p. 26).

[74] Finney preached in the High Street Congregational Church. This had been formed in 1834 by fourteen members from the Beneficent Congregational Church, and a wooden meeting house was built that year. By 1842 the congregation had increased to over two hundred. The minister was Leonard S. Parker, who had been a student at Oberlin. He recalled the great difficulty he had getting ordained over the church in December 1840 and the feeling of alienation from other ministers because of his suspect theology: "And when Mr. Finney aided me in a glorious revival there, not a brother in the ministry stood by me" (L. S. Parker, "Early Days," in *The Oberlin Jubilee, 1833–1883,* ed. W. G. Ballantine [Oberlin: Goodrich, 1883], p. 74; see also William R. Staples, *Annals of the Town of Providence* [Providence: Knowles and Vose, 1843], p. 635; Samuel Dunham, *An Historical Discourse Delivered at West Brookfield, Mass.* [Springfield, Mass.: Bowles and Goodrich, 1836], p. 34; and *NYE,* 13 February 1841, p. 27).

[75] The word "now" was not crossed out by Fairchild but does not appear in the published edition.

church. The number of inquirers had become too large, and the congregation to[**o**][76] much crowded, to call the inquirers forward, as I had done in some places; and I therefore requested them to **descend**, after the blessing was pronounced, to the **basement or** lecture room **of the church** below. The room was nearly as large as the whole audience room of the church, and would seat nearly as many **with the exception of those who might occupy** MS 736 **the gallery in the room above.** |The work increased and spread in every part of the city until the number of inquirers became so great, together with the young converts, who were always ready to go below with them, as **to fill** nearly or quite that large **basement** room. From night to night after preaching that room would be filled with rejoicing young converts and trembling, inquiring, **anxious** sinners.[77] This state of things continued for two months. I was then, as I thought, completely tired out; having labored **so very hard and** JHF 356 **so** incessantly for four months, two in Boston and two in Providence. |Beside, the time of year had come, or nearly come, for the opening of our Spring term in Oberlin. I therefore took my leave of Providence and started for home.[78]

There was one circumstance **connected with** Boston that I think it duty to relate **in this place**. A Unitarian woman had been converted in Boston who was an acquaintance of the Rev. Dr **Channing**.[79] Hearing of her conversion, **Dr Channing**, as she informed me **herself**, sent for her to visit him, as he was

[76]Here Matson had written the word "to," and it appears to have been corrected to "too" by Fairchild.

[77]A report from Providence at the end of January indicated that "the *whole church* at the last accounts, was filled by *enquirers*, instead of the basement, as has always been usual. 200 at a time come forward to be prayed for. the Universalists are in trepidation & dismay—losing their adherents" (Elizabeth S. S. Eaton to Amos B. Eaton, 31 January 1842, in Blake McKelvey, "Letters Postmarked Rochester, 1817–1879," *The Rochester Historical Society, Publication Fund Series* 21 [1943]: 75–76).

A report on the revivals in *The Oberlin Evangelist* about that time spoke of the work under Knapp in Boston and Mahan in Newark: "And a greater work still at Providence, R.I., under the preaching of Prof. Finney. This is attracting the attention of the whole city, and is extending into other towns" (*OE,* 16 February 1842, p. 31). Josiah Chapin wrote to Finney later: "About 80 hav[e] been added to our Church thus far—We have some cases of interest among our people" (Chapin to Finney, 4 May 1842, Finney Papers, microfilm, roll 4).

[78]Soon after Finney left, the Providence church was disturbed by the civil unrest in Rhode Island over the extension of the franchise and the rebellion led by Thomas Dorr.

> It has seriously effected very many who first indulged hope during the winter past, as well as older professing Christians. Bro Codding you may recollect as one of the young converts who conversed with you at some length upon the subject of the proper action of churches in regard to Slavery. He has withdrawn from our band because some of its members took up arms in defence of the state government in opposition to Dorr. Bro. Jackson, the Englishman, who was so much revived you will probably call to mind. He is very seriously effected, and refused to unite in prayer, or even pray himself, with a brother in the chh, who though he did not take up arms, yet justified it as right. Many others are similarly effected & a very serious injury has resulted to the cause of the Redeemer in Rho. Island & particularly Providence. None of our chh were among the insurgents, yet many are decidedly favorable to Mr. Dorr & his constitution, & refuse to be in subjection to any other (Josiah Chapin to Finney, 4 August 1842, Finney Papers, microfilm, roll 4).

See also George M. Dennison, *The Dorr War: Republicanism on Trial, 1831–1861* (Lexington: University of Kentucky Press, 1976).

[79]William Ellery Channing (1780–1842) was the leader of the Unitarians in Boston. He was the minister of the Federal Street Church from 1803 until his death. See *DAB.*

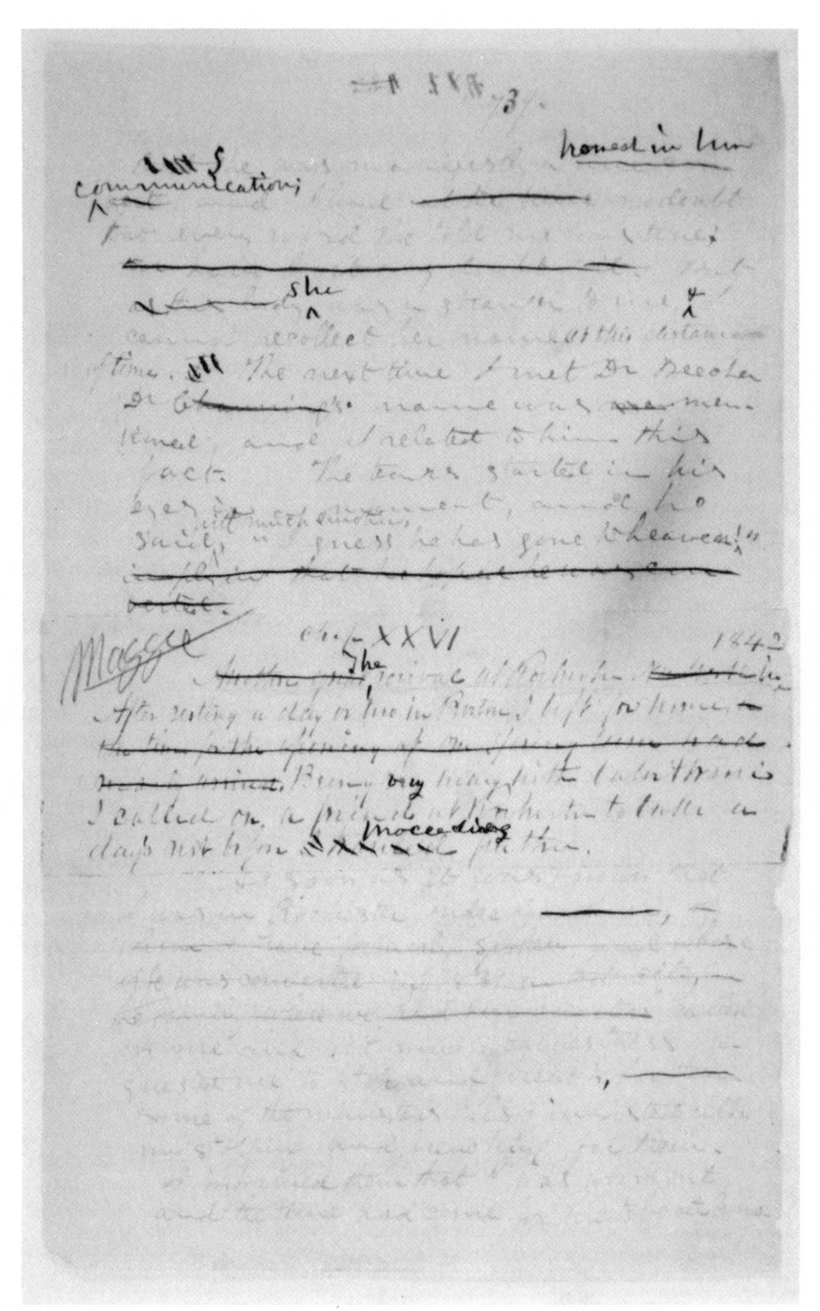

Page 739 of the Manuscript. This photo shows Dr. Channing's name and the piece of paper pasted onto the sheet starting the new chapter. "Maggie" was the typesetter. Courtesy Oberlin College Archives

in feeble health and could not well call on her. She complied with his request, and he wished her to tell him the exer|cises of her mind, and her Christian experience, and the circumstances of her conversion. She did so, and the Doctor manifested a great interest in her change of mind; and inquired of her if she had anything that I had written and published that he could read. **He said he knew what was transpiring in Boston, and felt a great interest to understand it better; and he wanted to know what my views were, and what I preached that seemed to interest the people so much.** She told him that she had a little work of mine which had been published, on the subject of sanctification.[80] He borrowed it, and told her that he would read it; and if she would call again in a week **she might have it, and** he should be happy to have farther conversation with her. At the close of the week she returned for her book, and the **D**octor said, "I am very much interested in this book, and in the views that are here set forth. I understand," says he, "that the **O**rthodox object to this view of sanctification, as it is presented by Mr. Finney; but I cannot see, if Christ is divine and truly God, why this view should be objected to. **If Christ is really God, I cannot see why people might not be sanctified by him in this life**; nor can I see any inconsistency in **Mr. Finney in** holding this as a part of the orthodox faith.[81] Yet I should like to see Mr. |Finney. Cannot you persuade him to call on me? for I cannot go and see *him*." **She promised him to deliver his message, and request me to call and see him.** She **did** call at my lodgings **immediately**; but I had left Boston for Providence. **I was absent, as I said, two months; and then called at Boston on my return homeward from Providence.**[82] This lady **hearing that I was in Boston the second time** called immediately to see me, and gave me the information **concerning Dr Channing that** I have related. But **she also informed me that** he had **left the city and** gone into the country on account of his health. **I never saw him. I was very sorry that I had not had the opportunity of an interview with that man, whom I had learned to respect for his talents and earnestness as the leader of the Unitarians in Boston. I had heard that Dr Channing was inquiring on the subject of religion, and disposed to reconsider the whole question of the divinity of Christ and of his own personal interest in him; and when this woman told me her story** I greatly regretted not having an opportunity to see him. But he died shortly after, and of his history **after he left Boston** I know nothing.[83] Nor can I vouch for the truth of what this lady said.

MS 737 / MS 738

[80] *Views of Sanctification* (Oberlin: Steele, 1840).

[81] In another reference to this statement by Channing, Finney represents him as saying: What is the ground of these objections, raised by those who are called Orthodox, against your views of sanctification? If the orthodox views of Christ are correct, and he is truly divine, then this result, as held by Oberlin men, *is just what ought to be expected.* A Savior really divine ought to be able not only to pardon but to cleanse from sin. . . . Every thing seems to turn on the question of his true divinity. And I marvel how men who hold to this divinity can yet object against his having such power to save (*OE,* 23 December 1857, p. 202).

[82] Finney was in Boston about the first week in February 1842.

[83] George Burgess wrote of Channing's receiving a letter in 1842 from Orestes A. Brownson, in which he declared the insufficiency, for the heart and for the truth, of a religion without a mediation. . . . It was almost the last voice which came to the ear of Channing. He visited the valleys of Berkshire, and it was at Lenox, on the anniversary

|**But**[84] she was manifestly **a true convert,** and I had **at the time** no doubt that every word she told me was true; **nor have I yet any doubt of it.** But **as this lady** was a stranger to me, I cannot recollect her name ‹at this distance of time.›[85]

MS 739
JHF 357

The next time I met Dr Beecher Dr **Channing**'s name was mentioned, and I related to him this fact. The tears started in his eyes in a moment, and he said with much emotion, "I guess he has gone to heaven!" **implying that he hoped he was converted.**

of West Indian emancipation, that he spoke for the last time to an assembly of his fellow-men. As if through all his negations, a gleam from the heaven of truth had shot in at sunset, he said that "the doctrine of the Word made flesh, shows us God uniting himself most intimately with our nature, manifesting himself in a human form, for the very end of making us partakers of his own perfection." "The doctrine of grace, as it is termed," he said, "reveals the Infinite Father imparting his Holy Spirit, the best gift he can impart, to the humblest human being who implores it." In the concluding paragraph, he uttered what, as a rhetorical apostrophe, would be almost profane, and as a prayer, would be at variance with the efforts of his life, "Come, Friend and Saviour of the race, who didst shed thy blood on the cross, to reconcile man to man, and earth to heaven!" A few days after, he died at Bennington (*Pages from the Ecclesiastical History of New England, During the Century Between 1740 and 1840* [Boston: Dow, 1847], pp. 119–20).

Channing died on 2 October 1842.

[84] The bottom half of MS 739 begins chapter XXVI.

[85] Finney added the phrase "at this distance of time." It may be the same incident that Asa Mahan recollected:

Dr Channing inquired of the celebrated seamen's chaplain in the city, Dr Taylor, whether the latter could designate any individuals, or class of individuals, whose inner and visible lives accorded with the revelations of the New Testament in respect to what believers are privileged to become. "There are many such," Dr Taylor replied. At Dr Channing's special request, Dr Taylor designated a lady whom he well knew, and who had for two or three years "walked in the light of God." At Dr C.'s written request, that lady called upon him. As soon as they met, the Doctor said to her, with much feeling, "I desire to hear from you about this *full redemption* of which so much is said in the churches in the city and country." The lady then detailed to him her own personal experience on the subject. . . . Dr Channing wept like a child while listening to that narrative, and said, as the lady took her leave, that he should take an opportunity to converse with her again on this subject. Immediately after this the Doctor left the city on his summer vacation, and died while absent. In an address which he delivered just before he died, on the subject of slavery, he made a devout reference to Christ as having made an atonement for our sins, as living in the world as "God manifest in the flesh," and as the foundation of all our hopes. The facts above stated—facts connected with Dr Taylor and the lady referred to—I give as given personally to me by these individuals themselves (A. Mahan, *Out of Darkness into Light* [London: Wesleyan-Methodist Book-Room, 1882], pp. 227–28).

MS 739
JHF 358

CHAPTER XXVI

‹*Another great* **revival** *at* **Rochester** *New York in 1842.*›

‹After[1] resting a day or two in Boston, I left for home, **as the time for the opening of our spring term had nearly arrived.** Being very weary with labor & travel I called on a friend at Rochester to take a days rest before **I traveled** further.›[2] As soon as it was known that I was in Rochester Judge **Gardiner**[3] called on me and with much earnestness requested me to stop and preach **for them.** Some of the ministers also insisted upon my stopping and preaching for them.[4] I informed them that I was worn out, and the time had

[1]The first half of MS 739 contains the end of chapter XXV. The section down to note 2 is in Finney's handwriting on a separate piece of paper pasted onto the sheet. The section covered over reads, "I spent a day or two at Boston at this time and came on toward home. When I arrived at Rochester I stopped at the house of a friend to rest being weary of my winter's labors and of my journey to Rochester. It was I think then the latter part of February."

[2]This ends the section in Finney's handwriting on a separate piece of paper pasted onto the page. Finney was in Boston on 7 February 1842. He planned to travel west via Syracuse, where he was to deliver a letter for Mrs. Anna Austin, and was in Rochester by 12 February. See Joseph H. Moses to Anna Austin, 7 February 1842, in Onondaga County Historical Society, Syracuse (information from Timothy E. Gorman); and Blake McKelvey, "Letters Postmarked Rochester, 1817–1879," *The Rochester Historical Society, Publication Fund Series* 21 (1943): 75–76.

[3]Here a section follows that Matson had written down and that appears to have been crossed out by Finney. It reads, "of whom I have formerly spoken, and whose wife was converted in 1831 in that city, in the family where we had our quarters." See MS 581.

[4]According to H. Pomeroy Brewster: "It was almost solely through Judge Gardiner's influence, though Rev. George Boardman of the 'Bethel' and Dr. Shaw joined in the effort, that Mr. Finney took any part in the revival of 1842" (H. Pomeroy Brewster, "The Magic of a Voice," *The Rochester Historical Society, Publication Fund Series* 4 [1925]: 282–83). Finney had been in Rochester the previous summer for the week of 4–11 July, attending the Rochester convention on the subject of holiness. He had then preached on the Sundays before and after the convention and during the week, and his preaching had created a demand for his return. See *OE,* 21 July 1841, p. 120; and 4 August 1841, p. 125; and George A. Avery to Levi Burnell, 30 July 1841, Letters Received by Oberlin College, 1822–1866, microfilm, roll 8.

Not all the ministers, however, welcomed him. In particular, Rev. Tryon Edwards of the First Presbyterian Church recalled:

> Much more than ordinary religious interest had been for some time manifest in the city, when Mr. Finney was invited, by a few lawyers and other friends, to visit the city. At that time he adopted his well known *perfection* views, and when, on his arrival, he wished, and apparently was expecting to preach in the First Presbyterian Church, as he had done at his first visit, its pastor, after full conversation with him as to his *perfection* views, declined his proposal, and in so doing was unanimously sustained by his strong and influential Session, some of the members of which had been converted under the preaching of Mr. Finney at his first visit, in 1831 (*NYE,* 25 January 1894, p. 6).

come for me to be at home. |However,[5] they were very urgent, and especially one of the ministers, whose wife was one of my spiritual daughters, **and** the Sarah **Brayton** of whom I have spoken as having been converted in Western **in Oneida County**.[6] I finally consented to stop and preach a sermon or two, and did so. But th**is only excited general attention, and** brought upon me a more importunate invitation to remain and hold a series of meetings. I **finally consented to do so**, and though wearied went on with **my labors. The Rev.** George Boardman[7] was **the** pastor of what was then called "The Bethel; or Washington st. church;"[8] and **the Rev.** Mr. Shaw **was pastor** of the Second or Brick church.[9] **Brother** Shaw was very anxious to unite with **Brother** Boardman, and have the meetings alternately **at each of their churches. Brother** Boardman was indisposed to take this course, saying that his congregation was weak, and needed the concentration of my labors at that point. I regretted this; but still I could not overrule it, and went on with my labors at Bethel, or Washington st. church. Soon after, **as the house in Washington st. could not hold the multitudes that desired to attend,** Dr Shaw secured the labors of **the** Rev. Jedediah Burchard in his church, **and went on with** a protracted effort there.[10] |**Brother Burchard's labors were better calculated to attract the more excitable ones of the community**

MS 740

MS 741
JHF 359

[5]MS 740 had originally been numbered 571 by Matson but was not used in sequence. Pages 740–62 were numbered 588–610 and renumbered 720–42 by Matson, and then changed to 740–62 by Finney.

[6]See MS 289–90. The minister was George Smith Boardman (1796–1877). He was a graduate of Union College and Princeton Theological Seminary and had been the minister of the Presbyterian church at Watertown, New York, from 1821 to 1837. He was one of the ministers assigned by the presbytery to supervise Finney's theological studies. He went to the Bethel Church in Rochester in 1837 and remained until June 1842. In 1843 he moved to Rome, New York. See *NYE,* 15 February 1877, p. 8; and P. H. Fowler, *Historical Sketch of Presbyterianism Within the Bounds of the Synod of Central New York* (Utica: Curtiss and Childs, 1877), p. 191. Evidently Boardman's church had sent for Finney earlier in January while Finney was in Providence, but Finney declined to go. See McKelvey, "Letters Postmarked Rochester, 1817–1879," pp. 73–75.

[7]The initial *S* was inserted in pencil in the manuscript between the names "George" and "Boardman," possibly by Dr. Charles P. Bush to whom Fairchild submitted this section of the manuscript for his comments. See MS 746, reverse.

[8]Bethel Free Church had been founded in 1836 by thirty-nine members of the First Presbyterian Church, many of them Finney converts; and a small meeting house was erected on the north bank of the Erie Canal next to the Washington Street bridge. It was designed as a place where moral and political issues such as slavery and temperance could be freely discussed and as a center of evangelism and reform, particularly among the boatmen and passengers on the canal. In 1842 its name was changed to Washington Street Church, and in 1858 the church moved to Plymouth Avenue North and was renamed Central Presbyterian Church. At the beginning of January 1842 the membership stood at 239. See Walter E. Hastings et al., eds., *A Century with Central Church, 1836–1936* (Rochester, 1936), pp. 1–6; and *NYE,* 17 August 1876, p. 6.

[9]James Boylan Shaw (1808–1890) was a graduate of Yale and had studied law in New York before attending Auburn Theological Seminary. He went to Rochester from Dunkirk in December 1840 and was to remain in Rochester for the rest of his life. He was a prominent minister in the Presbyterian church and moderator of the General Assembly in 1865. See Alfred Nevin, ed., *Encyclopaedia of the Presbyterian Church* (Philadelphia: Presbyterian Encyclopaedia Publishing Co., 1884), pp. 823–24; and *NYE,* 21 November 1895, p. 12.

[10]Jedediah Burchard (1791–1864) was a prominent revivalist who had been associated with Finney in their earlier labors. See p. 14 n. 57 (MS 20). Edwin Scrantom recorded in his diary under the date 4 March 1842: "Revd. Jedidiah Burchard commenced a protracted meeting with us. The opening appearances are fine. Revd. C. G. Finney is holding meetings in the Bethel Chh with success" (Diary in Rochester Historical Society).

than mine were. ‹In the meantime›[11] Judge **Gardiner** had united with **the** members of the bar, **together with other judges in the city,** in a written request to me to preach a course of sermons to lawyers, **a course** adapted to their ways of thinking.[12] Judge **Gardiner** was then one of the judges of the Court of **A**ppeals in the state **of New York,** and held a very high place in the estimation of the whole profession **as a lawyer and a judge**. I consented to deliver the course of lectures. I was aware of the half s**k**eptical state of mind in which those members of the bar were,—many of them at least, who were still unconverted. There was still left in the city a goodly number of pious lawyers, who had been converted in the revival of 1830 and '31. I began my course of lectures to lawyers by asking this question: "Do we *know* anything?"[13] **To this question I gave an answer,** and followed up the inquiry by lecturing evening after evening. My congregation became very select. Brother Burchard's meetings opened an interesting place for **the more**
MS 742 **excitable** class of community, |and made room for the lawyers and **for the more sober and intelligent class** in the house where I was preaching. It was filled every night **to its utmost capacity, insomuch that it was very difficult to get into the house at all unless they came early**. As I proceeded in my lectures from night to night I observed the interest constantly deepening. As Judge **Gardiner's**[14] wife was a particular friend of mine I had occasion to see **Judge Gardiner** himsel**f**[15] not unfrequently, and was very sure that the **W**ord was getting a strong hold of him. He remarked to me after I had delivered several lectures, "Mr. Finney, you have cleared the ground to my satisfaction thus far; but when you come to the question of the endless punishment of the wicked you will slip up,—you will fail to convince us on that question." I replied, "Wait and see, Judge." This hint made me the more careful when I came to that point to discuss it with **as much** thoroughness **as I was able**. The next day I met him, and he volunteered the remark at once, "Mr. Finney, I am convinced. Your dealing with that subject
MS 743 was a success; nothing can be said against it." The manner |in which he said this indicated that the subject had not merely convinced his intellect, but had deeply impressed him.

JHF 360 |I was going on from night to night, but **did** not **think** my somewhat new and select audience **were** yet prepared for me to call for any decision **and demonstration** on the part of inquirers. But I had arrived at a point where I thought it was time to draw the net ashore. I had been carefully laying it around the whole mass of lawyers, and hedging them in, as I supposed, by a train of reasoning that they could not resist. I was aware that lawyers **were**[16]

[11] Here Finney changed the word "But" to "In the meantime."

[12] This document is not in the Finney Papers.

[13] According to William C. Cochran, "On the first night he removed the Bible from the pulpit and said he would not replace it until they were convinced of their need for it, and announced as the text of his first lecture, 'Do we know anything?' " (Cochran, "Charles Grandison Finney," *The Oberlin Alumni Magazine* 25 [March 1929]: 171–72).

[14] Gardiner's name, apart from the initial, was crossed out in pencil by Charles P. Bush. See MS 746, reverse.

[15] The words "Judge Gardiner" and the "self" of "himself" were crossed out by Bush. See MS 746, reverse.

[16] The word "were" was not crossed out in the manuscript but appears as "are" in the published edition.

Addison Gardiner. The eminent Rochester judge who was converted during the Rochester campaign in 1842. In William F. Peck, *Semi-Centennial History of the City of Rochester* (Syracuse: Mason, 1884), opposite p. 370. Courtesy The Rochester Public Library.

accustomed to listen to argument, to feel the weight of a logically presented truth, and had no doubt **in my mind** that the great **mass** of them were thoroughly convinced **up to the point that** I had **reached**; consequently I had prepared a discourse **that** I intended **to reach** the point, and if it appeared to take effect I intended to call on them to commit themselves.[17] Judge **Gardiner** at the time I was there before, when his wife was converted, had opposed the anxious seat. I expected he would do so again, ˡas I knew he **was a very proud man, and** had strongly committed himself in what he had said against the use of the anxious seat. When I came to preach the sermon of which I have spoken, I observed that Judge **Gardiner** was not in the seat usually occupied **by him in those lectures**; and on looking around I could not see him anywhere among the members of the bar or judges. I felt MS 744

[17] Matson started the next sentence with the words "I have said that," but they appear to have been crossed out by Finney.

concerned about this, for I had prepared myself with reference to his case. I knew his influence was great, and that if he would take a decided stand it would have a very great influence upon all the legal profession in that city; **therefore I regretted greatly that he was not there.** However I soon observed that he had come into the gallery, and had found a seat just at the head of the gallery stairs, **and** sat wrapped **up** in his cloak. I went on with my discourse; but near the close of what I designed to say I observed that Judge **Gardiner** had gone from his seat. I felt distressed; for I concluded that as it was cold where he sat, and perhaps there was some confusion, it being near MS 745 the head of the stairs, |he had gone home;[18] and hence that the sermon which I had prepared with my eye upon him **was thrown away, at least upon *him*, and therefore as one of the course delivered to lawyers.**

There was a very large basement room in the Washington st. church, nearly as large as the audience room above. From this basement room JHF 361 there was a nar|row stairway into the audience room above, **that came** up just by the side of, and partly behind, the pulpit. Just as I was drawing my sermon to a close, and with my heart almost sinking with the fear that I was to fail in what I had hoped to secure that night, I felt some one pulling at the skirt of my coat. I looked around,—and **who should it be but** Judge **Gardiner?** He had gone down through the basement room, and up those narrow stairs, and crept up **on** the pulpit **stairs** far enough to reach me and pull me by the coat. When I turned around to him and beheld him with great surprize, he said to me, "Mr. Finney, won't you pray for me *by name*? and I will take the anxious MS 746 seat?" I had said nothing |about[19] an anxious seat at all. The congregation had observed this movement on the part of Judge **Gardiner** as he came up on the pulpit stairs; and when I announced to them what he said it produced a wonderful shock. There was a great gush of feeling in every part of the house. Many held down their heads and wept; others seemed to be engaged in earnest prayer. He crowded around in front of the pulpit, and knelt

[18]Here Matson had written down, "therefore he had gone out and gone home," but it appears to have been shortened by Finney to "he had gone home."

[19]On the reverse of MS 746 is a letter in pencil from James H. Fairchild to Rev. Charles P. Bush, secretary of the American Board of Commissioners for Foreign Missions, followed by his reply in pencil:

> Dear Doctor. Please read this & tell me how it will strike Judge G. & what to do with it—& return as soon as you can to
>
> Jas. H. Fairchild
> Newburgh Orange Co. N.Y.
> Care Wm. McCrea Esqr.
>
> Dec. 3rd 1875.
>
> Dear President. I hardly know what to say. It will bear a little more pruning & then I guess it is safe. It would be a pity to omit it. It is a grand incident. I saw you had left Gardiner's name in full in two places, & I drew my pencil over all but the G. Pardon the liberty, if it was too much.
>
> I have written you twice—once to care A. S. Barnes, once to Newburg only. I want your recommendation for Mr. Ament. Please send me such a document at once.
>
> Yrs C. P. Bush
>
> Dec 6. 75.
>
> This was received today

"Mr. Ament" is probably William Scott Ament (1851–1909), a graduate of Oberlin College in 1873, who was to become a well-known missionary in China.

immediately down. The lawyers arose almost **en masse**, and crowded into the aisles, and **crowded around** the open space in front, wherever they could get a place to kneel, **and as many knelt around Judge Gardiner as could. As** the movement had begun without my requesting it, I then publicly **requested that** any who were prepared to renounce their sins and give their hearts to God, and to accept Christ and his salvation, **should** come forward,—**that they should get** into the aisles, or wherever they could, and kneel down. There was a mighty movement. **The congregation was moved to its profoundest depths, and the movement was among the principal citizens of Rochester.** ˡWe prayed, and **afterwards** I dismissed the meeting. MS 747

But as I had been preaching every night and could not give up an evening to a meeting of inquiry, I appointed a meeting for the instruction of inquirers the next day at two O'clock in the basement of **that** church. When I went I was surprized to find the **basement** nearly full, and that the audience was composed almost exclusively of the **principal** citizens **of Rochester**. This meeting I continued from day to day, having an opportunity to converse freely with great numbers **of their principal people, who** ˡwere as teachable JHF 362 as children. I never attended a more interesting and affecting meeting of inquiry, I think, than that. A large number of the lawyers were converted, Judge **Gardiner**, I might say, at their head; as he had taken the lead in coming out on the side of Christ.[20] I remained there at that time two months. The revival became wonderfully interesting and powerful, and resulted in the conversion of **a** great number **of their most respectable citizens.**[21] It took a powerful hold in one of the Episcopal churches, ˡSt. Luke's, of which Dr MS 748 Whitehouse, the present **Bishop** of Illinois, was pastor.[22] When I was in

[20] Louis Chapin specifically mentions two other prominent lawyers who were converted at this time: "Fletcher M. Haight who was a leading lawyer, President of the city Bank & father of the late Governor Haight of California, and Thomas Kempshall who had been Mayor, Member of Congress & other offices though an extensive miller" (Chapin to G. F. Wright, 10 February 1890, Wright Papers, box 8).

[21] Edwin Scrantom wrote under the date 21 April 1842: "There has been a wonderful outpouring of God's Holy Spirit and such a precious time as we have had no one scarce ever saw or heard since the Day of Pentecost. Hundreds have professed" (Diary in Rochester Historical Society). One early report indicated that 350 had been converted, although only 16 of those joined the Bethel Church (Hastings, *Century with Central Church*, p. 5). A report in the *Rochester Democrat* of 4 April 1842 stated: "We should not be surprised to find that the whole number of conversions in the city during the last six weeks, exceeds two thousand. Men of all ranks, as well as females and children, are included in the number" (reprinted in *OE*, 27 April 1842, p. 70).

Charles P. Bush and Augustus H. Strong both give the number of converts as 1,000 (C. P. Bush, "Charles G. Finney: His Early Labors, Incidents, Converts," *NYE*, 26 August 1875, p. 4; and A. H. Strong, *Christ in Creation and Ethical Monism* [Philadelphia: Williams, 1899], p. 365). As a result of Burchard's labors that year, 118 were added to the Brick Church, and 83 more were added the next year (see *Fiftieth Anniversary of the Organization of the Brick Church, Rochester, N.Y.* [Rochester: Andrews, 1876], p. 19). It was later reported, "As the fruits of the revival in Rochester the past winter, 441 have been added to the Presbyterian, Baptist, Methodist and Episcopal churches" (*BR*, 15 July 1842, p. 111).

[22] Henry John Whitehouse (1803–1874) was a graduate of Columbia College and General Theological Seminary and was rector of Christ Church, Reading, in 1827. He went to St. Luke's, Rochester, in 1830, where he remained until 1844. After being at St. Thomas's Church, New York, he became assistant bishop of Illinois in 1851 and diocesan on the death of Bishop Philander Chase in 1852. "Bishop Whitehouse was one of the most accomplished prelates of the Episcopal Church, possessing versatility of talent with great learning. He was a brilliant orator and

Reading, Pa., several years before, Dr Whitehouse was preaching to an Episcopal congregation in that city; and, as one of his most intelligent ladies informed me, was greatly blessed in his soul in that revival. When I came to Rochester in 1830 he was then pastor of St. Luke's; and, as I was informed, encouraged his people to attend our meetings, and I was told that many of them were at that time converted. So also in this revival in 1842, I was informed that he encouraged his people, and *advised* them to attend **our** meetings. He was himself a very successful pastor, and had great influence in Rochester. I have been informed that in this revival in 1842 not less than seventy, and those almost all among the principal people of his congregation, were converted and confirmed in his church. **The revival made a very general sweep among that class of people at that time.**[23]

MS 749 |**To enter into anything like a detailed account of special cases of conversion in this revival would itself fill a considerable volume. There was one very** striking incident. I had insisted much in my instructions upon entire consecration to God, giving up all to **H**im, body and soul and possessions and everything to be forever thereafter used for his glory, as a condition of acceptance with God. As was my custom in revivals I made this as prominent as I well could. One day as I went into meeting one of the lawyers with whom I had formed some acquaintance, and who had been in deep anxiety of mind, I found waiting at the door of the church. As I went in he took out of his pocket a paper and handed me, remarking, "I deliver this to you as the servant of the Lord Jesus Christ." I put it in my pocket until after JHF 363 meet|ing. On examining it I found it to be a quit claim deed, made out in regular order and executed ready for delivery, in which he quit-claimed to the Lord Jesus Christ all ownership of himself and of everything he possessed. **He made out** the deed in due form, **and** with all the peculiarities and formalities MS 750 of such conveyances. I think I have **that deed |in my possession now somewhere** among my papers.[24] He appeared to be in solemn earnest, and so far as I could see was entirely intelligent in what he did. But I must not go farther into particulars **in this place.**[25]

As it regards the means used in this revival, I would say that the doctrines preached were those that I always preached everywhere, **laying the foundations deep in the law of God, in the total moral depravity of the unregenerate, the voluntariness of this depravity, its utter unreasonableness and infinite wickedness; the necessity of regeneration, or a total change of moral position and character under the teaching and persuading influence of the Holy Ghost; the necessity, nature, and universal sufficiency of the atonement of our Lord Jesus Christ; the**

conversationalist" (*Appletons' Cyclopaedia of American Biography*, vol. 6 [New York: Appleton, 1889], p. 479).

[23] Matson had written the following section after this, which appears to have been crossed out by Finney:

> But I said that I remained about two months, and was completely exhausted; having labored two months in Boston, two months in Providence, and two months in Rochester, almost night and day. I then came home, and went on with revival work, and with my College duties as best I could.

[24] This is not in the Finney Papers.

[25] The words "in this place" are in the original but were omitted from the published edition.

absolute deity of Christ, the personality and divinity of the Holy Ghost, and the divine authority of the Holy Scriptures as the only rule of faith and practice. The moral government of God was made prominent;—and the necessity of an unqualified and universal acceptance of God's will as a rule of life; the **unqualified** acceptance by faith of the Lord Jesus Christ as the Savior of the world, and in all his official relations and work; and the sanctification of the soul |through or by the truth,—these and kindred doctrines were dwelt MS 751 upon as time would permit and as the necessities of the people seemed to require.[26]

The measures were simply preaching the Gospel; and abundant prayer in private, in social circles, and in public prayer-meetings, much stress being always laid upon prayer as an essential means of promoting the revival. Sinners were not encouraged to expect the Holy Ghost to convert them while they were passive, and never told to wait God's time; but were taught unequivocally that their first and immediate duty was to submit themselves to God, to renounce their own will, their own way, and themselves, and instantly to deliver up all that they were and all that they had to their rightful owner, the Lord Jesus Christ. **No compromise was made with them, no telling them to pray for a new heart, no telling them to go and read their Bibles and wait God's time to convert them, no setting them to use means to move God in the matter. They were told here, as everywhere, that God was using means with *them*, and not they with *God*; that our meetings were all so many means which God was using to gain their consent.** They were taught here, as every|where in those revivals, that the only obstacle in MS 752 the way was their own stubborn will; that God was trying to gain their unqualified consent to give up their sins, and accept the Lord Jesus Christ as their righteousness and salvation. The point was frequently urged upon them to give their *consent*; and they were told that |the only difficulty was to get JHF 364 their *own* honest and **unqualified** *consent* to the terms upon which Christ would save them, and the lowest terms upon which they possibly could be saved.

Meetings of inquiry were held for the purpose of adapting instruction to those who were in different stages of conviction; and after conversing with them as long as I had time and strength, I was in the habit of *summing up* at

[26]The doctrine of sanctification was particularly a feature of the preaching at this time. *The Oberlin Evangelist* carried a notice:

> A brother in Rochester, in a letter ordering a hundred copies of Bro. Finney's work on Sanctification, says, "The Lord is doing a great work here, through Bro. Finney. The doctrine of sanctification is agitating the church to its center. Zion is being 'ploughed as a field.' The interest continues to increase, and we know not when the Lord will release Bro. Finney" (*OE*, 30 March 1842, p. 55).

Louis Chapin told G. F. Wright: "Mr Finney dwelled a good deal on his views of christian perfection which were not acceptable to all" (Chapin to Wright, 10 February 1890, Wright Papers, box 8). Tryon Edwards reckoned:

> The result of Mr. Finney's preaching and urging, as he did, his *perfection* views, was that the pastor of the Bethel Church was dismissed and the church was left in a divided and shattered state, and it was some years before, under new influences, it was so built up and strengthened that its members, uniting with some excellent colonists, from the other churches, formed what is now the strong Central Church of Rochester (*NYE*, 25 January 1894, p. 6).

last, and taking up representative cases, **as they will generally be found to be easily classified,** and meeting all their objections, answering all their questions, correcting all their errors, and pursuing such a course of remark as was calculated to strip them of every excuse and bring them face to face with the great question of present, unqualified, universal acceptance of the will of God in Christ Jesus. Faith in God, and God in Christ, was ever made prominent. MS 753 |They were informed that this faith ‹is›[27] not a mere *intellectual assent*, but ‹is› the *consent* or *trust* of the heart‹.[28] T›**hat faith** ‹is› a *voluntary, intelligent trust* in God as he ‹is› revealed in the Lord Jesus Christ. **Pains were taken to show the sinner that the entire responsibility ‹is› upon himself; that God ‹is› entirely clear, and ‹will› ever remain so if the sinner ‹are›[29] sent to hell.** The doctrine of the justice of endless punishment was fully insisted upon; and not only its *justice* but the *certainty* that sinners ‹will› be endlessly punished if they died in their sins, was strongly held forth.[30] On all these points the Gospel was so presented as to give forth no uncertain sound. ‹This was at least *my* constant aim & the aim of all who gave instruction.›[31] The nature of the sinner's dependence upon divine influence was explained and enforced, and made prominent. Sinners were taught that without the divine teaching and influence it ‹is› certain from their depraved state that they never would be reconciled to God; and yet that their want of reconciliation was simply their own hardness of heart or the stubbornness of their own wills, so that their dependence upon the Spirit of God ‹is› no excuse for their not being Christians at once. MS 754 |These points that I have noticed, and others which logically flow from them, were held forth in every aspect, so far as time would permit, **that could influence the human mind.**

JHF 365 |Sinners were never taught in those revivals that they needed to expect conversion in answer to their *own* prayers. They were told if they regarded iniquity in their hearts the Lord would not hear them; and that while they remained impenitent they *did* regard iniquity in their hearts. I do not mean that they were exhorted not to pray. They were informed that God required them to pray, but to pray in *faith*, to pray in the *spirit* of repentance; and that when they asked God to forgive them, they were to commit themselves unalterably to His will. They were taught expressly that mere impenitent and

[27] Matson wrote the word "was" here, but Finney changed it to "is." He also changed many of the other verbs in the past tense to the present in this section.

[28] Matson had written down a semicolon here and started the word "that" with a small *t*. Finney inserted the period and capital *T*.

[29] Finney changed the word "were" to "are" here in error.

[30] Fifty years later, Dr. Farley Porter recollected Finney preaching this doctrine:

> The torments amid the flames of a literal hell were described with lurid rhetoric which terrorized vast audiences. I can well remember some of these scenes and their effects upon others and upon myself. When a little boy, I have often gone home from one of these meetings with my throat swelled and dry, suffering all the tortures of a condemned murderer, afraid to go to bed and not able to sleep when I got there. I was never able to persuade myself that these horrible fears were the "conviction of sin," which we were told was the first stage of true conversion. With me it was then the dreadful belief that what I heard was really true, and a deep-seated childish sense of the injustice of such a law as I had been born to live under (Farley Porter, "Rochester in the Forties," *The Rochester Historical Society, Publication Fund Series* 4 [1925]: 265).

[31] Finney added this sentence.

unbelieving prayer **was**[32] an abomination to God; but that if they were truly disposed to offer acceptable prayer to God they could do it, for that there was nothing but their own obstinacy in the way of their offering acceptable prayer at once. They were never left to think that they could do their duty in any respect, could perform any duty whatever, unless they gave their hearts to God. To repent, to believe, to submit as inward acts of the mind, ˡwere the first duties to be performed; and until these were performed, no outward act whatever was doing their duty. That for them to pray for a new heart while they did not give themselves up to God, was to tempt God; that to pray for forgiveness until they truly repented, was to insult God, and to ask **Him** to do what **He** had no right to do; that to pray in unbelief, was to charge God with lying instead of doing their duty; and that all their unbelief was nothing but a blasphemous charging of God with lying. In short pains were taken to shut the sinner up to accepting Christ, his whole will, atonement, official work and official relations, **unqualifiedly,** cordially, and with fixed purpose of heart, renouncing all sin, all excuse-making, all unbelief, all hardness of heart, and every wicked thing in heart and life, *here*, and *now*, and *forever*. **After the evening in which Judge Gardiner came forward, of which I have spoken, instead of inviting the inquirers to come forward and take particular seats they were invited into the lecture room below. The house was too much crowded, and the aisles too compactly filled, to admit of using the anxious seat in the sense of calling ˡthem forward to particular seats.**[33] **These meetings were attended by throngs of young converts and inquirers every evening.**

MS 755

MS 756

In this revival there was no appearance of any fanaticism or rudeness, no rash conduct, and nothing that I recollect to which the most fastidious mind would naturally take exceptions.[34] I **was** always particularly interested in the salvation of lawyers, and all men of a legal profession. To that profession I was myself educated. I understood ˡpretty well their habits of reading and thinking, and knew that they were more certainly controlled by argument, by evidence, and by logical statements than any other class of men. I have always found **in every place** where I have labored, that when the Gospel was properly presented, they were the most accessible class of men; and I believe it is true that in proportion to their relative number in any community, more have been converted than of any other class. I have been particularly struck with this in the manner in which a clear presentation of the law and of the Gospel of God ˡwill carry the intelligence of judges, men who are in the habit of sitting and hearing testimony and weighing arguments on both sides. I have never, to my recollection, seen a case in which judges were not convinced of the truth of the Gospel, where they have attended meetings in the revivals which I have witnessed. I have often been very much

JHF 366

MS 757

[32]The word "was" appears in the original and is not crossed out, but it is changed in the published edition to "is."

[33]Here Matson had written down, "them to come forward to particular seats, and therefore as there was a good room below they were invited there." This appears to have been altered by Finney.

[34]The two sentences that follow were crossed out by Fairchild, but similar sentences were written in.

affected in conversing with members of the legal profession, by the manner in which they would consent to propositions to which persons of ill-disciplined minds would have objected. There was ‹one›[35] of the judges of the Court of Appeals **who** lived in Rochester, who seemed to be possessed of a chronic skepticism. He was a reader and a thinker, a man of great refinement and of great **legal** honesty. His wife having experienced religion under my ministry, was a particular friend of mine. I have had very thorough conversations with that man. **He is a gentleman, and a man of exquisite refinement and delicacy of feeling.** He always freely confessed to me that the arguments were conclusive, and that his intellect was carried **right along with** the preaching and the conversation. He said to me: "Mr. Finney, you always in

MS 758 your public discourses ¦carry me right along with you; but while I assent to the truth of all that you say, I do not *feel* right,—somehow my heart does not respond.[''] He was one of the loveliest of unconverted men, and it was both a grief and a pleasure to converse with him. His candor and intelligence made conversation with him on religious subjects a great pleasure; but his chronic

JHF 367 unbelief rendered it exceedingly painful. I ¦have conversed with him more than once when his whole mind seemed to be agitated to its lowest depths. And yet, so far as I know, he has never been converted. His praying and idolized wife has gone to her grave. His only child, a son, was drowned before his eyes. After these calamities had befallen him I wrote him a letter, referring to some conversations I had had with him, and trying to win him to a Source from which he could get consolation. He replied in all kindness, but dwelling upon his loss.[36] He said there could be no consolation that could meet a case like that. He was truly blind to all the consolation he could find in Christ. He could not conceive how he could ever accept this dispensation and be happy.

MS 759 **His wife was a rare woman. Few like her have I met anywhere, ¦in[37] point of intelligence, beauty of person, and all those accomplishments that render a lady fascinating.** He has lived in Rochester through ‹one› great revival after ‹another›;[38] and although his mouth was shut so that he had no excuse to make, and no refuge to which he could betake himself, still he has mysteriously remained in unbelief **so far as I know**. I have mentioned his case as an illustration of the manner in which the intelligence of the legal profession can be carried by the force of truth. When I come to speak of the next revival in Rochester in which I had a share, I shall have occasion to mention other instances that will illustrate the same point. ‹**Reader, pray for the judge just above mentioned.**›[39]

Several of the lawyers that were at this time converted in Rochester gave up their profession and went into the ministry. **Our brother Charles Torrey,**

[35]Matson had originally omitted the word "one" and then inserted it after, instead of before, "of." It was corrected by Finney.

[36]This letter is not in the Finney Papers.

[37]On the reverse of the manuscript sheet 759, in pencil, the numbers *45*, *9*, and *50* have been added up. This appears to be in the same handwriting as the entries on the reverse of MS 154 and 181.

[38]Matson had written the phrase "through great revival after revival," but Finney changed it to read, "through one great revival after another."

[39]Finney added this sentence.

who has been so frequently here, was one of the lawyers converted at that time;[40] **and strange to say,** Chancellor **Walworth**'s son, at that time a young lawyer in Rochester, **was another** who appeared at the time to be soundly converted.[41] For some reason with which I am not acquainted, he went to Europe and to Rome, and finally became a Roman Catholic priest. He has been for years laboring zealously ˡto promote revivals of religion among them, holding protracted meetings; and, as he told me himself when I met him in England, trying to accomplish in the Roman Catholic church what I was endeavoring to accomplish in the Protestant church.[42] Mr. **Walworth** seems to be an earnest minister of Christ, given **with**[43] heart and soul to the salvation of Roman Catholics. How far he ˡagrees with all their views I cannot say. When I was in England he was there and sought me out, and came very affectionately to see me; and we had just as pleasant an interview, so far as I

MS 760

JHF 368

[40]This was Charles William Torrey (1815–1884), a graduate of Union College in 1838. In 1842 he went to Auburn Theological Seminary, and he was ordained in 1845. For two years he was an agent for the American Board of Commissioners for Foreign Missions before becoming pastor of the Presbyterian church in Delaware, Ohio. He was there from 1847 to April 1850. In 1847 he was married to Eliza Fitch of Oberlin, by Finney. His son, Charles Theodore Torrey, was born in Oberlin in 1850 and later entered Oberlin College. The father continued in pastorates in Ohio. In 1865 he undertook an agency that collected funds for Oberlin College. See *The Congregational Year-Book* (Boston), 1885, p. 36; *OE,* 10 November 1847, p. 183; 13 May 1857, pp. 73–74; 27 May 1857, pp. 81–82; Alumni Records, file 28/1, "Charles T. Torrey," Oberlin College Archives; and Finney to the Friends of Oberlin College, 21 April 1865, Correspondence of Charles G. Finney, 1830–1875, Oberlin College Archives, microfilm.

[41]Reuben Hyde Walworth (1788–1867) was the last chancellor of New York. He had been a lawyer and a judge of the supreme court, but he was an unpopular chancellor and may have contributed to the abolishment of the office of chancellor in 1846. Walworth was a Presbyterian and was active in the reform movements of the day (see *DAB*).

His son, Clarence Augustus Walworth (1820–1900), graduated from Union College in 1838 and studied law in Canandaigua and Albany. He was admitted to the bar in 1841 and practiced law for a year in Rochester with the firm of Chapin and Walworth. He then studied for three years at the Protestant Episcopal General Theological Seminary in New York. But in 1845 he became a Roman Catholic and entered the Redemptorist order, going to Belgium and Holland to study. After two years of mission work in England, he returned to America in 1851. In association with Isaac T. Hecker he became one of the most prominent Redemptorist preachers in America. In 1858 he was one of the founders of the Paulists. From 1866 until his death he was a pastor in Albany. See *DAB*; and Jay P. Dolan, *Catholic Revivalism* (Notre Dame: University of Notre Dame Press, 1978). Walworth stated that he had already been converted during a revival at Union College in 1838: "A real, substantial, and lasting impression was made upon me which changed the whole current of my life" (quoted in Dolan, *Catholic Revivalism*, p. 69).

[42]The Redemptorists, or Congregation of the Most Holy Redeemer, were mainly involved in preaching, mission work, and conducting retreats, and they were influential in the spread of revivalism in the Catholic church. Walworth became one of the leading mission preachers in America. In a letter to his father from England, he wrote, describing his mission work, that he was "giving a spiritual retreat, that is, as you would say in America, a revival" (quoted in Dolan, *Catholic Revivalism*, p. 69).

In 1854 a writer in the New Haven *Church Review* spoke of the "Modern Papists" as understanding about "earnestness" in preaching:

> They have an Order of men, the "Redemptorists," who are the Revivalists of the System. Fathers Walworth, Hewitt, Hecker and Duffy, are among the Burchards and Finneys of that Church ("The Revival System: Its Good and Its Evil," *The Church Review and Ecclesiastical Register* [New Haven] 7 [October 1854]: 371).

[43]The word "with" was not crossed out in the manuscript, but the published edition has "up."

know, as we should have had if we had both been Protestants.[44] He said nothing of his peculiar views, but only that he was laboring among the Roman Catholics to promote revivals of religion **among them**. Many ministers have been the **result** of the great revivals in Rochester. It was a fact that often greatly interested me when laboring in that city, that lawyers would come to my room when they were pressed hard and were on the point of submission, for conversation and light on some **particular** point which they did not clearly apprehend; and I **have** observed again and again that when those points were cleared up they were ready at once to submit. Indeed, as a MS 761 general thing they ˡtake a more intelligent view of the whole plan of salvation than any other class of men to whom I have ever preached, or with whom I have ever conversed. Very many physicians have also been converted in the great revivals which I have witnessed. I think their studies incline them to skepticism, or to a form of materialism. Yet they are intelligent; and if the Gospel is thoroughly set before them stripped of those peculiar features which are embodied in hyper-Calvinism, they are easily convinced, and as readily converted, **and more so, than the less intelligent class of society.** Their studies as a general thing have not prepared them so readily to apprehend the moral government of God as those of the legal profession. But still I have found them open to conviction, and by no means a difficult class of persons to deal with, **as a minister of Christ** upon the great question of salvation.[45]

I have everywhere found that the peculiarities of hyper-Calvinism have been **the** stumbling block both of the church and of the world. A nature sinful in itself, a total inability to accept Christ and to obey God, condemnation to MS 762 eternal death for the sin of Adam ˡand[46] for a sinful nature,—and all the JHF 369 kindred and resultant dogmas of that peculiar ˡschool, have been the stumbling block of believers and the ruin of sinners. Universalism, Unitarianism, and indeed all forms of fundamental error have given way and fallen out of sight in the presence of **those** great revivals. I have learned again and again that a man needs only to be thoroughly convicted of sin by the Holy Ghost to give up at once and forever, and *gladly* give up, Universalism and Unitarianism. When I speak of the next great revival in Rochester, I shall **then** have occasion to speak more fully of the manner in which skeptics, if a right course is taken with them, are sometimes shut up to condemnation

[44]This was probably when Finney was in Worcester in the spring of 1850. Walworth was in England from late in 1848 to January 1851. During most of this time, he was at the parish of Our Blessed Lady and St. Alphonsus, at Hanley, Upton-on-Severn, nine miles south of Worcester. It was there that the Hornyhold-Gandolphi family, local wealthy Catholics, had introduced the Redemptorists to England in 1846, and Father J. B. Lans hired a room for the mission until the new St. Joseph's Church was built in 1850. Walworth was sent there and became the first minister of a Catholic church in Upton-on-Severn since the Reformation. See *The Catholic Directory and Ecclesiastical Register* (London), 1849, p. 42; 1850, p. 47; and 1851, p. 76; and information from J. O'Brien, C.SS.R., Redemptorist Archives, Clapham, London; and the Reverend J. R. Watkins, Upton-on-Severn, Worcester.

[45]Matson appears to have written the end of this sentence to read, "and by no means a difficult class of persons to deal with, in my relation to them as a minister of Christ dealing with them upon the great question of salvation." Finney appears to have altered it.

[46]The figure "–7" was added after the page number 762 by Fairchild to indicate to the printers to omit the next five pages and proceed to page 768.

‹by›[47] their own irresistible convictions, so that they will rejoice to find a door of mercy opened through the revelations that are made in the Scriptures. But this I leave to be introduced in the order **in which those great revivals occurred.**[48]

[47] Here Matson had written the word "from," but Finney crossed it out and inserted "by."
[48] See MS 932–42. Finney crossed out a section that followed from here to the bottom of the page when he started a new chapter at the top of the next page. It read, "After remaining at Rochester at this time two months, or thereabouts, I left for home, and on arriving addressed myself to my work here in the performance of my college and parochial."

MS 763

CHAPTER XXVII

‹*Return to Oberlin & labors there & again in New York city & in Boston*›

‹After[1] two months labor at Rochester I left for Oberlin & on arriving addressed myself to my work as professor & Pastor of the Church.[2] The work of God revived amongst our students & people & we had a continual work of grace at this place. There occurred a considerable number of›[3] conversions every week, and almost daily through the summer, ‹new cases were reported›[4] until I left in the fall to labor in the city of New York. This was in 1843.[5] One of our students, the Rev. Samuel Cochran,[6] was settled over a church in New

[1] Pages 763–98 were originally numbered 611–46, then renumbered 743–78 by Matson and changed to 763–98 by Finney. The chapter heading and the first section of page 763 down to n. 3 were written by Finney on a separate strip of paper pasted onto the top of the page. It covers up the previous page numbers and a portion of the text in Matson's handwriting. The section covered over reads, "duties. The Word of God revived here among the students, and we had a continual blessing. There were more or less." Some alterations to the text were made by Fairchild on this page before he decided to omit the whole section down to MS 767.

[2] Finney returned to Oberlin during the third week of April 1842. See *OE,* 13 April 1842, p. 63; and 27 April 1842, p. 71.

[3] This ends the section in Finney's handwriting.

[4] Finney added, "new cases were reported."

[5] Finney refers again to the Oberlin revival in the summer of 1842 in MS 766–68. It was actually in the fall of 1842 that he arrived in New York. He arrived on 11 November and started preaching on 13 November. See *NYE,* 10 November 1842, p. 178; and Samuel D. Cochran, "Notebook 1841–1847," 11 and 13 November 1842, George N. Allen Papers, file 30/67, box 2, Oberlin College Archives.

[6] Samuel Davies Cochran (1812–1904) had been a brilliant theological student at Oberlin College. He went to the Second Free Congregational Church in New York on Finney's recommendation in April of 1842. But because of the "Oberlin heresy," he could not be ordained in New York and had to return to Oberlin, where he was ordained on 23 August 1842. He remained with the church until August 1846 but was recalled there in 1848. In 1851 he went to the Free Presbyterian Church in Paterson, New Jersey. See *The Oberlin Alumni Magazine* 1 (November 1904): 56; and (December 1904): 69; W. C. Cochran, "Rev. Samuel D. Cochran, D.D.," *The Oberlin Alumni Magazine* 1 (February 1905): 117–19; Cochran, "Notebook 1841–1847"; Lewis Tappan to Hamilton Hill, 24 March 1842, Letters Received by Oberlin College, 1822–1866, microfilm, roll 8; *The Independent* (New York), 28 December 1848, p. 14; and *OE,* 21 May 1851, p. 87.

He subsequently had Congregational pastorates in Brooklyn, New York; Ann Arbor, Michigan; and Grinnell, Iowa, before becoming president of Thayer College in Kidder, Missouri, in 1870. He was a notable preacher and pastor and was prominent in Congregational affairs. See *The Independent,* 12 June 1856, p. 187; *The Congregational Quarterly* (Boston), 1860–1878; and J. Irving Manatt, "President Magoun and the Early Days of Iowa College," *The Independent,* 27 February 1896, p. 270.

York city;[7] and they had taken the theater on the corner of Broadway and Prince street, called Niblo's Garden theater, and were holding their public services there.[8] I remained there for several weeks,—I do not recollect how long.[9] Many very interesting cases of conversion oc-

[7]This was the Second Free Congregational Church. It had been formed by Lewis Tappan and others who were friendly to the Oberlin theology, as a result of a campaign conducted by Asa Mahan in the winter of 1841–1842. They started meeting in the hall of the Medical College in Crosby Street and were organized as a church on 22 April 1842 with thirty-six members. After three years a new church was built on Sullivan Street. It is not to be confused with the old Second Free Presbyterian Church, over which Rev. J. H. Martyn was the pastor. That church had become Congregational after Finney left and was known also as the Second Free Congregational Church until its name was changed in September 1844 to the First Free Congregational Church. The Broadway Tabernacle had been considered to be the First Congregational Church. See Jonathan Greenleaf, *A History of the Churches, of All Denominations, in the City of New York* (New York: French, 1846), pp. 359–60, 364–65; and Lewis Tappan Letters in *OE,* 2 March 1842, p. 38; and 11 May 1842, p. 79; see also 17 August 1842, p. 136.

The church enjoyed a number of revivals, and after five years, three hundred people had been converted. It was sometimes referred to as the "Sanctification Church" or the "Oberlin church" and was in many ways an outgrowth of Oberlin in New York. While Finney was there it was discussed whether *The Oberlin Evangelist* might be transferred to New York in association with the work there. See *NYE,* 10 November 1842, p. 178; *The Spiritual Magazine* (Putney, Vt.), 15 April 1846, p. 26; Lewis Tappan to Finney, 9 December 1842; and Tappan to H. C. Taylor, 2 December 1842, Letterbook, Tappan Papers, microfilm, roll 3; and *OE,* 28 February 1844, p. 39; 7 July 1847, p. 111; 24 November 1847, p. 197; and 5 January 1848, p. 5.

Cochran's church was one of a number of Free churches in the area that had become sympathetic to the Oberlin theology and were working together for a revival. Edward Weed, the minister of one of these churches at Paterson, New Jersey, wrote in a letter dated 6 September 1842:

> A powerful revival is going forward at Newark in Brother Parsons' church. Some 200 attend the inquiry meeting daily, and there is a good state of things in Brother Cochran's church in New York. Brother Finney is expected to spend the winter with them. The Holy Spirit seems to be hovering over this region, and the cloud of mercy begins to break (*Faith and Works; or, The Life of Edward Weed, Minister of the Gospel* [New York: Benedict, 1853], p. 105; see also Cochran, "Notebook 1841–1847," 1842–1843).

[8]William Niblo (1789–1878) had created his public gardens on the east side of Broadway, north of Prince Street, in 1824; and in 1827 a 1,200-seat theater was erected. When the new Niblo's Garden Theater was planned to be built on the same site two years later, the old theater was converted into a concert saloon, which "for a long time was used for various exhibitions, including concerts, spiritualistic meetings, and lectures." See *DAB*; and Thomas A. Brown, *A History of the New York Stage* (New York: Dodd, Mead, 1903), 1:175–76; 2:9.

It was Niblo's Saloon, rather than the Garden Theater, that had been hired by Lewis Tappan and his friends. Tappan stated that it "will hold 1500 comfortably." It was hired for six months and was ready to be opened for services on Sunday, 6 November. Finney preached his first sermons there on Sunday morning and evening, 13 November. Niblo's continued to be used until the end of March, 1843. See Lewis Tappan to Finney, 29 September 1842, Letterbook, Tappan Papers, microfilm, roll 3; *NYE,* 10 November 1842, p. 178; and Cochran, "Notebook 1841–1847," 6 to 13 November 1842, and 2 April 1843.

[9]Finney remained in New York about three months, leaving for Oberlin on 13 February 1843. See *OE,* 15 February 1843, p. 29; and 15 March 1843, p. 47; and Cochran, "Notebook 1841–1847," 13 February 1843. According to William C. Cochran,

> A professional stenographer was employed at one time to report his sermons in Niblo's Theatre, New York City. He succeeded very well for fifteen or twenty minutes, but when Mr. Finney began to warm up, and his words began to glow with feeling, he forgot entirely what he was there for and sat, with idle pencil, in open-mouthed astonishment. He could not be persuaded to try again (W. C. Cochran, *Charles Grandison Finney: Memorial Address* [Philadelphia: Lippincott, 1908], pp. 64–65).

However, about twenty-five of the lectures Finney gave on "Holiness of Christians in the Present

curred. But in a great city it is very difficult, and often impossible, to form any judgment of the extent of a revival.[10] The people come from every part of a great mass of souls, and get convicted and converted, and are then mixed up with a vast population; so that in all probability comparatively few of those that are really blessed are known at the time.

In this revival the present Governor of this state was hopefully converted.[11] He was then a youth of perhaps sixteen or eighteen years of age.[12] MS 764 **|One night—the house being very much crowded—I called for those who would submit themselves to God, as usu[a]l,[13] to come forward and take certain seats. While others were making their way slowly through the crowds in the aisle, I observed a young man coming across from a remote part of the house stepping on the tops of the slips. He had a very earnest look, and I was at the time quite impressed by the alacrity with which he came forward, stepping upon the backs of the seats.[14] He appeared exceedingly well as a young convert, and I had no doubt then that he was truly converted to Christ. Indeed, I have not**

Life" were taken down by S. D. Cochran, commencing on Tuesday, 29 November. Thirteen of these were published in *The Oberlin Evangelist* from 4 January to 16 August 1843 (Cochran, "Notebook 1841–1847," 29 November 1842; 13 February and 20 April 1843).

Finney also gave a series of lectures on the "Moral Government of God." A prospectus for eighteen of these lectures was advertised in *The New-York Evangelist* to begin on Sunday, 8 January, and continue on Tuesday, Wednesday, Friday, and Sunday evenings until completed. Lecture 15 was to be on regeneration and was scheduled for 27 January. Lewis Tappan took it down and sent it to the Brooklyn *Evening Star*. He also had five hundred copies of the lecture printed, and he sent them to people. This lecture was also published later in *The Preacher's Magazine* in London. Tappan had been visiting London at that time. See *NYE,* 12 January 1843, p. 7; Lewis Tappan Letters to H. C. Taylor, 18 February 1843; to William Harned, 20 March 1843; to Edward Weed, 20 March 1843; and to William Bradford, 14 April 1843, Letterbook, Tappan Papers, microfilm, roll 3; and *The Preacher's Magazine* (London) 5 (September 1843): 261–70.

[10] On 20 April 1843 Cochran reported at the first annual meeting of the church that fifty-nine had been added to the membership during the year, thirty-two by letter and twenty-seven on profession (Cochran, "Notebook 1841–1847," 20 April 1843). According to Lewis Tappan, Finney's effectiveness was limited, because

> the city has been so excited all winter, with the numerous lectures and debates on every sort of subject, that it has been more difficult than usual to get people together to hear plain sermons, especially from an *Oberlin* professor. The consequence is that thousands have lost a rich intellectual and moral treat (*OE,* 15 March 1843, p. 47).

[11] This was Jacob Dolson Cox, Jr. (1828–1900), the son of a building contractor in New York who had suffered severely in the 1837 financial crisis. The son, being unable to afford to go to college, was about to become apprenticed as a law clerk (see *DAB*). He was normally known as Dolson Cox; later he married Finney's daughter Helen.

[12] He was born on 27 October 1828 and was therefore at the time in his fifteenth year.

[13] Matson wrote the word "usul" here, but it was not altered in the manuscript.

[14] According to his grandson and biographer, William C. Cochran, the sermon had been on Hebrews 2:3, "How shall we escape if we neglect so great salvation?" Cox believed that "if he remained in his seat *one minute* his soul would be lost" (*Charles Grandison Finney,* p. 71). Cochran wrote further of this incident:

> His emotion was so great when he got there that he could not speak, nor even give his name. It was Jacob D. Cox. To all outward appearance this speechless emotion was the only immediate result of Mr. Finney's preaching; but, under the preaching and influence of Mr. Cochran, he was baptized, and joined the church the following fall (W. C. Cochran, "Early Life and Military Services of General Jacob Dolson Cox," *Bibliotheca Sacra* [Oberlin] 58 [July 1901]: 440–41).

He joined the church on 1 October 1843 (Cochran, "Notebook 1841–1847," 1 October 1843).

seriously doubted it since. He afterward came here to college, went through, and began the study of theology.[15] He began this study while I was in England the first time. But about that time he became bewildered, as I think, by reading President Edwards' treatise on the freedom of the will.[16] He came to study for the ministry. His mother, a very devout woman, was earnestly hoping that he would make a useful minister.[17] We all had high hopes and expectations of his future ˡusefulness, for he was a very promising young man. But he became so entangled in his metaphysical speculations as to call in question the freedom of the human will.[18] In this state of mind he saw clearly that he could not intelligently and with hope of success, present the Gospel to men. He therefore quit his theological studies and went to teaching school.[19] He had been in a law office as clerk before he came to Oberlin.

MS 765

[15]Dolson Cox went to Oberlin in July 1846 and spent a year in the preparatory department, entering as a college freshman in the fall of 1847. But in the fall of 1848 he had become engaged to Finney's daughter, Helen, whose first husband, William Cochran, brother of Samuel, had died the previous year. She had just given birth to a son in March 1848. Dolson was married to Helen at the end of the fall term in November 1849, just after the Finneys left for England, and they lived in the Finney home and looked after the younger children until the Finneys returned in May 1851.

Dolson was a brilliant student and managed to cover the last two years of his college course in one year, entering the middle class of the theological department in the fall of 1850. By the end of his first year he was so far ahead that he was almost ready to become a third-year theology student. See Eugene D. Schmiel, "The Career of Jacob Dolson Cox, 1828–1900: Soldier, Scholar, Statesman" (Ph.D. diss., Ohio State University, 1969), pp. 10–20.

[16]Jonathan Edwards, *A Careful and Strict Enquiry into the Modern Prevailing Notions of that Freedom of Will, which is supposed to be Essential to Moral Agency, Virtue and Vice, Reward and Punishment, Praise and Blame* (Boston: Kneeland, 1754). The book was frequently reissued by different publishers.

[17]His mother, Thedia Redelia (Kenyon) Cox (b. 1804), a descendant of Elder William Brewster of the *Mayflower*, and her two oldest daughters had started attending Cochran's meetings soon after they were commenced in Crosby Street, near their home. She was herself influenced by Finney in the revival, as was her second son, Kenyon. And according to W. C. Cochran, "So great was Mrs. Cox's love and regard for Mr. Finney that she named her youngest son, born January 16, 1846, Charles Finney Cox" (Cochran, "Life of Cox," pp. 438–41; and Cochran, "Charles Finney Cox," *The Oberlin Alumni Magazine* 8 [March 1912]: 170).

[18]Cox's rejection of the doctrine of free will is clearly indicated in correspondence he had after leaving Oberlin, with Thomas H. Robinson, a friend of his at the college, who had become a pastor in Harrisburg, Pennsylvania. In his first letter he wrote: "What, then, is our freedom? It is freedom from control by any other being. . . . The law of causality interferes in no way with our desires, for that law *is* simply this, that the strongest desire determines our acts" (Cox to Robinson, 11 April 1852, "Manifold Letter Book, No. 1,' Jacob Dolson Cox Papers, Oberlin College Archives, microfilm, roll 3). This was the position held by Jonathan Edwards. He described the will as always being determined by "the strongest motive" or "the greatest apparent good." See Jonathan Edwards, *Freedom of the Will*, ed. Paul Ramsey (New Haven: Yale University Press, 1957), pp. 141–42. Some years later Cox wrote to John M. Ellis:

> When I left O. I was fully determined to spare no labor to reach something like assurance in regard to that most vexed of all disputed questions, the freedom of the will, and although my study has been very desultory and much broken up, what I have been able to do in the way of reading and thought has confirmed the convictions I then had, instead of weakening them (Cox to Ellis, 26 December 1858, "Manifold Letter Book, No. 1," Cox Papers).

[19]William C. Cochran explained what happened. Finney had returned from England and was disturbed "to find a young man in his own family digging deep about the very foundations of religion."

Dolson was studying those problems,

"Of Providence, foreknowledge, will and fate—

Not finding his way out of his metaphysical speculations so as to feel clear in his mind to go forward and preach the Gospel, he finally adopted the profession of law.[20]

> Fixed fate, free will, foreknowledge absolute,"
>
> which every man who essays to be the religious guide of others should work out, at some time and in some way, for himself. He was debating these questions with himself and with others with intense earnestness. His whole future depended upon his finding sure ground on which to stand. It is possible that there was more of the *debater*, than the *seeker after truth*, in his manner, and that when he was *testing* doctrines he seemed rather to wish to *overthrow* them. Be that as it may, there came a day, late in the summer, when Mr. Finney said to him, after a particularly warm discussion, "Dolson, you are not *honest*. You do not *want* to see the truth." If he had stabbed the young man, he could not have hurt him more. In that awful moment he saw all his hopes and ambition dashed to earth. If theology was not a science permitting of free inquiry and intellectual apprehension, he could go no further. Whether it was or not, the word spoken had made it impossible for him to continue studying in Oberlin, or to remain in his father's house. No man, then, or thereafter, in all his long and useful life, had the right to call Jacob D. Cox, *dishonest*. Dependence upon a man who could think him so, was intolerable. Dr. Morgan, who was present and saw the deadly effect of the words uttered, said, with trembling voice, "Brother Finney, Brother Finney, you must not say that. I believe Dolson is honest"; and for these kind words uttered in the hour of greatest anguish he had ever known, General Cox held Dr. Morgan in loving remembrance ever after. But the blow had fallen. Dolson applied immediately for the position of Superintendent of Public Schools in Warren, Ohio, of which he chanced to hear, secured it, and left Oberlin with his wife, his adopted son, and a little girl of his own, then about a year old.
>
> If there had been more patience on one side, or less sensitiveness on the other, matters might not have reached this crisis; he might have solved *his* doubts as many another honest man has done, as Mr. Finney himself did after three years of anxious questioning, during which *he* was regarded as a dangerous infidel, and Jacob D. Cox might have been one of the most polished, cultured, and able preachers of his generation.

Cochran adds a footnote:

> In justice to Mr. Finney, it must be said that he probably never realized what a wound he had inflicted. He always manifested a fatherly solicitude for the young man and his family, called on him frequently when passing to and from his journeys East, tendered financial assistance when the pinch of poverty was felt, left his daughter, Julia, in their care for a year or more at a time, and expressed an ever-growing regard for his son-in-law. They discussed freely professional ethics, politics, the practical affairs of life; but Theology was never again the subject of their conversation ("Life of Cox," pp. 445–47).

Cox referred occasionally in his correspondence to this accusation of dishonesty. He wrote to J. A. R. Rogers:

> Had I not been constantly met with the declaration that it were damnable heresy for me to push my investigations fearlessly, looking only to my honesty and patience in study, to judge of the rectitude of my conclusions, instead of jud[g]ing my honesty *by* my conclusions; I might have been in the Pulpit today. The world needs preaching to, badly enough, but my terrible *lisp* in pronouncing Shibboleth, shut the door against me.

He reckoned that "to get out of Oberlin, is like coming to one's senses" (Cox to Rogers, 21 December 1854, Cox Papers, microfilm, roll 3; and see Schmiel, "Career of Cox," pp. 21–22).

[20]Cox started a law practice in Warren in the summer of 1853. Although he abandoned an orthodox belief in the inspiration of the Bible, he did not abandon his Christian faith, and he joined the Presbyterian church in Warren. Cox subsequently entered politics as a Republican, rose to the rank of major general in the Civil War, and became secretary of the interior in Grant's government. He was subsequently governor of Ohio, president of the Wabash Railway, dean of the Cincinnati Law School, and president of the University of Cincinnati. His wide-ranging interests led him to become distinguished in the field of microscopy and as an author and military

It will be remembered by those who have observed and noted such facts, that the winter of 1843 was one in which revivals very extensively prevailed. I started for home about the first of March, I think, and found sleighing all the way to Oberlin.[21] I found also, to my great satisfaction, that a continuous revival was prevailing through almost every town between here and New York. I hardly stopped at a place as we journeyed on in the stage ꜌without[22] learning that they were holding daily meetings for prayer, and that they were in the midst of a powerful revival.[23] MS 766

In looking back upon the extensive revivals ‹an› account of which I have given,[24] I can truly say that I have never read or heard of such extensive revivals of religion prevailing anywhere with so little to be lamented and so little that was truly objectionable. This fact is owing, no doubt, to the very general intelligence of the American people,

historian. He had been a trustee of Oberlin College since 1876, and in 1897 he retired there with his wife to live (Schmiel, "Career of Cox," pp. 24, 461). In 1871 Finney wrote to Cox:

> Dolson what are we to think of your spiritual state. When your mother read your last letter she sighed & said O, that he was an earnest Christian! She much admires you & dearly loves you. Will you tell us what we may think of your spiritual state so that if you should die suddenly as so many do we should not be in doubt as to your future & eternal state (Finney to J. D. Cox, 2 September 1871, Correspondence of Charles G. Finney, 1830–1875, Oberlin College Archives, microfilm).

[21] Finney left New York on 13 February and had arrived back in Oberlin by 1 March. See Mary Gutzlaff to Finney, 12 February 1843, Finney Papers, microfilm, roll 4; and *OE,* 15 February 1843, p. 29; and 15 March 1843, p. 49.

[22] MS 766 starts with a section that begins on the previous page and appears to have been crossed out by Finney. It reads: "—for at the time [MS 766] we had to come much of the way in the stage, for west of Rochester railroad ‹travel› was entirely suspended by the depth of the snow—I said that I scarcely stopped at any place."

[23] Finney elaborated further on this in a sermon in 1859:

> In 1842 a revival again took place in Rochester, overflowing as it had done before, and continued to extend. In 1843 it had spread from New York to Ohio. In March, 1843, I went over the country in that direction, and found the revival influence at work in every town at which I stopped. In all these places the awakening partook of substantially the same character; the same means were used,—believing prayer for a definite object was offered, and daily prayer-meetings were held. This revival was of wide extent. I have seen no estimate of the number of hopeful conversions in and about 1842 and 1843. But the number must have been large. In the single city of Albany, I have been informed by a minister who was then laboring there, there were over 3000 conversions. This revival was only the development of an awakening that had, the year before (that is in 1842), been very powerful in Boston, Providence, Rochester, and many other places where evangelists had assisted the able pastors in holding daily meetings, and using the appropriate means (Finney, *The Prevailing Prayer-Meeting* [London: Ward, 1859], pp. 23–24).

Richard Carwardine has pointed out that

> the winters of 1842–43 and 1843–44 brought enormous gains to all denominations, especially the Methodists. In these two years the M[ethodist] E[piscopal] C[hurch] added over a quarter of a million members, a staggering growth of nearly 30 percent. . . . William G. McLoughlin has placed the end of the Second Great Awakening in 1835, after the Finneyite climax of the early 1830s. But in strictly statistical terms the peak of the Awakening came in this adventist phase of 1843–44 (R. Carwardine, *Transatlantic Revivalism* [Westport, Conn.: Greenwood, 1978], p. 52).

[24] Here Matson had originally written the words "which I have thus given." He changed them to "the account of which I have given." Finney later changed the word "the" to "an."

especially of the people of the Northern states, where education is universal.

I have spoken of my return from Rochester in the Spring of '43,[25] and that winter[26] we had an interesting revival. I should have been a little more particular in noticing some of the characteristics of that revival. Sometime in July, I believe it was, a convention of ministers met in Rochester, N.Y, to consider the question, if I recollect right, of the sanctification of the Sabbath.[27] My friends in Rochester were very
MS 767 **anxious to have me attend, and I did so.[28] But the Sabbath be|fore I went I preached on the text, "Then shall ye seek me and shall find me, when ye search for me with all your heart."[29] The word made a profound impression. On Monday morning I started for Rochester.[30] But it was found, although I did not know till after I left, that the students were too much impressed to go on with their recitations. The teachers seeing the state of things suspended recitations for a few days; and they gave themselves up to prayer, and to attending to the great question of their salvation. The feeling was intense, and for a few days quite overwhelming. Conversions multiplied very rapidly. But some of the students got very ‹much›[31] excited; and one among them, a young Scotchman became quite insane. His insanity, however, lasted but a short time. Such was the state of things that my people requested me to return immediately to Oberlin. I did so; and no permanent evil resulted from the intense excitement that had prevailed for a few days while I was absent. The studies were suspended but a short time, and things went on as usual. The over-excited ones became calm. But a deep spirit of prayer continued through the Summer, with much spiritual progress among Christians; and a large number of our students were hopefully**
MS 768 **converted.[32] |There[33] was in this revival no heretical tendency, that I**

[25] See MS 763. It was 1842, not 1843.

[26] Fairchild altered the word "winter" to "summer." The revival Finney was speaking about was in the summer.

[27] The Rochester Sabbath Convention was held in the First Baptist Church in Rochester on 20 and 21 July 1842. See the report of the proceedings in *NYE,* 28 July 1842, pp. 118–19.

[28] He attended the convention on Wednesday, 20 July, and addressed the assembly in the evening. See *NYE,* 28 July 1842, p. 118.

[29] Jeremiah 29:13.

[30] This was Monday, 11 July. Finney had planned to be away for two weeks. He went with his wife via Buffalo, where he attended a "holy convocation" on Wednesday. See *OE,* 20 July 1842, p. 118; and 17 August 1842, p. 133; and Lydia Finney to Helen and Charles Finney, 19 July 1842, Finney Papers, microfilm, roll 4.

[31] Finney added the word "much."

[32] In a survey entitled "Religious History of Oberlin," the author, probably Henry Cowles, wrote of this revival:

> It came, not like the gentle dew, nor indeed as when the ordinary showers of summer refresh us, but more as when a water-spout breaks above us, and suddenly we find ourselves immersed in the floods of great waters. It came first and chiefly among the students. All suddenly, whole classes were borne down with burdens of prayer. It was a Sabbath. Prayer meetings were kept up all the vacant hours of the day and evening, and in every direction from the fields and forests around were heard voices of prayer all the ensuing night. The next day opened, and we are not aware that any thing else occupied the attention of the masses of students but prayer. Strong convictions of sin seemed to seize on some hitherto careless minds;—but the work was too transient to mature the

recollect, at all, or anything that could properly be called fanaticism. Indeed after I returned—and I think I was not absent a week, or certainly more than one Sabbath—things fell into the ordinary channel of a wholesome and powerful revival.

ᴵIn the fall of 1843 I was called again to Boston. **When I was there in '42, if I am not mistaken as to dates,** it was the time of the greatest excitement in Boston on the subject of the second Advent of Christ. **There was a tremendous movement in the public mind on that subject at that time.** Mr. Miller was there lecturing **on that subject**, and was holding daily Bible classes, in which he was giving instruction and inculcating his peculiar views.[34] **I never was anywhere that I recollect where I saw so** much that was wild and irrational **as in that excitement in Boston**. I attended Mr Miller's Bible class once or twice; after which I invited him to my room, and tried to convince him that he was in error. I called his attention to the construction which he put on **some of** the prophecies, and as I thought showed him that he was entirely mistaken in some of his fundamental views. He replied that I had adopted a course of investigation that would detect his errors, if he had any. ᴵI tried to show him that his fundamental error was already detected. The last time that I attended his Bible class he was inculcating the doctrine **which he based upon the prophecy in Daniel,** that Christ would come personally and destroy his enemies in 1843. He gave what he called an exposition of the prophecy of Daniel on the subject. He said the stone cut out of the mountain without hands, that rolled down and destroyed the image there spoken of,

JHF 370

MS 769

best results. Excitement so intense and unremitted doubtless overtasked the minds of a few, and this may have conduced to the reaction that followed. For some days, however, as our memory most distinctly testifies, there were extraordinary workings of divine power in the hearts of God's people, and more hopeful indications than had been seen for several years before.

So far as I could judge, the work closed almost as suddenly as it commenced, and it was long ere any more midsummer revivals blessed our Institution (*OE,* 8 June 1853, p. 92).

[33]The first paragraph of MS 768 was crossed out by Fairchild, and he inserted the chapter heading for chapter XXVII of the published edition.

[34]William Miller (1782–1849) was from Hampton, New York, and had been a farmer and a prominent man in local affairs before his conversion in 1816. This led to his becoming a Baptist preacher in 1833. Study of the Bible convinced him that Christ would soon be returning to earth. He started expounding his views in public in 1831, and in 1836 he published them in *Evidence from Scripture and History of the Second Coming of Christ, about the Year 1843*. He soon had a large following and was in great demand as a lecturer, and revivals attended his efforts. The "Millerite" movement gained considerable impetus through his association with Rev. Joshua V. Himes, minister of the Chardon Street Chapel in Boston. Himes promoted the movement by arranging conferences, publishing literature, and organizing lecturers. By the end of 1841 Miller had become a national figure. He was predicting the return of Christ in 1843. See *DAB*.

As a result of Miller's association with Himes, Boston became one of the centers of the movement. Miller first lectured there in 1839 and was so successful that a second series of lectures was held in the Marlborough Chapel. Rev. Charles Fitch was the minister there, and he became one of the outstanding promoters of the new doctrines. In 1840 Fitch left the Free church to become a lecturer for the cause. The Millerites organized their first general conference in Himes's church in October 1840, and by the summer of 1841 they procured a large room as a library and reading room. A sixth conference was organized in Himes's church starting on 30 November 1841. See Leroy Edwin Froom, *The Prophetic Faith of Our Fathers,* vol. 4 (Washington, D.C.: Review and Herald, 1954), p. 510; and Francis D. Nichol, *The Midnight Cry* (Washington, D.C.: Review and Herald, 1943), pp. 80–95.

was Christ. When he came to my room I called his attention to the fact that the prophet affirmed expressly that the stone was, not Christ, but the kingdom of God; and that the prophet there represented the church, or the kingdom of God **which was set up**, as demolishing the image. This was so JHF 371 plain that Mr. Miller was obliged to acknowledge that that was indeed a ˡfact; and that it was not Christ that was going to destroy those nations, but the kingdom of God. I then asked him if he supposed that the kingdom of God would destroy those nations in the sense in which he taught that they would be destroyed, with the sword, or with making war upon them. He said, **No**, he could not believe that. I then inquired, "Is it not **really** the governments MS 770 that **are to be overthrown**, instead of the destruction of the ˡpeople? **And** is not this to be done by the influence of the church of God in enlightening their minds by the Gospel? And if this is the meaning, where is the foundation for your teaching, that at a certain time Christ is coming in person to destroy all the peoples of the**se nations**?" I said to him: "Now this is fundamental to your teaching. This is the great point to which you call attention in your classes; and here is a manifest error, the very words of the prophet teaching the direct opposite to what you teach." **To this, as I said, he only replied, "Well, if I am in error, your course of investigation will detect it."** But it was vain to reason with him and his followers at that time. Believing, as they most certainly did, that the advent of Christ was at hand, it was no wonder that they were **greatly excited, and** too wild with excitement to be reasoned with to any purpose.[35]

When I arrived there in the fall of '43 **or '44**,[36] I found **a very curious state of things.** That particular form of excitement had blown over; but **I found existing among many of** the people **almost every conceivable form of error**. Indeed I have found that to be true of Boston of which Dr Beecher MS 771 assured me the first winter that I ˡlabored there. He said to me: "Mr. Finney, you cannot labor here as you do anywhere else. You have got to pursue a different course of instruction, and begin at the foundation; for Unitarianism is a system of denials, and under **their** teaching the foundations of Christianity are fallen away. You cannot take anything for granted; for hav**ing** destroyed the foundations, **as the Unitarians and Universalists have done,** the people are all afloat. The masses have no settled opinions, and every lo here **and** lo there **gets** a hearing; and almost any conceivable form of error may get a footing **here**."

JHF 372 ˡI have since found this to be true to a greater extent than in any other field in which I have ever labored. The masses in Boston are more unsettled in their religious convictions than in any other place that I have ever labored in, notwithstanding their intelligence; for they are surely a very intelligent people on all questions but that of religion. It is extremely difficult to make religious truths lodge in their minds, because the influence of Unitarian teaching has

[35] A copy of *Miller's Works* containing his *Views of Prophecy* and the *Evidences from Scripture*, published in Boston in 1841 by Joshua V. Himes, is in the Oberlin College Library. Finney's signature is on the first title page, and the flyleaf has the inscription: "Prof. Finney with Mr. Wm. Miller's respects."

[36] Finney arrived in Boston late in October 1843 and started preaching at the Marlborough Chapel on Sunday, 29 October. See *BR*, 26 October 1843, p. 171.

been to lead them to call in question all the principal doctrines of the Bible. Their system is one of denials. Their theology is negative. They deny almost everything, ˡand affirm almost nothing. In such a field error finds the ears of the people open; **and all sorts of most crazy** and irrational views on religious subjects **are** held by a great many people. MS 772

I have spoken of the Marlborough chapel, at that time the property of Brother Willard Sears.[37] I began my labors **there** at this time, and found a very singular state of things. **They had formed a** church composed **almost altogether** of radicals; and most of the members held extreme views on various subjects. **The church was mostly composed of that class of persons that** had come out from other orthodox churches and united in a church at Marlborough chapel. They were staunch, and many of them consistent, reformers. They were good people; but I cannot say that they were a *united* people. Their extreme views seemed to be an element of mutual repellence among them. Some of them were extreme **N**on-resistants, and held it to be wrong to use any physical force, or any physical means whatever, **of** controlling **even our** own children. Everything must be done by moral suasion. Upon the whole, however, they were a praying, earnest, Christian people. I found no particular ˡdifficulty in getting along with them; but at that time the Miller excitement, and various other causes, had been operating to beget a good deal of confusion among them. They were not at all in a prosperous state as a church.[38] A young man by the name of **Smith** had risen MS 773

[37] See MS 731–32. Although Sears was probably one of the members of the corporation who owned the chapel and may have been a large contributor, it was not until after the church dissolved in November 1843 that he, in company with a "Mr. Fawcett" (probably Samuel H. Fawcett, "a paver," in Boston), purchased the chapel. See Sears to Finney, 2 May 1844; and 18 August 1845, Finney Papers, microfilm, roll 4; and *Stimpson's Boston Directory* (Boston: Stimpson, 1845), p. 201.

[38] After Finney had been there a month, the Free church ceased operations. The following notice appeared in the *Boston Recorder*:

> At a meeting of the First Free Church worshipping in Marlborough Chapel, Nov. 28, 1843, it was voted nearly unanimously to dissolve the Church. Hereafter Prof. C. G. Finney will preach at the Chapel not in connexion with any Church, on the Sabbath and on Wednesday and Thursday evenings. The public are invited to attend (7 December 1843, p. 195).

Commenting on this article, the New England correspondent of *The New-York Evangelist* wrote:

> It is understood that Mr. Finney has been dealing plainly and faithfully with the several elements of discord there associated, and that this dissolution is in part, if not mainly, the result. . . . There are however, some things connected with the past history of that enterprise that the public ought to know. One is, that some two, three or more of the most eager and promising of the recipients of Mr. Mahan's *ism*, when he first preached in the chapel, have since run into such full grown antinomian perfectionism, that even that church has been obliged to cut them off from its communion.

The writer then speaks of some financial irregularities on the part of the Marlborough Chapel Corporation and ends by saying: "The dissolution of the church is just what any one familiar with the jarring nature of the elements composing it would have expected. The wonder is, that it has lived so long" (*NYE,* 21 December 1843, p. 202).

A portion of the church members went off to form the Garden Street Congregational Church under the pastoral charge of William R. Chapman. The remainder re-formed under the name Beulah Congregational Church. It was hoped that Finney would settle as pastor, but he declined.

> This church never settled a pastor, but continued to worship in the Marlboro Chapel, under the ministration chiefly of Perfectionists. . . . It could lay little claim to perfection, surely, for it was in a constant broil, and finally Mr. Finney himself, who did much to sustain them, advised them to "give up," telling them their disagreements

up among them who professed to be a prophet. I had many conversations
JHF 373 with him, and tried to convince him that he was all ˡwrong; and I labored with his followers to try to make them see that he was wrong. However, I found it impossible to do anything with him, or with them, until he finally committed himself on several points, and predicted that certain things would happen at certain dates. One was that his father would die on a certain day; **and on several points he committed himself to certain times.**

I then said to him: "Now we shall prove you. Now the truthfulness of your pretensions will be tested. If these things that you predict come to pass, and come to pass as you say they will at certain times, then we shall have **Bible authority for** believing that you are a prophet. But if they do not come to pass, it will prove that you are deceived." That he could not deny. As the
MS 774 good providence ˡof God would have it, these predictions related to events but a few weeks from the time the predictions were uttered. He had staked his reputation as a prophet upon the truth of these predictions, and awaited their fulfilment. Of course they every one of them failed, and he failed with them, **and shut up his mouth; and** I never heard anything more of his predictions. But he had confused a good many minds, and really neutralized their efforts **as Christians**; and I am not aware that those who were his followers ever regained their former influence as Christians.

During this winter the Lord gave my own soul a very thorough overhauling, and a fresh baptism of His Spirit. I boarded at the Marlborough hotel, and my room was in one corner of the chapel building. **I had my study there, and adjoining my study a bedroom.** My mind was greatly drawn out in prayer for a long time, as indeed it always has been when I have labored in Boston. I have been favored there uniformly with a great deal of the Spirit of
MS 775 prayer. But this winter in particular my mind was exceedingly exercised ˡon the question of personal holiness; and in respect to the state of the church, their want of power with God, **and** the weakness of the Orthodox churches in Boston,—the weakness of their faith, and their want of power in the midst of
JHF 374 such a community. The fact that they were ˡmaking little or no progress in overcoming the errors of that city, greatly affected my mind. I gave myself to a great deal of prayer. After my evening services I would retire as early as I well could; but rose up at four O'clock in the morning, because I could sleep no longer, and immediately went to the study and engaged in prayer. And so deeply was my mind exercised, and so absorbed in prayer, that I frequently continued from the time I arose at four O'clock till the gong called to breakfast at eight O'clock. My days were spent, so far as I could get time—**for I had a great deal of company coming constantly to see me**—in searching the Scriptures. I read nothing else all that winter but my Bible, and a great deal of it seemed new to me. Again the Lord took me as it were, from
MS 776 Genesis to Revelations. He led me to see the connection ˡof things—**how**

were a disgrace to themselves and to Christianity, or to that effect. They came to an end by no formal action, but *run out* (*The Independent,* 23 March 1854, p. 96).

In the summer of 1845 the Marlborough Chapel was converted for the use of a Chinese museum. See Sears to Finney, 20 March 1844; and 18 August 1845, Finney Papers, microfilm, roll 4; Lewis Tappan to Finney, 24 December 1843, Letterbook, Tappan Papers, microfilm, roll 3; and *BR,* 10 July 1845, p. 110.

things predicted in the Old Testament had come out in the New Testament—the promises, **the** threatenings, the prophecies and their fulfilment; —and indeed the whole Scripture seemed to me all ablaze with light, and not only light but it seemed as if God's Word was instinct with the very *life* of God.

After praying in this way for weeks and months, one morning while I was engaged in prayer the thought occurred to me, what if after all this teaching my will is not carried, and this teaching takes effect only in my sensibility? May it not be that my sensibility is affected by these revelations from reading the Bible, and that my heart is not really subdued by them? At this point several passages of Scripture occurred to me, such as this: "Line must be upon line, line upon line, precept upon precept, precept upon precept, here a little and there a little that they might go and fall backward, and be snared and taken."[39] The thought that I might be deceiving myself **by the states of my sensibility**, when it first occurred to me, stung me almost like an adder. It created a pang that I cannot describe. The passages of Scripture that occurred in that direction for a few moments greatly increased my distress. ꜌But directly I was enabled to fall back upon the perfect will of God. I said to the Lord, that if He saw it was wise and best, and that His honor demanded that I should be left to ꜌be deluded and go down to hell, I accepted His will;[40] and I said to Him "Do with me as seemeth good."[41] Just before this occurrence I had **had**[42] a great struggle to consecrate myself to God in a higher sense than I had ever before seen to be my duty, or conceived of as possible. I had often before laid my family all upon the altar of God, and left them to be disposed of at His discretion. But at this time that I now speak of, **and previously to my finally accepting the will of God,** I had had a great struggle about giving up my wife to the will of God. She was in very feeble health, and it was very evident that she could not live long. **I about that time had a dream about my wife that had opened the way for the struggle of which I speak. After that dream I attempted to lay her upon the altar, as I had often before done. But** I had never before seen so clearly what was implied in laying her and all that I possessed upon the altar of God; and for hours I struggled upon my knees to give her up unqualifiedly to the will of God. But I found myself unable to do it. I was so shocked and surprized at this that I perspired ꜌profusely with agony. I struggled and prayed until I was exhausted, and found myself entirely unable to give her altogether up to God's will, in such a way as to make no objection to His disposing of her as He pleased.

MS 777

JHF 375

MS 778

This troubled me much. I wrote to my wife, telling her what a struggle I

[39] Isaiah 28:13 reads, "But the word of the Lord was unto them precept upon precept, precept upon precept; line upon line, line upon line; here a little, and there a little; that they might go, and fall backward, and be broken, and snared, and taken."

[40] A penciled question mark in the margin against this part of the sentence appears to have been inserted by Lewis Tappan. See n. 43 below. A willingness to be damned for the glory of God was one of the tenets of the Hopkinsians to which Finney had earlier objected. See MS 472–73.

[41] Jeremiah 26:14 reads, "As for me, behold, I am in your hand: do with me as seemeth good and meet unto you."

[42] One of the words "had" here was omitted in the published edition, although there is no alteration in the manuscript.

d, and the concern that I felt at not being willing to commit her ualifiedly to the perfect will of God. This was but a very short time fore I had this temptation, as it now seems to me to have been, of which I have spoken, when those passages of Scripture came up distressingly to my mind, and when the bitterness almost of death seemed for a few moments to possess me at the thought that my religion might be of the Sensibility only, and that God's teaching might have taken effect only in my feeling. But as I said, I was enabled, after struggling for a few moments with this discouragement and bitterness, which I have since attributed to a fiery dart of Satan, to fall back in a deeper sense than I had ever done before upon the infinitely blessed and perfect will of God. I then told the Lord that I had such confidence in Him that I felt perfectly willing |to give myself, my wife and my family, and all, to be dis|posed of without any qualification according to His own views and will. That if He thought it best and wise to send me to hell, to do so, and I would consent to it.[43] As to my wife, I felt also entirely willing to lay her, body and soul, upon the altar, without the least misgiving in my mind in delivering her up to the perfect will of God. I then had a deeper view of what was implied in consecration to God than I ever had before. I spent a long time upon my knees in considering the matter all over, and giving up everything to the will of God: the interests of the church, the progress of religion, the conversion of the world, and the salvation or damnation of my own soul as the will of God might decide. Indeed I recollect that I went so far as to say to the Lord with all my heart, that He might do anything with me or mine to which His blessed will could consent. That I had such perfect confidence in His goodness and love, as to believe that He could consent to do nothing to which I could object. I felt a kind of holy boldness in telling Him to do with me just as seemed to Him good. That He could not do anything that was not perfectly wise and good; and therefore I had the best of grounds for accepting whatever He could |consent to in respect to me and mine. ‹So deep &› perfect ‹a› resting[44] in the will of God I had never before known.

JHF 376 MS 779 MS 780

What has appeared strange to me is this, that I could not get hold of my former hope; nor could I recollect with any freshness any of the former seasons of communion and divine assurance that I had experienced. I may say that I gave up my hope, and rested every thing upon a new foundation. I mean I gave up my hope from any past experience, and recollect telling the Lord that I did not know whether He intended to save me or not. Nor did I feel concerned to know. I was willing to abide the event. I said that if I found that He kept me, and worked in me by His Spirit, and was preparing me for heaven, working holiness and eternal life in my soul, I should take it for granted that He intended to save me; that if, on the other hand, I found myself empty of divine strength and light and love, I should conclude that He saw it wise and expedient to send |me to hell; and that in either event I would accept His will. My mind settled into a perfect stillness.

JHF 377

[43] A penciled question mark in the margin against this sentence appears to have been inserted by Lewis Tappan. See also n. 40 above.

[44] Here Matson had written "Such a perfect resting," but Finney changed it to read, "So deep and perfect a resting."

This was early in the morning; and through the whole of that |day I seemed to be in a state of perfect rest, body and soul. The question frequently arose in my mind during the day, "Do you still adhere to your consecration, and abide in the will of God?" I said without hesitation, "Yes, I take nothing back. I have no reason for taking anything back; I went no farther in pledges and professions than was reasonable. I have no reason for taking anything back;—I do not *want* to take anything back." The thought that I might be lost did not distress me. Indeed, think as I might during that whole day, I could not find in my mind the least fear, the least disturbing emotion. Nothing troubled me. I was neither elated nor depressed; I was neither, as I could see, joyful or sorrowful. My confidence in God was perfect; my acceptance of His will was perfect; and my mind was as calm as heaven. Just at evening the question arose in my mind, "What if God should send me[45] to hell,—what then?" "Why, I would not object to it." "But *can* He send a person to hell," was the next inquiry, "who accepts His will in the sense in which you do?" This inquiry was no sooner raised in my mind than settled. |I said, "No, it is impossible. Hell could be no hell to me if I accepted God's perfect will." This sprung a vein of joy in my mind that kept developing more and more for weeks and months, and indeed I may say for years.[46] For years my mind was too full of joy to feel much exercised with anxiety on any subject. My prayer that had been so fervent and protracted during so long a period, seemed all to run out into, "Thy will be done." It seemed as if my desires were all met. What I had been praying for for myself, I had received in a way that I least expected. Holiness to the Lord seemed to be inscribed on all the exercises of my mind. I had such strong faith that God would accomplish all His perfect will, |that I could not be *careful* about *anything*. The great anxieties about which my mind had been exercised during my seasons of agonizing prayer, seemed to be set aside; so that for a long time when I went to God to commune with Him—as I did very, very frequently—I would fall on my knees and find it impossible to ask for anything with any earnestness except that His |will might be done on earth as it was done in heaven. My prayers were swallowed up in that; and I often found myself smiling, as it were, in the face of God, and saying that I did not want anything. I was very sure that He would accomplish all His wise and good pleasure; and with that my soul was entirely satisfied.

MS 781

MS 782

JHF 378

MS 783

Here I lost that great struggle in which I had been engaged for so long a time, and began to preach to the congregation in accordance with this my new and enlarged experience. There was a considerable number in the church, and that attended my preaching, who understood me; and they saw from my preaching what had been, and what was, passing in my mind. I presume the people were more sensible than I was myself of the great change in my

[45]Here Fairchild changed the word "me" to "you," but it appears as "me" in the published edition.

[46]Lewis Tappan received a letter from Finney at this time and wrote in reply: "I rejoice that religion is to you an increasing source of enjoyment, and that the Holy Spirit has made new revelations to you. It would delight me greatly to know the nature of them" (Tappan to Finney, 23 January 1844). And Tappan commented to James A. Thome: "Br. Finney writes as if he were in a sweet state of mind" (Tappan to Thome, 20 January 1844, Letterbook, Tappan Papers, microfilm, roll 3).

manner of preaching. Of course my mind was too full of the subject to preach anything else except a full and present salvation in the Lord Jesus Christ. At this time it seemed as if my soul was wedded to Christ in a sense in which I had never had any thought or conception of before. The language of the Song MS 784 of Solomon was as natural to me as my breath. |I thought I could understand well the state of mind he was in when he wrote that song; and concluded then, as I have ever thought since, that that song was written by him after he had been reclaimed from his great backsliding. I not only had all the freshness of my first love, but a vast accession to it. Indeed the Lord lifted me so much above anything that I had experienced before, and taught me so much of the meaning of the Bible, of Christ's relations and power and willingness, that I JHF 379 often found myself saying to him, "I had not known |or conceived that any such thing was true." I then realized what is meant by the saying, that he "is able to do *exceeding abundantly* above all that we ask or think."[47] He did at that time teach me indefinitely above all that I had ever asked or thought. I had had no conception of the length and breadth, and height and depth, and efficiency of his grace. It seemed then to me that that passage, "My grace is sufficient for thee,"[48] meant so much that it was wonderful I had never understood it before. I found myself exclaiming, "Wonderful!" "Wonderful!" MS 785 "Wonderful!" as these revelations were |made to me. I could understand then what was meant by the prophet when he said, "His name shall be called Wonderful, Counsellor, the Mighty God, the everlasting Father, the Prince of peace."[49]

I spent nearly all the remaining part of the winter, till I was obliged to return home, in instructing the people in regard to the fulness there was in Christ.[50] But I found that I preached over the heads of the masses of the people. They did not understand me. There was, indeed, a goodly number that did; and they were wonderfully blessed in their souls, and made more progress in the divine life, as I have reason to believe, than in all their lives before. But the little church that was formed there was not composed of materials that could, to any considerable extent, work healthfully and efficiently together. The outside opposition to them was great. The mass even of professors of religion in the city did not sympathize with them at all.[51] The

[47] Ephesians 3:20.

[48] 2 Corinthians 12:9.

[49] Isaiah 9:6.

[50] On 5 February Finney wrote to the treasurer of Oberlin: "Will you request the O. Evangelist to say in their next No. that God willing I shall be at my post at Oberlin by the first of March. This notice was promised to my class that they may know when to return." The notice appeared in *OE,* 28 February 1844, p. 39.

On 13 February he wrote again to the treasurer, "The interest increases here so that I may not be at home so early as I anticipated." And on 22 February his meetings were advertised "Wednesday and Thursday evenings of each week, and on Sabbath day and evening," in *BR,* 22 February 1844, p. 31. See Finney to Hamilton Hill, 5 and 13 February 1844, Letters Received by Oberlin College, 1822–1866, microfilm, roll 9.

[51] Josiah Chapin, of Providence, wrote to Finney:

> I fear in the short time you have before the next term begins you will be able to do little in Boston such is the influence against you, among professors and others. The opposers of Oberlin say we are beginning to see the legitimate influence of their doctrine on sanctification (Chapin to Finney, 27 December 1843, Finney Papers, microfilm, roll 4).

people of the churches generally were in no state to receive my views of sanctification; and although there were *individuals* in nearly all the churches who were deeply interested and greatly blessed, |yet as a general thing the testimony that I bore was unintelligible to them. MS 786

Some of them could see where I was. One evening I recollect that Deacon **Proctor**[52] and Deacon **Safford**,[53] after hearing my preaching, and seeing the effect upon the congrega|tion, came up to me after I came out of the pulpit and said: "Why, you are a great ways ahead of us in this city, and a great ways ahead of our ministers. How can we get our ministers to come and hear these truths?" I replied: "I do not know. But I wish they could see things as I do; for it does seem to me infinitely important that there should be a higher standard of holiness in Boston." They **said it ‹was›;**[54] **and** seemed exceedingly anxious to have those truths laid before the people in general. They were good men, as the Boston people well know; but what pains they really took to get their ministers and people to attend, I cannot say.[55] JHF 380

I labored that winter mostly for a revival of religion among Christians. The Lord prepared me to do so by the great work **He** wrought in my own soul. Although I had had much of the divine life working within me; yet, as I said, so far did what I experienced |that winter exceed all that I had before experienced, that at times I could not realize that I had ever before been truly in communion with God. MS 787

To be sure I *had* been, often and for a long time; and this I knew when I reflected upon it, and remembered through what I had so often passed. It appeared to me that winter **as if it is** probable when we get to heaven, our **views,** and joys, and holy exercises, will so far surpass anything that we have ever experienced in this life, that we shall be hardly able to recognize the fact that we had any religion while in this world. I had in fact oftentimes

t had just been announced in *The Oberlin Evangelist* that Horace C. Taylor, who was the editor of he paper and was acting as postmaster in Oberlin, had been found guilty of embezzling funds, tealing from the Post Office, and procuring an abortion for a young woman whom he had educed. The woman was managing his household after the recent death of his wife. The scandal, oming so soon after the Oberlin lynching affair in which Taylor had taken a prominent part, was mmediately picked up by the papers and was attributed to the perfectionist doctrines held at Oberlin. See *OE,* 20 December 1843, p. 197; *NYE,* 21 December 1843, p. 203; *The New York Observer*, 23 December 1843, p. 202; and MS 716–29.

[52]John Cleveland Proctor (1786–1860) was a hardware dealer and was prominent in the eligious life of Boston. He had joined the Park Street Church in 1815 and was elected deacon in 819. In 1827 he was one of those who moved as a colony to form the Salem Church. In 1835 he vas a founder and deacon of the Franklin Street Church, which became the Central Congregational Church. In his later years he was a member of Mount Vernon and Shawmut hurches. He helped to organize the City Mission in Boston and was a regular supporter of the Old South Chapel prayer meeting. See *Stimpson's Boston Directory* (Boston: Stimpson, 1843), . 409; and *The Congregational Quarterly* 3 (January 1861): 66–67.

[53]Daniel Safford (1792–1856) was a deacon of Mount Vernon Congregational Church. He ad gone to Boston in 1812 and had rapidly become the leading blacksmith and wrought-iron nanufacturer in the city. He became a deacon of Park Street Church in 1835, and he was largely esponsible for getting Rev. E. N. Kirk to the city and for organizing the Mount Vernon Church or him in 1842. See Ann Eliza Safford, *A Memoir of Daniel Safford* (Boston: American Tract ociety, 1861).

[54]Here Finney changed the word "did" to "was."

[55]Lewis Tappan wrote to George W. Schuyler: "Br. Finney has been preaching at Boston this vinter. The ministers turn their backs upon him" (Tappan to Schuyler, 11 March 1844, Tappan apers, microfilm, roll 3).

experienced inexpressible joys, and very deep communion with God; but all this had fallen so into the shade, under my enlarged experience **that winter**, that frequently I would tell the Lord that I had never before had any conception of the wonderful things revealed in his blessed Gospel, and the wonderful grace there **was**[56] in Christ Jesus. This language, I knew when I reflected upon it, was *comparative*; but still all my former experiences for the time seemed to be sealed up, and almost lost sight of.

MS 788 JHF 381 |As the great excitement of that season subsided, my mind became more calm. I saw more clearly the different steps of my Christian experience, and came to recognize the connection of things as all wrought by God from beginning to end. But since then I have never had those great struggles, and long protracted seasons of agonizing prayer **before I could get hold of full rest in God**, that I had often experienced. **Since then** it is quite another thing to prevail with God in my own experience, from what it was before. I can come to God with more calmness, because with more perfect confidence. He enables me now to *rest* in **Him**, and let everything sink into **His** perfect will, with much more readiness than ever before the experience of that winter. I have felt since then a religious freedom, a religious buoyancy and delight in God and in **His Word**, a steadiness of faith, a Christian liberty and overflowing love, that I had only experienced, I may say *occasionally* before **that**. I do not mean that such exercises had been rare to me before, for they had been frequent and often repeated, but |never *abiding* as they have been since. My bondage seemed to be at that time entirely broken; and since then I have had the freedom of a child with a loving parent. It seems to me that I can find God *within* me in such a sense that I can rest upon **Him** and be quiet, lay my heart in **His** hand, and nestle down in **His** perfect will and have no carefulness or anxiety. MS 789

I speak of these exercises as *habitual* since that period; but I cannot affirm that they have been altogether unbroken, for in 1860, during a **fit** of sickness, I had a season of great depression and wonderful humiliation. But the Lord brought me out of it into an established peace and rest.[57]

[56]The word "was" was not changed in the manuscript, but the published version has "is."

[57]See MS 1026. Finney's illness lasted from the middle of December 1860 through the spring of 1861. He wrote of it to the Barlows, friends of his in England:

> My disease has tended strongly to dispondency. I have taken some new & experimental lessons on the subject of living by "naked faith." My nervous prostration has been made the occasion of deeper revellations of myself to myself than I ever had before. It has been a profitable time for me. It has seemed to me that I was the greatest sinner, my life taken altogether, with the light I have enjoyed, that perhaps the world can produce: & that I am the very weakest of all God's children. I used to think such language hyperbolical, but really I could use it litterally & in calm prose. But such experiences are useful. There seemed to be a veil drawn over my precious experiences of the past, & over all my success in the ministry, & only my sins, my short comings, my hatefulness could be seen by me. Up to *this* illness my experience has been different. When ill formerly, I have had strong faith, great rest of soul in Christ & not a doubt of my acceptance. This nervous prostration has been the occasion of a new experience & one that will enable [me] better to understand the case of nervous, desponding children of God. In my despondency it seemed to me that I had not well understood such cases, & that without knowing or intending it I had sometimes been cruel to them (Finney to Alice Barlow, 7 May 1861, Correspondence of Charles G. Finney, 1830–1875, Oberlin College Archives, microfilm).

A few years after this season of refreshing **in Boston of which I speak**, that beloved wife of whom I have spoken, died.[58] This was to me a great affliction. However I did not feel any murmuring, or the least resistance to the will of God. I gave her up to God without any resistance whatever that I can recollect. But it was to me a great sorrow. The night after she died |I was |lying in my **lonely bed**, and some Christian friends were sitting up in the parlor and watching out the night. I had been asleep for a little while and awoke, **and** the thought of my bereavement flashed over my mind with such power! My wife was gone! I should never hear her speak again, nor see her face! Her children were motherless! What should I do? My brain seemed to reel, as if my mind would swing from its pivot. I rose instantly from my bed exclaiming, "I shall be deranged if I cannot rest in God!" The Lord soon calmed my mind for that night; but still at times seasons of sorrow would come over me that were almost overwhelming.[59]

MS 790
JHF 382

One day I was upon my knees communing with God upon the subject, and all at once **He** seemed to say to me: "You loved your wife?" "Yes," I said. "Well, did you love her for her own sake, or for your sake? Did you love her, or yourself? If you loved her for her own sake, why do you sorrow that she is with me? Should not her happiness with me make you rejoice instead of mourn, if you loved her for her own sake?" "Did you love her," **He** seemed |to say to me, "for *my* sake? If you loved her for my sake, surely you would not grieve that she is with me. Why do you think of *your loss*, and lay so much stress upon that, instead of thinking of *her gain*? Can you be sorrowful when *she* is so joyful and happy? If you loved her for her own sake, would you not rejoice in her joy, and be happy in her happiness?" I can never describe the feelings that came over me when I seemed to be thus addressed. It produced an instantaneous change in the whole state of my mind **in regard to the loss of my wife**.

MS 791

From that moment sorrow on account of **the event** was gone forever. I no longer thought of **her** as dead, but as alive and in the midst of the glories of heaven. My faith was at this time so strong and my mind so enlightened, that it seemed as if I could enter into the very state of mind in which she was in heaven; and if there is any such thing as commun|ing with an absent spirit, or with one who is in heaven, I seemed to commune with her. Not that I ever supposed she was present in such a sense that I **at any time** communed |personally with her. But it seemed as if I knew what her state of mind was there, what profound, unbroken rest in the perfect will of God. I could see that that was heaven, and I experienced it in my own soul. **And** I have never to this day **got over** these views‹. T›hey frequently recur to me,—‹as›[60] the

JHF 383
MS 792

[58] Lydia Finney died of consumption in Oberlin on 18 December 1847. She was forty-three years old. See the obituary by Finney in *OE,* 5 January 1848, pp. 3–4; see also MS 800.

[59] In a sermon some months after his wife's death, Finney said that "it was some days before I could get over that numbness which the dreadful shock of her death gave me. . . . For a few days after my wife died, my sorrows seemed to increase upon me, until it seemed to me that I should go deranged" (*OE,* 6 June 1849, p. 90).

[60] Matson had written down, "these views so but that they frequently recur to me,—a sense of," but Finney altered it.

very state of mind in which the inhabitants of heaven are, and ‹I can see›[61] why they are in such a state of **mind**.

My wife had died in a heavenly frame of mind. Her rest in God was so perfect that it seemed to me that **after she was dead** she only entered into a fuller apprehension of the love and faithfulness of God, so as to confirm and perfect forever her trust in God and union with **His** will. These are experiences in which I have lived a great deal since that time. But in preaching I have found that nowhere can I preach those truths on which my own soul delights to live, and be understood, except it be by a very small number. **Much as that subject has been dwelt upon here,** I have never found that more than a very few of **our** people appreciate and receive those MS 793 views of God and Christ, and the fulness of his **pres[ent]**[62] |salvation, upon which my own soul still delights to feed. Every-where I am obliged to come down to where the people are, in order to make them understand me; and in every place where I have preached for many years, I have found the churches in so low a state as to be utterly incapable of apprehending and appreciating what I regard as the most precious truths of the whole Gospel.

When preaching to impenitent sinners I am obliged, of course, to go back to first principles. In my own experience I have so long passed these outposts and first principles, that I cannot live upon those truths. I however have to preach them to the impenitent to secure their conversion. When I preach the JHF 384 Gospel, I can preach the atonement, con|version, and many of the prominent views of the Gospel that are appreciated and accepted by those who are young in the religious life; and by those also who have been long in the church of God, and have made very little advancement in the knowledge of Christ. But it is only now and then that I find it really profitable to the people of God to MS 794 pour out to them |the fullness that my own soul sees in Christ. In this place there is a larger number of persons by far that understand me and devour that class of truths, than **in any other place that I ever saw**; but even here the majority of professors of religion do not understandingly embrace those truths. They do not object, they do not oppose; and so far as they understand they are convinced. But as a matter of experience they are ignorant of the power of the highest and most precious truths of the Gospel of salvation in Christ Jesus.

I said that this winter **of which I have spoken** in Boston was spent mostly in preaching to professed Christians, and that many of them were greatly blessed in their souls. **That winter** I felt very confident that unless the foundations could be relaid in some sense, and that unless the Christians in Boston took on a higher type of **the** Christian **religion**, they never could prevail against Unitarianism. I knew **they had been reasoning with them, and** that the **O**rthodox ministers had been preaching **O**rthodoxy as opposed MS 795 to Unitarianism for many years, and that all that could be accom|plished by discussion had been accomplished. But I felt that what Unitarians needed was to see **them** live **right** out the pure Gospel of Christ. They needed to hear

[61] Finney added the words "I can see."

[62] Matson had ended the page with the start of a word, "pres-", but the remainder of the word was not written at the top of the next page. He may have intended to write "present." It was not altered in the manuscript, but the published edition has "free."

them say, and prove what they said by their lives, that Jesus Christ was a divine Savior, and able to save them from all sin. Their professions of faith in Christ did not accord with their experiences. They could not say **right out** that they found Christ in their experience what they preached him to be. **In short, in their private and public testimony of the power of the grace of God in their own consciousness, they could not sustain their own Orthodoxy; but on the contrary, their constant confessions of bondage to sin contradicted their professions of faith in Christ. I saw more clearly than I ever had done before that Orthodoxy in Boston had very little power, and never could have much power till it took on entirely another type of Christian experience. That they** needed the testimony of God's living witnesses, **and** testimony of experience **and consciousness**, to convince the Unitarians; and **that** mere reasonings and arguments, however conclusive, **would** never overcome their errors and their prejudices. **And I still believe this to be true.** ˡThe **O**rthodox churches ˡthere are too formal; they are in bondage to certain ways; they are afraid of measures, **and** afraid to launch forth in all freedom in the use of means to save souls. They have always seemed to me to be in bondage in their prayers, insomuch that what I call the spirit of prayer I have seldom witnessed in Boston. **They are fastidious, and in a strait jacket; and until they can break over their notions of what is wise and expedient, and do what is necessary to break the ice and overcome the stagnation there is among them, they will never succeed in saving that city. The great part of the time there was a spiritual stagnation there.** The ministers, and deacons,[63] of the churches, though **I trust** good men, are afraid of what the Unitarians will say if, in their measures to promote religion they launch out in such a way as [**to**][64] wake the people up. Everything must be done in a certain way. The Holy Spirit is grieved by their yielding to such a bondage.

JHF 385
MS 796

However there are in Boston a great many most excellent people, praying people, people who prove their sincerity by their open-heartedness and open-handedness, and by helping forward every good word and work. But they need more courageous leaders. They need ˡministers of a higher experience, a larger faith, and a greater moral courage than they have generally had for many years.

MS 797

I have labored in Boston in five **different** powerful revivals of religion;[65] and I must express it as my sincere conviction that the greatest difficulty in the way of overcoming Unitarianism and all the forms of error there, is the *timidity* of Christians and churches. Knowing as they do that they are constantly exposed to the criticisms of the Unitarians, they have become over-cautious. Their faith has been depressed. And I do fear that the prevalence of Unitarianism and Universalism there, has kept them back from preaching and holding forth the danger of the impenitent as **P**resident Edwards presented it. The doctrine of endless punishment, the necessity of entire sanctification, or the giving up of all sin as a condition of salvation—

[63] Here the words "and elders" appear to have been crossed out by Finney.

[64] Here Matson had originally written " 'to break the ice' and," but he crossed it out. Fairchild supplied the word "to."

[65] In 1831–1832, 1841, 1843–1844, 1856–1857, and 1857–1858.

indeed the doctrines that are calculated to arouse **all the impenitent, and all the half-worldly Christians to bestir themselves**, are not, I fear, held forth with that frequency and power that are indispensable to the salvation of that city.

The little church at the Marlborough chapel, **as it was called**, were very MS 798 desirous that I should become their pastor. ¹I[66] left Boston and came home with this question before my mind.[67] Afterward Brother Sears came on, **as I afterward learned,** with a formal call in his pocket, to persuade me to go and take up my abode there. But when he arrived in Oberlin and consulted the brethren here, about the propriety of my going, they so much discouraged him that he did not lay the question before me at all.[68]

JHF 386 **¹This was not my last winter by any means in Boston. I have much more to say, in another place, of revivals there. As to the number of conversions in that city that winter, I cannot speak other than to say that they must have been upon the whole numerous, as I was visited in my room almost constantly from day to day by inquirers from different parts of the city. However, as I have said, I think the greater number of inquirers that winter were professors of religion, whose minds were stirred up mightily to inquire after a higher Christian life.[69]**

[66] After "798," Fairchild added "–800." This was an indication to the printers to proceed to page 801, omitting the intervening pages. He later altered the "800" to "814."

[67] Finney wrote to Lewis Tappan in New York about it on 21 December 1843, and Tappan replied:

> The principal objection that seems to me against the plan suggested of your taking the pastoral charge of a new chh at the M[arlborough] C[hapel] is, you cant be there more than half the time if so much, & will have all the discredit of what may be done in your absence, & Oberlin also.

But Tappan wanted Finney to go to Brooklyn and start a new church there (Tappan to Finney, 24 December 1843; and 23 January 1844, Letterbook, Tappan Papers, microfilm, roll 3; and Tappan to James A. Thome, October 1844, Letterbook, Tappan Papers, microfilm, roll 4).

[68] A formal call from the Beulah Congregational Church, dated 20 March 1844 and signed by Willard Sears, moderator, and John J. Cary, clerk, is in the Finney Papers, microfilm, roll 4.

[69] A section in Matson's handwriting follows after this in the manuscript at the bottom of the page. It was replaced by a similar section when Finney started a new chapter at the top of the next page: "The next fall, the fall of 1845, I was earnestly urged, as I had frequently been before, to visit the place and region of country where I was converted."

CHAPTER XXVIII

MS 799

‹Labors in Oberlin, in Michigan etc.›

‹The[1] next fall, the fall of 1845[2] I was invited & urged as I often had been to visit the place of my Spiritual nativity & labor as an Evangelist.›[3] I finally made up my mind to go. The time arrived for my leaving; and I packed my trunk, and made ready to start the next morning. I retired early, and before my wife came I fell asleep. I was soon awakened by ‹her› coughing.[4] I opened my eyes, and saw that she was coughing blood in a most terrific manner.[5] She had come in while I was

[1] Pages 799–814 were originally numbered 647–62 and renumbered 779–94 by Matson, then changed to 799–814 by Finney. The chapter heading of page 799 and the section down to n. 3 were added by Finney on a piece of paper pasted over the top section of the page, which covered up the earlier page numbers written by Matson and one line of the earlier text: "and labor there as an Evangelist." Fairchild omitted the whole of this chapter from the published edition.

[2] The next fall was in fact the fall of 1844. That fall and winter Finney stayed most of the time in Oberlin and was occupied in revival labors and writing for *The Oberlin Evangelist*. In January 1845 it was reported:

> Almost the whole people are moved, and the movement bears precious tokens of being the work of the Spirit of Love. The people of God have perhaps never been more deeply searched and humbled,—never brought into so sweet a frame of love to the brethren and love to all mankind (29 January 1845, p. 22).

On 12 February a notice appeared: "Prof. Finney's very pressing occupations in revival labors among the people of this place, have prevented him from furnishing the Sermon for the present paper" (*OE,* 12 February 1845, p. 31). As a result of the revival, forty-three of the sixty admitted to membership of the Oberlin Church at the March Communion Service were by profession (*OE,* 26 March 1845, p. 55).

In January 1845 Finney commenced writing an important series of "Letters on Revivals," which were published in *The Oberlin Evangelist* from 29 January through to 24 June 1846. This provided him with an opportunity to examine the course that revivals had taken and apply the lessons he had learned since he had published his *Lectures on Revivals of Religion* ten years earlier. An edition of these was published in Pulaski, New York, by W. E. Wright in 1845; and in 1861, William Bremner of Manchester, England, published a selection edited by Rev. John Moore. Abridged versions, under the title *Revival Fire,* were published around the turn of the century, and in 1979 Bethany Fellowship of Minneapolis brought out the complete series of thirty-two letters, compiled by Donald W. Dayton.

[3] This ends the section in Finney's handwriting. A list of "Invitations to C. G. Finney" records an invitation from "*many* persons" in Adams received by Finney some time in 1845 (manuscript in Finney Papers, file 2/2/2, box 7; see also Walter Webb to Finney, 26 October 1846, Finney Papers, microfilm, roll 4; and n. 10 below).

[4] Matson had written down, "by the coughing of my wife," but Finney altered it to read, "by her coughing."

[5] Matson wrote down after this, "and throwing it into the foot-tub that she had taken from under the wash stand." There is a question mark in pencil in the margin against this sentence that may have been inserted by Lewis Tappan. The sentence appears to have been crossed out by Finney.

sleeping, ‹&›[6] either a slight cough produced this bleeding, or the bleeding produced the cough, I know not which. But the exhibition was frightful. The blood was pouring from her mouth so fast as almost to choke her. It seemed to be with difficulty that she cleared her lungs from blood fast enough to keep from strangulation. It appeared as if she would bleed to death in a very short time. However, I took her in my arms, held her head over the foot-tub,[7] and soothed her as much as I could without giving any alarm to any of the members of the family. Indeed she did not appear to be frightened herself. Her soul was too much stayed upon God in implicit trust, to suffer her to be greatly MS 800 **|agitated. She knew she was of a consumptive family, and a strongly consumptive tendency, and probably was not greatly surprized at what had happened. For sometime it appeared as if she would die in my arms; but ‹soon›[8] the bleeding began to abate, and finally ceased altogether. After rinsing her mouth and throat with cold water, and wiping the blood from her as well as I could, I laid the precious woman in bed and myself by her side to watch her breathing, her pulse, and every symptom that showed itself. She grew more and more quiet till finally she fell asleep. She recovered from this, and never bled at the lungs again; but after struggling two years with the consumption she passed away.[9]**

But this terrific bleeding rendered it necessary that I should stay at-home and take care of her, so that I gave up all idea of going abroad that winter.[10] I gave myself up to nursing her, and preached and labored for

[6] Matson originally wrote, "to go to bed; and before she was ready to get into bed." Finney crossed it out and inserted the symbol *&*.

[7] Matson had originally written down, "held off her head from the foot-tub." He then altered it. A penciled question mark in the margin next to this sentence appears to have been inserted by Lewis Tappan.

[8] Finney changed the word "presently" to "soon."

[9] Finney mentioned in a sermon preached at Oberlin, "my poor sick wife." This was published in *OE,* 22 October 1845, p. 171. When Lewis Tappan read it he wrote to Finney: "While reading your sermon, from a late Oberlin Evangelist, to my family last evening I noticed the expression 'when I pray for my poor sick wife etc.' Now I know that you would not have thus alluded to her if she was not very sick" (Tappan to Finney, 10 November 1845, Letterbook, Tappan Papers, microfilm, roll 3).

Other letters to Lydia Finney about that time also referred to her illness and offered help and medical advice (see letters to Lydia Finney from Mrs. S. Boardman, 28 November 1845; and Mrs. A. C. Chapin, 11 December 1845, in Finney Papers, microfilm, roll 4). Lydia Finney died on 18 December 1847. See *OE,* 5 January 1848, pp. 3–4. George W. Hastings, who was living in Oberlin at the time, recalled:

> The most pathetic scene that I ever witnessed in the First Church of Oberlin, was on the occasion of the funeral of Mrs. Finney, whose funeral sermon Mr. Finney preached. He related their earlier acquaintance, her earnest desire and prayers for his conversion, her ideal domestic life. "And now," said the great man, as he wept aloud, "I feel as if a part of my person were being torn from me and buried up in yonder cemetery" (G. W. Hastings, "Earlier Days of Oberlin," *The Advance* [Chicago], 5 February 1903, p. 167).

[10] Mrs. L. Webb wrote from Adams to Lydia Finney in February 1846:

> We regretted very much the providence which deprived us of the labors of Mr. Finney as we had hoped much good might result from his being among us our church is in the same lifeless inactive state that it was when he was here our pulpit is not yet supplied (L. Webb to Lydia Finney, 5 February 1846, Finney Papers, microfilm, roll 4).

a revival of religion at-home. We had a very interesting state of things here all the winter; but as this was so common, and almost universal here, but little was said about it as being a revival of religion. Indeed it has for many ˡyears[11] been the case that our meetings of inquiry would be large, numbers would be converted from week to week, and there would be additions to the church at every communion of perhaps from ten to thirty or fifty, and it would hardly be spoken of here as being out of the ordinary course of things.[12] MS 801

I did not leave home to labor particularly as an Evangelist till the next winter.[13] The next winter I was pressed hard to go to Detroit. I

The next fall Walter Webb wrote from Adams to Finney:

> Among the numerous calls you have to spend your vacation in different sections of the country, we thought it not improper to press our claims. You know how anxious we were last fall that you should come and help us, and you recollect that it was owing to a particular providence of God that prevented you at the very time you were prepared to start for Adams. This result disappointed us very much (W. Webb to Finney, 26 October 1846, Finney Papers, microfilm, roll 4; spelling and punctuation altered for ease of reading).

[11]Here Fairchild originally started a new chapter, number XXVIII, entitled "*Labors in Michigan.*" He did some editorial work on it but later decided to leave the entire section from MS 799 to MS 814 out of the published edition.

[12]George W. Hastings, who arrived as a student in the fall of 1845, recollected: "Almost a continuous revival was manifest throughout the year, and there was seldom a communion that large numbers did not unite with the church" ("Earlier Days of Oberlin," p. 167). The revival was reported as being still in progress in March. On 15 March fifty-two were admitted into membership of the church. See *OE,* 1 April 1846, p. 55.

However, on 23 February, Stephen and Abby Kelley Foster, the "come-outer" abolitionists who denounced the churches, had visited Oberlin. They had difficulty getting any place to speak but were eventually allowed to use the chapel. After reporting the meeting, the editor of *The Oberlin Evangelist* wrote:

> We will only add that this visit of our friends occurred at a time when many souls among us were anxiously enquiring the way of salvation—when many were just entering upon the peculiar trials, vicissitudes and joys of a life of faith and consecration to God.—Under these circumstances there were many of our people who felt they could not endure to have their own minds or the minds of their children and friends diverted from the great interests of the revival—the salvation of souls around our own firesides and in the bosom of our own Institution and community (*OE,* 4 March 1846, p. 39; see also *The Liberator* [Boston], 17 April 1846, p. 61).

Finney wrote to Lewis Tappan on 19 March speaking of this event, and Tappan replied, "I heard of your revival & am sorry that couple wandered there & broke it up" (Tappan to Finney, 31 March 1846, Letterbook, Tappan Papers, microfilm, roll 3).

The Fosters themselves, in a letter to Parker Pillsbury, wrote: "Professor Finney said the Spirit of God left the place immediately on our entering it; and Professor Morgan publicly declared that they should not have opened the chapel for us, had it not been for the colored people" (*The Liberator,* 23 October 1846, p. 171). Lucy Stone, then a student at the college, who supported the Fosters, wrote to them on 25 March about the possibility of a return visit:

> That precious revival soon died away, and on the tenth of March it was so far extinct that Prof. Hudson could lecture on the character of the constitution, without any fear of "ruining souls." I inquired of the man who stayed at home to have a prayer-meeting, so that you might do no injury, if there was not danger of checking the religious influence, he said, he thought there was a very different state of things, from what there was, when Mr. & Mrs. Foster were here, he thought no harm would be done now (Lucy Stone to Stephen and Abby Foster, 25 March 1846, Abigail Kelley Foster Papers, American Antiquarian Society, Worcester, Mass.).

[13]This was the winter of 1846–1847. During the previous months, Finney had been working on the first volume of his *Systematic Theology,* which was published in Oberlin by J. M. Fitch in July 1846. See *OE,* 22 July 1846, p. 119; see also Mrs. C. O. Thompson to Lydia Finney, 12

went there to assist Brother Hammond, who was pastor of a Congregational church in that city.[14] The churches in that city were at that time Presbyterian as opposed to Congregational, and indeed pretty much throughout the state. Dr Duffield, pastor of the First Presbyterian church in Detroit, was a very persistent Presbyterian, and seemed not to take it kindly that I should come there to labor.[15] At any rate his influence was all on the other side; and he at that time had great influence in Detroit. However we had a precious work there. Some very striking cases of conversion occurred; but I was there but a very short time.[16] It was very difficult to secure such a state of feeling between the Congregationalists and persistent Presbyterians, as was essential to the promoting of a general revival. Indeed it was impossible. |Congregationalists[17] seemed to be regarded as interlopers; and I found it impossible to secure anything like union of effort or feeling in that city at that time.[18] Dr Duffield professed to be New School in his theology, and had been arraigned and tried in Pennsylvania for being such.[19] But

MS 802

October 1846, described in the Calendar of the Finney Papers; and Willard Sears to Finney, 14 February 1846, Finney Papers, microfilm, roll 4.

[14]Henry Laurens Hammond (1815–1893), a graduate of Oberlin College and Andover Theological Seminary, was minister at the Congregational Church, Detroit, from its foundation in 1844 to July of 1847. He was later editor of the *Congregational Herald* and treasurer of Chicago Theological Seminary. See Silas Farmer, *The History of Detroit and Michigan* (Detroit: Farmer, 1884), p. 613; *Oberlin College Necrology for 1892–1893*, Oberlin College Archives; and Donald W. Disbrow, "A Recent Find: The Hammond-Movius Papers," *Ypsilanti Gleanings*, Ypsilanti Historical Society Publications, April 1975, pp. 1–22.

The Congregational church had been formed on 20 December 1844 with only thirteen members. Hammond succeeded in getting help from David Hale of New York, the promoter of many Congregational causes, and in August 1846 they were able to open their first meeting house in the upper part of the city. Within a few years this was too small, and in 1854 they built a church to seat one thousand people, "one of the most commodious and beautiful church edifices in all the West" ("Congregationalism at Detroit," *The Independent* [New York], 26 October 1854, p. 340; Joseph P. Thompson, *Memoir of David Hale* [New York: John Wiley, 1850], pp. 514–15; and "First Congregational Church, Detroit, Mich.," *The Congregational Quarterly* [Boston] 3 [July 1861]: 266).

[15]George Duffield (1794–1868) went to the Presbyterian church in Detroit in 1838 and was there until his death. See *DAB*.

[16]Finney wrote later from Pontiac to Henry Cowles at Oberlin,

> I came here with *great reluctance*, after spending a week at Detroit. The interest there became such that I never left a place with so much reluctance. But I had suffered myself to be drawn into an engagement here from which they were so unwilling to release me, that I literally tore away & came here (Finney to Cowles, 8 February 1847, Correspondence of Charles G. Finney, 1830–1875, Oberlin College Archives, microfilm).

Silas Farmer recorded his visit: "On January 16, 1847, the noted revivalist, Rev. C. G. Finney, visited Detroit, and preached every evening for the week following. Several were added to the Society" (*History of Detroit*, p. 613).

[17]Fairchild had crossed out most of the page and added "–806" after 802, indicating to the printers to proceed to page 807 and omit the intervening pages. He later omitted the whole page from the published edition.

[18]Presbyterians and Congregationalists had worked well together under the Plan of Union until a new denominational consciousness emerged in the 1830s and 1840s. The plan favored Presbyterian organization, and the attempt to spread Congregationalism created a serious crisis and the eventual breakup of the Plan of Union. Hammond and Duffield were prominent in the controversy. See Frederick I. Kuhns, "The Breakup of the Plan of Union in Michigan," *Michigan History* 32, no. 2 (June 1948): 157–80.

[19]Duffield's trial before the Presbytery of Carlisle and the Synod of Philadelphia took place in

after all his philosophy had so mystified his mind that he took great exceptions to the truth as I presented it. He arrayed himself strongly against my preaching; and his great influence no doubt greatly circumscribed the work there that winter.[20] Before I left there, however, I was led to pray about that state of things in such a manner, as to feel confident that God would either change Dr Duffield's views, or in some way greatly abate his influence in that city and in that state. It appeared to me plain that ‹revival effort›[21] was not to be hedged in there; and that Dr Duffield would be obliged to take a different course, and the way would be opened for revival effort and for the free development of Congregationalism in that region. In its proper place I shall have occasion to notice the results of this state of things.[22]

But before I close my ǀnarrative of the occurrences at Detroit, I must relate one very interesting fact. There was at the time a very wealthy and influential merchant in that city by the name of ‹Chandler›.[23] He was himself a professor of religion; but his wife, a New York lady of great cultivation and personal beauty, was an impenitent woman.[24] There was also a prominent lawyer by the name of ‹Joy› living in that city, who at present, if he is alive, I believe lives in Chicago.[25] Mr. MS 803

1833. See Samuel J. Baird, *A History of the New School* (Philadelphia: Claxton, Remsen, and Heffelfinger, 1868), pp. 463–467.

[20] Many of the entries in Duffield's diary from January to October 1847 show his antagonism to Finney and the Oberlin theology. See "Diary" in Burton Historical Collections, Detroit Public Library; and L. G. Van Der Velde, "The Diary of George Duffield," *Mississippi Valley Historical Review* 24, no. 1 (June 1937): 21–34, 53–67. Duffield authored an attack on Finney's theology entitled *"A Warning Against Error" being the Report of a Committee, adopted by the Presbytery of Detroit, at their Session at Northville, Michigan; and approved by the Synod of Michigan at their Session at Kalamazoo, October 18, 1847*. This was republished in Detroit in 1849 under the title *The Theology of Professor Finney Reviewed and Put to the Test of the Sacred Scriptures*. Finney published a reply in the second volume of his *Systematic Theology*.

The Oberlin theology was one of the important contributing factors in causing a rift between Presbyterians and Congregationalists in Michigan. See L. G. Van Der Velde, "The Synod of Michigan and Movements For Social Reform, 1834–1869," *Church History* 5 (1936): 52–70; and the research of Frederick I. Kuhns in "The Operations of the American Home Missionary Society in the Old Northwest, 1826–1861" (Ph.D. diss., University of Chicago, 1947); and Kuhns, "New Light on the Plan of Union," *Journal of the Presbyterian Historial Society* 26, no. 1 (March 1948): 19–43.

[21] Finney changed the word "Congregationalism" to "revival effort."

[22] Finney does not appear to have made any further reference to this. But in his letter to Henry Cowles written soon after from Pontiac, he wrote:

> The Detroit presbytery, within whose bounds I am & in one of whose churches I am laboring, had their annual meeting about 20 miles from here last week. Three of their number were for passing resolutions against my laboring in their churches but Br. Duffield of D[et]roit & others opposed it. So they did nothing. I have written Br. Duffield a letter thanking him for the course he took & begging his Pres[bytery] to be careful what they do (Finney to Cowles, 8 February 1867, Correspondence of Charles G. Finney, 1830–1875, Oberlin College Archives, microfilm).

[23] Zachariah Chandler (1813–1879) was one of the richest men in Michigan. He was mayor of Detroit in 1851 and was a Republican senator from 1857 to 1875 (see Sister Mary K. George, *Zachariah Chandler: A Political Biography* [East Lansing: Michigan State University Press, 1969]). Finney crossed out the name "Chandler" but then wrote it in again.

[24] Chandler was married in December 1844 to Letitia Grace Douglass of New York.

[25] James Frederick Joy (1810–1896) made his name in railway litigation and then turned from law to building railroads. He became president of the Michigan Central Railroad Company. He and Chandler had been boyhood friends and were leading members of Duffield's church (see

Chandler of whom I have spoken has been for many years a member of the Senate of the United States. Mrs. Joy, the wife of this lawyer, was a very accomplished woman from New England. Her father, in his day, was one of the principal men in Massachusetts ‹I believe.›[26] Mrs. Joy soon became very anxious about her soul, attended the meetings of inquiry; and after a severe struggle of mind was hopefully, and I might say powerfully, converted. She and Mrs. Chandler were intimate friends, and she became very much interested in Mrs. Chandler. One evening I had preached on the text, "I pray thee have me excused."[27] The next morning Mr. Chandler called on me and said that his wife was powerfully convicted |by that sermon, and had spent a very restless night; and he desired me to call and see her. He said if I would go directly to his house he would go to his store[28]—he had a room there—and he would pray for his wife's conversion. I went immediately to his house, and as I rung the bell at the door, Mrs Chandler herself immediately opened it; for she and Mrs. Joy were both standing inside the door when I rung the bell. There was a female prayer-meeting in a private house in that neighborhood that morning; and Mrs. Joy knowing that Mrs. Chandler was convicted, had come over to go with her to that prayer-meeting. They were all dressed, with their furs on, ready to go, and had got as far as the door when I rung the bell. I was acquainted with Mrs. Joy, and as soon as I went in she introduced me to Mrs. Chandler, for with her I had not spoken. I took Mrs. Chandler by the hand and immediately told her my errand, that I had come to converse with her about her soul. I saw as I took her hand that she trembled all over. She turned back and invited me into the parlor, where I found a comfortable fire. Mrs. Joy did not follow us into the parlor, but passed right by into another room. Mrs. Chandler |asked me to sit. I told her, No; I wanted to know whether she would give her heart to God before I sat down. I saw from her appearance that she was deeply convicted; but she hesitated very much. I however pressed the subject on her. But I saw from all she said, and from everything around her, that she was a woman of worldly tendencies, ambitious and proud, and that the world had a terribly strong hold upon her. I finally sat down, and she sat down; and I pressed the subject home upon her as earnestly and thoroughly as I could. Her great struggle seemed to be to give up the world. She was manifestly an indulged wife; was young, beautiful, the idol of her husband and a great favorite in society, and very fond of dash and equipage and worldly amusements. Her father

MS 804

MS 805

DAB). Finney crossed out the name "Joy" but then wrote it in again. His capital *J* however was unclear. Someone made an attempt to clarify it in pencil, and the name was then penciled in clearly in the margin.

[26]Joy's first wife was Martha Alger Reed, daughter of Lieutenant Governor John Reed of Yarmouth, Massachusetts. She died in February 1850. See James Richard Joy, *Thomas Joy and His Descendants* (New York: printed for the Family, 1900), p. 49. Finney added the words "I believe."

[27]Luke 14:18 or 19.

[28]There is a penciled question mark in the margin of the manuscript against this sentence. It appears to have been inserted by Lewis Tappan.

was a prominent man in the city of New York; and she had been an indulged daughter, as she was at this time an indulged wife. Beside, she had manifestly great pride of heart. She was a lady in her education, in her deportment, and so far as I could see in every respect; a lady of most estimable character, so far as a lady can be such who is not a Christian. |She had manifestly never been dealt with personally and searchingly in respect to her own salvation. To be addressed, therefore, in the manner in which I conversed with her, searched her most ‹deeply.›[29] After conversing with her a considerable time, I pressed upon her the necessity and duty of kneeling down then and there, and renouncing the world and her sins, and giving up herself entirely to Christ. We knelt down, and I prayed for her, and tried in my prayer to lead her mind to Christ. I could hear her struggle and weep, and she seemed to be in the greatest anguish of mind. After I had prayed for her sometime, and she had agonized in that way she said, "I cannot submit," and was about to rise from her knees. I begged her not to rise, told her it would never do; and that I was afraid she would quench the Spirit of God if she then rejected mercy. She then gave up the idea of rising from her knees, and I prayed for her again. Her agonizing struggle continued, and seemed to increase. The conflict thickened, and the struggle of her |mind became fearful. But finally she said, "I will." She became calm; and after consecrating her to God in prayer we arose from our knees. She appeared to be calm and subdued. As soon as Mrs. Joy, who was in an adjoining room, and it appeared had been engaged in prayer for her, was aware of the state of things, she came suddenly into the room; and the scene between her and Mrs. Chandler was very affecting. I did not see Mrs. Chandler after this more than once or twice before I left the city; since which time I have never seen her, and for many years have not heard of her. She appeared at the time to be thoroughly subdued and converted. However I was aware that her temptations to take a worldly course of life were very strong, and I do not know whether she has been a devoted Christian woman or not. But that scene I shall not soon forget.[30] There were many other interesting cases, which, however, I must pass over. After spending a few weeks in Detroit, in compliance with the earnest request of the church at Pontiac I went there for a season.[31]

MS 806

MS 807

[29] Finney changed the word "tremendously" to "deeply."

[30] After reading this section of the manuscript, Lewis Tappan wrote to Finney:

> You speak of Senator Chandler & wife as subjects of divine grace. It may be so, but *his* career in Congress is so much like that of a bully, or a mere man of the world, that it will be supposed, by most persons who may read the Narrative, that his religion is of a suspicious stamp. Whether Mrs. C., in her house, in society, & in the church, manifests a [Christ]ian character I do not know (Tappan to Finney, 2 June 1868, Finney Papers, microfilm, roll 5).

[31] Finney had preached in the Pontiac church earlier in October. His brother-in-law, Samuel Andrews, was a farmer living nearby in West Bloomfield and may have provided the link with this area. However, John Bradford, an immigrant farmer from Scotland, was evidently "the moving spring in drawing Professor Finney, of Oberlin, to that district of Michigan . . . by means of whose efforts, he himself, and many Christians were greatly refreshed." See the obituary of Bradford in *The Christian News* (Glasgow), 19 July 1849, p. 3. See also the entry for 18 October

MS 808 'There I found a very trying and singular state of things. The place had been settled at first by a class of infidels, who were real scoffers at religion. But there were several pious women in the neighborhood; and after a great struggle they finally had prevailed to have religious meetings established, and had built a church and settled a minister.[32] There was then living in Pontiac the man who had been the pastor of the church immediately preceding the brother who was there at the time I went.[33] The young man who was pastor when I arrived was from New England. His name I do not now recollect.[34] With this former pastor the church had had a great difficulty. They had become very much divided in respect to him, and finally dismissed him.[35] But the circumstances had been such as to leave a very bad state of feeling between him and the church; and also between him and another elderly minister who lived close by the village, and who had labored a good deal as a missionary in that new country in establishing churches.[36] This former missionary had taken a very active part in the controversy MS 809 between the old pastor 'and the church; so that between him and the old pastor there was no ministerial, or even Christian, sympathy. Indeed I found the state of things about as unpromising and difficult to manage as I had ever met with anywhere. However I began to preach, and it was

1846 in the Sunday school record book in possession of the First Congregational Church, Pontiac; and O. Poppleton, "Report of the Memorial Committee—Oakland County," *Michigan Pioneer and Historical Society, Historical Collections* 18 (1891): 266–67. The letter inviting Finney to go to Pontiac, from a committee of the First Congregational Church, 23 December 1846, is missing from the Finney Papers.

[32]The first church in Pontiac, organized in 1823, was Presbyterian. Through the efforts of Rev. Isaac Ruggles, a Congregational church was organized in 1831, and the church built in 1834. Information from the records of the church provided by the minister, Rev. Dr. James G. Keough, Jr.

[33]The pastor "immediately preceding" was Nathaniel West, who was there from 1844 to early in 1846. But Finney is probably referring to Lemuel P. Bates, who had been the pastor from 1838 to 1840. See "The First 150 Years, 1831–1981: First Congregational Church, Pontiac, Michigan" (pamphlet produced by the church, 1981), p. 2. Information from Harold F. Worthley of The Congregational Library, Boston.

[34]He was Orlo Daniel Hine (1815–1890), a graduate of Yale Divinity School who had gone to Pontiac from a church in Vermont in March 1846. He was acting pastor of the Congregational church there until October 1851, when he went to North Woodstock, Connecticut. He was subsequently pastor in Lebanon, Connecticut, for more than thirty years. See *Obituary Record of Graduates of Yale University Deceased during the Academical Year ending in June, 1891* (n.p.), p. 21.

[35]Under the Plan of Union the Pontiac Congregational Church came within the jurisdiction of the Presbytery of Detroit and for some years had a close relationship with the Presbyterians. But in 1840 troubles in the Congregational church led to Bates being asked to resign. He was dismissed by the presbytery but was invited to become the minister of the Presbyterian church, which was by then located in Auburn but had become inactive. He and a number of his friends, who also left the Congregationalists, revived the Presbyterian church, relocated it in Pontiac, and built a meeting house in 1844 across the street from the Congregational church. He then led the Presbyterian church to withdraw from the New School Detroit Presbytery and join the Old School Presbyterians (information from records in the First Congregational Church).

[36]This was Isaac W. Ruggles (1783–1857), a Congregational home missionary, who had moved to Michigan in 1824 and was very active in setting up churches on the frontier. In 1845 he had retired to a farm near Pontiac. See MS 812; and see also his obituary in *The American Congregational Year-Book* (Boston) 5 (1858): 114–15. For his pioneering activities, see William W. Sweet, *Religion on the American Frontier, 1783–1850*, vol. 3, *The Congregationalists* (Chicago: University of Chicago Press, 1939).

soon evident that the Spirit of the Lord was greatly searching the church. I began there, according to my custom, to have the stumbling blocks removed, mutual confession and restitution attended to, and in short to re-convert the church and prepare the way for a general revival among the openly impenitent. The state of morals at that time in Pontiac was low.

The people were enterprizing, and the place was thrifty in a business point of view; but religion was at the lowest ebb. I saw that nothing effectual could be done until the old roots of bitterness were extracted, their divisions healed, and their animosities put away. I therefore addressed my preaching to the church and to professors of religion, and preached some as searching sermons to them as I could. That was the home of their then Lieutenant Governor Richardson.[37] His wife was a religious woman, ꜝbut had been drawn considerably into the great MS 810 controversy between their old pastor and the church. After preaching for a week or two I thought the way was prepared; and it was agreed to set apart a day for fasting, humiliation, and prayer. When the day arrived I preached to them from this text: "O the Hope of Israel, and the Savior thereof, why art thou to us as a stranger in the land, and as a wayfaring man that tarrieth but for a night?"[38] My mind was greatly affected with the application of this text to the then state of that people. In the afternoon we had a general prayer-meeting of the church. Soon after the meeting began it was evident to me that there was a very searching spirit upon the meeting. I was the guest of a Mr. Davis, who had taken a very prominent part in the controversy with their old pastor.[39] He was a man of strong feelings, and had been very hostile in his feelings to their old pastor, thinking him altogether out of the way. This old pastor lived a near neighbor to him. As we came home from the morning service I saw that Mr. Davis was very deeply affected. He said to me: ꜝ"Don't you think it would be well for me to go and make MS 811 confession to that minister? He was wrong," said he, "but I have had a very bad spirit toward him." I inquired: "Can you go and confess to him without reproaching him, leaving him to confess his own sins?" He said he could; and immediately left the house, went over, and as I understood made an humble confession without accusing him at all. He

[37]Origen Drew Richardson (1795–1876) was a lawyer in Woodstock, Vermont, until he moved to Pontiac in 1826. He continued to practice law there until 1854, when he moved to Omaha, Nebraska. He was lieutenant governor of Michigan in the early 1840s and was also a member of the Michigan legislature. See John A. Vinson, *The Richardson Memorial* (Portland, Maine: Brown Thurston, 1876), pp. 672–73; and Augustine C. Baldwin, "Oakland County—Its Bench and Bar Prior to 1840," *Michigan Pioneer and Historical Society, Historical Collections* 31 (1901): 156–157.

[38]Jeremiah 14:8 reads, "O the hope of Israel, the Saviour thereof in time of trouble, why shouldest thou be as a stranger in the land, and as a wayfaring man that turneth aside to tarry for a night?"

[39]This may have been Abner Davis, one of the early pioneers who had purchased land in Pontiac in 1821. See Thomas J. Drake, "History of Oakland County," *Michigan Pioneer and Historical Society, Historical Collections* 22 (1893): 420.

told him that he had entertained very unchristian feelings toward him, and asked his forgiveness.

As I said, soon after we assembled in the afternoon, it was evident that there was a spirit of great searching on the congregation. Their old pastor was present, as I believe he was every time we had held meeting. Soon after we had assembled I observed Mrs. Lieutenant-Governor Richardson rise from her seat and pass around the church ‹to›[40] the opposite side where her old pastor sat, and ‹she openly› confessed to him[41] that she had entertained very unchristian feelings toward him. MS 812 This produced a very general outburst of feeling. |I observed that the old pastor's face turned deadly pale. As soon as Mrs. Richardson turned away, there was quite a general movement from different parts of the house of persons going to his seat to confess to him. I saw how the work was going on, and felt confident that there would be a general breaking down.

From the manifest impression that was making upon their old pastor, I expected every moment to see him go on his knees and make confession. The pressure at this time upon the congregation was tremendous. I kept entirely still; and so also did the then pastor, the young man. But just at this moment the old missionary, whose name, I think, was Ruggles, arose and interposed an objection to what was going on. He objected to it, he said, because their old pastor,—calling him by name, would triumph, and say that they had justified him and condemned themselves. I did not believe then, nor do I now, that there was the least danger of that. I think if Father Ruggles, as they called him, had kept still, it would not have been ten minutes before he would MS 813 have |made as full a confession as they could have desired. However Father Ruggles felt too strongly committed against him to see anything done that could, by any possibility, be construed into a justification of his course, and a condemnation of the course which his church had pursued toward him. The moment Father Ruggles took this position a terrible reaction came over the meeting. All confession ceased; all tears were wiped away; and I never in any meeting in my life saw so manifest a quenching of the Holy Spirit's influences as was manifest there.

The reaction was instantaneous, terrible, and decisive. Up to that moment all their animosities were melting away; but this mistaken course of Father Ruggles arrested the whole tide of good feeling, turned it back upon its fountains, and the animosities sprang up again in much of their former strength. After looking at the desolation for a few days I returned to Detroit, where I was taken sick and for a number of days MS 814 was confined to my bed. The season had arrived |for opening our Spring term; and as soon as I was able to travel I returned home, and as usual commenced my labors here; and we had a very interesting revival through the Summer.

[40] Here Finney changed the word "on" to "to."

[41] Here Matson had written down, "and I think she fell upon her knees, and confessed to him." Finney altered it to read, "and she openly confessed to him."

That Summer I published the second volume of my Systematic Theology.[42] I wrote it out and published it, and attended to my college and pastoral duties. Most of the second volume I wrote at the rate of a lecture a day, and sent it to the printers; so that I would correct the proof of one lecture, and write another and send it to the press the same day.[43] But this with all my pastoral duties and intense labors in my classes, so used up my strength that on Commencement evening I was taken with the typhus fever.[44] For two months I was very sick, and came very, very near the gates of the grave.[45] Meanwhile my precious wife was failing of consumption. About the middle of December she passed away.[46] When she died my strength had not returned; and I stayed at home that winter, and did not perform much ministerial labor here or elsewhere.[47]

[42]The second volume (numbered vol. 3) of *Lectures on Systematic Theology* was published in Oberlin by J. M. Fitch in August 1847. See *OE,* 1 September 1847, p. 143.

[43]Finney stated elsewhere: "I myself wrote them under so great pressure, that I could not edit it properly, so that a portion of the labor was committed to other hands" (*The British Banner* [London], 2 April 1851, p. 220).

[44]Commencement was on Wednesday, 25 August 1847, when Finney gave the address to the graduating class of the theological department. (*OE,* 1 September 1847, p. 142.) Dr. Isaac Jennings, the physician who attended Finney, wrote a detailed account of his illness and the treatment. He said, "It was typhoid in some respects, but not genuine typhus." At that time doctors often did not distinguish between true typhus and typhoid or enteric fever. He stated, "Professor Finney took to his bed on 27th of August [1847] and kept it for about 8 weeks" (*OE,* 20 July 1848, p. 104).

[45]The fever was at its height during the last few days of August. His fifty-fifth birthday, on 29 August, occurred at the time of the worst sickness. He was so ill that his wife, Lydia, wrote down details of the progress of the fever and what Finney was saying. Her notes covering the week from 25 to 31 August were jotted down at the back of an undated notebook of Finney's, containing notes and outlines of lectures ("Charles G. Finney Lectures and Sermon Outlines, 1872–1875 and n.d.," Oberlin College Archives, microfilm). According to notices in *The Oberlin Evangelist,* Finney was still unwell at the end of September, but by mid-October he was recovering, and by the end of the year he was better. See *OE,* 29 September 1847, p. 159; 13 October 1847, p. 167; and 22 December 1847, p. 207.

Dr. Jennings, who treated Finney, practiced "orthopathy," which involved no interference with the recuperative powers of the body, no medicines, and only rest, diet, and careful nursing. For the first fourteen days Finney had no food and only small quantities of cold water. Dr. Homer Johnson, an orthodox doctor in Oberlin, was very critical of the diagnosis and treatment. He maintained that it was not typhus but one of a number of cases "of common remittent fevers" and that proper food and medicines would have produced a much quicker cure (*OE,* 6 December 1848, p. 184). See also Hebbel E. Hoff, "Isaac Jennings and the Magic Bullet," *Bulletin of the History of Medicine* 35, no. 1 (January–February 1961): 71–73.

[46]Lydia Finney died on 18 December 1847. Her end was hastened by an attack of typhoid fever. Finney wrote a sketch of her life and final illness in a letter to the editor of *The Oberlin Evangelist,* 5 January 1848, pp. 3–4.

[47]Finney also remained in Oberlin through the winter of 1848–1849. Matson started a new sentence at the bottom of the page—"As I was left a widower with"—which Finney crossed out when he replaced the next three pages with a new page 815, the start of a new chapter.

MS 815
JHF 386

CHAPTER XXIX

‹*Visit to England as an Evangelist in 1849.*›

‹After[1] my severe illness my strength returned but slowly. I resumed my labors as Pastor & Professor too so[o]n[2] to favor a rapid return of strength. For this reason I remained at home through the winter of 1847 & 8, not feeling able to perform the labors of an Evangelist abroad.[3] Meanwhile I had been repeatedly written to & urged to visit England &

MS 816

labor for the promotion of revivals,› ˡin[4] that country; and in the autumn of 1849 **my wife[5] and myself embarked for England, leaving our family in charge of my eldest daughter.[6]** After a stormy passage **in the Steamer Hermon** we arrived at Southampton early in November.[7] There we met the pastor of the church in Houghton, **Huntingdonshire,** a village situated midway between the market towns of Huntington and Saint Ives.[8] A Mr.

[1] Page 815 written by Finney, replaces three previous pages of the manuscript. The whole section was crossed out by Fairchild, who inserted a new beginning to the chapter, numbering it XXVIII.

[2] Finney spelled this word "son."

[3] A revival in Oberlin early in 1848 was reported in *OE*, 15 March 1848, p. 46.

[4] Pages 816–36 were originally numbered 666–86 and renumbered 798–818 by Matson. Finney then altered them to 816–36.

[5] Finney's second wife, Elizabeth (Ford) Atkinson (1799–1863), was the widow of William Atkinson, a prosperous mill owner and member of the Episcopal church in Rochester. He had died in 1843. Since 1841 she had run the Atkinson Female Seminary in Rochester and was prominent in religious and benevolent activities. She supported Finney's revivals there and was a convert to Oberlin perfectionism. She and Charles Finney were married on 13 November 1848 in Akron, Ohio, by Oberlin president Asa Mahan. See *NYE*, 3 December 1863, p. 1; *OE*, 22 November 1848, p. 175; and Leonard I. Sweet, *The Minister's Wife* (Philadelphia: Temple University Press, 1983), pp. 184–211.

[6] Finney's oldest daughter was Helen Clarissa (Finney) Cochran (1828–1911), then age twenty-one. Her first husband, William Cochran, a young Oberlin professor to whom she was married in May 1846, died in August 1847, leaving her with a son, William, who was born 29 March 1848. She was married again to another Oberlin student, Jacob Dolson Cox, on 29 November 1849 at the end of the college term, two months after her parents left for England. See William C. Cochran, "Helen Finney Cox," *The Oberlin Alumni Magazine* 8 (October 1911): 8–10. The Finneys left Oberlin on 26 September 1849 and were in New York by Sunday, 7 October, where Finney preached for Henry Ward Beecher. See *OE*, 10 October 1849, p. 167; and *NYE*, 11 October 1849, p. 178.

[7] This was the U.S. Mail steamer *Hermann,* belonging to the Ocean Steamship Company. It left New York on Saturday, 20 October 1849. See *The New York Daily Tribune*, 20 October 1849, p. 2; and 23 October 1849, p. 4; and Frank C. Bowen, *A Century of Atlantic Travel, 1830–1930* (London: Sampson Low, Manton, 1932), pp. 47–48.

[8] Houghton was one of two adjoining villages usually linked together and now called Houghton-cum-Wyton, lying on the River Ouse about three miles east of Huntingdon. The population of Houghton in 1849 was about five hundred. See *History, Gazetteer, and Directory of*

Potto Brown, a very benevolent man, of whom I shall have occasion to speak frequently, had sent Mr. James Harcourt, his pastor, to meet us at Southampton.[9] **We arrived in Southampton on Sunday morning.**[10] **We spent the Sabbath there, and on Monday passed through London by rail to Mr. Brown's‹, in Houghton.›**[11]

Mr. Potto Brown was by parentage and education a Quaker. He and a partner were engaged in the milling business,[12] and belonged to a congregation of Independents in Saint Ives.[13] **Of course they were dissenters.** They became greatly affected **with seeing** the state of things in their neighborhood **around about**. The Church, as it is called in England, seemed to them to be effecting very little for the salvation |of souls. There were no schools outside (MS 817) of the church schools for the education of **the masses of** the poor; and the mass of the people were greatly neglected. After much prayer and consultation with each other, they agreed to adopt measures for the education of the **masses of** children in the village where they lived, and in the villages around them; and to extend this influence as far as they could. They also agreed to apply their means to the best advantage in establishing worship, and in building up churches independent of the Establishment. **They began this work at Houghton, a village, as I have said, midway between Saint Ives and Huntington.** |Not long after this enterprize was commenced, **Brother** (JHF 387) Brown's partner died. His wife, I believe, had died before him; and his partner committed his family, consisting of several sons and daughters, to the

the County of Huntingdon (Huntingdon: Hatfield, 1854). Matson spelled "Huntingdon" as "Huntington" in the manuscript.

[9] Potto Brown (1797–1871) was a dominant figure in the Nonconformist religious and social life in the county. His flourishing flour-milling business provided the means for promoting many reform and benevolent enterprises. See *Potto Brown: The Village Philanthropist* (St. Ives: Goodman, 1878); and J. C. G. Binfield, "Nonconformity in the Eastern Counties, 1840–1885" (Ph.D. diss., Cambridge University, 1965). James Harcourt (1816–1896) was a Baptist minister. He was at Houghton from 1844 until 1850. See *Baptist Handbook* (London), 1897, pp. 171–72.

[10] 4 November 1849.

[11] Matson had written down, "by rail to Saint Ives, where we took a carriage to Mr. Brown's house, whose guests we were to be." Finney changed it. Finney expected to be stopping in London and delivering some letters, but

> Mr. Brown dispatched Mr. Harcourt . . . to Southhampton, with strict injunctions to take Mr. and Mrs. Finney in hand immediately on landing, and not to leave them for a moment until they were safely housed with him at Houghton. Mr. Brown took this course to ensure that no one should have the opportunity of waylaying Mr. Finney, to withdraw him to another part of the country (Robert W. Dixon, "Religious Life and Work," in *Potto Brown*, pp. 168–69; and Finney to P. J. Bolton, 10 November 1849, Antislavery Society Papers, Rhodes House Library, Oxford; this letter was found and transcribed by Louis Billington but is not catalogued and cannot now be located).

[12] His partner was Joseph Goodman (1799–1844). He learned the milling business with Potto Brown's father, William Brown, entering into partnership with Potto Brown and taking over the business in 1822. He later branched out into farming. He was actively involved in philanthropic and religious work, and he became superintendent of the Houghton Chapel Sunday school. See Albert Goodman, "Genealogical Book of the Ancestry of the Surrey Goodmans, the Descendants of Albert and Olivia Goodman," vol. 1 (c. 1910), typescript copy in the Huntingdon Record Office, Huntingdon.

[13] The Independent Chapel in St. Ives was originally a Presbyterian church that had been formed at the time of Charles I. Oliver Cromwell had been a member there. From 1820 it had been under the pastoral charge of Rev. Isaiah K. Holland. See Herbert E. Norris, *History of Saint Ives* (St. Ives: printed at "The Hunts County Guardian" Office, 1889), pp. 42–45; and MS 969.

Left: Potto Brown. The wealthy miller of Houghton who persuaded Finney to visit England. This statue is in the center of Houghton Village. Photograph by Jane E. Rosell.

Below: Houghton Chapel. The place where Finney first preached in England. In Henry Bell, *A Jubilee Memorial of the Union Chapel, Houghton, Huntingdon* (Cambridge: Cambridge University Press, 1890), frontispiece. Courtesy The British Library.

fraternal care of **Brother** Brown, who committed them to the training of a judicious widow lady in a neighboring village.[14] **Brother** Brown's partner at his death begged him not to neglect the work which they had projected; but to pursue it with vigor and singleness of eye. **Brother** Brown's heart was |in MS 818 the work. His partner left a large property to his children.[15] **Brother** Brown himself had but two children, **and they were** sons.[16] He was a man of simple habits, and expended but little money upon himself or his family. He employed a school teacher in the village where he resided,[17] and built a chapel there for public worship. They called a man to labor there as a minister who had hyper-Calvinistic views; and consequently he labored year after year with no results **that at all** met the **views** of **Brother** Brown.[18] **Brother** Brown had frequent conversations with his minister about the want of good results. He was paying his salary, and laying out his money in various ways to promote religion by means of Sabbath schools, and teachers, and laborers; but few or none were converted. **Brother Brown spread this thing before** his minister so frequently that he finally replied: "Mr. Brown, am I *God*, that I can convert souls? I preach to them the Gospel, and God does not convert them: am I to blame?" **Brother** Brown replied: "Whether you are God or no God, *we must have conversions. The people must be converted*."[19] So **he dismissed** this minister |**and employed another, the** Rev. James Harcourt.[20] Mr. MS 819

[14] Joseph Goodman's wife, Rose, died in January of 1843, and he died in October of 1844. The children, three daughters and four sons, went to live with Mary Ann (Clarke) Tebbutt (1800–1861), widow of Matthew Tebbutt, in Bluntisham, a village about seven miles northeast of Houghton. See Goodman, "Genealogical Book," pp. 117–29; and information from Margaret Tebbutt of Forest Row, Sussex.

[15] Joseph Goodman's property on his death was valued at £70,000, chiefly in the form of fen farms, which were divided among his children (Goodman, "Genealogical Book," p. 122).

[16] Bateman Brown (1823–1909) and George William Brown (1821–1901) both went into the milling business and became prominent local citizens. See Bateman Brown, *Reminiscences of Bateman Brown, J.P.* (Peterborough: Peterborough Advertising, 1905).

[17] Francis Cross was employed in 1837 to run the newly formed British School, which was under the auspices of the British and Foreign School Society. He became a prominent man in the village and "from an educational point of view, the 'Father of the Parish.'" He was in full sympathy with the religious efforts of Goodman and Brown, and he continued at the school until his death in 1867 at age fifty-four.

The school had a considerable reputation, and at one time there were about two hundred scholars coming from all around the county. Potto Brown also built schools for boys and girls at St. Ives. See Brown, *Reminiscences*, pp. 27, 35–36; Potto Brown to Finney, 29 March 1867, Finney Papers, microfilm, roll 5; Henry Bell, *Jubilee Memorial of the Union Chapel, Houghton, Huntingdon* (Cambridge: Cambridge University Press, 1890), pp. 39, 86; and p. 505 n. 12 (MS 853).

[18] Augustus Smith was appointed to preach in the villages in 1839, and the chapel was built in 1840. He later "embraced very high Calvinistic sentiments." In 1844 he became pastor of the Strict Baptist Chapel in St. Ives. He died in 1849. See Bell, *Jubilee Memorial*, p. 7; and Ralph F. Chambers, *Strict Baptist Chapels of England*, vol. 4 (London: Fauconberg, 1962), p. 107.

[19] G. Holden Pike related a story of what Potto Brown told a visiting preacher on one occasion:

> The smallness of result in the way of apparent conversions was a source of complaint with him. "During the last few years I have spent £1000 here, and there has not been a soul converted; now, if that money had been given to the Wesleyans there would have been a large number saved, for they convert them at the rate of ten shillings per head" (G. H. Pike, "Potto Brown and the Browns of Houghton," *The Sword and the Trowel* [London] 15 [1879]: 160; see also G. Holden Pike, *Charles Haddon Spurgeon* [London: Hodder and Stoughton, 1886], p. 23).

[20] It was not until after the dismissal of Augustus Smith and the arrival of James Harcourt in

Harcourt is an open-communion Baptist. **He is** a talented man, a rousing preacher, and an earnest laborer for souls. Under **Brother Harcourt's** preaching **they soon began to have** conversions, and the work went on hopefully. Their little church **at their little chapel** increased in numbers and in faith; **and the work spread gradually**; and the **little** leaven was extending **its influence** perceptibly **but gradually** on every side.

JHF 388 They soon extended their operations to neighboring vil|lages with good results. But still they did not know how to promote revivals of religion.[21] The children of his partner, who had been left under his charge, had grown up to be young men and women, and were not converted. There were three daughters and three sons, a fine family, with **a plenty** of property; but they were unconverted.[22] Mr. Brown had a large number of very interesting and influential friends in that county, for whose salvation he felt a very deep interest. He was also very anxious about **this Goodman family—for that was the name of his partner**—that they might be converted. For the MS 820 education |of his sons he had employed a teacher in his family; and a considerable number of young men of respectable families from neighboring towns had studied with his sons.[23] This little family school, to which the young men who were sons of his friends in various parts of the county had been invited, had created a strong bond of interest between **Brother** Brown and these families. **Brother** Harcourt's labors, for some reason, did not reach these families, **nor the Goodman family**.

He was successful among the poorer and lower classes, was zealous and devoted, and preached the Gospel. As Mr. Brown said, "He was a powerful minister of Jesus Christ." But still he wanted experience to reach the class of persons that Mr. Brown had more particularly on his own heart. **He and Brother Harcourt, his minister,** frequently talked the matter over, and inquired how they could reach that class of persons and draw them to Christ. **Brother** Harcourt said that he had done all that he could, and that something else must be done or he did not see that this class of persons would be reached at all.

Brother Harcourt had read my revival lectures, **which had been** MS 821 |**extensively circulated in England**; and he finally suggested to **Brother** Brown the propriety of writing to me to see if I would not **visit England and**

1844 that they formed a church of fifty-seven members. See Bell, *Jubilee Memorial,* pp. 19–21; and Houghton Chapel "Record Book," in possession of the chapel.

[21] R. W. Dixon said that "there were many conversions and a general revival of religion ensued" (*Potto Brown*, p. 216). Harcourt was helped by evangelists from other areas, notably Thomas Pulsford and Charles H. Roe. This revival was part of a nationwide movement, mainly among Nonconformists, that was largely inspired by the revivals in America. See Richard J. Carwardine, "The Evangelist System: Charles Roe, Thomas Pul[s]ford, and the Baptist Home Missionary Society," *The Baptist Quarterly* 28, no. 5 (January 1980): 209–25.

[22] At this time there were, in fact, seven children. The oldest boy, Joseph, died in 1857. The oldest daughter, Eliza, was married to the Reverend Henry Allon and was living in London. There are sketches of all the children in the "Genealogical Book" compiled by the youngest child, Albert.

[23] John Watson was employed as tutor. Among the pupils were Frederick Coote, a son of William Coote of St. Ives; George Clark, a son of John Clark of Houghton; Charles Tebbutt, a son of Mary Tebbutt of Bluntisham; and Robert Felkin from Nottingham, a first cousin of Charles Tebbutt. See Brown, *Reminiscences*, p. 29.

come to that place. This led to my receiving a very earnest request from Mr. Brown to visit them.[24] **Brother Brown** conversed with many people, and with some **of the** ministers; which led to my receiving divers letters of pressing invitation to visit England.[25]

|At first these letters made but little impression upon me, for I did not see how I could go to England. **Circumstances, however, transpired that led me to see that the way was open for me to leave this place**, at least for a season; and as I have said, in the **fall** of 1849 my wife and myself went to England. When we arrived there and had rested a few days, I began my labors in thei**r** village chapel.[26] I soon found that **Brother** Brown was altogether a remarkable man. Brought up a Quaker he was entirely catholic in his views. **He had not for a long time had any particular intercourse with them as a denomination, but had been** laboring in an independent way directly for the salvation of the people |around him. He had wealth, and his property was constantly and rapidly increasing. His history had reminded me many times of the proverb: "There is that scattereth and yet increaseth: there is that withholdeth more than is meet, **which** tendeth to poverty."[27] For religious purposes he would spend his money like a prince. The more he spent, the more he had to spend.

JHF 389

MS 822

I have said we were the guests of Brother Potto Brown. While we were there he threw his house open morning, noon, and evening, and invited his friends far and near to come and pay him a visit. They came in great numbers, so that his table was surrounded nearly every meal with divers persons who had been invited in that I might have conversation with them, and that they might attend our meetings. A revival immediately commenced, and spread among the people. The **Goodman family** were soon interested in religion, and converted to Christ.[28] The work spread among those that came **for conversation and to attend meetings** from the neighboring villages **round**

[24] See Potto Brown to Charles Finney, 13 February 1849, Finney Papers, microfilm, roll 4.

[25] See letters from C. H. Roe and Potto Brown to Finney, Finney Papers. The first letter from Roe is not in the Finney Papers.

[26] This was on Sunday, 11 November. See Elizabeth Finney to her sister, Henrietta Bissell, 25 December 1849, Finney Papers, microfilm, roll 4. The letters written from England by Mrs. Finney to her sister contain detailed descriptions of Finney's preaching and revival work.

[27] Proverbs 11:24.

[28] The involvement of the Goodman family in the revival and the activities of the church can be seen in the letters from Potto and Mary Brown and Mary Tebbutt in the Finney Papers, and in correspondence in the Goodman Family Papers, in the possession of Mr. Thomas Tebbutt, of Hadleigh, Suffolk. Albert Goodman, not yet ten years old at the time, claimed not to have been influenced by the revival. See Goodman, "Genealogical Book," p. 151.

In another account of this revival Finney wrote:

> Neville, the eldest son of the Goodman family, was soon converted, to the great relief and joy of Mr. Brown. The conversion of the younger Goodman children followed, one after the other, until I believe they were all converted. . . .
>
> Neville . . . about whom Mr. Brown had been so very anxious, was a zealous, whole-hearted convert, and soon began to preach the Gospel, to the great joy of Mr. Brown. The Goodmans were a lovely family, and Mr. Brown, their guardian, rejoiced over their conversion with the ardor of a Christian father. They have all done great honor to his guardianship, and to his prayers and efforts for their good (Finney to the Editor, 20 February 1873, *NYE,* 6 March 1873, p. 1).

In May 1861 two of the brothers, Henry and Albert, while on a six-month trip to the United States, visited the Finneys in Oberlin. See Goodman, "Genealogical Book," p. 161.

MS 823 **about.** They heard and gladly received the Word. And so extensive and thorough was the work among **Brother** Brown's particular friends, whose conversion he had been longing and praying for, that before I left **there** he said that every one of them was converted,—that the Lord had not left one of them out for whom he had felt anxiety, and for whose conversion he had been praying.

JHF 390 The conversion of this large number of persons scattered over the county, made a very favorable impression where they were known. The house of worship at Houghton was small, but it was packed **to its utmost capacity** at every meeting;[29] and the devotedness and engagedness of **Brother** Brown and his wife were most interesting and affecting. There seemed to be no bounds to their hospitality.[30] Their schoolmaster was a religious man, and would run in every day, and almost every meal, and sit down with us to enjoy the conversation. Gentlemen would come in from neighboring towns, from a distance of many miles, early enough to be there at breakfast. The young men MS 824 who had been educated with his sons, were invited and came; and I believe every one of them was converted. Thus **Brother Brown's** largest desires in regard to them were fulfilled; and very much more among the masses was done than he had expected. **Brother** Harcourt had at that time several preaching places beside Houghton in the neighboring villages **round about.**[31] **They were endeavoring to establish Sabbath Schools for dissenters and among the poor, and to get up prayer-meetings and preaching services, at three or more places,**[32] **in villages not far distant from Houghton.**[33] The savor of this work at Houghton continued for years. Mr. Harcourt informed me that he preached in a praying atmosphere, and with a melting state of feeling around him as long as he remained in Houghton.[34] **I shall have occasion in another place to speak of his**

[29]The chapel could hold four hundred people. Mrs. Finney wrote: "The chapel became too small to hold all that would come on a Sunday evening and Mr Brown had a large tent that would accommodate 1000 persons or perhaps more" (E. Finney to H. Bissell, 25 December 1849, Finney Papers, microfilm, roll 4).

[30]Potto Brown's wife was Mary (Bateman) Brown. She had also been a Quaker. They were married in 1822. In a letter of appreciation of Potto Brown, Finney wrote: "Mrs. Brown entered with all her heart into the work, and spared no pains to make everybody feel as much at home as possible at her house. A more laborious, unselfish, hospitable family of laborers for Christ I never saw" (Finney to the Editor, 20 February 1873, *NYE,* 6 March 1873, p. 1). Mary Brown died in 1854. Potto Brown married his second wife (also named Mary) while the Finneys were in England the second time, in 1859. See Goodman, "Genealogical Book," pp. 481–82.

[31]Matson had written down the words "a few of them" at the end of this sentence, but they appear to have been crossed out by Finney.

[32]Here Matson had written down, "I think, at three or more places at that time," but the words "I think" and "at that time" appear to have been crossed out by Finney.

[33]There were meetings particularly in Hemingford Grey, Hemingford Abbot, Hartford, and Woodhurst. Fifty members were admitted to the different branches of the church during the four months after Finney left. See Houghton Chapel "Record Book"; and Potto Brown to Finney, 3 June 1849, Finney Papers, microfilm, roll 4.

[34]One of the nearby ministers who had helped Finney at Houghton wrote some months later to Finney:

> The work is still going on well it appears to me that God blessed your labours particularly to the stirring up of professors. Bro. Harcourt has now a working church and preaches in a praying atmosphere, so that his labours are evidently far more

leaving Houghton for another field of labor, his great success in that

successful than ever they have been. religion among them seems to be quite a contagion (H. L. Tuck to Finney, 9 April 1850, Finney Papers, microfilm, roll 4).

Mrs. Finney also picked up this phrase, "Brother Harcourt has now a *working church*, and preaches in a praying atmosphere," quoting it in a letter to her sister, H. Bissell, 22 April 1850, Finney Papers, microfilm, roll 4. Ten years later it was reported in a local paper:

It was with the hope that Mr. Finney would be instrumental in the conversion of various individuals who were cared for, that induced a gentleman in that county to secure his services in 1848. The result was most satisfactory, and showed that the means used were wise. All the individuals were hopefully converted to God, and are found, to this day, in connexion with various Churches in the county, and among the most earnest and influential spirits in all religious and philanthropic movements ("The Rev. C. G. Finney," *The Eastern Counties Gazette* [St. Ives], 26 February 1859, p. 2).

Henry Ward Beecher, who was in England about that time and met Finney later in London, wrote that Finney had "labored for three weeks with remarkable success. In a population of 700, in two villages, probably a hundred conversions occurred; fifty have united with churches, and more are propounded" (*The Independent* [New York], 21 November 1850, p. 190).

There were, however, some doubts about the longer-term influence of the revival. R. W. Dixon, who later married one of the Goodman children, wrote about Finney's account:

His autobiography, while giving a good idea of the feeling produced, is probably somewhat exaggerated, for his personal references are known to be very inaccurate, and though no doubt written with a sincere desire to give a correct estimate—yet some allowance must be made for them as the reflex of excitement and of a most sanguine temperament. That the meetings were productive of great good, and left permanent results, is unquestionable. Large crowds from all around gathered to attend them. Mr. Brown's great tent was put up and filled. The sermons and prayers were deeply impressive, and after the public meetings enquirer's meetings were held, which were so largely attended that Mr. Finney had to ask the help of other ministers to talk with enquirers. Mr. Brown was highly gratified with the results. Some of those he was most anxious about derived lasting benefits from these revival efforts, and he knew that he had reason to be very thankful that the movement had been set on foot. He felt very grateful to Mr. Finney, joining him afterwards at many places where he laboured, to uphold him by his presence and prayers. Mr. Brown kept up a friendship with him, and they corresponded after Mr. Finney returned to America (*Potto Brown*, p. 169).

Henry Bell, a later minister at Houghton, wrote:

How far such religious efforts as Mr. Finney's resulted in abiding spiritual good to the Houghton Church, it is difficult to decide. No doubt at the time the result seemed very wonderful, but looking back upon this time, and to the services then held, whether those who are now living, and who took part in them are as thoroughly satisfied of their real value in building up the Christian cause as they were then, it is not for us to say.

The striking results which at the time seemed to be manifest from these and other revival efforts, were such as to lead Mr. Brown to imagine that if only the same kind of work could be done in other villages, a large central organisation might be formed to direct and support it. Unhappily for Houghton, Mr. Harcourt removed to Luton at the end of the year 1851, and from that time until a comparatively recent date, Houghton had no pastor of its own, although a succession of preachers were resident in the village (*Jubilee Memorial*, pp. 22–23; Harcount left at the end of 1850, not 1851).

A reviewer of Finney's *Memoirs* in *The British Quarterly Review* wrote:

We are compelled to say, however, that the strong statements of his autobiography—or, at any rate, some of them—are to be taken *cum grano*. Mr. Finney's very absorption in his work magnified it in his apprehensions. We happen to be somewhat minutely acquainted with some part of his work in England, and we are bound to say that particulars here stated concerning several families and individuals are, in some respects, not true at all, and in others greatly exaggerated.

The reviewer was probably the editor, Henry Allon, a Congregational minister in London. He was married to Eliza Goodman, a daughter of Joseph Goodman of Houghton, and he was in close touch with events there. He also had met Finney. See *The British Quarterly Review* (London) 63 (April 1876): 545. See also *The Patriot* (London), 30 May 1850, p. 342; and letters of Allon to Finney in the Finney Papers.

field, and his call to London, where I finally found him on my second visit to England.[35]

MS 825 |I did not remain long in Houghton at this time—several weeks, however.[36] Among the brethren who had written urging me to come to England was a Mr. Roe, a Baptist minister of Birmingham.[37] As soon as he was informed that I was in England, he came to Houghton and spent several days, attending the meetings and witnessing the results.

I said we arrived in Houghton early in November. About the middle of December we left Houghton and went to Birmingham to labor in the congregation of **Brother** Roe.[38] Here, soon after our arrival, we were introduced to **the** Rev. John Angell James, who was the principal dissenting minister in Birmingham.[39] He was a good and a great man, and wielded a very

[35]See MS 971. Harcourt moved to Luton, where he started on 1 December 1850. See *The Baptist Reporter and Missionary Intelligencer* (London), n.s., 8 (February 1851): 71.

[36]During his stay in Houghton, Finney visited London on two occasions. One day was spent with his wife sightseeing. But he was invited to help Rev. John Stevenson, minister of the Baptist Chapel in Borough Road, Southwark, who was holding meetings for revival and was being assisted by Asa Mahan, who had gone over from Oberlin to attend the Paris Peace Conference. See "Extracts from Prof. Finney's last letter home," 4 December 1849, Correspondence of Charles G. Finney, 1830–1875, Oberlin College Archives, microfilm; Finney to Angelina Atkinson and Julia Finney (1849), Finney Papers, microfilm, roll 4; and Edward H. Madden and James E. Hamilton, *Freedom and Grace* (Metuchen, N.J.: Scarecrow, 1982), p. 96.

Two of Finney's sermons during these visits, preached at Borough Road Chapel on 22 and 23 November 1849, were published with the title *A Fourth Voice from America*, by A. Weston of Manchester in 1849. These were also published in *The Penny Pulpit* (London), as well as was a third sermon preached there on 27 November. The first three "Voices" from America were sermons that had been preached by James Caughey when he was in England in 1847 and were published in Manchester by J. Ainsworth, 1847–1849.

[37]Charles Hill Roe (1800–1872) was an evangelist and secretary of the Baptist Home Missionary Society from 1835 until he settled in Heneage Street Chapel, Birmingham, in 1842. He emigrated to America in 1851 and became one of the founders of the University of Chicago. "Among the first in England . . . he caught the spirit of the revivals" from America. See Eliza R. Shannon, *A Minister's Life: Memoirs of Charles Hill Roe* (Chicago: Lakeside, 1900); and *The Baptist Magazine* (London) 65 (January 1873): 25–26.

[38]Finney wrote in another account of the work at Houghton:

> Houghton is midway between Huntingdon and St. Ives. These are market towns, and at that time were strongly barricaded against all efforts to promote revivals of religion. Mr. Brown was very anxious to have me labor in those towns. But the doors were not thrown open to me, and I was soon called away to Birmingham (*NYE,* 6 March 1873, p. 1).

Finney started at Heneage Street Chapel on Sunday, 9 December. He preached twice on Sundays and three or four times during the week. At the end of the second week he had an appointment to visit Leeds in Yorkshire. There he met with some of his English disciples, notably Edward H. Weeks and John Morris, and on Sunday, 23 December, he preached to "an immense congregation both morning & evening" (E. Finney to H. Bissell, 25 December 1849, Finney Papers, microfilm, roll 4; and see Finney to Charles P. Tebbutt, 16 December 1849, Goodman Family Papers; and E. H. Weeks to Finney, 26 May 1853, Letters Received by Oberlin College, 1822–1866, microfilm, roll 14).

Before returning to Birmingham, Finney attended the annual Christmas festival of the Leeds Temperance Society on Christmas afternoon, where he upheld the success of the temperance movement in America as an example to the British. See *Leeds Times,* 29 December 1849, p. 3. Finney's outspoken pronouncements on drinking in Britain were later to get wide publicity and cause him and the temperance reformers considerable embarrassment.

[39]John Angell James (1785–1859) was at Carr's Lane Church, Birmingham, from 1805 until his death. He was an elder statesman in the Congregational church and was internationally known for his writings and interest in promoting revival. He kept in close touch with the American movements. See R. W. Dale, *The Life and Letters of John Angell James* (London: Nisbet, 1861); J.

extensive influence in that city, and indeed throughout England. When my revival lectures were first published in England **Brother** James wrote an introduction to them, highly commending them.[40] **They were circulated very extensively among the dissenters. Ministers read them in their lecture rooms to their churches and commented upon them;**[41] **and throughout England, and Scotland, ˡand Wales there was quite an extensive religious movement at that time.**[42] But when I arrived in Birmingham, I ˡwas informed that after **Brother** James had publicly recommended them in meetings of ministers, and by his pen, he had been informed by men **of a certain stamp** on this side of the Atlantic, that those revivals that had occurred, under my ministry especially, had turned out very disastrously; and that to such an extent had these representations been made to him that he had taken back what he had said publicly in favor of those revival lectures.[43] However, when he saw me in Birmingham he called the Independent ministers **in Birmingham** to a breakfast at his house, and requested me to attend.[44] This is the common way of doing things in England. When we assembled at his house, after breakfast was concluded, he said to his ministerial brethren, that he had been impressed that they were falling greatly short of accomplishing the *end* of their ministry. That they were too well

MS 826

JHF 391

R. Kennedy, "The Life, Work, and Thought of John Angell James" (Ph.D. diss., Edinburgh University, 1956); and *DNB*.

[40]There had been previous editions published in England from January 1838 (see p. 375 n. 77 [MS 665]). This edition was *Lectures on Revivals of Religion with introductory prefaces by Rev. John Angell James, Rev. George Payne, and Rev. N. S. S. Beman with notes, and carefully revised by Rev. William Patton, D.D.* (London: Snow, 1839). The lectures were published on 5 August 1839 and had a substantial sale. One bookseller told John Keep six months later that he had sold more than 4,500 copies. See John Keep to Lydia Keep, 27 February 1840, transcription in R. S. Fletcher Papers, file 30/24, box 6, Oberlin College Archives.

[41]Rev. John Campbell of London was one who had read the *Lectures on Revivals* to his congregation. See Campbell, *Valedictory Services and Farewell Sermon of Professor Finney* (London: Snow, 1851), p. 25, reprinted in the Appendix of this volume.

[42]James wrote a letter dated 29 July 1839 to the editor of *The New-York Evangelist,* describing the revival efforts that had been made for several years. He pointed out: "The work has been materially aided and benefited, in several places, by the circulation of Finney's Lectures on Revivals. . . . Opinion, however, is much divided upon the work; but it is certain that it has quickened the movement which has been so happily commenced in many places." He went on to say: "A new and cheap edition of Finney revised and with notes, by Dr. Patton of New York, is just about to issue from the press, with many of the more exceptionable passages expunged. . . . I have no doubt that the sale will be extensive, and its influence considerable" (*NYE,* 31 August 1839, p. 138).

William Patton, a particular friend of James, was then on a visit to England with N. S. S. Beman. Patton and James also published at that time some of the writings of Jonathan Edwards under the title *Edwards on Revivals*. Speaking of these books, Patton's son wrote: "Such efforts did much to prepare the way for the subsequent success of Mr. Finney himself, when he visited England, as also for the evangelistic labors of Mr. Moody" (William W. Patton, *A Filial Tribute to the Memory of Rev. William Patton* [Washington, D.C., 1880], p. 18; see also Richard Carwardine, *Transatlantic Revivalism* [Westport, Conn.: Greenwood, 1978], pt. 2). For the influence of Finney's *Revival Lectures* in Scotland and Wales, MS 665–66; see p. 591 n. 6 (MS 989); and the Appendix, pp. 667–70.

[43]James publicly repudiated his recommendation at the autumnal meeting of the Congregational Union in Leeds in October of 1843. See W[illiam] L[amb] to Finney, March 1845, *OE,* 18 June 1845, p. 102; Dale, *Life of James*, p. 420; and *The Congregational Magazine* [London], 3d ser., 7 (December 1843): 953–54. See also n. 87 below.

[44]This was on the Friday after Christmas, 28 December 1849 (E. Finney to H. Bissell, 22 April 1850, Finney Papers, microfilm, roll 4).

satisfied to have the people attend meeting, pay the minister's salary, keep up MS 827 the Sabbath School, and with |an outward prosperity; while the conversions in most of the churches were very few, and after all the people were going to destruction. I was told by **Brother** Roe, **of whom I have spoken, and** with whom I was at that time commencing my labors, that there were in Mr. James' own congregation not less than fifteen hundred impenitent sinners. At the breakfast at Mr. James' he expressed himself very warmly, and said that something must be done. Finally the ministers agreed upon holding meetings, as soon as I could comply with their request, **alternately** in the different Independent churches, **preaching around in a circle among them.** But for some weeks I confined my labors to Mr. Roe's congregation, and there was a powerful revival. **It was a state of things that** they had never seen. The revival swept through the congregation with great power; and a very large proportion of the impenitent **in the congregation** were turned to Christ. **Brother** Roe entered heart and soul into the work. I found him a good and MS 828 true man. He was not at all sectarian or |prejudiced in his views; but he JHF 392 opened his heart to divine influence, and poured out himself in labors |for souls like a man in earnest. Day after day he would sit in the vestry of his church, and converse with inquirers **who were invited** to visit him, and direct them to Christ. His time was almost entirely taken up with this work for many days. His church was at the time one of the few close-communion churches in England, as nearly all the Baptists in England are open-communionists.[45] After the number of conversions had become large, the church began to examine converts for admission. They examined a large number, and were about to hold a communion.[46] I preached in the morning, and they were to hold their communion in the afternoon. When the morning service was closed **Brother** Roe requested the church to remain for a few moments. ‹**I & my D[ea]r**› **wife,**[47] **who had entered very warmly into the work, and exerted herself among the ladies of the congregation to her utmost,** retired after the morning service, and went to our lodgings at Mr. MS 829 Roe's, where we were guests. |**Bye and bye Brother** Roe came home, and **came smiling into our room**, saying, "What do you think our church have done?" **I replied** I **did not know**; for really it had not occurred to me to raise the inquiry what they were going to do when they were requested to stay. He replied, "They have voted unanimously to invite you and Mrs. Finney to our Communion this afternoon." Their close communion was more than they could **swallow** on such an occasion as that. However, on reflecti**ng on it my wife and I** concluded that we had better not accept their invitation, lest they

[45] In the eighteenth century most Baptist churches refused membership or Communion to anyone who was not baptized as a believer. Early in the nineteenth century a controversy over allowing other than Baptists to the Communion service led to the practice of "open" or mixed Communion spreading gradually throughout both Particular and General Baptist churches. Heneage Street was a General Baptist church. See W. T. Whitley, *A History of British Baptists* (London: Griffin, 1923), pp. 306–9.

[46] This was on 10 March, when thirty-six were admitted to the church. Twelve more were admitted on 12 April, and ten on 5 May. See *The Baptist Reporter and Missionary Intelligencer,* n.s., 7 (May 1850): 224; and (June 1850): 272.

[47] Matson had written down here, "My wife," but Finney crossed out the word "My" and wrote in "I & my Dr." Fairchild altered it further.

had taken the vote under a pressure that might create some reaction and regret among them afterwards; and as we were really fatigued, we excused ourselves, and remained at-home **that afternoon**.

As I had to preach again in the evening, I was glad to have the rest. I soon accepted the invitations of the ministers to labor in their several pulpits.[48] The congregations were everywhere crowded **and packed**; a great interest was excited; and the numbers that would **crowd** into the vestries after preaching under an invita|tion for inquirers **to take that room**, was large. Their largest vestries would be packed with inquirers, whenever a |call was made to resort thither for instruction.[49] As to means I used the same there that I had done in this country. Preaching, prayer, conversation, and meetings of inquiry were the means used. But I soon found that **Brother** James was receiving letters from various quarters, warning him against the influence of my labors. **He informed me of this, and of what had been written and said to him on this subject.** He had acquaintances on this side of the Atlantic; and some of them, as I understood him, had written him letters warning him against my influence. Besides, from various parts of his own country the same pressure was made upon him.[50] He was very frank with me, and told me how the matter stood; and I was as frank with him. I said to him: "Brother James, your responsibility is great. I am aware that your influence is great; and these letters show both your influence and your responsibility in regard |to these labors. You are led to think that I am heretical in my views. You hear my preaching **every night, and** whenever I preach; and you know whether I preach the Gospel or not." I had taken with me my two published volumes of Systematic theology. I said to him, "Have you heard me preach anything that is not Gospel?" He said, ["]No, not anything at all." "Well," said I, "now I have my Systematic Theology which I teach to my classes at-home, and which I everywhere preach; and I want you to **take and** read it." He was very earnest to do so. I soon saw that there was a very venerable looking gentleman with him from evening to evening at our meetings. They would attend meeting together; and when I called for inquirers they would go in and stand where they could get a place, and hear all that was said. Who this

MS 830

JHF 393

MS 831

[48] After being with Roe, Finney preached three sermons in Carr's Lane Chapel and round the different churches "for four or five weeks." He then confined his labors to Ebenezer Chapel, Steelhouse Lane, the second largest chapel in Birmingham, and at that time without a minister (E. Finney to H. Bissell, 22 April 1850, Finney Papers, microfilm, roll 4; and reports in *The Birmingham Mercury*, 19 January 1850, p. 8; and *The Inquirer* [London], 26 January 1850, p. 58; Henry Baker, *Historical Memoranda relating to the Society of Protestant Dissenters of the Independent Persuasion meeting in Ebenezer Chapel, Steel House Lane, Birmingham, etc., a Centenary Celebration 1803–1903* [Birmingham: Hudson, 1903]; and *The Independent*, 4 April 1850, p. 55).

[49] According to Henry Ward Beecher, "There was no lecture-room in the city that could hold the inquirers" (*The Independent*, 21 November 1850, p. 190). And Mrs. Finney wrote to her sister: "The inquirers were so numerous that a school room which would hold five hundred would be filled and sometimes all could not gain entrance" (E. Finney to H. Bissell, 22 April 1850, Finney Papers, microfilm, roll 4).

[50] James sent to Finney a letter from a London pastor dated 25 January 1850, which James had received, warning him against Finney's theology and showing concern about James's inviting Finney into his pulpit. James had obliterated the signature and address of the sender before showing it to Finney. The handwriting, however, reveals it to be that of Rev. John Waddington. He had heard Finney at the Borough Road Chapel in London. See [Waddington] to James, 25 January 1850; and James to Finney, 26 January 1850, Finney Papers, microfilm, roll 4.

venerable gentleman was I was not aware. For several nights in succession they came in this way; but Mr. James did not introduce me to the person that was with him, nor come near to speak with me at those meetings.

MS 832 |After things had gone on in this way for a week or two, **Brother** James JHF 394 and his venerable friend called at our lodgings. |He introduced me to Dr Redford, informing me at the same time that he was one of their most prominent theologians.[51] That he had more confidence in Dr Redford's theological acumen than he had in his own; and that he had requested him to visit Birmingham, attend the meetings, and especially to unite with him in reading my Theology. He said they had been reading it from day to day; and Dr Redford would like to have some conversation with me on certain points of theology. We conversed very freely on all the questions to which Dr Redford wished to call my attention; and Dr Redford said very frankly, "Brother James, I see no reason for regarding Mr. Finney in any respect as unsound. He has his own way of stating theological propositions; but I cannot see that he differs, on any essential point, ‹from› us."[52]

They had with them a little manual prepared by the Congregational Union MS 833 of England ‹**&**›[53] Wales, in |which was found a brief statement of their theological views.[54] They read to me certain portions of this manual; and in my turn I questioned them. I heard their explanations, and was satisfied there was a substantial agreement between us. Dr Redford remained **for sometime** longer at Birmingham. He then went home, and with my consent took with him my Systematic Theology; and said he would read it carefully through, and then write to me his views respecting it. I observed that he was indeed at-home in theology, was a scholar and a Christian, and a thoroughly educated theologian. I was therefore more than willing to have him criticize my Theology, that if there was anything that needed to be retracted or amended, he might point it out. I requested him to do so thoroughly and frankly, **and he said he would.** He took it home, gave himself up to a thorough examination of it, and read the volumes patiently and critically through. I then received a letter from him, expressing his strong approbation of my MS 834 theological views; saying there were a few |points upon which he would like JHF 395 to make some inquiries, and he wished |me, as soon as I could get away from Birmingham, to come and preach for him.[55] I continued in Birmingham, I

[51] George Redford (1785–1860) was a Nonconformist theologian and minister at Angel Street Chapel, Worcester, from 1826 to 1856. He was the founder of *The Congregational Magazine* and author of many books and articles on theology. See *DNB*; and William Urwick, *Nonconformity in Worcester* (London: Simpkin, Marshall, 1897). Redford had been one of those who had pioneered the use of protracted meetings in England in 1837. See Redford, "Means of Usefulness by Special Religious Services," *The Evangelical Magazine* (London), n.s., 16 (March 1838): 129–31; and letter from J. A. James in *NYE,* 31 August 1839, p. 183.

[52] Finney inserted the word "from" to replace the word "with."

[53] Finney inserted the symbol *&*.

[54] Redford had been appointed chairman of the Congregational Union in 1834, and about the same time he prepared the celebrated "Declaration of the Faith," which formed the basis for the later compilation *The Congregational Manual, Church Membership, Christian Baptism, the Lord's Supper, and the Declaration of Faith, Church Order, and Discipline* (London: Jackson, Walford, and Hodder, 1864). See "Dr. Redford," *The Christian Witness* (London), n.s., 2 (July 1860): 303.

[55] This letter is not in the Finney Papers. Mrs. Finney referred to it as being sent by Redford after he read the books "partly through." She quoted an appreciative extract: "Your system is

think, about three months.[56] There were a great many interesting conversions in that city; and yet the ministers were not then prepared to commit themselves heartily to the use of the necessary means to spread the revival universally over the city.[57] **I might mention a great many very interesting cases that occurred at Birmingham.** There was one of so interesting a character that I will call attention to it. I suppose it is generally known in this country that Unitarianism, in England was first developed and promulged in Birmingham. That was the home of old Dr Priestly, who was one of the principal, if not one of the first Unitarian ministers in England. His congregation I found still in existence in Birmingham, **presided over by a pastor.**[58] One evening before I left Birmingham I preached on this text: "Ye stiff-necked and uncircumcised in heart and ˡears, ye do always resist the Holy Ghost."[59] I dwelt first upon the divinity and personality of the Holy Ghost. I **then pointed out many ways in which men could and did strive with**

MS 835

well-arranged and carried out to its logical consequences in almost every particular" (E. Finney to H. Bissell, 22 April 1850, Finney Papers, microfilm, roll 4). After finishing the books, Redford wrote again, enclosing a separate paper with "the principal points on which difficulties suggest themselves." This was followed a few days later by another letter suggesting changes that would be needed if the books were to be republished in England, and again inviting Finney to Worcester (Redford to Finney, 1 March 1850; and 5 February 1850, Finney Papers, microfilm, roll 4; the date 5 February appears to have been a mistake and probably should have been 5 March; the paper enclosed with the first letter is in Miscellaneous Items, Finney Papers, microfilm, roll 8).

[56] Finney continued preaching in Ebenezer Chapel, Carr's Lane, and Heneage Street until he had to leave in the middle of the revival because of exhaustion. See letter from E. Finney to H. Bissell, 22 April 1850, Finney Papers, microfilm, roll 4.

[57] It was noted at the time in *The British Banner* (London):

> We understand that Mr. Finney has laboured chiefly in the chapel of the Rev. Peter Roe, and that he has not obtained very generally the sympathy of Evangelical ministers, who, while they wish him well, and concur in much of his sentiments, as well as admire his zeal, have yet doubts of the entire correctness of some of his views (13 March 1850, p. 189).

John Angell James wrote soon after to the Rev. William B. Sprague, a particular friend of his in America, that Finney "excited some considerable attention, but did not succeed to the extent of his expectations. Most of our ministers stood aloof from him. This I could not bring myself to do. He preached five or six times for me, and sometimes with great power" (Dale, *Life of James*, p. 546).

Peter Sibree, another Birmingham Congregational minister, later wrote: "His visit to our town was a great boon. Some in my congregation will eternally thank him" (*The British Banner,* 27 November 1856, p. 386). Robert W. Dale, the Nonconformist statesman and successor to J. A. James at Carr's Lane Chapel, was a student at the time at Spring Hill College in Birmingham. He heard Finney there and also in London later, during the vacation. He wrote, "I heard him often about three-and-twenty years ago, and I doubt whether he preached so effectively in any other part of England, with the exception, perhaps, of Huntingdonshire, as he preached in Birmingham" (editorial note in "Mr. Finney's Preaching," *The Congregationalist* [London] 4 [December 1875]: 725; and "Original Letters of Dr. R. W. Dale chiefly written to Mrs. Josiah Cash of Leamington, 1846–1870," manuscript in Birmingham Reference Library; reference from Dale W. Johnson). R. W. Dale was deeply influenced by Finney's preaching and writings. See Dale, *Nine Lectures on Preaching* (London: Hodder and Stoughton, 1877), pp. 96–97, 146, 149–50.

[58] Joseph Priestly (1733–1804), the theologian, philosopher, and scientist, was minister at the New Meeting-house, Birmingham, from 1780 to 1791. He went to America in 1793. When Finney was in Birmingham the minister there was John Kentish (1768–1853). However, he was virtually retired, and his colleague Samuel Bache (1804–1876), who was an eminent Unitarian, was effectively in charge. See *DNB*. The words "presided over by a pastor" were not crossed out by Fairchild in the manuscript but do not appear in the published version.

[59] Acts 7:51.

him. That his work was to teach and convince men of sin, and to teach them in regard to their duty, to plead the cause and claims of God with sinners and with all classes of men. I endeavored to show in how many ways, and on how many points, men resisted the divine teaching. That when convinced by the Holy Spirit, they **would** still persist in taking their own course; and that in all such cases they **were** resisting the Holy Spirit. The Lord gave me liberty that night to preach a very searching discourse. My object was to show **them**, that while **they were** pleading their dependence on the Holy Spirit they **were** constantly resisting him. I found in Birmingham, as I did everywhere in England, that the greatest stress was laid upon the influence of the Holy Spirit. But I nowhere found any clear discrimination

MS 836 between a *physical* influence of the Spirit, exerted directly ˡupon the soul itself, and that *moral, persuasive* influence which he in fact exerts over the minds of men. **The people of England were very jealous lest the Holy Spirit should be dishonored, and his influence overlooked. But I found there, as I had done in this country, a great want of discrimination in regard to the *manner* of his influence.** Consequently I found it frequently necessary to call the attention of the people to the work in which the Holy Spirit **was** really engaged, to explain to them the express teachings of Christ

JHF 396 upon this subject; and thus to lead them to see that they ˡwere not to wait for a *physical* influence, but to give themselves up to his *persuasive* influence, and obey his *teachings*. This was the object of my discourse that evening. After I arrived at our quarters, a lady who was present at the meeting, and who came into the family where we ‹were guests›,[60] remarked that she observed **the** Unitarian minister present in the congregation.[61] I remarked that that must

MS 837 have sounded strangely in the ears of a Unitarian. ˡ‹She[62] replied she hoped it would do him good. Not long after this **&** when I was laboring in London I rec[**eive**]d a letter from this minister giving an account of the great change wrought in his religious experience by means of that sermon. **I copy** this letter **verbatim** as follows.[63]

"**Stratford upon Avon Warwickshire,** Aug. **16th** 1850.

Rev. **&** dear Sir. Learning from the Banner that you are about to take your

[60] Here Finney changed the word "lodged" to "were guests." The Finneys were staying with a Mr. and Mrs. W. Phillips in Balsall Heath, about two miles out of the center of Birmingham. See "Mr. Finney in England," *The Independent,* 4 April 1850, p. 55; and W. Phillips to Finney, 10 April 1850, Finney Papers, microfilm, roll 4.

[61] Finney implies that the minister referred to was Priestly's successor at the New Meeting-house, but this was another Unitarian minister, James Cranbrook (see n. 81 below). Fairchild altered the phrase "the Unitarian minister" to "a Unitarian minister."

[62] MS 837 is the first of eight pages in Finney's handwriting. These pages replace the original pages 819–24.

[63] This letter is in the Finney Papers (microfilm, roll 4). In transcribing the letter, Finney made a number of changes. The more important ones are indicated in the footnotes. Fairchild made additional changes. The original letter is paragraphed by indenting on a new line. Although Finney did not insert the letter *P* to indicate new paragraphs in his transcription, he followed the paragraphing of the original letter in some places by starting a paragraph on a new line but without indenting. In other places he ignored the paragraphing or started a sentence on a new line where there is no new paragraph in the original. Where Finney's paragraphing corresponds with the original, the paragraphing has been retained here. It is interesting to note that Mrs. Finney also copied the whole of the letter soon after it was received and sent it to her sister in America (E. Finney to H. Bissell, 16 August 1850, Finney Papers, microfilm, roll 4).

departure from England I feel it would be somewhat ungrateful if I allow you to go without expressing the obligation I am conscious of being under to you for the benefit I received[64] from a sermon of yours preached in Steel house Lane Birmingham. I think it was the last sermon you preached **there, &** was on resisting the Holy Spirit, but I have never been able to find the text. Indeed in the interest of the points that most concerned me I thought no more about the text for two or three days after. In order that you may understand the benefit I received from the sermon it is necessary that I should recount briefly[65] my peculiar position at the time.

I was educated at one of our dissenting colleges for the ministry among the independents. I entered upon the ministry & continued to exercise it about seven years. During that time I gradually underwent a great change in[66] my theological views. The change was produced, I think, partly by philosophical speculations & partly in the deterioration that had taken place in my spiritual condition. ˡI would say with deepest sorrow my piety never recovered the tone it lost in my passage through college. I attribute all my sorˡrows principally to this. My speculations led me without ever having **even** read Dr. Williams' **B**ook on **D**ivine **S**overeignty & **E**quity to adopt fundamentally his views.[67] The reading of his book fully perfected my system.[68] Sin is a *defect* arising out of the *necessary defectability* of a creature when unsupplied with the grace of God. The fall of man[69] therefore, expresses nothing but the inevitably original imperfection of the human race. The great end of God's moral government is to correct this imperfection by education revellation[70] &c &c, & to ultimately perfect mans condition.[71] I had already & long previously adopted Dr. Jenkyns views of Spiritual influence.[72] Under the guidance of such principles you will understand without my explaining how sin became a mere misfortune temporarily permitted, or rather a necessary evil to be remedied by infinite wisdom & goodness. **H**ow eternal punishment became a[73] cruelty not for one moment to be thought of in the dispensations

MS 838
JHF 397

[64]In the original letter this word is "derived." The same error occurs a few lines later.

[65]This phrase is "revert briefly to" in the original letter.

[66]Finney had written "in" twice here. Fairchild crossed out the first one.

[67]Edward Williams, *An Essay on the Equity of Divine Government, and the Sovereignty of Divine Grace* (London: Burditt, 1809).

[68]The following section down to n. 71 in the original letter is in single quotation marks. It does not appear to be a quotation from Williams's book, although the ideas expressed and the language used are those of Williams.

[69]"The fall of man" is in double quotation marks in the original.

[70]The additional *l* in the word "revellation" is not in the original letter.

[71]This ends the section in quotation marks in the original.

[72]Thomas Williams Jenkyn (1794–1858), president of Coward College, obtained prominence among dissenters with the publication of his books on the Atonement and the Holy Spirit in 1837. They had a considerable influence in introducing what, in America, was the New School theology—a challenge to a limited atonement and to the Spirit's direct influence in conversion and sanctification. His book *On the Union of the Holy Spirit and the Church in Its Conversion of the World* (London: Snow, 1837) together with Finney's *Lectures* were having a great impact on thousands of the younger ministers. See *Christian Journal* (Glasgow), n.s., 7 (February 1844): 85–86; and Glyn Richards, "A History of the Theological Developments Among Nonconformists in Wales During the Nineteenth Century" (B.Litt. diss., Oxford University, 1956), p. 131. Jenkyn had been influenced in his doctrinal innovations by American theologians and, in particular, by N. S. S. Beman.

[73]Finney wrote "a" twice here.

of a good being—& how the atonement became a perfect absurdity founded upon unphilosophical views of sin. I became thoroughly Unitarian & in the beginning of the year 1848 I professed my Unitarianism & became minister
MS 839 of a church **in Birmingham**. ꜀The tendencies of my mind however were fortunately too logical for me long to be able to rest in Unitarianism. I pushed my conclusions to simple deism & then found they must go still further. For this I was not prepared. My whole soul started back in horror. I reviewed my principles. A revolution took place in my whole system of philosophy. The doctrine of responsibility was restored to me in its most strict & literal sense, & with it a deep consciousness of sin. I need not enter into minute details with reference to my struggles & mental sufferings. About two weeks[74] before I hea[**r**]d you I saw clearly I must some day or the other readopt the evangelical system. I never had doubted it was the system of the bible. I
JHF 398 became Unitarian upon purely rationalistic grounds. But ꜀now I found I must accept the bible or perish in darkness. You may imagine the agonies of spirit I had to endure. On the one hand were convictions becoming stronger every day, the sense of sin & the need of Christ obtaining a firmer hold over my heart—& the miserable condition of withholding the truth I knew from the
MS 840 people looking up to me for instruction. ꜀On the other hand if I professed myself, I, instantly, in the sight of all parties (especially with that great majority having no sympathy with such struggles) ruined my character by my apparent fickleness, & **through**[75] myself, my wife & children **(we were looking forward to the birth of the sixth)** upon the world. I could not make up my mind to this alternative. I had resolved to wait—gradually to prepare peoples minds for the change—& by exercising a more rigid economy for some months to make provision for our temporal wants during the period of transition. In this state of mind I heard your sermon. You will recollect it & easily comprehend the effect it produced. I felt the truth of your arguments—Your appeals came home irresistably to my heart—& that night on my way home I vowed before God, come what would I would at once consecrate myself afresh to that Saviour whose blood I had so recently learned to value, & whose value[76] I had done so much to dishonor. The result is through the kind influence of Mr. **James** I have lately become the minister
MS 841 of the church in this town. The peace of mind I now ꜀enjoy does indeed surpass all[77] understanding. I never before found such an absorbing pleasure in the work of the ministry. I enter fully into the significance of what Paul says, "If any man be in Christ **Jesus** he is a new creature."[78] I can not tell you therefore with how many feelings of gratitude your name will[79] be associated in my soul. I bless God for the kind providence that brought you **to Birmingham**. It seems to me now more than probable had I not heard you my newly awakened religious life would soon have been destroyed by

[74] In the original letter this word is "months."

[75] The original letter has the word "threw." Fairchild corrected the manuscript.

[76] The original letter has the word "name."

[77] Finney had written "all" twice. Fairchild crossed out the first one.

[78] 2 Corinthians 5:17. The original letter has the word "creation." The quotation marks are not in the original.

[79] The original letter adds the word "henceforth" after "will."

continued resistance to my deep convictions. My conscience would again have become hard|ened—& I should have died in my sins. Through the grace of God I shall trace up to you any usefulness God may hereafter crown my labors with. JHF 399

I should have told you all this before but I thought my history might then in some way become publick & that I shrink from all idea of. Your return to America guards me from this & I feel it would be unjust to withhold from |you[80] the knowledge of this fruit of your labors. MS 842

May God of his infinite mercy & grace grant you a long life of even greater usefulness than He has yet blessed you with will be the constant prayer of Dear Sir,

Yours very truly,

James Cranbrook."[81]

When I rec**[eive]**d this letter I was laboring with Rev. John Campbell **D.D.** in the old Tabernacle of Whitfield in London.[82] I handed it to him to read. He read it over with manifestly deep emotion & then exclaimed "There! that is worth coming to England for."

I have said that at the time of my short stay in Birmingham the minist[e]rs of the dissenting churches were not prepared to commit themselves to the work of promoting a general revival of religion which should morally renovate the whole city as we have seen revivals sweep through & renovate our American Towns & Cities from time to time. I must mention the reason. When the report of our great revivals from 1825 & onward reached England Scotland & Wales, a Spirit of enquiry was[83] awakened & when my Lectures on revivals were published they were soon Stereotyped in England, & soon after translated into the Welch & French languages. As I was soon |informed by letters the publication & circulation of those lectures almost immediately inauger-ated a revival movement in that country.[84] I have said that Rev. John MS 843

[80] Fairchild added the figure "–4" after page number 842 to indicate to the printers to proceed to page 845, omitting the pages in between.

[81] James Cranbrook (c. 1817–1869) was trained as an Independent minister at Highbury College from 1836 to 1840 and was minister of Congregational churches in Suffolk, Cambridgeshire, and Dublin before becoming the Unitarian minister at Newhall Hill, Birmingham, in 1848. After leaving Stratford-on-Avon in 1851, he went to Liscard in Cheshire and then to Edinburgh in 1865. In 1867 he caused a stir by openly advocating positivism and resigning from the Congregational church. He carried on lecturing and published his views until his death in 1869. See George E. Evans, *Midland Churches: A History of the Congregations on the Roll of the Midland Christian Union* (Dudley: "Herald" Printing Works, 1899), pp. 63–67; and John Waddington, *Congregational History,* vol. 5, *1850–1880* (London: Longman Green, 1880), pp. 518–22.

[82] John Campbell (1795–1867) was one of the most prominent London Congregational ministers, best known for his aggressive and controversial religious journalism. He moved from Scotland to London in 1829, where he was at the Tabernacle in Moorfields. After 1848 his health caused him to give up preaching, and he devoted his time increasingly to writing and editorial work (Robert Ferguson and A. Morton Brown, *Life and Labours of John Campbell, D.D.* [London: Bentley, 1867]; and *DNB*). Finney spelled the name "Whitefield" without the first *e* as Matson also did in MS 848 and 849.

[83] Finney had written "was" twice. Fairchild crossed out the first one before crossing the whole paragraph out to the bottom of the page.

[84] Letters to Finney from Congregational ministers in Wales and in Yorkshire, England, told of the revival movement and of the influence of Finney's *Revival Lectures*. Finney also received

Angel James one of the most influential of the dissenting Ministers wrote a commendatory preface to those lectures.[85] But as soon as the opposers of the revivals in this country learned of the influence those lectures were producing in England the[y] took steps to counteract their influence. They assured Mr James that those revivals in this country of which those lectures were the outcome had turned out disasterously to the Churches, & made such representations as to induce Mr James to recall his commendation of the lectures. Some of the opposers from this country, Mr Nettleton amongst others visited England & Scotland it would seem for the purpose of counteracting the influence of those lectures.[86] Their testimony regarding the revivals in[87] this country that were connected with my labors was such as to frighten the good brethren on that side of the ocean out of the revival movement that had been so hopefully inaugerated.[88] Thousands had in the mean

information from William Dawes and John Keep, who went to England from Oberlin in 1839–1840. See James Griffiths to Finney, 13 July 1840; and Congregational Ministers of North Wales to Finney, 27 February 1840, Finney Papers, microfilm, roll 4; and p. 376 n. 84 (MS 666); W[illiam] L[amb], J[ohn] M[orris], and E[dward] H[enry] W[eeks] to Finney, March 1845, *OE,* 18 June 1845, pp. 102–3; W. Dawes and J. Keep to Finney, dated 25 November 1840 in the calendar of the Finney Papers, microfilm, roll 4; and Anna Hill to Lydia Finney, 24 August 1840, typescript transcript in the Robert S. Fletcher Papers, file 30/24, box 5, Oberlin College Archives.

[85] See MS 825.

[86] James had written to Finney:

> The publication in this country, of your volume of sermons on Revivals produced on many minds at first a very strong excitement. It was extensively read by a certain class—and was on some accounts admired. . . . But it was by others, and even by some who first admired it, soon thought to be defective in evangelical unction, and somewhat contradictory on the subject of divine spiritual influence. . . . Soon after this Mr Nettleton and others of that school of theology were in this kingdom and your works were still more in disfavour (James to Finney, 29 January 1850, Finney Papers, microfilm, roll 4).

Nettleton had been in England from the spring of 1831 until August 1832, before Finney had given his lectures. He had, however, sought to counteract the prejudices that had arisen against American revivals by dissociating himself from the practice of the "anxious seat" and the excesses of the New Measures revivals, which he found had been widely reported. See Bennet Tyler, *Memoir of the Life and Character of Rev. Asahel Nettleton, D.D.*, 2d ed. (Hartford, Conn.: Robins and Smith, 1845), pp. 190–93.

[87] Finney had written the word "in" twice.

[88] William Lamb, the Congregational minister in Wakefield, Yorkshire, wrote to Finney in March 1845:

> Your works (especially that on Revivals) have had a vast influence upon all sections of the Christian church. You would perhaps meet with more condemnatory reviews &c. than commendatory. J[ames] of B[irmingham], who wrote an introductory essay to it, and whose name did more to give it notoriety than all beside, about twelve months ago, declared publicly at the Congregational Union that he was sorry he ever lent it the sanction of his name and should for the future caution his brethren against many of the sentiments it contained. Indeed there are very few who would sail in the same boat with Finney, but I am confident that book has made a broader and deeper impression upon the cause of Christ in these realms than any volume that has been published within the memory of man. Whilst most of the ministerial brotherhood have much to say by way of caution and little in commendation yet I can assure you that the little leaven is rapidly leavening the whole lump. Our periodical literature (sacred of course) is wonderfully transformed. Revivals, the prayer of faith, being filled with the Spirit, &c. are now topics upon which all have much to say, those who have most condemned your publications are considerably modified thereby (*OE,* 18 June 1845, p. 102).

time been converted. Before I visited that country the revival effort had ceased & the brethren were under the impression that those great ¦**& glorious revivals in this country had been rather a curse than a blessing to the churches.**[89] MS 844

I had left New York city & come to Oberlin. They heard no more of me through my lectures reported for the N. York Evangelist, & finally it had been reported in that country that I had become a heretic & then an infidel. These things I learned with amazement when I arrived in England in 1848.[90] **I do not know how extensively these reports of heresy & infidelity were believed in England, but the reports of the evil results of those revivals in this country had been wide spread & generally credited in that country. Hence the trepidation & fear that possessed the minds of the best men in Europe in regard to committing themselves to far reaching efforts to promote a general revival of religion in England in connection with my labors. I did the best I could under the circumstances & have no doubt of the integrity of the brethren on that side who hesitated to embark with me in an effort on a large scale to promote a wide-spread & thorough revival throughout protestant Europe. I have never doubted that had it not been for the misrepresentations from opposers on this side of the Atlantic a most sweeping far reaching & powerful revival would at that time have swept not only over Birmingham, but also over all England Wales and Scotland.›**

¦From[91] Birmingham I went to Worcester, I think about the middle of March, to labor with Dr Redford.[92] I have said that he had my Systematic Theology, **had read it through,** and had written to me that he wished to have some conversation with me on certain points. I had **taken** with me **from home** my reply to the criticisms **of Dr Hodge of Princeton, and also my reply to Dr Duffield; and my reply to the presbytery of Troy was, I think, at that time embodied in the work itself.**[93] **I handed Dr Redford, on my arrival, the pamphlets containing these replies.** He read them MS 845

See also John Jefferson, ed., *Christian Life, and Living by Faith, Exemplified in the Experience, Labours, and Letters of the Late William Lamb, Minister of the Gospel, Wakefield*, 2d ed. (London: Morgan and Chase, 1866), pp. 5, 275.

[89] When Lewis Tappan was in England in 1843 he found that John Angell James "had some prejudices against Oberlin and against Mr. Finney." Tappan gave James facts about Finney's preaching and some account of the 1842 Rochester revival, which he "thought was the best to disarm it." See Tappan, "Journal," 15 July 1843, p. 70; and 17 July 1843, p. 73, Tappan Papers, microfilm, roll 1; and *OE,* 27 September 1843, p. 155.

[90] Finney wrote the date "1848," but the final *8* was crossed out and replaced in pencil with the number 9. This may have been done by Fairchild. Finney had arrived in England in November 1849. See MS 816.

[91] Pages 845–49 were originally numbered 693–97 and renumbered 825–29 by Matson. Finney altered the numbers to 845–49.

[92] Finney went to Worcester, not to preach, but to rest at the home of John Hutchinson, "an old friend and spiritual child of Mr. Finneys," from New York. See MS 649. But as soon as he arrived there, "the request was made that he would commence a series of services at Dr Redfords chapel and in the Baptist chapel" (Elizabeth Finney to H. Bissell, 22 April 1850, Finney Papers, microfilm, roll 4). After a week's rest he commenced preaching.

[93] See pp. 404–5 nn. 92–96 (MS 703). The "Action of the Troy Presbytery" and Finney's reply are in *Lectures on Systematic Theology,* vol. 3 (Oberlin: Fitch, 1847), pp. 175–95.

through, and then called on me and said: "Those replies have cleared up all the questions on which I wished to converse; therefore I am fully satisfied that you are right." After that **he** in no instance, that I recollect, **ever** made a criticism upon any part of my theology. Those who have seen the English edition of that work, are aware that he wrote a preface to it, in which he commended it to the Christian public.[94] At the time I refer to, when he had read through my replies to those reviews, he expressed a strong desire that the work should be immediately published in England; and said that he thought the work was greatly needed there, and would do great good. His opinion had great weight ˡin England upon theological questions. Dr Campbell, I remember, affirmed in his newspaper that Dr Redford was the greatest theologian in Europe.[95] I remained in Worcester ˡseveral weeks and preached for Dr Redford, and also for a Baptist congregation in that city.[96] There were many very **interesting**[97] conversions **in that city**; and **for the time that I spent there** the work was **very powerful and** interesting indeed.[98]

MS 846

JHF 400

Some wealthy gentlemen in Worcester laid before me a proposition to this effect: They proposed to erect a movable tabernacle, or house of worship; one that could be taken down and transported from place to place upon the railway and at slight expense, **and** set up again with all its seats and all the **paraphernalia** of a house of worship. They proposed to build it one hundred and fifty feet square, with seats so constructed as to **hold** five or six thousand people. They said if I would consent to use it, and preach in it from place to place as circumstances might demand for six months, they would be at the expense of building it. But on consulting the ministers at that place they

[94] *Lectures on Systematic Theology*, ed. and rev., with an introduction by the Reverend George Redford (London: Tegg, 1851). Redford was asked by Finney to edit the volumes for the British edition. Redford's introduction was read by John Campbell during the farewell services for Finney at the Tabernacle. It appears in *Valedictory Services*; see Appendix, pp. 649–51).

[95] Campbell spoke of Redford in *The British Banner* as "one of the most competent men in England or in Europe," and as "a theologian second to none in these realms" (*The British Banner,* 4 September 1850, p. 602; and 2 April 1851, p. 219). Mrs. Finney wrote that Dr. Redford "is the great theologian among the Independents and of whom Dr Campbell says 'there is not a wiser man in all England' " (Elizabeth Finney to H. Bissell, 22 April 1850, Finney Papers, microfilm, roll 4).

[96] The Finneys were in Worcester from about the second week in March until 5 May 1850. See Elizabeth Finney to Angelina Atkinson and Julia Finney, 1 April 1850; and to H. Bissell, 22 April 1850, Finney Papers, microfilm, roll 4. Silver Street Baptist Church was under the pastoral charge of Rev. William Crowe, a Congregational missionary turned Baptist. See *The Baptist Magazine* 65 (January 1873): 27–28.

[97] The word "interesting" was not altered in the original, but the published version has "striking."

[98] Richard Joseland of Worcester sent Finney details of several interesting cases of conversion that had occurred and a copy of an article in the *Worcestershire Chronicle* on a case of restitution. See Joseland to Finney, 8 May 1850, Finney Papers, microfilm, roll 4; and *Worcestershire Chronicle* (Worcester), 8 May 1850, p. 4. Mrs. Finney's letters also described the effect of the preaching on all classes and on many people from the surrounding towns. There were so many at the inquiry meetings that the church had to be used and would be filled. "Dr Redford remarked he had never witnessed the like nor had he ever expected to witness such a scene" (E. Finney to H. Bissell, 13 May 1850; and 22 April 1850, Finney Papers, microfilm, roll 4). Henry Ward Beecher wrote of the work in Worcester: "The fruits were very great. Nor did the work cease upon Mr. F's departure, but continued for months under the labor of Dr. Redford" (*The Independent,* 21 November 1850, p. 190).

John Campbell. The Independent minister of Whitefield's Tabernacle and editor of *The British Banner* who supported Finney during his British tours. In Robert Ferguson and A. Morton Brown, *Life and Labours of John Campbell, D.D.* (London: Bentley, 1867), frontispiece. Courtesy The British Library.

advised me not to do it.[99] They thought it would be more useful |for me to occupy the pulpits in the already established congregations in different parts of England, than to go through England preaching in an independent way such as was proposed by those gentlemen. As I had reason to believe the ministers generally would disapprove of a course then so novel, I declined to pledge myself to occupy it. I have since thought that I probably made a mistake. For

MS 847

[99] In a letter dated 3 December 1850, Redford advised Finney not to take up the offer (Finney Papers, microfilm, roll 4). An undated copy of a letter in Redford's handwriting addressed to "Messrs Waters Williams & E. Evans Jnr." is in reply to their request for an "opinion upon the project of erecting a temporary place of worship with the view of engaging Mr Finney's services for a few months." The writers of the letter, whose initials only are copied, are "G[eorge] R[edford]," "W[illiam?] C[rowe?]," and "G. H." (perhaps Rev. George R. Hewlings, of Lady Huntingdon's Chapel, Bridport). After getting advice and discussing it, they came to the conclusion: "We do not think that it w[oul]d be desirable all things considered to carry the project into execution" (Anonymous Letters, no. 6, Finney Papers, microfilm, roll 6; and *Post Office Directory of Birmingham, with Staffordshire and Worcestershire* [London: Kelley, 1850], p. 500).

Whitefield's Tabernacle. This is the church in London where Finney preached for nine months during 1850 and 1851. In *The Home Missionary Magazine* (London) 8 (September 1827): opposite p. 281. Courtesy The British Library.

when I came to be acquainted with the congregations and places of public worship of the Independent churches, I found them generally so small, so badly ventilated, so **located, and so much in a straight-jacket in many respects**, so hedged in and circumscribed by *the Church*—I mean, of course, the ***established* Church**—that it has **always** since **I refused to accept that proposition** appeared to me doubtful whether I was right; as I have been of opinion that I could upon the whole have accomplished much greater good in England by **having** carried, as it were, my own place of worship with me—**have** gone where I pleased, and **secured** the **attendance** of the masses irrespective of denominations **altogether. I have no doubt that throngs** MS 848 **would have attended everywhere; greater than** ˡ**could possibly have got within such a building; and if** my strength were now as it was then, I should be strongly inclined to visit England again, and try an experiment of that kind.

JHF 401 Dr Redford was ˡgreatly affected by the work in Worcester; and at the May anniversaries in London he addressed the Congregational Union of England and Wales and gave a very interesting account of this work. ‹I attended those May meetings[100] **& was** about to **enter upon** labor with›[101] Dr John

[100]The Finneys left Worcester on 5 May and went to London, where Finney attended the meetings on 7 May and spoke at the afternoon soiree for an hour on the subject of revivals. See *The Congregational Year Book* (London), 1850, pp. 26–27; and John Stevenson to Asa Mahan, 10 May 1850, in *OE,* 5 June 1850, p. 94. Mrs. Finney wrote:

Campbell ‹**who**›[102] was a successor of Whitfield, and was pastor of the church at the Tabernacle in Finsbury, London,[103] and also of the Totenham—court ‹Road› chapel.[104] These chapels **were** both in London, and about three miles apart. They were built for, and occupied for years **by, Mr. Whitfield**. Dr Campbell was also at that time editor of the British Banner, the Christian Witness, and[105] of one or two other **magazines**.[106] His voice was such that he did not preach, but gave his time to the editing of those papers. He lived in the **house** in which Whitfield resided, **which was the parsonage;** and used the same library, I believe, that Whitfield ˡhad used. Whitfield's portrait hung **up** in his study in the Tabernacle. The savor of his name was still there; yet I must say that the spirit that had been upon him was not very apparent in the church **at that place** at the time I went there. I said that Dr Campbell did not preach. He still held the pastorate, resided in the parsonage, and drew the salary; but he supplied his pulpit by employing for a few weeks at a time, the most popular ministers that could be employed, to preach to his people. I began my labors there early in May.[107] Those who are acquainted with the workings of such a constant change in the ministry as they had had at the Tabernacle **for years**, would not expect religion in the church to be in a flourishing condition.

MS 849

Dr Campbell's house of worship was **of course** large. It was compactly seated, and could accommodate full three thousand persons. A friend of mine

> Dr Redford took this occasion to tell of the gratification he had felt in listening to Mr Finney his confidence in his honesty and *orthodoxy*—the success attending his preaching—the faithful and clear presentation of truth—the effect upon the congregation and with great emotion said, he had witnessed such scenes in his own congregation as he had never expected to see, in the conviction and conversion of souls—indeed he had never believed it possible for any mans preaching to produce such an effect (E. Finney to H. Bissell, 13 May 1850, Finney Papers, microfilm, roll 4).

[101] This sentence up to this point was inserted by Finney.

[102] Finney inserted the word "who."

[103] The Tabernacle, Moorfields, in the Borough of Finsbury, was built for George Whitefield in 1753. It was eighty feet square. In 1869 it was pulled down to make way for a new church. See *The Christian Witness,* 4 (May 1847): 203–14; and *The Congregational Year Book,* 1870, p. 380. Matson had spelled the name "Whitefield" here and in the other places in this section as "Whitfield."

[104] The Tottenham Court Chapel on Tottenham Court Road had been built in 1756 for George Whitefield. It was under the superintendence of Campbell's assistant, Rev. John W. Richardson. In 1890 it was pulled down, its foundations having become unsafe, and a new chapel was built on the site. Figures for the seating capacity of the old chapel vary. One account written in 1832 states: "This chapel is believed to be the largest place of worship in the kingdom, not immediately connected with the established church. . . . This chapel will seat between 4,000 and 5,000 persons." But this number was probably too high. The *Survey of London* gives the seating capacity as between 3,000 and 4,000; however, 2,500 may be more realistic. See *The Christian's Penny Magazine* (London), 20 October 1832, p. 153; London County Council, *Survey of London* (London: London County Council, 1949), pp. 67–74; and *The British Baptist Reporter and Missionary Intelligencer,* n.s., 14 (April 1857): 125.

Matson had written, "Totenham road chapel" and changed it to "Totenham-court road chapel." Finney then crossed out "road" and inserted "Road."

[105] The word "and" appears twice here in the manuscript.

[106] *The British Banner* was a weekly paper, and *The Christian Witness* a monthly journal. He also edited a monthly, *The Christian's Penny Magazine.* In 1858 Campbell gave up the editorship of the *Banner,* for he had started his own paper, *The British Standard.* From 1859 he also edited another weekly paper, *The British Ensign.*

[107] Finney began preaching at the Tabernacle on Sunday, 12 May.

took particular pains to ascertain which would hold the greatest number of people, the Tabernacle in Moorfields or Finsbury, or the great Exeter Hall,[108] ‹of which every body has heard.[109] It was ascertained that the Tabernacle would seat some hundreds more than Exeter Hall›.[110]

[108]The section from here to the bottom of the page was added by Finney after he had pasted a strip of paper onto the top of the next page for the start of a new chapter.

[109]Exeter Hall was opened in 1831 for holding religious and philanthropic meetings. It was the center for the great annual meetings of the benevolent societies, and it served the same function as the Chatham Street Chapel and the Broadway Tabernacle in New York. See "Exeter Hall and Its Associates," *The Scottish Review* (Glasgow) 5 (July 1857): 225–35.

[110]Vernon J. Charlesworth, the Baptist writer, who heard Finney in 1859, wrote a review of the *Memoirs* in which he said:

> The memory does not always treasure a strictly accurate record of the past, and this accounts for some of the statistical errors which are apparent to the English reader; as, for instance, when he says the Old Tabernacle in Moorfields "would hold several hundreds more than the great Exeter Hall" (*The Sword and the Trowel,* 12 [1876]: 213).

No accurate figures for the seating capacities are known, and estimates vary. The Exeter Hall was said to be "capable of containing with comfort from 3000 to 4000 persons." Whitefield's Tabernacle was said to have seating capacity for "about 4000 persons," but Finney's figure of "more than three thousand" (MS 863) is probably more accurate. See "Exeter Hall," *The Home Missionary Magazine* (London) 16 (June 1835): 246; Leonard W. Cowie, "Exeter Hall," *History Today* 18 (1968): 390–97; and A. G. L. Howland, "The Tabernacle in Moorfields: A Brief History," *The Tabernacle in Moorfields* (1909), p. 10.

William E. Lincoln, a student at the London University who participated in the meetings at the Tabernacle and who had read Finney's *Memoirs*, wrote: "Finney spoke in Exeter Hall and failed; he could not speak where the cheers and clappings and hear, hear of an English audience were let loose. In the pulpit, first of Borough Road chapel, and afterward in Whitfield's pulpit, he drew the attention of all England" (W. E. Lincoln, "A Reminiscence of Finney and Mahan," *The Oberlin News*, 23 February 1910, p. 2).

MS 850
JHF 402

CHAPTER XXX

‹*Labors in the Tabernacle, Moor Fields, London.*›

‹I[1] had accepted Dr. Campbells cordial invitation to supply his pulpit for a time[2] & accordingly›[3] After the May meetings **were over** I put in in earnest for a revival; though I said no such thing to Dr Campbell, or anybody else, for some weeks. I preached a course of sermons designed to convict the people of sin as deeply and as universally as possible.[4] I saw from Sabbath to Sabbath, and from evening to evening, that the Word was taking great effect. On Sabbath day I preached morning and evening; and I also preached on Tuesday, Wednesday, Thursday, and Friday evenings.[5] On Monday evening

[1]Pages 850–59 were originally numbered 698–707 and renumbered 830–39 by Matson. They were changed to 850–59 by Finney. The chapter heading and first two lines down to n. 3 are in Finney's handwriting on a separate piece of paper pasted onto the top of the sheet, obscuring the previous page numbers and a section of the text. The covered up section reads: "of which everybody has heard. He measured them both, and ascertained that the Tabernacle would seat a considerably larger number." The text continued below the pasted sheet: "than Exeter Hall. This measurement was made because it was desired to get the largest place that could be found in London at that time for preaching." Finney crossed out these words.

[2]Campbell's invitation to Finney is in a letter dated 28 March 1850, Finney Papers, microfilm, roll 4.

[3]This ends the section in Finney's handwriting. Matson wrote the next word, "After," with a capital, indicating the start of a new sentence. Finney did not alter it.

[4]A number of Finney's lectures and sermons delivered while he was in London from 12 May 1850 until his farewell sermon on 2 April 1851 were published. Finney had suggested to Campbell before he went to London that arrangements should be made for reporting his sermons and publishing them (see Campbell to Finney, 16 April 1850, Finney Papers, microfilm, roll 4). Forty-two were taken down by a stenographer, and they appeared in *The Penny Pulpit* weekly tract series, published by James Paul of London, between May 1850 and June 1853. Twenty-two of these were subsequently gathered together and reissued in book form by James Paul in about 1851 under the title *Sermons on Important Subjects*. Another thirty of Finney's sermons were listed as "preparing for publication in *The Penny Pulpit*" but never appeared. See *The Penny Pulpit* (London) 1,683 (April 1851): 168.

Another sermon preached in December 1850 at the Tabernacle was published in *The Christian News* (Glasgow), 3 July 1851, p. 74; and a sermon preached in January 1851 was edited by John Campbell and published by John Snow of London in 1851 under the title *Repentance: Its Nature, Grounds, Necessity, and Infinite Importance*. A number of these sermons were copied and reviewed in the religious press at the time.

[5]W. E. Lincoln wrote:

> When Finney went to Whitfield's chapel the congregation was small. I got Dr. Campbell to get cards printed. Finney thus headed them, "Life, Death, Heaven and Hell," with the place and times of service noted. Four of us, students and school teachers, distributed them through the surrounding houses. They came to hear (Lincoln, "A Reminiscence of Finney and Mahan," *The Oberlin News*, 23 February 1910, p. 2).

we had a general prayer meeting in the Tabernacle. At each of those meetings MS 851 I addressed **them** on the subject of prayer.[6] |‹Our congregations› [**were**][7] very large; and always on Sabbath and Sabbath evenings the house was crowded **to its utmost capacity**.

Religion had so declined throughout London at that time, that very few weekly sermons were preached; and I recollect that Dr Campbell said to me once, that he believed I preached to more people *during the week evenings* than all the rest of the ministers in London together. I have said that Dr Campbell had the salary belonging to the pastor in his congregation. But this salary he did not use for himself, at least more than a part of it; because he supplied the pulpit at his own expense, **and** performed such parochial duties as it was possible for him to perform under such a pressure of editorial labors. I found Dr Campbell to be an earnest, but a very belligerent man. He was always JHF 403 given to controversy. To use an American |expression, he was given to "pitching into" everybody and everything that did not **comport** with his views **of things.** In this way he did a great deal of good; and occasionally, I fear**ed**, MS 852 |**a good deal of** harm. After preaching for several weeks in the manner that I have described, I knew that it was time to call for inquirers. But Dr Campbell, I perceived, had no such idea in his mind. Indeed he had not sat where he could witness what was going on in the congregation as I could from the pulpit; and if he had done, he probably would not have understood it. They **have a** practice in that church **of** hold**ing** a **C**ommunion service every alternate Sabbath evening. On these occasions they would have a short sermon, then dismiss the congregation; and all would retire except those that had tickets for the **C**ommunion service, who would remain while that ordinance was celebrated.

On the Sabbath morning to which I have referred[8] I said to Dr Campbell: "You have a **C**ommunion service to-night, and I must have a meeting of inquiry **in the meantime**.[9] Have you any room anywhere on the premises to which I can invite inquirers after preaching?" He hesitated, and expressed MS 853 |doubts whether there were any that would attend such a meeting as that. However, as I pressed the **thing** upon him he replied: "Yes, there is the infant school room, to which you might invite them." I inquired how many persons it would accommodate. He replied, "From twenty to thirty, or perhaps forty."[10] "O," I said, "that is not half large enough. Have you not a

See also *The British Banner* (London), 5 June 1850, p. 381; and 26 March 1851, p. 211; reprinted in the Appendix, p. 643).

[6] After this Matson had written down: "On Saturday evening I held a meeting of inquiry every week. Our congregations were." Finney crossed it out.

[7] Finney added the words "Our congregations" after crossing them out on the previous page. He failed to insert the word "were," but Fairchild added it in the manuscript.

[8] This was 2 June, Finney's fourth Sunday at the Tabernacle. See Elizabeth Finney to her sister, Henrietta Bissell, 16 August 1850, Finney Papers, microfilm, roll 4.

[9] The words "in the meantime" were not altered in the manuscript but were changed to "at the same time" in the published edition.

[10] The Tabernacle had a comprehensive system of schools related to its work. The Infant School, for children from ages two to seven, was started by Campbell in October 1841,; and by 1847 it had about 130 infants "taught upon the Home and Colonial School system." The Infant School room, which had been occupied by the old Charity School, was alongside the church. See *The Christian Witness* (London) 4 (May 1847): 207.

larger room?" At this he expressed astonishment; and inquired if I thought that there was interest enough in the congregation to warrant any such invitation as I had intended to give. I told him there were *hundreds* of inquirers in the congregation. But at this he laughed, and said it was impossible. I asked him if he had not a larger room. "Why yes," he said, "there is ‹the British school› room.[11] But that will hold fifteen or sixteen hundred; of course you don't want that."[12] "Yes," said I, ¦"that is the very room. Where is it?" "O," said he, "surely you will not venture to appoint a meeting there. Not half as many would attend, I presume, as could get into the ¦infant school-room." Said he, "Mr. Finney, remember you are in England, and in London;—and that you are not acquainted with our people. You might get people to attend such a meeting, under such a call as you propose to make, in America; but you will not get people to attend here. Remember that our evening service is out before the sun is down at this time of year. And do you suppose that in the midst of London, under an invitation to those that are seeking the salvation of their souls and are anxious on that subject, that they will single themselves out right in the day time, and under such a call as that, publicly given, to attend such a meeting as that?" I replied to him: "Dr Campbell, I know what the state of the people is better than you do. The Gospel is as well adapted to the English people as to the American people; and I have no fears at all that the pride of the people will prevent their responding to such a call, any more than **that of** the people in America." JHF 404 MS 854

I insisted on having him tell me where that room was; and so to specify it that I could point it out to the people, and make the appeal that I intended to make. ¦After a good deal of discussion the **D**octor reluctantly consented; but told me expressly that I must take the responsibility on myself, that he would not share it. I replied that I expected to take the responsibility, and was prepared to do so. He then gave me particular directions about **the location of** the place, which was but a little distance from the Tabernacle. The people had to pass up Cowper st. toward **c**ity road a few rods, and turn through a narrow passage to the British school room building. We then went to meeting; and I preached in the morning, and again at evening,—that is, **I think** at six **O**'clock, if I recollect the hour. I preached a short sermon, and then informed the people what I desired. I called upon all who were anxious for their souls, and who were then disposed immediately to ¦make their peace with God, to attend a meeting for instruction adapted to their state of mind. I was very particular in regard to the class of persons invited. I said: "Professors of religion are not invited to attend this meeting. There is to be a Communion service here; let them remain here. ¦*Careless* sinners are not invited to this MS 855 JHF 405 MS 856

[11] Matson had written down, "a large room," but Finney changed it to "the British school room."

[12] British schools were at this time an important educational institution in the country. By the time of the 1851 census they were probably educating "upwards of 200,000" children. They were church-related schools under the auspices of the British and Foreign School Society. This particular school, largely supported by the Tabernacle church and congregation, was built in 1841 and by 1847 had about 850 scholars. According to Campbell, "the British Institution Room" was "an edifice into which, sitting and standing, from 1,000 to 1,200 people may be pressed." See *The Educational Record* (London) 2 (July 1854): 205–6; *The Christian Witness* 4 (May 1847): 206–7; and *The British Banner,* 28 August 1850, p. 580. See also p. 481 n. 17 (MS 818).

meeting. Those, and those only, are expected to attend who are not Christians; but who are anxious for the salvation of their souls, and wish instruction given them directly upon the question of their present duty to God." This I repeated **over** so as not to be misunderstood. Dr Campbell listened with great attention; and I presume he expected, since I had restricted my appeal to such a class, that very few, if any, would attend. I was determined not to have the mass of the people go into that room; and furthermore that those who did go, should go with the express understanding that they were inquiring sinners. I was particular on this point; not only for the sake of the *results* of the meeting, but to convince Dr Campbell that his view of the subject was a mistaken one. I felt entirely confident that there was a great amount of conviction in the congregation, and that hundreds were prepared to respond to such a call at once. I was perfectly confident that I was not premature in making such a call. I therefore proceeded very particularly MS 857 to point out the class of persons whom ǀI wished to attend, **and the place where,** and the manner in which they would find **it**. I then dismissed the meeting, and the congregation retired.

Dr Campbell nervously and anxiously looked out of the window to see which way the congregation went; and to his great astonishment Cowper st. was perfectly cr**amm**ed with people, **sidewalks and all,** pressing up to get into the British school-room. I passed out, and went up with the crowd, and waited at the entrance till the multitude went in. When I entered I found the room packed. Dr Campbell's impression was, that there were not less than JHF 406 fifteen or sixteen hundred ǀpresent.[13] It was a large room, seated with forms or benches, such as are often used in school-rooms. There was near the entrance a platform on which the speakers stood whenever they had public meetings, which was of frequent occurrence. I soon discovered that the congregation were pressed with conviction in such a manner that great care needed to be taken to prevent an explosion of irrepressible feeling. It was but MS 858 a very short time before Dr Campbell came in himself. Observing ǀsuch a crowd gather he was full of anxiety to be present; and consequently **pressed** through with his **C**ommunion services **in as few moments as possible**, and came into the meeting of inquiry. He looked amazed at the crowd present, and especially at the amount of feeling manifested. I addressed them for a short time on the question of immediate duty; and endeavored, as I always do, to make them understand that God required of them ***now* and *here*** to **submit** themselves[14] entirely to **H**is will, to ground their weapons of rebellion, make their submission to **H**im as their rightful Sovereign, and accept Jesus as their only Redeemer.

I had been in England long enough to feel the necessity of being very particular in giving them such instructions as would do away their idea of *waiting God's time*. London is, and long has been, cursed with hyper-**C**alvinistic preaching. I therefore aimed my remarks at the subversion of

[13] Campbell gave the figure as seven or eight hundred in his report of the meeting in *The British Banner*, 5 June 1850, p. 381. Elizabeth Finney estimated one thousand in a letter to her sister, 16 August 1850, Finney Papers, microfilm, roll 4.

[14] The published edition reads, "required of them then to yield themselves." Fairchild had not altered the word "*now*" in the manuscript.

those ideas in which I supposed many of them had been educated; for but few persons present, I supposed, belonged properly to Dr Campbell's ˡcongregation. Indeed, he had himself told me that the congregation which he saw from day to day was new to him,—that the masses who were thronging there were as much unknown to him as they were to me. I tried therefore in my instructions to guard them on the one hand against hyper-Calvinism, and on the other against that low Arminianism in which I supposed many of them had been educated. I then, after I had laid the Gospel net thoroughly around them, prepared to draw it ashore. As I was about to ask ˡthem to kneel down and commit themselves entirely and forever to Christ, a man cried out in the midst of the congregation, in the greatest distress of mind, that he had sinned away his day of grace. I saw that there was danger of an uproar, and I hushed it down as best I could, and called on the people to kneel down; but to keep so quiet, if possible, that they could hear every word of the prayer that I was about to offer. They did by a manifest effort keep so still as to hear what was said, although there was a great sobbing and weeping in every part of the house.

MS 859

JHF 407

ˡI[15] then dismissed the meeting. After this I held similar meetings, with similar results, frequently on Sabbath evening, while I remained with that congregation, which was in all nine months.[16] The interest rose and extended so far that the inquirers could not be accommodated in that large British school room; and frequently when I saw that the impression on the congregation was very general and deep, after giving them suitable instructions and bringing them face to face with the question of unqualified and present surrender of all to Christ, I would call on those that were prepared in mind to do this to stand up in their places while we offered them to God in prayer. The aisles in that house were so narrow and so packed, that it was impossible to use what **was** called the anxious seat, or for people to move about at all in the congregation **only as they commenced at the door and went out.**

MS 860

Frequently when I made these calls for people to arise and offer themselves while we offered them in prayer, many hundreds would arise; and on some occasions, if the house seated as **the measurement to which I have referred affirmed it to do,** not less than two thousand people **have arisen** when an appeal was made. Indeed it would appear from the pulpit as if nearly the ˡwhole congregation arose. And yet **I would make such discriminations as would lead them to understand that** I did not call upon church-members, but simply upon inquirers to stand up and commit themselves to God.

MS 861

[15] MS 860 and the next four pages appear to have been inserted in the place of an original page 708. They were numbered 708–12 and renumbered 840–44 by Matson. Finney then changed them to 860–64.

[16] Henry Ward Beecher wrote:

> On two occasions we were present, when, at the close of Sabbath evening's service more than a thousand persons presented themselves in an adjoining hall, as inquirers. Nor have we ever witnessed in any place, more solemnity, order, and unexceptional propriety in the conduct of meetings, than has prevailed under Mr. Finney at the Tabernacle (*The Independent* [New York], 21 November 1850, p. 190).

In the midst of this work a circumstance occurred which will illustrate the JHF 408 extent of the religious interest connected |with that congregation at that time. **When I say as connected with that congregation, however, I do not mean those that *belonged* there; but those that attended our meetings from different parts of the city during this great revival.**[17] The circumstance to which I allude was this. The dissenters in England had been for a good while endeavoring to persuade the government **and the parliament** to have more respect in their action, than they were wont to do, to the dissenting interest in that country. But they had always been answered in a way that implied that the dissenting interest was small as compared with that of the Established church. So much had been said on this subject that the government determined to take measures to ascertain the relative strength of the two parties, that is of the dissenters and Church of England. On a certain Saturday night, without any previous warning or notice whatever that should MS 862 lead the people anywhere |to understand or even suspect the movement, a **request** was secretly sent to every place of worship in the kingdom, requesting that individuals should be selected to stand at the doors of all the churches, and chapels, and places of worship in the whole kingdom on the next Sabbath morning, to take the census of all that entered houses of worship of every denomination. Such a notice was sent to Dr Campbell; but I did not know it till afterwards. **But** in obedience to directions he placed men at every door of the Tabernacle, with instructions to count every person that went in during the morning service. This was done, as I understood, throughout the whole of Great Britain. In this way they ascertained the relative strength of the two parties; in other words, **they ascertained** which had the most worshippers on Sabbath, the dissenters or the established church. I believe this census proved that the dissenters were in a majority.[18] But however this may be, **the number that entered the Tabernacle was very great. This occurred not long before I left England; and not until I was there the second time**[19] **was I aware of the facts as connected with Dr Campbell's Tabernacle. He** told me that the men stationed at the doors of the Tabernacle reported **many** thousands more than could at any one time MS 863 get into the house. |**I forget how many, but I know the number was enormously great. It was common on the Sabbath for great multitudes to throng around in the open space on the outside of the Tabernacle, and for as many as could to stand here and listen on the outside. But of the throng without people were constantly coming and going. Many would get within the doors, and either would not hear or were uncomfortable, and would go out again. None were counted except**

[17] Campbell wrote to Finney: "Your week-day Congregations were generally, at least two thirds, and, I believe, three fourths, entire strangers; so that while the speaker was stationary, the Assembly was rotatory; you were in effect preaching to portions of a hundred churches" (Campbell to Finney, 22 October 1850, Finney Papers, microfilm, roll 4).

[18] The census was held on Sunday, 30 March 1851. The dissenters were not in fact in a majority, but the census showed them to be substantially stronger than had previously been thought. "The strength of the Dissenters was very roughly that of the Established Church." See W. S. F. Pickering, "The 1851 Religious Census—a Useless Experiment?" *The British Journal of Sociology* 18 (1967): 394.

[19] In 1859.

those that came ‹within›[20] **the door; and as I said, these numbered many thousands more than the Tabernacle could hold.**[21] **The fact is that** the interest **at that time** was so great, **that had there been** a place of worship that would hold **twenty or even forty** thousand, **I have no doubt but that it** would have been just as full as the Tabernacle **that held somewhat more than three thousand.**

I mention this to give some little idea of the manner in which the work extended. |Where they all came **from** Dr Campbell did not know, and no one could tell; but that hundreds and thousands of them were converted, there is no reason to doubt. Indeed I saw and conversed with vast numbers, and labored in this way to the full |**extent** of my strength.

JHF 409

MS 864

On Saturday evening inquirers and converts would come to the study for conversation. Great numbers came every week, and conversions multiplied **beyond any possibility of keeping any account of them.** People came, as I learned, from every part of the city. Many people **have** walked several miles every Sabbath to attend **our** meetings. Soon I began to be accosted in the streets, **as I was** in different parts of the city, by people who knew me, and **who** had been greatly blessed in attending our meetings. **Thousands of persons knew *me* whom I had never seen, to know them.** Indeed the Word of God was blessed, greatly blessed in London at that time. **Dr Campbell was not himself personally popular with the people of London, and I was aware at the time that comparatively few of the converts would ever unite with his church. However, I believe about two hundred of them did join his church.**[22]

|One[23] day Dr Campbell requested me to go in and make a few remarks to the scholars in the British school room. I did so, and began by asking them what they proposed to do with their education, and dwelt upon their responsibility in that respect. I tried to show them how much good they might do, and how great a blessing their education would be to them and to the

MS 865

[20]Here Finney crossed out the word "in" and inserted "within."

[21]The audience "was carefully counted, both morning and evening, by two individuals at each entrance, who took each a separate account, afterwards comparing their computations. The attendance in the morning was 2,100, and in the evening, in round numbers, 3,200." These figures do not include Sunday school children who met elsewhere. The average attendance during the previous twelve months was given as 2,200. See "Census of Great Britain—1851," manuscript H.O.129, in Public Records Office, London; and Campbell, *Valedictory Services and Farewell Sermon of Professor Finney, with Critical Observation on his Preaching by John Campbell, D.D.* (London: Snow, 1851), p. 18; reprinted in the Appendix.

[22]By the end of August, Campbell reported, "far above a hundred individuals have offered themselves for the fellowship of the Church" (*The British Banner,* 28 August 1850, p. 580). The first admissions to the membership of the Tabernacle took place when the Finneys had left London the first time. Fifty-nine were admitted on 19 September and another fifty-three on 25 October. Campbell reckoned that "a goodly number of these, however, do not ascribe their conversion to his [Finney's] ministry, but most do their decision." He also reported, "Nor can I doubt that there are hundreds more the subjects of saving impressions, who have not yet come forward." See *The British Banner,* 25 September 1850, p. 651; and 30 October 1850, p. 738.

[23]MS 865, originally numbered 709, started with the words "did join his church." They were crossed out by Matson and written in at the end of the preceding page after he had inserted five new pages in place of the original page 708. This page and the next thirteen pages to 722 had to be renumbered 713–26. They were subsequently renumbered again by Matson 845–58 and then altered by Finney to 865–78.

world if they used it aright, and what a great curse it would be to them and to the world if they used it selfishly. The address was short; but that point was strongly urged upon them. Dr Campbell afterward remarked to me, that a goodly number—I forget now how many—had been received to the church who were at that time awakened and led to seek the salvation of their souls. He mentioned it as a remarkable fact, because, he said, he had no expectation that such a result would follow.[24] The fact is, that the ministers in England, as well as in this country, had lost sight, in a great measure, of the necessity of

MS 866 pressing *present obligation* home upon the consciences of the people. |"Why," said Dr Campbell when he told me of this, "I don't understand it. You did not say anything but what anybody else might have said just as well." "Yes," I

JHF 410 replied, "they *might* have said it; but *would* they |have said it? Would they have made as direct and pointed an appeal to the consciences of those young people as I did?" This is the difficulty. Ministers talk *about* sinners; and **they say** ***they*****, and** ***they*** **instead of** ***you*****. They address them in such a way as not to leave** the impression that God commands them *now* **and** ***here*** to repent; and thus they throw their ministry away. **People have sometimes called me crazy, because I addressed sinners as if I expected them** ***then*** **and** ***there*** **to become Christians. But if I believe the Gospel what else should I expect? ‹As I have before said, when›[25] I first began to preach my old pastor, Brother Gale, used to insist upon it that I would offend the people, and that they would not come to hear me. But he soon found out that the throngs that would continue to come were so great that no**

MS 867 house could hold them. |He then insisted that it would not wear, that the people would soon become disgusted and hardened and would not continue to attend my ministry. But this prediction as utterly failed as everything else that he used to urge upon me by way of objecting to my manner of preaching the Gospel. The fact is, ‹as I have said›[26] the education he had received at Princeton had totally unfitted him for the work of winning souls to Christ; and he had told me, soon after my conversion, that he did not know that he had ever been the instrument of converting a soul in his life. I did not wonder; for though a talented man, there was nothing in his mode of preaching until after the great change occurred in his mind of which I have spoken, that was calculated to convert anybody.[27] Indeed I **have** seldom heard a sermon that seemed to be constructed with the intention of bringing sinners at once face to face with their present duty to God. **Instead of this they have written essays, often, indeed, fine specimens of rhetoric and correct**

MS 868 **theology; but** you would scarcely get the idea from the sermons |that are heard either in this country or in England, that **the** ministers expected to be

[24]Dr. Campbell wrote to Finney in a letter about this address given on Whitmonday and of eight or nine who were converted as a result of it. See Campbell to Finney, 1 November 1850, Finney Papers, microfilm, roll 4.

[25]See MS 106. Finney added the words "As I have before said, when." These words replace the word "When" written by Matson and a paragraph sign inserted by Finney.

[26]Finney added the words "as I have said."

[27]See MS 107–9, 305–6.

instrumental in converting anybody in the house ‹**at that time.**›[28] **You would not get the idea that he expected it, or that he *intended* it.**

A fact was related to me **sometime** ago, that will illustrate what I have said. Two young men who were acquaintances, but had very different views of preaching the Gospel, were settled over congregations at no great distance from each other. One of them had a powerful revival in his congregation; the other had none. One was having continual accessions to his church, and the other none. **Meeting** one day, **the one** who had no accessions to his church inquired **what was** the cause of the difference between them; and asked if he might **not**[29] take one of his **brother's** sermons and preach it, and see if it had any different effect from his own. **It was consented to; and he took one of his neighbor's sermons, made himself familiar with the hand-writing,** and preached **it** to his people. It was a sermon, though written, yet constructed for the purpose of bringing sinners ꞁface to face with their duty to God. **He went on and preached it, and before he was through he observed several of his congregation in tears; and** at the close he saw that many were very much affected, and remained in their seats weeping. He there**upon**[30] made a profound apology; saying he hoped he had not hurt **any of** their feelings, for he did not intend it!

MS 869

When in London at this time, my own mind was greatly exercised in view of the moral desolation of that vast city. The**re were not** places of worship **enough** in the city as I learned, to accommodate **but** a small part of the inhabitants. But **while I was there** I was greatly interested in a movement that sprang up among the Episcoꞁpalians. Numbers of their ministers came in and attended our meetings. One of the rectors, a Mr. Allen, became very much engaged, and made up his mind that he would try to promote a revival in his own great parish.[31] As he afterwards informed me, he went around and established twenty prayer meetings in his parish at different ꞁpoints. He went to preaching with all his might directly to the people. The Lord greatly blessed his labors, and before I left **there** he informed me that not less than fifteen hundred persons had been hopefully converted in his parish.[32] Several

JHF 411

MS 870

[28] Finney added the words "at that time."

[29] Fairchild did not cross out the word "not" in the manuscript, but it does not appear in the published edition.

[30] The word "thereupon" was not changed in the manuscript, but the published edition has "therefore."

[31] Hugh Allen (1806–1877) was an Irishman and a graduate of Trinity College, Dublin. After ministering in Episcopal churches in the Isle of Man, Dublin, and the Manchester area, he went to St. Jude's Church, Whitechapel, in 1848. He was a powerful preacher and a radical Evangelical. In 1859 he gained notoriety through his clashes with the Tractarians that led to the famous riots in St. George's-in-the-East. That year he was appointed rector of St. George's the Martyr in Southwark. See Frederic Boase, *Modern English Biography,* vol. 1 (London: Cass, 1965), pp. 50–51; and *The Christian Cabinet* (London), 29 June 1859, p. 409. Information from the librarian, Church House, Westminster, London.

[32] Hugh Allen became one of the most popular Church of England preachers and built up one of the largest congregations in London. He cooperated with Nonconformists and was active in the temperance movement and the Christian Bond of Brotherhood. He also took a lead in promoting the special services that were organized for evangelism during the 1859 revival. See *The British Ensign* (London), 14 December 1859, p. 398; Joseph Johnson, *Popular Preachers of Our Time* (London: Cassell, Petter, and Galpin, 1864), pp. 270–76; and John Vine Hall, *The Author of "The Sinner's Friend": An Autobiography* (London: Nisbet, 1865), pp. 306, 311.

Elizabeth and Charles Finney. From a daguerreotype made in England in 1850. Courtesy Oberlin College Archives.

other Episcopal ministers got greatly stirred up and quickened in their souls, and went to holding protracted or continuous services. When I left London there were four or five different Episcopal churches that were holding daily meetings, and making efforts to promote a revival. In every instance, I believe, they were greatly blessed and refreshed. **Indeed the nine months' labors at that time performed in London, by the blessing of God made a mighty and lasting impression upon that city. It introduced new ideas into the minds of the people, thousands were awakened and converted, and multitudes of old professors stirred up and set to work.**[33] It was ten

[33] A reviewer of the *Memoirs* (probably Rev. Henry Allon) considered the results "greatly exaggerated." "Some of the details of alleged success at Moorfields, will, we suspect, be new to those who witnessed or participated in his labours" (*The British Quarterly Review* [London] 73 [April 1876]: 545). But reports at the time were enthusiastic. The London correspondent of *The Christian Journal* (Glasgow) wrote, "We doubt not that thousands will have cause to bless God throughout all eternity, that in his providence he permitted Mr. Finney to visit the Metropolis of England" (n.s., 2 [March 1851]: 137). Campbell himself wrote in a letter to a friend after Finney left:

years before I visited London again to labor; and **I found, as** I was told, that the work had never ceased; that it had been going on, and enlarging its borders, and ˡspreading in different directions. I found many of the converts, the second time I visited there, laboring in different parts of London in various ways, and with great success. **The results in Dr Campbell's congregation I shall have occasion to mention when I narrate the movements that occurred when I was there ten years afterwards.**[34] MS 871

I have said my mind was greatly exercised about the state of London. I was scarcely ever more drawn out in prayer for any city or place than I was for London. Sometimes when I prayed in public especially, it seemed, with the multitudes before me, as if I could not stop praying; and that the Spirit of prayer would almost draw me out of myself in pleadings for the people, and for the city at large. I had hardly more than arrived in England before I began to receive multitudes of invitations **to go** to preach for the purpose of taking up collections for different objects: to pay the pastor's salary, to help **them** pay for **their** chapel, or to raise money for the Sabbath School,—or for some object.[35] ˡ**It seemed as if the great idea of the people was to get great collections, and that this was the object in having me come to different parts of England;** and had I complied with their requests I could have done nothing else. But I declined to go in answer to any such call. I ˡtold them I had not come to England to get money for myself or for them. My object was *to win souls to Christ.*[36] **Consequently I did not spend my time in sight-** MS 872 JHF 412

The sensation he has produced is marvellous. . . . I have reason to believe that he has done great good, although much, very much less than from appearances the inexperienced may have been led to expect. Nothing is so deceptive as public preaching. . . . In his case, as in that of all other popular preachers, there is no proportion whatever between the appearance and the reality. The number of additions, however, which has resulted, has been large, and I trust the bulk of them will wear well (Robert Ferguson and A. Morton Brown, *Life and Labours of John Campbell, D.D.* [London: Bentley, 1867], pp. 430–31).

Joseph Adams later recollected: "In mighty London it must be something very extraordinary to create even a ripple of excitement; but this man, by the aid of the Spirit, produced a deep and widespread impression. His preaching drew immense crowds. . . . Thousands were converted as the result of his labors." Adams was converted through the meetings and witnessed the scene in the British schoolroom described in MS 855–59. He was later a student at Oberlin and boarded with the Finney family. See "Remarks of Rev. Joseph Adams," in *Reminiscences of Rev. Charles G. Finney* (Oberlin: Goodrich, 1876), p. 54.

[34] See MS 964. This sentence was not crossed out in the manuscript but was omitted in the published edition.

[35] A number of these letters are in the Finney Papers.

[36] The following appeared in *The British Banner*, in an article on Finney by John Campbell:

We cannot close without making a communication which may save much trouble to others as well as to Mr. Finney. He is continually assailed by applications to attend this meeting and that, to preach for this object and the other, in the city, and in the suburbs, and in the country. Of course, the answer in every case, is a negative. His hands at present are so full, and he is so borne down by the oppressive labours of the sphere he occupies, that any addition is out of the question. He has not come to England for the performance of multifarious labour, but for one special object from which nothing can detach him; and to that object he is giving himself with a uniformity, a devotion, and an energy, which leave neither time nor thought for anything else.

A fortnight back, Mr. Finney presented us with a written notice for the *Banner* to this effect, which, however, we withheld, deeming it better that the statement should come directly from ourselves (5 June 1850, p. 381).

seeing, or running here and there to attend to anything but the express business of winning souls to Christ.[37]

After I had preached for Dr Campbell **for** about four months and a half, I became very hoarse; and my wife's health also became much affected by the climate, and by our intense labors. And here I must commence more particularly a recital of what God did by her.

Up to this time she had attended and taken part only in **female** meetings; and those were so new a thing in England that she had done but little thus far

MS 873 in that way.[38] But while we were at Dr Campbell's a request was made ǀthat she **sh**ould attend a Tea-meeting—**which they are in the habit in England of having when they wish to get any particular class of persons together**—of poor women, without education and without religion. Such a meeting was called by some of the benevolent Christian gentlemen and ladies, and my wife was urgently requested to attend it. She consented, having no thought that gentlemen would remain in the meeting while she made her address. However, when she got there she found the place crowded; and in addition to the **females** a considerable number of gentlemen, who were greatly interested in the results of the meeting. She waited a little, expecting that they would retire. But as they remained, and expected her to take charge of the meeting, she arose, and I believe apologized for being called to speak in public, informing them that she had never been in the habit of doing so. She had then been my wife but a little more than a year, and had never been

MS 874 abroad with me to labor **for** revivals until we went to England. ǀShe made an address **to them** at this meeting, as she informed me after she came to our lodgings, of about three quarters of an hour **long**, and with very manifest good results. The poor women present seemed to be greatly moved and

[37] In fact, the first time the Finneys were in London, they "spent a day, two weeks since, in riding about London to visit its wonders." And there are other references to sightseeing in their correspondence and in Mrs. Finney's "Journal" kept during their second visit to Britain (Finney to Angelina Atkinson and Julia Finney, [? November 1849], supplement no. 23, Finney Papers, microfilm, roll 4). However, Henry Allon pointed out: "When he first visited London, to conduct services at Dr. Campbell's Tabernacle in Moorfields, he was never known to be curious about a single London attraction. We doubt whether he saw anything beyond the precincts of Finsbury and the way to it" (*The British Quarterly Review* 63 [April 1876]: 545). And Campbell himself remarked in the preface to the *Valedictory Services*: "He has left London with little more knowledge of it than he possessed on his arrival" (p. 4; see Appendix, p. 640).

[38] Mrs. Finney had addressed meetings for females on several occasions in Houghton and in the surrounding villages (see E. Finney to H. Bissell, 24 December 1849, Finney Papers, microfilm, roll 4). She also addressed meetings in Birmingham. She spoke to the Dorcasian Society there, an organization run by Cherry Street Methodist Church. An entry in the minute book of the society under the date 10 May 1850 reads:

> The dorcas meetings of the past Quarter had been favored by two visits from Mrs Finney, wife of the Rev C G Finney of Oberlin College America, her interesting conversation & deeply spiritual addresses made a powerful impression, & will long be remembered with feelings of great pleasure by the large number of Ladies who were privileged to be present on those occasions (Dorcasian Society Committee, "Minute Book, 1818–1861," manuscript in Central Hall Deposit, box 12, Birmingham Reference Library).

Mrs. Finney also held meetings with large crowds in Worcester. She wrote to her sister, "My Husband rejoices that I can make myself useful and so useful as not to be considered a mere apendage for his comfort" (E. Finney to H. Bissell, 13 May 1850; see also the letter from the deacons of Angel Street Church to Finney, 4 May 1850, Finney Papers, microfilm, roll 4).

interested; and when **my wife** had done speaking, some of the gentlemen present arose and expressed their great satisfaction at what they had heard. They said they had had prejudices against women speaking ˡin public; but they could see no objection to it under such circumstances, and they saw that it was manifestly calculated to do great good. They therefore requested her to attend other similar meetings, which she did. When she returned **to me** she told me what she had done, and said that she did not know but it would excite the prejudices of the people of England, and perhaps do more harm than good. I feared this myself, and so expressed myself to her. Yet I believe I did not advise her to keep still, and not attend any more such meetings; but after consider**ing it, ˡI on the other hand** encouraged it. From that time she became more and more accustomed, while we remained in England, to that kind of labor;[39] and after we returned home she continued to labor with her own sex **in connection with my labors** wherever we went **to labor for the promotion of revivals**. Upon this I shall have occasion to enlarge when I speak of the revivals in which she bore a very prominent **share in our labors**.

JHF 413

MS 875

There were a great number of most interesting cases of conversion in London at that time;[40] **of** almost all classes of society. I preached a great deal on confession and restitution; the results of which were truly wonderful. Almost every form of crime was thus searched out and confessed. Hundreds, and I believe thousands of pounds sterling were paid over to make restitution. **After I left London at this time Dr Campbell published a pamphlet or little book, in which he gave some account of my labors, and a copy of which I now possess; and ˡshould this which I am now writing ever be published, it might be interesting to insert at least extracts from this little book.**[41]

MS 876

But I said that both myself and wife became hoarse. Every one acquainted with London is aware that from early in November till the next March the city is very gloomy, **very damp, dark, smoky,** and has a miserable atmosphere either to breathe or to speak in.[42] We went there early in May. In

[39] She established a daily morning female prayer meeting at the Tabernacle about the middle of July 1850. It started with two people, and by mid-August there were usually twenty and sometimes as many as forty. In addition to presiding over that, she addressed meetings of mothers and other females there and in other places, "besides occasionally addressing Ragged and other schools, and Temperance Societies" (*The British Banner,* 2 April 1851, p. 219; and E. Finney to H. Bissell, 16 August 1850, Finney Papers, microfilm, roll 4).

[40] After this, Matson had written, "many males and females, and many." Above the word "males," written in small letters in pencil, was the word "men"; and above "females," the word "women" was written. These appear to have been inserted by Lewis Tappan. Finney crossed out the whole phrase.

[41] *Valedictory Services.* See Appendix. In addition to this pamphlet, much of which was first published in *The British Banner*, Campbell published other accounts of Finney's activities in the paper.

[42] Finney wrote back to Oberlin:

> Rain & smoke & dirt & the suffocating gases generated by millions of coal fires, & millions of human & of animal lungs, render the air quite unfit for respiration. . . . The utter & dangerous ignorance of men in *high places* of the laws of respiration & ventillation, of the nature & causes of atmospheric change, of the generation & effects of gases &c. &c. not only annoy me but absolutely endanger my life, & waste my strength (Finney to the Faculty of Oberlin College, 16 January 1851, Letters Received by Oberlin College, 1822–1866, microfilm, Oberlin College Archives).

September my friend Brown, **of whom I have spoken,** called on us **in London;** and seeing the state of health that we were both in, he said: "This will never do. You must go to France, or somewhere on the Continent where they cannot understand your language; for there is no rest for you in England as long as you are able to speak at all." After talking the matter over we concluded to take his advice, and go for a little while to France.[43] He handed me fifty pounds sterling to meet our expenses. We went to Paris, and various other places in |France. We sedulously avoided making any acquaintances, and kept ourselves as quiet |as possible. The influence of the change of climate upon my wife's health was very marked. She recovered her full tone of strength very rapidly. I gradually got over my hoarseness; and after an absence of about six weeks we returned to our labors in the Tabernacle, where we continued to labor till early in the next April we left for home.[44] I left England with great reluctance. But **circumstances had occurred here that** seemed to **render it necessary for the stability of our college** that I should return.[45] We had become greatly interested in the people of England, and desired very much to remain there and protract our labors. We sailed in a large packet ship, the Southampton from London.[46] On the day that we sailed a **great** multitude of people who had been interested in our labors, gathered upon the wharf. A great majority of them were young converts. The ship had to wait for the tide, **and to get all her emigrants on board;** and for several hours there was a vast crowd of people in the open space around the ship, |waiting to see us off. Tearing away **as we did** from such a multitude of loving hearts, completely overcame the strength of my wife. As soon as the ship was clear of the dock she retired to our state-room **with a violent headache, from which she did not recover for many hours.** I remained upon the deck and watched the waving of **their** handkerchiefs **and the holding up of their hats, and the various manifestations which they made,** until we were

JHF 414
MS 877
MS 878

[43]During his farewell sermon preached on Wednesday, 11 September, Finney complained of being very hoarse (*The Penny Pulpit* 1,581 [September–November 1850]: 45). Potto Brown had a longstanding connection through his milling business with the Darblay family of Corbeil, near Paris, and had been to France himself. See G. H. Pike, "Potto Brown, the Houghton Miller," *The British Workman* (London) 358 (October 1884): 231.

[44]The Finneys were in France for about two weeks at the end of September. They then went to Houghton for a month and to Dr. Redford's at Worcester, where Finney was busy revising his *Systematic Theology* for publication. He commenced again at the Tabernacle in London on Sunday, 1 December. But he was complaining of hoarseness again at the end of December (see Finney's sermon preached on 23 December 1850 in *The Penny Pulpit* 1,658 [December 1850–March 1851]: 305). However, he continued to preach until 2 April 1851.

[45]Asa Mahan had been asked to resign from the presidency of Oberlin College, and Finney was needed to succeed him. Furthermore, the theological department and plans for endowing the college were in danger of collapsing without Finney's presence. Finney had a series of letters from John Morgan, one of his colleagues on the faculty and acting pastor of the church in his absence. Over the months, he also received letters from the faculty; from John Keep, chairman of the board of trustees; from his family; and from Lewis Tappan, begging him to return (letters in Finney Papers, microfilm, roll 4).

[46]The *Southampton* was a 1,299-ton sailing packet of the Black X Line, which had come into service in 1849. See Robert G. Albion, *Square-Riggers on Schedule* (Princeton: Princeton University Press, 1938), pp. 282–83.

swept down the river **by the tide ‹aided›**[47] **by two steam tugs** out of sight.[48] Thus closed our labors in England, **the first time that we**[49] **visited there.**[50]

[47]Finney inserted the word "aided" in place of the word "and."

[48]They sailed on 7 April, arriving in New York on 26 April 1851. See *The New York Daily Tribune*, 28 April 1851, p. 8. On board was Francis B. Hurcomb, one of Finney's converts in London, who was on his way to study at Oberlin College. He later returned as an evangelist to the Church of England. Also on board, Finney met William M. Barbour, who was on his way to Oberlin College. He had been converted in Scotland through Rev. Fergus Ferguson, Sr., of Aberdeen, and Finney was very interested to get information from him about James Morison and the Evangelical Union. Barbour was later to become a professor at Bangor Seminary and Yale Divinity School. A. M. Hills remembered Barbour's once saying in a lecture that "President Finney was the first great thinker who had ever adequately and fully maintained, in all its bearings, the doctrine of THE FREEDOM OF THE WILL. He named him among the very foremost of the metaphysical thinkers of the world" (A. M. Hills, *Life of Charles G. Finney* [Cincinnati: Office of "God's Revivalist," 1902], p. 208). Also see Ann Potter to the Secretary of Oberlin College, 6 March 1908, Oberlin Alumni Records, file 28/1, box 126, folder "Francis B. Hurcomb," Oberlin College Archives; *Sermons by the Late Rev. Francis Burdett Hurcomb, Incumbent of West Ashby, Lincolnshire. With Prefatory Memoir by Rev. Frederick Arnold* (London: Pickering, 1877); Barbour to Fergus Ferguson, Sr., 10 April 1853, in *The Canada Evangelist* (Amherstberg) 3 (December 1853): 191; and *The Christian News*, 25 August 1888, p. 4.

[49]The word "together" was inserted here and written in the margin in pencil. It appears to be in Lewis Tappan's handwriting. Finney crossed it out.

[50]Matson had originally written down the following after this:

> We arrived in New York about the time of the May meetings. From there we came home, and had a very interesting state of things all summer. As usual the interest was quite extensive, especially among the students. In the fall of the year the pastor of the Tabernacle Church, which I had left in New York, wrote me an urgent request to come and labor with him the next winter. I knew they were in the habit of

Finney crossed out this section when he added a new chapter heading at the top of the next page.

MS 879
JHF 415

CHAPTER XXXI

‹*Labors at home again and Elsewhere.*›

‹We[1] arrived at Oberlin in May & had a very interesting revival, especially among our Students, that lasted all summer.[2] In the following Autumn I was invited to visit New York & labor in the Broadway

[1]The sheets originally numbered 723–25 in advance by Matson were used for MS 918–20. Pages 879–913 were originally numbered 727–61 and renumbered 859–93 by Matson. Finney changed them to 879–913. The chapter heading and the section down to n. 4 are in Finney's handwriting on a separate piece of paper pasted onto the top of the sheet, which covers up the previous page numbers (727 and 859). The additional strip pasted on extended the length of the page by an inch. Fairchild inserted a new sheet of paper between pages 878 and 879, starting chapter XXX and giving a brief summary of the contents of pages 879–81, which were omitted from the published edition.

[2]Having arrived in New York on Saturday, 26 April 1851, the Finneys remained there over three Sundays before returning to Oberlin. On Sunday, 4 May, Finney preached in the Broadway Tabernacle in the morning. He preached for Henry Ward Beecher at the Plymouth Church, Brooklyn, in the evening. On Tuesday, 6 May, he spoke at the anniversary of the American Foreign Antislavery Society at the Broadway Tabernacle and then preached in the tabernacle again the next Sunday morning and evening. The Finneys spent the following Sunday in Rochester, arriving back in Oberlin on 20 May to a great reception in the church. See *The Independent* (New York), 1 May 1851, p. 71; and 12 June 1851, p. 99; *The New York Daily Tribune*, 10 May 1851, p. 1; the *American and Foreign Antislavery Society, Annual Report* (New York), 1851, pp. 16–18; *OE*, 4 June 1851, p. 95; and "Reception of Professor Finney at Oberlin," *The Christian Witness* (London) 8 (August 1851): 398. This account had been sent by the Finneys to John Campbell, who published it. See John Campbell to Finney, 18 August 1851, Finney Papers, microfilm, roll 5.

Later, Finney attended the great Christian Antislavery Convention in Chicago, addressing the meeting on 3 July. And on 26 August, at the trustees' meeting held during commencement at Oberlin, he was elected president of the college. See *Christian Antislavery Convention: Minutes of the Convention Held July 3rd, 4th and 5th, 1851, at Chicago, Illinois* (Chicago: Office of Western Citizen, 1851), pp. 23–24; and Oberlin College Board of Trustees Minutes, 26 August 1851, Oberlin College Archives, microfilm.

During the spring of 1850, while the Finneys were in England, there had been one of the most powerful revivals ever known at Oberlin, at which about three hundred were converted (see *OE*, 27 February 1850, p. 39; and D. L. Leonard, *The Story of Oberlin* [Boston: Pilgrim, 1898], p. 210). The revival in the summer of 1851, after their return, was also notable. It was probably the first revival of any great power that had occurred during a summer term since 1842. It reached its peak at the end of September. A report stated:

> A very large number of youth are solemnly thinking and enquiring; many who have previously professed religion are searched and revived, and cases of hopeful conversion are frequent. We are not able to give numbers; but we see crowds coming forward in token of personal interest and anxiety for an effective and full salvation. Prof. Finney has preached daily for two weeks past, and with manifest tokens of divine power attending (*OE*, 8 October 1851, p. 166; and 8 June 1853, p. 92).

Fully 105 members were added at one time after this revival.

Tabernacle, the place of my former labors.[3] I knew they were in the habit of›[4] letting the Tabernacle to various societies to hold their Anniversaries, and for various lectures, especially during the winter season, and that we could do nothing there to promote a revival if the house was to be continually let for such purposes. I therefore wrote to Brother Thompson ‹the Pastor›[5] declining to accept of his invitation except upon the condition that, during my stay with him, the Tabernacle should not be let for other purposes. After a short time he replied that they had concluded *not* to let the Tabernacle during my laboring there to any of the Societies; and that they had raised a fund in their own congregation to meet the expenses of the congregation, so that they should be under no pecuniary necessity of letting it.[6] When the time arrived my wife and myself went down and commenced our labors.[7] But I soon found to my surprize that Brother Thompson objected wholly to putting up any posters about the city, giving notice of our meetings. I told him that I had never known that to be objected to in any place where I had labored in this country or in Europe; and that the custom was universal in ˡgreat cities to put up posters advertizing our meetings. But he persisted in refusing to have any such thing done; consequently our meetings were advertized in that great city only from the notices that were given from time to time in our meetings themselves.[8] Brother Thompson's own congregation was not large, although his house was so large. The people were inquiring continually when I was going to preach. Mr. Thompson himself generally preached once on the Sabbath. The people were anxious to

MS 880

[3]The invitation came from Joseph Thompson, the pastor, who saw Finney in Cleveland in the summer. See J. P. Thompson to Finney, 6 August 1851, Finney Papers, microfilm, roll 4. After Finney had resigned as pastor of the Broadway Tabernacle in 1837, the Free church worshiping there declined and finally disbanded. But in 1840 the building was purchased by David Hale, and a new Congregational church, effectively the first Congregational church in New York City, was formed. By 1851 it had grown to a membership of about four hundred. See "Broadway Tabernacle Church," *The Independent,* 6 March 1851, p. 38.

[4]This ends the section in Finney's handwriting.

[5]Finney inserted the words "the Pastor." Joseph Parrish Thompson (1819–1879) was a graduate of Yale and Andover Theological Seminary. After being at a Congregational church in New Haven he went to the Broadway Tabernacle in 1845. He became a prominent Congregational leader and author and was one of the founders and editors of *The Independent.* In 1871, because of declining health, he moved to Germany, where he died (see *DAB*). John Campbell in London wrote of him: "We recollect, indeed—with the exception of Professor Finney—of no man ever so expressing himself as did Mr. Thompson" (*The British Banner* [London], 10 November 1852, p. 779).

[6]Thompson's letter reads, "As an evidence of the good spirit of the brethren, I may mention that to guard against contingent losses from the omission of the ordinary uses of the house, a subscription has been made of some $1500" (J. P. Thompson to Finney, 6 August 1851, Finney Papers, microfilm, roll 4).

[7]Finney started preaching at the Broadway Tabernacle on Sunday, 19 October. See *The New York Daily Tribune*, 18 October 1851, p. 1.

[8]The meetings were, however, also advertised in *The New York Daily Tribune* from 18 October through 20 December 1851; in *NYE,* 6 November 1851, p. 179; and in *The Independent,* 13 November 1851, p. 186. An editorial in *The Independent*, probably written by Thompson, defending Finney and his meetings against attack, stated, "His labors in this city were conducted precisely as they were at the Tabernacle in London, excepting that no such extraordinary measures as 'placards' were resorted to in order to notify the public" (26 February 1852, p. 34).

know, as I was then a stranger to most of them, what part of the day I would preach. But he would seldom or never give any notice to the people as to what part of the day I would preach. If for a Sabbath or two in succession I preached in the morning, or in the afternoon, as the case might be, the people would come expecting to hear me. But several times he exchanged, and took that part of the day to preach himself that I had occupied the previous Sabbath. It was very difficult for me to get hold of the people. I never could account for this course pursued by Brother Thompson; but I ¦give the facts as they occurred. But soon after I began my labors I found that the men who had the financial affairs of the congregation in their hands began to let the Tabernacle on week evenings as they had formerly done. At first I supposed that these were to be merely exceptional cases. But I soon learned that the Societies that had had the use of the Tabernacle in former years, and those who had been in the habit of holding lectures there, etc., had informed the leading men in the Congregation that if they did not let them have the Tabernacle *that winter* as usual, they would go up town and hold their meetings, and not return there again. This overruled their decision not to let the house, and consequently it broke up in a great measure our weekly preaching services. On one Sabbath I had preached afternoon and evening to a very full house, and the congregation was very mellow, and everything looked as if we were on the point of having a great outburst of religious interest. But on going home I took cold, and on the next Monday morning found myself unable to rise from my bed.

MS 881

MS 882

¦I had appointed, if I remember right, to preach on Tuesday evening. But when the evening came I was still confined to my bed. I felt very anxious about it; but as Brother Thompson knew that I was sick, I supposed that he would be prepared to preach himself, or would get some one to take my place. However, for some reason he did no such thing. When the evening arrived he simply told the people, as they came thronging together, that I was unable to preach, and dismissed them and sent them away. After so far recovering as to be able to preach, I preached but very little; finding it, as I thought, impossible under the circumstances to promote a general revival.[9] I therefore left, and accepted an invitation to go to Hartford, Connecticut, and hold a series of meetings.[10] I was sent for by Brother William Patton, who was then a pastor of one of

[9]Reports of Finney's meetings indicated that there was considerable interest and some conversions, both among church members and also among people who were "transiently in the city." About fifty new members were added to the Broadway Tabernacle Church. See *NYE,* 20 November 1851, p. 186; *The Independent,* 11 December 1851, p. 202; and 26 February 1852, p. 34; and L. Nelson Nichols, *History of the Broadway Tabernacle of New York City* (New Haven: Tuttle, Morehouse, and Taylor, 1940), p. 105.

Looking back over his ministry at the Broadway Tabernacle, J. P. Thompson told the church:

> At intervals, glorious revivals have cheered our hearts with large and precious ingatherings. Most memorable was that occasion, when, to aid your pastor, you invited dear blessed Father Finney to preach again in the house that was built for him at the first. Those months were memorable in the fruits of grace (J. P. Thompson, *Broadway Tabernacle Church: Its History and Work* [New York, 1871], p. 46).

[10]Finney was in New York for ten or eleven weeks, preaching his last sermon on Sunday, 21 December 1851, in the evening. See *The New York Daily Tribune*, 20 December 1851, p. 1.

the Congregational churches of that city.[11] I began my labors there, **and very soon** a powerful revival influence was manifested among the people.[12]

But there was at this time an unhappy ˡstate of disagreement existing between Dr Hawes and Dr Bushnell.[13] The orthodoxy of Dr Bushnell, as is well-known, had been called in question. Dr Hawes was himself of opinion that Dr Bushnell's views were highly objectionable.[14] MS 883

However both Dr Hawes and Dr Bushnell attended our meetings, and manifested a great interest in the work which they saw had fairly begun. They invited me to preach in their churches, which I did. Still the lay brethren through the city felt as if the disagreement among the ministers was a stumbling block in the way; and there was a considerable urgency expressed **on the part of the laity** to have the ministers come more fraternally together, ˡand take a united stand before the people to promote the work.[15] JHF 416

[11]William Weston Patton (1821–1889) was the son of William Patton, who had edited an English edition of Finney's *Lectures on Revivals of Religion*. A graduate of Union Theological Seminary, he was a pastor in Boston from 1843 until he went to Hartford in 1846. He remained there until 1857, when he went to Chicago. He subsequently became editor of *The Advance*. He also did some lecturing at Oberlin College on theology. From 1877 until his death he was president of Howard University in Washington, D.C. Finney's reference here is to Patton's serving as pastor of the Fourth Congregational Church in Hartford. See *Appletons' Annual Cyclopaedia and Register of Important Events of the Year 1889* (New York: Appleton, 1890), p. 644.

[12]*The New-York Evangelist* of 1 January 1852 carried the notice: "Rev. C. G. Finney is now preaching in the Fourth Congregational church in Hartford (Rev. Mr. Patton's) in a series of meetings, having been invited there by the church. We hope his labors may have their accustomed blessing" (p. 3).

A written sermon dated 2 January 1852, which may have been preached by Finney in Hartford, was found by James R. Emmel in the Finney Papers. It is transcribed by him in "The Persuasive Techniques of Charles Grandison Finney as a Revivalist and Social Reform Speaker, 1820–1860" (Ph.D. diss., Pennsylvania State University, 1959), pp. 397–437.

[13]Joel Hawes was the minister of the First Church in Hartford. This was the first church to be formed in Connecticut, originating in 1636 with the first settlers. Hawes had been the minister since 1818. See Joel Hawes, *Historical Sketches of the First Church in Hartford: A Centennial Discourse Delivered in the First Church, June 26, 1836* (Hartford, Conn.: Hudson and Skinner, 1836).

Horace Bushnell (1802–1876) was a graduate of Yale Divinity School and went to Hartford to be pastor of the North Church in 1833. He made a name for himself through his early writings, which challenged the then-current belief in the necessity of revivals and stressed the possibility and need for children to be brought up never having been other than Christian. Then in 1848, as a result of a mystical experience, he challenged the orthodox doctrines of the Trinity and the Atonement in three lectures published the next year as *God in Christ*. This was to herald a new movement of liberalism in theology. He resigned his pastorate in 1859 through ill health but became famous as an innovative theologian and writer. See *DAB*.

[14]The publication of *God in Christ* in 1849 had brought a storm of controversy, and Bushnell came under attack from all quarters, Joel Hawes being in the forefront. Repeated attempts on the part of the Congregational associations to put Bushnell on trial resulted in the withdrawal of his church from the consociation. Hawes felt it to be his duty "to withdraw ministerial fellowship," a situation that was to continue for four years. See Edward A. Lawrence, *The Life of Rev. Joel Hawes, D.D.* (Hartford, Conn.: Hammersley, 1871), pp. 198–215.

[15]Attempts had been made earlier in the year to promote a revival in Hartford, but it was considered that the Bushnell controversy had

> produced a bad, though scarcely avoidable state of feeling in the city, breaking up harmony of sentiment and action among the pastors and churches. This has been a sore trial to those who have longed for the prosperity of Zion, and has been a chief obstacle in the way of a general revival of religion ("Letter from Connecticut," *The Independent*, 6 March 1851, p. 37).

The people generally did not sympathize with Dr Hawes' strong views in regard to the orthodoxy of Dr Bushnell. Being informed of this I in a fraternal spirit told Dr Hawes that he was in a false position, and that the MS 884 people felt tried with his laying ˡso great stress upon what he called the errors of Dr Bushnell, and that they very generally, I believed, did not justify him in the position that he occupied. Dr Hawes was a good man, and manifestly felt his responsibility in this matter very deeply.

One evening I had been preaching, I think, for Brother Patton, and the three Congregational ministers were present. After meeting they followed me to my lodgings, and Dr Hawes said: "Brother Finney, we are satisfied that the Spirit of the Lord is poured out here; and now what can we as ministers do to promote this work?" I told them freely what I thought. That a great responsibility rested upon them, and it seemed to me that it was for them to say whether the work should become general throughout the city or not. That if they could reconcile their differences, and come out before the churches and be united and take hold of the work, a great obstacle would be removed; and that I thought we might expect the work to spread rapidly on every hand. MS 885 ˡThey saw their position, for I talked quite plainly to them; and Dr Hawes and Dr Bushnell came to an understanding to lay aside their difficulties, and go on and promote the work. I should say here that I believe Brother Patton had never sympathized with the strong views held by Brother Hawes;[16] and I should also say that Dr Bushnell himself did not seem to have any controversy with Dr Hawes; and the obstacle to be removed from before the public seemed to be mostly ‹the unwillingness of› Dr Hawes ‹to› cordially co-operate[17] with the other ministers in the work.

Dr Hawes was too good a man to persist in anything that would prevent his JHF 417 doing whatever he could consistently ˡdo to promote the work. Therefore from that time we seemed to work together with a good measure of cordiality. The work spread into all the congregations, and went on very hopefully for a number of weeks.[18] But there was one peculiarity about that work that I have

[16] Patton initially felt obligated to dissociate himself from Bushnell, but he was "touched and won by the patience and somewhat saddened good-temper" of Bushnell, and a "warm friendship and alliance" grew up between them (Mary Bushnell Cheney, *Life and Letters of Horace Bushnell* [New York: Harper, 1880], p. 253).

[17] Matson had written down here, "seemed to be mostly that Dr Hawes should cordially cooperate," but Finney changed it.

[18] In February *The Independent* reported:

> We are happy to learn through a private letter, that there is a continually rising religious interest in Hartford, extending to most of the churches. Three of the Congregational churches, Dr. Hawes's, Dr. Bushnell's and Mr. Patton's, have united their efforts, and have engaged Mr. Finney to preach in the several congregations by turns. The fruits of brotherly union are happily apparent (12 February 1852, p. 27).

This, however, was only a temporary truce. All attempts on the part of Bushnell to come to an understanding with Hawes failed, "and everything went on as before" (Cheney, *Life of Bushnell*, pp. 253–54).

William Patton recalled that Dr. Bushnell invited Finney frequently to his home

> with special purpose to compare views on the subject of holiness. . . . Yet there the two grand men would sit and talk, hour after hour, totally disagreeing in their philosophy on certain mooted questions, but agreeing in their aims and burning desires and in their belief that Christians might claim and receive far higher blessings than were usually supposed to be any part of our earthly inheritance. . . . And he expressed

never forgotten. I believe every Sabbath that I was in that city it stormed furiously. Such a succession of stormy Sabbaths I almost never ¹witnessed. MS 886 However, our meetings were fully attended; and for a place like Hartford the work became powerful and extensive.[19]

Those who are acquainted with Hartford know how fastidious and precise **they** are in regard to all they do. They were afraid of any measures other than **simply** prayer-meetings, and preaching meetings, and meetings for inquiry. In other words it was out of the question to call on sinners to come forward and break away from the fear of man, and give themselves publicly to God. Dr Hawes was especially very much afraid of any such measures. Consequently I could do no such thing there. Indeed Dr Hawes was so much afraid of measures, that I recollect one night in attending a meeting of inquiry in his vestry **with him** the number of inquirers present was large, and at the close I called on those that were willing **then and there** to give themselves up to God, to kneel down. This startled Dr Hawes; and he remarked before they knelt down that none were requested to do so unless they did it cheerfully, of their own accord; **which, by the by, ¹I was aware that most of them would** MS 887 **very readily do.** They did kneel down, and we prayed with them. Dr Hawes remarked to me as the inquirers rose and were dismissed: "I have always felt the necessity of some such measure, but have been afraid to use it. I have always seen," said he, "that something was needed to bring **them** to a stand, and to induce them to act on their present convictions; but I have not had courage to **do** anything of the kind." I said to him that I had found some such measure indispensable to bring sinners to the point of submission.

In this revival *there was a great deal of praying*. The ¹young converts JHF 418 especially gave themselves to very much prayer. One evening, as I learned,

> to me a strong liking for Mr. Finney, as a minister of powerful mind and remarkable singleness of aim, saying once to me of him: "He is pure gold" ("A Tribute to Horace Bushnell, D.D," *The Independent,* 2 March 1876, p. 1).

In October of that year Bushnell traveled west for his health and visited Oberlin. He wrote home: "Our friends, the Finneys, are both glad as they can be to see me, and I am spending the night with them. I have had a most happy and blessed day here." Later in December in another letter to his wife he wrote:

> I am glad that you have had the pleasure of a call from Mr. Finney. I know not how it is, but I feel greatly drawn to this man, despite of the greatest dissimilarity of tastes and a method of soul, whether in thought or feeling, wholly unlike. I said I knew not how, but I do know. It is because I find God with him, and consciously receive nothing but good and genuine (he would say honest) impressions from him (Cheney, *Life of Bushnell*, pp. 268, 275).

[19] Finney may possibly have mistaken the winter when the Sabbaths were stormy. The winter of 1855–1856, when he was in Rochester, was notorious. A report from an American in an English paper read:

> We are now having one of the severest winters ever known in this country. In no part of it is there any exception to this remark. One marked peculiarity has characterised the providence of God in this particular. Our severest storms and intensest cold, for months past, have occurred upon our Sabbaths. In some of the Eastern papers, I see it stated, that out of twenty-five successive Sabbaths, all but two or three have been very stormy, and often so much so as to render an attendance upon public worship, to the mass of worshippers, almost impossible. . . . These facts, connected with others, have no doubt combined to render revivals of religion less frequent than in former years (Letter from "M.P.," dated Ohio, February 1856, in *The Christian Times* [London], 21 March 1856, p. 179; and see "Storms on Sunday," *Christian Watchman and Reflector* [Boston], 24 January 1856, p. 2).

one of the young converts after the evening services invited another **convert** to go home with him, and they would hold a season of prayer together. The Lord was with them, and the next evening they invited others, and the next evening more still, until the meeting became so large that they were obliged MS 888 to divide it. These meetings were held after the preaching service. |The second meeting soon became too large for the room, and that again was divided. And I understood **at the time** that these meetings multiplied until the young converts were almost universally in the habit of holding meetings for prayer in different places after the preaching service. Finally to these meetings they invited inquirers, and such as wished to be prayed *for*.[20] This led to quite an organized effort among the converts for the salvation of souls.

A very interesting state of things sprung up at this time in the public schools. As I was informed, **the** ministers had agreed that they would not visit the public schools and make any religious efforts there, because it excited jealousy on the part of different denominations. One morning a large number of lads, as I was told, when they came together were so affected that they could not study, and asked their teacher to pray for them. He was not a professor of religion, and sent for one of the pastors, informing him of the state of things, and requesting him to come and hold some religious service MS 889 with them. |But he declined, saying that there was an understanding among the pastors that they would not go to the public schools to hold any religious services, **lest it should excite denominational animosities**. He sent for another, and another, as I was informed; but they told him he must pray for the scholars himself. This **put him in a tight place**. But it resulted, I believe, in his giving his own heart to God, and in his taking measures for the conversion of the school. I understood there was a goodly number of the scholars in the various **C**ommon **S**chools that were converted at that time.

JHF 419 |Every one acquainted with the city of Hartford knows that its inhabitants are a very intelligent people, that all classes are educated, and that there is perhaps no city in the world where education of so high an order is so **universal** as it is in Hartford. When they came to receive **the converts**, some six hundred, I believe, united with their churches.[21] Dr Hawes said to me before I left: "What shall we do with these young converts? If we should form MS 890 them into a church by them|selves they would make admirable workers for

[20]Henry Clay Trumbull, the noted Sunday school leader and author, at that time a young railroad clerk, was one of the inquirers invited to one of those meetings. It was "a young men's prayer meeting, which is holden every evening in a room over the Post Office, commencing at the close of Mr. Finney's services." Trumbull was deeply influenced by Finney's teaching. See Philip E. Howard, *The Life Story of Henry Clay Trumbull* (Philadelphia: The Sunday School Times, 1905), pp. 88–89; and H. C. Trumbull, *My Four Religious Teachers: Charles G. Finney, David Hawley, Elias R. Beadle, Horace Bushnell* (Philadelphia: The Sunday School Co., 1903), pp. 23–24. In a report of the revival in *The Independent*, a correspondent wrote, "The overwhelming mass of inquirers are the young from fifteen to twenty-five" ("Tennent," letter dated Hartford, 3 March 1852, *The Independent,* 11 March 1852, p. 41).

[21]The following notice appeared in *The Oberlin Evangelist*: "We see it stated that at least *six hundred* have been admitted into the several churches of Hartford as the fruits of the revival enjoyed in the city last winter in connection with the labors of Pres. C. G. Finney" (7 July 1852, p. 110). Sixty-six were said to have united with the First Church of Joel Hawes. See George L. Walker, *History of the First Church in Hartford, 1633–1883*, (Hartford: Brown and Gross, 1884), p. 380.

the salvation of souls. If, however, we receive them to our churches, where we have so many elderly men and women who are always expected to take the lead in everything, their modesty will make them fall in behind these staid Christian men and women; and they will live as they have lived, and be inefficient as they have been." However, as I understood, the young converts of both sexes formed themselves into a kind of City Missionary Society, and organized for the purpose of making direct efforts to convert souls throughout the city. Such efforts as this, for instance, were made by numbers of them. One of the principal young ladies **in the city**, perhaps as well-known and as much respected as any lady in the city, undertook to reclaim, and if possible save, a class of young men who belonged to **high** and wealthy families, **and** had fallen into bad habits and into moral decay, **had lost their character and had a good deal fallen out of society** and lost the respect of the people.

ˡThe position and character of this young lady rendered it possible and proper for her to make such an effort without creating a suspicion of any impropriety on her part. She **took measures to get an** opportunity to converse with this class of young men; and as I understood **got** them together for religious **instruction, and** conversation, and prayer, and was very successful in reclaiming numbers of them. If I have been rightly informed th‹e› converts ‹of that revival› were[22] a great power in that city for good; and many of them remain there still, and are very active in promoting religion. MS 891

Mrs. Finney established prayer-meetings for ladies, which ˡwere held in the vestry of the churches. These meetings were largely attended, and became very interesting. The ladies were **very much** united and very much in earnest, and became a principal power, under God, in promoting **His** work there.[23] **The doctrines that I preached were what I had everywhere preached, and the measures that I used what I had everywhere used, ˡwith the exception of the anxious seat. After preaching, however, I invited inquirers, as I had in other places, to the vestry for particular instruction; and those meetings were often very large.[24] There were very many striking cases of conversion in this city, as was usual in all other places.** JHF 420 MS 892

We left there about the first of April, and went to the city of New York, on our way home.[25] There I preached a few times for **Brother** Henry Ward Beecher in Brooklyn;[26] and there was a growing and deepening religious

[22]Matson had written here "those young converts were," but Finney changed it to "the converts of that revival were."

[23]A report at the time stated, "Female prayer-meetings have been largely attended, in connection with which, as also otherwise, Mrs. Finney's labors have been invaluable" (*The Independent,* 11 March 1852, p. 41).

[24]A report stated, "Sometimes, particularly on Sabbath evenings, as many as four hundred have gone into the inquiry-meeting, even when the invitation has been guarded" (*The Independent,* 11 March 1852, p. 41).

[25]Finney was in New York by Thursday, 25 March, when he was preaching in Henry Ward Beecher's church. See Lewis Tappan, "Journal," 25 March 1852, Tappan Papers, microfilm, roll 2.

[26]Henry Ward Beecher (1813–1887), a son of Lyman Beecher, had attended Lane Theological Seminary just after the Lane Rebels had left. He had become the pastor of the newly organized Plymouth Church in Brooklyn in 1847 and was already famous as a preacher, with

influence **there** when I arrived and when I left.[27] But I preached but a few times, because my health gave way, and I was obliged to desist. We came home and went on with our labors here as usual, with the almost uniform results of a great degree of religious influence among our students, and extending more or less generally to the inhabitants.[28] **It had become so common to have large numbers of our students inquiring from week to week, and from month to month, that the inhabitants came to look** MS 893 ¹**upon it as a thing of course. There was no novelty in such a state of things, and therefore no such interest excited here by it as would have been excited in any other place. However, the good people always prayed earnestly for the forwarding of the work among the students; and there was always a goodly number of our people that would enter heart and soul into anything of this kind.**

The next winter we left Oberlin at the usual season **in the fall**,[29] and

weekly congregations averaging 2,500 persons in the recently built semicircular auditorium. He remained pastor there until his death. See *DAB*.

[27] It was noted by Lewis Tappan about the time the Finneys arrived in Brooklyn: "morning prayer meeting at Mr. Beecher's 1/4 before 8 & continue 45 minutes & a Union prayer meeting from 5 to 6 every pm. Considerable interest is felt—many converted—& [Christ]ians revived" (L. Tappan, "Journal," 25 March 1852, Tappan Papers, microfilm, roll 2). On 1 April 1852, *The Independent* reported: "Rev. Mr. Finney continues to preach here every evening. Inquiry meetings are held almost daily, and many are rejoicing in hope. The interest is thought to be increasing" (p. 54).

Finney left New York on 5 April. Ten days later it was announced that about eight morning prayer meetings had been established in different churches in Brooklyn. "More seriousness than was ever noticed in that city it is thought now pervades the whole Christian community. In nearly all the churches where special efforts have been made the Lord seems to be pouring out his Spirit." Another report a week later spoke of another prayer meeting being established, and the work spreading among the Sunday schools and other Presbyterian and Congregational churches (*NYE*, 8 April 1852, p. 58; *The Independent*, 15 April 1852, p. 54; and 22 April 1852, p. 66).

On Sunday, 2 May, sixty people were admitted into Beecher's church, fifty of those "on profession of faith." "The pastor announced that there would be an *extra* communion in June to receive others, fruits of the present revival. The religious awakening has reached the Sabbath-School and Bible classes, about forty of whom are indulging hope" (*The Independent*, 6 May 1852, p. 74). *The New-York Evangelist* reported about the same time: "The revival in this church is said to be increasing. More than one hundred have already been hopefully converted. All the meetings are largely attended" (6 May 1852, p. 74). A survey of Plymouth Church revivals over the years mentioned the revival in 1852 as being "especially fruitful in blessed results," 162 having joined the church, 103 of those being by profession (*American Congregational Year-Book for the Year 1855* [New York] 2 [1855]: 113–14).

[28] A notice in *The Oberlin Evangelist* in July stated:

> All along within the past three months the word of the Lord has been with power in the great congregation who sit under Pres. Finney's preaching. The Oberlin church numbers about *one thousand*; the congregation nearly *two thousand*, filling our spacious house full. . . . On several different Sabbaths, special means have been used to press convicted minds to real and immediate submission. The numbers embraced in this class were found to range variously from two to three hundred. This may give some general idea of the state of religious interest in this place.
>
> . . . Opportunities are now being afforded for the converts to profess Christ publicly. Ten were received May 1, and seventy more now stand propounded for admission to the church. Others still are waiting their opportunity (7 July 1852, p. 111).

The revival continued into the fall. Eighty-seven were admitted by profession into the church in July, with a further eighteen in September and twenty-seven in November. See *OE*, 8 December 1852, p. 197; and 6 July 1853, p. 111.

[29] The words "in the fall" were not crossed out by Fairchild in the manuscript but were omitted from the published edition.

started east to occupy a field of labor to which we had been invited.[30] While we were in Hartford ‹the previous winter›[31] we had a very pressing invitation to go to the city of Syracuse to labor. **The Methodist brethren had held a protracted meeting; and the kind and degree of excitement that had been manifested among them had excited opposition on the part of professors of other denominations, and a very unpleasant state of things had resulted as a consequence.**[32] **In this extremity** the minister of the Congregational church came down to Hartford to persuade me, if possible, to **go to Syracuse.**[33] |I could not see it my duty to go at that time, and thought no more about it. But ‹**as**› **we went east, at Rochester** we met this minister,[34] **who** was not then the pastor of the **little** Congregational church in the city of Syracuse. But he felt so much interest for them that he finally induced me to promise him that I would stop there, and spend at least one Sabbath. We did so, and found the little **Congregational** church very much discouraged. Their number was small. The church was mostly composed of persons of very radical views in regard to all the great questions of reform. The Presbyterian churches, and the other churches generally, did not sympathize at all with them, and it seemed as if the Congregational church must become extinct. I preached one Sabbath, and learned so much about the

MS 894

[30]The Finneys left Oberlin early in November 1852. A letter dated Cleveland, 12 November, stated: "Mr. Finney passed through here two days since to New York State. He contemplates laboring in the churches of Oneida County" (*The Independent,* 25 November 1852, p. 191).

[31]See MS 882–92. Finney added the words "the previous winter."

[32]A correspondent of *The New-York Evangelist* wrote about the revival in Syracuse:

> You will be glad to learn that during the winter several of the Methodist and Presbyterian churches in Syracuse have enjoyed more than usual religious interest. The extent of this work in the Methodist churches, I have not the means of knowing (1 April 1852, p. 54).

[33]This was probably Ovid Miner (1803–1891). He was a graduate of Auburn Theological Seminary and from 1837 to 1841 was minister of the Presbyterian church in Penn Yan, New York. He was dismissed from there because of his radical abolitionism and his sympathies with the Oberlin theology. However, a number of the church members who shared his views seceded and formed a Congregational church, and Miner continued for some years as pastor there. Then from 1846 to 1849 he was acting pastor of the Independent Congregational Church in Syracuse. He subsequently became a temperance and antislavery lecturer and was one of the founders of Hoyleton in Illinois. But he continued to take an interest in the Syracuse church, finally settling in the town after 1873. He was closely in touch with the activities of Oberlin College and "held strongly to the religious views of Mr. Finney" (*NYE,* 28 March 1895, p. 9; and see *The Congregational Year-Book* [Boston], 1892, p. 32; James H. Hotchkin, *A History of the Purchase and Settlement of Western New York* [New York: Dodd, 1848], pp. 397–98; Edgar F. Raines, "The American Missionary Association in Southern Illinois, 1856–1862: A Case History in the Abolition Movement," *Journal of the Illinois State Historical Society* 65, no. 3 [Autumn 1972]: 262; and *NYE,* 20 December 1849, p. 202). The files of *The Oberlin Evangelist* and letters from Miner in Treasurer's Office, file 7/1/5, box 29, Oberlin College Archives, and in Letters Received by Oberlin College, 1822–1866, microfilm, roll 11, indicate his close connection with Syracuse and with Oberlin. See also *Oneida Circular,* 21 April 1873, p. 131; and 28 April 1873, p. 139.

The Independent Church in Syracuse was not officially organized as a Congregational church until 1853, but it had been in existence at least since the early 1840s. Ovid Miner and the church had tried to get Finney to go there in 1848. See Hotchkin, *History of Western New York,* pp. 326–27; and O. Miner and the Independent Congregational Church of Syracuse to Finney, 8 May 1848, Finney Papers, microfilm, roll 4.

[34]Here Matson had written down, "But at Rochester as we went east, the next fall we met this minister." Finney altered it.

JHF 421 |state of things as to be induced to remain another Sabbath.[35] Soon I began to perceive a movement among the dry bones.[36]

Some of the leading members of the Congregational church began to make MS 895 confession to each other, |and public confession of their wanderings from God, and of other things that had created prejudice against them in the city. This conciliated the people around them, and they began to come, and soon their house of worship was too narrow to hold the people. I **however** had not expected to stay more than one Sabbath; **but** I could not see my way clear to leave; and I kept on from Sabbath to Sabbath. The interest continued to

[35]"An Old Syracusan" remembered:

> Visitors were sent out into every street and lane of the city to learn the real status of the people upon the subject of religion. . . . Many professing Christians on leaving their home in the East leave their church relations and interest in spiritual things for themselves and their families behind, and are not supposed to have ever enjoyed the privileges and blessings of the children of God. Just that condition was found to prevail in Syracuse. It was found that nearly one-third of the adult population had been members of Christian churches in their former homes, while not more than one-fourth of that number had identified themselves with the people of God here ("Some Old-Time Revivals," *The Journal* [Syracuse], 2 June 1894, p. 8).

[36]Finney wrote back to Oberlin early in January:

> The work of the Lord advances slowly but steadily & perceptibly. I found here perhaps, the most difficu[l]t field I ever labored in; owing in a great measure to the fact that Infidelity & Unitarianism Universalism &c, have taken the lead in reforms & the foundations have fallen away in the convictions of the many in regard to the fundamental truths of religion (Finney to Hamilton Hill, 7 January 1853, Letters Received by Oberlin College, 1822–1866, microfilm, roll 14).

In another letter to John Keep in February, Finney wrote:

> Upon this city has been concentrated on the one hand Gerrit Smith's Garrison's, Goodell's, Beria Green's, Foster's & all that kind of influence mingled & compounded with infidelity around, and with universalism around, & unitarianism professed but truly universalism Woman's rights conventions of the infidel school but all mixed up with apostates from Christianity & those who profess religion still. These on the one hand & the natural result a miserable conservatism on the other had in their action & reaction brought on a total loss of confidence in the fundamental truths of christianity & of the [Chris]tian system & especially in revival efforts & in revivals themselves. . . . For these reasons I made up my mind to stop here. At first people would not go to the Con. church. Nearly all were afraid of Oberlin. But the work has gone on in spite of all opposition & prejudice (Finney to John Keep, 14 February 1853, transcription in R. S. Fletcher Papers, file 30/24, box 6, Oberlin College Archives).

The Third Woman's Rights Convention had been held in Syracuse the previous September. Radical reformers like Samuel J. May, a Unitarian minister in Syracuse, and Gerrit Smith, the wealthy Peterborough reformer, took part. (Finney had just been in conflict with Gerrit Smith over what Finney considered to be Smith's sectarianism in his political actions.) But particularly prominent at the convention were Lucy Stone and Antoinette Brown, both former Oberlin students. Finney added a postscript to his letter to John Keep:

> From some things Br. Hudson said to me when here I think he must have met with *something* of what I have met *so much*, of a spirit of sheer *infidel reform*. A compounding of Parkerism, Mayism, Davisism, Spirit Rappings and all such stuff with true religion. I hear that Lucy Stone has become a skeptic, & I fear Antoinette Brown will do the same.

The views of Unitarian Theodore Parker and spiritualist Andrew Jackson Davis were popular among reformers. When Samuel J. May preached a series of sermons in the Unitarian Church in January in order to counteract Finney's teaching on the justice of future or endless punishment, J. Arnold was in the congregation at Finney's request taking notes. See *The Proceedings of the Woman's Rights Convention, Held at Syracuse, September 8th, 9th, and 10th, 1852* (Syracuse: Masters, 1852); Finney to Gerrit Smith, 13 September 1852; and Smith to Finney, 18 September 1852 (copy in Letterbook), Gerrit Smith Papers, George Arents Library, Syracuse University; and J. Arnold to Finney, 31 January 1853, Finney Papers, microfilm, roll 4.

increase and to spread. The Lord removed the obstacles, and brought Christian people nearer together. The Presbyterian churches were thrown open to our meetings, and conversions were multiplied on every side. However, as in some other cases, I directed my preaching very much to the Christian people. There had been very little sympathy existing between them; and a great work was needed among professors of religion before the way could be prepared outside of the churches.[37] Thus I continued to labor in the different churches until the Second Presbyterian church |was left without a pastor; after which we concentrated our meetings there in a great measure, and held on throughout the winter.[38] MS 896

Here again Mrs. Finney established her ladies' meetings with great success. She generally held them in the lecture room of the First Presbyterian Church, I think, a commodious and convenient room for such meetings.[39] A great many very interesting facts **transpired** in her meetings that winter. Christians of different denominations seemed to flow together after awhile, and all the difficulties that had existed among them seemed to be done away. **Neither of the Presbyterian churches had at that time any pastor. The First church had no pastor when I arrived there;**[40] **and the pastor of the Second church left after I went there. The Congregational church had no pastor;**[41] and hence none of them opened the doors **of their churches** to receive the converts.[42] I was very willing that this should be so, as I knew that

[37] A report at the end of January spoke of the work as

> gradual, but deep and widening. As yet it is mainly confined to the churches; the First Presbyterian, Park Presbyterian, the Congregational and the Second Baptist Churches participate in it. . . . Because it is a wicked place, and has been proverbial for excitement, Brother F. has felt in duty bound to labor on. His heart is encouraged, and so are the people of God in the city who enter into the work; and the number of such is constantly increasing (*The Independent,* 27 January 1853, p. 15).

Another report in March stated:

> The peculiarity of the case is, that both Mr. Finney's labors and their success have been almost entirely confined to professed Christians. Many of those in the Congregational Church, and the two Central Presbyterian Churches, have been greatly quickened and confirmed (*OE,* 30 March 1853, p. 53, reprinted from the *Religious Recorder* of Syracuse for 17 March).

[38] By the Second Presbyterian Church, Finney is referring to what was usually called the Park Church. This had been formed in 1847 with William W. Newell as minister, but he appears to have transferred to the First Ward Presbyterian Church earlier in 1852. Byron Sunderland (1819–1901) was then at Park Church until he received a call in January 1853 to the First Presbyterian Church in Washington City. See Joshua V. H. Clark, *Onondaga; or, Reminiscences of Earlier and Later Times,* vol. 2 (Syracuse: Stoddard and Babcock, 1849), p. 96; *NYE,* 1 April 1852, p. 54; and *The Independent,* 20 January 1852, p. 11.

[39] The First Presbyterian Church had been organized in 1826. A new meeting house had been built in 1849. See "Reminiscences of Syracuse from Personal Recollections of Timothy L. Cheney," *Annual Volume of the Onondaga Historical Association* (Syracuse), 1914, p. 126.

[40] The first pastor of the First Church was John Watson Adams, who had repeatedly tried to get Finney to hold revival meetings in Syracuse in 1830–1831. He died in April 1850 after a ministry of twenty-four years, which was considered at the time to have been the longest pastorate in any Presbyterian church in western New York. He was followed in 1851 by Charles King McHarg, who left in 1852. See Clark, *Onondaga,* p. 96; *NYE,* 27 July 1876, p. 4; and letters of J. W. Adams to Finney, Finney Papers, microfilm, roll 2.

[41] Ovid Miner had acted as pastor since 1846 but had left in 1849. See *The Congregational Year-Book,* 1892, p. 32.

[42] The Syracuse *Religious Herald* for 17 March reported on the revival in the Presbyterian churches: "It is quite apparent that the good influences that have prevailed in those churches have

MS 897 JHF 422 there was great danger, if they began ˡto ˡreceive the converts that jealousies would spring up and mar the work.

As we were about to leave in the Spring I gave out notice from the pulpit, on my own responsibility, that on the next Sabbath we should hold a Communion service; to which all Christians who truly loved the Lord Jesus Christ, and gave evidence of it in their lives, were invited. That was one of the most interesting Communion seasons I ever witnessed. The church was filled **almost or quite to its utmost capacity** with communicants. Two very aged ministers, **Father** Waldo[43] and **Father** Brainard,[44] attended and helped at the Communion service. There was a great melting in the congregation; and a more loving and joyful Communion of the people of God I think I never saw anywhere.[45]

After I left the churches all secured pastors **as soon as they could**.[46] I have

been greatly hindered by the fact that neither of them have a Pastor" (reprinted in *OE,* 30 March 1853, p. 53). Finney wrote at the time to Hamilton Hill in Oberlin:

> I hope to return to O[berlin] early in April. But they have no minister in either of the three churches & seem not likely to have. I don't know what to do. It is so very difficult to leave under such circumstances. The work of the Lord progresses without any abatement as I can see (Finney to H. Hill, 18 March 1853, Letters Received by Oberlin College, 1822–1866, microfilm, roll 4).

[43]Daniel Waldo (1762–1864), in his ninetieth year, was a well-known Congregational minister, familiarly known as "Father Waldo." He had been a prisoner in the Revolutionary War. After his graduation from Yale in 1788 he was a minister of churches in New England. When he was 93 he was made chaplain of the House of Representatives. He died in Syracuse at age 102. See *Appletons' Cyclopaedia of American Biography*, vol. 6 (New York: Appleton, 1889), p. 321.

[44]Israel Brainerd (1772–1854), age eighty-one years, was a Yale graduate and a classmate of Lyman Beecher. He had been pastor of the Congregational church in Verona, New York, from 1807 to 1836, where Finney had preached for him during the Rome revival in 1825. Brainerd's youngest daughter, Elizabeth, who was married to Rev. G. W. Thomson, wrote of Finney, "During life a warm friendship continued between him and my father, though the latter stood with the Conservatives; and most cordial was their meeting in after years, when both had passed the meridian, and could calmly survey the past." Brainerd died in his daughter's home in Syracuse in 1854. See F. B. Dexter, *Biographical Sketches of the Graduates of Yale College*, vol. 5 (New York: Holt, 1911), pp. 261–63; *The Independent,* 9 September 1854, p. 357; *NYE,* 16 November 1854, p. 184; 6 July 1876, p. 2; and Mrs. G. W. Thomson, "Early Labors of President Finney," *NYE,* 9 December 1875, p. 2.

[45]"An Old Syracusan" recollected:

> The farewell services were held in Park church, which was without a pastor at that time. The special feature of the day was the delightful communion service. The house was filled to its utmost capacity, and Mr. Finney, in his peculiarly tender and loving spirit, invited all present who felt that they really loved the Lord with all their heart, whether they had ever made a public confession of their faith or not, to partake of the feast which the Lord had spread, and invited them to partake. There were some, of course, who would criticise such a departure from the regular order, but the service could never be forgotten by any participant (*The Journal,* 2 June 1894, p. 8).

[46]The First Presbyterian Church obtained the services of Sherman B. Canfield. He had been a student at Oberlin with the first theological class in 1835 but left after a short time and, in spite of "imperfect education," was able to obtain a license to preach. He soon became a Presbyterian minister in Cleveland. But he turned conservative and repudiated the Oberlin theology. He was the author of *An Exposition of the Peculiarities, Difficulties, and Tendencies of Oberlin Perfectionism: Prepared by a Committee of the Presbytery of Cleveland* (Cleveland: Smead, 1841). He went to Syracuse from Cleveland in 1854, where he remained a much-loved pastor until his death in 1871. See *NYE,* 16 March 1871, pp. 4, 6; and 27 July 1876, p. 4; and James Barr Walker, *Experiences of Pioneer Life in the Early Settlements and Cities of the West* (Chicago: Sumner, 1881), pp. 159–61. Samuel C. Aikin, Finney's old friend from the Utica revival days, was also one of the committee who helped to produce the pamphlet against Oberlin perfectionism.

been informed that that revival resulted in great and permanent good. The Congregational church **afterwards** built them a larger house of worship; and **has** been, ˡI believe, ever since a healthy church and congregation.[47] The Presbyterian churches, and I believe the Baptist churches, were much strengthened in faith and increased in numbers. MS 898

The work was very deep there **amongst** a great many professors of religion. One very striking fact occurred which I will mention. There was a lady **living in the first Ward** by the name of **Childs**, the Christian wife of an unconverted husband.[48] She was a lady of great refinement, and beauty of character and person. Her husband was a merchant, a man of good moral character; **and as I should judge from what I heard him say, passionately fond of his wife**. She attended our meetings, and became very much convicted for a deeper work of grace in her soul. She called on me one day in a state of very anxious inquiry. I had a few moments' conversation with her, and directed her attention especially to the necessity of a thorough and universal consecration of herself and of her all to Christ. I told her that when she had ˡdone this she must believe for the sealing of the Holy Spirit. She had heard the doctrine of sanctification preached, and it had greatly interested her; and her ˡinquiry was how she should obtain it. I gave her the brief direction which I have mentioned, and she got up hastily and left me. Such a MS 899 JHF 423

The Park Church, having struggled with debts, was eventually able to install Samuel H. Hall in May 1855. In connection with his installation a correspondent wrote: "Our churches in the Central City are now all manned with able, active and earnest pastors. It has cost no little anxiety, labor, money and active movement to accomplish the successful establishment of our three Presbyterian societies" (*NYE,* 7 June 1855, p. 89).

The Congregational church had been independent but was organized as Plymouth Congregational Church on 24 September 1853 with thirty-one members; and in May 1854 it joined the newly formed Onondaga Association. On 26 September, Michael Epaphras Strieby (1815–1899) received and accepted a call. He had graduated from Oberlin College in 1838 and had been the minister of the Congregational church in Mount Vernon, New York. He remained as the acting minister in Syracuse until 1859, when he was ordained over the church. In 1864 he became a corresponding secretary of the American Missionary Association. In 1845 he had been made a trustee of Oberlin College, and he was later considered as a possible successor to Finney in the presidency. See *The Independent,* 18 August 1853, p. 131; and 18 May 1854, p. 155; *Manual of the Plymouth Congregational Church, of Syracuse, N.Y.* (Syracuse: Truair, Smith, 1872), pp. 29, 30; *The Congregational Year-Book,* 1900, p. 34; and John Morgan to Mark Hopkins, 26 February 1864, Morgan-Hopkins Correspondence, file 30/28, box 6, Oberlin College Archives.

[47] A new chapel seating four hundred was built in connection with their reorganization and came into use in February 1855. But by 1857 the membership had risen to 160 or 170, and the chapel was already too small. A new church was built in 1859. By then it was reported: "The Church has been blessed in its spiritual relation and endeavors. Harmony has prevailed among its members, and it has had a steady and somewhat uniform increase of numbers. . . . The names of 303 members have been enrolled on its catalogue" (*Manual of the Plymouth Church of Syracuse* [Syracuse: Masters, 1859], pp. 3–4). See also *The Independent,* 25 May 1854, p. 163; and *American Congregational Year-Book for the Year 1857* (New York) 4 (1857): 154.

[48] This was probably Martha B. Childs, wife of Noadiah M. Childs, a dry-goods and grocery merchant, whose home address was 455 Lodi Street in the First Ward. In 1859 she and a son, Franklin, were listed as being members of the Plymouth Congregational Church. The 1850 Census Schedule gives her husband's age as forty-four, and his real estate is valued at ten thousand dollars. Five children are listed. Martha Childs's age is given as thirty-nine. Information from Onondaga County Public Library, Syracuse; *Syracuse City Directory* (1857), p. 30; *Manual of the Plymouth Church of Syracuse* (1859), p. 14; and "Population Schedules of the Seventh Census of the United States, 1850," Onondaga County, City of Syracuse, Schedule 1, First Ward, p. 56, Dwelling 405, The National Archives and Records Service, microfilm, roll 569.

pressure was upon her mind that she seemed in haste to lay hold of the fulness there was in Christ. I do not think she was in my room more than five or ten minutes, and she left me like a person who has some pressing business on hand. In the afternoon she returned as full of the Holy Spirit, to all human appearance, as she could be. She said she hurried home from my room in the morning, and went immediately to her chamber, and cast herself down before God and made a thorough consecration of herself and of her all to Him. She said she had clearer apprehensions by far of what was meant by that than she had ever had before; and she made a full and complete resignation of herself and everything into the |hands of Christ. ‹H›er[49] mind became at once entirely calm, and she felt that she began *to fill up*[50] with the fulness of the Holy Spirit. In a very short time she seemed to be lifted up above herself, and her joy was so great that she could hardly refrain from shouting.

MS 900

As I said, she came down to see me again after dinner. I had some conversation with her, and saw that she was in danger of being over excited. I said as much as I dared to say to put her on her guard against this, and she went home. In the evening she attended our prayer and conference meeting; and as one after another was getting up to relate their Christian experience, she arose to tell what the Lord had done, and was doing, for her soul. Her face was literally radiant with religious joy. Every person present I presume, was struck with the halo that seemed to fill her countenance. She proceeded a little way in her narrative, and became incoherent as if she was forgetting herself. I understood |it in a moment, and stepped to her and speaking softly to her advised her to sit down. I then requested her friends to take her home, and advised my wife to go with her. She did so, and remained with her two or three days, until her excitement abated. Her joy was so great as to lift her quite above herself for several days, and she was really in danger of becoming entirely insane. However my wife remained with her, did not suffer her to see any company, and soothed and quieted her as best she could until her danger of insanity was quite past.

MS 901

A few days afterwards her husband called on me one morning with his sleigh, and asked me to take a ride with him. I did so, and found that his object was to talk with me about his wife. He said that she was brought up among the Friends, and when he married her he thought she was one of the most perfect women that he ever knew. But finally, he said, she became converted, and then he |observed a greater change in her than he thought was possible; for he thought her as perfectly moral in her outward life before as she could be. Nevertheless the change in her spirit and bearing at the time of her conversion was so manifest, he said, that no one could doubt it. "Since then," he said, |"I have thought her almost or quite perfect." "But," said he, "now she has manifestly passed through a greater change than ever. I see it in everything," said he. "There is such a spirit in her, such a change, such an energy in her religion, and such a fulness of joy and peace and love!" ‹He

MS 902

JHF 424

[49] Matson had written "She said her," but Finney altered it.
[50] Here Finney crossed out the word "within."

ıquired›,[51] "What shall I make of it? How am I to understand this? Do such hanges really take place in Christian people?"

I explained it to him as best I could. I tried to make him understand what he was by her education as a Quaker, and what her conversion had done for er; and then told him that this was a fresh baptism of the Holy Spirit that had o greatly changed her at that time. |**He was manifestly ‹much› surprized at he change‹s›[52] that had come over his wife, and especially this last one.** he has **now** passed away to heaven; but the savor of that anointing of the Ioly Spirit remained with her, as I have been informed, to the day of her eath.[53] MS 903

There **was** one circumstance that I have often heard **my wife** relate that ccurred in her meetings, that is worth ‹notice here.›[54] Her ladies' meetings vere composed of the more **cultivated and refined class of** ladies in the ifferent churches. Many of them were**, as my wife supposed,** fastidious. But **mong others** there was an elderly and uneducated old ‹woman›[55] that ttended their meetings, and that used to **get up and** speak, sometimes **a ood deal** to the annoyance of the ladies**, as my wife understood**. Somehow he had the impression that it was her *duty* to speak at every meeting; and ometimes she would get up and complain of the Lord that **He** laid it upon er to speak in meeting, while so many **fine** ladies of education were allowed) attend and take no part. She wondered why it was that God made it her uty to speak; while those fine ladies, who could speak so much to edification, vere |allowed to attend **those meetings** and "have no cross," as she expressed , "to take up." **What** she **said was** always **in** a whining and complaining manner›.[56] The part that she felt it her duty to take in every meeting a good eal annoyed and discouraged my wife. She saw that it did not interest the ıdies; and it seemed to her rather an element of **disgust**.[57] |But after things ad gone on in this way for **sometime**, one day this same old ‹woman› arose ı meeting, and a new spirit was upon her. **My wife said she observed her ise; and at first she felt sorry that she was going to occupy the time gain. But** as soon as she opened her mouth it was apparent to everybody ıat a great change had come over her. She had come to the meeting full of

MS 904

JHF 425

[51]Matson had written the words "Said he," but Finney changed them to "He inquired."

[52]Here Matson had written "He was manifestly wonderfully surprized at the change," but nney altered it.

[53]An obituary of Martha Childs indicates that it was not until March 1897 that she died, in ıglewood, New Jersey, which raises a question about the correct identification of this person. nney may have been mistaken about her death as already having taken place. The obituary says at she was a prominent church and charity worker, who had continued to live in Syracuse until ·o years before her death. "For thirty-four years she had been a member of the First :esbyterian church and always took an active interest in anything tending for its welfare" ewspaper clipping dated 25 March 1897 in Onondaga County Public Library). When the ymouth Church organized the Plymouth Society in 1858, her husband, N. M. Childs, was pointed a trustee (*The Journal,* 4 September 1858, p. 3; information from Onondaga County ıblic Library).

[54]Finney changed the word "relating" to "notice here."

[55]Matson had written the word "lady" here and in three other places, but Finney changed it in ıch case to "woman."

[56]Here Finney changed the expression "state of mind" to "manner."

[57]The word "disgust" was not altered in the manuscript, but the published edition has listurbance."

the Holy Ghost, and she poured out her fresh experience **in a manner tha made the ladies stare. My wife said that she saw in a moment that the** were greatly interested in what the old ‹woman› said; and she went forwar with an earnestness in relating what the Lord had done for her that carrie conviction to every mind. **The ladies** turned and leaned toward her to hea

MS 905 every ˡword that she said, the tears began to flow, and a great movement o the Spirit seemed to be visible at once throughout the **congregation. M wife has often remarked that** such a remarkable change **as that manifeste to those ladies,** wrought immense good **among them;** and **that** the ol ‹woman› became a favorite. After that they expected to hear from *her*; an were greatly delighted from meeting to meeting to hear her tell what the Lor had done, and was doing for her soul.

In that city, I found a Christian woman whom they called "Mothe Austin," a woman of most remarkable faith.[58] She was poor, and entirel dependent upon the charit**able assistance** of the **Christians in that city** fo subsistence.[59] She was an uneducated woman, and had been **raised** manifestl in a family of very little cultivation. But she had such faith as to secure th confidence of all who knew her. The conviction seemed to be univers among both Christians and unbelievers, that mother Austin was a saint. I d

MS 906 not think I ever witnessed greater faith ˡin its simplicity **and implicitnes** than was manifested by that woman. A great many facts were related to m respecting her that showed her trust in God, and in what a remarkabl manner God provided for her wants from day to day. She said to me on on occasion: "Brother Finney, it is impossible for me to suffer for any of th necessaries of life, because God has said to me, "Trust in the Lord and d good: so shalt thou dwell in the land, and verily thou shalt be fed."[60] Sh

JHF 426 related ‹to›[61] me many facts in her history, and ˡmany facts were related t me by others, illustrative of the power of her faith.

She said one Saturday evening a friend of hers, but an impenitent ma called to see her; and after conversing awhile he offered her as he went away five dollar bill. She said that she felt an inward admonition not to take it. Sh felt that it would be an act of self-righteousness on the part of that man, an might do him more harm than it would do her good. She therefore decline

MS 907 to take it, and he went away. ˡShe said she had just wood and food enough i the house to last over the Sabbath, and that was all; and she had no mear

[58] Anna Austin (1776–1858) was widely known for her remarkable Christian life. She was sa to have been unable to read until she was thirty-six years old, to have been subject to epileptic f until she was forty, and to have been addicted to every kind of vice until her conversion in h forty-sixth year. But she acquired a remarkable knowledge of the Scriptures and was sought aft by many people for her instruction and counsel. Finney probably had met her in Boston in 18 and may have called on her to deliver a letter on his way through Syracuse early in Februa 1842. At that time she was evidently addicted to tobacco and smoked a pipe, which prejudic Finney and others at Oberlin against her. She became a member of the Plymouth Church Syracuse (information from Anna Austin Papers, Onondaga County Historical Society, Syracus supplied by Timothy E. Gorman).

[59] She lived in a small house at 215 East Fayette Street. A life lease for the house was given her by the first mayor of Syracuse, Harvey Baldwin (*The Syracuse Directory*, 1857, p. 6; and An Austin Papers).

[60] Psalm 37:3.

[61] The word "to" appears to have been added by Finney.

whatever of obtaining any more. But still she was not at all afraid to trust God in such circumstances, as she had done **it** for so many years. On the Sabbath day there came a violent snow-storm. **It snowed terrifically all Sunday and Sunday night.** On Monday morning the snow was several feet deep, and the streets were blocked up so that there was no **passing** without **shoveling**. She had a young son that lived with her, they two composing the whole family.[62] They arose in the morning ‹& found themselves›[63] snowed in on every side. They made out to muster fuel enough for a little fire, and soon the boy began to inquire what they should have for breakfast. She said, "I do not know, my son; but the Lord will provide." She looked out, and nobody could pass the streets. The lad began to weep bitterly, and concluded that they should freeze and starve to death. However, she said she went on and made such preparations ˈas[64] she could to provide for breakfast, if any should come. I think she said she set her table, and made arrangements for her breakfast, believing that some would come in due season. Very soon she heard a loud talking in the streets, and went to the window to see what it was, and ‹behold›[65] a man in a single sleigh, and some men with him shoveling the snow so that the horse could get through. Up they came to her door, and behold! they had brought her a plenty of fuel and provisions, everything to make her ˈcomfortable for several days. But time would fail me to tell the **numbers of** instances in which she was helped in a manner as striking as this. Indeed, it was notorious through the city, so far as I could learn, that Mother Austin's faith was like a bank; and that she never suffered for want of the necessaries of life, because she drew on God.[66] MS 908 JHF 427

I never knew the number of converts at that time in Syracuse. Indeed I was never in the habit of ascertaining the number of hopeful[67] ˈ**conversions. I left all such things to be known when the secrets of all hearts shall be revealed.**[68] **However, the state of things in the Spring in that city** MS 909

[62]The 1850 Census Schedule also lists Joseph Austin living in the family. He was by then age thirty-three and a laborer ("Population Schedules of the Seventh Census of the United States, 1850," Onondaga County, City of Syracuse, Schedule 1, Second Ward, p. 276, Dwelling 1828, The National Archives and Records Service, microfilm, roll 569).

[63]Finney added the words "& found themselves."

[64]Fairchild added "–913" after page number 908 to indicate to the printers to proceed to page 914 and to omit the intervening pages.

[65]Finney changed the word "lo" to "behold."

[66]The section of the paragraph that follows to the bottom of the manuscript page was scored through in pencil. Fairchild may have done this with the intention of omitting it from the published version. It was, however, included.

[67]The word "converts" was added in pencil after the word "hopeful" at the bottom of the page. This appears to have been inserted by the typesetter. It ends the chapter in the published edition.

[68]It was noted at the time that Finney's supporters were careful not to make claims to immediate visible results nor to publish details of conversions. This was in contrast to earlier revivals. But it was also noted that the results were disappointing. William E. Knox, the Presbyterian minister in Rome, New York, wrote:

> His discourses are very much like those delivered upwards of twenty-five years ago with so great effect. Yet it must be confessed that his meetings from evening to evening are producing very little apparent result. I have attended some of them, and have been surprised, as have others, at the comparatively slight impression made on the audience; a fact going to show that a considerable change has taken place in the power of the preacher or the susceptibility of the people (*NYE,* 20 January 1853, p. 12; see also *OE,* 19 January 1853, p. 11).

religiously was the very opposite of what it had been the fall before; and if I am rightly informed they have never had so disastrous a state of things in that city since, or anything like it, as there was immediately previous to that revival. By those who have had any knowledge of the state of things in this country for the last thirty years, it will not be considered strange that everywhere where I was called to labor I had to overcome a great deal of prejudice in regard to my theological views. Hyper-Calvinistic views had obtained among Presbyterians and Congregationalists almost universally, up to the time that I began to preach. I saw that it was indispensable to introduce new views on several important questions, before anything like a successful effort could be made to convert the world. President Edwards' view of the bondage of the will, and the strange distinction he made between moral and natural ability and |inability, had greatly influenced the ministry, and taken possession of nearly all the pulpits in the Presbyterian and Congregational denominations. In most of the Baptist churches in the country they held to a higher and more absurd Calvinism than in the Presbyterian and Congregational churches. It is not wonderful, therefore, that the theology which I preached should have excited alarm and resistance. But after all it was the strange confusion that had taken possession of the minds of men in regard to our views of sanctification as taught in this place, that developed a great deal of prejudice in the land, and was many times a powerful obstacle to be overcome wherever I attempted to promote a revival. At Syracuse, as in every other place where I preached, the people were snuffing ‹for›[69] heresy; and it was not until their prejudices were absolutely *worn out* by attending our meetings, hearing what was said, and seeing that God evidently bore testimony to the truth as it was exhibited, that their prejudi|ces were so far overcome as to unite in forwarding the work. I have already said that it was the avowed object of certain leading minds to hedge me in, and if possible shut all the pulpits in the land against me. In this, however, they never succeeded; and it was always impossible for me to favorably respond to but a small portion of the pressing invitations I had to preach in almost every direction. However very much labor was needed, and very much caution and wisdom, to get over these prejudices that had been created, and secure union of effort among Christians to promote revivals of religion. I was no doubt in a sense responsible for much of the prejudice that existed. It fell to my lot, in the providence of God, to attack and expose many fallacies and false notions that existed in the churches, and that were paralyzing their efforts and rendering

MS 910

MS 911

Another later report mentioned that "not large numbers of the unconverted have attended the meetings." On the other hand the editor of *The Oberlin Evangelist* claimed that these reports underestimated the results and that "the Spirit of God descends in power; many backslidden are reclaimed; many deceived professors are converted; that hundreds are inquiring." However, he may have received this information from Finney's letters. See *OE,* 2 March 1853, p. 39; and 30 March 1853, pp. 53–54; and Finney to John Keep, 14 February 1853, transcription in R. S. Fletcher Papers, file 30/24, box 6, Oberlin College Archives.

[69] Finney added the word "for."

the preaching of the Gospel inefficacious. Indeed, as long as ministers would preach repentance, and then solemnly inform their hearers that they could not repent; |as long as they would preach faith, and then speak of faith as the gift of God in such a sense as that they could not exercise it; as long as they would represent faith as an *intellectual state* instead of a *voluntary trust*; as long as they would represent repentance as a feeling of godly sorrow, a state of the Sensibility, and consequently an involuntary state instead of a voluntary change of mind,—as long as these and kindred dogmas were held and taught, the Gospel was not really preached. What they *called* the Gospel was a stumbling block. As long as human nature was represented as in itself morally depraved, and, as a consequence, that sinners must wait for God to change their very *nature* before they could be Christians, what could be expected but a universal waiting on the part of sinners, and upon the part of Christians a universal throwing all the responsibility of the conversion of sinners upon God? As long as men were taught that for their sinful *nature* they were threatened with eternal dam|nation, and that the atonement of Christ was made only for the elect,—every one can see that all these and kindred dogmas were a snare and a stumbling block, and their legitimate influence was consequently manifesting itself in the wide-spread moral desolation that reigned.

MS 912

MS 913

It is not at all wonderful to me that, being commissioned, as I supposed myself to be, to attack and expose these errors let the consequence to myself be what it might, I should meet with just the opposition and prejudice that I did. However it is true that the opposition and prejudice were greatly increased in some instances, by the unwise and almost unaccountable opposition of men who professed to agree with me in my theological teaching. I have seldom been in any place where I felt the strong bands of prejudice on the part of those around me, more than I did for some weeks in Syracuse.[70]

[70] Matson had written down at the bottom of the page the following section after this: "As usual, after our labors in Syracuse were completed, we returned home and spent." Finney crossed this out when he entered a new chapter heading at the top of the next page.

MS 914
JHF 428

CHAPTER XXXII

‹*Labors* in Oberlin *Western & Rome.*›

‹As[1] usual, after our labors in Syracuse wer[e] completed we returned to Oberlin & spent & performed our usual labors with the usual results.[2] I always have expected›,[3] and I trust I always shall expect, to see the Word of the Lord take effect in this place, and in every place where it is truly and pointedly preached, and where such efforts are sustained by the prayers of God's people. The next winter at Christmas time we went again to Western, ‹Oneida county **N. York**›[4] where I have already related that I commenced my labors in the Autumn of 1825.[5] They were at ‹this›[6]

[1]The chapter heading and the first sentence of page number 914 down to n. 3 are in Finney's handwriting on a separate piece of paper pasted over the top of the page. The covering strip obscures the previous page numbers 762 and 894 in Matson's handwriting and a section that read: "the Summer, and performed our usual labors with the usual." Finney crossed out the rest of this section below the piece of paper. It reads, "results. I always have ex-." The rest of this word, "pected," on the next line he omitted deleting. The whole sentence was crossed out by Fairchild.

[2]The Finneys were back in Oberlin by 10 April 1853. See W. M. Barbour to Fergus Ferguson, 10 April 1853, in *The Canada Evangelist* (Amherstberg), 3 December 1853, p. 191. A report in *The Oberlin Evangelist* of 6 July 1853 reads:

> For the past three weeks there have been precious tokens of the Divine presence, an unusual number of youth having been solemnly impressed with divine truth and considerable numbers having given evidence of being savingly converted from their sins. It is indeed a time of solemn interest when the Lord is adding *daily* to his praying people such as shall be saved (p. 111).

A visitor in Oberlin on Sunday, 26 June, wrote:

> As usual, Oberlin is enjoying a revival, though without the use of any special services. Two months since about forty united on profession of their faith, and yesterday as many more stood up and entered into covenant with Jehovah. The afternoon was occupied with the reception of members and the administration of the Lord's Supper. At six o'clock there was an inquiry meeting, at which there were eighty present, though there had been scarcely a word addressed to the impenitent during the day. Some twenty or thirty neighborhood prayer-meetings were held during the evening (*OE,* 20 July 1853, p. 118).

It was pointed out that there had been "a daily prayer-meeting, sustained by a few, and that an obvious connection may be noticed between the interest and power of this meeting and the efficiency of the revival" (*OE,* 3 August 1853, p. 126). On 26 June, twenty-nine were admitted into membership of the church, and on 21 August, another twenty-one, mostly students. See *OE,* 31 August 1853, p. 143.

[3]This ends the section in Finney's handwriting.

[4]Finney added the words "Oneida county N. York."

[5]See MS 278–307. This was not the next winter. During November and December 1853 Finney held revival meetings in Cleveland. After returning to Oberlin at the end of December, he left again on 4 January 1854 for Cincinnati, where he held meetings until the middle of March, arriving back in Oberlin on the twenty-fourth. See *OE,* 18 January 1854, p. 13; 12 April 1854,

time again without a minister; and we spent several weeks there in very interesting labor, and with very marked **and interesting**[7] results. **The Brayton family, to which I have referred in my former notice of that place, had most of them passed away and gone to heaven. Father and Mother Brayton, their two eldest daughters, Sarah and Cynthia, and their youngest daughter, were all dead.**[8] |**Some very** striking things occurred in the revival **at** ‹this›[9] time **in that place. Not to go into particulars,** I will mention the case of one young man **‹that›**[10] **was quite striking.** He was the son of pious parents, and had long been made the subject of prayer. His parents were prominent members of the church. Indeed, his father was one of the elders of the church; and his mother was a godly, praying woman. When I commenced my labors there, to the great surprize and grief of his parents, and of the Christian people generally, he became exceedingly bitter against the preaching, and the meetings generally, and all that was done for the promotion of the revival. He committed himself with all the strength of his will against it; and affirmed, as I was told, that "neither Finney nor hell could convert him." He said many very hateful and profane things, **as I was told,** until his parents were deeply grieved; but I am not aware that he had ever been suspected of any outward immorality. MS 915

|**However,**[11] the Word of God pressed him from day to day till he could stand it no longer. He came one morning to my room. His appearance was truly startling. I cannot describe it. I seldom ever saw a person whose mind had made such an impression upon his countenance. He appeared to be almost insane; and he trembled in such a manner that when he |**sat down in** the room **you could literally feel the jar of** his trembling. I observed when I took his hand that it was very cold. His lips were blue; **and there was manifestly such a determination of blood to his brain as to deprive his extremities of blood to such an extent that** his appearance **seemed** quite alarming. The fact is, he had stood out against his convictions as long as he could endure it. MS 916 JHF 429

When he sat down I said to him: "My dear young man, what is the matter with you?" "O," said he, "I have committed the unpardonable sin." I replied,

p. 63; and Donald E. Pitzer, "Professional Revivalism in Nineteenth Century Ohio" (Ph.D. diss., Ohio State University, 1966), chap. 3.

During the summer and autumn of 1854, there was another revival in Oberlin, particularly among the students. The Finneys left Oberlin in November, arriving in Westernville on the thirtieth. See William Barbour's report, "From a Student at Oberlin," *The Canada Evangelist* 4 (August 1854): 122 (the place of publication of *The Canada Evangelist* changed to "Hamilton, C.W." in January 1854); *OE,* 22 November 1854, p. 191; and 28 February 1855, p. 35.

[6] Finney changed the word "that" to "this."

[7] The words "and interesting" were not crossed out by Fairchild in the manuscript but were omitted from the published edition.

[8] Matson had written down after this, at the bottom of the page: "Some very striking things occurred at that time in the revival in that place, especially," but he crossed it out.

[9] Finney crossed out the word "that" and inserted "this."

[10] Matson had written down the word "that." Finney crossed it out and inserted "this," but he subsequently crossed out "this" and inserted "that" again.

[11] Pages 916–17 were originally numbered 767–68 and were renumbered 896–97 by Matson. Finney changed them to 916–17. It appears that three earlier pages (764–66) were later removed. This page begins with the words "outward life," which were crossed out by Matson.

MS 917 "What makes you say so?"[12] "O," said he, "I *know* that I ꜝ**did**; and I did it *on purpose*." He then related this fact of himself. Said he, "Several years ago a book was put into my hands called, "The pirate's own book."[13] I read it, and it produced a most extraordinary effect upon my mind. It inspired me with a kind of terrible and infernal ambition to be the greatest pirate that ever lived. I made up my mind[14] to be at the head of all the highway robbers, and bandits, and pirates whose history was ever written.[15] "But," said he, "my religious education was in my way. The teaching and prayers of my parents seemed to rise up before me, so that I could not go forward. But I had heard that it was possible to grieve the Spirit of God away, and to quench his influence so that one would feel it no more. I had read also that it was possible MS 918 to sear my conscience, so that that would not trouble me; ꜝand[16] after my resolution was taken, my first business was to get rid of my religious convictions, so as to be able to go on and perpetrate all manner of robberies and murders without any compunction of conscience. I therefore set myself deliberately to blaspheme the Holy Ghost." He then told me in what manner he did this, and what he said to the Holy Ghost; but it was too blasphemous to repeat. **Indeed, so far as I have been able, I have thrown it entirely out of my recollection. But suffice it to say, it was something as bad as human, and I may say as infernal, ingenuity could conceive.** ‹He continued› "I then felt[17] **as if** it must be that the Spirit of God would leave me, and that my conscience would no more trouble me. After a little while I made up my mind that I would commit some crime and see how it would JHF 430 affect me. There was a school house across the way from ꜝour house; and one evening **about bedtime** I went **across the way** and set **the school house** on MS 919 fire. ꜝI[18] then went to my room and **went** to bed. Soon, however, the fire was discovered, **but too late to be extinguished**. I arose and mingled with the crowd that **assembled** to put it out; but all efforts were in vain, and it burnt to the ground." To burn a building in that way was**, in that state,** a state-prison offence. He was aware of this. I asked him if he had gone **any**[19] farther in the commission of crimes. He replied, "No." And I think he added, that he did not find his conscience at rest about it as he **hoped to have done**. I asked him

[12] Matson wrote this sentence in the margin. Fairchild crossed it out and reinserted it in between the lines of the text.

[13] *The Pirate's Own Book; or, Authentic Narratives of the Lives, Exploits, and Executions of the most Celebrated Sea Robbers, with historical sketches of the Joassamee, Spanish, Ladrone, West India, Malay, and Algerine Pirates* (Portland, Maine: Sanborn and Carter, 1837). This was a 432-page book with many illustrations, written by Charles Ellms.

[14] Matson had written down, " '. . . mind,' said he, 'to be. . . . ' " The "said he" appears to have been crossed out by Finney.

[15] Matson began the next sentence indented on a new line with new quotation marks probably indicating the start of a new paragraph. However, Finney inserted no paragraph sign.

[16] MS 918 was numbered 723 and renumbered 768 (instead of 769) and 898 by Matson, and then changed to 918 by Finney. Matson used sheets that had already been numbered 723–25 in advance but had not been used earlier after page 722 (MS 878).

[17] Matson had written the words "he said" after the word "felt," but Finney crossed them out and inserted the words "He continued" at the beginning of the sentence.

[18] Pages 919–20 were originally numbered 724–25, renumbered 769–70 and 899–900 by Matson, and changed to 919–20 by Finney.

[19] The word "any" was not crossed out in the manuscript but does not appear in the published edition.

if he had ever been suspected of having burnt it. He replied that he did not know that he had; but that other young men had been suspected, and talked about. I asked him what he proposed to do about it. He replied that he was going to the trustees to confess it; and he asked me if I would not accompany him. I went with him to one of the trustees, who lived **very** near‹by›;[20] and the young man asked me if I would not tell him the facts. |I did so. The (MS 920) trustee was a good man, and a great friend of the parents of this young man. The announcement affected [**him**] ‹deeply›.[21] The young man stood speechless before him. After conversing with the trustee for a little while, I said, "We will go and see the other trustees." The gentleman replied, "No, you need not go; I will see them myself, and tell them the whole story." He assured the young man that **they would forgive him.** That he himself would freely forgive him; and he presumed that the other trustees, and the people in the town, would forgive him, and not subject him or his parents to any expense about it.

I then returned to my room, and the young man went home. Still he was not at rest. As I was going to meeting in the evening he met me at the door and said, "I must make a *public* confession. Several young men have been suspected of this thing; and I want the people to know that I did it, and that I had |no[22] accomplice, that nobody but God and myself knew it." And he (MS 921) added: "Mr. Finney, won't *you* tell the people? I will be present, and say anything |that may be necessary to say if anybody should ask any questions; (JHF 431) but I do not feel as if I could open my mouth. You can tell them all about it." When the people were assembled I arose and related to them the facts. The family was so well-known, and so much beloved in the community, that the statement made a great impression. The people sobbed and wept all over the congregation. After he had made **a clear breast of it** he obtained peace. Of his religious history since I know not much. I have recently learned, however, that he retained his hold upon Christ, and did not seem to backslide. He went into the army during the **great** rebellion, and was slain at the battle of Fort Fisher. **Every one at all familiar with revivals of religion is aware that multitudes of cases are occurring from day to day and from week to week of most interesting conversions, conversions |that are particularly (MS 922) interesting to those upon the spot, and who are acquainted with the persons and circumstances. But to relate these conversions for the satisfaction of the public would interest them but very little, inasmuch as they know nothing of the persons, and feel no particular interest in their conversion more than in that of any others. In my Narrative I have not thought best to go into a detailed account of the conversion of persons not known to the general public, unless there was something very striking or interesting that brought out some great principle in the**

[20] Finney inserted the letters *by*.

[21] Here Matson had written down, "affected him very much indeed." Finney crossed out the words "him very much indeed" and wrote in the word "deeply." Fairchild reinserted the word "him."

[22] Pages 921–22 were originally numbered 901–2 by Matson and changed to 921–22 by Finney. They were inserted by Matson to replace a previous page 771. Fairchild added "–2" after 921 to indicate to the printers to omit the next page and to proceed to page 923.

administration of God's government. Should I go into detail, and notice what occurred from evening to evening and from day to day, my narrative would swell to many volumes. Indeed, should I give anything like a detailed account of any one of the great revivals in which I have labored, it would fill a large volume. Where, for instance, many hundreds, and in some cases some thousands of persons are converted in a revival, numbers of conversions are occurring every day of persons, and under circumstances,[23] |that thrill through the community where they are known, and make a most intense impression. But I have not thought it best to go into such detail at all, because however interesting those numerous cases may have been to those upon the spot and who were acquainted with the persons and circumstances, in general the public would take but comparatively little interest in the details. Indeed, I have been obliged, in writing out this Narrative, to give only an outline of what the Lord has done, without attempting to give such details as would swell my narrative beyond reasonable dimensions.

MS 923 |In[24] giving my narrative of revivals thus far I have passed over a great number of cases of crime **that came to my knowledge, ‹crimes›[25] of almost every description, that had been** committed by persons who came to me for advice, and told me the facts. In many instances in these revivals restitution, sometimes to the amount of many thousands of dollars, was made by those whose consciences troubled them, either because they had obtained **it** directly by fraud, or by some selfish over-reaching in their business relations. The winter that I first spent in Boston resulted in making a great many such revelations. I had preached there one Sabbath in the morning upon this text: "Whoso covereth his sins shall not prosper;" and in the afternoon on the remainder of the verse: "But whoso confesseth and forsaketh them, shall find mercy."[26] I recollect that the results of those two sermons were most extraordinary. For weeks after **that** persons of almost all ages and of both sexes came to me for spiritual advice, disclosing to me the fact that they had committed various frauds, and sins of almost every description. Some young MS 924 men had defrauded their employers |in business; and some women had stolen watches and almost every article of female apparel.[27] Indeed it seemed as if the Word of the Lord was sent home with such power at that time in that city, JHF 432 as to uncover a very |*den* of wickedness. It would certainly take me hours to mention the crimes that came to my personal knowledge through the confessions of those that had perpetrated them. But in every instance the persons seemed to be thoroughly penitent, and were willing to make restitution to the utmost of their ability.

[23] At the foot of page 922 Matson wrote "[over]" in brackets and continued this section on the reverse of the page.

[24] Pages 923–38 were originally numbered 772–87 and renumbered 903–18 by Matson. Finney changed them to 923–38.

[25] Finney added the word "crimes."

[26] Proverbs 28:13.

[27] One of these young men was A. S. Reeves, who wrote to Finney giving details of his stealing from employers and asking Finney's advice (Reeves to Finney, 9 November 1831, Finney Papers, microfilm, roll 3).

But to return from this digression to Westernville. The revival was of a very interesting character; and there was a goodly number of souls born to God. **The population, however, in that region is very much scattered; and there had been for many years an unhappy state of feeling among the inhabitants in regard to supporting a minister.**[28]

The conversion of one young lady there I remember with a good deal of interest. She was teaching the village ˡ**public** school. Her father was, I believe, a **skeptic**; and as I understood she was an only daughter, and a great favorite with her father. He was a man, if I was rightly informed, of considerable influence in the town, but did not at all attend our meetings. He lived on a farm away from the village. Indeed the village is very small, and the inhabitants are scattered through the valley of the Mohawk, and over the hills on each side; so that the great mass of inhabitants have to come a considerable distance to meeting. **The farms are large and the farmers wealthy, and consequently the inhabitants are scattered. Western is one of the most beautiful places for a country residence that I almost ever saw. But to speak of the conversion of this young lady.** I had heard that **she** did not attend our meetings much, and that she manifested a considerable opposition to the work. In passing the school house one day I **thought I would** step in **and** speak with her, **and I did** ‹**so**›.[29] ˡAt first she appeared surprized to see me come in. I had never been introduced to her, and should not have known her if I had not found her in that place. She knew me however, and at first appeared as if she recoiled from my presence. **I had heard her name, however; and** I took her very kindly by the hand and told her that I had dropped in to speak with her about her soul. "My child," I said, "how is it with you? Have you given your heart to God?" This I said while I held her hand. Her head fell, and she made no effort to withdraw her hand. I saw in a moment that a subduing influence came over her, and so deep and remarkable an influence that I felt ‹almost›[30] assured that she would submit to God right on the spot. ˡThe most that I expected when I went in was to have a few words with her that I hoped might set her to thinking, and to appoint a time to converse with her more at large. But **on speaking** the impression was at once so manifest, and she seemed to break down in her heart so readily, ˡthat **in** a few sentences quietly and softly spoken to her she seemed to give up her opposition, and to be in readiness to lay hold on the Lord Jesus Christ. I then asked her if I should say a few words to the scholars; and she said, yes, she

MS 925

MS 926

JHF 433

MS 927

[28]The Syracuse *Religious Recorder* reported:

> When brother F[inney] first reached W[esternville] there were but three or four brethren who were in the habit of coming together for prayer, and Mrs. F[inney] could find but one or two sisters of the church who thought they could engage in a female prayer-meeting. A general depression rested upon visible Zion, and all around was desolation. The church numbers not far from one hundred members, and out of all there were not more than half a dozen who could be brought forward to act, and general discouragement prevailed (reprinted in *OE,* 25 February 1855, p. 35).

Finney referred to the situation at the beginning of January: "The state of things has been about as bad as possible, but is changing fast for the better" (Finney to Gerrit Smith, 6 January 1855, Gerrit Smith Papers, George Arents Library, Syracuse University).

[29]Finney added the word "so."

[30]Finney added the word "almost."

wished I would. I did so, and then asked her if I should present herself and her scholars to God in prayer. She said she wished I would, and became very deeply affected in the presence of the school. We engaged in prayer, and it was a very solemn, melting time. The young lady from that time seemed to be subdued, and to have passed from death unto life. She did not live long before she passed, I trust, to heaven. These two seasons of my being in Western were about thirty years apart. Another generation had come to live in that place from that ‹which›[31] lived there in the first revival in which I labored there. I found, however, a few of the old members there. But the congregation was mostly new, and composed principally of youngerly people who had grown up after the first revival.

MS 928 As in the case of the first ǀrevival, so in this, the people in Rome heard what was passing in Westernville, and came up in considerable numbers to attend our meetings. This led, after a few weeks, to my going down and spending sometime in Rome.[32] The state of religion in Western has, I believe, been very much improved since this last revival.[33] The ordinances of the Gospel have been maintained, and I believe considerable progress has been made in the right direction. The Braytons have all gone from Western with the exception of one son and his family. That large and interesting family have melted away; but one of them being left in Western, one in Utica, and JHF 434 one son who was converted in the first revival ǀthere, and who has for many years been a minister, ‹& Pastor of the first Presbyterian church in Watertown N.Y.›[34]

After the first revival in Rome a good many of the people became satisfied that their old pastor, the Rev. Moses Gillett, was not quite MS 929 adequate to the performance of the duties devolvǀing upon him in the new condition of things. He had said to me before I left, in the first great revival there, that he had no sermons that were applicable at all to the altered situation of his people. Said he: "My sermons have been prepared entirely for another state of things. And now so far as my people are concerned, the Millennium has come; my people are nearly all converted." The house of worship was full to overflowing ‹of professed Christians.›[35] It resulted in forming another congregation.

[31] Here Finney changed the word "that" to "which."

[32] W. E. Knox, the minister at Rome, reported:

Early in the fall Rev. C. G. Finney commenced his labors in Western, seven miles distant. The circumstances of his former great success in this region in 1826, excited expectation in the minds of some of the churches, and aided in rekindling a spirit of prayer in our meetings. After considerable success in Western, Mr. Finney came to Rome the second week in February, and remained until the 1st of April (*NYE,* 10 May 1855, p. 74).

[33] By 1 February it was reckoned that

forty or fifty had given their hearts to Christ. Several family altars have been erected. Of course the church has been encouraged, and though it is by no means where it should be as a body, yet it offers now a very interesting field of labor to a minister of the gospel (*OE,* 28 February 1855, p. 35).

[34] Matson had originally written down, "been a minister, and did live in Albany." He crossed out "did" and added "has." Finney then crossed out the last phrase and added, "and Pastor of the first Presbyterian church in Watertown N.Y." This was Isaac Brayton. See MS 292.

[35] Finney added the words "of professed Christians."

Mr. Gillett took another field of labor, and many years since passed away to his reward.[36] **The two congregations worshipped separately for several years; but finally agreed to unite, and build them a large, commodious church that would accommodate both congregations.**[37]

The Autumn I was **there** ‹the first time›[38] and for many years after, the church was Congregational. But a few years before I was there the last time they had settled a Presbyterian **M**inister, a young man, **educated, I** |**believe, at Princeton.**[39] **He** felt **as if** the church ought to be Presbyterian instead of Congregational; **and he** proposed and recommended this to the church. **In some way he** succeeded in bringing it about, but to the great dissatisfaction of a large number of influential persons in the church. This created a very undesirable state of things in Rome; and when I arrived there from Western I was for the first time made acquainted with that very serious division **in regard to their changing their form of government**. Their pastor had lost the confidence and affection of a considerable number of very influential members of his church. When I learned the state of things I felt confident that but little could be done to promote a general revival, unless that difficulty could be healed. But it had been talked over so much, and the persons first concerned in it had so committed themselves, that I labored in vain to **get over** |**that difficulty**. It was not a thing to preach about; but in private conversation I tried to pluck up that root of bitterness. I found the parties did not view the facts alike. I kept preaching, however; and the Spirit of the Lord was poured out, conversions were occurring very frequently, and I trust great good was done.[40] But after endeavoring in vain to secure a union of feeling

MS 930

MS 931

[36]By 1830 the church membership had grown to 500, the population of the town being then 4,300. A Second Presbyterian Church was formed in January 1831. In July, Jacob Helffenstein was installed as pastor. He remained until ill health caused him to leave in 1833. The church then had a succession of ministers, among them Theodore Spencer, Herman Norton, and George S. Boardman. There were notable revivals in 1831 with the help of Jedediah Burchard and in 1841 with the help of Orson Parker. Boardman continued ministering there until 1847, when the two churches united. Moses Gillet left the First Church in September 1837 and supplied churches in Moscow and Sweden, New York. He retired to Rome in 1846, dying there in June 1848. See W. E. Knox, *Semi-Centennial. A Sermon, Preached in the First Presbyterian Church, Rome, N.Y., September 29, 1850* (Rome, N.Y.: Sandford, 1851), pp. 19–22; p. 156 n. 2 (MS 308); and MS 1054.

[37]Gillet left in September 1837. After his departure the church was supplied by three different ministers until 1841, when Selden Haynes was installed as pastor. He resigned in June 1846. The two churches were united in June 1847, and a new meeting house was opened in January 1852. See Knox, *Semi-Centennial*, pp. 21–23; and *NYE*, 20 January 1853, p. 12.

[38]Finney added the words "the first time." He was in Rome during the winter of 1825–1826. See MS 308–40.

[39]The First Church of Rome had been founded in 1800 as a Presbyterian church but became connected with the Oneida [Congregational] Association in 1812. In 1818, while retaining a Congregational form of government, it transferred to the Oneida Presbytery. As the minister put it, "Though nominally Congregational, we are really Presbyterian, 'with a defective organization' " (Knox, *Semi-Centennial*, p. 13).

The minister was William Eaton Knox (1820–1883). He is not listed among the alumni of either Princeton College or the theological seminary. He went to the First Church in May and was installed in August 1848. Knox had attended Finney's meetings in Syracuse the previous winter (1852–1853) and had apparently not been impressed by the results. See *NYE*, 20 January 1853, p. 12; and p. 535 n. 68 (MS 909).

[40]W. E. Knox reported on the good influence of the revival in Rome in a letter to *The New-York Evangelist*. He gave a figure of "between fifty and sixty conversions recently of young

and effort such as God would approve, I made up my mind to leave them, **and did so.**[41] I have heard since that some of the disaffected members of the church went and joined the church in Western, leaving the church in Rome altogether. ‹I presume the Pastor did what he deemed to be his duty in that controversy but the consequent divisions were exceedingly painful to me as I felt a peculiar interest in that church.›[42]

people" (10 May 1855, p. 74). But in a later letter published in *The Oberlin Evangelist* he revised that figure: "I think, on better investigation, it may safely be rated at seventy. These converts, almost without exception, appear well, and are evidently growing in religious experience and knowledge. A spirit of inquiry still remains to a considerable degree" (Knox to Henry Cowles, 25 May 1855, in *OE,* 6 June 1855, p. 95).

[41] The Finneys were in Rome for seven weeks. They had arrived there by Saturday, 10 February 1855. The *Utica Daily Gazette* for that day advertised that Finney was to preach in the Presbyterian church the next day. The following Sunday, Ralph Waldo Emerson, the transcendentalist writer, who was visiting Rome, was taken to hear him preach. He wrote:

> Today, I heard Mr Phinney, the noted revivalist preach. I did not suppose such a style of preaching still survived. A great parade of logic, to be sure, but all built on a cobweb of church traditions which a childs popgun or a doll's brush would go through. I could not help telling my kind entertainer, who wished me to admire "the intellectual treat," that I thought the preacher had extolled God's heart at the expense of his head. Neither did he once launch away from this ostentatious logic, did not once trust himself, or dive into any sentiment or imagination, so that I could not believe it more affecting to others than to me. Tis 25 years since I heard him once before. I did not like him then much better (Ralph Waldo Emerson, *Letters*, ed. Ralph L. Rusk, vol. 4 [New York: Columbia University Press, 1939], p. 493).

Finney preached his last sermon at Rome on 1 April. See Finney to Julia Finney, 10 February 1855, Finney Papers, microfilm, roll 4; *OE,* 6 June 1855, p. 95; and *NYE,* 10 May 1855, p. 74.

[42] Finney added this sentence at a later time. Just after Finney's *Memoirs* were published, P. H. Fowler wrote in his history of Presbyterianism in central New York:

> Sermons get out of date. Their repetition becomes anachronistic. The powerful preaching of 1826 is feeble in 1876. The receptivity for it has passed away. Mr. Finney shared the common experience. He himself never waned, but (save in exceptional communities and circumstances,) his pulpit fell off. I was cognizant of an illustration of this at Rome in 1855. As able and earnest then as he was when there in 1826, little or no response to his discourses came back. He ascribed it in his autobiography very erroneously and unjustly to the pastor; but the explanation of it was his *passé* matter and style. So manifest was this at the time, that his old friends in Utica, where considerable religious interest existed, deemed it unwise to invite him there (*Historical Sketch of Presbyterianism Within the Bounds of the Synod of Central New York* [Utica: Curtiss and Childs, 1877], pp. 284–85).

In fact, Finney did have invitations to Utica the next year. See "Invitations to C. G. Finney," Miscellaneous Items, Finney Papers, microfilm, roll 8.

In spite of Finney's criticism of him, Knox was very positive about the visit of the Finneys and reported after they left Rome:

> The effect of his labors has been happy on the church, a large number of whom have been much quickened in their religious experience, and stirred up to new zeal in the service of God; especially have the female members been sharers in this blessing, a result attributable in no small degree to the judicious and efficient influence exerted by Mrs. Finney. . . . At times during our meetings, a powerful impression of the truth appeared to rest upon the community at large. The result of Mr. Finney's visit has, on the whole, been a hopeful and happy one (*NYE,* 10 May 1855, p. 74).

At the end of May, Knox was in Oberlin and took the opportunity to write a letter to Henry Cowles, editor of *The Oberlin Evangelist,* expressing similar opinions on the value of the revival. See n. 40 above.

Finney crossed out the following section when he started a new chapter on the next page: "The next Autumn, which was in 1855, we were invited again to the city of Rochester to labor for the salvation of souls there. At first I had no mind to go, but after receiving several letters from there a messenger arrived with a pressing invitation, bearing the signatures."

MS 932
JHF 435

ǀ‹In[43] the Autumn of 1855, we were called again to the City of Rochester **N.Y.** to labor for souls. At first I had no mind to go, but a messenger arrived with a pressing request bearing the signatures of a large number of persons both professors of religion & nonprofessors.›[44] After much deliberation and prayer I **made up my mind to go**. We commenced our labors there, and it was very soon apparent that the Spirit of God was working among the people. Some Christians in that place, and especially the brother who came after me, had been praying most earnestly all summer for the outpouring of the Spirit there. A few souls had been wrestling with God until they felt that they were on the eve of a great revival.[45] When I stated my objections to going to labor in Rochester again, the brother who came after me set that all aside by saying: "*The Lord is going to send you to Rochester; and you will go to Rochester this winter, and we shall have a great revival.*" **But** I made up my mind with much hesitancy after all. But when I arrived there I was soon convinced that it was of God.[46] I began preaching in the different churches. The First Presbyterian church in that city was Old School, and they did not open their doors to our meeting.[47] ǀBut the Congregational church, and the **other two**[48] Presbyterian churches ‹with their **Pastors**›[49] took hold of the work, and entered into it with spirit and success.[50] **Since I first labored there in 1830 and '31 the**

MS 933

[43]The first section of MS 932 down to n. 44 is in Finney's handwriting on a separate piece of paper pasted onto the sheet. It obscures the previous page numbers 781 and 912 in Matson's handwriting and a section of the text that reads, "of a great number of persons both in and out of the churches, urging me very strongly to come and labor there." Finney crossed out the last word—"there"—which was left exposed below the covering strip. Finney had started a new chapter heading that read, "‹Chap. XXXIII. *Revivals again in Rochester N. York.*›" but crossed it out. Fairchild inserted a similar title as the start of chapter XXXII in the published version.

[44]This ends the section in Finney's handwriting. This request was signed by "the ministers and elders of the Second and Fourth Presbyterian Churches (New School), joined by some of the other denominations, and some citizens not connected with any church" (report in *The Congregationalist* [Boston], 21 March 1856, p. 45, reprinted in *American Congregational Year-Book for the Year 1857* [New York], p. 152). This report, signed "J.E.," was written by Rev. Jonathan Edwards. See n. 64 below. The request is not in the Finney Papers.

[45]According to one report, "During last December an oppressive sense of the coldness of Christians and of the heedlessness of the unforgiven was felt by a few, and about the time of the annual church fasts the feeling found expression of the necessity of special means to arouse the public mind to a sense of religious truths" (*The Independent* [New York], 15 May 1856, p. 155).

[46]The Finneys had left Oberlin on 24 December, and Finney started preaching in Rochester on Sunday, 30 December 1855. Louis Chapin wrote: "On his arrival here he went to board with a lawyer, Truman Hastings who soon after slip[p]ed down on an icy side walk & broke his leg. I then asked Mr. Finney to bring his wife & make their home at my house which they did for 96 days (without pay)." See *OE,* 2 January 1856, p. 7; *The Independent,* 15 May 1856, p. 155; and L. Chapin to G. F. Wright, 10 February 1890, Wright Papers, box 8.

[47]Finney refers to this in more detail in MS 939.

[48]The order of the words "other two" was not altered in the manuscript but was altered in the published version.

[49]Finney added the words "with their Pastors."

[50]These were the Second, or Brick Presbyterian, Church; the Fourth, or Washington Street, Church; and the new Plymouth Congregational Church. See MS 439. Finney started preaching alternately in these churches during the week and on Sundays. See *OE,* 30 January 1856, p. 23; and 26 March 1856, p. 55. It was reported that when he first arrived in Rochester, Finney found the church in a more apathetic state than he anticipated, with "no marked manifestation of interest or readiness" for revival efforts; and "he said that had he really understood the state of things he should hardly have come." For the first two or three weeks his sermons "were addressed exclusively to Christians, and were of a most thorough and searching character"

city had grown very largely in its proportions, in its wealth, and in every respect.[51] **The two great revivals that preceded this one had left in that city a very strong and predominant Christian influence.** The Baptist churches also entered into the work at this time; and the Methodist churches **went to work** in their own way to extend the work.[52] We held daily noon prayer meetings, which were largely attended, and in which a most excellent spirit prevailed.[53]

JHF 436 |Soon after I commenced my labors there a request was sent to me, signed by the members of the bar and several judges—two judges of the Court of Appeals, and I believe one or two judges of the Supreme Court who resided there—asking me to preach again a course of lectures to lawyers on the Moral Government of God.[54] I complied with their request.[55] I began my

(*American Congregational Year-Book for the Year 1857,* p. 152; and *The Independent,* 15 May 1856, p. 155).

[51]The population of Rochester in 1830, when a census was taken, was 10,863. In 1855 it was probably about 50,000. See *Directory of the City of Rochester* (Rochester: Morse, 1834), p. 5; W. F. Peck, *Semi-Centennial History of Rochester* (Syracuse: Mann, 1884), pp. 136, 140, 173; and *The Independent,* 15 September 1853, p. 147.

[52]The First and Second Baptist churches asked Finney to extend his labors to them at the end of February, and he started preaching there early in March. See MS 940; *The Independent,* 13 March 1856, p. 83; and *OE,* 26 March 1856, p. 55. The First Methodist Episcopal Church had been greatly increased as a result of the revival of 1831, and nine hundred members were reported in 1834. The Second Methodist Church was formed on the east side of the river in 1836. By 1855 there were three additional Methodist churches in the city. For a time during the revival the Methodists had the help of Rev. Dr. Redfield of New York. They carried on meetings separately from the union meetings held by the other churches. See Peck, *Semi-Centennial History,* pp. 268–72; *OE,* 26 March 1856, p. 56; and *The Independent,* 15 May 1856, p. 155.

[53]The morning union prayer meetings were held in rotation in the lecture rooms of the churches every day from 9:00 to 10:00. It was reported that three hundred usually attended. There was also a prayer meeting "for youth" at 8:00 "to accommodate the members of schools." Later, in April, these meetings were amalgamated and held at 8:00. See *OE,* 27 February 1856, p. 40; 26 March 1856, p. 55; *NYE,* 13 March 1856, p. 43; *The Independent,* 15 May 1856, p. 155; and *American Congregational Year-Book for the Year 1857,* p. 152.

Rev. J. H. McIlvaine's recollection in 1890 that a prayer meeting "averaging from eight hundred to a thousand persons, was maintained daily at ten o'clock in the morning for six months" is probably an exaggeration (see J. H. McIlvaine to G. F. Wright, 4 May 1890, Wright Papers, box 8). But by the middle of April the numbers had become so large that the lecture rooms, which held four or five hundred, were not large enough, and the churches had to be used. Kingman Nott, a student at the theological seminary, wrote about the 24 April meeting: "The church was almost full—six or eight hundred persons. . . . It has been agreed to continue the prayer meetings during the year" (Richard M. Nott, *Memoir of Abner Kingman Nott* [New York: Evans, 1882], p. 162).

[54]This undated document is in the Finney Papers. It is in the handwriting of Addison Gardiner and reads:

> The undersigned would be gratified, should the Rev. C. G. Finney find it compatible with his other engagements, to deliver a course of Lectures designed more particularly, for the members of the legal profession. The time & place of delivery, and the subject of the lectures respectively, to be selected by Mr. Finney, & announced in such manner as to give all who were inclined, an opportunity to attend them (Miscellaneous Items, Finney Papers, microfilm, roll 8; it is signed by Gardiner and fifteen other lawyers).

Addison Gardiner and his partner, Samuel Lee Selden (1800–1876), were the two judges of the court of appeals. Selden had also been a justice of the New York State supreme court since 1847. He succeeded Gardiner in the court of appeals in 1856. See *The National Cyclopaedia of American Biography,* vol. 4 (New York: White, 1897), p. 154.

Two of the others on the list, Joseph A. Eastman and John C. Chumasero, had been practicing law in Rochester when Finney was there in 1842 and were partners. Chumasero became a judge in the court of common pleas in 1863. Another was James C. Campbell, who had been a law

course to lawyers this time by preaching first on |the text: "Commending ourselves to every man's conscience in the sight of God."[56] I began by remarking that the text assumed that every man had a Conscience. I then gave a definition of Conscience, and proceeded to show what every man's conscience did truly affirm. That every man knew himself to be a sinner against God; that therefore he knew that God must condemn him as a sinner; and that every man knew that his own conscience condemned him as a sinner. I was aware that among the lawyers were some skeptics. Indeed one of them had a few months before declared that he would never again attend a Christian meeting. That he did not believe in the Christian religion, and he would not appear to do so. That it placed him in a false position; and his mind was made up to pay no more respect to the institutions of Christianity. I shaped my lectures from evening to evening with the design to convince the lawyers that if the Bible was not true there was no hope for them.[57] That their own consciences condemned them, |and they must be aware that God must condemn them; and how should they be forgiven? I endeavored to show that they could not infer that God would forgive them because He was *good*, for His goodness might *prevent* His forgiving them. It might not on the whole be wise and good to pardon such a world of sinners as we know ourselves to be. That left without the Bible to throw light upon that question, it was impossible for human reason to come to the conclusion that sinners could be saved. Admitting that God was infinitely benevolent, we could not infer from that that *any* sinners could be forgiven; but must infer from it, on the contrary, that *impenitent* sinners could not be forgiven. I

MS 934

MS 935

student in 1842. The others who signed had started practicing since Finney was there. George G. Munger had become a judge in 1855. John Norton Pomeroy (1828–1885) had grown up in Rochester. He was admitted to the bar in 1851 and was later to become well known as a writer of legal textbooks and a law lecturer in California (see *DAB*). Martin S. Newton was district attorney in Rochester from 1850–1853.

Others who signed were Oliver M. Benedict, Hiram F. and Jarvis M. Hatch, Hiram K. Jerome, Daniel Wood, Henry Sargent, and John Thompson, Jr. The last signature on the list is that of Lewis Henry Morgan (1818–1881), who had been practicing law in Rochester since 1851 and was soon to become famous as an ethnologist and the "Father of American Anthropology." See *DAB*. See also Peck, *Semi-Centennial History*, pp. 372–74; and *King's Rochester City Directory and Register, 1841* (Rochester: Welles and Hayes, 1840).

[55]The course of lectures was noticed in the *Congregational Journal*: "By invitation from the lawyers in the city, he is now giving them a course of lectures on the Divine Law—its sanctions, penalties, etc. He comes out in all his power, as he did twenty years ago" (reprinted in *NYE*, 13 March 1856, p. 43).

[56]2 Corinthians 4:2.

[57]Commenting on this passage in the *Memoirs*, H. Pomeroy Brewster told an audience at a Rochester Historical Society meeting in 1892:

> Some of you, I know, listened to these masterly efforts; and will recall their clear, terse arguments. His manner had nothing then, of the dramatic character, which at earlier times marked his sermons to the masses. He well knew that was not the time nor place for an exhibition of intellectual pyrotechnics and therefore concentrated the whole powers of his great mind to convince beyond question the minds of these men, leaving the rest to a higher power. Dr. Anderson, who was always present, never failed to accord Mr. Finney the highest possible praise, not only for "his magnificent logic," but more for "his candor and honesty in meeting frankly the questions involved" (Brewster, "The Magic of a Voice: Rochester Revivals of Rev. Charles G. Finney," *The Rochester Historical Society, Publication Fund Series* 4 [1925]: 286).

JHF 437 endeavored to clear the way so as to shut them ¦up to the Bible as revealing the only *rational* way in which they could expect salvation.

At the close of my first lecture I heard that the lawyer to whom I have referred, who had said he would never attend another Christian meeting, MS 936 remarked to a friend as ¦he went home, that he had been mistaken, that he was satisfied there was more in Christianity than he had supposed, and he did not see any way to escape the argument to which he had listened; and furthermore that he should attend all those lectures, and make up his mind in view of the facts and arguments that should be presented.

I continued to press this point upon their attention until I felt that they were effectually shut up to Christ, and the revelations made in the Gospel, as their only hope. But as yet I had not presented Christ, but left them shut up under the law, condemned by their own consciences, and sentenced to eternal death. This, as I expected, effectually prepared the way for a cordial reception of the blessed Gospel. When I came to bring out the Gospel as revealing the only possible or conceivable way of salvation for sinners, they gave way, as they had done under a former course of lectures in former years. They began MS 937 to break down, and a large proportion ¦of them were hopefully converted. **As the revival at this time, as well as at other times, took effect to a very large extent among the principal unconverted inhabitants of the city, it spread very generally through the city.** What was quite remarkable in the three revivals that I have witnessed in Rochester,—they all commenced and made their first progress among the higher classes of society. This was very favorable to the general spread of the work, and to the overcoming of opposition.

There were many very striking cases of conversion in this revival, as in the revival that preceded it. The work spread, and excited so much interest that it became the general topic of conversation throughout the city and the surrounding region of country. Merchants arranged to have their clerks attend, a part of them one day and a part the next day. The work became so general throughout the city that in all places of public resort, in stores and JHF 438 MS 938 public ¦houses, ¦in[58] banks, in the street and in public conveyances,—and everywhere, the work of salvation that was going on was the absorbing topic.[59] **I have never known the number of conversions that occurred**

[58] Fairchild added "−9" after page number 938 to indicate to the printers to omit page 938 and to proceed to 939.

[59] William C. Wilkinson, at that time one of the students at the university and later a well-known Baptist author, recollected:

> The interest was extraordinary. The city was taken possession of. Scarcely anything else was talked about. The atmosphere was full of a kind of electricity of spiritual power. The daily papers all reported the meetings at great length. Strangers casually visiting the city were unable to resist the infection of the prevailing religious influence. The railroads at one time, I remember, were obstructed by a snowstorm, which detained large numbers of passengers temporarily in the city. A large proportion of these were attracted into the meetings. The result was that a great many, during this brief interval, were converted. People accosted each other in the street, and began an exchange of question and reply on the subject of personal religion, as naturally and easily almost as in a time of commercial distress they would talk of the financial condition of the country; or to use an apter illustration, as in a time of epidemic disease

here in any of these great revivals; but the number must have been very arge in each of them, and I should think larger in the last than in either of the two former.[60] Men that had stood out in the former revivals, many of hem bowed to Christ in this, **and submitted themselves to God**. Some men who had been open Sabbath breakers, others that had been openly profane,—indeed, all classes of persons, from the highest to the lowest, from the richest o the poorest, were visited by the power of this revival and brought to Christ. I continued there throughout the winter, the revival increasing ontinually, **until in the Spring, just at the time when the current was the trongest and the divine influence seemed to be the most all-pervading, I had a carbuncle on my neck which finally laid me aside, and I was obliged to stop preaching and leave the city.**[61] **|‹At**[62] **this time the newly organized congregational church were without a Pastor.**[63] **While I was there & during the revival the Rev. Mr. Edwards was installed pastor of that church.**[64] **Rev. Dr. Shaw was Pastor of the Second Pres. Church, & Rev. Mr. Ellenwood was Pastor of the fourth, or Washington**

MS 939

they would talk of their own health and of that of their families and friends ("Charles G. Finney as a Preacher," *The Independent,* 9 September 1875, pp. 1–2).

Extracts of Finney's sermons and coverage of the meetings were reported particularly in the *Rochester Daily Union*. See James E. Johnson, "The Life of Charles G. Finney" (Ph.D. diss., Syracuse University, 1959), pp. 367–68; and n. 72 below.

[60] Augustus H. Strong, the Baptist theologian who was converted in this revival and was later president of the theological seminary in Rochester, reckoned that a thousand had been converted in the 1842 revival, "and a thousand more joined the churches" as a result of the revival in 1856 (A. H. Strong, *Christ in Creation and Ethical Monism* [Philadelphia: Williams, 1899], p. 365).

[61] The last line on the manuscript page, "obliged to stop preaching and leave the city," was added by Matson at the foot of the page from the top of what had been page 919, when Finney added eight new pages in his own handwriting. Finney became ill late in April and left Rochester on 4 May. He went to Brooklyn, New York, to rest for a while and then returned to Oberlin on 22 May. See *OE,* 21 May 1856, p. 87; and 4 June 1856, pp. 95–96.

[62] MS 939 is the first of eight pages in Finney's handwriting inserted between pages 918 and what had previously been 919. It was omitted by Fairchild, except for the last sentence, which he rewrote at the top of the next page. The eight pages were originally numbered 919–26 and changed to 939–46 by Finney.

[63] Finney had originally written, "At this time the newly erected congregational church were when I arrived without a Pastor," but he changed it. The Plymouth Congregational Church had been organized in April 1854. Their new church on the corner of Troup and Sophia Streets was considered to be "the most impressive house of worship in western New York when it was built." It had just been dedicated on 21 August 1855.

> Plymouth Church was seen by other Congregational Churches and leaders as a star of Congregational hopes, shining over the Presbyterian desert of western New York. It was located in the elite section of the city, possessing a congregation of business, professional and political leaders. Everything pointed to its eminence and influence (Charles D. Broadbent, "A Brief Pilgrimage: Plymouth Church of Rochester," *Rochester History* 40, no. 4 [October 1978]: 1, 3).

[64] Jonathan Edwards (1820–1894) was a graduate of Yale College and Andover Theological Seminary. He went to Rochester from Woburn, Massachusetts, in February 1856 and was installed at Plymouth Church on 18 April. "Dr. Shaw, assisted by Mr. Finney, conducted the exercises." He remained there until 1862, when he was called to Dedham, Massachusetts. He was related to the more famous Jonathan Edwards of Northampton. See *The Congregational Year-Book* (Boston), 1895, p. 25; *The Congregationalist,* 9 May 1856, p. 74; and Broadbent, "Brief Pilgrimage," pp. 4–6. A report at the time stated: "Mr. Edwards immediately on his arrival commenced revival work, cooperating with Mr. Finney. Plymouth church is crowded to overflowing, and hundreds go away not being able to obtain admittance, so great is the desire to hear the Gospel" (*The Independent,* 21 February 1856, p. 64).

Street Pres. Church.[65] I have said the first Pres. Church was old school. Its Pastor was the Rev. Dr. Mclevain.[66] He declined to take hold of the work & his church as a body did not appear to sympathize with it.[67] But a considerable number of its prominent men & several of its Elders attended our meetings & took a deep interest in the work. The Pastor of the third Pres. church Rev. Dr. Hall was also old school & declined to sympathize with the re[v]ival.[68] His church mainly followed his example & kept away from our meetings. But some of them attended & were much interested in the spirit's work.[69] Dr. Shaw & Rev. Mr.

[65]James Boylan Shaw (1808–1890) was a prominent New School Presbyterian minister and moderator of the 1865 General Assembly. He had apparently attended Yale College and studied law in New York. After pastorates in New York State, he went to the Brick Church in 1841 and remained there forty-seven years. See Alfred Nevin, ed., *Encyclopaedia of the Presbyterian Church in the United States of America* (Philadelphia: Presbyterian Encyclopaedia Publishing Co., 1884), pp. 823–24.

Frank Field Ellinwood (1826–1908) had gone to the Washington Street Church in 1854 from Belvidere, New Jersey. He was a graduate of Hamilton College and of Auburn and Princeton seminaries. He remained until ill health necessitated his resignation in 1865. In 1858 the church changed its name to the Central Presbyterian Church. See Peck, *Semi-Centennial History,* pp. 246–48; and *The Independent,* 2 November 1854, p. 346.

[66]Joshua Hall McIlvaine (1815–1897) was a graduate of Princeton College and Seminary. He went to the First Church in 1848, remaining until 1860, when he returned to Princeton Theological Seminary as a professor. He was later the founder of Evelyn College for Women at Princeton, where he was president until his death. He was also a philologist of some note. See *The National Cyclopaedia of American Biography,* vol. 5 (New York: White, 1907), p. 456. Finney appears to have spelled his name "Mclevain."

[67]In 1891, McIlvaine wrote to H. Pomeroy Brewster:

> Almost all the churches were opened to Mr. Finney, but I, being a true-blue old Scotch Sectarian, would not let him into the First Church, for which I have repented ever since.
>
> Judge Gardiner, Mrs. Benedict, another gentleman whose name I do not now recall, came to me begging and entreating that I would invite him. But I, in my blindness, stood firm, telling them they might break my heart, but they should not break my principles. The number of converts were incredible. Mr. Finney was heard to say: "If he could only get into First Church, he would have all Rochester converted;" and I do not doubt but he would. . . .
>
> Upon the whole, the blessing of that revival to Rochester, in my opinion, can never be over-estimated (Brewster, "Magic of a Voice," p. 284).

According to Louis Chapin, McIlvaine was said to have admitted later that "the error of his ministerial life was in not fellowshiping Mr Finney" (Louis Chapin to G. F. Wright, 10 February 1890, Wright Papers, box 8). McIlvaine also wrote to G. F. Wright: "I have long been convinced that I was totally wrong and have since taken occasion to say so to the church itself" (J. H. McIlvaine to G. F. Wright, 4 May 1890, Wright Papers, box 8).

[68]Albert Gallatin Hall had originally started work as a printer and was publisher of the *Rochester Observer.* He was at that time a member of the Third Presbyterian Church. But in 183[illegible] he was licensed to preach and was at Penfield, New York, until called to the Third Church in 1840. He was there until he died suddenly of cholera in 1871.

> In the division of the Presbyterian Church he ranged himself with all the fervor of his nature on the Old School side. He became very jealous of revival men and revival measures. They were carefully excluded from his pulpit, even though his church at the outset was the most radical and progressive of any in all the region. And in this course he was manifestly honest and consistent with his own decided convictions of truth and duty (*NYE,* 14 September 1871, p. 1).

[69]H. Pomeroy Brewster recollected in 1892:

> Dr. Hall never came to be in full accord with Mr. Finney, though I'm inclined to think that his views may have become a trifle modified, for at a later period (some time after 1856) when Mr. Finney chanced to be in Rochester over Sunday, a self-appointed committee consisting of Dr. Dewey and others went to Dr. Hall, who was then

Ellenwood went heart & soul into the movement & their churches as well as the congregational church were much blessed & their membership greatly enlarged.[70] Rev. Dr. Anderson Pres. of the **Baptist** University engaged ˡin the work with great cordiality, & as I understood **the great mass** of the Students in the university were converted at that time.[71] The **Pastors** of the two Baptist Churches took hold of the effort & I preached several times in their Churches.[72] MS 940

confined by illness at home, to consult what was best to do. Even then Mr. F. seems to have been something of an elephant on the hands of the good brethren. Dr. Dewey was saying, "We must do something; some one must open their doors for him," and Dr. Hall was protesting that he did not know what was best, when suddenly the door was opened and O. N. Bush came in and at once cut the gordian knot by saying: "You are too late for any argument, Doctor, for I have invited him to take your place as I knew you were sick." Dr. Dewey, my informant told me, fairly roared with laughter, while a sigh of relief came from all, not the least noticeable that of the conservative Dr. Hall (Brewster, "Magic of a Voice," p. 285).

[70] Some details of admissions to the churches were reported in the papers. The Plymouth Church received more than 100 new members in three months, most of them converts of the revival; and 111 were received into the Brick Church as a result of the revival. See *The Independent,* 5 June 1856, p. 179; and 19 June 1856, p. 195; and *Fiftieth Anniversary of the Organization of the Brick Church, Rochester, N.Y.* (Rochester: Andrews, 1876), p. 19.

The start of the sentence that follows was not altered by Fairchild in the manuscript but was written in, substantially the same, at the top of the next page.

[71] The university in Rochester had been started by the Baptists in 1850. There was a theological seminary in association with it. Martin Brewer Anderson (1815–1890) was the first president of the university, having been appointed in 1853. After a prominent and successful career, he retired in 1888. See Asahel C. Kendrick, *Martin B. Anderson, LL.D: A Biography* (Philadelphia: American Baptist Publication Society, 1895).

The revival had already begun in the university some weeks before Finney arrived in town, largely through the efforts the previous year of Kingman Nott, a senior student. The first conversion of a student occurred on Monday, 5 November. Nott continued his efforts when he returned to the theological seminary after the brief winter vacation. By 25 February he reckoned "four of our fellow-students have recently indulged a hope"; and a report in the *Genesee Evangelist* of 6 March noted that "several students of the University" had been converted. See Nott, *Abner Kingman Nott,* pp. 146–55; and *OE,* 26 March 1856, p. 56.

The following report appeared later in the *Genesee Evangelist*:

> This institution . . . is now enjoying its full share in the great blessings with which God has visited our city. A few individuals from among the students, by attending the daily meetings held in the churches of the city, were hopefully brought to Christ early in the winter; but since the day of fasting and prayer for Colleges [28 February], the University itself has become a new center of revival influence. Some ten or fifteen students are indulging hope of pardon and acceptance. President Anderson, Prof. Dewey, and other members of the faculty, seem to be most deeply interested in the work, both in the University and in the Churches (*The Independent,* 1 May 1856, p. 139).

See also *OE,* 27 February 1856, p. 39.

It was noted later, "In the revival in Rochester University last winter, only twenty remained without expressing the Christian's hope" (*The Independent,* 12 March 1857, p. 3). Finney's expression "the great mass" of the students was altered by Fairchild to "a large number." However, the numbers converted may not have been large. The total enrollment at the university that year was 138. The previous year when Nott had commenced his efforts, the enrollment was 118. He reckoned then that there were "only twenty or twenty-five irreligious students." See Nott, *Abner Kingman Nott,* p. 127; and Jesse L. Rosenberger, *Rochester: The Making of a University* (Rochester: University of Rochester, 1927), p. 138.

[72] The First Baptist Church was under the charge of Rev. Jacob R. Scott. The church had received 193 people into membership as a result of the revival of 1830–1831, more than doubling its membership. But in 1834 some of the more radical members left and formed the Second Baptist Church on the east side of the river. This church was devoted to the cause of

Mrs Finney was well acquainted in Rochester having lived there for many years, & having witnessed the two great revivals in which I had labored that preceeded this. She took an absorbing interest in this revival & labored as usual with great zeal & success.[73] As on former occasions, I found the people of Rochester like the Noble Bereans ready to "hear the word with all readiness of mind & to search the scriptures daily whether these things were so."[74] Many of the ladies in Rochester exerted their utmost influence to bring all classes to meeting & to Christ. Some of them would visit the stores & places of business, & use all their influence to secure the attendance, at our meetings, of the clerks & employees of those establishments.[75] Many men connected with the operations of the Rail Road were converted & finally much of the sabbath business of the Roads was suspended because of the great religious movement in the city & amongst the employees of the Roads.[76]

MS 941 'The blessed work of grace extended & increased until it seemed as if the whole city would be converted. As in the former revivals the work sp[r]ead

revivals and missions and took a stand against slavery and intemperance. They occupied the building that had been used by the Third Presbyterian Church when Finney was in Rochester in 1831. The minister was Rev. G. W. Howard. See Orlo J. Price, "One Hundred Years of Protestantism in Rochester," *The Rochester Historical Society, Publication Fund Series* 12 (1933): 279–80; and Peck, *Semi-Centennial History,* pp. 261–63.

[73] A prayer meeting for females was held at 3:00 every afternoon. See *The Independent*, 15 May 1856, p. 155; and *OE,* 26 March 1856, p. 55.

[74] Acts 17:11.

[75] The *Genesee Evangelist* of 17 April 1856 reported that a new impulse had been given to the work. "The great majority of those who are now concerned for their soul's welfare, are the young men in our stores. It is no unusual thing to see five or six clerks from one establishment at the morning prayer-meeting" (reprinted in *OE,* 7 May 1856, p. 75). Another report mentions the conversion of young men, "especially the clerks, and of these the wild and dissipated quite as much as the more quiet and sober" (*The Independent,* 15 May 1856, p. 155).

[76] By the 1850s Sunday trains had become a matter of great concern to the Christian public. Since railroads were first introduced in the 1830s there had been a dramatic growth. By 1856 there were probably more than five hundred companies operating over twenty-three thousand miles of railroad. This was a threefold increase since 1850. See *The United States Railroad Directory* (New York: Homans, 1856); and *American Railway Times* (Boston), 3 January 1856, p. 2.

There had been some concern about Sunday working as early as the 1840s, but in the summer of 1852 the Hudson River Railroad began running trains on Sundays. This was considered to be "the beginning of mischief." It was soon followed by a number of other companies. The New England states still observed the Sabbath, but by the end of 1854 it was noted: "As we leave New England, we find greater laxity. Upon most of the leading roads in New York, one or more Sunday trains are run, particularly upon the Harlem, Hudson River and Central. In the Western States, the New England custom generally prevails." Rochester was one of the stations on the New York Central Railroad (*The Independent,* 24 February 1853, p. 31; *OE,* 30 March 1853, p. 54; and *American Railroad Journal* [New York], 23 December 1854, pp. 801–2).

Pressure was put upon the companies and upon the traveling public to observe the Sabbath, and there was some success. In March 1856 it was reported: "The New York Central, the Hudson River, and the New York and Erie Railroads (and the Roanoke and Seaboard) have now their Sabbath days" (*The New York Observer*, 27 March 1856, p. 102). This encouraged *The New York Observer* to compile "a catalogue of Sabbath-keeping Railroads," and further reports appeared as more companies abandoned Sunday trains. See *The New York Observer*, 26 April 1856, p. 134; *The Independent,* 28 July 1856, p. 118; and *American Railroad Journal,* 7 June 1856, pp. 356–57. Over the course of the next two decades, however, Sunday observance declined, and "by the 1880s, most companies abandoned all pretense of curtailing Sunday operations" (Walter Licht, *Working for the Railroad: The Organization of Work in the Nineteenth Century* [Princeton: Princeton University Press, 1983], p. 180).

from this center to the ˡsurrounding Towns & Villages. It has been quite JHF 439 remarkable that revivals in Rochester have had so great an influence upon other Towns Cit[i]es & villages far & near.[77]

The means used to promote this revival were the same as had been used in each of the preceeding great revivals. The same doctrines were preached. The same measures were used, with results in all respect[s] similar to what had transpired in the former revivals. There was manifested, as there had previously been, an earnest & candid attention to the word preached. A most intelligent inquiry after the truth as it really is taught in the bible. I never preached anywhere with more pleasure than in Rochester. They are a highly

[77] A letter describing the revival drew attention to the way it had spread:

> At an early day in the progress of the work, the editor of one of our daily papers had a reporter attend, and take a sketch of the sermons, then another reporter came in, and we had services in two daily papers. These reports being read abroad, and in the places of business, and in families through the city, contributed to increase the interest. Large numbers of people from the towns around have been in the habit of riding in to spend a day and evening, to attend the meetings, and people from more distant places have come to spend days for the purpose of seeing and hearing what the Lord was doing. I have known of people coming from Buffalo, Lockport, Batavia, Brockport, Genesee, Canandaigua, Palmyra, Syracuse, Rome, Utica and I might name many other places for this purpose, and as they returned they have carried a revival interest with them which is being felt in many places now (*Christian Watchman and Reflector* [Boston], 27 March 1856, p. 1).

This revival in Rochester was looked upon as "the precursor, in the State of New York, of that great religious awakening, which in 1858, extended over the whole North and introduced a new era in religious operations." See Nott, *Abner Kingman Nott*, p. 154. See also W. C. Wilkinson, "Charles G. Finney as a Preacher," *The Independent*, 9 September 1875, p. 2.

Mrs. Finney wrote three years later:

> Here commenced the overflowing union morning prayer meetings—and these morning meetings have continued to this day. Persons came from the towns and cities round Rochester hearing of what God was doing for that place—went home and established similar meetings and revivals followed ("A Journal Kept by Mrs. Elizabeth Ford Atkinson Finney during a Visit to England in 1859–1860," p. 11, manuscript in Special Collections, Oberlin College Library).

Finney made the same point during the 1858–1859 revival:

> It has been supposed that this present movement originated in prayer-meetings established for business men in the city of New York. This is a great mistake. A spirit of revival had been growing for several years in many parts of the United States. The people of God saw the tide rising and the cloud gathering, and they said to each other they should soon see a general movement. In Rochester, Christians of all denominations,—Baptists, Congregationalists, and Presbyterians,—united in the work, and daily prayer-meetings and preaching were held in the different churches in succession—the meetings moving round from church to church in a circle. So much interest began to be manifested in these meetings, that information regarding them could no longer be withheld by the secular press. The facts lay too prominently on the face of society to be ignored by the secular press. They had ignored it in great measure, but a man who is a sceptic himself as I am informed, yet editor of a paper of great importance in Rochester, having a Roman Catholic reporter, sent him to take notes of the sermons every night, and they were published next morning. He also attended the prayer-meetings in the morning, I believe, and reported them. The public demanded this—it must be done—the papers must not ignore it—they must give the intelligence to the public. As soon as this was done, it aroused the masses in every town. The daily press reported the sermons, and that brought the movement into public notice. From that the revival spread in every direction. Daily prayer-meetings were commenced, which resulted in a great many others, and the awakening gave promise of becoming general. The next winter the work commenced in Boston, and became powerful (Finney, *The Prevailing Prayer-Meeting: A Sermon* [London: Ward, 1859], pp. 24–25).

intelligent people & have ever manifested a candor, an earnestness, & an appreciation of the truth excelling any thing I have seen on so large a scale in any other place. I have labored in other cities where the people were **as well** & even more highly educated than in Rochester. But in those cities the views & habits of the people were more stereotyped—they were more fastidious—MS 942 More afraid of measures ˡthan in Rochester. In New England I have found a high degree of general education but a timidity—a stiffness—a formality & stereotyped way of doing things that has rendered it impossible for the Holy Spirit to work with **such** freedom & power **as He does in Rochester. I have seen & passed through three great revivals in Rochester, & have been uniformly struck with the different type of those revivals from any thing that I have seen in New England.** When I was laboring in Hartford **Connecticut** I was visited by a minister from central New York who had witnessed the glorious revivals in that region. He attended our meetings & **witnessed** the type & progress of the work there. I said nothing to him of the formality of our prayer meetings or of the timidity of the people in the use of measures, but he remarked to me, "Why Bro. Finney your hands are tied, you are headged in by their fears & stereotyped way of doing everything. They have even put the Holy Ghost into a straight jacket." This was strong & to some may appear irreverent & profane but he intended no such thing. He was JHF 440 a godly, earnest, humble minister of Jesus ˡChrist, & expressed just what he saw & felt, & just what I saw & felt that the Holy Spirit was restrained greatly in his work by the **prejudices, the** fears & the selfwisdom of the people. **In** MS 943 **Rochester I have witnessed less of this ˡthan in any place in New England.**

Indeed I must say I do not think the people of New England can at all appreciate the restraints which they impose on the Holy spirit in working out the salvation of souls. Nor can they appreciate the power & purity of the revivals in those places where these fears, prejudices, restraints & selfwisdom do not exist. **The opposition to the revivals in western & central New York gotten up & persisted in by Dr. L. Beecher & Mr. Nettleton did very much to put New England into an attitude of mind very unfavorable to the free & full development of pure & powerful revivals of religion. But in Rochester there is an earnest intelligent freedom from such bondage & revivals there consequently take on a type & progress with a power compounded with the liberty with which the Holy Spirit pursues his work of love. The same is true here, & in many places where I have labored. And neither in Rochester nor elsewhere where this liberty has been employed, have I witnessed any tendency to wildness, extravagance or fanaticism as a consequence.** In an intelligent educated community great freedom may be given in the use of means without danger of disorder.

MS 944 ˡIndeed[78] wrong ideas of what constitutes disord›er[79] ‹are very prevalent. Most churches call any thing disorder to which they have not been

[78]Fairchild added "–6" after page number 944, indicating to the printers to omit the bottom section of this page and the next two pages and to proceed to page 947.

[79]The *er* of "disorder" appears to have been added by Matson.

accustomed. Their stereotyped ways are God's order in their view, & whatever differs from these is disorder & shocks their ideas of propriety. But in fact nothing is disorder that simply meets the necessities of the people from time to time. In religion, as in every thing else, good sense & a sound discretion will from time to time judiciously adapt means to ends. The measures needed will be naturally suggested to those who witness the state of things, & if prayerfully & cautiously used let great freedom be given to the influences of the Holy Spirit in all hearts.[80]

The reader will have observed that I have made but slight mention of open opposition to revivals since the failure of the opposition by Dr. Beecher & Mr. Nettleton. The revivals were of so pure & powerful a type, both at the time, & subsequent to that opposition, that opposers were awed & a feeling of general & almost universal confidence in them as the blessed fruits of the Holy Spirit has pervaded all classes. I have already related the reaction that came over the opposers of the revival in Auburn & how those opposers afterwards confessed their mistake & their sin & urged me to labor with them again.[81] ˡAt the time of the opposition of Dr. Beecher & Mr. Nettleton much was said & prophesied of an alarming & crushing reaction that would come over the people & churches where those revivals were witnessed. It was said that the people would become ashamed & disgusted when they looked back upon the scenes through which they had passed, & become so afraid of the repetition of such scenes as not to want or to have any more revivals for, at least, a generation. It was predicted by opposers that the reaction would be so great as to sweep the labors of evangelists from the field, & to give opposers in, & out of the Church, abundant occasion to triumph insomuch that the ministers & churches who labored in those revivals› would be[82] **‹ashamed & afraid to attempt such a movement again.**

MS 945

It is now more than 40 years since those revivals & that opposition existed and what & where is the reaction? There has been an overwhelming reaction now manifest to all men. But it has been on the other side. It has been in favor of the revivals & against the opposition. All men have become convinced that the course pursued by the promoters of those & su[b]sequent revivals was in the highest degree rational, biblical & blessed of God, & that the course pursued by the opposition was unwise, unjust & unchristian in a high degree.

ˡNotwithstanding the pains that have been taken to justify the course of the opposition the verdict of the churches & people where these revivals have prevailed, is almost unanimous in *their* favor & against the

MS 946

[80]G. F. Wright pointed out that James B. Shaw had listened to Finney's preaching in Auburn in 1827, and in subsequent years was repeatedly assisted by Finney. According to Dr. Shaw, the earlier as well as the later preaching of Finney was characterized by great propriety of manner; and when anything occurred which seemed otherwise, it was amply justified by the attendant circumstances as interpreted under the inspiration of the moment (G. F. Wright, *Charles Grandison Finney* [Boston and New York: Houghton Mifflin, 1891], p. 301).

[81]See MS 609–12.

[82]The words "would be" appear to have been inserted by Matson.

opposition. So true is this that for many years I have seen but little open opposition to revivals. I have found that even the unconverted had no confidence in the opposition that had been made to revivals. Reaction! Yes indeed there has been reaction. But it has been against opposers & opposition so that ministers would not dare now to follow the lead of such men as before led the opposition. And where is the fulfillment of those prophesies that the ministers & chur[che]s would be ashamed of what they had done, & that there would be no revivals in those churches again for a generation. How exactly opposite to these predictions have been the facts in the case. Blessed are the ministers & people who have no greater reason to be ashamed of what they have done than the promoters of those revivals have to be ashamed of the part they took in those blessed works of grace. God & history will sustain the Honor of those revivals, & already results have fully vindicated them & confounded their opposers. Let God have all the Praise & glory forever & let man lie low before him.›

MS 947
JHF 441

CHAPTER XXXIII

‹Revival in Boston in 18[5]6, & 7, & 8›

The[1] next Autumn we accepted an invitation to labor again in Boston. We began our labors at Park street, and the Spirit of God immediately manifested his willingness to save souls.[2] The first sermon that I preached was directed to the searching of the church; for I always began by trying to stir up a thorough and all-pervading interest among professors of religion; to secure the reclaiming of those that were backslidden, and search out those that were self-deceived, and if possible bring them to Christ. After the congregation was dismissed and the pastor was standing with me in the pulpit, he said to me, "Brother Finney, I wish to have you understand that I need to have this preaching as much as any member of this church. I have been very much dissatisfied with my religious state for a long time; and have sent for you on my own account, and for the sake of my own soul, as well as for the sake |of[3] the souls of the people." **As the work went on this brother became more and more deeply convicted, until one day he sent a note to my lodgings inviting me to his study that he might have some conversation with me. He then told me that he thought he had been self-deceived. That when**

MS 948

[1] The chapter heading of page 947 in Finney's handwriting is on a separate piece of paper pasted over the top of the sheet. It obscures the page numbers 788 and 919 in Matson's handwriting and 947 in Finney's handwriting and the first words of the page: "obliged to stop preaching and leave the city," which Finney crossed out. The chapter heading reads, "‹Chap XXXIII Revival in Boston in 1826, & 7, & 8›." Fairchild altered the date to "1856."

[2] Park Street was one of the Congregational churches where Finney had preached in the autumn of 1831. It was the first Trinitarian Congregational church to be established in Boston after Unitarianism had swept through the Orthodox churches in the late eighteenth century. Formed in 1809 with twenty-six members, it had become the largest Congregational church in Boston, with a membership of seven hundred. The minister was Andrew Leete Stone (1815–1892), who had gone there in 1849. In 1866 he moved to San Francisco. See MS 633; Edwin M. Bacon, *King's Dictionary of Boston* (Cambridge, Mass.: King, 1883), p. 351; *American Congregational Year-Book for the Year 1858* (New York), p. 71; and *The Congregational Year-Book* (Boston), 1893, pp. 37–38.

Finney started preaching on Sunday, 7 December 1856, and continued "during a temporary absence of Rev. Mr. Stone at the West." His first sermon was reported in *The Congregationalist* (Boston). He remained in Boston until 19 April 1857, usually preaching four evenings in the week and on Friday mornings, as well as twice on the Sabbath. His wife, Elizabeth, held meetings for women. See *The Congregationalist,* 12 December 1856, p. 198; and 24 April 1857, p. 66. Dr. H. L. Wayland, who heard Finney preach at this time, recollected: "His personal appearance was commanding. The pastor, the late Dr. Andrew L. Stone, was a man of fair stature; but he seemed insignificant as he stood beside the evangelist" ("Evangelists and—Evangelists," *The Homiletic Review* [New York], n.s., 35 [June 1898]: 493).

[3] Pages 948–62 were originally numbered 789–803 and renumbered 920–34 by Matson. Finney changed them to 948–62.

he was in College he passed through a change that he was led to think was conversion;[4] **but he was now satisfied that he was entirely mistaken, and that he had never been truly converted; and he wished me to give him the same directions that I would to any other person in his situation.** We had a protracted and very interesting conversation. **I found his convictions of sin very striking.** He seemed **then to** thoroughly give his heart to God. **That** evening **there was** a prayer and conference meeting **in the vestry of that church; and the pastor**, as I understood, related to the people his experience, and told them that he had been that day converted. MS 949 |**The next Sabbath in his sermon, I was informed that he did the same.** This of course produced a very deep impression upon the church and congregation, and upon the city quite extensively. Some of the pastors thought that it was injudicious for him to make a thing of that kind so public. But I did not regard it in that light. It manifestly was the best means he could JHF 442 use for the salvation of his people, and highly cal|culated to produce among professors of religion generally a very great searching of heart.[5]

The work was quite extensive that winter in Boston, and many very striking cases of conversion occurred. We labored there until Spring, and then thought it necessary to return to our labors **here.**[6] But it was very manifest

[4] Stone was a graduate of Yale College in 1837 and was then a student at Union Theological Seminary for two years (*The Congregational Year-Book,* 1893, p. 37).

[5] When Finney was about to embark for England in November 1858, Stone wrote a letter to Finney to be used as a testimonial, in which he said:

> My personal indebtedness to you is beyond all compass of expression—for good to my own soul—for more certain & copious views of the sufficiency of Christ for every soul's need—and for wise suggestions as to the way to preach Christ to my dying fellow men (A. L. Stone to Finney, 27 November 1858, Finney Papers, microfilm, roll 4).

[6] Finney preached mainly in Park Street Church, but in March 1857 he is reported as also preaching in the Shawmut and Somerset Street churches. He preached also in the Chestnut Street Congregational Church in Chelsea, a village on the northeast side of Boston. The pastor, Isaac P. Langworthy, was ill and had just obtained leave of absence for his health. See *The Congregationalist,* 6 March 1857, p. 38; 13 March 1857, p. 42; 20 March 1857, p. 46; and 27 March 1857, p. 50. Finney's meetings were not only reported in the Boston *Congregationalist*, in other local papers, and in *The Oberlin Evangelist,* but they were noticed nationally through papers such as *The Independent* (New York), *The New-York Evangelist,* and *The New York Observer*. Reports of his meetings also reached Britain. See, e.g., *The Christian News* (Glasgow), 30 May 1857, p. 362; *The Freeman* (London), 15 April 1857, p. 196; and *The British Standard* (London), 15 May 1857, p. 161.

Finney, in common with other observers, saw his Boston meetings as the continuation of a broadening revival movement. It had been given a powerful impetus in Rochester the previous winter, affecting New York, and now from Boston it spread through New England, leading to the national awakening the next year. A report of his meetings by a Boston correspondent in *The Independent* pointed out:

> Members of other churches in the city soon began to come in considerable numbers; then from the neighboring towns; and finally from distant places in New Hampshire and Maine, came ministers by scores, and private Christians by hundreds, if not thousands, to hear the word, and catch some of the sacred influences that evidently attended it (23 April 1857, p. 8).

See also *The Independent,* 2 April 1857, p. 3; and 16 April 1857, p. 1; *OE,* 15 April 1857, p. 63; *The British Standard,* 14 May 1858, p. 156; and Finney, *The Prevailing Prayer-Meeting* (London: Ward, 1859), pp. 24–25. A widely copied report that appeared at the height of the revival the next year reckoned:

> The first manifestation of the present general awakening was in New England, particularly in Connecticut and Massachusetts, from which the spirit of the revival

that the work in that city was by no means done; and we left with the promise that, the Lord willing, we would return and labor there the next winter. Accordingly the next Autumn we returned to Boston.[7] In the meantime **Brother** |**Kirk** had been writing some articles, which were published in the Congregationalist, opposing our return there.[8] He regarded my theology, especially on the subject of Sanctification, as unsound. **When I labored there the winter previous he was in Paris.**[9] **When he came home and found that I was expected there the next Autumn, he endeavored "to head it off," as I have said, by some articles in the newspaper.**[10] **However his purpose was not accomplished. But still** we felt at once that there was a jar **there** among the Christian people. Some of the leading members of his church, who the winter before had entered heart and soul into the work, stood aloof and did not come near our meetings; and it was evident that his whole influence, which was considerable at that time in the city, was against the work. This made some of his good people very sad.[11] **This was in the**

MS 950

> spread rapidly through the Middle and the Western States, or rather broke out simultaneously in all (reprinted, e.g., in *The Congregationalist,* 12 March 1858, p. 42).

The Finneys left Boston after Sunday, 19 April, when he preached for the last time in Park Street. Before returning to Oberlin, they spent some time in New York. They were probably staying with Mrs. Finney's brother, Hobart Ford, and his family in Brooklyn. The Finneys' daughter, Julia, had been there while her parents were in Boston. Finney was advertised to preach on Sunday, 3 May, in George B. Cheever's Church of the Puritans in New York. See *The Congregationalist,* 24 April 1857, p. 66; *The Independent,* 30 April 1857, p. 5; and letters of Finney to Julia Finney, January to March in Finney Papers, microfilm, roll 4.

[7]When Finney left Boston the previous April, a report of his last meeting included the remark: "It is not improbable, we learn, that he may, if desired, resume his labors here next winter" (*The Congregationalist,* 24 April 1857, p. 66). Finney left Oberlin again late in November after there had been another awakening in the college. He traveled via Cleveland, Buffalo, Rochester, and Albany, arriving in Boston on 2 December. His wife arrived two days later. See *OE,* 11 November 1857, p. 183; and Finney to Julia Finney, 4 and 5 December 1857, Finney Papers, microfilm, roll 4.

[8]Edward Norris Kirk (1802–1874) was the minister of the Mount Vernon Congregational Church and an outstanding Congregational leader. As a young man he had attended Princeton College and then worked in a lawyer's office until his conversion in 1822, when he entered Princeton Theological Seminary. His first pastorate was in Albany, where he soon achieved eminence as a preacher and revivalist. At that time he was a disciple of Finney and invited him to Albany to help in revival meetings. In 1842 Kirk moved to Boston, where the Mount Vernon Church was organized especially for him. It was under his ministry that John B. Gough, the temperance orator, and Dwight L. Moody, the evangelist, were converted. Theodore L. Cuyler, who knew Kirk well, reckoned: "As a revival preacher he deserves a place in the triumvirate with Finney and Moody." He remained at Mount Vernon until his death. See *Appletons' Cyclopaedia of American Biography,* vol. 3 (New York: Appleton, 1888), pp. 553–54; Z. R. Shipherd to Finney, 24 December 1827, Finney Papers, microfilm, roll 1; letters from Kirk to Finney in the Finney Papers; and T. L. Cuyler, "Edward N. Kirk," *The Independent,* 3 January 1878, p. 1. See also *DAB*. The articles to which Finney refers are not to be found in *The Congregationalist* at that time.

[9]Kirk went to France in January 1857 under the auspices of the American and Foreign Christian Union to set up an American chapel in Paris. He returned to Boston in October 1857. See *The Independent,* 22 January 1857, p. 4; 22 October 1857, p. 3; and 10 December 1857, p. 4.

[10]*The Independent* reported in October, before Kirk's return:

> There is a movement on the part of a number of orthodox churches and clergy of this city to secure the labors of Mr. Finney the approaching winter. We understand that Winter-street and Essex-street churches are the only ones which have expressed themselves as unfavorable to the project (15 October 1857, p. 2).

[11]Finney tried to get Kirk's cooperation but received a letter in which Kirk wrote:

MS 951 **winter of 1857 and '58; and** ˡit will be remembered **that it was** at this time **that** a great revival prevailed throughout all the Northern states. It swept over the land **in such a tremendous manner**, that **for some weeks** it was estimated that not less than fifty thousand conversions occurred **per** week.[12] This revival had some very peculiarly interesting features. It was carried on to a large extent through lay influence, so much so as almost to throw the ministers into the shade.[13] There had been a daily prayer meeting observed in Boston for several years **previous**;[14] and in the Autumn previous to the great outburst the daily prayer meeting had been established in Fulton st., New

> I did not request you to come to Boston to labor, and am entirely unable to regard myself as responsible for the results of your labors. . . .
>
> I told you when you were about to embark for Europe, that I would not invite you to labor with me until you or I was changed. I have seen no reason to alter that decision.
>
> We may talk this over in heaven. In this world I am persuaded it would do no good. And there we will drop the matter (Kirk to Finney, 1 March 1858, Finney Papers, microfilm, roll 4).

When Finney was in Scotland the next year, an article entitled "Mr. Finney's Career and Theology" was published in the Glasgow *Christian News*. The writer, Fergus Ferguson, Jr., pointed out that, while recent attacks against Finney's orthodoxy were being penned in Scotland, "he was laboring for months together with such men as Mr. Stone, and Dr. Kirk of Boston, and their numerous co-adjutors." This brought an immediate reply from Finney: "This is a mistake, so far as Mr. Kirk is concerned. How far Mr. Kirk of Boston might agree with or differ from me I am not aware. I have not laboured as an evangelist with him since he has occupied his present pulpit" (*The Christian News,* 10 September 1859, p. 5; and 17 September 1859, p. 5; and F. Ferguson, Jr., to Finney, September 1859, Finney Papers, microfilm, roll 5).

In 1866 Kirk wrote a letter of welcome to the Baptist evangelist, A. B. Earle: "I have long waited for an evangelist with whom I could cordially cooperate. After more than twenty years of waiting, God has granted me this desire of my heart" (Absolom B. Earle, *Bringing in the Sheaves* [Boston: Earle, 1868], p. 189). In 1871, when it was proposed that Finney visit Boston again, it appears that Kirk was by then willing to cooperate. See the letters of Willard Sears and N. Broughton, Jr., to Finney, January and February 1871, Finney Papers, microfilm, roll 6.

[12] The revival spanned a period of approximately nine months, from September 1857 through May 1858. Within that period it picked up increasing momentum in the early months of 1858 and crested in March of that year. Frank G. Beardsley in his *History of American Revivals* estimated that 100,000 people were converted between January and April 1858. See John D. Hannah, "The Layman's Prayer Revival of 1858," *Bibliotheca Sacra* 134 (January–March 1977): 63, 72.

[13] Finney wrote from Boston back to Oberlin on 11 March 1858:

> Such is the desire to pray & be prayed for that people prefer prayer meetings to preaching. At prayer meetings the people don't want exhortation nor talk but prayer. This is a very marked feature of this work at present. This I have formerly seen, but not so much of late years (Finney to H. Hill, 11 March 1858, Correspondence of Charles G. Finney, 1830–1875, Oberlin College Archives, microfilm).

[14] A daily prayer meeting had been started in Boston in March 1840 as a result of recent revivals. Deacon Daniel Safford of Park Street and a few others organized it in the Park Street Church to promote the revival. It had continued for ten years, when it was decided to include all denominations and form a union prayer meeting. This was commenced in the Old South Church in the autumn of 1850 and was held every weekday morning at 8:00 or 8:15 for an hour. It had been maintained over the years and had become well known. See *Old South Chapel Prayer Meeting: Its Origin and History* (Boston: Tilton, 1859); Isaac P. Langworthy, "Daniel Safford," *The Congregational Quarterly* (Boston) 3 (January 1861): 1–12; and "Morning Prayer Meetings," reprinted from *The American Missionary* in *The Congregationalist,* 2 October 1857, p. 157. This article was probably written by Lewis Tappan, who had visited Boston while Finney was there and was so impressed with the Old South prayer meetings that he started a similar meeting back in Brooklyn and wrote a tract entitled "Morning Prayer Meetings" to promote the idea. See Tappan, "Journal," 2 November 1856; and 7 April to 4 May 1857, Tappan Papers, microfilm, roll 2; and *The Congregationalist,* 24 April 1857, p. 16.

York, which has been continued to this day.[15] Indeed, daily prayer meetings were established throughout the length and breadth |of the ‹Northern **or free** states.›[16] I recollect in one of our prayer-meetings in Boston that winter a gentleman arose and said: "I am from Omaha **the capital of** Nebraska." "On my journey **e**ast I |have found a continuous prayer meeting all the way. We call it" said he, "about two thousand miles from Omaha to Boston; and here was a prayer meeting about two thousand miles in extent."[17]

JHF 443

MS 952

In Boston we had to struggle, as I have intimated, against this divisive influence, which set the religious interest a good deal back from where we had left it the **S**pring before.[18] However the work continued steadily to increase. **In** the midst of these **diverse circumstances** it was evident that the Lord intended to make a general sweep in Boston. Finally it was suggested that a business men's prayer meeting should be established at twelve **O**'clock in the chapel of the Old South church, which was very central for business men. ‹The **c**›hristian friend ‹whose guests we were›[19] secured the use of the room, and advertized the meeting.[20] ‹B›ut whether such a meeting would succeed

[15]The Fulton Street meeting was started by Jeremiah C. Lanphier in September 1857. He was a businessman who had been appointed to do lay missionary work in the vicinity of the North Dutch Reformed Church in Fulton Street. He saw the need for a prayer meeting to which businessmen could come and go in the middle of the day. It was initially arranged to be held weekly. Only six men came to the first meeting on 23 September, but by the third meeting, there were between forty and fifty. A decision was made to hold the meeting daily from that point on.
By the middle of October there were more than a hundred attending each day, and by the end of the year meetings were being held on all three floors of the consistory building and hundreds were being turned away. Prayer meetings soon started to be organized in many other places in New York and in other cities. By March 1858 there were said to be 150 meetings for prayer in New York and Brooklyn alone (Samuel I. Prime, *The Power of Prayer* [Edinburgh: Strahan, 1859], pp. 5–33).

[16]Matson had written the word "land," but Finney replaced it with "Northern or free states."

[17]*The Congregationalist* reported at that time:

> A gentleman from Ohio, recently in Boston, stated that by adding his personal observations to those of a friend, he could say, that from Omaha City, in Nebraska, to Washington, *there was a line of prayer meetings along the whole length of the road*; so that wherever a Christian traveler stopped to spend the evening, he could find a crowded prayer meeting, across the entire breadth of our vast republic (2 April 1858, p. 54).

[18]However, a correspondent reported in the *Religious Herald* of 18 December 1857:

> Mr. Finney has got his meetings somewhat systematised, and his services are much better attended than last year at this time. He has less prejudice to contend with, and the sobered state of the public mind, from embarrassment and trouble, is believed to be favorable to his labors and to the cause of religion (reprinted in *OE,* 6 January 1858, p. 7).

[19]Here Matson had written down, "A Christian friend of mine," but Finney changed it to "The christian friend whose guests we were." This was Edwin Lamson, a merchant and deacon of Park Street Church. The Finneys had been guests in his house at 5 Beacon Street when they were in Boston the previous winter (1856–1857). Finney arrived in Boston on 2 December 1857 ahead of Mrs. Finney and spent the next day moving into 9 Davis Street. See Edwin Lamson's letter, 21 July 1876, written the day before he died, in *Reminiscences of Rev. Charles G. Finney* (Oberlin: Goodrich, 1876), p. 39; *Boston Directory for the Year 1858* (Boston), p. 216; and Finney to Julia Finney, 4 December 1857, Finney Papers, microfilm, roll 4.

[20]Matson had written down after this, "Such meetings were already in progress in New York, and in many cities throughout the land; but. . . ." Finney crossed it out and changed the *b* of "but" to a capital letter. Lamson, with others who were in charge of the Old South morning prayer meeting, started the businessmen's meeting on 8 March 1858. They had wanted to get the use of a room in State Street, the business center of Boston, but in the end they decided to use the Old South Chapel. "For a day or two previous, placards were posted about the streets notifying the public that such a meeting would be held at twelve o'clock, and would continue for

MS 953 ¹in Boston at that time was considered doubtful. However this brother called the meeting; and to the surprize of almost everybody the place was not only crowded **to its utmost capacity,** but multitudes could not get in at all. This meeting was continued day after day with wonderful results. The place was from the first too strait for them, and other daily meetings were established in other parts of the city.[21]

Mrs. Finney held ladies' meetings daily at the large vestry of Park street. These meetings became so crowded that the ladies would fill the room **to its utmost capacity**, and then stand about the door on the outside as far as they could hear on every side.[22] One of our daily prayer-meetings was held at Park street church, which would be full whenever it was open for prayer; and this was the case with many other meetings in different parts of the city.[23] The population, large as it was, seemed to be moved **en masse**. The revival JHF 444 became too ¹general to keep any account at all of the number of conversions, MS 954 or to allow ¹of any estimate being made that would approximate ‹**to**›[24] the

one hour." See *Old South Chapel Prayer Meeting*, p. 121; and *The Massachusetts Spy* (Worcester), 10 March 1858, p. 2. And on the morning of Monday, 8 March, in the Old South Chapel vestry, the following notice "was suspended conspicuously upon the walls of the room":

> Business Men's prayer meeting in this house this day from 12 to 1 o'clock. Friend, stranger, traveler, come in and stay five, ten, or twenty minutes, or longer if possible. Come in (*The Congregationalist*, 12 March 1858, p. 42).

[21] After the businessmen's prayer meeting had been going for two days, it was reported to be "larger than ever before."

> The upper chapel was filled to overflowing, and then the lower chapel was opened and speedily packed as full as it could hold. The doors were then closed and the room leading to the lower chapel, was then crowded to overflowing. In each of the three rooms there were services—mostly earnest prayers, and singing.
>
> There were probably near a thousand men engaged in the services in the different rooms. The audiences were composed to a great extent of men in middle life (*Boston Morning Journal*, 11 March 1858, cutting in Finney Papers, file 2/2/2, box 9).

[22] Meetings for females had been started by Mrs. Finney the previous winter in Boston. Lewis Tappan wrote:

> During the winter and spring of 1857, when Rev. C. G. Finney was successfully laboring in Boston, in promoting the cause of Christ, Mrs. Finney was accustomed to lead a meeting of women which was held every morning immediately after the adjournment of the general morning prayer meeting in the Chapel. These meetings were greatly blessed. Several ladies took part in them, and participated with Mrs. Finney in carrying them forward (*The Congregationalist*, 2 October 1857, p. 175; see also n. 14 above).

During the winter of 1857–1858, a female prayer meeting was held in Park Street Church after the daily prayer meeting, from 4:00 to 4:30 P.M. (*The Congregationalist*, 26 February 1858, p. 34). Finney spoke about these meetings the next year:

> The present revival is characterised far above all precedent by the individual activity and labour of the female members of the churches. If the business men have had their daily meetings, so have the women; if the men have visited and conversed with individuals, so have the women. God has greatly used and greatly honoured the instrumentality of woman, and is still doing so. The ladies' meetings are now regarded as a most important branch of the great movement in many places.
>
> . . . In Boston, I have seen the vestries crowded to suffocation with ladies' prayer-meetings, and these ladies, comprising some of the most educated and talented to be found perhaps in the United States (Finney, *Prevailing Prayer-Meeting*, p. 29).

[23] The prayer meeting in Park Street vestry was held every afternoon from Monday to Friday at 3:00 for an hour. See *The Congregationalist*, 29 January 1858, p. 19. By March there were said to be eight major prayer meetings in progress in different churches in Boston (Hannah, "Layman's Prayer Revival," p. 66).

[24] Finney inserted the word "to," but Fairchild crossed it out.

truth. All classes of people were inquiring everywhere. Many of the Unitarians became greatly interested, and attended our meetings in large numbers.[25]

This revival is of so recent date that I need not enlarge upon it, because it became almost universal throughout the Northern states. A divine influence seemed to pervade the whole land. Slavery seemed to shut it out from the South. They were in such a state of irritation, of vexation, and of committal to their peculiar institution, which had come to be assailed on every side, that the Spirit of God seemed to be grieved away from them. There seemed to be no place found for him in the hearts of the Southern people at that time.[26] It was estimated that during this revival not less than five hundred thousand souls were converted in the **Northern states.[27] It extended all the way from our frontier settlements in the west, to our most eastern boundary on the Atlantic coast.** |[As[28] I hav]e said, it was carried on very much through the instrumentality of prayer meetings, personal visitation and conversation, by the distribution of tracts, and by the energetic efforts of the laity, **male and female.**[29] Ministers nowhere opposed it that I am aware of. I MS 955

[25]The participation of Unitarians in the revival was particularly noted at the time. Edward Everett Hale, the Unitarian minister at South Church, welcomed Finney's preaching at Park Street, and Unitarians were reported as joining in the prayer meetings. An article in the Unitarian *Christian Register* (Boston) made the comment:

> Boston has been comparatively quiet; and everywhere the demonstrations have been less violent and fanatical than usual in such excitements—less sectarian, bigoted, and marked by objectionable features of any nature. Hence Unitarians have been more disposed to join in them, and we may hope, the impressions made being more in accordance with reason, will be more permanent and practical (13 March 1858, p. 3).

See also *Christian Watchman and Reflector* (Boston), 15 April 1858, p. 2; *NYE,* 17 June 1858, p. 2; and Timothy L. Smith, *Revivalism and Social Reform in Mid-Nineteenth-Century America* (Nashville: Abingdon, 1957), pp. 70–71, 97–98.

[26]When reports of the awakening in *The New York Daily Tribune* stated that the revival had had very little effect in the southern states, a writer from Beaufort, South Carolina, wrote in to deny them and to give evidence that the impact was considerable. See *The New York Daily Tribune*, 24 April 1858, p. 6.

J. Edwin Orr has made the same point. Drawing largely on the book *Great Revivals and the Great Republic* (1904), by the southern Methodist Episcopal bishop, Warren A. Candler, Orr has argued that "abundant evidence" demonstrates that "the 1858 Revival swept the South in spite of the slavery issue" and that in the South it won as many converts proportionately to the population as in the North (J. E. Orr, *The Fervent Prayer: The Worldwide Impact of the Great Awakening of 1858* [Chicago: Moody Press, 1974], pp. 29–30).

[27]Orr's research into the additions to church membership and the reports of numbers of converts indicates that the figure of 500,000 is probably much too low and that 1 million is probably more likely. See Orr, *The Second Evangelical Awakening in Britain* (London: Marshall, Morgan, and Scott, 1949), pp. 36–37.

[28]A portion at the top of MS 955 has been torn away, removing the page numbers and the first few words of the page. The published edition starts a new paragraph here with the words "As I have said," but it is not known if Finney had inserted a paragraph sign. The number 955 has been penciled in and appears to be in the same handwriting as on MS 714 (see p. 413 n. 16) and MS 731 (see p. 424 n. 62).

[29]Finney elaborated on this point in a sermon in Scotland the next year:

> The present revival has employed the membership of the churches greatly beyond anything that has been done since the days of the apostles. The readers of my lectures on revivals know that I have all along insisted upon this, and that several of those lectures are devoted to this point, namely, the necessity and the consequences of the whole membership taking personally hold of the work of revival. The present work exceeds all the former, just because the means have been greatly multiplied. God has

believe they universally sympathized with it. But there was such a general confidence in ‹the prevalence of› prayer,[30] that the people very extensively seemed to prefer meetings for prayer to meetings for preaching. The general impression seemed to be, "We have had instruction until we are hardened; it is time for us to pray." The answers to prayer were ‹constant›,[31] and so striking as to arrest the attention of the people generally throughout the land. It was evident that in answer to prayer the windows of heaven were opened and the Spirit of God poured out like a flood. **I recollect very distinctly, that in praying for Boston I was led to lay hold of that class of promises in which God promises to open the windows of heaven and pour out His** MS 956 **Spirit like a flood |upon[32] the people, and like showers that water the earth, etc. It seemed to me clear that the revival would be according to the faith of God's people, and that if they would lay hold upon God's largest promises they would receive an unparallelled blessing.** The New York Tribune at that time published several extras filled with accounts of the progress of the revival in different parts of the United States.[33]

A circumstance occurred during this revival relating to the celebrated Theodore Parker, who held services in a large hall in Boston, and whose views of theology and religion are so well understood that I need not enter into particulars in regard to them.[34] During this winter a good

prepared the American church and ministry for the work, and by repeated and multiplied local revivals taught them how to work (*Prevailing Prayer-Meeting*, p. 27).

[30] Here Matson had written "an answer to prayer," but Finney crossed out "an answer to" and inserted "the prevalence of."

[31] Here Matson had written "very frequent," but Finney crossed it out and inserted "constant."

[32] Fairchild inserted "−7" after 956 to indicate to the printers to omit the next page and proceed to 958.

[33] In October 1857 Lanphier had called "on some of the editors of the religious papers *to have them notice* the interest that is *daily* manifested in our meetings" in the Dutch Reformed church. Then he called on the editors of the daily papers on 5 January. *The New York Daily Tribune* gave the first extended report, covering six columns, on 1 March 1858. Thereafter there were reports almost daily, usually covering two or three columns, until the end of March. The interest in the revival had become so widespread that an extra devoted entirely to the revival movement was published on 3 April. And the demand for that issue was so great that a second edition was published four days later. Finney spoke about this occurrence in Scotland in September 1859:

> It ought to be said that the editor and proprietor of the *New York Tribune* has done much that has extended this work. He employed a special and an able Christian editor to collect and arrange the revival intelligence, and that paper was instrumental in doing very much to extend the work. All honour to Mr Greely for the honourable course he pursued. I sent several copies of his paper to this country—papers made up altogether with revival intelligence—and have good reason to know that they were the means of exciting prayer, and a desire for a revival on this side of the Atlantic (*Prevailing Prayer-Meeting*, pp. 26–27).

See also Prime, *Power of Prayer*, pp. 11, 20.

The Reverend George Redford, then retired in Worcester, England, was one to whom Finney evidently sent copies of the papers. Redford wrote to Finney: "The chief object of my writing was to express the deep interest I feel in all that is going on among you & to thank you for the papers sent. . . . We deeply need such a revival in this country. Brother James & others are moving with the hope that it may come—in a few places there are some pleasing symptoms" (Redford to Finney, 25 May 1858, Finney Papers, microfilm, roll 4, misdated 1850 in the calendar). The revival continued to receive weekly coverage in *The Tribune* until the beginning of May 1858.

[34] Theodore Parker (1810–1860) was the most prominent and influential Unitarian clergyman in Boston. "The great American preacher," as he was sometimes called, was minister of the Twenty-Eighth Congregational Society of Boston. The society had taken possession of Music

many of the Christian people became very much exercised in their minds about the evil influence that he was exerting in Boston, and there was much prayer offered for him.[35] I called twice myself to see him, hoping to have an opportunity to converse with him; but in both instances he declined to see me, as was [repor]ted[36] to me on account of his health.[37] ¹But the spirit of prayer for him seemed to increase, and took on this type: that the Lord would convert him if He wisely could; but that if He could not do this, his evil influence might in some way be set aside. The minds of God's people labored so much upon this point, that a number of Christian gentlemen met by appointment in a certain place to lay this matter before God. I state the facts as they were told me by one of the gentlemen present. He said that after the meeting was opened they called on one of their number to lead in prayer; and he was led out in prayer in such a remarkable manner,—laid the whole subject so fully before God, and in such a spirit, as to lead them all with one heart and one soul to unite in laying the whole case before God. He said the man who led in prayer seemed almost to be inspired; to say just the right things, and in the right way and spirit, in leading them in prayer. They all felt as if their prayer would be answered; and so deep was this impression that although they had come together for a prayer ¹meeting,[38] after the first prayer was offered no one had a word to say.

MS 957

MS 958

Hall when it was built in 1852. This impressive building could hold three thousand people. See *DAB*; and John White Chadwick, *Theodore Parker, Preacher and Reformer* (Boston: Houghton Mifflin, 1900), p. 210.

[35]During Finney's previous visit to Boston the year before, the following notice appeared in *The New-York Evangelist*:

> Rev. Mr. Finney, the revivalist, has undertaken the conversion of Rev. Theodore Parker, and has secured the assistance of quite a number of Christians in prayer for that end. It is understood that Mr. Parker holds himself ready for improvement to any extent, and will not quarrel with the means, if the object is obtained (23 April 1857, p. 133).

During Finney's visit the next winter, a Boston paper noted:

> We understand there is a concerted action and agreement in all the Orthodox churches, and churches of other denominations to offer constant and fervent prayer, both public and private, for the conversion of Theodore Parker, which prayers are to be offered until the Lord shall answer them (*The Banner of Light* [Boston], 13 March 1858, p. 4).

[36]Library tape used to repair the edge of the paper has obscured part of this word, which appears to be "reported."

[37]Parker was suffering from consumption and was quite ill. Early in April he wrote to a woman who was attempting to convert him:

> Several persons have come to "labor with me," or have written me letters to convert me. They were commonly persons quite ignorant of the very things they tried to teach me; they claimed a divine illumination which I saw no proofs of, in them, in their lives, or their doctrines (Parker to Julia Bridges, 9 April 1858, published in John Weiss, *Life and Correspondence of Theodore Parker,* vol. 1 [New York: Appleton, 1864], p. 252).

[38]On the reverse of MS 958 is a letter written in pencil by J. H. Fairchild to Rev. Michael E. Strieby, at that time secretary of the American Missionary Association in New York:

> Dear Bro. S. Read this with Bro. W., & tell me whether it should go in. Another thing—. Can you ascertain for me the date of Mr. Finney's "lectures to Christians" which were published in the New York Evangelist, after his revival lectures? He states that they were given before he went to Oberlin, & that two of them presented the doctrine of Sanctification, I have always remembered (?) that it was after he went to O.

He said the impression was universal that they had prayed enough, that the answer to their prayer was certain, and that no more prayer was necessary; and no one of them felt inclined to offer any further petition to God about it. In some way this prayer-meeting came to the knowledge of Mr. Parker; and he said, and I believe wrote, some very strong things against it.[39] However he was very soon laid aside by illness, became unable to preach, went to Europe for his health, and there died.[40] Thus ended the evil influence of his preaching forever, except as the remembrance of it may influence future generations.

JHF 445 I have said there were some very striking instances of ˡconversion in this revival in Boston. One day I received an anonymous letter from a lady, asking

Return these Sheets as soon as you can, & oblige, Jas. H. Fairchild
Newburgh Orange Co. N.Y. Care W. McCrea, Esq.
Dec. 3. 1875.

"Bro. W." is George Whipple, joint secretary of the American Missionary Association with Strieby. They were both Oberlin graduates. Whipple had been a teacher there and knew Finney well. Strieby's reply to Fairchild reads:

New York, Dec. 8, 1875

Rev. J. H. Fairchild D. D.
My Dear Brother,

Bro. Pike kindly consented to examine the files of the Evangelist for the item of information you wished. He found that the Revival Lectures were printed in 1835, and that "Lectures on Christian Duties" were published in 1836 commencing with the first number of the year. "Rev. Mr. Finney's Return to Oberlin" is the title of an editorial which appeared in May 1836—stating that although he was installed in the Broadway Tabernacle this would not interfere with his work in Oberlin.

I hope this will answer your query. If not, we will search farther.

Yours truly
M. E. Strieby.

(Strieby to Fairchild, 8 December 1875, Fairchild Papers, microfilm, roll 2). "Bro. Pike" was the Rev. Gustavus D. Pike, the New York secretary of the American Missionary Association. See *The Congregational Quarterly* 17 (January 1875): 212.

[39]The prayer meeting that Parker heard about was the famous occasion on Saturday afternoon, 6 March 1858, in Park Street vestry:

From thirty to forty persons were assembled at this meeting, and nine or ten of them spoke and prayed, all in relation to Mr. Parker, and all in the same strain. They prayed that God would destroy his life; or, if not his life, his reason; that confusion and distraction might be sent into his study, so that he should not be able to finish his sermon for the next Sunday; or, if he were allowed to finish it, that he might be miraculously prevented from delivering it; that he might be confounded and brought to shame before the people; and lastly, if God did not please to grant these petitions, that he would miraculously influence Mr. Parker's audience to 'leave that house, and come up to this'!

Charles K. Whipple, the writer of this account, added: "Remember, *this* meeting chanced to be reported. No one knows how many more there were" (*The Liberator* [Boston], 24 September 1858, p. 156; see also *The Radical* [Boston] 1 [July 1866]: 437; and Weiss, *Life of Theodore Parker*, pp. 250–51).

In response to these prayer meetings Parker preached two sermons in Music Hall, one on 4 April entitled "A False and True Revival of Religion" and one on 11 April entitled "The Revival of Religion Which We Need." These were reported in the papers and were soon after published in pamphlet form by William L. Kent of Boston.

[40]Early in January 1859, Parker had a hemorrhage of the lungs and was told that his chance of recovery was one in ten, but he decided to take a trip to the West Indies and Europe. He left Boston on 3 February with his wife and in the company of Dr. Samuel G. and Julia Ward Howe. After traveling to Europe, he spent the winter in Rome, but he died in Florence on 10 May 1860. See Chadwick, *Theodore Parker*, pp. 351–72.

my advice in regard to the state of her soul.[41] Usually I took no notice whatever of anonymous letters. But the handwriting, the manifest talent displayed in the letter together with the unmistakable earnestness of the writer, led me to ˡgive it unwonted attention. She concluded by requesting me to answer it and to direct it to Mrs. M., and leave it with the sexton of the church where I was to preach that night, and she should get it. I was at this time preaching around from evening to evening in different churches.[42] I replied to this anonymous letter, that I could not give her the advice which she sought, because I was not well enough acquainted with her history, or with the real state of her mind. But I would venture to call her attention to one fact, which was very apparent not only in her letter but also in the fact of her not putting her name to it, that she was a very *proud* woman; and that that fact she needed thoroughly to consider. I left my reply with the sexton as she requested, and the next morning a lady called to see me. **As soon as I was alone with her in the parlor** she informed me that she was the lady that wrote that anonymous letter; and she had called to tell me that I was mistaken in thinking ˡthat she was proud. She said that [**she**][43] was far enough from that; but she was a member of the Episcopal church, and did not want to disgrace her church by revealing the fact that she was not converted. I replied: "It is *church* pride, then, that kept you from revealing your name." This touched her so deeply that she ‹arose›,[44] and in a manifest excitement left the room. I expected to see her no more; but that evening I found her after preaching among the inquirers in the vestry. **It was my custom all along, after preaching to invite inquirers into the vestry. The vestry was generally filled with inquirers, and often there were more than could get seats. I used to spend more or less time in these meetings in conversing in few words with individuals as I passed around, that I might be enabled the more intelligently to address to them the class of truths that I perceived they needed.** In passing around **at this meeting** I observed this lady. She was manifestly a **lady** of **first rate** intelligence and ˡeducation, and I could perceive that she belonged to **the first class of** society. But as yet I did not know her name; for our conversation that morning had not lasted ˡ**perhaps** more than a minute or two before she left the room as I have related. As I observed her in passing around I remarked to her quietly, "And *you* here?" "Yes," she replied; and dropped her head as if she felt deeply. I had a few words of kind conversation with her, and it passed for that evening. In these inquiry meetings I always **pressed them with** the

MS 959

MS 960

MS 961

JHF 446

[41] This letter is not in the Finney Papers.

[42] Finney's first sermon after arriving for the winter in Boston was preached in the Pine Street Church. Thereafter he divided his labors between Old South, Park Street, Salem Street, and Pine Street churches, preaching six times during the week and twice on Sundays. Later on he was reported as preaching also in the Shawmut Church and was advertised to preach in South Baptist Church, South Boston, as well as in churches in East Boston, Chelsea, and Charlestown. See *The Congregationalist,* 18 December 1857, p. 202; 29 January 1858, p. 19; *The Independent,* 7 January 1858, p. 1; 4 February 1858, p. 2; and see MS 963. A number of Finney's sermons were reported in *The Congregationalist* from 15 January to 5 March 1858.

[43] Matson had originally written "That she," but he crossed it out and wrote "She said that." Fairchild reinserted the word "she."

[44] Here Finney crossed out the words "got up" and inserted the word "arose."

necessity of immediate submission to Christ, and brought them face to face with that duty; and I then called on such as were prepared to commit themselves unalterably to Christ, to kneel down. I observed when I made this call that she was among the first **of the number** that made a movement to kneel **down**. The next morning she called on me again at an early hour. As soon as we were alone she opened her mind to me and said: "I see, ¹Mr.[45] Finney, that I have been very proud. I have come to tell you who I am, and to give you such facts in regard to my history that you may know what to say to me." She was, as I had supposed, a woman in high life, the wife of a wealthy gentleman who was himself a skeptic. She had made a profession of religion, but was unconverted. She was very frank in this interview, and threw her mind open to instruction very cordially; and either at that time or immediately after, she expressed hope in Christ and became a very earnest Christian. She is a remarkable writer, and could more nearly report my sermons without short-hand than any person I ever knew. She used to come,[46] and sit and write my sermons with a rapidity and an accuracy that was quite astonishing. She sent copies of her notes to a great many of her friends, and exerted herself to the utmost to secure the conversion of her friends in Boston and elsewhere. With this lady I ¹have[47] had much correspondence **since that time.**[48] She has always manifested that[49] same earnestness in religion that she did at that time. She has always some good work in hand; and is an earnest laborer for the poor, and for all classes that need her instruction, her sympathy, and her help. She has passed through many mental struggles, sur¹rounded as she is by such temptations to worldliness **and vanity**. But I trust that she has been, and will be, an ornament to the **cause** of Christ.

MS 962 [1]

MS 962 [2]

JHF 447

In this revival I had conversation with a large number of the higher classes in Boston, especially those that attended Episcopal worship. But I suppose we shall never know in this world anything like the number savingly affected during this great revival in Boston.[50] **The interest was**

[45]MS 962 [1] is the first of two consecutive pages numbered 962.

[46]Matson had written down after this, "with pen ink and paper," but it appears to have been crossed out by Finney.

[47]MS 962 [2] was numbered 804 and renumbered 935 by Matson; Finney incorrectly renumbered it 962, so a ½ was later added by Fairchild.

[48]This correspondence is not in the Finney Papers.

[49]Fairchild altered this word to "the" in the manuscript, but it appears as "that" in the published edition.

[50]John D. Hannah, in referring to an article in the *Christian Advocate and Journal* for 1 July 1858, has made the point: "What is known in Boston is that in one instance the Baptists, Methodists, and Congregationalists collectively listed fourteen hundred conversions" ("Layman's Prayer Revival," p. 72). The Park Street Church held their semicentennial celebration the next year, and it was stated there:

> In the years 1857 and 1858, under the labors of Rev. Charles G. Finney and Mrs. Finney, a deep and searching work of the Spirit was witnessed, in which many professors of religion renewed their experience and their hope, and probably not less than six hundred souls were converted, of whom about two hundred united with this church (*The Semi-Centennial Celebration of the Park Street Church and Society: Held on the Lord's Day, February 27, 1859* [Boston: Hoyt, 1861], pp. 144–45).

G. F. Wright, Finney's biographer, wrote in 1891 of the extensive revivals attending Finney's labors in Boston:

> It is the universal testimony of the members of Park Street Church surviving from that time that the conversions were characterized by greater permanence than were those

as great and general in that large city as any that I ever witnessed in any place that I recollect. Should I take time to give an account of one in ten ˡor[51] **even twenty of the interesting cases that came under my own observation, it would require a considerable volume to do them justice.** The revival extended from Boston to Charlestown and Chelsea. In short it spread on every side. I preached in East Boston[52] and Charlestown;[53] and for a considerable time in Chelsea, where the revival became very general and precious.[54]

MS 963

We continued to labor in Boston that winter until it was time for us to return to our labors **here** in the Spring. When we left **there** the work was in its full strength, without any apparent abatement at all. The church ‹**&** ministry in this country›[55] had become so very extensively engaged in promoting the revival, and such was the blessing of God attending the exertions of laymen as well as of ministers, that I made up my mind to return and spend another season in England, and see if the same influence would not

brought about in connection with the labors of any other revivalist whom they have had with them (Wright, *Charles Grandison Finney* [Boston and New York: Houghton Mifflin, 1891], p. 106).

[51] Fairchild added "–967" after page number 963, indicating to the printers to proceed to page 968 and to omit the intervening pages. Page 963 was originally numbered 805 and then renumbered 936 by Matson. Finney changed it to 963.

[52] The Congregational church in East Boston was the Maverick Church, which had been founded in 1837. The minister, R. W. Clark, had left in 1857, and the church was without a pastor. The membership was about 370. In 1859, T. N. Haskell became the minister. See *American Congregational Year-Book for the Years 1857–1859.*

[53] Charlestown, the area on the north side of Boston between the Mystic and Charles rivers, had two Congregational churches. The First Church, under James B. Miles, established a union prayer meeting at the end of January. The larger Winthrop Church was without a pastor. See *The Congregationalist,* 12 February 1858, p. 26; and *American Congregational Year-Book for the Year 1858.*

[54] Chelsea is a village northeast of Boston. The principal church where Finney preached was the Winnisimmet Congregational Church. The minister was Isaac P. Langworthy. The church had been formed in 1841, and Langworthy was the first pastor. By 1850 their meeting house had become too small, and Langworthy and a number of the members formed a new congregation and built the Chestnut Street Church, which could hold a thousand people. Langworthy had been away from the church for much of 1857, acting as secretary of the American Congregational Union, but he returned at the beginning of January 1858. Finney preached in both churches and also in the Broadway Congregational Church, where J. A. Copp was the minister. See *American Congregational Year-Book for the Year 1858,* pp. 149–50; *The Independent,* 21 January 1858, p. 3; and *The Congregationalist,* 12 March 1858, p. 42. Notices of Finney's meetings and the revival in Chelsea appeared in many of the local papers as well as in *The Oberlin Evangelist.* A report of the revival in the Winnisimmet Church, probably written by Langworthy, states:

> A precious revival of religion was enjoyed by this Church during the last Winter. More than ordinary interest appeared very soon after the pastor's return, the 1st of January. Inquiry meetings were attended by slowly increasing numbers, and some had already indulged hope. About the middle of February, the Rev. Mr. Finney commenced preaching in the church. He preached with great plainness, and power, four times a week, either in this or the Broadway church, for some seven weeks. Mrs. Finney, in the meantime, met a very large company of ladies, to whom she spoke, and with whom she prayed, the Lord blessing her labors abundantly. More than *sixty* persons, it is believed, passed the great change, during this religious interest, the most of whom have united with some Church of Christ. And many who had been professing Christians for years, were greatly revived and comforted, and will long remember the affectionate and faithful labors of Mr. and Mrs. F. (*American Congregational Year-Book for the Year 1859,* pp. 154–55).

[55] Finney added the words "& ministry in this country."

pervade that country.[56] **‹The Brethren of all evangelical denominations had so entered into the work & both Mrs Finney & myself were so exhausted that we left Boston & went to her brother in Brooklyn & spent a week or two there.[57] We then labored in Oberlin with success & the next fall went to England.›**[58]

[56]Finney added the section that follows to the end of the manuscript page when he started a new chapter heading at the top of the next page. Fairchild crossed it out.

[57]The Finneys had both been ill during much of the time they were in Boston that winter. At the beginning of January, Finney had to cancel all his meetings for a week because he developed boils and carbuncles and then "rheumatism in [his] chest." He was confined to bed for several days. Mrs. Finney nursed him and then became ill herself. By the end of January he felt so ill that he thought seriously of returning home. Soon after that he had an inflamed eye (Finney to Julia Finney, 13 and 23 January, and 15 February 1858, Finney Papers, microfilm, roll 4; see also *The Independent,* 28 January 1858, p. 1).

They left Boston on 8 April 1858 for Brooklyn. Mrs. Finney's brother was Hobart Ford, who ran a storage and lighterage business in Brooklyn and lived with his family at 44 Remsen Street. He had visited the Finneys in Boston in April. See *The Brooklyn City Directory, for the year ending May 1st 1858* (Brooklyn: Lain, 1858), p. 125; and Finney to Julia Finney, 15 February 1858, Finney Papers, microfilm, roll 4.

While Finney was in Brooklyn, he was invited to preach for George B. Cheever, the Congregational minister of the Church of the Puritans in New York. Advertisements for the meetings and notices of the work were carried in *The New York Daily Tribune* from 17 April through 1 May 1858. The church was in serious trouble as a result of the strong antislavery stance of the minister, and there was strong pressure to get Cheever to resign. Seth B. Hunt, one of the deacons, recalled:

> In Doctor Cheever's church, we got into a sad quarrel, and called in Mr. Finney as peace-maker. He gathered a company of us into Dr. C.'s parlor to pray with us. One sister who spoke in meetings, he prayed for (by name), that she might have "the grace of silence." He prayed that "Dr. — might know his own mind," and so on. After a while he added, "But Thou knowest, O Lord, that we have had enough of this! Amen" (*Reminiscences of Finney,* p. 36).

See also Cheever to Finney, 29 May 1858, Finney Papers, microfilm, roll 4; and *The Independent,* 14 January 1858, p. 2. Finney stood by Cheever in his denunciations of slavery. See *OE,* 15 September 1858, p. 146.

Dr. James W. Alexander, who heard Finney at that time, described one of the meetings that he and Rev. Theodore L. Cuyler attended. Finney's preaching reminded Alexander of the old Scottish preachers Ebenezer and Thomas Erskine and Robert Murray McCheyne: "He was able and tremendous against infidels. The interest, though intellectual, was intense. I find his plan and all the details graven on my memory" (*Forty Years' Familiar Letters of James W. Alexander, D.D.,* ed. John Hall, D.D., vol. 1 [New York: Scribner, 1860], p. 278; and T. L. Cuyler, "The Princeton Revival—President Finney," *NYE,* 10 February 1876, p. 1).

[58]The Finneys left Oberlin for England on 16 December. A "considerable degree of religious interest" was reported in Oberlin in October and November, with eight being admitted to the church on 31 October. See *OE,* 10 November 1858, p. 182.

CHAPTER XXXIV

MS 964
JHF 448

‹Labors in England till 1860.›

During[1] my absence from England a new pastor had been settled at the Tabernacle over the Congregation of Dr Campbell, and a new order of things had been introduced. Troubles had occurred in the congregation that had caused most of the converts of the revival when I was there to withdraw and go to other churches.[2] Before I speak of the labors that I at this time performed in England, I must notice some opposition that I met with the first time that I was there, that I have passed over. I have already spoken of the letters received by John Angell James when I was at Birmingham, both from this and the other side of the Atlantic.[3] When I arrived at London the letters were directed to Dr Campbell; but as they were nearly or quite all anonymous, he would have nothing to do with them. As soon as he saw that they were anonymous, and were about me, he would hand them to me, and would not read them unless I requested him to do so. They made no other impression upon him that I could see than to arouse his indignation. A little while before I left him, however, he received a copy of "The Presbyterian," published at that time, I believe, in Philadelphia, and edited, ˡas I afterwards learned, by Mr. Prime, since editor of the New York Observer.[4] The article was

MS 965

[1] Pages 964–85 were originally numbered 806–27 and renumbered 937–58 by Matson. They were changed to 964–85 by Finney. The chapter heading was written by Finney on a narrow strip of paper pasted onto the top of page 964. This obscured the previous pagination and most of a section that had been added by Finney at the top of the page. It read: "and in New York and then returned and labored in Oberlin with the usual results and the next autumn we left for England. This was 1858." The chapter title was crossed out by Fairchild, and the whole section from MS 964 to 967 was omitted in the published edition.

[2] Rev. John Corbin (1811–1890) was copastor with Campbell from 1853 until June 1856. He left because of "a want of congeniality between my own tastes and habits and those of the bulk of the people" ("John Corbin [Congregationalist]," 1875, p. 6, in Autobiographical Notices of contemporary divines, collected by Rev. Thomas Hunter, 1875–1876, MS 38.64 in Dr. Williams's Library, London). In February 1859, Rev. William Grigsby (1808–1876) went to the Tabernacle to help Campbell. He remained until his death. See *The Congregational Year Book* (London), 1877, p. 366. A notice of Finney's death stated that

> Dr. Campbell, who welcomed him to the Tabernacle of which he was the pastor, and praised and defended him in the *British Banner*, used afterwards to lament that he had done so, because the church there had been greatly injured by the hastily made converts of the revivalist preacher ("Death of Charles G. Finney," *The Christian World* [London], 10 September 1875, p. 600).

[3] See MS 826.

[4] Samuel Irenaeus Prime (1812–1885) was an influential Presbyterian minister and author. He was the well-known editor of *The New York Observer* from 1840 to 1874, but for a short period

designed to warn the British churches against me and my influence.[5] Among other severe things the writer said that as he hoped to be saved, and as he expected to answer it at the solemn judgment, he must say that there was no man living or dead that had done so much to injure the cause of revivals as I had done. That the churches where I had labored had wept tears of blood over the desolations that had resulted from those revivals. I give as nearly his words as I can recollect.[6] I do not know that this made any particular impression on Dr Campbell's mind other than to arouse his indignation. However I wrote a letter to the editor of the New York Evangelist, and inquired who this editor of the Presbyterian was, for then I did not know.[7] I also inquired where those churches were that had wept tears of blood over those revivals; and what evidence he had of any such thing. I then appealed to all the churches and brethren where I had labored, if they knew of any such disastrous |results from those revivals to write, and publish their letters, and let it be known throughout the world. I affirmed that I knew of no such results anywhere where I had labored. I made as strong an appeal as I could to all the churches and ministers where I had labored to say if they knew ought of the things with which he had charged me. That I

MS 966

from 1849 to 1851 he was away from that paper. From January 1850 for a year, he was assistant editor of *The Presbyterian*, the editor being Dr. William M. Engles (see Wendell Prime, *Samuel Irenaeus Prime, Autobiography and Memorials* [New York: Randolph, 1888], p. 232; *NYE*, 10 January 1850, p. 6; and *DAB*). Prime is known today as the author of *The Power of Prayer*, an account of the Fulton Street prayer meeting, which played such a prominent role in the revival of 1858. Finney was critical of his treatment of the causes of that revival and reckoned Prime had misunderstood the function of the businessmen's prayer meetings. See Finney, *The Prevailing Prayer-Meeting* (London: Ward, 1859), pp. 19–21.

[5] It appeared in *The Presbyterian* (Philadelphia), 20 July 1850, p. 112. Campbell may have been sent a copy of this paper, but the relevant part of the article was reprinted with favorable comments in *The Puritan Recorder* (Boston), 25 July 1850, p. 118, which Campbell, as editor of *The British Banner*, received as an exchange paper anyway. It is possible, therefore, that it was this reprint that Finney was shown. *The Puritan Recorder* came under attack from Campbell because of its antagonism toward Finney. See *The British Banner* (London), 4 September 1850, p. 602; see also *The Inquirer* (London), 7 September 1850, p. 573.

[6] The article entitled "Finney in London" quoted an extract from *The British Banner* of 5 June 1850, p. 381, in which Campbell gave a favorable account of Finney's preaching in Whitefield's Tabernacle. It went on to say:

> It is obvious from this, that Finney preaching is to have its run in London, as it had here. Similar accounts, even far more favourable, were given in the early years of his labours in this country; but the churches that *enjoyed* his ministrations have wept bloody tears of regret that he ever saw them. We presume that no man, now living or dead, has inflicted more injury upon the cause of religion, and especially upon revivals of religion, than Charles G. Finney. Thousands, who were once his admirers and friends, are now witness to the truth of this solemn and awful declaration. We make it in view of our accountability to God, as well as to those who read this paper; and if our friends in Great Britain should be tempted to try the experiment of Mr. Finney's gospel in their churches, they will find it eminently successful at first, and disastrous in the end. Like the little book in the Apocalypse, it may be sweet in the mouth, but it will disagree with them dreadfully after they swallow it (*The Presbyterian*, 20 July 1850, p. 112; reference from Keith J. Hardman).

[7] Finney wrote to Joshua Leavitt. The letter, which was eventually published, does not contain any inquiry about who the editor of *The Presbyterian* was, so Finney must have written an accompanying letter to Leavitt, or perhaps to Henry Ward Beecher, asking for this information. See nn. 8 and 11 below.

did not want them to say ought in my favor. But if they knew anything against me, or of the results of my labors, I wanted they should make it known, for I did not know it myself. This letter I directed to Brother Joshua Leavitt ‹the Editor of the New York evangelist›; and I waited, and received no notice of it.[8] He did not publish it, and I could not understand why. This was but a little while before I left London to return home; but the answer did not come as soon as I expected, by any means.[9] When I arrived in New York I found that the letter had been published, and several answers were given by brethren with whom I had labored.[10] This had taken place while I was on my passage home from London. On inquiring of Brother Leavitt why the letter had not been published sooner, he informed me that he received it from the office |just as he was starting on a journey, and by mistake he put it in his pocket instead of leaving it in the office to be published. Hence no more attention was paid to it until after he returned, and by chance found it in his pocket, and then he had it immediately published.[11] But as I had returned and was again in this country, but two or three letters had been written by my friends on this side and published. They

MS 967

[8]Although Finney probably saw the article in August, he did not write his letter until 12 December. He was, however, away from London recuperating from the middle of September until the end of November. See MS 877. Henry Ward Beecher was also in London, staying with Campbell at that time, and it was probably the same paper that he saw before he left for New York at the end of August. He deeply regretted its publication and promised Finney that he would "take an early opportunity to speak through the *Independent* on the interference of American Christians in this shameless manner." His letter in Finney's defense was published in *The Independent* (New York), 21 November 1850, p. 190. See also William C. Beecher and S. Scoville, *Biography of Rev. Henry Ward Beecher* (New York: Webster, 1888), p. 349; Beecher to Finney, 30 August 1850, Finney Papers, microfilm, roll 4; and *The British Banner,* 4 June 1851, p. 277.

Finney seems to have forgotten that Joshua Leavitt had not been editor of *The New-York Evangelist* since 1837. In 1848 he had joined *The Independent* and had become the office editor (see *DAB*). Finney's letter was in fact addressed "To the Editors of the Independent" and was published in the 17 April 1851 issue, p. 61. A copy was sent to *The New-York Evangelist* and appeared on the same day in that paper, p. 64.

[9]The Finneys sailed for New York on 5 April, arriving about three weeks later. See *OE,* 23 April 1851, p. 71; and *The New York Daily Tribune*, 28 April 1851, p. 8.

[10]Joseph P. Thompson, one of the editors of *The Independent* and minister of the Broadway Tabernacle, New York, wrote an editorial entitled "Revival Reminiscences" in reply to Finney's letter, which was published in the same issue, p. 62. There were also two other letters. One was from Dirck C. Lansing, dated 21 April 1851 and published in *The Independent,* 1 May 1851, p. 72. The other was from Josiah Hopkins, dated May 1851 and published in *NYE,* 12 June 1851, p. 93.

[11]The following statement appeared in *The Independent* of 15 May 1851 under the heading "Mr. Finney's Letter":

> We have been requested to state why the letter of Mr. Finney did not appear till four months after its date, and as the circumstance has given rise to evil surmises we hasten to make the explanation. The letter was sent under cover to Mr. Beecher, who gave it to Mr. Leavitt just as he (Mr. L.) was setting out upon a journey. Thus it got mislaid, and had passed out of mind till it was accidentally recalled. It came to the knowledge of the acting editor only one week before its publication. It was published really as soon as received. We meant that it should go in without date, and therefore made no explanation at the time. The surmise that it was withheld by design till the eve of Mr. Finney's arrival is wholly gratuitous, and so is every other surmise or conjecture about it. Mr. F. knew nothing of the circumstances. As the letter was sent to the *Evangelist* from this office, the same explanation will apply to our neighbor (p. 82).

supposing that now I had returned there was no use of writing further, those of them that were expecting to write said no more about it. How Mr. Prime came by such an idea of those revivals I cannot say; but I presume he came by it very much as Mr. Nettleton and Dr Beecher received their information.[12]

On our second visit to England we landed at Liverpool; and from thence went to Houghton, Huntingdonshire, to my good friend, Potto Brown's. We found him away from home in search of us. I had dropped him a line two or three days before we left New York, saying that we expected to take passage in the Persia. We arrived on Saturday morning[13] in Liver|pool[14] and went and spent the Sabbath with Brother William James, formerly of New York, an old and tried friend of mine.[15] Brother Brown had left home expecting to arrive in Liverpool

MS 968

[12] Fairchild crossed out this sentence on the manuscript before he decided to omit the whole page. After weeks of indecision about whether they should go to England, the Finneys finally left Oberlin on the evening of Wednesday, 15 December, spending Thursday in Rochester with Mrs. Finney's children. In view of these difficulties that Finney had encountered on his previous trip to England, he went the second time armed with letters of introduction and testimonials. He was given some of these in Rochester on the way to New York from Oberlin. They sailed from New York on the *Persia* on Wednesday, 22 December. See letters from Horace Bushnell, Andrew L. Stone, Laymen of Rochester, James B. Shaw, William Wisner, and Levi A. Ward, November–December 1858, Finney Papers, microfilm, roll 4; and "A Journal Kept by Mrs. Elizabeth Ford Atkinson Finney during a Visit to England in 1859–1860," p. 15, manuscript in Special Collections, Oberlin College Library. This journal gives a day-to-day account of the Finneys' labors in the British Isles.

[13] This was Saturday, 1 January 1859. See E. Finney, "Journal," p. 17.

[14] Fairchild crossed out the first three-quarters of MS 968 and added a new chapter heading and an introductory sentence.

[15] Finney seems to have confused the name here. "William" James was the minister in Rochester when Finney was there in 1830 (see MS 560). He had spent two years at a Scottish university after leaving Princeton but is not known to have been in England after that time nor to have been a resident of New York City. However, an address book used in connection with the visit of the Finneys to Britain has the following entry: "Daniel James Esq., Oakwood, Aigburth, Liverpool" ("Where is it?" Address Book, Finney Papers, file 2/2/2, box 7).

Daniel James (1801–1876) was a native of New York State. He became a partner in the New York firm of Phelps, Dodge and Co. and married Elizabeth Phelps, the oldest daughter of Anson G. Phelps. In 1831 he went to Liverpool to work in the English end of the business, importing cotton and exporting and dealing in metals. Phelps had written to Finney in 1831: "Mr. James, his wife, little son, and my daughter Harriet expect to sail for England, Providence permitting, 16 inst., and desire an interest in your prayers. Who can tell but you may one day visit them there?" (Phelps to Finney, 6 May 1831, Finney Papers, microfilm, roll 3; spelling and punctuation corrected for ease of reading). James took over the English business in 1834 under the name of Phelps, James and Co. and spent the rest of his life in Liverpool. His wife died in 1847, and on a visit to New York the next year he remarried. When he died he was considered to be the oldest and most respected merchant in England connected with Anglo-American trade. He was the father of Daniel Willis James, a later partner in the American branch and a noted philanthropist in his day. See *DAB*; Richard Lowitt, *A Merchant Prince of the Nineteenth Century, William E. Dodge* (New York: Columbia University Press, 1954); *Appletons' Cyclopaedia and Register of Important Events of the Year 1876* (New York), n.s., 1:621; Anson G. Phelps, "Diary" in New York Public Library; and Phelps to Finney, 26 March 1848, Finney Papers, microfilm, roll 4.

James was an elder in the church of Dr. Thomas Raffles, the great Liverpool Nonconformist minister. It is interesting to note that Raffles, who was an avid collector of autograph letters of eminent people, had in his collection two of Finney's letters. One of these was addressed to Daniel James during Finney's earlier visit to England (Thomas Raffles, "Original Letters—Authors," English manuscripts, box 377, John Rylands University Library of Manchester). Mrs. Finney, who was very anxious about whether she and her husband would be accepted in England,

in time to meet us. But we had left the ship and had gone, as I said, to Brother James', so that he failed to meet us. He however drove to all the principal hotels and inquired for us. He went on board the ship and tried to learn where we had gone; but they could give him no reliable information.[16] **He then concluded we had gone to London, and forthwith went there; and when he found we were not there he returned home on the same evening that we arrived at his house, but after our arrival. He had been two or three days running almost night and day. His object was to have us** labor in Houghton for a season before we committed ourselves to any other field **of labor**. Immediately on ‹our›[17] arrival I received a great number of letters from different parts of England, expressing great joy at our return **there,** and inviting us to come and labor in many different |fields. However I spent several weeks laboring in Houghton and ‹St› Ives,[18] where we saw precious revivals.[19] In ‹**St.**› Ives they had never had a revival before. In Houghton, **as I have before said,** we labored during our first visit **there**, and saw a very interesting work of grace. At this time we found at Saint Ives a very **curious** state of things. There was but one Independent church, the pastor of which had been there a good many years, but had not succeeded in doing much as a minister.[20] He was a mysterious sort of man. He was very fond of wine, and a great opposer of **temperance.**[21] We held our meetings **at Saint Ives** in a hall **that had been built for the accommodation of lectures on various subjects;** which would accommodate more people by far than the Congregational church. I sometimes preached, however, in the **Congregational** church; but it was a less desirable place to preach in than the hall, as it was a very small and incommodious house.[22]

MS 969

wrote in her journal, "Our reception from Mr James at Liverpool and our princely entertainment by them, the reception of Mr. F. by Dr. Raffles—his asking Mr Finney to preach and ourselves to dine—these things I look at as indications of the welcome before us" (p. 18).

[16]The Finneys had left their address with the steward, but he was not on the boat. One of the men thought they had gone to London. See E. Finney, "Journal," p. 18.

[17]Here Finney changed the word "my" to "our."

[18]Matson had written the word "Saint" here and elsewhere, but Finney sometimes changed it to "St." Fairchild restored "Saint."

[19]Finney started preaching in Houghton, where Rev. John Hart had become the minister, but on 15 January, Finney and his wife moved to the nearby market town of St. Ives. They stayed with Potto Brown's son Bateman and his wife. Finney began preaching there on Sunday, 16 January, but returned occasionally to Houghton to preach. See E. Finney, "Journal," pp. 19–21.

[20]Isaiah Knowles Holland was minister at the Independent Chapel from 1820 until his retirement in 1860. He died in 1873 (see *The Congregational Year Book,* 1874, pp. 332–33). Mrs. Finney noted in her journal on 8 January: "Mr. Holland of St Ives opens his pulpit—this is most unexpected—looks almost like a miracle to the friends" (p. 26).

[21]Fairchild changed this to "total abstinence."

[22]The old Independent Chapel, built in 1811, had deep galleries and could hold a thousand people. The Public Institution, a spacious hall, sixty by thirty feet, had been built in 1848. See *History, Gazetteer, and Directory of the County of Huntingdon* (Huntingdon: Hatfield, 1854), p. 401.

Finney started preaching in the Congregational church on Sunday, 16 January. The Institution was used for evening meetings during the week from Tuesday to Friday. On subsequent Sundays he preached in rotation in the Congregational and Methodist chapels. Mrs. Finney also started holding afternoon meetings for women in the Institution from Saturday, 22 January. See *The Eastern Counties Gazette* (St. Ives), 12 February 1859, p. 2; and 26 February 1859, p. 2; and E. Finney, "Journal," pp. 21–29.

MS 970 The revival took a powerful effect there, notwithstanding the position of the **Congregational** minister. He stood firmly against it until the interest became so great that he left the town, and was absent, I know not where, for several weeks.[23] Since that time the converts of the revival, together with my JHF 449 friend Brown, and some of the older members of the church, have put up a fine chapel, **as I understand, in that city;**[24] and the religious **state of things** has been exceedingly different from what it ever had been before.

I have said they had a new pastor in Dr Campbell's place at the Tabernacle in London. For some reason he was very much prejudiced against me, and did not invite me to preach[25] to his people. I have also spoken of Brother James Harcourt as being the pastor at Houghton at the time I first labored there.[26] The revival at that place had not only greatly quickened him, but it had given him new ideas of promoting revivals of religion. He remained at Houghton for some two or three MS 971 **years after I left there, and then was invited to a much wider field of labor, I believe in Luton. There he went to work and had a powerful revival of religion under his own ministry. He soon built up a large congregation, and came to be more publicly known by far than he ever had been before. This led to his being** called to London, to Borough Road Chapel.[27] Here I found him on my second visit to England. He had been waiting with anxiety **for** our return to England; and as soon as he heard we were there he used most strenuous efforts to secure our labors with him in London.[28] The church over which he presided in London had been torn to

[23] Reports of the meetings indicated an increased unity among the different denominations, an increased spirit of prayer, "a complete revolution in the experience and thinking of professing Christians," and "the conversion to God of not a few of the undecided."

> Beyond all question, to say nothing of the conversion of sinners, an incalculable amount of good has been effected—an impetus has been given to religious zeal and effort, which requires but to be well organized and judiciously directed by the ministers of the town, in order to produce yet higher, and happier, and permanent results (*The Eastern Counties Gazette,* 26 February 1859, p. 2).

See also *The Cambridge Independent Press*, 12 February 1859, p. 7; and 26 February 1859, p. 7. Potto Brown wrote to Finney in December 1860:

> You will recollect what a hindrance poor Mr. Holland used to be (as we thought) to the spread of the Gospel in our County, that difficulty has just ceased, he has resigned his pastorate and we are now endeavouring to unite ourselves with his people and so gain more strength and power for doing good (P. Brown to Finney, 16 December 1860, Finney Papers, microfilm, roll 5).

[24] Finney's use of the term "city" could be misleading. St. Ives was "the chief commercial town in the County of Huntingdon, containing about 4,000 inhabitants, and the centre of a large number of interesting country villages." The new Free church, which dominates the market place, was built in 1863 and became the center for the Nonconformist work in the area. See *The Cambridge Independent Press*, 26 February 1859, p. 7; and Herbert E. Norris, *History of St. Ives* (St. Ives: The Hunts County Guardian, 1889), pp. 42–44.

[25] Here Matson had written "come and preach," but the words "come and" appear to have been crossed out by Finney.

[26] See MS 816–24.

[27] Harcourt moved to Luton at the end of 1851. In 1855 he was called to Regent St. Lambeth, and he moved to the Borough Road Chapel, Southwark, in February 1857. The chapel, built in 1838, was the largest Baptist church in London. See *The History of the Southwark Baptist Church* (booklet published by the church, May 1955).

[28] In November 1858, while deciding whether to go to England, Finney had received a letter from Harcourt urging him to go there again. Harcourt then visited Finney in Houghton on 11

pieces by most ultra and fanatical views on the subject of Temperance. They had had a lovely pastor, whose heart had been almost broken by their feuds upon that subject, and had finally left the church in utter discouragement.[29] Their deacons had been compelled to resign, and the church was in a state of ¦disorganization,**—or perhaps, to use our American phrase, of *demoralization*.** MS 972 Brother Harcourt ‹**came to St Ives &**›[30] informed me[31] that unless the church could be converted, he was satisfied he never could succeed in doing much in that field.

As soon as we could leave Saint Ives we went to London to see what could be done **with Brother Harcourt's** church and congregation. We found them as he had represented, in so demoralized a state that it seemed questionable whether the church could ever be resuscitated and built up. However we went to work, my wife among the ladies of the Congregation; and I went to preaching, and searching them, to the utmost of my strength.[32] It was very soon perceptible that the Spirit of God was poured out, and that the church were very generally in a state of great conviction. The work deepened and spread till it reached, I believe, every house-hold belonging to that congregation. All the old members of the church were so searched that they made confession one ¦to another, and settled their difficulties; and **Brother** MS 973 Harcourt told me before I left that his church was entirely a new church. **That is, that they were so thoroughly overhauled that they were quite a new people;** that the blessing of God had been universal among them, so ¦that all their old animosities were healed; and that he had the greatest JHF 450 comfort in them. Indeed the work in that church was really most wonderful. I directed my labors for several weeks to the church itself. **Brother** Harcourt had been praying for them and laboring with them till he was almost discouraged; but the blessing at last came in such **a** fulness as **fully** to meet the longings of his heart. His people were reconverted and cemented together in love, and they learned to take hold of the work themselves.[33]

Some years after my return to this **place Brother** Harcourt came over and

January, with an invitation from his congregation. He again visited Finney in St. Ives the next week and twice later in February, as well as writing further letters. See E. Finney, "Journal," pp. 5, 20–29.

[29] Rev. T. C. Keen was pastor from 1855 until he resigned in January 1857. According to E. J. Poole-Connor, a later pastor of the church, "His pastorate was brief and troubled" (*History of the Southwark Baptist Church*, p. 10).

[30] Finney added the words "came to St Ives &."

[31] Matson had written down after this, "as soon as he saw me," but it appears that he crossed it out.

[32] Finney started laboring at Borough Road Chapel on Sunday, 27 February. His first sermon, "License, Bondage, and Liberty," on Romans 8:15, was published in *The Christian World*, 4 March 1859, pp. 379–80. He preached twice on Sundays and on the evenings of Tuesday to Friday each week. Mrs. Finney held a meeting for women from 3:00 to 4:00 every afternoon from Tuesday to Friday (E. Finney, "Journal," p. 30; and *The South London News, and Surrey, Kent, and Sussex Chronicle* [Lambeth], 26 March 1859, p. 1).

[33] A year later Finney said that Harcourt told him that "the work goes on and increases, and that not a week passes without conversions" (Finney, *The Freeness of the Gospel* [Manchester: Bremner, 1860], p. 158). And a report noted, "We are free from debt. . . . The cause of the Redeemer prospers amongst us" (*The British Baptist Reporter, and Missionary Intelligencer* [London], n.s., 17 [December 1860]: 379).

made us a visit. This was a little while after the death of my dear wife.[34] **He**
MS 974 **had over-worked, and was obliged to leave his church** ¹**for a considerable time; and he visited this country for rest.** He then told me that the work had continued in his church up to that time. That his people felt that if there were not more or less conversions every week, something was entirely wrong. They were frightened if the work was not perceptibly and constantly going forward. He said they stood by him, and he felt every Sabbath as if he was in the midst of a praying atmosphere. Indeed his report of the results of that revival up to the time of his leaving, was ‹deeply›[35] interesting. Considering what the church had been, and what it was after the revival, it is no wonder that **Brother** Harcourt's heart was as full as it could hold of thanksgiving to God for such a **great** blessing.[36]

In this place, as had been the case before at Dr Campbell's, there were great revelations made of iniquity that had been covered up for a long time among professors of religion.[37] These cases were frequently brought to my notice by persons coming to me to ask for advice. **This was** not only **true of**
MS 975 **some** professors ¹of religion, but **of** numbers that had never made a profession of religion, who became terribly convicted of sin. **The revelations that are often made in revivals of religion of the terrible things in which men have been engaged, frequently far exceed anything that would be so much as suspected by any who had never had any experience in this matter.**

The conversions in Brother Harcourt's congregation were numerous. I say his congregation, I mean, of course, those who attended his meetings; for I believe the number of professedly unconverted sinners was very small previous to my arrival. But the house immediately filled up, and was filled to its utmost capacity very soon after our meetings commenced.[38] **I do not know, and never shall know in this world, the**

[34] Finney's second wife, Elizabeth, died on 27 November 1863. See *NYE,* 3 December 1863, p. 1.

[35] Here Finney changed the word "wonderfully" to "deeply."

[36] Harcourt named the house in which he lived at 131 Southampton Street, Camberwell, in south London, "Oberlin Cottage." See "Where is it?" Address Book, Finney Papers, file 2/2/2, box 7; and *The Post Office London Suburban Directory*, 3d ed. (London: Kelly, 1865), p. 407.

[37] On 21 March Mrs. Finney noted in her journal, "Yesterday Mr Finney preached on "confession & covering sin"—The house was filled both morning and afternoon—conviction passed upon the congregation." And on 4 April she wrote, "The sermon on confession has wrought wonders—such an uncovering of sin—God is greatly blessing the truth" (p. 33).

[38] On the first Sunday that Finney started preaching at Borough Road, Mrs. Finney noted in her journal: " 'Congregation' large in the morning—seats in the aisles. . . . In the evening hundreds went away—house would not hold them. . . . House very solemn—More than 50 inquirers" (p. 30). Many of the notices and reports of the meetings that were carried in the local papers and the religious press emphasized the crowds that attended. See, e.g., *South London Observer and Borough Record* (Southwark), 5 March 1859, p. 2; and 26 March 1859, p. 2; *The South London News* (Lambeth), 26 March 1859, p. 3; and 2 April 1859, p. 2; *The Freeman* (London), 2 March 1859, p. 101; and 9 March 1859, p. 117; *The Nonconformist* (London), 2 March 1859, p. 116; and 23 March 1859, p. 223; *The Patriot* (London), 3 March 1859, p. 132; *The Christian World,* 11 March 1859, p. 389; *The British Baptist Reporter and Missionary Intelligencer,* n.s., 16 (April 1859): 124; and *The Beacon* (London), 27 April 1859, p. 329. The following notice appeared in a local paper with Anglican leanings, under the heading of "The Beacon":

> The great American revivalist, Professor Finney, known as the star of Oberlin College, is attracting eager audiences almost every evening in the Baptist Chapel, Borough-

numbers of conversions that occurred there, although after the church got into the work they multiplied on every side.[39] Soon after I began my labors at this time in London, a Dr Tregelles, a distinguished literary man and a professed theologian,[40] wrote to Dr Campbell, calling his attention to what he regarded as a great error ¦in my theology. In treat¦ing upon the conditions of salvation I had said in my Systematic Theology, that the Atonement of Christ was one of the conditions. I said **the *foundation* or *source* from which our salvation flowed was *the Love of God,***—that God's infinite love was the foundation or source from which the whole movement sprang; but that the *conditions upon which we could be saved* were the Atonement of Christ, faith, repentance, **sanctification, &c.**[41] To this statement Dr Tregelles took great exceptions.[42]

MS 976
JHF 451

Strange to tell, instead of going to my Theology and seeing just what I did say, Dr Campbell took it up in his paper and agreed with Dr Tregelles, and wrote several articles in opposition to what he supposed to be my views.[43] **I had explained in my Theology what I meant by the *foundation*[44] upon**

road, and we regret, for the sake of religious truth, that a very unseemly and shabby imitation of the Coal-hole half-penny candle and paper-lanthorn dodge, is being successfully resorted to in order to draw benighted wanderers into the Finney-fold (*Lambeth Observer and the South London Times* [Southwark], 19 March 1859, p. 2).

[39] At the farewell tea meeting on Monday, 18 April, which was "convened . . . for the purpose of giving an opportunity to those who have received benefit to make it known for mutual encouragement and for the glory of God," it was reported:

> From the statements that were made it is evident that the labours of Mr. and Mrs. Finney have been attended by the Divine blessing to a great extent. Many professors of religion have been quickened into new life, backsliders have been restored, and hardened sinners have been melted into penitence and led to Christ (*The Freeman,* 20 April 1859, p. 213).

[40] Samuel Prideaux Tregelles (1813–1875) was a well-known biblical scholar who had written extensively on the ancient texts and on the prophetic books of the Bible. He was then at work on his famous Greek text of the New Testament. Born of Quaker parents in Cornwall, he had settled in Plymouth and joined the Plymouth Brethren, although later in life he was said to have become a Presbyterian. See *DNB.*

[41] Fairchild crossed out the words "sanctification, &c."

[42] Tregelles was not referring to statements in Finney's *Systematic Theology*, as Finney indicated later. In fact, he had not read the book. He had read Finney's *Lectures to Professing Christians* twenty years earlier and was writing to Campbell, the editor of *The British Standard*, to inquire if Finney still held the views he advocated back then or whether he had renounced them. Tregelles wrote: "No 'revival' wrought by the Spirit of God can be based on doctrines which deny the true condition of fallen man, and which trench on the true substitutionary sacrifice of Christ 'the Lord our Righteousness.' "

Tregelles's letter dated 28 February 1859 and Finney's response three days later were published in *The British Standard* (London), 11 March 1859, p. 77. Finney said he had not changed his views "in the substance of them." He wrote, "Every year gives me a clearer apprehension of the great truths of the Gospel, and would modify more or less the manner of stating them." Another letter from Finney written nearly three weeks later, after a more thorough consideration of Tregelles's letter, was published by Campbell in *The British Standard,* 25 March 1859, p. 93. And a further reply from Tregelles and an editorial by Campbell were published on 1 April (pp. 100–101).

[43] Campbell did in fact go to Finney's *Systematic Theology*. In his first notice of the controversy, he wrote that he not only had reread the whole of the *Lectures to Professing Christians*, but "we went further, and had recourse to his great work, 'Systematic Theology,' to which he refers Dr. Tregelles, which we examined on the point in hand with the utmost care" (*The British Standard,* 1 April 1859, p. 100). Campbell wrote two further articles that appeared in *The British Standard,* 8 April 1859, p. 108; and 15 April 1859, p. 116.

[44] Finney underlined the words "*foundation*" and "*source*" in this and the next sentence.

which our salvation rested. I had said that ‹*love*›[45] was the *source* from which the whole movement proceeded. Dr Campbell did not go to my Theology to see that this was my own statement, nor did Dr Tregelles. They both of them strangely misunderstood my position, and got up in MS 977 England at this time ˡa good deal of opposition to my labors.[46] Dr Campbell, it appeared, after all had no doubt **at all** of my orthodoxy. Dr Redford insisted **upon it** that my statement of the matter was right, and that any other statement was far from being right.[47] However I paid no attention publicly to Dr Campbell's strictures on the subject. **They injured him a great deal more than they did myself. I was not at that time laboring in his congregation; and a great many of his readers,—perhaps falsely, but they in fact did impute to him other motives than concern for orthodoxy in what he wrote at that time.**

He afterwards wrote me a letter, which I have now in my possession, subscribing fully to my orthodoxy and to my views; but saying that unfortunately I made discriminations in my theology that common people did not understand.[48] The fact is, a great many people understood them better than the Doctor did himself. He had been educated in Scotland, and was after the straitest sect a Scotch theologian;[49] consequently my **N**ew School MS 978 statements of doctrine puzzled him, and it took him ˡ**sometime** to understand them. **When I preached for him, at first he would say, "Brother Finney, you *reason* too much with the people; it is of no use. Just make your statements. It is of no use to reason with them, for they will not understand you." I told him that they *would* understand me; and that he would see in the event that they had understood me. The fact is, that with him theology was to a great extent dogmatic.** I found when I first arrived in England that their theology was to a very great extent dogmatic. **They had, as everybody knows, a good many years ago come out from the Roman church**. They **then** had their thirty nine articles in the

[45]The underlined word "***love***" is in Finney's handwriting and replaces the word "it."

[46]In his first notice of the controversy, Campbell referred to a number of letters that he had received, all of which—"with one exception, from a Wesleyan minister,"—were critical of Finney's position as represented by Tregelles and of Finney's reply, which was "unanimously held to be unsatisfactory." Campbell published two such letters in *The British Standard,* 15 April 1859, p. 117; and 20 April 1859, p. 133. See *The British Standard,* 1 April 1859, p. 100.

[47]Campbell admitted that when Finney's *Systematic Theology* was first published he only had time "to look cursorily through it, and to read the Preface of Dr. Redford," on which he had relied for believing in the soundness of Finney's views. Although he now disagreed with Redford's judgment and criticized Finney's theology at many points, he included the whole of the preface in his second article, "that Mr. Finney might enjoy the full benefit of it, to which he was entitled" (*The British Standard,* 8 April 1859, p. 109; and 15 April 1859, pp. 116–17). He had drawn attention to the preface when the book first came out, and it was included in the *Valedictory Services* for the Finneys published in 1851. See Appendix, pp. 649–51. But Campbell had in fact read enough of Finney's *Lectures on Systematic Theology* to review the book in *The Christian Witness* soon after it was published. There, amid similar criticisms, he had stated, "On a careful examination of his views, it will be found that he does not differ so widely as might be supposed from the accredited Theology of England" (*The Christian Witness* [London] 9 [March 1852]: 130).

[48]This letter is not in the Finney Papers.

[49]Campbell had been at the University of St. Andrews and then in Glasgow at the university and the divinity hall of the Congregational church. See *DNB*.

established church, and their **Presbyterian** Confession of faith; and these they regarded as *authority*. They were not at all in the habit of trying to *prove* the positions taken in these "standards," as they were called; but dealt them out as dogmas. When I began to preach they were surprized that I *reasoned* with the people. Dr |Campbell did not approve it, and insisted that it would do no good. But the people felt otherwise; and it was |not uncommon for me to receive such intelligence as this, that my reasonings had convinced them of what they had always doubted; and that my preaching was *logical* instead of *dogmatic*, and therefore met the wants of the people. I had myself, before I was converted, felt greatly the want of instruction and logical preaching from the pulpit. **The only minister under whose instruction I had ever sat who was really a man of learning and ability, was Brother Gale; and he was a Princeton theologian, and failed altogether to meet my intellectual wants. I used to tell him so. I often told him before I was converted, that he seemed to begin in the middle of his discourse, so far as the congregation was concerned; that he assumed that we knew and admitted what we did not know and admit, and consequently the foundations not being laid in our minds he did not produce conviction.** This experience always had a great influence upon my own preaching. I knew how thinking men felt when a minister |took for granted the very things that needed proof. I therefore used to take great pains to meet the wants of persons who were in the state of mind **in which I had been before I was converted.** I knew what my difficulties had been; and therefore I endeavored to meet the intellectual wants of my hearers. JHF 452 MS 979 MS 980

I **told**[50] Dr Campbell this; but at first he had no faith that the people would understand me and appreciate my reasonings. But when he came to receive the converts, and to converse personally with them **about what they did understand**, he confessed to me again and again his surprize that they had so well understood my reasonings. "Why," he would say, "they are theologians." He was very frank **on this point**, and confessed to me[51] how erroneous his views had been upon that subject.

After I had finished my labors at Borough Road Chapel, we left London **and went back to Brother Brown‹'s at› Houghton.**[52] **We rested for a season there, and** such was the state of my |health that I thought I must return home. **However, after resting two or three weeks Dr Foster**, an excellent Christian man living in Huntington, urged us very much to go to his house and finish our rest, and let him **see if** he could **do anything** for me as a physician.[53] **I told him I took no medicine; but he thought by nursing he** MS 981

[50] Here Matson had written "I have told," but the word "told" appears to have been crossed out by Finney. He had probably meant to cross out the word "have." Fairchild altered it accordingly.

[51] Here Matson had written "again and again," but it appears that Finney crossed it out.

[52] Here Matson had written "and went back to Houghton where Brother Brown lives," but Finney changed the order of the words. Fairchild crossed it all out. The Finneys had a farewell tea meeting at Borough Road on Monday, 18 April, and went to Houghton three days later. See *The Revival Advocate and Record of the Churches* (London) 2 (May 1859): 528; and E. Finney, "Journal," pp. 37–39.

[53] Michael Foster (1810–1880) had graduated with high honors from the University College medical school in London and had begun practicing in Huntingdon (not "Huntington," as spelled by Matson) in 1834. He had a large country practice for more than forty years. He was also a

could do what was needed to be done. We accepted his invitation and went to his house.[54] He had a family of eight children, all unconverted. The oldest son was also a physician, **and a remarkably *clever* young man in the English sense of the term.**[55] He was a young man of remarkable talents, but a **most intensified** skeptic. He had embraced Comte's philosophy, and settled down in extreme views of atheism, or I should say, of **N**ihilism.[56] He seemed not to believe anything. **He had embraced that form of philosophy that runs everything into the ground; that comes to the conclusion that there is in fact no such thing as existence; that everything that appears**

MS 982 **to be is only a seeming, and that *seeming* |is nothing. This young man**

JHF 453 **was Dr Foster's eldest child, and** a very affectionate son; |but his skepticism had deeply wounded his father, and for his conversion he had come to feel an unutterable longing. **He had given me an account of his son's religious position before I went there; consequently I waited for an opportunity to get at the young man, and if possible annihilate his skepticism.**[57]

After remaining at the **D**octor's two or three weeks my health became such that I began to preach.[58] There never had been a revival in Huntington, and they really had no conception of what a revival would be. I occupied what

deacon of the Union Church and a leading citizen, becoming the first Nonconformist mayor of Huntingdon in 1868 and an alderman in 1874. He died of Parkinson's disease. See *Hunts Guardian and East Midland Spectator* (St. Ives), 17 January 1880, p. 2; *The Lancet* (London), 17 January 1880, p. 111; *Transactions of the Baptist Historical Society* (London) 7, nos. 3 and 4 (1921): 202; and Foster Family Papers in the possession of Sir Robert Foster, Great Glemham, Suffolk.

[54]The Finneys moved into his home on 13 May 1859. See E. Finney, "Journal," p. 41.

[55]Michael Foster (1830–1907), Dr. Foster's oldest son, was at this time twenty-nine years old and had graduated in medicine from University College, London, in 1858. He was living at home and was soon to start in medical practice with his father. He was later to become the eminent Cambridge physiologist Sir Michael Foster K.C.B., M.P. See Gerald L. Geison, *Michael Foster and the Rise of the Cambridge School of Physiology, 1870–1900* (Princeton: Princeton University Press, 1978); and *DNB*.

[56]The writings of French philosopher Auguste Comte (1798–1857) were having a considerable influence in England. His system sought to replace all religious and metaphysical speculation with a positive scientific attitude in which human beings in their social relationships were at the center. Although his "Religion of Humanity" never had many adherents, his philosophy of "Positivism" had a wide appeal and influenced many radical thinkers. It contributed significantly to the process of secularization and the rise of scientific humanism, which was to characterize much of Western society in the late nineteenth and twentieth centuries. See Terence R. Wright, *The Religion of Humanity: The Impact of Comtean Positivism on Victorian Britain* (Cambridge: Cambridge University Press, 1986). Mrs. Finney wrote in her journal: "Michael Foster, a son of Dr Fosters is a young man of talent but deeply imbued with the German Philosophy and German scepticism" (p. 42).

[57]Dr. Foster had spoken about Michael during a visit to the Finneys on 19 February, while they were in St. Ives. Three days later he visited again, accompanied by his son (E. Finney, "Journal," p. 29).

[58]According to Mrs. Finney's journal, Finney started preaching two days after going to Huntingdon. The "two or three weeks" were spent in Houghton with the Browns. See MS 981. They were in Houghton from 21 April until 13 May. In that time Finney preached twice in the Houghton Chapel. See E. Finney, "Journal," pp. 39–41. Finney had been invited to conduct meetings for revival by the Union Church in Huntingdon, a Baptist church, of which Dr. Foster was a deacon. The minister was Rev. Charles Clarke. The other Nonconformist churches in the town also cooperated. See Union Church Minister and Deacons to Finney, 21 January 1859, Finney Papers, microfilm, roll 4; and Nonconformist Ministers in Huntingdon to Finney, 30 March 1859, Finney Papers, microfilm, roll 5.

they called "Temperance Hall," the only large hall in the town.[59] It was **always full to its utmost capacity; and** the Spirit of the Lord was soon poured out upon the people. I soon found **an** opportunity to converse with young Dr **Foster**. I drew him out into some long walks, and entered fully into an investigation of his views;[60] and finally, under God, succeeded in bringing him to a perfect stand-still. He saw that all his ¦philosophy was **used up; and its foundations all fell away. I said to him: "My dear young man, now you see what all your skepticism amounts to, and that you are confounded like a fool in the presence of the truth of the Gospel." He admitted it, and became very anxious about his soul. Just at the time when his anxiety was ripening** I preached one Sabbath evening on the text: "The hail shall sweep away the refuges of lies, and the waters shall overflow the hiding places. Your covenant with death shall be disannulled, and your agreement with hell shall not stand."[61] **At the close of my discourse, in dwelling upon the hail's sweeping away the refuges of lies and the waters overflowing the hiding places, I drew a picture as vividly as I could of one of our American hail-storms; the like of which they never have in England, I suppose on account of its being so far North.**[62] **I had** spent my strength in searching out the refuges of lies, and exposing them; and concluded with **this** picture of the hail-storm, ¦and the descending torrent of rain that swept away what the hail had not demolished. The impression on the congregation was at the time very deep.[63] That night young Dr **Foster** could not sleep, **his agony was so great.** His father **hearing him up** went up to his room, and found him in the greatest consternation and agony of mind. **But I should have said, that the immediate reason of this great fear and agony was, that about ten O'clock at night there came up a fearful thunder storm, such as they seldom have in England, and such was his sense of guilt that he had an impression that a storm of hail was about to sweep him to hell.**[64] **Soon after** he became calm, and to all appearance passed from

MS 983

MS 984

[59] For the first week he preached in the Union Chapel. Then he moved to the Institution (as the "Temperance Hall" was usually called) on 22 May (E. Finney, "Journal," pp. 42–43).

[60] Mrs. Finney noted in her journal that the second day they were there, Finney went for a walk with Michael, while Mrs. Finney and Michael's parents prayed for him (p. 42).

[61] Isaiah 28:17–18. This sermon was preached on the evening of 29 May. See E. Finney, "Journal," p. 44.

[62] There is a question mark in ink in the margin against the last part of this sentence. It appears to be in Lewis Tappan's handwriting.

[63] Mrs. Finney noted in her journal, "It was a tremendous sermon—Many seemed in haste to receive Christ—hands stretched out by many before any test asked—Many inquirers it seemed as if they would not leave—men in tears—Michael stayed at the second meeting" (p. 44).

[64] Mrs. Finney wrote in her journal the next morning (Monday, 30 May):

> Last night God heard prayer so far that Michael could not sleep—I awoke in the night to pray for him & heard the voice of prayer in another room—this morning found Michael could not sleep—he retired about nine—at 12 his Mother heard a noise and found him up and partly dressed. He could not sleep—about one this night had a tremendous storm of *Hail*—thunder & lightning and for a time the rain fell in torrents. It seemed a wonderful coincidence after such a sermon—and the people so received it—Michael has promised to leave off smoking—His Father & Mother prayed with him & pressed him to pray—"God be merciful to me a sinner"—God hear this prayer. They do not yet get at the state of his heart—he is secretive—keeps all to himself (p. 45).

death unto life.[65] **Dr and Mrs. Foster's** prayers for their children were heard. The revival went through their family, and converted every one of them.[66] It was a joyful house, and one of the most lovely families that I ever had the privilege of residing in. We remained at his house while we continued our labors |in[67] Huntington. MS 985

The revival took a very general hold of the church, and of professors of religion in that town, and spread extensively among the unconverted; **but I know not the number of conversions that occurred. However the revival** greatly changed the religious aspect of **things in that** town.[68] There was then no Congregational |church there. There were two or three churches of the JHF 454

[65]Mrs. Finney later wrote in a letter to the Lamsons in Boston:

> We left Huntingdon Monday June 20th. The Saturday before we left—Mr F prayed with him & Michael promised God he would seek him, and would open his heart to his manifestations. Monday he told Mr Finney he had renounced his Infidelity. Since that we have seen him in London—& in Edinburgh twice—He told Mr Finney he was a changed man—and told his Father the same. His love for us is very interesting—he seeks us out at once when he comes where we are staying (E. Finney to Edwin and Mary Lamson, 6 January 1860, Correspondence of Charles G. Finney, 1830–1875, Oberlin College Archives, microfilm).

Letters written home by Michael while he was on a six months' voyage to the Red Sea in 1860 and 1861 have a religious tone to them, but he still had doubts that he never overcame. In later years he accepted the Darwinian theory of evolution and scientific naturalism and was indifferent to religion (letters of Michael Foster to his family, 1860–1861, Foster Family Papers; and Geison, *Michael Foster*, pp. 61–63).

[66]The Fosters eventually had ten children, three sons and seven daughters. Michael was the only one who survived his father. Dr. Foster later wrote to the Finneys:

> What a year of blessing to my family has this last been—Dear Anne converted & a *declared* follower—Now dear Emily converted & is to be proposed for church fellowship, only 12 years old—her experience is *clear*, simple—genuine—these both the result of your visit and abode with us—*thus the power of the Holy Ghost* resting upon Mr Finney's sermons & Mrs Finney's personal conversations—Then I feel no doubt of Willey's conversion though he is silent about joining the church—He is very prayerful, and very earnest in prayer—Then we hope Michael has become weary "of the husks that the swine do eat," and that the Lord has turned his face to "his Fathers home," and that my dear Wife has *grown in grace* very much—Oh so much and then *my life* in Christ is so much clearer & joyous (quoted in E. Finney to the Lamsons, 6 January 1860; see also Victor G. Plarr, *Plarr's Lives of the Fellows of the Royal College of Surgeons of England*, vol. 1 [Bristol: Wright, 1930], p. 413).

[67]After the page number 985, Fairchild added the figures "–6,7,8," indicating to the printers to proceed to page 989 and to omit the intervening pages. An asterisk and the word "over" two-thirds of the way down this page indicate an insertion written by Matson on the reverse of the page. This was numbered 986 by Finney.

[68]Just before Finney preached his last sermon there on 19 June, *The Eastern Counties Gazette* reported:

> He has been listened to with profound attention, by almost all classes, and we have no doubt in asserting that his visit has been profitable, not only to many of his audience, but to the Christian public, by uniting in closer bonds of union, and increasing their zeal and piety (18 June 1859, p. 3).

A summary of his labors in the minutes of the Union Church concludes: "That day only can reveal the amount of good which was done in the hearts of many who heard Mr. Finney, and have retired from our notice. Many now amongst us will long remember the time for all that was done to immortal souls—to God be all the glory" (entry between minutes of the meetings of 21 April 1859 and 2 August 1859 in "Minutes of Trinity Church, Huntingdon," in possession of the church). Rev. J. H. Millard, who had been the minister of the church when Finney was first in England, had doubts about the long-term effects: "It was a season of very solemn excitement, and some were led to take up the cross and follow Christ: though, perhaps, not so many as the more sanguine had ventured to hope" (J. H. Millard, *A Jubilee Memorial of Trinity Church, Huntingdon* [London: Smart and Allen, 1873], p. 101).

Establishment, one Methodist, and one Baptist, at that time in Huntington. Since then the converts of that revival, together with **Brother** Brown and his son and those Christians that were blest in the revival, have united and built, as I understand, a commodious chapel at Huntington, as they did at St. Ives.[69] |**I have said that when I was in England the first time Brother Brown had built a chapel at Houghton, and that there were two or three other places in the neighboring villages where his minister preached from time to time.**[70] **He** had pushed this work of evangelization with such energy, that when I arrived **there** the second time I found that he had seven churches in as many different villages in **that** neighborhood, and was employing preachers, and teachers, and laborers **for souls**, to the number of twenty.[71] **He is still pushing forward this work, and as I have related has succeeded with what help he could get, in building the two fine chapels at Saint Ives and at Huntington since I was last there. To how many other villages this work has been extended since I left I cannot say.**[72] **To the chapel at Saint Ives Brother Brown contributed three thousand pounds sterling; to the chapel in Huntington he also contributed three thousand pounds sterling, and his son about half that amount, I think.**[73] His means of doing good have fully kept pace with his princely ‹outlays for souls›.[74] When I first arrived in England he was running a hired flour mill with ten pair of stones;[75] the second time I was there, in addition to this **hired one** he was running a mill which he had built at Saint Ives, at an expense of **20** thousand pounds sterling, with sixteen pair of stones; **in addition to these he has since** built at Huntington another mill of the same capacity. Thus God pours into his coffers as fast as he pours out into the treasury of the Lord.[76]

MS 986

[69]The Union Chapel and an Independent mission in Huntingdon united to build the new Trinity Church, which was opened in 1868. See C. P. Petty, *A History of Trinity Church (Huntingdon) in the Nineteenth Century* (Huntingdon, 1956).

At this point in the manuscript an asterisk and the word "over" in Matson's handwriting indicate the insertion of a section on the reverse of MS 985. This section was numbered 986.

[70]See MS 824.

[71]Further churches to come into association with the Houghton Chapel were the Baptist church at Fenstanton and the chapel at Godmanchester. See Millard, *Jubilee Memorial*, pp. 92, 98.

[72]The work of evangelization among the villages was also being carried on in association with the Huntingdon church, and in 1861 the Hunts Association of Christian Churches was formed. By the time of Potto Brown's death in 1871, Trinity Church, Huntingdon, had taken over as the center for village evangelism, and churches were opened in six more villages. See Millard, *Jubilee Memorial*, p. 103; Petty, *History of Trinity Church*, p. 24; and Bateman Brown to Finney, 21 October 1871, Finney Papers, microfilm, roll 6.

[73]Bateman Brown in fact gave two thousand pounds toward the cost. He had been made chairman of the managing committee responsible for erecting the new chapel and in 1863 moved to Huntingdon, where he became active in the church and a prominent citizen. He was made a deacon in 1877. See Petty, *History of Trinity Church*, pp. 17–19.

[74]Finney replaced the word "donations" with "outlays for souls."

[75]This was the mill at Houghton. It was owned by Lady Olivia Sparrow, the local landowner. See *Potto Brown: The Village Philanthropist* (St. Ives: Goodman, 1878), p. 19.

[76]In 1873, Finney wrote an account of his visits to Houghton for *The New-York Evangelist*, in which he said:

> In my two visits to England I have reason to believe that many hundreds were converted to Christ,—I suppose I might without extravagance say thousands; and in both cases it was Mr. Brown more than any other, and all other influences together, aside from the Holy Spirit, that decided me to go. . . . How much England owes to his

From Huntington we returned to London, and labored for several weeks in the North eastern part of the city, in several chapels occupied by a branch of the Methodist church.[77] One of the places of worship was in Spitalsfield, the house having been originally built, I think, by the Huguenots.[78] It was a commodious place of worship, and we had a glorious ǀwork[79] of grace there.

MS 987

Some very striking providences occurred in that congregation while we held meetings there. One Sabbath evening I had invited them "to come forward around the altar," as the Methodists express it, and give their hearts to God.[80] One lady who was present refused to come forward, but was observed by those immediately around her to be in great agony of mind. They invited and urged her to go forward, but she declined. I had made a strong appeal to them not to hesitate; and as I frequently did, had warned them that might be their last opportunity. But for some reason this lady did not come forward. The next morning she was called to visit a friend who was dangerously ill at a distance from London, and she set off in the morning on the railroad to make this

> exertions for Christ, the Day of Judgment can alone reveal. Upon the whole, he was one of the most remarkable Christian men I ever knew.
>
> . . . I have seldom ever loved a human being as I did him; and cannot speak or write of him without tears. . . . To know him was a great blessing (Finney to the Editor, 20 February 1873, *NYE,* 6 March 1873, p. 1).

This ends MS 986, which is on the reverse of MS 985. The text continues on MS 985.

[77] The Finneys were invited to London by the Third London Circuit of the United Methodist Free Churches, largely through the efforts of a Methodist layman, Theodore Jones. See E. Finney, "Journal," pp. 31, 34, 39; and letters of Theodore Jones and Robert Bushell to Finney, May and June 1859, Finney Papers, microfilm, roll 5. The United Methodist Free Churches had been formed in 1857 by the amalgamation of the Wesleyan Methodist Association and the Wesleyan Reformers. They were groups that had broken away from Wesleyan Methodism in the 1830s and 1840s, in opposition to the increasing centralization of authority. They united in "an attempt to construct a system which would unite Connexionalism and Congregationalism, the cohesion of the one with the freedom of the other" (Joseph Kirsop, *Historic Sketches of Free Methodism* [London: Crombie, 1885], p. 47; and see also Oliver A. Beckerlegge, *The United Methodist Free Churches: A Study in Freedom* [London: Epworth, 1957]).

The Third London Circuit, in the east end of London, had fourteen churches and a membership of about 1,270. There was one circuit minister, Rev. Robert Bushell, most of the work being carried on by over thirty local preachers and eighty class leaders. See *The United Methodist Free Churches Magazine* (London), n.s., 2 (May 1859): 279; (September 1859): 516; and (November 1859): 618.

The Finneys arrived in London on Monday, 20 June, and rested for the rest of that week. Finney commenced preaching the next Sunday in Brown's Lane Chapel. He was subsequently advertised to preach "Every Tuesday Evening, at Jubilee-Street Chapel, Mile-end-Road. Every Wednesday Evening, at Brown's-Lane Chapel, Spitalfields. Every Thursday Evening, at St. George's Chapel, Cannon-street-road. Every Friday Evening, at Bath-Street Chapel, East India-road, Poplar." These were some of the largest chapels in the circuit. On Sundays he preached in turn in the Jubilee Street, St. George's, and Brown's Lane chapels. See *The Wesleyan Times* (London), 27 June 1859, p. 409; 18 July 1859, p. 461; and E. Finney, "Journal," p. 47.

[78] This was Brown's Lane Chapel. Built about 1719, it was successively occupied by Huguenots, German Lutherans, and Baptists and was taken over by the United Methodist Free Churches in 1852. See T. R. Hooper, "Baptists in a Huguenot Temple," *The Baptist Quarterly* 5, no. 3 (July 1930): 111–17.

[79] Page 987 was omitted from the published version except for the first four words, which were rewritten by Fairchild at the bottom of page 985. Pages 987–88 were originally numbered 828–29 and renumbered 959–60 by Matson. Finney changed them to 987–88.

[80] This was 26 June, the evening of the first Sunday that Finney preached in Brown's Lane. Mrs. Finney mentioned the incident in her journal (p. 47).

visit. She had been strongly exercised in her mind through the night, and her agony had been too great to permit her to sleep; but for some reason she could not be persuaded to submit. She started on this journey, and died on the railroad carriage before she arrived ‹at her destination.›[81] Her friends |in the congregation immediately reported this to me as a very striking and affecting fact.

MS 988

On the next Sabbath evening, when I made the call for them to come forward, I related this fact to the crowded congregation, and again warned them that that might be their last time.[82] There was then a man in the congregation who was in great distress of mind; which being observed by his friends they urged him till I think he went forward, but reluctantly. But when he had come forward, he refused to give his heart to God.[83] The brethren remained and prayed for him, if I recollect right, after the service was over, and took much pains to try to bring him to Christ, but in vain. He stood out against all their entreaties. The next day he died in an apoplectic fit.[84] These two very striking cases made a great impression upon the people that attended worship there.

I held services in several other chapels in that part of London; and we had a good work, which continued and increased till late in the summer.[85]

[81] Matson had written down, "on that morning," but Finney replaced those words with "at her destination."

[82] This was not the next Sabbath evening; it was the next Sabbath evening that he preached at Brown's Lane, which was 17 July (E. Finney, "Journal," p. 48).

[83] In Mrs. Finney's description of this incident to her stepdaughter, Julia, she said: "One man who sat near me said to some of the gentlemen who were leaders in the society, I feel enough to go forward to-night for prayers, but he did not" (E. Finney to Julia Finney, 20 and 21 July 1859, Finney Papers, microfilm, roll 5).

[84] Mrs. Finney wrote: "and on Monday night he expired in a fit" (E. Finney to Julia Finney, 20 and 21 July 1859, Finney Papers, microfilm, roll 5).

[85] Finney preached his last sermon in Brown's Lane Chapel on 7 August 1859; and on Tuesday, 9 August, the Finneys attended a farewell tea meeting. See E. Finney, "Journal," p. 49.

MS 989
JHF 455

CHAPTER XXXV

‹*Revival labors* at Edinburgh, Aberdeen, Scotland & *in* Bolton, *England*.›

While[1] I was at this time in London, I was invited very urgently to visit Edinburgh in Scotland; and about the middle of August we left London and took passage by steam up the coast, through the German ocean, to Edinburgh.[2] I had been urged to go there by the Rev. Dr Kirk of Edinburgh,[3] who belonged to that portion of the church in Scotland called the Evangelical Union church.[4] Their leading theologian was a Mr. Morrison, who presided over a theological school at Glasgow.[5] I found **Brother** Kirk an earnest man,

[1]Pages 989–1022 were originally numbered 830–63 and renumbered 961–94 by Matson. Finney changed them to 989–1022. A strip of paper pasted onto the top of page 989 with the chapter heading in Finney's handwriting covers up the previous page numbers 830 and 961 by Matson and 989 by Finney.

[2]The Finneys left London on Wednesday, 10 August 1859, and arrived in Edinburgh early in the morning on the twelfth. See "A Journal Kept by Mrs. Elizabeth Ford Atkinson Finney during a Visit to England in 1859–1860," p. 50, manuscript in Special Collections, Oberlin College Library.

[3]John Kirk (1813–1886) was brought up near Stirling, not far from the village of Muckhart, where his ancestors came from. He had been a blacksmith and had done missionary work before entering the ministry. He was minister of the Independent church in Hamilton from 1839 until 1845. While at Hamilton, his advocacy of the "new views" on the universality of the Holy Spirit's work led to a disruption in the Congregational denomination. A large portion of the churches broke away and joined the Evangelical Union. Kirk then moved to Edinburgh, where he became prominent as an editor and a leader in the revival and temperance movements. See Helen Kirk, *Memoirs of Rev. John Kirk, D.D.* (Edinburgh: Fairgrieve, 1888); and James Ross, *A History of Congregational Independency in Scotland* (Glasgow: Maclehose, 1900). Kirk's invitation to Finney is in a letter, dated in the calendar of the Finney Papers, 10 May 1859, Finney Papers, microfilm, roll 5.

[4]The Evangelical Union of Scotland (E.U.) had been formed in 1843, the same year as the disruption in the Church of Scotland. It originated as a movement away from the Calvinistic teaching of a limited atonement and was led by Rev. James Morison and others who had been expelled or had seceded from the United Presbyterian (Secession) Church. The union gained strength in 1845 through the addition of members and churches who had left the Congregational Union of Scotland for denying the irresistible work of the Holy Spirit. As a movement associated with revivals and reform and a more liberal theology, it soon became a denomination, with considerable influence. By 1896, when it amalgamated with the Congregational Union, it had more than ninety churches. Members of the Evangelical Union were often called "Morisonians." See Fergus Ferguson, *A History of the Evangelical Union from Its Origin to the Present Time* (Glasgow: Morison, 1876).

[5]James Morison (1816–1893) had been a minister in the United Presbyterian Church in Kilmarnock until 1843, when he was suspended for spreading the doctrine of a universal Atonement. He founded the Evangelical Union, and his teaching and writings, including his well-known commentaries, were influential in the swing away from Calvinism in Scotland. Morison was the minister of the North Dundas Street E. U. Church in Glasgow. The Evangelical Union

and a great lover of revival work. This Evangelical Union, or E. U. church, as they call it, had grown out of a revival effort made in Scotland at the time of the first publication of my revival lectures in that country.[6] A considerable number of Scotch ministers, and a much larger number of lay men, had been greatly stirred up, and had made many successful revival efforts; but had expended their strength very much in controversy upon the hyper-Calvinistic views maintained by the Scotch ǀPresbyterians. **We** remained three months in Edinburgh, preaching mostly in **Brother** Kirk's church, which was one of the largest places of worship in Edinburgh.[7] We had a very interesting revival in that place, and many souls were converted. Church members were greatly blessed, and **Brother** Kirk's hands were full day and night of labors among inquirers.[8] But I soon found that he was surrounded by a wall of prejudice. The Presbyterian churches were strongly opposed to this E. U. branch of the church; and I found myself hedged in as it respected openings ‹for›[9] labor **freely** in other churches.[10]

MS 990

Academy was started by Morison in Glasgow in 1843, and he remained the principal until his death. See William Adamson, *The Life of the Rev. James Morison, D.D.* (London: Hodder and Stoughton, 1898); Charles E. Kirsch, "The Theology of James Morison" (Ph.D. diss., Edinburgh University, 1939); and *DNB*. Matson spelled his name "Morrison."

[6] Finney's *Lectures* and *Sermons* were widely read in Scotland from 1839 and had considerable influence on Morison, Kirk, and other leaders of the revival movement and the Evangelical Union. The influence of Finney's *Lectures on Revivals* in bringing about the revival in Scotland is given paramount importance by John Kirk in a series of articles entitled "The Revival Movement of the last thirty years," *The Christian News* (Glasgow), July to October 1865. See also *Worthies of the Evangelical Union* (Glasgow: Morison, 1883); and Ferguson, *History of the Evangelical Union*, p. 7. An editorial, written soon after Finney arrived in Scotland, introducing him to the readers of *The Christian News*, announced:

> Almost all the revival spirit that has prevailed among our ministers and people is due in no small degree to the influence of his Lectures on Revivals, published amongst us at the commencement of our own revival period. He comes, among other things, to see the fruit of his own efforts, and the Spirit of God in him when that fruit is ripening to harvest ("Professor Finney in Scotland," *The Christian News*, 27 August 1859, p. 5).

[7] Brighton Street Church was at the end of "a gloomy *cul-de-sac*" leading off Lothian Street, on a site now occupied by part of the Edinburgh Museum. It was built in 1835 by a congregation of the Relief Church. In 1845 it was taken over by a newly formed Evangelical Union congregation, with John Kirk as pastor. The church could hold two thousand people. See James Grant, *Cassell's Old and New Edinburgh*, vol. 2 (London: Cassell, 1884), p. 326; and *Brighton Street Evangelical Union Congregational Church, Edinburgh. History of the Church and Report of Its Jubilee Service* (Edinburgh: Fairgrieve, 1894). Finney commenced preaching on Sunday, 21 August, and continued until 6 November 1859. See E. Finney, "Journal," pp. 50–53.

[8] The writer of a letter to *The Wesleyan Times* (London), published two months after Finney went to Edinburgh, reported:

> I may remark that those of us who have attended Professor Finney's meetings and watched their progress may say, with all safety, that we have never seen in so short a period of time, under the preaching of the Gospel, so many moved to earnest inquiry about the concerns of their souls, and so many intelligently yielding themselves up to the service of God. . . . Mr. Finney, Mr. Kirk, and other brethren assisting them, have not conversed with less than about 300 persons really anxious about spiritual matters; and we can say, with all confidence, that the great majority of these, so far as we can judge, have found peace to their souls (24 October 1859, p. 684).

Reports of Finney's meetings appeared in many of the Edinburgh papers as well as in *The Christian News*.

[9] Matson had written down the word "of." Finney replaced it with "for."

[10] Attention was drawn to the prejudice in an article in *The Wesleyan Times*, 17 October 1859, p. 670. This sparked a controversy in the pages of *The Wesleyan Times* and *The Christian News*.

John Kirk. One of the founders of the Evangelical Union in Scotland and minister of the Brighton Street Church in Edinburgh. In Helen Kirk, *Memoirs of Rev. John Kirk, D.D.* (Edinburgh: Fairgrieve, 1888), frontispiece. Courtesy The British Library.

I soon became convinced that in that state of things there was little hope of seeing a wide spread revival throughout the city. I had no doubt then, nor have I now, that thousands would have been converted had it not been for that prejudice against Brother Kirk and his views. He was at that time, and still is, one of the professors in the theological school at Glasgow. MS 991 JHF 456 |Brother Kirk's congregation proper was not large at the time that I went there; but it soon increased, so that his large house was filled. The Word of God took a powerful hold. I never made any inquiry as to the number of converts, so far as they were ascertained.[11] But I have said before, and here say again, that in a large city there is perhaps no such thing as ascertaining the number of converts. Brother Kirk was

Finney tried to dissociate himself from being identified with the "Morisonians" in a letter published in *The Wesleyan Times,* 31 October 1859, p. 700.

[11] By January, Kirk reported that, out of 600 inquirers, 120 were joining Brighton Street Church and many of the others were joining other churches in the city (*The Freeman* [London], 11 January 1860, p. 21).

at that time not only pastor **and** theological **professor, but also** editor of "The Christian News," which was published at Glasgow.[12] In that paper from time to time he represented my theological views, **which he heard me preach from day to day,** as identical with the views of their theological Seminary and of their church.[13] But on some points I found that I very considerably differed ‹from›[14] them.

Their views of faith as a mere intellectual state I could not receive. They explained away, in a manner to me utterly unintelligible, the doctrine of election; and on sundry points I found I did not agree with them.[15] |However **Brother** Kirk insisted that he accepted my views **entire** as he heard me preach, and that they were the views of the E. U. church. Thus insisting **upon it** that my views were identical with theirs, without intending it he shut the doors of the other pulpits against me, and doubtless kept multitudes of persons who otherwise would have come and heard me, from our meetings. **I had not then, and I have not now any doubt that had he said nothing in his paper respecting my views according with their views, other pulpits would have been thrown open, and very different results would have followed. The prejudice was so universal and strong against their views of doctrine, that to know, as they supposed they did, that I agreed with them, was enough to close up all the avenues to the hearts of the congregations of all the Presbyterian churches.**[16]

MS 992

[12]John Kirk had started *The Christian News* in August 1846, the first weekly religious newspaper to be published in Scotland. It became the vehicle of the Evangelical Union. See Kirk, *Memoirs of Rev. John Kirk*, p. 228. The paper gave extensive coverage of Finney's revival meetings while he was in Scotland.

[13]See *The Christian News,* 10 September 1859, p. 5; 15 October 1859, p. 5; 29 October 1859, p. 5; and 12 November 1859, p. 5. A number of these articles were probably written by Rev. Fergus Ferguson, Jr., of Glasgow. See Ferguson to Finney, 19 September 1859, Finney Papers, microfilm, roll 5.

[14]Matson had written "with," but Finney replaced it with "from."

[15]From early in his ministry Morison emphasized his disagreement with Finney over the nature of faith. As a result he was not keen for Finney to occupy his pulpit (see *The Question "What must I do to be saved?" Answered*, by "Philanthropos" [Kilmarnock: Muir, 1840], p. 20; and Morison to Finney, 8 November 1859, Finney Papers, microfilm, roll 5).

During Finney's first visit to England in 1850, Asa Mahan, who was also in Britain, had visited Morison in Glasgow. Finney had already heard then about the Evangelical Union teaching on election. He wrote to Morison:

> My Dear Brother. I did not expect to be in England so long as I have been without seeing you. . . . I have kept myself informed, to a considerable extent, of the progress of reform in Scotland, & have taken a deep interest in your own movements & writings. Br. Mahan saw you. . . . You perceive from my theology I hold *eternal* but *not unconditional election & reprobation*. I can not see how to escape this with[out] denying the attributes of God (Finney to Morison, 5 January 1851, James Morison Letters, Mitchell Library, Glasgow).

The difference in their views was given unwelcome prominence at this time in a pamphlet entitled *Finney Versus Morison; or, Oberlin Strictures on Morisonian Faith* (Glasgow: Wilson, 1859). The author was Rev. Alexander McArthur, a former Oberlin student and Evangelical Union minister on a visit from Canada. See also Morison's review of the pamphlet in *The Evangelical Repository* (Glasgow), 2d ser., 2 (December 1859): 159–63.

[16]Matson had written a section at the end of page 992, which he crossed out when he inserted an additional page after this. It read: "After remaining at Edinburgh three months, and seeing there a blessed work of grace, we accepted an invitation to go to Aberdeen; and in November we found ourselves in that city, near." Matson wrote an almost identical section at the end of page 993.

MS 993 ¦Mrs.[17] Finney's labors in this place were greatly blessed. Mrs. Kirk, the wife of the pastor, was a very earnest Christian lady;[18] and she took hold with my wife with all her might. They established a ladies' prayer meeting **at Bristo**[19] **Place**, which is continued to this day; reports of which have been made from year to year in the Christian News; and Mrs. Kirk published a small volume, giving an account of the establishment and progress of that meeting.[20] The answers to prayer that were vouchsafed there were wonderful. Requests have been sent from various parts of Scotland to them, **for them** to pray for various places, and persons, and objects. The history of that meeting has been one of uncommon encouragement.

From that sprang up similar meetings in various parts of Scotland; and these have put the **ladies** of Scotland very much in a new position in regard to personal efforts in revivals of religion. **They have been very much organized since then, and have been a great power for good in direct efforts to convert souls. Accounts of the progress of that meeting and its results, have been sent me, I believe from year to year since we returned from that country.**[21] **The establishment of that meeting introduced a new era, it would seem, in respect to the religious efforts made in Scotland, and especially in respect to the efforts on the part of females.**[22]

After remaining in Edinburgh three months, and seeing there a blessed JHF 457 work of grace, we accepted an invitation to ¦go to Aberdeen; and in MS 994 November we found ourselves in that city, which is near ¦the northern

[17] MS 993 was numbered 834 and renumbered 965 by Matson, then changed to 993 by Finney. This page was inserted between pages 833 and 834, requiring pages 834 and 835, which had been numbered in advance, to be renumbered.

[18] Helen (Bruce) Kirk was married to John Kirk in 1851. She was his second wife. Mrs. Finney wrote to the Lamsons in Boston:

> Mrs Kirk is only thirty—has five children—three of them she adopted in to her heart when she took the place of the second Mother—two of them are hers by birth—but her energy—industry and readiness to enter upon any work and labor of love makes her a beautiful example as a ministers wife (E. Finney to Edwin and Mary Lamson, 6 January 1860, Correspondence of Charles G. Finney, 1830–1875, Oberlin College Archives, microfilm).

See also Kirk, *Memoirs of Rev. John Kirk*; and "The Late Mrs. Helen Kirk," *The Christian News,* 20 April 1895, p. 3.

[19] Matson had written down the word "Bristol" here, but Finney changed it to "Bristo."

[20] Helen Kirk, *Woman and Prayer; or, The History of the Ladies' Union Prayer Meeting, Held in Bristo Place Hall, Edinburgh* (London: Ward, 1861). Mrs. Finney wrote in her journal under the date 7 September 1859: "We commenced our Ladies meetings Monday 22 of August and continued them every day except Saturday—We began with 70 and the next day nearly twice that number—Mrs Kirk & a Mrs McKinley take hold with a helping power—Mrs Kirk always present" (p. 51). And on 10 October she wrote, "Dear Mrs Kirk never fails to be present at each meeting—leads in the singing prays & generally says a few words—quite to the point" (p. 52). According to Helen Kirk, there were "about thirty" at the first meeting, and numbers ranged from about fifty to two hundred. See "Mrs Finney and Ladies' Meetings," *The Christian News,* 5 November 1859, p. 5.

[21] Accounts were published frequently in *The Christian News.*

[22] Helen Kirk made the point that private meetings of women for prayer had not been uncommon, "but for woman to come forward in a public capacity and confess Christ before a multitude, was so. Hence, a new feature of Christian activity was introduced. Woman was not so much tied up to privacy—a somewhat fresh and untried field was opened, in which it was a privilege for her to till, sow, and reap, as seemed good to her Lord" (Kirk, *Woman and Prayer,* p. 11).

James Barlow. The Lancashire mill owner who was host to the Finney's in Bolton. Engraving in *The Christian Portrait Gallery* (London: Morgan and Scott, 1890), p. 19. Courtesy The British Library.

extremity of Scotland.[23] We were invited there by a Mr. Ferguson, also a minister of the E. U. church, and an intimate friend of Brother Kirk.[24] He

[23]The Finneys went to Aberdeen by train on 11 November 1859 (E. Finney, "Journal," p. 53).
[24]Fergus Ferguson, Sr. (1799–1878), had been in business and was ordained as a Congregational minister in 1843. Expelled with Kirk and others from the Congregational Union,

had been very much irritated, and was at the time we arrived there, with the opposition that he met from the Presbyterian and Congregational churches. His congregation was still more closely hedged in by prejudice than **Brother** Kirk's. He was an earnest Christian man, but had been chafed exceedingly by the opposition which had enclosed him like a wall.[25] At first I could not get a hearing except with his own people; and I became a good deal discouraged, and so did Brother Ferguson himself.[26] At the time of this discouragement **Brother** Davison, a Congregational **M**inister of Bolton in Lancashire, **Eng.**, wrote me a very pressing letter to come and labor with him.[27] The state of things was so discouraging at Aberdeen that I gave him encouragement that I

MS 995 would go. But in the meantime the interest greatly increased in |Aberdeen, and other ministers and churches began to feel the influence of what was going on there. The Congregational minister invited me to preach in his church for a Sabbath, which I did.[28] A Mr. Brown in one of the Presbyterian churches also invited me to preach; but at the time my hands were too full to accept his invitation, though I intended to preach for him at another time.[29] Before this, I should have said, that the work in Mr. Ferguson's congregation had begun, and was getting into a very interesting state. Numbers had been converted, and a very interesting change was manifestly coming over his congregation and over that city. But in the meantime I had so committed myself to go to Bolton that I found I must go; and we left Aberdeen just before the Christmas holidays and went to Bolton. While I was with **Brother** Ferguson at Aberdeen, I was urged by his son, who was settled over one of the E. U. churches in Glasgow, to labor with him for a season.[30] This had

he started an Evangelical Union church in Aberdeen in 1846, where he remained until he retired in 1872. He had been a deacon in Kirk's church in Hamilton and is best known as David Livingstone's Sunday school teacher. See Fergus Ferguson, Jr., "The Late Rev. Fergus Ferguson of Aberdeen," *The Evangelical Repository,* 6th ser., 4 (June 1878): 249–58.

[25]Ferguson was minister of St. Paul's Church, where he was "studiously shunned by the ministers of the city. Sometimes he was hissed by respectable people on the street; others would spit as he passed by, and 'New views,' 'New lights,' 'New gas' would be called after him in derision" (Alexander Gammie, *The Churches of Aberdeen, Historical and Descriptive* [Aberdeen: Aberdeen Daily Journal Office, 1909], p. 253).

[26]The lack of cooperation experienced by Finney provoked correspondence in the *Aberdeen Free Press,* 2 December 1859, p. 8; and 9 December 1859, p. 5.

[27]William Hope Davison (1827–1894) was at Cheshunt College before becoming minister at Duke's Alley (later St. George's Road Church), Bolton, in 1852. Because of ill health he moved south in 1874 to Chatham. He became well known as an editor and publisher of Congregational literature. See *The Congregational Year Book* (London), 1895, pp. 200–202.

Davison's letter is not in the Finney Papers, but the historian of his church wrote: "Towards the end of the year [1859] the Pastor had upwards of 80 persons on his list of enquirers, and the labour had become so oppressive that he was obliged to seek assistance. This he found in the Rev. C. G. Finney and his Lady" (F. W. Peaples, *History of the St. George's Road Congregational Church and Its Connections* [Bolton: Tillotson, 1913], p. 64).

[28]Rev. David Arthur (1806–1890) was minister of George Street Congregational Chapel from 1841 until his retirement in 1874. See John Bullock, *Centenary Memorials of the First Congregational Church in Aberdeen* (Aberdeen: Murray, 1898). Finney preached there on 27 November to "a large and attentive audience" (E. Finney, "Journal," p. 57).

[29]John Crombie Brown (d. 1895, aged eighty-one years) was minister at the Belmont Street United Presbyterian Church from 1850 to 1863 and lecturer in botany at King's College, Aberdeen. See Robert Small, *History of the Congregations of the United Presbyterian Church, 1733 to 1900,* vol. 1 (Edinburgh: Small, 1904), pp. 8–9.

[30]Fergus Ferguson, Jr. (1824–1897), the son of Fergus Ferguson, Sr., was one of the nine

been ˡurged upon me before I left Edinburgh.[31] But I was unwilling to continue my labors longer with that denomination. Not that they were not good men, ˡand earnest workers for God; but their controversies had brought them into such relations to the surrounding churches as to shut me out from all sympathy and co-operation except with those of their peculiar views. I had been **used** in this country to labor freely with Presbyterians and Congregationalists; and I desired greatly to get a hearing among the Presbyterians and Congregationalists of Scotland. But in laboring with E. U. churches I found myself in a false position. What had been said in the Christian News, and the fact that I was laboring in that denomination, led to the inference that I agreed with them in their *peculiar* views, while in fact I did not. I thought it not my duty to continue any longer in this false position. I declined, therefore, to go to Glasgow.[32] Although I regarded the brother who invited me as one of the best of men, and his church as a godly, praying people; yet there were other godly, praying people in Glasgow, and a great many more of them than could be found in the E. U. church. I felt uneasy as being in a position to misrepresent myself. Although I had the strongest affection for those brethren **of that denomination**, so far as I became acquainted with them; yet I felt that in confining my labors to ˡthat denomination I was greatly restricting my own usefulness. We therefore left Aberdeen and **journeyed** by rail to Bolton, where we arrived on Christmas **eve**, **of** 1859.[33]

JHF 458

MS 996

MS 997

students expelled from the Congregational Theological Academy in Glasgow in 1844 for holding the "new views." He was ordained in 1845 over the Blackfriars' Street Evangelical Union Church, where he remained until his death. After the Evangelical Union united with the Congregationalists in 1896, he became the first president of the new Congregational Union. See William Adamson, *The Life of the Rev. Fergus Ferguson* (London: Simpkin, Marshall, 1900); and Harry Escott, *A History of Scottish Congregationalism* (Glasgow: Congregational Union of Scotland, 1960).

[31] While Finney was still in London he had been invited by Fergus Ferguson, Jr., to preach in Glasgow, and Finney had preached there on the occasion of the reopening of the Blackfriars' Street Church on 4 September 1859. He preached two sermons. The first, in the morning, was not so much a sermon as "a narratory address on the history of the American revivals." It lasted for an hour and twenty minutes and was delivered to "a very crowded house, as many as 1200 people occupying the seats and standing in the passages" (Fergus Ferguson, Jr., "The Late Professor Finney's Visit to Glasgow," *The Christian News,* 10 August 1895, pp. 3–4; letters from Ferguson to Finney in July 1859, Finney Papers, microfilm, roll 5; and William C. Wilkinson, *Modern Masters of Pulpit Discourse* [New York: Funk and Wagnalls, 1905], p. 286).

The address was taken down in shorthand by William T. McAuslane, the poet and journalist, at that time a reporter for the *North British Daily Mail.* It was partly published in *The Christian News,* 10 September 1859, p. 2, and issued as a separate pamphlet under the title *The Prevailing Prayer-Meeting* (London: Ward, 1859). The sermon in the evening was also published in *The Christian News* (17 September 1859, p. 2). Finney had further invitations from Ferguson to go again to Glasgow in letters dated 14 and 25 November, and 1 and 6 December 1859 (Finney Papers, microfilm, roll 5). When a son was born to the Fergusons on 13 June 1860, he was named Charles Finney Ferguson. See Adamson, *Life of Rev. Fergus Ferguson*, p. 127; and *The Christian News,* 16 June 1860, p. 6.

[32] An embarrassing situation had arisen in Glasgow over James Morison's refusal to invite Finney to conduct revival services in his church. The lack of wholehearted cooperation by the Glasgow Evangelical Union churches was probably a key factor in discouraging Finney from going there. See letters to Finney from James Morison and Fergus Ferguson, Jr., November and December 1859, Finney Papers, microfilm, roll 5.

[33] Fergus Ferguson, Jr., who reviewed the *Memoirs* of Finney when they were first published, wrote in reference to this section:

Bolton is a city of about thirty thousand inhabitants, lying a few miles from Manchester.[34] It is in the heart of the great manufacturing district of England. It lies within the circle of that immense population, that spreads itself out from Manchester, as a center in every direction. It is estimated that at least three millions of people live within a compass of sixty miles around about JHF 459 Manchester. In this place the work of the Lord commenced immedi|ately. We were received as guests by **Brother James Barlow**.[35] He belonged to the Methodist denomination; **but** was a man of sterling piety, **and** very unsectarian in his views and feelings. The next evening after we arrived he invited in a few friends for religious conversation and prayer;[36] and among **others a friend of his with his wife; and his wife, he informed me,** had been for **sometime** in an inquiring state of mind.[37] After we had had a little MS 998 |conversation we concluded to have a season of prayer. My wife knelt near this lady of whom I have spoken, and during prayer she observed that she was much affected. As we rose from our knees Mrs. Finney took her by the hand, and then beckoned to me across the room to come and speak with her.[38] The lady had been brought up, as I afterwards learned, a Quakeress; but had married a Methodist **man**. She had been for a long time uneasy about the

> The venerable author might perhaps have spared us this somewhat slighting notice. The fact is, that in this highly Calvinistic country there was so much opposition to himself on account of his well known deviations from *soi disant* orthodoxy, that we do not believe that he could have got a hearing at all, except under the wing of the Evangelical Union. . . .
>
> One point we are willing to concede . . . namely, that we of the Evangelical Union have been compelled to contend for thirty years and more against what he calls "a terrible wall of prejudice." Indeed, it is wonderful that we are in existence at all. It is much to our credit, we think, that we have braved and breasted that difficulty from which Mr. Finney ran away. Of course, we required to bear it or die; whereas he was under no such necessity. Therefore, it was perhaps better for him not to come to Glasgow, but to go to Bolton, where all the dissenters in the town worked with him, and where he had great success. We heard a Congregational minister say, the other day, that he had heard Finney at the time, both in London and Scotland, and he was quite sorry to see him preaching only to a hundred or two in the north, while thousands had hung upon his lips in the south (*The Evangelical Repository,* 6th ser., 3 [June 1877]: 286–87).

The Finneys left Aberdeen on Wednesday, 14 December, by train, arriving at Bolton at midnight. See E. Finney, "Journal," p. 60.

[34]The town of Bolton was made up of Great and Little Bolton. The population of Great Bolton in the census of 1851 was 39,925, and that of Little Bolton, 20,468 (*A New Alphabetical and Classified Directory of Manchester and Salford, Bolton,* etc. [Manchester: Whellan, 1853], p. 933).

[35]James Barlow (1821–1887), the son of a Lancashire farmer, was a partner in the cotton spinning firm of Barlow, Gooddy, and Jones. His conversion had taken place in Ireland the previous summer. He was to become prominent as a philanthropist and active in religious and reform movements, becoming treasurer of the British Temperance League from 1873 until his death. He was mayor of Bolton from 1867 to 1869. See Frederic Boase, *Modern English Biography,* vol. 4 (London: Cass, 1965), p. 270; and T. Bowman Stephenson, *James Barlow: A Memorial Tribute* (London: Woolmer, 1881).

[36]This was on Friday, 16 December. See E. Finney, "Journal," p. 61.

[37]These friends were Mr. and Mrs. Bell, according to Mrs. Finney, who described this incident in her journal. They were probably Joseph Bell, a cotton spinner, and his wife, Mary. In the 1851 census schedule their ages are both given as fifty (E. Finney, "Journal," p. 61; *The Bolton Chronicle*, 4 August 1860, p. 5; information from Bolton Reference Library; and *Directory of Manchester and Salford, Bolton,* etc., p. 966).

[38]Mrs. Finney wrote in her journal, "I led her into the dining room & motioned Mr F to follow me" (p. 61).

state of her soul; but had never been brought face to face with the question of present, instantaneous submission. I responded to the call of my wife, and went across the room and spoke with her. I saw in a moment that her distress of mind was profound. I therefore asked her if she would **not let me see her alone for a short time.** She readily complied, and we crossed the hall into another room; and then I brought her face to face, at once, **to**[39] the question of instant submission and acceptance of Christ. I asked her if she would *then* and *there* **renounce all iniquity, and** renounce herself, |and everything else, MS 999 and give her heart to Christ. She replied, "I must do it sometime; and I may as well do it now **as ever.**" We knelt immediately down; and so far as human knowledge can go, **I judged then, and judge now, that** she did truly submit to God. After she had submitted we returned to the parlor; and the scene between herself and her husband was very affecting. **He was an earnest Christian man, but had somehow failed in giving his wife just the instruction that she needed.** As soon as **he saw her** come[40] into the room he saw such a change manifested in her countenance, that they seemed spontaneously to clasp each other in their arms and **melt**[41] down before the Lord.[42]

We **had hardly got** seated before the son of Mr. **Barlow** came into the parlor, announcing that one of the servants |was deeply moved.[43] In a very JHF 460 short time that one also gave evidence of submission to Christ. Then I learned that another was weeping in the kitchen, and went immediately to her; and after a little conversation and instruction, |she too appeared to give her heart MS 1000 to God.[44] Thus the work had begun. Mrs. **Barlow** herself had been in a **very**[45] doubting and discouraged state of mind for years; and she, too, appeared to melt down, and get into a different state of mind almost immediately.[46] The report of what the Lord was doing was soon spread

[39]The word "to" was not altered in the manuscript but was changed to "with" in the published version.

[40]The words "he saw her come" were not altered in the manuscript but were changed to "she came" in the published version.

[41]The word "melt" was not altered in the manuscript but appears as "knelt" in the published version.

[42]Mrs. Finney noted in her journal two weeks later: "Mrs. Bell grows fast. Her Husband says he is astonished at her letters and faithfulness in conversation with her friends." Later in January, Mrs. Finney wrote, "Mrs. Bell says she is so benefited by the meetings for Mothers." Then, by early March, Mrs. Bell was leading the afternoon ladies' prayer meeting. See E. Finney, "Journal," pp. 63, 68, 74, 78.

[43]This was probably Thomas Barlow (1845–1945), the oldest son, at that time a boy of fifteen years, who was later to become an eminent London pediatrician. See Helen Barlow, ed., *Sir Thomas Barlow, Bt., K.C.V.O., M.D., F.R.C.P., F.R.S., 1845–1945* (London: Dawsons of Pall Mall, 1965); and *DNB*.

[44]These were Lizzy, the servant girl, and Sarah, the cook (E. Finney, "Journal," p. 62). The story of these conversions was told by Mrs. Finney in a letter to Edwin and Mary Lamson of Boston, dated 6 January 1860 (Correspondence of Charles G. Finney, 1830–1875, Oberlin College Archives, microfilm).

[45]The word "very" was not crossed out in the manuscript but was left out of the published edition.

[46]Alice (Barnes) Barlow (1825–1888) was the daughter of James Barnes of Edgworth. She was married to James Barlow in 1845 and had five children, the youngest of whom was to be named Annie Elizabeth Finney Barlow. Mrs. Finney noted in her journal that, although Mr. and Mrs.

abroad; and people came in daily, and almost hourly, for conversation. The first week of January had been appointed to be observed as a week of prayer, as it has been since from year to year; and the different denominations agreed to hold Union meetings during that week.[47]

Our first meeting was in the chapel occupied by **Brother** Davison, who had sent for me to come to Bolton.[48] He was an Independent, what we in this country call a Congregationalist. His chapel was filled the first night. The meeting was opened by a Methodist minister;[49] who prayed with great fervency, and with a liberty that plainly indicated to me that the Spirit of God MS 1001 was upon the congregation, and that we should have a powerful meeting. |I was invited to follow him with some remarks. I did so, and occupied a little space in speaking upon the subject of prayer. I tried to impress upon them as a fact that prayer would be immediately answered if they took the stumbling blocks out of the way, and offered the prayer of faith. The Word seemed to thrill through the hearts of Christians. Indeed I have seldom addressed congregations upon any subject that seemed to produce a more powerful and salutary effect, than **upon** the subject of prayer. I find it so everywhere. Praying people are immediately stirred up by it to lay hold of God for a blessing. They were in this place. That was a powerful meeting.[50]

Through the whole of that week **of prayer** the Spirit of prayer seemed to JHF 461 be increasing, and our meetings had greater and |greater power. About the third or fourth day of our meetings, I should think, it fell to the turn of a **Brother** Best, also a Congregational minister at Bolton, to have the meeting in his chapel.[51] There, for the first time, I called for inquirers. After MS 1002 addressing the congregation for **some|time** in a strain calculated to lead to

Barlow had been members of the Methodist church for many years when Mr. Barlow was converted in Ireland,

> his wife feeling the want of a Savior that they might again find sympathy in the same things looked forward anxiously for our coming with the hope that she too should be converted—On Friday Mrs Barlow had a long conversation with Mr Finney told him all that was in her heart and her hope of now becoming a true child. After a long struggle she submitted herself to God (E. Finney, "Journal," pp. 60–61).

Alice Barlow was all her life prone to depression and never seemed to find real peace. See the correspondence between the Finneys and the Barlows in the Finney Papers. See also "James Barlow, Esq., J.P.," *The Bolton Journal*, 1 June 1878, p. 7; 29 September 1888, p. 5; and information from Helen Barlow.

[47]The special week of prayer was held, in fact, during the second week of January 1860.

[48]This was not Finney's first meeting in Bolton; he had been holding revival meetings there since 18 December. This was the first at which he preached for the special meetings arranged for each day at the different Nonconformist churches during the week of prayer. The meeting in Davison's Chapel was on Tuesday evening, 10 January, and was reported in *The Bolton Chronicle* and *The Bolton Independent*.

[49]The meeting was presided over by Rev. Henry H. Cheetle.

[50]A correspondent of the *New-York Evangelist* wrote: "There had been for some months a remarkable spirit of prayer prevailing, and a visit from Professor Finney and his excellent wife was the chief means of ripening the Churches for the crisis" (*NYE*, 12 April 1860, p. 3). This correspondent was probably Miss Mary Allen of Rochester, New York, who was in Bolton at the time. See Mary B. Allen King, *Looking Backward; or, Memories of the Past* (New York: Randolph, 1870), p. 425.

[51]Robert Best (1823–1887) had been a student at Homerton Theological College and had had pastorates in Kirkham and Fleetwood in Lancashire before going to Mawdsley Street Chapel, Bolton, in 1852. He remained there until his death. See James Johnston, *Memoir of the Rev. Robert Best* (Bolton: Blackshaw, 1888). This meeting was on Thursday, 12 January.

that point, I called for inquirers, and his vestry was thronged with them. We had a **powerful** meeting with them; and many of them, I trust, submitted to God. There was a Temperance hall in the city, which would accommodate more people than any of the chapels.[52] After this week of prayer the brethren secured the hall for preaching; and I began to preach there twice on the Sabbath, and four evenings in the week. Soon the interest became very general. The hall would be crowded every night **to its utmost capacity,** so that **no** person could get so much as within the door.[53] The Spirit of God was poured out copiously.

I then recommended to the brethren to canvass the whole city. To go two and two, and visit every house; and if permitted, to pray in every house in the city. They immediately and courageously rallied to perform this work. They got great numbers of bills, and tracts, and posters, and all sorts of invitations printed, and began the ˡwork of canvassing.[54] The Congregationalists and Methodists took hold of the work with great earnestness.[55] MS 1003

The Methodists are very strong in Bolton, and always have been since the day of Wesley.[56] It was one of Wesley's favorite fields of labor; and they have always had there **a powerful** ministry and **powerful** churches. Their influence was far in the ascendancy there over all other religious denominations. I found among them both ministers and lay men who were most excellent and earnest laborers for Christ.[57] But the Congregationalists too

[52]The Temperance Hall had recently been enlarged and a gallery added so that it could hold up to three thousand people (see *The Bolton Chronicle*, 3 December 1859, p. 5; and 21 January 1860, p. 7). Finney started preaching there Friday, 18 January 1860 (E. Finney, "Journal," p. 66).

[53]The correspondent of the *New-York Evangelist* reported: "He preaches in a temperance hall that will seat about three thousand; it is decently filled each night, and on the Sabbath and Sabbath evening, hundreds come that are unable to find admittance. Sometimes there will be ten or twelve ministers on the platform with him" (*NYE,* 12 April 1860, p. 3).

[54]Finney inserted here the phrase "like men in earnest" but appears to have crossed it out.

[55]The Bolton Evangelical Revival Committee was formed about the second week of March, and the town was divided into thirteen districts, with people appointed to visit in each district. See "Bolton Evangelical Revival Committee, 1860," records in Bolton Reference Library. The campaign followed a similar plan that had been adopted in New York in the spring of 1857, when two thousand visitors, in teams of two for each block, covered the whole city. Jeremiah Lanphier had been appointed in July 1857 to superintend the work among the poor in the Fulton Street area. A similar plan had been successfully tried in Hartford, Detroit, Buffalo, and other places, and also in Boston while Finney was there in February 1858. See Timothy L. Smith, *Revivalism and Social Reform in Mid-Nineteenth-Century America* (Nashville: Abingdon, 1957), p. 66; "Religious Efforts for Cities," *Christian Watchman and Reflector* (Boston), 4 February 1858, p. 2; and, in the same paper, "Evangelization in Boston," 11 February 1858, p. 2.

[56]John Wesley (1703–1791), the founder of Methodism.

[57]The correspondent of the *New-York Evangelist* wrote:

> The Wesleyan Methodists of Bolton, with their pastors, have heartily cooperated with the Finney's, and the conversions have been altogether of the Methodist type. Moreover, such immense addition as have been made to the membership and resources of Methodism, that steps have been taken to erect two additional Wesleyan places of worship, which are to cost £12,000 (*NYE,* 12 April 1860, p. 3).

Among the converts were "many connected with the Independent Methodist Sabbath School who had been long convinced, but were now savingly converted" (Stephen Rothwell, *Memorials of the Independent Methodist Chapel, Folds Road, Bolton* [Bolton: Winterburn, 1887], p. 191).

One of the Methodists particularly involved was Rev. Thornley Smith, minister of Fletcher Street Chapel. He had been present in the Methodist Chapel in St. Ives, at the very first meeting that Finney attended in England, after he arrived for his first tour. Smith was later to become

entered into the work with great spirit and energy; and while I remained there at least, all sectarianism seemed to be buried.[58] They gave the town a JHF 462 thorough canvassing; and the canvassers met once or twice ꜝa week to make their reports, and to consider farther arrangements for pushing the work. It was very common to see a Methodist and a Congregationalist hand in hand, and heart in heart, going from house to house with tracts, and praying MS 1004 wherever they were permitted in every house, and ꜝwarning **them** to flee from the wrath to come, and urging them to come to Christ.[59] Of course in such a state of things as this the work would spread rapidly among the unconverted. All classes of persons, high and low, rich and poor, male and female, became interested. I was in the habit every evening I preached,[60] of calling upon inquirers to come forward and take seats in front of the stand

prominent in the Holiness Movement and an intimate friend and associate of Asa Mahan. See Thornley Smith, *A Christian Mother: Memoirs of Mrs. Thornley Smith* (London: Hodder and Stoughton, 1885); and *The Watchman and Wesleyan Advertiser* (London), 19 April 1876, p. 127.

[58] The union of Christians of every denomination in the work was a feature particularly noted in many of the local papers. "Minor differences are for the time entirely lost to view, and men who have never supposed before that they could work together, now find themselves, without a semblance of difference, heartily engaged in a common cause, and in every practical respect one" (*The Bolton Chronicle*, 25 February 1860, p. 8; see also 28 January 1860, p. 5; *The Bolton Independent*, 7 January 1860, p. 3; and *The Bolton Guardian*, 7 April 1860, p. 3).

[59] *The Bolton Chronicle* reported:

> House to house visitation is being actively and systematically carried on. The whole of Little Bolton and Haulgh, and a large part of Great Bolton, have been already visited by those who have at heart the moral and spiritual elevation of their fellow-townsmen; and it is intended that no house or family shall be left uncared for. Thus far, the visitors have generally been received with great kindness on the part of both rich and poor, and the unobtrusive and benevolent spirit in which they have set about their mission, has even won upon those who are most opposed to the movement (10 March 1860, p. 5).

The written reports submitted by the visitors confirm that they were well received. They found many who had already heard Finney preach and had benefited, and many others who promised to go to the meetings. Most of the families were glad to have been visited and to have been given the literature. The main opposition came from the Roman Catholics (handwritten reports in "Bolton Evangelical Revival Committee, 1860," records).

One woman, Betty Smith, wrote an amusing account of a visit by two of the women canvassers. It was published in *The Bowtun Loominary*, a satirical paper written in the local Lancashire dialect. The paper objected strongly to "Finneyism." Betty Smith was not pleased when one of the women told her that the minister of the church where she and her husband attended was unconverted.

> Unconverted! aw says, Heaw dun yoa know that?
>
> Awve bin towd so, hoo says.
>
> Well, aw says, tell thoose uz towd yoa that it would look better on um if they'd study th'ninth commandment a bit closer, un gie oer bearin false witness ogen their nayburs. Un if they belung to yoar lot, for goodness sake make some labbur on um, or the dule [devil] ull as shure get howd on um as yoar stondin theere.

Betty Smith did go with her husband to hear Finney,

> un aw mun say that after yerrin him four toimes awm satisfied that there's mooar rail Christianity i' that peawson's little finger, uz th'ladies said wur unconverted, than there is i' aw his whole kerkus. . . .
>
> Good lorjus days! Mestur Hedditur, if Finneyism be true religion, wot a miserable, waik, namby-pamby, crouchin cringin, vinegar-faced, lanterun jawed set o foak we should be ("Betty Smith on Finneyism," *The Bowtun Loominary, Tumfowt Telegraph, un Lankishire Lookin-Glass* [Bolton], 7 April 1860, pp. 105–6.

[60] Matson had written down, "every evening, as I preached, " but the word "as" appears to have been crossed out by Finney. He omitted, however, to cross out the comma.

where I stood to preach. Great numbers would come forward, **and** crowd as best they could through the dense masses that **stood in**[61] every nook and corner of the house. The hall was not only large on its ground floor, but had a gallery, which was always thronged **to its utmost capacity**. After the inquirers had come forward we **always** engaged in a prayer meeting, having several prayers in succession while the inquirers knelt before the Lord. The Methodist brethren were very much engaged, and for **sometime** were quite noisy and demonstrative **in that direction** in their prayers when sinners came forward. For **sometime** I said ˡnothing about this, lest I should throw them off and lead them to grieve the Spirit. I saw that their impression was, that the greater the excitement the more rapidly would the work go forward. They therefore would pound the benches, pray exceedingly loud, and sometimes more than one at a time. I was aware that this distracted the inquirers, and prevented their becoming truly converted; and although the number of inquirers was great and constantly increasing, yet conversions did not multiply as fast as I had been in the habit of seeing them, even where the number of inquirers was much less. MS 1005

After letting things pass on so for two or three weeks until the Methodist brethren had become acquainted with ˡme, and I with them, **after** calling the inquirers forward **one evening** I suggested that we should take a different course. I told them that I thought the inquirers needed more opportunity to think than they had when there was so much noise. That they needed instruction, and needed to be led by one voice ˡin prayer **at a time**; and that there should not be any confusion, or anything bordering on it, if we expected them to listen and become intelligently converted. I asked them if they would not try for a short time to follow my advice in that respect, and see what the result would be. They did so; and at first I could see that they were a little in bondage when they attempted to pray, and a little discouraged because it so crossed their ideas of what constituted powerful meetings. However they soon seemed to recover from this, because I think they were convinced that although there was less apparent excitement in our prayer meetings, yet there were many more converted from evening to evening.[62] JHF 463 MS 1006

The fame of this work spread abroad, and soon **they** began to come in large numbers from Manchester to Bolton to attend our meetings; and this, as was always the case, created a considerable excitement in that city, and a desire to have me come thither as soon as I could.[63]

[61]The words "stood in" were not altered in the manuscript, but the published version has "filled."

[62]Rev. John. H. Beech, one of the Methodist ministers in Bolton, wrote an account of Finney's visit, in which he commented on Finney's *Memoirs*:

> An interesting autobiographical record of much of his life has been published, from which it appears he entertained low views of the intelligence of Methodist preachers. But as he apparently knew little of them, he may be easily forgiven. Ignorance and error are frequent companions (J. H. Beech, *Outer Life of a Methodist Preacher, and Sermons* [London: Simpkin, Marshall, 1884], p. 162; reference from Peter Howard).

[63]Mrs. Finney noted in her journal on 2 February the presence of "Mr & Mrs Morris from Manchester"; and a fortnight later, "Five gentlemen at dinner, Mr. Dunn, Mr Thompson and others from Manchester." The Reverend James P. Dunn was a Wesleyan Methodist, and the Reverend Patrick Thomson, a Congregationalist. Then on Saturday, 17 March, Mrs. Finney wrote: "The desire for Mr Finney to come to Manchester has been presented and the corn

MS 1007 However I remained in |Bolton I think about three months, perhaps more.[64] The work became so powerful that it broke in upon all classes, and every description of persons. **It extended to the factories, or Cotton Mills, as they were called.**[65] Brother **Barlow** had an extensive **Mill** in Bolton, and employed a great many hands, **male** and **female.**[66] **I called** with him down to his mill once or twice, and held meetings with his operatives. The first time we went we had a powerful meeting. I remained with them till I was much fatigued, and then returned home, leaving Brother **Barlow** still to pray with and instruct them. When he came home he reported that not less than sixty appeared clearly to be converted that evening among his own hands.[67] **Thus**[68]
JHF 464 meet|ings were continued till nearly all his hands expressed hope in Christ.

exchange is mentioned as the place for the union meetings. Mr Barlow objects to the place—Mr Weeks and Mr McDonald were over yesterday as a committee" (E. Finney, "Journal," pp. 69, 73, 79). Rev. George B. McDonald was minister of the Oldham Street Wesleyan Methodist Chapel in Manchester. Edward Henry Weeks was the Congregational minister of Harpurhey on the north side of Manchester. He had been a disciple of Finney's for many years and had visited Bolton soon after the arrival of the Finneys in December. See "E.H.W." to Finney, March 1845, in *OE,* 18 June 1845, pp. 102–3; Weeks to Finney, 11 March 1859, Finney Papers, microfilm, roll 5; and E. Finney, "Journal," p. 62.

[64]The Finneys were in Bolton from 15 December 1859 to 1 April 1860.

[65]Bolton was second only to Manchester as a cotton manufacturing town. There were more than eighty mills and factories. Mary Allen King recollected, "From a hill, a mile out of the town, might be counted one thousand chimneys, from one to three hundred feet high, conveying smoke from engines connected with factories" (*Looking Backward*, p. 427).

[66]The firm of Barlow, Gooddy, and Jones ran the Albert Mill in Little Bolton. They employed a thousand men and women to weave cotton fabrics and to make such things as "Marseilles" quilting, gentlemen's vests, and calico shirts. See E. Finney to Edwin and Mary Lamson, 6 January 1860, Correspondence of Charles G. Finney, 1830–1875, Oberlin College Archives, microfilm. On Friday, 6 January, Mr. Barlow gave a tea for his work people. Mrs. Finney noted in her journal, "1000 present—Mr Barlow made a good address—many wept—good done." And on 17 January she noted, "In Mr Barlows mill a good work has commenced" (pp. 64, 66). *The Bolton Chronicle* for 21 January reported:

> A singular scene was witnessed last night, at the mill of Messrs Barlow, Gooddy, and Jones. The engines were stopped at half past five; labour ceased; and several hundreds of the hands assembled in a room on the lower storey, where a prayer meeting was held, in the course of which revival addresses were delivered by Mr. Barlow and some of his *employés* ("A Revival Meeting in a Cotton Mill," p. 5).

By the middle of February it was reported, "Meetings have been held nightly in Messrs Barlow, Goody, and Jones's mill in Higher Bridge-street, and the intensest interest has attached to them, inasmuch as the awakenings and conversions have been often from 50 to 80" (*The Bolton Chronicle*, 18 February 1860, p. 5).

[67]Mrs. Finney described this meeting in a letter to Mrs. Helen Kirk in Edinburgh. It was on Monday, 13 February.

> After an address and prayers, the people were dismissed. God had been very manifestly present. Many felt deeply. They lingered, and Mr Barlow said, "If any wish for conversation, they can remain." About one hundred came back. Mr Finney said, "I wish to understand your whereabouts. Those who have been Christians for some time may take this seat." About four moved to the right. Then he requested "those who had recently been converted to take the same seat." About twenty went over. By this time there was loud weeping. He made some remarks, telling them what Christ requested of them—what he would do for them. He requested all who wanted salvation . . . to kneel. They all knelt while prayer was offered for them. . . . Sixty-two professed, that night, to find the Saviour. The next night, 38. The meetings were continued each night, and each night God visited and redeemed some souls (E. Finney to Helen Kirk, 18 February 1860, in *The Christian News,* 25 February 1860, p. 5).

After the meeting, Mrs. Finney noted in her journal, "Mr Barlow came home shouting glory" (p. 72).

There were a great many very striking cases of conviction and conversion at the time. Although I kept cool myself, and endeavored to keep the people in an attitude in which they would listen to instruction, ¹and would act MS 1008 understandingly in everything they did; still in some instances persons for a few days were too much excited for the healthy action of their minds, though I do not recollect any case of real insanity. One night as I was standing on the platform and preaching, a man in the congregation rose up and crowded his way up **on** the platform and said to the congregation, "I have committed a robbery." He began to make a confession, interrupting me as I was preaching. I saw that he was over-excited; and **B**rother Davison who sat on the platform stepped up and whispered to him, and took him down into a side-room and conversed with him. He found that he had committed a crime for which he was liable to be transported. He gave him advice, and I heard no more of it that evening. Afterwards the facts came **out**[69] more fully to my knowledge. But in a few days the man obtained a hope.

One evening I preached on confession and restitution, and it created a most tremendous movement among business men.[70] One man told me the next day ¹that he had been and made restitution I think of fifteen hundred MS 1009 pounds,[71] in a case where he thought he had not acted upon the principle of loving his neighbor as himself. The consciences of men under such circumstances are exceedingly tender. The gentleman to whom I have just referred, told me that a dear friend of his had died and left him to settle his estate. He had done so, and simply received what the law gave him for his labor and expense. But he said that **on** hearing that sermon, it occurred to him that as a friend and a Christian brother, he could better afford to settle that estate without charging **them** anything, than **they** could afford to allow him ¹the legal fees. The Spirit of God that was upon him led him to feel it so JHF 465 keenly that he immediately went and refunded the money.[72]

[68]The word "Thus" was not altered in the manuscript, but the published version has "These."

[69]The word "out" was not crossed out in the manuscript but does not appear in the published edition.

[70]This sermon was preached on Sunday, 15 January. Mrs. Finney noted in her journal: "Mr Finney preached in the Hall afternoon & evening—a perfect jam—everyplace filled. Ante room, stairs, lobby. Subject covering sin—evening Confessing & forsaking" (p. 66). The sermon was reported in *The Bolton Chronicle:*

> the lesson inculcated in [the sermon] being the necessity of personal reparation being made as far as possible and at any cost, to those who have been injured, by those who have committed the injury. In the course of the argument, which was elaborate and profound, many illustrations of the power of conscience, and of reparation made under conviction of sin, were given from the preacher's own experience. In connection with this subject, it may not be out of place for us to notice here, that several interesting cases of restitution have recently occurred in our own town, which are traceable directly to the influence which has flowed from the present series of special services (21 January 1860, p. 7).

[71]The word "sterling" had been written here by Matson, but he crossed it out.

[72]Cases of restitution continued to receive publicity in *The Bolton Chronicle* and other papers. The *Chronicle* for 11 February 1860 reported that

> not a week has passed in which cases of restitution have not occurred, some of them of a most remarkable character. Only the other day, £5 was put into the hands of a gentleman connected prominently with the services, for restitution to one from whom it had been wrongly obtained. In this way many hundreds of pounds have been restored—in one case in a sum as large as £300 (p. 5).

There was a case in Rochester, in New York, that I have forgotten to mention, but that may just as well be mentioned in this place, of the same MS 1010 kind. An extremely tender conscience led a man to see and feel |keenly on the subject of acting on the principle of loving our neighbor as ourselves, and doing to others as we would that they should do to us. A man of considerable property was converted in one of the revivals in Rochester in which I labored, who had been transacting some business for a widow lady in a village not far distant from Rochester. The business consisted in the transfer of some real estate for which he had been paid for his services some fifteen or sixteen hundred dollars.[73] As soon as he was converted he thought of this case; and upon reflection he thought he had not done by that widow lady and those fatherless children, as he would wish another to do by his widow and fatherless children should he die.[74] He therefore went over to see her, and stated to her the present view of the subject as it lay before his own mind. She replied that she did not see it in that light at all. That she had considered herself very much obliged to him indeed, that he had transacted her business MS 1011 in such a way as to make for her all she could ask or expect. She de|clined therefore to receive the money which he offered to refund. After thinking of it a little he told her that he was dissatisfied, and wished that she would call in some of her most trust-worthy neighbors, and the‹y›[75] would state the question to them. She did so, called in some Christian friends, gentlemen of business, and they laid the whole matter before them. They said that the affair was a business transaction, and it was evident that he had transacted the business to the acceptance of the family and to their advantage; and they saw no reason why he should refund the money. He heard what they had to say; JHF 466 but before he left the town he called on the lady |again and said, "My mind is not at ease. If I should die and leave my wife a widow and children fatherless, and a friend of mine should transact such a piece of business for them, I should feel as if he might do it gratuitously, inasmuch as it was for a widow

The next week it was noted: "The 'restitutions' continue to pour in almost daily, and Mr. Finney has been generally requested to allow the 'restitution sermon' to be published, in the hope that the influence attaching to its delivery may be perpetuated" (18 February 1860, p. 5).

A month later the *Chronicle* reported: "On the evening of Thursday [22 March], Mr. Finney preached a third discourse on 'Confession and Restitution,' and the Hall was crowded to excess." The report then went on to give a résumé of the sermon, from Proverbs 28:13 (24 March 1860, p. 5).

Further examples of restitution were given by the *New-York Evangelist* from a letter "written by a lady, recently returned from Europe. During her tour she was much interested in the revival movements about her, and visited the Rev. Mr. Finney, who was then preaching at Bolton and Manchester." The writer (probably Mary Allen) said that "there was over three thousand pounds restored in the city of Bolton in one week." But that may have been an exaggeration, for Mrs. Finney wrote to her sister, Henrietta Bissell, "It was ascertained that restitution was made to the amount of 1000 lb Sterling" (E. Finney to H. Bissell, 6 June 1860, Finney Papers, microfilm, roll 5; and *NYE,* 16 August 1860, p. 4). See also *The Bolton Independent*, 21 January 1860, p. 2; *The Bolton Guardian*, 24 March 1860, p. 3; and *The Revival* (London), 17 March 1860, p. 84.

[73] This is probably the same case that was mentioned by Louis Chapin in a letter to G. F. Wright. It was during the 1830–1831 revival, and the sum mentioned by him was $1,500 (L. Chapin to G. F. Wright, 10 February 1890, Wright Papers, box 8).

[74] Matson had at first written down "orphan" in this sentence but in both places changed it to "fatherless."

[75] Matson had written the word "then" here, but the *n* appears to have been altered to a *y* by Finney.

and fatherless children." Said he, "I cannot take any other view of it than this." |Whereupon he laid the money upon her table, and **b‹a›d**[76] **her** MS 1012 **goodbye.**[77]

Another case occurs to me now, which illustrates the manner in which the Spirit of God will work in the minds of men when their heart **is** open to his influence. In preaching in one of the large cities on a certain occasion, I was dwelling upon the dishonesties of business, and the over-reaching **policies** of men; and how they justi**fied** themselves in violations of the golden rule. **If I recollect right I was preaching on the golden rule,—but I am not certain; at any rate I made that rule very prominent in what I was saying.** Before I was through with my discourse a gentleman arose in the middle of the house and asked me if he might **ask** a question. He then supposed a case; and after he had stated it, asked me if that case would come under the rule that I had propounded. I said, "Yes, I think that it clearly would." He sat down and said no more; but I afterwards learned that he went away and made restitution to the amount of thirty thousand dollars.

|I could relate great numbers of instances in which persons have been led MS 1013 to act in the same manner, under the powerfully searching influences of the Spirit of God. But to return from this digression, **to Bolton.** The work went on **there** and spread, until one of the ministers who had been engaged in **engineering** the movement of canvassing the town, said publicly **in my presence,** that they found that the revival had reached every family in the city; and that every family had been visited, **I think he said more than once. Indeed they kept up the visitation whilst I remained there, and ‹thoroughly›**[78] **canvassed the city.**[79]

If we had had any place of worship **that could have held the inhabitants of the city,** we should probably have had ten thousand persons **there** from evening to evening. All we could do was to fill the hall as full as it could crowd, and then use such other means as we could to reach the multitudes in other places of worship.[80]

[76] Matson had written the word "bid" here, but the *i* appears to have been altered to an *a* by Finney. Fairchild crossed it out.

[77] It was probably this case among others that was referred to in a report of the revival: "One Lawyer sent $1500, 50 miles, to the widow & children of a man whom he had wronged to that amount. A number of persons in the Village have received letters enclosing money, saying that the writer had wronged them to that amount" ("Copy of a letter from a gentleman in Utica to a Clergyman in Boston," 7 February 1831, in Clark Collection, Congregational Library, Boston). And it was noted in the papers at the time of the revival in Rochester that there were "a great many instances in which restitution has been made for injuries that had been done" (*BR,* 16 February 1831, p. 27). See also *Christian Advocate and Journal and Zion's Herald* (New York), 4 March 1831, p. 106.

[78] Finney inserted the word "thoroughly."

[79] *The Bolton Guardian* reported at the time the Finneys finished at Bolton:

> From information given us by a good authority, it appears that upwards of 2000 persons have been brought to the stage of inquiry, and not less than 1200 have been converted. Of the latter number, nearly three-fourths had previously made a profession of religion, but had never possessed the root of the matter. It is, of course, impossible to estimate the thousands who have had some of their errors corrected, and will hereafter lead a better, if not a renewed life (7 April 1860, p. 3).

[80] The dense crowds attending the hall, particularly on Sundays, and the hundreds having to turn away, were remarked on in the newspaper reports. "The addresses delivered by Mr. Finney

JHF 467 MS 1014 ǀI recollect a striking case of conversion among the great ǀMill-owners there.[81] I had been told of one of them that was a very miserly man. He had a great thirst for riches, and had been spoken of as being a very hopeless case. The revival had reached a large number of that class of men; but this man had seemed to stand out, and his worldly-mindedness and his miserly spirit had seemed to eat him up. But contrary to my expectations, and to the expectations of others, he in his turn called on me. I invited him to my room, and had a very serious conversation with him. He acknowledged to me that he had been a great miser; and that he had once said to God that if He would give him another hundred thousand pounds[82] he would be willing to be eternally damned. **He said that so great was his love of money that he willingly consented to be damned if God would give him another hundred thousand pounds.** I was very much shocked at this; but could see clearly that he was terribly convicted of the sinfulness of that state of mind.

MS 1015 ǀI then repeated to him a part of the sixth chapter of Matthew, where Christ warns men against laying up treasures on earth, and recommends them to lay up treasures in heaven. I finally came to that verse, "But seek first the kingdom of God and His righteousness, and all these things shall be added unto you."[83] He leaned toward me, and appeared to be as much interested as if it were all new to him. When I repeated to him this verse he said to me with the utmost earnestness, "Do you believe *that*?" I said, "Be sure I believe it. It is the Word of God." "Well then," said he, "I'll go it," and sprang upon his feet in the utmost excitement. "If that is true," said he, "I will give up all to Christ at once." We knelt immediately down, and I presented his case to God in prayer; and he seemed to break **all** down like a child. From that time he appeared to be a very **altered** man.[84] His miserly feelings all seemed to melt MS 1016 away. He took hold of that work like a man in earnest, and ǀwent and hired at his own cost a city **Missionary**, and set him to work to win souls to Christ.[85]

JHF 468 At this place also Mrs. Finney's meetings were very ǀlargely attended. She

create such interest that even the Temperance Hall is not near large enough to contain those anxious to hear them on the Sunday" (*The Bolton Chronicle*, 18 February 1860, p. 5; see also 28 January 1860, p. 5; and 11 February 1860, p. 5).

Mrs. Finney noted the same thing in her journal, Sunday by Sunday, from 22 January through to 18 March. She wrote remarks such as: "a dense mass of human being"; "The crowd was even greater than ever—At six the house was well filled—though the services did not commence til ¼ to 8"; "crowded again"; "Hall filled—many standing"; "The house was more densely packed than ever"; "perfect jam of a congregation"; "Evening the house seemed more densely packed than ever"; "The usual jam at the Hall"; "The Hall just as full as usual" (pp. 67–79).

[81] This was probably John Sharples of the firm of Sharples and Horrocks, flax spinners and linen manufacturers, employers of three hundred persons. He visited Finney on the morning of 7 February before breakfast "and did not leave until he had fully submitted to God" (E. Finney, "Journal," p. 70; and *Directory of Manchester and Salford, Bolton,* etc., pp. 956, 969).

[82] Matson had written the word "sterling" here and at the end of the next sentence, which he crossed out.

[83] Matthew 6:33.

[84] Mrs. Finney noted: "as I went to my breakfast I met him in the Hall, had come to submit himself to God. . . . This evening Sermon, 'Glorifying God.' Mr. Sharples present—on the inquirers seat—pride humbled. His friend Mr. Bell with him" (E. Finney, "Journal," pp. 70–71).

[85] John Sharples was for some years an alderman of the borough and died in Manchester in 1886 at age seventy. See James Clegg, *Annals of Bolton* (Bolton: The Chronicle Office, 1888), p. 222.

held them, as she always did **her meetings**, in the day-time; and sometimes I was informed that at her meeting of ladies, Temperance Hall would be nearly full. The Christian ladies of different denominations took hold with her and encouraged her; and great good, I trust, was done through the instrumentality of those ladies' meetings.[86]

My wife and myself were both of us a good deal exhausted by these labors.[87] But in April we went to Manchester.[88] In Manchester the Congregational interest, as I was informed, rather predominates over that of other denominations. As is well-known, the manufacturing districts have a stronger democratic element than other parts of England. Congregationalism, therefore, is more **popular** in Manchester than in any other city that I visited. I had not been long there, however, before I saw that there was a great lack of ˡmutual confidence among the brethren **there**. I could see that there was a jar among the leaders **in that movement**; and frequently to my grief I heard expressions that indicated a want of real heart-union in the work. This I was soon convinced was a great difficulty to be overcome; and that if it could not be overcome, the work could never be as general there as it had been in Bolton. There soon was manifest a dissatisfaction with some of the men who had been selected to engineer the work,—**to get out the bills, do the necessary printing,** and provide for carrying on the general movement.[89]

MS 1017

[86] An account of the women's prayer meetings stated "that previous to the visit of Mr and Mrs Finney to Bolton, a copy of the tract, 'Mrs Finney and the Ladies' Prayer Meeting,' was sent to the Rev. Mr Davison, who, through the liberality of James Barlow, Esq., had 1000 copies printed and distributed. This prepared the way for the Prayer Meeting" (*The Tea Meeting: Mrs Finney and The Women of Bolton* [Manchester: Bremner, 1860], p. 2; this was a report of the farewell meeting for Mrs. Finney, attended by about one thousand women). Reports of the meetings in *The Bolton Chronicle* and entries in Mrs. Finney's journal indicate that she started off with twenty or thirty women and ended up with meetings of six or seven hundred.

[87] The Finneys held their last meeting at Bolton on Sunday, 1 April, and then went to Houghton to Potto Brown's for a rest. See *The Bolton Chronicle*, 7 April 1860, p. 5; and letters of Mr. and Mrs. Finney to the Barlows in Bolton, 5 and 9 April 1860, Correspondence of Charles G. Finney, 1830–1875, Oberlin College Archives, microfilm.

Rev. W. H. Davison later became editor of *The Preacher's Monthly* and appears to have been responsible for an 1882 review of a new edition of Finney's *Memoirs*. He wrote:

> Probably, had it been entrusted to one of Mr. Finney's old friends, we might have had some life-like sketch of him, with the glow, and colour, and action which characterize life. In writing, as manuscripts in our possession show, Mr. Finney was apt to become hard and rigid. He was a lawyer by nature—a born logician—and he seemed to live under the burden of a necessity to do honour to the syllogism wherever that was possible. In writing these chapters of autobiography, he seems to have felt himself obliged to keep out as much as possible the emotion which thrilled his deep, warm heart. The self-repression is extreme. He passes over in single sentences, interesting scenes and circumstances which, fairly told, would fill entire chapters. Having been associated with him in labours referred to in this volume for months, the present writer is able to testify that the half has not been told. . . . He was at times like one possessed; but he never allowed mere animal excitement to displace the Truth (*The Preacher's Monthly* [London], n.s., 4 [July 1882]: 63–64).

[88] At Manchester, Finney started preaching on 22 April in Grosvenor Street Chapel, which was the oldest Independent congregation in Manchester. Under the influence of Rev. William Roby it had become the place of worship for many of the leading Manchester families. The church was built in 1807. The pastor, Rev. Patrick Thomson, had been there since 1854 (*The Manchester Evening News*, 18 March 1910, p. 3; and *The Congregational Year Book* [London], 1872, pp. 351–53).

[89] The meetings were advertised "by placards on the walls of the city," according to Rev. James

Charles Finney, 1860. A photograph taken just after his return from England, showing him wearing a fur-lined overcoat he brought back with him (referred to in W. J. Keep to G. M. Jones, 18 April 1908, copy in Robert Samuel Fletcher Papers, box 18, Oberlin College Archives). Courtesy Oberlin College Archives.

Everett (J. Everett, "Diary," vol. 9, 29 April 1860, p. 2568, manuscript in John Rylands University Library of Manchester). They were also well advertised in local papers. *The Manchester Guardian* and *The Manchester Daily Examiner* carried advertisements on most days from 18 April through to the end of July, and they were advertised each week in the *Manchester Weekly Advertiser*. Mrs. Finney's ladies' meetings were advertised in the same way.

This grieved the Spirit and crippled the work. And although from the very first the Spirit of God attended the Word; yet the work never so thoroughly overcame the sectarian feeling and disagreements of the brethren generally, that it could spread over the city in the way it had done at Bolton. When I went to that city I expected that the Methodist and Congregational brethren would work harmoniously together, as they ˡhad[90] at Bolton; but in this I found myself mistaken. Not only was there a want of cordiality and sympathy between the Methodists and Congregationalists; but also a great lack of confidence and sympathy amongst the Congregationalists themselves. However our meetings were very ˡinteresting, and great numbers of inquirers were found on every side; and whenever a meeting was appointed for inquirers, large numbers would attend. Still what I longed to see was a general overflowing of the Spirit's influences in Manchester, as we had witnessed it in Bolton.[91] **After laboring in Manchester proper for several weeks, we made a stand at Salford—which is, indeed, a part of Manchester.[92] I spent most of my time after that in Salford and Pendleton.[93] But for some reason there seemed to be a lack of earnestness and cordiality in the minister at Salford.[94] He did not seem to know how to get into the work. One evening I recollect that I preached from this text: "If ye will not lay it to heart, to give glory to my name, I will curse ˡyour blessings."[95] I had seen, as I thought, on the part of the minister, a want of confidence in the reality and extent of the work that was going on. He seemed to be partially blind in regard to the Spirit's work. But he was very deeply convicted of sin, of having failed to give glory to God for what He had done. After service, on retiring to the vestry for my**

MS 1018

JHF 469

MS 1019

[90] Fairchild crossed out the last section of this page and wrote "–19" after the page number 1018 to indicate to the printers to omit page 1019 and to proceed to page 1020.

[91] Finney preached in Grosvenor Street Chapel until Friday, 11 May. He preached twice on Sundays and four times during the week. Mrs. Finney held meetings for women five times during the week. "About 130 persons on the average remain after service" (report by "S.C." [probably Samuel Clarkson], *The Revival,* 14 July 1860, p. 13). On Sunday, 5 May, Finney also started preaching in the Free Trade Hall. This hall was considered to be the largest in the country, even larger than the Exeter Hall. It could seat four thousand comfortably and could hold more than seven thousand if some remained standing. It was built in 1856 to replace an earlier one on the same site. In 1940 it was bombed but was rebuilt (see "The New Free Trade Hall, Manchester," newspaper cutting dated October 1856, Cutting Book, Manchester Public Library; and *The Manchester Guardian*, 16 November 1951, pp. 5–8). Finney preached there on Sunday afternoons until 9 June.

[92] Salford is the district about a mile to the west of Manchester, across the River Irwell. Finney moved there to Chapel Street Chapel on 14 May. This was an Independent church. The meeting house was built in 1819 and could seat nine hundred ("Chapel-Street Congregational Church," *The Salford Weekly News*, 30 January 1875, p. 3).

[93] Pendleton is on the north side of Salford and is a suburb of Manchester, two miles to the northwest. The Pendleton Congregational Church in Broad Street was an offshoot of Chapel Street Chapel, Salford, in 1836. It was under the pastoral charge of Rev. Stephenson St. N. Dobson, who had gone there in 1858. His predecessor, Albert E. Pearce, had tried to get Finney to go there during Finney's previous visit to England in 1851. The church, built in 1846, could seat 550 people ("Pendleton Congregational Church," *The Salford Weekly News*, 20 March 1875, p. 3; and James Gwyther to Finney, 3 February 1851, Finney Papers, microfilm, roll 4).

[94] The minister was Samuel Clarkson (1820–1886). He had been at Spring Hill College and had had pastorates in Sheffield and Bridgnorth before going to Salford in 1854. He remained there until 1861, when he moved to Exeter (*The Congregational Year Book,* 1887, pp. 181–82).

[95] Malachi 2:2.

overcoat he was greatly moved, and exclaimed, "O how you have made me feel!" I trust he was a good man; but somehow or other he did not get so into the work as to have the Spirit of discernment, so as to perceive clearly what the Lord was doing. As an illustration, the last time that I preached I appointed in his vestry, by his consent, a meeting for young converts the next evening; and told them that I wished them to see and converse with the pastor. I learned afterwards that this meeting he totally forgot. That converts assembled in large numbers around the door of the vestry, and waited, and waited; and he finally never came. Not long after that he was dismissed from his charge, for MS 1020 **what reason I am not apprized.** ˡThe difficulty was, there was not a good spirit manifested at that time by the leading men in that movement. I did not learn the cause—perhaps it was something in me.[96] But although I am sure that large numbers of persons were converted, for I saw and conversed with a great number myself that were powerfully convicted, and to all appearance converted; yet the barriers did not break down so as to give the Word of the Lord, and the Spirit of the Lord, free course among the people.[97] When we came away a meeting was called for those who had been particularly blessed during those meetings; and the number in attendance was, I believe, very much larger than was expected by the ministers themselves. I am confident that they were surprized at the numbers present, and at the spirit of that

[96]Finney's preaching and manner came in for some criticism. Rev. James Everett, one of the leaders among the Reformed Methodists, was in Manchester on 29 April and went to hear Finney at Grosvenor Street Chapel. He noted in his diary:

> He had made a favourable impression on my mind as a *writer*; but I was sadly disappointed with him as a *preacher*. . . . His matter was thoroughly common-place, and his style no less so; his voice and manner harsh, nasal, stiff, and severe. He had a long string of particulars,—as "Sin is *sometimes hidden*"—"sometimes," "sometimes," &c. &c. &c in an almost interminable chain, mostly in a single sentence or two, without point or amplification, relieved by three or four anecdotes, which effected but little in the way of illustration. It would have been a bald, sapless affair, from a poor local preacher, without any pretentions to ministerial character; but from the President of a college, it was absolutely discreditable. Intellect, power, feeling, were wanting; while repetitions occupied, at least one third of the time. How often the public are carried away with a *name*! (29 April 1860, p. 2568).

Another writer compared Finney with James Caughey and H. Grattan Guinness, who had been in Manchester shortly before and had been a disappointment.

> His meetings were often crowded, and several times he preached in the Free Trade Hall. He was said to be very successful; as was also his wife, who laboured with him, in holding meetings for females. Being anxious to know if he were any better than his predecessors, I went one evening to hear him preach on "The constraining love of Christ." I certainly did not expect to hear a written discourse, which varied little in character from a moral essay; and was still less prepared to find it in substance a mere tirade against Calvinism. I came away with a worse opinion of revivalists than ever ("Popular Preaching," *The Christian Bond of Brotherhood Magazine* [London] 1 [June 1861]: 119).

[97]There were reports and testimonies to the value of the meetings, but two of these, published in *The Revival* over the initials "S.C." (probably Samuel Clarkson), drew attention to the unfavorable time of the year, business preoccupation, interruptions from Sunday school festivities, and other hindrances, as well as sectarian prejudices that prevented the revival from spreading. See *The Revival,* 7 July 1860, p. 4; and 14 July 1860, p. 13; see also 18 August 1860, p. 51; *The Bolton Chronicle*, 4 August 1860, p. 5; Lizzie Willson to Elizabeth Finney, 7 October 1860; and Peter Spence to Elizabeth and Charles G. Finney, 14 November 1860, Finney Papers, microfilm, roll 5.

meeting. Indeed I do not think that any of the ministers there were aware of the extent of that work, for they did not generally attend our meetings. They did not follow them from place to place, and were seldom seen in **our** meetings of inquiry. We continued in Manchester till about the first of August; and the revival continued to increase and spread up to that time.[98] ꜔But the strength of both myself and my wife had become exhausted **so much that** some of the leading brethren[99] proposed to us to suspend our labors, and go down into Wales **and spend a few weeks** and rest, and then return to Manchester and resume our labors. What they proposed was, to secure a large hall **in which to hold our meetings**, and thus to go on with our meetings in an independent way. They thought, and I thought myself, that we should secure a greater amount of good in that way than by laboring with any particular congregation. **Indeed, I found it to be true in England wherever I tried it, that the best way to promote revivals of religion was to hold independent meetings; that is, meetings in large halls, where they can be obtained, to which all denominations may come.** Denominational lines are much more strongly marked in that country than they are ꜔in this. It is very difficult to get the Church of England **people** to attend a dissenting place of worship. The Methodists will not generally and freely attend worship with other denominations. Indeed, the same is true ꜔of[100] all denominations in England, and in Scotland. Sectarian lines are much more distinctly drawn, and the member**ship** of the different churches keep more closely within the lines

MS 1021

JHF 470

MS 1022

[98]Toward the close of his time in Manchester, Finney wrote to John Kirk in Edinburgh:

> The work of grace here has gone on increasing, in connection with our meetings from week to week, and of late more rapidly than ever. The numbers converted no one can tell. Many have professed conversion, but as they are not looked after by ministers I fear for many of them. As it was in London, so it is here: the great mass of the converts are not known to the ministers, and only a part of them will find their way to unite with churches soon. The number of inquirers has for many weeks been large. Last Sabbath evening we must have had nearly or quite three hundred. . . . This city greatly needs a general revival. To human view it appears to be a great pity not to follow up this well begun, and growing revival of religion (Finney to Kirk, 26 July 1860, in Kirk, *Memoirs of Rev. John Kirk,* p. 325).

There were reports of Finney's sermons in the *Salford Weekly News*, 26 May 1860, p. 2; and 16 June 1860, p. 2. Also a *Memorial Volume of Revival Sermons* was published jointly by William Bremner of Manchester and the Christian News Office in Glasgow. These were thirteen of the sermons that Finney preached in the Free Trade Hall and Chapel Street Chapel, Salford, from 6 May to 29 July 1860. The first in the book, entitled "Life's Great Question," which was the first sermon that Finney delivered in the Free Trade Hall, had been published as a penny pamphlet by Bremner the week after it was delivered. See the advertisement in *The Manchester Guardian*, 10 May 1860, p. 1. No copy of the *Memorial Volume* has been located, but it was advertised with a list of the contents in *The Christian News,* 8 September 1860, p. 8; and also in *The Day-Star* (Glasgow) 17 (September 1861): opposite p. 180. Lizzie Willson of Manchester spoke of it in a letter to Mrs. Finney: "Fourteen of Mr. Finney's sermons are published, handsomely bound, entitled The Memorial Volume of his visit to Manchester. I am going to get it to morrow" (L. Willson to E. Finney, 7 October 1860, Finney Papers, microfilm, roll 5). The last sermon in the *Memorial Volume* was also published separately under the title *The Freeness of the Gospel* (the copy in Oberlin College Library is paginated 147–60). That was the last sermon that Finney preached in England, on the evening of 29 July, in Chapel Street Chapel, Salford.

[99]In his letter to John Kirk, Finney speaks of these brethren as "laymen" (Finney to Kirk, 26 July 1860, in Kirk, *Memoirs of Rev. John Kirk,* p. 325).

[100]Fairchild wrote "–3" after the page number 1022 to indicate to the printers to omit page 1023 and to proceed to page 1024.

of their own denomination, than in this country. **The fact is, that society in England** ***is dove-tailed together.*** **And** I am persuaded that the true way to labor for **souls** there is to have no particular connection with any distinct denomination; but to preach the true **Gospel**, and make a stand in halls, or even in streets when the weather is favorable, where no denominational feelings and peculiarities can straiten the influences of the Spirit of God. On the second of August we left Manchester and went down to Liverpool.[101] A goodly number of our friends went down with us, and remained over night. On the morning of the third we left in the Persia for New York.[102] We found that large numbers of our friends had assembled from different parts of England, to bid us good bye. We took an affectionate and an affecting leave of them, ‹**&**[103] the glorious old steamer rushed out to sea **&** we were on our way home.›

[101]Mrs. Finney held her last ladies' meeting on Saturday, 28 July, in Salford, and Finney preached his last sermon there on Sunday evening, 29 July. On the evening of Monday, 30 July, there was a farewell tea meeting for the Finneys held in the Roby Schoolroom, Picadilly, in Manchester, at which testimony was given to the valuable results of their efforts. Finney received a testimonial of one hundred guineas, and thirty guineas were presented to Mrs. Finney (see *The Manchester Daily Examiner and Times*, 1 August 1860, p. 3. A guinea was a gold coin worth twenty-one shillings, or £1.05.). On Thursday, 2 August, they paid a farewell visit to the Barlows in Bolton. They left Manchester for Liverpool the next evening. See *The Bolton Chronicle*, 4 August 1860, p. 5.

[102]The *Northern Press* gives the sailing date for the *Persia* as 4 August (*Northern Press and Liverpool and Manchester Advertiser* [Liverpool], 11 August 1860, p. 7).

[103]At the bottom of page 1022 the word "over" is written in Finney's handwriting. Fairchild drew attention to the word by encircling it in ink and drawing the symbol of a finger pointing. The remainder of the sentence is written by Finney on the reverse of the manuscript page.

CHAPTER XXXVI

MS 1023
JHF 471

‹Return to Oberlin & a glorious revival here.›

I[1] should have said that I had been strongly urged, for reasons that existed here, to come immediately home; and this urgency had been increasing upon me for several weeks before we left Manchester. It was thought by persons here that the state of things in our church demanded my presence.[2] Had it not been for this pressure, we should have remained longer in England. I thought then, and think now, that the work would have greatly increased, not only at Manchester, but throughout all that part of England, could we have remained another

[1] Pages 1023–28 were originally numbered 864–69 and renumbered 995–1000 by Matson. Finney changed them to 1023–28. The chapter heading was inserted by Finney at the top of page 1023. Matson had written the following at the start of the page: "and the glorious steamer rushed out to sea, and we were on our way home." There is a question mark in pencil in the margin against the beginning of this portion of the sentence. It appears to have been inserted by Lewis Tappan. Finney crossed out the sentence and rewrote it, adding the word "old" on the reverse of the previous page when he started the new chapter heading. Fairchild omitted the whole page from the published version and started chapter XXXVI on the next page.

[2] From early in 1860 Finney had been receiving letters concerning the state of religion in Oberlin. After he had left America for England, the nationwide interest in religion during the great awakening of 1858 had given place to excitement over slavery. The Oberlin community had become engrossed in the subject, particularly through the famous Oberlin-Wellington Rescue case. In December 1858 twenty-one Oberlin citizens and members of the college had been put in jail for preventing a black youth being taken back into slavery under the Fugitive Slave Act. This was followed by the execution of John Brown. One of his associates, who had been living in Oberlin, was killed in the raid on Harper's Ferry, and another was executed. See R. S. Fletcher, *A History of Oberlin College from Its Foundation Through the Civil War* (Oberlin: Oberlin College, 1943), pp. 402–15.

There was some revival of interest in religion in the winter of 1859–1860. Daily prayer meetings were crowded, but energy was being dissipated through internal problems in the church. Finney heard of the agitation for a copastor and the failure to secure Rev. Michael Strieby of Syracuse for the post. Then there was a division of the church and the formation of a second Congregational church. But perhaps more disturbing was another division in the church caused by an outbreak of fanaticism. A group of church members had been seeking the "gift of the Holy Ghost," and one of them, a son of one of the deacons, was thought to have become insane and was committed to a mental asylum. He later escaped. Others were considered to be fanatical or "on the borders of insanity." This group was critical of the lack of spirituality in the rest of the church and particularly of Rev. John Morgan, Finney's colleague on the faculty, who was standing in for him as pastor. All parties were eager for Finney's return. See letters to Finney from Henry Cowles, 22 November 1859 and 30 January 1860; John Keep, 14 and 17 May 1860; Uriah Thompson, 31 January and 2 February 1860; Permelia Hall, 3 June 1860; A. M. Crane, 8 June 1860; and John Morgan, 10 August 1860, Finney Papers microfilm, roll 5. There was also strong pressure from the faculty on Finney to return and take up his responsibilities at the college. See E. H. Fairchild to Finney, 10 July 1860; and Oberlin College Faculty and Resident Trustees to Finney, 21 July 1860, Finney Papers, microfilm, roll 5.

year or two. We were invited, and urged strongly, to go to many places, to towns and cities, in that region.[3] But as I said, we were over-ruled by the intelligence from this place, and left England with great reluctance, hoping that sometime we might return.

MS 1024 **ˡThe first and second day out from Liverpool it rained almost incessantly. I was a good deal on deck and took a severe cold, which subjected me to a very painful attack of lumbago.[4] This continued with a good deal of severity until we arrived in New York. I was so lame on our arrival in New York that I could not immediately travel by land to Oberlin.[5] However I soon recovered, and we came on to Oberlin and**

[3] Finney had had deputations and urgent invitations particularly from Bury and Rochdale, towns near Bolton, and also from Birmingham (see Elizabeth Finney, "A Journal Kept by Mrs. Elizabeth Ford Atkinson Finney during a Visit to England in 1859–1860," pp. 68–69, 71–72, 79, manuscript in Special Collections, Oberlin College Library; and *The Bolton Chronicle*, 4 August 1860, p. 5). A deputation from Rochdale went to Finney on 20 March. One of those who went, John Ashworth, the Methodist businessman and founder of the Chapel for the Destitute, recorded the scene:

> Being shown into the library, we had only to wait a few minutes, when he made his appearance in a printed morning dress. After a mutual introduction all sat down.
> "What is your errand, gentlemen?" asked Mr. Finney.
> "We come from Rochdale," was the reply, "and the friends are anxious to have you a few nights with them. We have a very large chapel, and no doubt it will be crowded to hear you."
> "Is your chapel well ventilated?"
> "Yes, very," we reply.
> "The Manchester people are urging me to give them three nights in the Corn Exchange, before I return to America, which will be in a few days."
> "We understand you are wanted there," we observed.
> "But I cannot come to you and go to Manchester?"
> "Well, perhaps you will give us the preference."
> "Indeed! indeed! Let us kneel down and pray about this matter," said Mr. Finney.
> We knelt down, and I do not think either of us will ever forget that moment. Mr. Finney began first, and said,—
> "Lord, here are two selfish men come from Rochdale to request me to go to that town to preach; they say they know I am requested to go to Manchester. I cannot go to both, and they want me to give Rochdale the preference; they care nothing about Manchester souls, only about Rochdale souls; but, Lord, souls are souls, equal in value everywhere: teach these two men that souls are souls."
> Then laying his hand on my shoulder, he said, "Pray, brother."
> What I said I cannot tell, but I know I was very short. He then laid his hand on my companion, "Pray, brother."
> He also was very brief, and we arose from our knees with no little confusion. After a considerable pause Mr. Finney rose up, paced quickly about the room, and abruptly said, "I feel I have nothing to do at Rochdale" (A. L. Calman, *Life and Labours of John Ashworth* [Manchester: Tubbs and Brook, 1875], pp. 63–68; reference from Hillel Schwartz).

[4] Mrs. Finney, in a letter written on board the *Persia* on 8 August, to James and Alice Barlow in Bolton, England, mentioned that her husband "has had an attack of lumbago." A letter also from Finney to James Barlow written on 12 September from Oberlin mentions that, after parting from them on the boat, "I kept about for one day & then came on the lumbago from which I have not yet recovered" (E. Finney to James and Alice Barlow, 8 August 1860; and Finney to James Barlow, 12 September 1860, Correspondence of Rev. Charles G. Finney, 1830–1875, Oberlin College Archives, microfilm).

[5] The Finneys landed in New York about 15 August and went to Brooklyn to stay with Mrs. Finney's brother, Hobart Ford. They remained there until the end of August. See *The New York Daily Tribune*, 16 August 1860, p. 8; and Finney to Edwin Lamson, 18 August 1860, Correspondence of Charles G. Finney, 1830–1875, Oberlin College Archives, microfilm.

First Congregational Church, Oberlin. Built in 1842–43 the church remains essentially the same today. Finney was pastor of the church from 1837 to 1872. In J. H. Fairchild, *Oberlin: The Colony and the College, 1833–1883* (Oberlin: Goodrich, 1883), opposite p. 104. Courtesy Oberlin College Archives.

immediately commenced our labors for a revival of religion in this place.[6]

We had had very little rest in England for a year and a half; and those who are used to sea voyages will not wonder that, **with the lumbago upon me,** I did not rest much during our voyage home. Indeed we arrived **here** a good deal exhausted. I was myself hardly able to preach at all. However the state of things was such, and the time of year such, that I could not, as I supposed,

[6]The Finneys returned to Oberlin via Albany and Rochester, where Mrs. Finney stayed for a week. From there Finney went to Clifton Springs for a few days, "but it was no place he said for him to rest and so he came back" (E. Finney to James and Alice Barlow, 14 September 1860, Correspondence of Charles G. Finney, 1830–1875, Oberlin College Archives, microfilm). They arrived in Oberlin on 5 September, and by 14 September Mrs. Finney was writing to the Barlows in England:

> The people here are delighted to hear Mr Finney again—they drink in his words and the truths he preaches as if they were hungry. The word takes hold . . . We have a daily morning prayer meeting—and there is much earnest pleading with God for a great outpouring of the Spirit in this place and for the world, that it may be blessed (E. Finney to James and Alice Barlow, 14 September 1860, Correspondence of Charles G. Finney, 1830–1875, Oberlin College Archives, microfilm).

afford to rest.[7] There were many new students here, and strangers had been moving into the place; so that there was a large number of impenitent persons residing here at that time. The **Faculty**[8] were of opinion that an effort must be made immediately to revive religion in the churches, ˡand to secure the conversion of the unconverted students. During my absence in England the congregation had become so large that the house could not, with any comfort contain them; and after considering the matter, the church concluded to divide and form a Second Congregational Church. They did so; the new church worshipping in the College Chapel, and the First Church continuing to occupy their usual place of worship.[9] The Second Church invited me to preach a part of the time to them in the College Chapel. But that would **not** hold **perhaps much** more than half as many as the church; and I could not

MS 1025

[7] It was reported by one of the students that Finney had returned "in excellent health, and with his remarkable powers of mind and expression apparently improved. Immediately on his arrival here he began holding a series of daily religious meetings, preaching a strong and earnest discourse each alternate day" (Alvord B. Nettleton, "Oberlin College," *The University Quarterly* [New Haven] 2, no. 1 [January 1861]: 179).

[8] Fairchild, who was one of the faculty, altered this word to "brethren."

[9] By 1860 the membership of the Congregational church in Oberlin had risen to 1,545, being by far the largest Congregational church in America. The meeting house, which was the largest church in the West when it was built in 1842–1843, had seating for 1,600 and could be made to accommodate 500 more. But by 1856 the average attendance on a Sunday was said to be 2,200. See *The Congregational Quarterly* (Boston) 3 (January 1861): 100; J. H. Fairchild, *Oberlin: The Colony and the College, 1833–1883* (Oberlin: Goodrich, 1883), p. 104; and *OE,* 18 June 1856, p. 103.

It had been the aim from the founding of the Oberlin colony to have only one community church, to which all Evangelical Christians could belong. Finney was against division in any form and opposed it whenever it came up for discussion. He was in favor of enlarging the existing structure, even though that was considered impractical. While Finney was in Oberlin it was thought that the organization of a second Congregational church would have been impossible. It was therefore decided to act in his absence, although he was informed of what was happening. Except for one dissenting vote, the church was unanimous in the decision, and the new church was organized on 3 May 1860. See John M. Ellis, "Address," *The Oberlin Weekly News*, 8 May 1885, p. 2; D. L. Leonard, "Historical Address," *The Oberlin News*, 11 May 1900, p. 8; and Mrs. William Kincaid, "Oberlin in the Individual," in *The Fiftieth Anniversary of the Second Congregational Church, Oberlin, Ohio* (Oberlin: Second Congregational Church, 1910), p. 76.

It was said that on Finney's return from England, Professor John M. Ellis, one of the leaders in the organization of the Second Church, called on him to explain why it had been done,

> assuring him that it was not on account of any unfriendly feelings or dissatisfaction whatever with the First Church or its affairs, but that, as the church had become so large, and the meeting-house so crowded, they thought it wise and best that a portion should withdraw and give others, who so much needed to hear Prof. Finney's preaching, an opportunity. With that inimitable Finney look that used to carry such tremendous force of logic and argument with it, Prof. Finney replied: "John, you folks that have gone off to form this Second Church need my preaching more than anybody else!" It is said that with this the interview presently came to a close ("What President Finney Thought of It," *The Oberlin News*, 11 May 1900, p. 1).

The Second Church met in the college chapel until a building was erected in 1870. Although Finney never countenanced the new church or had anything much to do with it, he urged the First Church to contribute liberally toward the cost of the new building. He is said to have entered its pulpit only once. That was in July 1875, when he preached a memorable sermon. It was the last time he ever stood in a pulpit. However, there are recollections of his being in Second Church on other occasions. See Leonard, "Historical Address," *The Oberlin News,* 18 May 1900, p. 8; George B. Siddall, "The Second Church Choir" in *The Fifieth Anniversary*, p. 59; Hiram Mead, "Charles Grandison Finney," *The Congregational Quarterly,* 19 (January 1877): 27; and Roselle T. Cross, "Memories of Charles G. Finney," typescript, n.d., p. 4, Alumni Records file 28/9, folder, "Roselle Theodore Cross," Oberlin College Archives.

think it my duty to divide my labors, and preach part of the time to one congregation and part of the time to the other; and therefore took measures immediately to secure a revival of religion, holding our meetings at the large church. The Second Church people came in and labored as best they could; but the preaching devolved almost altogether upon myself.

|We held daily prayer meetings in the church, which were largely attended. JHF 472 The body of the church would generally be full. At these meetings I labored hard to secure the legitimate results of a prayer meeting |judiciously managed. MS 1026 Besides preaching twice on Sabbath, and holding a meeting of inquiry in the evening of every Sabbath, I preached several **times** ‹**on**› week ‹**evenings each week.**›[10] In addition to these labors I was obliged to use up my strength **by** conversing with inquirers, who were almost constantly visiting me when I was out of meeting. These labors increased in intensity and pressure from week to week.[11] The revival became very general throughout the place, and seemed to bid fair to make a clean sweep of the unconverted in the place.[12] But after continuing these labors for four months until I had very little rest day or night, I came home one Sabbath afternoon from one of the most powerful and interesting meetings I ever **saw**, and was taken with a severe chill; and from that time I was confined to my bed between two and three months.[13]

Being obliged to change the preaching, it was found in **that** case, as it always has been so far as my experience has gone, that the change of preaching soon let down the tone of the revival; and not suddenly, but gradually it ceased. **However it did not re-act in |the sense in which great** MS 1027 **and badly managed religious excitements do re-act.** There was not, that I am aware of, any reaction **at all**. But the conversions grew less frequent, and

[10] Here Matson had written down, "I preached several times a week." Finney changed it.

[11] Mrs. Finney wrote to the Barlows at the end of December 1860 and early in January 1861 that her husband had "been doing more work here—four times more work than he ever did in any place in England."

> His labors here have been beyond everything I have ever known him to do[.] He said it seemed as if he had super human strength—he has attended three meetings a day often, and conversed with inquirers till nine at night—Beside he has dictated eight sermons for the press since his class teaching has been suspended (E. Finney to the Barlows, 22 December 1860 and 8 January 1861, Correspondence of Charles G. Finney, 1830–1875, Oberlin College Archives, microfilm).

The sermons were published in *The Oberlin Evangelist* from 2 January to 24 April 1861. See *OE,* 10 October 1860, p. 164.

[12] On 22 December Mrs. Finney wrote to the Barlows:

> Our revival here continues and is greatly increasing in power—the whole town seems moved at the presence of God and such breaking down and humbling of the church I have never seen in Oberlin—I suppose several hundred persons have been converted (E. Finney to James and Alice Barlow, 22 December 1860, Correspondence of Charles G. Finney, 1830–1875, Oberlin College Archives, microfilm).

[13] Mrs. Finney wrote on Saturday, 22 December, to the Barlows: "Last Sunday after preaching twice and holding an inquiry meeting he had a slight chill—his sleep was very disturbed and very little during the night." Then a letter arrived from Oshkosh, Wisconsin, dated 21 December, announcing that Jenny, the wife of Finney's son, Norton, was dying, and he was needed there. So Finney set out on the journey on Wednesday, 26 December. But he only got as far as Chicago and was so ill that he had to return. Mrs. Finney wrote, "Since that his nerves have been in a very shattered condition." See E. Finney to the Barlows, 22 December 1860 and 8 January 1861, Correspondence of Charles G. Finney, 1830–1875, Oberlin College Archives, microfilm; and Charles G. Finney, Jr., to Finney, 21 December 1860, Finney Papers, microfilm, roll 5.

from week to week the ‹weekday›[14] meetings gradually fell off in their attendance; so that by the time I was able to preach again I found the state of religion interesting, but not what we here call a revival of religion.[15] However, the next Summer, as has been almost universally the case, a goodly number of our students were converted, and there was a very interesting state of religion **all the Summer.**[16]

During the Summer months there is a great pressure upon the people here. **Every family almost take boarders, and the female part of the family have as much as they can do.** The students are engaged in preparing for the Anniversaries of their various College Societies, for their examinations, and for Commencement; and of course during the Summer term there is a great deal of excitement unfa|vorable to the progress of a revival of religion. We have much more of this excite|ment in later years than we had when we first commenced here. College Societies have increased in number, and the class exhibitions and **everything that is exciting** have been multiplied **a good deal for several years**; so that it has become more and more difficult to secure a powerful revival during the Summer term. ‹This ought not to be.›[17]

JHF 473
MS 1028

Before I went to England the last time I saw that an impression seemed to be growing in Oberlin that during term time we could **not attend to the work of revival, and could** not expect to have a revival; and that our revivals must be expected to occur during the long vacations in the winter. This was not deliberately avowed by any one **here**; and yet it was plain that that was **fast** coming to be the impression. But I had come **here,** and resided here, for the sake of the students, to secure their conversion and sanctification; and it was only because there was so great a number of them here, which gave me so good an opportunity to work upon ‹so many›[18] young minds in the process of education, that I had remained here from year to year. I had frequently

[14] Finney added the word "weekday."

[15] Notices in *The Oberlin Evangelist* from 10 October 1860 to 16 January 1861 indicated that the revival was still continuing. On 27 February it was reported: "The religious interest cannot be considered general, but affects individuals and classes. There have been cases of hopeful conversion every week through the winter; during the last month more especially among the young men." "Ingatherings at Oberlin" listed ninety-eight as having been admitted to the two Congregational churches by profession of faith since 1 November (*OE,* 27 February 1861, pp. 37, 39).

Finney's health gradually improved through the spring of 1861. He went to church for the first time on 12 May. Soon after that he was able to resume the preparation of sermons for *The Oberlin Evangelist.* However, he was not well enough to preach (E. Finney to the Lamsons, 5 and 7 February 1861; Finney to Alice Barlow, 7 May 1861, Correspondence of Charles G. Finney, 1830–1875, Oberlin College Archives, microfilm; Finney to Julia Finney, 16 May 1861, Finney Papers, microfilm, roll 5; and *OE,* 22 May 1861, p. 87).

[16] During the summer Finney was able to meet his theological class two or three times a week, but he was still not well enough to preach. On 5 August he wrote: "The state of religion here is interesting. Conversions frequently occurring but no general revival. The war excitement has greatly diverted attention & my ill health has kept my mouth closed" (Finney to Edwin Lamson, 5 August 1861, Correspondence of Charles G. Finney, 1830–1875, Oberlin College Archives, microfilm). *The Oberlin Evangelist* reported on 20 November 1861: "For several months past, there have been manifest indications of the presence of the Divine Spirit in this place, especially among the students. . . . Hopeful conversions have been occurring frequently, and the religious aspect assumes a deepening interest" (p. 191).

[17] Finney added the sentence "This ought not to be."

[18] Finney added the words "so many."

ˡalmost[19] made up my mind to leave and give myself wholly to the work of an Evangelist. But the plea always used with me had been, that we could not do much in this country in promoting revivals anywhere except at that season of the year when we have our long vacation. Furthermore, that my health would not enable me to sustain revival labor the year around; and that therefore I could do more good here during the term time—that is, in the Spring, Summer, and early Autumn—than I could anywhere else. This I myself believed to be true; and therefore had continued to labor here during term time, for many years after my heart strongly urged me to give up my whole time in laboring as an Evangelist. MS 1030

When I was **this** last **time** in England, and receiv**ed there** urgent letters to return, I **brought up this subject in my reply** of the impression to which I have alluded **that seemed to be growing here** that we could not expect revivals in term time; and said **to them**, that if that was going to be the prevalent idea it was ˡnot the place for me, for during our long vacation ˡour students were gone of course, and it was for their salvation principally that I remained. I had been greatly afflicted too, by finding when an efford[20] was made to secure the conversion of the students during term time, that the first I would know some excursion would be planned, some amusement **and pleasure-seeking, or some exciting thing planned and brought into execution** that would counteract all that **I, and those that were laboring with me with the same design,** could do to secure the conversion of the students. I never supposed that that was the *design*; but such was the *result*, insomuch that previous to going to England the last time I had become almost discouraged in making efforts to secure revivals of religion during term time. In my replies to letters received while I was in England, I was very free and full upon this point in saying, that unless there could be a change **upon this point,**[21] Oberlin was not my field of labor any longer.[22] JHF 474 MS 1031

Our fall term is properly our harvest here. It begins about the first of September, when we have a large number of new students, ˡand many of these unconverted ones. I have always felt, as a good many others have **here** and I believe the Faculty **have realized**, that during that term was the time to secure the conversion of our new students. **In the fall of our return, as I have related,** this was secured to a very great extent. The idea that during term time we could not expect a revival of religion, seemed to be exploded; **and** the people took hold **for a revival,** and we had a powerful **one.** MS 1032

[19] Finney numbered this page 1030 instead of 1029, in error. Pages 1030–33 were originally numbered 870–73 and renumbered 1001–4 by Matson. Finney changed them to 1030–33.

[20] This word is written "efford" in the manuscript but was unchanged by Fairchild. It was corrected to "effort" in the published version.

[21] The words "upon this point" were not altered in the manuscript but were omitted from the published version.

[22] Finney wrote letters in reply to John Keep on 4 June 1860 and to John Morgan on 14 June 1860, which were read before a joint meeting of the faculty and resident trustees. In their reply to Finney they took up all the points that he had raised, and they presented a strong case for his continuing at Oberlin. E. H. Fairchild, one of the faculty, also wrote independently to Finney and dealt specifically with the problems of promoting revivals in term-time (Faculty and Resident Trustees to Finney, 21 July 1860; and E. H. Fairchild to Finney, 10 July 1860, Finney Papers, microfilm, roll 5).

Since then we have been much less hindered in our revival efforts in term time by **excursions, and parties of pleasure, and running after worldly amusements**, than we had been for a few years before **my last going to England.** Our revival efforts have taken effect among the students from year to year, because they were aimed to secure the conversion especially of the students. **The inhabitants have been changing a good deal, almost as much as the change of our students. As I have said, the first fall after my**
MS 1033 **return from England, that is the fall of 1860, ¦there was quite a large number of our citizens converted, as well as many students. But the change in the inhabitants here is so great that** we very frequently need a sweeping revival through the whole town, among the house holders as well as the students, to keep up a healthy tone of piety **in the families where the**
JHF 475 **students board.** A goodly num¦ber of our students learn to work themselves in promoting revivals, and are very efficient in laboring for the conversion of their fellow-students. The young men's prayer-meetings have been greatly blessed. The young people's meetings, where **the sexes** meet for a general prayer meeting, have also been **greatly** blessed. The efforts of **lay men and women generally** in the church, have been increasingly blessed from year to year. **As for myself, I have over-labored nearly every fall term since 1860; and as a consequence have been confined from one to three months to the house, and mostly to my bed.**[23] We have had more or less of
MS 1034 a revival continually, summer and winter, ¦since[24] 1860[.][25] ‹**A**›lthough[26]

[23]By the summer of 1861, Finney was recovering from his long sickness, but he became seriously ill again at the beginning of September with shingles. He was in bed for two months, and it was 9 February before he could resume preaching—the first he had done in fourteen months. In March he was able to lecture to his theological class. He had been preaching for a month when once again his health broke down, and it was 11 July before he was again able to preach. However, he was over the worst, and his health continued to improve, so that by the time of his seventieth birthday, on 29 August 1862, he was better than he had been for two years. His health remained reasonably good over the next three years in spite of some setbacks. The excitement of commencement time each year usually exhausted him, but he was able to lay aside the responsibilities of the presidency of the college just before commencement in August 1865. He was not seriously ill again until the end of January 1866. Details of Finney's health and his preaching appear in letters from him and from his wife in the Oberlin College Archives and in notices and reports in *The Oberlin Evangelist*, 1861, 1862; *The Lorain County News* (Oberlin) 1861–1866; and William E. Bigglestone, ed., *The Journal of Russell T. Hall, 1863* (Oberlin. Grady, 1983).

On 27 November 1863 his wife, Elizabeth, died of consumption. Although this was a shock, Finney's health was not affected. On 9 October 1865 he was married for the third time—to a widow, Rebecca (Allen) Rayl, assistant principal of the female department of Oberlin College, the ceremony being performed by Asa Mahan, then president of Adrian College in Michigan (Finney to Edwin and Mary Lamson, 10 December 1863, Correspondence of Charles G. Finney, 1830–1875, Oberlin College Archives, microfilm; and *The Lorain County News,* 11 October 1865, p. 2).

[24]MS 1034 was originally numbered 873 in error. Pages 1034–40 were numbered 873–79 and renumbered 1005–11 by Matson. Finney then changed them to 1034–40.

[25]Periods of increased religious interest were noted by *The Lorain County News*, the local paper, more particularly in the fall and winter each year than in the summer, with the period from October 1865 to April 1866 being the most extensive since the winter of 1860–1861—"like revival times of 30 years ago" (*The Lorain County News,* 3 January 1866, p. 3; and 7 February 1866, p. 3). At the end of January 1866, the height of this revival, Finney's health broke down yet again, and he was then confined to his bed for three months. By the next fall, however, he was helping to promote one of the most remarkable revivals ever known at Oberlin (Finney to John Moody, 2 May 1866, Finney Papers, microfilm, roll 5).

continually pressed by churches, east and west, to come and labor as an Evangelist, I have not dared to comply with their request. **With home comforts and nursing I can still perform a good deal of ministerial labor; but I find that I cannot bear excitement in the evening without preventing my sleep.** I have been able, by the blessing of God, to perform a good deal of labor here; but **as I said** I felt inadequate to the exposure and labor of attempting to secure revivals abroad. Last winter, 1866 and '67, the revival was more powerful among the inhabitants than it had been since 1860.[27] However, as heretofore I broke down in the midst, and was unable to attend any more meetings.[28] The brethren, however, went forward with the work. **The lay membership took hold with such vigor and persistency that the work** continued with great interest until Spring. **The brethren that preached laid out their strength as best they could, and by the blessing**

[26] Matson had started a new sentence at the beginning of the page, "Since 1860, although . . . ," but Finney changed the *a* of "although" to a capital *A*.

[27] While the revival was "in the full tide of its glorious progress," a newspaper report concluded: "Never will this winter be forgotten by this generation; memorable it must stand for its glorious work of grace." It described the beginning of the revival:

> President Finney, breaking down little by little each year under pulpit labors, had set his heart on a great revival that should renovate Oberlin before he laid aside his work. Early in the winter he had said to his congregation, with tearful eyes, that after such a result he could feel to say, "Lord, now lettest thou thy servant depart in peace." And first among all human means must be counted the resistless arguments, the probing rebukes, the wonderfully winning appeals of his sermons. Frequently do we hear the remark that never has his preaching been more powerful. Assuredly few now resident in Oberlin remember when it had such response among us (*The Lorain County News,* 13 February 1867, p. 3).

Religious interest was increasing through December 1866, and by the end of the year it was reported: "Three daily prayer meetings, beside the many other weekly and semi-weekly meetings, are now held and well attended" (*The Lorain County News,* 26 December 1866, p. 3). The most noticeable feature was the work among the citizens of the town, particularly the business community. Through the months of January and February the revival was at its height, with special meetings for businessmen and clerks. By the end of March it was noticed: "Though the attendance is somewhat diminished with the spring work the interest continues to an unusual degree. Among the students who have come in since the new term began it is now more particularly manifest and new conversions are daily noted" (27 March 1867, p. 3).

A meeting for the admission of members to the First Congregational Church was held on Sunday, 10 March.

> *One hundred and eight* stood up in the aisle to cast in their lot with the church, a larger number than ever united with it at one time before, . . . Eighty-eight of these united upon "profession" and many of those who presented letters date their renewal and return from a backslidden life to the gracious influences of the winter's revival. It was noticeable that a much larger proportion than usual of the new members were residents of town as distinguished from students, and, in several instances, almost whole families were included in the list as the names were called (*The Lorain County News,* 13 March 1867, p. 3).

[28] At the beginning of January, Finney became ill and was unable to preach for two weeks, but he was preaching again during the height of the revival in February. Then early in March he broke down again and was unable to attend the memorable meetings on 10 March for the admission of converts. He was confined to his bed, and it was 14 April before he could preach again. His health was then better for the rest of the year, when he was writing his narrative of revivals. See *The Lorain County News,* 16 January 1867, p. 3; 3 April 1867, p. 3; 17 April 1867, p. 3; Finney to John Moody, 14 January 1867, Finney Papers, microfilm, roll 5; and Finney to James and Alice Barlow, 8 January 1868, Correspondence of Charles G. Finney, 1830–1875, Oberlin College Archives, microfilm.

MS 1035 **of God a great and permanent good was secured. |This[29] Summer ‹1867›[30] and Autumn we have been very much hindered in our revival effort by the discussion of the question of Freemasonry, and of secret societies generally.[31] The discussion and action of the churches, however, have been confined almost entirely to the question of Freemasonry. When we first settled this place, and when this college was first established, ‹we›[32] had a rule excluding from membership those that belonged to secret societies.[33] But the churches never had any rule on this subject. There were no secret societies in the place; and until recently there never have been, to my knowledge. However, within a year or two past a Masonic lodge was formed here.[34] But I knew nothing of it till last Spring, when a young man who belonged to the lodge proposed himself for admission to the church. I think that he had been examined by the church, and that the church had voted to have him propounded, before it was known that he was a freemason. When I**
MS 1036 **understood that he was a freemason, having |Elder Bernard's book entitled, "Light on Masonry," in which the whole thing is revealed, I gave the young man that book, expecting of course that when he had read that he would want nothing more to do with Masonry.[35] I dreaded**

[29]The section from here to MS 1050 on the anti-Masonic controversy in Oberlin was omitted by Fairchild from the published version. According to D. L. Leonard, before Fairchild started editing the manuscript he sent it to "a connection of Fin[ney]'s," probably Truman Hastings, "who said that chap[ter was] unwise & w[oul]d better be omit[ted]." When Fairchild read the section, "deeming it out of place and a serious blemish," he concluded it was not wise to use it (D. L. Leonard, "Notes upon Talks with Pres. Fairchild," bk. 2, p. 15, 10 June 1897, R. S. Fletcher Papers, file 30/24, box 1, Oberlin College Archives; Leonard, "A Legacy from President Fairchild. X," in *The Oberlin News*, 20 March 1903, p. 4; and Introduction, p. xl). Fairchild himself had taken a prominent part in the controversy.

[30]Finney inserted the date 1867.

[31]The discussion about secret societies came prominently before the public in Oberlin on 7 April 1867, when J. H. Fairchild preached a sermon in the Second Church on "the evils of secret organizations in their relation to society in general." A report stated: "The positive opinion with which the Oberlin 'philosophy' has always regarded secret societies of all kinds is well known. Lately the question has been agitated anew, the occasion being found in the application of members of such societies for admission to the churches" (*The Lorain County News,* 10 April 1867, p. 3).

[32]Here Matson had written the word "it," but Finney changed it to "we."

[33]Finney is referring to a rule governing the admission of students to the college that mainly forbade membership of college fraternities but by its wording included all secret societies. See William E. Bigglestone, *Oberlin: From War to Jubilee, 1866–1883* (Oberlin: Grady, 1983), p. 48.

[34]Early in February 1867 it was noted that the Masons had formed a lodge in Oberlin and had acquired premises. They began to use their new hall at the end of March. Up until that time the Masons had mainly met in Elyria. See *The Lorain County News,* 6 February 1867, p. 3; and 3 April 1867, p. 3.

[35]David Bernard, *Light on Masonry: a collection of all the most important documents on the subject of speculative free masonry: embracing the reports of the Western committees in relation to the abduction of William Morgan . . . with all the degrees of the order conferred in a master's lodge, as written by Captain William Morgan; . . .* (Utica: Williams, 1829). According to James J. Tyler, William L. Cummings, in his "Bibliography of Anti-Masonry," published in *Nocalore,* 4, no. 1 (1934): 49–50, refers to this book: "Five editions were printed in 1829. The 18th edition, with an alleged exposure of Odd Fellowship was published at Dayton, Ohio, in 1878. This book may well be termed, 'The Bible of the Anti-Masons,' most of the works against Masonry published since being largely reprints from Bernard's book." See James J. Tyler, "The Last Crusade of Rev. Charles G. Finney," in *1950 Proceedings of the M. W. Grand Lodge of . . . Free and Accepted Masons of the state of Ohio* (n.p., n.d.), appendix, p. 170.

to have the subject brought into the church, or anything said about it. The young man informed me that he had read the book, but I had no opportunity to converse with him with regard to the impression it made on his mind. But I felt it could not be possible that after reading that book through he would feel as if he could attend a lodge any more.

Soon after another young man proposed himself for church membership, who was a member of the lodge. It was objected to by several members of the church, and consequently he could not be received. The same occurred at about the same time at the Second church. Some one or more members of the lodge proposed to unite with that church, and they took the same action that the First Church did. A minority voted against it, when, according to Congregational |usage they could not be MS 1037 received. But this forced the question of Masonry upon the churches. It was found on inquiry that there were a few in each church who had been Masons when they were young, but for many years had paid no attention to it, and did not approve their establishing a lodge in this place. The churches felt no inclination to meddle with this class of persons. As they had ceased to have any fellowship or to co-operate with Masons, nothing was said or thought of, so far as I know, in the churches about taking any action in respect to them.[36] But the question was, What should we do in regard to receiving new members that were Masons,—I mean, that were *active, adhering, co-operating Masons* at the *present time.*[37] Committees were appointed in both churches to examine the subject, and make report to the churches as to the nature and tendencies of Masonry.[38]

Professor Morgan was the chairman of the Committee in the First church, and Professor Dascomb and Brother Jabez Burrell were the other members of the Committee.[39] Various causes hindered |their MS 1038

[36]In a letter to Rev. A. Ritchie, the corresponding secretary of the Western Tract and Book Society, Finney wrote:

> When we began the discussion of the subject we found to our surprise that we had three Royal Arch masons in our church. One of them went over to the Episcopalians without asking for a letter. Another, did not deny having taken the oath belonging to that degree, but denied its obligation. The third denies that he ever took the oath & affirms that any man who would adhere to that oath or to the oath of the master's degree, should be excluded from the church (Finney to A. Ritchie, 10 November 1868, Finney Papers, microfilm, roll 5).

[37]The underlining here appears to have been added by Finney.

[38]This was in the summer of 1867. The two churches initially formed a joint committee. See *The Lorain County News,* 23 October 1867, p. 2.

[39]James Dascomb (1808–1880) was the professor of chemistry, physiology, and botany at Oberlin College. A graduate of medicine from Dartmouth College in 1833, he went the next year as one of the first teachers at the newly formed Oberlin Collegiate Institute. He also acted as the first physician in the colony. He was considered to have been a stable, level-headed, and conservative influence during the fervent radicalism of the early years in Oberlin. Many improvements to the village were due to his thoughtfulness, and First Church was built under his supervision. He resigned his professorship in 1878. See James H. Fairchild, "Prof. James Dascomb," *Oberlin Review,* 22 April 1880, pp. 195–97; Elton S. Cook, "Dr. James Dascomb," *Journal of Chemical Education* 12 (March 1935): 111–14.

Jabez Lyman Burrell (1806–1900) was an Oberlin resident and a deacon of the First Church. Originally from Sheffield, Massachusetts, he lived in Sheffield, Ohio, until he moved to Oberlin in 1845. He had intended to enter the ministry and had studied under John J. Shipherd in Elyria,

making a report immediately. The difficulty of getting the books that were necessary to a thorough examination of the subject, the want of time and the health of Brother Morgan, and the great labors of the Committee in other directions delayed their making a report until after the Commencement.[40] Just at the time when I wanted to make special efforts for a revival, during the fall term as usual, this question was thrown upon the churches for discussion. The committees of both churches reported strongly against Masonry as an institution, as immoral in its nature and tendency. Meetings were appointed for discussion; and some of the brethren who had been Masons wished an opportunity to reply to the report made by the Committee in the First Church, and such an opportunity was given to them to their satisfaction. They said what they could, some of them, in justification of Masonry; or rather, represented what they regarded as its best side. However, with the exception of the few Masons that were in the church nobody seemed MS 1039 at all inclined to justify Masonry,—if indeed the |Masons did themselves; for I believe they all declared that spoke, that they did not wish to justify it, or defend it, but simply to justify themselves in holding the relation to it that they did.

As I said the churches—that is the two Congregational churches—with very few exceptions, and those, persons that had belonged to the fraternity, condemned the institution as immoral in its nature and tendency, and dangerous to government and to society. Both churches held meetings for discussion weekly, or oftener, through the fall term; consequently but little was done for the direct promotion of a revival of religion.[41] However, conversions were occurring from week to week,

but his health was poor and he went into business. He was one of the first trustees of Oberlin College and a considerable benefactor, giving his large house in Sheffield to be used as a branch of the manual labor school and later giving the house he had built in Oberlin to the college along with coal lands in Illinois. About the time of the Masonic discussions he went into the Aurora Oil business (obituary in *The Oberlin News*, 26 January 1900, p. 1; Alumni Records, file 28/3, box 10, Oberlin College Archives; and *The Lorain County News,* 27 November 1867, p. 3).

As well as being the professor of biblical literature in the college, John Morgan was assistant pastor to Finney in the church. He was asked by First Church "to prepare a somewhat exhaustive essay" on the subject of secret societies and to present it before them.

> This essay was very decided in its tone against the principle of secret association, in general, but strong against masonry in particular on account of its "blasphemous oaths, its puerile ceremonies, and its murderous history."
>
> The essay elicited much discussion, and finally Pres. Finney, Senior pastor of the church, appointed a Sabbath in which to discuss the moral and spiritual aspect of the whole subject (*The Lorain County News,* 23 October 1867, p. 2).

[40]Commencement was on Wednesday, 28 August. The joint committees initially advised the churches that the applicants who were Masons should be admitted to church membership, but they "took the ground that masonry was unfavorable, though not necessarily fatal to piety." This was then put to the churches for discussion. But the churches were unable to accept this proposal, and it was referred back with the proposed amendments to the joint committee, which was unable to come to agreement. The two committees therefore put separate proposals to their churches. The First Church committee finally presented its proposals on 20 November. The committee members at that time were George Clark, James Dascomb, and Jabez W. Merrill (*The Lorain County News,* 23 October 1867, p. 2; and 8 January 1868, p. 2).

[41]Toward the end of October 1867 "a very encouraging state of religious feeling" was being reported. It was noted in the local paper on 23 October: "The prospect now is that the Masonic question will be superceded by a revival. Pres. Finney's sermon on Sunday was a powerful one

and have been all through the fall term and until this time, January 1868.›[42]

The great question in these churches upon which there was a difference of opinion, was *not* whether Masonry was an evil thing; nor was it whether intelligent, adhering, and active Masons *ought* to be *received* to our churches. But it was this: ‹Is› it wise to *say so.*[43] Was it wise to have a *rule excluding them from fellowship*, when, after taking so much time and ˡexpending so much labor as to develop their views th[or]oughly[44] and ascertain that they were truly and intelligently adhering Masons, persons that justified the institution understanding what it is, and avowed their determination to co-operate with it understanding the tendency of such co-operation—whether it was wise to say *beforehand* that in view of these considerations they should not be received. I believe it was agreed on all hands that they *would not be received* by the churches, in any case where these facts were ascertained. And the discussion for several weeks hung upon that point,—whether it was best to say that under such circumstances we should not receive them; or whether it was best *not* to say it, but *do* it, as the several cases came up. MS 1040

Those that were in favor of such a rule gave as a reason, among others, for wishing to have the rule, that without such a rule the question would be thrown right back upon the church for discussion again, should any one present himself for membership, and a minority should oppose his uniting with the church. It would then bring the question right back ˡupon[45] the church for discussion, as it had been at this time. For myself I was not able to attend their discussions;[46] and if I had been able, I should not have been willing to have gone into the discussions, taking one side or the other. I felt it my duty, however, as pastor of the church, from time to time, when I found that they lacked instruction on some particular points, to preach to them and give them the instructions that I supposed they needed. I have reason to believe that these sermons settled many minds.[47] I gave no opinion, however, MS 1042

and large numbers 'came forward' in response to his invitation." However, two months later it was reported under the heading "Masonry Again": "Extra meetings have been held in both Congregational Churches every week, and sometimes twice a week, for nearly two months." See *The Independent* (New York), 31 October 1867, p. 4; *The Lorain County News,* 23 October 1867, p. 3; and 25 December 1867, p. 2.

[42]Finney added the date "1868."

[43]Here Matson had written down, "Was it wise to say so." Finney altered it to read, "Is it wise to *say so.*" The word "say" was underlined twice.

[44]This word is spelled "thoughly" in the manuscript.

[45]MS 1042 was numbered incorrectly by Finney. Pages 1042–50 were originally numbered 880–88 and renumbered 1012–20 by Matson. Finney changed them to 1042–50.

[46]The local paper noted in the middle of December, "Pres. Finney has been unable to preach to his congregation for a few Sabbaths by reason of illness. Last Sabbath afternoon however he once more made his appearance in the pulpit and preached with unabated power" (*The Lorain County News,* 18 December 1867, p. 3).

[47]On 6 October, after there had been considerable discussion, Finney preached to his congregation both morning and afternoon on the subject.

> The conclusion he arrived at was the same as that of Prof. Morgan, and there is no doubt that he carried the minds of the great mass of his hearers with him. Let it be

until the last time that I preached, upon the question of passing the rule to which I have referred. I then stated my preference for the rule, and gave my reasons.

The Second Church on the Friday previous to my preaching for the last time on the subject, had passed a final rule, excluding, as I understood it, from church fellowship any that might apply, who, after due labor being bestowed and time taken to enlighten them, still adhered to the institution.[48] |I recommended to the First church to concur in this resolution; or to pass one of similar import, which they had already before them. They did so on the next Tuesday.[49] But the week after the Second Church rescinded their last resolution, considering it after all unwise to have such a rule on the subject.[50] ‹A large minority protested against the repeal.›[51] It should be understood, however, by all persons here and elsewhere who take any interest in the matter, that Christian people here, with very few exceptions, are entirely opposed to Masonry as a vile and evil institution. The substance of their convictions are expressed in their resolutions; and it should be understood that on all the resolutions except the last—I mean the one excluding from membership intelligent and adhering Masons—the people are nearly a unit. Perhaps it will be thought—if any should ever read this—that that was a trifling distinction upon which so much time

MS 1043

> known that the whole subject was approached and discussed in the kindest spirit with many cautions to the people against uncharitableness and harsh judgments (*The Lorain County News,* 23 October 1867, p. 2).

After his illness Finney spent another whole day, Sunday, 22 December, preaching on the subject. See *The Lorain County News,* 25 December 1867, p. 2.

[48]The Second Church held a meeting on Thursday, 26 December, and the next day *The Lorain County News* published an extra giving the results of the meeting. It consisted of "prefatory remarks," expressing opposition to Masonry, and five resolutions. The first four resolutions laid down the conditions for church membership and the procedures to be taken in examining candidates. The fifth resolution reads:

> If, after due time has been taken to enlighten the candidate, and develop his views and spirit, he seems at heart to endorse the Institution, and with an intelligent apprehension of the nature of Masonry, persistently adheres to it, we hold that he cannot in the nature of the case give the requisite evidence of present piety, and cannot be admitted to church fellowship (*The Lorain County News,* 1 January 1868, p. 2).

See also *Extra*, 27 December 1867 (copy in Miscellaneous Items, Finney Papers, microfilm, roll 8).

[49]The resolution they already had before them, put forward by their committee on 20 November, reads:

> That in receiving members, if any candidate be connected with this Secret Organization, we will in the spirit of Christ use all hopeful endeavors to convince him of his error; but if, after such labor, he shall decide to continue *active* connection with it, we will regret his decision, but cannot "bid him God-speed" by giving him the right hand of fellowship and entering into covenant with him (*The Lorain County News,* 8 January 1868, p. 2).

It was passed at a meeting of the First Church on Tuesday, 31 December, by 180 votes to 97. See D. L. Leonard, *The Story of Oberlin* (Boston: Pilgrim, 1898), p. 210.

[50]It was at a meeting of the Second Church on Monday, 6 January 1868, that the fifth resolution was repealed "because it had been widely misinterpreted and was not necessary to a clear exposition of the convictions of the majority." This was at the instigation of James Fairchild and his brother, Henry, who were against rigidly excluding Masons (*The Lorain County News,* 8 January 1868, p. 3; and Bigglestone, *Oberlin*, p. 49).

[51]Finney added this sentence.

was spent. I regarded it as such myself; and said repeatedly to individuals, I cared but little whether they had such a rule or not. Provided the action of the church was right, it mattered but little, in ˡmy estimation, whether they rejected them under a rule, or without a rule. But on mature deliberation, after seeing how the matter stood, and the many reasons for having the rule, my mind came to the conclusion that to have such a rule might save us a great deal of discussion and trouble in the future; and that it was best to say what we really meant, that freemasons might know beforehand, that if they *intended at all events to adhere* to the institution they need not make application for admission to the church. I thought it upon the whole unwise to leave the matter in such a shape that they might hope to get into the church although they were resolved to adhere to the institution, make an effort to do so, and finally find that the church would not receive them. I thought it would be better to let it be known beforehand that the church could not receive them after ascertaining that they were intelligent, adhering Masons. MS 1044

That to say so beforehand would avoid being reproached with any appearance of insincerity in leaving our action in such a way as to encourage Masons to offer ˡthemselves, when in fact we did not mean to receive them if they were intelligent, adhering Masons. My former connection with a Masonic lodge, and my reading on the subject since I withdrew from them, enabled me to supply in a great measure, in my sermons, the place of the books in which Masonry had been revealed. But few such books could be found, as a great deal of pains have been taken, as is well-known, to destroy those books.[52] MS 1045

Soon after I was twenty one years old, being at school in Connecticut, an old uncle advised me to become a Mason.[53] I did so, and took the first three degrees of the Order.[54] Although at the time I regarded the ceremony as silly; still there was nothing that struck me as particularly immoral until I took the oath in the Master's degree, in which "I promised to keep a brother Master Mason's secrets when committed to me as such, inviolate, murder and treason alone excepted, and those left to my freewill and accord." That promise I knew to be improper and dangerous. ˡBut still I had no religion, and was extremely ignorant of the truths of religion. On my going to study law, in Adams, Jefferson County, I joined the lodge there, and became Secretary of the lodge.[55] I MS 1046

[52]One of the books preserved in the Oberlin College Library that bears Finney's signature on the title page is John G. Stearns, *An Inquiry into the Nature and Tendency of Speculative Freemasonry,* 6th ed. (Utica: Seward and Thurber, 1858).

[53]This was Cyrus Finney (1771–1840), the youngest brother of Finney's father, who lived in Warren, Connecticut. Finney lived on his farm while he attended the Warren Academy. See Howard Finney, *Finney-Phinney Families in America* (Richmond, Va.: Byrd, 1957), pp. 44–45; and p. 6 n. 22 (MS 9).

[54]Finney joined the Meridian Sun Lodge No. 32, in Warren. He took the first degree of Entered Apprentice on 26 February 1816, and the degrees of Fellow Craft and Master Mason on 6 March 1816. See Tyler, "Last Crusade," p. 164.

[55]The lodge in Adams was the Rising Sun Lodge, No. 125. His first visit there was on 18 June 1818. He visited occasionally until 24 February 1820, when he was made "Secretary, *pro tem,*"

took no more degrees, but continued in an active relation to the lodge until I was converted to Christ. During the period of my conviction I do not know that I so much as thought of Freemasonry, my mind was so much taken up with making my peace with God. However, soon after I was converted the time came around for attendance upon the lodge.[56] But the ceremonies distressed me. I found to my surprize that I could have no fellowship with them at all. All their oaths and proceedings appeared to me to savor so much of profanity, that my new nature

MS 1047 **recoiled from them, and could have no fellowship with them. |I retired distressed, and felt as if I had been in an atmosphere not congenial with my spiritual life. I laid the question before God in prayer, ‹& after a severe struggle›[57] I requested a dismission from the lodge, informing them that I could not conscientiously continue my membership with them. With manifest reluctance they ‹finally› gave me an honorable discharge.[58] This created some excitement about the institution in the**

and after that attended regularly. On 14 December 1820 he was admitted to membership of the lodge by ballot and was also elected secretary. In December 1821 he handed over his role as secretary to Charles C. Sears, whom he had introduced to the lodge. Information from the lodge minute books, which are in Finney's handwriting during the time he was secretary, is given in Tyler, "Last Crusade," p. 164; and "Mr. Finney—His Misstatements—His Masonic History from the Records," *The National and Freemason* (New York), 20 June 1868, p. 394.

[56]The following section was written down after this by Matson: "I went in as usual. The Master of the lodge was a skeptic, and asked me to open the lodge with prayer, instead of opening it himself, as he usually had done. I did so. I both opened and closed the lodge that night with prayer, at his request." Finney crossed out this section and made some alterations later on, probably as the result of an editorial that appeared in *The National and Freemason* in June 1868. The editorial was written in response to the first of a series of articles on Freemasonry, which were being written by Finney for *The Independent*. In the first article Finney had given a similar account of his involvement in Freemasonry as he had written here. The editor of *The National and Freemason*, however, referring to the records of the lodge at Adams, disputed Finney's details of how often he had attended and who the master of the lodge was. This led Finney to write to Samuel Bond in Adams for help to substantiate his account. In reference to a quotation from the editorial, Finney wrote to Bond:

> At the time I was converted Eliphalet Edmonds a notorious Deist was master of the Lodge. Benj. Wright, I believe, after he was converted was master of the Lodge & after he became an elder, but of this I am not certain. In my first article I state to the best of my recollection of course, that I attended the Lodge but twice after my conversion. This quotation represents me as attending three times, Jan. 3d 1822, June 10th 1822 & Oct. 30th 1823. [In fact, it also states he was present on 10 January 1822.] He says I was discharged at my own request May 6th 1824. Now I cannot recollect attending Lodge but twice, after my conversion, and my impression was that they were both soon after my conversion [which was on 10 October 1821]. If my memory is not at fault, I requested a dismission at my second attendance. My discharge may not have been made out & delivered to me until the 6th of May when I was about to leave town. . . . I may be mistaken in regard to the number of times I attended Lodge before I finally got my discharge (Finney to Samuel Bond, 30 June 1868, copy in Mrs. Rebecca Finney's handwriting, Finney Papers, microfilm, roll 5).

When Finney came later to revise his articles in *The Independent* for republication in book form, he added: "At this distance of time I can not be certain whether the deist to whom I refer, Eliphalet Edmunds, was Master of the lodge when I first joined. My best recollection is that Captain Goodell was Master when I first joined the lodge at Adams, and that Judge Edmunds was Master at the time of my conversion to Christ" (Finney, *The Character Claims, and Practical Workings of Freemasonry* [Cincinnati: Western Tract and Book Society, 1869], pp. v–vi).

[57]Matson had started this sentence, "I then laid the question before God in prayer, and at the next meeting of the lodge," but Finney altered it.

[58]Finney added the word "finally." His discharge, signed by George Andrus, secretary of the

place at the time. And I have always supposed with design to keep me in such relation to the institution as they desired, they got up a Masonic celebration and proposed to me to deliver an oration on the occasion. I decidedly declined to do so, informing those that presented the request that I could not conscientiously do it.[59] However, I remained silent; and nobody out of that place, wherever I went, I presume, suspected that I had ever been a freemason. I did not suppose at that time that I should ever be called upon to bear any public testimony against it. But not many years later William Morgan published his book, ¹in which he faithfully revealed the secrets of Masonry ‹as far as I had knowledge of it›.[60] This, as is well-known, resulted in his murder.[61] Other publications to the same effect immediately followed, and Masonry was no longer a secret, but all its interior was thoroughly laid open to the public. When I was questioned whether that was a true revelation of Masonry, I unhesitantly said, "Yes; so far as I have been, it is a faithful representation of it." I did not consider myself under the least obligation any longer to try to keep a thing secret which was open to the gaze of all the world. It was no longer a secret. I could not deny that Masonry was thoroughly revealed without telling a falsehood, without deliberately lying. I could not even set up the pretence that it was not revealed, or appear to disbelieve that it was truly revealed, without equivocation and lying. Furthermore, consideration and farther light upon the subject had convinced me that it was my *duty* to cast off such MS 1048

lodge, quotes the minutes of 6 May: "On motion, voted that Br. Charles G. Finney be honorably discharged from this Lodge, pursuant to his request" (State of New York, Rising Sun Lodge No. 125 to Finney, 7 May 1824, Finney Papers, microfilm, roll 1).

[59]The editor of *The National and Freemason* questioned whether there had ever been any such celebration, as it was not recorded in the minutes of the lodge. But Finney wrote to Samuel Bond:

> I don't know whether there is any record of this, but I do know that a celebration was held, that I was requested to be the speaker on the occasion; that I declined & that Abner Morton delivered the oration & that he read it to me in the room I then occupied in Mr. Morton's old store, before he delivered it. I did not attend the meeting. Do none of you remember this? (Finney to Bond, 30 June 1868, Finney Papers, microfilm, roll 5).

[60]Finney added the words "as far as I had knowledge of it." This book by William Morgan was *Illustrations of Masonry, by one of the fraternity, who has devoted thirty years to the subject* (Batavia, New York: Miller, 1826). It was reissued in many editions and was widely copied in anti-Masonic literature.

[61]William Morgan (?1774–?1826) was a stonemason living in Batavia, New York, when he disappeared in 1826. His exposure of Freemasonry was about to be published when he was abducted by Masons and allegedly murdered. No proof of his murder was ever completely established, but his disappearance, and the subsequent court cases, together with a whole series of other incidents and cover-ups, brought Masonry into considerable disrepute. The prevalence of Masonry that came to light among civil and political leaders soon caused a significant political stir, and a movement to abolish the institution gained considerable popular support. Thousands of Masons seceded and many lodges were closed, and there was such a decline in Masonic activity that Finney thought: "Forty years ago, we supposed that it was dead, and had no idea that it could ever revive. But, strange to tell, while we were busy in getting rid of slavery, Freemasonry has revived, and extended its bounds most alarmingly" (Finney, "Freemasonry.—I," *The Independent,* 9 April 1868, p. 1; Ronald P. Formisano and Kathleen S. Kutolowski, "Antimasonry and Masonry: The Genesis of a Protest, 1826–1827," *American Quarterly* 29 [Summer 1977]: 139–65; and *DAB*).

profane oaths, that I had been induced to take by fraud, being told that MS 1049 there would be nothing in my oaths that ˡwould be inconsistent with my obligations to God or man, or in other words, that would be inconsistent with my religious or civil obligations. Furthermore, I considered it immoral in me to allow myself to be still under Masonic obligation to do many things which Masons promise and swear to do.

The revelations made of the nature and tendency of Masonry in connection with Morgan's publication and consequent murder, had shown that the institution was eminently dangerous to civil government; and finally the history of Masonry, as it now stands before the world, is such as to convince me of the utter incompatibility of intelligent freemasonry with the Christian religion.

I should say that although our discussions on Masonry have been exciting, still in general a Christian spirit has prevailed; and in the First church, as I am informed, particularly, the closing debate and final vote were conducted in an excellent spirit. I trust that nothing has occurred that will produce any permanent jar and division amongst us.

MS 1050 **ˡWe have from the first had very frequent discussions on many points, oftentimes protracted discussions, and discussions in which, at their close, we were not all agreed. But we adopted the principle of accepting, so far as our action was concerned, the decision of the majority; and the minority has acquiesced so far as to raise no opposition to the judgment and action of the majority. We have supposed that anything inconsistent with this was revolutionary, and if carried out would create endless divisions. I trust that in this case the same course will be taken, and that no evil will result. We could not avoid the discussion; and upon the whole, as to the great question of the nature and tendency of Masonry, we are a unit.**[62] Thus I have brought my

[62]The agitation at Oberlin coincided with a wider movement beginning to be felt in the country. On 31 October and 1 November 1867 a convention was held at Aurora, Illinois, organized by Jonathan Blanchard, president of Wheaton College, to launch a campaign against secret societies. There the National Christian Association came into being and a national convention was planned for the next spring, Oberlin being suggested as the venue. Blanchard himself was in Oberlin on Sunday, 15 December, and spoke in both Congregational churches. "Fresh from the Aurora Convention it is not surprising that he handled a controverted subject without gloves" (*The Lorain County News,* 18 December 1867, p. 3; J. Blanchard, "The Aurora Christian Convention," *The Independent,* 21 November 1867, p. 1; and Clarence N. Roberts, "The Crusade Against Secret Societies," *Journal of the Illinois State Historical Society* 64 [Winter 1971]: 383–84).

The convention the next May was in fact held in Pittsburgh, and John Morgan and Jabez Burrell were two of the five delegates from the First Church in Oberlin. J. H. Fairchild was one of three delegates from the Second Church, and he gave one of the main addresses. See *The Lorain County News,* 22 April 1868, p. 3; and 6 May 1868, p. 3; and *The Independent,* 28 May 1868, p. 6. By this time *The Independent* had begun to publish a series of articles by Finney on Freemasonry. Beginning on 9 April 1868, twelve numbers had appeared by 2 July. Being allowed no more space by the editor, Finney revised the articles, added another eight numbers, and they were republished early the next year as *Character Claims, and Practical Writings of Freemasonry.* These articles revealed an enormous interest in the subject. Finney started receiving dozens of letters from all over the country, many of them requests for anti-Masonic literature. More than two hundred letters relating to Masonry are in the Finney Papers.

Finney and the Oberlin community continued to be actively involved in the campaign, and in 1872 the annual meeting of the National Christian Association was held in Oberlin. Finney's

revival narrative **up** to this time, the 13th of Jan. 1868. Yesterday, Sabbath **Jan. 12th**, we had a very solemn day in the First church. I preached all day upon resisting the Holy Ghost. At the close of the afternoon service **first** I called upon all professors of religion who were willing to commit themselves against all resistance offered to the teachings ˡof[63] the Holy Spirit, to rise up and unite with us in prayer under the solemnity of this promise. Nearly all the professors of religion, **I should think,** rose up without hesitation. I then called upon those that were not converted to rise up, and take the same stand. I had been endeavoring to show **that they had *always* been resisting the Holy Ghost**; that they were stiff-necked and uncircumcised in heart and ears, and had always resisted the Holy Ghost. I asked those of them who were willing **then and there** to pledge themselves to do this no more, and to accept the teachings of the Holy Spirit and give themselves ˡto Christ, also to rise up, and we would make them subjects of prayer. So far as I could see from the pulpit, nearly every person in the house stood up under these calls. We then had a very solemn season of prayer, and dismissed the meeting.[64]

MS 1052 [1]

JHF 476

In regard to my revival record, which for the present at least I must leave here, I would say, that I have recorded only a few of the interesting and striking things which I remember to have ˡoccurred[65] in the *principal* revivals in which I have labored. I have written under the fear of being too full in my narrative, and of making too large a book. I have said but little of the opposition that has been offered to those revivals; and should have said nothing had it not been for the desire I have to rectify the impression that has so extensively prevailed, that

MS 1052 [2]

writings were extensively used, and his zeal for the cause contributed greatly to the crusade, but because of his health he was unable to be more actively involved. After his death in 1875 the movement began to lose its appeal, and much of the crusading energy was taken up in the temperance movement and the antisaloon war. See Bigglestone, *Oberlin*, p. 51; and Charles C. Cole, "Finney's Fight Against the Masons," *Ohio State Archaeological and Historical Quarterly* 59, no. 3 (1950): 270–86.

[63] MS 1052 was numbered 889 and renumbered 1021 by Matson. In error, Finney changed it to 1052.

[64] This ends the published version. Fairchild crossed out the remainder of this page.

On 8 January, under the heading "A Truce," the local paper reported: "By common consent the question of Masonry is to be dropped in the Oberlin churches for the present, that the gospel may receive some attention, at least on the Sabbath" (*The Lorain County News,* 8 January 1868, p. 2). And on 16 January there was a notice in the New York *Independent*: "A good degree of religious interest exists in the college, and upward of thirty students have been hopefully converted." But soon after this Finney was ill again and took to his bed. It was Sunday, 1 March, before he was again in the pulpit (16 January 1868, p. 5; and 19 March 1868, p. 4; and Finney to E. P. Marvin, 5 February 1868, Finney Papers, file 2/2/2, box 9).

During April there was considerably increased revival activity in Oberlin, with the young people's meeting having to be transferred from First Church chapel to the college chapel because of the large numbers attending. This revival was part of a widespread movement throughout the United States. Accounts of local revivals had started to become more numerous in the religious press earlier in the year, and by the third week of March *The Independent*, which gave details weekly of the numbers of conversions being reported, announced: "Our exchange papers report more than 14,000 conversions" (26 March 1868, p. 4). The level of activity kept up through April, but by the middle of May it was noted that there was "some falling off in the number of revivals" (21 May 1868, p. 4). The revival similarly declined in Oberlin until the next fall.

[65] MS 1052 [2] was numbered 890 and renumbered 1022 by Matson and then changed to 1052 by Finney. The fraction ½ was added in pencil, apparently by Lewis Tappan. This page was edited by Fairchild but was omitted from the published version.

there have been great disorders connected with the revivals in which I have labored. I have wished to have it understood that that impression is erroneous; and have aimed to give a few hints only in relation to the source of this erroneous impression. I should not have mentioned Dr Beecher ‹&›[66] Brother Nettleton as ever having arrayed themselves against the revival in central New York, but for the fact that their letters in opposition to it have been made public. *They were deceived.* That everybody knows who shared in those revivals, and was well-acquainted with the facts. In the neighborhood where those revivals occurred, there were |always[67] some who were ready to listen to false reports and give them publicity. However, I wish it distinctly understood, I say again, that I have said nothing of the opposition that those revivals encountered, more than I have deemed necessary to do away the false impression respecting them to which I have so often alluded. And here I wish to say at the conclusion of my record, that I have seen none of the evils which have been complained of. I have never witnessed those disastrous reactions, nor do I know where they have occurred. I have never known that those churches where those revivals occurred have "wept tears of blood," or any other tears, over any disastrous reaction that came over them.[68] A few cases occurred where those revivals resulted in division. In Auburn, for instance, as I have related, a number of leading men in Dr Lansing's congregation went off and formed a new congregation.[69] But Dr Lansing stood firm in his place; and never was so much beloved, I venture to say, by his people |‹as[70] after that revival.

MS 1053

MS 1054

Br. Gilletts church in Rome New York as I have said was afterwards divided into two.[71] That was owing in part, no doubt, to the fact that their meeting house was too small & old fashioned to well accommodate the greatly enlarged church & congregation, & partly to the fact that Br. Gillett was an old man, his sermons, as he said to me which were the product of his whole ministry, were none of them suited to the new order of things in his congregation. There were many of his people who felt solemnly impressed with the necessity of having a younger man to lead on the converts & the much altered state of society to more advanced ground than could be expected of a man of B[r.][72] Gilletts age. In the great revival Br. Gillett proved himself to be a noble Christian man & minister, & had as I beli[e]ve the confidence & affection of his people in an eminent degree. With all the reasons for the division I am not acquainted.[73]

[66]Here Matson had written "or," but Finney changed it to an ampersand.

[67]MS 1053 was numbered 891 and renumbered 1023 by Matson. Finney changed it to 1053.

[68]See MS 965.

[69]See MS 390–91.

[70]MS 1054 is the first of two pages in Finney's handwriting added in December 1868 that replace a previous ending to the manuscript. They were not altered by Fairchild but were omitted from the published edition.

[71]See MS 928–29.

[72]The manuscript is torn at this point.

[73]On 12 January 1831, Maria Roberts had written to Mrs. Finney from Rome:

In some few instances I have known divisions to arise because the pastor did not so enter into the work as to secure & retain the confidence of his people. They were led to feel that he would not follow up the work that had been wrough[t] so as to secure the best results. But this has been my experience as a whole, after I have labored both as an Evangelist & as Pastor for more than ¦forty five years. I have observed that uniformly where pastors have gone into revival work with honest earnestness & have cordially & without jealousy cooperated with an evangelist the revival has greatly strengthened his hands & increased his influence in his Church & congregation. At this date Dec. 1868, I would add that we have had a precious revival as usual during our fall Term. Our students are now just gone home, & many to their winter teaching during our winter vacation. Our church is in an interesting state & many seem to be struggling not only for a higher personal experience but for the conversion of the residue of the unconverted amongst us.›[74]

MS 1055

After the services of a very solemn and eventful day (on account of a case of discipline which has excited much interest, also the division of our Church,) I sit down to tell you something relative to our condition as a people. this day after much deliberation our Church has been divided, and we have been publicly set apart, organized as a Church and received by the Presbytery. between eighty and ninety have thus voluntarily dedicated themselves anew to God. it was indeed a very solemn day. we are now but a little band of brothers and sisters, and are almost as sheep without a shepherd, but we trust the Lord in his good providence will send us one to break unto us the bread of life, and to feed this little flock. . . . Our former dear Pastor had relapsed into his Old School views and feelings, and you will readily perceive that we could not walk together because we were not agreed. some individuals felt that something more *must* be done for the advancement of the Redeemers kingdom. most of the members of the Presbytery advised to it, viz. Messrs Frost, Gale, Aikin, Lansing, Coe, Butts, Merrick, Burrett, Foote, etc etc. the division was made with pretty general unity of feeling with the exception of two or three families. we feel that we have a great work before us (Maria Roberts to Lydia Finney, 12 January 1831, Finney Papers, microfilm, roll 2).

[74] In mid-November the local paper had reported:

There has been a steadily increasing religious interest in the several churches and prayer meetings for some weeks past. . . . Last Sabbath the interest culminated in a remarkable manner. Mr. Finney preached from the text, "Come unto me all ye that labor," a most tender and rich invitation, and the response was immediate and wonderful. Some three hundred or more came forward for prayers, filling all the body slips far back under the galleries. . . . In the evening a large number gathered at the inquiry meeting and confirmed their resolutions and consecrations. We have to regret that the Churches were not awake earlier in the term to give the work greater scope, and to give time for a more perfect establishment of the new converts. Prayer and labor are now directed to this end and especially to the spreading of the work through every part of this place (*The Lorain County News,* 18 November 1868, p. 3).

Conclusion to the First Edition

Those who have read the preceding pages, will naturally inquire in reference to the closing years of a life so full of labor and of usefulness. The narrative, completed with the beginning of 1868, leaves Mr. Finney still pastor of the First church in Oberlin, and lecturer in the seminary. The responsibilities of pastor he continued to sustain, with the help of his associate, some four or five years longer, preaching, as his health would admit, usually once each Sabbath. At the same time, as professor of Pastoral Theology, he gave a course of lectures each summer term, on the pastoral work, on Christian experience, or on revivals. He resigned the pastorate in 1872, but still retained his connection with the seminary, and completed his last course of lectures in July 1875, only a few days before his death. He preached, from time to time, as his strength permitted; and during the last month of his life, he preached one Sabbath morning in the First church, and another in the Second.

Notwithstanding the abundant and exhausting labors of his long public life, the burden of years seemed to rest lightly upon him. He still stood erect, as a young man, retained his faculties to a remarkable degree, and exhibited to the end the quickness of thought, and feeling, and imagination, which always characterized him. His life and character perhaps never seemed richer in the fruits and the beauty of goodness, than in these closing years and months. His public labors were of course very limited, but the quiet power of his life was felt as a benediction upon the community, which, during forty years, he had done so much to guide and mold and bless.

His last day on earth was a quiet Sabbath, which he enjoyed in the midst of his family, walking out with his wife at sunset, to listen to the music, at the opening of the evening service in the church near by. Upon retiring he was seized with pains which seemed to indicate some affection of the heart; and after a few hours of suffering, as the morning dawned, he died, August 16th, 1875, lacking two weeks of having completed his eighty-third year.

The foregoing narrative gives him chiefly in one line of his work, and one view of his character. It presents him in the ruling purpose, and even passion of his life, as an evangelist, a preacher of righteousness. His work as a theologian, a leader of thought, in the development and expression of a true Christian philosophy, and as an instructor, in quickening and forming the thought of others, has been less conspicuous, and in his own view doubtless entirely subordinate; but in the view of many, scarcely less fruitful of good to the church and the world. To set forth the results of his life in these respects, would require another volume, which will probably never be written; but other generations will reap the benefits, without knowing the source whence they have sprung.

THE END.

I apprehend that we have not a hundredth part of
Mr. Finney's wondrous life in his wondrous book.

Rev. Charles C. Foote
in *Reminiscences of Charles G. Finney*
(Oberlin: Goodrich, 1876), p. 52.

Appendix

The following is the text of the pamphlet referred to by Finney in MS 875–76.

Valedictory Services and Farewell Sermon of Professor Finney,
of the Oberlin Institute, United States.
With Critical Observations on His Preaching.

by
John Campbell, D.D.

London: John Snow, 35, Paternoster-Row, 1851

PREFACE.

There is always something due to the instruments of eminent usefulness in the cause of God. To honour the servant is, in effect, to honour the Master. Among such instruments a very high place is due to the Rev. C. G. Finney, who has left behind him, in England, an impression such as was never made by any other American among the British Churches. The visit of the celebrated Dr. Mason was memorable in the circles of genius; British Biography has accorded to that most eloquent man a niche in her temple in connection with the record of the life of one of her most illustrious sons; but we have yet to learn that Dr. Mason was the means of turning even one soul to God. In his case attention was fixed on himself rather than on his Master. It is, however, but justice to say, that Dr. Mason came not to the Mother Country for the purpose of labour but of repose, that he might recover the health he had lost in the work of his Master. It was otherwise with Mr. Finney, who came with the express purpose of sounding the Gospel trumpet, that he might both animate the living and quicken the dead; and, we presume, he is the first American minister that ever visited England solely with that view,—unless an exception must be made for that amiable, and, in his way, celebrated enthusiast, Lorenzo Doe. The just and beautiful conception of Burke, relative to Howard and his philanthropic pilgrimages, is most strikingly applicable to Finney. The great Orator said of the former, "He visited all Europe and the East, not to survey the sumptuousness of palaces, or the stateliness of temples; not to make accurate measurements of the remains of ancient grandeur, nor to form a scale of the curiosity of modern art; not to collect medals, or to collate manuscripts:" so may we say of Mr. Finney; he came not for these things, but to point lost men to the Cross of Christ. He has left London with little more knowledge of it than he possessed on his arrival.

It was under the influence of these feelings, of what is due to men by whom it pleases God to bless their fellows, that the present publication was projected. Although in itself small, yet from its subject, and its relation to the highest of all causes, it is precious, and, notwithstanding its frail aspect, it will survive when all who have been concerned in it will have mouldered into dust. It will tell the generation to come of an event which, in connection with the cause of God, was considered at the time as far from unimportant. It will, moreover, explain the history of a volume from the pen of Mr. Finney, which has just been added to the catalogue of English Theology.

The Observations on his Preaching first appeared in the *British Banner*, as also the account of the Valedictory Services. The Sermon, which was delivered amid the heavy pressure of manifold engagements, and not without a measure of personal indisposition, was taken by a Special Reporter, and revised by the Preacher himself.

J.C.

TABERNACLE-HOUSE, LONDON,
April 4, 1851.

CRITICAL OBSERVATIONS.

Now that Mr. Finney's course has reached its close, it may be permitted us to utter a thought or two relative to a man for whom we have conceived a very high regard, and in whose labours and history we feel the deepest interest. Well, we cannot say that we are much gratified by the idea of Mr. Finney's returning to college duties, and the general ministry of a rural charge. We do not consider that such is the place for the man; and we must be allowed to think that fifteen years ago a mistake was committed when he became located in the midst of academic bowers. In our view, there are few living men to whom such an element is less suited. He is made for the millions,—his place is the pulpit rather than the Professor's chair. He is a heaven-born sovereign of the people. The people he loves, and the mass of the people all but idolise him. He seems specially created for oral labour. The structure of his mind is altogether peculiar. The logical faculty is developed in an unusual degree, and hence there is a tendency to argument in excess. He reasons on and on to the extreme of redundancy, often labouring to explain that which requires no further explanation, and to prove what needs no further proof. He is, moreover, strongly addicted to the metaphysical and analytical, and hence whatever he touches becomes more or less arrayed in a dialectical costume. These peculiarities might, at first sight, seem somewhat to unfit him for pulpit labour among the millions: but it is otherwise; he succeeds either through, or in spite of them. Whether he be understood or not, he is listened to, and complaints are not generally heard on the score of his being unintelligible. These rare gifts are of signal service in enabling Mr. Finney to fathom the deepest recesses of the human heart, and to throw light on the darkest portions of human character. For moral anatomy he has no equal among the multitude of great and successful ministers whom it has been our lot to hear. An assembly often quivers under him as does the living subject under the knife of the operator, whom experience has rendered skilful and habit made callous. Multitudes have stood amazed at themselves, as presented in the mirror he exhibits to their astonished view. This peculiar power alone would have rendered Mr. Finney remarkable among public instructors; but this is only one feature of his very complex and multifarious character as a preacher. His declamatory are fully equal to his logical powers. In this walk, we think, he has no superior. He thunders and lightens when his subject requires it, in a manner to shake the heart of an assembly, rousing the most apathetic, and awing the most careless. He would have ranked as a prince among that class of zealous and most useful men whom a godless world has scornfully denominated—Ranters!

But even this is not all; he possesses another quality seldom found in combination with the foregoing; he is occasionally, although but seldom, strongly pathetic,—the voice falters, and the eyes become suffused with tears. Thus, then, Mr. Finney largely combines in himself the qualities necessary to constitute the three great classes of public speaking, and is capable, with proper application, of the highest success in them all; but we believe it is only justice to his great character to say, that he never thought five minutes upon the subject. Whatever he is, he is from nature and the gifts of God; art has done nothing for him. The result of the whole is, an extraordinary range of mental and moral contact with the assembly. There is something for men of every class; all, in turns are gratified, and all are occasionally disappointed, according as throughout the discourse the one quality or the other may predominate. Sometimes during an entire sermon he is dry and logical in the extreme, addressing himself to pure intellect, making no provision whatever for either heart or fancy. At other times, both are regaled in a very high degree, as an interdict is then placed on the logical faculty; and there have been a few discourses, also touching and pathetic throughout. In these respects he is the most varied of preachers, and in all respects the most unequal.

There is another peculiarity about the public speaking of Mr. Finney, which renders it noticeable, and even striking. The style of address, the accent and intonation, and the whole air, is American, and such as presents a striking contrast to that of England. At first, it is unpleasant to the English ear; but that ear soon comes to like it, and at length is charmed with it. The general cast of his preaching is simple even to plainness, and good taste is occasionally violated for the purpose of illustration. The whole air of the man, and of his address, is deeply marked by homeliness and simplicity. As everything beyond the mere outline of his discourse is extemporaneous, there is an utter absence of obvious effort, whether of thought or language. The elaborate, the exquisite, and the ornate, have no place in his pulpit performances. Nature is everywhere apparent in her modest, every-day garb. There is no exhibition,—no speaking for speaking's sake. Mr. Finney may say with Whitefield (whom, in many respects, he resembles), "I use market language." There is no room for display of any description. Self seems annihilated. The subject is everything, and the salvation of men is the supreme concern. To crown all,

Mr. Finney, beyond the great run of public speakers, is endowed with a voice of remarkable clearness. Its faintest accents were heard in the remotest corner of the edifice where he has been labouring, although eighty feet square, while it is capable of acquiring the swell of the martial trumpet. It is not sweet,—not melodious, but possesses a penetrating clearness of tone, with a distinctness of enunciation, which would render him audible in the largest edifice in Europe. He finds his account exceedingly in this attribute. When he has spoken three hours, there is often no symptom whatever either of hoarseness or fatigue. Indeed, he has appeared to us, not seldom, the only person who was not exhausted! It is certainly a pity that a man so singularly endowed for evangelical labour should be chained down by the dull routine of college duties. If we mistake not, there are a thousand men to be found in the United States, that would perform Mr. Finney's professorial duties as well, perhaps in many respects better, than he; but we doubt if, amongst the three-and-twenty millions of American citizens, and the forty thousand ministers, more or less, that labour among them, there are many, if one, that possess all the qualifications above enumerated. Thus much for the attributes of Mr. Finney as a public instructor; and the opinion is given after hearing him incessantly for months.

But what may be said of the effects of his labours? For, after all, this is the point both with him and with the Church of God. On this point we have little to say at present, in addition to the very copious statements already made in our columns. The attendance, and the visible impression of his labours, have grown rather than diminished up to the present hour. There has, of course, been a great and constant change going on in the audience; but still the crowds are unabated, and the number of inquirers has considerably increased. We are not yet in a position to speak with particularity on the subject of conversion in connection with his second visit. In the former case, it was not till his departure that the effects became fully apparent; and, perhaps, it will be largely so again.

Mr. Finney's mode of dealing with men is peculiar, such as, at times, to subject him to the charge of not preaching the Gospel. What he does, however, is done upon principle. He gave, last Lord's-day morning, a most masterly defence of his own course in descanting on the words of the Prophet, "Break up the fallow ground, and sow not among thorns." Mr. Finney is not disobedient to the heavenly voice; he breaks up the fallow ground, as with a steam-plough, turning-up, crushing, and destroying whatever of roots or weeds may stand in the way.

Of his theology, after what we have said on former occasions, we need here say nothing beyond re-asserting its radical soundness on all the great points of Evangelism. His mode of statement, at times, are not such as a sound, erudite English divine would approve or adopt; he may be occasionally the victim of his own logical subtlety, his statements may sometimes appear to be rash, and his deductions daring, but he always and quickly rights himself, and, with a powerful hand, never fails to vindicate the ways of God to man. On the subject of man's responsibility, he has, in our view, no equal; never was it our lot to see the human spirit so completely divested of every plea, and so shut up to the faith! He may often, with justice, be charged with a limited or defective exhibition of the grace of God. We have heard sermons from him, in which the name of Christ was never mentioned, nor his work so much as referred to,—sermons which might have been preached by a Jew or a Turk; but, in setting forth the claims of justice, he has no superior and few equals; and, when he does preach the Gospel, it flows like the river of the water of life!

But our space forbids enlargement, which is needless, as Mr. Finney will shortly speak for himself deliberately, and upon a large scale. As we stated before, Mr. Tegg has purchased the copyright of Mr. Finney's great work on Theology, which, during his residence in London, he has carried through the press, severely revising, and, to a considerable extent, re-writing it. In a few days, that goodly volume of nearly a thousand pages will be before the public, who will then be in a position to judge for themselves.

It is but proper to say, that the extraordinary audiences of Mr. Finney, through so long a period, have not been the sole fruit of mere pulpit attraction. He has been sustained as never was preacher before in this Metropolis nor in these lands. In addition to the aids he derived from the journals under our conduct, other means have been adopted on an unusual scale to awaken public attention. In addition to the issue of two large Addresses, written by the Pastor, of eight thousand copies each, distributed from house to house throughout the surrounding neighbourhood, the young men of the Tabernacle have laboured most laudably, and even heroically, to excite the attention of the careless, and to bring them to hear the Word of Life. They actually subscribed among themselves between thirty and forty pounds to work the Press! Fifty thousand copies of another Address, prepared by the Pastor, were circulated by them and the young females throughout the city, and large numbers of other addresses. Besides all this, large bills were extensively posted, and not only so, but carried on the shoulders of men throughout the numerous thoroughfares. There can be no doubt that these measures had a mighty effect in calling together the best sort of material to work upon—the unsophisticated, the men not Gospel proof and sermon hardened, the men with whom Whitefield and Wesley dealt, and who formed the staple of their original converts. These boards, which were borne through the streets, created considerable scandal to not a few worthy people, who are not quite so wise as the children of this generation. And there were not wanting those to blame both the Pastor of the Tabernacle and Mr. Finney, although neither of them had aught more to do with the matter than the Presidents of France and the United States. Neither of them so much as even knew of the thing till it had been some time in operation; but we believe, looking at the subject not through the medium of a diseased decorum, but of common sense, and even of sound discretion, they felt less disposed to censure than to applaud the deed. Would that the spirit which prompted it may extend throughout the length and breadth of the land: Delicacy and propriety are, in their places, virtues to be highly prized; but delicacy may be false and cruel; propriety may be spurious and fatal; and, through an undue regard to them, immortal men may be suffered to go down to hell through a dread of violating the proprieties of an ungodly world and a slumbering Church!

VALEDICTORY SERVICE.

It is now our painful duty to announce the close of the evangelical labours, for the present, in England, of Mr. Finney. To complete our previous notices of this distinguished stranger, we shall, therefore, add the facts which have attended the termination of his services. Last Lord's-day morning he preached from James ii. 22,—"Seest thou how faith wrought with his works, and by works was made perfect?" The weather was favourable to attendance, and the congregation accordingly was large, although both the services of the day were signalised by one of those things which generally tend somewhat to winnow metropolitan assemblies,—collections were made at both times, for the Christian Instruction Society. The subject of faith in relation to works was one with which Mr. Finney is peculiarly fitted to deal, and accordingly it was wrought out with consummate ability.

The subject was such, of course, as to admit of little originality in its mode of treatment, and it was selected, not for exhibition, but for usefulness. The primary object was to state the truth comprised in the given text, and to press home its consequences. But only to have done this would not have been fully to meet the demands of the occasion, in a day of general, superficial, cheap, and easy profession. The subject is one of immense importance in the economy of redemption, as entering fully into the very essence of true religion. It is a point on which millions have erred to their own eternal undoing. The error comprises two extremes; men on the one hand have relied on a faith that produces no works, and on the other they have rested on works that did not proceed from faith—works which had no regard to the Gospel of Jesus Christ. Either extreme is alike certainly fatal to all who are the subjects of it. To prevent the occurrence of either evil is, therefore, the business of the public teacher; but this is not enough,—it is also a matter of the utmost moment to recover such as are fallen into one or other of these errors; and accordingly this was not forgotten by Mr. Finney, who, with characteristic penetration, distinguished between things that differ, and, with his accustomed point and vigour, pressed home the great lessons upon all whom the several matters concerned. The refuge of lies was swept away as with a hurricane, while the honest and earnest—those betaking themselves to works of faith and labours of love—had much to encourage and fortify them. The Evangelical System was strikingly exhibited in all its grace and loveliness. The tendency of all such discourses must be to purify real religion and to elevate it. In the evening, Mr. Finney took for his text Acts xxiv. 24, 25. On this occasion the house was much crowded, and the preacher rose with the occasion. He has repeatedly equalled, but never exceeded, the power of the discourse then delivered. Blending a good deal of mental and moral philosophy, which was rendered subservient to theology, he came exceedingly close to the conscience of the audience. One copious passage fell with a weight on the assembly superior to anything we ever heard him utter, putting us in remembrance of some of those outbursts of intellect and emotion which were wont to characterize the preaching of Dr. Chalmers on great occasions, and which frequently signalize the pulpit labours of Mr. Parsons. After about an hour and a half of a mingled stream of argument and address, the preacher paused, giving place to the Pastor; who addressed the assembly on certain matters of arrangement. This was followed by devotional services; when the congregation was dismissed, it being intimated that all who chose to remain for a further address might do so. Accordingly, overborne by heat and fatigue, a multitude withdrew; but when they were gone scarcely a sitting seemed to be left vacant, curiously exemplifying how closely human beings may be packed together.

It may be observed, that, as last Lord's day was that appointed for taking the census, the audience was carefully counted, both morning and evening, by two individuals at each entrance, who took each a separate account, afterwards comparing their computations. The attendance in the morning was 2,100, and in the evening, in round numbers, 3,200; these numbers refer to adults, as the Sunday-schools were not present either morning or evening, there being for these a separate service.

The tea-meeting, at which upwards of 600 sat down, took place in the Royal British Institution, Cowper-street, City-road; Mr. and Mrs. Finney, of course, being present. We say Mrs. Finney—for the wife of the great Evangelist accompanies him. Not having had occasion till now to mention this excellent lady, it may be proper to say a word concerning her. This may be considered due to her own personal worth, and useful as serving to open her way elsewhere to humble efforts at public usefulness. Mrs. Finney is a woman of wholly kindred spirit with her husband; she sees everything in the same light, estimates all matters by the same standard, and by the same means seeks the same ends. Her heart is strongly set on the advancement of the kingdom of God; and to that end, like him, she perseveringly labours. She established the daily morning female prayer-meeting, which has been held in the Tabernacle for the last nine months, and over which she has, while in London, uniformly presided. In addition to this, she has on a number of occasions addressed meetings of mothers and other females in the Tabernacle and in other places, besides occasionally addressing Ragged and other schools, and Temperance Societies. In this and other ways Mrs. Finney is in a high degree a helpmate for her husband.

The tea-meeting occupied from five to seven o'clock; when, for the accommodation of the friends assembled, and others who were expected to join, although unable to attend the tea-meeting, the assembly adjourned to the Tabernacle, which was very considerably filled, both in the pews and in the galleries. After the devotional exercises, in which Dr. Brown, of Cheltenham, offered prayer, the Pastor, in the chair, having addressed the meeting on subjects which had been suggested by the occasion, turning to Mr. Finney, said:

"My dear Friend, you must now for a moment allow my character of President to merge into that of representative of a body of people among us to whom you are peculiarly dear. You will, therefore, please to consider me as their embodiment. Whatever I now feel, speak, and do, you will kindly consider as felt, spoken, and done by them. They are anxious to assure you, that by them you will never be forgotten; and they are very unwilling that they should be forgotten by you. They have, therefore, devised a means by which, in some measure, to prevent this: they have provided the copy you see in my hands of the "English Hexapla," comprising the Greek Text of the New Testament, with six translations subjoined, on which is inscribed the following:

> 'Presented to the Rev. C. G. Finney, as a token of respect and affection, by his friends in the Tabernacle, London, March 31, 1851, on his departure for his native land.'

"Permit me, then, my dear Brother, to present to you this book in their names, as a memorial of your British visit and of your London friends. The thing and the deed are both to be considered solely as monumental—as '*in memoriam.*' It will serve at times to remind you of another clime and of other men than those of the New World. It will also serve to apprise your posterity that their ancestor visited the Fatherland in 1851, and that there it pleased God to give him favour in the eyes of many of the excellent of the earth, and to honour him through the conversion of souls to add to their numbers. Accept, then, the book as a token of love. Such it is—nothing more—nothing less. The question of its pecuniary value was wholly excluded from their thoughts, as it will be wholly excluded from yours. Its character is altogether spiritual; its object is entirely moral; you will accept it in the same spirit in which it is given, with the strong desire, with the earnest prayer on their part that you may continue for many years to publish its truth with increasing success, fidelity, and power, and that through life, and at the close of life, its doctrines may be your support and your consolation."[1]

Dr. Campbell, then turning to Mrs. Finney, said:

"My dear Friend, will you permit me to beg that you will apply to yourself what has just been uttered respecting your husband. As every way one, you cannot be separated, and assuredly it is not in the wish or the intention of those whom I now represent to attempt it. But, although one, you have your distinct personal identities, attributes, characters, and claims. I have, then, to assure you, on their behalf, that you are very highly esteemed, not simply for your husband's sake, but for your own. Those who have been privileged to hold intercourse with you, and to share your friendship, highly prize your worth, and greatly respect your character. They have also witnessed with delight your anxiety to be useful, and the efforts you have made for that purpose, both amongst ourselves and throughout the locality. They will long remember you, and they desire that you should not wholly forget them. To prevent this, as far as may be, they adopt the same method towards yourself as your husband. I hold in my hands, the condensed "Commentary" of Ingram Cobbin, the best production of its class in the English tongue, bearing an inscription, the exact counterpart of that presented to your husband:

> 'Presented to Mrs. C. G. Finney, as a token of respect and affection, by her friends in the Tabernacle, London, March 31, 1851, on her departure for her native land.'

"Allow me, then, my dear Friend, to place this in your hands, and to beg your acceptance of it as a token of Christian affection. When far away from

[1]This book is in the Oberlin College Library, Special Collections.

the white cliffs of Albion, it will remind you of intercourse which was profitable to others, and, it is to be hoped, pleasant to yourself. It will remind you of a place where prayer was wont to be made, in which you had long the privilege to lead or join. It will tell your children and your children's children, that their revered mother was once in England, and had friends in the Mother Country who prized her worth, and were stimulated by her zeal."

Turning to the audience, the Chairman said: "In looking to these two beautiful and invaluable volumes, I am strikingly reminded of the fact of the decease of both the men whose honoured names are inseparably connected with them—Samuel Bagster, as the projector of the "English Hexapla," and Ingram Cobbin, as the author of the condensed "Commentary." In connection with the subject of the Scriptures, Bagster and Cobbin are by far the two most remarkable men of their own time. Bagster founded the most complete Bible establishment the world has seen; and for intense, prolonged, and useful labour, on the Sacred Scriptures, Ingram Cobbin had no equal among his contemporaries. Cobbin is no more; he rests from his labours, and his works follow him. The turf was only just placed on his honoured grave, when it was announced that Bagster had followed him. The venerable publisher died last week, and is still unburied. Peace to their ashes, and honour to their memories! My friends will excuse this digression, and, perhaps, consider that it is not wholly impertinent to the occasion. There is something due to the memories of those who have been distinguished as the benefactors of mankind upon a scale which embraces all nations, and which will extend to a distant posterity; and more especially is it meet and grateful, while inscribing tablets to the worth of the living, that we should pay a passing tribute to the wisdom and the virtues of the dead who have aided us in our enterprise.

"But let me now, before I close, ascend for a moment from the particular and personal to more general views, and endeavour to impress upon you the fact, that this is not simply a night of friendly valediction. It is also, or it ought to be, a night of solemn individual self-inquisition. A voice is now sounding in the ears of the assembly: 'Let them assuredly know that a prophet has been among them!'

"You have for a long period been receiving from the lips of a stranger instructions the most precious, warnings the most solemn, enforced by considerations the most tender. You have been plied with every consideration that love, knowledge, and experience could devise. All the resources of Scripture, fact, and argument have been brought to bear upon you, with a view to detach you from the world, and bring you to the Lord. In no other spot in Europe, perhaps, no other on the earth, during the same long period, has there been such an amount of evangelical labour put forth upon such a multitude of people. Six nights a week the doors of this edifice have been thrown open; its walls have literally never cooled: and what is to be the issue? So far as Mr. Finney is concerned, this stupendous effort of pulpit toil is now at an end. Another service, and he is on the mighty waters, speeding his way for the land of the Pilgrim Fathers, to meet with the bulk of you no more till you meet in the solemn Judgment! What is the day to declare? What will eternity reveal? Who among you are to prove his joy at the final audit? When the Lord shall write up the people, of whom will it be heard, this man, and that man, and the other, were born there? Concerning whom shall he say, 'Here am I, and the children whom thou hast given me?' May the result to him, to you, and to all that have heard him, be glory and joy for evermore!

"It was my wish for many years that Mr. Finney should visit the shores of England. His works had come before him, and, when his Lectures on Revivals appeared, I read them with avidity, and, as a portion of you will remember, for three months, from week to week, at special meetings, I read and expounded them in this edifice. Their value was not in my estimation at all lessened by their peculiarities, and by what might be called, not without truth, their occasional extravagance, both of thought and of language. These I considered, and still consider, but as the dust in the balance—as spots in the sun! The volume, as a whole, I have ever viewed as of extraordinary importance. The more I pondered, the more I perceived its inherent excellence. The book excited a very strong desire in me to see the man, and still more to hear him. The man I have seen, the man I have heard, and in both the expectations excited by the book have been more than realized. But I have not only seen and heard him: after the manner of the ancients, we have eaten salt together. You all know the adage, If you would know a man, you must live with him. Mr. Finney and I have lived together for the space of some nine months; a period which, I suppose, will be admitted sufficient for the purpose in question. I think I may, therefore, say I have a tolerable knowledge of him, and that it is but simple justice to say that to increase knowledge has been only to increase regard. Throughout that long period, we have seen in him much to love and much to admire. I shall never cease to prize his friendship, and to think of him with unalloyed satisfaction and high pleasure. His virtues partake not a little of the old Roman, while his manners are strongly Republican. In everything good the reality exceeds the appearance, and, as the observation becomes closer, the esteem ascends.

"But it is incumbent on me, on the present occasion, to say something on the subject of Mr. Finney's Theology; circumstances render this imperative. My own creed is, I believe, generally considered sound. I swear by the Sacred Scriptures, their plenary inspiration, and their supreme authority, holding, with a firm grasp, those views of their import which have ever characterised the Nonconformists of England. This is by me confessed; it is my boast and glory! While I call no man on earth master, I hesitate not to declare my very general concurrence with that illustrious body of men, the most distinguished class of Britain's sons, the Puritans and Nonconformists of England. Such are my views and my avowal of them. Now there are those—and among them people of sense and worth—who think that Mr. Finney and I preach very different gospels. These have expressed their sorrow and amazement that he should have so long occupied the pulpit of this ancient edifice. Those worthy people are much mistaken, if they refer to *principles:* I am not aware of any tenet of Revelation connected with the hope of man on which we differ. We may differ in our views of many Scriptures, and in our modes of stating many truths, and the proportions in which such truths ought to be combined and presented. On these points we may differ; we do differ; but that difference, while a fact, is a proof of nothing but itself. I may think Mr. Finney would be improved, in some respects, by leaning a little more in my direction; and it is just possible my friend will conclude, that I should be improved by leaning a little more in his; and who is to decide? However, I believe we are both right. Were I to commence Evangelist to-morrow, I would most assuredly, to a great extent, run in the vein of Mr. Finney, the propriety, the expediency, and the necessity of which have been thoroughly made out under my own observation. On the other hand, were Mr. Finney to become a settled pastor to-morrow, I think it is just possible that he would pursue the course which is now pursued by the bulk of the best of English ministers. For special efforts I think his method incomparable; for settled pastorship I should deem it very defective. I view the ministrations of Mr. Finney as partaking of a special character; I look upon them as admirably adapted, as special means, to accomplish a special end. The thing, however, is not to be determined by prior reasoning, it must be tested by its harmony with the Divine examples, and by its results as indicative of Divine approbation. I have encountered considerable obloquy in some quarters, on account of the course I have pursued with respect to Mr. Finney; but assuredly none of these things move me. So far as I can judge, with the amplest means of ascertaining the fact, his creed is as sound, in all radical matters, as that of John Owen. Even his opponents being judges, Mr. Finney's faults have been mainly of a negative character. The regrets which have been felt—and regrets in which I have occasionally shared—have arisen, not from what he has said, but from what he did not say. When he has been, with his own peculiar vigour, 'breaking up the fallow ground' of the human heart, it has been lamented that he did not, at the same time, both plough and sow; but Mr. Finney had his reasons for his course, although these reasons were not always understood. What he did not state it was presumed he denied; but I need not tell the bulk of you, that when Mr. Finney did preach the Gospel, no man ever preached it more fully or more purely. The noble specimen of yesterday morning is still fresh in your memory.

"I reflect with the utmost satisfaction on the course I have pursued respecting Mr. Finney, and cannot doubt but it has the approval of the Master of us both. Would that everything else I have done in connection with His cause were as sure to obtain from his lips—'Well done!' I have not hesitated, both with tongue and pen, to defend Mr. Finney, and to promote the success of his labours to the utmost of my power. In all I have done I do rejoice, and will rejoice. I ask, on Mr. Finney's behalf, candour and inquiry. Let this be granted, and I seek no more. For a long period I have stood alone in the face of the public in the character of advocate; now, however, I find myself in the company of such as I highly value, and such as serve largely to fortify me as the advocate of our American friend and his potent labours. Dr. Redford, of Worcester, as a theologian second to none in these realms, has boldly prefixed his name to the English edition of Mr. Finney's "Theology," just about to appear under the respectable auspices of Mr. Tegg. Dr. Redford has prefixed to the volume a preface, which I now hold in my hand, and a portion of which I will read to you:

" 'The Editor having had the pleasure and honour of forming a personal acquaintance with the Author soon after his arrival in this country, did not long remain ignorant of his Theological Lectures. After the first hasty perusal of them, he ventured strongly to recommend their publication, both for the sake of making the British churches better acquainted with the Author's doctrinal views, and also on account of the direct benefit which students, and other inquirers into the theory of Gospel doctrines, would be likely to derive from a work so argumentative, and so unlike all the works on systematic and dogmatic theology known to the English schools. After due consultation and deliberation, the Author pressed upon the Editor the work of revision, and placed the Lectures in his hands with the request, that he would read them carefully, and suggest such alterations as he might deem desirable to adapt the work to the English reader; and then submit the whole to the Author's adoption or rejection.'

"'There is another important circumstance with which the reader should be made acquainted, which will enhance the value of this edition, and render it highly preferable to the American,—it is this: on the publication of these Lectures, they attracted the attention of many able theologians in America, and were severely attacked by the periodical press. The Author replied at considerable length to the most learned and distinguished of his critics, fairly and fully meeting every objection that had been urged against his views. The present edition incorporates the substance of these objections, with the replies of the Author.

"'The Editor, however, would not have ventured to recommend the publication of these Lectures in this country, if he had not deemed them, as a whole, eminently deserving the attention and examination of British theologians. When they first came into his hands they struck him as so pleasingly unlike all the other systems of dogmatic theology and moral philosophy it had ever been his lot to peruse, so thorough in their grappling with difficulties, and often so successful in the solution of them; so skilfully adjusted to modern metaphysical speculations, and so comprehensive of what is valuable in them; so manifestly the production of a masculine intellect and independent thinker, that he was not only pleased with the air of freshness and originality thrown over old themes of dry and elaborate discussion, but greatly benefited and instructed by some of the Author's views of important moral and theological questions. It may not be the same with all the Author's English readers; but assuredly few will rise from the perusal of the whole work without confessing that, at least, they have seen some points in a new and impressive light, have been constrained to think more closely of the opinions they hold, and in other respects have been benefited by the perusal.

"'As a contribution to theological science, in an age when vague speculation and philosophical theories are bewildering many among all denominations of Christians, this work will be considered by all competent judges to be both valuable and seasonable. Upon several important and difficult subjects the Author has thrown a clear and valuable light, which will guide many a student through perplexities and difficulties which he had long sought unsuccessfully to explain. The Editor frankly confesses, that when a student he would gladly have bartered half the books in his library to have gained a single perusal of these Lectures; and he cannot refrain from expressing the belief, that no young student of theology will ever regret the purchase or perusal of Mr. Finney's Lectures.

"'One recommendation he begs respectfully to offer to all readers, whether old or young; it is this, suspend your judgment of the Author and his theology until you have gone completely through his work. On many subjects, at the outset of the discussion, startling propositions may be found which will clash with your settled opinions; but if you will calmly and patiently await the Author's explanation, and observe how he qualifies some strong or novel assertions, you will most probably find in the issue, that you have less reason than you supposed to object to his statements.

"'In many respects, Mr. Finney's theological and moral system will be found to differ both from the Calvinistic and Arminian. In fact, it is a system of his own, if not in its separate portions, yet in its construction; and, as a whole, is at least unique and compact,—a system which the Author has wrought out for himself with little other aid than what he has derived from the fount itself of heavenly truth, and his own clear and strong perception of the immutable moral principles and laws by which the glorious Author of the universe governs all his intellectual creatures.'

"Now, my friends, what say you to this? Is not this going as far as I ever went on the subject of Mr. Finney's Theology? This seems a tolerable testimony to be borne by such a man as Dr. Redford to a Republican heretic! But, seriously, Mr. Finney is a man of no human school; he has framed his own chart, and made his own compass; but, notwithstanding this, it will be found, that he is a safe guide on the ocean to eternity! For his special work, what many worthy people have deemed his defects are really his excellences, and constitute, in no small degree, his strength. To point out the advantages which have arisen from them would take more time than we can now afford, and therefore I shall not attempt it. Suffice it to say, that in this way he has commanded attention, excited inquiry, and awakened fears for the world to come, which could not have been awakened by a simple, polished, stereotype exhibition of the common salvation, as it is generally administered in these realms. Of the acceptance of his ministry in this city I need say nothing; the result is before the world. No such experiment has been made on the population of this great Metropolis in our times; and, so far as numbers and continued attendance are concerned, the experiment has been complete. Had a Council of the Ancients, of wise and experienced men in matters appertaining to Metropolitan Religion, at the close of March, last year, been convened, and their opinion solicited as to the likelihood of success, it is highly probable, that, with one consent, they would have predicted its utter failure,—they would have foretold the impossibility of any man whatever commanding audiences such as he has commanded so frequently, and through so long a series of months. Had these reverend councillors, before they began to deal with the question, been permitted to hear Mr. Finney deliver one of his 'fallow-ground' manifestoes, they, of a certainty, would have predicted, that, before two months, he would have fairly scattered the largest congregation in London, and have been in a position to present the keys to the masters of the concern, to prevent further damage to the edifice. So blind is man, and so difficult is it to ascertain the springs which govern the human mind.

"I must close my observations by reciting to you the draft of the Letter which it is proposed to hand to Mr. Finney, as expressive of the sentiments you entertain towards him, which, if it meet your approval, will be signed by the Pastor and Office-bearers, and communicated to our friend. The proposed draft is as follows:

" 'Dear and Honoured Sir,—We cannot suffer you to return to the land of your Fathers without expressing to you the pleasure we have derived from your visit. Your spirit and speech, while they have ofttimes not a little contributed to reprove and to condemn, have also served to animate and cheer us. Your enlightened zeal for the salvation of men has been rendered instrumental in firing many hearts that required to be animated, and in giving fresh impulse even to those that were previously valiant for the truth. Your vigorous, pungent, and faithful ministrations have greatly tended to quicken believers; while your broad, luminous, and impressive exhibitions of the great doctrine of Repentance towards God have been made extensively the means of awakening the careless to a sense of their danger, and of leading them to flee from the wrath to come. We have witnessed with delight, often not unmingled with astonishment, your *self-consuming* and *unwearied efforts* for the salvation of the perishing, and *greatly rejoice in the manifold tokens of success* on all sides which are already apparent, while there is the utmost reason to look on what is known as only the *first fruits* of *a coming harvest.*

" 'But, beloved Brother! while rejoicing in the profit which has redounded to ourselves as a flock, to many of our families, to a portion of our congregation, and residents in our immediate locality, we reflect with special satisfaction on the benefit which we have grounds to believe will result to other Churches in our neighbourhood, and throughout the City. There is on all hands proof abundant that your labour in the Lord has not been in vain; but that your visit to England has been one of the most useful periods of your laborious life.

" 'You will, therefore, dear and honoured Sir, accept this expression of our sincere and most cordial thanks for all your intense endeavours to advance the Kingdom of God in our midst, together with the assurance of our grateful esteem. You leave our country bearing with you the affectionate confidence of multitudes, who will pray for journeying mercies to you, both by land and sea; and that, with your dear and much-esteemed companion, Mrs. Finney you may reach your home in safety, and find all well.

" 'Wishing you and yours grace, mercy, and peace, and every blessing of the New Covenant we remain, dear and honoured Sir, on behalf o[f] the Church and congregation assembling in thi[s] house, yours most truly in the bonds of the Gospel.' "

Mr. Edward Selby then moved the following resolution:

"That the draft of Letter now read be transcribed, signed by the Pastor and Officers, and transmitted to Mr. Finney."

Mr. Henry Child, with great cordiality, rose to second the resolution. They did not exactly agree with their friend Mr. Finney on all points; but they believed he had preached to them the glorious Gospel of Christ, and that in the way in which he had been taught by the Holy Spirit. They were satisfied he was doing God's work, and it was impossible that independent mind should on all points see with one another; it was only the noodles of the earth who saw eye to eye on every matter, and subscribed unreservedly to creeds and catechisms, and even to the dots of the i's and the crosses of the t's.

The resolution was then put to the meeting, upstanding, and carried unanimously; but on the contrary being put, a number still stood: this, however, was explained, amidst considerable merriment, by a gentleman, who called out from the crowd,—"We are only standing because we are obliged to do so."

Mr. Finney then rose to reply, and was received with the most enthusiastic applause, which was suppressed by the Pastor, on the ground that it incommoded Mr. Finney. After a few introductory remarks with reference to the novelty of the position he occupied, he proceeded to detail the circumstances which led him to visit this country. His ancestors were English. New England was peopled by the English, from whom he was descended. In New England they had all our names, customs, and, to a large extent, held our views. In England he felt at home in almost every respect, so far as the people were concerned. His Lectures on Revivals—the book which had been published in this country,—were delivered some twelve or thirteen years ago, and were reported at the time by the Editor of the *New York Evangelist,* and were published in successive numbers of that journal. He thought it necessary to state that he did not see those Lectures until they were in print; but that before they were gathered up into a volume, he had just glanced through them to correct any serious errors that he might happen to meet with. This volume was published in England by Mr. Tegg. The consequence was, that many persons interested in the subject wrote to him from all parts of the United Kingdom, and this correspondence gave rise to a desire in his mind to visit England. About this time his health so failed as to compel him to desist from his labours as Evangelist, and he accordingly took the pastoral oversight of a church in New York, and has continued to sustain the pastoral office ever since. His church and congregation at Oberlin was one of the largest in America. He understood, therefore, very well, what Dr. Campbell meant by the difference between the labours of an evangelist and those of a pastor. He had laboured eighteen years as a pastor, but it was always on the condition that a portion of the year should be devoted to his labours as an evangelist. He could not tell them how much he had been affected by the numbers of persons from all parts of the United Kingdom whom he had met in America, and who testified to the benefit they had derived from the perusal of his works,—more especially of his Lectures; and it was the interest which these circumstances had excited that induced him to come. For a time he was prevented by the state of his health, and then by his public duties; but for the last twelve years he had been constantly entertaining the idea of coming, and he had accordingly taken the first opportunity at which God had seemed to open the way. On arriving in England, as Dr. Campbell had said, he passed straight through London, and went down into Huntingdonshire. He soon afterwards came up, and preached several sermons at the Borough-road Chapel. Then he returned to the Provinces, and laboured first in Huntingdonshire, then in Birmingham, and subsequently in Worcester. Various rumours were circulated respecting him, and the first minister he saw told him that reports were circulated that he (Mr. Finney) had become an infidel! Now, this minister had himself been rescued from infidelity by the perusal of his works! Before he had been long in Birmingham, Mr. James received various letters calling in question his orthodoxy; some said he was a Unitarian, some a low Arminian, and some a Perfectionist; and all united in warning Mr. James lest he should aid in the diffusion of heresy! But he appealed to Mr. James, whose position in the matter had assumed importance, at once to satisfy himself, and forthwith to pronounce upon the matter. Mr. James had abundant opportunities of hearing him, but, not satisfied with this, he handed him two volumes of his "Theology," wherein the said errors were reported to be found. These volumes Mr. James and Dr. Redford, of Worcester—in whose logical and theological acumen Mr. James had great confidence—submitted to three days' careful examination. So satisfied were they with their general soundness and accuracy, that Dr. Redford urged their publication in this country for the benefit of the British public. Subsequently, he went to preach for Dr. Redford; when the subject again came up, and he handed his volumes to the Doctor, with a request that he would go through them, and make such criticism and corrections as would enable him to make himself understood to British theologians. This Dr. Redford did; and, without his solicitation, had also, at the instance of the publisher, consented to have his name appear on the title-page as Editor.

Dr. Campbell: "It ought to be known that I advised Mr. Finney to get Dr. Redford, who had read the work, to write a preface; but he said, 'Let the book go alone, and stand on its own merits.' Mr. Tegg, however, knew his business better, and secured it."

Mr. Finney: "The present publication by Mr. Tegg contains only a part of my Theological system, which was necessary to meet the necessities of my theological class in their preparation for theological examination; and further, the Oberlin edition, as Dr. Campbell observes, was not very nicely got up. In fact, the firm to whom the printing was entrusted had but just commenced business, and this was the first book they ever produced. I myself wrote them under so great a pressure, that I could not edit it properly, so that that portion of the labour was committed to other hands. I wrote them at the rate of one a day, in the midst of all my other duties, and therefore it is not to be wondered at if they needed revision. I have no doubt you may find errors, even in the present English edition; but those who know what I have been doing here, will find sufficient excuse in the multiplicity and continuity of my engagements. I may just observe, that, although I am not pecuniarily interested in the sale of this work, which is the property of the Publisher, yet I am interested—and deeply interested—in its being read. I want people to read it, and to judge for themselves.

"But I never meant to speak so much of myself. The fact is, I never attended a meeting of this kind before, or any meeting of which I was myself so much the subject. As to the manner in which I have been received in this country, I may say that I have been greatly affected by the way in which I have been treated, especially by those ministers and others with whom I have become personally acquainted. I have felt myself more and more at home amongst you, and more and more united to all Christians. Let me say with respect to Dr. Campbell,—as he spoke of me so freely,—that Mr. James said to me, 'I want to have you see Dr. Campbell. I think you will find in him a kindred spirit in the work in which you are engaged.' Dr. Redford also said, 'I want you to go to the Tabernacle, for Dr. Campbell will stand by you.' He also intimated that Dr. Campbell was 'not afraid.' (Great laughter.) Now, I wanted to find a man who could stand fire. (Increased laughter.) I know that a minister, to stand by me under such circumstances, must have some brass in his face, and some firmness in his heart, and a strong determination to stand for the sake of truth. I have now lived nine months in the Doctor's family,—and I always love to live with the pastor with whom I labour, that I may get at his heart daily, and he at mine, so that if there be any running to and fro and talking, we may understand each other,—I have been, as I said, nine months in his house, and I can most cheerfully reciprocate what he has said of me,—'the more I know him, the more I love him.' That he would agree with me in all things I never expected. I have my own views, and I express them freely; and I allow my brethren to do the same. I do not say I will not tolerate them because they do not agree with me; for if they do not agree with me, it is because I do not agree with them. Nevertheless, I call no man a heretic who maintains the fundamental truths of the Gospel, and such a man I cordially love. If he holds the fundamental truths of the Gospel, I bid him God-speed. I have published my views with pen and voice, and expect others to do the same. However some may prefer to see every truth together and adhere unreservedly to a stereotyped orthodoxy, independent minds cannot do so, so long as the progress of mind is what it is. Again; it is all the more honourable to religion when it is found that men holding diverse views can bid each other God-speed in the great work. Because they have the same aim they unite; and, if they do not exactly agree, yet they do not quarrel.

"I have my own way of doing things, and can do them in no other man's way. Of course, a man must be crazy to undertake the pastoral office, and set about the work as a mere Evangelist would. I plough my own church up afresh every year, but I do not confine myself to that species of labour. My discourses have embraced a very extensive range, which, of course, I should neither have had time nor inclination to accomplish had I been simply an Evangelist.

"For my dear wife, to whom, with myself, you have presented these beautiful volumes,—for which I most cordially thank you,—I may say, that we have found warm and loving hearts here. We have met with a greeting which has greatly delighted us in Dr. Campbell's family. We have seen the hand of God in that family, and we shall never forget it as long as we remember anything."

Mr. Finney concluded his address by a pathetic appeal to the young Converts, whom he urged to come forward and announce themselves to Dr. Campbell and his officers. This, he said, was simple justice to them, that they might glorify God for the success which had attended their efforts. He then went into copious details of his own emotions towards the spot on which he was converted, and described his deep grief at finding the beautiful grove transformed into a simple field. He could not take his leave of them on that occasion, as he hoped to address them once more on Wednesday (this evening). He would not indulge in any appeal to their sensibilities. When he left them his heart would still remain with them; his body departed, but his heart remained; and when he was pushing away o'er the mighty deep, he asked them to pray that the Lord would bless and preserve them, and give the winds and the waves a charge concerning them, that they injure them not.

Dr. Brown, of Cheltenham, who had been an interested auditor during the lengthened service, on the stroke of ten o'clock, received intimation from the Pastor, that the few closing minutes would be accorded to him; and the Doctor, in standing up, intimated that the eyes of multitudes in all parts of the kingdom were now being directed towards this spot, and that they were anxiously waiting the result of these special movements, apprising the converts, that they, in a great measure, held the honour of the movement and of those concerned in it in their own hands. In confirmation of this, he stated a most touching fact which occurred in Dorsetshire, and which came under his own eye—the case of a wife whose persecutions from her husband were severe in the extreme, but who combined the utmost meekness with the most unflinching firmness, the result of which was completely to overcome her husband; who became, in the end, himself a companion in her pilgrimage, and a man of exemplary piety and eminent usefulness. The fact gave a beautiful finish to the interesting services.

It may be proper to state, that, with one or two exceptions, the numerous expressions of intense interest and sympathy with which the addresses were interspersed, to economise space have been suppressed in the Report. Altogether the service was one which will be long remembered.

FAREWELL SERMON.

"Wherefore I take you to record this day, that I am pure from the blood of all men for I have not shunned to declare unto you all the counsel of God," Acts xx. 26, 7

I speak to-night, as you are aware, from these words at Dr. Campbell's particular request. Much as I have laboured as an Evangelist, and numerous a are the times I have been called to part with those amongst whom I have been preaching, yet I have never hitherto allowed myself to address them from thi text, or, in fact, from any other portion of the chapter in which it is found; and when Dr. Campbell asked me to preach from it, I told him I did not feel as if could. There are so many affecting things grouped together in this chapter respecting the Apostle, that I have been afraid, lest, if I preached from the text, that some one should think I meant to compare myself, in some point with the Apostle. Nothing, however, could be further from my thoughts

The first inquiry to which we are naturally led by the text, is, What i intended by the assertion of the Apostle, that he is "pure from the blood of al men?" This may be explained by a reference to what we find in Ezekiel iii. 17 and elsewhere the same sentiment occurs expressed in similar terms: "Son c man, I have made thee a watchman unto the house of Israel: therefore hea the word at my mouth, and give them warning from me. When I say unto th wicked, Thou shalt surely die; and thou givest him not warning, nor speakes to warn the wicked from his wicked way, to save his life; the same wicked ma shall die in his iniquity; but his blood will I require at thine hand. Yet if thou warn the wicked, and he turn not from his wickedness, nor from his wicked way, he shall die in his iniquity; but thou hast delivered thy soul. Again, when a righteous man doth turn from his righteousness, and commit iniquity, and I lay a stumbling-block before him, he shall die; because thou hast not given him warning, he shall die in his sin, and his righteousness which he hath done shall not be remembered; but his blood will I require at thine hand. Nevertheless if thou warn the righteous man, that the righteous sin not, and he doth not sin, he shall surely live, because he is warned; also thou hast delivered thy soul."

Here, then, is the principle involved in the language used by the Apostle. The reference to "blood" of course is figurative, and must be regarded as the blood of the soul. To be guiltless or clear of the blood of men is to be clear of the charge of unfaithfulness to them. The Apostle means that *he* is not to blame if those who have sat under his ministry are lost. He has discharged his duty, and such as were lost were themselves answerable. In further remarking from these words, the following is the train of thought I design to pursue:

I. THE SOUL IS OF INFINITE VALUE.
II. IT CANNOT BE LOST, WITHOUT INFINITE GUILT TO SOME ONE.
III. I SHALL NOTICE SOME OF THE CONDITIONS UPON WHICH THOSE WHO ARE HELD RESPONSIBLE FOR THE SOUL WILL OR WILL NOT BE FOUND CLEAR OF THEIR BLOOD IF THEY ARE LOST.
IV. I SHALL OFFER SOME GENERAL REMARKS.

With respect to the infinite value of the soul, it is a theme so vast, that whenever the mind gives itself up to dwell upon it, it seems to be overcome with the attempt to conceive of so vast a thing. It is a thought familiar to you all, that everything that is really valuable must either belong to the mind itself or to something which is valuable as a means of promoting the welfare of mind. Nothing can be valuable in itself but the well-being of mind. If you take all mind out of the universe, what is there left that is valuable? All things, painful or pleasurable, belong to mind, and especially is this true of moral agents. It is, of course, of their souls I speak; for of mere brute beasts, as we know but little, we can say but little about them. When we speak of the souls of men we refer to what we know to be immortal. They must live for ever; when they have once begun to be, they will never cease to be. Beginning to be they will grow older and older, live onward and onward, as long as God shall live. Think of that! But I must not extend here.

Another consideration is, that, from the very nature of mind, it must be either happy or miserable, and one of these must be ever increasing in quantity. The capability of the finite mind is for ever increasing. By a natural law, this must be the case. The means of its happiness or misery,—its thoughts, knowledge, character,—all these things are developing onward and onward for ever and for ever, and consequently the power of mind,—its capacity for enjoyment or misery,—is always enlarging, and its cup is ever full in a future world.

But I must not enlarge on this thought. I dwelt at considerable length on it one evening when I preached on "The Infinite Worth of the Soul," and for that reason I shall not enlarge on it, but proceed in the next place to suggest some thoughts which I then suggested. When we consider the fact, that from the point where we commence existence the soul goes on enlarging in capacity either of enjoyment or misery,—that this capacity is ever full, and goes on increasing as long as eternity endures, it is easy to see that a period must arrive when the amount of enjoyment or suffering, which can be predicated of any individual soul, is greater in amount than can be computed by the aggregate mind of all the creatures of God. Were every finite mind merged in one, and that mind to put forth its utmost conception, it could neither compute nor conceive of an amount so great either of enjoyment or suffering as will actually be enjoyed or suffered at some period of its existence by every immortal soul in the universe, and this is only the beginning of joy or sorrow; for when any one individual, say the last that has gone to heaven, has enjoyed more than all heaven had enjoyed at the commencement of its bliss, or than all the inhabitants of heaven could conceive of up to that time; still beyond roll the waves of eternity, onward and onward, and the soul has not one moment less to exist than at first: and stretch your conceptions as you may, to the utmost limit of finite capacity, and still enjoyment or suffering has but begun, and there is no computing it; it is ever increasing in quantity, yet never infinite, though vast beyond comprehension. If you are to live for ever, and your existence runs on till the elements are melted with fervent heat, and the universe is rolled together as a scroll, and passes away with a great noise,—the time must come when you can say of yourself, looking back o'er the lengthened ages through which you have lived,—the vast cycles which have rolled away,—remembering all your sorrows or joys,—you may say, "I have either enjoyed more or suffered more now, in my own personal experience, than all the creatures of God had enjoyed or suffered when I came to this place.["] But when you have said that, a soul in heaven might say, Why I know more of God now than all heaven knew, when I came here! Just think of that! Think that the youngest child in this congregation must arrive at a period of its existence, when looking round on the vast throngs which surrounds the heavenly throne, it will be able to say, "I am older now than the aggregate age of all the children of God and of all angels in heaven, when I first came here. I am older than they all then were. I have had more experience and know more about God than they all then knew. Yes! I have received mercies and favours from God Himself now, more than they all had received when I came here, and they all have been progressing as fast as I have, and they are as far a head of me now as they were then, and yet I myself, perhaps the last of all that came here, I know more of God than they all knew, I am older than they all were when I came here. My cup of joy, which is always full and running over, has run over more than they all had enjoyed before I came here." Well, what of that? You have only just begun. Right beyond is an eternity still just as real,—just as extensive as it was the moment you entered here. The waves of life are rolling, and rolling, and rolling,—there is neither shore, nor bound, nor bottom, nor height, nor depth,—there is an infinity on every side.

Paul,—how many years has he been in heaven, with his spiritual children gathered around him—all those who were converted under his ministry? Thousands of them could now tell him, "Why I know more, a thousand times, about God and about heaven, than you and all the Church of God knew, when I came here." Go forward to any period; let any computation be made. Let your mind stretch itself to the utmost limits of its capacity—what then? You have only set your foot on the threshold of Eternity, and are no nearer the end. When your cup has enlarged and enlarged, so that oceans and oceans and oceans have been enjoyed and overflowed—what then? You are rising and rising and rising, but as God is absolutely infinite, you will continue to rise; but notwithstanding you are always rising towards Him, you will always remain infinitely below Him.

Now turn it over on the other hand to the individual who goes on sinning and sinning and sinning. There was a first sin,—there was a time when sin first took hold of him, and remorse caused the first pang in his little conscience,—when his little mind was pressed, and he resisted,—when the tear was forced into his little eye, and his little conscience twinged. Ah! that was the first twinge, but by-and-by he sinned and sinned and sinned again and again, and so he went on till now. Think of such an individual launching into Eternity, where all restraint on his sinfulness is taken off. His bodily appetites and propensities which he sought to indulge, are now no more. His friendships are gone for ever. He has received all the good he ever will receive. He has passed God's mercy, rejected His Gospel, abused His Spirit, and is sinning still. With increasing vigour he rushes on in his awful course. Ah! think of the many twinges, sorrows, agonies, and hours of remorse even in this world; but in a future world where conscience will do its duty perfectly, where there will be no diverting it, where the eyes will be opened to the truth, and cannot be shut, but must behold the everlasting loss of the soul, where he blasphemes God and looks upwards sinning on and on. Ah! sinner, think! You will be able to say, "I have now committed a greater number of sins than all the sinners in hell, and in all the rest of the universe had, before I was born! All the devils in hell put together, and all the wicked men in hell at the time I came here, had not committed so many sins in the aggregate, as I have myself since I have been here.["] This period must certainly arrive. To be sure, the others have gone far a head of you still; but notwithstanding this, what I have said of you is perfectly true. Ah! who can tell the deep agonies and tears,—who can compute or conceive of them! What but an infinite mind could look at them without being overcome and wailing out through the agony of eternal despair to think they were not holy. There is no contemplating the idea of immortality from any point of view, or believing in it without its weighing upon the spirit. What mortal can look at it?—what angel or other being can look at its vast and infinite import, without feeling as if his nerves were on fire with such a conception? But I must not enlarge upon this, or I shall keep you here all night.

In the next place, not one of these souls of such great and infinite value can be lost, without somebody incurring infinite responsibility and infinite guilt. God is, in a threefold sense, the owner of these souls. He has created them all—He has preserved them all—and when they had sold themselves, He has redeemed them all by the precious blood of Jesus Christ. Therefore He has a threefold claim on them, and if they cost Him so much, He will not see them lost without making an inquisition for blood. The souls of those He thus redeemed cost Him far more than the material universe. He spoke, and the energy of His word gave existence to the material universe, and created system upon system. He could thus people space with worlds and systems, but He could not thus easily redeem the sinful myriads who were spiritually dead, and who had incurred the penalty of His Divine law, and this could not be done by His simple fiat. Oh! no. This is a different work. It cost Him much, indeed, to redeem these souls. The Word which called them into existence was powerful and infinite; but to redeem them, to release them from the penalty of the Divine law, to make an atonement, to throw open the door of mercy, so that God could be just, and yet the justifier of the ungodly—this was a great work, and cost the Son of God more than thirty years intense suffering and labour, missionary labour, trouble, persecution, misapprehension, and finally, it cost him life!—He must die an ignominious death, and go down to the grave with the accusation of blasphemy resting upon Him. Ah! under the charge of blasphemy, the Son of God must die!—Under the charge of blasphemy, for you and for me? God the Father, must give His only begotten and well-beloved Son, in whom He was well pleased, to die. What a sacrifice was this! What a view we have here, of His amazing self-denial. Think of that. To see the whole family of heaven, every creature in heaven, with the Father, Son, and Holy Spirit,—all combining to carry on, with the greatest self-denial, this effort to save the souls of sinful and perishing men! What a testimony is this to its value! What are we to think of God's opinion of the value of the soul? Think what self-denial! Think of the Father, as it were, fitting out His only begotten and well-beloved Son, as a missionary to this world. Just think of it! What must the inhabitants of heaven have thought to see Him fitted out as a missionary to save this dying world! We talk about the missionaries, and self-denial, and get up meetings when missionaries are going off, to express our sympathy, to sing hymns to God, and pray together, and give them our blessing and our prayer,—but what must have been the state of things when it was published in heaven for the first time, that the Son of God was going as a missionary to this world to save these rebels by His blood? You would suppose that there would have been tears in heaven—there would have been tears of grief and unspeakable joy,—astonishment of the angelic hosts at the love of God, wonder at the whole thing when published in heaven, as a new thing; for it must have been, at some time or other, a new thing,—it must have filled them with astonishment and joy and sympathy unutterable. How many millions of hearts were then drawn into sympathy with this wonderful undertaking.

Now, mark; God has made provision for the salvation of every immortal soul, although it was condemned to die. Every man is enjoined to take care of his soul. He is asked what he will give in exchange for it, and reminded that it will profit him nothing to gain the whole world, if he loses it. Every man is bound to look well to it, and make it his first business to secure it from eternal death. He is to seek first "the kingdom of God and His righteousness," and everything else shall be thrown in. He shall lose nothing by it, if he is careful not to lose his soul. This charge He has given to every man solemnly. Take care you do not lose it, while God thus prizes it infinitely, and has given His Son to die for it. He loves it with an everlasting love, but He cannot save it without your concurrence. You are free; and He must have your consent,—your heart,—your sympathy. Take care that you do not lose it. It is impossible for Him, from the nature of the case, to save it without your co-operation and consent. Take care, then, and set about it. Let it be your first great concern to take care of, and to save this immortal soul!

He has also given us charge in respect to the souls of those around us. This refers especially to ministers: "Son of man," He says, "I have set you as a watchman to the house of Israel;" you must "hear the word of My mouth, and if I say to the wicked man, Thou shalt surely die, if thou warn not the wicked man to flee from his way, and he flee not, he shall die in his iniquity; but his blood will I require at *thy* hands: but if thou warn him, and he flee not, he shall die in his iniquity; but his blood will I require at *his* hands, and thou shalt deliver thy soul." He has also given a solemn charge to the Church in this point, to watch over, to pray, to warn, to exhort, and labour for the souls of those around them. Christian parents, teachers, brothers, sisters,—all classes of Christians: "What I say unto you, I say unto all,—watch;" and not only watch for your own souls, but see what can be done for the souls of those with whom you have to do. Again; God has charged all men to love their neighbours as themselves, and to take care of *their* souls, as well as of their own. Every person,—even the wicked man,—is bound to love his neighbours, and to see to it that he never neglects his own soul, or the souls of those who may be under his influence.

But I pass, in the third place, to notice in a few words, the conditions upon which all who have this responsibility can be clear of the blood of souls. This cannot be said of us, unless we do all that we consistently can do. If we neglect our own souls, we are guilty of our own blood; and if we do not do our duty to others, we are also guilty of theirs.

I shall now advert, in a few words, to the different classes of persons, and the duties of their different relations. Ministers and teachers must be "instant in season and out of season," teaching the truth, the whole truth, and nothing but the truth; labouring in a right way, and with a right spirit; laying themselves on the altar, and not shunning to "declare the whole counsel of God;" selecting such truths as the people seem most to need; powerfully appealing to the hearts and consciences of those amongst whom they live. They are bound also, to live in such a manner as to show everybody that they themselves believe and practise what they preach to others. We must live the truth out of the pulpit, as well as declare the truth in the pulpit, and preach by our spirit, temper, life, and all that we do, that we may be clear of the blood of souls.

But there are other classes who have also serious responsibilities with regard to this matter: Church officers should consider their responsibility. Let them remember it is great, and that they cannot be made clear of the blood of souls if they do not sustain their important relation as they ought to sustain it.

Again: take parents, and see how great are their responsibilities. Only think of their exerting a greater influence over their children, perhaps, than all the world besides. They will do more for or against the souls of their children than, perhaps, everything else combined; and if they do not do their duty, their hands will be red with the blood of their children at that day. See that unfaithful mother's hands,—how red they are! What! has she been murdering her children? or, to say the least, has she been neglecting to labour for the conversion of her children? What has she been about? I have not time, of course, to descend into all the relations of life; but let what I have said suggest to you the relations of Sabbath-school teachers and missionaries, brothers, sisters, friends, young converts, and older Christians. Let me say to all of you, that you have each of you great and peculiar responsibilities, and no man can be guiltless of the blood of souls who does not do his duty, labouring faithfully, as God has given him opportunity and power to present God's offers of salvation to men. But, of course, it is especially expected of ministers, that they shall warn, exhort, and rebuke with all long-suffering.

But having said thus much upon the three leading thoughts, I shall now proceed to make some general remarks. And the first remark is this,—to have a clear conscience is a point of inestimable importance. What an infinite consolation to God the Father, Son, and Holy Spirit, must be the reflection, that nothing has been omitted that enlightened benevolence demanded for the salvation of immortal souls,—that nothing has been done which enlightened benevolence forbade, to throw obstacles in the way of their salvation,—that He has consulted His infinite intelligence, and in all things done the best that Infinite power and love could do to prevent the loss of any immortal soul. So that when God looks around upon the universe, and beholds the sufferings of the wicked,—when He listens to their wailings, just think of the consolation He will have of being able to exclaim, "I am clear of their blood,—I call the universe to record that I am clear!" This must be one of the great objects of the general Judgment, that God,—if I may use such an expression,—may clear up His character and vindicate His conduct in the presence of the entire universe, and bring it with one consent to pronounce a sentence of deserved condemnation upon the wicked!

It is easy to see, that so complicated is the vast machinery,—so little do we know of the vast multitude of the things which make up this world's history, and the history of the universe,—that *now* we cannot, of course, pronounce upon God's conduct any further than that our limited intelligence declares He must be right. At a period when there will be time enough,—when suns and moons have ceased to rise and set,—when years have ceased to mark the cycles which roll away,—when men have ceased to die, and shall put on immortality, and have time to consider the matter,—God, having recorded in His infinite mind all the facts, bringing up all the transactions of the entire universe, will then explain in a clear light all the reasons which have actuated Him in our creation, preservation, and in all His providential arrangements. All His disinterestedness and self-denial will come out. Every mouth will then be stopped,—everything will be cleared up, so that it shall not be possible for any being in the universe to open his mouth and add another word as to the propriety of what has been done: "Every mouth shall be stopped, and all the world become guilty before God!" Now, if this be so, when God has disclosed it all, and brought home to the intelligence of the whole universe the question of what is right in the case, and has received the unanimous consent of the entire universe of his creatures that He is infinitely far from the least fault in this matter,—when He has placed the thing in such a light that there can be no doubting as to anything He has done,—as to His propriety, benevolence, and affection,—then He will know that they know as He now knows, and will eternally know, that He has done all that infinite love and power could do, to save those souls to which He attaches a value so infinite.

Again; suppose God's conscience condemned Him, and suppose that He being a moral agent could accuse Himself of anything which was unbecoming, any want of faithfulness or benevolence, or of anything which His infinitely pure mind could pronounce wrong? It would fill that infinite mind of His with unutterable regrets, sorrow, and pangs of remorse, to see eternity rolling onward and onward, and the amount of misery accumulating, and accumulating, and accumulating, till no mind but His could comprehend the extent of it; and if He could only accuse Himself of the least wrong in all this, it would fill His own mind with a pang that would really make an Infinite hell. There will, however, be no such thing, but right over against this there will be the eternal consciousness of being clear; and when it is found that the souls are lost, and the inquiry is made—Here is murder! Ten hundred thousand millions of immortal souls—yes, more in number than can be computed! Here is murder! murder! Those souls are slain! Who has done this? Who has committed all these murders? God the Father says, "I am clear,"—and the Son says, "I am clear,"—and the Holy Ghost says, "I am clear!" and now inquisition must be made, Who has been guilty of this deed? What deeds of death are here! What dreadful things are done! Who has done them?

Once more: Paul said to those to whom he had preached, that they knew very well from their own observation that he was clear of their blood, and he called on them themselves to witness to it, and to make a record of it. I call upon you to take knowledge, and record the testimony, that I may use it in the solemn judgment—that I may take with me your testimony, and confront you with it then, that I may be clear of the blood of you all.

Again: this parting, on the other hand, must be dreadful indeed to a minister who has been unfaithful—who has, on his conscience, a direct and powerful accusation of his unfaithfulness. Suppose it says, "You have been seeking your own popularity and filthy lucre. You have been indolent. You have truckled to a false and most pernicious public sentiment, and bowed down to an ungodly fastidiousness. You have not rightly represented God and Christ. You have concealed things which you feared would give offence. You have been seeking your own character, reputation, and advancement, more than the honour and glory of God.["] Why, suppose he was obliged to confess this, while his conscience strongly accused him of it! Oh! how would he feel to die confessing this? What would he say on meeting those souls in the solemn judgment? How solemn it must be for Paul or for any minister to meet right face to face the masses to whom they have proclaimed the whole counsel of God! What a meeting this must be! Oh! beloved, we shall meet again, directly at the bar of God; and what shall we meet for? I, to give an account of my ministry, and the manner in which I have dealt with your souls, and you to give an account of the manner in which you have received or rejected the counsel of God; and now, beloved, are we prepared for the trial, when the Judge of all the Earth shall sit on his great white throne and come forth with so terrible a majesty?—when heaven and earth shall flee from his presence, the books shall then be opened, and the dead shall be judged out of those books? The sea shall then yield up its dead. Whenever I have been at sea these words have come home to me with solemn emphasis. In a few days I shall be again on the bosom of the mighty deep, and they will, doubtless, occur to me again and again.

Ah! it will be a solemn time both for ministers and for hearers, for saints and for sinners, for parents and for children, for old and for young! Each must give an account for himself, and what a responsibility is this! I have been a pastor now, as I said on Monday, about eighteen years, besides labouring a great deal in the capacity of an Evangelist; and thousands have sat under my ministry; here and there I have known them pass into eternity before me; but thousands and thousands will also come after me; we must all be congregated at that day: and I know very well it is one thing to appeal to men, but vastly different to walk right up to the Almighty and take his judgment on the entire matter. When it comes to this—when all the secrets of our hearts are laid open to the bottom of our deepest thoughts, and brought out and exhibited—when every motive of my heart, when every sermon is thoroughly scanned, and every circumstance and thought of every day! Ah! that will be a solemn time for me, when scores of thousands in America and in Britain will face me! But I am not going to say all that Paul said.

It must be an awful thing for congregations to meet their ministers,—those who have had pastors and those who have had occasional preachers,—it must be an awful thing for them to meet! Just think of it. I have often thought that the relation of pastor and people is one of the most solemn relations of life. Just think what it will be for ministers to meet their people. God will surely make inquisition for blood. He must require this at some one's hands. Who is to blame? Will God see this, think you, and make no inquiry about it? Who has done this deed, shed this blood, and helped to fill the courts of hell with moanings and lamentations?

As I have said, the Father, Son, and Holy Ghost will say, "We have not done it." The Prophets and Apostles will say, "We have not done it." Who then has done it? First, the sinner himself; secondly, unfaithful ministers; thirdly, unfaithful deacons and other office-bearers in the Church; fourthly, unfaithful parents; unfaithful children have done it; unfaithful brothers and sisters have done it; unfaithful Sabbath-school teachers have done it,—all unfaithful men have contributed towards it. See them there! They are dripping with blood! It is clear who has done it; you need not ask who it is, every man can see that for himself. Who has done it? Those on the left hand, there—they are the men! There they are; does it need proof? See that murderer standing over his victim with the weapon reeking in his hand; he has just done the deed, and the blood is still upon him! Ah! see that unfaithful minister coming up; he cannot lift up his head. He has come with those who have sat under his ministry, and heard his pretty oratory, seen his graceful gestures, and his trimming to please their fancy. Ah! there comes that ungodly minister! How afraid he was to say hell, or to let us know there was such a place! Do you recollect how he trimmed and opposed this thing that thing and the other? Do you recollect how he was almost always against all reform and all progress in religion? Do you remember it? Hear them talk. Ah! that was our minister; see how he looks down; what is he afraid of? Is he afraid to see the eye of the Judge, as it glances through and through him? Ah! that unfaithful minister pretended to preach the Gospel! He pretended to deal faithfully with our souls; but how much blood there is upon him! What an awful thing it must be!

I have hundreds of times, in my own experience, been greatly searched with the truths which I have preached myself; and in reading the Bible I have been thousands of times pressed close by such passages as these, to look them right in the face and say, Am I clear of their blood? And in looking over the many fields where the providence of God has called me to labour, I have heard of this man and of that man being dead; how has it led me to exclaim, Have I done my duty to that man?—was I faithful to him, or was I indolent, ambitious, and unfaithful? I have often thought of this, and I speak it not boastingly; I can say so far as concerns myself, that I have never kept back what I thought the people needed most of all, either because I was afraid of them on the one hand, or from any other reason whatsoever. I never had courage to keep it back. People have said to me, How dare you preach as you do? How dare I preach as I do? Why I dare not preach any otherwise. I have not the courage to disobey God, and rush to the judgment covered with the blood of the souls of men. No! I have no such courage as that. Which should I fear, God or man? How much intellect must a man have who fears rather to walk up to the sinner and tell him the truth, than to walk up to God and give an account of his unfaithful stewardship? Why, such a man must be an infidel. Afraid of man rather than of God!

When we shall meet in the judgment, those who have been sinners will find themselves utterly without excuse, and they will have observed that their own blood must be upon their own heads. It is also clear that there is somebody guilty,—cruelly guilty,—of not praying and labouring for them as they ought to have done. Whatever occurs at the judgment, I have often wondered whether the strong feelings which must then exist will find vent in the natural expression of them. I have often wondered whether,—when the unfaithful minister, for instance, meets the multitude with whom he has dealt unfaithfully,—whether they will really be allowed to hurl their curses upon him. If they are in their senses, they will be wicked enough, and have reason enough! But will the Judge allow them? They will, perhaps, have more reason to curse him than all the world besides,—more reason to say to him, Oh! thou most cursed amongst men, hast thou not trifled with thine office, and with our souls? Did we not look up to thee, as a teacher of religion, and yield ourselves up in confidence to thee, and now thou hast led us to hell! Oh! if such feelings as must exist are allowed to find expression, is it too much to say that they will hiss, and groan, and gnash their teeth at that man to all eternity!

But let me turn this over! What a meeting it will be, when Ministers, Prophets, Apostles, Moses, Elijah, Elisha, Joshua, Jeremiah, Ezekiel, and all the minor Prophets, all the Apostles, shall assemble in heaven; I have thought a great many times of the wonderful convention that assembled once during the time of our Saviour's residence upon earth. It was the most wonderful meeting probably that ever took place in this universe. We read that Christ took James and Peter and John, and went up into a mountain, and was transfigured before them; and his raiment became white as snow, and there appeared also Moses and Elias,—the two great representatives of the Old Dispensation. There was Moses, the great deliverer of the Law. There, too, was Elijah, the great representative of the race of Prophets; and Jesus Christ, the Head and Captain of the Lord's hosts, and the Saviour of the world! with whom Moses and Elias, of the Ancient Church (the Old Dispensation), were commissioned to attend this convention, and the three Apostles, Peter, James, and John. What an assembly! And they spoke with Christ about His advent, and what He should accomplish by His death and His resurrection. What a sight was that! No wonder the thing was so overcoming to these representatives of the Church Militant! The Church on earth, as represented, was quite overcome. They could not stand such glory as was caused by Christ being transfigured before them, and by the sight of the two representatives of the Church triumphant in glory. They were confounded. They said it was good for them to be there. They were intoxicated with joy, and said, "Let us make three tabernacles, one for thee, and one for Moses, and one for Elias; for it is good to be here." The poor Apostles were hardly able to bear so much: it almost bewildered them. We are told they knew not what they said.

Now just think, beloved, for a little, of how it will appear by-and-by. There had been Moses greeting for thousands of years those who had come to heaven through his instrumentality. All knew Moses; and, doubtless, when any saint goes to heaven in these days, as soon as he can get a little time from gazing on the wonders and glories of Jesus, he searches out him amongst the crowds of ancient worthies. Whitefield, too, is gone, and with and after him the crowds who sat where you now sit, when he was standing where I now stand, and they will doubtless know each other. What a happiness for them all, to meet and mingle their joys,—pastors and people, evangelists and the multitudes to whom they have preached,—the whole of the Church of God will be gathered home. Since I have been in London, how many I have heard of departing for a better world! There is Dr. Pye Smith, and several other ministers, with whose names and works I had become acquainted in America, but they are gone, and others are following on and on; fathers and mothers, sisters and brothers, have been taken even from the midst of this flock since I have laboured amongst you. What a glorious idea, that when we meet there it will not be to part,—that is, those of us who have washed our robes and made them white in the blood of the Lamb,—we shall meet, to say farewell no more!

The last three verses of the chapter I did not read: "When he had thus spoken,"—after he had preached his sermon,—"he kneeled down, and prayed with them all. And they all wept sore, and fell on Paul's neck, and kissed him, sorrowing most of all for the words which he spake, that they should see his face no more. And they accompanied him unto the ship." What a beautiful parting it was! How deeply affecting it must have been, when we take into consideration all the circumstances of the case!

But I must not detain you longer; I have only to say this, before I sit down.

May I not ask you, with all humility, who have been my hearers since I have been in London, as a matter of justice, to record to-night this fact,—that according to the best of my ability I have dealt faithfully with your souls? May I?—may I not challenge you to bear this testimony in your conscience; and let it be borne in mind till the solemn judgment, that so far as I have had ability I have kept nothing back which I thought you needed, and which I have had ability and time to say? I do not say this boastingly, as God is judge between us; but I fear that some of you I shall have to leave in your sins! But do let me ask, Have you not begun the work of preparing for the great judgment? You have heard the solemn appeals and warnings which have issued from this pulpit,—will you not think and act? Will you, my dear friends, rid me of all responsibility by saying, "Yes! yes!—and if I perish it is not your fault, you have dealt faithfully with me, and I consent that it may be recorded in heaven, at the solemn judgment, that you are clear."

I want to be able to carry this, not in my own conscience only, for I know that my record must be carried on high. It is in vain for me or you to justify ourselves; the record must be on high. Probably I may see none of you, it is certain I shall see but few of you, again till the solemn judgment. Ah! what a meeting must that be!

It is not my custom to preach farewell sermons, but to tear away, and let God do the judging and recording, and seal it up to the solemn judgment. The last leaf of the transactions connected with my ministry here is just about to be folded and put away; the last record is just about to be made and put away, laid aside among the records of eternity, to be exhibited when you and I shall stand before God,—when there will be no darkness, no excusing, no shuffling, no false pleas, no false thing, but oceans of light will be poured upon you.

May God search my own heart and prepare me for that solemn season! May He prepare you for it too! And now may I be allowed to call on heaven and earth to record upon your souls that, so far as I have had ability, I have set before you life and death, blessing and cursing, the Gospel, and the law as the rule of life; and opened to you, as far as I have been able, the gate of mercy, and shown you the heart of Jesus Christ, and will you have Him? But I must not say another word.

APPENDIX.

The Editor happening one day, in conference with Mr. Finney, to refer to the Welch Independent Churches, apprised that gentleman that his Lectures had been translated into the Welch language,—an intimation which brought out the fact that Mr. Finney had had some correspondence with the ministers of those churches, relative to this matter, and that he had some of the communications among his papers. The Editor on reading the same, and considering them important as facts connected with the history of the labours of his honoured guest, as also of religion in Wales, requested copies of the same; and now that on issuing the present pages he finds that there is space to spare, he deems it proper, as well as highly pertinent to the subject of the publication, to set them forth.[2] The first, which is from North Wales, runs as follows:

"TO THE REV. C. G. FINNEY.

"Rev. and dear Brother,

"We, the undersigned Ministers of the Congregational Denomination in North Wales, being assembled at a Meeting held at Mostyn, Flintshire, on the occasion of the departure of our much-esteemed brother, the Rev. Benjamin W. Chidlaw, of Cincinnati, Ohio, avail ourselves of the opportunity of forwarding to you our Christian regards.

"Although we are on another continent far apart, your name is familiar to us: with your Christian labours we are also acquainted, and we bless God that you have been so eminently successful as an instrument in His hands in the conversion of souls.

"Your work on 'Revivals' has been translated into our native language, and under the blessing of God has been the means of rousing the dormant energies of our churches. Your 'Sermons on Important Subjects' are also in course of translation, and will shortly issue from the press. We humbly trust and pray that their publication may be followed by the same desirable and happy effects.

"We have great pleasure in being enabled to inform you that the Lord's work is progressing rapidly in the northern counties of the Principality of Wales. We have been greatly refreshed by the evident tokens of the presence of the Holy Spirit in our churches. Within the last two years, several thousand souls have been added to our churches, and the increase is still proceeding onward.

"We have also great pleasure in informing you that this happy state of things is to be attributed, in a great measure, to the reading of your works. This, combined with the readiness with which the Total Abstinence principle was received and acted upon, both by ministers and people, and the zeal with which we engaged in its propagation,[3] we believe to have been the means, under the Divine blessing, of producing life, prosperity, and joy in our churches.

"We sincerely and deeply regret that an afflictive Providence has incapacitated you from your public ministrations. We deeply sympathise with you, under this affliction. Our prayer is, and shall be, directed to our gracious Lord, that he may be pleased to produce good out of evil,—turn the cup of bitterness into sweetness, and reveal His goodness, not only to you personally, but to his Church in general, by a means of what we cannot but view as a public calamity.

"Accept our most affectionate Christian regards. It is not likely we shall meet each other face to face in this world, but we look forward confidently to another and a brighter day, when we shall meet in heaven, as faithful soldiers of the Cross, and partake of the spoils of victory. Hail, glorious day!

"Signed at Mostyn, Flintshire, North Wales, February 27, 1840.

"Michael Jones, Llannwehllyn, near Bala.
"William Rees, Denbigh.

[2]The original letters are in the Finney Papers (microfilm, roll 4). There have been a number of minor changes made, the more important of which are given in the footnotes.

[3]The rest of this sentence in the original reads: "is the means which under the Divine Blessing we believe to have been the cause of producing life, prosperity and joy in our Churches."

"Jonathan Davis, Pennel.[4]
"Thomas Griffiths, Rhydlydon.
"Richard Jones, Ruthya.
"Thomas Ridge, Hangwyfan.
"Lewis Everett, Llanrwst.
"Hugh Pugh, Mostyn.
"Ellis Hughes, Holywell.
"Isaac Harvies, Mold."

From this it will be seen that Mr. Finney's Sermons also were translated into the Welch language. These Discourses have had a most extensive circulation in England, although they have not commanded the same public attention as his Lectures, in the blaze of which the lustre of his other writings, published in England, have been lost.

This frank and interesting letter, shows the power of the printing-press in diffusing truth and extending the labours of men. When Mr. Finney was pouring forth these vigorous effusions in New York, he little dreamed that the echoes of his voice would resound in the valleys of Wales,—entering the ear, penetrating the hearts of a multitude of fervent men, who should respond to his appeals, adopt his counsels, and betake themselves to the labours which have had so happy a result. The next communication is from South Wales, and comprise the resolutions which follows:

"*St. David's, July* 13*th,* 1840.

"Reverend Sir,

"It is gratifying to me to be employed in transmitting to you the following Resolution of the Conference, at an annual assembly of the Independent Ministers in the counties of Carmarthen, Pembroke, and Cardigan, South Wales, held on the 4th[5] of June, 1840, at Brynberian, Pembrokeshire; viz.,—

" 'That the Chairman be requested to write to the Reverend Charles G. Finney, of America, offering him the cordial thanks of this Conference for the publication of his valuable 'Lectures on Revivals,' and to state to him that those Lectures have proved the means, under the blessing of God, of awakening in the minds of many ministers, and also in many churches, a feeling which has led them to seek the revival[6] of pure religion in a more suitable manner than they had done before.'

"There were present at the Conference between forty and fifty ministers, many of whom professed to feel, in an unusual degree, the importance of the work, and their responsibilities as ministers. It was also stated, that a like feeling seemed to prevail, in some measure, in the churches generally, which[7] was ascribed to the perusal[8] of the above Lectures, as a[9] means, accompanied by the powerful influences of the Holy Spirit. A far greater number has been added to the churches in the Principality, during the last year, than in any

[4]The name is spelled "Davies" in the original.
[5]The original has here "3rd & 4th."
[6]The words "the revival" have replaced the word "revivals."
[7]The word "which" has replaced the words "and this happy change" in the original.
[8]The original has "reading."
[9]The word "a" is not in the original.

former year; and we are willing to hope that it is the beginning of a new era in the cause of the Redeemer in Wales.

"Thus, dear Sir, does our Divine Master seem to honour you with usefulness in promoting His blessed cause, not only in your own country, but also in distant parts of the world.

"That it may please Him to prolong your valuable life for many years yet to come, and grant you the enjoyment of health and strength to labour in His vineyard, and that all your efforts may be attended with continued tokens of His approbation, is the sincere wish and prayer of, dear Sir, your unknown, yet very respectful brother in the Lord,

(Signed) "JAMES GRIFFITHS,
"St. David's, Pembrokeshire."

We have much pleasure in appending these testimonies, so interesting in themselves, and to Mr. Finney's labours as honourable, as we have reason to know their communication was highly gratifying to his feelings.

An example, moreover, is here set to individuals and public bodies in one nation, of the duty which they owe to men who have rendered them service in another nation. We know not if any action has been taken, for example, by Ecclesiastical bodies with respect to the Rev. Albert Barnes; but certainly nothing could be more graceful, nothing more worthy and illustrative of the spirit of England, than the transmission of expressions of the sense of obligation which is entertained towards that excellent man for his labours as a Commentator on the Sacred Scriptures.

Sources and Selected Bibliography

Research for this book has brought to light a wealth of material on Charles G. Finney. Because the memoirs are limited mainly to Finney's experiences in revivals of religion, only selected sources have been directly used for the annotations. However, the sources given here are not restricted to items in the footnotes. Details are given of all known sources of Finney manuscripts as well as of material written by Finney in published works. The primary material, in particular, has been useful in elucidating the text and filling out the narrative.

Secondary literature on Finney is very extensive. Much useful research has been published, but there is a considerable amount that remains unpublished. Listed below are dissertations and theses that deal with Finney and the movements in which he figures. The more important of the published works are listed in the bibliography. In addition, the footnotes include a large amount of material that is not listed here.

MANUSCRIPTS

Manuscript of the Memoirs

The manuscript of the memoirs is in the collection "Letters and Papers of Charles Grandison Finney" in the archives of Oberlin College, Oberlin, Ohio. It appears not to have been seen by scholars until it came into the possession of the college about 1930. It was then studied by Robert S. Fletcher, the professor of history and author of the comprehensive two-volume *History of Oberlin College* noted below, and it has been used by some students and historians since then. But little of the material in the manuscript that was excluded from the first published edition of the *Memoirs* has found its way into print. Few scholars seem to have had the opportunity of working thoroughly through the manuscript. There is, however, one notable exception. The renewed interest in Finney's writings in some circles in recent years, represented by publications from Bethany House Publishers has, in part, been due to the work of Gordon C. Olson. He has made use of the original manuscript, for example, in his compilation *Quotations from the Writings and Experiences of Revivalist Charles G. Finney* (Chicago: Bible Research Fellowship, 1967). More recently Louis G. Parkhurst, Jr., has also published some sections in his compilation of Finney material, for example, in *Charles G. Finney's Answers to Prayer* (Minneapolis, Bethany House, 1983), and Finney's *Principles of Liberty* (Minneapolis: Bethany House, 1983). Historians in general, however, have remained unaware of what the original manuscript contains.

In 1976 a microfilm was made of the original document, but because of the faintness of some of the writing, the archivist at Oberlin College, William E. Bigglestone, considered that the quality was not good enough to make the microfilm generally available for scholars. Copies were, however, made available for use in the preparation of this edition. But the complexity of the document, having several handwritings and different inks, required a careful examination of the original.

The Finney Papers

In addition to the manuscript of the memoirs, the Finney Papers at Oberlin contain the bulk of the manuscript material of Finney. The most useful for this study was the main correspondence, containing some 2,500 letters written to Finney during his life. Among this group are about 70 letters written by Finney from 1831 to 1874—many of them to his family in later years. This correspondence, together with more than 700 sermon outlines, lecture notes, and miscellaneous papers, has been microfilmed as the "Charles Grandison Finney Papers." It is worth noting that, between the time the calendar of the papers was prepared in 1939 and the microfilm was made in 1958, some 160 of the letters written to Finney disappeared and have never been found. Among the miscellaneous items on roll 8 of the microfilm are copies of the two important letters written by Finney to the editor of the Baptist *Examiner and Chronicle* in 1873 about the revival in Gouverneur. These letters do not appear to have been published.

The Finney Papers further contain folders of account books, receipts, business papers, marriage certificates, newspaper clippings, and other miscellaneous papers that have not been microfilmed. These include Finney's license to preach, dated 30 December 1823, and the manuscript entitled "Diary," used as an account book from 1814 to 1820.

Additional material acquired since the microfilming of the main correspondence includes two important groups of manuscripts: twenty-four letters written between 1860 and 1875 by Charles and Elizabeth Finney to James and Alice Barlow of Bolton, England; and twenty letters from Finney written between 1860 to 1870 to Edwin and Mary Lamson of Boston. These letters, together with Finney correspondence contained in other collections at Oberlin, have been microfilmed under the title "Correspondence of Charles G. Finney, 1830–1875."

The contents of six of Finney's lecture notebooks have also been microfilmed under the title "Charles G. Finney Lectures and Sermon Outlines, 1872–1875 and n.d." At the back of the undated notebook are the entries in Lydia Finney's handwriting dated 25–31 August 1847, giving a day-to-day account of Finney's progress during the height of his severe typhus illness. No doubt Lydia wanted to be sure of capturing his last words, should he die.

Since the microfilm of the correspondence was made, five letters (and a fragment of a sixth letter) from Finney to Edward P. Marvin, dated between

1868 and 1874, and three letters to Jacob Helffenstein have been received at Oberlin. The letters to Helffenstein are an important group, for they contain two of the few surviving letters written by Finney to his collaborators in the early revival movements. Helffenstein published extracts of these letters in his article listed below.

Other Manuscript Collections at Oberlin

On the microfilm of the Finney correspondence are forty-five letters written by Finney that are in other collections at Oberlin. Among these are seventeen of the eighteen letters in the Treasurer's Office File (the main secretarial correspondence of the college in the early years). This collection has also been microfilmed under the title "Letters Received by Oberlin College, 1822–1866." It contains a large amount of material bearing upon Finney and his connection with the college. It also contains many letters written to Finney that he passed over to the secretary and many addressed to him as president. These letters and the ones written by Finney himself deal mainly with the affairs of the college. But Finney often included in his letters remarks about the revivals in which he was engaged.

The archives also house the records of the Oberlin churches, the alumni records, collections of letters and diaries, and other materials relating to the college and the town, all of which have been of value. Of particular interest are reminiscences written about 1918 by many former students at the request of P. D. Sherman, secretary of Oberlin College, in connection with a proposed history of the college (which was never written). The trustee, faculty, and prudential committees' record books are also on microfilm.

The papers of notable individuals connected with Oberlin and with Finney are valuable resources. The papers of James Harris Fairchild, George Frederick Wright, and Robert Samuel Fletcher are particularly useful. The correspondence in the Fairchild Papers, including the letters exchanged by Fairchild and his future wife between 1838 and 1841, has been microfilmed. The Wright Papers contain important letters from people whom Wright approached in gathering material for his biography of Finney noted below. Wright used some of this material for his book, but there are many interesting details that were not included. The Fletcher Papers are a mine of valuable Finney and Oberlin material, including transcriptions of some of the letters that have come up missing and letters from other collections seen by Fletcher but not now available. These include the transcription of a letter of Finney written from Syracuse to John Keep, 14 February 1853. The papers also contain the notebooks of talks that D. L. Leonard had with J. H. Fairchild between 1894 and 1897 in connection with writing his book *The Story of Oberlin* noted below. These provide a valuable supplement to Fairchild's writings on Oberlin, including one of the few references to the woman and child that Finney lived with before his conversion.

Oberlin College also holds papers of Finney's sons-in-law Jacob Dolson Cox and James Monroe and of his grandson William Cox Cochran. The correspondence in the Cox Papers has been microfilmed, but the five Finney letters there and the three in the Monroe Papers are also included on the Finney correspondence microfilm.

In all, the Oberlin College Archives holds some 162 Finney letters. Most of these are original autographs, but some of them are copies or transcriptions, and a number of the letters written in the last years of his life (when his sight was failing) are in the handwriting of his third wife, Rebecca. The Oberlin collections also contain letters by all three of Finney's wives. In addition to the detailed letters in the Finney Papers written by Elizabeth, the second Mrs. Finney, while she and her husband were in Britain in the 1850s, the special collections in Oberlin College Library include the journal she kept during their second visit in 1859–1860. This has also been microfilmed.

Finney Manuscripts in Other Archives and Collections

It is somewhat frustrating that so few of the letters that Finney wrote during the early years of his revival activities have come to light. Apart from two of the letters to Jacob Helffenstein, dated 9 December 1828 and 8 March 1832, now in the Finney Papers, only twenty-three other manuscript letters written by Finney before he went to Oberlin in 1835 are known to exist. Five of those are also in the Finney Papers, and of the remaining eighteen, eight were written to Theodore Dwight Weld and are in the Weld-Grimke Papers in the William L. Clements Library, University of Michigan. Altogether, this group, which also contains two other letters written to Weld in 1836 and 1837, constitutes the most significant collection of early Finney letters. Five of these were published by G. H. Barnes and D. L. Dumond in their edition of the Weld-Grimke letters listed in the bibliography. The transcriptions, however, are not always accurate.

In addition to the ten letters to Weld, there are fifty-four other Finney manuscript letters known outside of Oberlin College. Sixteen of these are in the American Missionary Association Papers at Dillard University, New Orleans. They are mostly concerned with Oberlin students and financial affairs of the association. Among them is the only known manuscript letter that Finney wrote to Lewis Tappan. The Lewis Tappan Papers in the Library of Congress, Washington, D.C., have no original Finney letters, although there is important information relating to Finney and Oberlin in the diaries and letterbooks of Tappan, as well as newspaper clippings and correspondence from other people. These papers are on microfilm. The Gerrit Smith Papers in Syracuse University Library, Syracuse, New York, in addition to valuable material on early Oberlin, have five Finney letters.

Apart from these groups of letters, no substantial collection of Finney manuscripts is known to exist. Some important letters, however, are scattered through a number of archives and private collections.

The University of Rochester Library, Rochester, New York, has a letter from Finney to Edward N. Kirk, dated Rochester, 1 November 1830; and the American Antiquarian Society, in Worcester, Massachusetts, has one to George B. Cheever from New York, dated 15 March 1833. Another of the early letters from Boston, dated 13 November 1831 and written to Fanny

(Thomas) Gulick, is in the Houghton Library of Harvard University, which also has a letter from Finney to Charles Sumner, dated 22 April 1869.

A number of Finney letters have turned up in autograph collections. Simon Gratz (1838–1925), the public schools administrator, whose massive collection of sixty-six thousand autograph manuscripts is in the Historical Society of Pennsylvania Library, Philadelphia, collected three Finney letters. One of these, in the "American Clergy" collection, was an early letter, dated 9 April 1831, to George S. Boardman. The other two are dated 18 August 1836 to Joshua Seixas, in the "American Prose" collection, and 13 September 1856 to [John?] Gulliver, in the "University and College Presidents" collection.

The Dreer Collection of Autograph Letters of American Clergy, also housed in the Historical Society of Pennsylvania, has a letter from Finney to [Albert] Barnes, [Thomas] Braynard (i.e., Brainerd), [John] Jenkins, and [John] Chambers, dated 12 February 1856. And the great English Nonconformist minister Thomas Raftes, in his massive collection of autograph letters, had two of Finney's: one dated 11 December 1849 to "S. Evans" (this was probably Benjamin Evans, a Baptist minister in Scarborough—Finney was turning down an invitation to preach); the other was to Daniel Lanes, dated 26 January 1851.

Other letters appear in the following collections: The Lane Seminary Records in the Cincinnati Historical Society contain Finney's recommendation of John Morgan, dated New York, 9 May 1833, appended to the bottom of a recommendation from Joshua Leavitt. William Bigglestone has drawn our attention to a letter from C. T. Carrier to Robert Stuart, 13 March 1843, which has recommendations of Oberlin students for missionary work from the Oberlin College faculty. Finney's recommendation is among these. This letter is on National Archives Microfilm ME: Michigan Superintendency of Indian Affairs and Mackinac Indian Agency, letters received, roll 54.

The Mitchell Library, Glasgow, Scotland, has an important letter from Finney to James Morison, dated 5 January 1851, in the Morison collection; and the National Library of Wales, Aberystwyth, has two letters to Thomas Rees in the Rees Manuscripts, in which Finney declines invitations to preach in Wales during his British tours.

The Massachusetts Historical Society in Boston has a letter to Joseph E. Worcester, dated 6 October 1855; Yale University Library has three letters written by Finney to William L. Kingsley in the 1860s in the James Luce Kingsley Family Papers; the University of California in Berkeley has a letter to Mary Atkins dated 30 January 1867 in the Atkins Family Papers; and Drew University Library, Madison, New Jersey, has a letter to Walter and Phoebe Palmer, dated 31 December 1867, in the Palmer Collection.

Two of Finney's letters have turned up in private hands. The Goodman Family Papers, in the possession of Thomas Tebbutt of Hadleigh, in Suffolk, England, contain, among many important letters of the Goodman and Brown families that deal with Finney's revivals in England, two letters of Finney, one to Charles P. Tebbutt, dated 16 [December] 1869; the other to Potto Brown, dated 1 October 1857.

Some collections of Finney letters have not been available to us for study. The Race Street Church in Philadelphia has three of the early letters of

Finney written to the consistory of the German Reformed Church between 1829 and 1832; and the Bernice P. Bishop Museum in Honolulu, Hawaii, has three letters from Finney to the Judd family dating from 1827 to 1836.

Some further letters of Finney that are known to have been in existence cannot now be found. Whitney R. Cross in *The Burned-over District* (see bibliography below), p. 153 n. 5, refers to "Daniel Nash and Charles G. Finney, Western, Feb. 3, 1826, to John Fine (enclosure to Absolum Peters)," in the American Home Missionary Society Papers. It is apparently missing from the papers, now housed in the Dillard University Library, New Orleans. The Rhodes House Library in Oxford also has, somewhere, a letter from Finney to P. J. Bolton, dated 10 November 1849. It was found by Louis Billington in a bundle of papers that were not catalogued and was transcribed by him, but a subsequent search has not brought it to light.

About 1956 a collection of letters from Finney to John Moore, an English Methodist, was sent by his granddaughter, Miss G. D. Moore, to the London Bible College. She also sent there two engravings or photographs of Finney, one containing a lock of his hair, and a copy of Finney's *Memoirs* presented by one of Finney's daughters to Miss Moore's father, Charles Grandison Moore, who was named after Finney. None of these items has been found. At the time, the London Bible College was using premises also occupied by the Evangelical Library, and it is possible that they were all transferred there and are somewhere in the library. It is probably an extract from one of these letters that appears in John Moore's edition of Finney's *Letters on Revivals of Religion* (1861), listed below, and it may be another of these that appeared in James Hughes's article on Thomas Aubrey listed below. A copy of another letter from Finney to John Moore, dated 19 March 1851, in Moore's handwriting, with a note "*Original Copy* in the hands of Crane Fishwich Esqi-Scoston Lanceshire," is among the Moore Family Papers, in the possession of Richard Dupuis.

There are some miscellaneous Finney letters and manuscripts in other archives. The Hamilton College Library, in Clinton, New York, houses the manuscript "Autobiography" by Alexander Bryan Johnson. On page 251 Johnson transcribed part of a letter he received from Finney in December 1827 or January 1828 while he was president of the Oneida Evangelical Society. An extract appears in Charles L. Todd and Robert Sonkin, *Alexander Bryan Johnson: Philosophical Banker* (Syracuse: Syracuse University Press, 1977), p. 158.

The printed questionnaire sent to Finney by Childs and Peterson, Philadelphia publishers, in connection with compiling *A Critical Dictionary of English Literature and British and American Authors* (1859–71), edited by S. A. Aubone, is preserved in the Historical Society of Pennsylvania Library, in Philadelphia. The rather scanty information given by Finney refers to "contributions to periodical literature published mostly in the *Oberlin Quarterly Review.* Also in *The Oberlin Evangelist.* Occasional articles in some other papers." It is not known what these other articles are.

James J. Tyler, in his article listed below, states that the Records of the Rising Sun Lodge, No. 125, in Adams, New York, are in Finney's handwriting, entered while he was acting as secretary in 1819.

Sources and Selected Bibliography

The letter of Sylvester Finney to J. L. Edwards, commissioner of pensions, dated Oberlin, 23 March 1838, is signed by Finney's father, Sylvester, but the text of the letter is in Charles's handwriting. The letter is in Pension Application File S.16114 in the Military Archives Division, National Archives and Records Service, Washington, D.C. The National Archives also houses the Judiciary Committee, Petitions, in the House of Representatives Papers. Among the petitions for the immediate abolition of slavery is one signed by eighty-four Oberlin citizens, referred to the committee in January 1862. Heading the list is Finney's signature. The brief text of the petition is not in Finney's handwriting, but *The Oberlin Evangelist,* 15 January 1862, p. 16, states, "The form of petition . . . is from the pen of President Finney."

Leonard Sweet has noted in *The Minister's Wife* (listed below), p. 264 n. 79, that there are entries of Charles and Lydia Finney in Sarah T. Seward's Album, "a repository of messages, mementos, poems, and good wishes from her friends. The MS copy is in R[ochester] P[ublic] L[ibrary]."

Finney's "Last Will and Testament," dated 8 March 1872, in his own handwriting, is in the Court of Common Pleas, Probate Division, Lorain County, Elyria, Ohio. It is on Estate Film 20, Case No. 1886.

Additional Manuscript Material

Material relating to Finney exists in many other manuscript sources, including the following:

American Unitarian Association, Correspondence Files in Andover-Harvard Theological Library. The copy of the important letter from Ephraim Perkins to A. Bancroft has a strong attack on Finney.

Austin, Ana. Papers in Onondaga County Historical Society, Syracuse.

Bolton Evangelical Revival Committee, 1860. Records in Bolton Reference Library, Bolton, Lancashire.

Bragdon Family Papers. University of Rochester Library. Contain letters written by John J. Shipherd.

Chambers, E. P. "Incidents of Early Days. Recounted by E. P. Chambers." Typescript paper read to the Knox County Historical Society, in Knox College Library, Galesburg, Illinois.

Churchill, Charles. "Book of Memoranda" and "Notebook of sermons preached by Charles G. Finney in Auburn, 1831." Silas Churchill Papers, Presbyterian Historical Society, Philadelphia.

Clark Collection. The Congregational Library, Boston. "Copy of a letter from a gentleman in Utica to a clergyman in Boston," dated 7 February 1831.

Coan, Fidelia and Titus. Letters, 1830–1872. New York Historical Society Library.

Dale, Robert W. Letters to Mrs. Cash. Birmingham Reference Library. Letters written in 1850 by a student who heard Finney preach.

Dorcasian Society Committee. "Minute Book, 1818–1861." Central Hall Deposit, Box 12, Birmingham Reference Library.

Duffield, George. Diary. Burton Historical Collections, Detroit Public Library, Detroit.

Ely, Herman. Collection in New York Historical Society Library. Box 1, Folder A, has an unsigned account of Finney's labors in Rochester dated 26 December 1830.

Everett, James. Diaries, 1784–1866. John Rylands University Library of Manchester. Vol. 9 reports Finney's sermon in Manchester in 1860.

Finney Genealogy. Connecticut Historical Society Library, Hartford, Envelope 32101, labeled "Finney."

Fitch, Asa. Diary. Yale University Library. Vol. D has details of Finney in Troy in 1826.

Foster, Abby Kelley. Papers in American Antiquarian Society, Worcester, Massachusetts. Letter of Lucy Stone to Abby and Stephen Foster, dated 25 March 1846.

Foster Family Papers. In possession of Sir Robert Foster, Great Glenham, Suffolk. Contain papers of Michael Foster of Huntingdon and his son Sir Michael Foster.

Gale, George W. "Autobiography." Knox College Library, Galesburg, Illinois. The original manuscript in Gale's handwriting covers only the section from 1827 to 1834; the rest of the original is said to have been destroyed. A typescript of the whole manuscript was prepared from a handwritten copy by Margaret Gale Hitchcock. This was published as *Autobiography (to 1834) of George Washington Gale (1789–1861), Founder of Galesburg, Illinois, and Knox College* (New York: privately printed, 1964). There are, however, differences between all the versions.

Hooker, Edward W. Papers on Burchardism. Congregational Library, Boston. Contain important material on Finney's relations with Jedediah Burchard.

King Family Papers. University of Rochester Library, Box 2. Contain Brandford King's diary, giving details of Finney in Rochester in 1830 and 1831.

Marsh, James. Collection in University of Vermont Library, Burlington. Has letters referring to Burchard and Finney. They were published with some minor changes in John J. Duffy, ed., *Coleridge's American Disciples* (Amherst: University of Massachusetts Press, 1973).

Nettleton, Asahel. Papers. Hartford Seminary, Hartford, Connecticut. Contain many important letters relating to Finney, but some of them are in very poor condition.

Phelps, Anson G. Diary, 1806–1807, 1816–1853. New York Public Library, microfilm.

Porter Family Papers. University of Rochester Library. A number of references to Finney are scattered through the collection. The letters of Samuel D. Porter are particularly important.

Scranton, Edwin. Diary and scrapbooks, 1835–1880. Rochester Historical Society Library. References to Finney and Burchard appear in 1842.

Tappan, Lewis. Papers, 1809–1903. Library of Congress, Washington, D.C. Microfilm has important journals and letterbooks, with much material on Finney and Oberlin.

Sources and Selected Bibliography

Doctoral Dissertations, Theses, and Unpublished Papers

There are several hundred dissertations and theses that deal more or less directly with Finney and the times in which he lived. The items listed below include those that deal mainly with Finney himself. Dissertations in English that have been published substantially as they were originally presented are not included here.

Aheimer, Shirley Irene Shoben. "The Opportunism of Charles G. Finney." M.A. thesis, Duquesne University, Pittsburgh, 1976.

Asa, Robert Lynn. "The Theology and Methodology of Charles G. Finney as a Prototype for Modern Mass Evangelism." Ph.D. diss., Southern Baptist Theological Seminary, Louisville, Ky., 1983.

Binfield, John Clyde Goodfellow. "Nonconformity in the Eastern Counties, 1840–1885, with Reference to Its Social Background." Ph.D. diss., Cambridge University, 1965.

Bonkowski, Elizabeth Leitch. "The Church and the City: Protestant Concern for Urban Problems, 1800–1840." Ph.D. diss., Boston University Graduate School, 1973.

Brown, Raymond. "Evangelical Ideas of Perfection." Ph.D. diss., Cambridge University, 1964.

Bussey, Oscar. "The Religious Awakening of 1858–60 in Great Britain and Ireland." Ph.D. diss., Edinburgh University, 1947.

Cafone, James Michael. "The Role of the Holy Spirit in the Theology of Charles Grandison Finney." S.T.D. diss., Catholic University of America, Washington, D.C., 1979.

Carpenter, Nollie Wilbur, Jr. "A Socio-Etiological Study of Revivals in Early Nineteenth Century America." Th.D. diss., New Orleans Baptist Theological Seminary, 1953.

Cheesebro, Roy Alan. "The Preaching of Charles G. Finney." Ph.D. diss., Yale University, 1948.

Cler, Albert. *Charles Finney: Sa conversion, sa théorie du réveil, et son activité.* Bachelier en théologie, thèse, Université de Paris, Faculté de Théologie Protestante, 1899 (Cahors: A. Coueslant, 1899).

Clitheroe, Eric Lawton. "The Mormon Doctrine of Salvation and the Nineteenth Century Background." Ph.D. diss., Edinburgh University, 1936.

Cowley, W. H. "Notes on the Life of John Monteith, 1788–1868." Typescript, 1975, Hamilton College Library, Clinton, N.Y.

Davis, Hugh Houck. "The Reform Career of Joshua Leavitt, 1794–1873." Ph.D. diss., Ohio State University, 1969.

Eckelberry, Roscoe H. "A Study of Religious Influences in Higher Education in Ohio." M.A. thesis, Ohio State University, 1923.

Ehlke, Margaret S. "Enthusiastic Religion and the Lives of Titus and Fidelia Coan, Missionaries to Hilo." M.A. thesis, University of Hawaii, Honolulu, 1986.

Emmel, James Robert. "The Persuasive Techniques of Charles Grandison Finney as a Revivalist and Social Reform Speaker, 1820–1860." Ph.D. diss., Pennsylvania State University, 1959.

Evans, Robert Philip. "The Contribution of Foreigners to the French Protestant Revival, 1815–1850." Ph.D. diss., University of Manchester, 1971.

Frantz, John Brenneman. "Revivalism in the German Reformed Church in America to 1850, with Emphasis on the Eastern Synod." Ph.D. diss., University of Pennsylvania, 1961.

Frazee, John Elmer. "Lyman Beecher, Theologian and Social Reformer." Ph.D. diss., Edinburgh University, 1937.

Gaddis, Merrill Elmer. "Christian Perfectionism in America." Ph.D. diss., University of Chicago, 1929.

Goodman, Albert. "Genealogical Book of the Ancestry of the Surrey Goodmans, the Descendants of Albert and Olivia Goodman." Typescript, c. 1910, Huntingdon Record Office, Huntingdon.

Gouverneur, First Baptist Church. "Souvenir Journal Celebrating the 100th Anniversary of the First Baptist Church of Gouverneur, N.Y." Mimeographed MS, 1971, Gouverneur Historical Society, Gouverneur, N.Y.

Griffin, Charles James Grant. "Charles Finney's Prayer: A Dramatistic Interpretation of Charles Grandison Finney's Lectures on Revivals of Religion, 1834–1835." Ph.D. diss., University of Missouri, Columbia, 1983.

Grimshaw, Ivan G. "Religious Revivals in the Light of Modern Psychological Theory." Ph.D. diss., Edinburgh University, 1933.

Grover, Norman L. "The Church and Social Action: The Idea of the Church and Its Relation to Christian Social Strategy in Charles G. Finney, Horace Bushnell, and Washington Gladden." Ph.D. diss., Yale University, 1957.

Hamilton, James E. "A Comparison of the Moral Theories of Charles Finney and Asa Mahan." Ph.D. diss., State University of New York, Buffalo, 1972.

———. "Philosophy and Revival in Edwards and Finney." Paper given at the Oxford Conference on Revivals, July 1976.

Hamilton, Neil Quinn. "Charles Grandison Finney and Two Problems in Evangelism." Th.M. thesis, Princeton Theological Seminary, 1953.

Hardesty, Nancy Ann. "'Your Daughters Shall Prophesy': Revivalism and Feminism in the Age of Finney." Ph.D. diss., University of Chicago, 1976.

Harpester, Donald Earl. "Controversy in the German Reformed Church in Pennsylvania, with Emphasis on Nineteenth-Century Philadelphia." Ph.D. diss., Pennsylvania State University, 1976.

Hendricks, Tyler Owen. "Charles Finney and the Utica Revival of 1826: The Social Effect of a New Religious Paradigm." Ph.D. diss., Vanderbilt University, Nashville, 1983.

Henry, Carl F. H. "Charles Grandison Finney: His Life and Ministry." Paper from the publicity chairman of the Finney Sesquicentennial Memorial Conference, 1942. Typescript copy in Herbert J. Taylor Papers, Billy Graham Center, Wheaton, Ill.

Hollon, David Leslie. "Love as Holiness: An Examination of Charles G. Finney's Theology of Sanctification, 1830–1860." Ph.D. diss., Southern Baptist Theological Seminary, Louisville, Ky., 1984.

Joachim, Melvin Julius. "Comparative Study of Typical Revivals in America During the Nineteenth Century." S.T.B. thesis, Biblical Seminary, New York, 1931.

Johnson, James E. "The Life of Charles Grandison Finney." Ph.D. diss., Syracuse University, 1959.

Kaltenback, Jacques. *Étude psychologique des plus anciens réveils religieux aux États-Unis.* Bachelier en théologie, thèse, Université de Toulouse, Faculté de Théologie Protestante du Montauban, 1905 (Geneva: Kündig, 1905).

Keeling, James H. "A History of the First Presbyterian Church of Le Ray, Evans Mills, Jefferson Co., N.Y. For Its One Hundred and Twenty-fifth Anniversary, 1814–1939." Typescript, Presbyterian Historical Society, Philadelphia.

Kennedy, Jack Reynolds. "The Life, Work, and Thought of John Angell James (1785–1859)." Ph.D. diss., Edinburgh University, 1956.

Kirsch, Charles E. "The Theology of James Morison." Ph.D. diss., Edinburgh University, 1939.

Kuhas, Frederick I. "The Operations of the American Home Missionary Society in the Old Northwest, 1826–1861." Ph.D. diss., University of Chicago, 1947.

Lamb, Wallace E. "George Washington Gale." Ed.D. diss., Syracuse University, 1949.

Lansing, Grace Moffett. "Charles G. Finney." Typescript, 1942, Documents Room, Watertown Public Library, Watertown, N.Y.

Larson, Arlin T. "A College's Purposes: The Idea of Education at Oberlin College." D.Min. diss., University of Chicago, 1976.

Lee, James William. "The Development of Theology at Oberlin." Ph.D. diss., Drew University, Madison, N.J., 1953.

Lenn, David Jeffrey. "The Kingdom of God in America." Ph.D. diss., Boston College, 1981.

Lobue, Wayne Nicholas. "Religious Romanticism and Social Revitalization: The Oberlin Perfectionists." Ph.D. diss., University of Kansas, 1972.

Luker, Richard Michael. "The Western Reserve and a Legacy for Higher Education: Faculty Self-Governance at Oberlin College Under the Finney Compact." Ed.D. diss., University of Akron, 1985.

Lyrene, Edward Charles, Jr. "The Role of Prayer in American Revival Movements, 1740–1860." Ph.D. diss., Southern Baptist Theological Seminary, Louisville, Ky., 1985.

Lythberg, Richard W. "The Evangelism of Charles Finney." B.D. thesis, Northern Baptist Theological Seminary, Lombard, Ill., 1959.

McClelland, William Lester. "Church and Ministry in the Life and Thought of Charles G. Finney." Ph.D. diss., Princeton Theological Seminary, 1967.

McElroy, James Logan. "Social Reform in the Burned-over District: Rochester, New York, as a Test Case, 1830–1854." Ph.D. diss., State University of New York at Binghamton, 1974.

McMillan, David K. "To Witness We Are Living: A Study of Charles Finney and the Revival of Religion in and about Utica, New York, During the Winter and Spring of 1826." B.D. thesis, Union Theological Seminary, New York, 1961.

———. Working draft of monograph on James Richards and Charles Finney, 1983, circulated privately.

Mattson, John Stanley. "Charles Grandison Finney and the Emerging Tradition of 'New Measure' Revivalism." Ph.D. diss., University of North Carolina, Chapel Hill, 1970.

May, Sherry Pierpont. "Asahel Nettleton: Nineteenth Century American Revivalist." Ph.D. diss., Drew University, Madison, N.J., 1969.

Miles, John Lester. "Perfectionism." Th.M. thesis, Dallas Theological Seminary, 1942.

Myers, John Lytle. "The Agency System of the Anti-Slavery Movement, 1832–37, and Its Antecedents in Other Benevolent and Reform Societies." Ph.D. diss., University of Michigan, 1961.

Newberg, Eric Nelson. "The Civil War in Zion: Charles Grandison Finney and the Popularization of American Protestantism During the Second Great Awakening, 1795–1835." M.A. thesis, Pacific School of Religion, Berkeley, Calif., 1974.

Ogden-Malout, Susan Marie. "American Revivalism and Temperance Drama: Evangelical Protestant Ritual and Theatre in Rochester, New York, 1830–1845." Ph.D. diss., Northwestern University, Evanston, Ill., 1981.

Olive, Howard. "The Development of the Evangelistic Invitation." M.Th. thesis, Southern Baptist Theological Seminary, Louisville, Ky., 1958.

Opie, John. "Conversion and Revivalism: An Internal History from Jonathan Edwards Through Charles Grandison Finney." Ph.D. diss., University of Chicago, 1964.

Pitzer, Donald E. "Professional Revivalism in Nineteenth-Century Ohio." Ph.D. diss., Ohio State University, 1966.

Rader, Paul A. "A Study of the Doctrine of Sanctification in the Life and Thought of Charles G. Finney." B.D. thesis, Asbury Theological Seminary, Wilmore, Ky., 1959.

Rice, Arthur Harry. "Henry B. Stanton as a Political Abolitionist." Ed.D. diss., Columbia University, 1968.

Rice, Robert Jay, "Religious Revivalism and British Methodism, 1855–1865." Ph.D. diss., University of Illinois, 1979.

Richards, Glynn. "A Study of the Theological Developments Among Nonconformists in Wales During the Nineteenth Century." B.Litt. thesis, Oxford University, 1956.

Rivierre, Fernand. *La prédication du réveil: Charles Finney.* Bachelier en théologie, Université de Toulouse, Faculté de Théologie Protestante de Montauban, 1902 (Montauban: Granié, 1902).

Rosell, Garth M. "Charles Grandison Finney and the Rise of the Benevolence Empire." Ph.D. diss., University of Minnesota, 1971.

———. "The Millennial Roots of Early Nineteenth Century Reform: An Examination of Charles Finney's Theology of Social Action." Essay read at the Johns Hopkins/Harwichport Seminar on American Religious History, Cape Cod, Mass., Summer 1973.

Rovick, Norman. "The Impact of Religious Revivalism upon Five Selected Ohio Colleges of the Mid-Nineteenth Century." M.A. thesis, Ohio State University, 1965.

St. Amant, Penrose. "The Rise and Early Development of the Princeton School of Theology." Ph.D. diss., Edinburgh University, 1952.

Salstrand, George August Emmanuel. "Charles G. Finney: Evangelist, Educator, Theologian." Th.M. thesis, Northern Baptist Theological Seminary, Lombard, Ill., 1942.

Schmiel, Eugene David. "The Career of Jacob Dolson Cox, 1828–1900: Soldier, Scholar, Statesman." Ph.D. diss., Ohio State University, 1969.

Scott, Donald Moore. "Watchman on the Walls of Zion: Evangelicals and American Society, 1800–1860." Ph.D. diss., University of Wisconsin, 1968.

Sequestra, Jean. *Charles Finney et les pécheurs travaillés: Étude sur la méthode qu'il sait pour les amener à la conversion.* Bachelier en théologie, thèse, Université de France, Académie de Toulouse, Faculté de Théologie Protestante de Montauban, 1890 (Mazamet: Carayol, 1890).

Shields, Robert Wylie. "A Psychological Study of the Effects of Contemporary Nonconformist Revivals." Ph.D. diss., University of London, 1950.

Shipley, Mark. "A Shower of Religion at Rochester: The Charles Grandison Finney Revival, 1830–1831." Typescript, Graduate History Course 285D, Spring 1969, University of California, Berkeley.

Skyrm, Richard Dean. "Oberlin Conservatory: A Century of Musical Growth and Influence." D.M.A. diss., University of Southern California, 1962.

Strauss, Preston Franklin. "The Revivals of Religion in the State of New York (1825–1835) Under the Leadership of Charles G. Finney." Typescript, c. 1935, Princeton Theological Seminary Library.

Talpos, Vasile F. "The Importance of Evangelism in Ministerial Training: A Critical Analysis of the Contribution of Selected Nineteenth Century Christian Educators." Ph.D. diss., Southern Baptist Theological Seminary, Louisville, Ky., 1983.

Taylor, Richard Shelley. "The Doctrine of Sin in the Theology of Charles Grandison Finney." Ph.D. diss., Boston University School of Theology, 1953.

Taylor, Roger. "Methods of Revivalism: Studies in Post-Reformation Religious Revivals." M.A. thesis, Leeds University, Leeds, Yorkshire, 1959.

Tufft, John R. "The Influence of the Theology of Charles G. Finney on the Presbyterian Church in the United States of America." S.T.M. thesis, Biblical Seminary, New York, 1949.

Von Glahn, George Andrew. "Natural Eloquence and the Democratic Gospel: The Idea of an American Rhetoric from the Second Great Awakening to Cooper's Natty Bumppo." Ph.D. diss., University of North Carolina, Chapel Hill, 1969.

Vulgamore, Melvin L. "Social Reform in the Theology of Charles Grandison Finney." Ph.D. diss., Boston University Graduate School, 1963.

Walzer, William C. "Charles Grandison Finney and the Presbyterian Revivals of Central and Western New York." Ph.D. diss., University of Chicago, 1945.

Warburton, T. Rennie. "A Comparative Study of Minority Religious Groups, with Special Reference to Holiness and Related Movements in Britain in the Past Fifty Years." Ph.D. diss., University of London, 1966.

Warford, Malcolm Lyle. "Piety, Politics, and Pedagogy: An Evangelical Protestant Tradition in Higher Education at Lane, Oberlin, and Berea, 1834–1904." Ed.D. diss., Columbia University, 1973.

Watt, David H. "A Transforming Faith: Essays on the History of American Evangelicalism in the Middle Decades of the Twentieth Century." Ph.D. diss., Harvard University, 1987.

Wauzzinski, Robert Alan. "God and Mammon: The Interrelationship of Protestant Evangelicalism and the Industrial Revolution in America, 1820–1914." Ph.D. diss., University of Pittsburgh, 1985.

Weddle, David LeRoy. "The New Man: A Study of the Significance of Conversion for the Theological Definition of the Self in Jonathan Edwards and Charles G. Finney." Ph.D. diss., Harvard University, 1973.

Wellman, Judith M. "The Burned-over District Revisited: Benevolent Reform and Abolitionism in Mexico, Paris, and Ithaca, New York, 1825–1842." Ph.D. diss., University of Virginia, 1974.

Weston, Garth. "The Baptists of North-West England, 1750–1850." Ph.D. diss., University of Sheffield, 1969.

White, John Wesley. "The Influence of North American Evangelism in Great Britain Between 1830 and 1914 on the Origin and Development of the Ecumenical Movement." Ph.D. diss., Oxford University, 1963.

Whitesell, Faris Daniel. "Finney and His Theology." Th.D. diss., Northern Baptist Theological Seminary, Lombard, Ill., 1931.

Williams, Ben. "Charles G. Finney's Revivalism and the Early Abolition Movement." M.A. thesis, Harding Graduate School of Religion, Memphis, Tenn., 1972.

Wood, Raymond Lee. "Lyman Beecher, 1775–1863: A Biographical Study." Ph.D. diss., Yale University, 1961.

Zikmund, Barbara Brown. "Asa Mahan and Oberlin Perfectionism." Ph.D. diss., Duke University, 1969.

PRINTED SOURCES

Publications Containing Finney Letters

Almost as important as the manuscript letters of Finney that have survived are the letters he wrote that have found their way into print. The following list contains all that are known to the editors:

Brainerd, Mary. *The Life of Rev. Thomas Brainerd, D.D.* Philadelphia: Lippincott, 1870, pp. 52–55. Contains Finney's letter to his convert Thomas Brainerd, dated Philadelphia, 21 October 1828. This letter was widely republished (e.g., in *NYE,* 23 September 1875, p. 4) and has recently appeared again in Louis G. Parkhurst's compilation *Principles of Victory,* pp. 23–24 (see below).

Bristol, Sherlock. *The Pioneer Preacher: An Autobiography.* London: Wheeler, 1891, p. 121. Has an extract from a letter to Bristol from Finney and the other members of the Oberlin College faculty, written probably about 1843.

Cuyler, Theodore L. "Under the Catalpa." *NYE,* 14 May 1891, p. 1. Has an extract from a letter that Finney wrote in February 1873 inviting Cuyler to succeed him in the pulpit at Oberlin.

Dodd, Henry M. "The Conversion of Zenas Finney." *NYE,* 9 March 1876, p. 8. Contains an extract of a letter from Finney to his brother, Zenas, dated 19 June 1874, and an extract of a letter to H. M. Dodd, probably of the same date.

Finney, Charles, G. *Innocent Amusements.* A tract published about 1873 in Boston by the Willard Tract Repository. Contains a letter to Dr. Charles Cullis. An extract of this letter is republished in Charles G. Finney, *Power from on High: A Selection of Articles on the Spirit-filled Life* (London: Victory Press, 1944), pp. 58–59.

_______. *Letters on Revivals of Religion, Addressed to Ministers of the Gospel.* Edited by John Moore. Manchester: Bremner, 1861, p. 10. Contains an extract of what was probably a letter written by Finney to John Moore, in which he speaks of his having to resort, "with great reluctance," to the use of tea and coffee at the age of fifty-eight.

_______. *A Sermon Preached in the Presbyterian Church at Troy, March 4, 1827.* Troy, N.Y.: Tuttle and Richards, 1827, p. 2. Prints Finney's letter to members of the Presbytery of Troy, dated Troy, 30 March 1827.

Fowler, Philemon H. *Historical Sketch of Presbyterianism Within the Bounds of the Synod of Cental New York.* Utica: Curtiss and Childs, 1877, pp. 258–59, 268–69, 283. Contains extracts from one or more letters of Finney, possibly written to Fowler and giving information about Finney's life.

[Griffiths, Julia.] *Autographs for Freedom.* Boston: Jewett, 1853, p. 74. Publishes Finney's letter dated 24 September 1852 to "the President of the Rochester Ladies Antislavery Society," who was Julia Griffiths, the compiler of the book. The letter was also reprinted with slight changes in Wilson Armistead, *A Cloud of Witnesses Against Slavery and Oppression* (London: Tweedie, 1853), p. 106.

Headley, Phineas C. *Evangelists in the Church.* Boston: Hoyt, 1875, pp. 152, 167, 170–71. Gives extracts from letters written by Finney to Headley around 1875. The date of one extract (pp. 170–71) about Daniel Nash is the last known letter that Finney wrote.

Hopkins, Josiah. *The Christian's Instructer.* Auburn, N.Y.: Ivison, 1833, pp. 3–4. Has Finney's letter to the publishers dated 9 March 1833, recommending the book.

Hughes, James. "Reminiscences of the Late Rev. Thomas Aubrey." *The City-Road Magazine* (London) 1 (1871): 299. Has a letter from Finney dated 23 February 1860 written to an unidentified recipient, whom internal evidence indicates was John Moore.

Jennings, Isaac. *Medical Reform.* Oberlin: Fitch and Jennings, 1847, pp. v–vi. Publishes Finney's letter to Jennings, dated 5 January 1847, recommending the book.

Kirk, Helen. *Memoirs of the Rev. John Kirk, D.D.* Edinburgh: Fairgrieve, 1888, pp. 325–26. Publishes a letter from Finney to Kirk, dated Manchester, 26 July 1860.

[Moore, Stanley J.] *"Heartily Yours": The Life-Story of Charles G. Moore, by His Son.* Harrogate: "Out and Out," 1922, pp. 10–11. Gives extracts of a letter from Finney to Charles G. Moore, dated 18 April 1873.

Morgan, John. *The Gift of the Holy Ghost.* Oberlin: Goodrich, 1875. Prints an introduction by Finney dated 5 July 1875.

[Orvis, William B.] *Christ Coming in His Kingdom.* A printed leaflet probably distributed by the publisher, N. Tibbals of New York, advertising the book as "Just Published!" (1869), gives reviews and includes extracts from two letters that Finney wrote to Orvis. There is a copy of the pamphlet with a letter from Orvis dated 18 January 1871 in the James Monroe Papers, Oberlin College Archives.

"A Religious Revival in Reading, 1829." *Historical Review of Berks County* 15 (October 1849): 148–50. Publishes three important letters from Finney to Louis Richards, written in 1872 about the revival in Reading, Pennsylvania.

Shannon, Eliza Roe. *A Minister's Life: Memoirs of Charles Hill Roe.* Chicago: Lakeside Press, 1900, pp. 69–70. Gives extracts from a letter that Finney wrote to Roe about April 1850.

[Tappan, Lewis.] *The Life of Arthur Tappan.* New York: Hurd and Houghton, 1870, p. 42. Gives an extract from a letter that Finney wrote to Lewis Tappan about 1870. This book also has a section of what was probably Lewis Tappan's copy of Finney's manuscript of the memoirs (pp. 238–40).

Van Santvoord, C., and Lewis, Tayler. *Memoirs of Eliphelet Nott, D.D.* New York: Sheldon, 1876, p. 226. Contains an extract of a letter that Finney wrote to Tayler Lewis in May 1874.

A number of Finney's letters were published in periodicals. The following publications contain those that have so far come to light:

The Antislavery Watchman (London), 1 November 1853, pp. 15–16, published an article, "Professor Finney and the Fugitive Slave Law," containing a letter from Finney to F. W. Chesson, the editor of the paper, dated 26 September 1853.

The British Banner (London), 21 August 1850, p. 572, published a letter from Finney to the editor, John Campbell, dated 15 August 1850. This paper is a valuable source on the activities of the Finneys in Britain during their first tour.

The British Standard (London), 21 January 1859, p. 20, has an extract of a letter from Finney to the editor, John Campbell, dated 17 January 1859. This was widely republished. See, for example, *The Christian World* (London), 28 January 1859, p. 342; *The Wesleyan Times* (London), 24 January 1859, p. 55; and *NYE,* 10 March 1859, p. 4. *The British Standard* also has three other letters from Finney to Campbell: one dated 14 February 1859, published on 18 February 1859, p. 3, and reprinted in the *Scarborough Mercury,* 26 February 1859, p. 4; one dated 3 March 1859, published on 11 March 1859, p. 77, and reprinted in *The Watchman* (London), 23 March 1859, p. 94; and one dated 22 March 1859, published on 25 March 1859, p. 93, drawing attention to printer's errors in the previous letter. This one was reprinted in part in *The Watchman* (London), 30 March 1859, p. 103. *The British Standard* is an important source on Finney's second tour in Britain.

The Christian News (Glasgow), 17 September 1859, p. 5, published an important letter of Finney to the editor, John Kirk, dated 10 September 1859, in which Finney, for the first time, spoke out against Nettleton. *The Christian News,* 2 January 1864, p. 3, published a letter to John Kirk dated Oberlin, 3 December 1863, in which Finney spoke about the death of his second wife, Elizabeth. This periodical is the most important source for Finney's activities in Scotland.

The Emancipator (New York), extra of 25 June 1833, published the letter from twelve prominent reformers, including Finney, to the secretary and board of managers of the American Colonization Society, dated 7 March 1833, challenging the society on its policies. The letter was reprinted in *The Liberator* (Boston), 13 July 1833, p. 109, and in *The Antislavery Reporter* (London) 1 (July 1833): 26.

The Independent (New York), 17 June 1852, p. 99, published an advertisement by J. Ball and Co. entitled "Restoring and Preserving Sight." It contained a letter from Finney dated 1 December 1851 testifying to the value of using "eye cups" and giving details of his eyesight. At that point he had worn glasses for about ten years. On 26 November 1857, p. 2, a letter appears from Finney to a subscriber to the Theological Fund, dated 7 November 1857. It was republished in *OE,* 9 December 1857, pp. 194–95. An interesting letter on Finney's views on coeducation, entitled "The Joint Education of the Sexes," dated 31 December 1867, appeared in *The Independent* for 9 January 1868, p. 1. This paper also contains several articles by Finney and much other material concerning his revival activities and theology.

The Lorain County News (Oberlin) published letters of Finney on 11 November 1863, p. 2; and 11 January 1872, p. 2. This paper covers Finney's activities in Oberlin from 1860.

The New York Evangelist published important letters of Finney on 17 April 1851, p. 64, about the problems he was having in England; and on 6 March 1873, p. 1, on Potto Brown. This weekly newspaper is one of the most important sources of Finney material from 1830 onward.

The Oberlin Evangelist (1839–1862) is the richest periodical source for Finney material. As well as written and reported sermons, many of which were republished in book form, it printed several series of letters written to the churches. A number of other letters by Finney on various subjects, as well as book reviews, occurred from time to time.

The Oberlin Weekly News, 26 March 1874, p. 2, has a letter to the paper written by Finney and dated 24 March 1874. It was a call for civil service reform in view of new laws introduced to appoint postmasters.

Radical Abolitionist (New York) 1 (January 1856): 1 published a letter from Finney to William Goodell, 27 November 1855, approving his paper.

The Wesleyan Times (London), 31 October 1859, p. 700, had a letter from Finney to the editor dated 25 October 1859.

The Western Recorder (Utica), 6 July 1825, p. 54, published Finney's letter dated 10 June 1824 to "The Presiding Officer of the Female Missionary Society of the Western District of New York." This is the earliest known letter written by Finney. It was copied in *The Religious Intelligencer* (New Haven), 17 July 1824, p. 111; and *Boston Recorder and Telegraph,* 17 July 1824, p. 114. *The Western Recorder* (1824–1833) covers Finney's early revivals.

The Witness (Ithaca, N.Y.), 20 August 1837, p. 2, has an important letter from Finney to John H. Noyes, dated 3 April 1837.

Selected Bibliography

Much of the basic bibliography on Finney was collected by James E. Johnson for his doctoral dissertation listed above. Useful bibliographies appear above in most of the dissertations and theses on Finney and also in Keith J. Hardman's biography of Finney listed below. A fairly complete list of Finney's writings (other than periodical material), together with locations, appears in *The National Union Catalog Pre-1956 Imprints* (London: Mansell Publishing; Chicago: American Library Association, 1968–1981), 173:48–52; with more recent editions of Finney's works listed in the supplements. The bibliography here lists some of the more important primary and secondary material.

Abzug, Robert H. *Passionate Liberator: Theodore Dwight Weld and the Dilemma of Reform.* New York: Oxford University Press, 1980.

Aiken, Samuel C. Letter to the editor of *The Cleveland Herald,* 24 February 1865, reprinted in *The Lorain County News* (Oberlin), 8 March 1865, p. 1.

Aikman, Robert. "President Finney." *The Independent* (New York), 2 September 1875, p. 1.

Ashworth, Jesse. "Charles G. Finney." *The Primitive Methodist Quarterly Review* (London), n.s., 8 (July 1886): 385–406.

[Atwater, Lyman H.] "Influence of the New Divinity on Religion." *The Biblical Repertory and Princeton Review* 14 (January 1842): 1–45.

———. "Revivals of the Century." *The Presbyterian Quarterly and Princeton Review,* n.s., 5 (October 1876): 690–719.

B., F. B. "Revival Recollections." *Oneida Circular,* 13 January to 12 May 1873.

Baird, Samuel J. *A History of the New School, and of the questions involved in the Disruption of the Presbyterian Church in 1838.* Philadelphia: Claxton, Remsen, and Haffelfinger, 1868.

Ballantine, William Gay, ed. *The Oberlin Jubilee, 1833–1883.* Oberlin: Goodrich, 1883.

Barnes, Mrs. G. S. "Recollections of President Finney: His Rebukes—The Missionary Fever—Mrs. Finney." *The Independent* (New York), 29 August 1895, pp. 1154–55.

Barnes, Gilbert H. *The Antislavery Impulse.* Introduction by William G. McLoughlin. New York: Harcourt, Brace and World, 1964.

Bartlett, David W. *Modern Agitators; or, Pen Portraits of Living American Reformers.* New York: Miller, Orton and Mulligan, 1856.

Beardsley, Frank G. *A Mighty Winner of Souls, Charles G. Finney: A Study in Evangelism.* New York: American Tract Society, 1937.

[Beecher, Henry Ward.] "Mr. Finney in England." *The Independent* (New York), 21 November 1850, p. 190.

Beecher, Lyman. *The Autobiography of Lyman Beecher.* Edited by Barbara M. Cross. Cambridge, Mass.: Harvard University Press, Belknap Press, 1961.

Bell, Marion L. *Crusade in the City: Revivalism in Nineteenth-Century Philadelphia.* Lewisburg, Pa.: Bucknell University Press, 1977.

Bigglestone, William E. *Oberlin: From War to Jubilee, 1866–1883.* Oberlin: Grady Publishing, 1983.

Binfield, Clyde. *George Williams and the Y.M.C.A.: A Study in Victorian Social Attitudes.* London: Heinemann, 1973.

Boardman, George Nye. *A History of New England Theology.* New York: Randolph, 1899.

———. "President Finney as a Theologian." *The Advance* (Chicago), 13 March 1879, pp. 161–62.

Boardman, William Edwin. *The Higher Christian Life.* London: Sampson Low, 1859.

Boreham, F. W. *A Casket of Cameos: More Texts That Made History.* London: Epworth Press, 1924.

Brand, James, and Ellis, John M. *Memorial Addresses on the Occasion of the One Hundredth Anniversary of the Birth of President Charles G. Finney.* Oberlin: Goodrich, 1893.

Brewster, Harold Pomeroy. "The Magic of a Voice: Rochester Revivals of Rev. Charles G. Finney." *Rochester Historical Society; Publication Fund Series* 4 (1925): 273–90.

Bruner, Frederick Dale. *A Theology of the Holy Spirit: The Pentecostal Experience and the New Testament Witness.* London: Hodder and Stoughton, 1971.

Buckham, John Wright. "The New England Theologians." *The American Journal of Theology* 24, no. 1 (January 1920): 19–29.

Bush, Charles P. "Charles G. Finney, His Early Labors, Incidents, Converts." *NYE,* 26 August 1875, pp. 4–5.

Cairns, Earle E. *An Endless Line of Splendor: Revivals and Their Leaders, from the Great Awakening to the Present.* Wheaton, Ill.: Tyndale House, 1986.

Calman, A. L. *Life and Labours of John Ashworth.* Manchester: Tubbs and Brook, 1875.

Candler, Warren A. *Great Revivals and the Great Republic.* Nashville: Publishing House of the Methodist Episcopal Church South, 1904.

Carwardine, Richard J. "The Evangelist System: Charles Roe, Thomas Pul[s]ford, and the Baptist Home Missionary Society." *The Baptist Quarterly* 28, no. 5 (January 1980): 209–25.

———. "The Second Great Awakening in the Urban Centers: An Examination of Methodism and the 'New Measures.'" *The Journal of American History* 59, no. 2 (September 1972): 327–40.

———. *Transatlantic Revivalism: Popular Evangelicalism in Britain and America, 1790–1865.* Westport, Conn.: Greenwood Press, 1978.

———. "The Welsh Evangelical Community and 'Finney's Revival.'" *The Journal of Ecclesiastical History* 29, no. 4 (October 1978): 463–80.

Case, Lora. *Hudson of Long Ago. Progress of Hudson During the Past Century. Personal Reminiscences of an Aged Pioneer. Reminiscences Written in 1897.* Hudson, Ohio: The Hudson Library and Historical Society, 1963.

Chapman, John Wilbur. *Revivals and Missions.* New York: Lentil, 1900.

"Charles G. Finney: A Symposium." *The Watchman-Examiner* (New York), 15 January 1931.

Cheeseman, [Lewis]. *Differences Between Old and New School Presbyterians.* Rochester: Darrow, 1848.

Churchill, Alfred Vance. "Midwestern: Early Oberlin Personalities." *Northwest Ohio Quarterly* 23, no. 4 (Autumn 1951): 211–31.

Clark, Franklin C. "The Bristol Branch of the Finney Family." *New England Historical and Genealogical Register* 60 (1906): 67–73, 155–59.

Clarke, Charles. *Pioneers of Revival.* London: Fountain Trust, 1971.

Cochran, Samuel D. "Modern Evangelists and Special Efforts to Convert and Save Sinners." *The Congregational Review* (Boston) 11 (May 1871): 253–69.

Cochran, William Cox. "Charles Grandison Finney." *Oberlin Alumni Magazine* 25 (February 1929): 137–39; (March 1929): 171–72.

———. *Charles Grandison Finney: Memorial Address Delivered at the Dedication of the Finney Memorial Chapel, Oberlin, June 21, 1908.* Philadelphia: Lippincott, 1908.

———. "Some Interviews with Charles G. Finney." *Oberlin Alumni Magazine* 24 (March 1928): 7–8.

Cole, Charles C. "The Evangelist as Theological Disputant: Charles Grandison Finney and Some Others." *Ohio State Archaeological and Historical Quarterly* 62 (1953): 219–33.

———. "Finney's Fight Against the Masons." *Ohio State Archaeological and Historical Quarterly* 59, no. 3 (1950): 270–86.

———. "The Free Church Movement in New York City." *New York History* 34 (1953): 284–97.

———. "The New Lebanon Convention." *New York History* 31 (October 1950): 385–97.

——— *The Social Ideas of the Northern Evangelists.* New York: Columbia University Press, 1954.

Cook, Paul E. G. "Finney on Revival." In *One Steadfast High Intent. Puritan and Reformed Studies Conference Report for 1966.* London: *The Evangelical Magazine,* 1966, pp. 4–16.

C[ox], H[elen] F[inney]. "Charles Finney." In *Lives of the Leaders of Our Church Universal,* edited by Ferdinand Piper, pp. 730–40. Philadelphia: Presbyterian Board of Publication, 1879. This sketch of Finney was written by his daughter, Helen. She complained to George Frederick Wright: "The article . . . was so garbled in the printing that I have been ashamed to have my friends see it. The proof sheets were never submitted to me, and unwarrantable liberties were taken with the manuscript, such as speaking of my father as "Charles" all the way through, where I had said uniformly "Mr. Finney"—besides the usual misprints & mistakes in reading the manuscript" (Helen Cox to G. F. Wright, 17 October 1889, Wright Papers, box 7).

Cox, Jacob Dolson, III. *Building an American Industry: The Story of the Cleveland Twist Drill Company and Its Founder, an Autobiography.* Cleveland: Cleveland Twist Drill Co., 1951. Anecdotes of Finney by his grandson.

Cragin, George. "The Free Church of Old Times." *The Free Church Circular* (Oneida, N.Y.), 7 February to 26 March 1850. A critical look at the Free-church movement and Finney's part in it by one of Finney's early converts who later defected to perfectionism and the Oneida Community.

———. "The Late Charles G. Finney." *Oneida Circular,* 30 August 1875, p. 277.

———. "Revivals in New York City." *Oneida Circular,* 16 June 1873 to 9 March 1874. Recollections of the Finney revivals in New York.

Cross, Roselle Theodore. "The Finney Centennial." *The Advance* (Chicago), 25 August 1892, p. 668.

Cross, Whitney, R. *The Burned-over District: The Social and Intellectual History of Enthusiastic Religion in Western New York, 1800–1850.* Ithaca, N.Y.: Cornell University Press, 1950.

Cuyler, Theodore L. "Pen Pictures of Eminent Preachers: Rev. Charles G. Finney." *The Treasury* (New York) 9, no. 6 (October 1891): 377, 379.

Dale, Robert W., ed. *The Life and Letters of John Angell James, including an unfinished autobiography.* London: Nisbet, 1861.

———. "Mr. Finney's Preaching." *The Congregationalist* (London) 4 (December 1875): 725–28.

Dall, Caroline H. "Charles G. Finney of Oberlin." *The Independent* (New York), 27 January 1876, p. 67.

———. *The College, the Market, and the Court; or, Woman's relation to education, labor, and law.* 2d ed. Boston: Lee and Shepard, 1868.

Dayton, Donald W. *Discovering an Evangelical Heritage.* New York: Harper and Row, 1976.

Dike, Samuel W. "A Study of New England Revivals." *American Journal of Sociology* 15 (November 1909): 361–78.

Dix, John Ross. *Pen Pictures of Popular English Preachers.* London: Partridge and Oakey, 1851.

Doe, Walter P., comp. *Eminent Authors on Effective Revival Preaching.* Providence, R.I.: Greene, 1876.

Dolan, Jay P. *Catholic Revivalism: The American Experience, 1830–1900.* Notre Dame, Ind.: University of Notre Dame Press, 1978.

Drummond, Lewis A. *Charles Grandison Finney and the Birth of Modern Evangelism.* London: Hodder and Stoughton, 1983.

Duffield, George. "Review of Finney's Theology." *The Biblical Repository and Classical Review,* 3d ser., 4 (1848): 212–52, 412–53, 711–46; 5 (1869): 96–129.

Dunn, James D. G. "Spirit-Baptism and Pentecostalism." *Scottish Journal of Theology* 23, no. 4 (November 1970): 397–407.

Ellis, John M. "Finney's Influence upon Theology." *The Advance* (Chicago), 25 August 1892, p. 669.

"An Era of Revivals." *OE,* 15 April 1857, p. 66; 29 April 1857, p. 68.

Essig, James David. "The Lord's Free Man: Charles G. Finney and His Abolitionism." *Civil War History* 24, no. 1 (March 1978): 25–45.

The Examiner and Chronicle (New York), 20 February 1873, p. 4; 27 February 1873, p. 4; 13 March 1873, p. 4. Articles on Finney and the Gouverneur Baptist Church.

Fairchild, Edward Henry. *Historical Sketch of Oberlin College.* Springfield, Mass.: Republic Printing, 1868.

Fairchild, James Harris. "The Doctrine of Sanctification at Oberlin." *The Congregational Quarterly* (Boston) 18 (April 1876): 237–59.

———. *Oberlin: Its Origin, Progress, and Results.* Oberlin: Butler, 1871.

———. *Oberlin: The Colony and the College, 1833–1883.* Oberlin: Goodrich, 1883.

———. "The Revival Wave of Fifty Years Ago." *Jubilee Notes* (Oberlin), March 1883, pp. 2–3.

———. "Sketch of the Life of C. G. Finney." *The Oberlin Weekly News,* 19 August 1875, p. 5. Given at his funeral, 18 August 1875.

Ferguson, Fergus, Jr. *A History of the Evangelical Union, from its Origin to the Present Time.* Glasgow: Morison, 1876.

———. "The Late Professor Finney's Visit to Glasgow." *The Christian News* (Glasgow), 10 August 1895, pp. 3–4.

———. "Memoirs of Rev. Charles G. Finney." *The Evangelical Repository,* 6th ser., 3 (June 1877): 279–88.

———. "Mr. Finney's Career and Theology." *The Christian News* (Glasgow), 10 September 1859, p. 5.

Ferguson, Robert, and Brown, A. Morton. *Life and Labours of John Campbell, D.D.* London: Bentley, 1867.

[Field, Henry M.] "Rev. Charles G. Finney." *NYE,* 10 February 1876, p. 4. Editorial.

Finney, Adelbert Howard, Sr. *Finney-Phinney Families in America.* Richmond, Va.: Byrd, 1957.

Finney, Charles G. *The Heart of Truth: Finney's Lectures on Theology.* Minneapolis: Bethany Fellowship, 1976.

———. *Lectures on Revivals of Religion.* Edited by William G. McLoughlin. Cambridge, Mass.: Harvard University Press, Belknap Press, 1960.

———. *Lectures on Systematic Theology.* London: William Tegg, 1851.

_______. "Mr. Finney's Journal." *The Eighth Annual Report of the Trustees of the Female Missionary Society of the Western District.* Utica, 1824, pp. 17–19.

_______. *Power from on High.* London: Victory Press, 1954.

_______. *Principles of Liberty: More Great Themes on Romans from the Writings of Charles G. Finney.* Compiled and edited by Louis Gifford Parkhurst, Jr. Minneapolis: Bethany House, 1983.

_______. *Principles of Prayer.* Compiled and edited by Louis Gifford Parkhurst, Jr. Minneapolis: Bethany House, 1980.

_______. *Principles of Victory: Great Themes from Romans, by One of America's Foremost Evangelists and Bible Teachers.* Compiled and edited by Louis Gifford Parkhurst, Jr. Minneapolis: Bethany House, 1981.

_______. *The Promise of the Spirit.* Compiled and edited by Timothy L. Smith. Minneapolis: Bethany Fellowship, 1980.

_______. *Reflections on Renewal.* Compiled by Donald Dayton. Minneapolis: Bethany Fellowship, 1979.

_______. *Reminiscences of Rev. Charles G. Finney: Speeches and Sketches at the gathering of his Friends and Pupils in Oberlin, July 28th, 1876, together with President Fairchild's Memorial Sermon.* Oberlin: Goodrich, 1876.

Finney, Elizabeth Ford Atkinson. *The Tea Meeting: Mrs. Finney and the Women of Bolton.* Manchester: Bremner, 1860.

Fletcher, Robert Samuel. *A History of Oberlin College from Its Foundation Through the Civil War.* Oberlin: Oberlin College, 1943.

_______. "The Pastoral Theology of Charles G. Finney." *Ohio Presbyterian Historical Society Proceedings* 3 (June 1941): 28–33.

Foster, Frank Hugh. *A Genetic History of the New England Theology.* Chicago: University of Chicago Press, 1907.

Fowler, Henry. *The American Pulpit: Sketches, Biographical and Descriptive of Living American Preachers.* New York: Fairchild, 1856.

Gaustad, Edwin S. "Charles Grandison Finney." *Mid-Stream* 8, no. 3 (Spring 1909): 80–91.

Gillett, E. H. *History of the Presbyterian Church in the United States of America.* Philadelphia: Presbyterian Publication Committee, 1864.

Gresham, John Leroy, Jr. *Charles G. Finney's Doctrine of the Baptism of the Holy Spirit.* Peabody, Mass.: Hendricksen, 1987.

Hall, Russell T. *The Journal of Russell T. Hall, 1863.* Introduction and notes by William E. Bigglestone. Oberlin: Grady, 1985.

Hamilton, James E. "Academic Orthodoxy and the Arminianizing of American Theology." *Wesleyan Theological Journal* 9 (Spring 1974): 52–59.

_______. "Finney: An Appreciation." *Christianity Today* 19 (8 August 1975): 13–16.

Hamilton, James E., and Madden, Edward H. "Edwards, Finney, and Mahan on the Derivation of Duties." *Journal of the History of Philosophy* 13, no. 3 (July 1975): 347–60.

Hammond, John L. *The Politics of Benevolence: Revival Religion and American Voting Behavior.* Norwood, N.J.: Ablex Publishing, 1979.

Hardesty, Nancy A. *Women Called to Witness: Evangelical Feminism in the Nineteenth Century.* Nashville: Abingdon, 1984.
Hardman, Keith J. "Charles G. Finney, the Benevolent Empire, and the Free Church Movement in New York City." *New York History* 67, no. 4 (October 1986): 412–35.
———. *Charles Grandison Finney, 1792–1875: Revivalist and Reformer.* Syracuse: Syracuse University Press, 1987.
H[eadley, Phineas C.]. "Early Life of C. G. Finney." *NYE,* 23 May 1850, p. 81.
———. "Revival Intelligence, Adams." *NYE,* 11 February 1869, p. 4.
Helffenstein, Jacob. "C. G. Finney on 'New Measures': View of a Contemporary Minister." *NYE,* 20 July 1876, p. 6.
Hewitt, Nancy A. *Women's Activism and Social Change: Rochester, New York, 1822–1872.* Ithaca, N.Y.: Cornell University Press, 1984.
Heydenburk, David H. "Alumni Letters." *Oberlin Alumni Magazine* 38, no. 7 (May 1942): 1.
Hills, Aaron Merritt. *Life of Charles G. Finney.* Cincinnati: Office of "God's Revivalist," 1902.
Hodgson, Francis. *An Examination of the System of New Divinity or New School Theology.* New York: Lane, 1840.
Hoffman, Fred W. *Revival Times in America.* Boston: Wild, 1956.
Hogeland, Rondel W. "Co-education of the Sexes at Oberlin College: A Study of Social Ideas in Mid-Nineteenth-Century America." *Journal of Social History* 6, no. 2 (Winter 1972-1973): 160–76.
Hopkins, Josiah. Letter to the Editor, Seneca Falls, May 1851. *NYE,* 12 June 1851, p. 93.
Hosford, Frances J. "Finney and His Children." *Oberlin Alumni Magazine* 30 (July 1934): 299–302.
———. "Finney the Inscrutable." *Oberlin Alumni Magazine* 30 (May 1934): 233–36.
———. *A Living Stone: The Story of the First Church in Oberlin.* Oberlin, 1933.
———. "Oberlin No-Myths." *Oberlin Alumni Magazine* 30 (March 1934): 171–73.
Hotchkin, James H. *A History of the Purchase and Settlement of Western New York; and of the Rise, Progress and Present State of the Presbyterian Church in That Section.* New York: Dodd, 1848.
Hudson, William. "Finney, the American Evangelist." *The City-Road Magazine* (London) 6 (1876): 252–56.
James, William. *Varieties of Religious Experience.* London: Longmans, Green, 1952.
Johnson, James E. "Charles G. Finney and a Theology of Revivalism." *Church History* 38, no. 3 (September 1969): 1–21.
———. "Charles G. Finney and Oberlin Perfectionism." *Journal of the Presbyterian Historical Society* 6, no. 1 (March 1968): 42–57; no. 2 (June 1968): 128–38.
———. "Charles G. Finney and the Great 'Western' Revivals." *Fides et Historia* 6, no. 2 (Spring 1974): 13–30.

Johnson, Paul E. *A Shopkeeper's Millennium: Society and Revivals in Rochester, New York, 1815–1837.* New York: Hill and Wang, 1978.
Johnston, Adelia A. F. "Significant Events and Noted People." *Oberlin Alumni Magazine* 6 (November 1903): 51–63.
Kellogg, Louisa A. "The True Ideal for a College." *Jubilee Notes* (Oberlin), June 1883, pp. 38–39.
Kent, John. *Holding the Fort: Studies in Victorian Revivalism.* London: Epworth Press, 1978.
Kimball, David. "Rev. Charles G. Finney." *The Independent* (New York), 14 May 1868, p. 6.
King, Henry Churchill. "The Oberlin Inheritance." *Oberlin Alumni Magazine* 7 (July 1911): 354–73.
———. *Personal and Ideal Elements in Education.* New York: Macmillan, 1904.
King, Mary B. Allen. *Looking Backward; or, Memories of the Past.* New York: Randolph, 1870.
Kirk, Helen. *Woman and Prayer; or, The History of the Ladies' Union Prayer Meeting held in Bristol Place Hall, Edinburgh.* London: Ward, 1861.
Kirk, John. "The Revival Movement of the Last Thirty Years." *The Christian News,* 8 July to 14 October 1865.
Ladd, Celia R. *Personal Recollections of President Finney.* Spring Arbor, Mich., n.d. A tract written about 1875.
Lansing, Dirck C. Letter to the Editor, Brooklyn, 21 April 1851. *The Independent* (New York), 1 May 1851, p. 72.
Lawson, J. Gilchrist. *Deeper Experiences of Famous Christians.* Chicago: Glad Tidings Publishing, 1911.
Leonard, Delavan L. *The Story of Oberlin: The Institution, the Community, the Idea, the Movement.* Boston: Pilgrim Press, 1898.
Lesick, Lawrence Thomas. *The Lane Rebels: Evangelicalism and Antislavery in Antebellum America.* Metuchen, N.J.: Scarecrow Press, 1980.
Lincoln, William E. "A Reminiscence of Finney and Mahan." *Oberlin News,* 23 February 1910, p. 2.
Loud, Grover C. *Evangelized America.* New York: MacVeagh, 1928.
Loveland, Anne C. "Evangelicalism and 'Immediate Emancipation' in American Antislavery Thought." *Journal of Southern History* 32 (May 1966): 172–88.
McArthur, Alexander. *Finney versus Morison; or, Oberlin Strictures on Morisonian Faith. Compiled from the "Oberlin Evangelist," the organ of Oberlin Institute, Ohio, U.S.* Glasgow: Wilson, 1859.
McGiffert, Arthur Cushman, Jr. "Charles Grandison Finney: Frontier Preacher and Teacher, 1792–1875." *Christendom* 7, no. 4 (Autumn 1942): 486–506.
McGraw, James. *Great Evangelical Preachers of Yesterday.* New York: Abingdon, 1961.
McKay, Johnston R. "An American Evangelist in Great Britain." *Bulletin of the British Association for American Studies* 6 (February 1958): 3–8.
———. "The Impact of American Religion on Great Britain." *The Expository Times* 71, no. 1 (October 1959): 19–21.

McLoughlin, William G. "C. G. Finney: The Revivalist as Culture Hero." *Journal of American Culture* 5, no. 2 (Summer 1982): 80–90.

———. *Modern Revivalism: Charles Grandison Finney to Billy Graham.* New York: Ronald Press, 1959.

McPherson, Anna Talbot. *Spiritual Secrets of Famous Christians.* Grand Rapids: Zondervan, 1964.

Madden, Edward H., and Hamilton, James E. *Freedom and Grace: The Life of Asa Mahan.* Metuchen, N.J.: Scarecrow Press, 1982.

Mahan, Asa. *Autobiography: Intellectual, Moral, and Spiritual.* London: Woolmer, 1882.

———. "Rev. C. G. Finney." *The Banner of Holiness* (London), 30 September 1875, pp. 22–24.

———. "The Sequel." *Divine Life* (London) 4 (March 1881): 163–65.

Marsh, James B. T. "Memories of Mr. Finney." *The Independent* (New York), 17 August 1876, pp. 6–7.

Matson, Henrietta. *Recollections of Rev. Charles G. Finney.* Nashville: Pentecostal Publishing, n.d.

Matson, Henry. "Mr. Finney." *Oberlin Review,* 17 November 1875, pp. 207–8.

Mead, Hiram. "Charles Grandison Finney." *The Congregational Quarterly* (Boston) 19 (January 1877): 1–28.

Meyer, D. H. *The Instructed Conscience: The Shaping of the American National Ethic.* Philadelphia: University of Pennsylvania Press, 1972.

Miller, Perry. *The Life of the Mind in America.* London: Gollancig, 1966.

Moore, Robert, Jr. "Charles Finney and the 'Altar Call.'" *The Banner of Truth* (London) 82–83 (July–August 1970): 29–34.

Moorhead, James H. "Charles Finney and the Modernization of America." *Journal of Presbyterian History* 62, no. 2 (Summer 1984): 95–110.

———. "Social Reform and the Divided Conscience of Antebellum Protestantism." *Church History* 48, no. 4 (December 1979): 416–30.

Morrison, Howard Alexander. "The Finney Takeover of the Second Great Awakening During the Oneida Revivals of 1825–1827." *New York History* 59, no. 1 (January 1978): 27–53. "Mr. Finney—His Misstatements—His Masonic History from the Records." *The National and Freemason* (New York), 20 June 1868, pp. 393–94.

Nichols, Leon Nelson. *History of the Broadway Tabernacle of New York City.* New Haven: Tuttle, Morehouse, 1940.

Noble, William F. P. *1776–1876. A Century of Gospel-Work: A History of the Growth of Evangelical Religion in the United States.* Philadelphia: Watts, 1876.

[Oneida Association.] *Pastoral Letter of the Ministers of the Oneida Association, to the Churches Under Their Care, on the Subject of Revivals of Religion.* Utica: Ariel Works, 1827.

[Oneida Presbytery.] *A Narrative of the Revival of Religion in the County of Oneida; particularly in the Bounds of the Presbytery of Oneida, in the year 1826.* Utica: Hastings and Tracy, 1826. Reprint, Princeton: D. A. Borrenstein, 1827.

Opie, John. "Finney's Failure of Nerve: The Untimely Demise of Evangelical Theology." *Journal of Presbyterian History* 51, no. 2 (Summer 1973): 155–73.

Orr, J. Edwin. *The Fervent Prayer: The Worldwide Impact of the Great Awakening of 1858.* Chicago: Moody Press, 1974.

———. *The Light of the Nations: Evangelical Revival and Advance in the Nineteenth Century.* London: Paternoster Press, 1965.

———. *The Second Evangelical Awakening: An Account of the Second Worldwide Evangelical Revival Beginning in the Mid-Nineteenth Century.* London: Marshall, Morgan and Scott, 1955.

———. *The Second Evangelical Awakening in Britain.* London: Marshall, Morgan and Scott, 1949.

Packer, James I. "Puritan Evangelism." *The Banner of Truth* (London) 4 (February 1957): 4–13.

Parker, Orson. *The Fire and the Hammer; or, Revivals, and how to promote them, together with a biographical sketch of the author.* Boston: Earle, 1877.

Parker, Robert A. *A Yankee Saint: John Humphrey Noyes and the Oneida Community.* New York: Putnam's, 1935.

Parker, Russell D. "The Philosophy of Charles G. Finney: Higher Law and Revivalism." *Ohio History* 82, nos. 3–4 (Summer–Autumn 1973): 142–53.

Paton, Lewis Bayles, ed. *Recent Christian Progress: Studies in Christian Thought and Work During the Last Seventy-Five Years.* New York: Macmillan, 1909.

Perkins, Ephraim. *A "Bunker Hill" Contest,* A.D. *1826.* Utica: Printed for the author, 1826.

Petersen, Owen. *A Divine Discontent: The Life of Nathan S. S. Beman.* Macon, Ga.: Mercer University Press, 1986.

Pierson, Arthur Tappan. *Evangelistic Work in Principle and Practice.* London: Dickinson, 1888.

———. *Forward Movements of the Last Half Century.* New York: Funk and Wagnalls, 1900.

———. "The Great Spiritual Movements of the Century." *The Christian and Missionary Alliance* (New York) 18 (8 January 1897): 33–34.

Potto Brown: The Village Philanthropist. St. Ives, Hunts: Albert Goodman, 1978.

Prall, John P. "Rev. C. G. Finney in New York: A Reminiscence." *NYE,* 16 September 1875, pp. 2, 4.

Pratney, Winkie. *Revival.* Springdale, Pa.: Whitaker House, 1984.

Price, Orlo J. "One Hundred Years of Protestantism in Rochester." *Rochester Historical Society, Publication Fund Series,* vol. 12, 1933, pp. 241–393.

———. "The Significance of the Early Religious History of Rochester." *Rochester Historical Society, Publication Fund Series,* vol. 3, 1924, pp. 165–87.

Quimby, Rollin Walker. "Charles Grandison Finney: Herald of Modern Revivalism." *Speech Monographs* 20, no. 4 (November 1953): 293–99.

Rand, Asa. *The New Divinity Tried, Being an Examination of a Sermon Delivered by the Rev. C. G. Finney, on Making a New Heart.* Boston: Light and Harris, 1832.

Reed, Andrew, and Matheson, James. *A Narrative of the Visit to the American Churches, by the Deputation from the Congregational Union of England and Wales.* London: Jackson and Walford, 1835.

Rees, Thomas. *History of Protestant Nonconformity in Wales: From its rise in 1633 to the present time.* London: Snow, 1883.

"Rev. C. G. Finney." *The Christian Witness* (London) 7 (October 1850): 473–76.

Ryan, Mary P. *Cradle of the Middle Class: The Family in Oneida County, New York, 1790–1865.* New York: Cambridge University Press, 1981.

———. "A Women's Awakening: Evangelical Religion and the Families of Utica, New York, 1800–1840." *American Quarterly* 30, no. 5 (Winter 1978): 602–23.

Sargant, William. *Battle for the Mind: A Physiology of Conversion and Brainwashing.* London: Heinemann, 1957.

Scharpff, Paulus. *History of Evangelism.* Translated by Helga Bender. Grand Rapids: Eerdmans, 1966.

Scott, Donald M. *From Office to Profession: The New England Ministry, 1750–1850.* Philadelphia: University of Pennsylvania Press, 1978.

Seitz, Don C. *Uncommon Americans: Pencil Portraits of Men and Women Who Have Broken the Rules.* Indianapolis: Bobbs-Merrill, 1925.

Seldes, Gilbert. *The Stammering Century.* New York: Day, 1928.

Senex. "Revival Sketches." *The Advance* (Chicago), 5 December 1867 to 23 April 1868. These sketches in all likelihood were written by Truman Hastings.

Shaw, William B. "A College That Pioneered: Oberlin, 1833–1908." *Outlook* (New York), 13 June 1908, pp. 336–41.

Shearman, Julia. "Oberlin College, its history and its work." *The Christian* (London), 4 August 1870, pp. 13–14.

Sheppard, Nathan. *Heroic Stature.* Philadelphia: American Baptist Publishing Society, 1897.

Shumway, Arthur L., and Brower, C. de W. *Oberliniana: A Jubilee Volume of Semi-Historical Anecdotes with the past and present of Oberlin College.* Cleveland: Home Publishing, 1883.

Skinner, Warren, "Specimen of Revival Preaching." *Christian Intelligencer and Eastern Chronicle* (Portland, Maine), 14 August 1829, p. 129. The first known report of a sermon by Finney, probably preached in Brownville, New York, in 1825.

Smith, Thornley. "Personal Recollections of the Rev. Charles G. Finney." *The Watchman and Wesleyan Advertiser* (London), 19 April 1876, p. 127.

Smith, Timothy L. "The Doctrine of the Sanctifying Spirit: Charles G. Finney's Synthesis of Wesleyan and Covenant Theology." *Wesleyan Theological Journal* 13 (Spring 1978): 92–113.

———. *Revivalism and Social Reform: American Protestantism on the Eve of the Civil War.* Baltimore: Johns Hopkins University Press, 1980.

_______. "Righteousness and Hope: Christian Holiness and the Millennial Vision in America, 1800–1900." *American Quarterly* 31, no. 1 (Spring 1979): 21–45.

Smith, Wilson. *Professors and Public Ethics: Studies of Northern Moral Philosophers Before the Civil War.* Ithaca, N.Y.: American Historical Association, 1956.

Snider, Denton Jacques. *A Writer of Books in His Genesis.* St. Louis, Mo.: Sigma Publishing, c. 1910.

Stanton, Henry B. *Random Recollections.* New York: Harper, 1887.

Stanton, Robert L. "Finney and Moody: A Parallel." *The Independent* (New York), 23 August 1877, pp. 2–3.

_______. "The Great Preacher." *The Independent* (New York), 23 September 1875, pp. 5–6.

_______. "Oberlin and the Finney Memorial." *The Independent* (New York), 26 August 1876, pp. 6–7.

Steel, Richard. "The Late Rev. C. G. Finney." *NYE,* 9 September 1875, p. 1.

Stone, Lucy. "In Memoriam." *The Woman's Journal* (Boston), 21 August 1875, p. 269.

Strong, Augustus Hopkins. *Christ in Creation and Ethical Monism.* Philadelphia: Roger Williams, 1899.

Strong, Josiah. *The Next Great Awakening.* New York: Baker and Taylor, 1902.

Sweet, Leonard I. *The Minister's Wife: Her Role in Nineteenth Century American Evangelicalism.* Philadelphia: Temple University Press, 1983.

_______. "The View of Man Inherent in New Measures Revivalism." *Church History* 45, no. 2 (June 1976): 206–21.

_______, ed. *The Evangelical Tradition in America.* Macon, Ga.: Mercer University Press, 1984.

Sweet, William Warren. *Makers of Christianity from John Cotton to Lyman Abbott.* New York: Holt, 1937.

Swing, Albert Temple. *James Harris Fairchild; or, Sixty-Eight Years with a Christian College.* Chicago: Revell, 1907.

_______. "Late President Finney." *Oberlin Weekly News,* 26 August 1875, p. 5.

_______. "President Finney and an Oberlin Theology." *Bibliotheca Sacra* (Oberlin) 57 (July 1900): 465–81.

Synan, Harold Vinson. *The Holiness-Pentecostal Movement in the United States.* Grand Rapids: Eerdmans, 1971.

Thomas, Benjamin Platt. *Theodore Weld, Crusader for Freedom.* New Brunswick, N.J.: Rutgers University Press, 1950.

Thome, James A. "Baptism of the Holy Ghost." *Divine Life* (London) 4 (March 1881): 163.

Thompson, Charles Lemuel. *Times of Refreshing: A History of American Revivals from 1740–1877, with the Philosophy and Methods.* Chicago: Palmer, 1877.

Thompson, Joseph P. *The Last Sabbath in the Broadway Tabernacle: A Historical Discourse.* New York: Calkins and Stiles, 1857.

———. "Revival Reminiscences." *The Independent* (New York), 17 April 1857, p. 62.

Thomson, Mrs. G. W. "Early Labors of President Finney." *NYE,* 9 December 1875, p. 2.

Thornbury, John F. "Asahel Nettleton's Conflict with Finneyism." *Baptist Reformation Review* 6, no. 2 (Summer 1977): 12–20.

———. *God Sent Revival: The Story of Asahel Nettleton and the Second Great Awakening.* Welwyn, Herts: Evangelical Press, 1977.

[Tilton, Theodore.] "Lights and Shades at Oberlin." *The Independent* (New York), 21 January 1869, p. 4.

———. "Oberlin." *The Independent* (New York), 13 December 1866, p. 4.

Torrey, Reuben Archer. *How to Promote and Conduct a Successful Revival, with Suggestive Outlines.* London: Melrose, 1901.

Trumbull, Henry Clay. *My Four Religion Teachers: Charles G. Finney, David Hawley, Elias R. Beadle, Horace Bushnell.* Philadelphia: The Sunday School Co., 1903.

Tyler, Alice Felt. *Freedom's Ferment: Phases of American Social History to 1860.* Minneapolis: University of Minnesota Press, 1944.

[Tyler, Bennet.] *Letters on the Origin and Progress of New Haven Theology. From a New England minister to one at the South.* New York: Carter and Collier, 1837.

———. *Memoir of the Life and Character of Asahel Nettleton, D.D.* Hartford, Conn.: Robins and Smith, 1844.

———. *Nettleton and His Labours.* 2d ed. Edinburgh: Clark, 1860.

Tyler, Clive. "Charles Finney and the Disappearance of Revival." *Reformation Today* (Haywards Heath, Sussex) 18 (March–April 1974): 16–27.

Tyler, James J. "The Last Crusade of Rev. Charles G. Finney." *1950 Proceedings of the M. W. Grand Lodge of . . . Free and Accepted Masons of the State of Ohio.* Appendix, pp. 164–72.

Vulgamore, Melvin L. "Charles G. Finney: Catalyst in the Dissolution of American Calvinism." *Reformed Review* 17, no. 4 (June 1964): 33–42.

Wallis, Arthur R. *Rain from Heaven: Revival in Scripture and History.* London: Hodder and Stoughton, 1979.

Walters, Ronald G. *American Reformers, 1815–1860.* New York: Hill and Wang, 1978.

Ward, Susan Hayes. *The History of the Broadway Tabernacle Church.* New York: The Trow Print, 1901.

Warfield, Benjamin B. *Perfectionism.* New York: Oxford University Press, 1931.

W[atts], E[dmund]. "Reminiscences of Rev. C. G. Finney." *NYE,* 2 September 1875, p. 2.

Weddell, J. W. "Charles G. Finney, Lawyer, Evangelist. The Forerunner of the Modern Man's Movement in the Churches." *Review and Expositor* 15, no. 2 (April 1918): 142–47.

Weddle, David L. "The Law and the Revival: A 'New Divinity' for the Settlements." *Church History* 47, no. 2 (June 1978): 196–214.

———. *The Law as Gospel: Revival and Reform in the Theology of Charles G. Finney.* Metuchen, N.J.: Scarecrow Press, 1985.

Weisberger, Bernard A. *They Gathered at the River: The Story of the Great Revivalists and Their Impact upon Religion in America.* Boston: Little, Brown, 1958.

Whittaker, Colin. *Seven Great Prayer Warriors.* London: Marshall Pickering, 1987.

Wilkinson, William C. "Charles G. Finney as a Preacher." *The Independent* (New York), 9 September 1875, pp. 1–2.

———. *Modern Masters of Pulpit Discourse.* New York: Funk and Wagnalls, 1905.

Willard, Frances E. *Glimpses of Fifty Years: The Autobiography of an American Woman.* Chicago: Woman's Temperance Publishing Association, 1889.

Willson, Seelye A. "An Oberlin Preacher Who Spoke His Mind." *Magazine of Western History* 9, no. 3 (January 1889): 249–51.

Winship, Albert Edward. *Great American Educators, with Chapters on American Education.* New York: Werner School Book Co., 1900.

[Wisner, Benjamin Blydenburg.] *Review of "The New Divinity Tried"; or, An Examination of Rev. Mr. Rand's Strictures on a Sermon by the Rev. C. G. Finney, on Making a New Heart.* Boston: Peirce and Parker, 1832.

Wolf, Richard C. "Charles G. Finney: Mr. Oberlin, 1835–1875." *Oberlin Alumni Magazine* 71 (September–October 1975): 2–14.

Wood, James. *Old and New Theology; or, An exhibition of differences with regard to Scripture doctrines which have recently agitated and now divided the Presbyterian Church.* Philadelphia: Wm. S. Martien, 1838.

The Worthies of the Evangelical Union. Glasgow: Morison, 1883.

[Wright, George Frederick.] "The Alleged Collapse of New England Theology." *Bibliotheca Sacra* (Oberlin) 65 (October 1908): 601–10.

———. *Charles Grandison Finney.* Boston and New York: Houghton, Mifflin, 1891.

———. "Dr. Hodge's Misrepresentation of President Finney's System of Theology." *Bibliotheca Sacra* (Andover), 2d ser., 33 (April 1876): 381–92.

———. "Oberlin College." *New England Magazine,* n.s., 23 (September 1900): 65–84.

———. "President Finney and Oberlin." *The Advance* (Chicago), 25 August 1892, pp. 668–69.

———. "President Finney's System of Theology in its relation to the so-called New England Theology." *Bibliotheca Sacra,* 2d ser., 34 (October 1877): 708–41.

Wright, Walter E. C. "Oberlin's Contribution to Ethics." *Bibliotheca Sacra* (Oberlin) 57 (July 1900): 429–44.

Wyatt-Brown, Bertram. *Lewis Tappan and the Evangelical War Against Slavery.* Cleveland: Press of Western Reserve University, 1969.

Yrigoyen, Charles, Jr. "The Second Great Awakening and Finney's Revival in Reading." *Historical Review of Berks County* 38 (Spring 1973): 65–73.

Index

References in **bold** include a brief biographical summary. Throughout, CGF = Charles Grandison Finney.

Index

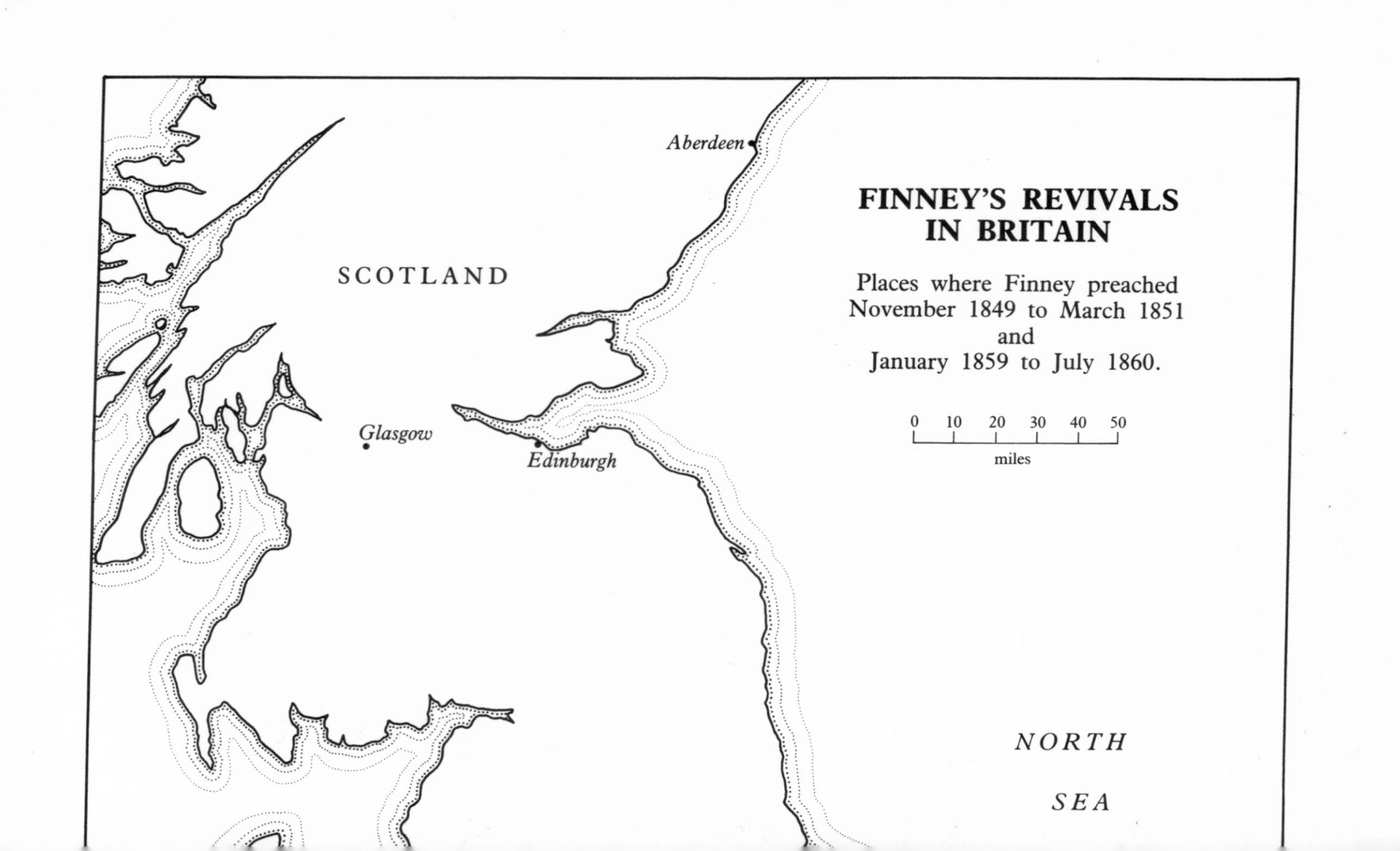
FINNEY'S REVIVALS
IN BRITAIN
Places where Finney preached
November 1849 to March 1851
and
January 1859 to July 1860.
0 10 20 30 40 50
miles
Aberdeen
SCOTLAND
Glasgow
Edinburgh
NORTH
SEA